Praise for John Milton Cooper, Jr.'s

WOODROW WILSON

"Cooper's much-anticipated biography finally gives Wilson his due. The preeminent living historian of Wilson and his era, Cooper has studied the man and his times for decades. . . . He now presents us with his magnum opus. The book is deeply, indeed exhaustively researched, and beautifully, often movingly narrated. It is far and away the best biography of the twenty-eighth president we have, and as such it is unlikely to be surpassed." —*The Boston Globe*

"Cooper clearly admires his subject but is not blind to his faults. His is a nuanced portrait of the twenty-eighth president. . . . It also offers lessons for another intellectual professor-turned-president, who combines principle with pragmatism. He, Wilson, and Teddy Roosevelt are the only presidents to receive a Nobel Peace Prize while still in office." —*The Plain Dealer*

"This biography doesn't solve all of the long-running arguments arising from Wilson's paradoxes. But it does offer a definitive portrait of him for our own paradoxical times."
—*The Journal of American History*

"John Cooper is what a biographer should be: a serious historian who has a gift for storytelling. . . . Cooper reanimates history. He captures Wilson's humanity as well as his mind. The book is dazzling and incisive." —*The Advocate* (Baton Rouge)

"A gripping story full of revelations about its subject as well as a recounting of the deep sadness of [Wilson's] unfinished work. . . . Cooper's biography stands as an impressive monument."
—*The New Leader*

"Cooper's new biography—thorough, nuanced, and striking just the right balance between Wilson's private and public lives—will become the standard to which others will be compared. . . . We are all in Cooper's debt for this clear, vigorous, three-dimensional portrait of a president who for nearly a century has often been reduced to cliché." *—The Providence Journal*

"In this spellbinding new biography, sure to take its place as the definitive one-volume life, John Milton Cooper rescues Woodrow Wilson from historical caricature. Crafted with a scholarship and eloquence worthy of its subject, Cooper's Wilson is intensely moving, sometimes infuriating, and surprisingly contemporary. Above all, it lives." —Richard Norton Smith, author of *Patriarch: George Washington and the New American Nation*

"A landmark work, the best one-volume biography ever written about the twenty-eighth president, and political history at its finest. With great deftness, Cooper describes and evaluates Wilson's personality and intellect, in ways that will surprise many readers. He thereby illuminates the idealism and the tragedy, the insight and the blindness, of one of the monumental figures in the nation's history." —Sean Wilentz, author of *The Rise of American Democracy: Jefferson to Lincoln*

"There is no more accomplished Woodrow Wilson scholar than John Milton Cooper, and this magisterial, judicious, deeply researched book—the culmination of decades of study—shows the author at the zenith of his powers. Cooper's book demonstrates Wilson's importance to our own generation, and his powerful judgments will shape the way we view the twenty-eighth president for a very long time." —Michael Beschloss, author of *Presidential Courage*

"Woodrow Wilson continues to intrigue—and divide—us. At once an idealist expressing the noblest of liberal sentiments and a racist, an intellectual and a skilled politician, a man capable of great kindness and great vindictiveness—John Milton Cooper's masterly biography describes him warts and all. A full and fascinating study of the man and his turbulent times."
—Margaret MacMillan, author of *Paris 1919*

"A riveting account of one of America's most intellectually magnetic, yet also enigmatic, presidents. John Milton Cooper does a superb job of portraying the aspirations of Wilson's idealistic internationalism while at the same time detailing the realistic pitfalls that helped undermine it. Cooper has provided a fascinating read for those who want to understand a presidency that helped set the tone for U.S. foreign policy in the twentieth century."
—James A. Baker III,
sixty-first U.S. Secretary of State

"Of all the important presidents of the twentieth century, Woodrow Wilson has always been the least-known and seemed the least-knowable. Now John Milton Cooper has written a crisp, clear-eyed account of the life of this extraordinary but deeply flawed leader who began his career as a dynamic, far-seeing reformer and ended it shortsighted and delusional. It is a Shakespearean story, beautifully and sensitively told by one of our finest historians."
—Geoffrey C. Ward, author of
A First-Class Temperament:
The Emergence of
Franklin Delano Roosevelt

John Milton Cooper, Jr.

WOODROW WILSON

John Milton Cooper, Jr., is E. Gordon Fox Professor of American
Institutions at the University of Wisconsin–Madison, where he
has taught since 1970. He is a graduate of Princeton University
and took his M.A. and Ph.D. at Columbia University. He is
the author of five previous books, including *The Warrior and the
Priest: Woodrow Wilson and Theodore Roosevelt* and *Breaking the
Heart of the World: Woodrow Wilson and the Fight for the League of
Nations*. He has held fellowships from the Guggenheim Foundation and the National Endowment for the Humanities and has
been a Policy Scholar at the Woodrow Wilson International Center for Scholars. He has served as Fulbright Professor of American history at Moscow State University, and for fifteen years he
was a member of the Editorial Advisory Committee to *The Papers
of Woodrow Wilson*. He appeared on and was a consultant to the
television biography of Theodore Roosevelt and was chief historian to the television biography of Woodrow Wilson, both of
which appeared on the Public Broadcasting Service's *American
Experience*. He lives in Madison, Wisconsin, and Harpswell,
Maine.

WOODROW WILSON

WOODROW WILSON

A Biography

John Milton Cooper, Jr.

VINTAGE BOOKS
A DIVISION OF RANDOM HOUSE, INC.
NEW YORK

FIRST VINTAGE BOOKS EDITION, APRIL 2011

Copyright © 2009 by John Milton Cooper, Jr.

All rights reserved. Published in the United States by Vintage Books,
a division of Random House, Inc., New York, and in Canada
by Random House of Canada Limited, Toronto. Originally published in hardcover
in the United States by Alfred A. Knopf, a division of Random House, Inc.,
New York, in 2009.

Vintage and colophon are registered trademarks of Random House, Inc.

The Library of Congress has cataloged the Knopf edition as follows:
Cooper, John Milton.
Woodrow Wilson: a biography / by John Milton Cooper.
p.   cm.
Includes bibliographical references and index.
1. Wilson, Woodrow, 1856–1924. 2. Presidents—United States—Biography.
3. United States—Politics and government—1913–1921. I. Title.
E767.C695 2009
973.91'3092—dc22
[B] 2009019097

Vintage ISBN: 978-0-307-27790-9

Author photograph © John Cooper
Book design by Soonyoung Kwon

www.vintageanchor.com

Printed in the United States of America
10 9 8 7 6 5 4 3 2 1

To the memory of my sister,

Jere Louise Cooper Marteau, 1946–2001

Contents

PROLOGUE "THIS MAN'S MIND AND SPIRIT"   3

1 TOMMY   13

2 WOODROW   33

3 PROFESSOR   56

4 BOLD LEADER   79

5 ACADEMIC CIVIL WAR   102

6 GOVERNOR   120

7 NOMINEE   140

8 THE GREAT CAMPAIGN   159

9 PREPARATION   182

10 BEGINNINGS   198

11 TAKEN AT THE FLOOD   213

12 TRIUMPH AND TRAGEDY   237

13 IRONY AND THE GIFT OF FATE   262

14 THE SHOCK OF RECOGNITION   285

15 SECOND FLOOD TIDE   307

16 TO RUN AGAIN   334

17 PEACE AND WAR   362

18 WAGING WAR   390

19 VICTORY   425

20 COVENANT   454

21 PEACEMAKING ABROAD AND AT HOME   476

22 THE LEAGUE FIGHT   506

23 DISABILITY   535

24 DOWNFALL   561

25 TWILIGHT   579

Notes   601

Sources and Acknowledgments   669

Index   677

WOODROW WILSON

"THIS MAN'S MIND AND SPIRIT"

Each year, in the morning on December 28, a military honor guard carrying the American flag presents a wreath that bears the words "The President." Accompanying the honor guard are members of the clergy, who carry a cross and say a prayer. The clergy are present because the wreath-laying ceremony takes place in front of a tomb in the Washington National Cathedral. Since the day is only a week after the winter solstice, the low angle of the morning sun causes bright colors from the stained glass windows to play across the floor of the alcove where the tomb is located, over the stone sarcophagus, and on the words carved on the walls. The alcove contains two flags, the Stars and Stripes and the orange and black–shielded ensign of Princeton University. The wreath laying takes place on the birthday, and at the final resting place, of the thirteenth president of Princeton and twenty-eighth president of the United States, Woodrow Wilson.

The ceremony and the tomb capture much about this man. The military presence is fitting because Wilson led the nation through World War I. The religious setting is equally fitting because no president impressed people more strongly as a man of faith than Wilson did. His resting place makes him the only president buried in the sanctuary of a church and the only one buried in Washington. The university flag attests to his career in higher education before he entered public life. Wilson remains the only professional academic and the only holder of the Ph.D. degree to become president. The inscriptions on the alcove walls come from his speeches as president and afterward. Wilson made words central to all that he did as a scholar, teacher, educational administrator, and political leader; he was the next to last president to write his own speeches. No other president has combined such varied and divergent elements of learning, eloquence, religion, and war.

In 1927, three years after Wilson's death, Winston Churchill declared, "Writing with every sense of respect, it seems no exaggeration to pronounce that the action of the United States with its repercussions on the history of the world depended, during the awful period of Armageddon, on the workings of this man's mind and spirit to the exclusion of every other factor; and that he played a part in the fate of nations incomparably more direct and personal than any other man." Churchill was referring to the part that Wilson played in World War I and above all, his decision in 1917 to intervene on the side of the Allies. That was the biggest decision Wilson ever made, and much of what has happened in the world since then has flowed from that decision. Unlike the other American wars of the last century, this one came neither in response to a direct attack on the nation's soil, as with World War II and Pearl Harbor and the attacks of September 11, nor as a war of choice, as with the Gulf War and the Iraq War, nor as a smaller episode in a grand global struggle, as with the Korean War and the Vietnam War. Many have argued that the United States joined the Allies in 1917 because great underlying forces and interests involving money, ties of blood and culture, and threats to security and cherished values were "really" at work. Perhaps so, perhaps not, but one incontrovertible fact remains: the United States entered World War I because Woodrow Wilson decided to take the country in.[1]

Despite his deep religious faith, he did not go to war in 1917 because he thought God was telling him to do it. When someone telegraphed him to demand, "In the name of God and humanity, declare war on Germany," Wilson's stenographer wrote in his diary that the president scoffed, "War isn't declared in the name of God; it is a human affair entirely." To Wilson, as an educated, orthodox Christian, the notion that any person could presume to know God's will was blasphemy. Likewise, as someone born and raised in the least evangelical and most God-centered of Protestant denominations, the Presbyterian, the notion of a personal relationship with the Almighty was foreign to him. Three months after the outbreak of World War I in Europe and at a time when he was enduring agonies of grief after the death of his first wife, he told a YMCA gathering, "For one, I am not fond of thinking about Christianity as a means of saving individual souls."[2]

Wilson practiced a severe separation not only between church and state but also between religion and society. Unlike his greatest rival, Theodore Roosevelt, he never compared politics with preaching. Unlike the other great leader of his Democratic Party, William Jennings Bryan, he never supported the greatest moral reform crusade of their time—prohibition. Also unlike Bryan, he saw no conflict between modern science and the

Bible, and he despised early manifestations of what came to be called Fundamentalism. By the same token, however, he had little truck with the major liberal religious reform movement, the Social Gospel. Wilson remained a strong Presbyterian, but his second wife was an Episcopalian who continued to worship in her own church. He was the first president to visit the pope in the Vatican. He counted Catholics and Jews among his closest political associates, and he appointed and fought to confirm the first Jew to the Supreme Court, Louis D. Brandeis.

A person with that kind of religious background and outlook could never be either of the two things that many people would charge him with being—a secular messiah or a naïve, woolly-headed idealist. Wilson was bold, extremely sure of himself, and often stubborn, and he did think of himself as an instrument of God's will. But according to his beliefs, every person was an instrument of God's will, and even his own defeats and disappointments were manifestations of the purposes of the Almighty. Such an outlook left no room for messianic delusions. It did leave room for idealism, but that did not distinguish him from the other leading politicians of his time. Except for a few crass machine types and hard-bitten conservatives, all the major figures in public life during the first two decades of the twentieth century proclaimed themselves idealists. Roosevelt and Bryan did so proudly, and nothing infuriated Roosevelt more than to hear Wilson called an idealist. Moreover, this was, as Richard Hofstadter characterized it, "the age of reform." Prohibition, woman suffrage, anti-vice campaigns, social settlement houses, educational uplift, and an embracing set of political movements loosely gathered under the umbrella of "progressivism" were the order of the day. In that context, Wilson came off as one of the most careful, hardheaded, and sophisticated idealists of his time.

His circumspection extended to foreign as well as domestic affairs. By his own admission, he did not enter the White House with much of what he called "preparation" in foreign affairs. As a scholar, he had studied and written almost exclusively about domestic politics, and the only office he had held before coming to Washington was a state governorship. Even before the outbreak of World War I, two years into his presidency, he began to deal with problems abroad, particularly fallout from the violent revolution next door in Mexico. Wilson had to learn diplomacy on the job, and he made mistakes, particularly in Mexico, where he originally did harbor some facile notions about promoting democracy. He learned hard lessons there, which he applied later in dealing with both the world war and the Bolshevik Revolution in Russia.

Like others at the time, Wilson invested American intervention in the world war with larger ideological significance and purpose. But he had no illusions about leading a worldwide crusade to impose democracy. The most famous phrase from his speech to Congress in 1917 asking for war read, "The world must be made safe for democracy"—perhaps the most significant choice of the passive voice by any president. A year later, speaking to foreign journalists, he declared, "There isn't any one kind of government which we have the right to impose upon any nation. So that I am not fighting for democracy except for those peoples that want democracy." Wilson did not coin the term *self-determination*—that came from the British prime minister David Lloyd George, who also coined the phrase "war to end all wars," words Wilson probably never uttered. Later, he did sparingly adopt "self-determination," but always as something to be applied carefully and contingently, never as a general principle for all times and places.[3]

Wilson's most renowned policy statement, the Fourteen Points, addressed specific problems of the time as much as larger conditions. Half of the points addressed general matters—such as open covenants of peace, freedom of the seas, and an international organization to maintain peace, all carefully couched as aims to be pursued over time. The other half dealt with specific issues of the war—such as the restoration of Belgium, an independent Poland, the integrity of Russia, and the matter of autonomy— but not necessarily in specific terms—so, for example, there is no mention of independence for subject peoples of the Austro-Hungarian and Ottoman empires. Wilson's moral authority and America's lesser taint of imperialism made the soberly stated Fourteen Points a rallying ground for liberals and progressives throughout the world, but if he could have heard the ways later generations would use "Wilsonian" as an epithet to scorn naïve efforts to spread democracy in the world, he might have echoed Marx's disclaimer that he was no Marxist, just Karl Marx: he was no Wilsonian, just Woodrow Wilson.

In World War I, he fought a limited war, though not in the usual sense of a war fought with limited means and in a limited geographic area. He fought with all the means at his disposal for limited aims—something less than total, crushing victory. This was a delicate task, but he succeeded to a remarkable extent. In just over a year and a half, the United States raised an army of more than 4 million men and armed and sent 2 million of them to fight on the Western Front. This miracle of mobilization foiled the hopes of the Germans and allayed the fears of the Allies that the war would be over before the Yanks could arrive. Feats of industrial, agricultural, and logistic transportation organization speeded the arrival of those "doughboys." Those accomplishments dovetailed with the president's liberal program to persuade the Germans to sue for peace in November 1918 rather than fight on to the bitter end, as they would do a quarter century later. This was Wilson's greatest triumph. He shortened World War I, and hundreds of thousands, perhaps millions, of people owed their lives to him.

Tragically, his greatest triumph sowed the seeds of his greatest defeat. For the men and women who wanted to build a new, just, peaceful world order, World War I ended in the worst possible way—neither as a compromise accepted by equals nor as an edict imposed upon the defeated foe. One of those alternatives might have offered Wilson a chance to make his ideas of peace work. Instead, he tried to thrash out the best settlement he could through arduous negotiations at the peace conference in Paris in 1919. Those negotiations wore him out physically and emotionally and produced the Treaty of Versailles, which left sore winners and unrepentant losers. This peace settlement might have had a chance to work if the victors had stuck by it in years to come, but they soon showed they would not. The first of the victors to renege was the United States, which never ratified the Treaty of Versailles and never joined the organization that Wilson helped establish to maintain the peace, the League of Nations.

The decisions he made in waging war and making peace have stirred almost as much argument as his decision to enter the war. The Fourteen Points drew fire as obstacles to total victory, and such attacks would spawn the next generation's misguided consensus that World War II must end only with "unconditional surrender." Wilson's part in the peace negotiations at Paris has drawn fire as a quixotic quest after the mirage of collective security through the League of Nations, an allegedly utopian, or "Wilsonian," endeavor that traded vague dreams for harsh realities and derailed a more realistic settlement, which might have lasted. Worst of all, arguments about the political fight at home over the treaty and membership in the League have cast him as a stubborn, self-righteous spoiler who blocked reasonable compromises. That view of him has often overlooked or minimized one glaring fact: in the middle of this fight, he suffered a stroke that left him an invalid for his last year and a half in office. Wilson's stroke caused the worst crisis of presidential disability in American history, and it had a Dr. Jekyll and Mr. Hyde effect on him. Out of a dynamic, resourceful leader emerged an emotionally unstable, delusional creature.

At the time of his death, four years after suffering his stroke, many eulogies compared Wilson to the figure from classical Greek mythology,

Icarus, who perished because he flew too close to the sun. The comparison was apt up to a point. In 1914, he told his Princeton classmates at their thirty-fifth reunion, "There is nothing that succeeds in life like boldness, provided you believe you are on the right side." Boldness and thinking big marked Wilson all his life, and those qualities helped make him the only president who rose to the top in two professions entirely removed from public affairs. As a scholar, he became the leading American political scientist of his time and one of a tiny cohort of truly great students of politics of any era. As an academic administrator, he began to transform Princeton from a socially select but intellectually somnolent men's college into one of the world's leading universities. In later years, a joke would go around Princeton that the proverbial visitor from another planet might think that only two people had ever gone there—Woodrow Wilson and F. Scott Fitzgerald. The joke made an unintended point: those men were the two leading alumni whose fame and accomplishments were bound up with the college itself and who stood for opposite but persistent sides of its character and reputation—the place of serious intellectual endeavor and the snobbish, glamorous "country club."4

In politics, Wilson became a dynamic reformer as governor of New Jersey and an instant front-runner for his party's presidential nomination. As a domestic president, he emerged as one of the greatest legislative leaders ever to occupy the White House. His legislative accomplishments included the Federal Reserve, the income tax, the Federal Trade Commission, the first child labor law, the first federal aid to farmers, and the first law mandating an eight-hour workday for industrial workers, as well as the appointment of Brandeis to the Supreme Court. As a foreign policy president, he intervened in the world war, led the country through the war, pushed his peace program, and wrote his plans for a new world order into the peace treaty. Yet Wilson never saw himself as someone who did what doomed Icarus—he never saw himself as overreaching. His greatest inspiration as a student of politics came from Edmund Burke, and he steeped himself in Burke's anti-theoretical, organic conception of politics. He could admire lonely crusaders and inspired visionaries, but only from afar. He was a man of this world, who practiced the art of the possible and went in for practical, down-to-earth ideas. When his big schemes failed, as with the League of Nations and earlier at Princeton, he came close to winning, and he lost more through bad luck than through attempting too much.

No president ever made such a swift transition from private life to politics. Two years before he entered the White House, Wilson had never held or run for any public office, and he had rarely taken any active part in politics. Moreover, his background was one that many have found particularly unsuitable for participation in public affairs or business—the "ivory tower" of academia. When Wilson first entered politics, reporters often asked him how his background had prepared him for politics and opponents sometimes sneered at him as a "professor" or "schoolmaster." He had ready responses to those questions and charges. After academic politics, he joked, the "real thing" was so much easier to deal with. As for being a teacher, he embraced the title, and he made educating the public the central tenet in his concept of leadership.

Wilson's academic background shaped his performance as president in major ways. Writing and lecturing were excellent preparation for public persuasion. Dealing with individuals and small groups as a college president readied him for wheeling and dealing with politicians and interest groups. In the White House, he practiced the "collegial" leadership that he brought from the university, a style that flew in the face of the twentieth century's later images of the strong president, derived mainly from Franklin Roosevelt and Lyndon Johnson, with a touch of Theodore Roosevelt thrown in—that is, a hyperactive, meddlesome, manipulative bully. Wilson treated his cabinet members and agency heads like responsible adults who knew their departments better than he did, and he gladly delegated authority to them. He set overall policy directions, but usually after freewheeling discussion in cabinet meetings, which he did not try to dominate. His practice of delegation proved its worth after his stroke, when the government functioned reasonably well with little or no guidance from the top. The practice also had bad effects, as when Wilson condoned ill-conceived initiatives by subordinates and allowed untoward actions without his knowledge.

Most of his subordinates liked the latitude he gave them, but they and other politicians often found him a strange sort. Wilson enjoyed being with people and got along well with individuals and small groups. He was no "effete" intellectual. In 1914, he told an audience of journalists that he disliked notions "that I am a cold and removed person who has a thinking machine inside. . . . You may not believe it, but I sometimes feel like a fire from a far from extinct volcano, and if the lava does not boil over it is because you are not high enough to see into the basin and see the cauldron boil."5 Wilson certainly passed most of the tests expected of a "regular guy." In his youth, he played baseball, and he remained an avid fan throughout his life. As a professor, he helped coach football, and as a college president, he helped save the game from being banned. He never smoked, but he liked to take an occasional drink of Scotch whisky. He was a sexually ardent lover to the two women whom he married and, possibly, to another during his first marriage. Yet Wilson was not naturally gregarious the way politicians usually are. He probably spent more time alone than any other president. When he made big decisions, he would listen to advice and discuss matters with the cabinet, but he would also seclude himself and think the matter through strictly on his own.

In the White House, Wilson retained the working habits of a professor. He liked to study questions, read memoranda and papers, and write notes to himself and drafts of ideas that might or might not find their way into his speeches. Some of the people close to him griped about Wilson's solitary habits and claimed that they weakened him politically. Plausible as such complaints might sound, they were nearly always wrong. With only a few exceptions, Wilson profited from his penchant for sequestering himself and thinking things through. The proof of this pudding was in his spectacular legislative accomplishments and his reelection despite the relative weakness of his party.

Besides luck and a natural talent for leadership, Wilson owed much of his success as president to something else that he brought with him from academic life. His study of politics always revolved around a central question and its corollary: how does power really work, and how, in a democratic system, can power be made to work more efficiently, with more accountability to the people? He compared the American separation of powers with parliamentary governments, which he found more efficient and more accountable, and he advocated adopting parliamentary practices in the United States. As part of that advocacy, he became the champion of a normally unloved institution—the political party—and he called for government through parties that acted "responsibly"—that is, efficiently and accountably—as the remedy for many of the nation's troubles. When he entered politics, he enjoyed the opportunity to put his ideas and approaches to work; in particular, he acted like a prime minister and functioned as a party leader. Other circumstances helped him rack up his legislative achievements and win reelection, but he owed much of his success to his practice of party government.

Wilson was not a president for all seasons. Peculiar political circumstances—particularly divisions in both parties between progressives and conservatives—allowed this outsider to leap into the front ranks in a way that would not have happened in ordinary times. The superheated reform sentiment of the times aided him enormously in compiling his legislative record and winning a second term. The earth-shaking events of the world war and revolutionary upheavals opened incredible opportunities for international leadership. Nor was Wilson a perfect president. Two things will always mar his place in history: race and civil liberties. He turned a stone face and deaf ear to the struggles and tribulations of African Americans. Though a southerner by birth and upbringing, he was not an obsessed white supremacist like most whites from his native region in that era. Yet in keeping with his practice of delegating authority, he allowed some of his cabinet secretaries to try to introduce segregation into the federal workplace, and he permitted them to reduce the number of African Americans employed by the government. When vicious racial violence broke out during and after the war, he said nothing, except once, when he belatedly but eloquently denounced lynching. Wilson essentially resembled the great majority of white northerners of his time in ignoring racial problems and wishing they would go away.

During the war, Wilson presided over an administration that committed egregious violations of civil liberties. He pushed for passage of the Espionage Act, which punished dissident opinions, and he refused to rein in his postmaster general, who indiscriminately denied use of the mails to dissenting publications, particularly left-wing ones. He likewise acquiesced in his attorney general's crackdown on radical labor unions. Wilson did not order those actions himself, but he was aware of them. The worst violations of civil liberties came after the war, with the "Red scare." By then, Wilson had suffered his stroke, and he knew nothing about the central role that another of his attorneys general was playing in those events. Still, it remains a mystery why such a farseeing, thoughtful person as Wilson would let any of that occur. Likewise, it remains puzzling why someone so sensitive to economic, religious, and ethnic injustices could be so indifferent, often willfully so, to the toxic state of race relations in his country.

In the end, much about Wilson remains troubling. He shared his shortcomings with Abraham Lincoln, who likewise approved massive violations of freedom of speech and the press, and Thomas Jefferson, a slave owner who fathered children by a slave mistress, and Franklin Roosevelt, who approved an even worse violation of civil liberties, the internment of Japanese Americans during World War II. A consideration of Wilson poses the same ultimate question as does that of those other towering figures in the presidential pantheon: do his sins of omission and commission outweigh the good he did, or do his great words and deeds overshadow his transgressions? Likewise, as with Jefferson, who similarly left office under the cloud of a foreign policy failure, the fiasco of the embargo, does a final failure offset earlier eloquence and accomplishment? Behind Woodrow Wilson's distinctive and often caricatured features—his long nose, big jaw, and pince-nez eyeglasses—lay one of the deepest and most daring souls ever to inhabit the White House. His was also a flawed soul rendered worse by the failing of his body, which consigned his presidency to an inglorious ending. His tomb in the National Cathedral speaks to the Christian faith that helped to form this man's mind and spirit and would forgive him his trespasses.

TOMMY

In December 1912, Woodrow Wilson's name, picture, and story were all over the newspapers and magazines. Everybody, it seemed, wanted to meet the man who had been elected president of the United States the month before. Office seekers and advice givers figuratively, sometimes literally, banged on his door. Each mail delivery brought invitations to attend ceremonies in his honor around the country. The president-elect evaded the callers for a while by sailing away with his family for an island vacation. He declined invitations to events—except one. He could not resist making a sentimental journey to Staunton, Virginia, the town of his birth, for a celebration of his fifty-sixth birthday.

The trip lived up to all expectations for warmth and festivity. The whole town turned out for a parade, and the guest of honor spoke at two events. For him, the highlight of the occasion came when he spent the night of his birthday sleeping in the same bed, in the same room, in the same house where he had been born. Also during the visit, he went to see the only member of his family who still lived in the town, an elderly aunt on his mother's side of the family who was slightly deaf. She remembered him from his childhood, but she had not followed his life and career since then, and she did not even call him by the name he had been using since his early twenties. "Well, Tommy, what are you doing now?" she asked. "I've been elected President, Aunt Janie," he shouted into her ear trumpet. "Well, well," she answered. "President of what?"[1]

When Thomas Woodrow Wilson was born, on December 28, 1856, in Staunton, his birth was big news in this town of just under 4,000 people.[2] He was the third child and first son of the Reverend Joseph Ruggles Wilson, minister of Staunton's leading church, the First Presbyterian Church. He was born in the house that the church provided for the minister, which Presbyterians call a manse, and this manse stood among the newest and finest houses in the town. Staunton is in the Shenandoah Valley, then a diversified agricultural area with a focus on wheat growing and comparatively few plantations and slaves. It drew its population largely from the Scotch-Irish who had migrated southward from Pennsylvania and Maryland. They had made the valley strongly Presbyterian.

The boy's father, thirty-four-year-old Joseph Wilson, was himself the son of Scotch-Irish immigrants, and he had been born and raised in Ohio. In his youth, he had worked as a printer on the newspaper edited by his father, who had also served as a representative in the Ohio legislature and as a state judge. He had sent Joseph, his youngest son, to Jefferson (now Washington and Jefferson) College in Pennsylvania, where he graduated as valedictorian of his class in 1844. Joseph Wilson had taught school for a year before going to seminary, first in Ohio and then in New Jersey, at Princeton. He had taken his first pulpit in Pennsylvania while teaching rhetoric part-time at Jefferson College. Teaching had drawn him to Virginia in 1851, when he became professor of chemistry and natural sciences at Hampden-Sydney College. Preaching, however, was his heart's desire, and he served as a temporary, or supply, minister while at Hampden-Sydney. In December 1854, two years before his son's birth, Joseph Wilson had received the call to Staunton, and the following June he had moved there with his family to fill the pulpit of its large, prosperous Presbyterian church.3

The new minister did not fit the prevalent stereotype of the stern pastor. He was outgoing and witty, much given to puns. He smoked cigars and a pipe heavily, played billiards incessantly, dressed well, and took an occasional drink of Scotch whisky. He was tall and handsome, with warm brown eyes, and he endeared himself particularly to his female parishioners. According to one relative, Joseph Wilson's first son believed "that if he just had his father's face and figure, it wouldn't make any difference what he *said.*" Yet Joseph Wilson did care about what he said and how he said it. Having taught rhetoric, he was well versed in secular as well as religious speaking, and he followed the contemporary oratorical stars of American politics, especially Daniel Webster. Perhaps not surprisingly, Joseph Wilson remained fascinated with worldly success and would try to push his first son toward that goal.4

In those days, a truly successful Presbyterian minister needed intellect and an intellectual pedigree. With their intricate Calvinist theology, the Presbyterians laid great stress on learning and analysis, but Joseph Wilson had little taste or patience for the intricacies of that theology. Likewise, as the son of a self-made man and Scotch-Irish immigrant, he enjoyed no particular standing in Presbyterian circles. But he did have one advantage: he had married well.

Joseph Wilson's wife was Janet Woodrow, the English-born daughter of a Scottish-born and -educated Presbyterian minister. Janet, or Jessie, as her family called her, was eight years younger than her husband, whom she had married in 1849 at the age of nineteen. Her father, Thomas Woodrow, had graduated from the University of Glasgow and its seminary and counted among his ancestors eminent seventeenth-century Scottish divines. When Jessie was five, her family immigrated to the United States from England, enduring a rough ocean crossing, which her mother did not long survive. They eventually settled in Ohio as well, where Jessie and her four older siblings were raised by their mother's sister; their father had remarried when Jessie was thirteen and had gradually distanced himself from his first family. Those experiences had left Jessie Woodrow a shy, timid, sometimes self-pitying young woman. She also lacked her future husband's good looks. The few surviving photographs of her suggest that it was from her that her son got his long jaw and angular features. He also inherited her blue-gray eyes, which reportedly changed color according to his mood, as had hers.[5]

In Presbyterian circles, everyone regarded the Woodrows as enjoying a higher status than the Wilsons. This sense of superiority was not just a matter of background. Jessie's older brother, James, or Jimmy, Woodrow was a rising star in their little Presbyterian firmament. A friend of Joseph Wilson's at Jefferson College, Jimmy Woodrow had studied first at Harvard, with the leading American scientist Louis Agassiz, and then in Germany, at Heidelberg. In 1861, at the age of thirty-three, he would become a professor at the South's leading Presbyterian seminary, the Columbia Theological Seminary, then located in South Carolina. The Woodrow connection was something that Joseph Wilson cherished.

The young couple had two daughters before their son was born: Marion Williamson Wilson, born in Pennsylvania in 1851, and Anne, or Annie, Josephine Wilson, born at Hampden-Sydney in 1853. As happy as the Wilsons were with the births of their daughters, they made a great deal more of the birth of their first son. In the first surviving description of him, when he was four months old, Jessie Wilson told her father that he was "a fine healthy fellow . . . and just as fat as he can be. Every one tells us, he is a *beautiful* boy. What is best of all, he is just as *good* as he can be—as little trouble as it is possible for a baby to be. You may be sure Joseph is very proud of his fine little son. . . . Our boy is named 'Thomas Woodrow.'"[6]

. . .

The Woodrow connection played an indispensable part in Joseph Wilson's rise in his denominational world. In August 1857, he preached at James Woodrow's wedding, at the First Presbyterian Church in Augusta, Georgia. His sermon evidently went over well, because the church issued a call to him the following December. Joseph Wilson was moving up in his world. With more than 12,000 residents, Augusta counted for much in its region's economy, particularly the lucrative cotton trade. The church there had more members and bigger buildings than Staunton's First Presbyterian, and its manse was larger and grander and provided more slaves to serve the minister and his wife and children.[7] Joseph Wilson also parlayed his professional advancement still further with a shrewd political move. In May 1858, he invited the president of Oglethorpe University, where James Woodrow was then teaching, to take part in his installation service. A few months later, possibly with some prompting from James Woodrow, the president repaid the compliment by conferring an honorary doctorate of divinity on Joseph Wilson. No title sounded sweeter or more august to Presbyterian ears than Reverend Doctor, and for the rest of his life he would go by the title Dr. Wilson.

The family's move to Georgia made their son truly a child of the South. Located across the Savannah River from South Carolina, Augusta was the unofficial capital of the region known as the black belt, at first because of the color of its soil. The richness of the soil had made this part of South Carolina and Georgia, together with the lands stretching westward to the Mississippi River, a singularly attractive place for producing the most profitable commodity in the world at that time, cotton, which had fueled a half-century-long economic boom. But this form of economic development exacted a high price from the labor force, which planters paid by using large numbers of slaves to work the plantations, thereby giving an ironic racial twist to the name of the region. At the time of the Wilson family's move to Augusta, slaves made up just under a third of the city's residents, but in the surrounding county they constituted half the population.[8]

The Wilson family soon felt a huge consequence of their move to Augusta. According to his own account, their son's first lasting memory from childhood went back to November 1860, just before his fourth birthday, "hearing some one pass and say that Mr. Lincoln was elected and there was to be war. Catching the intense tones of his excited voice, I remember running in to ask my father what it meant." Lincoln's victory at the polls set off a chain of cataclysmic events. Six weeks later, South Carolina moved to secede from the Union, and the rest of the black belt, or Deep South, states quickly followed suit, including Georgia, on January 19,

1861. Though not a politician, Joseph Wilson was in the thick of the events that led to secession and the ensuing four years of civil war.⁹

The southern wings of all the major Protestant denominations except the Episcopalians likewise seceded from their national organizations. Despite his Ohio birth and upbringing, Joseph Wilson fervently embraced the cause of the South. When the southern presbyteries withdrew from the Presbyterian Church of the United States of America during the summer of 1861, he offered his church as the meeting place for the newly formed General Assembly of the Presbyterian Church in the Confederate States of America, which convened there the following December. That body elected him to its third-ranking office, permanent clerk, and in 1865 he moved up to the second-ranking spot, stated clerk, managing the organization's finances and serving as its parliamentarian and record keeper. At the war's end, the southern Presbyterians dropped the reference to the Confederacy from their denominational name but did not rejoin their northern brethren. Joseph Wilson would remain stated clerk of this denomination for thirty-three years. He also saw active service in the Confederate cause. He joined a group of influential citizens of Augusta in a home defense unit and made at least one trip to the Confederate capital, Richmond, Virginia, to inspect hospitals and confer with high-ranking officials, and he also served briefly as an army chaplain.¹⁰

The war and the denominational split caused a family rift as well. The break was worse with the Wilsons than with the Woodrows. Joseph Wilson's father had earlier taken anti-slavery stands, and two of his brothers became Union generals. Joseph Wilson did not resume relations with his extended family after the war, and his son would not get to know his Wilson relatives until he was a grown man. On the Woodrow side, things were different. James Woodrow's move to the Columbia Seminary in 1861 had placed him in the citadel of secession. During the war he put his scientific training to use as chief chemist of the Confederacy, which meant that he oversaw munitions manufacturing for the Confederate armies. His and Jessie's father, Thomas Woodrow, remained in Ohio and sided with the northern Presbyterians, but after the war Joseph Wilson invited his father-in-law to preach in Augusta, and his son grew up knowing his Woodrow relatives from the North.¹¹

The war came home to the Wilson family in Augusta when wounded Confederate soldiers began to arrive. In 1863, the government took over the church to use as a military hospital and its grounds to use as a temporary detention camp for captured Union soldiers on their way to the notorious Confederate prison camp at Andersonville. Fortunately for Augusta, the enemy bypassed the city the next year when William Tecumseh Sherman's army made its March to the Sea, but Union forces did occupy Augusta at the end of the war.

The early 1860s were an often exciting, sometimes frightening, time to be a young boy there, but what effect this Civil War childhood had on the Wilsons' son is hard to judge. He almost certainly saw and heard wounded and dying soldiers in the town and in his father's church and prisoners of war in the churchyard. At the end of the war, he watched a conquering army occupy his hometown, and he saw the captured former Confederate president, Jefferson Davis, being transported to prison. Yet those sights and sounds do not seem to have affected him deeply. "To *me* the Civil War and its terrible scenes are but a memory of a short day," he wrote in a note to himself when he was in his early twenties. Nor did his boyhood experiences fill him with repugnance toward fighting or war. He may or may not have gotten into fights as a boy, but he certainly liked the idea of fighting, and like many other boys he would dream about adventure in arms. Later, when he was about to become president, he remarked that he "thought there was no more glorious way to die than in battle." If the Civil War left a psychological imprint on the boy or the man, it was buried so deep as to be imponderable.[12]

Except for the war, he seems to have had a happy, healthy childhood. His mother later confessed to him, "I always wanted to call you Woodrow from the first." But they called him Tommy, and that was the name he would use until his early twenties. His older sisters reportedly adored their little brother, and his mother unquestionably played the biggest role in his early life, while his father was often away. Her son wrote to his wife, "I remember how I clung to her (a laughed-at 'mamma's boy') till I was a great big fellow; but love of the best womanhood came to me and entered my heart through those apron-strings." As an urban minister's son, he had a more sheltered upbringing than did the mischief-filled, rough-and-tumble southern white boys depicted in Mark Twain's stories. One of his friends in Augusta later recalled him as "a dignified boy" who on horseback was "a conservative rider . . . very careful and very orderly." He and his friends organized a baseball club after the war, and the same friend remembered him as "not active or especially strong, although his figure was well knit and he was what you would call a 'stocky' boy." Yet like Tom Sawyer, Tommy Wilson had a rich, elaborate fantasy life and enjoyed a certain amount of mischief; he once recalled that he had liked cockfighting, evidently using the family rooster.[13]

Tommy's closeness to his mother did not spring from any need for shelter from boyhood's knocks and scrapes. Rather, what was most important was that his "love of the best womanhood" had come from her. The next sentence in his letter to his wife read: "If I had not lived with such a mother I could not have won and seemed to deserve—in part, perhaps, deserved, through transmitted virtues—such a wife—the strength, the support, the human source of my life." Throughout his life, Wilson would spend more time with women and enjoy female companionship more than most men of his era. He would value women not only as wives and lovers but also as friends and confidants with whom he could share his deepest thoughts and emotions.[14]

In those early years, his mother did help to shelter him from one significant childhood travail. Tommy Wilson did not appear at first to be very bright. He was slow in learning to read. His presidential physician, Cary T. Grayson, later claimed that Wilson told him that he had not learned his letters until he was nine, and one of his daughters said that he did not read comfortably until he was twelve. It is not clear just what Tommy's problem was. He told Dr. Grayson that his mother and his sisters would read to him by the hour, "and he would listen as long as anyone chose to read." The story smacks of rationalization, although it hints at how protective Jessie Wilson was of Tommy. He was her favorite of all her children, and he enjoyed his primacy even after the birth of a second son, in 1867. Born when Tommy was ten, Joseph (Josie) Ruggles Wilson, Jr., was the last of the family's children. People later described Josie Wilson as a smaller, brown-eyed, less sparkling version of his older brother. Josie would never enjoy the attention and solicitude that Tommy received from both his parents.[15]

Tommy's difficulty with reading most likely stemmed from some physical cause. His vision may have contributed to the problem. As an adult, Wilson would wear glasses to correct astigmatism and farsightedness, but he did not begin to wear them until after college. A better explanation may be that he suffered from some kind of developmental disorder. At the age of thirty-nine, when he suffered from semiparalysis in his right hand, Wilson easily shifted to writing with his left hand, producing the same neat script with almost no practice. Such ambidexterity, which can manifest itself in childhood as a lack of preference for either hand, often accompanies slowness in speaking and reading.[16]

Young Tommy Wilson may also have suffered from a form of dyslexia, a condition that would not begin to be identified for another thirty years. Several known facts support this explanation. He never became a rapid or voracious reader, and he developed ways to compensate for that shortcoming. As a freshman in college, he wrote in his diary, "I sometimes wish that I could read a little faster but I do not know that it would be an advantage." His brother-in-law Stockton Axson later remembered Wilson saying in his thirties, "I wonder if I am the slowest reader in the world." As an adolescent, Tommy eased the burden of writing by teaching himself shorthand. When he was sixteen, he began a two-year correspondence course in the Graham method. As a writer, Wilson would later confess that he composed entire paragraphs and even longer passages in his mind before putting them down on paper. As a speaker, he would deliver long, well-organized addresses from the sketchiest of notes—usually just a few shorthand jottings—or no notes at all. Other known facts, however, work against the notion that he suffered from dyslexia. He soon did learn to read, and he never made the grammar and spelling mistakes that often plague dyslexics. Foreign languages also pose problems for dyslexics, but in college he earned good grades in Latin and Greek and French, and he used German in his scholarly work, although he never became fluent in any foreign language.[17]

In any case, this experience left the boy with no discernible psychological scars, much of the credit for which belonged to his parents. His mother took the lead at first, giving her son more than comfort and protection. The letters she wrote to him after he went away to college show how fervently she believed in his gifts. In one, she told him, "I hope you will lay aside all *timidity*—and make the most of all your powers, my darling." One of the few people who appreciated the deep imprint Jessie Wilson left on her son was David Bryant, one of the family's African American servants in Wilmington, North Carolina, who would tell one of Wilson's biographers, "Outside Mr. Tommy was his father's boy. But inside he was his mother all over."[18]

Almost everyone recognized his father's influence. After the Civil War ended, Joseph Wilson began to play a bigger role in his son's life. From the time Tommy was eight or nine until he went off to college, he spent a lot of time in his father's company. "He was good fun," Wilson recalled in his fifties; "he was a good comrade; . . . and by constant association with him, I saw the world and the tasks of the world through his eyes." Even after Tommy started school, he spent Mondays, which was a minister's day off, with his father, who took him to see sights he thought "might interest or educate a boy." Afterward, his father would have Tommy write an essay about what he had seen. After his son had read the essay aloud, Dr. Wilson would say, "Now put down your paper and tell me in your own words what you saw." Tommy would then give a shorter, more direct account, and his father would respond, "Now write it down that way."[19]

After he mastered his letters, Tommy helped Dr. Wilson with his duties as stated clerk of the southern Presbyterians. He would attend the meetings and help keep the minutes and review parliamentary procedure.

Those experiences may have given Tommy a taste for debate and organization, but the type of politics that he witnessed in those denominational gatherings was more like what he would later find in college faculties— usually self-righteous and self-important, frequently petty, often grudge-ridden. As for his interest in "real-world" politics, it seems to have grown out of his father's having him study speeches by celebrated orators with an eye to improving them and out of the surrounding environment. Later, Tommy remarked to a college friend, "As usual politics is the all-engrossing topic of conversation. Southerners seem born with an interest in public affairs though it is too often of late a very ignorant interest."[20]

As those Monday jaunts and the essay writing suggest, Joseph Wilson gave Tommy more than companionship. His son later called him the "best teacher I ever had," and his father did spend much of their time together teaching the boy, particularly about the use of words. The core of his teaching consisted, in his son's recollection, of an analogy to firearms: "When you frame a sentence don't do it as if you were loading a shotgun, but as if you were loading a rifle. . . . [S]hoot with a single bullet and hit that one thing alone." The son remembered his parental instruction as nothing but joyful and loving. The elder Wilson began his letters with "My darling son" or "My darling boy" when Tommy was in college and even afterward, the letters themselves reading like elaborations of Polonius's advice to Laertes in *Hamlet*. In one, he admonished, "Let the esteem you have won be only as a stimulant to fresh exertion." In other letters, he exhorted, "Study *manner*, dearest Tommy, as much as matter. *Both* are essential." His father also bucked Tommy up when he encountered setbacks. "You are manly. You are true. You are most lovable in every way and deserving of confidence." Plainly, Joseph and Tommy Wilson regarded each other with warmth and happiness and love. One of his nieces supposedly declared, "Uncle Joseph never loved anyone except Cousin Woodrow."[21]

From Tommy's late teens on, Joseph Wilson's circumstances conspired to make his older son the main object of his hopes and dreams. In 1870, the ambitious clergyman took another step upward in his southern Presbyterian world. The family left Augusta for Columbia, South Carolina, where Dr. Wilson became a professor at the Columbia Theological Seminary. With just over 9,000 residents, Columbia was smaller than Augusta, but it was the capital of the state and the home of the state university, as well as the seat of the Presbyterians' most prestigious seminary in the South, where James Woodrow was on the faculty. This was a plum assignment for Joseph Wilson. The idyll lasted less than four years. Joseph Wilson was a popular teacher, but he entangled himself in the kind of political snare that often afflicts churches and faculties. Students balked when he tried to require them to attend his chapel services rather than the services at other churches in town.[22] Wilson consequently resigned from the seminary faculty and moved to a well-paid pulpit in Wilmington, North Carolina. He would spend the rest of his working life on a gradual downhill slide in professional esteem.

Not surprisingly, Joseph Wilson would yearn for Tommy to redeem his own thwarted ambitions. Indeed, the boy was beginning to show promise as a vehicle for his father's hopes. Columbia had broadened Tommy's horizons. From the time he was thirteen until he first left for college three years later, Tommy lived in an environment that was as much academic as it was clerical. Moreover, thanks mainly to having on its faculty James Woodrow and George Howe, a New England–born and –educated theologian whose son married Tommy's sister Annie, this environment was sophisticated in intellectual matters and liberal in religious thinking.

The schools Tommy attended did not challenge his mind, but his imaginative life continued to flourish, with his fantasies now turning to armed exploits at sea. He fantasized about organizing his friends into such units as the "Royal Lance Guards," assigning them ranks, and giving them knighthoods, and he fancied himself "Lord Thomas W. Wilson, duke of Eagleton, Admiral of the blue."[23] He continued to play baseball, and music offered another diversion. He also became an accomplished singer, a tenor, and music, both sacred and secular, would remain his main artistic interest outside literature for the rest of his life.

Tommy Wilson also grew fascinated with the subject that would become his life's work. A cousin recounted that he showed her a picture in his room of the British prime minister William Ewart Gladstone and "remarked that when he was a man he intended to be a statesman such as this hero of his." A friend in Columbia chided him, "Never mind Tom you just wait till you and me get to be members of the US Senate." It might seem surprising that as the son, grandson, and nephew of Presbyterian ministers, he did not want to become one too. Some evidence suggests that his father wanted him to follow in his footsteps, perhaps to assuage his own disappointments over his career setbacks. But it is more likely that Joseph Wilson never pushed Tommy toward the ministry and viewed his son's nascent interest in politics with relish, not regret.[24]

Not choosing the ministry as his vocation implied no want of religious commitment on Tommy's part. He took the serious step of joining the church when he was fifteen, which evidently required a personal decision to accept Christ as his savior, as young Presbyterians were expected to do.

Tommy resembled his father more than he did James Woodrow and others on the seminary faculty in having little taste for Calvinist theology or metaphysical speculation. Religious books would rarely figure in his reading. When he was twenty-four, he confessed to a friend that his reading had been "very unusual in kind. I've been looking into some Biblical discussion, thus coming at least to the outskirts of theology." He added, "As an antidote to Biblical criticism I've been reading aloud to my sister and cousin a novel by Thomas Hardy." Eight years later, on his thirty-third birthday, he would record in a private journal, "I used to wonder vaguely that I did not have the same deep-reaching spiritual difficulties that I read of other young men having. I *saw* the intellectual difficulties, but I was not *troubled* by them: they seemed to have no connection with my faith in the essentials of the religion I had been taught."[25]

Still, Tommy Wilson's upbringing in one of the most liberal and sophisticated religious and intellectual environments in America at that time gave him familiarity with the basic concepts of Protestant thought, Lutheran as well as Calvinist. He believed that Christians were instruments of God's will and must fulfill their predestined part, but his upbringing among learned Presbyterians stood in stark opposition to evangelicals who stressed emotional commitment and personal salvation. Attitudes and approaches borrowed from evangelical Protestantism had spawned the pre–Civil War moral reform movements, such as the temperance and anti-slavery crusades. Those attitudes would flourish again in such varied incarnations as the Protestant Social Gospel, anti-liquor and anti-vice crusades, and an overall evangelical style of political reform. Yet despite a deep religious faith and a look and manner that would later strike some observers as preacherish, the man Tommy Wilson grew up to be would not adopt those approaches. It was not this preacher's-son-turned-president but rather his greatest rival, himself a religious skeptic, who would call their office a "bully pulpit." Wilson did not call the presidency by that name, nor did he think about it and politics that way, largely because his religious upbringing had inoculated him against such notions.

Tommy Wilson's upbringing also inoculated him to a degree against the influence of the larger environment around him—the South. With an Ohio-born father, an English-born mother, and foreign-born grandparents, he did not have deep roots in the South or any place in the United States, and he raised the question of his southern identity whenever he opened his mouth. By the time he went north to college, at the age of eighteen, he lacked the distinguishing characteristic of his native region—a southern accent. The close-knit nature of the Wilson family may have insulated him somewhat from his surroundings, but Tommy had plenty of exposure to southern-accented playmates and schoolmates, together with the family's African American servants and the general populace of Augusta and Columbia. In adolescence, he seems to have consciously rid himself of a southern accent, training himself to speak with a broad *a*, which he considered more pleasing and more refined. He would also try, without success, to get his Georgia-born and -raised fiancée, Ellen Axson, to rid herself of her southern accent.[26]

Yet Tommy Wilson was still a southerner. A friend during his freshman year in college remembered him as "very full of the South and quite secessionist. One night we sat up until dawn talking about [the Civil War], he taking the southern side and getting quite bitter about it." As an adult, he would avow that "a boy never gets over his boyhood, and never can change those subtle influences which have become a part of him, . . . [so] that the only place in the country, the only place in the world, where nothing has to be explained to me is the South."[27] Being a southerner made him identify with a defeated, impoverished, disadvantaged region. As the son of a well-regarded and well-paid minister, he never knew poverty or social inferiority firsthand, but his local advantages paled in comparison with the wealth and status that he encountered when he went north to college. His southern allegiance also fixed his choice of party identification. Wilson would remain a Democrat throughout many years of residence in the North, but unlike many northern Democrats, he would never carry disaffection with the party's later turn toward agrarian reform and evangelical-style politics to the point of switching parties or turning into a disgruntled conservative. Identification with his underdog native region would help to keep him on the side of reform.

Tommy Wilson could not have been a young white southerner without encountering race. He grew up surrounded by African Americans. His family had not owned slaves because the common practice was for Presbyterian churches to lease slaves, usually from parishioners, for their ministers' use. Tommy and those slaves and, later, servants had known each other well. In moving to Columbia, the Wilson family moved to a city and a state where a majority of the population was African American, and while they lived there, African Americans served in Congress, held statewide offices, and made up a majority in the state legislature, as they would for nearly all the years of Reconstruction. Yet African Americans remained invisible to Wilson. References to people of color almost never appear in any of the documents or recollections of Tommy's early years. Later, he told a friend of how some blacks had seemed awestruck when he practiced oratory in the pulpit of his father's church in Wilmington. "I'm

Southern," he commented, "but I have very little ease with coloured people or they with me. Why is it? For I care enormously about them." Wilson's later dealings with matters of race suggest otherwise.[28]

Tommy Wilson's youth in the South ended after his first foray into college education. In the fall of 1873, at the age of sixteen, he entered Davidson College in North Carolina. Small and struggling, like other southern colleges, Davidson was a spartan place, with each student having to draw his own water, cut his own wood, and light the fire in his room. The student body numbered only between 100 and 150. Tommy got good grades, except in mathematics, and did a lot of reading on his own. He made friends, took a leading part in the literary and debating society, and played on the baseball team. He spent just one year at Davidson. Why he left is not clear, but contrary to some later reports, ill health does not seem to have been the reason for his withdrawal. He spent the next year at his family's new home in Wilmington, where he read, helped around the house, practiced oratory, and improved his shorthand skills. He wrote to his shorthand school, "I am studying for entering Princeton College, where I expect to be next session." The "diffident youth" evidently planned to expand his horizons beyond the bounds of his native South.[29]

The official name of the institution that eighteen-year-old Tommy Wilson wanted to enter was the College of New Jersey, but from early on it had gone by the name of the town in west-central New Jersey where it was located, Princeton, which by the 1870s boasted a population of about 3,500 people. It was one of nine American colleges founded before the American Revolution, and its main building, Nassau Hall, dating from 1756, was the second-oldest college building in the United States. During the Revolution, Nassau Hall came under fire before and after the battle of Princeton, and it later served briefly as the meeting place of the Continental Congress.[30]

Princeton's history was as illustrious as it was long. The college's early presidents included the theologian Jonathan Edwards and the Scottish-born and -educated divine John Witherspoon, who was a signer of the Declaration of Independence. Its early alumni included three other signers of the Declaration; nine delegates to the Constitutional Convention; the nation's notorious third vice president, Aaron Burr; and most notable of all, the co-author of *The Federalist Papers*, co-framer of the Bill of Rights, and fourth president, James Madison. Equally important to the members of a Presbyterian minister's family, Princeton was the first college in America founded by their denomination. Its founders had named Nassau Hall for William, prince of Orange and count of Nassau, the king who secured Protestant succession to the English throne, and the students had adopted orange and black as their college colors.

When Tommy Wilson entered Princeton, in 1875, the college was staging a comeback. Until recently, a succession of lackluster presidents had not upheld the standard set by the early leaders, and more recent alumni had not been as stellar as those from the early years. Princeton had also suffered from the Civil War. Before the war, the college had drawn students from the South, but sectional tensions and the war had constricted and then cut off this source of students. Circumstances had begun to improve only in 1868, with the appointment of an able new president, James McCosh, who had immediately begun to upgrade intellectual standards and recruit students. The class Tommy Wilson entered was the largest in the college's history, and the place was a good fit for him. With an unbroken succession of minister presidents, Princeton had not strayed far from its denominational roots and embodied the learned, sophisticated, liberal brand of Presbyterianism in which he had grown up. Happily for him, the college allowed plenty of time for reading and solitude. For all of McCosh's learning and intellectual rigor, he had not made Princeton academically demanding for its students.[31]

Tommy Wilson quickly made friends and fitted in socially, but his classes did not challenge him. Princeton's curriculum during the first two years consisted entirely, as in most colleges, of prescribed subjects, mainly the classics, and the classroom experience featured incessant daily drill. Yet the academic situation seemed to suit Tommy Wilson. "He was not a hard student and had no ambition to stand high," recalled his classmate Robert McCarter. Instead, he "read a great deal—good books." Another classmate, Robert (Bob) Bridges, who became his closest friend at Princeton, remembered that "what he called 'the play of the mind' was as exhilarating to him as the play of the body to an athlete. It was as natural for him as an undergraduate to talk about [Edmund] Burke . . . as it was for the rest of us to allude to [James Fenimore] Cooper or [the popular boys' novelist] Mayne Reid."[32]

He paid scant regard to what went on in class. He confessed in his shorthand diary that he cut class to read Thomas Babington Macaulay's *History of England:* "It has all the fascination for me of a novel." Yet he experienced an intellectual awakening. Soon after he arrived at Princeton, he wrote home excitedly, "Father, I have made a discovery; I have found that I have a mind." His diary entries crackled with excitement at his discoveries and reflections, and his growing sense of his intellectual powers filled him with doubt as well as confidence. "I have come to the conclusion," he wrote, ". . . that my mind is a very ordinary one indeed. I am nothing as far as intellect goes. But I can plod and work." Despite his unconcern for classes, he got good grades. In a class that averaged 180 students during his four years at Princeton, he always ranked in the highest quarter, though never among the "honor men," who were limited to the top twenty-one students.33

His academic performance also came in spite of his preoccupation with sports, which were beginning to emerge on the college scene. Princeton played its first schedule of football games against other colleges during Tommy's sophomore year. Although he was big enough to make the team in those days, having grown to his full height of five feet eleven inches, with a medium build, he did not try to play, but he did become an avid fan of the game. Baseball remained his favorite sport, and at the end of his freshman year he noted, "This is the first day this week that I have not played baseball." He also joined an eating club, called the Alligators. In a photograph of the Alligators taken during Wilson's senior year, he is the most recognizable figure because he is the only one to make the jaunty gesture of doffing his hat.34

Of the three celebrated temptations of college men—tobacco, alcohol, and sex—Tommy Wilson made no mention in his diaries. One of his daughters told his first biographer that she remembered "hearing her father say that he had never smoked because the old Doctor [Joseph Wilson] had done enough of it for the two." His ambitions and training as a speaker may also have led him to consider smoking a hazard to his voice, as did some aspiring orators of his generation. Later, Wilson did become a moderate drinker—like his father, of Scotch whisky—but alcohol did not flow as freely at Princeton in the 1870s as it subsequently would. Nor did sex—at least in the form of the romantic associations permissible among proper young men and women of that time—loom large. He later tried to explain away a post-college romance to his fiancée this way: "I was just fresh from Princeton where for four years I had been leading what was, to all intents and purposes, a monastic life."35

Tommy Wilson found outlets for "the play of the mind" in speaking and writing. Of Princeton's two venerable debating societies, he joined Whig, where the debate topics featured his favorite subject—politics. In his freshman year he began to reflect on what he saw as the shortcomings of the system of government in the United States as compared with Britain's parliamentary institutions, noting, "How much happier [?] she [the United States] would be now if she had England's form of government instead of the miserable delusion of a republic. A republic too founded upon the notion of abstract liberty!"36 That preference for British institutions and practices most likely stemmed from pride in his mother's English birth and his family's Scottish heritage, combined with his southerner's resentment toward the triumphant North. Rejection of universal suffrage for men was becoming a widely held article of faith among "better" people throughout the country, and it was one of his father's strongest convictions.

Wilson would soon change some of those views, especially the bias against republics and universal suffrage. But that early statement contained two significant elements of his later political thought. One was the penchant for comparing the British and American systems of government, and the other was his scorn for "the notion of abstract liberty," which showed how early and how thoroughly he had absorbed Edmund Burke's fundamental approach to politics—the rejection of notions of applying general principles and sweeping theories to public life and the belief that institutions and parties must emerge organically from human experience.

His political views were already changing by the end of his freshman year. Twelve years later, he told a fellow scholar, "Ever since I have had independent judgments of my own I have been a Federalist (!)" By "a Federalist," he meant the rejection of prevailing southern state-rights and limited-government views and the espousal of a strong, centralized national government, along the lines expounded by Alexander Hamilton, who would become his favorite among the founders of the Republic. Wilson also claimed that the "mixture of elements in me—full identification with the South, non-Southern blood, and Federalist principles"—instilled "a detachment of my affectionate, reminiscent sympathies from my historical judgments."37

In his sophomore year, Wilson began writing for publication at Princeton. In 1876, the faculty approved student petitions to start a campus newspaper, which took the name *The Princetonian*. This student paper became young Wilson's major activity in addition to his participation in Whig. His first contribution was a long letter signed "W," which deplored "the fact that very little attention is paid to oratory in Princeton College." He came into his own during his last two years. He had already moved into the most desirable housing on campus, the newly opened Witherspoon Hall, where he joined a coterie of student leaders known as the Witherspoon Gang. Overlapping with his eating club, the Alligators, the Witherspoon Gang included such close friends as Bob Bridges, who would later distinguish himself as a poet and editor of *Scribner's Magazine*; Charles (Charlie) Talcott, a future lawyer who shared Wilson's interest in politics and would later serve in Congress; and Hiram "the Cow" Woods, who would become a physician and professor of medicine in Baltimore.38 Another future lawyer who roomed in Witherspoon, wrote for the *Prince-*

tonian, and belonged to the Alligators, Mahlon (May) Pitney was not such a close friend of Wilson's. Pitney would also serve in Congress and would become a justice of the U.S. Supreme Court, appointed by Wilson's Republican predecessor.

During those final years at Princeton, Tommy still read on his own, although he devoted more time during his junior year to writing for *The Princetonian*. His harping on Princeton's deficiencies in oratorical training took on a sharper edge, while he ridiculed charges that football was dangerous and brutal. In his senior year, he ascended to the top position, managing editor. Another editor in 1879 was his successor in the next class, a tall, gifted mathematician named Henry (Harry) Burchard Fine, who would later become a dean and Wilson's right-hand man during his presidency of Princeton.

"He ran a good paper," Tommy's classmate Robert McCarter recalled long afterward. "I can remember him now running around with a memo pad, taking shorthand notes; he worked hard." Wilson left his stamp on *The Princetonian*. In contrast to his predecessor as managing editor, he included almost no references to religion and instead covered and commented on student activities and athletics. His editorials reflected his major interests, particularly speaking. In one, he pleaded for more opportunities for debate, because "debate is the chief field of oratory outside of the pulpit. . . . Oratory is persuasion, not the declaiming of essays."[39] Those editorials may also have been part of a self-serving and none-too-subtle campaign on Wilson's part for a prominent speaking role at his graduation: he was describing the kind of orator that he was striving to be.

One essay from this time, which was not published, gives the first evidence of this young man's newfound detachment and independent judgment. Titled "Some Thoughts on the Present State of Public Affairs," this work deplores "the entire and almost fatal separation of power and responsibility." What sets this essay apart from Tommy's earlier musings is an about-face on universal suffrage, which he now called "the blessing that it is capable of becoming." Acknowledging the view that universal suffrage had lowered the tone of American politics, he argued, "This is one side of universal suffrage: look at the other. While it is indisputably true that people can comprehend great truths, is it not as true that people can comprehend these truths and that they must be educated into an acceptance of them?"[40] Young Wilson was becoming a convinced democrat, and he was beginning to grasp what would become the central tenet of his concept of leadership—education of the public.

By contrast, Joseph Wilson told his son, "Either a limitation of suffrage or anarchy in twenty-five years or sooner. I do not refer to the

Negroes any more than to the ignorant Northern voters." Conflict between the young man's growing independence of thought and filial loyalty caused him to pass up a chance at the highest oratorical honor at Princeton. He refused to take part in the Lynde debate because he would have had to argue publicly in favor of universal suffrage; he lamely claimed to his father that the subject did not interest him. Wilson was not elected to be a class officer, either. That may have been because other classmates resented the Alligators and the Witherspoon Gang as a privileged clique that dominated college affairs. If so, that was ironic, because the Princeton class of 1879 included young men from New York and Chicago such as Cleveland Dodge and Cyrus McCormick, whose families were far richer and more socially prominent than the families of Wilson and his friends. The college was small enough for all the students to know each other, but Wilson was not particularly friendly with his upper-crust classmates. Nor was he chosen to be valedictorian. The faculty selected William F. Magie, who later recalled, "Wilson ought to have had it." The faculty evidently resented Wilson's outspoken criticisms of them and the curriculum in *The Princetonian*, together with his thinly veiled campaign for the valedictorian's spot.[41]

Editing the college paper and speaking at Whig cut down on Wilson's outside reading, but not completely. In fact, he began a more purposeful program of self-education, which led him to discover a major intellectual influence. Five years later, he noted, "My reading in constitutional law and history had begun to widen about a year before I left Princeton," when he had come upon the writings of the recently deceased English political commentator Walter Bagehot. Of those writings, he wrote that his "appetite for the investigation was whetted by my admiration . . . and finally demanded a comparative examination of our own constitution as it exists outside of the books and stripped of 'the refinements of the literary theory.'" Those writings appealed to Wilson because his previous steeping in Burke's anti-theoretical approach to politics had made him receptive to Bagehot's approach to politics and government. Like the child in Hans Christian Andersen's fairy tale about the emperor's new clothes, this Englishman had been an unrelenting empiricist who insisted upon seeing things as they were, not as they were supposed to be. He had set aside formal institutions and insisted on probing how politics really worked, wanting to know where power resided, who exercised it, and to what ends. Likewise, Bagehot's direct, pungent writing style caught Wilson's fancy.[42]

This new intellectual influence also helped bring about some immediate results for Wilson's study of politics. At the middle of his senior year, he composed an essay titled "Cabinet Government in the United States," and in April 1879 a Boston magazine, the *International Review*—whose editor was a young instructor in history at Harvard named Henry Cabot Lodge—accepted it for publication. Appearing in the magazine's August 1879 issue, "Cabinet Government" was more polished, mature, and thoughtful than anything Wilson had written before. He opened by noting a "marked and alarming decline in statesmanship," but he argued that its "real cause" lay not in universal suffrage but "in the absorption of all power by a legislature which is practically irresponsible for its acts." This irresponsibility sprang, in turn, from Congress's suppression of "thorough, exhaustive, and open discussions" in favor of "dangerous and unwholesome" domination by committees that operated in secret. To remedy this evil, he proposed to give seats in Congress to cabinet members, thereby introducing *"responsible Cabinet government* in the United States" and opening the way for freer, more open discussion in Congress. Wilson's solution would deprive "factious government, . . . [p]arty trickery, legislative chicanery . . . of the very air that they breathe—the air of secrecy, of concealment," and would restore the fundamental principle "that *debate* is the essential function of a popular representative body" and absolutely indispensable to its role in educating the public.[43]

Wilson also maintained that having cabinet members sit and debate in Congress would forge a link between the executive and legislative branches and thus promote efficiency and lessen corruption. Although he conceded that a cabinet system might bring its own defects and dangers, knitting together executive and legislative powers still struck him as a positive good because it would overcome the "complete separation of the executive and the legislative." He scoffed at those who would sound "the alarm-bell of *centralization*," inasmuch as congressional committees already exercised "despotic authority." The present defects in American government were not, he claimed, "self-adjusting": without action by "the people from whom springs all authority, . . . our dangers may overwhelm us, our political maladies may prove incurable."[44]

"Cabinet Government" would have done credit to an older writer, much less a twenty-two-year-old college senior. The essay is not perfect. The analysis does have a hasty, all-embracing quality, and the tone often suggests an alarmist speech rather than a dispassionate dissection. Such ideas as seating cabinet members in Congress and comparing American and British practices were not original with Wilson, and his writing sometimes lapses into floweriness and convolution. Yet despite those shortcomings, he had come by his thoughts on his own and poured his own thoughts and writings since adolescence into the essay. "Cabinet Government" was also his declaration of intellectual independence. He was embracing both democracy and Hamiltonian federalism, and he was rejecting the limited, noninterventionist government views that were purveyed in high-toned journals and college classrooms, including Princeton's. "Cabinet Government" was a plea to make politics and government matter more, so that those arenas could become challenging, worthy fields of endeavor for him and others like him.[45]

Publishing his essay in a well-regarded journal complicated Wilson's plans for what he would do after graduation. Four years later, he wrote to his fiancée, Ellen Axson, "The profession I chose was politics; the profession I entered was the law. I entered the one because I thought it would lead to the other." In fact, his choice was not so straightforward. His political ambition evidently remained unchanged. As Robert Bridges later recalled, Wilson regularly joked, "When I meet you in the Senate, I'll argue that out with you." Law was the part of his choice that had grown problematic. For years both Wilson and his father had assumed that he would become a lawyer after college. Yet he yearned to follow the path that allowed young men from wealthy, socially prominent families to gain office at an early age. His new editor, Lodge, was already active in Massachusetts politics and would go to Congress within a decade and would become a senator at the age of forty-two. Lodge's closest friend, Theodore Roosevelt, an upper-class New Yorker, would enter the New York State legislature only a year out of Harvard and become president at the same age at which Lodge entered the Senate. Without such wealth and connections, Wilson could foresee for himself only a long grind at the law to earn a living, which he thought would unfit him for meaningful, broad-gauged public service.[46]

That was only part of the problem. Publishing essays in student publications and now the *International Review* whetted his desire to write. As he also later told Ellen Axson, "[M]y predilections, ever since I had any that were definite, have always turned very strongly towards a literary life, notwithstanding my decided taste for oratory. . . . I want to contribute to our literature what no American has ever contributed, studies in the philosophy of our institutions, not the abstract and occult, but the practical and suggestive, philosophy which is at the core of our governmental methods; their use, their meanings, 'the spirit that makes them workable.'"[47] The quotation came from Bagehot, and Wilson wanted to be an American Bagehot. Over the next six years, he would devote himself to explaining how American politics and government really worked and how to make them work better. During his four years at Princeton, he had experienced an intellectual awakening that was changing his life and taking him away from being Tommy Wilson.

2

WOODROW

In the fall of 1879, twenty-two-year-old Thomas Woodrow Wilson followed the path of many young college graduates when he bowed to family pressure in preparing himself for a career. Dr. Wilson had long assumed that his older son would become a lawyer, and he had aimed much admonition and advice toward that end. Unlike his Princeton friends and classmates, Wilson did not follow the usual path of the time, which was to read law under an established attorney's tutelage. Instead, he enrolled in the law school of the University of Virginia. This seemed an academically more respectable way to enter the legal profession, but law school and Wilson were a mismatch from the start—and the fault lay with the student, not the institution.

The University of Virginia still bore the impress of its founder, Thomas Jefferson. Even fifty years after young Wilson entered the law school, according to Jefferson's leading biographer, "they still talked of Mr. Jefferson as though he were in the next room." Much about the place did strike a responsive chord with this youthful would-be statesman. The university had an intellectual seriousness he had not found at Princeton. "Study is made a serious business and the loafer is the exception," Wilson wrote to Robert Bridges. He found the teaching at Virginia much better than any he had encountered before: "The course in Law is certainly as fine a one as could be desired," he told Bridges. Professor John Barbee Minor, whom he called "a *perfect* teacher," would be the only instructor whom Wilson would praise in any of the four colleges and universities that he eventually attended; he would later rank Minor among the greatest teachers he ever had, surpassed only by his father. "And the place is cosmopolitan," he added, "—at least as far as the South is concerned . . . and one feels that the intellectual forces of the South are forming here."[1]

At Virginia, Wilson made some good friends, sang in the glee club, joined a fraternity, and continued to occupy himself with writing and debate. In an essay he had written the preceding summer, "Self-Government in France," he contrasted the convulsions of French politics with the gradual achievement of self-government in Britain and America. Openly borrowing from Alexis de Tocqueville's *L'ancien régime*, he concluded that France's "liberties are insecure. They rest upon habits of revolution." Wilson was stressing the relativity of institutions, and in leaning on Tocqueville, he chose the most insightful interpreter yet of the French Revolution. In another essay, "Congressional Government," he called the American Constitution "a cornerstone, not a complete building. It is a root, not a perfect vine." He defended political parties against currently fashionable denigrations, dubbing party government "the best that human wisdom has yet been able to devise," and he again called for bridging the separation of powers by having the president choose the cabinet from among members of Congress. In that essay, he coined the phrase that would become the title of his first and most influential book, and he showed his lack of reverence for the Constitution and took for granted that a Hamiltonian centralist position was the only one worth considering.[2]

During his first year in law school, Wilson published some other essays in *The Virginia University Magazine*. In one, he maintained that it was "next to impossible" for new ideas to flourish "in agricultural communities or rural neighborhoods. . . . *Trade*, indeed, is the great nurse of liberal ideas." Saying that at Jefferson's university was tantamount to pulling the beard of the Sage of Monticello in his own house. He uttered an even more daring declaration of apostasy when he wrote, "I yield to no one in precedence in love of the South. But *because* I love the South, I rejoice in the failure of the Confederacy." Successful secession would have perpetuated slavery, which was "enervating our Southern society and exhausting our Southern energies. . . . Even the damnable cruelty and folly of reconstruction was to be preferred to helpless independence."[3]

The debating club at Virginia, the Jefferson Society, was where Wilson had his first real encounter with rivalry and jealousy. In 1879, the society's other star speaker was William Cabell Bruce, a handsome nineteen-year-old scion of a distinguished Virginia family. The two young contenders disliked each other from the start. Many years later, Bruce dismissed Wilson as a socially stunted Presbyterian minister's son and noted, "In all my life, I think, I have never known any one so covetous of fame as he was, or so confident that he would attain it." For his part, Wilson later confessed to his fiancée, "I admire my friend (?) Bruce's striking face and brilliant talents, but the words would stick in my throat if I were to try to tell him so, because I thoroughly dislike the man."[4] It was when he encountered Bruce that Wilson told a cousin that if he had had his father's looks, it would not have mattered what he said.

The pair collided head-on in April 1880, when they competed in the Jefferson Society's annual oratorical contest. The question assigned for debate was "Is the Roman Catholic element in the United States a menace to American institutions?" Bruce drew the affirmative, Wilson the negative, stands that allowed these polar opposites to draw on their respective strengths. At his energetic, gesticulating, fiery best, Bruce painted a lurid picture of the menace posed by Catholics, especially the Irish. Wilson, an eyewitness later recalled, "did not use oratory. He adopted the English style. No gestures. No step forward." He maintained that "the vitality of Anglo-Saxon institutions . . . had stood the test of centuries" and America's vital, superior culture would easily assimilate Catholics."[5] After two days of deliberation, the judges, three professors at the law school, awarded the first prize to Bruce and a consolation prize to Wilson.

Most members of the Jefferson Society regarded Wilson as the better speaker, but one of them recalled long afterward that Bruce excelled in "brilliant oratorical flights" and in "[p]owerful summary of affirmative facts in unanswerable logic." Bruce and Wilson reacted differently to what happened. One of Wilson's friends recalled that Bruce "seemed nettled and sour because the judges had not immediately awarded him the medal." After the judges' decision, another friend remembered that Wilson admitted to being fairly beaten but added, "Bruce beat me in this, but I will beat him in life, for I'm a worker, he is not." The wounds from this encounter left a smoldering resentment. In the last year of his life, Wilson would warn a Democratic Party official about Bruce: "He is by nature envious and intensely jealous, and cannot take part in disinterested service of any kind."[6]

Dealing with Bruce and knowing that he would meet others like him did not endear the young man to the law. After three months at Virginia, he confessed to a Princeton classmate, "I am most terribly bored by the noble study of Law sometimes." It was like eating "that other immortal article of food, *Hash*, when served with such endless frequency." Wilson wanted to be studying and writing about politics. In February 1880, he told Bridges that his "brightest dream" was "the great work of disseminating political truth and purifying the politics of our own country. . . . [W]hen I get out of this treadmill of the law I intend to devote every scrap of leisure time to the study of that great and delightful subject." Joseph Wilson did not share his son's dream. He warned him against "a mere literary career such as you seem to dream about now and then. At any rate, *far, far,* better conquer the law, even through all its wretched twistings and technical paths of thorn."[7]

This time witnessed the closest approach to an open clash that ever occurred between father and son. The words "a mere literary career" sparked another smoldering resentment in Wilson. It would flare up thirteen years later, when he published an essay titled "Mere Literature," in which he figuratively flung his father's words and views back in his face. He remained a dutiful son who respected and loved his father, but their relationship was changing as the son began to have his own ideas about his future. He also changed his name. During his first year at Virginia, he gave up calling himself Tommy in favor of Woodrow. Such experimentation with names was common among young men of that era. He would still be Tommy to his old Princeton cohorts, but family and new friends would now call him Woodrow. The shorter, alliterative pairing, Woodrow Wilson, had a nice literary ring to it.

His attitude toward assignments and classes did not change. He dutifully read and made shorthand notes in his texts, but he found a new reason for cutting classes: he was falling in love. His affections settled on his first cousin, Harriet (Hattie) Woodrow, who was a student at the Augusta Female Seminary in nearby Staunton. A vivacious young woman of nineteen with brown hair and blue eyes, Hattie was the daughter of Thomas Woodrow, Jr., one of Jessie Wilson's brothers who had stayed in Ohio. Years later, Hattie remembered that she had taken walks with Woodrow and participated in a group singing around the piano: "I think of him as a rather mature, dignified, serious minded young man—yet with a keen sense of humor." Wilson got into academic trouble in the spring of 1880 when he cut several classes to attend Hattie's graduation ceremony.[8]

The second year of law school proved even less palatable because Hattie had gone home to Ohio, and he had to content himself with writing to her. Classwork bored him as much as before, and after he came down with a persistent cold in December 1880, he bowed to his mother's entreaties to come home. He insisted to Bridges that his plans remained unchanged: "My *end* is a commanding influence in the councils (and counsels) of my country—and *means* to be employed are writing and speaking." He lived for the next year and a half with his parents in Wilmington, where he spent much of his time practicing oratory in the pulpit of his father's church and writing essays. He read law and prepared himself for bar examinations, but he studied on his own rather than under the tutelage of an established lawyer. He taught Latin to his brother, helped with household chores, and played with his young nieces. He began wearing eyeglasses—the pince-nez that would become a hallmark of his appearance—and he grew a large, flowing mustache, which together with his newly thick sideburns softened the impression made by his long jaw and angular features. In February 1881, the *New York Evening Post* published an essay by him titled "Stray Thoughts from the South," in which he condemned Reconstruction for having "held the South back from her natural destiny of regeneration" but applauded the South's "happy extension" of commerce and manufacturing, "such as the unnatural system of slave labor alone kept her from establishing long ago."[9] In getting the piece published, it helped that Bridges was now working for the *Evening Post*.

He also continued to court Hattie Woodrow. Physical separation and social convention required his courtship to be epistolary and oblique. He wrote long, rambling letters in which he dropped broad hints about deeper feelings. After he returned to Wilmington, he told her, "I simply love you well enough to love to write to you even when I have to write stupidly." Later, he used expressions such as "You know that I love you dearly" and "You know how much [love] I send—just as much as you desire."[10] How Hattie responded to such hints of love is not known. If she hinted that she did not return his affections, he failed to take the hint and pushed his suit to a disastrous conclusion.

A moment of truth—and melodrama—came on the night of September 25, 1881. On a visit to the Woodrow home in Chillicothe, Ohio, Wilson got Hattie to leave the dance floor at a party so that he could declare his love and propose marriage. She turned him down, saying they were too closely related. Distraught, he left the party and insisted on moving to a local hotel for the night and departing from Chillicothe the next day. From the hotel, he scribbled an anguished note on a torn piece of paper. "Now, Hattie," he implored, "for my sake, *and for your own*, reconsider the dismissal you gave me to-night. I cannot sleep tonight—so give me the consolation of thinking, while waiting for the morning that there is still one faint hope left to save me from the terror of despair." Hattie stood her ground. Her refusal to marry him because they were first cousins was an excuse to spare his feelings. She did not love him, and the next day, as Wilson waited at the train station and poured his heart out to Hattie's younger brother, he met Edward Welles, the man she did love and would soon marry. The incident plainly hurt Wilson. Hattie's letters to him were among the few pieces of correspondence in his life that this compulsive saver of papers would not keep. Two years later, he told Ellen Axson that Hattie had been "heartless," and he maintained, "I had been mistaken in thinking that she was *capable of loving*."[11]

Like other young men who make fools of themselves in love, Wilson was rationalizing. He soon got over his hurt feelings. A few months later, he told Bridges, "Of course I am not such a weakling as to allow myself to be unmanned even by a disappointment such as this," although he admitted that it had delayed his plans to begin practicing law. Yet he gave no sign of being in a hurry to hang out his shingle as a lawyer, and he told Bridges he was "intellectually busy in the same desultory manner as of old. I've read all sorts of books besides law books."[12]

Wilson also wrote his first book-length work at this time, which he called "Government by Debate." As the title suggests, he was revisiting the ground he had covered in "Cabinet Government" and the unpublished "Congressional Government." In fact, much of this work repeats his previous arguments and his Bagehot-derived observation that the Constitution "has had a great growth. It is now neither in theory or in fact what its framers are thought to have intended it to be." He did lay a new stress on "reason" as opposed to "passion," which would become a central element in his political thought. This stress on reason did not lead him down paths of conservatism, because he called for "regulation of its [America's] vast and innumerable industries" and "the restraint of monopolies." As a piece of writing, "Government by Debate" bounced between scholarly analysis and political exhortation and was long on rhetoric and short on specifics. Wilson was clearly having trouble making the shift from writing essays to writing a book. "Government by Debate" fell flat with publishers, three of which turned it down. A portion of the manuscript finally appeared as an article titled "Committee or Cabinet Government?" in the January 1884 issue of *The Overland Monthly*.[13]

By the time that magazine article appeared, Wilson's life had taken several significant turns. In May 1882, he began his law practice, in Atlanta. This city was the boomtown of the post–Civil War South, the capital of Georgia, and the unofficial but generally recognized capital of the "New South," where Henry Grady, the editor of its leading newspaper, the *Constitution*, beat the drum for the South's commercial and industrial renaissance. Wilson heartily endorsed the economic side of the New South vision, and he had earlier identified himself as a member of "that younger generation of Southern men who are just now coming to years of influence . . . [who are] full of the progressive spirit."[14] The impetus to move to Atlanta had come in January 1882, when Edward I. Renick, a classmate at Virginia, invited Wilson to share a law office and take a room in the boardinghouse where he lived. The arrangement worked well. They made a division of labor in which Renick did the office work and Wilson handled the court appearances. In October 1882, Wilson passed the Georgia bar examination with the highest score among the test takers, and he was admitted to practice in the federal district court the following February.

Unfortunately, the fledgling attorneys lacked work. Wilson argued only two or three cases in court during his time in Atlanta, and he and Renick had little other business. The two young men whiled away idle hours in the office reading Virgil's *Aeneid* aloud to each other, and Wilson read Tocqueville's *Democracy in America* and biographies of Alexander Hamilton and John C. Calhoun, in which he wrote marginal notes. "I allow myself my afternoons for writing," he told Bridges.[15] As an outlet for public speaking, he and Renick organized a branch of the New York Free Trade Club, at which they discussed questions of political economy and promoted opinions opposing tariff protection. Wilson went to observe sessions of the Georgia legislature a few times, but he made no effort to get involved in local politics or take part in election campaigns.

A fortuitous event allowed him to address a significant audience on a weighty subject. In September 1882, the Tariff Commission, an investigatory body created by Congress, held hearings in Atlanta. Covering the commission as a reporter for the New York *World* was a friend of Renick's, Walter Hines Page. This lanky, cigar-smoking North Carolina native, who was a year older than Wilson, arranged for him to testify before the commission. In his thirty-minute talk, the young lawyer called the tariff "one of the leading questions of political discussion" and advocated "a tariff for revenue merely." He doubted that he made much of an impression on the commissioners, but he was grateful for the exposure, particularly Page's report in the *World* that "[n]o argument of dignity was made to-day except by Mr. Woodrow Wilson."[16] That was a bit of puffery, but Page prided himself on being a talent spotter, and he marked Wilson as someone to watch and keep in touch with. Their paths would cross again, and they would play important roles in each other's lives.

Wilson could have enjoyed himself in Atlanta, but he did not. He evidently complained from the outset about his situation, because his father resumed writing letters of advice and admonition. Joseph Wilson counseled his son to overcome "your law-distaste" and exhorted him to "fight the future with a *brave* front not only but also with a smiling [one]." Wilson almost never argued with his father, but he lamented to Bridges "the dreadful drudgery which attends the initiation into our profession." His discontent grew to include his fellow lawyers and his newly adopted hometown. He might identify with the New South as an intellectual proposition, but confronting the reality of it and trying to make his way in

its heartland filled him with disgust. "Here the chief end of man is certainly to make money," Wilson told a Princeton classmate, "and money
cannot be made except by the most vulgar methods." Worse, he confessed
to a friend from Virginia, he found that "the practice of law, when conducted for purposes of gain, is antagonistic to the best interests of the
intellectual life," which was "the natural bent of my mind. . . . I can never
be happy unless I am enabled to lead an intellectual life; and who can lead
an intellectual life in ignorant Georgia?"[17]

In the spring of 1883, Wilson decided to abandon his law practice and
pursue graduate study in order to become a college professor. Leaving a
legal career for teaching had been on his mind even before he went to
Atlanta. He had mentioned it to Harriet Woodrow at the time of his ill-
fated proposal to her, and just after he moved to Atlanta, he told Bridges
that he wanted to go into college teaching. Bridges tried to talk him out of
the idea, warning him, as he recalled later, "that the material results of the
course you propose to follow appear even more slowly than in the law."
Still, the decision was a wrench. He believed he was turning his back on
his heartfelt dream of holding office. He claimed to Bridges that he was
not forsaking politics completely: "I want to make myself an *outside force in
politics.* No man can safely *enter* political life nowadays who has not an
independent fortune, or at least independent means of support: this I have
not: therefore the most I can hope to become is a speaker and writer of the
highest authority on political subjects. This I *may* become in a chair of
political science, with leisure and incentive to study, and with summer
vacations for travel and observation." The following fall, he told Ellen
Axson, "The law is more than ever before a jealous mistress. Whoever
thinks, as I thought, that he can practice law successfully and study history
and politics at the same time is wofully mistaken."[18]

Yearning to write and lead "an intellectual life" was what pulled him
away from the law. In the same letter to Ellen Axson, he confessed his
"unquenchable desire to excel" in both political and *"imaginative"* writing,
by which he meant "something (!) that will freshen the energies of tired
people and make the sad laugh and take heart again." College teaching
was not the only or necessarily the best alternative to the law for fulfilling
that desire. He had earlier told Bridges, "I sometimes find myself regretting that I too had not gone into journalism." Bridges had started writing
for the high-toned, influential magazine *The Nation,* and that kind of work
would have given Wilson greater opportunity to study, observe, write
about, and influence politics than a college professorship. But Wilson
shied away from journalism. He saw himself as a slow learner and method-

ical thinker who was not naturally given to ready observation and description. Conversely, college teaching attracted him because it would allow him to live in a milieu that he found conducive to "an intellectual life."[19]

Wilson may also have chosen college teaching because of his family's opinion. When he informed his father of his wishes early in 1883, Dr. Wilson urged him to stick with the law, but added, "I will not object to any decision you may come to, and will do my utmost to secure you a position." His parents sought advice from the family's arbiter in matters academic, James Woodrow, who urged that his nephew attend the graduate school at the Johns Hopkins University. The better colleges were increasingly looking for faculty from "the Johns Hopkins," James Woodrow explained, and a fellowship there would give their son excellent visibility in the changing job market.[20] When Wilson applied for a fellowship in April 1883, he was told that all of the slots for the next year had been filled; his father then agreed to pay his son's expenses.

Before Wilson left Atlanta, he made two further changes in his life. One was mundane, but it would have a big impact on the way he did his work. In June 1883, he bought his first typewriter, a Caligraph, which cost the substantial sum of $87, and thereby jumped aboard the technological bandwagon of the time. Typewriters had been on the market for less than a decade and did not yet feature either standard keyboards or common mechanisms for producing capital letters. Nonetheless, the typewriter gave Wilson another means with which to overcome his slowness in reading and writing, and he quickly learned to use it, typing with two fingers on each hand. In later years, he produced most of his correspondence, even intimate letters, on a succession of typewriters. He would also compose on the typewriter his manuscripts for publication and speeches that required a prepared text, often working from shorthand notes.[21]

The other big change in Wilson's life was that he had fallen in love again. On April 8, 1883, he met Ellen Louise Axson. "The first time I saw your face to note was in church," he recalled a few months later. It was a fitting place for them to meet, since she was the daughter of the Reverend Samuel Edward Axson, a friend and colleague of his father's and a member of a family that stood even higher than the Woodrows in Presbyterian circles. Wilson had gone to Rome, Georgia, to do legal work for his mother in a dispute over the estate of one of her brothers. On Sunday he attended the church where Ellen's father was minister. He probably did not pay much attention to the service because, he told Ellen later, "I remember thinking 'what a bright, pretty face; what splendid, mischievous, laughing eyes! I'll lay a wager that this demure little lady has lots of fun in her!'"

After the service, he further recounted, "I took another good look at you, and concluded that it would be a very clever plan to inquire your name and seek an introduction."[22]

If this was not love at first sight, it came close. Ellen Axson, who would celebrate her twenty-third birthday the following month, was an attractive young woman. She stood five feet three inches tall, weighed about 115 pounds, and had a slightly rounded face, dark blond hair, and haunting, expressive brown eyes. When Wilson called on the Axsons after the service, his first conversation with Ellen did not proceed beyond pleasantries because her father talked about church matters. The young man fared better on his next visit to Rome, at the end of May. He got Ellen to go for a carriage ride and a walk up a hill. "Passion," he later confessed, ". . . had pretty nearly gotten the better of [me] by the time we had climbed to the top of that hill." After this visit, he confided to his mother that he was in love with Ellen Axson and intended to ask her to marry him. On a walk during his next visit, he recalled, "I was quite conscious that I was very much in love with my companion, and I was desperately intent upon finding out what my chances were of winning her." He told her about his plans to be a teacher, including "the narrowness of my means," all "with a diplomatic purpose, in order to ascertain whether *she* was inclined to regard such an alliance as a very dreary and uninviting prospect for any maiden free to choose." Soon afterward, as they sat together in a hammock at a picnic, "I declared that you were the only woman I had ever met to whom I felt that I could open all my thoughts[.] I meant much more than I dared to say."[23]

Within the conventions that governed courtship between respectable middle-class people of the time, especially ministers' children, the young man made his intentions unmistakable. This time, Wilson was giving his heart to someone who was prepared to receive it. For her part, Ellen remembered feeling during their walk "a quiet little glow and thrill of admiration, tingling out of my very finger-tips," as she got her "first glimpse of your [Wilson's] aims in life," especially his "generous enthusiasm" about attempting to do great things and striving to be "one who could live the best and *fullest* life." Yet Ellen had a reputation among her female friends as a "man-hater." She had rejected at least three marriage proposals, in part because no man had yet come up to her standards. Her husband must be, she had once told a friend, "good, nice, handsome, splendid, delightful, intelligent and interesting." Woodrow Wilson filled the bill except in the matter of being handsome, but with his mustache and sideburns he cut an attractive figure.[24]

Ellen may have had other reasons for her reluctance to marry. She had a deep, searching mind and a complex personality. From childhood, she had shown great intelligence, excelling in school and leading her class at the Rome Female Seminary. Unlike Wilson, she had a flair for mathematics, as well as foreign languages, and she showed exceptional talent at drawing and painting. She also had a taste for philosophy and the deeper aspects of religious thought. Her dearest wish was to continue her education, but her father could not afford to send her to college, a circumstance that outraged her best friend, who told her, "Ellie, I feel *bound* to believe that you won't always live in Rome."[25]

Ellen was clearly expressing her own yearnings when she said she recognized that Wilson wanted to "live the best and *fullest* life." For her, such a life had seemed to grow even further out of reach when her mother, Margaret Jane Hoyt Axson, died in November 1881, soon after giving birth to her fourth child, a daughter. Ellen had lost the parent who understood her best and sympathized with her aspirations, and Samuel Axson's wife's death shattered his fragile mental composure. Showing signs of the severe depression that would later also afflict Ellen and two of her siblings, he was unable to work or cope with people for long periods of time. The burden of keeping the family together fell on Ellen, who now had to look after her father and her younger brothers, Stockton and Edward, who were fourteen and five. Her infant sister, Margaret (Madge), was put for the time being in the care of their mother's sister. In the midst of this ordeal of managing the household, watching over her increasingly unstable father, and looking after her brothers, Woodrow Wilson must have struck Ellen like a ray of hope. Even his poor financial prospects as a consequence of his going to graduate school may have seemed like an advantage, since the situation could allow her time to sort out her life.[26]

The romance between these two young Presbyterians had a happy though madcap ending. Wilson began to write serious, intimate letters to "Miss Ellie Lou." In July, he told her that "I had longed to meet some woman of my own age who had acquired a genuine love for intellectual pursuits without becoming bookish, without losing her feminine charm. . . . See, therefore, what a delightful lesson you have taught me!" He faced the problem of how and where to make his move. After pulling up stakes in Atlanta, he went to Wilmington and then accompanied his mother, brother, sister Annie, and her children to the mountains of North Carolina, planning to leave from there for Johns Hopkins at the middle of September. Ellen also went to North Carolina in early September, and Wilson desperately angled to get together with her so that he might have the chance to declare his love.[27]

The fateful encounter almost did not take place. Ellen's father's illness took a turn for the worse, and she decided to return to Rome. Her letters to Wilson about her change of plans went astray, and they met only by a coincidence. In order to return home, Ellen had to wait for several hours between trains in a hotel in Asheville on September 14. Wilson, who was to leave for Johns Hopkins two days later, chanced to be in Asheville that day. As he walked down the street where the hotel stood, he looked through a window and recognized Ellen by the way she wore her hair. Rushing into the hotel, he persuaded her to postpone her trip until he had to leave. The couple walked and talked and went for a drive in the mountains. Wilson took Ellen to meet his mother, and when the time came for him to leave, he told her that he loved her and asked her to marry him. Flustered, Ellen said yes. "I had no smallest idea how much I loved you," she wrote him a few days later, "until I found how wretched I was made at the thought of your leaving . . . and felt my heart give a great suffocating throb." For Wilson, there could have been no better send-off for his venture into "an intellectual life" and no sweeter token of the transformation signaled by his newly adopted name. Ellen's letters to him would now begin "My darling Woodrow."[28]

Journeying northward to Baltimore in September 1883 to begin graduate study at Johns Hopkins was another big change for Wilson. Baltimore, with around 360,000 residents, was much larger than any city in the South and had a population that was mixed in religion and ethnicity as well as race. Not yet a decade old in 1883, Hopkins, as it was commonly called, was modeled on a German university and occupied a few drab edifices in downtown Baltimore. The student body consisted largely of men pursuing the Ph.D. degree in academic subjects. Wilson made friends with his fellow graduate students in the seminary in history and political science and at the boardinghouse where he lived, went to the theater, and under Ellen's influence, took an interest in the visual arts for the first time. The university drew a stream of visiting intellectual luminaries, of whom the most interesting to Wilson was James Bryce, a professor at Oxford and a member of Parliament in Britain. He told Ellen that he marveled at the "strength and dash and mastery about the man which are captivating."[29] This was the first of what would turn out to be several encounters with Bryce over the next four decades.

The seminary in history and political science offered Wilson an outlet for public speaking. Students and faculty gathered for weekly Friday-evening meetings around a large table covered with a red tablecloth in what Wilson described to Ellen as "a large cheerful room," during which students read papers "upon special subjects political and social." From the beginning, he shone in those sessions. The seminary also staged debates on current issues, including one in which Wilson argued against a Republican-sponsored bill in Congress for the provision of federal aid to public schools, particularly in the South. The minutes of the seminary noted that he called it "both *unconstitutional . . .* and *politically inexpedient.*" That was a good characterization of his position: the critical words were *politically inexpedient,* and he almost certainly stressed what he considered the unwise nature of the proposal more than the constitutional limitations. His mostly northern fellow students teased Wilson about his southern background and views by greeting him as Colonel.[30]

Once more, Wilson could have been happier than he was. The fault again lay more with him than with the institution, but not entirely. Six weeks after he arrived at Hopkins, he told Ellen that he wanted "to get a special training in historical research and an insight into the most modern literary and political thoughts and methods" so that he might achieve his "ambition to become an invigorating and enlightening power in the world of political thought and [that] a master in some of the less serious branches of literary art may be the more easy of accomplishment." But he had discovered that no one at Hopkins seemed to care about how to express thoughts: "*Style* is not much studied here; *ideas* are supposed to be everything—their vehicle comparatively nothing." He was balking at the ruling intellectual dispensation of Johns Hopkins—the German model of rigorous, painstaking "scientific" research in all fields, based on the belief that the steady, progressive accumulation of knowledge would yield precise, measurable standards and explanations. He told Ellen that his professors "wanted to set everybody under their authority to working on what they called 'institutional history,' . . . and other rumaging [*sic*] work of a like dry kind, which seemed very tiresome in comparison with the grand excursions amongst imperial policies which I had planned for myself." He also disliked carrying a heavy load of courses on top of work for the seminary, admitting to Ellen, "I have a distinct dread (partly instinctive and partly instilled by my home training) of too much reading."[31]

Wilson likewise had scant respect for his professors. The three faculty members in his field were Herbert Baxter Adams, who had earned a doctorate at Heidelberg before becoming Hopkins's first professor of history and political science; Richard T. Ely, who also held a doctorate from Heidelberg and worked in economics; and John Franklin Jameson, who had just received Hopkins's first Ph.D. in history. Wilson quickly took their measure, telling Ellen in November, "I have been much disappointed to find that the department of history and politics is more weakly manned as regards its corps of instructors than any other department of the Univer-

sity." Wilson found Adams "insincere and superficial," Ely "full of information but apparently much too full to have any movement which is not
an impulse," and Jameson "merely a satellite" of Adams.[32] Further contact
did not improve those impressions. Wilson's judgment was not wide of the
mark. Adams and Ely subsequently built reputations as academic organizers, whereas only Jameson would do much original work as a scholar.

Physical separation from his fiancée also hurt him keenly. He settled
again for an epistolary romance, but because he and Ellen had already
committed themselves to each other, he could write freely, frankly, and
revealingly to her, and he did so to a greater degree than he would to anyone else in his life. During the three decades of their engagement and
marriage, the couple would write more than 1,400 letters to each other—
the most remarkable set of letters between a president and his spouse,
except for the correspondence between John and Abigail Adams. They
usually wrote letters to each other every day or two; this period before
they were married, between September 1883 and June 1885, yielded well
over a third of their letters (306 by Wilson and 280 by Ellen).

As an engaged couple, they wrote about many things—family, friends,
respective doings, art, music, physical surroundings, hopes, dreams, plans,
thoughts. But from first to last, these letters were expressions of love.
"Why, my darling, I can't tell you how completely I am yours, in my every
thought," Wilson declared in his first letter from Baltimore. "I did not
know myself how much I loved you until I found out that you love me."
Ellen—who soon insisted that he call her that instead of Ellie Lou, which
she disliked—responded, "*I love you*. Ah, my darling, I have no words—
will never find them—to tell how much; nor how very, very happy it
makes me to hear you say—and repeat it—that you love me." Each one's
tone of passionate love for the other never faltered. In her last letter
before their wedding, Ellen quoted from one of Elizabeth Barrett Browning's *Sonnets from the Portuguese* and avowed, "When I feel that you give
me such a love as that, my heart is flooded with a deep peace—a perfect
joy in loving and . . . being loved, such as no other thought can give."[33]

Since Wilson seemed more comfortable with the written word, his
letters were usually longer than hers, although the literary quality of her
letters does not suffer in comparison. At least twice a week during his first
two months at Hopkins, he sent her letters that covered many pages with
his neat handwriting. The longest and most revealing of these is dated
October 30, 1883. Avowing that "there can be no greater delight in my
life, my love, than making you the keeper [of] all my secrets, the sharer of
all my hopes, *because I am sure of your love*," he filled nineteen pages about
his "*object*" in studying at Hopkins, his original political ambition, his dis-

appointment with the law, his settling for "becoming an *outside* force in politics," his literary aspirations ("an unquenchable desire to excel in two distinct and almost opposite kinds of writing: political and *imaginative*"), his description of the meetings of the seminary, his assessment of his own abilities, and his mixed desires and doubts about "reaching the heights to which I aspire." He said that writing "this profuse epistle . . . had done me lots of good. I've worked off any amount of stored-up steam."[34]

Some of Wilson's discontent found a constructive outlet when he went to see Professor Adams and, as he told Ellen, "made a clean breast" of his distaste for "institutional" research. To his surprise, Adams "received my confidence with sympathy . . . and bade me go on with my 'constitutional' studies." Wilson began research for the project he really wanted to undertake—a book about Congress. "My desire and ambition are," he told Ellen, "to treat the American constitution as Mr. Bagehot (do you remember Mr. Bagehot, about whom I talked to you one night on the veranda at Asheville?—) has treated the English constitution," although he admitted, "I am not vain enough to expect to produce anything so brilliant or so valuable as Bagehot's book." In January 1884, Wilson had to interrupt writing this new work in order to make an emergency visit to Ellen in Savannah. Her father's mental state had apparently turned violent, forcing the Axsons to commit him to a state asylum. After the visit, Wilson returned to Baltimore doubly determined to write his book and marry Ellen as soon as he could.[35]

The nine months from January through September 1884 would give him the most concentrated, least interrupted, most satisfying experience of writing he ever had. Evidently not yet completely comfortable composing directly on the typewriter, he first wrote and revised a draft in longhand and then typed a copy on his Caligraph. In early April, he submitted some chapters to the Boston publishing house Houghton Mifflin, which gave an encouraging though noncommittal response. In May, he read parts of those chapters to the seminary and submitted them as part of his fellowship application, which was successful this time. He wrote the last three chapters over the summer at his parents' home in Wilmington.[36]

In early October 1884, Wilson sent the revised manuscript to Houghton Mifflin. On November 26, after what seemed to him an interminable wait, the publishers accepted the book. "They have actually offered me as good terms as if I were already a well-known writer!" he exulted to Ellen. "The success is of such proportions as almost to take my breath away—it has distanced my biggest hopes." By mid-December, he was reading proofs, and on January 23, 1885, he received the first bound copies of the book, one of which he immediately sent to Ellen. "It is a very nicely gotten up, and attractive looking book, is it not?" she wrote back. "It's truly delightful to behold it—almost as delightful as to read it. It seems to me, darling, that it sounds better than ever 'in print.' The style is really wonderful; not the most fascinating novel could 'hold' one more closely." Lovers are prone to exaggerate, but Ellen did not overestimate her fiancé's book by much. *Congressional Government* would be the best book that Wilson ever wrote. Some people thought that this first book by an unknown twenty-eight-year-old was the feat of a prodigy, but it was not. Wilson had been working on this subject for more than five years, and he had found his voice and viewpoint in ways that he had not been able to do before. Rereading Bagehot's *English Constitution* during the summer of 1883 had helped, as had his successful wooing of Ellen Axson—requited love had concentrated his mind wonderfully.[37]

Congressional Government has a different tone from that of his earlier efforts. "I have abandoned the evangelical for the exegetical—so to speak!" he told Bridges. From its opening sentences, *Congressional Government* purports to present a dispassionate look at the American system. "The most striking contrast in modern politics is not between presidential and monarchical governments," Wilson asserted, "but between Congressional and Parliamentary governments. Congressional government is Committee government; Parliamentary government is government by a responsible Cabinet Ministry." Elucidating the contrast between these two systems is the "chief aim" of the book, which Wilson pursues through the next 330 pages. He briskly argues that the American system of checks and balances has grown outmoded, that the government is a living organism in which the Constitution is "only the sap-centre," that the major development was centralization of power in Congress at the expense of both the states and the other branches of the federal government, and that this centralization stemmed from the ways in which "the whole face of that world has changed."[38]

In his treatment of the House of Representatives, Wilson again painted his portrait of a body dominated by standing committees that meet in secret and stifle meaningful debate on the floor, but he leavened that familiar mix of criticisms with a more extensive comparison than anyone had yet made between the ways of Congress and the British and French parliamentary practices. He broke fresh ground when he contrasted the methods by which Congress and Parliament handle the tasks of raising revenue and funding executive departments and when he described the Senate. Rejecting what he regarded as an excess of both condemnation and praise of that body, he judged senators to be no better than congressmen because they all rise out of the same pool of talent: "No stream can be purer than its sources." He regretted that the Senate was not spawning "a new order of statesmanship to suit the altered conditions of government," and he argued that it also suffered from domination by committees, absence of debate, lack of party leadership, and divorce from executive responsibility.[39]

Another fresh contribution was his consideration of the executive branch. The president, in Wilson's view, falls victim to the same fundamental flaw as the houses of Congress. "The business of the President, occasionally great, is usually not much above routine. Most of the time it is *mere* administration, mere obedience of directions from the masters of policy, the Standing Committees." This subordinate role is "the practical result of the piecing of authority, the cutting of it up into small bits," which fragments responsibility. "*Power and strict accountability for its use* are the essential constituents of good government," Wilson declared. "The best rulers are always those to whom great power is intrusted in such a manner as to make them feel that they will surely be abundantly honored and recompensed for a just and patriotic use of it, and to make them know that nothing can shield them from full retribution for every abuse of it."[40] It sounded as if he was arguing for a stronger presidency, but he did not say so directly.

Wilson did not entirely forsake evangelism for exegesis. At the end, he argued that the demands of physical and economic progress require still greater and more efficient centralization of power. Therein lay the problem: "As at present constituted, the federal government lacks strength because its powers are divided, lacks promptness because its processes are roundabout, lacks efficiency because its responsibility is indistinct and its action without competent direction." The cure lay in taking a leaf from British practice and requiring those who talked in the legislature to execute their policies. Wilson did not think such a result would be easy to achieve in America, and he closed with a call for "fearless criticism," scrutiny "without sentiment," and assessment "by the standards of common sense."[41]

The book's reception exceeded Wilson's wildest dreams. Some critical, even hostile, reviews dismissed it as long on rhetoric and short on solutions, but there were few of those. The most gratifying review came in *The Nation*, from Gamaliel Bradford, an influential political writer whom Wilson admired and read regularly. Bradford called *Congressional Government* "one of the most important books, dealing with political subjects, which have ever issued from the American press." He found the book, which was "evidently modeled on Mr. Bagehot's 'English Constitution,'" so good that "it will, though the praise is so high as to be almost extravagant, bear comparison to that inestimable work." In the longer view, *Congressional Government* came in for additional criticism and regard. A year after its publication, *The Atlantic Monthly* published an article by A. Lawrence Lowell, a Boston lawyer and part-time instructor at Harvard, who took exception to Wilson's borrowing from British models and castigated him for not appreciating the need to restrain the power of the majority. Those two points—misplaced Anglophilia and unchecked majoritarianism— formed the main lines of attack on *Congressional Government* for several years after its publication.[42]

Wilson responded to those criticisms with good-humored silence, although he did stick to his guns in prefaces to later editions of the book. In the case of his critic in *The Atlantic*, he took direct action. As Lowell recalled, "A few weeks later there appeared at my office a tall, lantern-jawed young man just my age. He greeted me with the words: 'I'm Woodrow Wilson. I've come to heal a quarrel, not make one.'" He availed himself of *The Atlantic*'s offer to respond to Lowell's criticism: he insisted that the written Constitution, though useful in fostering "conservatism" to check public opinion, did not make the situation in the United States fundamentally different from that in Britain, and he continued to call for responsible party government. "The grave social and economic problems," Wilson argued, "now putting themselves forward as the result of the tremendous growth of our population, and the consequent sharp competition for the means of livelihood indicated that our system is already aging, and that any clumsiness, looseness, or irresponsibility in governmental action must prove a source of grave and increasing peril."[43]

The early critics were not particularly perceptive about the book's shortcomings. The allegation of Anglophilia did not stick because Wilson simply measured Congress and Parliament by standards of efficiency and accountability. The charge of majoritarianism carried greater weight. At the time, however—given persistent inertia, divided party control, and gridlock on Capitol Hill—that did not seem like much of a danger. A stronger criticism was that in his analysis he had mistaken the political deadlock between the major parties and fumbling over old and new issues for endemic structural flaws. Those conditions would soon change, first with the Republicans' imposition of party discipline in the House under Speaker Thomas B. "Czar" Reed in 1889 and then with the major party realignment over economic issues in 1896. Actually, Wilson observed that the present state of affairs had come to pass as a result of changing conditions and that the political system was an evolving, ever-adapting organism. When he stressed party discipline and leadership as cures for current ills, he was anticipating what would soon come to pass.

It was and remains a remarkable book. In the century and a quarter after its publication, *Congressional Government* would never go out of print. Part of the book's longevity has obviously sprung from its author's becoming president of the United States, but there is more to it than that. In *Congressional Government*, Wilson put his finger on enduring problems engendered by the separation of powers and the fragmentation of responsibility in the American system. Masterful Speakers of the House such as Reed, Joseph G. Cannon, and Sam Rayburn might periodically tame that rambunctious chamber, but entrenched committee chairs would limit even their ability to impose discipline. The Senate would fare even worse; it would be plagued by seniority and virtually limitless debate and brought in line only rarely through leadership of genius, as with Lyndon Johnson.

Wilson's achievement was all the more remarkable because of the way he wrote the book. He never made the short trip from Baltimore to Washington to observe Congress in person and would not set foot in the Capitol until 1898. This lack of curiosity seems strange because he had gone to observe the legislature in Georgia and had attended campaign events there and in North Carolina as recently as the summer before the publication of *Congressional Government*. Lowell later believed he had an explanation when he claimed that Wilson "lacked a scientific mind" and saw everything "through the haze of his own preconceptions." That judgment contained a kernel of truth. Wilson admitted to Ellen shortly after the book's publication, "I have no patience for the tedious toil of what is known as 'research'; I have a passion for interpreting great thoughts to the world."[44]

Yet it is doubtful whether firsthand observation and more primary research would have improved *Congressional Government*. Ironically, for all his worship of British empiricism and disdain for "literary theory," Wilson followed the path that he professed to scorn. Though not exactly a theorist, he did belong to the class of thinkers who take an idea and develop it. He recognized and regretted that he worked that way. "The fault of my mind is that it is creative, without being patient and docile in learning *how* to create," he told Ellen. He likened himself to a pianist who did not like to learn music or a soldier who wanted to lead without learning how to follow. This approach to scholarship also helps to explain why Wilson never wrote as good a book again. With *Congressional Government*, he had gone about as far as he could go with the inspiration from Bagehot. In order to do other work of this caliber, he would need a new inspiration.[45]

Life did not stand still while Wilson was writing his book and basking in the glory of its reception. The Axson family's ordeal had worsened in the spring of 1884, and Ellen's situation looked grim. Confinement in the Georgia state mental hospital had not helped her father, and his deterioration raised the question of what would become of his four children. Only Ellen was in a position to contribute to their support, which she decided to do by seeking a teaching job. The prospect filled Wilson with chagrin. He wished "most earnestly to keep my darling from its wearing, harassing trials," and he bemoaned that "I have never yet been of any use to anyone: I have yet to become a bread-winner." He wanted to marry Ellen immediately, but his father advised against it and admonished, "Imitate her, my son, in the sacrifice she is making for independence."[46]

Wilson tried to do that. Through his sister Marion, who was married to Anderson Ross Kennedy, a Presbyterian minister in Little Rock, Arkansas, he learned of a possible opening at the University of Arkansas. Wilson told Ellen he did not like the university's being "*co-educational*, admitting women to its classes, and even to its faculty," and going for this post would also mean taking a "foot-hold of places lower down" in the academic world, but "a good offer is not to be despised whencesoever it comes." Ellen knew what he craved, and she discouraged him from going to Arkansas. In any event, the prospect of a professorship there fell through in early summer. Then a turn of events brought both tragedy and salvation to Ellen and her siblings. On May 28, 1884, Samuel Axson died suddenly in the state mental hospital, probably a suicide. The news shook Ellen so badly that she told Wilson, "I sometimes wish I could go to sleep and never, never wake again." Her fiancé rushed to Georgia as soon as he could get away from Hopkins and spent two weeks with her and her seventeen-year-old brother Stockton, whom he met for the first time. Years later, Stockton Axson recalled that his sister's fiancé "was so very cordial that I lost my heart to him at once."[47] This was the beginning of what would become the closest and longest-lasting friendship of Wilson's life.

The tragedy had a true silver lining. Samuel Axson left his children an estate of $12,000, a substantial sum at that time. When Ellen learned about the inheritance, her brother recalled, she blurted out, "Now that we are *rich*, you can go to college and I can go to the Art League." For Stockton, college meant Davidson, while Ellen intended to go to New York to study at the Art Students League so that she might develop her talent as a painter under the best possible tutelage, a decision that Wilson reacted to with mixed feelings. Since he was going to spend another year at Hopkins, he was in no position to object, but he confessed that he was disappointed by "the indefinite postponement of our marriage. . . . I cannot live or work at my best until I have, not your love only, but your self, your companionship, as well."[48] He came as close as propriety permitted to confessing his sexual desires.

The couple spent two weeks together in September and early October when Ellen stayed with the Wilsons in Wilmington and he traveled with her to New York, with a sightseeing stopover in Washington. In New York, Wilson escorted Ellen to her boardinghouse. She reveled in her work at the Art Students League, and she enjoyed New York's cultural attractions, especially the museums and theater. Those months formed a happy interlude in her life as she developed a new sense of herself and her artistic gifts.

Yet she felt no pangs about giving up this independent life for marriage. After Wilson spent a week with her in New York over Christmas in 1884, he nerved himself to ask whether she really wanted to abandon it to marry him: "I *hate* selfishness, it hurts me more than I can tell you to think that I am asking you to give up what has formed so much of your life and constituted so much of your delight." Ellen put his fears to rest: "Sweetheart, I would never give you a divided allegiance; I owe you my little *all* of love, of life and service, and it is all my joy to give it. Believe me, dear, it is an absolutely pure joy—there is in it *no* alloy, I have *never* felt the *slightest* pang of regret for what I must 'give up.' *Don't* think there is any sacrifice involved, my darling, I assure you again there is *none whatever.*"[49]

Wilson was right when he told Ellen that he could not work at his best apart from her. Except for the success of *Congressional Government*, his second year at Hopkins pleased him even less than the first, and he was a bit at loose ends. Even before the book was accepted for publication, he decided not to try for a doctorate. He told Ellen he would "profit much more substantively from a line of reading of my own choosing," although he did concede "that a degree would render me a little more *marketable.*" With another graduate student, he did join a collaborative project initiated by Richard Ely to produce a textbook to be titled "History of Political Economy in the United States," a collection of accounts of American writers on political economy. Wilson plunged into the work, and by May 1885 he had completed his section of the volume—seventy legal-size pages on seven political economists. The book never would be published, most likely because Ely never wrote his part of it.[50]

Wilson was also looking for a job, which turned out to be easier than he anticipated. His fondest wish was to go back to Princeton as a member of the faculty, but nothing opened up there. In the meantime, another institution snapped him up, a newly founded and well-publicized college for women scheduled to begin classes in the fall of 1885: Bryn Mawr. Although the prospect of teaching there excited Wilson, Ellen raised the inevitable question: "*But* do you think there *is* much reputation to be made in a *girls school,*—or [if] it please you, a 'woman's college'?" He responded: "I have none of the same objections . . . that I have to a *co-educational* institution: and the question of the higher education of women is certain to be settled in the affirmative, in this country at least, whether my sympathy be enlisted or not." He would, "of course, *prefer* to teach young men," but Bryn Mawr offered better opportunities "than elsewhere for original work: and, after all, it's my *writing*, not my teaching, that must win me my reputation."[51] Wilson accepted an offer at the rank of associate in history with a salary of $1,500. Herbert Adams also held out the prospect of a part-time lectureship at Johns Hopkins, which would pay an additional $500.

Yet Wilson was having second thoughts about academic life. Before the Bryn Mawr prospect arose, he told Ellen, "I want to be near the world. I want to *know* the world; to retain all my sympathy with it—even with its crudenesses. I am *afraid* of being made a mere student." Later, he told her he worried about "avoiding the danger peculiar to a professor's position, the danger of being accounted a *doctrinaire*. I must make all my writings so conspicuously practical that the sneer will be palpably absurd." Now that the Democrats had regained the presidency with Grover Cleveland's victory in the 1884 election, he made inquiries about a position in the State Department. Journalism offered another possibility. In March 1885, the editor of a New York newspaper approached him about working as a Washington correspondent. He admitted to Ellen that he was intrigued by the "chance such work would give me for my favourite studies, in Washington, the place of places for the purpose."[52]

That journalistic feeler turned out to be a last temptation before Wilson entered academic life. He rejected that path, he explained to Ellen, because writing "strictly scientific study of institutions" was the only "field of journalism that I care to enter ever. . . . I should *like* an occupation which would leave me foot-loose, living on my wits, as it were." But his internal voice of prudence said no: "This excellent, conservative mentor says reprovingly, 'Wilson keep your head! Don't let your love of active affairs tempt you to hover on their outskirts. You know well enough that you can't *enter* them ever. If you understood the practical side of government and extracted a bit of its philosophy as a college pupil, there's no reason why you should not hope to do more and better of the same as a professor if only you keep out of scholastic ruts and retain your sympathetic consciousness of the conditions of the practical world.'"[53]

One last, happy task remained before Wilson could embark on his career as a professor. At the end of May 1885, he and Ellen separately made their way southward. On the evening of June 24, 1885, they were married in Savannah, Georgia. Out of respect for her father's recent death, the ceremony took place in the manse rather than in the sanctuary of her grandfather's church, with no flowers or music and only immediate family and a few friends in attendance. As befitted this union of two distinguished Presbyterian families, Ellen's grandfather Isaac Stockton Axson and Joseph Ruggles Wilson jointly performed the ceremony.[54] When the couple journeyed northward in September 1885 to Bryn Mawr, the new Mrs. Woodrow Wilson was two months pregnant, and her twenty-eight-year-old husband was eager to get on with the business of living.

3

PROFESSOR

When he began his teaching career at Bryn Mawr College in September 1885, Woodrow Wilson did not hold the title of professor—that would come two years later—but he would be a professor for the next twenty-five years. The Bryn Mawr campus occupied a former farm and as yet had only a few buildings. After spending a month at a boardinghouse, the Wilsons moved into a frame house newly built for faculty and their families. Bryn Mawr's first students, thirty-six members of the class of 1889 and five graduate "fellows," arrived on September 23, 1885. The faculty numbered only seven, five men and two women, all of whom held a Ph.D. except Wilson.[1]

The teaching load was heavy. Wilson had to offer all the courses in history and political science, five each semester, but he threw himself into his work with gusto. Even in areas where he was not well prepared, he declined to slip into well-worn grooves and developed his own approaches, stressing individuals, governments, and comparisons. Wilson proved from the outset to be a lucid, engaging lecturer. Decades later, a former student remembered him as "the most interesting and inspiring college lecturer I have ever heard" and others commented on his smiles and jokes, which were often lost on earnest students, but one former student believed "that he did not enjoy teaching young women" and seemed to see them "not as of a *lower* sort of intelligence so much as of a *different* sort from himself." It is not clear whether such views affected his teaching. He did complain to Bridges, "I very much fear that teaching young women (who never challenge my authority in any position I may take) is slowly relaxing my mental muscle." But he also told a friend from Virginia that he felt "thankful for so comfortable a berth—where the classes are docile, intelligent, and willing,—where the administration is honest, straightforward, and liberal." In his journal, he noted about student passivity, "Perhaps it is some of it due to undergraduateism, not all to femininity."[2]

Any restiveness Wilson felt at Bryn Mawr stemmed from his not feeling fully reconciled to academic life. After a year of teaching, he told his Princeton friend Charlie Talcott that he felt "the disadvantages of the *closet*. I want to keep close to the *practical* and the *practicable* in politics . . . in order that I may study *affairs*, rather than doctrine." His lack of total commitment to academic life had an impact on his dealings with graduate students. Two of the graduate fellows who studied with him, Jane Marie Bancroft and Lucy Maynard Salmon, had unhappy experiences, in part because he believed he had to dominate them and they did not want to be dominated by him or anybody else. Both women were older than Wilson; Bancroft was already a professor of French and dean of women at Northwestern University and held a Ph.D. in history from Syracuse University. Salmon, an experienced teacher, later told Wilson's first biographer that she had resolved "to express no opinions, to be entirely passive, and colorless, and to be a good listener." That was hard for Salmon, who judged him "singularly ill-adapted to teaching women," but she admitted that the real fault lay in his not having "an inquiring, adventurous mind, . . . never going out into the bypaths and seeking new facts or treasures."[3] Salmon was committed to scholarly research and inquiry, and Wilson was not.

Wilson liked the undergraduates at Bryn Mawr, although he told Stockton Axson that he had had to shave off his mustache so that they could see his mouth and know whether he was serious or joking. As a married man with a pregnant wife, he did not socialize outside the classroom as much as the bachelor professors did, but he did take up tennis, playing with students and other faculty members. The small rooms and lack of privacy in the faculty house bothered the young couple, who found the situation unsatisfactory for the birth of their child. In April 1886, Ellen journeyed to the home of her aunt in Gainesville, Georgia, arriving only a day before the birth of her daughter, who was christened Margaret, for Ellen's mother, and Woodrow, for Wilson's mother's family. Ellen stayed in Georgia through the rest of the academic year and into the summer, when Wilson joined her and saw his daughter for the first time. By the beginning of 1887, Ellen was pregnant again, and in the summer the Wilsons returned to Gainesville, where their second daughter was born in August. They christened her Jessie, for Wilson's mother, and again Woodrow. When they returned to Bryn Mawr in the fall of 1887, they moved into a rented Baptist parsonage near the campus. The Wilson household now included Ellen's eleven-year-old brother Eddie and her cousin Mary Hoyt, who would attend Bryn Mawr.4

Despite the heavy teaching load, Wilson signed a contract with the textbook publisher D. C. Heath to write a college survey of politics and government. He also changed his mind and decided to try for the doctorate. Professor Adams again proved accommodating by not requiring Wilson to return for further classes at Hopkins; in May 1886, Wilson, after sparse and sporadic preparation, passed the examinations easily. "Hurrah— a thousands times hurrah," he exulted to Ellen, "—*I'm through, I'm through*—the degree is secured! Oh, the relief of it!" With the Ph.D. in hand, he got a three-year contract to serve as associate professor at a salary of $2,000 and a promise from the Bryn Mawr administration to lighten his teaching load by appointing an assistant to take over some of his courses. Wilson had wanted a doctoral degree mainly because he still had his sights set on Princeton. In the spring of 1886, he spoke at a Princeton alumni banquet in New York, where he bored his listeners by talking about the college as a "gymnasium" for exercising "men's minds." The incident made some people at Princeton think that Wilson was too heavy and dull to teach there, but he continued to conspire with Bridges to gauge his chances at Old Nassau.5 In 1887, Adams finally came through with a part-time appointment at Johns Hopkins to lecture on comparative politics and public administration.

During his third year at Bryn Mawr, despite the promotion, the pay raise, and the promise of an assistant, Wilson began complaining about his students and expressing renewed doubts about academic life. Because women were barred from voting and holding office almost everywhere in the United States, he declared, "[l]ecturing to young women of the present generation on the history and principles of politics is about as appropriate and profitable as would be lecturing to stone-masons on the evolution of fashion and dress."6 He still sympathized with women's aspirations for greater independence and education. He and Ellen had brought her cousin Mary Hoyt to study at Bryn Mawr, and Mary would stay on to finish her degree after the Wilsons departed. The Wilsons' three daughters would attend women's colleges, and when Jessie grew dissatisfied at Women's College of Maryland, she considered transferring to Bryn Mawr, with her father's support.

All the while, Wilson's reputation was growing in academic circles. James Bryce invited him to contribute a chapter to his forthcoming book, *The American Commonwealth;* he declined because he did not think he knew enough about the suggested subject, woman suffrage. In June 1888, Wesleyan University in Middletown, Connecticut, offered him a full professorship at a higher salary, $2,500, with a lighter teaching load and an arrangement to continue his lecturing at Hopkins.[7]

Accepting the offer from Wesleyan required Wilson to get out of his contract at Bryn Mawr. He told the president, James E. Rhoads, "[M]y duty to my little family makes it even more imperative that I should seek rapid advancement in my profession in point of salary, amount and character of work, &c." He also claimed that Bryn Mawr's failure to hire an assistant for him meant that his contract was no longer binding. Rhoads and the Bryn Mawr trustees tried to hold him to the contract; he responded by consulting a lawyer, and the trustees relented. Wilson felt triumphant as he prepared to move. "I have for a long time been hungry for a class of *men*," he told Bridges.[8]

Wilson also looked forward to having more time for his writing. Yet in spite of Bryn Mawr's teaching load and his marriage and new fatherhood, he had completed most of the government textbook and produced essays on various subjects. In one essay, "The Study of Administration," he pioneered the new field of political science that later came to be called public administration—the study of how laws are administered after they are made. "It is getting harder to *run* a constitution than to frame one," he asserted. Unlike Prussia and Napoleonic France, where administration had developed naturally under absolutist regimes, Britain and the United States faced the problem of balancing accountability to public opinion with the creation of a strong, efficient civil service. That would require borrowing from alien political cultures, but, he argued, "[i]f I see a murderous fellow sharpening a knife cleverly, I can borrow his way of sharpening a knife without borrowing his probable intent to commit murder."[9]

Next, Wilson turned to other and, to his mind, bigger questions. In December 1885, he wrote in a note to himself, "I have conceived the (perhaps whimsical) purpose of combining Montesquieu, Burke, and Bagehot" and, thereby, achieving a "SYNTHESIS" of thought about the nature of democracy. He tried out some of his ideas in an essay in which he called democracy a doctrine that had never "arrogated to itself absolute truth . . . but was eventually convicted of being only relatively true, and nutritious only under certain conditions and for certain persons." Democracy worked both in "little Switzerland and big America," though not in France or Spain or Latin America, because it was "a form of state life for a nation in the adult age of its political development." In May 1886, he sent Horace Scudder at Houghton Mifflin a twelve-page letter in which he outlined "a very ambitious" program, noting and commenting on topics he wished to cover: "*Political Morality* . . . the democratic state is . . . a moral person with a very peculiar, delicate constitution"; "*Political*

Progress. What . . . *is* political progress . . . and how can its conditions be supplied?"; *"Political Expediency.* A big subject, and as important as big, hitherto largely neglected, save from the boss's point of view"; *"Political Prejudice* . . . its *good* offices as well as its bad"; and, finally, *"Practical Politics."* He intended to develop this "vast subject" over several years and eventually distill his best thoughts into a single volume.[10]

That was an ambitious plan, especially coming from a twenty-nine-year-old scholar who was then only on the verge of receiving his Ph.D. To his Princeton friend Hiram Woods, Wilson confessed "an intellectual self-confidence, possibly out of all due proportion to my intellectual strength, which has made me feel that in matters in which I had qualified myself to speak I could never be any man's follower." He needed such self-confidence because research and writing did not come easily to him. "Composition is no child's play with me," he told Ellen. "I can't write just what comes into my head: I have to stop and perfect both expression and thought."[11] After they married, Ellen helped him by reading not only his manuscripts but also foreign texts. With her gift for languages, she quickly learned German, and she read, selected, and translated material for him.

Looking at current affairs, he expounded on the need for party realignment in order to come to grips with such pressing issues as the tariff and monetary standards, and he claimed that "the difference between democracy and socialism is not an essential difference, but only a practice difference." In using government to address social and economic problems, socialists rushed in where democrats trod warily, but with the growth of huge corporations, he asked, "[M]ust not government lay aside all timid scruple and boldly make itself an agency for social reform as well as for political control?" He went further in his lectures at Johns Hopkins in 1888: "Government does not stop with the protection of life, liberty, and property, as some have suggested; it goes on to serve every convenience of society. . . . The state is *not a body corporate,—it is a body politic*; and rules of good business are not always rules of good politics. . . . Business-*like* the administration of government should be—but it is not business. *It is organic life.*"[12]

This sympathetic attitude toward socialism presaged an important breakthrough in Wilson's political thought. Also at Hopkins in 1888, he divided the nature of government into two functions, constituent and ministrant. Constituent functions are *"necessary to the civic organization of society,—which are not optional* with government, even in the eyes of the strictest *laissez-faire."* Ministrant functions are activities undertaken "by way of advancing the general interests of society,—functions which *are* optional, being necessary only according to standards of *convenience* or *expediency.*"[13] This definition of the functions of government allowed Wilson to move beyond asking *how* power worked so that he could begin to ask *why* political systems take the forms that they do. His identification and delineation of constituent and ministrant functions would provide the basic structure for the textbook published in 1889 as *The State*, and his latitudinarian, relativistic views about the permissible activities of government would receive further elaboration in that book. Likewise, his analogy likening political life to organic life would provide the basis for his interpretation of the growth and functions of states through the lens of evolutionary thought.

Another significant change in Wilson's life occurred on April 15, 1888, when his mother died. He left at once for Clarksville, Tennessee, where his parents had been living, and spent a week with his father, brother, and sisters. From there he wrote grief-filled letters to Ellen, in which he recalled his mother and his childhood with her, including his depiction of himself as "a laughed-at 'mamma's boy.'" Work helped Wilson get through this anguished time, as did the move a few months later to Wesleyan, where he again quickly demonstrated his prowess as a lecturer. "I can see him now with his hands forward, the tips of his fingers just touching the table, his face animated," one student later remembered, and another recalled, "He had a contagious interest—his eyes flashed."[14] At Wesleyan, Wilson could concentrate more on his specialty, and he used chapters of *The State* in his lectures. Outside the classroom, he organized the Wesleyan House of Commons, a debating society modeled on the ones he had participated in at Princeton and Virginia, and he found an outlet for his love of sports by helping to coach Wesleyan's fledgling football and baseball teams.

As southerners, he and Ellen had felt some trepidation in venturing so far north, but the college and the town suited them. With the larger income they were able to rent a bigger house—and Ellen could gather more of the Axson family together again under one roof. Already living with them was her brother Eddie, and in 1889 her brother Stockton joined them, enrolling at Wesleyan to study English literature. The Wilsons also found the religious situation in Middletown to their liking. Since Presbyterian churches were scarce in New England, they joined the First Congregational Church of Middletown, whose pastor was a superb preacher and became a close friend. When Ellen became pregnant for the third time, early in 1889, she did not retreat to Georgia, in part because she was receiving excellent care from a female physician in Middletown. This proved to be the most difficult of Ellen's pregnancies, but the doctor's care helped her through the last weeks. On October 16, 1889, she gave birth to another daughter, whom they christened Eleanor Randolph, after Ellen's aunt and uncle. Wilson and Ellen may have been hoping for a son, but because this pregnancy had taken such a toll on Ellen, they did not try to have any more children.

Happy as Wilson affected to be with his male students at Wesleyan, he did not find them an improvement over his female undergraduates at Bryn Mawr. "My source of stimulation is my connection with the Johns Hopkins," he told Scudder.[15] While giving his lectures there in 1889, he met Frederick Jackson Turner, a graduate student from Wisconsin, who was taking Wilson's class and staying at the same boardinghouse. Turner and another graduate student, Charles Homer Haskins, soon became fast friends of Wilson's. Both men went on to become outstanding historians, and Wilson would keep in touch with them, especially Turner.

Wilson never regarded Wesleyan as anything more than a way station on the road to Princeton, and in 1889 Francis Landey Patton, McCosh's successor as president, tentatively offered him a position teaching political economy and public law. Wilson demurred because it would oblige him to spread himself thin. Some Princeton faculty members then objected that Wilson was, as Bridges reported, "a little heterodox (shades of Calvin and Witherspoon protect us) . . . [and] too learned and deep to interest his students."[16] Patton, who was an orthodox, old-fashioned Presbyterian cleric and dilatory by temperament, shelved the matter.

Fortunately for Wilson, Bridges kept working on his behalf, and some influential younger alumni interested themselves in bringing him to Princeton. Two of them were Wilson's wealthy classmates Cleveland Dodge and Cyrus McCormick. Although they had not known Wilson well at Princeton, they felt a strong sense of class solidarity, and as products of the McCosh era they wanted to promote the college's academic prestige. McCormick was already a trustee, as was Moses (Momo) Taylor Pyne, another extremely wealthy man, who had been two classes ahead of them and was on his way to becoming the most powerful member of the board. At some point, these men offered to make up any additional salary for Wilson, and Patton and the trustees relented. On February 13, 1890, Pyne telegraphed Wilson to offer him a professorship at a salary of $3,000, with the promise that his classes would soon be limited to public law, his preferred field.

The victory had some sour notes. Wilson was already making $3,000, and Patton would not guarantee that he could continue to lecture at Hopkins. The president also took the new recruit down a peg by telling him that some at Princeton had objected to the way "you minimise the supernatural, & make such unqualified application of the doctrine of naturalistic evolution." Patton reminded him that the trustees "mean to keep this College on the old ground of loyalty to the Christian religion . . . & they would not regard with favour such a conception of academic freedom or teaching as would leave in doubt the very direct bearing of historical Christianity as a revealed religion upon the great problems of civilization." Wilson shrugged off the reproof. He told a friend that Princeton had "the size and progressiveness without the unbearable and dwarfing academic Pharaisaism [*sic*] of Harvard or the narrow college pride of Yale," and he called Patton "a thoroughly wide-awake and delightful man."[17]

Ironically, it was Wilson's growing reputation as a scholar that almost prevented him from going to Princeton. Patton's criticism accurately reflected what Wilson had been saying in his lectures at Hopkins and what he had written in *The State*. "It is now plain that [democracy's] inspiration is of man, and not of God," he also declared. "The constitution of govt. is not a matter of inspiration." Wilson further demonstrated his renown and his ambition when he reviewed James Bryce's newly published and much-heralded book, *The American Commonwealth*, in the leading journal in his field, *Political Science Quarterly*. Although he called Bryce's book "a great work, worthy of the heartiest praise," particularly for its clarity, its author having "breathed the air of practical politics," he judged it inferior to Tocqueville's *Democracy in America* in style and philosophy. Bryce conveyed the facts, he said, "not the principles derived from them." Though praising the book's "invaluable" contributions, he regretted that Bryce, "who has given us a great deal, might have given us everything."[18]

He also had a personal problem with *The American Commonwealth*. Bryce frequently cited and quoted from *Congressional Government*, but his treatment of Congress virtually plagiarized Wilson's book. "How remorselessly 'Congressional Government' (a small volume by myself) is swallowed up in Part I of Bryce!" he noted privately to the editor of *Political Science Quarterly*. "Was I not 'nice' not to say anything about it?" Instead, criticizing Bryce as he did allowed him to stake his own claim "to yield an answer to the all-important question: What is democracy that it should be possible, nay natural, to some nations, impossible as yet to others?" Answering that question would lead to "the most significant thing to be discovered concerning democracy," and that was what Wilson meant to do.[19]

The State marked his first step toward his grand work of interpretation and synthesis. He began with the proposition that government rests "ultimately on *force*" and that the potential use of force "gives it its right to rule." In essence, government depends "upon the organic character and development of the community." There is, therefore, "no universal law, but for each nation a law of its own which bears evident marks of having been developed along with the national character." Sovereignty really embodies only the "will of an organized, independent community," and laws follow "standards of policy only, not absolute standards of right and wrong." Government is much more than "a necessary evil. It is no more of an evil than society itself. It is the organic body of society: without it society would be hardly more than an abstraction." That being the case, "we ought all to regard ourselves and act as *socialists*, believers in the wholesomeness and beneficence of the body politic." He toned down that apparent radicalism by adding that there is "one rule . . . which cannot be departed from under any circumstances, and that is the rule of historical continuity. In politics nothing radically novel may safely be attempted. . . . Nothing may be done by leaps." Because it was a textbook, *The State* was not widely reviewed, but in the judgment of several scholars it was Wilson's finest published work on politics.[20]

By the time he went to Wesleyan, Wilson was in demand as a lecturer at colleges and universities and as a speaker to civic groups, and in June 1890 he gave a commencement address at the University of Tennessee, the title of which was "Leaders of Men." Reflecting on the differences between thought and action, he observed, "The seer, whose function is imaginative interpretation is the man of science; the leader is the mechanic." Statesmen he likened to riverboat captains: "Politics must follow the actual winding of the channel; if it steer by the stars it will run aground." The leader must do the work of "gathering as best he can, the thoughts that are completed, that are perceived, that have hold upon the common mind . . . and combining all these into words of progress, into acts of recognition and completion. Who shall say that is not an excellent function? Who shall doubt or dispraise the titles of leadership?"[21] The passion of unrequited yearning for Wilson's first love—politics—shone through in the speech, and a listener might have wondered whether the speaker would rather be piloting the riverboat than studying the stars.

For Wilson, the move to Princeton in the fall of 1890 was a homecoming. In the eleven years since his graduation, the student body had nearly doubled, and younger men had joined the faculty, including the top student in Wilson's own class, William F. Magie, now a professor of physics, and the leading man in the next class, Wilson's friend from *The Princetonian*, Henry Fine, who had become a professor of mathematics. Yet Princeton's upward trajectory in the academic world had stalled, and in 1887 the trustees had blocked McCosh's move to change the institution's name from the College of New Jersey to Princeton University because they regarded the use of the word *university* as a move in a more secular direction. When McCosh retired the following year, the trustees picked the conservative and less dynamic Patton to succeed him.

The stalled academic progress at Princeton did not seem to bother Wilson. He quickly established himself as the most popular lecturer on campus. His course in public law, which was open to juniors and seniors, drew more than half the members of those classes during his first year at Princeton and still more during his second year. The new professor joked about his reputation for seriousness, telling an alumni group, "So clean-shaven is my solemnity, that at the Irish end of the town, I've been taken for a Catholic priest." One student later recalled, "Speaking from a mere skeleton of notes, he hammered in his teaching with an up-and-down, full-armed gesture. Thus he was a perpendicular lecturer, his talking nose and his oscillating Adam's apple moving up and down with speech, along with his pump-handle gestures. . . . He was essentially the lecturer rather than the teacher." He would spend the first fifteen minutes of each session dictating concepts and information that he required the students to take down. As a result, another student recalled, "Very little reading was necessary for Wilson's course. The students trusted their lecture notes to get them by."[22]

Making his courses easy undoubtedly contributed to his popularity, but light reading and spoon-fed lectures were the norm at Princeton, buttressing its reputation as a "picnic" among leading colleges. Wilson gained a big undergraduate following also because of his manifest empathy with the students. Two of them who went on to become writers explained his attractiveness as a matter of his caring about them. The journalist Ernest Poole remembered that he came to their rooms to talk and recommend such books as *How the Other Half Lives*, Jacob Riis's account of life in the slums of New York's Lower East Side, which "gave me an exciting sense of new life stirring in our land." The novelist and playwright Booth Tarkington recalled the same thing: "I think we felt that Wilson understood us, and understood us more favorably than any other man on the faculty." His friendliness toward students extended beyond studies. He again played a part in extracurricular activities, particularly speaking and debate, and gave talks in chapel, as all faculty members were required to do, although he touched only lightly on religious subjects. He also immersed himself in college sports. He admired rowing and deplored Princeton's lack of the proper conditions for crew. Baseball remained his favorite sport, but he increasingly threw himself into the promotion of football, though now as a business manager and fan, not as a coach. He publicly defended football against charges that it was brutal and distracted students from academic pursuits. "Foot-ball is a manly game," he told an alumni group. "Athletics are a safety valve for animal spirits."[23]

Still, some shadows darkened Wilson's joy at Princeton. As much as he savored lecturing, he recognized the limitations of current university teaching. In 1894, he published an article titled "University Training and Citizenship," in which he argued that universities must induce their students to read "widely and intelligently. . . . For it is reading, not set lectures, that will prepare a soil for culture." To reach that goal, colleges should bring in a "considerable number of young tutors" to guide the students "in groups of manageable numbers, suggesting the reading of each group." This was the germ of the major reform in teaching that Wilson would introduce later as president of Princeton. Indeed, from the moment he came back, he had ideas for improving his alma mater. One such idea was to inject new blood into the faculty. Most of his fellow professors were also alumni, but unlike Wilson, few of them had studied or taught anywhere else. He shared the discontent of some younger faculty members with the prevailing parochialism, but he saw the problem as a matter of sectional as well as academic and religious narrowness—not just too many Princetonians and Presbyterians but also "too many men from the Northeast."[24]

Wilson particularly wanted to add men with broader perspectives in the fields closest to his own. During his first year at Princeton, he tried to recruit his Hopkins friend Albert Shaw—a midwesterner by background who was on the faculty at Cornell and editing a new magazine, *The American Review of Reviews*—to teach economics. Patton initially backed Wilson's effort, but conservative trustees shot down Shaw's candidacy because of his economic views. The opponents were, Wilson told Shaw, "businessmen, the moneyed men of the corporation. . . . Hard-headed, narrow men,—that's the breed." In 1896, he tried to recruit another friend from Hopkins, Frederick Jackson Turner, whose pathbreaking essay "The Significance of the Frontier in American History" had made him a rising star in his field. Once more, Patton ostensibly encouraged Wilson, but the trustees rejected Turner's candidacy, claiming that there was not enough money to create a separate professorship in American history. Wilson felt ill-used because Patton failed to inform him of the trustees' decision for three weeks. "I have been treated like an employee rather than a colleague," he exploded to Patton.[25] The president tried to mollify him with his usual sweet talk, but Wilson never again felt as warmly toward Patton or gave him the benefit of the doubt as he had done before.

Wilson's most ambitious project for changing Princeton was to start a law school. It would be, he explained, "an institutional law school, so to speak, in which law shall be taught in its historical and philosophical aspects, critically rather than technically, . . . as it is taught in the better European universities." During his first three years on Princeton's faculty, he spoke repeatedly to alumni groups about his plan and expounded the need for broader education for all the professions. "I believe that no medical or law or theological school ought to be a separate institution," he avowed. "It ought to be organically and in a situation part of a university." He called the narrowly trained specialist "the natural enemy of society."[26] Yet nothing came of this scheme. A nationwide depression in 1893 made funds hard to raise, and Patton did not bestir himself. After 1893, Wilson abandoned the idea and concentrated more on his own writing and undergraduate teaching. Yet the vision of instituting a liberal education for the professions and of integrating theoretical with practical education would remain central to his definition of a great university.

Setbacks did not unduly cloud Wilson's happiness at Princeton. For six years in a row, a student body poll chose him most popular professor, and most of the faculty held him in equally high regard. He served on such important committees as those dealing with student discipline, athletics, and the library, and the faculty chose him more often than anyone else to represent them in communicating with the trustees. Even Patton and older, more conservative faculty members could not gainsay his eminence—because he was getting job offers from other institutions. In 1892, the University of Illinois offered him its presidency at a salary of $6,000. Ellen shrewdly advised her husband to exploit the offer, and she urged him to consult with other university presidents, especially Daniel Coit Gilman at Hopkins, as a bit of self-advertising. The possibility also arose of his being offered the presidency of the University of Wisconsin. "It would be *such* fun for you to have this one too," Ellen exulted. "I should like to keep the Princeton trustees in the hottest kind of water on your account until they were shaken out of their selfish lethargy in the matter of salaries."[27]

Wilson's most tempting outside offer came in 1898, when the University of Virginia asked him to become its president. "Mr. Jefferson's University" had operated for almost three quarters of a century without a president, but by the 1890s the Board of Visitors had conceded that they needed one. Wilson was the first choice of the board and the faculty, strongly seconded by the governor. He responded to the offer by telling a Virginia friend that "almost every affection drew me towards the State and the institution I love" and to accept what "will probably turn out to be the highest honour of my life-time." But he did not hesitate to use the offer to improve his situation at Princeton, and he got sympathetic trustees to agitate to keep him. Patton professed himself eager to retain Wilson but insisted, "I cannot see that it is my duty to take the initiative."[28] Instead, Wilson's friends among the trustees, particularly Cyrus McCormick, arranged for him to receive an additional $2,500 a year for the next five years. Wilson thereupon turned down the Virginia offer, explaining that moral bonds held him at Princeton, together with the need to continue his writing.

Wilson was also happier with his home life and his circle of friends during his years as a professor at Princeton than at any other time in his life. His immediate family—Ellen and their three daughters, Margaret, Jessie, and Eleanor (Nell)—formed the core in a ring of concentric circles of love and friendship. Wilson and Ellen loved each other deeply and passionately. In a letter to her, he bemoaned "the riotous elements in my own blood," but he found ample outlets for his physical desires within their marriage, once reminding her, "The other thing I had thought of may occur to you independently: will you not bring the little bundle of *rubbers* in the bottom drawer of the washstand?"[29] She shared more than a bed with her husband. She was also his adviser and confidant. She interested herself in his work, and he gladly discussed with her his thinking about nearly everything. She often showed a keener insight than he did into such people at Princeton as Patton and various trustees. Above all, she understood him better than anyone else ever would.

Ellen managed the household and made sure that Wilson had plenty of time for his work. He spent long hours in his study turning out a stream of books, magazine articles, and speeches. Yet he did not impress people as driven or excessively absorbed in his work. He still played tennis, and he took up the new craze of bicycling. His brother-in-law Stockton Axson also recalled that Wilson "loved to 'loaf and invite his soul.'" His faculty friend Bliss Perry attributed Wilson's combination of productivity and apparent leisure to his highly disciplined habits, particularly his now almost exclusive use of the typewriter, and his "gift of intense concentration."[30]

He did not let the pressures of work make him an absentee or distant figure at home. The second Wilson daughter, Jessie, told his first biographer that her father loved to tell stories and was a "remarkable mimic," doing various dialects, including Irish and African American—betraying touches of ethnic and racial prejudice, though innocently intended. Often he would "seize one of the little girls and dance around the room, or up and down the hall with her, in a wild spirit of gaiety." He divided the family into its "proper members"—Ellen and Jessie—and its "vulgar members"—Nell and himself—with Margaret in between. His nephew George Howe similarly remembered his uncle's "playful nature, playful both of mind and body," and how he would dance with the girls after dinner, with "Aunt Ellie" calling out when they got too rambunctious, "Woodrow, what is the matter with you?"[31]

The Wilson daughters were each very different from the other in appearance and personality. The oldest, Margaret, was the smallest and the most musically gifted. She had a melodious voice and was a good student; she left the Women's College of Maryland after two years to go to New York, where she studied voice and tried, with mixed success, to become an opera singer. Margaret inherited her father's looks, and when she was in her twenties, she started wearing the same kind of eyeglasses, making her look like a female version of him. Jessie was the beauty of the family, with honey-blond hair and large blue eyes; she was an even better student than Margaret, attending the same college, where she earned a Phi Beta Kappa key. She was also the most deeply religious of the three daughters and felt a strong attraction to social reform. She and Margaret became ardent advocates of woman suffrage and often argued the issue with their father at the dinner table. Nell, the youngest, was dark-haired and dark-eyed, with a resemblance to her father that was softer than Margaret's. She was the least studious of the three; her higher education consisted of two years of finishing school in North Carolina. As the liveliest and least inhibited of the daughters, she became her father's favorite. She eagerly joined in his high jinks and made him laugh. According to Stockton Axson, Nell and her father played tag in the halls of the White House.[32]

The immediate family circle extended beyond the couple and their daughters. Ever since her mother's death, Ellen had wanted to bring the Axsons back together, and in Princeton she finally got her wish. After Stockton joined the Princeton faculty in 1897, he came to the Wilson house almost daily. Her brother Eddie continued to live with them during his four years as a student at Princeton, where he was a member of the class of 1897. And in 1893, Ellen had brought her twelve-year-old sister, Madge, to live with them, the rebellious tomboy adding to a household already lively with sprites. George Howe, Eddie's classmate at Princeton, lived with the family from 1893 to 1897, and Wilson's cousin Helen Woodrow Bones lived with them while she attended a women's college in Princeton. George Howe's mother, Wilson's sister Annie, was a frequent visitor, as was Wilson's father. Following the custom in southern families, relatives nearly always came for extended stays. Sadly, Wilson's other sister, Marion, had died in 1890, and he saw little of her children.

Several circles of friends radiated around the family. Everyone on the Princeton faculty knew everyone else and socialized to some extent. With some of his colleagues Wilson had pleasant but mainly businesslike relations, as with the physicist William F. Magie, his onetime classmate. He was closer to Harry Fine, who lived across the street and still called him Tommy. With Bliss Perry, Wilson enjoyed both a personal and a literary friendship until Perry left Princeton in 1899 to become editor of *The Atlantic Monthly*. Highest of all in Wilson's affections stood a new friend, the philosophy professor John (Jack) Grier Hibben, who was four years younger than Wilson and had joined the faculty a year after him. Madge Axson later counted Hibben among the small circle of men who—along with Wilson's father, Stockton Axson, and Bridges—"belonged in the inner citadel of his heart." Hibben's wife, Jennie, also became close to the Wilson family. In addition, there were frequent visitors from out of town, such as Bob Bridges and Walter Page.[33]

Church played less of a role in Wilson and Ellen's lives than it had earlier. It was seven years before they transferred their letter of membership from the church in Middletown to one in Princeton, where they rejected the older, long-established First Presbyterian Church in favor of its nearby dissident offshoot, the Second Presbyterian Church. After he became president of Princeton, Wilson transferred the family membership to the First, which in the meantime, with Hibben's influence, had reconciled its differences with the Second. The family recited grace before meals and said nightly prayers, and they read from the Bible together, although more often they read aloud from literary works, with Thackeray's *Vanity Fair* being a favorite.

During their first years in Princeton, the family lived in a rented frame house about a mile west of the campus. In 1895, Wilson took out a loan that permitted him to buy the lot next door and start construction on a house. Ellen designed the building, a large, elegant structure in the fashionable half-timber style. It cost $12,000 to build, with another $3,000 for the land—large sums of money at that time. In order to bridge the gap between the loan and the costs, Wilson took on additional outside speaking engagements. "I wanted to pos[t]pone building," Ellen explained to a friend, "but he had gotten his heart set on it and has agreed to lecture this fall for the University Extension Society to make up the deficit."[34] Having encountered and overcome some of the typical snags and frustrations of home building, the Wilson family moved into their new house in February 1896.

Wilson paid a physical price for the extra work he was doing. Looking back at her husband's lecturing efforts, Ellen told Frederick Jackson Turner, "Mr. Wilson makes $1500 every year; and last year when we were building, and he really tired himself, he made $4000 extra;—and almost killed himself doing it!"[35] In May 1896, he suffered his first serious health problem. Up to that point in his life, his only complaint had been recurring digestion problems, for which he sometimes used a stomach pump— a commonly prescribed remedy at the time—to remove acids and inject small amounts of coal. Now, without warning, he found that severe pain and numbness left him barely able to use his right hand. His doctors could not discover a cause and vaguely mentioned "neuritis" and "writer's cramp" and prescribed rest. With Hibben's help, Ellen arranged for her husband to take a two-month holiday in England and managed his affairs in his absence. While he was abroad, he wrote letters home in his neat handwriting, using his left hand until he gradually recovered the use of his right. He enjoyed the holiday, visiting Bagehot's grave and thrilling to the sights of London and, especially, Oxford. He mixed in a little work by renewing his acquaintance with James Bryce, trying to get him to come to lecture at Princeton. The rest cure evidently worked, because Wilson resumed his typical pace of activity in the fall.

This episode may have been a sign of a deeper problem. With the benefit of knowledge of the massive stroke he suffered more than twenty years later, some interpreters have speculated that the pain and weakness in Wilson's hand stemmed from a small stroke, caused by an occlusion in his right carotid artery. The transient nature of the semiparalysis was consistent with such a small stroke, and his family history, particularly his father's condition as he aged, likewise hinted at cardiovascular problems. But any diagnosis can only be speculative. Wilson would have no comparable problems for another ten years. Whatever its cause, this episode came as an unwelcome reminder of vulnerability and mortality.[36]

Wilson's physical problem came at a singularly inopportune time. Though not yet forty, he was the brightest star on the Princeton faculty, and his reputation was growing in academic circles and among the broader public. In the fall of 1896, he got an opportunity to shine before a most distinguished audience. It was the 150th anniversary of the charter of the College of New Jersey, and the trustees agreed to stage an elaborate sesquicentennial celebration in October and to use the occasion finally to change the institution's name to Princeton University. One faculty member, classics professor Andrew Fleming West, made most of the arrangements for what became an impressive affair that featured academic processions and stately ceremonies. West pulled off a coup when he secured the attendance of the president of the United States, Grover Cleveland. (Princeton and West made such a favorable impression on Cleveland that he decided to retire to the town when he left the White House the following year.) The highest place of honor at the celebration fell to Wilson, who was the undisputed choice to deliver the major address.

He titled the address "Princeton in the Nation's Service," but contrary to what that title seemed to imply and what later generations presumed the speech to say, it was not a call for students to enter public service or for the newly renamed university to outfit them for careers in the political arena. Its first half evoked the history of Princeton, and the second half pleaded for enlightened conservatism. The first half dwelled almost exclusively on John Witherspoon, "your thorough Presbyterian," but noted that Princeton's founders had not wanted "a sectarian school." In the second half, Wilson affirmed, "There is nothing so conservative of life as growth: when that stops, decay sets in and the end comes on apace." His conservatism was academic and intellectual rather than political, decrying the shift toward universities' spawning "your learned radical, bred in the schools," and exalting "the scientific spirit of the age," which has "bred in us a spirit of experiment and contempt for the past." Instead of trying to extend science beyond its proper sphere, Princeton "must turn back once more to the region of practicable ideals." Wilson closed by saluting a "place where ideals are kept in the heart in an air they can breathe; but no fool's paradise," and he asked, "Who shall show us the way to this place?"[37]

"Princeton in the Nation's Service" was an oratorical triumph. "And *such* an ovation as Woodrow received!" Ellen exulted to her cousin Mary Hoyt. "I never imagined anything like it. And think of *so* delighting *such* an audience, the most distinguished, everyone says, that has ever been assembled in America." Wifely adoration aside, Ellen's description captured the mood of the occasion. A faculty friend of Wilson's later recalled that someone who entertained notions about succeeding Patton as president of Princeton said this speech had made him abandon those hopes.[38] Whether Wilson had similar aspirations is not known, but the offer from Virginia a few months later would almost certainly plant the idea deeper in the minds of others, most notably such patrons of his among the trustees as McCormick and Pyne.

· · ·

During most of the 1890s, Wilson took little interest in politics. In 1893, he declined to write a magazine article about a hot current issue because "I am estopped by ignorance." There were exceptions to his detachment. In 1895, he spoke at a rally in Princeton for the Democratic candidate for governor of New Jersey, and in 1896 he addressed a meeting in Baltimore to protest shenanigans by the city's political machine. At that meeting, Wilson shared the platform with the dashing young Republican politician and New York City police commissioner Theodore Roosevelt. This was the first time that the two men met. They hit it off well, and Roosevelt had dinner with Wilson when he visited Princeton a year later. Wilson was in England during the first part of the 1896 presidential campaign—the epic clash between William McKinley, the Republican who backed the monetary gold standard, and William Jennings Bryan, the anti-Cleveland insurgent Democrat who stood for free silver and measures aimed at curbing the power of big business. Wilson confessed to Ellen, "It looks as if *I* would have to vote for *McKinley!*"[39] Fortunately for him, a splinter gold Democratic ticket offered a way to avoid such apostasy.

Wilson was beginning to take a new direction in his political thought. Ever since he first laid plans to write his grand synthesis, which he now called "Philosophy of Politics," he had been circling around Edmund Burke's conception of the nature of politics. Rereading Burke's writings in 1893 brought the intellectual breakthrough that enabled Wilson to recognize his deep affinity for that conception of politics. "If I should claim any man as my master," he told a friend, "that man would be Burke." In an essay, he lauded Burke's work for containing "no page of abstract thinking" and his perception "that questions of government are moral questions, and that questions of morals cannot always be squared with rules of logic, but run through as many ranges of variety as the circumstances of life itself." Wilson further argued, "The politics of the English-speaking peoples has never been speculative; it has always been profoundly practical and utilitarian. Speculative politics treats man and situations as they are supposed to be; practical politics treats them (upon no general plan, but in detail) as they are found to be at the moment of actual contact."[40]

Wilson probably did not recognize his affinity for Burke earlier and seize upon this insight to move forward with his "Philosophy of Politics" because he was focusing on other things. In addition to teaching and lecturing, he wrote a volume in the *Epochs of American History* series, edited by Professor Albert Bushnell Hart of Harvard. Titled *Division and Reunion, 1829–1889*, it was a work of synthesis, not original research, and in it Wilson followed the lead of Turner in stressing the influence of the frontier. He depicted the Old South in a kindly light, viewing slavery as generally benign, taking issue only with the breaking up of slave families and the institution's economic inefficiencies, but he had no patience with secession. The book received generally good reviews, although some historians criticized its sketchiness in parts and its slighting of the moral dimension of slavery. In the 1890s, he was also writing for a number of better-paying magazines, such as Albert Shaw's *Review of Reviews; The Forum*, which was edited by Walter Page; *Scribner's*, where Bridges had become editor; and *The Atlantic*, edited then by Horace Scudder, who had earlier accepted *Congressional Government* at Houghton Mifflin, and after 1899 by Bliss Perry.

The most interesting of these articles were "A Calendar of Great Americans" and "Mere Literature." In "Calendar," he praised Alexander Hamilton, Andrew Jackson, and Abraham Lincoln but dismissed Jefferson as "a great man, but not a great American" because his political thought was un-American in being "abstract, sentimental, rationalistic, rather than practical." In "Mere Literature," he took revenge on the dismissal of a book by a philologist at Johns Hopkins as "mere literature" and, possibly unconsciously, on his father's scoffing at his wanting "a merely literary career." The phrase "mere literature" epitomized "the irreverent invention of a scientific age," which had tried to turn universities into "agencies of Philistinism."41

Literary success and disengagement from current affairs did not entirely quell Wilson's yearning to play an active part in politics. He mentioned to Ellen "the road I used to burn to travel," declaring that he was "yet fairly restless and impatient with ambition, as of old." Seeing contemporaries make their way in politics drew varying reactions. When President Cleveland appointed the Atlanta lawyer and newspaper owner Hoke Smith secretary of the interior in 1893, Wilson told Shaw, "I . . . despise him as heartily as all the other men I knew at the Atlanta bar did." In a magazine article, he depicted Smith as a typical product of the bar: "Their training is narrow, their apprehension specialized; their conceptions of justice are technical, their standards of policy too self-regardful."42 That sounds like a restatement of Wilson's own reasoning when he abandoned the law. Others in politics were not so easy to brush aside. Wilson's first editor, Henry Cabot Lodge, had become a Republican congressman and then a senator from Massachusetts, while Lodge's close friend and Wilson's new acquaintance, Theodore Roosevelt, was enjoying a meteoric rise after having served spectacularly in the Spanish-American War.

Wilson crossed paths with Roosevelt a number of times. After Roosevelt's election as governor of New York, Roosevelt sought Wilson's advice about politics, and Wilson sought Roosevelt's about academic appointments. Wilson found in Roosevelt, he told Ellen, "a very sane, *academic* side . . . not known by everybody so much as to exist." Publicly, he praised Roosevelt as "too big a man to have it make any difference to him whether he was in office or out." When he was vice president, Roosevelt invited professors from Harvard, Yale, and Princeton to talk about interesting young men from their colleges who might go into politics. Wilson was the professor from Princeton, and during the summer of 1901 he spent part of a weekend at Roosevelt's home at Oyster Bay on Long Island. Roosevelt and Lodge evidently figured in conversations in the Wilson household, for Ellen wrote to her husband after driving past Lodge's estate in Massachusetts, "He seems to be, like Roosevelt, one of fortune's all round favourites."[43]

Some of those yearnings for the political arena may have sprung from Wilson's physical problem in 1896. Stockton Axson believed that his brother-in-law changed after that episode: "He had always been a purposeful man, but now he was a man of fixed and resolute purpose." He explained to Wilson's first biographer that "a subtle change came over Mr. Wilson after the return from the trip to Europe in 1896," and he no longer sat and talked for hours with Axson and Joseph Wilson. "Old Dr. Wilson often complained that Woodrow was getting away from his old interests." His brother-in-law struck Axson as "torn between the desire to live a studious and scholarly life, doing creative work and a life of action." Wilson once said to him, "I get so tired of a talking profession."[44]

Wilson began to take a greater interest in current affairs as the decade drew to a close. In 1897, he decried "leaderless government . . . in which no man stands at the helm to steer." In 1898, he cast aside his detachment in response to the Spanish-American War. Bliss Perry later recalled, "In those days Wilson was much more of a 'militarist' than I. I thought he romanticized the army and the navy too much." Axson similarly recalled, "During and immediately after the war he was belligerent—regretted he was not free to enlist in the armed forces and fight—read each day's news with the eagerness of a boy." Breaking with fellow Democrats, he publicly argued that America should take Hawaii, Guam, and the Philippines as colonies in order to prevent Germany or Russia from taking them. Moreover, he declared, "As long as we have only domestic subjects we have no real leaders."[45]

When the Democrats charged the Republicans with "imperialism" during the 1900 presidential campaign, Wilson supported McKinley's foreign policy and welcomed the political changes that he saw emerging in its wake. In a preface to a new edition of *Congressional Government*, he argued that the president was gaining new powers and that "new prizes in public service may attract a new order of talent," especially in carrying "the novel burdens we have shouldered." In an essay in *The Atlantic*, he maintained that possession of the Philippines "put us in the very presence of the forces that will make the politics of the twentieth century radically unlike the politics of the nineteenth" and that Americans must help "undeveloped peoples, still in the childhood of their natural growth[,] . . . inducting them into the rudiments of justice and freedom." If those arguments sounded like Rudyard Kipling's "White Man's Burden," it was probably no accident. Ellen and Wilson had recently added Kipling to their short list of favorite poets, and Wilson would carry Kipling's poem "If" in his wallet for years.[46]

His embrace of imperialism dovetailed with his rekindled interest in active politics. Early in 1898, Wilson observed Congress in session for the first time. "I have sat and watched the Houses a good deal in the afternoons," he told Ellen, "and the old longing for public life comes upon me in a flood as I watch. Perhaps I should be safer somewhere else, where I should be kept from a too keen and constant discontent with my calling." He also met the powerful Republican Speaker of the House, Thomas B. Reed, whom he found "not only agreeable but even attractive." Reed flattered Wilson by telling him "he had read 'Congressional Government' and had been astonished to find how admirably one outside affairs had been able to group the features of our 'government by helter-skelter.' "[47] Except for the occasional meetings with Roosevelt, nothing came of these renewed longings for active politics.

He did make some lucrative forays into the literary marketplace. In 1895 and 1896, he wrote a brief serialized biography of George Washington for *Harper's*, with illustrations by the artist Howard Pyle, which was later published as a book. Wilson received $300 for each of the six installments, thereby earning more than half as much as his annual Princeton salary at the time. *George Washington* was a bad book, written in an affected style with the saccharine, moralizing tone of contemporary children's books such as *Black Beauty* and *Little Lord Fauntleroy*. In 1900, *Harper's* offered Wilson $1,000 apiece—an "immense sum," he told Bridges—for twelve installments of a history of the United States, which would subsequently be published in five lavishly produced volumes as *A History of the American People*. Though better written than *George Washington*, these volumes amounted to—in the words of a Princeton faculty member—"a gilt-edged pot boiler."[48] Regardless, they earned him nearly $30,000, over and above the $12,000 for the magazine installments.

Having sated his need for money, he turned again to his "Philosophy of Politics" ("P.o.P."). Early in 1902, he told Turner that he had "to do the work I really seem to have been cut out for. I was forty-five three weeks ago, and between forty-five and fifty-five, I take it, is when a man ought to do the work into which he expects to put most of himself."[49] What might Wilson have produced if he had stuck with "P.o.P."? Might he have wrought what Burke himself had never done, a comprehensive examination of politics as an art or science that did not stem from theory and ideology but grew out of life and experience? No one before Wilson had ever written such a book, and no one has written one since. His essays and comments anticipated the mid-twentieth-century reaction among liberal intellectuals against metaphysical politics and world-altering systems of thought. If Wilson had run with his insights the way he had in *Congressional Government*, he might have written a still greater book, a unique masterpiece of reflection on the meaning and conduct of political life.

He did not stick with "P.o.P" because circumstances and other ambitions intervened to set his life and career on a different course. Affairs at Princeton were heating up as the twentieth century approached. Patton's indolent habits and conservative views dashed the high hopes raised in 1896 by the sesquicentennial celebration and the renaming of the institution. Jack Hibben and Andrew West began to foment opposition to the Patton regime. "We have had several informal gatherings of the Faculty malcontents on West[']s porch," Hibben reported to Wilson in 1899. "The excitement of the early days of the summer has subsided, and a sullen resentment seems to have taken its place in reference to the powers that be." Wilson shared their discontent, telling Ellen, "I *know* that Dr. P. cannot be depended upon for anything at all." When Patton hired a replacement for Bliss Perry, Wilson exploded to Ellen, "How complete it all is: . . . not a name added to our list, or prestige; money saved and second-rate men promoted!"[50]

The situation slowly began to change. In 1900, the trustees authorized the establishment of a graduate school with West as dean, although this new arm of the university existed only on paper. Also in 1900, faculty dissidents overcame Patton's objections and formed a committee to investigate undergraduate education, with a view to raising standards; they found allies among the trustees, including Moses Pyne, Cyrus McCormick, and Cornelius Cuyler, wealthy businessmen accustomed to efficiency and action. Patton's days as president of Princeton were clearly numbered, particularly after faculty dissidents began meeting privately with some of the trustees in the spring of 1902. Wilson attended several of these sessions, and he helped draw up a plan to create a joint faculty-trustee executive committee that would effectively supplant Patton.

Princeton's president could read the handwriting on the wall. As soon as he learned of the plan for the executive committee, Patton talked about resigning, and he cleverly inveigled the trustees into giving him a pension of $10,000 a year for six years. When the trustees met on June 9, Patton submitted his resignation and recommended Wilson as his successor. The trustees then unanimously elected Wilson president of Princeton. "I never saw so many men of many minds so promptly, without debate, without hesitation at the mere mention of a name," one of the trustees told Wilson, ". . . & when the vote was announced we agreed that it was an act of Providence."[51] This unanimity and seeming spontaneity masked a bit of maneuvering. Others had reportedly entertained hopes of succeeding Patton, including West. Patton reportedly swung around to Wilson because he and Wilson had maintained pleasant personal relations and he hated West for plotting against him. It also seems likely that Wilson's friends and patrons among the trustees had prepared to put his name forward and push his election.

Wilson affected surprise. The day after the election, he told the alumni gathered for class reunions, "This thing has come to me as a thunderbolt out of a clear sky." Yet Perry's wife wrote to Ellen, "[I]t makes me homesick and blue to think that the event we had so often talked about and wished for has come to pass and we are outsiders, not there to enjoy it." Ellen expressed some regrets to her cousin Florence Hoyt about how Wilson's "literary work must suffer greatly,—just how much remains to [be] seen, and we must leave our dear home and sweet, almost ideal life when he was [a] simple 'man of letters.'" If Wilson felt that way too, he hid his misgivings well. Speaking briefly at commencement ceremonies the following day, he gave a foretaste of what could be expected from him. "There are things which we hope to add to this university," he declared, "and there are things which we hope will never be subtracted from it. We hope that men will open their hearts to us and will enable us to crown this university with a great graduate college."[52] Woodrow Wilson was forecasting the greatest challenges, accomplishments, and conflicts of this new turn in his life.

4

BOLD LEADER

Princeton University inaugurated Woodrow Wilson on October 25, 1902. He considered his ranking as the university's thirteenth president a good omen because, unlike many people, he believed that thirteen was his lucky number—it was the sum of the number of letters in his first and last names. The inaugural ceremony was a gala event, which preceded a mid-day dinner for the attendees, a football game, and an evening dinner given by Wilson's class of '79. An injury prevented President Theodore Roosevelt from attending, but earlier, on hearing of the trustees' action, he had told a mutual friend, "Woodrow Wilson is a perfect trump. I am overjoyed at his election." Ex-president Cleveland, now a resident of Princeton and a trustee of the university, did attend, as did Abraham Lincoln's only surviving child, Robert Todd Lincoln. Other luminaries included the financier J. P. Morgan, former Speaker of the House of Representatives Thomas B. Reed, and the novelist William Dean Howells, together with such magazine editors as Wilson's friends Bridges of *Scribner's*, Perry of *The Atlantic*, and Page, who had recently started his own monthly, *The World's Work*, as well as George Harvey of *Harper's Weekly*, who had worked earlier with Wilson on his *History of the American People*.[1]

The pomp and circumstance of the academic procession recalled the spectacle six years before at Princeton's sesquicentennial celebration. But unlike that event, this was not an all-male or all-white affair. At Wilson's initiative, three female representatives of women's colleges joined the procession, as did an African American—the renowned principal of the Tuskegee Institute in Alabama, Booker T. Washington. The Tuskegee principal's views on race relations seemed to match Wilson's own thinking about gradual improvement in race relations. In 1897, he had written, "Even the race problem of the South will no doubt work itself out in the slowness of time. . . . Time is the only legislator in such matters." Not everyone in Wilson's family thought that way. As their daughter Jessie remembered, "Mrs. Wilson felt much more strongly about the color line than did Mr. Wilson." She also recalled that one of Ellen's aunts felt "scandalized" by Washington's presence at the inauguration "and said if she had known he was to be there she wouldn't have gone." Wilson said that he thought Washington's "speech was the very best at the dinner afterwards bar none."[2]

Wilson titled the speech that he delivered at the inaugural ceremony, on the steps of Nassau Hall, "Princeton for the Nation's Service." By changing just one word in the title of his sesquicentennial speech, he invited comparison with that earlier oratorical feat. Wilson asserted that as the nation's "affairs grow more and more complex[,] . . . [i]t needs efficient and enlightened men. The universities of the country must take part in supplying them." He laid greatest stress on the general education of undergraduates through "disciplinary" studies, such as classics, mathematics, and science, which would form a core curriculum. Without naming Harvard or its president, Charles William Eliot, who was not present, he was rejecting the free-elective system that Eliot had instituted there. Wilson also insisted that the leading professors, "those who guide special study and research[, should not be] altogether excused from undergraduate instruction." Moreover, Princeton should build a residential graduate college "at the very heart, the geographical heart, of the university," thus mingling graduate and undergraduate education in such ways as to produce leaders for America in a "new age, . . . in which, it seems, we must lead the world."[3]

"Princeton for the Nation's Service" was not as good a speech as its similarly titled predecessor. Wilson was more abstract and self-consciously oratorical, seldom mentioning Princeton by name, and offered the Graduate College as his only concrete proposal. All the same, he received thunderous applause, and the press reported the speech widely and approvingly. Particularly impressed was George Harvey of *Harper's Weekly*. A conservative Democrat and political associate of Cleveland's, he regarded himself as a political talent spotter, and he later said he had marked Wilson as a presidential possibility after hearing the speech.[4]

Before the inauguration, Wilson told Ellen, "I feel like a new prime minister getting ready to address his constituents." He also told her, "Fortunately, I never worked out the argument on liberal studies, which is the theme of my inaugural, before, never before having treated myself as a professional 'educator,' and so the matter is not stale but fresh and interesting." Actually, according to Stockton Axson, five years earlier Wilson had spelled out to him the three steps needed to make Princeton a place where "things of the mind" were paramount: first, reorganize the curriculum to combine electives with prescribed courses; second, adapt "the Oxford tutorial system to our American plan"; and third, divide the student body into smaller units, with unmarried faculty living among them.[5] This prefiguration of major reform sounds apocryphal, but he had given talks to alumni groups stressing the need to combine the advantages of the college and the university.

Although he exaggerated the lack of thinking he had devoted to the subject of education, he revealed habits of mind that would shape his leadership as a university president and later as a governor and as president of the United States. Wilson liked to prepare, to think things through by himself and get his bearings on a subject, and he liked to work from the general to the particular. Money presented the biggest obstacle to his plans. Axson recalled that on the day Wilson was chosen president, "he seemed a little nervous" and told Axson, "We cannot reform the University immediately. Funds will have to be found."[6] Still, he did not let such worries deter him from revealing a character trait that previously had found outlets only in his imaginings—a penchant for bold action. In situations where he had a choice, he would nearly always pick the grander, riskier course.

During the summer of 1902, Wilson prepared a report on the state of affairs at Princeton, which he had presented to the trustees four days before his inauguration. In that report he called the university's situation "in many respects, critical" and declared that "it is insufficiently capitalized for its business." The quality of the faculty was suffering from low pay, and the curriculum needed "a radical change of method." Such "essentially reading subjects" as philosophy, literature, history, politics, and economics required, with modification, "the English tutorial system." To institute such a system, he proposed hiring fifty young men on yearly contracts for a maximum of five years. The regular faculty likewise required more and more distinguished professors, and the sciences badly needed better facilities. Such changes would require upping Princeton's present resources of $3.8 million to more than $6 million. "No institution can have freedom in its development which does not stand at the top in a place of leadership," Wilson argued. "If Princeton should ever come to be generally thought of as standing below Harvard and Yale in academic development her opportunity for leadership and even for independent action within her own sphere would be gone. . . . Either we may withdraw from the university competition and devote ourselves to making what we are solid and distinguished, or we must find money enough to make Princeton in fact a great university."[7]

He also listed steps to take toward making Princeton a leading university. First and most important was a Graduate College, the residential facility for the Graduate School, for which the dean, Andrew West, had already presented a design to the trustees. Wilson saw no need for a medical school, but he did recommend a "school of jurisprudence"—his earlier idea for a different kind of law school—and an "electrical school" to teach advanced engineering. He estimated the cost of these new ventures at $6.6 million; almost half of that sum would go to the Graduate College. Wilson closed the report by stressing how imperative it was to accomplish the tasks he had outlined: "I do not hesitate to say that the reputation and the very success of the University are staked on obtaining them soon."[8]

He was staking out a bold vision for Princeton, but for the time being he moved slowly and looked for money. He spent part of the summer of 1902 visiting haunts of the wealthy on the north shore of Massachusetts and in Maine to cultivate such potential donors as J. P. Morgan. Like other university presidents of the time, he also stalked the biggest educational benefactor of all, the steel tycoon Andrew Carnegie. Fund-raising was the part of his new job that he liked least. "To ask for money is unpalatable to any man's spirit," he confessed in a draft of a fund-raising letter, "even though he ask, not for himself, but for the best cause in the world."[9]

Home life also distracted him during his first months as president. Joseph Wilson had come to live with his older son's family earlier in 1902. "He was ill much of the time and a large part of the nursing devolved upon Ellen," her cousin Mary Hoyt recalled; Wilson's sister Annie Howe also came to help. Wilson spent as much time as he could with his father, reading and singing hymns to him. Joseph Wilson died on January 21, 1903. "The blow of my father's death has been very hard to me, and my spirits come back with difficulty," he told one of his Princeton classmates. To Roosevelt, who had invited him to stay at the White House, he added, "I am for the time being in no spirits for pleasure. I feel, therefore, that I am relieving you of a sad guest in asking you not to expect me."[10]

Wilson's cautious start also stemmed from his collegiality, another leadership trait that he would carry with him into public office. He knew what he did not know, and he wanted to assemble a staff of able, loyal lieutenants to advise and assist him. Science formed the biggest gap in his knowledge, and the natural choice both to handle the sciences and to be his second in command in university affairs was his friend from their undergraduate days—Harry Fine. In June 1903, Wilson chose Fine to be dean of the faculty, the second-ranking officer of the university. The lanky, deliberate mathematician made a natural complement to Wilson, and he was one of the first people to recognize how Wilson worked as a leader. He later told Wilson's first biographer, "[I]t seems to have been his method throughout his life to make up his mind himself in regard to the larger policies of administration without much consultation with other people. Upon details he was always eager for advice." Fine called him "a man of certainty" once he had made up his mind, observing that this trait "made him enemies, . . . yet it was one of the most powerful factors in his success. To be certain of anything in a world of doubt is to have one of the most powerful weapons that ever comes to the hand of man."[11] Fine excelled at picking promising scientists, and Wilson took part in recruiting them and other prospective faculty members, usually with a personal interview. He shone in these encounters with recruits, and his persuasiveness played a big role in enticing them to come to Princeton.

Wilson also relied heavily on Jack Hibben. He appointed Hibben to head the most important faculty committees and leaned on him in dealing with administrative details, conferring with him daily. Later, when he fell ill and took a leave of absence, he named Hibben acting president.

As dean of the Graduate School, Andrew West remained an independent power. Wilson seems to have distrusted West at the outset of his presidency; Bliss Perry later recalled him saying soon after he became president, "If West begins to intrigue against me as he did against Patton, *we must see who is master.*"[12] Despite those misgivings, he found West friendly and cooperative, and the priority he placed on building a graduate college and improving graduate education guaranteed harmony between the two men for a while.

During his first three years as president, Wilson concentrated on the changes that were easiest to make—beefing up the faculty and revamping the curriculum. In pursuing those goals, he revealed still another aspect of leadership that would carry over to public office: he made speeches to people he considered his key constituents—Princeton alumni. This was the part of the job he liked most. He hit the alumni circuit far more than Patton had done and sought to build a base of support for what he wanted to do. He also spoke at other colleges and universities and to educational groups in an effort to bolster Princeton's visibility and broadcast his vision to a wider public. Securing a better faculty involved increasing the university's size and recruiting distinguished scholars and scientists. The faculty grew from 108 at the beginning of Wilson's presidency to 172 eight years later and became less inbred, with Princeton degree holders dropping as a share of the total from two thirds to less than half. Wilson also scrapped all notions about Presbyterian orthodoxy and hired the first Catholic and the first Jewish faculty members.[13]

Faculty affairs caused the first friction between him and others at

Princeton. Unlike Patton, who had solicited names for new hires from the trustees' Curriculum Committee, Wilson often acted on his own. Some trustees complained, but he continued to initiate appointments, submitting them afterward to the committee for pro forma approval. He likewise pruned dead wood from the faculty ranks. Most of the lesser lights were older men whom he could ignore or let retire, but in several cases he pushed full professors into retirement because of bad classroom performance. This practice left hard feelings, but he made dismissals stick and proved that he was in earnest about faculty standards.

Another aspect of improving the faculty dovetailed with reform of the curriculum. Princeton lagged behind other colleges and universities in establishing academic departments and organizing its curriculum along disciplinary lines, and Wilson changed that by organizing courses into "groups," such as philosophy, classics, mathematics, English literature, and the natural sciences, with distribution requirements among the groups to ensure that students took "a well-considered liberal curriculum."[14] He also announced that the faculty would be organized into eleven departments, and he appointed chairmen, including West in Classics and Fine in Mathematics. His own department was to be called History and Politics. When the department later split in two, the second half remained Politics; it did not become Political Science, a term Wilson sometimes used but disliked.

Nor was Wilson a detached overseer of student life. As he once noted, "Sometimes, when I go through the campus of Princeton at night, and see the brilliant display of lighted windows, I know perfectly well what is going on in those rooms. I have lived in those rooms myself." He continued to teach throughout his presidency because he did not want "to lose this direct contact with the men, or the intellectual stimulation which comes from class room work." He usually taught two courses each year, both in the second semester. He also remained approachable to students outside class, and he befriended several of the more serious and personable ones. Two such students were Raymond Fosdick and Norman Thomas, of the class of 1905; both were minister's sons from small towns, serious scholars but lively, sociable young men with potential for leadership.[15] In them, Wilson could see a later generation's embodiment of himself. Such young men represented his ideal student, but he knew how exceptional they were and how little the prevailing atmosphere encouraged other students to be like them. A lack of seriousness about studies still bedeviled Princeton, and its "picnic" reputation and plethora of easy courses, locally known as pipes, had increased in recent years.

Presbyterianism's grip on Princeton had loosened, but the influences that were replacing it among the students boded no intellectual improvement. As part of a larger social trend, more and more sons of the wealthy were going to boarding schools and prestigious colleges. Matriculation at these colleges had become an upper-middle-class rite of passage that featured social connections, attendance at football games, and the frenetic pursuit of leisure and excitement. Princeton's prevailing undergraduate style of dress—dirty corduroy trousers and a black sweater—tended to mask differences in wealth, but social distinctions were growing. McCosh had barred the Greek-letter fraternities that were proliferating on other campuses, but starting with the founding of the Ivy Club in 1879, "eating clubs" had come to play the same role of discriminating among students and introducing a universally acknowledged social hierarchy. After 1895, the eating clubs expanded in number and social importance, and President Patton had once allegedly boasted that he ran the best country club in America.[16]

In seeking to promote intellectual seriousness at Princeton, Wilson had his work cut out for him. Although he would later fight against social discrimination, especially by the clubs, that was not his original or primary aim. His focus during his first years as president of Princeton was overwhelmingly, relentlessly intellectual. Besides putting the new curriculum and departmental organization in place and stalking prospective donors, particularly Andrew Carnegie, he continued to speak out about his vision of liberal education and Princeton's leadership in the world. He also dealt with student affairs, including a case of a student who was caught cheating. The young man's mother had reportedly come to plead for her son, claiming that she was about to undergo a serious operation and his expulsion might kill her. "You force me to say a hard thing," Ellen's cousin Mary Hoyt remembered Wilson saying, "but if I had to choose between your life or my life or anybody's life and the good of this college, I should choose the good of the college." Mary Hoyt also remembered Ellen telling her, "And he came home so white and ill that he could eat no lunch."[17]

By his third year as president, Wilson felt ready to prescribe stronger medicine to remedy the lack of intellectual seriousness. In February 1905, in a report to the trustees, he recommended the "tutorial system" that he had long advocated, which would combine the "advantage of the small college" with the "advantage of the great university [that] lies in its stimulating life." He proposed to bring in a new corps of teachers to deal with "small groups of students, whose guides, counsellors, and friends they will be in their work," and thereby "make a reading man of [the student] instead of a mere pupil receiving instruction." Though intentionally short on specifics about this new system, he could not avoid the subject of money. He estimated that $2.5 million would be needed. "But," he argued, "no more distinguished gift could be made to American education." At the same time, he launched a committee of fifty wealthy alumni, headed by Cleveland Dodge, to raise the needed funds, and he went hunting for the men who would do the teaching. In a magazine article titled "The Princeton Preceptorial System," Wilson proposed to gather faculty and students "into a common body . . . among whom a real community of interest, pursuit, and feeling will prevail."[18]

His enthusiasm drove the project forward. He interviewed nearly all of the candidates himself, thereby exposing them to his persuasiveness. Appointed in June 1905, the initial cohort of what the students dubbed the "fifty preceptor guys to make us wise" actually numbered forty-four, with two more, in mathematics, appointed in September. By any measure, it was a remarkable group. Thirty-seven of the preceptors held doctorates, only three of which were from Princeton, and many would go on to distinguished academic careers, most often at Princeton. Given the normally glacial pace of change and ingrained resistance to innovation prevailing in most academic institutions, Wilson pulled off a remarkable coup in getting the preceptorial system up and running so fast. Even more remarkable was its instant, unqualified success. All interested parties praised the experiment. The faculty was delighted, and as one of the three Princeton Ph.D.'s among the preceptors recalled, "This infusion of new blood was the best thing that ever happened to Princeton. The place was too inbred." Even the undergraduates got caught up in the excitement; one who had been a freshman in 1905 recalled "that the intellectual life of Princeton was immediately quickened."[19]

Some of this seemed too good to be true, and it was. The system depended on the character and enthusiasm of the preceptors. Not all of them lived up to expectations, and small group tutorials did not work well in all fields. Fine recognized early that, except in mathematics, this approach did not apply to the sciences, and he diverted his preceptorial funds to laboratory instruction. The preceptorial system really depended on the inspiration provided by Wilson, and its greatest drawback was that the stimulation would wear off after this first blush of enthusiasm and would cool down in the absence of such inspired leadership. Nevertheless, the system did lift intellectual standards and expectations for years to come.

It also gave Princeton lots of good publicity and made it more attractive to applicants who were bright, ambitious, and well connected. In 1907, there would be rumors that President Roosevelt's second son, Kermit, might forsake his father's and older brother's alma mater, Harvard, for Princeton. Those rumors proved unfounded, but they gave a hint of how Princeton's reputation was blossoming. The preceptorial system made Wilson the best-known college president in the country, and newspapers and magazines carried numerous stories about this dynamic academic leader. Such publicity was heady stuff, and it came on top of other successes. Yet Wilson did not neglect the more mundane, practical aspects of a university president. Financially, Princeton's budget increased and ran deficits, a circumstance that evidently did not bother him greatly. He took an active interest in the university's buildings, possibly under Ellen's influence, and worked closely with Ralph Adams Cram, the country's leading exponent of Gothic Revival architecture, on the design and construction of classrooms and dormitories. It was during his presidency that the campus began to acquire the features that have given Princeton its distinctive look.

Nor did the athletic side of the university suffer under his leadership. Wilson remained a devoted fan of the football team, and in 1905 he joined with twelve other university presidents in an initiative of President Roosevelt's to fend off agitation for the abolition of college football by reforming the rules of the game. That year, Princeton also opened its first golf course, and the next year saw the dedication of the most significant athletic facility built under Wilson's presidency—Carnegie Lake. This lake, for rowing, was the only gift Wilson was able to wheedle out of the Scottish-born philanthropist, despite playing upon Witherspoon's, McCosh's, and Princeton's Caledonian heritage. He had hoped for a library or money for the preceptorial system. Instead, in keeping with his pacifism and belief that football was warlike, Carnegie paid for a lake in order to promote rowing as a major college sport.

Wilson's new job left him with little time for writing, except on educational issues. He did express some political opinions, but only privately or in passing in speeches on educational subjects. "I am of the class of men who are described as *imperialists*," he declared early in 1903, although he also confessed to "an intense sympathy with the men on the other side." Another time, he asserted that "the great incubus upon this country is its provincialism," and he condemned the provincialism of urbanites for lacking "an imaginative sympathy" for the lot of farmers. Yet he stuck to his anti-Bryan guns. "The trouble is that Bryan has caught the spirit and instincts of the finer aspects of American life," Wilson told Roland Morris, a former student who was a Bryan supporter, "but, Morris, the man has no brains. It is a great pity that a man with his power of leadership should have no mental rudder." Wilson's private views on race did not show much breadth of sympathy—or foresight—either. At the beginning of his third year as president, he answered an inquiry about the possibility of an African American applying to Princeton this way: "I would say that, while there is nothing in the law of the University to prevent a negro's entering, the whole temper and tradition of the place are such that no negro has ever applied for admission, and . . . [it] seems extremely unlikely that the question will ever assume a practical form."[20]

Wilson's family life was happy and harmonious during the first years of his Princeton presidency, with one tragic exception. Ellen did not enjoy having to exchange her beloved house on Library Place for Prospect House, the president's house on campus, especially after some students tore down a new fence around the grounds. But she and their daughters and her sister, Madge, adjusted to their new lives. Margaret, Jessie, and Nell followed Madge to the girls' school in the town of Princeton, founded by Harry Fine's sister, and Margaret and Jessie subsequently went away to college. The lively, attractive Madge became the object of much attention from the preceptors, and in 1910 she married one of them, a special favorite of Wilson's whom he made a dean, Edward (Ed) Graham Elliott. Ellen's brother Stockton had meanwhile established himself as a popular teacher at Princeton, although he periodically took leaves for "nervous exhaustion," most likely depression. The tragic exception to this pattern of domestic happiness came at the end of April 1905, when Ellen's brother Eddie and his wife and young son were killed in a ferryboat accident in South Carolina. Their deaths devastated Ellen, who fell into a depression that lasted several months and left a shadow of sadness over her for the rest of her life. As self-therapy, she read deeply in philosophy to assuage her doubts about religion, and she resumed drawing and painting.[21]

Ellen Wilson needed to summon up emotional reserves as the year 1905 drew to a close. On December 2, Princeton hosted the Army-Navy game, attended by the president of the United States. The Wilsons entertained the official party at a pregame lunch, and Madge later recalled Roosevelt shouting "Miss Axson!" at her and thumping the table with his fists as he delivered loud pleasantries. When she excused herself to meet her date for the game, the young man asked what the commotion was about. "That was just the President of the United States engaged in mild banter," Madge snapped, "and if that's the way Presidents behave, I hope to the Lord I never meet another!" At the game, Navy came from behind at the end to hold Army to a tie, but for some spectators the high point came when, as one preceptor recalled, "Roosevelt and Wilson cross[ed] the field together between the halves, Roosevelt exuberant, smiling, delighted, waving his hat, acknowledging the plaudits of the multitudes and tugging along the University president who followed 'with conscious step of purity and pride,' if not reluctant, at least not equally ebullient."[22]

As events transpired, Wilson was then almost halfway through his tenure as president of Princeton and at the pinnacle of accomplishment and joy in that office. "We have seen academic life at its best," Fine later remarked to Edward Elliott. "Never again can we hope to attain the conditions that marked the first half of Woodrow's regime." Six months later, on the morning of May 28, 1906, Wilson awoke to find that he was blind in his left eye. Accompanied by his friend Jack Hibben, he traveled to Philadelphia, where George de Schweinitz, an ophthalmologist, found that he had suffered a hemorrhage in the eye. He diagnosed its cause as arteriosclerosis—hardening of the arteries—and advised Wilson to give up all active work. A second physician, Alfred Stengel, an internist, agreed with the diagnosis but reassured Wilson that the disease was in an early stage and that a three-month rest would make him fit to work again. He did gradually regain partial vision in that eye.[23]

The incident shook Ellen, who was still grieving over Eddie's death, even more than it did her husband. "It is hardening of the arteries," she told Florence Hoyt, "due to the prolonged high pressure on brain and nerves. He has lived too tensely. . . . Of course, it is an awful thing—a dying by inches, and incurable." At the time, physicians had no way to treat arteriosclerosis except to prescribe rest. Wilson arranged to take a leave of absence, naming Hibben acting president, and he spent most of the summer of 1906 in England, particularly in the Lake District, first with Ellen and later by himself, hiking regularly, sometimes fourteen miles a day. On one of his hikes, he met a local artist named Fred Yates, who soon became a close friend and later painted portraits of Wilson and Ellen. By early September, he could report to Ellen that two eminent physicians in Edinburgh, an ophthalmologist and an internist, believed he could return to work with "proper moderation."[24] Wilson would make gestures at moderation, such as promising to limit outside speaking engagements and taking a winter vacation, in Bermuda, at the beginning of 1907. Otherwise, he reacted to this physical setback by becoming even more focused, purposeful, and driven.

Two major items remained on Wilson's agenda for transforming Princeton into one of the nation's leading universities. One was to reorganize the undergraduates into residential units, where they would be overseen and taught by members of the faculty, after the fashion of the colleges at

Oxford and Cambridge. The other was to build a graduate college and locate it in the center of the campus. Wilson tackled both problems as soon as he got back to New Jersey in the fall of 1906. Of the two, he would have preferred to deal first with the undergraduate college. The center-piece in this design was a scheme that had gelled in Wilson's mind during that summer of 1906—what came to be called the Quadrangle Plan, or the Quad Plan, for short. Instead, events intervened to bring the Graduate College to the fore temporarily. In October 1906, Andrew West, the dean of the Graduate School, received an offer to serve as president of the Massachusetts Institute of Technology. West later said that he told Wilson he was "discouraged at the delays in furthering the cause of the Graduate College and at his attitude toward me. President Wilson became indig-nant and said he had given me full support and that my attitude was not justified." After a meeting of the trustees' Graduate School Committee, they and the president urged the dean to stay, and West agreed. Everyone papered over the incidents with professions of harmony, but this was the first open clash between West and Wilson. It marked the beginning of a struggle for direction and control of graduate education at Princeton.[25]

With the matter of West's offer settled, Wilson could turn his atten-tion to the Quad Plan. Late in 1906, he unveiled a preliminary sketch of his vision at a meeting of the trustees. The eating clubs, with their "social competition," struck him as "peculiarly hostile" to intellectual life, and he proposed to remedy the situation by having students "live together, not in clubs but in colleges."[26] He also suggested that some clubs might become colleges. This presentation of the Quad Plan marked his first major mis-step as president of Princeton. As with the preceptorial system, he had not consulted anyone in advance, but this time his vision did not carry the day. The trustees appointed a committee that would take five months to study the question before making a recommendation. In the meantime, Grover Cleveland worried that the plan might interfere with development of the Graduate School, and another trustee asked why they could not simply require the eating clubs to take in all upperclassmen. Wilson tried to reas-sure Cleveland but dismissed the other trustee's question because it struck him as missing the point, which was not the clubs' social discrimination.

He also had mixed success in selling the Quad Plan to faculty inti-mates. After a meeting at Prospect House, Fine enthusiastically told him, "Yes, Tommy, I think that it will do the trick." Hibben, however, said nothing one way or the other. Undeterred, Wilson announced to the trustees' Graduate School Committee at the end of May 1907 that the Quad Plan involved "a thing more hopeful and of deeper consequence than anything we have hitherto turned our counsels to." Princeton's recent advances would be "in vain if the processes of disintegration and of distorted social ambition . . . are not checked and remedied by some radical change." The eating clubs were also pernicious, in his view, because they had "no intellectual purposes or ideals of any kind at their foundation." He made this argument to the Graduate School Committee because West was now proposing that the Graduate College be built at an off-campus site, separated from the undergraduate classrooms and dormitories. Wilson argued that such a move would be contrary to the larger purposes behind the Quad Plan: "nothing will so steady and invigorate the process of transformation as the close neighborhood, the unmistakable example, and the daily influence of the Graduate College."[27]

To the full board of trustees, he declared, "We have witnessed in the last few years the creation of a new Princeton," and now consummation of its drive to the top among American universities demanded the creation of residential colleges. "The clubs simply happen to stand in the way. . . . We are not seeking to form better clubs, but academic communities."[28] His eloquence appeared to carry the day, although he had also done his homework, meeting several times with the Graduate School Committee and enlisting Fine's aid in persuading committee members. Just one trustee voted against the plan, but in fact the trustees approved the Quad Plan only in principle. Wilson was not yet home free.

At the time, however, he felt so good that he allowed himself to crow a bit. Two weeks after the trustees' meeting, he received an honorary degree and spoke at Harvard. Wilson teased his hosts about the differences in their backgrounds—Massachusetts versus Virginia, Puritan versus Scotch-Irish—and drew upon those differences to observe that their respective universities were academic competitors: "Now we at Princeton are in the arena and you at Harvard are in the arena." Harvard championed the free-elective system, while Princeton was "seeking to combine men in a common discipline."[29] He welcomed the contest and left no doubt who he believed would win. Wilson was once more bearding a lion in his den. The Harvard president who conferred the honorary degree was Charles W. Eliot, the father of the free-elective system, and this upstart from Princeton was attacking the man's brainchild and challenging his university's primacy in American higher education.

Wilson's cocky tone may have reflected some success that he was enjoying in another area. The publicity he had garnered as president of Princeton had given him a chance to flirt again with his first love—politics. The magazine editor George Harvey had indeed marked him as a good prospect to shoulder the banner of the conservative Cleveland wing of the Democratic Party. A year earlier, in February 1906, the Lotos

Club—a prestigious New York City literary club whose members were prominent artists, journalists, and publishers—had given a dinner at which Wilson was a guest and speaker, and on that occasion Harvey had called on the Democrats to choose a leader "who combines the activities of the present with the sober influences of the past . . . Woodrow Wilson of Virginia and New Jersey." Wilson professed to be embarrassed by Harvey's remarks and the editor's endorsement in *Harper's Weekly.* Yet he did not laugh off this "nomination." Shortly afterward, he told a Democratic newspaper editor that he hoped their party would nominate "someone who held views and a position like my own" and reject "rash and revolutionary proposals."[30]

Probably through Harvey's influence, Wilson spoke in April 1906 at the annual Jefferson Day dinner held by the New York Democratic Club, a conservative group allied with the city's Democratic political machine, Tammany Hall. He soft-pedaled his long-standing rejection of Jefferson's limited-government state-rights views, lambasted socialism, and scorned wrongheaded government interference with business and labor. Frequent bursts of applause at the dinner, together with reactions that Harvey gathered, showed that the editor's new political prospect had made a hit. During the year following that speech, Wilson kept a foot in politics. Late in 1906, he spoke out against the income tax because he said it discriminated against the rich and because "I know of only one legitimate object of taxation, and that is to pay the expenses of the Government." In March 1907, he took a slap at Roosevelt and the president's platform, by declaring, "[W]hat we need is not a square deal, but no deal at all—an old-fashioned equality and harmony of conditions."[31]

Early in 1907, Wilson allowed Democrats in the New Jersey legislature to place his name in nomination for the office of U.S. senator. This was strictly a gesture, since the Democrats were in the minority. His backing came from party bosses and offended reformers. Wilson told a conservative Princeton alumnus, Adrian Joline, that he agreed with a pro-business, anti-Bryan speech Joline had recently given, adding, "Would that we could do something, at once dignified and effective, to knock Mr. Bryan once and for all into a cocked hat!"[32] That sentence would come back to haunt him, as would his sponsorship by the New Jersey bosses. This initial foray into politics would give him an embarrassing conservative past to live down.

More immediate problems vexed Wilson in 1907 as a backlash arose against the Quad Plan. Students and alumni who were attached to the clubs predictably saw the plan as a threat to their cherished institutions, and the trustees' timing—they met during the week of commencement and reunions and announced their support for the plan on a night when many students and alumni were enjoying parties at the clubs—seemed calculated to raise suspicion and ire. Opponents seethed in private over the summer and would burst into the open in the fall. In July, West told Wilson that the Quad Plan and the way he had introduced it were "both wrong—not inexpedient merely—but morally wrong. . . . If the spirit of Princeton is to be killed, I have little interest in the details of its funeral." In September, Henry van Dyke—a Presbyterian minister, popular poet and magazine writer, and professor of English—wrote in the *Princeton Alumni Weekly* that the Quad Plan was "distinctly an un-American plan. It threatens not only to break up the classes, but also to put the Princeton spirit out of date."[33] In October, Tommy Wilson's old paper, now called *The Daily Princetonian*, also came out against the plan.

Opposition from conservatives such as West and van Dyke was to be expected. What Wilson had not expected was the stand Jack Hibben took. In tense conversations early in July, Hibben told Wilson that he did not agree with him on the Quad Plan. These encounters upset both men, although they strove to handle their disagreement with respect and friendship. Wilson assured "my dear Jack" that they would still "at every step know each other's love." Otherwise, opposition to the Quad Plan roused a combative streak that had lain mostly dormant in Wilson since his youth. "The fight is on," he told Cleveland Dodge.[34] Letters of support that poured in from alumni, particularly younger men who had suffered rejection by the clubs, stiffened his resolve, as did expressions of support from other faculty members. But this combativeness worried some of his supporters among the faculty and board of trustees, who thought Wilson seemed tense and obsessive.

The showdown came when the faculty met to consider the Quad Plan in September. Some of Wilson's supporters had gotten together beforehand, and one introduced a resolution calling for the appointment of a committee to implement the plan. Van Dyke offered a substitute resolution to refer the matter to a joint faculty-trustee committee for further study, and Hibben seconded the motion. The faculty then agreed to adjourn and take up the resolutions the following week. Hibben's action struck the faculty like a thunderbolt and hit Wilson like a body blow. Ellen recalled that when she heard the news, she burst into tears and blurted out, "Oh, he *might* have let someone else second the motion!" Why Hibben did it is not known. Signs of strain had occasionally cropped up earlier in their friendship, and differences in temperament—Wilson's driving intensity and Hibben's bent toward conciliation—had made some around Princeton regard them as an odd couple. Also, theirs had never been a friendship of equals, and both Hibben and his strong-minded wife may have grown to resent what they regarded as Wilson's domineering ways.35

Nothing up to that time had ever hurt Wilson so deeply as what he regarded as Hibben's betrayal, and subsequent events would keep the wound raw. Three years later, he told a confidant about the anguish he felt on seeing Hibben at a ceremony at Nassau Hall: "Why will that wound not heal over in my stubborn heart?" With the exception of Stockton Axson, who was a family member, Wilson never had such a close male friend in his life, no one whom he could freely and unreservedly tell he loved. His daughter Margaret would later tell a family friend, "The two major tragedies in Father's life were his failure to carry over the League of Nations and the break with Mr. Hibben."36 Never again would Wilson open his heart this way to anyone, except sometimes to Axson and to the women who were closest to him.

Wounded feelings did not prevent him from rising to the occasion in the faculty debate over the Quad Plan, however. He spoke with such eloquence that even West applauded him. Unfortunately, no one recorded what he said; there is only one preceptor's recollection that he had affirmed, "Truth is no invalid." Wilson's eloquence helped him prevail with the divided faculty, although he almost certainly had the votes to win anyway. Those who favored van Dyke's motion to shelve consideration of the Quad Plan were alumni with attachments to the "old Princeton"; the only possible surprise was Wilson's classmate William Magie. Otherwise, the opposition included such familiar faces as West, van Dyke, Patton, and now Hibben. The president's supporters were an equally predictable assortment that included Axson, Fine, and all but one of the preceptors.37

The Quad Plan would almost certainly have prevailed if the faculty had gotten a chance to vote on it, and opponents were already talking about compromise. But the trustees rendered their consideration and talk of compromise moot when they met in October and passed three resolutions withdrawing their earlier approval. They softened the blow by adopting a further resolution that allowed Wilson to continue to try to sell his ideas to the Princeton community. For all practical purposes, this was the end of the Quad Plan. It was a stunning defeat, and Wilson should have seen it coming. His earlier successes had masked the fragile nature of his support among the trustees. Three years earlier, one supporter on the board had advised him to nominate other like-minded men and not to "elect two or three more very rich men simply because they are rich men."[38] Wilson had secured Dodge and other supporters as trustees, and they would form his hard core of support on the board. Otherwise, most of its members were "very rich men" chosen mainly for their wealth and alumni loyalty, and some of them had begun to have second thoughts soon after they approved the Quad Plan in June.

Why Wilson failed to heed the straws in the wind probably spoke more to his physical and emotional state than to anything else. His agitation and rigidity may have stemmed from his reaction to his illness the previous summer. His impatience to see the Quad Plan enacted and his combativeness toward critics and opponents bordered on obsession. Fine believed, he later told Wilson's first biographer, that "undoubtedly Wilson was too impatient and that if he had been willing to put the new plan in force gradually, he could perhaps have carried it, but he wanted it all at once." Wilson evidently recognized that he was rushing things. Before the trustees met, he drafted a statement affirming, "So great and complex a reform cannot be hastened either in its discussion or in its execution," but he extended this olive branch too late. Alumni opposition to the Quad Plan seemed to be growing. The editor of the *Princeton Alumni Weekly*, which was not an official university publication, opposed the plan and offered a forum for public attacks, which, together with private communications, moved the trustees to vote as they did. Their minutes did not record how each of them voted on the resolutions rescinding approval of the plan, but they did note that Moses Pyne moved the main resolutions. The most influential member of the board had evidently turned against Wilson.[39]

He tried to make the best of the situation. Right after the meeting, he drafted, in his shorthand, a stinging letter of resignation, telling the trustees that they had made "it plain to me that you will not feel able to support me any further in the only matters in which I feel that I can lead and be of service to you." He did not finish the draft and told a supporter, "I refrained from resigning because I saw at last that I did not have the right to place the University in danger of going to pieces." Instead, he put an optimistic gloss on the trustees' action in an interview with the New York *Evening Sun:* "I do not consider that the trustees are opposed to the quad system on principle, but merely reversed their former decision . . . as they thought that the university and alumni were not sufficiently informed or prepared for the new plan." That statement infuriated Pyne, who had words with Wilson. "They wish me to be silent," Wilson told a trustee who was a supporter, "and I have got nothing out of the transaction except complete defeat and mortification." If Pyne thought he could muzzle Wilson, he misjudged his man. "The difference between a strong man and a weak one," Wilson told a student group soon afterward, "is that the former does not give up after a defeat."[40]

The encounter with Pyne in October 1907 marked the opening skirmish in Wilson's continuing advocacy of the Quad Plan, which soon merged with the fight over the Graduate College. He would have the same main antagonist in both fights—not West, but Pyne. The dapper, handsome, high-voiced Momo Pyne epitomized the breed of "very rich men" Wilson had been warned about earlier. Heir to a large fortune made mostly in railroads, Pyne was just a year older than Wilson and had been two classes ahead of him at Princeton. He had retired early from active work to live at his elegant estate, called Drumthwacket, not far from the campus. He devoted his energies mainly to Princeton, where he had been a trustee since 1884. Previously a strong supporter of Wilson's, Pyne did not turn against him all at once in the fight over the Quad Plan. Two months after the trustees' decision, he worried that Wilson was working too hard and told him, "As one of your warmest friends, please allow me to protest against this."[41] Still, Pyne never again admired or trusted Wilson as he had done previously.

Wilson did not jump at once into the renewed fight over the Quad Plan because other matters occupied him at the end of 1907. This had been one of his best years for attracting academic stars to the Princeton faculty, and politics continued to provide an interesting diversion. He also delivered eight lectures at Columbia University, which gave him a chance to revisit the territory of *Congressional Government*. He spoke from short-hand outlines, and a stenographer produced a transcript of the lectures, which he revised for publication in 1908 as a book titled *Constitutional Government in the United States*. "A constitutional government is one whose powers have been adapted to the interests of its people and to the maintenance of individual liberty," he declared, and he advocated "conservative change, . . . a process, not of revolution, but of modification . . . nor by way of desperate search for remedies for existing evils."[42]

Despite those statements, *Constitutional Government* was not a conservative manifesto. Wilson included few direct comments on contemporary concerns and produced, instead, a work that stood somewhere between a revision of *Congressional Government* (which he had never undertaken) and a foreshadowing of what he might have done in "Philosophy of Politics." Wilson again revealed that he had no use for absolutist state-rights, limited-government views. Among the founders of the Republic, he praised only two Federalists—John Marshall and Alexander Hamilton—

and, without naming Jefferson, he eschewed what he regarded as Jefferson's political legacy by scorning "the Whig theory of political dynamics, which was a sort of unconscious copy of the Newtonian theory of the universe. . . . The trouble with the theory is that government is not a machine, but a living thing. . . . It is accountable to Darwin, not to Newton. It is modified by its environment, necessitated by its tasks, shaped to its functions by the sheer pressure of life."[43]

Much of this book reads like *Congressional Government* revisited, but with a different choice of subjects and a difficult emphasis. About the presidency, he affirmed, "There is no national party choice except that of President. No one else represents the people as a whole, exercising a national choice. . . . He can dominate his party by being spokesman for the real sentiment and purpose of the country, by giving direction to opinion." Wilson also noted that in foreign affairs the president's power is "very absolute." Congress pleased him no more than it had twenty years earlier. In the House, the Speaker had become "an autocrat," replacing the previously all-powerful committees, but the effect remained the same—stifling debate. Meanwhile, the Senate had become "the chamber of debate and individual privilege." To remedy these defects, Wilson now looked to the president: with his ability "to appeal to the nation," he could become the real legislative leader.[44]

Wilson also discussed courts and the states in *Constitutional Government*. He praised the power of courts "to restrain the government," but he worried about the influence of money, asking, "*Are* our courts as available for the poor man as for the rich?" He also declared, "The Constitution was not meant to hold the government back to the time of horses and wagons." He praised the states for saving the nation from excessive centralization, but he also once more dismissed the "old theory of State sovereignty" as having been settled by the "stern arbitrament" of the Civil War. In closing, Wilson argued that "only by the external authority of party" could the separation and dispersal of powers be bridged in order to gain "some coherence to the action of political forces." He ridiculed "the distinction that we make between 'politicians' and 'statesmen,'" and he praised those who "attempt the hazardous and little honored business of party management." Fortunately, he asserted, Americans now seemed to regard "parties once more as instruments for progressive action, as means for handling the affairs of a new age."[45]

Constitutional Government did not make the same splash as *Congressional Government*. Reviews were mixed, and it would never be as widely read, nor would it remain continuously in print, as *Congressional Government* has. To some extent, the difference in the two books' reception and reputation was deserved. *Constitutional Government* lacked the focus and freshness of *Congressional Government.* It suffered from mixed inspirations and mixed tones—sometimes sharp like Bagehot, sometimes reflective like Burke, sometimes diffuse like Bryce. Yet those defects did not detract from the book's strengths. *Constitutional Government* covered a larger canvas, and it spoke much better to possible cures for current ills. It also raised questions about how far its author had really gone down the road to conservatism.

Little else that Wilson said in 1907 would have made anyone doubt his allegiance to the right wing of the Democratic Party. At one point, he took a slam at both Roosevelt and Bryan by warning against radicalism and haste: "We are undertaking to regulate before we have made thorough analysis of the conditions to be rectified." He also objected to the new forms of direct democracy that were coming out of the West—the initiative and referendum—and he still opposed woman suffrage. His daughter Jessie later recalled that when she came home from college a convinced suffragist, she took issue with her father and said to him, "You have the vote, but there is only one of you and there are four of us, and we are unrepresented." Wilson's public and private utterances in 1907 marked his longest stretch toward conservatism. During the summer, he wrote a statement of his political convictions, "A Credo," in which he argued against "the danger of attempting what government is not fitted to do" and called for strict separation of powers in the federal government, especially insulation of the courts from pressures by the president or Congress. Yet he said nothing about state-rights, and he condemned overactive government as unwise and inexpedient, not as morally or constitutionally impermissible. He also again called the president "the only active officer of the government who is chosen by the whole people. He alone, therefore, speaks for them as a direct representative of the nation."[46]

One other influence held Wilson back from resuming the fight over the Quad Plan at the end of 1907. In late November, he suffered another attack of pain and numbness in his right hand, similar to the one he had suffered eleven years before.[47] This latest episode of what his doctors again called "neuritis" prompted Wilson to bow to urgings to take another winter vacation. He again traveled by himself, to spend half of January and most of February 1908 in Bermuda, where he rode his bicycle and spent time thinking and writing, including revising the transcripts of his lectures for *Constitutional Government.* He also enjoyed the company of some of the people he encountered there, among them the writer Mark Twain.

But of all Bermuda's seasonal denizens, the one who interested Wilson most was a tall, slender woman in her mid-forties from Pittsfield, Massachusetts, named Mary Allen Hulbert Peck. Long estranged from her husband, Mrs. Peck had spent winters in Bermuda since the early 1890s and had become a social fixture there. Wilson must have liked her almost at first sight, because on his first visit to Bermuda, a year earlier, he had told her, "It is not often that I can have the privilege of meeting anyone whom I can so entirely admire and enjoy." After he returned to Princeton, he sent her a volume of Bagehot's writings and a collection of his own essays, and he wrote to her of "an instinctive sympathy between us." Such expressions were common for Wilson; he was in the habit of corresponding on familiar terms with women. Ellen encouraged those relationships and did not accompany him on his winter trips to Bermuda in 1907 and 1908 or his summer visit to England and Scotland in 1908 because she recognized her own tendencies toward depression, especially after Eddie's death. "Since he has married a wife who is not gay," Florence Hoyt remembered her saying, "I must provide him with friends who are."[48]

Wilson did not write to Mrs. Peck again before he returned to Bermuda in 1908, but he rushed to see her as soon as his ship docked. During the next six weeks, he spent a great deal of time with her, sometimes in the company of others but often with her alone. He was plainly smitten with the vivacious, attractive Mary Peck. At one point, he wrote in shorthand on a document, "My precious one, my beloved Mary." He may have fallen for her now because of the emotional void left by the break with Jack Hibben. A year later, he would say to her, "What a fool I am to go back to that so often! Can my heart *never* be cured of its hurt?" She would also be the one to whom he would later confide how his "stubborn heart" would not heal from that wound.[49]

The recent defeat of the Quad Plan may also have made him feel emotionally vulnerable. Over the next two years, his feelings for Mary Peck would wax and wane, growing particularly intense during the times when he was suffering strain and setbacks in the fight over that plan and the negotiations for the Graduate College. He did not begin writing regularly to Mrs. Peck until the fall of 1908, after he and Ellen visited her in Pittsfield on their way to Williams College, where a friend and supporter from the Princeton faculty, Harry Garfield, was being inaugurated as president. After that visit, he started writing her letters in which he bared his heart and mind in a way he had not done with anyone except Ellen twenty years earlier. Mary Peck was not on Bermuda when Wilson returned for winter vacation early in 1909, and he saw her afterward mainly on visits to New York, where she moved around that time. For

Wilson, the relationship seems to have peaked in intensity at the beginning of 1910. He did not see Mary Peck much after that, although he continued writing her revealing letters for another five years.

One question has always hung over the encounter between Wilson and Mrs. Peck—how far did it go? Was this more than an intense, confiding friendship between a man and a woman (from 1909 on, Wilson began his letters "Dearest Friend")? Did this relationship qualify as an affair? The only people who knew—Woodrow Wilson and Mary Peck—never said. No one, therefore, can say for certain what happened between them, but that would not stop speculation. Some interpreters have concluded that this was not a full-fledged affair. Some, wishing to view Wilson's behavior charitably, have maintained that he was a moral man who did not want to hurt his wife, whom he still loved deeply. Wilson himself supported this view when he wrote to Ellen in 1908 about Grover Cleveland's admitted sexual dalliances, calling them Cleveland's "early moral weaknesses" and hinting that they "had returned" in his later years. Others, viewing Wilson harshly, have maintained that such a supposedly unattractive prig was incapable of having a sexual fling. When stories about Mrs. Peck began to circulate during the 1912 presidential campaign, Theodore Roosevelt, who was by then a bitter rival, brushed the talk aside with the sneer, "You can't convince the American people that a man is a Romeo who looks so much like the apothecary's clerk."[50]

Some interpreters have concluded that it was a real, sexual affair. Wilson may have been over fifty, but the sexual desires he had shown earlier for Ellen had not cooled. A few years later, when he courted the woman who became his second wife, he would demonstrate again just how much physical passion he could feel. Moreover, from the start, Ellen suspected something untoward between her husband and Mrs. Peck. She evidently said some harsh and hurt-filled things to him just before he went abroad by himself during the summer of 1908. "'Emotional love,' ah, dearest," Wilson wrote to Ellen from England, "that was a cutting and cruel judgment and utterly false; but as natural as false; but I never blamed you for it or wondered at it. . . . My darling! I have never been worthy of you,—but I love you with all my poor, mixed, inexplicable nature,—with everything fine and tender in me."[51] He wrote her several more letters in the same vein that summer; revealingly, perhaps, this was the only time that he did not save Ellen's letters.

On Ellen's side, shortly before Wilson's death a friend of Cary Grayson's, the White House physician, noted in his diary, "Mrs. Wilson—the first—also talked about . . . [Mrs. Peck] to Cary and among other things said that the 'Peck' affair was the only unhappiness he had caused her during their married life—not that there was anything wrong or improper—about it, for there was not, but just that a brilliant mind and an attractive woman had some-how fascinated—temporarily—Mr. Wilson's mind and she (Mrs. Wilson) did not want to share his confidence of his inner mind with anyone."[52]

Wilson's guilt-filled protests did not stop him from carrying on an intimate correspondence with Mary Peck and seeing more of her. Something happened between them in 1908 that made Wilson feel guiltier still. Seven years later, after Ellen's death, when Wilson became engaged to Edith Bolling Galt, stories about Mrs. Peck surfaced again, and there were threats that some of his letters to her would be published. In an agony of remorse, Wilson drafted a shorthand statement in which he declared, "These letters disclose a passage of folly and gross impertinence in my life. I am deeply ashamed and repentant. Neither in act nor even in thought was the purity or honor of the lady concerned touched or sullied, and my offense she had generously forgiven." He made a clean breast of the business with Edith Galt, writing to her, "I dreaded the revelation which seemed to be threatened because I knew that it would give a tragically false impression of what I really have been and am,—because it might make the contemptible error and madness of a few months seem a stain upon a whole life."[53]

For her part, Mary Peck behaved with restraint and dignity. Despite her divorce in 1911 and dire financial need, she never betrayed what had passed between her and Wilson. She never published anything about him until after his death, when she wrote some magazine articles and a gossipy memoir, which were more about her than him.

When Wilson returned from Bermuda at the end of February 1908, guilt and anguish about the relationship with Mrs. Peck lay in the future. At that moment, he returned, as he usually did from his holidays abroad, full of fighting spirit—in this case for the Quad Plan. Two weeks after his return, he defended it to an alumni group in Chicago and avowed, "I am a good fighter gentlemen,—on the whole I would rather fight than not, but I have made it a rule never to fight in my own family. I so thoroughly believe that the Princeton feeling is a family feeling."[54] Which way things would go—toward a fight or toward "a family feeling"—would soon become clear.

5

ACADEMIC CIVIL WAR

When Wilson renewed his effort to push the Quad Plan in 1908, he found not "a family feeling" but an academic civil war that for two years would pit student against student, professor against professor, alumnus against alumnus, trustee against trustee, and dean against president. "The quality of the fight on the personal side was incredibly [*sic*] bitter," recalled Stockton Axson. "It was taken up by the women, wives of Trustees[,] of the faculty[,] of the alumni[,] with all the intensity which women have subsequently shown in actual politics." That misogynistic gibe by a lifelong bachelor may be taken with a grain of salt, but in fact the distaff side of this academic family did lend a special edge to the fight. Jack Hibben's wife, Jennie, evidently harbored bitter feelings toward Wilson and badgered her mild-mannered husband, making sure that he continued to oppose him. Ellen Wilson reciprocated with malice toward their former best friend. Early in 1912, when the trustees finally picked Hibben as her husband's successor, Ellen wrote him sarcastically to salute "your very unusual loyalty and availability."[1]

The summer of 1908 provided a brief respite in the fight. Wilson's time in England and Scotland refreshed him, despite the strained feelings between him and Ellen over Mrs. Peck. Fred Yates, their artist friend in the Lake District, reported to Ellen, "He was like a boy last night in his light heartedness. You wouldn't think he ever had a care—it has done him good to come over—and he returns with a new grip of things." As before, Wilson spent much of his time bicycling. He wore short pants, a peaked cap, and a rain cape, and he carried *The Oxford Book of English Verse*. He did unburden himself about Hibben to Yates, who told Ellen, "I think there is no pain like the disloyalty of a man that one has trusted through a life time."[2]

Yet the time away was just a respite; upon his return from abroad Wilson faced Princeton's civil war—and on more than one front. In 1908, the question of the location of the proposed Graduate College burgeoned into a major controversy. This fight, unlike the one over the Quad Plan, struck some observers as overly personal. Bad blood between Andrew West and Wilson had become a painful fact of life at Princeton. Given their contrasts in temperament, outlook, and aims, a clash between them may have been likely, if not foreordained. They had been friends during Wilson's first years on the Princeton faculty, and they had some things in common. West, too, was a Presbyterian minister's son with one parent born in England, and he was likewise a cultural Anglophile and an admirer of Oxford and Cambridge. Also a loyal, devoted Princetonian, class of 1874, he had similarly chafed under the dilatory Patton regime and worked to raise academic standards. Yet even a casual acquaintance with the two men would reveal how different they were. Wilson's trim physique and solitary industriousness contrasted sharply with West's portly build and relentless sociability. It would be wrong, however, to overstress purely personal elements in their clash. A deep gulf in experience, values, and vision separated Wilson from West. The dean of the Graduate School had never attended such a school himself. His doctorate was an honorary degree from Princeton, awarded because he had been a personal favorite of McCosh's. His only academic experience outside Princeton had been at high schools in Cincinnati and New Jersey, and he remained a schoolmaster at heart, delighting in drilling students on fine points of Latin grammar, playing favorites among the students, rewarding and going easy on the sons of trustees and other prominent men. As one preceptor remembered, "He liked social distinctions and social amenities."[3]

When and why West first turned against Wilson is not entirely clear. He had legitimate complaints about the neglect of his plans for the Graduate College, but his enmity seems to have run deeper than would have been expected if those complaints had been the sole cause. He and Wilson held diametrically opposed visions for graduate education and the Graduate College, although the men did not clash during the first four years of Wilson's presidency. In 1903, Wilson had written an approving preface to a university publication in which he praised the dean's published plan for an elaborate, costly Graduate College, maintaining that this was not to be "a pleasing fancy of an English college" and insisting that "this little community of scholars set at the heart of Princeton" would furnish "the real means by which a group of graduate students are most apt to stimulate and set the pace for the whole University."4 That same year, at Princeton's expense, the dean spent several months in England visiting the colleges at Oxford and Cambridge.

The turning point for West probably came in 1905, when he took a stab at a trial run at implementing his vision of the future Graduate College. He took over Merwick, a large house with spacious grounds located half a mile from the campus, which Moses Pyne had secretly bought, to serve as a residence for graduate students. The dean often presided over meals and social functions in the evening, and the students afterward carried lighted candles to escort him to his house across the street. At dinner, the students wore formal dress under their academic gowns, recited grace in Latin, and ate sumptuous meals. Most of the residents knocked off from their studies around four in the afternoon and played sports or bridge. Merwick offered a more refined version of the amenities that the more fortunate juniors and seniors found in the clubs. Small wonder that West excoriated the Quad Plan as inimical to the clubs and the "spirit of Princeton."5

These opposing visions of the Graduate College explain why the battle between Wilson and West came to focus on the location of the college. Once he had tasted the delights of Merwick, the dean demanded an off-campus site, whereas Wilson never budged in his insistence that the facility should be located in the heart of the university. For some observers, this fight over location seemed petty and puzzling. Stockton Axson later recalled one of the trustees saying that "he could not see for the life of him why there was all this fighting . . . [over] where a boarding house should be located."6 This notion that the fight over location was a tempest in a teapot—a viewpoint that would later work against Wilson—was mistaken. The quarrel over where to build the Graduate College involved starkly opposed visions of both the environment and the aims of graduate education at Princeton and, thereby, the prevailing tone of the entire university.

Also, a struggle for power was lurking just offstage. When the trustees established the Graduate School, they gave the dean a large measure of autonomy as a means of circumventing President Patton. West was given the power to approve courses, admit students, award fellowships, and select the faculty Oversight Committee, and he reported directly to the trustees, not the president. Many at Princeton chafed at the arrangement. One graduate student recalled the dean as "authoritarian and devious, simply not to be trusted. He played favorites in awarding fellowships, and even tampered with amounts of scholarship and fellowship funds already granted."7 The academic stars whom Wilson and Fine had attracted to Princeton disliked the situation, too. Even the location issue had a bearing on the power struggle. Wilson's preferred location for the Graduate College was a tract on the campus between Prospect House, where the president lived, and 1879 Hall, where he had his office. Being thereby constantly under Wilson's eye, West would not help being under his thumb. Thus the two men clashed openly over the location in May 1907, but a committee of trustees sidestepped the issue, deciding that it was not expedient to choose a site at that time—a postponement that left West more embittered than ever.

Nearly a year passed before the question of the location of the Graduate College reared its head again. In April 1908, the trustees' committee voted in favor of the site between Prospect and 1879, but West soon introduced a new wrinkle. He claimed that shortly before Grover Cleveland's death in June he and the ex-president had inspected several possible sites and when they came to one adjoining a golf course, which was even farther from the campus than Merwick, Cleveland struck his cane on the ground and exclaimed, "Here is the best site, if you can get it!"[8] This reported blessing gave the dean a new weapon in the fight over the location of the Graduate College.

Wilson seemed oblivious to this turn in the Graduate College controversy, and he turned his attention again to the Quad Plan. When he resumed speaking about it in the fall of 1908, he sounded a new note of political and social reform. In October, at Haverford College's seventy-fifth-anniversary celebration, he asked his fellow college presidents whether it was "their ambition to be presidents of country clubs." He avowed, "Country clubs are very admirable things; but their presidencies do not afford careers." A month later, speaking at a high school in Jersey City, New Jersey, he regretted that only 18 percent of Princeton's students came from schools like that one: "The section from the public schools represents the great rank and file of our nation, and I want to see our colleges benefited and vitalized by the increment of blood and gristle from the very backbone of our civilization."[9]

Casting aspersions on country clubs and lauding "the great rank and file of our nation" provided the first public signs of a major shift in Wilson's approach to political issues outside the university. He was forsaking his flirtation with the conservative Democrats and joining their foes, the insurgents and reformers who were now calling themselves "progressives." In speeches in the spring of 1908, he again condemned the rush to regulate business, and he dismissed the Sherman Anti-Trust Act for being "as clumsy as it has been ineffectual." Those were the next to the last truly conservative utterances to come out of Wilson's mouth. His final foray on that side occurred when Princeton faculty members gathered informally to debate a resolution approving "the Roosevelt Policies." Wilson attacked the policies, but when a young preceptor vigorously rebutted his argument, he seemed to enjoy it—most likely because he secretly admired the expression of views that he was coming to hold himself.[10]

When, how, and why Woodrow Wilson became a progressive would become hotly debated questions after he entered politics. Foes on both sides would denounce him for opportunism: erstwhile conservative patrons would scorn him for ingratitude and for pandering to passing popular fancies; skeptical progressives would suspect him of belated and halfhearted adherence to their side. Opportunism unquestionably played a part in swaying Wilson toward progressivism. The popularity of Roosevelt's anti-trust and regulatory policies, growing reformist insurgency in both parties, and repeated defeats of conservative Democrats—all pointed to the direction in which the political winds were blowing. In November 1907, Wilson obliquely confessed to being an opportunist: "A politician, a man engaged in party contests, must be an opportunist. Let us give up saying that word as if it contained a slur. If you want to win in party action, I take it for granted that you want to lure the majority to your side. I never heard of any man in his senses who was fishing for a minority."[11] His tilt toward progressivism did contain an element of disingenuousness in that he did not tell his conservative Democratic sponsors that he no longer agreed with them. Instead, he soft-pedaled his newly evolving views and continued to welcome their efforts to boost his entry into politics.

In 1908, George Harvey mounted a drive to get Wilson the Democratic presidential nomination and got some backing from Tammany Hall. Wilson affected not to take the matter seriously, but that summer, while he was in Scotland, he stayed within reach of the telegraph at the time of the convention. Remote as he regarded his own prospects that year, the idea of running for president excited him. After the election—in which Bryan was the Democratic nominee and went down to his third defeat—Wilson told Mary Peck that the Democrats needed someone who could match Bryan's devotion "to principles, to ideas, to definite programmes and not to personal preferment, . . . a man with a cause, not a candidacy. It's a desperate situation,—for what man of that kind will be willing to risk the appearance of personal ambition?" He eschewed any such ambition for himself: "Certainly I do not want the presidency! The more closely I see it the less I covet it."[12] That is just the sort of ritual disclaimer typically made by a man with the presidential bee in his bonnet.

Wilson's opportunism and disingenuousness showed only that he was an ambitious man with a healthy regard for his prospects, and those qualities did not tell the whole story of how and why he became a progressive.

Other influences were also propelling him in that direction. Several interpreters have concluded that the battles at Princeton over the Quad Plan and the Graduate College helped change his politics—that the clubs' social exclusiveness and the influence of private wealth over the location of the Graduate College made Wilson more progressive in state and national politics. Certainly the tales he heard from former students and their parents about the pain and suffering inflicted by Bicker—the clubs' selection process—moved him, and he resented the way some of the rich men among the alumni and trustees threw their weight around. The trouble with that view of Wilson's turn toward progressivism is that it puts the cart before the horse; his changing political views were what influenced the stands he took at Princeton. Before 1908, he had based his arguments for the Quad Plan and the location of the Graduate College almost solely on intellectual grounds, and only after he started espousing progressive political views did he condemn the clubs' snobbery and the influence of rich men over the university.[13]

Wilson's intellect played a critical part in his political shift. Even at the height of his attempted espousal of Democratic conservatism, he could not hide his approval of strong, centralized government, as he showed in *Constitutional Government*. Given the public outcry against the arrogance of big business, misery among the rural and urban poor, and the corruption of political machines, progressivism made a good fit for a believer in governmental activism. Likewise, his party affiliation was more than a flag of convenience: it showed his loyalty to his southern origins and his feeling for the hinterlands and the hardworking folk who lived there. Two and a half decades of living in the Northeast and often hobnobbing with people of wealth and social prominence had not brought him to identify with them and their part of the country. In *Constitutional Government*, he lauded "the South and the West with their simpler life, their more scattered people, their fields of grain, their mines of metal, their little towns. . . . No country ought ever to be judged from its seething centres."[14] He was sounding like a Bryanite Democrat.

When Wilson turned toward progressivism, he was not yet a practicing politician. Instead of taking stands on current issues, he was able to proceed the way he preferred, which was to stake out his general position before he got down to specifics. He did this in speeches over the course of 1909. Although he still called himself a conservative, he repeated his long-held view that growth and adaptation were truly conservative, adding, "All the renewal of a nation comes out of the general mass of its people. Nations have no choice, in respect of power and capacity, but to be democratic." In expounding his approach to leadership, he again drew upon his favorite nautical analogy: "Because although you steer by the North Star, when you have lost the bearings of your compass, you nevertheless must steer in a pathway on the sea,—you are not bound for the North Star. The man who insists on theory insists that there is a way to the North Star." He also reiterated his belief in "expediency," maintaining that it, not theory, dictated what laws and reforms were needed.[15] Wilson was clearly drawing on his earlier political thinking to establish the core principles and strategic approach that would guide his emerging progressivism.

His anti-theoretical conception of politics and his metaphor of organic growth sprang from insights he had previously drawn from Burke, as did his renewed espousal of "expediency," which lent philosophical sanction to opportunism. The novel element was the radically democratic twist he now gave to these views. His affinity for strong, activist government and his permissive views about the "ministrant" functions of government always contained the potential for moving in a reformist direction, and this new vision of social renewal from below made such a move nearly impossible to resist. Political opponents would later point to Wilson's gradual, occasionally hesitant embrace of some reform measures as proof of a halfhearted, insincere conversion to progressivism. They misread the way his mind worked. Despite his rejection of theory and his disdain for "literary politicians," Wilson was a true intellectual. Ideas mattered to him, and he had always grasped for broad insights and perspectives before getting down to cases. His most significant step on the road to progressivism was the intellectual leap he made at the outset, when he embraced a thoroughly democratic vision. Once he decided where he stood on the big questions of political direction and leadership strategy, such matters as which reform measures to champion and when to champion them involved only reading changing political circumstances—matters of "expediency."

Wilson showed some of his new attitudes late in 1908 and early in 1909. In one speech, he called the "present conflict in this country . . . a contest between those few men in whose hands the wealth of the land is concentrated, and the rest of us." In another, he attacked "the men who are using their wealth for predatory purpose." He retreated to safer ground in a magazine article attacking the Republican Party's high tariff record, which all Democrats deplored, but he defended tariff protection in principle as a boost to economic development and condemned the way the Republicans had perverted protective tariffs, making them into nothing more than a "system of patronage." He told a group of New Jersey Democrats, "Most of the old formulas of our politics are worn threadbare and have lost their significance," and he urged them, "whenever national action is necessary, [to] be shy, not of governmental power, but of . . . its use to the wrong ends."16

One area where Wilson's thinking did not change was race relations. During his trip abroad in the summer of 1908, the daughter of his artist friend Fred Yates recorded in her diary that Wilson deplored Roosevelt's recent appointment of an African American to a prominent government post in South Carolina as "too much for them [whites] to stand. And intermarriage would degrade the white nations, for in Africa the blacks were the only race who did not rise. . . . Social intercourse would bring about intermarriage." Publicly, Wilson took more moderate stands. Speaking at an African American church in Princeton, he maintained that "the so-called 'negro problem' is a problem, not of color, but capacity; not a racial, but an economic problem," and he praised the work done by Booker T. Washington's school at Tuskegee "and many smaller institutions conducted along similar lines." A few months later, Wilson discouraged an African American from applying to Princeton. "Regret to say that it is altogether inadvisable for a colored man to enter Princeton," he wrote in a memorandum. "Appreciate his desire to do so, but strongly recommend his securing education at a Southern [Negro] institution."17 These views kept Wilson in harmony with Democrats of all stripes and a growing number of Republicans.

He obviously was not keeping the promise that he had made after his health crisis of 1906 to cut down on outside speaking and take things easy. Within a year, he had resumed his heavy schedule of speechmaking around the country, on top of working the alumni circuit to promote the Quad Plan. The stepped-up activity did not seem to affect his health. The one complaint that bothered Wilson much at this time involved his digestion. Off and on in the twenty-five years since his days at Johns Hopkins, he had suffered from stomach pains and various problems with eating, but he did not change his diet. The Wilson family continued to eat the fried, grease-laden southern-style cooking he and Ellen had grown up with. His doctors treated him with remedies that were in vogue in those days, which included having him periodically pump out his stomach. Such practices, since abandoned by the medical profession for their lack of therapeutic value, evidently did him neither good nor harm. Later, when he became president, his physician discontinued them.18

One thing that may have helped Wilson was a new administrative regime at Princeton. In 1909, he appointed a business manager and named Edward Elliott dean of students. He turned over much of the internal running of the university to Fine, already dean of the faculty, naming him dean of science as well. This division of labor, in which the president would concentrate more on general policy and external relations while a strong second in command would oversee internal management, foreshadowed the practice that most American colleges and universities of any size would adopt later in the twentieth century. The new arrangement allowed Wilson to devote much of his time to advocacy of the Quad Plan before the alumni. Throughout 1909, he not only hammered away at his previous arguments, but he also expanded his vision of the stakes involved and continued to give a new progressive twist to his stands. In one speech, he denounced colleges and universities that "encouraged social stratification and made a bid for the exclusive patronage of the rich," and he asked, "Could Abraham Lincoln have been of more or less service to this country had he attended one of our universities?"[19]

It might seem ironic—even hypocritical—that at the same time Wilson was saying those things publicly he was privately asking for money from two of the richest men in the country. In February 1909, he wrote an anguished letter to Carnegie's financial agent asking for funds with which to establish the Quad Plan: "If I cannot do this thing I have spoken of, I must turn to something else than mere college administration, forced, not by my colleagues, but by my mind and convictions and the impossibility of continuing at an undertaking I do not believe in." And he asked John D. Rockefeller's daughter about the possibility of approaching her father. Nothing came of these overtures, and the experience hurt Wilson. That summer, in a letter to Mary Peck, he lashed out at "the restless, rich, empty-headed people the very sight of whom makes me cynical. . . . They and their kind are the worst enemies of Princeton, and create for me the tasks which are likely to wear my life out. But enough of them,—let them pass and be d—— forgotten."[20]

The Wilson family spent the summer of 1909 at an artists' colony in Lyme, Connecticut, where Ellen had gone earlier to pursue her painting. The vacation evidently did Wilson good, because he returned to Princeton that fall bent on pressing forward. He told alumni in Baltimore that because the university could attract distinguished faculty and graduate students, "a little Princeton has given place to a big Princeton." As ever, the essential means to continue to build that "big Princeton" were the Quad Plan and a properly located Graduate College. Wilson persisted in seeking money for the Quad Plan, and using Cleveland Dodge as an intermediary, he again approached Rockefeller. Earlier, he had partially wrested control of graduate education from West, but he still regarded the location of the Graduate College as critical to his goals. West had upset the earlier decision in favor of an on-campus site by bringing in a pledge for $500,000 for construction of the Graduate College. The pledge came from William Cooper Procter, class of 1883, a member of the family that owned Procter and Gamble, the nation's leading manufacturer of soaps and cleansers, and it had two stipulations: that Princeton must match the sum within a year and that the new facility not be built at the on-campus site. When Procter visited Princeton in June 1909, he insisted on either Merwick or the golf course site that Cleveland had reportedly favored. At the same time, Ralph Adams Cram, the architect who was designing Princeton's new Gothic Revival buildings, had switched his allegiance to the golf course site, because the prospect of a larger, grander building appealed to his aesthetic ambitions; that summer, Wilson had gone to Boston to try to get him to change his mind. Cram played no further role in the controversy, but his defection was a blow to Wilson.[21]

Over the summer, Wilson had also attempted to get rid of West, by recommending him for the presidency of Clark University, but that scheme did not pan out. Efforts at conciliation and compromise failed, and Pyne went over to West's side. In October the trustees voted 14 to 10 to accept the Procter gift and build the Graduate College on the golf course site. Wilson felt so upset after the trustees' meeting that he telephoned Mary Peck long-distance in New York and then poured out his hurt and discouragement in a letter: "Suffice it to say that, after a week-long struggle, the Trustees adopted a plan of that arch-intriguer West's." Once again, "money talked louder than I did." He wanted to resign, he said, but he owed it to his supporters to fight on. "I admit, to *you*, that I am very low in my mind, filled with scorn and disappointment, and fighting to hold my tongue from words that might make all breaches irreparable."[22]

For the next two months, Wilson struggled to be patient. He tried to patch things up with Pyne, and he proposed a compromise: building two facilities for graduate students, one on campus, using the earlier bequest and other money, and another, smaller establishment on the golf course, using Procter's gift. Pyne said nothing to Wilson to discourage him, but he evidently told Procter to stand his ground. When Wilson met with Procter on December 22, he spent more than an hour laying out the details and observing that less than 10 percent of the faculty favored an off-campus site for the Graduate College, but Procter responded that the trustees had already accepted his offer. Right after that meeting, Wilson told Pyne, "The acceptance of this gift has taken the guidance of the University out of my hands entirely,—and I seem to have come to the end." Instead, he decided to force a showdown over Procter's gift. On Christmas day, he told Pyne, "This is a very solemn matter, my dear Momo, but the issue is clear. Neither my conscience nor my self-respect will permit me to avoid it. . . . I must ask [the trustees] to give the University, at whatever cost, its freedom of choice in matters which so nearly touch its life and development."[23]

Some trustees still wanted to accept Procter's offer, but the members of the faculty's Graduate School Committee, with the exception of Hibben, sent Wilson a strongly worded letter backing the president's position. Pyne remained outwardly noncommittal, but his pose was a ruse. Behind the scenes he was plotting with Procter to drop a bombshell. When the two men met in New York in January 1910, Pyne drafted a letter for Procter in which the manufacturer no longer required that his $500,000 be matched and pledged the whole amount for construction at the golf course site. Pyne read the letter aloud at the next meeting of the trustees' Graduate School Committee, which, Pyne told Procter, "took the ground entirely from under their feet." Wilson responded, Pyne recounted, "that the Faculty did not care where the College was placed;—anywhere in Mercer County would suit them, provided it was carried out under proper ideals." Pyne chortled that Wilson "was confused and self-contradictory, and I never saw a man more embarrassed or in a more unpleasant position where it was impossible for him to extricate himself from the numerous contradictory statements he has made."[24]

Wilson's behavior did not show him at his best, and he often did not respond quickly to changing circumstances. But he and his supporters appeared to take the incident in stride, and from this point on naked conflict was the order of the day. Later in January, Pyne outlined a scheme to force Wilson's resignation by having Procter publicly withdraw his offer while privately keeping it open and having West step down as dean. In that way, Wilson's opponents would be, Pyne believed, "ready to start in with the new administration when it comes, and it cannot be long in coming when these facts are known to the public." Procter was willing to go along with this scheme because, he told Pyne, "restoration of proper feeling in the Board, Faculty, and Alumni cannot begin while Woodrow remains."[25] Meanwhile, possibly at Pyne's instigation, the *Princeton Alumni Weekly* turned its issues of January 26 and February 2 into an anti-Wilson forum.

Two could play the game of going public. In a letter responding to an inquiry from a *New York Times* editorial writer, Wilson explained his stand on the Graduate College issue in terms of "the same artificial and unsound social standards that already dominate the life of the undergraduates," affirming that "[m]y own ideals for the University are those of genuine democracy and serious scholarship." Based partly on that letter, an editorial appeared in *The New York Times* in early February that took Wilson's side and portrayed him as fighting against "mutually exclusive social cliques, stolid groups of wealth and fashion, devoted to non-essentials and the smatterings of culture."[26]

Things seemed to go Wilson's way after this spate of publicity. Procter withdrew his offer, and Wilson exulted to Dodge, "At last we are free to govern the University as our judgments and consciences dictate! I have an unspeakable sense of relief."[27] When the trustees met, the Graduate School Committee presented a report that favored an on-campus site for the Graduate College but expressed the hope that Procter might change his mind. With the board's acceptance of this report, Wilson felt sure enough of his ground to discuss plans to get rid of West, broaching the subject with some of his trustee supporters and with the faculty's Committee on the Graduate School, minus Hibben, who had just resigned from that committee. Whether motivated by prudence or cold feet, the professors shied away from trying to force West out, and Wilson did not press the issue.

Academic communities have always been poor places in which to keep secrets, and word of faculty members' second thoughts about moving against West soon reached Wilson's opponents. Pyne chortled at reports that some faculty members "may come over to our side. In that case Wilson's side would have its back broken." Trustees on Wilson's side, by contrast, busied themselves with further efforts to find a compromise on the site issue. Wilson went along with those efforts, meeting with Procter before speaking to an alumni group in St. Louis. "Mr. Procter behaved very well but committed himself to absolutely nothing," he reported to a supporter. Wilson also expounded his position in speeches to alumni. In New York, he called the present situation "critical in respect of Princeton's standing among American universities." It had taken the lead "in a new age of reconstruction" that had brought it "to the budding point, to the blooming point," and now it must "take that step which would complete our title to be called a university and develop a great graduate school." In the academic world, Princeton's only choice was "which part of the procession we will form—the van or the rear. When you have once taken up the torch of leadership you cannot lay it down without extinguishing it."[28]

Wilson's eloquence was wasted on his opponents. Pyne and his supporters blocked all attempts to refer the site question to the faculty. Wilson responded by escalating the public conflict. "Immediately after the Board meeting I started for Pittsburgh, where I let myself go, as you may have noticed by the papers," he told Mary Peck. He was referring to the speech to alumni in which he charged that churches and colleges were dissociating themselves from the people: "They serve the classes, not the masses. . . . Where does the strength of the nation come from? Not from the men of wealth. . . . It comes from the great mass of the unknown, of the unrecognized." He asked again whether Lincoln could have done as well if he had gone to college, and he pledged, "I shall not be satisfied—and I hope you will not be—[until] the American people shall know that the men in the colleges are saturated with the same thought that pulses through the body politic." Never before had he injected his political opinions so blatantly into a speech about Princeton. This talk attracted the kind of attention from the press that was usually accorded to utterances by major politicians, and the "muckraking" journalist David Graham Phillips and the Social Gospel clergyman Washington Gladden were among those who wrote to commend him.[29]

The next month brought the conflict to an unexpected end. Early in May, Pyne and another trustee went to see West and informed him of a compromise plan that would allow the Graduate College to be built on the golf course but would remove West as dean. West reluctantly acceded to the plan, but then fortune suddenly smiled on him. He received word that Isaac Wyman of Salem, Massachusetts, a wealthy member of the Princeton class of 1848, was ill and might be dying. Wilson had tried unsuccessfully to meet Wyman in 1902 on his first fund-raising trip, and West had later succeeded in seeing him. The cantankerous old bachelor had challenged the dean's persuasive skills until he learned of West's plans for the Graduate College, although he would not make an immediate donation. On May 18, West got word that Wyman had died. Four days later, Wyman's lawyers telegraphed West and Wilson with the news that the bulk of the estate would go to Princeton for a graduate college, with West named as executor. No one knew exactly how much money was involved. Rumors placed the sum as high as $10 million, but most sources placed it around $2 million. Even at the lower estimate, it was a huge bequest. Assuming Procter's offer could be revived, it would permit the Graduate College to be built on a grand scale and with a substantial endowment that would attract both professors and graduate students.[30]

Wilson knew at once that he had lost the fight, and he took his defeat gracefully. Ellen's sister, Madge, remembered waking in the night when she heard his voice in the adjoining bedroom: "I couldn't hear what he was saying, but I was startled by a note of tenseness." Through the open door, she could see Wilson talking on the telephone and Ellen leaning back in a chair, "obviously close to tears." When Wilson saw Madge, he explained what had happened and said grimly, "I could lick a half-million, but I'm licked by ten millions." Nell Wilson recalled coming down to breakfast the next morning to find her father laughing in the dining room. When she asked him what was so funny, he told her about the Wyman bequest and said, "We've beaten the living, but we can't beat the dead—the game is up." He telephoned West and asked him to come to Prospect House. When the dean arrived, he recalled the president's saying, "You know I have set my face like flint against the site on the Golf Links. But the magnitude of the bequest alters the perspective. You have a great work ahead of you and I shall give you my full support." During the last week in May, Wilson told his supporters he was conceding. He did not plan to resign, but he admitted to a friend, "I must say that my judgment is a good deal perplexed in the matter."[31]

During the next few weeks, Wilson continued to feel perplexed. He worried about having, he told Mary Peck, "to drudge on here, trying to wring something out of an all but intolerable situation, . . . it all seems, sometimes, as if one should wake up and find it a bad dream." In June, commencement found him in a dark mood. What later became a famous photograph shows him in his academic gown striding forward with his long jaw set in a grim expression. Far from depicting the typical Wilson, that picture caught him at a moment of defeat and inner turmoil. Soon after commencement, he said to Stockton Axson, "I can stay here indefinitely, but the question in my mind is what is the use. I am not interested in simply administering a club. Unless I can develop something I cannot get thoroughly interested. I believe I can be elected Governor of New Jersey and the question I am debating in my own mind is whether or not I shall take that step."[32] This was not the first time politics had seemed to beckon him to greener pastures, and adversaries at Princeton were in no mood to make life easy for him. It seemed likely that he would leave sooner rather than later. Effectively, his presidency of Princeton had come to an end.

In the decades to come, Wilson's academic presidency would undergo repeated scrutiny, principally in terms of two questions: First, what clues did his performance in this office give to how he would fare in politics, especially in the White House? Second, what did he accomplish at Princeton, and what did his performance say about the future of that university and higher education? The first of these questions would receive far more attention, much of it sharply critical of Wilson. A common line would be that his behavior, particularly in the Graduate College controversy, showed him to be a self-righteous zealot who ignored or resented criticism and refused to compromise. Some have also argued that in this fight, as later, a stroke warped his behavior. Some of those interpretations would lump together dissimilar situations and personality traits and strain to find commonalities where few or none existed. Still, this search for similarities and patterns has been inescapable, and it has sometimes yielded insights into how Wilson functioned as a leader in both the academic and the political realms.[33]

The main pattern that shone through was what he said himself to Axson: "Unless I can improve something I cannot get thoroughly interested." Throughout his presidency of Princeton, Wilson repeatedly chose the path of boldness. He showed this proclivity most clearly with the preceptorial system and the Quad Plan. The main flaws that he displayed in these affairs were the defects of his boldness and innovation—namely, impatience and insufficient preparation. Those flaws did not hamper him with the preceptorial system, where he was adding resources and advantages, but they proved fatal with the Quad Plan, where he was taking away resources and where he underestimated the depth of the opposition. Worse, he did not at first seem to grasp the difference between the two situations, in part because his reaction to the blow to his health may have intensified his impatience. In his political career, his boldness and itch to develop would serve him splendidly until close to the end. Then, as at Princeton, he would pay a price for not preparing the ground and not explaining his position soon enough.

The Graduate College fight was different. It was not something he initiated; faculty supporters, especially Fine, helped push him into it, and he had to strike out defensively from start to finish. There, too, his main flaw lay in lack of preparation—in this case, in opposing the off-campus site. He did not prepare the way sufficiently in two areas. One was fundraising: as with the Quad Plan, Wilson should have lined up financial backing before taking his stand. That would become the cardinal rule for college and university presidents later in the twentieth century. Although this was a new aspect of academic leadership in Wilson's time, he did recognize how important money was, and he can be faulted for not overcoming his distaste for what he called "begging." That was the one advantage, besides blind luck, that West had over him—the dean positively enjoyed asking for money.

The other way in which Wilson failed to smooth the path sufficiently lay in not explaining why the location of the Graduate College was critical to his vision of a new, intellectually serious Princeton. The lack of such an explanation was the reason some observers could dismiss the issue as just a squabble about a "boarding house for graduate students." When he finally did state his position fully, as he did to the alumni in the spring of 1910, he made a compelling case. Wilson seems to have learned from this defeat. In the future, he would make timely exposition of his thinking—education of the public—central to his political career. The one great exception would come with the League of Nations, when, as in the Graduate College fight, he only belatedly took his case to the people. As it was, he almost won the fight over the Graduate College. Only an unexpected event stopped him just short of victory.

Wilson certainly thought his Princeton presidency prepared him for politics. Besides the public visibility and administrative experience that the office gave him, he believed that it taught him valuable, hard-won political lessons. In later years, he would often compare academic politics with the "real" thing. "After dealing with college politicians," Wilson commented during his first year as governor of New Jersey, "I find that the men with whom I am dealing . . . now seem like amateurs." When he campaigned for president in 1912, he observed that "politicians in the field of politics . . . play their hand rather openly," whereas "the college politician does it carefully. He plays it very shrewdly, and he has such a gift of speech that he could make black sound as if it were white any time that he chooses." Even after he became president, his mind strayed back to Princeton. His later confidant, Edward M. House, recorded on one occasion that Wilson told him "he had nightmares, and that he thought he was seeing some of his Princeton enemies." On another occasion, House wrote, "Whenever we have no governmental business to discuss, somehow or other, we drift into his life at Princeton and his troubles there, showing, as I have said before, how deeply the iron entered his soul."[34]

This experience also left so deep a mark on Wilson because of what he believed it meant for Princeton. When, as governor, he walked across the campus in the fall of 1911, he became aware, as he told Mary Peck, "at every turn of how the University . . . has turned away from me. . . . I went about from familiar place to place with a lump in my throat, and would have felt better if I could have *cried.*" The year after he lost the fight over the Graduate College brought more wormwood and gall as Pyne engineered Hibben's succession as president and West basked in glory at the opening of his grand new Graduate College. Early in 1913, House recorded in his diary, "[Wilson] said that Princeton was really for sale."[35]

He grieved over his beloved school's having forsaken the path of greatness in order to worship false gods. To some extent, his dark thoughts were justified. West never regained the full measure of his earlier autonomy, and the Wyman bequest ultimately turned out to be less than $800,000. Still, the dean reigned in splendor in his new buildings and resumed his old game of playing favorites and making life difficult for serious graduate students. The "country club" side of Princeton soon received powerful reinforcement, first in the person of a golden-haired, aristocratic athletic idol, Hobart (Hobey) Amory Hare Baker, of the class of 1914, and then in the writings of F. Scott Fitzgerald, class of 1917. They and others helped to brand Princeton with an image of glamorous pleasure seeking and social snobbery that would endure for decades and never fully wear off.

Yet Wilson had not labored in vain. Fine judged his legacy correctly when he told Wilson's first biographer in 1925, "[W]hen all is said and in spite of controversies and other difficulties, Wilson *made* Princeton. . . . He gave it the intellectual stimulus."[36] As it turned out, Hibben's regime did not bring total defeat for Wilson's aims, and under succeeding presidents Princeton would continue a steady ascent in academic prestige, so that by the middle of the twentieth century it would rank among the handful of most highly regarded universities in the nation.

Wilson did deserve the greatest credit for putting the university on that path. There was nothing foreordained about it. As he pointed out, Princeton did not enjoy the advantage of size that other major universities enjoyed, nor did it have the urban location and the ready-made ties to other institutions conferred by professional schools that most other major universities also enjoyed. Of all the colleges founded before the American Revolution, Princeton was unique in beginning the metamorphosis into a modern university as early as it did and without such extrinsic advantages. Other prestigious small colleges, including the newly founded women's colleges, were likewise adapting themselves to this new academic world of research and professionalization, but only Princeton rushed to make the leap to a full-fledged university and vied for the top spot among these newfangled institutions. That was Wilson's doing. It would take several decades for his vision to be fully realized, but Princeton University would never have become what it is today without his initial inspiration.

It is tempting to close the judgment on Wilson's presidency of Princeton by lauding him for his vision and early labors while faulting him for trying to do too much too soon. In that view, his academic career does seem to prefigure his political career; the same judgment encapsulates the near-universal estimate of what he achieved early in domestic affairs and then tried and failed to do with the League of Nations. But the question is not so easily laid to rest. Wilson at Princeton, it must be remembered, was operating at a moment of flux and possibility in the development of American higher education. Universities were a fresh import to the country. Some of the best of them were brand-new creations, such as Johns Hopkins, Cornell, Chicago, and Stanford. Even the state universities that emerged as scholarly and scientific powerhouses, such as Wisconsin, Michigan, and California (at Berkeley), were just a few decades removed from their origins as small, meagerly funded colleges. The situation was ripe for dynamic, visionary leadership, as had already been shown by Daniel Coit Gilman at Hopkins, Charles W. Eliot at Harvard, Andrew D. White at Cornell, and William Rainey Harper at Chicago—the kind of men Thorstein Veblen dubbed "captains of erudition." Princeton might have been a relative latecomer to this academic revolution, but not by much, and there was still room at the top for an institution led by someone with vision and boldness.

Wilson possessed both qualities in abundance. As a visionary, he grasped the essential problem of transforming the old-style small college into a modern university—combining intimate instruction of undergraduates with pioneering scholarly and scientific research by professors and graduate students. Wilson aimed all three of his main programs—the preceptorial system, the Quad Plan, and the location of the Graduate College—at perfecting that combination. Other universities soon followed his lead in one way or another. In the 1920s and 1930s, first Harvard, with its houses, and then Yale, with its colleges, adopted versions of the Quad Plan. In the 1930s and 1940s, Chicago, under Robert M. Hutchins, conducted a campaign to make its undergraduates more intellectually serious by downgrading varsity sports and other extracurricular diversions. Every other major university would mingle graduate students with undergraduates rather than separate them, after West's model. At Princeton, Wilson had within his grasp the chance to do all of those things first, and he came close to achieving his aims. If he had won his academic civil war, American higher education would have had an undisputed champion. Yet if he had won, he would have had to stay at Princeton and continue to remake the university in his own image. Andrew West's windfall liberated Woodrow Wilson from academic life and opened a larger career for him in politics.

6

GOVERNOR

As an academic political scientist, Woodrow Wilson seldom studied state politics, and he rarely wrote about the office of governor. Likewise, except for speaking about it a couple of times in the mid-1890s, he did not involve himself in local or state politics. In 1910, Wilson had been living in New Jersey for twenty years, but he had seen little of his adopted state. Speaking engagements as president of Princeton sometimes took him to Jersey City, Morristown, or Newark, but he visited few other places in the state, and he had never set foot inside the capitol in nearby Trenton. It might seem odd, then, even ironic, that he first entered active politics by running for and winning the governorship of New Jersey. In fact, it turned out to be an ideal way for him to begin his political career. Circumstances seemed to conspire to propel this fifty-three-year-old neophyte on a meteoric rise in both state and national politics. He became a political star practically overnight and a hot prospect for his party's presidential nomination almost as soon as the ballots were counted in New Jersey in November 1910.

Irony abounded, especially in the way Wilson won the Democratic nomination for governor. This freshly minted progressive and future reformer at the state and national level owed his start in politics to conservatives, machines, and bosses. As before, George Harvey got the ball rolling. The magazine editor owned a seaside home in New Jersey, which gave him good connections in conservative Democratic circles at the state as well as the national level. For several years, he had worked to interest the foremost leader of the New Jersey Democrats in Wilson. This was James Smith, a wealthy onetime U.S. senator. Widely known as Sugar Jim for his services as senator to the sugar-refining industry, Smith fit the popular image of the political boss. He was a big, smooth-faced Irish American with expensive tastes and a hearty manner. Politics was a family business: his son-in-law, James Nugent, was the boss of Newark's Democratic machine and his second in command in the state party. No two figures roused greater enmity among New Jersey's fledgling progressive Democrats.[1]

Yet it was Smith and, to a lesser extent, Nugent who made Wilson the Democrats' choice for governor. The Princeton president and the party bosses engaged in a lengthy and elaborate mating dance. Nineteen ten was starting to look like a good political year for Democrats at both the state and the national levels. In Washington, the Republicans were teetering on the brink of civil war as progressives, led by Robert M. La Follette, now a senator from Wisconsin, openly rebelled against the Taft administration over the recently passed Payne-Aldrich tariff and other issues. In Trenton, the Republicans were similarly suffering from internal strain as local progressives challenged their party's conservative leadership. In these circumstances, Smith and Nugent liked the idea of having an attractive, respectable new face at the top of their ticket. Harvey, whose horn-rimmed glasses and slicked-down hair made him look like an owl, again put Wilson's name in play with Smith. In January 1910, he assured Wilson that "the nomination for governor shall be tendered to you on a silver platter, without your turning a hand to obtain it."[2] Rumors about Wilson's nomination began to circulate in the spring, and he talked about the idea with Ellen and some of his supporters on the Princeton board of trustees.

Curiously, however, the road to Wilson's gubernatorial nomination really began in Chicago. Smith was there in June 1910, at a luncheon with the city's Democratic boss, Roger Sullivan, when some lawyers and businessmen with Princeton connections talked up Wilson. That talk led to a meeting at the middle of July between Wilson and party leaders, where he impressed them, although Smith did not like his favoring local option on liquor sales. He also struck some of the party men as unfamiliar with state issues, but he reportedly assured them that he would not try to interfere with the Democratic organization. Three days after that meeting, Wilson issued a public statement in which he asserted that if "a decided majority of the thoughtful Democrats of the State" wanted him to run for governor, "I should deem it my duty, as well as an honor and a privilege, to do so."[3] In other words, his hat was in the ring.

He was not yet home free, however. Nugent wanted a different candidate, but he promised to defer to the "Big Fellow." In August, Wilson drafted a set of suggestions for the New Jersey Democrats' platform, expressing progressive ideas. He also made some public pronouncements to cover divergent political bases, such as insisting that he was "the warm friend of organized labor" but also praising corporations "as indispensable to modern business enterprise." Coming out in the open as an aspiring politician gave Wilson mixed feelings. "I feel very queer adventuring upon the sea of politics," he told a Princeton friend, "and my voyage may be brief."4 He also chafed under an injunction from the bosses that he not talk to reporters, although he acknowledged that it allowed him to duck the liquor question.

Wilson did not have to put up with enforced silence for long. The state Democratic convention opened in Trenton on September 14. Smith arrived, accompanied by Harvey, and ensconced himself in room 100 of the Trenton House, the hotel where party bosses customarily resided. From there he and Nugent worked through the night to round up the votes needed to nominate Wilson. The party's progressives were furious at having a political unknown shoved down their throats by the bosses, but Wilson was duly nominated. A few minutes after five o'clock in the afternoon on September 15, 1910, he strode into the auditorium where the delegates were meeting. Many of the progressives sat in sullen silence while machine supporters and Princeton students shouted and cheered. Few of those present knew what to expect from their new nominee for governor, and few had ever seen him or heard him speak. "God, look at that jaw!" one man reportedly exclaimed.5

Wilson began his acceptance speech by claiming, "I did not seek this nomination." Therefore, he vowed, if he was elected governor, there would be "absolutely no pledge of any kind to prevent me from serving the people of the State with singleness of purpose." On the major issues, Wilson declared, "I take the three great questions before us to be reorganization and economy in [government] administration, the equalization of taxation and the control of corporations." Other important issues included employers' liability for workplace injuries, corrupt practices in elections, and conservation of natural resources. Wilson sounded a conservative note when he asserted, "We shall not act either justly or wisely if we attack established interests as public enemies." But he also called for the establishment of a public service commission to regulate rates for utilities and transportation, to be modeled on the one La Follette's progressives had instituted in Wisconsin. In closing, Wilson proclaimed, "We are witnessing a renaissance of public spirit, a re-awakening of sober public opinion, a revival of the power of the people." At that point, he offered to stop, noting that the delegates must be tired after putting in so many hours of work. Cries arose from the floor: "Go on!" He then repeated his promise to serve only the people and his demand for a public service commission, and he declared that the state needed to control corporations. Appealing to the "ideal" of America as a haven for equal rights, he urged the delegates, "Let us devote the Democratic party to the recovery of these rights."⁶

The speech was a triumph. Joseph Tumulty, a young Irish American assemblyman from Jersey City who was one of the leading progressive foes of the bosses, later recalled that many delegates stood with tears running down their cheeks and left the auditorium charged with crusading zeal. As for Tumulty himself, another delegate reported to Wilson that after the speech he "threw his arms about me & said '. . . this is one of the happiest days of my life—the Wisconsin R. R. law!—the best in the country—if Wilson stands for legislation of that caliber, Jim Smith will find that he has a "lemon." ' "⁷ Tumulty instantly became one of Wilson's most ardent backers and went on to serve as the governor's and president's right-hand man.

Wilson's speech and the progressives' response did not bother the party bosses because they were sure they could control their handpicked nominee. Four days after the convention, a group of them visited him at Prospect House. Standing on the portico and gazing at the tree-lined campus, Smith asked James Kerney, the editor of the *Trenton Evening Times*, "[C]an you imagine anyone being damn fool enough to give this up for the heartaches of politics?" As Nell Wilson later recalled, the politicians seemed ill at ease in the university president's book-lined study. "Do you read *all* these books, Professor?" Smith reportedly asked. "Not every day," Wilson answered. His jocularity broke the ice, and, he told Nell later, "[T]hey treated me like a school boy once they got over the professorial atmosphere." The politicians spent three hours instructing their pupil on campaign plans, and he now impressed them with his familiarity with local affairs and people. "We were charmed by the reception he had given us," Kerney wrote later. "When he unbent he could be the most urbane and delightful of companions."⁸

On the campaign trail, Wilson struck some observers as a bit stiff and formal in his first speeches, more professorial than political. That may have been the case, since he was a rookie on the stump with a lot to learn about modern political campaigns, especially how much they cost. He originally thought that he could pay all his expenses from his own pocket. He was still drawing his Princeton salary, and after the election he planned to earn $500 from speaking fees to cover expenses. In fact, he left overall financial matters to Harvey and Jim Smith, who later claimed to have personally contributed $50,000 to the campaign. In all, according to one estimate, the Democratic managers spent $119,000 during the campaign, which was big money in those days.⁹

Wilson quickly became a pungent, hard-hitting stump speaker. He stressed partisanship and national issues from the outset. "I am a Democrat by conviction because I am persuaded that it is the party through which the salvation of the country must come," he asserted in a newspaper interview early in October. "The Republican party has been guilty of forming an unholy alliance with the vast moneyed interests of the country." At the same time, he declared in a speech in Long Branch, "Between a real Democrat and a really progressive [Republican] insurgent there is very little difference. What has been happening to these insurgents is that they have been catching the Democratic infection."[10]

He did not neglect state issues. At the outset of the campaign, his Republican opponent presented him with a golden opportunity to play to his greatest strengths. Dominant since the mid-1890s, the New Jersey Republicans had experienced a much stronger progressive insurgency than the Democrats. Four years earlier, "New Idea" Republicans had mounted an intraparty revolt. They had attacked their party's alliances with big business and pushed for the kind of reform in taxation that Wilson advocated in 1910. The New Idea men had gone down to defeat before the conservative machine, but they remained a force to be reckoned with. In 1910, the Republicans bowed in their direction by picking a moderate progressive as their gubernatorial nominee. He was Vivian M. Lewis, a good-looking and respected lawyer who was the state commissioner of banking and insurance. Lewis opened his campaign by likewise calling for a powerful public service commission and endorsing a favorite progressive idea, the direct primary to pick party nominees. He promised to observe the "constitutional limitations" on the governor's authority and never to "coerce the Legislature into subordinating its judgment to my own." Those words helped ensure his defeat, because Wilson immediately announced, "I cannot be that kind of a constitutional Governor. . . . If you elect me, you will elect . . . an unconstitutional Governor."[11]

Wilson was having the time of his life as he crisscrossed New Jersey by train and automobile, going places he had never gone before, giving two or three speeches a day, translating ideas from his academic study of politics into campaign discourse. In Atlantic City, he asserted that government was not "an intellectual matter." Rather, people must use such "splendid, handsome passions" as love, honor, and patriotism to restrain and block such base passions as hatred and envy. In Flemington, he defended party government. He wanted to smash the "secret power" of machines. "But I am not here to break up parties," he declared, for they are indispensable instruments for addressing complicated issues and channeling popular opinion into constructive action. In Newton, he argued that government was needed "to protect the unprotected classes, the classes that cannot look out for themselves."[12] Yet gratifying as it was to express his ideas, he had an election to win. Wilson needed to overcome two liabilities. One was his party label. Though weakened by factional strife, the Republicans were still by far the stronger party in New Jersey, and Wilson had to persuade many Republicans to vote for him. The other, more glaring liability was his sponsorship by Smith and the bosses.

George Record, the irascible transplanted Maine Yankee who led the New Idea Republicans, presented him with a golden opportunity to overcome both of those liabilities. Record harped on the way Wilson had gotten his party's nomination, and he challenged the Democratic candidate to debate him on state issues. Wilson accepted on the condition that the Republicans endorse Record as their spokesman. Predictably, the Republican leaders balked, and Wilson declined to debate but added that he would publicly answer any written questions that Record put to him. On October 17, Record sent a sharply worded public letter that posed nineteen questions on subjects ranging from the powers of a public service commission to primaries to the popular election of senators to corrupt election practices to workmen's compensation. The letter contained a denunciation of machines and asked, "Do you admit that such a system exists as I have described it? If so, how do you propose to abolish it?" Record also asked whether Wilson would overthrow the Democratic bosses and demand that candidates for the legislature pledge themselves to progressive reforms.[13]

This letter allowed Wilson to show his greatest qualities as a campaigner: boldness and articulateness. A week later, in a carefully crafted letter of his own, Wilson quoted Record's questions in their entirety, followed by his answers. To most of them, particularly the ones about state reforms, he simply said yes. To some, such as the direct primary, he said he favored even stronger measures than Record proposed. Only to the last question, about requiring candidates to favor progressive measures, did he answer no, stating that it was up to voters to assess candidates. The questions about the boss system afforded Wilson a chance to admit its existence and propose to abolish it by passing new laws, by electing "men who will refuse to submit to it and bend all their energies to break it up, and by pitiless publicity," a phrase that would become one of his favorite slogans. As to whether he would fight the Democratic bosses, he shot back, "Certainly!" He claimed to be already reorganizing his own party, and he avowed, "I should deem myself forever disgraced should I in even the slightest degree cooperate in any such system or any such transaction as you describe in your characterization of the 'boss' system."[14]

Record knew at once that he had met his match. "That letter will elect

Wilson governor," he was quoted as saying. Years later, he added, "If he had been a small man, such a set of questions would have finished him off, but he had boldness and courage and he could rise to a great emergency." Wilson's letter became the sensation of the campaign and allowed him to finish the campaign with a flourish. In his closing speech, he sounded like Theodore Roosevelt as he affirmed, "We have begun a fight that it may be will take many a generation to complete—the fight against special privilege, but you know that men are not put into this world to go the path of ease; they are put into this world to go the path of pain and struggle. . . . We have given our lives to the enterprise, and that is richer and the moral is greater."[15]

The only discordant note in the final weeks of the campaign came out of Princeton. On October 20, Pyne and his followers on the board of trustees forced Wilson to resign as president. Wilson had planned to step down anyway, but he and his supporters had hoped he could wait until after the election. As he told a friend, he was glad the campaign "absolutely dominated my thoughts. Otherwise I believe that I should have broken down under the mortification of what I discovered last week to be the real feelings of the Pyne party toward me."[16] He refused to accept any further salary from Princeton, although he and his family did continue to live at Prospect until the following January.

On November 8, 1910, the voters of New Jersey elected Woodrow Wilson governor by a wide margin. He polled 233,682 votes to Lewis's 184,626, 54 percent to 43 percent. Only one gubernatorial candidate in the state's history had won a bigger majority, a Republican who rode Roosevelt's coattails in 1904. Wilson carried fifteen counties to Lewis's six, all of which were Republican strongholds, and he came close to winning four of those. He ran ahead of other Democratic candidates, but the party also did well, picking up four congressional seats and sweeping the state assembly, gaining forty-one of the sixty seats. Democrats did not win control of the state senate, but their margin in the assembly gave them enough votes to choose a U.S. senator when the legislature met in January. As the returns came in on November 8, a crowd that included many students gathered in Princeton and marched to Prospect House. Visibly moved, Wilson thanked the throng, but for once he was at a loss for words: "I think I have said all I know in my speeches in the campaign."[17]

Wilson would have liked the "honeymoon" typically accorded newly elected officials, especially because he wanted time to think and plan, but he did not get his wish. The spoiler was Sugar Jim Smith. Ever since he had sponsored Wilson as his choice for governor, rumors had persisted that he wanted an attractive candidate who would help the party gain enough seats in the state legislature to send him back to the U.S. Senate. When the two men met a week after the election, the boss evidently did not raise the question of his candidacy, but he later claimed that the governor-elect had dismissed the state's nonbinding senatorial primary as a "farce" and called the man who had won it a "disgrace." This was James E. "Farmer Jim" Martine, a perennial aspirant for office and one of New Jersey's few supporters of the Bryan wing of the Democratic party.[18]

Within days, however, Wilson changed his mind about the Senate seat. Though professing high regard for Smith personally, Wilson told Harvey that "his election would be intolerable to the very people who elected me and gave us a majority in the legislature. . . . It was no Democratic victory. It was a victory of the 'progressives' of both parties, who are determined to live no longer under either of the political organizations that have controlled the two parties of the State." That fact ruled Smith out for the Senate seat and meant that "ridiculous though it undoubtedly is,—I think we shall have to stand by Mr. Martine."[19] Wilson urged Harvey to get Smith to bow out. He reminded the editor that their party faced both opportunity and peril, and he raised the specter of a Roosevelt revival—the prospect that frightened conservative Democrats most.

Wilson started to line up support. Joe Tumulty took him to meet with several legislators and with the Jersey City boss, who said he owed Smith his personal support but would not feel "hurt" if others opposed him. On December 6, Wilson made one last effort to avert a clash by traveling to Newark to see Smith at his home. "You have a chance to be the biggest man in the state by not running for the Senate," Wilson reportedly told him and added that he, Wilson, could not ignore the results of the primary. Smith refused to step aside and asked if Wilson would be satisfied simply to announce his opposition and then leave the choice to the legislature. "No," Wilson answered. "I shall actively oppose you with every honorable means in my power." He warned that he would go public with his opposition if Smith did not reconsider within the next two days. When the deadline passed, the governor-elect issued a statement to the press noting that the voters in the primary had chosen Martine: "For me, that vote is conclusive. I think it should be for every member of the Legislature."[20]

Wilson braced for a fight. To Mary Peck he predicted "hard sledding," and to a Princeton friend he called Smith a "tough customer." During the rest of December, he met with legislators at Prospect House and in New York City. Early in January, he decided to appoint Tumulty his secretary, and with Tumulty's guidance he continued to lobby legislators before and after his inauguration, on January 17, 1911. He also resorted to a favorite tactic, which he brought from his Princeton presidency: he spoke directly to his constituents. On January 5, he addressed a big rally in Jersey City, where he charged that Smith represented "a system of political control . . . a systematic, but covert alliance—between business and politics." He likened his move toward breaking up that alliance by opposing Smith to "cut[ting] off a wart," and on the eve of his inauguration he dismissed Smith's candidacy as "a colossal blunder in political judgment."[21]

Wilson read the situation right. The big boss turned out to be a paper tiger. After the legislature convened, Smith journeyed once more to Trenton and ensconced himself in the same hotel room where he had previously labored to secure Wilson's nomination for governor, but this time he had no magic to work. At the party caucus, nine Democrats from the state senate and twenty-four from the assembly supported Martine; only fourteen backed Smith. Because the New Jersey constitution required a majority of the members of both houses voting together to choose a senator, the caucus canvass left Martine only eight votes short of the forty-one needed to elect him. By the time the legislators were ready to cast the first ballot in the joint session of the legislature on January 24, switches had given Martine forty votes, one short of victory, and Smith threw in the towel, releasing his supporters. The next day the joint session elected Martine with forty-seven votes, which included all but four of the Democrats. Wilson greeted the outcome with mixed feelings. "My victory last week was overwhelmingly complete," he told Mary Peck. "The whole country is marvelling at it, and I am getting more credit than I deserve. I . . . [pitied] Smith at the last. . . . It is a pitiless game, in which, it would seem, one takes one's life in one's hands,—and for me it has only begun!"[22]

The Smith affair may have spoiled Wilson's political honeymoon, but it gave him a big boost as governor. The fight burnished his credentials as a progressive in New Jersey and it drew nationwide coverage in the press. The country's leading Democratic newspaper, the New York *World*, anointed this new governor a special hero because a similar fight was taking place in New York, where the leader of Tammany Hall was also trying to grab a Senate seat for himself. "New York needs a Woodrow Wilson," proclaimed *The World*. Wilson welcomed the publicity, although one aspect of this attention bothered him. "Thought of the presidency annoys me in a way," he told Mary Peck. "I do not *want* to be President. There is too little play in it, too little time for one's friends, too much distasteful publicity and fuss and frills."[23] Again, the gentleman did protest too much. The eyes of the nation were on Wilson, and he was never going to be just another governor.

The fight with Smith gave him a chance to know and master his party's men in the New Jersey legislature and thereby get his legislative program off to a fast start. Despite his complaints about the time that the Smith affair took, he did not let it distract him from planning what he wanted to do once he took office. Soon after the election, he gave some foretastes of his intentions. "Pitiless publicity is the sovereign cure for ills of government," he asserted in a newspaper interview. In a speech to the national governors' conference, he described his new office with a paraphrase of what he had said about the presidency in *Constitutional Government*: "There is no one in any legislature, who represents the whole commonwealth—no one connected with legislation who does, except the Governor." Therefore, for the governor to appeal to the people over the heads of the legislators was "no executive usurpation."[24]

Family affairs and practical matters also required attention. As usual, most of the responsibility fell to Ellen, particularly the Wilsons' move out of Prospect House. Just before they left, they held a wedding reception for their niece, Annie Howe, the daughter of Woodrow's sister of the same name, who was married in the First Presbyterian Church on the last day of 1910. The immediate family circle had shrunk now. Ellen's sister, Madge, had married Edward Elliott in September, and her brother Stockton had suffered a nervous breakdown over the summer and was in a sanatorium in Connecticut.[25]

Still another element added to the upheaval. For the first time in more than twenty years the Wilsons did not have a home of their own. New Jersey did not provide a governor's mansion, although there was a summer residence, at Sea Girt on the Atlantic coast, where the Wilsons spent the warmer months of 1911 and 1912.[26] In the meantime, Ellen put most of their possessions in storage, and she and her husband and daughters moved into a suite of rooms in the Princeton Inn. The following fall, they rented a house in Princeton at 25 Cleveland Lane, just a block from the home they had built on Library Place. The street was named after Grover Cleveland, who had lived a few doors away, as did Andrew West. It was from the rooms at the inn and from this house that Wilson commuted twelve miles to the governor's office in the capitol at Trenton.

Running that office also required attention to practical matters, and that was where Tumulty proved to be a godsend. He functioned as the governor's chief administrative and legislative assistant and liaison to the press. Thirty-one-year-old Joseph Patrick Tumulty was a trim, neat man of medium height with a smooth, round face that made him look like a young priest. He was the son of an Irish immigrant and a Union veteran who had been wounded in the Battle of the Wilderness and later struggled to establish himself as the owner of a corner grocery store. His mother, also Irish-born, could not read or write, but she had pushed her children to go to school. Joe, the seventh of nine who survived, was a graduate of St. Peter's College in Jersey City. His opposition to the political machine did not bar him from knowing and savoring all sides of public life. He loved the game of politics and reveled in trading gossip and inside information with reporters and politicians. His gregariousness and attention to small matters made him a perfect complement to Wilson, who still liked to spend time by himself pondering political questions in their larger dimensions. The two men quickly developed a smooth working relationship, one that was warm and informal. Wilson did not call his secretary Joe. When others were present he called him Tumulty, but when they were alone he often addressed him as "my dear boy." Tumulty, in turn, called his boss Governor.[27]

From his own study of the issues and the campaign encounter with Record, Wilson had a good idea of what he wanted on his legislative agenda. Nevertheless, he took the unusual step of reaching across party lines to enlist Record's advice and support. First, he met privately with Record, and then, the day before his inauguration, he presided over a conclave at a New York hotel that included, besides Record, several legislators, newspaper editors and publishers, and veteran reformers. The group agreed that election reform, public utility regulation, and employers' liability laws should be top priorities, and Wilson assigned Record the task of drafting new legislation dealing with primaries and corrupt election practices. One of the legislators at the meeting leaked news of the deliberations to Smith. The boss's forces, in turn, denounced Wilson for secret dealings and perfidy to the party by ceding power over legislation to Record and other Republicans. Wilson shot back with a statement to the press that Record was "one of the best informed men in this State with regard to the details involved in the reforms proposed" and that the conference "was non-partisan in its purpose and meant in the public interest."[28] The new governor was getting his own dose of "pitiless publicity."

On January 17, Wilson set the tone for his governorship with a hard-hitting inaugural address. Although he offered a bit of reassurance to conservatives by observing that corporations were not "unholy inventions of rascally rich men," he affirmed that "wise regulation, wise adjustment," was nothing less than "an imperative obligation." Turning to specifics, he said employers' liability came first "because it is the adjustment for which justice cries loudest." He likewise called for stronger corporate regulation, a new public service commission, tax reform, and conservation of natural resources. Beyond that, in order to get "to the root of the whole matter," the legislature needed "genuine representatives, who will serve your real interests," and the only way to get that was through "the direct primary, the direct choice of representatives by the people." He did not close the speech, as most speakers would, with a stirring peroration but listed further measures, including consideration of initiative, referendum, and recall legislation, corrupt-practices and campaign-finance reform, and the investigation of how cold storage rates affect food prices.[29]

Wilson then moved into the governor's office and went to work. Although this was a big change from academic life, he adjusted quickly. "He seemed to be perfectly at home from the start and the duties seemed easy and pleasant to him," one of his stenographers, Ida Taylor, later told Wilson's first biographer. "He was an indefatigable worker and spent long hours at his desk." He attended to correspondence first thing in the morning, dictating to one of the staff, sometimes from shorthand notes he had made. He once reportedly tried using a dictating machine but was amused at how unnatural he thought his voice sounded and did not take to it. Wilson also continued to do much of his own typing. After attending to correspondence, the governor spent most of the rest of the day with appointments. He maintained an open-door policy, never turning away a caller, at least until he was elected president. By his fourth week in office, Wilson could tell Mary Peck that "when I am at them the things I deal with day by day do not pall upon me at all. I take them, on the contrary, with zest and unflagging interest."[30]

One aspect of the governorship did not interest Wilson—patronage. He resented the waste of time and energy involved in dealing with rival claimants for jobs, and he left this duty largely to Tumulty. Wilson did make some first-rate appointments. These included Record, whom he named to the Board of Assessors; Samuel Kalish, the first Jew to serve as a justice of the New Jersey Supreme Court; and Winthrop Daniels, a former faculty colleague from Princeton, whom he would appoint to the Public Utility Commission. By contrast, Wilson genuinely enjoyed personal interaction with legislators and other politicians. In one-on-one encounters, he again demonstrated the persuasive powers that he had exercised as president of Princeton. In group settings, he bared his playful side. At an outing with state senators in Atlantic City in April 1911, the governor and the senators joined in singing and dancing after a fried-chicken supper, and he led them in the cakewalk. "Such are the processes of high politics!" he joked to Mrs. Peck. "This is what it costs to be a leader."[31]

Such frolicking also served a serious purpose. It helped Wilson do the part of his new job he cared about most—legislative leadership. As soon as the senatorial election was settled, he started pushing the legislature to enact the measures he had enumerated in his inaugural address. The primary became the storm center of this legislative offensive. Record drafted a far-reaching measure that required primaries for all elected officials and delegates to the parties' national conventions; it also required that legislators vote for the man who won their party's primary for U.S. senator and restricted the activities of state conventions to drafting platforms. Wilson enlisted a Democratic assemblyman and former student of his from Princeton, Elmer Geran, to introduce the measure.[32] Smith-Nugent Democrats charged once more that Wilson was turning their party over to that insidious radical Record.

The governor responded with inside and outside strategies. Throughout February 1911, he met repeatedly with legislators, listened to their comments and criticisms, and eventually agreed to accept some amendments to what everyone was calling the Geran bill. Meanwhile, he spoke around the state in favor of his reform program. Besides the primary, he touted other measures, such as the proposed Public Utility Commission, noting pointedly their adherence to the Wisconsin models "introduced by that very able and very energetic man, Mr. La Follette." Wilson also drew upon his ideas about the nature of politics to ask, "If your tree is dying, is it revolution to restore the purity of its sap and to purify the soil that will sustain it? Is this process of restoration a process of disturbance? No! It is a process of life; it is a process of renewal; it is a process of redemption."[33] The speaking engagements tired him, but Wilson enjoyed himself.

The showdown came in March. "Things are getting intense and interesting again," Wilson observed to Mary Peck, adding that "my spirits rise as the crisis approaches." He stepped up his speaking schedule, and back in Trenton he made another bold move. "Why not invite me to the caucus?" he reportedly said to the Democratic leader in the state assembly. "It is unprecedented, I know. Perhaps it's even unconstitutional; but then I'm an unconstitutional governor." On March 6, when he attended the assembly Democratic caucus, one member challenged the constitutionality of his presence. "Since you appeal to the constitution," Wilson reportedly replied, "I think I can satisfy you." He pulled a copy of the New Jersey constitution from his pocket and read the clause that authorized the governor to communicate with the legislature and recommend *such measures as he may deem expedient.*"[34] He then spent two hours explaining features of the legislation dealing with the Public Utility Commission, corrupt practices, and employers' liability, as well as the Geran bill. The assemblymen easily reached agreement to support the first three measures, but they wanted more time to consider the Geran bill.

A week later, on March 13, Wilson again went before the caucus. During the three-hour meeting, he spoke for more than an hour to plead for the Geran bill. One legislator recalled soon afterward, "I have never known anything like that speech. Such beautiful Saxon English, such suppressed emotion, such direct personal appeal. . . . It was like listening to music. And the whole thing was merely an appeal to our better unselfish natures." A machine Democrat retorted that all those present owed their places to political organizations, and the governor acknowledged that he owed his own nomination to the party organization, but he "owed his election to the people only, and he would refuse to acknowledge any obligation that transcends his obligation to the people who elected him." That answer and others impressed the legislators even more than his speech. One of them reportedly asked, "Where did this schoolmaster learn so much about politics—not only legislation, but practical politics?" Another agreed that "he acted like a small boy playing his favorite game; he certainly enjoyed the proceeding to the full." The assembly Democrats voted to support the Geran bill, 27 to 11.[35]

Wilson was winning, but the game was not over. Smith's son-in-law, Nugent, worked the halls of the capitol, lobbying against the primary. Between Democratic holdouts and Republicans, there were enough votes in the assembly to defeat the Geran bill. But Nugent underestimated Wilson. On March 20, the governor invited Nugent to his office and asked him, in his capacity as the state Democratic chairman, to support the bill. When Nugent refused, Wilson claimed that he had the votes lined up to pass it. "I do not know by what means you got them," Nugent replied. "What do you mean?" Wilson asked. "The talk is that you got them by patronage," Nugent responded. Wilson stood up and waved Nugent out: "Good afternoon, Mr. Nugent." Nugent made a crack that Wilson was no gentleman, and Wilson repeated, "Good afternoon, Mr. Nugent." In a public statement, the governor recounted the incident and commented, "I invited him here and he insulted me." Privately, he told Mary Peck, "It was a most unpleasant incident which I did not enjoy at all; but apparently it did a lot of good. . . . I feel debased to the level of the men whom I feel obliged to snub. But it all comes in the day's work." There was some truth in Nugent's charge. As he had done earlier in the fight with Smith, Tumulty was using patronage, this time to line up support for the Geran bill, and he acted with the governor's implicit approval, if not his detailed knowledge.[36]

Besides patronage and favorable publicity, Wilson had one other card to play. Wittingly or not, he had done a shrewd thing by enlisting Record to write the primary law. Drawing upon his background with the New Idea movement, Record now persuaded two progressive-leaning Republican assemblymen to announce that they would vote for the Geran bill. That move broke the back of the opposition. The bill passed the assembly on March 21 by a vote of 34 to 25. Thirty-one Democrats and three Republicans voted in favor, while ten Democrats and fifteen Republicans voted against it. Ironically, the bill had an easier time in the Republican-controlled senate. Both Democrats and Republicans in that chamber were less dependent upon their party's machines and were not inclined to be obstructionist. Revised somewhat but not weakened, the Geran bill passed the senate unanimously on April 13. After assembly concurrence, again unanimous, the bill went to the governor for his signature on April 20.[37]

Victory in the fight over the primary law smoothed the way for the passage of the rest of Wilson's program. Record drafted a corrupt-practices bill based on the Oregon law that many regarded as the model progressive legislation in this area. He had to bargain with Republican leaders in the state senate, but a strong bill emerged and passed easily in both chambers. Utility regulation likewise had an easy time in the assembly, and one provision allowed the new Public Utility Commission to use the physical valuation of a company's property as the basis for its rates, a scheme that ranked among the farthest-reaching regulatory proposals of the time. Wilson later had to accept a watered-down version that came out of the senate. These measures, together with the primary law, constituted what were known as the governor's bills and made up the program that Wilson had advanced during the campaign and in his inaugural address.[38]

Nor did those laws exhaust the accomplishments of the 1911 legislative session. A number of reformers and civic associations wanted to allow municipalities to adopt the new city commission form of government, which enjoyed wide popularity in progressive circles. After some initial hesitation, Wilson threw his weight behind municipal-reform legislation that included provisions for a local initiative, referendum, and recall, as well as the city commission. The bosses put up a fight against this measure, but Wilson and the reformers got a reasonably strong law in the end. Fittingly for a man with his professional background, the governor supported education reform, and the legislature enacted a set of laws that created a new state Board of Education with the power to conduct inspections and enforce standards, regulate districts' borrowing authority, and require special classes for students with handicaps. At the governor's urging, the legislature also enacted new food-storage and -inspection laws, strengthened oversight of factory working conditions, and limited labor by women and children.39

Wilson's only defeat occurred when he asked the legislature to ratify an amendment to the U.S. Constitution passed by Congress in 1909 to permit the levying of income taxes. Unlike the election of a U.S. senator, ratification of an amendment to the Constitution required separate approval by each chamber. The assembly promptly complied with the request, but the Republican-controlled senate refused to go along. Almost two years would pass before New Jersey would ratify the income tax amendment. By then, Wilson had been elected president and had carried enough Democrats with him to control both houses of the state legislature.

Despite that defeat, he racked up an impressive record as a legislative leader and a progressive. "I got absolutely everything I strove for,—and more besides," he exulted to Mary Peck when the legislature adjourned late in April. He called it "as complete a victory as has ever been won, I venture to say, in the history of the country. I wrote the platform, I had the measures formulated to my mind, I kept the pressure of opinion constantly on the legislature, and the programme was carried out to its last detail."40 Pride did not blind Wilson to the secrets of his success. He correctly credited the spirit of the times for much of what he had been able to do. Progressivism was a rapidly rising tide in American politics, and Wilson was not the only governor to push through this kind of reform program in the ten years since La Follette had begun battling Wisconsin's bosses in order to make government more accountable and business better regulated. Nineteen eleven stood out as a particularly dramatic juncture in this march of political and economic reform. In Wisconsin, La Follette's forces were filling out a second ambitious reform agenda, which resembled Wilson's. In California, a band of Republican progressives led by their newly elected governor, Hiram Johnson, pushed through a comparable program, although one that would stress direct popular measures such as the initiative and recall far more than Wilson's did. The accomplishments of this academic-turned-governor were part of a bigger picture, and some of the other reform leaders were men with whom he would cross paths and swords in coming years.

Still, Wilson unquestionably earned most of his success on his own. Given New Jersey's history as a boss-laden, conservative-leaning state, it would have been easy for him to fall far short of such sweeping accomplishments. A vivid illustration of what could have happened lay just across the Hudson River. In New York, the Democrats had likewise ridden the reform wave in 1910 to win the governorship and control of the legislature for the first time since the mid-1890s. Yet despite the Empire State's previous experience with dynamic governors such as Roosevelt and Charles Evans Hughes and its moderately reformist record, the situation there deteriorated into a hopeless wrangle between progressive Democrats and Tammany Hall. The progressives did succeed in keeping the Tammany boss from becoming a U.S. senator, but the machine blocked most reform legislation. The New York *World* was prophetically right when it said that its state needed a Woodrow Wilson.

The former president of Princeton brought to his governor's office a potent mix of personal and intellectual gifts. He planned his strategy and then kept the legislators at their jobs and focused on the task at hand. His success depended on foresight, force, and perseverance, traits that he would soon show again as a legislative leader in Washington. He also put into practice ideas that he had developed earlier about how to be such a leader. He did act like a prime minister. By meeting so often with legislators, he acted as if he were one of them. By joining his party's caucus, he became its leader. In effect, he was finding a practical application for the proposals he had advanced years before when he wrote about giving cabinet members seats in Congress. All this worked well, and it offered the first demonstration of how readily Woodrow Wilson could translate the study of politics into the practice of politics.

This smashing success in New Jersey in 1911 launched his political career in the best possible way. His legislative accomplishments as governor won him his spurs in the hottest political arena of the time. Even before he attracted the limelight in the fight with Smith, talk about higher office was in the air, and a Wilson presidential boomlet started even before the end of the legislative session. Yet his governorship would witness no further triumphs. He had no way of knowing it, but when the legislators left Trenton in April 1911, his best days in the statehouse were behind him. The nearly two years that remained in Wilson's governorship would be an anticlimax. Part of the letdown would spring from his presidential campaign, which increasingly occupied his attention and took him away from New Jersey.

The distractions of national politics did not fully explain his poor showing. His wider visibility and the state's pride in having a potential presidential nominee might have enhanced his effectiveness as governor. A more potent influence behind the falloff was revenge by the bosses. Smith, who had reportedly left Trenton in tears after the collapse of his senate candidacy, was a spent force, but his son-in-law, Nugent, continued to fight Wilson even after the legislative session. In July, at a restaurant near the governor's summer residence at Sea Girt, Nugent sent a bottle of wine to a table where several officers of the New Jersey National Guard were eating and said to them and everyone else in the restaurant: "I propose a toast to the Governor of New Jersey, the commander-in-chief of the militia. He is an ingrate and he is a liar. Do I drink alone?" An embarrassed silence fell over the room. Reports varied in claiming that Nugent was drunk and that others joined him in the toast, but several of the officers walked out. Cries immediately arose for Nugent to be ousted as state Democratic chairman. After conferring with Wilson, several members of the state committee called a meeting in order to remove Nugent as state party chairman, which they did on August 10.[41]

From that time on, civil war raged among New Jersey's Democrats. Wilson took advantage of the new primary law to attempt to shore up his support in the legislature. He spent most of September campaigning for supporters and against what he dubbed "the reactionary element, the element of the opposition." He also declared, "I must mention names. Politics, when it means the service of a great people, is not a milk and water business." The results of the primary gratified the governor for the most part. His candidates for the legislature won nominations throughout the state, except in Newark, where machine-backed candidates prevailed. That did not deter Wilson from using the state party convention to draft a platform calling for stronger business and workplace regulation, legislative redistricting, and reform of the state's government machinery, tax system, and jury procedures. On the convention floor, the delegates greeted him with applause and shouted, "Three cheers for Governor Wilson, the next President of the United States."[42]

These victories were sweet, but they were only half the battle. Wilson barnstormed through the state in October and early November, giving at least one speech a day and sometimes as many as three. Besides boosting his candidates, he addressed state and national issues. He called himself "a modern radical" because, he said, he wanted "to bring my thinking up to the facts and not drag the facts back to my antiquated thinking." He also urged Democrats to keep "the progressive wave that is sweeping through this Nation" in control of the party: "The Democratic party holds its lease of power on those terms and only upon those terms."[43] New Jersey's voters responded to his appeal only up to a point. Democratic legislative candidates outpolled Republicans statewide. The governor's supporters won in most places, and the Democrats picked up seats in the state senate, though not enough to gain control. In Newark, Nugent's machine deliberately failed to get out the vote for its own candidates for the assembly, thereby turning over control of that chamber, and now both houses of the legislature, to the Republicans. The outcome was a bitter disappointment to Wilson and did not bode well for the rest of his governorship.

When the next session of the legislature convened in January 1912, he trimmed his sails by proposing a more modest program of governmental and tax reform and the creation of a state board of health. He hoped that the good relations he had developed the preceding year with some Republican senators might ensure cooperation, but that was not to be. The governor was now a leading contender for the Democratic presidential nomination, and New Jersey Republicans were not going to do him any favors. Not only did they refuse to act on any of his proposals, but they passed bills of their own that he felt obliged to veto. Wilson found the experience frustrating, but he still found professional politicians easier and pleasanter to deal with than academic ones.

His daughter Nell later recalled that her father met these troubles "with philosophic understanding and calm. And this was not like the Princeton controversy, where his old friends and his heart were involved."[44] He needed understanding and calm in the early months of 1912. This low point in his governorship was also a low point in his personal and larger political fortunes. After an impressive start, his drive for the presidential nomination had stalled, and meanwhile his old foes at Princeton had just installed Hibben as his successor, and West was about to open the new Graduate College.

Some events did relieve the gloom. In February 1912, President William Howard Taft nominated Wilson's friend and Princeton classmate Mahlon Pitney to serve as a justice of the Supreme Court. Pitney had served in Congress and in New Jersey's senate and supreme court, where he had earned a reputation as a political and judicial conservative. He came under attack in the U.S. Senate from some progressive Republicans and Democrats, and Wilson came to his aid by making telephone calls to Democratic senators in Washington. One journalist recalled that the two men sat together in the governor's office when he made the calls, "calling each other Tommy and May—reminiscent of their days together at Princeton."[45] Wilson also enlisted local party figures to work on Senator Martine, whose support of the nominee was doubtful.

Other aspects of the governorship also gave Wilson pleasure. Summers took the family to a seaside resort for long periods. A nearby golf course gave him a chance to pursue this newfound pastime, and he even enjoyed some of the ceremonial duties of his office. One of these required him to ride horseback as he reviewed the New Jersey National Guard on parade. Wilson had not ridden much since his youth, and he cut a decidedly civilian figure in top hat and tailcoat. Yet observers commented on how smartly he sat on his horse.

In some ways, he and, even more so, Ellen found the summers at Sea Girt a trial. There, the Wilsons had a hard time maintaining their customary separation between work life and home life. First at the Princeton Inn and then in the house on Cleveland Lane, family life went on in much the same way as before Wilson entered politics. He would have dinner with Ellen and Margaret and Jessie and Nell, and afterward they would read aloud together or sing around the piano. This routine sprang not only from their desire for privacy but also from Wilson's attitude toward his work in both academic and public life. As Stockton Axson later observed, his brother-in-law had a "creative, literary type of mind" that would be absorbed "with a tremendous theme, an epic." He therefore wanted his time away from work "simply to relax, not have business follow him." Because he wanted "to let his mind play, to give it a thorough rest, he talks small talk with the members of his family, he recites limericks and makes puns and tells anecdotes."[46]

Sea Girt, however, was a different story. Railroad tracks close by, the National Guard parade ground next door, swarms of visitors to the beach, and a constant parade of politicians—all these made it what Ellen Wilson's biographer called "a veritable gold fish bowl."[47] But the New Jersey governor's summer residence witnessed the turn of fortune that would always make Wilson remember the place with special fondness. The Wilsons were back at Sea Girt at the end of June 1912 when the Democrats met for their national convention in Baltimore. Here, they and Tumulty rode an emotional roller-coaster as seemingly endless rounds of balloting first seemed to doom Wilson's chances for the presidential nomination and then finally brought victory. Troubles in New Jersey and unpleasant reminders from Princeton now faded as Wilson set out on the greatest adventure of his life.

7

NOMINEE

Woodrow Wilson became a main contender for the Democratic Party nomination for president as soon as he was elected governor of New Jersey. This was an unusual turn of events. According to the political logic of the time, two other Democrats should have led the field for the presidential nomination: the governor-elect of New York and the governor of Ohio, states with much larger numbers of electoral votes. A governor or former governor of New York had run as the nominee of one of the two major parties in five of the last ten presidential elections, and the winning candidate for president in all but three of the last ten elections had been a native of Ohio, two of them governors. Yet the hottest prospect for the Democratic presidential nomination in 1912 came from a relatively small and politically undistinguished state, and the freshest new face in the party belonged to a neophyte freshly removed from academia.

Wilson owed his standing to a conjunction of luck, current issues, and changes in the political environment. The Democratic governors of the big swing states did not cut a strong figure in national politics. The New Yorker, John A. Dix, was indolent and colorless, while the Ohioan, Judson Harmon, was known mainly as an opponent of prohibition. Also, those governors came from the conservative side of the party, and Bryan's ideological sway among Democrats, together with the rising tide of progressive sentiment, effectively ruled out any presidential nominee from the conservative side. Wilson's well-publicized battles against privilege at Princeton had mitigated some of his vulnerability on those grounds even before he had taken on the New Jersey bosses. Moreover, a reputation earned outside the political arena had acquired newfound potency thanks to the proliferation of popular magazines and newspapers—the new "mass media." Roosevelt had already demonstrated how fame gained in other pursuits could help lead to political preferment. Wilson could not match

Roosevelt's war-hero status or glamorous exploits as a hunter and rancher, but as a well-regarded former university president he stood out from the political pack.

The movement to gain him the nomination started in the opening months of 1911. An early impetus came from New Jersey Democrats, who relished the prospect of promoting one of their own to the White House, but a serious contender needed wider support, which Wilson had from the outset. Besides Harvey and the conservatives, whom the governor now began to hold at arm's length, there was a trio of backers representing men who shared Wilson's background as an expatriate southerner who had sought his fortune in the North. First to jump in was Walter Page, now a successful magazine and book editor in New York.[1] Next was Walter McCorkle, a native Virginian who practiced law on Wall Street and was president of the Southern Society of New York, an organization of expatriates at whose meetings Wilson had often spoken. Last came William F. McCombs, a native of Arkansas who had been a student of Wilson's at Princeton, practiced law, and dabbled in New York politics. The three met on February 24, 1911, to discuss such campaign aspects as publicity for the candidate, out-of-state speaking tours, contacts with Democrats in Congress, and fund-raising. This meeting was the genesis of the Wilson presidential movement.

Wilson met with his new triumvirate for the first time a month later, at Page's apartment in New York. Up to this point, he had felt detached from the activity on his behalf, and this meeting with his backers did not hearten him. They told him he needed to make a speaking tour in the West, and they had hired one of Page's magazine writers, Frank Parker Stockbridge, to arrange this trip and handle publicity. "It is all a very strange business for me," Wilson reported to Mary Peck, "and not very palateable [*sic*]. I feel an almost unconquerable shyness about it." Having a publicity manager on the western tour likewise bothered him: "Already he is giving me no end of trouble to supply him with 'copy.'"[2]

His actions belied his professed ambivalence. He had already begun his own campaign to try to win over Bryan, who earlier had sought the governor-elect's views on a "political matter" and said, "The fact that you were against us in 1896 raised a question in my mind in regard to your views on public questions but your attitude in the Senatorial case has tended to reassure me." The two men met for the first time in March. Ellen Wilson once more showed her acuity in guiding her husband's career by arranging the meeting. When Wilson was out of town, she learned that Bryan would be giving a nonpolitical talk at the Princeton Theological Seminary. She telegraphed her husband to come back at once, and she invited Bryan to dinner with their family. The couple did their best to charm Bryan, who evidently reciprocated. Wilson confessed to Mary Peck that he now had "a very different impression of him" and was struck by Bryan's "force of sincerity and conviction. . . . A truly captivating man, I must admit." Two or three years later, Ellen reportedly told a friend, "[T]hat dinner put Mr. Wilson in the White House."[3]

That was an exaggeration, but this first meeting did open a courtship. Early in April, Wilson spoke after Bryan at a political dinner in New Jersey. "I have never been matched with Mr. Bryan, or any other speaker his equal before," he told Mary Peck, "and had my deep misgivings as to how I should stand the comparison." His performance showed that he could hold his own with the nation's champion orator. "Unless there was a general conspiracy to lie to me," he reported to Mary Peck, "I spoke as well as Mr. Bryan did, and moved my audience more. Ellen said I was 'more of an orator' than she had ever seen me before: that is, that I put more colour and emotion into what I said than usual." Bryan did not say anything about the speech, but in his own talk, Wilson reported, "Mr. Bryan paid me a very handsome tribute of generous praise, which my sanguine friends thought quite significant and were immensely pleased at; for of course no Democrat can win whom Mr. Bryan does *not* approve."[4]

In seeking the Democratic presidential nomination Wilson had three principal tasks. First, he had to make himself better known throughout the country. Second, he had to convince Democrats in the Bryan wing of the party that he was one of them. Finally, he had to burnish his credentials as a progressive. Given the Democrats' unbroken string of drubbings in the last four presidential elections, appealing beyond the bounds of the party was essential to winning the presidency. Wilson's experience in New Jersey had shown that progressivism offered the best chance to cast a broader net.

These tasks played to his strengths. Attracting publicity was never a problem for him. He had already earned a national reputation as president of Princeton, and now, as a crusading reform governor and dragon slayer in his fight with the bosses, he drew attention from people who wanted to size up this new boy on the political block. The experienced Frank Stockbridge knew how to ensure that local and national press gave the governor good coverage, which he supplemented by arranging personal interviews. The substantive side of the mission—appealing to Bryanites and progressives—fell entirely on Wilson's shoulders, and this neophyte showed that he was ready for the political big league.

He was already using language that Bryan's followers liked to hear. Early in 1911, he called himself a radical and avowed, "[T]he so-called radicalism of our time is nothing else than an effort to release the energies of our time." At a business convention in Atlanta, where he was when Ellen summoned him home to meet Bryan, he shared the program with the two men who would eventually be his main opponents in the election. Ex-president Roosevelt spoke the night before, and President Taft was to speak right after Wilson. According to Taft's military aide, Archie Butt, the governor held the audience spellbound for forty minutes with "a most polished and masterly address. . . . The President said it was the polished utterance of a politician. But he has got to be reckoned with." Wilson also thought he did well, telling Mary Peck, "On the whole the reception accorded me was finer than that accorded either Mr. Roosevelt or Mr. Taft." People in Atlanta talked about nominating him for president. It must have been particularly gratifying to receive such acclaim in the place where he had suffered through his brief, unsatisfying stint as a lawyer.5

Wilson expanded on his progressive themes during the spring of 1911. In a speech to a national Democratic gathering in Indianapolis, he lambasted the Republicans for favoring big business and the wealthy, and he coined a phrase he would use again later when he declared, "The men who understand the life of the country are the men who are on the make, and not the men who are made; because the men who are on the make are in contact with the actual conditions of struggle." He also stuck up for labor unions, praised factory-safety and workmen's compensation laws, and ridiculed the standard conservative line that such laws and union organizing interfered with freedom of contract: "[Workers] must work upon the terms offered them or starve. Is that freedom of contract?"6 Curiously, although he was speaking on Thomas Jefferson's birthday, Wilson made only perfunctory mention of the Sage of Monticello.

Jefferson posed a problem for Wilson both intellectually and politically. He had always ranked this man among his least favorite founders of the Republic, and he had never been able to swallow the legacies of state rights and limited government that conservative Democrats drew from him. Hamilton remained his favorite among the founders, and he had enjoyed a recent study of him by F. S. Oliver, an English businessman, more than any other book he had read in a long time. These views involved more than historical and intellectual preferences. At this time, Republicans generally reviled Jefferson because of the way secessionists had invoked his legacy at the time of the Civil War. Sophisticated Republicans such as Roosevelt and Henry Cabot Lodge went further, excoriating him in addition for having neglected military preparedness and for lowering the tone of politics to crass commercialism and self-interest. In his influential book published two years earlier, *The Promise of American*

Life, the progressive writer Herbert Croly had refined such arguments into an indictment of Jefferson's legacy as the worst obstacle to the development of transcendent nationalism and genuine idealism in American politics. Conversely, Hamilton came in for high marks in these circles on the same grounds. On the other side of the party divide, nearly all Democrats worshipped Jefferson as fervently as ever. Bryanites exalted him as the champion of the common people and the apostle of greater democracy. If Bryan's approval was essential for the Democratic nomination, so, in a sense, was Jefferson's.[7]

Wilson had begun to address this problem a while earlier. During the gubernatorial campaign, he had defined a "Progressive Democrat" as someone "who will try to carry forward in the service of a new age, in the spirit of Thomas Jefferson." On the western tour that Stockbridge arranged, he expanded on this argument. Speaking to the Jefferson Club in Los Angeles, he argued that "every true Jeffersonian" must strive to translate the founder's ideals into the language of the present time, and he claimed that "the Jeffersonian spirit" demanded support of such innovations as the primary and the referendum.[8] Such measured praise marked the limit of Wilson's embrace of Jefferson up to this point. He would go further later.

The western trip, which took up the month of May, began immediately after the end of the New Jersey legislative session. This was the most relaxed speaking tour Wilson ever made in his political career, more like a vacation than a campaign. The first and last parts of the trip, which took him across the Great Plains and the Rockies, featured only a few speeches, separated by long intervals of train travel. Princeton and Bryn Mawr alumni entertained him, and he visited with several cousins, including his old flame Hattie Woodrow Welles. He gave more speeches when he reached the West Coast, which he was visiting for the first time, and in all of his appearances he endorsed reform measures and refused to shy away from the word *radical*. He often praised the initiative, referendum, and recall, and in a newspaper interview he saluted "more freedom of action here in the West; you are younger and there exists a sort of brotherhood of pioneering." In one speech on the return leg, he declared that the nation's strength came from its ordinary people, not "its leading men. . . . You never heard of a tree deriving its energy from its buds or its flowers, but from its roots." In another speech, he declared that the doors of opportunity were "shut and double bolted and we know who has locked them and bolted them"—it was "the concentration of money" that choked off opportunity to all but a pre-selected few."[9]

Wilson got a warm reception everywhere, and the tour gave him a preview of the presidential campaign trail. He also used the trip to continue to woo Bryan. On his way back, he visited Bryan's adopted hometown, Lincoln, Nebraska, where he paid tribute to "the great Nebraskan, W. J. Bryan," and, referring to the name of Bryan's home, called him the "sage of Fairview." The object of this adulation was not present, because business had called him away, but his younger brother and political sidekick, Charles, was part of the welcoming committee. Charles Bryan took Wilson to Fairview, where Bryan's wife, Mary, received him. Also on the journey east, he met with his backers in Washington, D.C., where he had dinner with Page, McCorkle, McCombs, and Stockbridge. He told them he wanted to eschew "the usual methods" of politics, but he conceded, "I am far too well acquainted with practical [considerations] to think that the matter can be allowed to take care of itself." McCombs—who was the youngest of the group, unmarried, and independently wealthy—volunteered to take charge.[10]

The new manager did his job ably, up to a point. McCombs lavished nearly manic energy on coordinating Wilson's supporters in various states. He set up an office in New York and gathered a staff. He recognized the need to deal with politicians around the country, maintain an organization, and not just rely on publicity and the eloquence of the would-be candidate. But his contribution carried a stiff price. He began pestering Wilson to refrain from calling himself a radical and to cultivate leading businessmen and "stick to a few fundamentals." McCombs also grew possessive of Wilson and domineering in his management of the campaign. He forced Stockbridge out and became jealous of anyone who was attracted to Wilson's candidacy. His behavior would grow worse during the months leading up to the 1912 Democratic convention and may well have sprung from a deep-seated psychological disorder.[11]

Unfortunately for McCombs but fortunately for the Wilson presidential campaign, his jealousy was justified in one case. Late in the summer of 1911, yet another expatriate southerner in New York climbed aboard the bandwagon and gradually began to augment and then supplant McCombs's leadership. He was William Gibbs McAdoo. A tall man with sharp features and a dark complexion and hair, the forty-seven-year-old McAdoo had the air of the successful businessman that he was. He was a native of Georgia who had studied law at the University of Tennessee and practiced in that state until moving to New York in the early 1890s. In New York, he switched careers to organize, promote, and head the company that built and operated a new railway link beneath the Hudson River between lower Manhattan and New Jersey, known familiarly as the Hudson Tubes. Difficulties raising money to build the Tubes had left McAdoo

with an abiding dislike for the financial barons of Wall Street. He became
a hero in New York when he reversed the railroad magnate William
Henry Vanderbilt's notorious sneer, "The public be damned," adopting
for the Tubes the motto "The public be pleased." Those attitudes,
together with boyhood memories of hard times in the South after the
Civil War, set McAdoo apart from the conservatism that prevailed among
New York's leading businessmen. This newcomer proved to be a quick
learner in politics, and he had a steadiness and resolve that McCombs
lacked.[12]

McAdoo's qualities proved sorely needed in the months that stretched
between the fall of 1911 and the Democratic National Convention in the
summer of 1912. This was a time of troubles for Wilson's bid for the nomination, with opposition coming from bosses in New Jersey, conservatives,
and political rivals. The governor's foes at home did their greatest mischief now. Ever since his earlier fights with Smith and Nugent, they had
bad-mouthed him to machine leaders in other states, especially New York,
and they conspired to spoil his shot at the presidential nomination. His
party's losing control of the lower house of the state legislature led to the
stalemate of the 1912 legislative session, which broke the governor's string
of successes and helped to slow the momentum of his presidential bid outside New Jersey.

Conservatives inside and outside the Democratic Party also became a
thorn in Wilson's side. He heeded McCombs's warning not to appear
overly radical, and in October, speaking in Madison, Wisconsin, Robert
La Follette's hometown, he stated, "The diagnosis is radical, but the cure
is remedial; the cure is conservative. I do not, for my part, think that remedies applied should be applied upon a great theoretical scale." Yet he stuck
to his guns on the issue of financial concentration, excoriating a bill introduced in Congress by conservative Republicans as a move toward greater
consolidation and a threat to small banks. At the national governors' conference, he publicly sparred with a fellow Democrat, the governor of
Alabama, who cast aspersions on majority rule. As that spat indicated,
conservative views still prevailed among many Democrats, particularly,
but not exclusively, in the South. "The South is a very conservative
region," he told Mary Peck, ". . . and I am *not* conservative. I am a radical."
He worried that his southern supporters might "make a mistake and
repent it too late."[13] He was right to worry. His Dixie roots were not
enough to induce all of his fellow southern whites to flock to his standard,
and opposition from his native region soon proved to be a major obstacle
on the road to the nomination.

The first conservative assaults came from another quarter, however.

The New York *Sun*, the leading conservative Republican newspaper, had disliked Wilson from even before his governorship, and in December 1911 and January 1912 this paper published two potentially damaging disclosures about him. Both matters had roots in Wilson's presidency of Princeton. First, the *Sun* revealed that shortly before being elected governor, Wilson had applied for a $4,000 annual pension from a fund recently established by Andrew Carnegie for retired college professors and administrators. Both his age—fifty-three, not the usually mandated sixty-five—and the sponsor of the fund exposed him to scathing attacks. "The Carnegie Foundation was created for indigent teachers and not for indigent politicians," thundered one anti-Wilson newspaper. "I cannot understand how a real Democrat could touch such money," declared a radical Massachusetts party activist.[14]

This disclosure tarnished Wilson's progressive credentials. He immediately issued a statement explaining that Carnegie pensions were also awarded "on the ground of length and quality of service." He added, "I have no private means to depend upon. A man who goes into politics bound by the principles of honor puts his family and all who may be dependent upon him for support at the mercy of any incalculable turn of the wheel of fortune." Although he still felt justified in having applied for the pension, he noted that the Carnegie trustees had declined his request and "I have not renewed the application." Money worries did weigh on the family. Ellen told a friend that "his income from his books averages less than $1000 a year,—all of which goes for life insurance. . . . When he was a mere professor he could and did make some money writing and lecturing, so that we even built a home for ourselves,—but for the past ten years he has given his pen and his voice to the public service absolutely free, gratis, for nothing!"[15] In the meantime, Wilson did accept a personal gift of $4,000 raised by wealthy Princeton friends.

The brouhaha eventually calmed down, but in a letter to Mary Peck he blamed the situation on "certain big business interests in N.Y., who know that I could not be managed to their mind," together with the nominally Democratic newspaper tycoon William Randolph Hearst, who opposed him "for personal reasons." Wilson felt "set about by vindictive men, determined to destroy my character, by fair means or foul." He also feared that old enemies at Princeton were conspiring with his political foes, and a skeleton from that closet did come back to haunt him. On January 8, 1912, *The Sun* published the letter written almost five years earlier by Wilson to a conservative alumnus that closed with the sentence "Would that we could do something, at once dignified and effective, to knock Mr. Bryan once and for all into a cocked hat!"[16] When he wrote those words, he was still consorting with other conservative Democrats and trying to curry favor with this wealthy alumnus, Adrian Joline. Wilson began to change his political stance soon afterward, and Joline became one of his bitterest opponents in the fights over the Quad Plan and the Graduate College. Joline started circulating the letter in the spring of 1911, and one of his friends leaked it to *The Sun*.

This transparent attempt to discredit Wilson with Bryan and his followers fooled nobody, but it caused some tense moments. McCombs panicked and charged that a conspiracy was afoot, masterminded by Wall Street tycoons. Bryan took the matter in stride. It helped that he happened to be in Raleigh, North Carolina, when the news broke and staying with his close friend Josephus Daniels, a newspaper editor and prominent Democrat who backed Wilson. Daniels worked on Bryan and traveled with him to Washington, where the New Jersey governor was scheduled to speak on January 8 at the Democrats' biggest annual event, the Jackson Day dinner. One Democrat who sought to mollify Bryan remembered him saying, "If the big financial interests think they are going to make a rift in the Progressive ranks of the Democratic Party by such tactics, they are mistaken."[17]

Wilson reacted in a similar manner. He drafted a statement to the press praising Bryan but decided against issuing it. "We must not appear to place ourselves on the defensive," an adviser recalled him saying. "I will cover the situation tonight in my address." In his Jackson Day speech, he praised Bryan for having "the steadfast vision of what it was that was the matter" and having based his career unfailingly on principle. He urged Democrats to "move against the trusts" and remain faithful to "that vision which sees that no society is renewed from the top and every society is renewed from the bottom." The speech did the trick. Bryan put his hand on Wilson's shoulder and said to him, "That was splendid, splendid." Other Democrats rushed to congratulate him, and as he told Mary Peck, "I was made the lion of the occasion,—to my great surprise; and the effect of it all (for it was a national affair) seems to have been to strengthen the probabilities of my nomination many-fold."[18]

One more problem from the conservative side vexed Wilson in January 1912. This involved George Harvey and his cohort Henry Watterson, editor of the Louisville *Courier-Journal*. In December, Wilson had dinner with the two men in New York, and they discussed the political situation. At the end of the evening, Harvey asked for "a perfectly frank answer" to the question of whether his support was embarrassing Wilson, who answered that it might be. Wilson quickly regretted his frankness and, not having thanked Harvey for his support, said, "Forgive me, and forget my manners." Harvey affected to accept the apology, but he did not forgive his onetime protégé for his apostasy from Democratic conservatism. Harvey dropped the slogan "For President: Woodrow Wilson," which he had been running on the cover of *Harper's Weekly*. He also fed stories to newspapers about a "break" between him and Wilson and released a misleading statement to the press accusing Wilson of acting on his own initiative to brush him off. This attack backfired because Watterson wrote a letter to *The New York Times* in which he inadvertently confirmed that Harvey had initiated the affair. Meanwhile, Bryan sprang to Wilson's defense. In his magazine, *The Commoner*, he asserted that the attacks "are proving the sincerity of his [Wilson's] present position. . . . [T]he venom of his adversaries removes all doubt as to the REALITY of the change."[19]

In retrospect, this incident and the others would shrink in importance compared with the biggest test Wilson faced in his quest for the nomination—challenges from rival aspirants. His apparent ease in marching toward the party's top prize was deceptive. Novelty at first enhanced his attractiveness, while the Democrats' losing record in recent presidential contests initially made more-established politicians shy away. Both of those circumstances had changed by the end of 1911. Wilson's novelty may have been wearing off, and mounting political troubles for the Taft administration—together with open warfare in Republican ranks—made the Democrats' presidential prospects look unexpectedly bright.

The biggest question hanging over the party was whether its top national officeholder would make a bid for the nomination. He was the Speaker of the House of Representatives, James Beauchamp Clark of Missouri. Clark, who went by the nickname Champ, was sixty-one years old in 1911. Active in Democratic politics for four decades, he had served in the House, with one interruption, for the past eighteen years, becoming minority leader in 1907 and Speaker after the party won control in 1910. An educated man who had practiced and taught law and had briefly been a college president, Clark nevertheless gave the appearance of being Wilson's polar opposite. Folksy and taciturn, he had once endorsed a patent medicine in a speech on the floor of the House, and he had gotten ahead in politics in part by letting people underestimate him. To the press, Clark seemed the epitome of the small-town party hack, a public image that was both unfortunate and unfair. In his years as minority leader, Clark had welded the House Democrats into a disciplined, progressive force, and on all the important issues he was a loyal Bryanite. That record prompted many observers to predict that Bryan would endorse Clark for the nomination after the Speaker announced his candidacy late in the fall of 1911.

Champ Clark was a formidable contender, as Wilson and his backers soon discovered.[20]

Nor was Clark the only serious challenger. The Democrats' second-ranking national officeholder also entered the race for the nomination. He was the majority leader in the House, Oscar W. Underwood of Alabama. At first, his candidacy seemed to be just another home-state "favorite son" bid, but in the early months of 1912 Underwood began to gather support throughout the South. His attractiveness was testimony to the weakness in the South that worried Wilson.

Wilson drew fire from opposite ends of the political spectrum in the South. So-called Bourbon Democrats—conservatives who led the political machines in their states—recoiled from his "radical" progressive views. Agrarian radicals—such as Tom Watson of Georgia, once a leading Populist, and James K. Vardaman of Mississippi—rejected him on account of his anti-Bryan past. The common denominator of this opposition was the belief that this expatriate was no longer a "real" southerner. Wilson's opponents viewed him as someone who had adopted alien Yankee ways—either the radical progressivism that irked the Bourbons or the friendliness toward urbanites and big business that irked the agrarian radicals. His southern supporters tended to be more progressive types, such as Josephus Daniels and, ironically, Wilson's old but not fond acquaintance at the Atlanta bar, Hoke Smith. The fault line separating his supporters and opponents in the former Confederacy ran mainly between reconstructed and unreconstructed white southerners.[21]

Another irony made it clear that Underwood's backers did not so much love him more as they loved Wilson less. The forty-nine-year-old congressman was arguably no more a "real" southerner than the New Jersey governor. He was a native of Louisville, Kentucky, and had spent part of his boyhood in Minnesota. Only after attending the University of Virginia—his time there briefly overlapping with Wilson's, although the two men never knew each other—did he move to the Deep South, where, like Wilson, he had set up a law practice in a New South boomtown, in Underwood's case the rising manufacturing center of Birmingham, Alabama. After his election to Congress in the mid-1890s, Underwood became a spokesman for his city's business interests. Smooth-faced and affable, he owed his rise among House Democrats to his pleasant manner and his championship of tariff reform. His candidacy for the nomination was a blessing in disguise for Wilson. Besides keeping Bourbons from backing Clark, as some of them probably would have done, it kept sectional feeling strong. Southerners wanted one of their own to be the nominee, and an expatriate might be better than an outsider.

The race for the nomination got going in earnest when William Randolph Hearst came out for Clark at the end of January 1912. This was another case of loving Wilson less. The "personal reasons" cited by Wilson to account for Hearst's opposition evidently dated back to the beginning of his term as governor. According to later recollections, the newspaper tycoon had made a roundabout approach to Wilson, who responded, "Tell Mr. Hearst to go to hell." Wilson reportedly also remarked, "God knows I want the Democratic presidential nomination and I am going to do everything legitimately to get it, but if I am to grovel at Hearst's feet, I will never have it."[22] Wilson had made a dangerous enemy. Hearst's newspapers enjoyed a wide readership, particularly among working-class people in big cities. Those papers started to blacken the governor's name by reprinting derogatory comments about recent immigrants from southern and eastern Europe that appeared in Wilson's *History of the American People*. Conversely, Tom Watson attacked him as a tool of the Catholic church because Joe Tumulty was his secretary, and as soft on race because he had spoken to African American audiences.

The four months from February to the end of May 1912 marked a time of trial and discouragement for Wilson. His bid for the nomination met one setback after another, with only a few bright moments to relieve the gloom. In 1912, neither party chose a majority of its convention delegates through primaries, although several states did pick their delegates that way. Those primaries provided indications of how well candidates were doing and helped or hurt them in the race to gain other delegates. Wilson skipped the first of the primaries, in Missouri, because it was Clark's home state. The Speaker won handily there, despite some factional divisions. The governor prevailed in primaries in Wisconsin, Kansas, and Oklahoma, but he skipped Alabama because it was Underwood's home state. Meanwhile, Underwood drew support throughout the South. A heavy blow to Wilson's candidacy fell early in April in Illinois, where Clark beat him in the primary by a two-to-one margin. Soon afterward, the Speaker carried Bryan's adopted home state, Nebraska, although with only a plurality. The news was not good in the nonprimary states either. In New York, despite the efforts of such supporters as a young Democratic state senator named Franklin D. Roosevelt, Tammany chose a delegation that was hostile to Wilson. In May, Underwood swept primaries in several southern states, including one where Wilson had strong personal ties, Georgia; in another state where he had strong ties, South Carolina, he did eke out a victory. Meanwhile, Clark won primaries in western and northeastern states, and many observers predicted that he would be the nominee.[23]

The defeats were embarrassing to Wilson. He believed in primaries and had brought them to New Jersey; plus, he was running as the most progressive candidate and the one with the broadest appeal. Republicans had a ready, if disparaging, answer to the question of why Wilson had failed to do better. With them—conservatives and progressives alike—it was an article of faith that the Democrats were fundamentally unsound, triply tainted by the legacies of slavery and secession, by the corrupt influence of city machines, and by the cranky notions of farmer radicals. In the South, memories of the Civil War, with race lurking in the background, undermined Wilson's appeal. In northern states such as Illinois and New York, Hearst's attacks and Clark's ties to party organizations turned politicians and voters against him. Finally, Clark had a record on economic issues, which mattered more to Bryanites than political reform, and he stood unsullied by any earlier conservative flirtations.[24]

Wilson's high-toned but hard-hitting reformist style would have worked better with Republicans. In fact, at that moment Theodore Roosevelt was showing how strong such an appeal was. "My hat is in the ring," the ex-president announced in February 1912. He elbowed aside La Follette, who had previously carried the insurgent progressive banner against Taft, to run for the nomination against his own handpicked successor. Roosevelt denounced bosses and big business, advocated political and economic reform measures, and demanded that the will of the people be heard. He won all but one of the primaries he entered, even beating the president in his home state of Ohio. This turn of events hurt Wilson's prospects. The spectacular internecine fight in the other party—especially because it involved such a famous and colorful figure as Roosevelt—distracted public attention from the contest for the Democratic nomination. Moreover, the damage that Roosevelt's fight with Taft did to their party vastly improved Democratic prospects in November, so that the Democrats looked likely to win no matter whom they nominated. Why, then, turn to an unconventional newcomer when they could send a tried-and-true party man to the White House?

Wilson's poor showing in the primaries did not stem from lack of effort. When he spoke in various states during the first half of 1912, he gave a compelling exposition of his political thinking. He continued to hit away at the theme of unleashing the economic energies of ordinary people. In a newspaper interview, he echoed Bryan's well-known refrain from the 1896 Cross of Gold speech: "Who are the business men of the country? Are not the farmers business men? . . . Is not every employer of labor, every purchaser of material and every master of any enterprise, big or little, and every man in every profession a business man?" He also invoked sacred symbols, appropriating Lincoln's memory as an example of how high common folk could rise, and he traveled farther down the road to Monticello, avowing, "I turn, with ever renewed admiration, to that great founder of the Democratic party, Thomas Jefferson." Wilson likewise painted his own vision of a vigorous government led by a dynamic president. Several times, he implicitly or explicitly praised Roosevelt's assertive style, and he maintained, "Government must regulate business, because that is the foundation of every other relationship, particularly of the political relationship."[25]

By the time Wilson uttered those words, his prospects of leading the nation looked dim. Not only had the primaries gone against him around the country, but he also had to fight on his home turf. Vengeful to the end, Smith and Nugent endorsed Clark and mounted a campaign to deny the governor delegates to the convention. After some initial reluctance, Wilson came out swinging. He made speeches around the state, and in a public letter to the party faithful he asked, "Shall the Democrats of New Jersey send delegates to Baltimore who are free men, or are the special interests again to name men to represent them? . . . [D]o you wish to support government conducted by public opinion, rather than by private understanding and management, or do you wish to slip back into the slough of the old despair and disgrace?" Distraction from the hard-fought contest between Roosevelt and Taft in the Republican primary did not help. Wilson and Roosevelt crossed paths in Princeton, when the ex-president spoke in front of the Nassau Inn the day before the New Jersey primary and Wilson stood in the crowd across the street, in front of the First Presbyterian Church. In his own speech, on the steps of his rented house an hour later, he commented on "two very militant gentlemen" whose fight was making it hard for people to concentrate on the issues.[26] Still, the primary, on May 28, went Wilson's way. The up-and-coming new boss in Jersey City, Frank Hague, failed to deliver for Clark, and Nugent's Newark returned the only non-Wilson delegates—four of them.

Sweetening that outcome was an editorial endorsement two days later from the New York *World*. For *The World*, it was partly a matter of loving Clark a lot less. The paper had earlier called his nomination "*Democratic suicide*" and feared that it would open the way to another term for Roosevelt, whom the editorial called "the most cunning and adroit demagogue that modern civilization has produced since Napoleon III." Wilson seemed a bit too Bryanite for *The World*'s taste, but that shortcoming was "vastly overbalanced by his elements of strength." Wilson had proved "his political courage and fearlessness" and shown himself to be "the sort of a man who ought to be President." This good news from New Jersey and

The World did not hearten Wilson. He told Mary Peck, "I have not the least idea of being nominated, because . . . the outcome is in the hands of professional case-hardened politicians who serve only their own interests and who know I will not serve them except as I might serve the party in general. I have no deep stakes involved in the game."[27]

Wilson was bracing himself to face an impending disappointment. But his prospects were not quite as bleak as he thought. Despite the primary defeats, his candidacy had attracted widespread support. In addition to *The World*, a number of important newspapers and magazines endorsed his nomination, such as Page's *The World's Work, The Independent, The Nation, The Outlook*, the *New York Evening Post, The Kansas City Star*, and Daniels's Raleigh *News and Observer*. Protestant church leaders and journals embraced him as one of their own, as did teachers around the country. Wilson college clubs had more than 100 chapters by the time of the convention, with 10,000 members. Most important, Wilson had a strong, well-financed organization behind him. His wealthy Princeton friends contributed $85,000, of which $51,000 came from Cleveland Dodge, while other big donors chipped in an additional $65,000. Tensions between McCombs and McAdoo did not prevent them from resourcefully working the political circuit. They played the southern cards skillfully, gaining second-choice support from Underwood backers and extracting promises from his managers not to withdraw in favor of Clark. Moreover, Bryan declined to endorse Clark, and some people thought he might try to exploit a deadlocked convention to gain another nomination for himself. In short, Wilson's situation was serious but not hopeless.[28]

The year 1912 witnessed two of the most exciting national political conventions in American history. The first to meet and by far the more dramatic was the Republican gathering at the middle of June in Chicago. Nothing could match that convention's furious exchanges on and off the floor between the Roosevelt and Taft forces, charges of a "steal" from the ex-president and his supporters, and the walkout by his delegates, who promised to start a third party. Roosevelt spoke to those delegates in person. In the most impassioned speech of his life, he pledged to carry the battle forward with the new party: "We fight in honorable fashion for the good of mankind; fearless of the future; unheeding of our individual hearts; with unflinching hearts and undimmed eyes; we stand at Armageddon, and we battle for the Lord." Wilson's reaction to these events was guarded and quizzical. Even before the Republican convention, he had soured on Roosevelt and what he called "his present insane distemper of egotism!"[29]

The Republican split brought both peril and opportunity to Wilson's cause. At first glance, this development worsened things for him by making victory for the Democrats now seem well-nigh certain. All they had to do was hang together, so the conventional wisdom went, and they would win no matter who headed their ticket. At a deeper level, however, Roosevelt's bolt vastly expanded the stakes of the election. Some of the ex-president's friends thought he got carried away with his emotions, while others shared Wilson's view that he was at least slightly mad. Neither was true. Despite the sound and fury of the Republican convention and the pretext offered by the "steal," there was long-pondered, deeply thought-out method in Roosevelt's madness. He had convinced himself that the current battles over the control of big business and the extension of democracy were repeating the sectional conflict half a century earlier over slavery. He intended his new party to play the role previously played by Lincoln's Republicans—of standing up and fighting for freedom and national unity—and to emerge as a major, lasting political force.[30]

Wilson shared these views, though with a different twist. In February, he had alluded to Lincoln's "fearless analysis" that the nation could not endure half-slave and half-free. "[T]hat statement ought be made now," Wilson declared, "—that *as our economic affairs are now organized they cannot go on.*" The present division of the country was more intricate and difficult, but it was "something that can, by clear thinking, be dealt with and successfully dealt with, and no man who is a friend of this country predicts any deeper sorts of trouble." Now Roosevelt's actions threatened to inject dangerous passions into the present conflict and reshape the face of American politics. If the Democrats nominated a party regular like Clark or a southerner like Underwood, they would follow the Republicans in discrediting themselves in the eyes of progressive-minded voters, thus expanding Roosevelt's new venture into a major party—so Roosevelt and his supporters believed and hoped. His son Kermit told their distant cousin Franklin, who was married to the ex-president's niece Eleanor, "Pop is praying for the nomination of Champ Clark."[31]

The delegates who convened in Baltimore on June 25, 1912, came close to giving the ex-president his heart's desire. On the first ballot, Clark led Wilson by 440½ to 324, with Governor Harmon of Ohio next at 148 and Underwood fourth at 117½; another 57 votes were scattered among four candidates, including 31 for Governor Thomas R. Marshall of Indiana. On the next eight ballots, Wilson and Clark each picked up a few votes. The standoff broke on the tenth ballot. Persistent rumors predicted that Tammany would switch from Harmon to Clark, and that happened when the machine's boss, Charles Murphy, cast the state's 90 votes for the

Speaker. That shift gave a majority of the delegates to Clark, who reportedly was writing his telegram of acceptance and expected to be nominated on one of the next few ballots, and Wilson was ready to concede.[32]

If this had been a Republican convention, it would have been all over; only a majority was required for that party's nomination. If this had been a normal Democratic convention, it would also have been all over. The party did require two thirds for nomination, but not since 1844 had a candidate won a majority and not gone on to win the nomination. But this was far from a normal Democratic convention. Though nowhere near as explosive as the Republicans' recent fracas in Chicago, this one witnessed plenty of fireworks. Before the proceedings opened, Bryan had telegraphed the candidates to demand that they oppose anyone for temporary chairman of the convention who was "conspicuously identified with the reactionary element of the party." He was taking a slap at Alton Parker, the party's conservative nominee in the race against Roosevelt in 1904, who enjoyed the backing of Tammany and other northern machines. McCombs drafted a reply for Wilson that straddled the issue, just as Clark's reply did. When the governor received McCombs's draft, in his bedroom at Sea Girt, he said, "I cannot sign this." Sitting on the edge of a bed, he wrote his own reply on a pad of paper. "You are quite right," he told Bryan. "No one will doubt where my sympathies lie." Parker won the convention chairmanship with votes from the Clark forces, thereby adding weight to the rumors about a deal with Tammany. Further fights followed over the seating of delegates and the rules for voting. Bryan stirred up more controversy when he introduced a resolution on the floor demanding that delegates allied with Wall Street moguls not be seated. It was a quixotic gesture that angered even some of his staunchest allies, but it kept progressive sentiment squarely at the fore of the convention.[33]

Those fights offered a prelude to what transpired next. Tammany's switch on the tenth ballot infuriated Bryan, who began to maneuver against Clark. According to Tumulty's recollection, Bryan telephoned Wilson to tell him that his only chance was to declare that he would not accept the nomination with Tammany's help. Tumulty and Wilson decided that there was nothing to lose, and the governor sent a telephone message stating, "For myself, I have no hesitation in making that declaration." Then, possibly at Ellen's instigation, he sent a second message saying he would not make that declaration public. McCombs later claimed he had not delivered either message to Bryan. Whatever happened, Bryan took to the warpath against Tammany. During the calling of the roll for the fourteenth ballot, he declared on the floor that he could not vote for any candidate who would "accept the high honor of the presidential nomination at the hands of Mr. Murphy." He then switched his previously instructed vote for Clark to Wilson.[34] This marked the beginning of the turn of Wilson's fortunes.

At Sea Girt, the governor tried to deal at long distance with what was happening in Baltimore. He tried to stay calm by playing golf and reading John Morley's *Life of Gladstone*. But as he later confessed to Mrs. Peck, "While the convention was in session there was hardly a minute between breakfast and midnight when some one of our little corps was not at the telephone on some business connected with the convention." One telephone call came early in the morning of June 29 from a distraught McCombs, who said all was lost. According to William McAdoo's recollection, McCombs went to pieces, and the two men got into an argument after the call. McAdoo then telephoned Wilson and talked him out of quitting. In Sea Girt, everyone around the breakfast table was dispirited—except Wilson. When he noticed a catalog from a coffin company in the morning mail, he commented, "They've got their catalogue here by the first mail." But he was not ready to attend his own political funeral. Later in the day, reporters asked him what answer he might give to a telegram from Clark's manager asking him to withdraw. "There will be none," the governor said.[35]

From then on, Wilson's prospects improved, though at a snail's pace. This convention offered a foretaste of the party's fratricidal, seemingly interminable gatherings in the next decade. Behind the open debates about progressivism and bosses there were rumblings of the social and cultural conflict between country and city, "native" and immigrant, Protestant and Catholic, that would come close to destroying the Democrats in the 1920s. But in 1912, those conflicts had not yet come to the forefront. Also, an undemocratic rule and old-fashioned wheeling and dealing still prevailed. The two-thirds rule, which, like most progressive Democrats, Wilson opposed, saved him from defeat. Behind-the-scenes horse trading finally brought him victory.

During the long, hot days and nights in Baltimore, Wilson's managers worked tirelessly to get votes. McAdoo later claimed that he had a total of four hours' sleep during the last three days of balloting. More than McCombs, who turned into a nervous wreck, it was McAdoo who played the biggest part in putting Wilson over the top. He and others worked several angles successfully. One was to gain Indiana's votes by promising the vice-presidential nomination to Governor Marshall; that suited the state's party boss, who wanted to get rid of the governor. Another tactic was to cling to the ironclad agreement with the Underwood forces not to withdraw in Clark's favor. Wilson's managers offered Underwood the vice-presidential nomination, which he declined, and they promised to switch their votes to him if Wilson withdrew. Finally and mysteriously, the managers persuaded the Chicago boss, Roger Sullivan, to shift a large bloc of Illinois votes from Clark to Wilson. McAdoo and others cultivated Sullivan, who had clashed with Hearst's allies and Clark's supporters in Illinois. Also, Sullivan was reportedly afraid that a prolonged deadlock might result in Bryan's nomination. The Illinois switch came on the morning of July 2, on the forty-second ballot. It took four more ballots, and another of McCombs's panic attacks, before Wilson finally reached the magic two thirds and became the Democrats' nominee for president.[36]

A telephone call at two forty-eight in the afternoon brought official word of the nomination to Sea Girt. Wilson was alone in the library when the call came. He went upstairs to tell Ellen, who was planning a family trip to their favorite spot, Rydal Mount, in England's Lake District, in the event he was not nominated. She knew what was going to happen when she heard his footsteps on the stair. "Well, dear, I guess we won't go to Mount Rydal [sic] this Summer after all," he told her, and she answered, "I don't care a bit, for I know lots of other places just as good." The couple came downstairs, with Mrs. Wilson on her husband's arm. Reporters noticed that Wilson's eyes were moist, while Ellen was smiling. The men of the press stood in silence, holding their hats in their hands. Then the governor made a statement: "The honor is as great as can come to any man by the nomination of a party, especially in the circumstances, and I hope I appreciate it at its true value; but just [at] this moment I feel the tremendous responsibility it involves even more than I feel the honor. I hope with all my heart that the party will never have reason to regret it."[37]

That downbeat note was not just a bit of modesty for public consumption. Tumulty had hired a band to play outside, and Nell Wilson remembered, "Father asked him if he had instructed them to slink away in case of defeat." Someone in the crowd said, "Governor, you don't seem a bit excited." Wilson answered, "I can't effervesce in the face of responsibility." Four days later, he told Mary Peck, "I am wondering how all this happened to come to me, and whether, when [the] test is over, I shall have been found to be in any sense worthy. It is awesome to be so believed in and trusted."[38] Such faith and trust were going to be needed as Woodrow Wilson went out to do battle with the most formidable opponent he could face in an election that promised to be one of the most momentous in the nation's history.

8

THE GREAT CAMPAIGN

The election of 1912 witnessed one of the greatest presidential campaigns in American history, featuring a past president, a present president, and a future president: Theodore Roosevelt, William Howard Taft, and Woodrow Wilson. Coincidentally, these men were graduates of three of the country's oldest and most prestigious universities—Harvard for Roosevelt, Yale for Taft, and Princeton for Wilson. Also running was the country's most appealing radical politician, the Socialist Party's Eugene Victor Debs. From the outset, knowledgeable observers agreed that the real contest was between Roosevelt and Wilson. The fight between this pair held the center ring of the main tent of this electoral circus. It pitted the most colorful presidential politician since Andrew Jackson against the most articulate presidential politician since Thomas Jefferson. Woodrow Wilson could not have asked for a tougher or worthier opponent. If he won this fight, he could take pride in having beaten the heavyweight champion of politics.[1]

By another coincidence, Roosevelt and Wilson accepted their respective parties' nominations on the same day, August 7, 1912. Roosevelt's new Progressive Party met in the same hall in Chicago where the Republicans had gathered two months before. This convention struck many who were there as more like a religious revival than a political conclave. The delegates sang "Onward, Christian Soldiers," "Battle Hymn of the Republic," and words set to the tune commonly used in Protestant churches for the doxology. Roosevelt broke precedent by appearing in person at the opening of the convention to deliver his "Confession of Faith." He denounced the Republicans as hidebound reactionaries and "Professor Wilson" and the Democrats as wedded to "an archaic construction of the States'-rights doctrine" and quack economic remedies derived from Bryan's free-silver notions. He rejected "class government" by both "the rich few" and "the needy many": the country needed a transcendent vision of the national interest that would "give the right trend to our democracy, a trend which will take it away from mere greedy shortsighted materialism." He closed by repeating his famous shout: "We stand at Armageddon, and we battle for the Lord." Curiously, however, when the Progressives nominated him with great fanfare the next day, he said only a few words thanking the delegates for the honor.[2]

Wilson's acceptance of his party's nomination, which occurred a few hours earlier, was a tamer affair. He observed the formality of waiting for a party delegation to come and inform him of his nomination, a practice dating back more than three quarters of a century, to the first party conventions, which had taken place before railroads and telegraphs, when it had presumably taken some time to learn that one had received the party's nomination. In fact, the business of a delegation traveling to inform the nominee had long since become an artificial ritual, but it did give the nominee time to prepare an acceptance speech, which traditionally served to kick off the campaign. Wilson performed that duty when a committee of Democrats journeyed to Sea Girt on August 7.

Standing on the porch of the governor's summer residence, he thanked the committee for this "great honor" and then delivered a strongly progressive message. "We stand in the presence of an awakened nation, impatient of partisan make-believe," Wilson announced. "The nation has awakened to a sense of neglected ideals and neglected duties." In this "new age," it would require "self-restraint not to attempt too much, and yet it would be cowardly to attempt too little." He praised the Democratic platform, especially the planks on the tariff, the trusts, banking reform, and labor, as well as those on presidential primaries, popular election of senators, and disclosure of campaign spending. On the tariff, he again refused to condemn protection in principle and urged caution. On the trusts, he did not condemn bigness in itself: "Big business is not dangerous because it is big." Rather, new laws were needed to curb and prevent monopoly. He called banking reform a "complicated and difficult question" and confessed that he did not "know enough about this subject to be dogmatic about it." On labor, he declared, "No law that safeguards [workers'] life, that improve[s] the physical and moral conditions under which they live . . . can properly be regarded as class legislation or as anything but a measure taken in the interest of the whole people." He closed by demanding "unentangled government, a government that cannot be used for private purposes, either in business or in politics; a government that will not tolerate the use of the organization of a great party to serve the personal aims and ambitions of any individual. . . . It is a great conception, and I am free to serve it, as are you."[3]

As the slam at "personal aims and ambitions" indicated, Wilson was taking aim at Roosevelt. Each man had been sizing up the other for some time. Their once-friendly, mutually admiring acquaintance was long since dead. For several years, Roosevelt had been casting aspersions on Wilson as an impractical academic who purveyed outmoded and pernicious notions and had been belittling his conversion to progressivism. Several times during 1911, progressive Republicans and even Roosevelt's oldest son suggested to him that a Democratic victory in 1912 under Wilson might offer a good alternative to Taft and their party's conservatives. Roosevelt spurned such suggestions. In October 1911, he had told Governor Hiram Johnson of California that the Democrats were hopeless because "even those among them who are not foolish, like Woodrow Wilson, are not sincere . . . but are playing politics for advantage, and are quite capable of tricking the progressives by leading them into a quarrel over States' rights as against National duties."[4]

Wilson's attitude was more complicated. From the time he started to come out as a progressive, he publicly praised Roosevelt, despite his recent aspersion on the ex-president's alleged egotism. In October 1910, during his gubernatorial campaign, he had discussed with a Princeton faculty colleague the recent espousal by Roosevelt of the "New Nationalism," a phrase and idea borrowed from Herbert Croly's *Promise of American Life*. In a campaign speech, Wilson praised the New Nationalism and dismissed fears of centralized government. When he emerged on the national scene, reporters often compared him to Roosevelt, and at the end of 1911, when it began to look as if he and Roosevelt might become opponents in the presidential election, he told Mrs. Peck, "*That* would make the campaign worth while."[5]

Neither man rushed into the fray. Roosevelt faced the task of building a party and a campaign from scratch. Wilson was more fortunate in having an established party behind him, and one that smelled victory. Even before the ceremony on August 7, the governor had begun receiving visits and getting advice from leading Democrats. A sullen Champ Clark made an obligatory call and perfunctorily pledged his support. Oscar Underwood was more genial and voluble on his visit. The organizational work fell to McCombs, whose uncertain nerves compelled him to bow out for a while, and increasingly to McAdoo. Veteran party operatives likewise pitched in. After the acceptance ceremony, Wilson occasionally commuted to Trenton and received visitors in the governor's office.[6]

Wilson was mulling over how to approach the campaign, and he was weighing the challenge he faced from Roosevelt. His daughter Nell later recalled, "Father gave a delicious imitation of Teddy delivering his hysterical slogan, 'We stand at Armageddon and battle for the Lord,' and added, 'Good old Teddy—what a help he is.'" For all his joviality, Wilson regarded Roosevelt with the utmost seriousness. "Do not be too confident of the result," he told Mary Peck. "I feel that Roosevelt's strength is altogether incalculable. . . . He appeals to . . . [people's] imaginations; I do not. He is a real, vivid person, whom they have seen and shouted themselves hoarse over and voted for, millions strong; I am a vague, conjectural personality made up more of opinions and academic prepossessions than of human traits and red corpuscles. We shall see what will happen!" He thought the popular stereotypes reversed their real selves, with Roosevelt the cool calculator and him the passionately committed politician. Taking Roosevelt on "would be a splendid adventure and it would make me solemnly glad to undertake it."[7]

Wilson never thought about doing anything else but appealing to public opinion. Nell also remembered, "Father did not deny Roosevelt's popularity and influence, but he said, 'Are people interested in personalities rather than in principles? If that is true they will not vote for me.'" Another alternative might have been for Wilson to play things safe and rely upon having an undivided party behind him. Bryan advised against such a strategy, reminding Wilson that "our only hope is in *holding our progressives* and winning over progressive Republicans."[8] Wilson agreed, and he got potent reinforcement in this approach when a man whom he had not met before came to see him at Sea Girt on August 28, 1912.

The caller was the well-known "people's attorney" and reformer from Boston, Louis D. Brandeis. Just a month older than Wilson, the craggy-faced, mournful-eyed Brandeis was the son of Czech Jewish immigrants who had come to America in the wake of the failed revolutions of 1848. Like Wilson, Brandeis was a southern expatriate. He had been born in Louisville, Kentucky, although his parents were abolitionists and supporters of the Union. Unlike Wilson, he spoke with a southern accent all his life, but he had also gone north in 1875, to complete his education, in his case at Harvard Law School. Settling in Boston, Brandeis had become a highly successful attorney and seemed to fit in well with the city's Brahmin establishment. Yet he continued to view the economy and society from the standpoint of an outsider, and after the mid-1890s he had defended workers and small businesses. In 1908 he successfully argued before the Supreme Court in favor of Oregon's law limiting the hours women could work. He was also a friend and political adviser to the insurgent Republican leader Robert La Follette of Wisconsin.[9]

Brandeis came to see Wilson as a man on a mission. His study of economics and his defense of workers and small businesses had made him a fierce opponent of the trusts, and he was appalled at the stand Roosevelt had forced on the Progressives in favor of regulating rather than breaking up the trusts. He told reporters at Sea Girt that the right course was "to eliminate the evil and introduce good as a substitute," which meant "to regulate competition instead of monopoly." The two men talked for three hours, over lunch and afterward, and claimed to reporters that they had had a meeting of the minds. Brandeis later recalled that he had spent much of the time in an effort to wean Wilson from his belief that punishing guilty individuals would solve the trust problem, arguing instead for attacking the system that permitted such wrongdoing and fostering conditions that encouraged competition.[10] Brandeis seems to have been persuasive, because Wilson did address the trust issue in those terms during the rest of the campaign.

It would be wrong to think that Wilson's concern about the trusts originated with Brandeis. He had been criticizing the shortcomings of the existing anti-trust law for some time, and his visitor supplied tactical rather than strategic advice for the upcoming campaign, something Wilson would later call upon him for again. Brandeis put his finger on the issue where Roosevelt was most vulnerable and offered plans for attacking him there. Also, Brandeis's emphasis on freedom may have planted the seed in Wilson's mind to stress that word and concept and eventually counter Roosevelt's New Nationalism with his own "New Freedom." In all, this meeting proved important to the way Wilson waged his campaign, although it probably was not essential to his winning the election. He was both gracious and accurate when he told Brandeis right after the election, "You were yourself a great part of the victory."[11]

Wilson followed this new plan of attack five days later when he gave his first major speech since accepting the nomination. At a Labor Day rally in Buffalo, he commended the "social program" in the platform of Roosevelt's new party, "the bringing about of social justice," but he condemned its trust program "because once the government regulates the monopoly, then monopoly will see to it that it regulates the government." Worse, the party's program wanted to play "Providence for you," and he feared "a government of experts. God forbid that in a democratic country we should resign that task and give the government over to experts. . . . Because if we don't understand the job we are not a free people." That objection hinted at another of Roosevelt's vulnerable points—the widespread belief that he was a power-hungry potential despot. Wilson noted that people said he was "disqualified for politics" because he was a schoolteacher: "But there is one thing a schoolteacher learns that he never forgets, namely, that it is his business to learn all he can and then communicate it to others." Likewise, his party, the Democrats, did not seek to legalize monopoly, and they were "the only organized force by which you can set your government free."[12]

No one expected Roosevelt to take such charges lying down, and he did not disappoint expectations. Speaking in Fargo, North Dakota, four days later, he maintained that the past two decades' attempts to break up the trusts had failed, and he quoted a celebrated remark by the greatest of the trust magnates, J. Pierpont Morgan: "You can't unscramble the eggs in an omelet." Taft had tried to unscramble the eggs with anti-trust prosecutions and had failed, and now Wilson wanted to try the same futile approach. He scoffed at Wilson's aspersion on "government by experts" and extolled his own program as a "definite and concrete" approach to the trust problem, in contrast to Wilson's "vague, puzzled, and hopeless purpose feebly to continue the present policy."[13] This rejoinder opened a debate on the trust question that would last for most of the month of September 1912.

Roosevelt's reply contained the germ of the attack that he was about to launch at Wilson. If the trust issue was his Achilles heel, then Wilson's was his onetime flirtation with conservative Democrats, which left lingering suspicions about the depth and sincerity of his progressivism. Roosevelt had also been taking his opponent's mark and looking for a point of attack. One of his press aides on the campaign train recalled, "It was Wilson, Wilson, Wilson, all the time in the private car, and nothing but Wilson and his record in the Colonel's talks. We believed we were on the way to drive Wilson into one of his characteristic explosions, with [a] result that could only be detrimental to his campaign."[14] Why they thought they could provoke Wilson is not clear. The governor did not have a record of "characteristic explosions"; the idea that he did may have come from some stories about quarrels at Princeton, exaggerated and distorted in the retelling. At any event, three days after Roosevelt spoke, he found the opening he wanted.

On September 9, Wilson gave a speech in New York that contained the sentence "The history of liberty is a history of the limitation of governmental power, not the increase of it." In the body of the speech, that statement was part of an exhortation to keep government in touch with the people. By itself, however, as many newspapers quoted the sentence, it seemed to show that Wilson still clung to conservative Democratic state rights, limited-government views. Roosevelt wasted no time in exploiting the opening. In a speech in San Francisco on September 14, he quoted that sentence and called it "the key to Mr. Wilson's position," which he dismissed as "a bit of outworn academic doctrine which was kept in the schoolroom and the professorial study for a generation after it had been abandoned by all who had experience of actual life." He scorned Wilson's position as outmoded laissez-faire economics and proudly proclaimed his own intention "to use the whole power of government" to combat "an unregulated and purely individualistic industrialism."[15] Roosevelt was damning Wilson as a heartless, outmoded conservative and an impractical academic out of touch with the real world while presenting his own position in the most attractive light.

Wilson, with his penchant for extemporaneous speaking and his inexperience in national politics, with its far greater press coverage, opened himself to misrepresentations. Roosevelt had learned his lesson the hard way in 1910, when his remarks about recalling judicial decisions had been similarly quoted out of context; now he supplied the press with advance texts of his speeches. During one of his campaign trips, Wilson asked reporters who had covered Roosevelt how the ex-president managed to produce those texts. "I wish I could do that," one reporter said Wilson confessed. "I've tried to do it over and over again, but I can't." He thought prepared texts spoiled the spontaneity of his speaking. Only on the most formal occasions, such as the acceptance speech in August and major state addresses he delivered as president, would he write an address and read from a prepared text. Otherwise, he persisted in speaking from sketchy notes, usually in shorthand, or using no notes at all. As president, however, he would remedy the problem by having a team of stenographers quickly prepare transcripts of his speeches.[16]

Nevertheless, Roosevelt's counterattack proved a boon to Wilson. On his first extended campaign tour—a grueling five-day railroad trip that took him around a large swath of the Midwest at the middle of September—he began to spell out his economic views. In Sioux City, Iowa, he argued, "Now a trust is not merely a business that has grown big. . . . A trust is an arrangement to get rid of competition, and a big business is a business that has survived competition by conquering in the field of intelligence and economy. I am for big business, I am against trusts." But, he noted, "the third party says that trusts are inevitable; that is the only way of efficiency. I would say parenthetically that they don't know what they are talking about." In other speeches, he denied that monopoly was inevitable—"I absolutely deny that we have lost the power to set ourselves free"—and explained that regulated competition would open the marketplace to new-comers: "We are going to say to the newcomers, 'It depends upon your genius, upon your initiative.'"[17]

Roosevelt's aspersions on Wilson's progressivism provided still richer grist for his mill. On Wilson's second campaign tour—another five-day train trip immediately afterward, this one through the Northeast—he expounded on his political beliefs. In a speech in Pennsylvania, he explic-itly rejected Jefferson's limited-government views and threw Roosevelt's accusation back in his face: "Because we won't take the dictum of a leader who thinks he knows exactly what ought to be done by everybody, we are accused of wishing to minimize the powers of the Government of the United States. I am not afraid of the utmost exercise of the powers of the government of Pennsylvania, or of the Union, provided they are exercised with patriotism and intelligence and really in the interest of the people who are living under them." In another speech, he used the story from Lewis Carroll's *Through the Looking-Glass* about Alice's running as hard as she can just to stay in the same place to explain his progressivism: "I am, therefore, a progressive because we have not kept up with our own changes of conditions, either in the economic field or the political field." He also affirmed that modern life often left individuals helpless in the face of great obstacles and, "therefore, law in our day must come to the assis-tance of the individual."[18]

On that campaign swing, Wilson had two important meetings, both in Boston on September 27. The first was a chance encounter that stirred up some nice publicity. When he arrived at the Copley Plaza Hotel, he learned that President Taft was in the building, preparing to give a speech. He asked to call on the president, and the two men met in a private room on the fifth floor. According to press reports, the president asked the gov-ernor if campaigning had worn him out. "It hasn't done that, but it has nearly done so," Wilson answered and asked in turn, "How's your voice, is it holding out?" Taft said that it was and put the same question to Wilson. "It's pretty fine, but now and then it gets a bit husky," Wilson answered. Taft then observed, "Well, there are three men that can sympathize with you, Mr. Bryan, Mr. Roosevelt, and myself. We have been through it all." Afterward, Wilson told reporters, "It was a very delightful meeting. I am very fond of President Taft." He also made a joke about the president's renowned girth, saying that he knew the bed in his hotel room would be big enough "because it was built especially for the President."[19] This was the only face-to-face encounter between any of the candidates in 1912.

Wilson could afford to joke about Taft. No one believed the president had a chance of winning, not even Taft himself. Some people believed that he was staying in the race out of spite, to ensure Roosevelt's defeat by splitting the Republican vote. Taft did harbor deep feelings of hurt and resentment toward his onetime friend and patron, but in not bowing out he also believed he was pursuing a greater political aim. At the time of the convention, he had confided to a supporter, "If I win the nomination and Roosevelt bolts, it means a long hard fight with probable defeat. But I can stand defeat if we retain the regular Republican party as a nucleus for future conservative action." In his campaign speeches, Taft attacked Roosevelt and preached a conservative sermon. Two days after his encounter with Wilson, he admonished, "A National Government cannot create good times. It cannot make the rain to fall, the sun to shine, or the crops to grow, but it can, by pursuing a meddlesome policy, attempting to change economic conditions, and frightening the investment of capital, prevent a prosperity and a revival of business which might otherwise have taken place."[20] Such sentiments were new for Taft, who had earlier been a moderate progressive, and they sounded like the limited-government views then usually associated with conservative Democrats. This marked an early step toward the ideological transformation of the Republican Party during the rest of the twentieth century.

Wilson's other meeting in Boston on September 27 was with Brandeis. He asked the attorney to give him fresh proposals for dealing with the trusts. First in a lengthy talk and a few days later in two long memoranda, Brandeis outlined a legislative program. His proposals included, first, the removal of uncertainties in the current anti-trust law by facilitating court enforcement and establishing an agency to aid in enforcement and, second, the enumeration of prohibited practices and remedies for those practices. The remedies included withdrawing government business from convicted firms and attacking those firms' patents. At first, Wilson planned to use Brandeis's ideas in a letter to the press on anti-trust policy, but he decided instead to incorporate them into his speeches. Even before he received the memoranda, he revealed Brandeis's influence when he announced in a speech the same day that they met, "[T]here is a point of bigness—as every businessman in this country knows, though some will not admit it . . . where you pass the point of efficiency and get to the point of clumsiness and unwieldiness." He also warned that the country was nearing "the time when the combined power of high finance would be greater than the power of the government."[21]

Wilson was starting to hit his full stride as a campaigner. In the first half of October, he made his longest and most intensive tour, a nine-day trip in which he revisited the Midwest and went as far west as Colorado. In Indi-

anapolis, he coined his own great slogan when he urged people "to organize the forces of liberty in our time to make conquest of a new freedom."
Americans had a choice: either submit to "legalized monopoly" or else
"open again the fields of competition, so that new men with brains, new
men with capital, new men with energy in their veins, may build up enterprises in America." In Omaha, he poked fun at people who "have regarded
me as a very remote and academic person. They don't know how much
human nature there is in me to give me trouble all my life." He particularly relished meeting "the plainest sort of men. . . . And when they call me
'Kid' or 'Woody,' and all the rest of it, I know that I am all right." In Lincoln, which he called "the Mecca of progressive Democracy," he stayed
overnight at Bryan's home, where the two men talked late into the night
about the campaign, and they attended church together the next day.
Despite the strains of train travel and constant speechmaking, he enjoyed
talking with the reporters who accompanied him; it was on this western
trip that he quizzed them on how Roosevelt got out advance texts of his
speeches. The reporters found him more down-to-earth, humorous, and
given to cussing than they had expected. When he heard about a New
York paper refusing to support a Tammany-backed candidate, he scoffed,
"There's no use in being so damned ladylike."[22]

On this campaign swing, Wilson grew relentless in attacking Roosevelt and seeking to undercut his appeal. He praised insurgent Republicans and reminded people that La Follette, "that sturdy little giant in
Wisconsin," refused to support Roosevelt and what Wilson always called
the "third party," the "new party," or the "irregular, the variegated
Republicans"—never the Progressives. He also called Roosevelt "a very,
very erratic comet on the horizon" and accused him of harboring delusions of being the nation's savior. Reciting the famous rhyme about the
purple cow, he said he felt the same way about such would-be saviors: "I
never saw one, I never hope to see one, but I'll tell you, I would rather see
one than be one." Not all of his campaigning was negative, however. In
Abraham Lincoln's adopted hometown, he apologized for speaking while
the World Series was going on and appealed to memories of "the Great
Emancipator. We are going to repudiate all this [monopolistic] slavery as
emphatically as we repudiated the other." This oratorical effort came at a
cost. Early on the trip, he strained his voice: "The trouble with me is I talk
too damn much," he told Mary Peck.[23]

Wilson was not the only candidate who strained his voice. Taft's quip
about the three men in the country who could sympathize with his laryn-
geal problem applied even more aptly to their mutual adversary. Roosevelt
was not a polished, disciplined speaker like Wilson or Bryan, and early in

October he also started to suffer from the rigors of making himself heard to the crowds. This physical problem came on top of other troubles. Vigorous and blustery as ever, he kept up a campaign schedule that was even more grueling than the governor's. As he crisscrossed the eastern half of the country, he hammered away at his messages of trust regulation and strong government, but he did not talk much about his basic message of transcendent nationalism to overcome class division. This emphasis testified to how effectively Wilson was fending off Roosevelt's attacks and putting the ex-president himself on the defensive. Speaking in a cracking voice on October 12, he denied being pro-monopoly: "Free competition and monopoly—they're all the same thing unless you improve the condition of workers. . . . What I am interested in is getting the hand of government put on all of them."[24] Later, he issued a statement that endorsed strengthening the anti-trust laws along lines similar to those Brandeis had recommended to Wilson.

In a twisted way, both candidates found relief for their strained voices. On October 14 in Milwaukee, a mentally deranged bartender shot Roosevelt in the chest. The ex-president's practice of preparing speeches in advance helped save his life. The manuscript pages and his steel-reinforced spectacle case, both of which were in his jacket pocket, absorbed much of the impact of the bullet. True to form, Roosevelt insisted on going ahead with the speech. After informing the audience that he had just been wounded, he declared, "I have altogether too important things to think of to feel any concern over my own death; and now I cannot speak to you insincerely within five minutes of being shot." He said the incident showed the need to overcome the division between the "Havenots" and the "Haves," and he likened his present political crusade to the time when he had led his troops in the Spanish-American War, another battle "for the good of our common country." Those lines read like a dying declaration, and some historians have speculated that he was disappointed that he did not die after uttering those words. But he kept on talking and grew incoherent from shock and loss of blood until supporters led him off the stage. Roosevelt spent several days in a Chicago hospital and then convalesced at home for another two weeks. He gave one last speech, at a rally at Madison Square Garden, but for all practical purposes the attempt on his life ended his campaign.[25]

Wilson responded to this dramatic turn of events with a gesture that was at once generous and shrewd. After conferring with McAdoo and other campaign managers, the governor announced that he would suspend his campaign as soon as he fulfilled a few more obligations. McAdoo and most of the managers evidently opposed this move, but he overruled them. His daughter Nell later recalled, "He laughed when he told us of his decision. I couldn't see why it was funny, and when I questioned him, he said, 'Teddy will have apoplexy when he hears of this.' We were told that it did enrage him, but he made no comment of any sort."[26] The gesture looked good to the public and gave him time for rest and preparation.

Wilson's speeches after the announcement of the campaign suspension showed him at his best. On October 17, he saluted Roosevelt as "that gallant gentleman" who had done "so much to wake up the country to the problems that now have to be settled." He again praised La Follette and wished that he himself had joined the progressive ranks much sooner than he did. He revived an earlier catchphrase when he called for laws and government to "look after the men who are on the make rather than the men who are already made," but he also eschewed class warfare and sounded like Roosevelt when he maintained that "we must overcome class prejudice by making classes understand one another and see that there is a common interest which transcends every particular interest in the United States." Talking about himself, he affirmed, "If I am fit to be your President, it is only because I understand you. . . . I do not wish to be your master. I wish to be your spokesman."[27]

After those speeches, Wilson enjoyed a nine-day respite from the campaign trail. He spent part of the time dealing with two touchy issues, the first of which was race relations. Since July, some African American spokesmen and their white sympathizers, most notably Oswald Garrison Villard, editor of the *New York Evening Post* and grandson of the abolitionist William Lloyd Garrison, had been conferring with the Democratic nominee about the possibility of black support for him and his party. Some African American leaders had grown disgusted with long-standing Republican efforts to distance themselves from blacks and seek support from southern whites. Taft had made overtures toward the white South early in his administration, and Roosevelt had allowed the Progressives to organize in the South as a lily-white party. In response, Bishop Alexander Walters of the African Methodist Episcopal Zion Church had switched parties and now headed the National Colored Democratic League. Likewise, W. E. B. DuBois, the editor of *The Crisis*, the magazine of the recently organized National Association for the Advancement of Colored People, endorsed Wilson in August: "He will not advance the cause of the oligarchy in the South, he will not seek further means of 'Jim Crow' insult, he will not dismiss black men from office, and he will remember that the Negro in the United States has a right to be heard."[28]

Wilson responded warily. He stalled Villard and Walters until finally, on October 21, he sent a letter assuring African Americans of "my earnest wish to see justice done them in every matter, and not mere grudging justice, but justice executed with liberality and cordial good feeling. . . . My sympathy with them is of long standing, and I want to assure them through you that should I become President of the United States they may count upon me for absolute fair dealing and for everything by which I could assist in advancing the interest of their race in the United States."[29] Those guarded words were as far as Wilson was willing to go; he declined to make any further statement. This encounter foreshadowed the heartache and disappointment that would be felt after he entered the White House, when most of what DuBois said would not happen did come to pass.

The other touchy issue was woman suffrage. Here a real difference separated the two major candidates. The most renowned woman in the country, the social worker Jane Addams, had seconded Roosevelt's nomination at the Progressive convention, and the party platform and the nominee had endorsed woman suffrage. Roosevelt admitted privately that he did not feel strongly about the issue, and he rarely mentioned it in his speeches. Still, he was the first leading male politician to come out for woman suffrage. Wilson, despite having taught at a women's college and having two suffragist daughters, tried to duck the issue, claiming it was a state matter. He had to confront it publicly only once during the campaign, when, on October 19, a militant suffragist interrupted a speech and demanded to know what he thought about men's exclusive right to vote. Wilson answered that this was "not a question that is dealt with by the National Government at all." His answer did not satisfy the suffragist, who shouted, "I am speaking to you as an American, Mr. Wilson." Police carted her off to jail so that he could resume.[30]

Party affairs and the campaign organization also required the candidate's attention. New Jersey and New York remained trouble spots for the Democrats. In September, Sugar Jim Smith entered the primary for New Jersey's other U.S. Senate seat, but Wilson spoke against him and he lost. Across the Hudson, anti-Tammany reformers were trying to dump Governor Dix from the ticket; Wilson sympathized strongly with them but did not openly take sides. The reformers did succeed in replacing Dix, although Tammany's hold on the party remained strong. At the national headquarters, tensions between McAdoo and an ailing McCombs continued unabated, but others helped keep the organization running fairly smoothly, including two Texans. One was Congressman Albert S. Burleson, a hard-bitten political operator who oversaw speaking assignments for the campaign and coordinated publicity. The other was

Edward M. House, a wealthy expatriate Texan who held the honorary title of Colonel. House made himself and his spacious apartment available to the candidate and other managers, and his soft, ingratiating manner smoothed matters over at headquarters and led Wilson to warm to him.[31]

By and large, the managers mounted an effective campaign. They arranged the candidate's speaking tours, and they produced leaflets and brochures and delved into the new medium of motion pictures, making and distributing a campaign film. Their only failure was in fund-raising. Despite strenuous appeals to make this a campaign financed by "the people," less than a third of the money raised came from small donors. The rest came from big contributors. Charles R. Crane, the Chicago plumbing-fixture tycoon and longtime backer of progressive causes, was the biggest, with $40,000; Cleveland Dodge, Wilson's Princeton classmate and supporter from the board of trustees, was the second largest, with $35,000. Other big contributors included such leaders of the New York Jewish community as Henry Morgenthau, Jacob Schiff, and Samuel Untermyer, as well as a newcomer to their ranks, Bernard Baruch. Wilson drew the line at contributions from notorious trust magnates, but otherwise this champion of progressivism took money from the kind of people he was denouncing on the hustings.[32]

He wrapped up his campaign with a week of speechmaking in Pennsylvania, New York, and New Jersey. On October 28, he praised the middle class as the place "from which the energies of America have sprung" but whose members felt "a great weight above them—a weight of concentrated capital and of organized control—against which they are throwing themselves in vain." He also declared, "We do not want a big brother government. . . . I do not want a government that will take care of me. I want a government that will make other men take their hands off so that I can take care of myself." This final round ended with a big rally at Madison Square Garden and some barnstorming by automobile around New Jersey, where his car hit a bump and threw him up against the roof, giving him a scalp wound that bled a lot and required a doctor's attention and a bandage. "It was a very hard blow," he told reporters. "There is no doubt about that. But, fortunately, I am hard-headed."[33]

On November 5, Wilson voted in the morning at a fire station in Princeton. He spent the rest of the day walking with companions around the town and the campus. He pointed to the boardinghouse where he had lived as a freshman, his room in Witherspoon, and, in Nassau Hall, James Madison's diploma—"the diploma of the only Princeton man who has been elected President."[34] At the end of the afternoon, he went back to the house on Cleveland Lane, where his sister Annie Howe and Stockton

Axson joined him and Ellen and their daughters for supper. Afterward, they sat in front of the fire, and as they often did, they read poetry aloud, mostly Robert Browning.

They did not have to wait long to know the outcome of the election. Around eight-thirty, early returns came in on a teletype machine set up in the library of the house. The reports showed a sweep for Wilson and the Democrats in New York and other northeastern states, and soon after nine o'clock newspapers and wire services called the election for him. When the grandfather clock in the library chimed ten, Ellen put her hands on her husband's shoulders and kissed him. "Let me be the first to congratulate you," she said. In response to Nell's excitement, her father said, "Now Daughter, there is no cause of elation." Congratulatory telegrams began to pour in, including a terse one from Roosevelt and a warmer one from Taft. On the campus, President Hibben ordered the bell in Nassau Hall to toll, and a crowd of students carrying torches marched to Cleveland Lane. Wilson stood on a chair in the entrance so that, he joked, "you couldn't see the patch on my head." But one observer noted that he spoke "with great emotion and tears in his eyes." He told the students, "When I see the crowds gather it carries me back to the days when I labored among you." For himself, he said, "I have no feeling of triumph, but a feeling of solemn responsibility."[35]

The election returns gave Wilson reason to feel both triumphant and circumspect. He won the popular vote decisively: 6,294,327 to Roosevelt's 4,120,207 and Taft's 3,486,343. His Electoral College victory was overwhelming: forty states in all regions of the country, for a total of 435 electoral votes. Roosevelt took six states: California (where Wilson got 2 electoral votes), Michigan, Minnesota, Pennsylvania, South Dakota, and Washington, for a total of 88. Taft won Utah and Vermont, for a total of 8 electoral votes. Wilson's party shared in the sweep. Democrats won additional governorships, raised their majority in the House, and picked up ten seats in the Senate to win control of that chamber for the first time in eighteen years. Yet all was not as sweet as it seemed. Wilson's share of the popular vote was only 42 percent. He won majorities only in the former Confederate states. His total fell 100,000 votes short of Bryan's showing in 1908. All Wilson and the Democrats did in 1912 was maintain their grip on their previous minority share of the electorate.[36]

The returns brought no joy to the opposition. Roosevelt's second-place finish was impressive; it was the only time a third-party candidate had ever finished ahead of the nominee of one of the major parties. But that showing was largely a personal victory, since Roosevelt ran well ahead of all other Progressive candidates. Progressives did well only on the West

Coast, a bright spot that owed to their having taken over the formerly Republican apparatus in California and, to a lesser extent, Washington. Roosevelt apparently did not attract new voters. The combined Roosevelt-Taft total fell 69,000 votes short of Taft's showing in 1908. All Roosevelt had done was split the Republicans' previous majority share of the electorate. Taft's third-place finish, carrying only two states with a minuscule share of electoral votes, was personally galling, but he could take some comfort in coming in second in eighteen states, including several in the West and New York, Roosevelt's home state. The Republicans had stood firm in the face of the Progressives, and they finished ahead of them in most places, despite weakness at the top of the ticket. The only surprise in the results was the performance of the man the major contenders largely ignored, the Socialist candidate, Eugene Debs. He racked up 901,873 votes, more than double his total in 1908. At 6 percent of the vote, this would stand as the best showing a Socialist or any left-wing party candidate would make at any time in American history.[37] With that exception, the results in 1912 reflected politics as usual.

Why such an exciting and momentous campaign produced such an unremarkable outcome has remained a puzzle. It did not stem from want of effort by the major candidates. Until mid-October, Roosevelt and Wilson poured their best persuasive energies into their campaigns. They offered contrasting styles on the stump. Roosevelt's vivid personality buttressed an approach that derived from Protestant evangelism. Though not an orthodox believer, he had dubbed his former office a "bully pulpit" and often called his oratory "preaching." He hammered away at a few basic themes and often appealed to voters' emotions. Wilson's previous profession led people, including Wilson himself, to call him a schoolmaster, and he did move gracefully among a variety of themes to appeal to voters' intellect. Yet his oratory also sprang from the pulpit. His model was, not surprisingly, the basically educational preaching that Presbyterians favored.

The content of the two men's politics, unlike their images, did not strike many observers as offering much of a contrast. Woman suffrage, which did not loom large in the campaign, was the only issue on which they took clear-cut opposing stands. On the two questions that did loom large, the trusts and the size and strength of government, it was hard to see where they differed. Wilson talked about "big business" and "trusts"; Roosevelt talked about "good trusts" and "bad trusts." Both would leave the former alone and break up the latter. If monopoly became unavoidable in an industry, both held out nationalization as a possible last resort. Roosevelt's attacks on Wilson's governmental views fell flat—not, as Roosevelt believed, because Wilson was an adroit speaker who could twist arguments but because they were not true. Both men had admired Hamilton since their youth, and neither could top the other in admiration for strong, centralized, activist, interventionist government. Their respective party platforms differed, aside from woman suffrage, in the Progressives' endorsement of tariff protection and their emphasis on industrial labor and in the Democrats' greater sympathy for farmers. During the campaign, Wilson obviated most of those differences by refusing to renounce the principle of protection and advocating aid to labor. Small wonder that twelve years later the journalist William Allen White rendered the most widely accepted judgment on the 1912 campaign: "Between the New Nationalism and the New Freedom was that fantastic imaginary gulf that has existed between tweedle-dum and tweedle-dee."[38]

This widely perceived lack of difference between the candidates explained much of the inertia among voters. Roosevelt and Wilson had each tried to chip away at the other's support. In July, after Wilson's nomination and before the Progressive convention, it had looked as if Republican progressives might defect in large numbers to the Democratic candidate. The new party's convention and Roosevelt's performance there and on the campaign trail had arrested that drift.[39] But the Progressive nominee had failed to attract progressive Democrats. With both candidates taking the same stands on the main issues, voters had little incentive to cross old party lines. With his attacks on Wilson as a state-rights Democrat, Roosevelt was appealing to memories and prejudices that went back to the Civil War, which had ended less than fifty years before. Those memories and prejudices also threw up a formidable obstacle to any future effort by Wilson to build a majority coalition and win reelection against an undivided opposition.

Their opponents' split cast a shadow over the Democrats and their victory. A question haunted them: could Wilson have beaten Roosevelt in a two-man race? No one doubted that he could have trounced Taft, but nearly everyone assumed that he would have lost to Roosevelt. The ex-president's huge popularity and his impressive second-place finish reinforced that view. But could Wilson have beaten Roosevelt by himself? Two states offered a test case. In California, Governor Hiram Johnson, Roosevelt's running mate, hijacked the Republican organization and kept Taft's name off the ballot. Roosevelt won the contest there by only 174 votes out of a total of half a million cast. Four years earlier, Taft had car-

ried California with 55 percent of the vote to Bryan's 33 percent. In South
Dakota, local Progressives kept Taft off the ballot, and Roosevelt ran
almost 10,000 votes ahead of Wilson. South Dakota was the only state
Roosevelt carried with a majority, 50.5 percent, but in 1908 Taft had won
that state with 59 percent of the vote to Bryan's 35 percent. Such showings
in strongly Republican states, coupled with Roosevelt's third-place fin-
ishes elsewhere, especially in New York, raised doubts about the ex-
president's ability to beat Wilson in a two-man race.[40]

The perceived lack of difference between the two major candidates
also cast a shadow over their de facto debate. That perception, particularly
as expressed in White's crack about tweedledum and tweedledee, was doubly misleading: it ignored the deep differences that did separate Roosevelt
and Wilson, and it missed the intellectual depth and sophistication and
political significance of their debate. Some aspects of the campaign helped
mask their differences. The need both men felt to attack each other did
not facilitate a full exposition of their ideas, while the hiatus after the
assassination attempt on Roosevelt cut down on his and Wilson's opportunities to expound their thinking. Still, White should have known better.
He was one of the most acute observers of his time, and by the time he
rendered his verdict he had enjoyed a perspective enhanced by the passage
of time and the opportunity to witness the later conflict between Roosevelt and Wilson. Similarly, subsequent generations of historians have
had little excuse for failing to recognize what really transpired.

The differences between Roosevelt and Wilson were like a nested
Russian doll, in which each figure contains another one within it. Of the
main issues on the surface, only the size and strength of government was a
red herring. The trust question, for all the two men's apparent similarities, really did divide them. They might agree in distinguishing between
businesses that grew through efficient competition (Wilson's "big business," Roosevelt's "good trusts") and those that used illegitimate, anti-
competitive methods (Wilson's "trusts," Roosevelt's "bad trusts"), but they
disagreed about whether there were more of one or the other. Roosevelt
thought that bigness by and large promoted efficiency, whereas Wilson,
like Brandeis, believed that bigness usually stifled efficiency. That difference in assessment led to a sharp disagreement about where to go next.
For Roosevelt, the government needed to oversee a mature economy,
manage a distribution of power that was not likely to change, and ensure
that people affected by that power—workers and consumers—were protected from abuses. For Wilson, government had to reopen the marketplace to fresh players, intervene to restore competition, and ensure that

smaller players and their workers got a fair shot at getting ahead. Despite their public images to the contrary, it was Roosevelt who held an essentially static view of the economy and Wilson who held an essentially dynamic view.[41]

Those divergent convictions contained within them equally divergent views of society and political leadership. Each candidate drew his social views from his own background. Roosevelt was an aristocrat, born into a family of old wealth and exalted, long-established social position in the nation's greatest metropolis. For all his carping at his upper-crust peers and sincere espousal of democratic values, he viewed society from the top, and he feared upheaval and possible revolution from the lower orders. Those perspectives were what prompted him to preach his New Nationalism— a vision of transcendent national interest that would inspire people to put aside selfish, parochial interests. It was what he meant by getting away from "the greed of the Haves and the envy of the Havenots." Social betterment for him was analogous to military service, an enterprise in which each citizen would sacrifice and everyone would work together for the common good. It was a noble vision, and it was fundamentally aristocratic and conservative.

Wilson, on the other hand, was a product of the middle class, a man born and raised in the hinterlands who had sought his fortune in the environs of the metropolis. For all his prestigious education and hobnobbing with the wealthy and socially prominent, he still viewed society through the eyes of a striving outsider, and he did not fear upheaval or revolution. Those perspectives were what prompted him to expound his New Freedom— a vision of constant renewal from below, in which people would rise by dint of effort and ability. This was what he meant by praising "men who are on the make" and scorning "big brother government." Social betterment for him was analogous to the growth of a tree, which is refreshed and kept vital from its roots. It was an equally noble vision, and it was fundamentally democratic and liberal.

These conflicting social views encapsulated, in turn, different models of leadership. For Roosevelt, despite his likening himself to a military commander after he was shot, leadership consisted of evangelism. He reconciled his conservatism with his democratic views through the conviction that people can be inspired to rise above their narrow, selfish interests. Oddly for someone who was a devotee of modern science and something of a religious skeptic, Roosevelt adhered to orthodox Christian beliefs that people must be "born again," that they must become better through leaps of faith and pursue new lives of service and sacrifice. *Inspiration* was the right word for his approach; its Latin root is *inspirare*, "to breathe into." Roosevelt wanted to breathe something finer and nobler into his followers.

For Wilson, leadership consisted of education. He believed that people could grasp what was best for themselves and ought to be able to follow their dreams and desires with a little guidance. Oddly for someone who had grown up in the bosom of Presbyterian Calvinism, Wilson adhered to the more modern, secular belief that people can be trusted, within limits and with some guidance, to lead honest, constructive lives. *Education* was the right word for his approach; its Latin root is *educare*, "to draw out." Wilson wanted either to draw out the inner potential of his followers or to draw them out of their ignorance onto more enlightened paths.

The root of those differences—the final, irreducible doll in the nest—lay in divergent conceptions of human nature. Roosevelt held a pessimistic attitude toward human nature akin to the religious conception of original sin. For him, people left to themselves and pursuing their own interests would not produce either a good society or a strong, united nation capable of playing a great role in the world. This view has a long historical pedigree, stretching back many centuries to classical philosophy and early Christian teachings. Although he frequently called himself a radical, Roosevelt was at heart and by philosophy a conservative. Wilson, by contrast, had an optimistic attitude toward human nature akin to secular notions of innate human goodness and worth. For him, people left to themselves, safeguarded against predatory elements and pursuing their own interests, would produce both a good society and a vital, self-renewing nation. This view has a shorter historical pedigree, stretching back a few centuries to European and British, especially Scottish, Enlightenment thought. Although he also called himself a radical, Wilson was at heart and by philosophy a liberal.

It was a shame that Roosevelt and Wilson never met in a face-to-face debate, with a format that would have allowed each to develop his own views and challenge the other's arguments. Such debates had taken place only occasionally in American history. The most notable examples had taken place during the great confrontations in the Senate over slavery and the nature of the Union during the three decades that led to the Civil War and when Abraham Lincoln and Stephen Douglas squared off against each other in the Senate race in Illinois in 1858. Such debates had never occurred in a presidential election, and these competing speaking tours gave the closest approach to one that had ever come to pass. This race pitted against each other two men who were true intellectuals, who had equal and often similar, though not identical, gifts of mind and temperament, and who strove to persuade voters by expounding their ideas. Intellectually and philosophically, it seems that this was as good as it gets in a presidential campaign.

The 1912 race between Roosevelt and Wilson was at heart more than a debate. It formed the opening round in a battle that would grow stronger and more heated, especially when foreign affairs entered the picture after 1914. The true precedent and analogy to their adversarial relationship was the long-running clash a century earlier between Jefferson and Hamilton, with their conflicting visions of the nation's future. Roosevelt and Wilson were their twentieth-century successors. Roosevelt, despite his distaste for plutocracy and "materialism," was the true heir to Hamilton. Something deeper than nationalism and affection for strong government dictated the affinity between those two men. It was their shared pessimistic view of human nature and their belief in the need to overcome people's limitations through an attachment to a higher good. Wilson, despite his early disdain for Jefferson and continuing admiration for Hamilton, was the true heir to Jefferson. Something deeper than political expediency dictated Wilson's late-blooming affinity for Jefferson. It was Wilson's recognition that they shared the same optimistic view of human nature and the belief in the importance of creating an environment in which people can freely use their energies in the pursuit of their own happiness.

American politics might have followed a different, more interesting, and more constructive path if Wilson and Roosevelt had left legacies like those of Jefferson and Hamilton. Things turned out otherwise on both sides. For conservatives and Republicans, it was Taft, not Roosevelt, who pointed out the ideological path of the future. The link between approval of big business and revulsion from big government would take several decades to mature, and it would owe much to the trauma suffered by businessmen and Republicans in the 1930s, during the Great Depression. Roosevelt's brand of statist-oriented, commercially skeptical conservatism would grow less and less welcome in his former party. Instead, by a quirk of fate, his big-government views and concern for the welfare of workers and consumers would find a home among Democrats.

This ideological crossover would happen, in part, because the next Democratic president after Wilson would be Roosevelt's distant cousin and the husband of his niece, Franklin Delano Roosevelt. The second Roosevelt had adopted "Uncle Ted" as his role model early and absorbed much of his approach to politics. At the same time, Franklin Roosevelt was Wilson's political heir and a veteran of his administration. His eclectic, unintellectual temperament, together with the challenge of combating the Depression, afforded him lots of ideological latitude in drawing upon the visions of both his kinsman and his party predecessor. After the 1930s, with the exception of one slowly withering wing of the Republican Party, strong-government views along both Theodore Roosevelt's and Woodrow Wilson's lines would become the sole property of the Democrats. The result would be ideological mishmash, shallowness, and sterility in domestic political debate. Nothing would again match the depth and sophistication of what passed between Wilson and the first Roosevelt.[42]

In November 1912, the continuing conflict between these two men and their ideological legacies lay in the unseen future. For the man who won the election, the opportunities and the burdens of the presidency began to come in a rush. The flood of mail and telegrams that brought congratulations quickly gave way to an avalanche of men offering advice on policy and angling for office. Exhausted from the campaign, Wilson retreated to Bermuda for a month. This time, Ellen and their daughters accompanied him. The respite gave the president-elect more than rest and relaxation. It also afforded him time to do what he liked to do most—think, reflect, plan, prepare. When the family returned at the middle of December, Wilson was ready to tackle the twin tasks of finishing out his term in Trenton and choosing a crew and charting the course for his new ship of state in Washington. He also took time out for a backward-looking, sentimental journey.

At the end of December 1912, he and his wife made that two-day trip to Staunton, Virginia. The town pulled out all the stops to welcome back a native son who had risen to the highest office in the land. There were bands, cheering crowds, and another torchlight parade. On December 28, his birthday, Wilson gave two speeches, both of them a bit rambling, mixing sentiment with foretastes of politics to come. At the school where he had visited Hattie Woodrow, which was now called Mary Baldwin Seminary, he recalled visiting "five cousins" of whom he was "very fond." He said he hoped that, as a native Virginian who was governor of a northern state and about to become president of the United States, he might become an "instrument in drawing together the hearts of all men in the United States in the service of a nation that has neither region, nor section, nor North, nor South." He did not believe he faced an easy task in Washington. The capital contained many who did not appreciate the new responsibilities that government must assume and would "have to be mastered in order that they shall be made the instruments of justice and mercy. This is not a rosewater affair. This is an office in which a man must put on his war paint. Fortunately, I have not such a visage as to mind marring it; and I don't care whether the war paint is becoming or not."[43]

At an evening banquet sponsored by leading Virginia Democrats, Wilson hailed "my native place" and saluted "the standards established in the olden time in the great Commonwealth of Virginia. It is as if a man came back to drink at some of the original fountains of political impulse and inspiration in this country." The compliment carried a sting. The men in Washington who had "to be mastered" included not just conservative Republicans. He noted that the leaders of Virginia's Democratic machine—"I dare say one of them is present tonight"—had told him that "they thought I had some screw loose or that I was rather wild" and had opposed his nomination for president. He reminded them that he had advocated "nothing but the original doctrines of liberty as understood in America," and he pointed to the Virginia Bill of Rights. He added, "So I am not in the least afraid of being regarded as a heretic, provided you know the standards of orthodoxy."[44] The Democrats were in for an exciting ride with their new president.

For all the celebration and fanfare, the highlight and purpose of the visit were personal. "I remember that I have played many times in the yard of that little house opposite,"[45] Wilson said at the seminary, referring to the manse where he had been born fifty-six years before. The boy who was called Tommy Wilson had gone far in the intervening years. He had come back as Woodrow Wilson, husband, father, scholar, teacher, writer, speaker, university president, governor, and now soon-to-be president of the United States. This native of Staunton stood on the brink of the most challenging, fulfilling, and heartrending time of his life.

9

PREPARATION

A few days after the presidential election, Woodrow Wilson talked with a former colleague from the Princeton faculty, the biologist Edward Grant Conklin. As Conklin later recalled their conversation, Wilson said to him, "It would be an irony of fate if my administration had to deal chiefly with foreign problems, for all my preparation has been in domestic matters."[1] The first part of that remark proved prophetic because, following the outbreak of war in Europe in August 1914, Wilson did suffer that "irony of fate," but the second part of the remark was especially revealing of Wilson's character. When he talked about "preparation" he touched on the heart of his approach to politics. For him, "preparation" meant less the two years of practical political experience—a remarkably thin background for someone on the verge of entering the White House—and more the study of politics that had absorbed him since his days as a college student. He began his formal preparation for his presidency soon after the election returns had come in. Unlike most other politicians, Wilson did not surround himself with people when he made decisions. A decade as a college president and a governor had not changed the habits he had formed in his youth and strengthened as a professor. He still liked to be alone when pondering alternatives and sifting through ideas. Those were the activities he had engaged in during his monthlong sojourn with his family on Bermuda.

Two matters loomed largest in his preparation for the presidency: appointments and policy. He had a cabinet and other important positions to fill, and he had begun to receive advice and think about appointments even before he left for Bermuda. A new acquaintance proved useful in sorting out competing claims and assessing strengths, weaknesses, and political ramifications in various possibilities: Edward M. House. With his slight build and mild manner, House seemed to belie his origins in rough-

and-tumble Texas and his honorific title of Colonel. In some ways, he did belie that background. He was the son of an Englishman who had immigrated to Texas while it was still part of Mexico and had later amassed a large fortune. As a youth, House had gone to school in England and Connecticut before attending college at Cornell. Back in Texas, he had become active in Democratic politics and acquired a reputation as a kingmaker and power behind the throne of several governors. More recently, since retiring from business and moving to New York, House had cast about for ways to play a similar role in national Democratic politics and had involved himself in an intermittent, conciliatory way at the Wilson campaign headquarters.[2] He also ingratiated himself with the candidate by supplying him with a bodyguard during the campaign, Captain Bill McDonald, a former Texas Ranger who was also a crack pistol shot.

Wilson spent an hour and a half at House's apartment on New York's Upper East Side the day he sailed for Bermuda. "Cabinet material was discussed," House recorded in his diary. House suggested McAdoo for secretary of the Treasury and Albert Burleson for postmaster general. Wilson favored Josephus Daniels for the post office spot, but House had said, "I thought he was not aggressive enough and that the position needed a man who was also in touch with Congress. [Wilson] agreed that this was true." For attorney general, House recorded, "We practically eliminated Brandeis for this position," and for secretary of state he noted that he supported Wilson's leaning toward Bryan.[3]

Wilson seems to have deputized House to look into prospective cabinet officers and talk with Democratic leaders in Congress. Writing to Wilson about various possibilities for attorney general, House lavished special praise on James McReynolds, a Tennessean who was an experienced anti-trust prosecutor. He also had lunch with Brandeis, whom he praised to Wilson as "more than a lawyer" and dismissed criticism of him, but House noted, "There comes to the surface, now and then, one of those curious Hebrew traits of mind that makes one hold something in reserve." On a trip to Washington, the colonel sounded out leading Democrats on Capitol Hill, most of whom favored Bryan as secretary of state. House talked about banking reform with Representative Carter Glass of Virginia, chairman of the House Banking and Currency Committee, who said he would follow Wilson's lead but did not favor "central control."[4] Glass's attitude portended problems with banking reform.

Wilson kept his own counsel while he was in Bermuda, but he was clearly pondering what he would do in the White House. He wanted to accomplish something no incoming president had ever done: he wanted to introduce a comprehensive program of legislation at the outset of his administration. Before he left for Bermuda, he announced that he would call into session the newly elected Congress—where Democrats enjoyed a top-heavy majority in the House and a narrower margin of control in the Senate—on April 15, 1913, six weeks after his inauguration. Under the Constitution, this Congress did not have to convene until December 1913. The new president was signaling that he meant to break with politics as usual.

As House's report from Washington indicated, their party's senior men on Capitol Hill expected the new president to take the lead in proposing and drafting major legislation. This was a big change. Previously, when either party had won control of both the White House and Congress, legislative priorities had usually emerged slowly and collaboratively, and congressional leaders had often played a bigger role than the president. Even that recent paragon of presidential activism, Theodore Roosevelt, had bided his time before trying to push significant legislation through Congress. Taft had called Congress into session at the beginning of his administration and asked for reform and downward revision of the tariff. That effort had turned into a fiasco, and it did not offer an appealing precedent for major legislative initiatives by an incoming president. Wilson's eagerness to take this path testified to his self-confidence and sense of preparation. Congressional Democrats' willingness to follow him testified to their gratitude at finally having been led out of the political wilderness.

When his steamship docked in New York on December 16, reporters found Wilson tanned and in good spirits. He had enjoyed a restful vacation, he told them, "and we all feel ready for anything." When asked about appointments, he refused to discuss the matter—a vow of silence he would keep for another month—and he stayed mum on major policy issues as well. He was forthcoming on two subjects: New Jersey politics and the general tone of his presidency. Back at his desk in Trenton the next day, the governor gave out a statement saying that he would stay active in state affairs and would keep up the fight against the bosses. Speaking to the Southern Society of New York that evening, Wilson declared, "America is not what it was when the Civil War was fought. We have come into a new age. There can be no sectionalism about the thinking of the American people from this time on."[5]

Those four matters—appointments, policy, New Jersey politics, and presidential tone—would occupy Wilson for the remaining two and a half months before his inauguration. Behind the scenes and in public, he would deal with them simultaneously. He still preferred to tackle questions one at a time, and he often joked about his "single-track mind," yet already as a college president and as a governor he had rarely been able to follow that bent. Now he was getting a foretaste of the many and varied questions that would come at him all at once in the White House.

Appointments held the least appeal for him. The day after his speech to the Southern Society, he had lunch with House in New York. They discussed ambassadorships, including the possibility of one for McCombs, and cabinet posts, including Bryan for secretary of state and Brandeis for attorney general. House continued to throw cold water on Brandeis and sing the praises of McReynolds. Wilson offered Bryan the post of secretary of state when the Great Commoner visited him in Trenton on December 21. Bryan later recalled that he told the president-elect that as a matter of conscience he could not serve alcohol at his house or at official functions and Wilson raised no objections. In a handwritten letter four days later, Bryan noted, "I am thinking of increasing pleasure of association with McAdoo." This was the first indication that McAdoo would become secretary of the Treasury. In this almost offhand manner, Wilson filled the two top posts in his cabinet.[6]

As Democrats had predicted, Bryan weighed in with advice on other cabinet appointments. For secretary of the interior, he suggested the mayor of Cleveland, Newton D. Baker: "He is a man of ideals and capacity." He praised Josephus Daniels as being "of the Salt of the Earth" but did not say which post he thought his friend should fill. "As to the Atty. Gen.," Bryan wrote, "I share your high opinion of Brandeis & I do not know that a better man can be found. He has a standing among reformers & I am sure all progressives would be pleased." Bryan offered an additional, less flattering reason for favoring Brandeis: "It is more important that he be *at heart* with the people *against the special interests* than that he be a brilliant lawyer—brilliant lawyers can be hired but the right kind of man for Atty Gen is not so easy to find."[7] Wilson does not seem to have responded to these suggestions. He would not turn his attention to filling the rest of the cabinet until January, and although he had picked McAdoo for the Treasury post, he would not make the offer until the beginning of February.

Setting the tone for his presidency was a more appetizing task. Starting with the speech to the Southern Society of New York, Wilson delivered messages that had two main aims, one partly retrospective, the other prospective. Looking back, he continued to rebut Roosevelt's campaign charges that he, Wilson, was a limited-government, state-rights man only posing as a progressive. When he eschewed sectionalism in the speech to the Southern Society and bearded Virginia's conservative leaders during his birthday jaunt to Staunton, he underlined his claims to be an emancipated, up-to-date progressive. Looking forward, Wilson opened a long-term campaign to win over Roosevelt's third-party followers and build a majority behind himself and his party. He pursued both aims by dwelling on his newly coined slogan, the New Freedom, and he published a book with that title, which wove together some of his campaign speeches. In speeches during the first part of January 1913, he also expanded on his progressive vision. In one, he sounded like Roosevelt when he maintained that "men are no longer to be catalogued, . . . no longer to be put in classes," and he sounded like himself and Bryan when he demanded a turning away from the widespread belief "that a poor man has less chance to get justice administered to him than a rich man. God forbid that should be generally true. But so long as that is believed, the belief constitutes a threatening fact."[8] To seize upon this new temper and combat perceptions of injustice, he called for action in four areas: conservation of natural resources, equal access to raw materials, equal access to credit, and reform of the tariff.

When he pointed to the four areas in which he meant to take action, Wilson was tipping his hand to the major policies he intended to pursue. The first area—conservation of natural resources—was a gesture toward the Roosevelt following, because this was their most cherished issue. Wilson would appoint a conservationist as secretary of the interior, and his administration would compile a good record in this area. Except for the establishment of the National Park Service and consolidation of the parks under that agency in 1916, however, there would be no significant legislative initiatives. The second area—equal access to raw materials—was partly an appeal to westerners, who chafed under the domination of big outside-owned mining and timber interests, and was partly an oblique way of raising the anti-trust issue, which had loomed so large in the campaign. That was a complex problem to tackle: anti-trusters disagreed among themselves about whether to seek new laws or try administrative regulation. Finding common ground would require patience, diligence, and expert advice, and the anti-trust issue would become the last of the major issues that Wilson would address during the first part of his presidency.

The third area—equal access to credit—was another way of saying banking reform. It was the issue on which Wilson had received the most advice and had seen the most lobbying since the election—almost as much as on appointments. Carter Glass, the chairman of the House Banking Committee, wrote to Wilson several times before and after his trip to Bermuda, and on December 26 he traveled to Princeton to confer, accompanied by his adviser, Professor H. Parker Willis of George Washington

University. Wilson, who was in bed with a cold, looked over a draft plan for a reserve system drawn up by Willis. According to Glass, the president-elect wanted "some body of *supervisory* control."9 The congressman was willing to have government oversight of the banking system, but he did not want a central bank. Their discussions on this matter highlighted the main point of contention in banking reform—the degree and the kind of central control—and showed that Wilson wanted supervisory control. Banking reform would prove to be as complicated as the anti-trust issue and even more contentious. It would become the hardest-fought of Wilson's major legislative initiatives.

The last area—reform of the tariff—meant lowering rates. That would prove to be the easiest of Wilson's main legislative initiatives. For a quarter of a century, the tariff had pitted the two parties against each other more than any other issue. Among Republicans—except for some, but not all, insurgent progressives—high tariffs were an article of faith, especially regarding industrial products and some raw materials. Among Democrats—except for a scattering of deviations, such as Louisiana sugar growers and some western mining and ranching interests—lower tariffs were just as strong an article of faith and overrode even the enmity between Bryanites and conservatives. Taft's recent attempt to lower the tariff had broken the pattern, but his failure, along with an earlier stumble by Grover Cleveland, seemed to jinx any effort at downward revision. Still, with the Democrats in control of the White House and Congress, a renewed push in that direction seemed inescapable. As a corollary, if the effort succeeded, government revenues would decline, thereby providing an excuse to do what most Democrats, together with Progressives and progressive Republicans, wanted to do anyway—enact an income tax. Impending ratification of the Sixteenth Amendment by three quarters of the states would provide the required constitutional sanction, and a push in the next Congress to enact legislation to levy an income tax seemed well-nigh certain.

In the meantime, while preparing for his presidency, Wilson was still governor of New Jersey. Of all the tasks that occupied him between the election in November 1912 and his inauguration on March 4, 1913, this was the one he could have ducked. Thanks in part to the Republican-Progressive split, the Democrats had not only regained control of the New Jersey assembly in the November elections, but they had also won a majority in the state senate. Overall control of the legislature assured that Congressman William (Billy) Hughes, the victor of the 1912 Democratic primary in which Jim Smith had staged his ill-fated attempt at a comeback, would be chosen to fill the state's second seat in the U.S. Senate. Even more important, control of the state senate meant that a Democrat would succeed Wilson as governor. Because New Jersey did not have a lieutenant governor, the president of the senate was required to fill a governor's unexpired term. When the legislature met in January, the new Democratic majority chose James Fielder, a Wilson supporter, as its president. Wilson could have resigned at that point, but he did not: he believed he had unfinished business as governor.

He did not have as easy a time as many expected. Assembly Democrats rebuffed his choice for speaker, and he had to fight the machine over his choice for state treasurer. Nevertheless, when he addressed the legislature on January 14, 1913, the governor presented a list of proposals designed to round out his program. The main measures were reform of securities to discourage fraud and monopoly, changes in the jury system to reduce political manipulation, and a constitutional convention to streamline and democratize the state's government. He also again urged ratification of the Sixteenth Amendment, to allow an income tax, and the Seventeenth Amendment, to require popular election of U.S. senators. As before, Wilson employed a combination of cajolery and charm to bring the legislators around. Securities reform passed fairly easily, although some observers questioned whether the new law accomplished much, and the legislature also ratified the amendments to the Constitution. Those actions betokened a brief revival of the governor's honeymoon with the legislators. At the end of January, at a dinner with state senators in Atlantic City, the governor grew a bit misty-eyed as he reminisced about their times together and told them it was going to be "a great wrench" to leave. Near midnight, as the dinner ended, he proposed a walk on the Atlantic City boardwalk. "The Senate accepted the proposition en masse," reported *The New York Times*, "and led by the Governor the twenty-one Senators marched along the walk before the brisk breeze until the Governor's 'right face,' when they wheeled and returned." The entourage covered two miles in a little over half an hour.[10]

All did not remain fun and games with the legislature. The assembly passed a bill to call a constitutional convention, but the senators dragged their feet until after Wilson left for Washington and then defeated the bill. Jury reform turned into a fiasco. Machine forces were able to water down a bill embodying Wilson's ideas and attached a provision to require a referendum before any changes could take effect. The matter was not resolved when Wilson stepped down. Later, despite personal intervention by the president, the affair ended in a muddle, with the voters approving a much-weakened law in November 1913. Those wrangles marked the beginning of the resurgence of the machine forces, still led by Nugent, who was now joined by Frank Hague of Jersey City.[11]

Wilson put a good face on the last days of his governorship. He resigned on February 25, 1913. At Fielder's swearing-in ceremony, he called the governorship the greatest privilege of his life and expressed confidence in his successor. He had the satisfaction of seeing Fielder elected governor the following November, but that was almost the only post-gubernatorial victory he enjoyed. Between the renewed strength of the Democratic machine and the reversion of voters to Republican majorities under conservative control, New Jersey would not become a model progressive state like Wisconsin or Oregon. Moreover, despite repeated pledges to stay in touch with the state, Wilson would take little part in state affairs after 1913, except for an unsuccessful attempt in 1915 to get voters there to adopt woman suffrage. There was some truth to the acid line in John Dos Passos's novel *U.S.A.*: "so he left the State of New Jersey halfreformed."[12]

Meanwhile, Wilson was somewhat reluctantly tackling presidential appointments. He met with House ten more times during the last seven weeks before his inauguration, mostly at House's apartment in New York, where he stayed overnight five times. Except when the president-elect had a ceremonial dinner to attend, he would dine with House and spend the evening and the next morning discussing appointments and, occasionally, policy. The two men sometimes interrupted their discussions to attend a Broadway play, often a light comedy, Wilson's favorite form of theater. Telephone calls and letters from House supplemented the face-to-face meetings. In addition, Ellen Wilson visited the colonel once in New York and talked with him about appointments. These meetings between Wilson and House had a twofold significance. They were the times when Wilson thought about whom to appoint to cabinet posts and ambassadorships. They were also the times when he and House formed what House later called the "intimate" bond that became one of the two most important relationships of Wilson's presidency.[13]

Contrary to his normally orderly nature, Wilson went about cabinet making in a haphazard, almost sloppy way. From the outset, familiar names figured in the discussions. Early in January, the colonel drew up a list of possible cabinet picks; it included Bryan, McAdoo, and McReynolds at the State, Treasury, and Justice departments, with Brandeis, Page, and Daniels as possibilities for other departments. Also on the list or discussed were David F. Houston, who was chancellor of Washington University in St. Louis and a special friend of House's, and William C. Redfield, an anti-

Tammany Democratic congressman from New York.[14] All except Brandeis and Page eventually wound up with cabinet posts; Page would become ambassador to Great Britain, and Brandeis would later be appointed to the Supreme Court.

It was one thing for Wilson to think up names; it was another thing for him to make appointments. McAdoo got the nod for the Treasury post at the beginning of February, but the offer came after second thoughts that included naming him postmaster general or governor general of the Philippines. The attorney generalship continued to be a headache. Pressures from progressives and Wilson's own admiration for Brandeis resurrected the candidacy of "the people's attorney." Strong opposition from lawyers, financiers, and some Democrats, abetted by House, helped block him, but Wilson still wanted to appoint him in some capacity, possibly as secretary of commerce. The colonel found an ally in Tumulty, who was evidently swayed by a campaign against Brandeis by some Massachusetts Democrats. They finally prevailed upon Wilson to appoint Redfield instead to head the Commerce Department.[15]

Even with Brandeis out, there was still a scramble for the attorney generalship. One candidate was A. Mitchell Palmer, a Democratic congressman from Pennsylvania who had a strong progressive record and was openly angling for the job. Unfortunately for his chances, Bryan did not like him and had a new candidate of his own in Joseph W. Folk, another progressive and a former governor of Missouri. Also working against Palmer were stories that during the deadlock at the convention Palmer had dallied with a scheme to supplant Wilson for the nomination. This time, Wilson gave in to House's persistent advocacy and offered McReynolds the attorney generalship on February 15. Palmer could have joined the cabinet when Wilson offered him the secretaryship of war a week later. After briefly thinking it over, he declined, however, citing religious grounds: "As a Quaker Secretary, I should consider myself a living illustration of a horrible incongruity." House had a different take on Palmer's motives. "He wants to be Attorney General to advance his own fortunes," the colonel recorded, "as he thinks it would be possible for him to obtain a lucrative practice after four years of service." In the meantime, the War Department post had to be filled. Curiously, Wilson called in a New Jersey lawyer and judge, Lindley M. Garrison, whom he had not met before, and offered him the job.[16]

The other armed services secretaryship, the navy, came to be filled almost as casually. Of the men who had worked for his nomination, Wilson most liked and respected Josephus Daniels, and he initially thought of the North Carolina editor for the postmaster generalship. House and others maintained that this post should go to someone better versed in the tougher aspects of party politics. Wilson bowed to those objections, and just over a week before the inauguration he offered Daniels the secretaryship of the navy. Congressional politics helped sway the postmaster general appointment. Underwood, the House Democratic leader, came to see Wilson in Trenton after the election and argued that Albert Burleson of Texas, who was a ranking member of the House Appropriations Committee, should be in the cabinet because he enjoyed "the implicit confidence of the Democratic members of the House and Senate." The post office was the logical place for Burleson, and Wilson made the offer the same day that he wrote to Daniels.[17]

Walter Page and David Houston appeared as possibilities for the secretaryships of agriculture and the interior. After seeing Wilson for the first time in January, House recorded in his diary, "I gave Houston unqualified praise but was somewhat more guarded in regard to Page." The colonel pushed Houston because, before going to Washington University, he had been president of the University of Texas, and House had come to regard him as a protégé. Page remained under consideration, with Wilson shifting him and Houston back and forth between the two departments. House's patronage paid off for Houston, who was offered the agriculture secretaryship early in February. Page would have received the interior post if House had not continued to lobby against him and successfully pushed for Franklin K. Lane, a Californian who was serving on the Interstate Commerce Commission. Wilson did not meet Lane until the inauguration. The final cabinet slot was the head of the newly created Department of Labor. The only person considered, William B. Wilson, was, like Palmer, a Democratic congressman from Pennsylvania. Wilson was also a former officer of the mine workers' union and was close to the president of the American Federation of Labor, Samuel Gompers.[18]

Two other appointments vexed Wilson. The first was the question of what to do with his nominal party chairman, the increasingly unstable McCombs. Wilson refused to appoint him to the cabinet; instead, he offered McCombs the ambassadorship to the Austro-Hungarian Empire. After brooding over the matter for a month, McCombs declined and said he might take the ambassadorship to France but then declined that post too; he would fester for another three years as titular head of the party, increasingly isolated and embittered. The second troubling question about appointments was what to do with Tumulty. The governor's secretary yearned to fill the same post in the White House, but he was not a shoo-in for the job. Anti-Catholic prejudice still dogged Tumulty, and the president-elect received a raft of letters opposing his appointment, some of them scurrilous. Those prejudices carried no weight with Wilson, but he did worry about Tumulty's political background. House recorded Wilson's saying that "the trouble with Tumulty is that he cannot see beyond Hudson County, his vision is too narrow."[19] Fortunately for Tumulty, Ellen and House lobbied on his behalf, and at the beginning of February, Wilson agreed to appoint him. Overnight, Tumulty stepped in to advise and confer with House on filling the cabinet.

Wilson's method of making major appointments provided a foretaste of his method as president. Previous presidential cabinet making had also witnessed scurrying and confusion, but nothing in recent decades had seen anything like this. Most of Wilson's predecessors had mainly rewarded important factions and constituencies in their respective parties, nearly always in consultation with important state and congressional leaders. Roosevelt had broken away from that pattern to choose able men who were personally close to him, such as Taft and Elihu Root, for some—but not all—of his cabinet positions. Taft had followed Roosevelt's practice to a degree—though not often enough to satisfy his predecessor and patron. Because the Democrats had been out of power for sixteen years, Wilson faced a far different situation. His party had neither the clearly defined interests to appease nor a deep bench of qualified people to choose from. In this situation, Wilson bounced around among competing claims of friendship or service to him (Tumulty, Daniels, McAdoo), party standing (Bryan, Burleson), interest group representation (W. B. Wilson, possibly Redfield), and advice from House (Houston, Lane, McReynolds), as well as making a stab in the dark (Garrison). Consistently choosing first-rate lieutenants would not be his strong suit, and at times he would tolerate mediocre performance and even disloyalty from high-ranking subordinates. Why Wilson behaved this way in making appointments and later in overseeing subordinates remains puzzling. It may have reflected his essentially solitary approach to leadership, which made him care less about advisers and lieutenants: in making major decisions, he would consult with and receive advice from the men around him, but he would rely strictly on his own judgment.

Another foretaste of Wilson's presidency lay in his relationship with House. A deep affinity had arisen quickly between these men. Wilson supposedly once said, "Mr. House is my second personality. He is my independent self. His thoughts and mine are one."[20] He did seem to treat House like a second self. In picking his cabinet, he not only leaned heavily on the colonel, whom he had barely known before the election, but he also offered him a place in the cabinet. The colonel pleaded delicate health and preferred to remain a free agent and adviser.

Wilson and House made an odd couple. Wilson was an intellectual, and in the midst of public life he still liked to spend time alone thinking and writing. House, like Andrew West, was compulsively sociable, and he never read or wrote much: his anonymously published novel, *Philip Dru, Administrator*, was largely ghostwritten, and he dictated his diary to his secretary. This attraction of opposites harked back to Wilson's friendship with Hibben, and House's gentle, soothing manner may have reminded Wilson of Hibben. The colonel was also an accomplished flatterer, and he quickly learned how to play on his new friend's sensibilities. Josephus Daniels later recalled that before House saw the president, he would ask cabinet members, "What is the Old Man thinking about so-and-so" and then repeat what he heard as his own views: "Wilson was astounded to find that their minds ran in the same channel, and that made him think that he and House were almost one man in their thoughts."[21]

Yet it is not entirely clear what the relationship amounted to. Nearly all of the testimony about it comes from House's side, including the "second personality . . . independent self" remark attributed to Wilson. House's voluminous and highly informative diary has to be read with caution, particularly regarding his influence on Wilson. Only once did Wilson set down his opinion of House. Two and a half years into his presidency, writing to the woman who would become his second wife, he praised "dear House . . . for he is capable of utter self-forgetfulness and loyalty and devotion. And he is wise. He can give prudent and far seeing counsel. . . . But you are right in thinking that intellectually he is not a great man. His mind is not of the first class. He is a counselor, not a statesman. And he has the faults of his qualities."[22] Fond though he obviously was of House, Wilson recognized his friend's shortcomings—with one exception.

The flaw in the president's perceptiveness lay in his thinking that House was "self-forgetful" and gave disinterested advice. In his surreptitious way, the colonel aspired to be more than a "counselor"—he wanted to be a "statesman." His real reason for shunning office was, as he admitted, his belief that as a "free lance" with a "roving commission" he could have greater influence.[23] He began to attempt to exert influence from the outset. Not confining his advice to appointments, he also ventured opinions on policy matters, particularly banking reform. House fancied himself a progressive, but his advice on domestic policy usually had a conservative bent. Early in Wilson's administration, however, House picked foreign policy as his special bailiwick, and that was where he would seek to exert his greatest influence.

The colonel also couched his advice on appointments in ways that would promote his own influence. These included not only pushing his protégé Houston and his acquaintances McReynolds and Lane but also giving slanted advice about the men he opposed. His persistent resistance to Brandeis probably did not stem, despite one of his remarks, from anti-Semitism. He had Jewish acquaintances in New York, and he would later become friendly with the journalist Walter Lippmann. Rather, House seems to have wanted to keep Brandeis out of the cabinet because the lawyer was a powerful intellect who struck sympathetic chords with Wilson. He resisted a cabinet post for Page with equal persistence, probably because the energetic, opinionated editor had known Wilson longer than anyone else involved in his presidential bid. (Sending Page abroad was another matter; the idea of an ambassadorial appointment for him would originate with House.) With the top cabinet appointments, Bryan and McAdoo, the colonel bowed to the inevitable, but in succeeding months he would never pass up an opportunity to get in a dig at Bryan.[24] Two years later, when Bryan resigned from his post as secretary of state, House would urge Wilson not to replace him with anyone of comparable independence of mind and political stature.

Few people would be neutral in their opinion of Colonel House and his reputed influence, either during or after Wilson's presidency. To his admirers, he would become a fount of wisdom and a salutary softener of Wilson's rigidity and self-righteousness. To his detractors, he would become a sinister player and a subverter of Wilson's nobler inclinations. Both views would be greatly overdrawn. House would be neither a dispenser of saving grace nor an evil genius. The cabinet appointments that he pushed proved to be a mixed bag, and his views on domestic policy cut little ice. The colonel's foreign policy influence would be another story, one that would unfold over almost the entire course of the Wilson presidency. House would play his greatest role as a personal, often close, presence. Like Hibben before him, he furnished a soothing companionship and acted as a friend who appeared happy to be dominated by Wilson. Unlike Hibben, he felt no need to get out of Wilson's shadow. Just the reverse—he played upon his subordination and maintained a façade of what Wilson saw as "loyalty and devotion." The relationship between these two men would wax early and then wane to a degree, but it would remain a constant until midway through Wilson's second term. With just one exception, this would be the most important relationship of his presidency.

For someone who complained about having a one-track mind, Wilson took the multiple demands of preparing for his presidency and completing his governorship in stride. In February, his cousin Helen Woodrow Bones, who had lived with the family in Princeton and would live with them again in the White House, commented to her sister on how little "Cousin Woodrow" had changed: "The nicest thing about this President of ours is that we forget that he is President . . . because he is so simple and unaffected, so humble, I might almost say. I don't believe Lincoln could have been any more simple and unpretentious."[25]

Wilson appeared so little changed because he retained not only the manners and working habits he had formed during his years as a professor but also the same basic outlook toward politics. Nothing better illustrated how much he was bringing to the presidency from his study of politics than his response to a vote in the Senate a little more than a month before his inauguration. On February 1, 1913, an odd coalition of Democrats and conservative Republicans approved an amendment to the Constitution limiting the president to a single six-year term. Bryan had championed this measure for nearly twenty years, and he had gotten it inserted into the 1912 Democratic platform. Now, in reaction to Roosevelt's recent bolt and future prospects, Taft threw his weight behind the measure, and his supporters supplied the necessary margin in the Senate. Two days later, Palmer, who still harbored hopes of becoming attorney general, took it upon himself to solicit Wilson's opinion. The president-elect fired back a ten-page letter in which he not only lambasted the proposed amendment and the reasoning behind it but also stated his view of presidential powers and accountability. In writing this letter, he did not consult with anyone, but it was not a hasty response. Six weeks earlier, he had composed a statement on the subject in his shorthand, and now he had his secretary type a draft of it, which he edited in his own hand.[26]

Claiming to come to the issue "from a perfectly impersonal view" and with no thought about a second term for himself, he maintained that a four-year term was too long for a do-nothing president and too short for one who attempted "a great work of reform," but six years would also be too long for the duds and too short for the reformers. The president was "expected by the nation to be a leader of his party as well as the chief executive officer of the government. . . . He must be the prime minister, as much concerned with the guidance of legislation as with the just and orderly execution of the law," as well as the only leader in foreign affairs. The president therefore needed "all the power he can get from the support and convictions and opinions of his countrymen" and should enjoy "that power until his work is done." Wilson acknowledged the fear of excessive aggrandizement of power, and to avoid that he proposed a solution: "Put the present customary limitation to two terms into the constitution, if you do not trust the people to take care of themselves, but make it two terms." He ended with a plea: "If we want our Presidents to fight our battles for us, we should give them the means, the legitimate means. . . . Strip them of everything else but the right to appeal to the people; but leave them that; suffer them to be leaders; absolutely prevent them from being bosses."[27]

Wilson was applying ideas from *Congressional Government* and *Constitutional Government* to current affairs, and he was again giving the lie to any notion that he did not fully share progressives' desires for vigorous, popularly accountable government. The drive to pass the amendment might have been an effort to derail Roosevelt, but Wilson refused to go along with it. Instead, he was promising to be another Roosevelt, if not more so. The only gesture he was willing to make in an anti-Roosevelt direction was the backhanded endorsement of a two-term limit, which would go into the Constitution nearly four decades later in a posthumous slap at another president named Roosevelt.

This political squall soon blew over. Palmer advised against publication of Wilson's letter. He thought it might give the impression of a rift with Bryan, but he promised to share it with Henry D. Clayton, the chairman of the House Judiciary Committee. Meanwhile, at Wilson's request, House showed a copy of the letter to Bryan, who wrote to Clayton that he would favor postponing application of the amendment until 1921, the end of a possible second term for Wilson. The Judiciary Committee shelved the amendment, and it was not seriously proposed again.[28]

Another reason Wilson could seem so little changed was that his wife was managing the practical side of things. Public life had worn on Ellen Wilson. The move to Washington would mark the third time in two years that the family had changed its place of residence, not counting the summer decampments to Sea Girt. In addition to the responsibilities involved in managing the household and the moves, the burden of public appearances, interviews, and correspondence weighed heavily on Ellen. In January, she hired a secretary for the first time—Helen Woodrow Bones. Politically, she continued to advise her husband behind the scenes. Besides pressing him to name Tumulty as his secretary, she appears to have assuaged his doubts about appointing Bryan as secretary of state.

Help in the upcoming move to the White House came from President Taft, who harbored no hard feelings from the campaign. Early in January, he wrote to Ellen about the domestic staff. He advised the Wilsons to retain Elizabeth Jaffray, a Canadian-born widow, as head housekeeper, and Arthur Brooks, "the most trustworthy colored man in the District of

Columbia," as the president's valet and personal clerk. "Mrs. Jaffray and Brooks work very well together," Taft added. "Brooks is especially useful in looking after the wines and cigars to prevent their waste by waiters and others at entertainments." Taft likewise assured Wilson that the presidential salary and expense allowances were more than adequate: "I have been able to save from my four years about $100,000." Following Taft's advice, the Wilsons retained both staff members, and the new president would find that he, too, could save money in the White House.[29]

The family had mixed feelings about the impending revolution in their lives. Leaving Princeton was hard for them. The evening before the move, a crowd of more than 1,000 townspeople marched from Nassau Street to the house on Cleveland Lane. They carried torches, a band played, and the president of the local bank presented a silver loving cup to the president-elect of the United States. The Wilsons left Princeton the day before the inauguration. The weather was sunny and not too cold, and the family walked to the railroad station that adjoined the campus at the foot of Blair Arch. Friends and neighbors waved and greeted them along the way. At the station, a crowd gathered around the train, which had added seven cars to transport hundreds of Princeton undergraduates, including the college band, to Washington. As the train pulled out, Wilson stood on the rear platform and joined the crowd in singing "Old Nassau," waving his silk hat in unison with the crowd. He was leaving the place where he had lived longer than any other place in his life, where he had pursued his first career and begun his second career. Now he was going out, as he said to Mary Peck, "to new adventures amongst strangers."[30]

BEGINNINGS

The Wilson family arrived in Washington on the afternoon of March 3, 1913. They spent a quiet evening, which included a brief visit to the White House and dinner by themselves in their hotel room. They stayed away from most of the public events of the day, such as a big parade for woman suffrage and a host of parties thrown by jubilant Democrats. The next morning, Wilson met briefly with Bryan and the incoming vice president, Thomas R. Marshall, and at ten o'clock he joined Taft at the White House for the traditional ride down Pennsylvania Avenue to the Capitol. There, the two men went into the Senate chamber for the swearing in of the vice president and then walked outside to the platform erected at the front of the Capitol, on the eastern side, for the main event. After repeated cheers for the new president and his family, Wilson stepped up to take the oath of office from Chief Justice Edward White. After taking the oath, Wilson kissed the Bible that he had put his hand on, the same Bible that he had used two years before when he was sworn in as governor. Woodrow Wilson was now president.[1]

He opened his inaugural address with a telling gesture. Noticing that police had cleared a space in front of the platform, he directed, "Let the people come forward." Those words offered a nice prelude to a carefully crafted speech that balanced partisan and national appeals with a blend of specifics and generalities. "My fellow citizens," Wilson began, "there has been a change of government." Democrats now controlled all the elected branches, but, he asserted, "The success of a party means little except when the nation is using that party for a large and definite purpose." His party's purpose was "to cleanse, to reconsider, to restore, to correct the evil without impairing the good. Our work is a work of restoration." After that brief bow toward conservatives came a list of progressive priorities— tariff, tax, and banking reform; conservation; agricultural organization and efficiency—all intended to bring justice and protection to ordinary citizens. He closed by proclaiming, "Men's hearts wait upon us, men's lives hang in the balance; men's hopes call upon us to say what we will do. Who shall live up to the great trust? Who dares fail to try? I summon all honest, all patriotic, all forward-looking men to my side. God helping me, I will not fail them, if they will but counsel and sustain me."[2]

Wilson's inaugural address afforded a national audience its first taste of his eloquence—his blend of stirring appeals, exalted purpose, and divergent ideas—and gave an accurate forecast of the legislative and ideological direction his administration would take. Before he got down to pursuing his goals, however, other matters required his attention. On a practical level, he and Ellen and their daughters needed to settle into their new, though necessarily temporary, home. The new president and First Lady set an unostentatious tone. In keeping with their personal preferences and the incoming administration's reformist posture, they did not sponsor a ball on the night of the inauguration, although Democrats and wealthy socialites staged another round of private parties. On their first evening in the White House, the couple had a family dinner in the State Dining Room, after which they gathered at the windows to watch a fireworks display on the Mall.[3]

Despite her best efforts, Ellen Wilson found herself swept up in a whirl of duties and projects. Official entertaining began the day after the inauguration with a series of receptions, each for several hundred invited guests, together with smaller teas. The next week, the Wilson family and Secretary of State Bryan and his wife received the diplomatic corps. During the three months following the inauguration, the number of official receptions totaled forty-one, with average attendance exceeding 600. In addition, old friends and family members, including Stockton Axson and Wilson's brother, Josie, came to stay for a few days at a time. One weekend guest in May, at Ellen's invitation, was Mary Hulbert, as the former Mrs. Peck now called herself. Some of the entertainment included musical performances, and the Wilsons often went to the theater or to one of the new "movie" houses.

Having three unmarried daughters in their twenties added to the social mix. Margaret was often away, pursuing her singing career, but Jessie and Nell were at home and had serious suitors. Early in 1912, Nell had become engaged to Benjamin (Ben) Mandeville King, an engineer and lumberman. The elder Wilsons liked King, but they asked the couple to keep the engagement secret because the press was poking into their private lives. Later in the year, Jessie met and fell in love with Francis (Frank) Bowes Sayre, a new graduate of Harvard Law School, and they had also become secretly engaged. Between official functions and family affairs, the spring of 1913 was a lively season at the White House. No one could know it then, but those months would mark the social high point of Wilson's eight years as president.[4]

Ellen Wilson occupied herself with more than the social side of presidential life. The White House itself offered an outlet for her talents in art and architecture; she supervised the renovation of the third floor, which was completed during the summer of 1913, while she was away. She chose the decorations and furnishings for the new rooms, particularly favoring fabrics woven by women in the southern Appalachians. Urban renewal also became a cause of hers. Women active in the National Civic Federation interested her in working to clean up the neighborhoods where many of Washington's African American residents lived, particularly the notorious alleys within a few blocks of the Capitol. The First Lady not only joined a private effort to build better housing but also lobbied Congress for slum-clearance legislation, which was introduced the following year. The pace of these activities took a physical toll, and the navy physician assigned to the White House, Cary T. Grayson, urged her to slow down and leave Washington for the summer.

Remarkably, Ellen did not let her new activities come between her and her husband. She had been advising Wilson and reading his writings for nearly thirty years, and busy as they both were, they found time for each other. During their first week in the White House, they began to go for late-afternoon rides in the presidential limousine, often staying out as long as two hours. The whole family took one all-day drive on a Saturday, causing a small stir by showing up unannounced for lunch at a Baltimore hotel. Although Wilson never learned to drive, car rides would remain his favorite form of relaxation for the rest of his life.[5]

For the new president, settling into work appeared to pose few challenges. Wilson had joked earlier about the presidency being just a magnified governorship, and in that remark he predicted much of the way he would handle the office. Tumulty played the same role in Washington that he had played in Trenton. His title was secretary, rather than chief of staff, because, except for clerks, stenographers, military and naval aides, and Dr. Grayson, Tumulty was the staff. He managed the office and controlled the appointment calendar; no one got to see the president without his clearance. He and Wilson ran a tight schedule, with each caller usually getting no more than fifteen minutes. Tumulty managed party, press, and now congressional relations. Senators, congressmen, reporters, and even cabinet members quickly learned to contact him first. The secretary likewise read and summarized newspaper and magazine stories for the president, clipping items and writing short memoranda to call matters to his attention. Wilson normally arrived at the Oval Office at nine o'clock. As before, he spent the first hour handling the mail, dictating replies to Charles Swem, who had also been his personal stenographer in Trenton, or to another stenographer. The president would then spend three hours with visitors, go upstairs for a private lunch, and resume appointments for another two hours. He usually knocked off work at four in the afternoon, in time for a drive with Ellen or, later, at Dr. Grayson's suggestion, a game of golf.[6]

Such short, unruffled workdays seemed better suited to a more easy-going chief executive than the ambitious, activist president Wilson soon showed he was. Yet he was able to maintain these working habits through most of his two terms in office, including the war years. Only the frenetic, unrelenting demands of the peace negotiations in 1919 would derail this approach to his presidential duties.

His powers of concentration and disciplined habits were what allowed him to work this way. Nearly every journalist who interviewed him commented on the atmosphere of quiet control in his office. In June 1914, the young radical journalist John Reed described the contrast between Wilson and the last strong president: "There was none of that violent slamming of doors, clamor of voices, secretaries rushing to and fro, and the sense of great national issues being settled in the antechamber that characterized Mr. Roosevelt's term in the White House. The window curtains swayed in a warm breeze; things were unhurried, yet the feeling in that room was of powerful organization, as if no moment were wasted—as if an immense amount of work was being done." About the president himself, Reed noted, "I never met a man who gave such an impression of quietness inside. . . . Wilson's power emanates from it."[7]

Wilson continued to do much of his work himself. He would be the next to last president to write his own speeches (Herbert Hoover would be the last); it never occurred to him not to. On less formal occasions, he still spoke without notes or from a few jottings in his shorthand. On more formal occasions—as were increasingly the case—he would make an outline and notes in shorthand and then produce a draft on his own typewriter. He also typed correspondence that he regarded as especially intimate or important, such as letters to Colonel House and Mary Hulbert. He wrote those letters and some of the speeches in off-hours in an upstairs study, which was lined with books and piled with papers and offered a quiet refuge. The professor still lurked within the president.

Wilson acted like a bit of both in handling the press. At Tumulty's suggestion, he held regularly scheduled press conferences, often twice a week, becoming the first president to do so. His first meeting with reporters occurred on March 15, 1913. At twelve-forty-five in the afternoon, more than 100 journalists crowded into the president's office. Some of those present later remembered him as stiff in manner and terse and not at all forthcoming in answering their questions. A week later, at his second press conference, Wilson apologized for his earlier performance and made a fresh start. To relieve the crowding, he moved the gathering to the East Room, and he began with a talk that echoed both his campaign speeches and his lectures at Princeton. He claimed that newspapers could improve the atmosphere of public opinion, which, he asserted, "has got to come, not from Washington, but from the country. You have got to write from the country in and not from Washington out." Wilson asked the correspondents to "go into partnership with me, that you lend me your assistance as nobody else can, and, then, after you have brought this precious freight of opinion into Washington, let us try and make true gold here that will go out from Washington."[8]

There is no record of the exchange between Wilson and the reporters at those first two meetings; thereafter, the president had Swem take down what was said. These press conferences featured brisk exchanges between the president and his questioners, with Wilson usually responding in a sentence or two, and he often showed flashes of anger, but also of wit. He held sixty-four press conferences in 1913 and another sixty-four in 1914. All his remarks were off the record, although he sometimes permitted reporters to quote him, and a few angered him by leaking things he said.

The light, bantering tone set at the early press conferences persisted, although it is unclear whether Wilson really felt so jovial toward the reporters. Like most presidents, he fumed in private about the way the press treated him. Rumors of dissension within his administration annoyed him, and reports about his wife and daughters infuriated him so much that he dressed down the reporters at the beginning of a press conference in March 1914: "Gentlemen, I want to say something to you this afternoon. . . . I am a public character for the time being, but the ladies of my household are not servants of the government and they are not public characters. I deeply resent the treatment they are receiving at the hands of newspapers at this time. . . . Now, put yourselves in my place and give me the best cooperation in this that you can, and then we can dismiss a painful subject and go to our afternoon's business."[9]

Reporters did not always enjoy the repartee either. One of them later recalled, "The President gave the impression that he was matching his wits against ours, as a sort of mental practice with the object of being able to make responses which seemed to answer the questions but which imparted little or nothing in the way of information."[10] As with Wilson's complaints about the press, such journalistic carping about him was endemic to their relationship. Wilson's manner with the press, particularly the joviality and evasiveness, strongly resembled Franklin Roosevelt's performance twenty years later. With both presidents, the off-the-record setting facilitated the behavior. After the 1950s, with the advent of public press conferences carried live on television, there would be greater formality and accountability, but the relationship would remain fundamentally adversarial.

In 1915, the press conferences would grow a little less frequent, and in July he would cancel them. The stated reason was the pressure of foreign affairs, but some reporters believed that was just an excuse for doing something Wilson wanted to do anyway. Both explanations may be correct. The sinking of the ocean liner *Lusitania* by a German submarine, killing more than 100 Americans, had raised the specter of the United States' being drawn into the world war, and Secretary of State Bryan had just resigned in protest against Wilson's diplomatic responses to Germany. At the same time, the president was wooing the woman who would become his second wife, and rumors of his amorous escapades were already bubbling up. High policy and personal circumstance seem to have conspired to make regularly scheduled meetings with reporters less appetizing to Wilson.[11]

Questions have also arisen about whether abandonment of the press conferences sprang from Wilson's basically solitary temperament, but that is unlikely. If those meetings had been truly distasteful to him, the time to stop them would have been in the fall of 1914, following Ellen's death, one of the two worst times in his life. But he met the reporters as usual then. Even after he had stopped holding press conferences, he granted long interviews with individual journalists, such as one with Ray Stannard Baker in 1916. Those interviews helped writers such as Baker, Samuel G. Blythe, and Ida Tarbell produce penetrating and favorable magazine articles about him. Moreover, Tumulty persuaded the president to resume holding press conferences late in 1916. Unfortunately, the renewed submarine crisis and intervention in the war led to their abandonment again. Wilson would hold just one more press conference, in July 1919, when he returned from the peace negotiations in Paris. Soon afterward, the stroke he suffered would rule out any public appearances. In all, his relations with the press would be sometimes fruitful and harmonious but ultimately ill-starred.

· · ·

Relations with his cabinet resembled those with the press, but with a better outcome. Wilson held his first cabinet meeting the day after the inauguration. From then until November 1913, they met twice a week, on
Tuesdays and Fridays. Thereafter, Wilson cut back on the frequency to
once a week, with individual conferences taking the place of the second
meeting. The cabinet gathered around a long mahogany table in a room
in the West Wing next to the president's office. Wilson sat at one end of
the table, with the heads of the two ranking departments, Secretary of
State Bryan and Secretary of the Treasury McAdoo, on his right and left.
Secretary of the Navy Daniels later recalled that from the outset, Wilson
"act[ed] as if being chief executive were no new experience to him." He
found the president's manner "matter-of-fact" and described him as "the
moderator." Wilson would present a point and go around the table for
responses and discussion. He never took votes but treated these meetings,
"as he often said, more like a Quaker meeting" and would conclude, "It
seems to me the sense of the meeting is so and so."[12] If any of the cabinet
members had served on the Princeton faculty, they would have found all
this familiar.

Another one of the new president's practices with the cabinet also
recalled his academic leadership. Once more, Wilson delegated. Just as he
had deferred at Princeton to Harry Fine's expertise in the sciences, he now
assumed that his department heads knew their areas better than he
did, and he allowed them to run their agencies with little interference.
This approach offered a sharp contrast to what was then and later taken
to be the model for a strong president. Theodore Roosevelt had set
an example of hyperactive meddling in every aspect of his administration; in the future, his cousin Franklin and Lyndon Johnson would do the
same, throwing in manipulation and bullying. By contrast, Wilson would
endorse bold financial initiatives by McAdoo and would initially bow to
Secretary of Agriculture David Houston's opposition to government aid
to farmers. This approach had the advantage of promoting an efficient,
smooth-running government; it would show its greatest value after Wilson's stroke in 1919, when the administration could function without him.
Its great disadvantage lay in permitting cabinet members to take unfortunate actions at times, as when they repressed civil liberties at home after
the country went to war.

One ill consequence of Wilson's permissiveness emerged at the beginning of his administration. More than half of the cabinet hailed from the
South, and nearly all of the congressional leadership was southern. Journalists frequently commented on Washington's newly Dixiefied political

atmosphere—an atmosphere that was not entirely to Wilson's liking. Before the inauguration, he had publicly urged sectional reconciliation, and afterward he gave private encouragement to the proposal offered by the civil rights activist Oswald Garrison Villard that a government commission investigate race relations. Despite such talk and gestures, Wilson raised no objection early in April when Postmaster General Burleson echoed widespread southern white anger at racial mingling in federal offices, particularly in the case of black supervisors overseeing white clerks. "The President said he had made no promises to negroes, except to do them justice," Daniels recorded in his diary, "and he did not wish to see them have less positions than they have now, but he wishes the matter adjusted in a way to make the least friction."[13]

Burleson and McAdoo started to make arrangements to segregate offices, rest rooms, and eating facilities at the Post Office, Treasury Department, and Bureau of Printing and Engraving. McAdoo tried to create an all-black division in his department, but the project fell through, ironically because southern senators refused to confirm the African American Democrat chosen to head the office. More outspoken racists on Capitol Hill, spearheaded by Senator James K. Vardaman of Mississippi, fought Wilson's appointments to positions in the District of Columbia that were traditionally filled by African Americans. The appointments Wilson did make were exceptions to a general reduction in the number of black-held positions in the government during his administration, including lower-level positions.[14]

Plans to segregate federal departments stirred up strong protests from the National Association for the Advancement of Colored People. Villard, who was a founder, took the organization's case directly to the president. "I cannot exaggerate the effect this has had upon colored people at large," he wrote Wilson. Negroes had taken "from your 'New Freedom' the belief that your democracy was not limited by race or color." Wilson answered testily, "It is as far as possible from being a movement *against* negroes."[15] He also backed away from his earlier encouragement of the race commission idea, pleading the press of other business.

The controversy festered through the summer and into the fall of 1913. The black press—together with the *New York Evening Post* (which Villard owned) and *The Nation* (which then was affiliated with the *Evening Post* and edited by an uncle of Villard's) and some northern Democrats—loudly criticized the segregation and appointment policies, and the segregation practices were put on hold. In October, an *Evening Post* reporter had a private meeting with Wilson to assess the situation for Villard. The president, he reported, probably did believe that blacks were inferior, but the views of the congressional leaders were much worse, and they would block any appointment to a post in which a black person "is to be in command of white people—especially of white women." In this newly charged atmosphere, white bureaucrats could give free rein to their prejudices. In November, Wilson met with critics of the policies. Their spokesman, the fiery Boston editor William Monroe Trotter, an African American, delivered a lengthy indictment and challenged the president. Wilson lamely answered, "I am not familiar with it all," and admitted, "Now, mistakes have probably been made, but those mistakes can be corrected."[16] This would not be Wilson's last confrontation with Trotter, and it was not the end of the controversy.

The segregation controversy did not strain Wilson's relations with the cabinet, but their honeymoon did not last. By the fall of 1913, some secretaries were complaining about the lack of serious discussion at cabinet meetings and the lack of consultation by the president. Some of them later offered an explanation for why Wilson clammed up at their meetings: they believed it was because Secretary of the Interior Lane was leaking information from the Cabinet Room to the press. Lane was an inveterate gossip, but there is no direct evidence that Wilson reacted to his or others' indiscretions. Moreover, important matters still did get discussed at cabinet meetings, as when Wilson repeatedly talked in February and March 1917 about whether to enter the war—the most momentous decision he ever made. A better explanation for cabinet members' complaints lies in their hunger to feel important, which has affected most presidents' relations with their cabinets. Another explanation for those complaints lies in the temperamental differences that separated those men from Wilson. His habit of secluding himself when he pondered policies and made decisions did not sit well with more gregarious types, who wanted lots of talk and advice seeking. Those temperamental differences would underlie most of the complaints, which usually came from naturally sociable men, such as House, McAdoo, and sometimes Tumulty, who also thought the president ought to be following their advice on particular matters.[17]

It seems odd that House should have complained about a lack of discussion of great issues. If there was anyone in whom the Wilson did seem to confide, House was that person. He met with the president on seventeen occasions during his first year in office. Fifteen of those meetings took place in the White House, where House was an overnight guest twice. The two men also corresponded regularly, and at least twice they talked by long-distance telephone, which was not a common practice in those days. Wilson evidently felt comfortable discussing just about everything with House. Ellen Wilson also continued to take a shine to the Texan, and she discussed family finances with him. Curiously, House shied away from some contacts, as when he made an excuse for staying away from the inaugural ceremony.

Meetings between the two men followed a pattern that was partly political and partly seasonal. Ten of the first year's meetings took place between March and May 1913, and no others occurred until late October. House, like many wealthy Americans with cosmopolitan aspirations, made an annual journey to Europe in late spring that lasted for several weeks. Also, he and his family retreated for the summer to a seaside estate on the north shore of Massachusetts. Despite being a native Texan, he claimed that his health could not stand the summer heat of New York, much less that of Washington. He did maintain home-state ties by making a yearly visit to mend political fences and oversee his property. He struck some people in New York as a bit of a professional Texan, and one acquaintance noted that the heading on his stationery always read "Edward M. House, Austin, Texas."[18] During the first year of Wilson's administration, much of what he discussed with House centered on appointments and party matters, particularly the vexing question of what to do with McCombs. Domestic policy came up fairly often because this was the time when Wilson was launching his big legislative initiatives, and foreign affairs also came up.

House's collecting cabinet members' complaints about the president probably stemmed from his relish for gossip and his willingness to lend a sympathetic ear. He would later disparage Wilson regularly in his diary for not mingling with other people, but at this point he still seemed a bit awed by the president, especially by his analytic powers. House also harbored a big scheme of his own, which he was gradually unveiling. In recent years he had become interested in foreign affairs, and in his novel he had spun a vision in which the world's great powers, led by the United States, band together to maintain peace and order—a refined imperialism that resembled views held by Roosevelt and others close to him. In December 1913, House disclosed his gambit to a visiting British diplomat, recording in his diary that he wanted "to bring about an understanding between France, Germany, England and the United States regarding a reduction of armaments, both military and naval. I said it was an ambitious undertaking but was so well worth while that I intended to try it."[19] Ten days later, at a meeting with Wilson, he introduced the plan, and he would persist in pushing this scheme with the president during the spring of 1914.

. . .

House was not the only person beyond the family circle who became close to Wilson. During the spring and summer of 1913, the president made a new intimate friend—his physician, Cary Grayson. As Grayson later recalled, he first met the incoming president the day before the inauguration, when Taft introduced them by saying, "Mr. Wilson, here is an excellent fellow that I hope you will get to know. I regret to say that he is a Democrat and a Virginian, but that's a matter that can't be helped."[20] The next day, Grayson was on hand to treat Wilson's sister Annie Howe when she fell on some steps at the White House and cut her forehead. That encounter and Taft's recommendation prompted the new president to ask the navy to assign the short, thirty-four-year-old lieutenant to the post of White House physician.

Similarities in their backgrounds and the doctor's quiet charm soon gained him a place in the affections of both Wilson and Ellen. After Ellen and other family members left Washington in June—on Grayson's recommendation that Ellen get away—Wilson invited the bachelor physician to move in with him at the White House. The two men spent evenings on the porch, where Wilson would unwind by talking about nonofficial matters, sometimes reminiscing about his early life. On Sundays, the president took his Episcopalian physician with him to the Central Presbyterian Church, which he and his family regularly attended. "The doctor goes to church with me," Wilson reported to Ellen, "and is very sedate and an excellent imitation of a Presbyterian."[21]

Wilson's presidency afforded him something he had never had before—a full-time physician to attend to his health. Grayson was not a highly trained graduate of a university-affiliated medical school; he had learned most of his skills in the navy, serving briefly aboard ship and mostly at the Naval Dispensary in Washington. And he had had some White House medical assignments under Roosevelt and Taft.

Grayson found his new patient in reasonably good health. Politics still seemed to agree with him. "Father looked extraordinarily well and vital during these weeks," his daughter Nell later recalled of the first days in the White House. Grayson's main concerns lay with Wilson's diet and exercise. He got the president to abandon such practices as eating charcoal and pumping his stomach, and he got him to eat more vegetables. He also encouraged Wilson to play more golf and usually accompanied him on the links. Like automobile rides, golf relaxed the president and took his mind off problems, and he played the game avidly. Despite his earlier facility with tennis and baseball, he never became a good golfer, possibly because impaired vision in his left eye as a result of the 1906 hemorrhage prevented him from placing shots accurately.[22]

. . .

Appointments continued to be a headache. Rival Democratic leaders and members of inter- and intrastate factions were jockeying to snare jobs for their faithful. Party infighting remained especially fierce in New York, where Tammany regulars and reformers battled in 1913 over both the New York City mayoralty race and the state's gubernatorial race. A plum federal appointment, collector of the port of New York, drew Wilson into the fray. He made a choice worthy of King Solomon by appointing his friend Dudley Field Malone, who was both a reformer and the son-in-law of a Tammany leader. The president also used House as an emissary to the feuding New Yorkers; it was in this capacity that he supposedly made the statement, to be relayed to them, "Mr. House is my second personality. He is my independent self. His thoughts and mine are one."[23]

Diplomatic appointments gave the new president almost as many headaches as domestic political patronage. Wilson had originally wanted to name distinguished nonpolitical figures to major ambassadorships—academics such as Harry Fine to Germany and Harvard's ex-president Charles W. Eliot to China and his editor friend Page to Britain. He was able to persuade Page to go, and a leading scholar of Asian affairs, Paul S. Reinsch of the University of Wisconsin, did accept the China post. Otherwise, Wilson fell back on the time-honored practice of picking big campaign contributors. The post in Berlin went to James W. Gerard, a wealthy Tammany-affiliated lawyer. Because McCombs dithered for months before saying no to the post in Paris, the outgoing Republican appointee would stay until after the outbreak of the world war, when a rich Ohio manufacturer and former congressman, William G. Sharp, finally filled that ambassadorship. Most of the appointees to major European capitals were of a similar ilk.

Another problem in making diplomatic appointments involved the secretary of state. Bryan was an unreconstructed spoilsman, and he filled lower-ranking posts abroad, particularly those in Latin America—most of which were at the ministerial, not the ambassadorial, level—with "deserving Democrats." Wilson did resist a complete partisan housecleaning; he continued Roosevelt's and Taft's practice of staffing the consular service and subministerial foreign service by means of merit systems. Overall, the incoming administration did not distinguish itself with its diplomatic personnel.[24]

Given such fumbling and lack of concern for qualifications, it was just as well that the diplomatic front was comparatively quiet. Yet Wilson was not entirely free from foreign concerns. Mexico landed on his desk the moment he arrived in the White House. Less than three weeks before his inauguration, there was a bloody coup that Mexicans call the Ten Tragic Days, in which an army general, Victoriano Huerta, overthrew and sanctioned the murder of the reformist moderate president, Francisco Madero. Taft's ambassador, Henry Lane Wilson, sympathized with the coup and was urging recognition of the Huerta regime, as were a number of American businessmen with large holdings in Mexico. Partly because these events occurred so late in his administration, Taft left the question of whether to recognize Huerta to his successor. For his part, Wilson resisted pleas from business interests, relayed through House. Instead, on March 12, he issued a policy statement that stressed his desire "to cultivate the friendship and deserve the confidence of our sister republics of Central and South America" but warned that this would be possible "only when supported in turn by the orderly processes of just government based upon law and not upon arbitrary and irregular force." Without naming Huerta, he declared, "We can have no sympathy with those who seek the power of government to advance their own personal interests or ambitions."[25]

That statement in the second week of his presidency marked Wilson's first step into an entanglement that would last for years. It also revealed part of his initial underlying approach to foreign affairs. Since his outburst of imperialist enthusiasm almost fifteen years before, Wilson had paid little attention to foreign affairs and had given every appearance of falling into step with the Democrats' anti-imperialist, anti-militarist pronouncements set down by Bryan. When he chose Bryan to be secretary of state, Wilson raised no objections to the Commoner's pacifist foreign policy views, and he gave his blessing to the secretary's pursuit of his favorite scheme—a plan for compulsory delay when nations could not resolve disputes peacefully, often called cooling-off treaties. Yet Wilson's first foreign policy pronouncement as president sounded like Roosevelt's famous Corollary to the Monroe Doctrine of eight years before, which had proclaimed a United States "police power" over the nations of Latin America. It seems a bit of the imperialist was lurking within this new Democratic president.

Still, the official stance of the Democrats was anti-imperialist, and Wilson hewed to the party line in his other early pronouncements and moves. Previously, as the party's principal, and often only, spokesman in foreign affairs, Bryan had long attacked Republican diplomatic and military policies, and in recent years he had zeroed in on the Taft administration's enlistment of bankers and investment houses to promote American interests in Latin America and Asia. Not only fellow Democrats but also some Republican insurgents, most notably La Follette, had joined in heaping scorn on "dollar diplomacy." Now that he was secretary of state, Bryan could undo part of that diplomacy—the proposed American participation in an international syndicate of bankers that would lend money to China for railroad construction. The project offended Bryan's domestic politics as well, because the American banks in the syndicate were Wall Street firms, headed by the house of Morgan. The secretary brought the matter before the cabinet on March 12, and he found that most of the other members and the president strongly agreed with him. Six days later, Wilson issued a statement to the press in which he rejected the loan for appearing "to touch very nearly the administrative independence of China itself; and this administration does not feel that it ought, even by implication, to be a party to those conditions."[26]

Wilson further showed his concern for China when he made the United States the first nation to extend diplomatic recognition to the shaky new republican government that had been set up in the wake of the revolution that had toppled the Ch'ing dynasty. After discussions in the cabinet, Bryan informed ambassadors of other nations of the decision to recognize the Chinese Republic. Wilson drafted a formal message of recognition early in April, and the American chargé d'affaires in Peking delivered this message to the Chinese government on May 2. It included a statement by the president welcoming "the new China" and expressing confidence "that in perfecting a republican form of government the Chinese nation will attain to the highest degree of development and well being."[27]

Such uplifting words suited Wilson's and Bryan's wishes to present a vivid contrast to previous Republican policies, but they had little practical effect. At home, Democrats and some Republican insurgents applauded the rejection of the loan plan, and in China diplomatic recognition was popular. But American withdrawal from the railroad loan opened the way to further financial incursions by Japan and, in the view of many students of East Asian affairs, weakened China's ability to resist pressures from Tokyo. At the same time, thanks to domestic politics, the United States faced troubles of its own with Japan. In the 1912 campaign, Democrats and Progressives in California had vied with each other in appealing to anti-Asian prejudices, primarily those aimed at recent Japanese immigrants. In March 1913, California's legislature began debating measures to combat this "menace," particularly laws that would prohibit land ownership by persons ineligible for citizenship—that is, Japanese immigrants. Wilson, who had endorsed the exclusion of Asian immigrants during the campaign, told a leading California Democrat that he hoped any discriminatory actions "might be so modulated and managed as to offend the susceptibilities of a friendly nation as little as possible."[28]

That hope led the Wilson administration down a thorny path. Bryan acted as an emissary to Governor Hiram Johnson and other California leaders. The secretary of state made two trips across the country in the spring of 1913 to deal directly with Johnson and others in Sacramento. These efforts at domestic diplomacy failed. The California legislature passed a law forbidding land ownership by Japanese immigrants, and public indignation exploded in Japan, ultimately causing the cabinet there to fall. In May, a war scare flared briefly after reports of possible Japanese naval action. Secretary of War Garrison angered some fellow cabinet members by insisting on a tough response. The controversy blew over, thanks to Wilson's and Bryan's sweet-talking the Japanese and the unwillingness of leaders in Tokyo to push the matter to a full-fledged crisis. Still, the incident sowed resentment in the minds of many Japanese and created problems that would later trouble Wilson.[29]

Between Mexico and Japan, the new president spent a great deal of time on diplomatic matters. Foreign affairs offered a partial exception to Wilson's practice of delegating to cabinet members. Five years earlier, in *Constitutional Government*, he had asserted, "The initiative in foreign affairs, which the President possesses without any restriction whatever, is virtually the power to control them absolutely." Sounding a Rooseveltian note, he had added that the president "can never be the mere domestic figure" of bygone days but must "be one of the great powers of the world."[30] This greater involvement in foreign affairs did not spring from lack of confidence in Bryan. The Great Commoner drew criticism in some quarters for serving grape juice instead of alcohol at official functions, which some Republicans scorned as "grape juice diplomacy," and he continued to earn money lecturing on the Chautauqua circuit. Wilson raised no objections to those practices, and the only evidence of his casting aspersions on Bryan comes from the diary of Colonel House, who was probably trying to sow discord.

Wilson showed little hesitation about plunging into foreign affairs. He seemed bold and confident despite his lack of experience. For him, foreign affairs went along with press relations, political appointments, and working with the cabinet: these constituted the normal business of governing, matters that any president had to manage. For him, the acid test of leadership always lay in great initiatives to change the order of things. For him as president of the United States, that test lay in legislation. The enactment of major new laws loomed ahead as his biggest and fondest challenge.

TAKEN AT THE FLOOD

As a legislative leader in the White House, Woodrow Wilson repeated his performance as a college president and state governor. Once again, he got off to a fast start and pushed for major changes at once. Once again, he racked up big successes at the outset. In fact, he would succeed in pushing his programs through Congress throughout his first term as president. Taken together, his feats in enacting the New Freedom would rank him among the greatest legislative presidents in the twentieth century, perhaps in all of American history. His only rivals would be Franklin Roosevelt with the New Deal in the 1930s and Lyndon Johnson with the Great Society in the 1960s. In some ways, he wrought even more impressive feats than those men would. Unlike the second Roosevelt, he was not dealing with a desperate national emergency; unlike the second Johnson, he did not enjoy long experience, intimate knowledge, and mastery of the ways of Congress.

No one could have accomplished as much as Wilson did without help and luck. Congressional Democrats were willing to follow him, although their conflicting ideas and interests sometimes made them difficult to pull together. His party's leaders in the respective chambers, Congressman Underwood of Alabama and Senator John W. Kern of Indiana, proved able and cooperative. Speaker Champ Clark remained a bit sulky and passive, but he was no obstructionist. Bryan drew on his years of ideological primacy and his network of connections among Democrats to provide an important bridge to Capitol Hill. Brandeis continued to supply strategic policy advice at critical junctures. The larger political environment likewise smiled on Wilson. With the exception of Mexico, foreign problems would not greatly distract him from domestic matters. More important, the dominance of progressive issues in the 1912 campaign ensured that much of Wilson's program had gained, to use a favorite word of his, taken from Edmund Burke, "expediency"—these were ideas whose time had come. Thanks to overwhelming reform sentiment and the defeat and departure of old guard Republicans, Wilson would face less of the conservative obstructionism that had hobbled and stymied Roosevelt's and Taft's initiatives.

Ever since he won the election, he had been planning to break the custom, started by Jefferson, whereby the president did not appear in person before Congress. On April 6, 1913, the White House announced that President Wilson would deliver his first speech since the inauguration before a joint session of Congress. The news brought protests from strict Jeffersonians in his own party, who called the move "federalistic." Wilson laughed at the comparison and told Daniels that "the only federalistic thing about it was delivering the message in person." When he stood at the rostrum of the House chamber in the Capitol on April 8, he began, "I am very glad indeed to have this opportunity to address the two Houses directly and to verify for myself the impression that the President of the United States is a person, not a mere department of the government hailing Congress from some isolated island of jealous power, sending messages, not speaking naturally and with his own voice—that he is a human being trying to co-operate with other human beings in a common service."[1]

Wilson protested a bit too much when he disclaimed "federalistic" motives. As a long-standing critic of the separation of powers, he meant to make more than a symbolic break with that aspect of Jefferson's legacy. He was doing something that the country's most renowned admirer of Hamilton and greatest denigrator of Jefferson had not dared to do. His daughter Nell recalled her mother saying on the ride back to the White House from the Capitol, "That's the sort of thing Roosevelt would have loved to do if he had thought of it." Her father laughed and answered, "Yes, I think I put one over on Teddy."[2] Wilson meant to out-Roosevelt Roosevelt by working closely with Congress and taking command over legislation.

The question of how to exercise legislative leadership appeared to present him with a fateful choice between progressivism and partisanship. Postmaster General Burleson later recounted that the president talked to him shortly after the inauguration about lower-level federal appointments and party relations: "Now, Burleson, I want to say to you that my administration is going to be a progressive administration. I am not going to advise with reactionary or standpat Senators or Representatives in making these appointments." Burleson, who said he felt "depressed" and "paralyzed" upon hearing that, advised playing along with the Democrats in Congress on "little offices" and other small matters, and he stuck to his guns for two hours. Wilson finally said, "All right, Burleson, I will think about the matter." A week later, the president began to relent, and he soon left minor patronage to Burleson's discretion. A year later, after he had racked up some of his legislative triumphs, Burleson recalled him conceding, "What you told me about the old standpatters is true. They at least will stand by the party and the administration. I can rely on them better than I can on some of my own crowd."[3]

This face-off between dreamy idealist and the hard-bitten politico makes a nice story, and some elements of it ring true. Wilson did dislike his party's conservatives, and he had flaunted his progressivism repeatedly since the election. But it is wrong to think that a man who had lauded party government for more than thirty years would need to be tutored about the leaders in Congress. The presence of Bryan and Burleson in the cabinet testified to Wilson's undiminished regard for party affairs. Burleson acknowledged this when he told Ray Stannard Baker that "he felt he had been appointed in some degree as an intermediary between Wilson and Congress." At all events, the two men came to work so well together on party matters that the president and other cabinet members took to calling Burleson "the Cardinal."[4]

The president's newfound coziness with the postmaster general and party barons on Capitol Hill did not mean that he had abandoned his intentions to make the Democrats more progressive. Wilson believed he could have it both ways. He resumed his rhetorical campaign to set out his ideological direction. In one speech, he maintained that anyone who claims special privileges "forfeits the title of Americanism," and in another he gloried in paying attention to "the cool large spaces of the United States" rather than the sound and fury of Washington. Wilson did not use the term, but he was mounting Roosevelt's bully pulpit. Yet he knew it would take more than preaching to make good on his progressive promises. Before the inauguration, he had conferred with committee chairmen and party leaders in both houses of Congress, and he met with them frequently during his first months in the White House. By all accounts, he came across in those meetings as friendly but firm. On their part, his congressional visitors often felt, an English observer noted, "conscious of an intellectual inferiority, of a narrower point of view, of limitations in their knowledge, of less elevated purposes and motives."[5] The following year, the English caricaturist Max Beerbohm captured this contrast in a drawing titled "Professor Wilson Visiting Congress," which shows a slender, bespectacled Wilson in academic garb lecturing to a bunch of large, paunchy, mainly walrus-mustached men. Political cartoonists in American newspapers likewise often depicted the president in a cap and gown or as a schoolmaster with congressmen and senators as squirming schoolboys.

Charges soon arose in the press that he was dictating to Congress. Wilson resented such allegations. "I do not know how to wield a big stick," he protested, "but I do know how to put my mind at the service of others for the accomplishment of a common purpose. They are using me; I am not driving them." The gentleman again protested too much, but he did engage in genuine consultation with congressional leaders. As a result of those consultations and his own inclinations, Wilson decided to push the tariff as the lead item on the agenda, but he staked out his position in general terms and remained flexible. In that initial speech before Congress, he addressed the tariff but kept his remarks brief, referring only to the goal of altering the present system and stating that remedies might "at some points seem heroic."[6]

Choosing to lead off with tariff revision brought several advantages. The Democrats were largely united in wanting to lower rates, and the tariff promised to be the easiest measure on Wilson's agenda to enact. Likewise, tariff making was a long-practiced legislative art, so that the men on Capitol Hill could presumably handle the item much on their own, with little pressure and interference from the White House. Moreover, although the tariff contained a host of intricate schedules, it did not present the legal, technical, and philosophical challenges inherent in the other major items on the president's agenda: banking reform and anti-trust legislation. Finally, the tariff presented this Democratic president and his majorities in Congress with an unparalleled opportunity to prove their strength and effectiveness.

Twice before in the last two decades, presidents and congresses of both parties had tried and failed to lower the tariff. Grover Cleveland and the Democrats had fumbled in 1894 with the Wilson-Gorman tariff, and in 1909, Taft and the Republicans had similarly failed, with the Payne-Aldrich tariff. Both of those efforts had followed the same pattern: the House, where, constitutionally, revenue bills had to originate, passed a version that lowered rates. Then protectionist senators, aided by a swarm of lobbyists, passed a version loaded down with amendments that wiped out or, in the case of the Payne-Aldrich tariff, even reversed most of the downward revisions. The Senate version largely prevailed, and the president ultimately caved in, either allowing the bill to become law without his signature, as Cleveland did, or pretending that it was satisfactory, as with Taft. If President Wilson could break this pattern, he would win a big personal victory and establish his and his party's governing credentials.

At first, history seemed to be repeating itself in 1913. In the House, Underwood served as both majority leader and chairman of the Ways and Means Committee, and he speedily produced a bill that reduced the average tariff rate by 10 percent and removed protection altogether from a large number of products. In addition, the bill contained a provision to levy income taxes: 1 percent on income over $4,000 (substantial earnings at the time) and in steps to a maximum of 4 percent over $100,000. On May 8, just one month after Wilson's appearance before Congress, the House passed the Underwood bill without amendment, by a vote of 281 to 139. Just five Democrats, four of them from sugar-dominated Louisiana districts, broke ranks; four Progressives, two Republicans, and one independent supported the bill.

Then repetition of history seemed to show its sour side. The Senate presented Wilson and other tariff reformers with a veritable minefield. There, the Democrats held only a small majority—six seats—and Louisiana's two Democratic senators were almost certain to oppose any downward revision. Several Democrats who represented western states with mineral, beet sugar, and wool interests also seemed likely to defect. Ominously, too, the chairman of the Finance Committee was Furnifold Simmons of North Carolina, a conservative who had earlier helped Republicans gut tariff-revision bills. As matters transpired, the chairman bore out Cardinal Burleson's prediction that old-line Democrats would stand by the party: Simmons stuck to a pledge to follow the president's leadership. Still, like any good historian, Wilson could see what might happen, and he acted quickly to avert looming dangers. Even before the Underwood bill passed, he started meeting with and writing to individual Democratic senators, particularly westerners, turning on his charm and power of persuasion. Despite those efforts, one of the westerners, Thomas J. Walsh of Montana, announced that he might have to vote against parts of the bill. Meanwhile, as in earlier tariff fights, lobbyists were pulling out all the stops in their efforts to influence senators. Trying to attract public attention, Wilson told the press that the people were "voiceless in these matters, while great bodies of astute men seek to create an artificial opinion and to overcome the interests of the public for their private profit. . . . Only public opinion can check and destroy it."7

That statement was vintage Wilson. He was once more appealing directly to constituents, and as before, the appeal at first appeared to backfire. Usually supportive newspapers such as *The New York Times* and Democratic senators objected to the allegations. Republican senators thought they saw an opportunity to make mischief by demanding an investigation. Wilson called their bluff by urging Democrats to support the investigation, which the Senate quickly approved, along with a requirement that senators disclose any of their own interests that might be affected by changes in the tariff. During the first week of June, the Judiciary Committee witnessed a parade of senators revealing stock- and land-holdings and confessing to previous efforts to protect those interests. Then the committee delved into the lobbyists themselves and discovered that during the past twenty years, sugar interests had spent $5 million to influence legislation and had contributed to the Democratic campaign in 1912. Wilson seemed vindicated. "The country is indebted to President Wilson for exploding the bomb that blew the lid off the congressional lobby," declared the Senate's arch-progressive, Robert La Follette. "Congress sneered. The interests cried demagogue. The public believed. The case is proved."[8] Denouncing the lobbyists played much the same role for Wilson's presidency as the fight with Sugar Jim Smith had played for his governorship.

After those hearings, Senate debate on the tariff turned into a slow grind. The Finance Committee reduced rates further, and the Democratic caucus held firm in support of the measure, with only the two Louisianians in dissent. Republicans attacked on two fronts. Conservatives, joined by some insurgents, trotted out their party's well-worn justifications of protection, such as its supposed benefits for jobs and wages. They recognized that they did not have the votes to stop the tariff revision, but the maneuvering was delaying consideration of banking-reform legislation, which was making its way through the House. Meanwhile, insurgent Republicans attacked the income tax provision for not going far enough. In late August, La Follette persuaded four Democrats to demand that their caucus adopt his amendment to raise rates to 10 percent on the highest income. The Finance Committee countered with a compromise that raised the rate on income of more than $100,000 to 7 percent. Simmons appealed to Bryan and Wilson for help, and the president, who was on a short visit to his family's summer quarters in New Hampshire, wrote back to support the committee's proposals as "reasonable and well considered. I should think that they would commend themselves to the caucus."[9] Wilson's letter, together with Bryan's arm-twisting, sufficed to unite the Democrats behind the committee compromise.

Final passage came fairly soon. Republicans made a last-ditch effort to save the duties on wool, and insurgents tried to tack on an inheritance tax. On September 9, the Senate passed the Simmons bill by a vote of 44 to 37. Among the Democrats, only the Louisiana senators voted no; one Republican insurgent, La Follette, voted yes, as did the lone Progressive senator, Miles Poindexter of Washington. A conference committee ironed out differences between the versions, mainly keeping the lower rates in the Simmons bill, and both chambers passed the final version on an almost straight party-line vote. On October 3, the president staged a ceremony at the White House to sign the Underwood-Simmons tariff. He used two gold pens, which he presented to the respective chairmen, and he lauded their work and expressed gratitude for having played a part himself, quoting Shakespeare: "If it be a sin to covet honor, then I am the most offending soul alive."[10]

Only one thing kept the ceremony from being perfect: Ellen and the Wilson daughters were not there. They were still vacationing in New Hampshire, and on October 3, Ellen made a brief trip to New York to shop for Jessie's wedding, which was to take place at the White House in November. When Ellen read newspaper reports of the ceremony, she exulted, "[N]ow at last everybody in the civilized world knows that you are a great man[,] a great leader of men."[11] Her husband had won a great victory, succeeding where his predecessors had failed and doing so as a party leader. The theorist of party government had become the practitioner of party government. Hardly any Republicans voted for the tariff despite the inclusion of the income tax. Insurgents had a ready excuse in their claim that the tax did not go far enough; some of their lack of support also stemmed from their being ignored by the president. Conversely, it was a sign of future trouble that the insurgents made little effort to reach across party lines, as they had done in the past. Another sign of trouble was that the easiest item on Wilson's legislative agenda had taken so much time and effort to pass. At the time, however, all signs looked good. Tariff reform gave the new president a big boost toward his goal of seeing the rest of his reform program enacted.

The item that was now second on Wilson's agenda, banking reform, presented different and tougher challenges. A near consensus favored doing something to strengthen the country's financial structure, but that consensus presented the biggest challenge. If just about everybody agreed that something needed to be achieved, few agreed on exactly what that something should be. Broadly speaking, the divergent approaches to the problem attracted support from different constituencies and their political representatives.

The first approach, supported by big investment firms on Wall Street and in other metropolitan centers of the Northeast and Midwest, favored a privately controlled central bank that would hold government deposits and act as a reserve for smaller banks. Such central banks operated in Britain, France, and Germany; one had functioned in the United States before Andrew Jackson smashed it in the "Bank War" of the 1830s. In recent years, J. P. Morgan had acted informally as a central banker, particularly during financial panics in 1893 and 1907. Conservative Republicans

supported this approach to reform and had taken a step in this direction in
1908 by passing the Aldrich-Vreeland Act, which provided for moves
toward a single private reserve bank with fifteen branches. That move had
angered Democrats and progressive Republicans.

Apart from rejecting a private central bank, those opponents of the
Aldrich-Vreeland Act agreed on little else. Bankers and larger business
interests in the South and West had long resented domination by Wall
Street and other big financial centers. They, too, wanted privately controlled reserves, but they favored a second approach—namely, a system of
regional banks. More conservative southern Democrats supported this
approach, and Congressman Glass had begun to discuss ideas along those
lines with Wilson soon after the election. His Banking Committee had
recently drawn up a bill that embodied a decentralized version of the
Aldrich-Vreeland system.

Farmers and smaller business interests in the South and West supported a third approach, which also favored a regional system, but they
did not want access to credit controlled by local bankers and big opera-
tors. Other southern and western Democrats, mainly Bryan and his followers, took their party's Jacksonian anti-bank heritage seriously, and they
favored government-controlled regional reserve banks. Some insurgent
Republicans also supported this approach. Finally, urban intellectuals and
reform-inclined lawyers and economists believed that only a national
approach could slay the "money trust" and constructively address the
country's credit and financial needs. More sophisticated Republican insurgents, such as La Follette, and some of Roosevelt's Progressives were calling for a single government institution to provide reserves and oversee
banking. In short, two conflicting principles—private versus public control and decentralization versus centralization—created a veritable Gor-
dian knot that a successful program of banking reform would have to cut.

Wilson not only had to put together a congressional majority, but he
also had to wrestle with thorny technical problems in seeking to reform a
diverse, complex array of institutions spread throughout a vast nation. In
June, he described the difficulty to Mary Hulbert this way: "It is not like
the tariff, about which opinion has been forming long years through.
There are almost as many judgments as there are men. To form a single
plan and a single intention about it seems at times a task so various and so
elusive that it is hard to keep one's heart from failing."[12] By the time he
wrote those words, Wilson had been struggling for weeks to reconcile
Glass's plan for decentralized private banks with Bryan's demand for public control.

Bryan had a friend and powerful ally in the chairman of the Senate

Banking and Currency Committee, Robert Owen of Oklahoma, who resented having been left out of the talks before the inauguration and adamantly opposed the Glass bill. Secretary of the Treasury McAdoo had stepped in with a plan that, like Aldrich-Vreeland, called for a central bank with fifteen branches but would be part of his department and administered by a board of political appointees. Glass had counterattacked by enlisting support for his bill from prominent New York bankers. Meanwhile, House was passing along criticisms of public control by some of those same financiers, with murmurs of his own agreement with them. Buckling under this onslaught, McAdoo had withdrawn his plan and said he favored the Glass bill. On June 17, Wilson brought the congressman, the senator, and the secretary together for a meeting at the White House. In a long, heated discussion, Glass and Owen stuck to their guns, but McAdoo shifted again, this time back to public control, or, as he told House, "the right measure . . . which puts the Government in the saddle." Faced with an impasse and the secretary's shifting stands, Wilson ended the meeting without a decision and said he would think the matter over.[13]

Again he leaned on his most valued adviser on economic issues—Brandeis. The president had asked the Boston attorney to come to the White House on June 11 and thrash out the issues with him. As he had done earlier, Brandeis afterward wrote a memorandum that summarized their discussion and reiterated his advice. He urged balancing speed with "full and free discussion" and assurance that "limiting the power of the money trust" would make money available to businesses throughout the country. He also warned, "The conflict between the policies of the Administration and the desires of the financiers and of big business, is an irreconcilable one. Concessions to big business interests must in the end prove futile." As earlier, Brandeis appears to have been pushing Wilson down a path he already wanted to take. The president insisted to reporters that he had not decided on specifics but added, "About the main lines, I have had a considerable opinion."[14] Although he did not say so, the opinion was that bankers should not be on the central board of the new system.

On June 18, Wilson summoned Glass, Owen, and McAdoo back to the White House and told them that he wanted the board to be an exclusively governmental agency, with money issued by the regional banks to be backed as a government obligation. Two days later, he met with the Democrats on the House Banking Committee and made it clear to them that he was committed to passing a banking bill that contained those provisions. On June 23, he underlined his commitment to publicly controlled banking reform by going to the Capitol to deliver his second address to a joint session of Congress. Following the model of his tariff speech, Wilson kept his message brief and general and again struck notes that appealed to different sides in the debate. "We are about to set them [businessmen] free," he proclaimed but hastened to add, "It is not enough to strike the shackles from business." Government had a strong role to play in preventing "the concentration anywhere in a few hands of the monetary resources of the country," and it must control the new reserve system.[15]

Banking interests and conservative newspapers mounted furious attacks, with the New York *Sun* complaining that the proposal "is covered all over with the slime of Bryanism." Wilson made a gesture toward the financial community by meeting with representatives of the American Bankers' Association at the White House on June 25, joined by Glass, Owen, and McAdoo. When the bankers pushed for official representation on the new system's central board, Wilson asked them, "Which of you gentlemen thinks that railroads should select members of the Interstate Commerce Commission?" He did make one concession—the establishment of an advisory council chosen by the regional banks. The next day, Glass and Owen introduced the revised plan, called the Federal Reserve, in their respective chambers.[16]

The next attack came from the opposite flank. In the House, a band of southern and western agrarian Democrats bridled at what they saw as a sellout to the "money trust." They correctly grasped that the one element of private control in the plan—the role of bankers in the regional reserve banks—meant giving those bankers the power to create currency and manipulate credit. These agrarians called instead for further investigation of the "money trust" and extension of credit to farmers by allowing them to borrow against their crops. That scheme, known as rural credits, harked back to an idea of the Populists in the 1890s. Late in July, agrarians on the House Banking Committee offered amendments to the Federal Reserve bill that would expand the board to include representatives of agriculture and "industrial labor" and make $700 million available for loans to farmers. Wilson, who privately sympathized with the idea of rural credits, met with some of the agrarians and appeased them with promises to strengthen the next item on his legislative agenda: anti-trust legislation. This attack from the left did not bother him unduly, and he thought the trouble would disappear when the bill cleared the committees in which the troublemakers were ensconced. Then, he told Ellen, "I believe we shall have comparatively plain sailing."[17]

That prediction proved premature. After more meetings and some cajoling by the president, the Banking Committee rejected the agrarians' amendments and approved the bill on August 5. The Democratic caucus followed suit three weeks later, but only after concessions from the White

House on agricultural lending and a threatened agrarian revolt. It took intervention by Bryan to quell that revolt. In a public letter on August 22, he reiterated the president's promise of strong anti-trust legislation and implored his friends in the House to stand by the president. In the meantime, bankers redoubled their opposition. The American Bankers' Association met in late August and endorsed a set of counterproposals that amounted to a rejection of public control and reaffirmation of Aldrich-Vreeland. Their stand seemed to bear out Brandeis's judgment that their differences with the Wilson administration were "irreconcilable." Floor debate began in the House after Labor Day, and on September 18 representatives passed the Federal Reserve bill by the overwhelming margin of 285 to 85. Only three Democrats—southern agrarians—defected, while twenty-three Republicans, mostly insurgents, and ten Progressives voted in favor. It was a great victory for Wilson, but it had taken a long, hot summer of wrangling, coddling, arm-twisting, lobbying, and threatening to get this far.[18]

And it was only half the battle. Ahead loomed the Senate. Wilson tried again to put an optimistic face on the situation. He told Ellen that there would be "no insuperable difficulty in handling the situation, so far as I can see." The president's distance vision was defective. His party had a much smaller majority in the Senate, and three first-term Democrats on the Banking Committee were joining Republicans in dragging out hearings on the Federal Reserve plan. Each of them—Gilbert Hitchcock of Nebraska, James O'Gorman of New York, and James Reed of Missouri—had his own political and personal reasons for making trouble, and their openly flouted obstructionism strained Wilson's prized self-control. At the end of September, he told Mary Hulbert of his concern that a "man of my temperament and my limitations . . . may lose his patience and suffer the weakness of exasperation. It is against these that I have constantly to guard myself."[19]

Guard himself he did—barely. He made noises about denouncing the banking lobby, as he had done earlier with the tariff lobby, and he reportedly asked the Senate Democratic caucus to discipline Hitchcock, O'Gorman, and Reed. Eventually, however, he took a softer approach. On October 16, he invited the three recalcitrant senators to the White House and turned on his charm and persuasiveness. The overture seemed to work: newspapers reported that the senators had a pleasant meeting and remained open to changes in the banking bill. The president affirmed the newfound good feelings on October 20 in a public letter to Underwood: "I have met and had conferences with members of Senate Committee on Banking and Currency, both Democrats and Republicans. As a result of those conferences, I feel confident that a report on the bill may be expected not later than the first week in November. . . . The passage of the bill is assured."[20]

What happened next must have put Wilson in mind of the woes of Job. On October 23—at the request of the three dissident Democrats and one Republican on the Banking Committee—Frank A. Vanderlip, president of the National City Bank of New York, appeared before the committee to present a last-ditch alternative to the Federal Reserve plan: the "Vanderlip plan" would set up a Federal Reserve bank with twelve branches, all under the control of the government. The plan immediately attracted support from some progressives, who warmed to the government-control feature, and conservatives, who still wanted a central bank. Wilson bristled at the move. Vanderlip claimed to be working along the same lines as Wilson and requested a meeting so that he and two of his colleagues could explain the plan. The president shot back, "I am at a loss to understand how you have come to think of the plan which you presented to the Senate Committee on Banking and Currency yesterday as 'being along the lines of my own thought.' It is so far from being along the lines of my thought in this matter that it would be quite useless for me to discuss it with you." Wilson also summoned Senate Democratic leaders to a meeting at the White House, at which he warned them that he would not accept any plan dictated by bankers.[21]

He and his loyalists hung tough. After more haggling, the Banking Committee reported on two measures. One was the House-approved Federal Reserve bill, supported by Democrats, including O'Gorman and Reed; the other was a modified version of the Vanderlip plan, backed by the Republicans and Hitchcock. Floor debate in the Senate opened on December 2 and featured mainly conservative Republican attacks on the Federal Reserve as disguised "Bryanism." Their arguments evidently made an impact, because the Democratic caucus bowed to Republican preferences by increasing the level of gold reserves in the new system. That was the only modification adopted. On December 19, the Senate narrowly beat back the modified Vanderlip plan, 44 to 41; only Hitchcock joined the Republicans in voting for this alternative. The Senate then passed the Federal Reserve bill by a vote of 54 to 34. Every Democrat, including Hitchcock, supported it, as did six Republicans and the lone Progressive. A conference committee quickly ironed out differences, and the two houses approved the final version on December 22 and 23.[22]

Just hours after the final vote, the president staged another White House ceremony. This time, Ellen would be present, along with other family members, cabinet officers, congressional Democrats, and reporters. All watched as Wilson signed the Federal Reserve Act into law and presented gold pens—to Glass, Owen, and McAdoo. He praised the two legislators, along with their committee members, and he thanked the Republicans who supported the bill. "All great measures under our system are of necessity party measures," he noted, ". . . but this cannot be called a partisan measure." Nor would this measure benefit one class at the expense of any other but was simply finishing "a work which I think will be of lasting benefit to the business of the country."[23]

Wilson toned down the note of triumph because a sigh of relief was more fitting. Creating the Federal Reserve had been a longer, harder-fought, more complicated struggle than lowering the tariff. Downplaying partisanship was gracious, although Wilson had again worked almost exclusively with Democrats. Eschewing class politics was wise, and it served his larger ideological purposes of setting a new tone for his party. Yet he could have been pardoned if he had chosen to crow. This was the greatest legislative triumph of Wilson's presidency, and it showed his style of leadership at its best. He picked the destination and stayed on course. He avoided details and showed flexibility and patience.

Wilson also did something no president had ever done before: he kept Congress on the job without a break. Before then, senators and representatives had rarely spent more than half the year in the capital. Even during the Civil War, Lincoln had not kept them at work continuously. Moreover, in those days before air-conditioning, Washington's hot, humid summers made long sessions an ordeal on Capitol Hill. Wilson stayed in town, too, except for brief trips to visit his family, and shared in the discomfort. In fact, he would keep the senators and representatives on the job for another nine months, until the fall of 1914. This Congress would stay at work longer than any other in American history.[24] Small wonder the political cartoonists often drew Wilson as a schoolmaster keeping his charges chained to their desks.

The Federal Reserve Act brought off the feat of having something in it for everybody. Three of the four contending approaches found fulfillment under the new system. Public control prevailed, though not totally, while centralization and decentralization each found a place. The Federal Reserve would be a government agency with a chairman and board of governors appointed by the president. This was not, however, the awesome institution that later became "the Fed," with chairmen who mixed the roles of Delphic oracle and economics czar. That development would begin in another twenty years, as a result of reforms under the New Deal. Ironically, those reforms would make the Federal Reserve look more like the Vanderlip plan. Greater power in the original system resided, as most observers recognized at the time, in the regional banks. These, too, were government agencies, with boards appointed by the president, but the board members would be mostly bankers, and their assets would be the deposits of member banks. As Glass recognized, his approach lost little substance in the give-and-take of June 1913. Even the apparent losers in this fight—advocates of a privately controlled central bank—came out well: financial necessity dictated that one of the regional banks be located in New York, on Wall Street.[25]

Choosing the locations of the regional banks brought some ironic twists. The Federal Reserve Act divided the country into twelve districts, whose boundaries demarcated distinct economic regions. Locations were picked to ensure that anyone in a district could travel to its bank by overnight train. For the states and cities chosen, the banks were rich political plums, better than federal courthouses, almost as good as big customhouses. Some cities were inescapable choices, such as New York, although that particular choice rewarded the obstreperous Senator O'Gorman. One selection may have been at least partly political: the bank for the district covering the northern part of the Great Plains, which could have been located in either Omaha or Kansas City. Unfortunately for Omaha, that city was Senator Hitchcock's hometown. Instead, the bank went to Kansas City, which was Senator Reed's adopted hometown, thereby making Missouri the only state to have two Federal Reserve banks (the other one being in St. Louis). Ironically, Hitchcock would later metamorphose into an administration supporter, whereas Reed, after gripping the president's coattails when he ran for reelection in 1916, would become one of Wilson's bitterest enemies. Even the greatest political triumph can have surprising sequels.

One last major issue remained on Wilson's legislative agenda—an antitrust solution. By 1913, this issue had acquired even more "expediency" than banking reform. The previous year, all three major presidential contenders had argued that something had to be done about the huge concentrations of economic power in private hands, but careful analysis revealed sharp disagreements about what approach to take. Roosevelt's diagnosis of the problem as "conduct, not size" and the solution of government oversight and regulation had attracted scant support, even among his Progressive followers, but it did plant the seed of a regulatory, rather than a legal, approach. Taft and Wilson had favored a legal approach, but not the same one. Taft had maintained that vigorous enforcement of the existing anti-trust law, the Sherman Act, would do the job, an approach that had attracted little support even among Republicans; many conservatives disliked the anti-trust law, and insurgents were so alienated that they gave him little credit for effective action despite his success in dissolving such monopolies as Standard Oil and American Tobacco. Wilson had reaped the greatest political profit by attacking the Sherman Act as inadequate, thereby appealing to widespread convictions that the anti-trust laws needed to be strengthened. Now that he was president, he needed to come up with such a law and, presumably, a better approach to the trust problem.[26]

At first, Wilson seemed hesitant about how to proceed. He vetoed an effort by Attorney General McReynolds to use the new income tax as a tool to punish the "tobacco trust" and other firms convicted under the Sherman Act. Yet he backed moves by McReynolds against American Telephone and Telegraph, United States Steel, and the New Haven Railroad, a Morgan holding. The president did not speak out on the anti-trust issue until the end of 1913, but his praise of tariff revision for unleashing enterprise and of banking reform for attacking the "money trust," as well as his promises to congressional Democrats of a strong anti-trust law, showed that his ardor for the New Freedom had not cooled. Wilson's hesitancy seems to have sprung from the process of learning his way, from his not wanting to overload the legislative agenda, and from his feeling distracted by other matters, particularly Mexico. After Congress passed the banking bill, he predicted "many another struggle until the middle of next summer" over the anti-trust problem. In November, when the Federal Reserve bill appeared to be breaking free in the Senate, Wilson turned to this question. After conferring with congressional leaders, he affirmed in his first State of the Union address, on December 2, "I think that all thoughtful observers will agree that the immediate service we owe the business communities of the country is to prevent private monopoly more effectually than it has yet been prevented."[27] He called for new legislation to supplement and clarify the Sherman Act but said the subject was so complicated that it required a separate address to Congress.

With the trust problem, as with banking reform, Wilson faced a variety of proposed solutions and a plethora of conflicting advice. In the Senate, La Follette offered a bill, drafted with Brandeis's help, that called for broad revisions in the anti-trust law; other bills in both houses called for prison terms for persons convicted of violating the Sherman Act, strict control of railroad stock, and regulation of financial markets. At the same time, Secretary of Commerce William Redfield was urging the president to soft-pedal the anti-trust issue and reassure a nervous business community, and Colonel House was dropping similar hints. Wilson confronted the situation in typical fashion. He thought the issue over by himself during the two-week vacation that he and Ellen took in the Gulf Coast city of Pass Christian, Mississippi, after Christmas. This time, he did not confer with Brandeis directly, but he was receiving advance copies of the lawyer's series of articles on "Breaking the Money Trust," which were appearing in *Harper's Weekly*. When he returned to the White House, on January 13, 1914, Wilson was ready to move.

While he was away, he had written the speech he had promised to Congress. He read a draft to the cabinet as soon as he got back to Washington and met with members of the Commerce Committees of the two houses to discuss legislative plans. On January 20, he went before a joint session to speak about the anti-trust issue. His opening was pure Burke: "Legislation is a business of interpretation, not of origination; and it is now plain what the opinion is to which we must give effect in this matter. It is not recent or hasty opinion. It springs out of the experience of a whole generation." Into this vision of "expediency," he mixed reassurance toward business. "The antagonism between business and government is over," he announced, but he also favored a long-sought goal of Bryanite Democrats and insurgent Republicans, the prohibition of interlocking directorates. He likewise backed another of their schemes: empowering the Interstate Commerce Commission to oversee railroad finances, and he endorsed an idea previously favored mainly by Progressives: an interstate trade commission. He hedged by saying that such a commission would be used "only as an indispensable instrument of information and publicity," but he also affirmed, "Other questions remain, which will need very thoughtful and practical treatment."[28]

That last bit of ambiguity gave him the flexibility he wanted, and he would need all he could muster. For one thing, he would be grappling not just with other people's divergent ideas but also with his own. He would also face even more challenging legislative hurdles with this issue than he had with the previous two New Freedom measures. Those measures had needed only to go through single committees in each chamber—Ways and Means in the House and Finance in the Senate for the tariff and the income tax, Banking in both the House and the Senate for the Federal Reserve—and congressional Democratic leaders had shrewdly folded the income tax into the tariff bill. None of those advantages obtained with anti-trust measures. Proposals for a new law to supplement the Sherman Act would go before the Judiciary Committee in each chamber, whereas trade commission bills would go before the respective Commerce Committees. Finally, other issues and interests were intruding on the picture. In particular, some Democrats and insurgent Republicans wanted to take Wilson up on the issue of strengthening the Interstate Commerce Commission's oversight of railroads, while labor unions were clambering for Congress to lift restrictions that courts had placed on them under the Sherman Act.[29]

At first, Wilson again deferred to the men on Capitol Hill. The House Judiciary Committee, chaired by Henry D. Clayton of Alabama, drew up a bill that made officers and directors of companies subject to criminal prosecution for violating anti-trust laws, but the main thrust of the bill lay in its definition of unfair trade practices, such as predatory pricing, the acquisition of stock to reduce competition, and the creation of interlocking directorates among large firms doing business with one another. The press immediately dubbed the committee's measure, which was introduced on the House floor on April 14, the Clayton bill. Its legalistic approach enjoyed broad support among Bryanite Democrats and insurgent Republicans. The previous twenty years of prosecutions under the Sherman Anti-Trust Act had elicited disappointment, frustration, and fury among their agrarian and small-business constituencies. Much of the problem, as they saw it, stemmed from the brevity and vagueness of the law, which practically invited the courts to define what prohibited "combinations in restraint of trade" really were. The Supreme Court had handed down a string of decisions that gave great latitude to businesses, and in its *Standard Oil* ruling in 1911 the Court had promulgated a "rule of reason" that made explicit what had been plainly implicit—namely, that the justices arrogated to themselves near-total discretion in applying the anti-trust law. It was understandable, therefore, that Democrats and insurgents demanded that such judicial discretion be curbed with new, sharply defined anti-trust laws.

Still, the Clayton bill drew a lot of fire. Business groups predictably denounced it as dangerous and hostile, and they pointed to the severe recession that had started at the end of 1913 as proof that measures adopted and proposed by Wilson and the Democrats were ruining the economy. Such charges left Wilson unmoved, and he refused to rein in reform efforts and send Congress home. Attacks also came from anti-trusters who wanted to see more practices prohibited and stiffer penalties imposed, and from Democrats who pushed for an expanded role for the Interstate Commerce Commission in the financing of railroads and the regulation of stock exchanges. In this atmosphere, and with prodding from Wilson, the House Democratic caucus voted on May 12 to bind members to the Clayton bill. After perfunctory debate, the House passed the bill on June 5, by a vote of 275 to 54. Every Democrat but one supported it, joined by forty-one Republicans and fifteen Progressives.[30]

By the time the House passed the Clayton bill, the focus of attention and the argument had shifted. Most of the floor debate concerned not trade practices but labor unions. Starting with the 1894 conviction of Eugene Debs and his American Railway Union for "combination in restraint of trade," which was upheld by the Supreme Court, unions had suffered under a succession of decisions that imposed restrictions on their activities. Exemption from anti-trust laws had been the top legislative goal of the American Federation of Labor for more than a decade, and many Democrats were anxious to grant the AFL its wish. Bryan had courted union support ever since his first run for president in 1896. By his third run, in 1908, his appeal had grown so strong that Samuel Gompers, the resolutely nonpartisan head of the AFL, could not stop his organization from endorsing the Democratic nominee. Wilson had likewise wooed labor in 1912 and had won a big share of the union vote. In response, Gompers and other labor leaders put pressure on him and congressional Democrats to grant them their coveted immunity under the anti-trust laws.

Since the beginning of 1914, the AFL had engaged in such intense lobbying that some House Democrats were afraid the bill might not pass without labor's approval. Wilson, however, did not satisfy labor's demands immediately or fully. He personally sympathized with workers, and in 1913 he had privately deplored employers' brutal actions against striking miners in West Virginia and Colorado. He also supported laws to protect merchant seamen and had intervened with senators to urge that they move legislation on that matter. Then, when the Clayton bill went to the House floor in April 1914, he confronted the unions' demands for an anti-trust exemption. The president met with members of the Judiciary Committee on April 13 and agreed to conciliate labor, but it was unclear what he would do. He reportedly agreed to provisions requiring jury trials in criminal contempt cases and narrowing the scope of court injunctions in labor disputes, together with language stating that labor unions and farm organizations did not constitute conspiracies in restraint of trade. He also decided to oppose further concessions, evidently because he took umbrage at the AFL's heavy-handed tactics and doubted the legal wisdom and constitutionality of full exemption.[31]

Wilson's halfway house between anti-trust prosecutions of unions and full exemption shaped the final provisions of what became the Clayton Anti-Trust Act. Union and farm-organization leaders renewed their lobbying efforts, but to little avail. The only noteworthy change made in the Senate came when a Republican insurgent, Albert Cummins of Iowa, got a sentence added to the section affirming the legality of farm and labor organizations, which read, "The labor of a human being is not an article of commerce." In all, organized labor got no more in the final bill than such verbal reassurance and the jury-trial and injunction-limiting provisions. Nevertheless, Samuel Gompers put a bright face on the outcome. In July, he saluted the Clayton bill as labor's "Magna Carta," and in October he effusively thanked Wilson for sending him one of the pens used in signing the Clayton Act, "the labor provisions of which are indeed a magnificent piece of legislation, according to the working people of our country the rational, constitutional and inherent rights of which they have too long been denied."[32] Gompers was engaging in flummery to make the best of half a loaf, but the moment had great significance. These provisions of the Clayton Anti-Trust Act marked a milestone in the continuing courtship of organized labor and the Democratic Party.

In contrast to its earlier conduct in dealing with the tariff revision and the Federal Reserve, the Senate now did not linger long over the anti-trust measure. Conservatives on the Judiciary Committee struck out the criminal penalties in the Clayton bill and watered down other sections with qualifying language. On the floor, a group of southern and western "radicals," led by the irascible James Reed, tried to restore those penalties and add draconian provisions outlawing holding companies and limiting the size of businesses. They did not succeed. On September 2, the Senate passed the Judiciary Committee's version by a vote of 46 to 16. A conference committee labored for three weeks to reconcile the two chambers' bills and generally adopted the Senate version. On October 5, the Senate passed the final bill by a vote of 35 to 24. The House concurred three days later by a vote of 244 to 54. By then, the anti-trust bill had become a legislative orphan. It came to be known as the Clayton Act even though its namesake had left Congress to become a federal judge before the House passed the bill. Wilson did not involve himself in the Senate's debate and action, and this time he invited no one to the White House and held no public ceremony when he signed the anti-trust bill into law on October 15, 1914.[33]

The president had reasons—tragic reasons—for not involving himself in those last debates and votes. They ranged from the global—the outbreak of the world war in Europe in August 1914—to the personal—the death of Ellen at the same time. But even before those devastating events, other matters had diverted him from the anti-trust measure. By the time the House passed the Clayton bill in June, the focus of attention had shifted to a trade commission bill. In his speech to Congress in January, Wilson had left the door open to two kinds of agencies. One would be a purely investigatory body, such as the Interstate Commerce Commission had been before gaining rate-making powers under Roosevelt. The other would be something like the more recent ICC, a regulatory agency empowered to initiate actions, make rules, and enforce orders. The investigatory body appealed to more conservative Democrats and to Attorney General McReynolds, who did not want another agency infringing on his department's anti-trust prosecutions.

In March, the House Commerce Committee produced a measure called the Covington bill, after Representative James Covington of Maryland, which would create a trade commission authorized only to investigate conduct by businesses and recommend procedures to them for complying with existing laws. Meanwhile, the regulatory agency, though associated with Roosevelt, was gaining support among people who deplored his approval of bigness in business, most notably Brandeis. A protégé of Brandeis's, George Rublee, drafted a measure for introduction by another Democrat on the Commerce Committee, Raymond Stevens of New Hampshire, which would add provisions to the committee bill, giving the commission enforcement powers.[34]

Wilson initially leaned toward the investigatory body, but in April he received a letter that may have helped to change his mind. It came from Norman Hapgood, a well-known progressive journalist who was friendly with both him and Brandeis, who commended Rublee as "one of the best minds for this kind of thinking." Hapgood told the president that "a half hour spent with Mr. Rublee would not seem to you wasted." Rublee would later fancy himself the father of what became the Federal Trade Commission because he believed that when they met, he converted Wilson to his concept of the regulatory agency. In fact, as with Brandeis's influence at the outset of the 1912 campaign, this was a case of helping Wilson down a path he already meant to follow.[35]

Wilson had decided to back the regulatory agency before he met Rublee, and he had another reason for the switch, besides the attractiveness of the idea and the Brandeis connection: political calculation. On June 2, he told a Democratic senator, Henry Hollis of New Hampshire, that he and his colleagues could not hesitate and hold back because Progressives were going to attack them on anti-trust regulation, "as Mr. Roosevelt has kindly apprised us." Brandeis and his associates seemed to him to have come up with "a better way of dealing" with regulation: "The rest of it seems to me rather plain sailing." The remark about Roosevelt referred to the ex-president's opening salvos in the campaign for the congressional elections in November 1914. Wilson's great rival was once more charging him and his party with making halfhearted, ineffective stabs at solving major problems, while the sharpest criticisms of the Covington bill in the House were coming from the leader of the tiny band of Progressives, Victor Murdock of Kansas. By backing the regulatory agency, Wilson could kill several birds with one well-aimed stone. In the upcoming campaign, he could blunt attacks by Roosevelt and the Progressives. In Congress, he could reach across party lines and gain support from Progressives and insurgent Republicans such as La Follette. In the longer run, he might induce Progressives and insurgents to support him in 1916.[36]

On June 10, Wilson called to the White House Hollis, Stevens, Brandeis, and Rublee, whom he was meeting for the first time. Rublee presented the main argument, and Brandeis backed him up. By the end of the meeting, Rublee recalled, "it was clear to all of us that the president had accepted the idea. He seemed much interested and quite worked up." Brandeis went immediately to the Capitol and talked with members of the Senate Commerce Committee, most of whom, Democrats and Republicans alike, favored a strong agency, and they quickly approved their version of the Stevens bill, now called the Federal Trade Commission bill, on June 13. Then the troubles started. When floor debate began in July, a motley collection of Republican conservatives and insurgents and Bryanite Democrats mounted a fierce attack, concentrating their fire on the section of the bill that empowered the commission to identify and move against unfair trade practices, and they tried to attach amendments that imposed narrow definitions of such practices and restricted action against them. The bill's supporters wavered but stood their ground. Wilson wrote the chairman of the Commerce Committee to demand "elasticity without any real indefiniteness, so that we may adjust our regulation to actual conditions."[37] Presidential firmness carried the day. On September 2, the Senate passed the Federal Trade Commission bill, 46 to 16. All Democrats present voted in favor, as did seven insurgent Republicans and the sole Progressive.

Wilson exerted similar pressure in the House to get the measure approved. On August 5—the day before Ellen died—he wrote to the chairman of the Commerce Committee to argue for retaining the enforcement section: "It seems to me a feasible and very wise means of accomplishing the things that it seems impossible in the complicated circumstances of business to accomplish by any attempted definition." It thereby admirably advanced "the effort to regulate competition without making terms with monopoly." The president's view prevailed, although the House passed an amendment that broadened court review of commission rulings. The conference committee largely followed the House version. On September 8, the Senate passed the conference bill, 43 to 5, with all Democrats present again in favor. Two days later, the House concurred in a voice vote. Wilson quietly signed the bill into law on September 26.[38]

Together, the Clayton Anti-Trust Act and the Federal Trade Commission Act comprised Wilson's anti-trust program. By mid-October, the president could muster enough emotional resilience to say something publicly about those acts for use in the campaign for the congressional elections that was then under way. Thanks to the FTC, he maintained, unfair methods of competition could not be used to build up monopolies. Thanks to the Clayton Act, interlocking directorates could not sustain monopolies. Democrats had remained true to their cardinal principle: "that we should have no dealings with monopoly, but reject it altogether, while our opponents were ready to adopt it into the realm of law and seek merely to regulate it and moderate it in its operation. It is our purpose to destroy monopoly and maintain competition as the only efficient instrument of business liberty." Wilson likewise lauded the Clayton Act for doing justice to the worker: "His labor is no longer to be treated as if it were merely an inanimate object of commerce to be dealt with as an object of sale and barter."[39]

Fine words exalted legislation that fell short of its stated goals. The labor provisions helped unions less than either the president and his party or the AFL pretended. The insistence of the House on broader court review of FTC rulings would significantly weaken the agency's powers, and a series of questionable early appointments would further hobble its effectiveness. The FTC would not emerge as a truly strong regulatory body with an anti-trust thrust until the 1930s. Then, under the next Democratic president, new legislation would strengthen its powers, and stronger commissioners would come on board.[40]

Those shortcomings in the labor provisions of the Clayton Act and in the functioning of the FTC have led some interpreters to agree with Roosevelt. Wilson really was, they have claimed, a halfhearted progressive who still harbored a conservative's distaste for "class legislation" and preference for limited government. Such claims are wrong. Twenty-three years later, that next Democratic president would likewise be loath to give organized labor everything it demanded and would pronounce on big business and big labor "a plague on both your houses!" The first Roosevelt similarly disappointed ardent advocates of regulation when he had agreed to broader court review of rate setting by the ICC. Fatigue and emotional strain almost certainly affected Wilson's acquiescence in comparable court review of FTC rulings. Such personal factors probably also played a part in his early choices for the commission, although he often showed weakness in making first-rate appointments. At all events, the FTC was a brand-new agency venturing into uncharted waters. It could not help getting off to what its historian has called "a rocky start," and it would take time to find its way no matter who was at its helm.[41]

There has been a further twist to the view of Wilson as a reluctant, halfhearted progressive. That is the claim that his seemingly on-again, off-again espousal of the FTC showed that he was fitfully moving away from the less statist, more legalistic stance embodied in the New Freedom and toward eventual espousal of Roosevelt's New Nationalism. One usually incisive observer at the time thought so. In his new magazine, *The New Republic*, Herbert Croly, Roosevelt's chief intellectual adviser, declared, "In this Trade Commission act is contained the possibility of a radical reversal of many American notions about trusts, legislative power, and legal procedure. . . . It seems to contradict every principle of the party which enacted it." Croly and the interpreters who have followed him misread the political situation and Wilson's thinking. He might have been courting Progressive support in Congress and votes in the future, but an agency and an approach favored by Brandeis in no way endorsed the vision of collective bigness in Roosevelt's New Nationalism. As for Wilson himself, approval of strong, activist, centralized government, coupled with rejection of formalism and legalism in favor of organicism and administrative adaptation, had been a hallmark of his thought long before he entered politics. The historian of the FTC has characterized the president's changing attitude in 1914 as "expedient and ambivalent, but not unprincipled." Wilson might not have liked being called ambivalent, but otherwise he would have cheerfully accepted that judgment.[42]

Curiously, the neglected stepchild of the New Freedom anti-trust program, the Clayton Act, would have greater lasting impact. Anti-trust prosecutions would wax and wane after 1914. The need for cooperation between government and business during World War I would dampen the Wilson administration's anti-trust ardor. In the 1920s, pro-business Republican administrations would pursue few prosecutions under either the Sherman Act or the Clayton Act. With the Democrats' resurgence in the '30s, however, the two acts would take on new life as a disciplinary tool, much as the FTC was originally intended to be. Thereafter, even Republican administrations would find this act and its predecessor useful measures of public policy. Here was another surprising sequel to something that at the time looked like less of a legislative triumph than its more glamorous companion.

With the passage of the Clayton Act and the creation of the FTC, Wilson's initial legislative program was complete. The Sixty-third Congress could finally adjourn in October 1914, having met continuously for nearly eighteen months. This Congress had done more than set an endurance record. It had enacted a set of laws that would profoundly change American life. The men in the two chambers took great credit for these feats, but they knew they would have done far less without creative, wise, and indefatigable leadership from the White House. The hero of the hour was Wilson. He had not done everything right, even by his own lights, and he had not satisfied everyone who was presumably on his side. Nor had the world stopped while he and his legislative cohorts were going about their business. Everything they did occurred within a larger context that was already casting lights and shadows on their deeds. Yet when all was said and done, Wilson had emerged triumphant. He had set the course, taken the flood tide of progressivism, and reached the desired destination. It would be both ironic and tragic that he would have scant occasion to savor what he had wrought.

TRIUMPH AND TRAGEDY

When Woodrow Wilson talked about his "single-track mind," he was really describing his preferred method of working. If he could have had his way, he would have taken time to think in advance, prepare to deal with either one task or a related set of tasks, and stick to his game plan. As president, he came closest to working that way during the first year and a half, when he concentrated on the New Freedom legislative program. Seldom again would he enjoy the luxury of focusing so much on tasks of his own choosing. Even during those months, other matters constantly intruded. The biggest unsought distraction came from south of the border, where Mexico was melting into civil war. Other affairs in that region, such as turmoil in the Caribbean and Central America, made further claims on his attention. He also chose to take up some foreign policy matters, such as relations with Britain and thoughts about regional order and security in the Americas, and he began to speak about larger diplomatic designs. Domestic issues likewise demanded attention, often unpleasantly, as in the case of agitation over racial equality and woman suffrage. Finally, family life occupied his mind and his heart, at first happily and then tragically.

The new president showed some of his best and worst traits as a leader when he dealt with Mexico. Displaying both elementary prudence and his scholarly background, Wilson tried to get as much information and sound interpretation as he could. This was no easy task. There was clashing advice from the outset. From Mexico City, Ambassador Henry Lane Wilson and the American business community demanded recognition of the Huerta regime as the only way to restore order and protect American lives and property. Similar messages, more gently phrased, came from European governments, which had hastened to recognize Huerta. In April, when the president first brought up Mexico at a cabinet meeting, Josephus Daniels recorded in his diary that Secretary of War Garrison maintained that "it was doubtful whether the Mexicans could ever organize a government," but it might be "well to recognize a brute like Huerta so as to have some form of government which could be recognized and dealt with." Garrison added that lots of people on both sides of the border wanted America to intervene, but Secretary of the Interior Lane doubted "there were 500 people in Mexico who wished intervention."[1]

As Lane's retort indicated, there were equally strong views on the opposite side. Not even advocates of recognition found much good to say about Huerta, and in the opinion of most members of the cabinet, Daniels recorded, "the chief cause of this whole situation was a contest between English and American Oil Companies to see which would control."[2] Bryan opposed doing much to defend American property in Mexico, and he tried to squelch thoughts of intervention. Postmaster General Burleson, who was from Texas, believed that anti-Huerta forces in northern Mexico might welcome intervention, but he strongly opposed the idea. Besides airing conflicting views, that cabinet meeting showed how the subject of intervention was inexorably intruding on the discussion of Mexico.

Wilson contented himself at first with listening. Early in May, Colonel House suggested that a military move into Mexico would not be costly and urged the president to deal with Huerta. Soon afterward, at the behest of Cleveland Dodge, he met with a lawyer who represented mining and railroad interests in Mexico, Delbert Haff, who recapitulated his analysis and recommendations in a long memorandum. Haff called American intervention "a national calamity . . . to be avoided by the greatest care and by all honorable means," and he observed that Mexicans hated Americans because of history and "the natural antipathy between the Latin and the Anglo-Saxon." Anti-Huerta sentiment was widespread, but the organized opponents in the north, who called themselves Constitutionalists, were not strong. Predictably, Haff advocated protecting American investments and recommended offering recognition if Huerta promised to hold early elections, but Haff did not recommend demanding his resignation, because the real danger lay in disorder and anarchy.[3]

Those arguments swayed the president enough to draft a shorthand note incorporating this offer, presumably to be sent to Ambassador Wilson in Mexico City. Meanwhile, others who represented business interests were lobbying the State Department to mediate among the contending Mexican factions. That idea appealed to Bryan's peacemaking inclination and determination to avoid intervention. Wilson hesitated to pursue either course, presumably because he still did not think he had a firm grasp of the situation. Adding to the uncertainty was growing distrust of the ambassador. Starting in March, the New York *World* mounted a campaign against Henry Lane Wilson, replete with charges of his complicity in the coup that had overthrown and murdered President Madero. Those charges, together with the ambassador's inflated estimates of Huerta's strength, eroded the president's and the secretary of state's faith in him as someone who could carry out their policies. At a press conference in May, Wilson asked, "Did you ever know a situation that had more question marks around it? . . . Nobody in the world has any certain information that I have yet found."[4]

He decided to send his own man to Mexico. His choice struck many as odd: the journalist William Bayard Hale, who had written laudatory articles about Wilson as governor for Walter Page's *World's Work* and more recently had cobbled together Wilson's campaign speeches in the book *The New Freedom*. Hale had never been to Mexico and did not speak Spanish, but he had the president's trust and enjoyed a reputation as a first-rate reporter. For the next three months, from early June to late August 1913, Hale sent lengthy, insightful dispatches from Mexico City. He characterized Huerta as "an ape-like old man" who was usually "[d]runk or half-drunk (he is never sober)" but also resourceful, gritty, and brave. Hale likewise confirmed the president's suspicions of Ambassador Wilson. Hale did not make contact with the Constitutionalists, but he did accurately describe their guerrilla warfare, which denied Huerta's forces control of the countryside, and he confirmed their dominance in the north and near Mexico City.[5]

The president's restraint and circumspection lasted through the summer and fall of 1913. Pressure to do something about the growing disorder mounted, and not all of it came from business interests. Thousands of Americans lived and worked in Mexico as clerks, teachers, nurses, plumbers, and builders, people whom Hale called "Americans of our own type and with our own sentiments and ideals."[6] But recognizing the Huerta regime did not appear to offer the only or best way to combat disorder and protect those Americans. Not just the moral cloud hanging over Huerta's seizure of power argued against recognition; so did his regime's weak hold on much of the country. Wilson needed to find an alternative and figure out how to pursue it.

At the end of July, he summoned the American ambassador home. When the two namesakes met at the White House on August 3, the president politely heard his visitor out and then dismissed him. The next day, he announced the appointment of a special envoy to meet with Huerta. As before with Hale, he made an unusual, perhaps dubious choice: John Lind, a former Democratic governor of Minnesota and a friend of Bryan's. Lind, too, spoke no Spanish and knew next to nothing about Mexico. In his letter of instruction to the former governor, Wilson sounded another Rooseveltian note when he said the United States did not "feel at liberty any longer to stand inactively by" in the face of disorder: the situation was not compatible with Mexico's international obligations, "civilized development . . . [and] the maintenance of tolerable political and economic conditions in Central America." Specifically, the envoy was to demand immediate cessation of fighting, early and free elections, and Huerta's departure.[7]

Lind's mission got nowhere. Huerta blustered, declaring that he would refuse to receive the envoy, but he and his foreign minister did have several meetings with Lind. The talks were unproductive, but this envoy also produced insightful reports on conditions, particularly an assessment of social and economic conflicts and the relative strength of contending factions. After two weeks, the foreign minister broke off the talks, and Lind left for home. With the collapse of the Lind mission, the president decided to go before Congress on August 27 to talk about conditions in Mexico. "Those conditions touch us very nearly," he affirmed. The right conditions in Mexico would mean "an enlargement of the field of self-government" and thus realize "the hopes and rights of a nation . . . so long suppressed and disappointed." Warning against impatience, he affirmed, "We can afford to exercise the self-restraint of a really great nation which realizes its own strength and scorns to misuse it." He predicted that civil strife in Mexico was likely to worsen and promised to protect citizens there. He also ruled out arms sales and pledged continued American efforts to help bring peace.[8]

This was Wilson's first foreign policy speech as president. In it, he sought to serve several ends. Politically, he wanted to drum up public and congressional support and fend off criticism. Diplomatically, he wanted to send signals to the Mexicans by eschewing intervention and arms sales—something the anti-Huerta forces desired—for now. In the longer run, he pointed toward a larger design to guide his administration's policies abroad. This speech contained the earliest expressions of themes that would come to be hallmarks of Wilsonian foreign policy. His tone was unmistakably idealistic, particularly the reference to the "field of self-government." His model for international conduct drew upon his philosophy of personal conduct—"the self-restraint of a really great nation"—combined with its justification—"realizes its own strength and scorns to misuse it." Those words and images reached back to his childhood and foreshadowed some of his striking future pronouncements. This speech marked his opening gambit in laying down the vision that would shape both his own policies and his party's posture toward international affairs.

Meanwhile, Mexico festered. "The apparent situation changes like quicksilver," Wilson told Ellen in September, "but the real situation, I fancy, remains the same, and is likely to yield to absent treatment." It would have turned out better for his peace of mind and historical reputation if he had continued to heed those counsels of self-restraint and "absent treatment." A presidential election was scheduled in Mexico for October 26, but earlier that month the leader of the Constitutionalists, Venustiano Carranza, refused to participate, and his forces briefly seemed on the verge of taking Mexico City. Huerta responded by dissolving the Mexican congress, arresting most of the members, and declaring himself dictator. Complicating matters, the newly arrived British ambassador, Sir Lionel Carden, presented his credentials to Huerta three days later and started making statements to the press in support of the regime. These moves infuriated Wilson. After stewing over the situation, he drafted a diplomatic note to be sent to all nations, asserting that the United States "is and must continue to be of paramount influence in the Western Hemisphere" and must act under the Monroe Doctrine "to assist in maintaining Mexico's independence of foreign financial power."[9] In the end, Wilson scrapped that note in favor of one to Mexico simply demanding Huerta's departure.

Wilson's comment about "foreign financial power" harked back to earlier claims in the cabinet about British oil interests in Mexico. Many, including the president, thought Carden was under the thumb of the oil magnate Lord Cowdray, whose company had extensive holdings in Mexico. Fortunately, amicable relations prevailed, thanks mainly to a visit to Washington in November by a high-ranking Foreign Office official, Sir William Tyrrell, who was filling in for the ailing British ambassador. Colonel House laid the groundwork for a meeting on November 13 at the White House, at which Wilson stressed his unshakable opposition to Huerta and affirmed his support for dropping discriminatory tolls to be levied when the Panama Canal opened, something the British were demanding. Thereafter, the Foreign Office reined in and soon replaced Carden, and Britain reverted to its established policy of deferring to the United States in the Western Hemisphere.[10]

With that complication removed, Wilson turned to finding a way to get rid of Huerta. In his State of the Union address to Congress on

December 2, 1913, he called Mexico the "one cloud upon our horizon" and avowed, "There can be no certain prospect of peace in America until General Huerta has surrendered his usurped authority." But he did not believe that the United States would be "obliged to alter our policy of watchful waiting." Privately, he seemed to hanker to do more than watch and wait. At the end of October, House noted that Wilson wanted to blockade Mexican ports and send troops into northern Mexico: "It is his purpose to send six battleships at once."[11] Wilson seems to have been venting frustration rather than setting policy. Yet such sentiments disclosed an interventionist streak in him, and these remarks eerily predicted much of what he would eventually do.

Still, steps short of intervention might bring Huerta down. The most promising seemed to be something Wilson had previously ruled out— selling arms to the Constitutionalists. Talks opened with Carranza during November in the Mexican border town of Nogales, Arizona, with Hale representing Wilson. The envoy found Carranza, who held the title first chief, impressive but difficult to deal with. Carranza demanded freedom to buy arms with no strings attached, and he adamantly rejected any kind of American intervention. The talks broke off acrimoniously, but Wilson decided at the end of January 1914 to recognize the Constitutionalists officially as belligerents opposed to Huerta, and on February 3 he lifted the arms embargo. This move did not produce the expected result. Huerta's forces held out, and Mexican conservatives continued to rally to their side. Meanwhile, dissension was mounting in the Constitutionalists' ranks. Carranza's chief deputy, the blustery, violence-prone Francisco "Pancho" Villa, was conspiring to overthrow the first chief, and each man seemed more interested in stalemating the other than in fighting Huerta. In these circumstances, Wilson came to believe that intervention was his only option.[12]

An excuse to go in presented itself on April 9. Mexican troops in the Huerta-controlled port of Tampico arrested some American sailors who had gone ashore. The Mexican general in charge quickly released the sailors and apologized, but Rear Admiral Henry T. Mayo, the commander of the naval squadron, stiffly demanded the raising of the Stars and Stripes, accompanied by a twenty-one-gun salute. The Mexicans understandably balked, and a tense situation ensued. The incident would have caused little commotion if Wilson had not decided to seize upon it. Months later, after Huerta finally fell, he stated off the record at a press conference that "a situation arose that made it necessary for the dignity of the United States that we should take some decisive step; and the main thing to accomplish was a vital thing. We got Huerta. That was the end of

Huerta. That was what I had in mind. It could not be done without taking Vera Cruz."[13]

The reference to "taking Vera Cruz" was to the military action that Wilson ordered. He was giving in to his interventionist urge because he saw an opportunity to shape events. The Constitutionalists were now bouncing back, and Lind, whom Wilson had again sent to Mexico, reported that cutting Huerta off from ports such as Veracruz would seal his doom. In an interview with a magazine journalist, the president claimed that a "new order, which will have its foundations on human liberty and human rights, shall prevail." On April 20, Wilson went to Capitol Hill to speak to Congress again about Mexico. After recounting what had happened at Tampico and on other occasions, he claimed that such incidents could "lead directly and inevitably to armed conflict." Dismissing Huerta as an illegitimate authority who controlled little of the country, he contended that action against him would not mean war against Mexico, and he asked Congress to approve the use of the armed forces.[14] That evening, the House voted overwhelmingly to authorize the president to enforce demands on Huerta, and Wilson closeted himself with the secretaries of war and the navy and their top officers to plan a naval blockade and possible landing at Veracruz. During the night, a report from that city reached the State Department with the news that a large shipment of arms for the Huerta forces would arrive the next day from Europe. Wilson authorized Secretary of the Navy Daniels to order landings at Veracruz to seize the customhouse and intercept the munitions.

Just before noon on April 21, marines and sailors went ashore and took over the customhouse without incident. Soon afterward, however, Mexican troops and naval cadets opened fire from surrounding buildings. The Mexicans brought in artillery to bombard the Americans, and a naval vessel offshore returned fire. The next morning, the main U.S. fleet, including five battleships, steamed into the harbor. Three thousand additional men landed during the morning and quickly gained control of Veracruz. The two days' fighting left 152 to 175 Mexicans dead and 195 to 250 wounded, with 17 Americans killed and 61 wounded. Outrage flared throughout Mexico. Huerta immediately broke off diplomatic relations, and Carranza likewise denounced "the invasion of our territory." It looked as if the only question now was whether the situation would lead to full-scale war. At a White House meeting on the evening of April 24, Garrison argued strongly for intervention and Bryan argued equally strongly against. The decision lay in the president's hands.[15]

He acted quickly. Someone at the press conference on April 23 recalled that Wilson looked "preternaturally pale, almost parchmenty...."

The death of American sailors and marines owing to an order of his seemed to affect him like an ailment. He was positively shaken." The president gave no hint of his intentions, except when a reporter asked whether he regarded his moves in Mexico "as in the nature of a private act"—meaning not an act of war—and he responded, "Yes, sir, so far as they have gone."[16] He had already decided that military action would go no further. He scrapped plans for the naval blockade and a possible military expedition against Mexico City. On April 25, he eagerly accepted an offer by the ambassadors of Argentina, Brazil, and Chile to mediate the affair. The "ABC" mediators convened a conference at Niagara Falls, New York, in May. Tortuous negotiations ensued—with Carranza refusing to participate—before a face-saving formula emerged in the form of a mutual withdrawal from Veracruz by Huerta and the American forces. Huerta resigned and went into exile in July, and a triumphant Carranza rode on horseback into Mexico City on August 20. It was a good outcome from Wilson's standpoint, but he would soon learn that his imbroglio in Mexico had not ended.

Why Wilson reversed himself so abruptly and completely has prompted various explanations. Some observers have agreed that the deaths of the servicemen woke him up to the gravity of what he had done, a view that has merit, up to a point. Then and later, sending young men to die in combat affected Wilson profoundly. After Veracruz, he would never again seem so cavalier and enthusiastic about military intervention. This marked the end of that part of the Rooseveltian tendency in his foreign policy thinking. But Veracruz did not convert Wilson to pacifism. Instead, he would cling to another part of his Rooseveltian tendency. He still believed that the United States, as one of the great powers, must take an activist, involved part in world politics, a part that included potential use of armed force. Hereafter, Wilson might be more chastened in his ardor for America to play such a role, but his basic thought did not change.

Other interpreters have maintained that near-universal condemnation of the Veracruz incursion at home and abroad forced Wilson to change course. Republicans such as Taft and Elihu Root were particularly scathing in their denunciations of the president and his secretary of state as a pair of bungling clowns, while peace and socialist groups condemned Wilson as an aggressor.[17] Wilson was as sensitive to public opinion as the next politician, but he did not retreat before a barrage of criticism: he had changed course before he had any chance to gauge reactions. His about-face stemmed, instead, from self-criticism. He knew he had blundered. He had expected Huerta's forces to crumble, and discounting strong evidence to the contrary, he had expected their opponents to welcome a decisive move to bring him down. His response to the Veracruz affair marked the beginning of a diplomatic self-education that would intensify in response to the world war.

From this time on, Wilson did not waver in his resolve to aid revolutionary and democratic forces in Mexico and keep American hands off if at all possible. In May, he had resisted appeals by Garrison to send more troops to Veracruz, and he had given an interview to the New York *World* in which he again condemned Huerta and his privileged backers and praised Emiliano Zapata and others for seeking economic justice. During the negotiations at Niagara Falls, despite Carranza's noncooperation, he had insisted on terms that would favor the Constitutionalists. In August, he told Garrison, "There are in my judgment no conceivable circumstances which would make it right for us to direct by force or by threat of force the internal processes of what is a profound revolution, a revolution as profound as that which occurred in France. All the world has been shocked ever since the time of that revolution in France that Europe should have undertaken to nullify what was done there, no matter what the excesses then committed."[18]

Coming from a self-proclaimed disciple of Edmund Burke, those were remarkable words. They did not mean Wilson had renounced his adherence to Burke's organic, anti-ideological approach to politics, but they did mean that what he called the "progressive Democrat" in him was shaping his views not only at home but abroad as well. Mexico was giving him and the world the first experience in dealing with revolutions among downtrodden peoples, with attendant mixtures of nationalism, radicalism, and violence. The experience would stand him in good stead when he confronted a more cataclysmic revolution of this kind in Russia.[19]

The same strengths, virtues, and defects that Wilson showed with Mexico marked the rest of his pre–world war diplomacy. Mexico did not eclipse attention to the rest of Latin America. Bryan in particular wanted to strike an idealistic note there that offered a shining contrast to previous Republican interventionism and "dollar diplomacy." In August 1913, he had talked to Wilson about America's being "a Good Samaritan" toward Central America and helping its nations. As proof of the administration's good intentions, Bryan negotiated with Colombia over the secession of Panama in 1903 and the alleged American part in the "revolution" that led to Panama's cession of the Canal Zone. After some haggling, a treaty emerged that included a $25 million indemnity to Colombia and a statement by the United States of "sincere regret" over past incidents. That statement infuriated Roosevelt, who had long felt touchy about his role in the Panama affair. The ex-president denounced this treaty as "a crime against the United States, an attack on the honor of the United States, which, if true, would convict the United States, of infamy." His friend Henry Cabot Lodge spearheaded opposition in the Senate, and together with fellow Republicans, he prevented the treaty from coming to a vote.[20]

Wilson wholeheartedly endorsed both the gesture toward Colombia and the idea of a new look in Latin American policy. In October 1913, he went to Mobile, Alabama, to speak to the Southern Commercial Congress, which was attended by Latin American diplomats. "The future, ladies and gentlemen," he announced, "is going to be very different for this hemisphere from the past." Regretting past insults and depredations suffered by countries to the south, he admitted, "We must prove ourselves their friends and champions upon terms of equality and honor." He called for solidarity in the hemisphere, based upon rising above material interests, and he pledged that the United States would "never again seek one additional foot of territory by conquest." He was promising to follow the same policies at home and abroad, and he linked his vision for the hemisphere to his New Freedom program: "I would rather belong to a poor nation that was free than to a rich nation that had ceased to be in love with liberty. But we shall not be poor if we love liberty, because the nation that loves liberty truly sets every man free to do his best and be his best."[21]

This vision soon bore fruit in the project for a Pan-American pact. Originally the brainchild of a Democratic peace activist, Representative James L. Slayden of Texas, the project came to Wilson's attention through Colonel House, who suggested at the end of 1914 that such a pact could serve as a model for a broader plan to enforce world peace. House noted that the idea excited Wilson, who proceeded to type a draft for a pact that covered four points: a "solemn covenant" of mutual guarantee "of undisturbed and undisputed territorial integrity and of complete political independence under republican forms of government"; arbitration of current disputes by three-nation panels; exclusive government manufacture and control of armaments; and, in the case of future disputes not affecting "honour, independence, or vital interests," a one-year delay together with investigation and arbitration. Negotiations later foundered on opposition from Chile, which had long-standing border disputes, and fears by other Latin American nations of United States domination and aggression. Although nothing came of the Pan-American pact, its provisions contained language and ideas that Wilson would use in the Covenant of the League of Nations, and it pointed the way for Franklin Roosevelt's Good

Neighbor policy in the 1930s and hemispheric security pacts at the outset of World War II.[22]

The vision of hemispheric solidarity and a Pan-American pact presented the benign face of Wilson's Latin American policy. That policy also had less attractive features. In Central America and the Caribbean, the president showed few, if any, qualms about intervention. Nor, surprisingly, did his secretary of state. As the nation's leading opponent of imperialism since 1898 and a persistent critic of Republican incursions in that region, Bryan could and should have acted—as he did in Mexico—as a brake on intervention, but he did not. In fact, during his two years at the head of his department, he showed equal or greater relish than his chief for going forcibly into countries there.

The issue of intervention first arose in Nicaragua. The Taft administration had sent marines there to quell chronic unrest, but matters remained unresolved when Wilson came into office. Bryan quickly decided to continue the previous policy, explaining to the Senate Foreign Relations Committee that the country would otherwise fall into chaos. He also asserted, "Those Latin republics are our political children, so to speak." Bryan negotiated a treaty that included the right to intervene, a provision that was later withdrawn in the face of Senate opposition. Eventually, under strong prodding from the United States—which included sending in more marines and posting warships off its coasts—Nicaragua settled into a brief interlude of stability. But the whole business stirred resentment in the other Central American countries and stymied efforts to build better relations.[23]

The Nicaraguan intervention was smaller and shorter lived than other similar moves in the Caribbean. Two countries on the island of Hispaniola, Haiti and the Dominican Republic, witnessed the administration's largest and longest-lasting actions in the Western Hemisphere. The United States had occupied the Dominican Republic for four years under Roosevelt and intervened again briefly under Taft. Wilson faced a confusing situation there, which he and Bryan spent months trying to figure out. Bryan's rewarding "deserving Democrats" with diplomatic posts hurt most in that nation because American diplomats provided both inadequate information and poor representation. In July 1914, the president laid down what came to be called the Wilson plan for the Dominican Republic. It called for an immediate cease-fire between warring groups and the formation of a provisional government with free elections under American supervision. At first, the plan seemed to work, but fighting soon resumed. In May 1916, the United States mounted military operations that escalated into a full-fledged occupation and protectorate that would last until 1924. These actions could not have gone forward without the president's approval, but Wilson was not much involved in them.[24]

The administration found itself simultaneously entangled in neighboring Haiti, where total anarchy appeared imminent. After some hesitation, Bryan proposed, and Wilson approved, an American takeover of Haitian customhouses at the middle of 1914. This limited intervention did not solve the problem. Wilson then proposed American-supervised elections, but local complications prevented them. When fresh violence erupted in July 1915, claiming American lives, the president's patience ran out. "I suppose there is nothing for it but to take the bull by the horns and restore order," he said privately.[25] This decision set in motion steps toward an even more thoroughgoing military occupation and even longer control than in the Dominican Republic. American marines would not leave, and Haiti would not regain full sovereignty, until 1934.

These incursions into Nicaragua, the Dominican Republic, and Haiti formed the high-water mark of United States intervention in the Caribbean. Why did the nation reach this point under the professed idealist Woodrow Wilson, aided and abetted by the arch anti-imperialist William Jennings Bryan? At the time, socialists and some progressives denounced these moves as imperialistic and explained them as the workings of the same nefarious forces that Wilson himself had feared in Mexico—the influence of big business and finance. Later critics would deride him as a woolly-headed idealist and starchy moralist, with the leading historian of the Wilson administration dubbing these moves "missionary diplomacy" and maintaining that they sprang from a religious-based mania to spread democracy abroad—a mania that impelled the president to try to foist American-style institutions on other nations.[26]

Both of those lines of criticism miss the mark in explaining Wilson's interventionism in Latin America. This president, who deeply and sometimes unfairly suspected "material interests," was not listening to them and was not about to do their bidding. Likewise, his idealism was like his religious faith, deep-seated and ever-present but also largely taken for granted. Particular circumstances counted more than grand designs in his decisions to go into Nicaragua, the Dominican Republic, and Haiti. What later critics would fault Wilson for slighting—security considerations— weighed heavily in his mind. Protecting approaches and territory adjacent to the soon-to-be-opened Panama Canal appeared to leave few options other than trying to impose stability in the region. Those considerations gained added gravity after the outbreak of the war in Europe in August 1914, an event that largely explained why he paid so little heed to the later phases of operations in the Dominican Republic and Haiti. In addition, Veracruz did not seem to have totally quashed his interventionist urge. At bottom, Wilson and Bryan shared with the vast majority of their country-men a callousness toward and an ignorance of their neighbors to the south, but those flaws were not products of their religiosity and idealism.

In other parts of the world, such as Asia, the president and the secre-tary of state behaved with more restraint and consistency. Despite their early enthusiasm for the semblance of democracy in China and their dis-avowal of "dollar diplomacy" there, Wilson and Bryan largely followed their Republican predecessors in not seriously challenging Japanese influ-ence. They did break with the past in the Philippines. In every election since 1900, Democratic party platforms had pledged Philippine inde-pendence. Wilson had doubts about that pledge in 1912, but he chose not to buck the party. Once in office, he backed away from setting a deadline for getting out, but he did stick by the promise to grant autonomy and eventual independence. In October 1913, he announced that Filipinos would immediately have a majority in the appointive upper house of their legislature as well as in the elective lower house, an action that gave them a much larger share in their government.

The New Freedom legislation crowded the Philippines off the legisla-tive agenda until October 1914, when the House overwhelmingly passed a measure to grant independence, but Republicans blocked Senate approval during the short session after the 1914 elections. Congress took up another measure in 1916, but Republicans, who had increased their num-bers in the 1914 elections, stood virtually unanimous in opposing any deadline for independence. Catholic interests, fearing confiscation of church property under an independent Philippine government, persuaded thirty Irish American Democrats to join the Republicans in blocking any deadline. Stripped of a date for independence, the measure won final pas-sage in both houses at the end of August 1916. Satisfied with the outcome, Wilson declared that it was "high time that we did this act of justice which we have now done." This law—known as the Jones Act, after the chairman of the House Insular Affairs Committee—marked one of the biggest mile-stones on the road to Philippine independence.[27]

Europe offered an example of restraint and consistency where Wilson did choose to buck his party. When he took office, he found a diplomatic dispute simmering over tolls to be levied when the Panama Canal opened. In 1912, Congress had passed, and Taft had signed, a law that exempted from all tolls American vessels engaged in shipping between American ports, and authorized lower tolls for all American ships. The British, who had the world's largest merchant fleet, had immediately protested, maintaining that this law violated the Hay-Pauncefote Treaty of 1901, under which they had ceded to the United States exclusive rights to maintain and fortify a canal in return for equal treatment of ships of all nations. Wilson and the Democrats had endorsed the tolls exemption during the campaign, but the president quickly repented. Soon after taking office, he told the British ambassador, his old acquaintance James Bryce, that he planned to take up the matter after the tariff was out of the way. He did not mention the tolls issue in his State of the Union speech in December 1913, but shortly afterward he told Ambassador Page that he would ask Congress to repeal the exemption, "and I am not without hope that I can accomplish both at this session."[28]

In February 1914, he publicly called the tolls exemption "a very mistaken policy" that was "economically unjust," benefited "only a monopoly," and violated the Hay-Pauncefote Treaty. The situation grew tense when House Democratic leader Underwood announced that he would oppose repeal as a breach of the party's campaign pledge. The president responded by going to the Capitol on March 5 to speak to a joint session of Congress. "No communication I have addressed to Congress carried with it graver or more far-reaching implications to the interest of the country," he declared, and he asked for repeal "in support of the foreign policy of the administration. I shall not know how to deal with other matters of even greater delicacy and nearer consequences if you do not grant it to me in ungrudging measure." Making this an issue of loyalty was a risky strategy, which seemed to backfire when Speaker Clark joined Underwood in opposing him. Wilson refused to compromise and instructed Burleson to use patronage to bring wavering Democrats into line. The strategy worked. On March 31, the House approved a repeal bill, 247 to 162, with only Clark, Underwood, and some big-city Irish American Democrats breaking ranks. The Senate followed suit on June 11, approving the measure by a vote of 50 to 35.[29]

None of Wilson's other victories in this season of legislative triumphs tasted so sweet. Here, he did something different from the New Freedom legislation. He was not pulling his party together to deliver things that its leader and followers had long wanted. Instead, he was taking the party in a new direction and defying some of his strongest congressional allies. "There is nothing that succeeds in life like boldness," Wilson told Princeton classmates just after the final vote, "provided you believe you are on the right side." This victory boded well for future confrontations with party leaders. "I realized the political risks in undertaking to obtain a repeal of the tolls exemption," he wrote to Bryce, "but I do not know of anything I ever undertook with more willingness or zest." Winning this fight provided a fine capstone to Wilson's early foreign policy program, and it had the unforeseen benefit of putting relations with Britain on a good footing for dealing with "matters of greater delicacy and nearer consequences," which he had uncannily predicted.[30]

One other aspect of Wilson's European diplomacy in the first half of 1914 showed a kind of boldness and laid groundwork for dealing with future trials. This was Colonel House's self-named "Great Adventure"— his project to bring Britain, Germany, and the United States together to maintain international peace and order. The Texan worked with the German ambassador in Washington to make contacts in Berlin, which was his first stop on a European trip that lasted from late May until the middle of July. In the German capital, House found "jingoism run stark mad," as he reported to Wilson. "Unless someone acting for you can bring about an understanding there is some day to be an awful calamity." The colonel saw several German leaders and had an audience at Potsdam with Kaiser Wilhelm, who reportedly agreed that America must lead the way. "I made it plain, however," House noted, "that it was the policy of our Government to have no alliances of any character, but that we were willing to do our share towards promoting international peace." Next, House went by way of Paris to London, where he found an eager accomplice in Ambassador Page, and met the foreign secretary, Sir Edward Grey. At the beginning of July, he reported that Grey asked him to communicate with the Germans "in regard to a better understanding between the Nations of Europe, and to try to get a reply before I leave." House sent an ecstatic message to the kaiser, but he got no reply before he departed on July 21.[31] By the time his ship landed, the diplomatic crisis that led to the world war was in full swing.

How much stock Wilson put in House's efforts is difficult to judge. He told the colonel that the report of the audience at Potsdam "gives me a thrill of deep pleasure. You have, I hope and believe, begun a great thing and I rejoice with all my heart." Later, he expressed his thankfulness "to have a friend who so thoroughly understands me to interpret me to those whom it is important and inform and enlighten with regard to what we are really seeking to accomplish." Those words may have been little more than a characteristically sentimental expression of feelings to someone whose big scheme appealed to his own fanciful tendencies. House actually reported little of what he discussed in the European capitals, and when he got back to America he did not rush to see Wilson. When they finally met, at the end of August, House recorded that he had spoken "of the great work there was to do for humanity in the readjustment of the wreckage that would come from the European war."[32] The colonel's "Great Adventure" had started at a tragically inopportune moment, but he continued to dream big dreams about what he might accomplish through his friend in the White House.

Other matters on the home front also occupied Wilson during his first year and a half in office. Some burning social issues demanded his attention largely against his will. Racial justice continued to dog him as white southerners denounced the administration's few black appointments. When Wilson reappointed Robert H. Terrell, a respected black judge in the District of Columbia, howls of protest arose on Capitol Hill. He explained to one southern senator that he believed Terrell was well qualified and that during the 1912 campaign he had told some black leaders that he felt "morally bound to see to it that they were not put to any greater disadvantage than they suffered under previous Democratic administrations."[33] This lame excuse neither squared with the facts nor satisfied the more rabid racists.

Another issue from the campaign likewise dogged him—woman suffrage. When Wilson received delegations of female suffragists at the White House, he drew a line between his personal views and stands he could take as president and leader of his party. In June 1914, he told one delegation, "It is my personal conviction that this is a matter for settlement by the states and not by the federal government." Two of his visitors questioned him about whether that view did not leave room for women to seek the vote through an amendment. "Certainly it does," Wilson answered. "There is good room." Pressed further, he responded, "I do not think it is quite proper that I submit myself to cross-examination."[34] He felt genuinely ambivalent and uncomfortable. Anti-suffrage sentiment ran high among Democrats, especially southerners and members of urban ethnic groups, yet Wilson had taught at a leading women's college and had suffragist daughters. Political expediency and personal preference left his views in flux.

On two other pressing social issues—immigration restriction and prohibition—he felt no ambivalence, although he treated each one differently. Perhaps in part because he was the son and grandson of immigrants, he resisted efforts to curtail immigration from southern and eastern Europe. In May 1914, he extolled immigrants at a memorial service for the sailors killed at Veracruz. The president observed that some of the fallen had come from "several national stocks. . . . But they were not Irishmen or Frenchmen or Hebrews or Italians any more. They were not when they went to Vera Cruz: they were Americans, every one of them."[35] Political calculation may have colored his views, inasmuch as the Democrats enjoyed a large and growing following in the Northeast and Midwest among recent immigrants and second-generation Americans. Expedient or not, Wilson's views impelled him to veto literacy tests designed to keep out immigrants from southern and eastern Europe. In February 1917, Congress overrode the last of those vetoes and imposed the first of a series of twentieth-century bars to immigration.

Prohibition drew no sympathy from him either, but it gave him political headaches, and he tried to duck it. An infrequent, moderate drinker himself, Wilson never liked the idea of legislating morality. Unfortunately, in running for the presidential nomination, he had occasionally appealed to prohibitionist groups, and those appeals came back to haunt him when dry forces used his remarks in their campaigns. At one point, Tumulty asked, "How did you come to write that, Governor? . . . Were you crazy when you wrote it?" Wilson answered, "I declare I don't know. . . . I hate to look at it." Mainly, he stayed silent on the subject and avoided the issue—with one exception. In October 1919, a veto of enforcement legislation under the recently ratified Eighteenth Amendment, which established nationwide prohibition, went out in his name. Congress overrode this veto too, and the law took effect as the Volstead Act.[36]

Other domestic issues that bothered Wilson were, to an extent, of his own making. In hitching his own and his party's fortunes to the progressive bandwagon, he stirred expectations for sweeping reforms and invited criticism for failing to deliver. Two measures in particular opened him to attack: prohibiting child labor and extending financial aid to farmers. On child labor, Wilson talked and acted equivocally. Shortly before taking office, he expressed sympathy for outlawing child labor but questioned the constitutionality of federal action. When the House passed the Palmer bill to prohibit child labor in February 1915—by a wide margin: 232 for and 44 against—he took no stand, and the bill did not come to a vote in the Senate before the end of the session on March 4.

Financial aid to farmers—rural credits—found him similarly torn. Although he fought off moves to attach provisions for agricultural lending to the Federal Reserve Act, in his State of the Union speech in December 1913 he promised support in making "substantial credit resources available as a foundation for joint, concerted local action in their [farmers'] own behalf in getting the capital they must use."[37] Secretary of Agriculture David Houston adamantly opposed direct government loans to farmers, however, and for the time being Wilson deferred to his judgment.

Pro-farmer Democrats on Capitol Hill refused to let the matter drop. In the spring of 1914, they introduced a measure to create a system of land banks, corresponding to the Federal Reserve banks, with authority to issue up to $50 million a year for farm mortgages. Party leaders warned that the bill would pass overwhelmingly in the House unless the president intervened, and he sent a letter to the Democratic caucus opposing the bill and hinting at a veto. That slowed momentum behind the bill, but in February 1915, the House and the Senate passed it. The session expired before a conference could resolve the differences and a final vote could be taken. It is not clear where Wilson's true sentiments lay. He seemed to be resisting rural-credits legislation mainly because a valued lieutenant opposed it and it did not seem "expedient."[38]

Wilson had other reasons for applying the brakes to drives for such legislation. During the severe recession that began at the end of 1913, the stock market had plunged and unemployment shot up, particularly in industrial areas of the Northeast and Midwest. Business groups and Republicans, quick to blame the downturn on the Democrats' reforms, demanded abandonment of the anti-trust program. Wilson was of two minds about how to respond. He never considered dropping the anti-trust bills or soft-pedaling his progressivism, but he did make soothing noises toward business. In June 1914, he told a gathering of journalists that once his program was finished, "business can and will get what it can get in no other way—rest, recuperation, and a successful adjustment." Practical political considerations also weighed heavily against pushing reform further. In September, he told a Democratic congressman that he looked forward to such projects as the buildup of overseas shipping, the promotion of foreign commerce, and the conservation of natural resources, "to which we could turn without any controversy." At the same time, House said about the president, "He feared the country would expect him to continue as he had up to now, which was impossible."[39]

Wilson did send one unmistakable signal that he was not wavering in his progressive convictions. The brief, lame-duck session of the Sixty-third Congress passed a final piece of reform legislation at the beginning of 1915. This was the La Follette Seamen's Act. Andrew Furuseth, president of the International Seamen's Union, had lobbied long and hard to get laws passed to improve safety and working conditions for merchant sailors and to free them from notoriously oppressive labor contracts. The sinking of the *Titanic* in April 1912 had heightened public awareness, and at the outset of his administration Wilson had approved La Follette's bill to aid seamen. Complicating passage, however, were objections from foreign governments that the bill violated international treaties and would spoil the work of a conference that was to meet in London late in 1913 to draft a convention on safety at sea. At the behest of the State Department, Wilson stalled final congressional action on La Follette's bill until after the Senate had given its consent to the convention, which it did on December 16, 1914. La Follette and other backers then redoubled their efforts, and the bill won Senate approval on February 27, 1915.[40]

Wilson now faced a quandary. Bryan urged him to exercise a pocket veto—refrain from signing the bill and let it die with the end of the Congress on March 4—on grounds that the bill would disrupt trade and require the renegotiation of more than twenty treaties. On March 2, La Follette and Robert Owen changed Bryan's mind by taking Furuseth to meet the secretary and plead his cause. That evening, La Follette brought Furuseth to see the president. After his visitors left, Wilson told Tumulty, "I have just experienced a great half-hour, the tensest since I came to the White House." He signed the bill into law on March 4, admitting to a sympathetic Democrat that he had weighed "the arguments on both sides with a good deal of anxiety, and finally determined to sign it because it seemed the only chance to get something like justice for a class of workmen who have been too much neglected by our laws."[41]

One reason opponents could cast doubt on Wilson's progressivism was that he was not sharing his thinking with the public as much as he had done earlier. Yet he recognized that he needed to make a stronger personal impression on the public. In the spring of 1914, he admitted to the Washington press corps his concern that people thought he was "a cold and removed person who has a thinking machine inside. . . . You may not believe it, but I sometimes feel like a fire from a far from extinct volcano." He said he never thought of himself as president, and he wanted to give the public "a wink, as much as to say, 'It is only "me" that is inside this thing.'" He also did some Roosevelt-style preaching on personal virtues. He told a group of Princeton alumni, "Service is not merely getting out and being busy and butting into people's affairs, and giving gratuitous advice. . . . You cannot serve your friend unless you know what his needs are, and you cannot know what his needs are unless you know him inside out." To his fellow Princetonians he asserted, "The great malady of public life is cowardice. Most men are not untrue, but they are afraid."[42]

Those remarks served as a warm-up for his 1914 Fourth of July address at Independence Hall in Philadelphia, where he declared that liberty must be translated "into definite action." At home, Americans must "put hope into the hearts of the men who work and toil every day." Abroad, they must answer the question, "What are we going to do with the influence and power of this great Nation?" He closed with a stirring vision: "My dream is that, as the years go on and the world knows more and more of America, it will also drink at these fountains of youth and renewal; that it will also turn to America for those moral inspirations which lie at the basis of freedom; . . . and that America will come into the full light of the day when all shall know that she puts human rights above all other rights, and that her flag is the flag, not only of America, but of humanity."43 These were the most visionary words he had yet uttered as president, and they foretold his own "great adventure" in world affairs.

Just about everything seemed to be going right for Woodrow Wilson as the summer of 1914 began. Several people remarked on how good he looked then and how the presidency seemed to agree with him. He had been healthy most of the time since his inauguration. His skin was tan from his golf games with Dr. Grayson, and he found time for reading. He admitted to devouring detective stories, and during the summer of 1914 the books he borrowed from the Library of Congress included such influential works in progressive circles as Graham Wallas's *Human Nature in Politics* and Walter Lippmann's *Preface to Politics*.44

Home life had gone well for the Wilsons in the White House once Ellen adjusted to the social demands. Actually, all five of them seldom lived together there after the spring of 1913. Margaret had already left home to pursue her musical studies in New York, although she came back for frequent visits. She, Jessie, and Nell joined their mother in Cornish, New Hampshire, during the summer and early fall of that year, where the Wilsons rented Harlakenden, a 200-acre estate with a large Georgian house overlooking the Connecticut River. Cornish provided Ellen with an idyllic interlude. Besides quiet and beautiful surroundings, she found a group of artists nearby with whom she exchanged visits and discussed their work. She had taken up her painting again while Wilson was governor and had begun exhibiting her work in 1912. To avoid trading on her husband's name, she signed her paintings "E. A. Wilson," and with dealers she used the pseudonym Edward Wilson. At Cornish, she completed more paintings, five of which were chosen for the annual exhibition of the Association of Women Painters and Sculptors in New York. Adding to Ellen's happiness that summer were visits from old friends and the frequent presence of Jessie's fiancé, Frank Sayre.45

The only disagreeable note during this interlude was Wilson's absence. He managed just three short visits to Cornish. Ellen and Nell went back to Washington for a week in late August, in part to maintain their perfect record of attending Wilson's appearances before Congress. The separation pained both Ellen and Woodrow, and they tried to fill the void by writing the kind of letters they had written as young lovers three decades earlier. "How incomparably sweet and dear you are!" he wrote at the end of July. "Your letters warm my heart and give me so vivid a realization of you that even this barren house seems full of you." She replied, "Your wonderful, adorable Sunday letter has just come and made me fairly drunk with happiness. I would give anything to be able to express my love as perfectly as you do, dear heart."[46] Clearly, whatever hurt and rift had once come between them had long since healed, and their love burned as bright as ever. They wrote to each other several times a week and shared accounts of everything that was going on. She avidly followed the news and commented regularly on issues and personalities. He revealed his thoughts and feelings about the affairs of state that were swirling around him. These letters between them in 1913 likewise provide great insight into his mind and spirit.

The family's return to the White House in mid-October brought a burst of activity. November 25 was Jessie's wedding date, and much remained to be done. The White House staff pitched in with its wonted efficiency, and all was ready when the day arrived. The ceremony took place in the East Room, with Margaret and Nell among the bridesmaids. Performing the ceremony were two clergymen, Dr. Sylvester Beach, pastor of the First Presbyterian Church in Princeton, and the Reverend John Nevin Sayre, an Episcopalian and a social reformer who was the bridegroom's brother. With her golden hair, fine features, and rosy complexion, Jessie made a radiant bride. After her father gave her away, he stepped back and held Ellen's hand during the rest of the ceremony.

By all accounts, it was a gala occasion. Much of official Washington came, including cabinet officers, diplomats, and members of Congress. Most of the Wilsons' extended family were also there, although one sad absence was Ellen's brother Stockton, who was again hospitalized for depression. A lively reception followed the ceremony. "It was just like a big family party in the South," said Margaret Howe, the wife of Wilson's nephew. The Marine Band played dance tunes, including the newly popular turkey trot. Many of the diplomats danced with Margaret, who caught Jessie's bouquet—an event that did not turn out to be an omen of the next wedding. The belle of the ball, according to the newspapers, was Nell. "You know Nell, as we call Eleanor Wilson, is just crazy about dancing," Margaret Howe recounted.[47] Wilson did not dance, but he looked on and laughed and joked. For him and Ellen, the occasion was also bittersweet, for the first of their children had broken from the family circle.

Any sadness the father of the bride felt at the time of the wedding would have found some relief at a sporting event four days later. The family went to New York on November 28 to see Frank and Jessie off to Europe on their honeymoon. Wilson and Ellen stayed overnight with the

Houses and attended the theater. The next day, Wilson went to the Polo Grounds to attend his first Army-Navy game as president. It was rainy and misty, and Army dominated play, winning 22 to 9. "At the game many people of distinction came to our box to pay respects to the President," House noted. The dignitaries included Senator O'Gorman, and seeing this sometime nemesis play up to him in front of the photographers may have been particularly sweet for Wilson.[48] So, too, may have been memories of another Army-Navy game eight years before, when he had played host and supporting actor to the political star who had since become his greatest rival—Roosevelt.

Football was not the only athletic contest Wilson enjoyed as president. Living in Washington meant he could often follow baseball, his favorite sport. He gladly continued the custom, begun in 1910 by Taft, of throwing out the first ball at the opening game of the Major League season. On April 10, 1913, he tossed the first ball, and he attended a three-game series later that month. He missed opening day in 1914 because it came two days after the fighting at Veracruz. In October 1915, he would become the first president to attend the World Series, and he threw out the first ball at the second game. In his second term, Wilson would make it to only one game, a Red Cross benefit in 1918. Sportswriters often commented on how well pitched his tosses were.

Baseball, along with vaudeville shows and movies, offered him welcome respite in the spring of 1914. Matters at home were troubling him. Since February, Ellen had shown signs of ebbing energy, and Margaret often filled in for her mother at social functions. Early in March, Ellen took what Wilson described as "an ugly fall" when she slipped on a polished floor in her bedroom and was "recovering slowly from the shock and general shaking up it gave her." Her slow recovery concerned her husband so much that he canceled a trip to New York to see House at the beginning of April. At the middle of the month, she spent a week at White Sulphur Springs, West Virginia, accompanied by Nell and Dr. Grayson. The trip seemed to help.[49] She started making arrangements for another summer at Harlakenden, and on April 20 she sat in the gallery of the House chamber, as she always did when her husband spoke to Congress.

Ellen's frail health came at a particularly inopportune moment, for a family crisis was brewing, thanks to their youngest daughter's romantic inclinations. Nell had fallen madly in love with William Gibbs McAdoo, the secretary of the Treasury. She broke her engagement to Ben King in February and told her parents about McAdoo, who was out of town but took up the matter with the Wilsons when he returned. They were much less happy with this fiancé than they had been with his predecessor or with Frank Sayre. The fifty-year-old McAdoo was only seven years younger than Wilson, and he was more than twice Nell's age. A widower for the past three years, he had seven children from his first marriage, two of them older than Nell. For her, however, any such drawbacks paled in the presence of his dark, burly good looks, superabundant energy, and aura of manly strength. The elder Wilsons could not resist the couple's being, as Ellen put it, "simply *mad* over each other," and they gave their consent. Reporters had been on to the romance for some time, and Washington newspapers announced the engagement on their front pages on March 13.⁵⁰

The wedding took place at the White House on the evening of May 7, 1914. It was a small affair held in the Blue Room. Fewer than 100 guests were present, mostly family members. The official reason for their not having a larger, more festive event, according to *The New York Times*, was that "[t]hese days are burdened with grave responsibilities for the President; public business of great and growing importance presses upon him." Wilson felt even sadder at this breach in his family circle. "Ah! How desperately my heart aches that she is gone," he wrote three days later to Mary Hulbert. "She is simply part of me, the only delightful part; and I feel the loneliness more than I dare admit to myself." He did not embellish his grief. Of his daughters, Nell was his favorite. She shared her father's playful streak and sense of fun, and she was the one who could always make him laugh.⁵¹

Besides losing his favorite daughter, Wilson was gaining a problematic son-in-law. McAdoo was the most dynamic member of the cabinet, and the president owed him debts of gratitude for the role he had played in 1912. He would call his new son-in-law Mac, but he would never feel entirely comfortable with him. In his memoirs, published after Wilson's death, McAdoo recounted how he had once told Wilson a joke about an old black man who said, when a circus performer landed a balloon in his field, "Howdy do, Marse Jesus; how's your pa?" Wilson, as McAdoo recalled, did not like the joke, but not because of its racism: He "did not laugh; he did not even smile. He looked at me silently for a moment, and then said: 'Mac, that story is sacrilegious.'" Another time, McAdoo recalled, Wilson was reading something he had written and asked, "Mac, why do you write *under* the circumstances?" He then explained gently that *circum* refers to an enclosure: "You can be *in* a circumstance but not *under* it. The correct expression is 'in the circumstances.'"⁵²

It did not help relations between the two men that, unlike others in the family, McAdoo failed to respect the sharp line his father-in-law drew between work and private life. Without naming him, Stockton Axson was describing McAdoo when he later wrote:

> Now, suppose a member of the family, a dear and valued relative, also full of his schemes, his plans, which he sees as the business-man, the man of affairs, the man of action—not the man of meditation, not the artist, not the literary man; suppose he insists on talking business. . . . It rasps the older man, the literary man—why can't we drop business? At first he answers graciously by trying to avoid the topic. Then his tone takes a little edge on. Then he adopts the worst of all his defenses—silence. The silence of Woodrow Wilson is worse than the oaths of some men, more withering.[53]

The tension was not lost on McAdoo. In his memoirs he claimed he had known the president, whom he continued to call Governor, better than any other member of the cabinet. "But in another sense I hardly knew him at all. There were wide and fertile ranges of his spirit that were closed to me; and, I think, to everyone else except the first Mrs. Wilson. As far as I am aware, she was the only human being who knew him perfectly."[54]

He was about to lose that source of love and understanding. The real reason for Nell's small and simple wedding was Ellen's health. The apparent upturn in her condition did not last. Grayson urged her to go to Har-lakenden, and Wilson asked Jessie and Frank to get the house ready for the family to arrive later in the summer. Although she seemed to rally a few times, Ellen was dying. She had Bright's disease, a condition related to tuberculosis that was destroying her kidneys. It is not clear when her doctors made the diagnosis, but they did not tell her or her husband. On July 12, Wilson wrote to Mary Hulbert, "Ellen is slowly (ah, how slowly!) coming to her strength again." It was a false hope. By late July, Grayson was attending her constantly. Woodrow sat by her bedside every night. The news that Jessie was expecting her first child cheered Ellen, who managed to fuss about whether her daughter was taking proper care of herself. On August 3, Grayson informed the president that he should gather the members of the family. Margaret came at once, and Frank and Jessie arrived two days later. Sadly, neither Ellen's sister, Madge, nor her brother Stockton, who were on the West Coast, where they were both living, arrived in time.[55]

Ellen knew the end was near. In the morning of August 6, she asked her husband if he could get Congress to act on her project to clean up Washington's alleyways. Tumulty took the request to the Capitol, arranged for immediate passage by both houses, and brought back the news early in the afternoon. Ellen was drifting in and out of consciousness. In the morning, Woodrow had told her, "Jessie has arrived." She smiled and replied, "I understand." Several times, she awoke and asked, "Is your father looking well?" In the afternoon, when the news about her bill arrived from Capitol Hill, Ellen smiled again. She motioned to Grayson and said, "Doctor, if I go away, promise me you will take good care of my husband." Those were her last words. She lay unconscious while Margaret, Jessie, and Nell sat beside her bed and Wilson held her hand. At five o'clock, her breathing stopped. With tears streaming down his cheeks, her husband asked, "Is it over?" Grayson nodded. Wilson got up and went to an open window. "Oh, my God," he cried out, "what am I to do?"[56]

Ellen's death dealt him a cruel blow. For more than thirty years, Ellen had been his closest, wisest adviser. She had exercised a stronger, more salutary influence over him than anyone else. She had rarely let her family-inherited disposition toward severe depression affect him or their daughters. She had seen Wilson through and forgiven him for his infatuation with Mrs. Peck. Ellen had given him so much, and he was a far better man for her gifts. He had gone further and accomplished more in the worlds of scholarship, education, politics, and government than he could have done without her. And he knew it. Five years later, when he himself lay in a bed in the White House after suffering a stroke, Nell was reading to him and thought he had gone to sleep. As she later recalled, "Suddenly, he opened his eyes and smiled at me, the live, happy smile of the old days." After some reminiscences, he said to her, "I owe everything to your mother—you know that don't you?" He talked about their lives together, and Nell said to him, "I wish I could hand her torch to my own children." Her father answered, "You can—tell them about her. That is enough."[57]

Now Ellen was gone. Wilson had lost her at the moment when the world was cascading into the most terrible war yet in history. His only other recorded words at the time are in a note he typed the next day to Mary Hulbert: "God has stricken me almost beyond what I can bear."[58]

13

IRONY AND THE GIFT OF FATE

The guns of August 1914 began to boom as Ellen Wilson lay dying. The news from Europe startled and shocked Americans. To some, the war looked like a great natural disaster. Henry James called it the "plunge of civilization into this abyss of blood and darkness," while Theodore Roosevelt said it was "on a giant scale like the disaster to the *Titanic*." Others reached for their Bibles, dubbing the war Armageddon, after the final nation-shattering miracle in the book of Revelation. Woodrow Wilson felt devastated by grief after his wife's death, but he had to snatch moments from his mourning to respond to this world calamity. Now his inner anguish added to his sense of a lack of preparation to make his having to deal mainly with foreign affairs "an irony of fate."[1]

Ellen's funeral, on August 10, 1914, was a simple service in the East Room of the White House—the scene of Jessie's wedding nine months before—conducted by Dr. Beach of Princeton and Dr. James Taylor, pastor of Washington's Central Presbyterian Church. The service included prayers and readings from scripture but no music. Only family members, the cabinet, and a delegation from Congress were invited. After the service, Wilson; his brother, Joseph; his nephew George Howe; and Stockton Axson accompanied the casket to Union Station, where other family members joined them. Wilson and their daughters had decided that Ellen should be buried in the Axson family plot in Rome, Georgia. As the train made its way through Virginia, North and South Carolina, and Georgia, people lined the tracks to watch. At Rome, six of Ellen's cousins and the husbands of two others carried her casket into the church where her father had preached. The service included her favorite hymns and a eulogy by the pastor. At the grave site, a thunderstorm broke as the service began, and Wilson wept as his wife's body was lowered into the ground.[2]

Except for those tears, he bore himself stoically during the funeral services and burial. Privately, he confessed to Mary Hulbert, "I never understood before what a broken heart meant, and did for a man. It just means that he lives by the compulsion of duty only. . . . Every night finds me exhausted,—dead in heart and body." That "compulsion of duty" helped him shoulder his burden of grief. The most pressing duties arose from the war in Europe. The nation's diplomatic response was to proclaim neutrality, but there were urgent problems involving travel and trade. Thousands of Americans stranded across the Atlantic clamored for assistance getting home, and the president asked Congress for money to help cover their expenses. In London, Ambassador Page enlisted the services of an American businessman living there, Herbert Hoover, and the efficient way in which Hoover tackled the job launched his public career. Yet for most Americans, this war was a calamity that was happening to somebody else far away. Page, who would soon sing a different song, wrote to Wilson, "Again and ever I thank Heaven for the Atlantic ocean."[3]

The president did not share those feelings of remoteness from the war. In a statement to the press on August 18, he warned his countrymen not to become "divided in camps of hostile opinion, hot against each other," because of their ties to the nations at war. He urged instead, "The United States must be neutral in fact as well as in name during these times that are to try men's souls. We must be impartial in thought as well as in action, must put a curb upon our sentiments."[4] As he implied when he talked about curbing sentiments, he was speaking from his own inner turmoil, and he was also evoking the vision of his Fourth of July speech. The twin tragedies of the war and his wife's death made his designs for America's role in the world deeply personal and heartfelt.

Disrupted trade presented the first serious confrontation with the war's ramifications. Heavy selling by Europeans caused the biggest losses on the New York Stock Exchange since the panic of 1907, and McAdoo allowed the exchange to close temporarily. Equally heavy selling of debt instruments held by Europeans caused a fall in the dollar's exchange value and set off a run on gold. Wilson encouraged McAdoo to issue emergency currency, thereby averting all but a handful of bank failures. In the broader economy, they sought to forestall undue interruptions in the flow of exports, as interruptions could hurt such vital Democratic constituencies as southern cotton growers and western lead and copper miners. A shortage of ships appeared to pose a special danger, and the administration proposed to buy German vessels stranded in American ports to fill the predicted shortfall. This "ship-purchase" plan roused objections from the

British, who saw it as a breach of neutrality, and it ran into roadblocks on Capitol Hill, where sour feelings at the end of the congressional session prevented bills from reaching the floor in either chamber.[5]

Yet the horrendous cloud of carnage had a silver lining for the United States. Financial dislocations and export uncertainties at the war's out-break worsened the already bad state of the economy, but only in the short run. By the end of 1914, massive orders from warring nations for muni-tions and other military-related products and agricultural commodities would begin to reverse the yearlong recession and fuel a boom that would last into the next decade. Because the British dominated on the seas, only the Allies were able to buy from America, a situation that would later bring unanticipated dangers and add fuel to the economic boon. The boost to the economy almost failed to come to pass, however, thanks to a well-meant gesture. In anticipation of big war orders, the British and French governments engaged J. P. Morgan and Company to float a $100 million loan for them. The move raised Bryan's hackles. He reflexively distrusted anything involving Morgan or other big Wall Street firms, and he had long believed that lending money to nations at war was immoral and unneutral. "Money is the worst of all contrabands because it com-mands everything else," he told Wilson and argued that refusing to lend to the belligerents would shorten the war and set a noble example. Wilson assented, and on August 15 Bryan declared to the press, "[I]n the judg-ment of this government loans by American bankers to any foreign nation which is at war is inconsistent with the true spirit of neutrality."[6]

Why Wilson went along with Bryan's policy is not entirely clear. He did not discuss the matter with Bryan face-to-face, although they probably talked about it over the telephone. He may have been showing his usual deference toward a cabinet member in that man's area of responsibility, and he may have shared a fellow progressive's distrust of the influence of Wall Street. He may also have agreed with Bryan's intuition that loans to belligerents could have untoward consequences and likewise wanted to do something that might promote peace. Yet such a sweeping gesture and expression of faith in influence through example were not in character for him, and he had learned hard lessons during the previous year and a half about the difficulty of influencing other people and their governments. The distractions of grief may have affected Wilson's judgment.

The ban on loans did not stand for long. Credit is the lifeblood of international trade, and the Allied governments were not about to let it be cut off. In September, France proposed a $10 million loan through a dif-ferent Wall Street firm, Frank Vanderlip's National City Bank of New York. The French ambassador, Jean-Jules Jusserand, approached Bryan personally and told him the loan ban was prejudicial toward his government and its side in the war. As Vanderlip later recalled, Jusserand's argument shook Bryan, and in ensuing negotiations he agreed to call the loan a "commercial credit" and let it go forward so long as there was no publicity. Reporters soon got wind of the change, however. When they questioned the president at a press conference on October 15, he refused to discuss the matter and claimed nothing had changed. Wilson was employing the same sophistry Bryan had bought into, and that was the end of the loan ban. By early 1915, major financial houses were floating multimillion-dollar loans to belligerent governments and initiating an ever-tightening financial entanglement with the world war.[7]

Another, still more potent, entanglement involved merchant ships. The British began at once to impose a naval blockade of Germany and the other Central powers, but an accident of geography threatened to undermine the effectiveness of this move. The Rhine—the main artery for waterborne German commerce—empties into the North Sea in the Netherlands, and in peacetime more goods bound to and from Germany flowed through Rotterdam than through any other port. Now, with the outbreak of the war, shipments to that neutral Dutch port rose sharply, along with shipments to ports in neutral Scandinavian countries adjacent to Germany. The British were determined to close those loopholes, even at the cost of clashes with the largest neutral trading nation, the United States. Wilson first faced this aspect of the war at the end of September, when Britain published an expanded contraband list that included such unprecedented items as the important American exports of cotton and copper. The State Department drafted a diplomatic note strongly protesting the action and forwarded it to the president. House, who happened to be visiting, noted that he found the draft "exceedingly undiplomatic and . . . urged the President not to permit it to be sent." He also suggested that Wilson have him confer with the British ambassador, who was by then Sir Cecil Spring-Rice.[8]

The colonel met with the ambassador the next day and apprised him of how seriously the American government regarded this expansion of the contraband list. Meanwhile, Wilson used his literary skills to soften the draft, and a shortened, revised note went to Ambassador Page for presentation to the British. In coming years, many interpreters would make much of this episode, alleging that House and Wilson showed an unneutral bias in favor of the Allies and passed up a golden opportunity to oppose their blockade. Such allegations are wrong because the revised note, though more politely phrased, made the same points as the original draft. This decision and others regarding responses to the blockade in

1914 sprang mainly from a desire to avoid trouble. Fittingly, Bryan, whom no one ever accused of harboring unneutral sentiments, approved of the decision. This episode also revealed another element in Wilson's thinking: his fear of being drawn into the war. He read House a passage from his own *History of the American People* about how public anger had made it impossible for President Madison to avoid going to war in 1812 and said, "Madison and I are the only two Princeton men that have become President. The circumstances of the War of 1812 and now run parallel." Stockton Axson also recalled that when they returned from Ellen's burial, Wilson told him, "I am afraid something will happen on the high seas that will make it impossible for us to keep out of the war."[9]

Intentionally or not, invocation of the War of 1812 sent a useful signal to the British. House repeated Wilson's statement to Spring-Rice, who passed the story on to the foreign secretary, Sir Edward Grey, and quoted the president as saying about Madison, "I only hope I shall be wiser." This signal buttressed Grey's already set determination to avoid conflict with the Americans. Earlier than most leaders in London and Paris, he recognized how dependent the Allies were on munitions and other supplies from the United States. The British removed cotton from the contraband list for the present, and they began preemptively buying up cotton and other commodities, both to keep them out of German hands and to mitigate any economic damage in the United States. For their part, Wilson and his advisers decided against further protests and suggestions regarding the blockade, and they said nothing when Britain escalated the naval war by mining shipping lanes in the North Sea in November 1914. Matters subsided into little more than small frictions until after the beginning of the next year.[10]

The visit of House's, in which he conferred with the president on the subject of the blockade, was one of thirteen that he made between August 1914 and January 1915. As in the first year of Wilson's presidency, when he came to Washington, he usually stayed at the White House for two or three days. He continued to advise Wilson on party affairs and to meet with Democrats on and off Capitol Hill, but he increasingly pursued his bent toward foreign affairs. Besides Spring-Rice, he likewise met and corresponded frequently with the German ambassador, Count Johann-Heinrich von Bernstorff. These months marked the high point in the closeness between House and Wilson. The colonel was one of the few people outside his family with whom the president shared his agony of soul. "He said he was broken in spirit by Mrs. Wilson's death and was not fit to be President because he did not think straight any longer, and had no heart in what he was doing," House noted.[11]

The soft-spoken Texan came as a godsend in this ordeal. Stockton Axson and other family members spent as much time as they could with Wilson, and Dr. Grayson offered pleasant, undemanding companionship. But the colonel was the only male friend of his own age with whom Wilson shared both work and personal feelings. House's warm, easygoing presence, sensitive reading of moods, and availability made the president's life more bearable during these awful months. But House's help came at a price. For all his genuine sympathy, the colonel dispensed aid to the president in the spirit of protecting a valuable investment and repairing an irreplaceable instrument. He had his own ends to serve, and he intended to use Wilson as his means toward those ends. House was as determined as ever to pursue his grand design for a great-power directorate to manage world affairs. But Wilson's level of engagement did not satisfy him, and he worked to make the president pay more attention to the European situation. House also continued to try to undermine Bryan, and he got the president to agree not to tell the secretary about House's big project. They talked about the colonel going abroad to assess conditions, but House thought that such a mission might be premature and advised Wilson "to keep the threads in your hands as now and not push unduly."[12] That meant keeping "the threads" in House's hands, and he would soon decide that the situation was ready for him.

As time passed after Ellen's death, Wilson appeared to bear his grief better. In December he told a friend, referring to two political opponents, that such men as Lodge and Gardner "do not annoy me." Partisan squabbles likewise did not bother him, and he avoided reading the newspapers so as to maintain his composure. "*Somebody* must keep cool while our people grow hotter with discussing the war and all that it involves! There seems to be this advantage in having suffered the keenest, most mortal blow one can receive, that nothing else seems capable of hurting you!" The men he named were two Massachusetts Republicans, Senator Henry Cabot Lodge and his son-in-law, Representative Augustus (Gussie) Peabody Gardner, and he mentioned them because they had taken the lead in fomenting the first political controversy to arise out of the war. This pair of patrician conservatives had been making their accustomed summer grand tour in Europe when the war broke out. After they returned, Gussie Gardner, who tended to be more outspoken than his haughty father-in-law, declared that he had come back "entirely convinced that the German cause is unholy, and moreover a menace to civilization." He charged that American armed forces were pitifully inadequate to meet the dangers that would arise out of the war.[13]

Wilson responded by joking publicly that Gardner's charges were harmless "mental exercise" and the sort of talk he had been hearing since he was a boy of ten. This dismissal did not dispose of the problem. Lodge and other Republicans were working with Roosevelt to mount an attack when Congress reconvened in December. Some observers predicted that their efforts would reunite Republicans and Progressives in common cause against Wilson. The president met the challenge in his second State of the Union address, on December 8, 1914, when he defended modest increases in the army and navy. Reportedly looking Gardner straight in the eye, he declared, "More than this, proposed at this time, permit me to say, would mean merely that we had lost our self-possession, that we had been thrown off our balance by a war with which we have nothing to do, whose causes can not touch us, whose very existence affords us opportunities of friendship and disinterested service which should make us ashamed of any thought of hostility or fearful preparation for trouble." The move succeeded brilliantly. Democrats rallied to his side, and Republicans displayed their disunity. Insurgents such as La Follette dismissed talk of strengthening the armed forces, as did some conservatives, particularly Taft, who enjoyed taking a swipe at Roosevelt.[14] In fact, Wilson succeeded too well. Within months, he would have to eat his words about "a war with which we have nothing to do" and reverse himself on the preparedness issue.

When he overstated the nation's remoteness from the war, Wilson had other motives besides repelling a political attack. He was again trying to cool down public feelings. He had good reason to reiterate such counsels of calm and coolness. Gardner's calling Germany's cause "unholy" expressed a widely shared sentiment. Germany's violation of Belgian neutrality and its conquest of that little country had whipped up a storm of condemnation around the world, including in the United States. Roosevelt, in particular, denounced Germany and cheered the Allies in the fall of 1914. Privately, Taft and some other Republicans felt the same way, as did Colonel House. In November, a poll of newspaper editors by *The Literary Digest* found a quarter of them expressing the same sentiment, as compared with about 5 percent who sympathized with the Central powers.[15]

With his Scottish heritage, English-born mother, Anglophilic literary tastes, and long-standing admiration for British political institutions, Wilson could easily have shared such pro-Allied sentiments. In fact, he did harbor some of them. At the end of August, House recorded that Wilson expressed an opinion "to the effect that if Germany won it would change the course of our civilization and make the United States a military nation," and he condemned the Germans' actions in Belgium. Around the same time, Spring-Rice reported to Grey that Wilson had said, "Every thing that I love most in the world is at stake," and about the Germans, "If they succeed, we shall be forced to take such measures of defence here as would be fatal to our form of Government and American ideals." As with his response to the blockade, some interpreters would later seize upon such statements as proof that Wilson was unneutral and pro-Allied. Actually, those views had little impact on his policies and basic approach to the war. He declined to protest against alleged German atrocities in Belgium, as Roosevelt and some others were demanding, and he told Bryan he did not know "in sufficient detail the actual facts . . . [and] the time for clearing up all these matters will come when the war is over and the nations gather in sober counsel again."[16]

Such pro-Allied and anti-German sentiments, combined with determination to keep the war at arm's length, were in tune with broader public opinion. *The Literary Digest* claimed that sympathy for belligerents was "that of a detached observer," and a journalist later compared such sympathizers to baseball fans cheering from the bleachers. The first political trouble to arise out of public sympathy for belligerents came from the other side. Pro–Central powers sentiment flourished almost entirely among people of German extraction, whose sympathies were sharply focused and well organized. More than a decade before, the major brewing companies—with such names as Anheuser-Busch, Pabst, and Schlitz—had formed and financed the National German-American Alliance to lobby against prohibition. Soon after the outbreak of the war, the German embassy had taken over this organization and used it to agitate for a prohibition on the shipment of munitions to belligerents. The rationale for such an arms embargo had what *The New Republic* called "catchy reasonableness"—the idea that America should not add to the killing and destruction. But its main effect—and the reason the Germans were pushing it—would be to cut off the Allies from a vital source of munitions.[17]

Bryan, despite having backed a similar scheme with his abortive ban on loans, took the lead in opposing an arms embargo as unneutral. He and Wilson persuaded Democratic leaders on Capitol Hill to keep embargo resolutions bottled up in committee. They also received strong backing from Lodge and other Republican senators. On the other side stood perennially dissident Democrats such as Gilbert Hitchcock of Nebraska, together with La Follette, Albert Cummins, and other Republican insurgents, many of whose states contained substantial German American constituencies. On February 15, 1915, those dissidents and insurgents mustered thirty-seven votes in the Senate for an amendment to a ship-purchase bill that would have barred shipments of munitions. Such support for the arms embargo spelled trouble for Wilson if he sought congressional support for tough diplomacy toward Germany.[18]

Also at the beginning of 1915, the president was having problems on Capitol Hill on another war-related issue—purchase of foreign-owned ships stranded by the war for use by a government-owned corporation in the transatlantic trade. During the three months of this lame-duck session of Congress, Wilson tried to exercise the party leadership that had worked so well for the past two years. In January, at the Democrats' Jackson Day dinner, he breathed some of Old Hickory's fire as he denounced "any group of men [who] should dare to break the solidarity of the Democratic team for any purpose or from any motive" and admonished the party to "march with the discipline and with the zest of a conquering host." This time his magic did not work. The House passed a ship-purchase bill on February 17, by a vote of 215 to 122, but the other chamber did not follow suit. Seven Democrats refused to support the administration's bill, and all but four Republicans opposed the measure. They balked at an expansion of government power, and some of them cited British threats to seize converted German vessels. Wilson might have gotten a bill through if he had been willing to promise that the government would not purchase ships owned by belligerents, but for him that was half a loaf not worth having. Asked at a press conference on February 2 about accepting changes in the bill, he shot back, "No changes of any sort that are not consistent with the principle of the bill." The ship-purchase bill did not come up for a vote before the Congress expired on March 4. It was Wilson's first real defeat as president.[19]

Disappointment on Capitol Hill added to the emotional strain Wilson had been laboring under since Ellen's death, and on one occasion during this time he failed to maintain his prized self-control. That was on November 12, 1914, when he again met with a delegation headed by the Boston editor William Monroe Trotter, who opened with a fierce statement: "Only two years ago you were heralded as perhaps the second Lincoln, and now the Afro-American leaders who supported you are hounded as false leaders and traitors to their race. What a change segregation has wrought!" As he had done earlier, Wilson responded with bland assurances and evasions, claiming that "it takes the world generations to outlive all its prejudices" and nobody could be "cocksure about what should be done." Trotter lashed back, "We are not here as wards. We are not here as dependents. We are here as full-fledged American citizens." Trotter charged that the government's effort at segregation sprang only from prejudice, and he reminded the president of black support he had received in

1912. "Please leave me out," Wilson snapped back. "Let me say this, if you will, that if this organization wishes to approach me again, it must choose another spokesman. . . . You are an American citizen, as fully an American citizen as I am, but you are the only American citizen that has ever come into this office who has talked to me with a tone with a background of passion that was evident." Trotter rejoined, "I am from a part of the people, Mr. President." Wilson answered, "You have spoiled the whole cause for which you came."[20]

None of the exchange between Trotter and Wilson was made public. Trotter's opening statement was published in the *Chicago Defender*, but not in the white press. Mainstream papers did quote him saying after the meeting, "What the President told us was entirely disappointing. His statement that segregation was intended to prevent racial friction is not supported by the facts." Wilson knew he had mishandled the encounter. The secretary of the navy recalled that the president told him soon afterward, "Daniels, never raise an incident into an issue. . . . I was damn fool enough to lose my temper and to point them to the door. What I ought to have done would have been to have listened, restrained my resentment, and, when they had finished, to have said to them that, of course, their petition would receive consideration. They would have withdrawn quietly and no more would have been heard about the matter. But I lost my temper and played the fool."[21]

His remorse was sad and revealing. It was sad that he did not respond to what Trotter was telling him and did not grasp the facts of racial injustice that the editor was laying before him. By even friendly accounts, Trotter could be abrasive and imperious, but those qualities did not detract from the truth and power of his message. Wilson's regret involved only the way he had handled himself. He had lost his self-control; he had surrendered to the "passion" he accused Trotter of bringing into the president's office. More was involved here than Wilson's usual desire to avoid issues involving race. It was revealing that he suffered this breakdown of self-control not long after Ellen's death. Nothing like it would happen again while he was president, except in smaller, less conspicuous ways after he suffered his stroke. He rarely let personal turmoil and heartache affect his conduct of public affairs, at least not consciously. Except possibly for the ban on loans, this was almost the only time when the shadow of grief may have clouded the intelligence and discipline he relied upon to guide him as president.

Wilson tried to make partial amends for his exchange with Trotter. A month later he received a delegation from the University Commission on the Southern Race Question, an organization of white racial moderates, and told them that "as a southern man" he sincerely desired "the good of the Negro and the advancement of his race on all sound and sensible lines."[22]

Feeble as those words were, they might have helped if he had left matters there. Instead, he soon allowed himself to be dragged into an affair that made his racial views look worse than they were. At the beginning of 1915, the National Association for the Advancement of Colored People was protesting against and trying to prevent showings of D. W. Griffith's newly released *Birth of a Nation*. Though a pathbreaking masterpiece of cinematography, this movie presents a lurid racist picture of the post–Civil War South and glorifies the Ku Klux Klan of that era. *The Birth of a Nation* took its story from *The Clansman*, a novel by Thomas Dixon, who had briefly been a fellow student with Wilson at Johns Hopkins in the 1880s. As a ploy to gain publicity and counter NAACP protests, Dixon called at the White House and disingenuously asked his old acquaintance to show the film there. Dixon bragged afterward that he had hidden "the real purpose of my film," which was to spread southern white racial attitudes in the North: "What I told the President was that I would show him the birth of a new art—the launching of the mightiest engine for moulding public opinion in the history of the world."[23]

Wilson fell into the trap. On February 18, Dixon and a projection crew gave the president, his family, cabinet officers, and their wives a showing of *The Birth of a Nation* in the East Room of the White House. How Wilson reacted is a matter of dispute. Twenty-two years later, a magazine writer alleged that he said about the film, "It is like writing history with lightning. And my only regret is that it is all so terribly true." It is extremely doubtful that Wilson uttered those words, and Dixon did not quote them later in his memoirs. Sixty-two years later, the last person then living who had been at the showing recalled that the president did not seem to pay much attention to the movie and left when it was over without saying a word. Regardless of what he did or did not say, Dixon and Griffith soon touted the event and insinuated that *The Birth of a Nation* enjoyed a presidential seal of approval.[24]

Far from dampening protests, these antics only fanned the controversy. The NAACP stepped up its campaign, and the incident caused political embarrassment. Two months later, Tumulty forwarded a clipping about protests in Boston organized by Trotter and advised the president to write a note saying he did not endorse the film. Wilson said he would if he did not appear to be responding to agitation "stirred up by that unspeakable fellow" Trotter. He found a way to do this when he drafted a statement for Tumulty to send under his own name to a Massachusetts Democrat: "It is true that 'The Birth of a Nation' was produced before the President and his family at the White House, but the President was entirely unaware of the character of the play before it was presented and has at no time expressed his approbation of it. Its exhibition at the White House was a courtesy extended to an old acquaintance." Three years later, he told Tumulty that the movie was "a very unfortunate production" and he wished it would not be shown "in communities where there are so many colored people."[25] Once more, he deplored stirring up emotions and showing bad manners rather than deploring the racist messages of Dixon's novel and Griffith's movie. Even more than segregation policies, Wilson's involvement with *The Birth of a Nation* would make him anathema to African Americans.

Another lapse in judgment during this time may also have owed something to his emotional turmoil. In this case it stemmed from the death of Justice Horace Lurton of the Supreme Court, in July 1914. Wilson and House had evidently agreed that Attorney General McReynolds should fill the first vacancy on the Court and that the colonel's fellow Texan Thomas W. Gregory should become attorney general—as he did with McReynolds's elevation. From Europe, House wrote to remind him of those choices. Whether Ellen's illness and death and the outbreak of the war affected him when he appointed McReynolds to the Court is difficult to determine. Earlier, he had sometimes acted casually, almost thoughtlessly, in picking cabinet members and other officials, and this may have been another example of that weakness. McReynolds would make life unpleasant for fellow justices and bedevil presidents for more than twenty years, and appointing him would turn out to be one of the worst blunders Wilson committed as president. It was doubly unfortunate because McReynolds's views of constitutional interpretation were totally at odds with his own, which stressed growth and adaptation rather than the imposition of rigidly held ideas. In his other two appointments to the Supreme Court, he would choose men whose thinking was much closer to his own.

Politically, the end of 1914 marked a difficult time for Wilson at home as well as abroad. The legislative triumphs of the preceding year and a half brought scant reward to his party in that November's elections. In the House, Democrats lost forty-eight seats, though they still retained control. A few seats turned over in the Senate, but the party margins remained unchanged, with Democrats still holding a small majority. Most of the losses in the House and in governorships occurred in the Northeast and Midwest, particularly in New York, Ohio, and Illinois. Those states cast the big electoral votes, and Wilson had carried them in 1912. These results did not bode well for a run in 1916.

Yet Democrats were not the biggest losers in November 1914. Progressives lost everywhere except California, where Governor Hiram Johnson and his machine retained control. Republican insurgents likewise fared badly, even in Wisconsin, where La Follette's followers lost to resurgent conservatives. Those outcomes appeared to vindicate the old guard Republicans' reasoning in 1912—that progressivism was a passing fad and economic misfortune under the Democrats would bring voters to their senses. Roosevelt now agreed. "The fundamental trouble was that the country was sick and tired of reform," he told William Allen White. Voters had "felt the pinch of poverty; . . . and compared with this they did not care a rap for social justice or industrial justice or clean politics or decency in public life."[26] That conclusion, together with his growing obsession with the world war, would lead Roosevelt to do everything he could to scuttle the Progressives and reunite with the Republicans.

Wilson read the returns in just the opposite light. The results discouraged him at first, but he soon saw a brighter side. He took satisfaction from Democrats' winning new House and Senate seats in mountain and West Coast states, apparently by picking up formerly Progressive votes. "A party that has been called sectional is becoming national," he exulted to a friend. "The sweep of its power and influence is immensely broadened. *That* puts tonic in my lungs." He quickly sounded a new battle cry of progressivism. In December, he declared in the State of the Union address that Americans "do not wish to curtail the activities of this Government; they wish, rather, to enlarge them." In January, at the Jackson Day dinner at which he spoke about "march[ing] with the discipline and with the zest of a conquering host," he maintained, "The Democratic party, and only the Democratic party, has carried out the policies which the progressive people of this country have desired." Wilson was warming once more to party and progressive politics. "[T]here is a real fight on," he said privately, adding that "it is no time for mere manners. . . . I cannot fight rottenness with rosewater."[27]

If he looked forward to concentrating on domestic politics, he was not reckoning with the world war. The beginning of 1915 marked the moment when it became the central, lasting fact of his presidency. In January, a diplomatic flap seemed about to erupt when the British threatened to seize the S.S. *Dacia*, a formerly German vessel purchased by an American businessman, but the affair blew over when, by coincidence, the French intercepted the ship. Britain's ally Japan also caused friction, by following up its conquest of German-held areas in China with a sweeping set of demands for hegemony in much of northern China. Wilson agreed to send stiff diplomatic notes of protest, thereby setting off tensions with Japan that would last for the rest of his presidency.[28]

Far more serious trouble arose from the other side in the war. On February 4, 1915, the German Admiralty declared the waters surrounding Britain "a war zone." Starting two weeks hence, the Germans announced, all merchant ships, neutral or belligerent, would be legitimate targets for attack and sinking by submarines. This "submarine declaration" by Germany stemmed from a combination of frustration and enthusiasm in Berlin. Lack of action by their surface ships irked the German naval high command, and submarines—with the ability to sneak beneath enemy ships and attack without warning—seemed to offer a golden opportunity to get into the war at sea and achieve positive results. In their enthusiasm, however, the champions of undersea warfare overlooked some big drawbacks. As yet, Germany had only thirty slow-moving submarines, and no more than a third of those could be deployed at any time. Moreover, by attacking and sinking merchant ships, Germany was committing the one act that could cause a diplomatic crisis with the United States. This submarine declaration was really a bluff, and one that carried enormous risks.[29]

Wilson reacted cautiously. At a cabinet meeting the next day, Secretary of War Garrison wanted to take a tough line, and he thought the president agreed with him. At his next press conference, however, Wilson told reporters he was waiting for more information from Berlin. He and Bryan approved a note that went to Germany on February 10, which asserted that sinking ships without warning was "an act so unprecedented in naval warfare" that the Germans should not contemplate it, and if they did, the United States would hold them to "a strict accountability for such acts of their naval authorities." Those words sounded tough, and many interpreters would later point to them as further evidence of Wilson's bias against Germany and in favor of the Allies. Actually, the note was a counterbluff. It did not specify what was meant by "strict accountability" or what might be done to hold the Germans to that standard. Wilson found the whole business nerve-racking and told Mary Hulbert that keeping a cool head involved "a nervous expenditure such as I never dreamed of."[30]

As these events were unfolding, he was not just reacting to challenges thrown at him by the belligerents. For some time, he had been thinking more broadly about the best way to end the conflict and how to bring far-reaching reform to international affairs. In a confidential interview in December 1914 with Herbert Brougham of *The New York Times*, he admitted that he did not believe Germany was solely to blame for the war, and he asserted that neither side ought to win a big victory. He did not think American interests would suffer if the Allies won, but such a victory did not strike him as the best outcome: "I think that the chances of a just and lasting peace, and of the only possible peace that will be lasting, will be happiest if no nation gets the decision by arms; and the danger of an unjust peace, one that will be sure to invite further calamities, will be if some one nation or group of nations succeeds in enforcing its will upon the others." Two years later, he would publicly reiterate and expand this line of thinking and use the same phrases when he would attempt to end the war with "a peace without victory."[31]

In February 1915, he outlined another, equally significant part of that later call for a compromise peace. Stockton Axson recalled that Wilson spelled out a four-point program for instituting a new world order. His first point was: "No nation shall ever again be permitted to acquire an inch of land by conquest." Second, everyone must recognize "the reality of equal rights between small nations and great." Third, the manufacture of munitions must no longer remain in private hands. The final and most important point was: "There must be an association of nations, all bound together for the protection and integrity of each, so that any one nation breaking from the bond will bring upon herself war; that is to say, punishment, automatically." Wilson would publicly restate these ideas and again use similar phrases when he called for "peace without victory."[32] He would reiterate them again in 1918 in his Fourteen Points address, and in 1919 he would make them the heart of the Covenant of the League of Nations.

Even as he responded to the Germans' submarine declaration and shared his thoughts with Axson, Wilson was sending out his first feeler on mediation of the war. In January, House informed him that the time was ripe for the trip to Europe they had talked about the month before. The two men met at the White House, devised a private code for communicating by telegram, and had an emotional leave-taking. "The President's eyes were moist when he said his last words of farewell," House wrote. On January 31, the colonel sailed on the largest and most luxurious ship afloat, the British liner *Lusitania*. He carried with him a letter from Wilson giving him "my commission to go, as my personal representative . . . without any official standing or authority," and stating that his talks were not meant "to urge action upon another government." Wilson said his "single object" was to help the warring nations take "the first step towards discussing and determining the conditions of peace" by ascertaining on each side "what is the real disposition, the real wish, the real purpose of the other." Two years later, Wilson would put forward the same idea and use similar words when, as a prelude to "peace without victory," he would ask the belligerents to state their terms for ending the war.[33]

It is difficult to judge how much stock he took in this effort and what House was expected to accomplish. Nor is it clear what House did accomplish, beyond cozying up to Sir Edward Grey and conveying the impression that Wilson was more pro-Allied than he really was. House would spend the next four months on the other side of the Atlantic, reporting on his conversations in the belligerent capitals and, in the last month, taking a strongly pro-Allied line. Despite his affection for House, Wilson would not take everything he said at face value, and upon his return the colonel would not enjoy the same degree of intimacy with Wilson as before.

The submarine challenge left the president little time to think about trying to end the war or reform international affairs. The Germans started using their new weapon during the latter part of February 1915. The British retaliated by tightening their blockade further, now including foodstuffs among the list of contraband—another potential blow to American exports. Submarines torpedoed a few American ships, including a freighter carrying grain and an oil tanker, during March and April, but for the most part their commanders obeyed secret orders to spare vessels flying the Stars and Stripes. That was no great sacrifice because the United States did not have many ships plying the North Atlantic. A potentially more dangerous issue involved the safety of American citizens traveling as passengers and crewmen on vessels of Allied countries. The danger became real at the end of March, when a submarine sank a small British passenger ship, the *Falaba*, and one of the those who perished was an American engineer, Leon Thresher. The Wilson administration now faced its first serious controversy with Germany over the submarine issue.

Wilson had feared such an incident. At the beginning of March, he had issued a statement to the press warning that the war might soon test Americans' self-control and urging citizens "to think, to purpose, and to act with patience, with disinterested fairness, and without excitement." The sinking of the *Falaba* and the death of Thresher confirmed the president's forebodings. "I do not like this case," he told Bryan. "It is full of disturbing possibilities." He believed that the Germans had violated international law and that the United States would probably have to demand that its citizens' lives not be endangered. Bryan reacted differently. He did not want to respond quickly to the Germans, and he worried about "whether an American citizen can, by putting his business above his regard for his country, assume for his own advantage unnecessary risks and thus involve his country in international complications." He was sure that "the almost unanimous desire of our country is that we shall not become involved in this war" and that one man, "acting purely for himself and his own interests, and without consulting his government," should not be allowed to put the country at risk of war.[34]

Wilson did not immediately push the question of a diplomatic response. Instead, he delivered a series of foreboding speeches in April in an effort to prepare the public for trying times. At a meeting of the Associated Press in New York, he avowed, "I am not speaking in a selfish spirit when I say that our whole duty, for the present, at any rate, is summed up in this motto: 'America first.' Let us think of America before we think of Europe, in order that we may be Europe's friend when the day of tested friendship comes." America must remain neutral, he declared, "because there is something better to do than fight; there is a distinction waiting for this country that no nation has ever yet got. That is the distinction of absolute self-control and self-mastery." Wilson was staking out the position that he would cling to not just for the next two months but for the next two years, in spite of conflicts within and without his administration and with great political consequences. Ironically, in "America first" he coined the motto of the isolationists who would later oppose him and the next Democratic president.[35]

When he turned to the diplomatic response to the *Falaba* incident, his thinking did not mesh with Bryan's. He proposed sending a note that assumed that Germany would abide by international law "with regard to the safety of non-combatants and of the citizens of neutral countries" and suggested that submarines conform to established practices of providing for their safety—all to be stated in restrained but firm protest. He wanted the note to be predicated "not on the loss of this single man's life, but on the interests of mankind." Bryan was not satisfied. He urged a public effort at mediation because the United States might be drawn into the war, and he again asked, was it right "to risk the provoking of war on account of one man?"[36] Wilson opposed mediation as unwise at that time, but when he and Bryan thrashed things out at a cabinet meeting, he conceded that it might be better not to send a note. Wilson was trying to devise a strategy to deal with small-scale incidents such as the British seizure of cargo or ships and German submarine attacks like the one on the *Falaba*—situations resembling events a century earlier that had dragged Madison into war. Whether that strategy would have worked can be only a matter for speculation because a huge incident was about to transform America's whole stance toward the world war.

Fortunately for him and the country, at the time that Wilson faced these growing challenges his personal life was undergoing a transformation—

dramatically and for the better. Family and friends had tried to distract him from his grief. In January, Jessie came to the White House to give birth to his and Ellen's first grandchild, Francis Bowes Sayre, Jr. Nell and McAdoo came for dinner at least once a week, and Helen Woodrow Bones, Wilson's cousin and Ellen's former secretary, continued to live in the White House. Grayson played golf with him nearly every day, weather permitting, and persuaded him to go for rides in one of the limousines and for an occasional cruise on the presidential yacht, the *Mayflower.* Time and distractions did begin to dull the pain of his wounded spirit, and he was privately talking about running for reelection, if only to keep Bryan from making another bid for the White House. The secretary of state would be a bad president, Wilson told a friend—in one of his few criticisms of Bryan recorded anywhere besides House's diary—because he was too trusting and was "a spoilsman to the core and a determined enemy of civil service reform."37

That determination to run again, together with his renewed zest for progressivism and political combat, were signs that he might be returning to his old self. Also in January, House noted that when Nell got her father to stand in front of a portrait of himself, "he made all sorts of contortions, sticking his tongue in his cheek, twisting his mouth into different positions, rolling his eyes, dropping his jaw, and doing everything a clown would do at a circus." Yet there were signs to the contrary as well. One was that this devotee of English novelists and poets had lost his taste for reading. "Even books have grown meaningless to me," he told a friend. "I read detective stories to forget, as a man would get drunk!" Wilson was not likely to drown his sorrows in alcohol, and he did not turn to another readily available and more respectable source of solace—religion— although in January 1915 he made a rare confession about his religious beliefs: "My life would not be worth living if it were not for the driving power of religion, for *faith*, pure and simple. I have seen all my life the arguments against it without ever having been moved by them." He felt sorry, he said, for "people who *believe* only so far as they *understand*—that seems to me presumptuous and sets their understanding as the standard of the universe."38

With that kind of faith, it is not surprising that Wilson did not turn to religion in his grief. Privately, after his outcries at the time of Ellen's death, he mentioned God only in conventional and unreligious comments, as when he said to Bryan, "God knows I have searched my mind and conscience." Publicly, he gave just one speech that touched on religion. That was in October 1914, on his first trip outside Washington after Ellen's death, when he addressed the Pittsburgh chapter of the Young

Men's Christian Association. He applauded faith like theirs, which expressed itself in good works and social reform, but he also said that he did not like to think of Christianity "as a means of saving individual souls."[39] He was being true to his Presbyterian upbringing, which stressed the workings of God in the world in large ways, not as solace to individuals for life's agonies. He was also being true to a personal faith that was deep and steady but something he took for granted and seldom thought about in good times or bad. That aspect of his religious attitude would change as he continued to confront the world war, when he would be dealing with the fate of millions of people, not personal tribulations.

Wilson found his greatest solace, predictably, in female companionship. This companionship came mainly in the form of letters, especially when he poured out his heart to Mary Hulbert, as he often did. His letters carried emotional intimacy but never a hint of romance or desire for physical intimacy; whatever passion had once burned between them had long since cooled, on Wilson's side at least. Such friendships of emotional warmth on a plane of equality between a man and a woman were unusual in those days and might have caused comment if they had become publicly known. Long-standing social taboos against courtship and remarriage by widowed men and women were weakening, but individuals were expected to observe a "decent interval of time." For someone who had lost his spouse so recently to fall in love again was unthinkable. Yet that is what Wilson did.

The relationship began as the offshoot of another couple's romance. Grayson had been patiently courting Alice Gertrude Gordon, a fellow Virginian who had moved to New York and went by the nickname Altrude. She had a close friend who lived in Washington, a widow named Edith Bolling Galt, who was also a Virginian and a friend of Grayson's. In the fall of 1914, the doctor confided in Mrs. Galt about his feelings for Altrude and talked about life in the White House after Ellen Wilson's death. As Mrs. Galt later recalled, Grayson was worried about Helen Bones, who seemed lonely in Washington. He soon introduced the two women to each other, and they struck up a friendship, taking rides in Mrs. Galt's car and walking on bridle paths in Rock Creek Park and taking tea afterward at Mrs. Galt's house. Helen recounted how her aunt, Wilson's mother, had raised her after her own mother died; she also described how Wilson and Ellen had taken her and other young relatives into their home and sent them to college.

Edith Galt first met Wilson on a sunny afternoon in March 1915. As she later recounted the story, Helen had insisted on their using one of the presidential limousines and returning to the White House for tea after their walk. The paths in the park were muddy that day, and Edith protested against the plan to return to the White House: "Oh, I couldn't do that; my shoes are a sight, and I should be taken for a tramp." Helen brushed aside her objections. Cousin Woodrow, she said, would be out playing golf with Grayson, and he had been urging her to have people come to visit. When they got off the elevator on the second floor, Edith found herself face-to-face with the president, who had just come back from the golf course with Grayson. His and the doctor's shoes were as muddy as hers and Helen's. "We all laughed at our plight, but I would have been less than feminine than I must confess to be, had I not been secretly glad that I had worn a smart black tailored suit which [the fashion house of] Worth had made for me in Paris, and a tricot hat which I thought completed a very good-looking ensemble." Edith also recalled noticing that the president's golf clothes "were *not* smart." The women had their shoes cleaned, the men changed their clothes, and the foursome gathered for tea in front of a fire in the oval sitting room on the second floor.[40]

For Woodrow Wilson, history was repeating itself. Thirty-two years earlier, he had fallen in love with Ellen Axson practically from the moment he first laid eyes on her. Now he would react the same way with Edith Galt. The forty-two-year-old widow was a tall woman, with a shapely though not slender figure, gray eyes, dark hair, and a glowing complexion. Her Virginia roots stretched back to 1607 and the original settlement at Jamestown, including among her ancestors Pocahontas and John Rolfe. Over the intervening generations, her family had belonged to the planter class of the Tidewater, and they had connections with one of Virginia's grandest names, the Randolphs. Like many such families, the Bollings lost most of their money in the Civil War. Edith's father, a graduate of the University of Virginia Law School, relocated, becoming a judge in Wytheville, a town at the foot of the Blue Ridge Mountains near the North Carolina border, where Edith was born in October 1872. A lively young woman with a talent for music but little liking for books, she had received a somewhat spotty education, although she did attend two boarding schools. In her teens and early twenties, she began traveling to Washington to visit her oldest sister, who had married a member of the Galt family, which owned the city's most distinguished jewelry store. In the course of those visits, Edith met her brother-in-law's cousin, Norman Galt, who also worked in the family business, and they were married in 1896.[41]

The Galts' marriage lasted just eleven years. Outwardly, it appeared happy enough. As the wife of a prominent businessman, Edith enjoyed an assured though not elevated place in Washington society. She had been raised a devout Episcopalian, and she attended church regularly. Inwardly, some strains may have existed between the couple, possibly involving a tendency toward depression on Edith's part. They had had one child, a son who was born in 1903 but lived only three days. The jewelry store also posed problems. Norman Galt had taken sole ownership, but soon afterward, in January 1908, he died unexpectedly and without having paid the debts he had incurred to buy out his relatives. "I had no experience in business affairs," Edith later wrote, "and hardly knew an asset from a liability." Nevertheless, with the help of an experienced manager, she kept the store going. After a few prosperous years, she was able to delegate active management to others, and she began to enjoy herself.[42]

If not a merry widow, Edith certainly was a liberated one. She played golf, obtained the first driver's license issued to a woman in the District of Columbia, attended the theater and concerts, had one or two romances, and traveled widely, to Europe and around the United States, often accompanied by Altrude Gordon. As her comment about her own and the president's attire indicated, she had a flair for fashion. In sum, Mrs. Galt was a stylish, worldly, independent woman; in those respects, she resembled Mary Hulbert. Between that resemblance and her good looks, Edith Galt might well have been expected to catch the eye of the lonely widower who lived in the White House.

Catch his eye she did. Grayson recalled that one day they had been riding in a limousine when Wilson saw Mrs. Galt, whom he had not yet met, walking on the street and asked, "Who is that beautiful lady?" The story sounds apocryphal, but when Wilson did meet her, he was immediately smitten. She accepted an invitation to join Wilson, Grayson, Helen Bones, and a visitor from out of town for dinner on March 23. "I am just home from the White House where I spent the evening and dined informally with the President," she told her sister-in-law. "He is *perfectly* charming and one of the easiest and most delightful hosts I have ever known." After dinner, she and Helen went upstairs with Wilson to the oval sitting room, where they again sat in front of the fire, and he told "interesting stories" and, at Helen's request, read three English poems, "and as a reader he is unequalled." Two weeks later, she accepted another invitation, this time for a drive with Helen and the president. He sat in the front seat with the chauffeur and did not say much. After a quiet dinner, however, he talked about his childhood and his father. "The evening ended all too soon," Edith recalled, adding, incorrectly, "for it was the first time I had felt the warm personality of Woodrow Wilson. A boylike simplicity dwelt in the background of an official life."43

Wilson saw Mrs. Galt several more times during the month of April. She came to dinner and took rides again and went to the opening-day game of the baseball season, where she sat behind him in the presidential party. At the end of the month, Wilson began writing to her almost daily. He would use his shorthand to draft a letter, which he would then write, not type—a sure sign of how deeply he felt. For him, it was a short step from epistolary intimacy to a face-to-face declaration of love. He took the step on May 4, right after returning from a trip to Williamstown, Massachusetts, for the christening of his grandson. As Edith later recalled, the two of them were sitting alone on the South Portico porch after dinner with Helen, Wilson's daughter Margaret, and his sister Annie Howe. Drawing his chair closer to hers, he told her he loved her. She remembered that she felt almost shocked and blurted out, "Oh, you can't love me, for you don't really know me; and it is less than a year since your wife died."44

As Edith recounted the story, he replied, "Yes, I know that you feel that; but, little girl, in this place time is not measured by weeks, or months, or years, but by deep human experiences; and since her death I have lived a lifetime of loneliness and heartache. I was afraid, knowing you, I would shock you; but I would be less than a gentleman if I continued to make opportunities to see you without telling you what I have already told my daughters and Helen: that I want you to be my wife." He explained that because he was a public personage and the White House a public place, her visits were bound to stir up gossip. "It is for this reason I have talked to the girls about it, so that they can safeguard you and make it possible for me to see you. They have all been wonderful about it, and they love you for your own sake, but would anyway for mine." Edith recalled that they talked for more than an hour. She told Wilson that if he had to have an immediate answer, it would be no, but she agreed to keep seeing him. He then accompanied her home in a limousine.45

This account leaves a mistaken impression of Edith's feelings and behavior. She evidently did decline Wilson's proposal of marriage: an initial refusal was the proper response from a gently bred woman of that time, even when she planned to say yes. Likewise, it was untoward for such a recently widowed man to ask a woman to marry him. In fact, Edith was not so discouraging as she later claimed. That night, after midnight, she wrote a letter to him, opening with a poem that began with the lines

Your dear love fills me with a bliss untold,
Perfect, divine
I did not know the human heart could hold
Such a joy as mine.

In her own words, Edith told him, "Ever since you went away my whole being is awake and vibrant! . . . I am a woman—and the thought that you have *need* of me—is sweet!" Those were not the words of a woman who intended to keep a man waiting for long.[46]

Requited love brought out the best in Wilson. Thirty years earlier, Ellen's love had helped him write *Congressional Government* and launch his academic career. Now this new love would invigorate him to meet fresh challenges as president. In the morning of May 7, he wrote to Edith, "Ah, my precious friend and comrade, what happiness it was to be with you last night! While your hand rested in mine I felt as if I could stand up and shout for the strength and joy that was in me. . . . I knew where I could get the solace that would ease the strain and felt fit for any adventure of the spirit."[47]

14

THE SHOCK OF RECOGNITION

Friday, May 7, 1915, was in its time what Sunday, December 7, 1941, and Tuesday, September 11, 2001, would be in their times. Interviewing Americans ten years later, the journalist Mark Sullivan found that this day had burned itself into people's memories. Everyone he talked to remembered the sinking of the *Lusitania;* they remembered what they had thought and felt when they heard the news; they remembered where they had been; they remembered what they had done for the rest of the day. This sudden destruction of the world's fastest and grandest ocean liner inevitably recalled the sinking of the *Titanic* almost exactly three years before. But this great ship went down not because she had grazed an iceberg but because a German submarine had fired a torpedo into her hull. The liner sank in eighteen minutes, killing 1,198 people, of whom 128 were Americans. The event instantly transformed the stance of the United States toward the war. It brought the shock of recognition: gone were notions of viewing from afar a tragedy that was happening to somebody else; gone were ideas about enduring and managing a gradual accumulation of small incidents caused by blockades and sporadic submarine attacks.[1]

This traumatic recognition of how close and threatening the war now was spawned contradictory opinions. Nearly every person who spoke out expressed outrage. Roosevelt and Lodge stopped barely short of calling for war, but not many went so far. New York newspapers conducted the closest thing to a public opinion poll that was possible at the time, asking every editor in the country to telegraph his opinion of what the United States should do. Out of the thousand who responded, only six called for war. The lack of belligerence was not surprising. Newspaper and magazine coverage of the carnage on the Western Front and the recent use of poison gas left no room for illusions about the horrors of this war. Wilson summed up the public reaction best when he said to Bryan, "I wish with all my heart I saw a way to carry out the double wish of our people, to maintain a firm front in respect of what we demand of Germany and yet do nothing that might by any possibility involve us in the war."[2]

The news of the sinking of the *Lusitania* shook the president. The first report reached the White House early in the afternoon, just as he was about to leave for his daily round of golf. He canceled the game and stayed to hear more news, leaving only to take a ride in the limousine. A cable with more information arrived in the evening, just after dinner. Soon afterward, reporters noticed the president walking by himself out the main entrance to the White House. He crossed Pennsylvania Avenue and Lafayette Square and walked several blocks up Sixteenth Street and back down Fifteenth Street, ignoring the rain that was falling. "I was pacing the streets to get my mind in hand," he told Edith Galt the next morning. Typically for him at a stressful time, but unlike most other politicians, he did not see or talk with anyone.[3]

Over the weekend the president made a show of leading life as usual. On Saturday, he played golf and took a long ride. Whether Edith Galt accompanied him on the ride is not clear, but she came to dinner. The couple spent time alone afterward, and he handed her a love letter he had written that morning. On Sunday, Wilson went to church, but he departed from his usual practice of not working on the Sabbath to spend much of the day in his study. He started to draft a diplomatic note to Germany, and he made shorthand notes and wrote out two long letters to Edith. His only public reference to the incident came in a statement he had Tumulty give to the press on Saturday night, saying that he viewed the situation with utmost seriousness and was considering how to respond.[4]

Wilson began to involve others in the situation on Monday. He and Bryan exchanged several notes. Bryan broached the idea of warning American citizens not to travel on ships of belligerent countries. Wilson expressed no opinion of that idea, but he did say that they must weigh how their actions looked abroad. His stenographer, Charles Swem, noted that the president said he would not let the country be stampeded into anything and that he brushed aside a telegram imploring him, in the name of God, to declare war. The president said, "War isn't declared in the name of God; it is a human affair entirely."[5] He did not meet with cabinet members, and Edith Galt was his only visitor during the day, for a private lunch, at which they talked ardently of their love for each other.

Even before the sinking of the *Lusitania*, Wilson had planned to use a speech in Philadelphia on May 10 to continue to set the tone of America's response to the war. Because his audience included 4,000 newly naturalized citizens, the occasion lent itself to the subject. Mostly, he reiterated well-worn ideas of his about America's "constant and repeated rebirth" through immigration and its standing as "a great hope of the human race." He urged his listeners "not only always to think first of America, but always, also, to think of humanity." He did not mention the *Lusitania*, but he did say, "The example of America must be the example, not merely of peace because it will not fight, but of peace because peace is the healing and elevating influence of the world, and strife is not. There is such a thing as a man being too proud to fight. There is such a thing as a nation being so right that it does not need to convince others by force that it is right."[6]

The words "too proud to fight" would live on as one of Wilson's best-remembered phrases—to his chagrin. In uttering those words, he evidently did not think he was saying anything remarkable. They expressed a personal philosophy instilled in him since childhood, particularly by his mother. In the preceding weeks, he had been counseling calm and self-control in facing challenges posed by the war. He told Edith the next day that he did not remember what he had said in Philadelphia because he was thinking of her: "I did not know before I got up very clearly what I was going to say, nor remember what I had said when I sat down." That was a bit of sweet sophistry. Even before he heard any public reactions to the speech, Wilson knew he had blundered with "too proud to fight." At a press conference the next day, he claimed he had not been talking about policy and had expressed "a personal attitude, that was all." He allowed reporters to paraphrase, though not quote, his retraction. Frank Parker Stockbridge, his press secretary in 1911, recalled that Wilson told him, "That was just one of the foolish things a man does. I have a bad habit of thinking out loud. That thought occurred to me while I was speaking, and I let it out. I should have kept it in or developed it further." Of all the words he uttered in his public career, "too proud to fight" were probably the ones he most wished had never passed his lips.[7]

Actions, not words, caused him more immediate concern. Just how hard it would be to satisfy the "double wish" became painfully clear when he brought the *Lusitania* problem before the cabinet on May 11. Two days earlier, House had asserted in an impassioned telegram from London, "Think we can no longer remain neutral spectators. . . . We are being weighed in the balance, and our position amongst the nations is being assessed by mankind." Wilson opened the cabinet meeting by reading that telegram, and he read aloud his draft of a diplomatic note. In the discussion, Bryan grew emotional and accused other cabinet members of not being neutral, and Wilson reportedly reproved him. He was not really put out with Bryan. "Both in mind and heart I was deeply moved by what you said in Cabinet this morning," he wrote when he sent along the draft of the note, which demanded an apology and reparations for the sinking of the *Lusitania* as well as the earlier attack on the *Falaba* and warned that the United States would take "any necessary act in sustaining the rights of its citizens or in safeguarding the sacred duties of international law."[8]

Bryan showed great persistence in pushing his views on how to deal with the protest to Germany. The following day, he sent Wilson two handwritten letters containing suggestions to mitigate the risk of war and avoid siding with either set of belligerents. He also proposed to protest the Allied blockade and issue a supplemental statement that would invoke the principle of his compulsory delay, or a cooling-off treaty. Germany had not agreed to such a treaty with the United States, but he argued that it had endorsed the underlying principle. Wilson ignored the protest to the Allies, but he liked the idea of a supplemental statement and proposed to accompany the diplomatic note with a "tip" to the press, a draft of which he sent to Bryan. In this "tip," he noted that Germany had endorsed the principle of compulsory delay and expressed confidence that the Germans would either respond favorably to the note or submit the dispute to some process of arbitration.[9]

Wilson did not carry through with this move, seemingly scuttling it within hours. He told Bryan he had heard something from the German embassy that convinced him that such a statement would spoil the chance to resolve the dispute satisfactorily. That was not true. Instead, the "tip" fell victim to backstabbing intrigue. When Bryan described the move to Robert Lansing, the counselor of the State Department (the department's second-ranking official), Lansing said he approved. Immediately afterward, however, Lansing went behind his boss's back to inform Secretary of War Garrison, who was the most bellicose member of the cabinet. Garrison told Lansing to see Tumulty, who also reacted unfavorably to the "tip." In turn, Tumulty informed Postmaster General Burleson, and the two of them went to see the president. Wilson defended the press statement, but Tumulty maintained that it would give the appearance of double-dealing. When Wilson read the statement to them, Burleson did not think it was so bad, but Tumulty stood his ground, and Wilson finally agreed not to issue it and sent the note as it stood. It is doubtful that Tumulty's arguments swayed him and more likely that he had begun to have second thoughts of his own.[10]

In fact, Wilson had not completely scuttled the plan. He planted stories claiming that the mood of the administration was hopeful of a satisfactory reply from Berlin and a peaceful outcome to the situation. The stories, written by David Lawrence, who had gone to Princeton and was close to Wilson, appeared on May 14 and 15 in the *New York Evening Post* and *The New York Times*. Two weeks later, Wilson tried sending a stronger peace signal. He appears to have met with Bernstorff, the German ambassador, on May 28, before he received a reply to his diplomatic note. Bernstorff reported to Berlin that the president's thinking about peace terms included, besides a return to the pre-war status quo, "[t]he freedom of the seas to such an extent that it would be equal to neutralization of the seas" and "[a]djustments of colonial possessions."[11] This seems to have been the first time Wilson used the term "freedom of the seas," a phrase and an idea that would appear repeatedly in his pronouncements about post-war international order.

In the meantime, the president awaited Germany's reply to the *Lusitania* note. This waiting period marked the beginning of a sequence that would repeat itself several times over the next eleven months. It would be like a tennis game in extreme slow motion: first, the United States would send a diplomatic note; next, after a time, Germany would reply; then the United States would volley again. While this game took place, debate and conflict over the latest move would wax and wane on each side, often heightened by events on the battlefield or the seas.

Affairs of state did not keep Wilson from affairs of the heart. He invited Edith Galt and Altrude Gordon to accompany him, his daughter Margaret, his sister Annie Howe, Helen Bones, Grayson, and Tumulty on a cruise aboard the *Mayflower*. They sailed for New York, where Wilson was to give a speech and review the Atlantic fleet. A round of festivities greeted them on May 17. The president spoke at a luncheon given by the mayor and reviewed a parade, and Secretary of the Navy Daniels gave a dinner aboard the Navy Department's official yacht. The following day, the president reviewed the fleet in the Hudson River. As the *Mayflower* steamed past, each warship fired a salute and played an anthem. Edith and Wilson had little time alone together, although she reveled in "the absolute abstraction and [in] forgetting there was *anyone* else in the launch but *you*." Back in Washington, they resumed writing notes and meeting for rides and dinner. Wilson was growing impatient. Age had not cooled his physical desires; at fifty-eight he had the sexual appetite of a man half his age. Edith seems to have acted like a proper lady and resisted his advances. After spending two hours with her in the backseat of the presidential limousine with the curtains drawn, Wilson wrote the next morning, "For God's sake try to find out whether you really love me or not. You owe it to yourself and you owe it to the great love I have given you, without stint or measure."[12]

Edith was more upset with herself than with Wilson. "I have promised not to raise barriers and not to think defeat possible," she told him the next day. "I will patiently keep those promises, for I love you, and your love for me has made the whole world new." For her, his allure was inseparable from his office, as she later admitted in her memoirs.[13] On his side, he played upon the presidency in wooing her. He shared secrets of state with her and gave her glimpses of inner workings at the highest level of government. Some of this was standard practice for him. He was used to divulging his deepest thoughts and feelings to female friends, and he was accustomed to baring his soul to a woman he loved, as he had done with Ellen almost as soon as he had met her. The lack of privacy surrounding a president—ever-present Secret Service agents and staff and servants and an inquisitive press—restricted opportunities for intimacy, but they made do as well as they could.

The day after the scene in the limousine, the German reply to the *Lusitania* note arrived and set off a second, even more trying, round in the diplomatic tennis game over the submarines. Although the Germans issued secret orders to spare large passenger liners from submarine attack, their official reply was haughty and evasive. Press reaction in the United States was uniformly negative. Wilson again kept to himself, except to deliver an address at Arlington National Cemetery on May 30, Decoration Day. Having learned his lesson from "too proud to fight," he refrained from saying anything that might be taken as a comment on the current situation. When the cabinet met on June 1, everyone expressed disappointment at the German reply. Bryan had not changed his mind and once more argued against a quick response and for further inquiry into the *Lusitania*'s sinking. Wilson did not agree, but he did not totally reject this approach. He met again with the German ambassador for what Bernstorff described as "an extraordinarily friendly exchange of views," in which Wilson promised that if Germany would give up submarine warfare, he would press the British to end their food blockade.[14] That overture did not satisfy Bryan, who wrote Wilson a lengthy letter in which he noted that the *Lusitania* was alleged to have carried munitions and urged redoubled efforts to find a peaceful resolution.

As before, Wilson decided from the outset to make a strong protest. He spent two days working on a new diplomatic note to Germany. On June 4, he read his draft at a cabinet meeting. He charged that the sinking of the *Lusitania* involved "principles of humanity" that lifted the incident "out of the class of ordinary subjects of diplomacy," and he avowed that the loss of so many innocent lives imposed a "grave responsibility" on the United States. Another inconclusive discussion followed, with none of the cabinet members expressing his position clearly. By contrast, two senior Democrats from Capitol Hill showed no such hesitancy. The same day as the cabinet meeting, Thomas S. Martin, chairman of the Senate Appropriations Committee, and Henry (Hal) De La Warr Flood, chairman of the House Foreign Affairs Committee, both Virginians, went to see Bryan, who reported that they strongly opposed war and knew from talking with their colleagues that neither the House nor the Senate would vote for a declaration of war. Wilson responded that Bryan's report of what they said "made a deep impression on me, and I have no doubt echoes a great part of public opinion," and he made his comment about the people's "double wish."[15]

This expression of sentiment among congressional Democrats prompted Bryan to make one last stab at softening the diplomatic note. The next day, he suggested to Wilson "three matters which, to my mind, are necessary to prevent war with Germany": invoking the principle of compulsory delay, barring passenger ships from carrying munitions, and simultaneously protesting British blockade practices. Wilson immediately rejected those proposals, though "with deep misgiving." He liked the idea of keeping Americans off ships carrying munitions, but he could not see "the way to do it without hopelessly weakening our protest," and he wanted to keep any dealings with Britain separate from the submarine controversy.[16]

That exchange with Bryan took place on a Saturday. The weekend brought Wilson no respite. When he saw Edith Galt the next day, he showed her his latest draft of the diplomatic note, and he confided in her what one of the gravest consequences of that note would be. "Then, I did want to ask you more about the resignation of 'W.J.B.',," she wrote to him, "but saw the subject troubled you so would not let myself discuss it." That Saturday, he had learned that Bryan intended to resign rather than sign the new diplomatic note to Germany. Bryan had decided to tell McAdoo first, because he was Wilson's son-in-law. McAdoo later recalled that Bryan was nervous and haggard when he came to his house and admitted he had not been sleeping well. McAdoo tried unsuccessfully to talk him out of resigning, pointing out that a sign of disunity might lead to war—"the very result which you say you are so anxious to avoid." He suggested that Bryan and his wife spend the weekend away from the city and speak with him again on Monday. "Meanwhile I will see the President and tell him of our conversation." McAdoo then went to the White House and related everything to Wilson. According to his recollection, the president was not surprised at Bryan's intention but wanted to keep him in the cabinet if possible.[17]

The next day, Wilson again broke his custom of not working on the Sabbath and sought out Tumulty for advice. They talked over lunch, and Tumulty urged him to accept Bryan's resignation at once. So, too, facetiously, did Edith Galt. "I think it will be a blessing to get rid of him," she told Wilson, "and [I] might as well frankly say I would like to be appointed in his place, for then I should have to have daily conferences with you."[18] Wilson also met with McAdoo and Houston, his secretary of agriculture, in the afternoon and talked about possible successors to Bryan. The latter spent Saturday night and Sunday at the estate of a Democratic senator outside Washington, but time for reflection did not change his mind, as he told McAdoo on Monday. He wrote a lengthy final letter to Wilson suggesting changes to soften the note to Germany, and in the afternoon he went with McAdoo to the White House to inform the president in person of his intention to resign.

Wilson sat facing Bryan for more than an hour in his office. He remained calm, but Bryan grew agitated and at one point his hand shook so much that he spilled water from a glass as he was trying to drink. Wilson repeatedly urged Bryan to stay on, but the secretary would have none of it. The president was risking war, he maintained, and was letting other nations dictate America's policies. At one point, Bryan remarked in a quavering voice, "Colonel House has been Secretary of State, not I, and I have never had your full confidence." House, after hearing of this charge, wrote that Wilson "tried to minimize what I have done, but was not very successful for facts were against him, although Mr. Bryan knew but a small part of my work. The President said he had only shown him a few of my messages, and excused himself for this by saying how utterly impossible it would be to let Mr. Bryan know his whole mind."[19] House was getting in another dig at Bryan and exaggerating his own importance.

Wilson did not want Bryan to go. His resignation would not only send a signal of disunity to Germany but would also split the Democratic Party. Beyond such diplomatic and political considerations, he genuinely valued Bryan. He had worked more closely with him than with any other cabinet member. During the last two years, they had seen each other almost daily when they were in Washington, and they had exchanged a steady stream of notes and telephone calls. "No two officials ever got along more amicably," Bryan later recalled. "I was in charge of the department and the President and I never differed on a matter of policy until the controversy over American citizens riding on belligerent ships." Wilson agreed. At the meeting with McAdoo and Houston the day before, Robert Lansing's name had come up as a possible successor to Bryan, and, as Houston recalled, the president "remarked that Lansing would not do, that he was not a big enough man, did not have enough imagination, and would not sufficiently vigorously combat or question his [Wilson's] views, and that he was lacking in initiative."[20] In other words, he was no William Jennings Bryan.

There was more to this resignation than met the eye. The stated reason—policy disagreement—was not so straightforward as it appeared. Wilson was taking a harder line toward Germany than Bryan thought right or safe, but the president was also making peaceable overtures. It was also odd that Bryan signed the first *Lusitania* note and only balked at the second protest. The strain of risking war was taking a toll on him emotionally and physically, but his reasons for resigning went deeper. Bryan was facing a political identity crisis. He believed he must leave in order to remain faithful to his most cherished view of himself. His daughter Grace later recounted that when her father came home from his meeting with the president, his face was flushed, his walk was unsteady, and he seemed to be in "great emotional agony." Lying on a sofa, he told her and her mother, "We have come to a parting of the ways. The President does not seem to realize that a great part of America lies on the other side of the Alleghany Mountains. . . . By resigning I will be free to assist them in their struggle against entering this heart-breaking conflict on either side." The next day, after his resignation was made public, Bryan said, "I believe that I can do more on the outside to prevent war than I can do on the inside. . . . I can work to direct public opinion so it will not exert pressure for extreme action."[21]

Woodrow Wilson would never have said or thought those things. He, too, believed that the "real America" lay outside the Northeast, and he had a similar faith in the potency of public opinion. As governor, he had appealed to people over the heads of the legislature. As president, he would soon make another speaking tour to appeal to the citizenry over the heads of Congress. But Wilson's model of public persuasion was education, whereas Bryan's was evangelism. Likewise, Wilson never exalted a leader's role as a speaker above that of actually wielding power. He would never have dreamed of trading a place at or near the center of power for a perch on the stump. That difference was what Wilson had been getting at in January when he said he thought Bryan would make a bad president. He repeated that judgment when he told Edith Galt a few days after Bryan's resignation, "No stranger man ever lived, and his naïveté takes my breath away."[22]

Wilson handled Bryan's departure with dignity. He wrote a warmly worded letter accepting Bryan's equally warmly worded resignation, and Bryan attended a last cabinet meeting after the announcement of his departure. Behind his mask of cordiality, however, Wilson was apprehensive; he knew Bryan's departure brought both danger and opportunity. Its timing—in the middle of a diplomatic crisis—brought down on Bryan's head an expected deluge of abuse, even from fellow Democrats, but Wilson recognized that Bryan was poised to pounce at any perceived sign of belligerence, and he would soon come out swinging against proposed increases in the army and navy. Stockton Axson, who was staying at the White House at the time, recalled that at breakfast one day Wilson, "piercing me with that sharp look which he sometimes had," said about Bryan, "He is *absolutely* sincere. That is what makes him dangerous."[23]

Yet Bryan's attack from the pacifist flank highlighted Wilson's stance as champion of the "double wish." The terms *hawk* and *dove* would not be used for another fifty years, but the cartoonist Rollin Kirby of the New York *World* captured their essence when he drew Wilson standing between Bryan, who is holding a birdcage with a dove of peace inside, and Roosevelt, who is wearing a cowboy outfit and shooting off a pair of six-guns.

Others besides Democrats rallied to Wilson's side. Taft praised the president's position publicly and privately told a friend, "I have very little sympathy with such statements as those of . . . Theodore Roosevelt, which are calculated to make his [Wilson's] course more difficult." According to Tumulty, Wilson held up two fingers to symbolize his appreciation of Taft's support.[24]

The second *Lusitania* note went out on June 9, over the signature of Lansing as acting secretary of state. While he waited for the German reply, Wilson faced the task of choosing a successor to Bryan. Houston later recalled that the president thought House might be a good choice but ruled him out because of his frail health. He sent McAdoo to consult with the colonel, who had just returned from Europe. According to House, McAdoo floated the names of Houston and Wilson's old friend and Princeton supporter Thomas Jones. "I asked McAdoo why the President did not consider Lansing. He replied that he [Wilson] did not think he was big enough. I told McAdoo to say to the President that, in my opinion, it would be better to have a man with not too many ideas of his own." The colonel pressed this backhanded case for Lansing by letter and in person. In the letter, he conceded that he had met the man only once, "and while his mentality did not impress me unduly," he thought he would do. The meeting, their first in nearly five months, took place on June 24, when the president stopped over in New York on his way to Harlakenden—

where Edith Galt was joining members of the Wilson family. Wilson and House discussed Lansing, and Wilson said he had decided to appoint him because, as House recorded, the president was "practically his own Secretary of State and Lansing would not be troublesome by obtruding or injecting his own views."[25]

Wilson announced Lansing's appointment the next day. He may have been simply following the path of least resistance. Lansing was already the number two person in the State Department, and at a critical time like this the country needed a secretary of state. Yet this would be one of the worst appointments Wilson would make as president. With his perfectly barbered white hair and mustache and impeccably tailored suits, Robert Lansing looked like a theater director's idea of a secretary of state. That appearance and his technical knowledge of international law and diplomatic procedure were his chief qualifications. Privately, Lansing held pro-Allied views not too different from Roosevelt's or House's, but he kept those opinions to himself. He could be furtive and underhanded, as he had shown in going behind Bryan's back over the *Lusitania* "tip." Wilson's treating him like a clerk during the next four years would understandably breed resentment and aggravate Lansing's inclinations to try to undermine the president.[26]

On his side, Wilson would give in to his own inclinations toward lone-handedness, which he had largely held in check since entering politics. In pushing Lansing, House almost certainly believed that he was increasing his own influence, but Edith Galt had already begun to replace him as Wilson's most intimate adviser. House would remain close to Wilson, but he would be a sounding board and valued negotiator rather than a source of counsel. No one would replace Bryan as a strong, quasi-independent force in making foreign policy. That would be doubly unfortunate because in dealing with the world war, there would no longer be a forceful voice close to the president's ear warning against the risks of intervention. Doubt and restraint would have to come from Wilson himself, seldom from his advisers. From mid-1915 onward, he would make foreign policy decisions and set directions almost entirely on his own.

Courting Edith Galt continued to provide welcome diversion from public business. Wilson told House about her during his visit on June 24. "What would you think of my getting married again?" Wilson asked. He explained that he had met a wonderful woman and needed female companionship. He also felt sure Ellen would have approved, "for she had talked to me about it and I am sure I would be following her wishes." Grayson and Attorney General Gregory had already told House about

Edith, but he did not let on, nor would he tell Grayson that Wilson confided in him. House gave his approval because, he noted, "I feel that his
health demands it and I also feel that Woodrow Wilson is the greatest
asset the world has." He did suggest that the president wait for a year
before remarrying.[27]

Wilson spent three weeks at Harlakenden with Edith, Grayson, family members—and the ever-present Secret Service detail. "When we
walked together," Edith recalled in her memoir, "we would try to forget
that lurking behind every tree was a Secret Service man." The party took
rides in the limousines and gathered around the fireplace after dinner.
While Wilson worked on papers sent from Washington, in the next room
Grayson, Frank Sayre, Jessie, and Margaret would take turns reading from
his *History of the American People*, sometimes asking him for comments.
Edith remembered Wilson rejoining at one point, "Do you youngsters
realize that . . . right now I am in the midst of so much history in the making that I cannot turn my mind back to that time? Besides, I have never
been proud of that History. I wrote it only to teach myself something
about our country." He said that the lavish payments for its serialization in
Harper's had come "like a windfall" and then explained how the term *windfall* came from the old English custom of tenants on an estate enjoying the
right to gather wood blown down by the wind.[28]

The couple made the most of the time they could snatch away from
the rest of the party. On one of their walks early in the visit, Edith
accepted Wilson's renewed proposal of marriage, and they became
secretly engaged. They enjoyed some physical intimacy, although probably not as much as they wanted. Despite their lack of privacy, Wilson
enjoyed himself. "I am well and am profiting immensely by my delightful
vacation," he told House, "the first real one I have had since I went into
politics."[29] The idyll ended temporarily when Wilson returned to Washington for a few days at the middle of July. The German reply to the second *Lusitania* protest had arrived, and once more the government in
Berlin had taken a stand that struck many in America as haughty and evasive. Yet there were also strong signs of anti-war sentiment, thanks in part
to Bryan's recent oratorical barnstorming. Before returning to Washington, Wilson began drafting a third note to Germany, and he telegraphed a
statement for Tumulty to release to the press assuring that the president
would be returning to Washington to confer with the cabinet.

When Wilson met with the cabinet on July 20, he found that Bryan's
departure had changed things less than expected—except that pressure
now was coming mostly from the opposite side. Bellicose, blustery Garrison arrived with his own draft of a reply to Germany and did most of the

talking. Wilson responded by saying again that the American people wanted the government to issue a firm response but also to avoid war. Other cabinet members chimed in to support the president. In a note largely along the lines he had drafted, Wilson demanded an end to surprise attacks at sea but avoided an ultimatum. Despite that forbearance, he told Edith he feared war might come, and he worried about what that would mean for millions of people who "so confidingly depend on me to keep them out of the hor[r]ors of this war."[30]

Garrison did not come away from this encounter empty-handed. Wilson remained sensitive to the other side of the "double wish"—the need to strike a strong pose on the international stage. He now decided that he must put more military muscle behind his diplomatic stance toward Germany and the other belligerents. The day after the cabinet meeting, he drafted a statement for Tumulty to release to the press a few days later, announcing that the president was consulting with the secretaries of war and the navy about changes and increases in the armed forces. He wanted the navy "to stand upon an equality with the most efficient and serviceable," and he wanted the army to have "proper training of the citizens of the United States to arms." Wilson insisted that he was taking this action "regardless of present conditions or controversies" and that he intended to consult with the congressional Armed Services Committees.[31] The same day, he asked Garrison and Daniels to provide specific recommendations.

No matter how much Wilson might try to soft-pedal this move, he was making an about-face from his earlier rejection of increased military preparedness. Nor did anybody doubt that he was responding to the country's changed stance toward the world conflict and repeated attacks by bellicose critics. Tumulty admitted as much when he released the statement, telling reporters, "It will pocket Roosevelt completely."[32] That was wishful thinking. The ex-president, Lodge, and others speedily denounced any new defense program from this administration as too little too late. Even more dangerous for Wilson were attacks coming from within his own party. As expected, Bryan quickly denounced any talk of strengthening the army and navy as a step toward war, and his followers on Capitol Hill soon followed suit. By reversing course on preparedness, Wilson was picking the biggest fight yet in his political life.

The way Garrison and Daniels responded to Wilson's request for recommended increases gave a foretaste of how thorny and complicated things would become. Roosevelt and his circle claimed that Daniels was a satellite of Bryan and singularly unfit to run the navy. Some ranking officers similarly scoffed at him as a country bumpkin who did not appreciate their needs and special culture. Daniels's own deputy, thirty-three-year-

old Assistant Secretary of the Navy Franklin Roosevelt, shared those attitudes; he often lampooned his boss behind his back and sometimes leaked
damaging information to his wife's "Uncle Ted" and Senator Lodge. Far
from a rube, however, Daniels was a shrewd, experienced political operator gifted with a thick skin and an equable temperament; he likewise possessed the insight to detect a glimmer of merit in Franklin Roosevelt and
put up with him despite the young man's often flighty manner, furtive
condescension, and occasional disloyalty. Daniels also felt the strongest
personal loyalty to Wilson of any cabinet member except McAdoo. After
some dickering with the navy's planning arm, the General Board, Daniels
presented the president with a five-year, $500 million program that called
for 6 new battleships, 10 cruisers, 50 destroyers, and 100 submarines. This
was to Wilson's liking, and in October he approved the proposals without
change.[33]

The army program was another matter. Garrison basked in praise
from the administration's combative critics, and he felt little personal loyalty to the president. Earlier in 1915, he had made noises about resigning
if he did not get his way. "If Garrison mentions it again," House had
recorded in his diary in June, "[Wilson] would let him go." Garrison initially submitted only a sketchy outline of a big new reserve force, and
then, without Wilson's knowledge or approval, he publicly broached the
idea in a magazine article. The Army War College eventually produced a
concrete plan, which called for expansion of the regular army by nearly a
third, to more than 141,000 officers and men, and a 400,000-man reserve
force, separate from the state-controlled National Guard, to be called the
Continental Army. Wilson warily approved this program at the end of
October, but he found Garrison even more irksome than before, privately
calling him "a solemn, conceited ass!"[34]

Before he dealt with the preparedness fight and the next round in the submarine controversy, he returned to Harlakenden, where Edith was staying
for one more week. The couple renewed their routine of walks and rides,
and on sunny days they would sit on the terrace while Wilson went
through the official mail and, as Edith later recalled, "each morning we
worked together on what it contained." When Edith departed as planned
for visits with friends and family, Wilson missed her painfully: "I long for
you so passionately, that I am as restless as a caged tiger if I cannot at least be
pouring out my heart to you when I am come to my desk at all, before and
after business." Pour out his heart he did, in two or three letters a day. He
also continued doing what he had begun on the terrace at Harlakenden—
sharing secrets of state and matters of high policy. Wilson would enclose

other people's letters with his own, particularly letters from Page and House. For her part, Edith felt no hesitancy in commenting on those letters and their writers. She agreed with Wilson that Page had gone overboard in his pro-British sentiments and that it might be wise to bring him home for a visit. About House, whom she had not yet met, she ventured reservations: "I can't help feeling he is not a very strong character. . . . [H]e does look like a weak vessel and I think he writes like one very often."35

Edith's comments about House contained equal measures of perceptiveness and jealousy. She was reacting to the smarmy, sycophantic tone the colonel often used in addressing Wilson, and she was resenting anyone who might presume to be closer to him than she was. She also made critical remarks about Tumulty, whom she had met and talked about with Wilson. Wilson responded by defending both men. It was in his letter answering Edith's reservations about House that he admitted that the colonel was "intellectually . . . not a great man" and called him "a counselor, not a statesman." But he also assured her, "You are going to love House some day,—if only because he loves me and would give, I believe, his life for me." In the same letter, he said about Tumulty, "You know that he was not brought up as we were; you feel his lack of breeding. . . . *But* the majority, the great majority of the people who come to the office are not of our kind, and our sort of a gentleman would not understand them or know how to handle them."36

Edith would come to accept Tumulty because she recognized how useful he was to Wilson, but she would never feel as warmly toward him as Ellen had. Nor would she come to love House. The part the colonel would soon play in helping her through a rough patch in their courtship would reconcile her to him a bit, but she would never fully trust or accept him. She would not try to come between Wilson and House because she did not need to. Her presence in Wilson's life in itself diminished the colonel's influence. House apparently recognized the change. "It seems the President is wholly absorbed in this love affair and is neglecting practically everything else," he noted sourly at the end of July. It was after this time that House began noting his own complaints, as well as those of others, about Wilson's not seeking advice or listening to people. The colonel would never again enjoy the intimacy that Wilson had formerly shared with him.37

With Edith gone, Harlakenden held fewer charms for Wilson, and he returned to Washington a week after her departure. He had to deal with affairs in Mexico and the Caribbean, and the British had just tightened their blockade further by again declaring cotton contraband. This move brought angry protests from southern senators and congressmen and required Wilson and Tumulty to work to placate them. The British foreign secretary, Grey, remained sensitive to American opinion, particularly this vital Democratic constituency, and his government mitigated the economic damage by buying up much of that year's cotton crop. Serious as those matters were, however, they paled in comparison to a fresh flare-up of the submarine crisis. On August 19, a German submarine torpedoed and sank the British liner *Arabic*, killing forty-four people, including two Americans. This incident rubbed raw the wound left by the *Lusitania*. Roosevelt and Bryan predictably piped up from their respective corners, but the general mood of the public seemed squarely behind the president.[38] As before, Wilson made a show of calm and business as usual. He brushed aside demands to call Congress into session. Also, as he had done after the sinking of the *Lusitania*, he kept to himself, although this time he did not have Edith nearby for advice and comfort.

The *Arabic* incident put the president in a bind. The firm line he had taken in his three *Lusitania* protests to Germany left him little room to back down. Yet few people wanted war; for his part, Wilson still wanted to foster a nonpunitive outcome to the dispute and build a better world, and remaining neutral would put him in a position to achieve those goals. To that end, he got little help from his advisers. Page irritated him by sending agitated reports of British demands that the United States stand up to the Germans, and House continued to counsel against softness in responding to the incident, even at the risk of war. After much agonizing, Wilson hit upon the expedient of a deliberate news leak. On August 23, newspapers published reports that "speculation in Government circles" predicted that the president might break relations with Germany. The "highest authority" stated that he would take such action if the facts of the case showed that the Germans had "disregarded his solemn warning in the last note on the Lusitania tragedy." He also had Lansing tell Bernstorff how gravely the president regarded the situation. These moves got results. Debates rose in Berlin, and the chancellor journeyed to the kaiser's castle at Pless, in Silesia, to put the matter before him. The outcome was a public promise not to sink liners without warning, although there was no disavowal of the sinking of the *Arabic* or the *Lusitania*.[39]

Equivocal though this so-called *Arabic* pledge was, it set off an outburst of jubilation. Newspapers across the country hailed the president as the savior of peace. In the *New York Evening Post*, Oswald Garrison Villard, who bitterly resented the recent segregation efforts, emblazoned Wilson's portrait and gushed about him in a front-page editorial: "Without mobilizing a single regiment or assembling a fleet, . . . he has compelled the surrender of the proudest, most arrogant, best armed of nations."[40] If this seemed too good to be true, Wilson thought it was, and events soon confirmed his doubts. On September 4, a submarine sank the British liner *Hesperian*. Fortunately, because no Americans were killed in this attack and the circumstances were ambiguous—the Germans claimed the *Hesperian* had tried to ram the submarine—it did not reignite the dispute. Still, it served as a reminder of how fragile and fraught with danger the situation remained.

Wilson was fortunate not to have a full-fledged diplomatic emergency on his hands in September 1915 because he had to deal with a romantic one, in his courtship of Edith Galt. After she returned to Washington on September 3, they resumed their routine of rides in the limousine, dinners at the White House, and the exchange of frequent, passion-filled letters. Edith agreed to announce their engagement soon, but fearing the political ramifications, she still wanted to marry Wilson after the election, more than a year in the future. Others worried about the political effects of a marriage, too. Rumors of the president's romance were beginning to circulate, and members of the cabinet were fussing about the situation. A group of them met and decided to tap Daniels for the assignment of talking to Wilson. Daniels later recalled that he recoiled at once from the "dangerous high and exalted mission of Minister Plenipotentiary and Envoy Extraordinary to the Court of Cupid . . . in the performance of which my official head might suffer decapitation." Instead, McAdoo made a clumsy stab at confronting his father-in law by resurrecting concerns about Mary Hulbert, the former Mrs. Peck. He told Wilson he had heard that the president had sent $15,000 to her, and he added a story he had probably made up about having received an anonymous letter saying that she was showing Wilson's letters around Los Angeles, where she now lived.[41]

Wilson responded in two ways. At some point, he wrote two shorthand drafts titled "Analysis and Statement of Admission." He opened the first draft with "Even while it lasted I knew and made explicit what it *did not* mean," and added, "It did not last but friendship and genuine admiration ensued." In the second draft, he characterized his letters to Mary Hulbert as "a passage of folly and gross impertinence in my life," and added, "I am deeply ashamed and repentant." He insisted that nothing untoward had happened between them while admitting, "But none of this lessens the blame or the deep humiliating grief and shame I suffer, that I should have so erred and forgotten the standards of honorable behavior by which I should have been bound." Whether he meant to turn those drafts into a letter to Edith is not clear. Instead, on Saturday, September 18, he wrote a short note: "There is something, personal to myself, and I am going to take the extraordinary liberty of asking that I may come to your house this evening at 8, instead of your coming here to dinner." When he went there, he told her about Mrs. Peck and abjectly begged forgiveness. What Edith said is not known, but Wilson agonized through what he told her were "conflicting emotions that have surged like a storm through me all night long."[42]

He did not have to stay in that storm. Almost as soon as he wrote those words, he received a letter that Edith had written at dawn. After spending the night sitting in her big chair by the window, she declared, "I now see straight—straight into the heart of things—and am ready to fol- low the road 'where love leads.' . . . This is my pledge, Dearest One, I will stand by you—not for duty, not for pity, not for honor—but for love— trusting, protecting, comprehending Love." She felt so tired she could put her head down and sleep at her writing desk, "but nothing could bring me real rest until I had pledged you my love and my allegiance."[43]

The relief Wilson felt was almost painful. "Your note has just come and I could shout aloud for the joy and privilege of receiving such a pledge, conceived by such a heart," he wrote to her at once. He and Edith could now resume their romance where they had left off. After this, he began going to her house almost every evening and often stayed until midnight. The Secret Service agents noticed a new bounciness about the president when he walked back to the White House. As he waited for traf- fic to pass, he would dance a few steps and whistle or sing a vaudeville tune. One tune that an agent remembered him singing as his feet tapped out the rhythm was "Oh you beautiful doll! You great big beautiful doll! Let me put my arms around you, I can hardly live without you."[44]

The romantic crisis might have been over, but its political ramifica- tions remained. Wilson asked House to come to Washington, and on Sep- tember 22 the two men met for the first time in nearly three months. After going over the diplomatic situation, House noted, "The President at once took up his most intimate personal affairs. I could see that he did it with reluctance, but with a determination to have it over." Wilson told House about Mrs. Peck and the anonymous report to McAdoo of threats to publish his letters to her. The colonel discounted McAdoo's fears and thought any attempt at blackmail most unlikely. Turning to the subject of Mrs. Galt, a relieved Wilson asked his advice about when to announce their engagement and when to have the wedding. He also asked Edith to meet with House, and two days later they had tea together at the White

House. The colonel talked about the president's accomplishments and said that Wilson probably would not run again. Edith, in turn, played his own game of flattery, going on about the president's great affection and respect for him, to which House responded, "I thought if our plans carried true, the President would easily outrank any American that had yet lived; that the war was the greatest event in human history excepting the birth of Jesus Christ." Whether this conversation completely won Edith over is open to question, although she told Wilson that evening that she had found House "just as nice and fine as you pictured him" and she now had faith in his judgment.45

This conversation and others removed the last barriers to disclosing their engagement and planning an early wedding. The announcement, which Wilson wrote on his typewriter while Edith peered over his shoulder, came on October 6. The following day, papers carried the news, along with a formal photograph of Edith that the White House had supplied in advance.46 That day, many people got their first look at the new First Lady–to–be when she accompanied the president to Philadelphia for the second game of the World Series. One photograph caught the couple wreathed in smiles after Wilson tossed out the first pitch. Edith was fashionably dressed, as always, with a fur-trimmed coat and corsage, gloves, and a wide-brimmed hat. Appearing in the Sunday rotogravure section of newspapers over the next two weeks, that photograph introduced Mrs. Galt to the public at large with a radiant image that made her a political asset.

Politics, as well as romance, was on the president's mind in October 1915. If House really thought his friend might not run again, for once his mind was not working in tandem with Wilson's. On the same day he announced the engagement, the president gave another statement to the press: "I intend to vote for woman suffrage in New Jersey because I believe the time has come to extend that privilege to the women of the state."47 He insisted that he spoke only as a private citizen and reiterated his view that suffrage was a state matter. This endorsement was not enough to carry the day in a referendum two weeks later, but suffrage leaders expressed gratitude to the president for the gesture. Breaking his Sphinx-like silence on woman suffrage marked the beginning of more active political involvement on Wilson's part. He also started giving speeches again, but mindful of the "too proud to fight" fiasco, he stuck mostly to generalities.

He needed to watch his tongue especially because he was still entangled in delicate diplomacy over the submarine issue. He and Lansing continued to press the Germans to disavow the sinking of the *Arabic* and pay compensation. Without Wilson's knowledge, Lansing made threats of a diplomatic break to the German ambassador at a time when the president was writing to House, "*I* feel under bonds to [the country] to show patience to the utmost. My chief puzzle is to determine when patience ceases to be a virtue." Yet when Wilson saw House on September 22, he said that perhaps the United States should go to war in order to combat German militarism. The colonel's surprise was well taken: such Roo-seveltian thinking was out of character for Wilson and revealed how exas-perated he felt. Fortunately, the Germans chose not to try the president's patience much further. On October 5, Bernstorff presented Lansing with a letter that partially disavowed the attack on the *Arabic* and promised to pay an indemnity. With that, the submarine controversy subsided to its familiarly slow but ever-menacing simmer.[48]

At the same time, the political controversy over military preparedness was threatening to boil over. Bryan particularly denounced increases in the army and navy in speeches around the country in the fall of 1915. He drew big, enthusiastic crowds, and pledges of solidarity poured in from his followers in Congress. The most potent of his cohorts promised to be Representative Claude Kitchin of North Carolina. The usually coopera-tive Underwood was no longer Democratic leader in the House because he had been elected to the Senate in 1914; Kitchin would succeed him as party leader and chairman of the Ways and Means Committee, which gave him power to name new members to committees. Between the pres-ence of anti-preparedness Democrats on the Armed Services Committees and the party's reduced majority in the House, Wilson's program faced hard going. His opponents got reinforcement in the press from Villard. The editor lambasted the preparedness increases in the *New York Evening Post* and in *The Nation*, and he served as a liaison among opponents inside and outside Congress.[49]

Wilson strove to counter the congressional opposition by cultivating the chairmen of the Armed Services Committees and by playing up to Speaker Clark. He also began to speak out on preparedness. Early in October, in brief remarks to the Naval Consulting Board, a civilian advi-sory group headed by the inventor Thomas A. Edison, he asserted, "I think the whole nation is convinced that we ought to be prepared, not for war, but for defense." Later he declared, "Force everywhere speaks out with a loud and imperious voice." In this changed world, America needed stronger, more efficient armed forces, "not for war, but only for defense." Although he was calling for bigger armed forces, he reiterated, "There is no fear amongst us." Yet he also warned against "alien sympathies, which came from men who loved other countries better than they loved America."⁵⁰

Those speeches served as a warm-up for a major counterattack in the preparedness fight and a broader political campaign, which came in his State of the Union address on December 7, 1915. Wilson acknowledged that during the preceding year the world war had "extended its threatening and sinister scope," but he pledged to "keep the processes of peace alive," particularly in the Western Hemisphere. Professing goodwill toward neighboring nations, he promised not to impose any government upon them: "This is Pan-Americanism. It has none of the spirit of empire in it." That noble vision seemed at odds with recent intervention in the Caribbean, but Wilson used it as a way to justify his military policy. "Great democracies are not belligerent," he declared. "We regard war merely as a means of asserting the rights of a people against aggression." The United States would maintain no more of a military establishment than necessary, as his program of increases in the army and navy would do. Because the preparedness and shipping programs would be costly, he urged raising the needed sums through taxes, particularly income taxes. He also proposed federal aid to vocational and agricultural education, a rural-credits plan for farm-mortgage lending, and stronger railroad regulation. Unfortunately, he again referred to disloyal people, particularly those immigrants who "seek to make this proud country once more a hotbed of European passion."⁵¹

This State of the Union address, his third, was not one of Wilson's best speeches. As he had done before, he rambled as he covered diverse matters. This speech also suffered from a mixture of messages as Wilson sought to take a firm stand in military and foreign policy but also to give assurances of peaceful intentions. He made up for some of those deficiencies in other speeches during the next few days. To the Democratic National Committee, he declared that Mexicans could "raise hell. . . . It is their government, and it is their hell." To a business group in Columbus, Ohio, he sounded the basic New Freedom theme that the average man was "the backbone of the country," and he said he wanted the world war to end in a peace in which "the instrumentalities of justice will be exalted above the instrumentalities of force."⁵² This was the closest he had come to divulging his agreement with those who were advocating some kind of league of nations. Those speeches in December 1915 flaunted a fresh political assertiveness. Wilson alluded to the upcoming campaign without explicitly announcing that he would run again. Still, hints here and elsewhere were hard to miss; he was clearly gearing up for a new round of action.

Only one thing remained before he plunged in. On Saturday, December 18, 1915, Edith Bolling Galt and Woodrow Wilson were married. In deference to the circumstances—a second marriage for both of them and the relatively recent death of Wilson's first wife—the ceremony took place at Edith's home, on Twentieth Street, rather than at the White House. The guests included only family members: Edith's mother, brothers, and sisters; Wilson's brother, sister, and daughters; his cousin Helen Bones; and Stockton Axson. This restriction gave Edith an excuse not to invite House, although she did include Grayson and Altrude Gordon, as well as her family's servants. As at Jessie's wedding two years earlier, both an Episcopal and a Presbyterian clergyman officiated: Herbert Scott Smith, rector of St. Margaret's Church, where Edith attended, and James Taylor of the Central Presbyterian Church. The ceremony, which took place at eight-thirty in the evening, was short and simple. There were no attendants, and the bride's mother gave her away. After having supper with their guests, the newlyweds sped away in an unmarked car to elude reporters and boarded a private railroad car that took them to Hot Springs, Virginia, for a three-week honeymoon. When the train pulled into the station the next morning, a Secret Service agent noticed the president dancing a jig, clicking his heels in the air, and again singing, "Oh you beautiful doll! You great big beautiful doll!"[53]

The honeymoon was suitably idyllic. The couple stayed in the finest suite at the famed Homestead hotel. They played golf most mornings and went for automobile rides in the afternoon, often getting out to take long walks. Although official business followed Wilson, he and Edith enjoyed plenty of time alone together—but the end came sooner than the honeymooners wanted. On January 2, 1916, reports reached Washington that a German submarine had sunk the British liner *Persia*, killing two Americans. On advice from Tumulty and Lansing, the president returned to Washington the next day. "The President looked very well after his trip and seemed to be in a fine mood, although it was plainly evident that the PERSIA affair weighed on him," Tumulty noted.[54] It was good for Wilson that his marriage and honeymoon had buoyed his spirits. The new year, 1916, was about to bring the greatest challenge—and fulfillment—yet in his life.

SECOND FLOOD TIDE

Woodrow Wilson needed the emotional lift that he felt when he returned from his honeymoon in January 1916, for his political prospects looked bleak. A year earlier, in his grief and gloom following Ellen's death, he had doubted whether he could live up to people's expectations, especially whether he could repeat his earlier feats as a legislative leader. Since then, the sinking of the *Lusitania* and the seething submarine controversy had promised to make such prospects look dimmer still by diverting attention from domestic concerns. His "irony of fate" had come home to roost with a vengeance—and that was not the worst of it. Bryan's defection and vociferous opposition to a tough diplomatic stance toward Germany and increased military preparedness raised the specter of civil war among Democrats—the same kind of internecine strife that had fractured the Republicans four years earlier and doomed the reelection bid of Wilson's predecessor. Now the tables appeared to be turning. Roosevelt's mounting hostility toward Wilson's foreign policy and his envy and loathing of Wilson personally made it increasingly likely that a reunited opposition would confront the president and his party in the fall elections. Despite newfound happiness at home, 1916 seemed to bode ill for the man in the White House.

Submarine attacks demanded immediate attention. Not only the sinking of the *Persia* but also the earlier sinking of an Italian liner, the *Ancona*, apparently by an Austrian submarine, was reheating the diplomatic pot. Now that Congress was back in session, sentiments on both sides found fresh outlets, and anti-war Democrats were bruiting about Bryan's demand to keep Americans off the ships of belligerent countries. Wilson shared their sentiments to a degree. "If my re-election as President depends upon my getting into war," Tumulty recorded him saying on January 4, "I don't want to be President. . . . I have had lots of time to think about this war and the effect of our country getting into it." He cared more about what people would think of him in ten years than what they thought now. He appreciated their desire for action, "but I will not be rushed into war, no matter if every damned congressman and senator stands up on his hind legs and proclaims me a coward."[1]

Luckily, the Germans and Austrians had little stomach for a new quarrel, and they apologized for sinking the *Ancona* and the *Persia*. But Lansing was determined to get the Germans to disavow the *Lusitania* sinking as well. He pushed the Germans hard, and some in Berlin seemed willing to accept a diplomatic break with the United States, which would have been a likely prelude to war. Learning about the situation in Germany through House, who was again in Europe, Wilson reined Lansing in at the beginning of February. Meanwhile, prominent Democrats on Capitol Hill publicly rejected all talk of a break with Germany. At the middle of February, Wilson accepted a partial acknowledgment of liability for the *Lusitania* and an implicit agreement to defer claims for a post-war settlement. This was the quiet, anticlimactic end to a long wrangle, but it did not resolve the submarine controversy or lift the threat of war.[2]

Lansing was able to bear down on the Germans because Wilson was away from Washington for part of this time. The political fight over military preparedness was almost as pressing as the diplomatic controversy over the submarines. At the middle of January, Tumulty warned, "I cannot impress upon you too forcibly the importance of an appeal to the country on the question of military preparedness." Tumulty's sources on Capitol Hill told him that support for preparedness was weak in both houses and public sentiment was indifferent and confused. Between Bryan's pacifism and Roosevelt's militarism, people did not know what to think, and the president needed to enlighten them by presenting sober, responsible arguments for an increase in armaments. "If your leadership in this matter is rejected," Tumulty warned, "the Democratic party may as well go out of the business of government."[3] That argument fell on receptive ears, and after discussing the idea with the cabinet, Wilson authorized Tumulty to inform the press that the president was going to make a speaking tour about preparedness.

Before he embarked on the tour, he spoke in New York on January 27—and showed how sorely out of practice he was. Wilson rambled among several subjects, barely touching on preparedness. He announced that he had changed his mind and now favored a tariff commission to investigate and advise on rates, and he grew personal, repeating his earlier confession about having "volcanic forces . . . concealed under a most grave and reverend exterior." He admitted that he had also changed his mind about preparedness and sounded a familiar note from his writings about politics: "The minute I stop changing my mind as President, with the change of all the circumstances in the world, I will be a back number." Two days later, in his first speeches on the tour, he regained his wonted focus and force. "I believe in peace. I love peace," he declared, but he warned, "The world is on fire, and there is tinder everywhere." Therefore, it had become "absolutely necessary that this country should prepare herself, not for war, not for anything that smacks in the least of aggression, but for adequate national defense." He promised to uphold both peace and honor, but he confessed that he was dealing with "things that I cannot control—the actions of others."[4]

Those speeches set the pattern for the tour. During the following week, broken by his customary observance of the Sabbath, he gave fifteen speeches, talking several times each day, including brief remarks from the rear platform of his train. Accompanied by Edith, Tumulty, and a retinue of reporters, he traveled as far west as Kansas, speaking along the way in Illinois, Wisconsin, and Iowa, and, on the return leg, in Missouri and Illinois again. The itinerary took him to the reputed strongholds of anti-war sentiment, and the tour harked back to his forays around New Jersey as governor to advocate his reform program. But now that he was president, it also took on the trappings of his 1912 campaign. Big crowds gathered almost everywhere he appeared—15,000 in Milwaukee, 18,000 in Des Moines—and parades escorted him to his appearances. These events afforded many people their first look at the new First Lady, who was frequently photographed beaming at her husband's side. Yet not everyone warmed to Wilson's message. In Kansas, the reception matched the winter weather. The Republican governor, who opposed increased preparedness, gleefully reported that the newspapermen on the train "said that the president's reception was the coldest he received any place." In most places, however, including heavily German Wisconsin, the audiences cheered wildly and applauded the president's message.[5]

In making this tour, Wilson was exercising an aspect of political leadership that he prized, excelled at, and enjoyed. He was educating the public: explaining his programs and sharing his larger thoughts. These speeches allowed him to restate his grand vision of America's role in the world. "America has no reason for being unless her destiny and her duty be ideal," he avowed in Milwaukee. They also allowed him to draw a sharp line between himself and, as he said in Des Moines, "some men amongst us preaching peace who go much further than I can go"—a thinly veiled reference to Bryan and his cohorts. Apparently repudiating "too proud to fight," he proclaimed that he would not "pay the price of self-respect." In

St. Louis, he warned that "one reckless commander of a submarine . . .
might set the world on fire," and he declared that America's navy "ought,
in my judgment, to be incomparably the greatest navy in the world."[6]

Whether this speaking tour helped Wilson with his troubles within
his party is questionable. The anti-preparedness stalwarts stood firm.
Bryan complained about the "slush" in Wilson's speeches and hinted at
opposing his renomination for president. Kitchin reported to Bryan that
the speeches changed no minds on Capitol Hill because "they sounded
too much like Roosevelt." Kitchin's assessment was accurate but misleading. Many congressional Democrats wanted to remain loyal to the president without appearing militaristic. Republicans, except for some
insurgents, most notably senators La Follette and George W. Norris of
Nebraska, tended to support increased preparedness.[7]

In this situation, Wilson could exercise another of his favorite aspects
of leadership: consulting and bargaining with legislators. Throughout the
fall of 1915, he had been talking with the chairmen and key members of
the Military Affairs and Naval Affairs Committees. Patient explanation
and cultivation worked well with the navy bill. Die-hard Bryanites
remained opposed and denounced construction of new warships as a boon
to the steel trust. Their opposition notwithstanding, by the beginning of
1916 the navy bill appeared to be on its way to eventual passage. Some difficult times would come in the House later, when Kitchin and his followers temporarily succeeded in cutting new battleship and cruiser
construction. Wilson stuck to his guns, however, and the Senate restored
the ship authorizations. The senators also mollified critics by adding a
provision to establish a government-owned factory to produce armor
plate, thereby taking business and profits away from the steel industry. In
final form, the navy bill gave the president everything he asked for.[8]

The army bill presented a tougher challenge at the outset. Opposition
to it flared up early and focused on Garrison's proposed reserve force, the
Continental Army. In the eyes of opponents, this plan raised the age-old
specter of a large standing army, like the ones then fighting in Europe.
The Continental Army also drew fire from the state militias—the
National Guard—which saw themselves being supplanted and diminished
in importance. They had a potent lobby and enjoyed close ties with many
senators and congressmen, and their influence extended well beyond the
anti-preparedness phalanx. The key person with whom Wilson had to
deal on the army bill was Representative James Hay of Virginia, chairman
of the Military Affairs Committee. Like most Virginia Democrats, Hay
was not an avid Bryanite, but he did have a long record of resisting Republican efforts to enlarge and modernize the army, and Garrison's overbear-

Joseph Ruggles Wilson: The father whose good looks his son wished he had inherited

Janet Woodrow Wilson: The mother whom many thought her son resembled physically and emotionally

Tommy Wilson, 1873: The earliest known photograph of Wilson, age sixteen

Thomas Woodrow Wilson, 1879: About to graduate from the College of New Jersey, known then familiarly as "Princeton" and later renamed Princeton University

(Top) The Alligators, Princeton, 1879: An eating club that Wilson joined as a sophomore—he is the student doffing his hat.

(Bottom) The Johns Hopkins Glee Club, 1883: Wilson, as a first-year graduate student, is in the back row, with the flowing mustache.

(Left) Ellen Louise Axson, 1881: The Presbyterian minister's daughter from Rome, Georgia, with whom Wilson fell in love almost at first sight
(Right) Ellen Louise Axson, 1883: At the time of her engagement to Wilson, who was about to depart for Johns Hopkins

Jessie and Margaret Woodrow Wilson, early 1890s: The older two of the three Wilson daughters

Princeton faculty members with Grover Cleveland, early 1900s: Retired to Princeton after leaving the White House and a trustee of the university, Cleveland sits directly behind Wilson; to the left in the row above Cleveland sit Wilson's two closest friends, John Grier Hibben *(far left)* and his brother-in-law Stockton Axson *(middle left)*.

An academic procession at Princeton with Andrew Carnegie: Despite assiduous wooing that stressed Princeton's Scottish heritage, Wilson succeeded only in getting Carnegie to endow a lake for rowing.

Defeat, 1910: Wilson on his way to his last commencement as president of Princeton, just after learning his opponents had received a large bequest, prompting him to say, "We have beaten the living, but we can't beat the dead."

With Mrs. Peck, 1908: On Bermuda, where Wilson met the divorced Mary Allen Hulbert Peck and entered into a relationship that included emotional intimacy and may or may not have become a short-lived affair

(*Left*) On the road to the White House, 1912: On the golf course at Sea Girt, New Jersey, with Joseph P. Tumulty (*middle*), his ever-loyal secretary and political helpmeet, Wilson hears news from the Democratic National Convention in Baltimore, where he was about to win the nomination for president. (*Bottom*) The nominee and his family, 1912: Wilson and Ellen at Sea Girt, soon after learning of his nomination; behind them stand (*left to right*) Jessie, Eleanor (Nell), and Margaret.

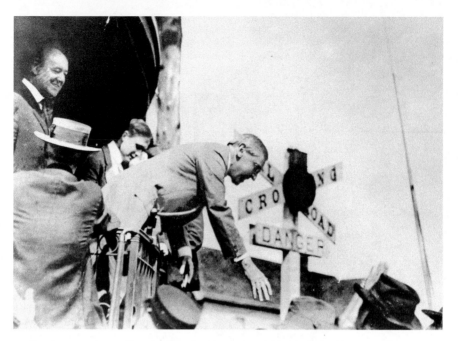

On the campaign trail, 1912: No aloof academic, Wilson relished being on the campaign trail, as he had shown earlier while running for governor of New Jersey.

The First Lady and her daughters, 1913: Ellen Wilson on the White House portico with Jessie, Margaret, and Nell

President Wilson, 1913: At his desk in his office at the White House, already deep into the business of leadership

The Scholar in Politics, 1913: "President Wilson Visits Congress," by the English caricaturist Max Beerbohm. Editorial cartoonists often depicted Wilson in a mortarboard cap and an academic gown, sometimes kindly, sometimes not. (DEPARTMENT OF RARE BOOKS AND SPECIAL COLLECTIONS, FIRESTONE LIBRARY, PRINCETON UNIVERSITY)

With Secretary of State William Jennings Bryan, 1913: Despite differences in background and temperament, Wilson and Bryan worked well together until the sinking of the *Lusitania* raised the threat of the United States' being dragged into World War I.

With Colonel House, 1914: The outwardly mild-mannered Texan Edward M. House formed an intimate bond with Wilson immediately after Wilson's election to the presidency and kept a diary that emphasized his own influence. Wilson wears a black armband because this photograph was taken shortly after Ellen's death.

Edith Bolling Galt, 1915: The official engagement photograph of the stylish Washington widow whom Wilson wooed and wed in 1915

Wilson, by John Singer Sargent, 1917: While he sat for this portrait, Wilson found conversing with the painter hard work, and Edith disliked the finished product. But his closest friend from their student days at Princeton, Bob Bridges, told "Tommy" that he liked it "hugely. I can see you getting ready to tell a story."

Wilson, by Sir William Orpen, 1919: The official artist
of the British delegation painted this portrait toward the
end of the peace conference. Some people, including
Colonel House, preferred this to the portrait by Sargent.

(*Left*) At a baseball game with Edith Galt, autumn 1915: For their first outing in public after announcing their engagement, Wilson chose to take Edith to a baseball game, which also attested to his lifelong love of that sport. (*Bottom*) Peacemaking, 1919: The "Big Four" in the study of Wilson's temporary quarters in Paris: (*seated, left to right*) Premier Vittorio Orlando of Italy, Prime Minister David Lloyd George of Great Britain, Premier Georges Clemenceau of France, and President Wilson; (*standing, left to right*) Count Luigi Aldrovandi, the official Italian interpreter; Sir Maurice Hankey, secretary to the British cabinet and official note-taker; and Professor Paul Mantoux, the official French interpreter

(*Top*) Final colloquy at Versailles, 1919: Wilson in an exchange with Clemenceau just after the signing of the Treaty of Versailles; between them stands Dr. Cary T. Grayson (in uniform), Wilson's physician; behind Clemenceau stands Ray Stannard Baker (in straw hat), press secretary to the American delegation to the peace conference and later Wilson's biographer; behind Wilson, leaning over, stands Arthur James Balfour, the British foreign secretary. (*Bottom*) The ravages of the League fight, 1919: At the end of his aborted speaking tour, Wilson walking through Union Station in Washington, four days before he suffered a massive stroke

Wilson with Isaac Scott, 1923: Living as an invalid on S Street in Washington after leaving the White House, Wilson depended heavily on Edith; her brother John Randolph Bolling, who served as his secretary; and Isaac Scott, his valet.

Wilson on his birthday, December 28, 1923: The last photograph taken of Wilson, riding in the open-topped Rolls-Royce given him by a group of wealthy friends and admirers; he died a little more than a month later.

ing manner had also rubbed him the wrong way. Yet Hay was a good party man, and he had earlier promised to support the army bill, including the Continental Army. Once Congress convened and his committee held hearings, however, Hay backed away from that pledge. Garrison's officious manner again offended him, and he began to apprehend the threat posed to the National Guard, which he favored. In mid-January, Hay presented an alternative plan, which would expand the National Guard to 425,000 men, about the same size as the proposed Continental Army, and give the president additional powers to "federalize" it—to call it into national service.[9] Garrison exploded when he heard about that plan and once again threatened to resign. This standoff awaited the president's return from his speaking tour.

The choice between these two men and their respective plans was not a hard one for Wilson. He had never felt close to Garrison, and since Bryan's resignation he had found the secretary of war's pretensions to premier-like status in the cabinet increasingly irksome. Garrison made the choice easier by drawing a line in the sand against not only Hay's National Guard plan but also efforts in the Senate to speed up the proposed timetable for Philippine independence. Disagreement on either matter would be, Garrison told the president, "not only divergent but utterly irreconcilable." This was tough talk, but thanks to having made his speaking tour, Wilson had less to fear now from Garrison's presumed following among preparedness advocates. In consultation with Tumulty, he drafted an artful reply to Garrison. He sidestepped the Philippine matter and stated that it would be "a very serious mistake to shut the door" on Hay's alternative to the Continental Army. He also reminded Garrison that he did not "at all agree with . . . favoring compulsory enlistment for training": a draft, the political hot potato that no major figure but Roosevelt would touch. Garrison responded by offering his resignation, and Wilson allowed him to go "because it is so evidently your desire to do so."[10] He directed Tumulty to release their exchange of letters to the press, together with the preceding correspondence about the Continental Army.

Garrison's resignation had the air-clearing effect Wilson hoped for. Hay thanked him on behalf of his committee and pledged their cooperation, and the choice of Garrison's successor enhanced these newfound good feelings. At the beginning of March, Wilson named Newton D. Baker, the mayor of Cleveland, whom Wilson had earlier tried to enlist to serve as his secretary or fill a cabinet post. A short man with horn-rimmed glasses, Baker enjoyed a stellar reputation among Democrats and other progressives. His appointment raised some controversy when reporters unearthed statements in which he called himself a pacifist and opposed increased preparedness. Those revelations actually helped smooth the way for the army bill in the House, however, where it passed later in March by the lopsided margin of 402 to 2, with even Kitchin and other Bryanites voting in favor. The Senate subsequently resurrected a modified Continental Army and added a government-owned factory to manufacture nitrates for munitions—another scheme to take profits away from big business. In May, with Wilson mediating between the chambers, the House bill largely prevailed, but the nitrate plant stayed in, with the president's backing. This was a huge legislative victory. Wilson had won a huge political fight and, thereby, taken a giant step toward proving that he, not Bryan, was master of the Democratic Party.[11]

Before he won that fight, however, he had to beat back another, still graver, threat from Bryan and his followers on Capitol Hill. During the second half of February, panic swept through Congress in reaction to rumors of impending intervention in the world war. The spark that ignited the hysteria emanated from other negotiations that Lansing had been conducting since the beginning of the year. Recurring tensions with Germany over the submarines, combined with persistent though less threatening friction with Britain over the blockade, impelled Lansing to grasp at an expedient to solve the underlying problems finally. With Wilson's approval, he broached the idea of what he called a modus vivendi—a scheme whereby the Germans would abandon surprise submarine attacks and the British would stop arming their merchant ships. Reporters soon got wind of the idea, and support for it grew in the press and in Congress. The British, however, bristled at the scheme, and the Germans appeared bent on using their submarines without restraint. House cabled from London to urge delay until his return: "I cannot emphasize the importance of this." After discussion in the cabinet the next day, Wilson had Lansing announce withdrawal of the modus vivendi.[12]

Many representatives and senators believed that the administration was abandoning a promising idea and risking war. Representative Jeff McLemore of Texas, a Bryanite, introduced a resolution in the House to warn citizens not to travel on armed merchant vessels, while Senator Thomas Gore of Oklahoma, another Bryanite, demanded a vote on a resolution he had introduced earlier to forbid Americans to travel on ships of belligerent nations. In an effort to head off a confrontation, Wilson asked three leading congressional Democrats—Senator William J. Stone of Missouri, chairman of the Foreign Relations Committee; Senator John W. Kern of Indiana, the majority leader; and Representative Hal Flood of Virginia, chairman of the Foreign Affairs Committee—to come to the White House late in the afternoon of February 21. The meeting did not go well. The president condemned the Gore and McLemore resolutions, affirmed Britain's right to arm ships, and maintained his tough line against German submarine attacks. According to one newspaper account, Senator Stone reacted by beating his fist on a table and asking, "Mr. President, would you draw a shutter over my eyes and my intellect? You have no right to ask me to follow such a course."[13] Despite that outburst, Stone and the others agreed to try to calm fears among their colleagues.

Their efforts did not succeed. In the House, pressure grew for a vote on the McLemore resolution, with predictions that it would pass handily. Speaker Clark and majority leader Kitchin asked for a meeting of their own with the president. On the morning on February 25, Wilson met with them, accompanied by Flood, for what came to be called the Sunrise Conference. The Speaker warned that the McLemore resolution might pass by a two- or three-to-one margin, and he or one of the others asked what would happen if a submarine attacked an armed ship with Americans aboard. "I believe we should sever diplomatic relations," Wilson answered. Pressed further, he added that Germany would then declare war, which might lead to an earlier end to the world war. Clark objected to that remark and warned that the president could count on his support only so long as he believed the administration was not seeking war. According to one newspaper account, Wilson retorted that people had jeered and sneered at him for his efforts to keep the peace: "In God's name, could anyone have done more than I to show a desire for peace."[14]

Meanwhile, on February 24, with assistance from Tumulty, he had sent Senator Stone a public letter in which he affirmed that he would do everything possible to stay out of the war but stuck to his hard line on the submarines. He would not accept any abridgment of American citizens' rights: "Once accept a single abatement of right and many other humiliations would follow." Diplomacy as well as party politics moved him to take this line. Reports from Berlin indicated that the Germans were on the verge of expanding their submarine attacks, and the president was trying to warn them off. Next, he decided to force a showdown in the House. Addressing a public letter on February 29 to the second-ranking Democrat on the House Rules Committee, in the absence of the chairman (who was out of town), he asked for an early vote on the McLemore resolution. It was a bold stroke—too bold for his party's congressional leaders, who trooped to the White House to urge delay. Wilson stood his ground and tightened the screws by dispatching the most politically potent cabinet members, Burleson and McAdoo, to the Capitol. They carried with them a handwritten letter from the president asking congressmen to relieve "the present embarrassment of the Administration" by defeating the

McLemore resolution: "No other course would meet the necessities of the case."[15]

These moves did the trick. The Senate acted first. That same day, March 2, Gore intensified the debate by charging that at the Sunrise Conference the president had said he wanted war. Wilson fired back by labeling such reports "too grotesquely false to deserve credence for a moment." The next day, Senate debate degenerated into a muddle when Gore perversely struck a critical "not" from his resolution to make it state that submarine attacks "*would* constitute a just and sufficient cause of war." Just 14 senators voted against tabling—in effect voting for—the resolution. Only 2 Democrats, James O'Gorman of New York and George Chamberlain of Oregon, joined 12 Republicans, nearly all of them midwesterners and westerners who opposed increased preparedness. Several Democrats who favored the resolution, including Stone and Gore himself, voted to table it. Some claimed the situation was too confused, while others said they did not want to embarrass the president. In all, 68 senators—48 Democrats, 19 Republicans, and the 1 Progressive—voted to table the Gore resolution.[16]

The House disposed of the McLemore resolution in a more straightforward way. During seven hours of debate on March 7, a parade of Democrats declared that they favored the idea behind the resolution but would vote to table it because, as one said, "the question presented in this context is whether we shall stand by the President in this crisis or not." The motion to table carried almost two to one: 276 to 142. Only 32 Democrats opposed tabling, while 181 backed the administration, including Kitchin and others close to Bryan. Also voting to table were 94 Republicans and 1 Progressive. By contrast, 104 Republicans, 5 Progressives, and the House's lone Socialist opposed tabling. The Republican split was mainly sectional, with the number of northeasterners for tabling and the number of midwesterners against nearly equal; many of the midwesterners represented districts with substantial numbers of German Americans. This division embarrassed Republican hard-liners toward Germany, such as Lodge, who up to now had appeared to speak for their party on the issue. The Progressives' votes were even more embarrassing to Roosevelt.[17]

These votes in Congress marked a political triumph for Wilson, and everyone knew whom he had beaten. Bryan had rushed to Washington to rally his cohorts on Capitol Hill behind the resolutions, and he was particularly active, along with German American organizations, in lobbying congressmen before the House vote. Wilson closely followed the debates from the White House, but he refrained from public comment. He did talk privately about Bryan on the day of the House vote, during a late-afternoon drive with Edith and House, who had just returned from Britain. "He seems to have come to a parting of the ways with Mr. Bryan," House wrote. "We thought that the real cause of Bryan's displeasure was that the President is standing for a second term."[18] Bryan put a good face on what happened in the Capitol, stating that the debates showed that Congress and the people did not want war. He was whistling in the dark. The votes proved that Wilson was undisputed master of the Democratic Party, and Bryan knew it. The House votes on the army bill later in March would reaffirm the president's primacy.

Behind this whole business lay some tortuous, delicate diplomacy that Wilson did not believe he could disclose. The reason House had insisted so vehemently on dropping the modus vivendi was that he was on his second wartime mission to Europe and in the midst of negotiations that he thought could change the course of history. As soon as his ship docked in New York, on March 5, the colonel took the train to Washington, and he met with the president the next day. He carried with him a document he had drawn up two weeks earlier with Foreign Secretary Grey. Later known as the House-Grey Memorandum, the document stated, purportedly in Grey's words, "Colonel House told me that President Wilson was ready, upon hearing from France and England that the moment was opportune, to propose that a Conference should be summoned to put an end to the war. Should the Allies accept this proposal and should Germany refuse it, the United States would probably enter the war against Germany." The memorandum also offered assurances that this conference "would secure peace on terms not unfavourable to the Allies; and that, if it failed to secure peace, the United States would leave the Conference as a belligerent on the side of the Allies." The "not unfavourable" peace terms included restoration of Belgium, return of Alsace and Lorraine to France, and a warm-water outlet to the sea for Russia.[19]

On its face, the House-Grey Memorandum encapsulated a breathtakingly bold initiative to end the war by means of mediation or intervention by the United States. It appeared to justify House's growing reputation as a visionary strategist and adroit diplomatist. His self-styled "Great Adventure" seemed to be bearing fruit with actions that could bring untold good to the world and, as he kept telling Wilson, would make the president's name shine brightly down through the ages. Yet as in so much involving House, the difficulty lies in figuring out what this scheme really amounted to. Did other people take the plan as seriously as House did? Most important, did he intend this memorandum to be an invitation to mediation or a pretext for intervention?[20]

The colonel showed himself at his best and his worst on the mission. He spent nearly two months shuttling among the capitals of the main belligerents, London, Paris, and Berlin, but he passed the bulk of his time in London. In each city, he operated almost entirely on his own, communicating directly with Wilson by letter or by telegram in the private code the two men had devised a year earlier. He treated the American ambassadors there correctly, but he tried to involve only one of them in his contacts with foreign officials: in London, he attempted to draw in Page, who had been a friend of his in southern expatriate circles in New York and whose appointment he had helped to arrange. Page, however, had grown so ardently pro-Allied that he told House bluntly that he would have no part in his schemes. Page scorned the venture as "mere aloof moonshine." Nor was this House's first clash with Page. On the colonel's mission to Europe the previous year, he had enlisted a junior diplomat in the embassy, Clifford Carver, to work behind Page's back, and they took to referring to the ambassador in their correspondence as P.O.P.—Poor Old Page. This was an example of the antics that later prompted Daniels's son Jonathan to say of House, "He was an intimate man even when he was cutting a throat."[21]

In his dealings with the British, the colonel began to display the skill and sensitivity as a negotiator that led some to admire him as America's ablest diplomat. The main object of his attentions and persuasion was Grey. With this hawk-nosed, nature-loving, melancholy widower, the colonel forged a bond that resembled the one between him and Wilson. His letters to Grey and diary entries about meetings with him took on the same intimate, ingratiating tone he used with the president. The colonel also met and got on well with other British leaders, including the strongman of the cabinet and soon-to-be prime minister, David Lloyd George, and the man who would later succeed Grey as foreign secretary, Arthur James Balfour. But nothing approached his closeness to Grey, without which the House-Grey Memorandum would not have come to pass. Therein lay one of the major flaws in this undertaking. As he often did with Wilson, House let his personal feelings and sense of his own importance get out of hand. In Grey's case, he seemed to forget that he was dealing with the diplomatic leader of a foreign power—someone who had his nation's interests to maintain and who operated under powerful constraints. House did not deceive himself about Grey's affection for him, but he did exaggerate both the foreign secretary's commitment to this scheme and his willingness and ability to sway others in his government.[22]

Another defect in this undertaking lay in the way House represented it to the Allies and to Wilson. In both London and Paris, he stressed how his plan might facilitate American intervention. The French foreign minister, Jules-Martin Cambon, noted that House told him that if France cooperated, "inevitably America will enter the war, *before the end of the year,* and will align herself on the side of the Allies. . . . This statement from Colonel House astonished me. I had him repeat it and, after having noted it in English, I had him read it. He said to me: 'exactly.'" To Wilson, House reported simply—in a letter, not a telegram—that he had "most interesting and satisfactory talks" with Cambon, "quite freely outlining the entire situation as it seems to me." House also talked differently to Allied leaders and Wilson on the subject of peace terms. Just before he left on this mission, he assured the president that he would not get into issues involving territorial demands or financial indemnities. Wilson likewise instructed House to avoid such matters and stated, "The only possible guarantees . . . are (a) military and naval disarmament and (b) a league of nations to secure each nation against aggression and maintain the absolute freedom of the seas." In fairness to House, it should be noted that Wilson's only other guidance was encapsulated in these words: "You ask me for instructions as to what attitude and tone you are to take at the several capitals. I feel that you do not need any."23

Yet House plunged into just the matters that Wilson had instructed him, and he had pledged, to avoid. The references in the House-Grey Memorandum to Belgium, Alsace-Lorraine, and Russia came after extensive discussion of those and comparable subjects, including an independent Poland, a dissolved Ottoman Empire, a consideration of Italian ambitions at the expense of the Austro-Hungarian Empire, and the disposition of German colonies in Africa. As for the items Wilson specified, House dropped "freedom of the seas" as soon as the British predictably scorned this "German" notion, he did not raise disarmament, and he talked about a league of nations rarely and only with Grey. In his letters to Wilson, House did not tell the president much about what he was discussing and mainly touted British and sometimes French receptivity toward mediation. "A great opportunity is yours, my friend," he exulted from Paris, "the greatest perhaps that has ever come to any man. The way out seems clear to me, and when I can lay the facts before you, I believe it will be clear to you also."24

The same day that he gushed to Wilson from Paris, House met again with Cambon and the French premier, Aristide Briand, to whom he sang a different tune. He assured them of American intentions to intervene either peaceably or militarily, in order to secure a peace that would favor the Allies. He also discussed Alsace-Lorraine, Turkey, and Armenia, and said he wanted Britain, France, and the United States to work together after the war. Cambon noted that House also stressed "the secrecy which he wanted to surround his statements." His statements were so secret that he would not share them with his friend and boss, the president. Small wonder that Jonathan Daniels would also later call him "that devious son-of-a-bitch Colonel House" and "a porcelain chamber pot full of shit."[25]

What did the respective parties—Wilson and the British—make of these doings of House's? The colonel noted, after delivering the memorandum to Wilson on March 6, "[T]he president placed his arm around my shoulders and said: 'I cannot adequately express to you my admiration and gratitude for what you have done.'" When House showed him the memorandum, Wilson "accepted it *in toto* only suggesting that the word 'probably' be inserted in the ninth line after the word ['would'] and before the word 'leave[']."[26]

A world of difference supposedly hung on that word *probably*, inserted in the clause "the United States would leave the Conference as a belligerent on the side of the Allies." Lloyd George would later claim that Grey believed this addition "completely changed the character of the proposal" and therefore did not communicate it to the other Allies: "The world was once more sacrificed to the timidity of statesmanship." That claim was totally wrong. The memorandum stated earlier that "the United States would probably enter the war against Germany." So Wilson's reiteration of *probably* simply underlined the plain meaning of the document. Nor did Grey react to *probably*, and he did pass the memorandum on to at least one Ally when he gave a copy to the French ambassador. The British had no reason to be surprised by Wilson's insertion. Their soon-to-be-famous intelligence operation, Room 40 of the Admiralty, was tapping the American embassy's cables and had broken both the regular diplomatic codes and House and Wilson's amateurish "private" cipher. The British therefore knew that House was representing the situation differently to them and to Wilson. This Texan was playing poker with people who could read his cards. Also, Grey did pursue the matter further later in March, when he presented the memorandum to the cabinet War Committee; it was rejected there by nearly everybody, especially Lloyd George, with only Grey himself meekly suggesting the possibility of considering the plan.[27]

Wilson's *probably* was significant only as a window onto his thinking about House's scheme. It showed that he did not regard that part of the House-Grey Memorandum as a veiled promise to come into the war but, rather, as an objective description of the state of relations with Germany. Despite his words of affectionate praise for House, he did not view the memorandum in the same world-shaking light that the colonel did. Other matters—such as the conflicts on Capitol Hill over preparedness and travel on armed ships, together with flare-ups in Mexico and in the submarine crisis—would relegate House's scheme to the back burner. Ironically, the biggest effect of the House-Grey Memorandum on Wilson may have been to enhance the colonel's standing in his eyes as a negotiator.

For Wilson, the month of March 1916 brought troubles in the proverbial threes. The first had been having to beat back the congressional revolt over travel on belligerent ships. The last would be the most dangerous round yet in the submarine dispute. In between, the violence in Mexico spilled over into the United States. In the predawn hours of March 9, Pancho Villa led a force of several hundred Mexicans in an attack on the border town of Columbus, New Mexico. Their main target was Camp Furlong, a U.S. Army garrison, which was caught by surprise because commanders in the area had discounted warnings of a possible raid. At the garrison, Villa and his men mistook the stables for the barracks and killed a number of horses. Their mistake gave the Americans time to set up machine guns and bring the Mexicans under heavy fire. Falling back, the marauders rampaged through the small, ramshackle town of Columbus. Yelling "Viva Villa!" and "Viva Mexico!" they shot wildly into houses and at any civilians they saw and set the town's hotel on fire. Within an hour, a detachment of U.S. cavalry arrived from another post and chased the raiders back across the border. The fighting lasted less than three hours. It left eight American civilians and seven American soldiers dead and two civilians and five soldiers wounded; sixty-seven Mexicans were killed, and seven were wounded and taken prisoner.[28]

News of the attack reached the White House within two hours. Wilson immediately decided to send a military force across the border in pursuit of Villa and his band. Lansing informed the diplomatic representative of the Mexican Constitutionalists of the president's intention, and messages went out to the department's agents who were assigned to keep in touch with the Constitutionalist leader, Carranza. The cabinet met the following day and discussed the incident; everyone present supported the president's decision, although there was discussion of asking Carranza's permission to enter Mexico—an idea that was rejected. After the meeting, Wilson had Tumulty issue a two-sentence statement to the press: "An adequate force will be sent at once in pursuit of Villa with the single object of capturing him and putting a stop to his forays. This can and will be done in entirely friendly aid of the constituted authorities in Mexico and with scrupulous respect for the sovereignty of that Republic."[29]

That statement captured the dilemma Wilson faced. On the one hand, this was an attack on American soil—the first one since the War of 1812—and it had to be answered forcefully. Outrage predictably flared on

Capitol Hill and in newspapers across the country, but Wilson did not wait to gauge opinion when he told reporters that he was sending troops. Immediately after the cabinet meeting on March 10, an order went out from the War Department for a force under the command of Brigadier General John J. Pershing to pursue the marauders who had attacked Columbus. On the other hand, even a limited invasion, which was the way Mexicans of all persuasions would see Pershing's pursuit, might ignite a nationalist backlash. That was Villa's main motive behind this provocation— to foment outrage among his countrymen in order to strengthen his hand in his fight with Carranza. For Wilson, such a reaction would undo his months of restraint in the face of demands for intervention and his low-keyed encouragement of democracy and order in Mexico, for which Carranza's side seemed to offer the best hope. References to "constituted authorities" and "scrupulous regard" for sovereignty in the War Department orders were meant to reassure the Constitutionalists.[30] Likewise, Pershing's orders forbade any clashes with Carranza's forces and stipulated withdrawal as soon as Mexicans could deal with Villa.

What followed was a frustrating and nerve-racking year of diplomatic and military controversy. Once more, there was danger of full-scale war between the United States and Mexico. The flash point lay not with Villa but in relations with Carranza, who proved as difficult as ever to deal with. At the outset, it looked as if he might refuse to sanction American forces entering Mexico. Yet despite his lofty talk about Mexican sovereignty, Carranza put up no real resistance. After all, the Constitutionalists would profit from Villa's death or capture so long as they themselves did not appear to be American puppets. General Pershing's force of, initially, 4,000 officers and men, which came to be called the Punitive Expedition, crossed the border on March 15 and quickly drove deep into Mexico.[31]

The deeper the expedition penetrated, the more Mexicans suspected that the dreaded Yanquis were bent on conquest, thereby increasing the chances for clashes with civilians or Constitutionalist troops. An incident occurred early in April when a mob attacked a cavalry unit in the town of Parral. In the ensuing melee, two Americans were killed and six wounded, while somewhere between 40 and 100 Mexicans died. For a while, it looked as if Pershing might fight with Constitutionalist forces in the area. A month later, a band of Mexican irregulars crossed the Rio Grande and attacked two settlements in Texas, killing a boy and taking two prisoners. American cavalry units pursued those raiders 180 miles into Mexico and killed some bandits. The most frightening incident took place on June 21 near the town of Carrizal, when two U.S. Cavalry units attacked Constitutionalist troops and were beaten back. Fourteen Americans were killed and twenty-three captured, and thirty Mexicans died and forty-three were wounded. The situation was growing intolerable. At Wilson's initiative and with Carranza's concurrence, a mediation commission was appointed, consisting of three representatives of each country. The mediators met first in New London, Connecticut, and later in Philadelphia and Atlantic City, New Jersey, for eight months of fractious, wearying negotiations. At long last, early in 1917, those negotiations led to withdrawal of the Punitive Expedition and diplomatic recognition of Carranza's government.

The pursuit of Villa turned into a farce. Many Americans viewed him through the distorting lens of an ethnic stereotype: Pancho seemed to personify the lazy but wily, capriciously violent but slightly comical Mexican *bandido* later featured in innumerable Hollywood films; actually, for all his criminality and cruelty, he was a serious revolutionary leader. An American force that eventually numbered more than 7,000—equipped with the latest in military technology, including motor vehicles and airplanes—chased Villa through northern Mexico for months and never caught him. He regrouped his forces and captured the capital of Chihuahua in September 1916 and did not begin to lose his power until Carranza's forces inflicted a decisive defeat on his forces in January 1917. Villa lived on until 1923, when he met the fate of most of the leaders of Mexico's revolution, including Carranza—assassination. The best that can be said for the Punitive Expedition is that it provided the U.S. Army with timely experience in the field and that its commander, the obdurate Black Jack Pershing, kept his reputation intact and remained in line for higher command.[32]

Wilson resisted intense pressure to go to war in Mexico. On March 15, the day the expedition crossed the border, Tumulty told him that members of the cabinet did not believe he was acting forcefully enough. Wilson answered, "I shall be held responsible for every drop of blood that may be spent in the enterprise of intervention," and he told Tumulty to say to those cabinet members "that *'there won't be any war with Mexico if I can prevent it,'* no matter how loud the gentlemen on the hill yell for it and demand it." He was not going to send "some poor farmer's boy, or the son of some poor widow" to fight "unless I have exhausted every means to keep out of this mess." He also worried about the Mexicans, who were fighting "the age-old struggle of a people to come into their own. . . . Poor Mexico, with its pitiful men, women, and children, fighting to gain a foothold in their own land." As for talk about valor, he maintained, "Valour is self-respecting. Valour is circumspect. Valour strikes only when it is right to strike." Tumulty's recollection almost certainly embellished what Wilson said, but those remarks—with their echoes of "too proud to fight"—captured Wilson's state of mind as American forces went into Mexico.33

The armed clashes in Mexico did not change his thinking. On May 11, after the raid in Texas and the ensuing war scare, he talked off the record with the journalist Ray Stannard Baker, who noted, "He said his Mexican policy was based upon two of the most deeply seated convictions of his life: first his shame as an American over the first Mexican war & his resolution that while he was president there should be no such predatory war; Second upon his belief . . . that a people had the right 'to do as they damned pleased with their own affairs' (He used the word 'damned')." He also felt ashamed over the part played by the American ambassador in the overthrow of Madero in 1913 and thought the worst source of trouble lay with Americans "who wanted the oil & metals of Mexico & were seeking intervention to get them." In addition, he gave Baker a novel reason not to go to war with Mexico—namely, that he "[d]id not want one hand tied behind him at the very moment the nation might need all its forces to meet the German situation"—and he believed that pacifying Mexico would take at least half a million troops.34

When he talked to Tumulty and Baker, Wilson was airing his views in strict confidence, but he also voiced such thoughts publicly. Speaking in New York at the end of June, after the Carrizal incident, he charged that "a war of conquest in Mexico" would bring no glory and any "violence by a powerful nation against this weak and distracted neighbor" would add no distinction to the United States. He observed that the letters he was getting contained "but one prayer . . . 'Mr. President, do not allow anybody to persuade you that the people of this country want war with anybody.'" He related that when he got off the train that had brought him to New York, the engineer had said to him, "Mr. President, keep us out of Mexico." He also noted that Napoleon had once said that force never accomplished anything permanent.35

Those convictions and the resolve to stick to them prevented the Mexican situation from escalating into war. In the upcoming presidential campaign, Democrats would trumpet the slogan "He kept us out of war." Many people at the time and nearly all interpreters since then have assumed the slogan referred to the war in Europe. In fact, campaign material would mention Mexico more often, and Wilson did deserve credit for staying out of war there. He may have let his domestic progressive prejudices get out of hand when he saw only nefarious financial influences behind agitation for intervention, but he did not mistake how strong and widespread popular opposition was. In New York, when he asked whether war with Mexico would bring glory to America, his listeners—more than

600 journalists and businessmen—shouted, "No!" In coming days, a flood of approving letters and telegrams swamped the White House mail room. Contrary to what critics such as Roosevelt charged, Wilson's reluctance to go to war did not spring from any trace of timidity or tinge of pacifism. He believed it took more courage to stay out of war than to go in, and no pacifist could have said valor meant striking "when it is right to strike." House noted that Wilson's "determination not to allow Germany to force him into intervention in Mexico could account for this."[36] The comment to Baker also showed that he was thinking along those lines, and at the same time that he was reluctant to go to war in Mexico, he came close to risking war with Germany.

On March 24, a German submarine torpedoed the *Sussex*, a French steamer carrying passengers and cargo in the English Channel. Though heavily damaged, the *Sussex* did not sink and was towed into port at Boulogne. Eighty people were killed or injured, including four Americans who were hurt. On a much smaller scale, the incident was eerily reminiscent of the *Lusitania*. Wilson greeted the news with the same outward show of calm as he had shown earlier. He and Edith played golf together on Saturday morning and went for a long automobile ride in the afternoon. On Sunday, the president attended church, took another drive with the First Lady, and had dinner at her mother's house.[37] Newspapers also carried the news that his daughter Jessie had given birth to her second child, a daughter, who was named Eleanor Axson Sayre.

The major difference in the way Wilson approached this crisis—besides having Edith openly and constantly at his side—lay with his advisers. In place of Bryan's implacable inclination toward peace now came peremptory advice from Lansing to follow a course that would lead to war. "I do not see how we can avoid taking some decisive action," he told the president. "We can no longer temporize in the matter of submarine warfare." House was on the scene too, as he rushed to Washington to try, in his softer way, to push in the same direction. He countered Wilson's worries about war by offering to go to Europe again to coordinate planning with the Allies for the peace settlement; Wilson seemed "visibly pleased at my suggestion and I believe will now be more inclined to act." The colonel again overestimated his influence. As usual, Wilson kept his own counsel. Lansing drafted a diplomatic note that had a harsh tone and presented two alternatives: severing diplomatic relations at once or threatening to do so unless the Germans abandoned submarine attacks against all merchant ships. When the cabinet discussed the situation two days later, everyone reportedly agreed that an ultimatum was called for. After taking an overnight cruise with Edith on the *Mayflower*, Wilson worked all weekend—including again, unusually for him, on Sunday—to produce his own draft. He softened Lansing's language but still condemned sneak submarine attacks as inhuman and contrary to international law, and threatened to break relations unless such attacks ceased.[38]

This draft sparked almost as much internal dissension as the first *Lusitania* notes had done, but with the opposite slant. On April 11, House met with Wilson and Edith and objected to the draft as only opening the way for more argument with the Germans. Wilson stood firm, but he cut out a sentence about hoping for an amicable outcome and added the word *immediately* to the demand for cessation of submarine attacks without warning. According to House, Edith also thought the draft was weak. Wilson denied that it was, and he reminded them that he had promised Senator Stone that he would not break relations without informing Congress first. Lansing likewise tried to inject a more threatening tone, and he again resorted to his old tricks. He did not pass on to Wilson a message from the German foreign minister to Bernstorff that hinted at conciliation, and he did not tell Wilson about a meeting at which the ambassador was conciliatory.[39]

At the same time, the president had to deal with Congress and the public. On April 13, he gave a Jefferson Day speech to Democrats in Washington. Again, mindful of "too proud to fight," he stuck mostly to domestic matters, sounding a strongly progressive note, and touched only once, cryptically, on foreign affairs: "God forbid that we should ever become directly or indirectly embroiled in quarrels not of our own choosing. . . . But if we should ever be drawn in, are you ready to go in only where the interests of America are concerned with the interests of mankind and to draw out the moment the interest centers in America and is narrowed from the wide circle of humanity?"[40] Yet he knew he had to be more specific with Congress. He honored the letter of his promise to Stone, though just barely. The diplomatic note to Germany was sent at the end of the day on April 18, and at ten o'clock the next morning he met with Stone, Congressman Flood, and the ranking Republicans on their committees to tell them the contents of the note.

At noon on that day, Wilson went to the Capitol and delivered a sixteen-minute address to a joint session of Congress. Comparing the attack on the *Sussex* to the sinking of the *Lusitania* as "singularly tragical and unjustifiable," he declared that he had regretfully decided to threaten to break relations because he recognized "that we are in some sort and by the force of circumstances the responsible spokesmen of the rights of humanity, and that we cannot remain silent while those rights seem in process of being swept utterly away in the maelstrom of this terrible war." The assembled senators and representatives sat in silence throughout the speech, and only at the end was there a little applause, mostly from Democrats. In view of the earlier congressional agitation over travel on belligerent ships, the subdued mood seemed strange. Bryan again came to Washington to rally anti-war congressmen and senators, but he departed after only a day, in a mood of resignation. Predictably, Roosevelt blamed the current crisis on Wilson's previous weakness in dealing with the submarine threat.[41]

Everything now depended on what the Germans decided to do. To nearly universal surprise and relief, they backed down. Heated debates raged within imperial, military, and naval circles. The chancellor, who favored conciliation, threatened to resign. The head of the navy unexpectedly weighed in against unrestricted submarine warfare. He argued that the time was not yet ripe for an all-out campaign and that coming to terms with the Americans would cause trouble for the British blockade. Germany replied with two notes: the first, on May 4, dealt with submarine warfare, and the second, on May 8, apologized for the *Sussex* attack. The first note pledged to limit submarines to established rules of warfare, which forbade attacks without warning, but it equivocated by stating that the United States should help to get the British to modify the blockade and by reserving the right to resume submarine attacks if that did not happen.[42]

Many Americans objected to the haughty tone of the German response and its conditions, but Wilson responded to the positive signals while downplaying the unsatisfactory parts. Again breaking his rule of not working on the Sabbath, he spent Sunday, May 7—the anniversary of the sinking of the *Lusitania*—drafting a reply to the May 4 note. The president expressed his government's "satisfaction" at the Germans' decision, and he added that the United States took it for granted that Germany's new policy did not depend on American negotiations with other nations. Lansing got him to remove the word *satisfaction* and tone down the reply to a bald statement.[43] This version of the reply went to Germany on May 8 and was released to the press the next day. The Germans acquiesced, and the yearlong submarine crisis was over—for the time being.

It was a triumph for Wilson. Whether he really hoped to bring the Germans to heel is not clear. His decision to force their hand was reluctant, and it did not spring from a shrewd reading of their intentions. Neither the embassy in Berlin nor House's informal network was particularly astute in assessing crosscurrents of opinion in Berlin or at the military headquarters. Wilson may have felt resigned to having to go to war, but unlike House and Lansing, he did not welcome that prospect. He may simply have gotten lucky, but he had shown great patience in seeking a way to satisfy the "double wish." Ironically, he had succeeded by finally choosing one half over the other—gaining satisfaction from Germany even while risking war. Choruses of praise arose from newspapers and private citizens throughout the country. Wilson deserved their praise, although not as much as he did for keeping out of war in Mexico. This diplomatic triumph would alter the balance of relations with the belligerents. The German naval leader's hopeful prediction of trouble between the United States and the Allies would soon come true. More important for Wilson, this triumph cleared the way for new initiatives abroad, fewer distractions on the domestic front, and a clearer path toward another four years in the White House.

He did not exult at his good fortune. Besides knowing how differently the confrontation might have gone, Wilson was painfully aware of how fragile and unstable American neutrality remained. On May 8, the same day that his reply to Germany went out, he met at the White House with a group of anti-preparedness leaders, who included the renowned social worker Lillian Wald, the young socialist writer Max Eastman, and the radical Progressive Amos Pinchot. After listening patiently to their arguments and defending his preparedness program, the president asserted, "This is a year of madness. . . . Now, in these circumstances, it is America's duty to keep her head." He wanted not only to keep the bad influences of European power politics out of the Western Hemisphere but also to create a new effort to maintain world peace, in which the United States would "play our proportional part in manifesting the force that is going to be back of that. Now, in the last analysis, the peace of society is obtained by force. . . . And if you say we shall not have any war, you have got to have force to make that 'shall' bite."[44]

He was edging toward unveiling what he had hinted at earlier: his belief in the league of nations idea. Three days later, in his off-the-record interview with Baker, he said he was thinking about what he could do to promote peace and asked whether he should disclose his ideas to the League to Enforce Peace. That organization, headed by Taft and increasingly known by its initials, LEP (pronounced "el-ee-pee"), had invited the president to speak at its annual dinner in Washington on May 27. Ignoring House's advice to the contrary, he accepted the invitation and found himself sharing the speaker's platform with Lodge, who a year earlier had called for "great nations . . . united" to enforce peace. Wilson struck a properly circumspect pose. He declined to endorse or comment on the

LEP's program and talked instead about how the world war had changed so much. "With its cause and effects we are not concerned," he maintained, but only with its profound impact on America: "We are participants, whether we would or not, in the life of the world. The interests of all nations are our own also."[45]

One cause of the war did concern Wilson: "secret counsels" that had forged alliances and resorted to force. The shock and surprise of the war's onset had shown "that the peace of the world must henceforth rest upon a new and more wholesome diplomacy." The world's "great nations" must decide what is "fundamental to their common interest, and as to some feasible method of acting in concert when any nation or group of nations seeks to disturb those fundamental things." This was an unequivocal endorsement of the league idea. Wilson went further, declaring, "We [Americans] believe in these fundamental things: First, that every people has a right to choose the sovereignty under which they shall live. . . . Second, that the small states of the world have a right to enjoy the same respect for their sovereignty and for their territorial integrity that great and powerful nations expect and insist upon. And, third, that the world has a right to be free from every disturbance of its peace that has its origin in aggression and disregard of the rights of peoples and nations." He vowed "that the United States is willing to become a partner in any feasible association of nations formed in order to realize those objects and make them secure against violation."[46]

Wilson's circumspect pose could not hide his wonted boldness. Despite endorsing the LEP's central idea—international enforcement—he said nothing about arbitration or international courts, which Taft and the organization's other activists, mainly lawyers, stressed. Wilson's second and third "fundamental things" foreshadowed Article X of the Covenant of the League of Nations, which he would call its "heart," and he even foreshadowed the language of that article when he called for "a virtual guarantee of territorial integrity and political independence." He was showing from the outset that he wanted an essentially political league, which differed from the judicial body that LEP leaders envisioned, and he was enunciating the concept that would later come to be called collective security. Likewise, when he deplored "secret counsels" and advocated "a right to choose . . . sovereignty," he was foreshadowing elements of his Fourteen Points and other major policy statements, as he did further when he demanded "the inviolate security of the highway of the seas for the common and unhindered use of all the nations of the world." These ideas would later come to be known as open diplomacy, self-determination, and freedom of the seas. These ideas, together with his demand for equal rights for small nations, put him at odds with some of the LEP leaders and Lodge, who envisioned a great-power directorate to run the world. Furthermore, these ideas put him more in line with liberal and left-wing thinkers on both sides of the Atlantic who wanted sweeping reforms to replace the balance of power, institute disarmament, and promote freedom for subject peoples.47

Wilson knew he had taken a bold step. Both Bryan and Roosevelt had been attacking the LEP, though for opposite reasons. Bryan had invoked traditional American isolation, with genuflections to Washington's Farewell Address and Jefferson's injunction against "entangling alliances," and he had condemned the league idea as imperialistic and warmongering. Those arguments had drawn support from some Democrats and Republican insurgents. Wilson strove to reassure his party brethren in his next speech, a Decoration Day address three days later at Arlington National Cemetery. "I shall never consent to an entangling alliance," he avowed, "but I would gladly assent to a disentangling alliance—an alliance which would disentangle the peoples of the world from those combinations in which they seek their own separate and private interests and unite the peoples of the world to preserve the peace of the world upon a basis of common right and justice." He was aiming that rhetorical reversal at skeptical Democrats, but he was not retreating. A few days later, he drafted the Democratic platform on which he would run for reelection. In one section, he lifted both the ideas and many of the same words from his speech to the LEP, declaring, "[W]e believe that the time has come when it is the duty of the United States to join with other nations of the world in any feasible association that will effectively serve these principles."48

Wilson's attempt to bring Democrats on board a more activist, outward-looking foreign policy was an even bolder move than espousal of the league idea. In domestic affairs, he had been going further down a trail that others, especially Bryan, had blazed before him, and he had been taking the party in directions in which most of its members wanted to go. By contrast, in foreign policy he was trying to wean them from a heritage of resistance to overseas commitments and opposition to bigger armed forces—a heritage that Bryan was now distilling into self-conscious isolationism. Left to themselves, a majority of Democrats would most likely have followed the Great Commoner's lead rather than accept the president's new course. There was peril for Wilson, but he had advantages. As he had already shown in the preparedness fight, he could appeal to party and patriotic solidarity. Equally important, this was an election year, and the Democrats' hopes of remaining in power rested with him. Finally, he had long since proved to the more progressive Democrats, who gave the party its ideological lifeblood, that he was one of them and could deliver legislation and appointments that gave them their hearts' desires.

Domestic issues necessarily took a backseat for Wilson during the first half of 1916, but he did not forget them. In January, he made three moves that signaled a second and more progressive installment of the New Freedom. He reversed himself on two issues on which earlier he had not favored action. One was the tariff. As he had already publicly stated, he now supported an independent commission to investigate and advise on tariff rates, an idea formerly favored mainly by Roosevelt and his Progressives. The other was rural credits. He now brushed aside Secretary of Agriculture Houston's objections and supported his government lending program for farmers. When the plan's principal Democratic sponsors, Senator Henry Hollis of New Hampshire and Representative Asbury Lever of South Carolina, came to see him in the White House in late January, the congressman proposed a figure of $3 million. Wilson stunned his visitors by saying, "I have only one criticism of Lever's proposition, and that is that he is too modest in his amount." His visitors quickly agreed to double the sum.[49]

Wilson's final move in January 1916 dramatically gave the strongest proof of his undiminished progressive zeal. On January 28, without warning, he nominated Louis Brandeis to a seat on the Supreme Court. The death of Justice Joseph Lamar three weeks earlier had created the vacancy. It probably helped that House, who had worked assiduously against appointments for Brandeis, was in Europe. Wilson evidently did not consider anyone else. He discussed the nomination only briefly with McAdoo and Attorney General Gregory, who were both enthusiastic, and he mentioned it to Samuel Gompers, the head of the American Federation of Labor, who assured him of the unions' support. Wilson bypassed the custom of honoring "senatorial courtesy" by not consulting with Lodge and John W. Weeks, the two conservative Republicans who represented Brandeis's adopted home state of Massachusetts. He did consult with La Follette, who assured him of progressive Republican support. The news of Brandeis's nomination landed like a bombshell on Capitol Hill. As Taft's friend and Washington informant Gus Karger reported to the ex-president, "When Brandeis's nomination came in yesterday, the Senate simply gasped. . . . There wasn't any more excitement at the Capitol when Congress passed the Spanish War resolution."[50]

Those moves in January served as openers to a new legislative campaign. In March, Wilson urged his party's leaders in Congress to push an ambitious program, and the House Democratic caucus committed itself to new taxation, a tariff commission, shipping regulation, and rural credits. Of those measures, rural credits unexpectedly proved the easiest to pass. Bills cleared both houses in May by lopsided margins, with most Republicans not voting. The tariff commission took longer to pass but excited little debate, as did a bill to establish a commission to regulate maritime shipping. Those measures drew scant attention because by the beginning of the summer the presidential campaign and more heated domestic issues would overshadow them.[51]

One domestic matter did stir up a major conflict from the outset—the Brandeis nomination. True to predictions, conservatives and legal traditionalists were apoplectic. Fifty-one leading citizens of Boston, where Brandeis lived and practiced law, issued a public letter that pronounced him lacking the proper temperament to sit on the Supreme Court. Most of the signers were Boston Brahmins, including Harvard's president, A. Lawrence Lowell. Not everyone at Harvard agreed with Lowell, however. Former president Charles W. Eliot publicly supported Brandeis, as did Roscoe Pound, the dean of the law school, together with nine of the school's eleven faculty members. A petition in support of Brandeis drew more than 700 signatures from Harvard students. On the other side, seven former presidents of the American Bar Association, including Taft, called Brandeis "unfit" for the Court. In view of Brandeis's progressive activism and unorthodox legal thinking, such opposition was to be expected.[52]

Another element in the opposition was anti-Semitism. If confirmed by the Senate, Brandeis would become the first Jew to serve on the Supreme Court and thereby attain the highest public office in the United States yet held by a Jew. No prominent opponent ever publicly stated that Brandeis should not be on the Supreme Court because of his religion, but privately many of them thought so and said so. The use of the word *unfit* by the president of the bar association also carried a connotation of prejudice. Equally disturbing, in the Senate, La Follette proved to be a poor judge of sentiment among his fellow Republican insurgents. Two who served on the Judiciary Committee, Albert Cummins of Iowa and John Works of California, announced their opposition to the nomination. Some Democrats on the committee also seemed lukewarm. Brandeis did not testify at the Judiciary Committee hearings, although he played an active role behind the scenes in managing the public relations aspect of his nomination. The hearings became a parade of character witnesses for and against him, and his nomination appeared to be stalled in the committee. Some of his supporters privately accused Wilson of failing to act and not wanting the nomination to go through.

Those suspicions were unfounded. Early in May, Wilson intervened with another deft exercise in legislative leadership. Behind the scenes, he worked with Attorney General Gregory and the chairman of the Senate Judiciary Committee, Gregory's friend and fellow Texan Charles A. Culberson, to move things along. By prearrangement, Culberson wrote to ask the president to give his reasons for choosing Brandeis. Wilson responded on May 5 with a long letter, which the chairman read to the committee and released to the press. Calling Brandeis "singularly qualified by learning, by gifts, and by character," the president dismissed the charges leveled against this nominee as "intrinsically incredible. . . . He is a friend of all just men and a lover of the right, and he knows more than how to talk about the right—he knows how to set it forward in the face of its enemies." Wilson recounted Brandeis's stellar record as a lawyer and praised "his impartial, orderly, and constructive mind, his rare analytical powers, his deep human sympathy. . . . This friend of justice and of men will ornament the high court of which we are all so justly proud."[53]

Wilson's letter was a masterstroke, but his nominee was not out of the woods. One Democrat on the Judiciary Committee, James Reed of Missouri, had a history of giving the president trouble, and another, John K. Shields of Tennessee, was no friend of his either. Two others, Wilson's nemesis at the Atlanta bar but more recently his supporter, Hoke Smith of Georgia, and Lee Overman of North Carolina, were also wavering. In response, Wilson had McAdoo, Burleson, and Gregory apply patronage pressure, and he personally courted Shields and Overman. In the latter case, Wilson invited Overman to accompany the presidential party on a trip to North Carolina, and he publicly praised the senator when the train stopped in his hometown.

These tactics worked. On May 24, the Judiciary Committee reported favorably on Brandeis's nomination. The vote was 10 to 8, strictly along party lines. Besides Cummins and Works, another Republican insurgent, William E. Borah of Idaho, also voted no. On June 1, the full Senate acted without debate in executive session, approving the nomination by a vote of 47 to 22. Only one Democrat, the aged, cranky Francis Newlands of Nevada, voted against Brandeis. Only two Republicans, La Follette and Norris, and the lone Progressive, Miles Poindexter of Washington, crossed party lines to vote in favor. This was an early sign of Republicans' coming alignment against progressive measures. At the time, however, only joy abounded in reform circles. The president refrained from public comment, but he said privately, "I never signed a commission with such satisfaction as I signed his." Brandeis's friend and supporter Norman Hap-

good recalled that the president told him, "I can never live up to my Brandeis appointment. There is nobody else who represents the greatest technical ability and professional success with complete devotion to the
people's interest."54 He was right. Besides striking a blow against religious
prejudice, he had made his finest and most important appointment. In
itself, this was one of Wilson's greatest contributions to American public
life. He had made his deepest bow yet toward progressivism, and he had
thrown out a fitting opener to his bid for reelection.

Wilson was at the top of his form as a leader. By the middle of 1916, he
had turned the troubles that had faced him into a tide that was leading him
on to fortune. He was also happy in his personal life, and he owed most of
his happiness to Edith. The newlyweds had settled into a comfortable
routine at the White House. They usually woke early for a snack and a
round of golf, followed by breakfast at eight. An hour later, the stenographer Charles Swem would come to the upstairs study to take dictation.
Edith often stayed to listen. "It was a delight and an education to hear the
lucid answers that came with apparently no effort from a mind so well-
stored," she recalled in her memoirs. Then, while her husband spent the
morning in his office, she would tend to household management with
Mrs. Jaffray and work on her own correspondence with her secretary,
Edith Benham. The couple would have lunch together, usually with
guests, and following his afternoon stint in the office, they would take a
ride. On Saturdays, they often took longer rides, sometimes as far as
Harpers Ferry, West Virginia, or they might go on an overnight or weekend cruise on the *Mayflower*. They saw friends and family as before, and
Edith got on well with Wilson's daughters and other relatives. Grayson
remained a special friend, and on May 24 the Wilsons and McAdoos journeyed to New York for his wedding to Altrude Gordon.55

Private and official life frequently dovetailed, to Edith's delight. She
enjoyed public functions. Her first White House occasion was in January,
when she and the president greeted 3,328 guests at a diplomatic reception.
State dinners followed at regular intervals. Edith had a keen fashion sense
and chose her ensembles with care on these gala occasions. She accompanied Wilson on the preparedness speaking tour in January and February,
and she was with him when he gave most of his speeches at other times.
She also paid attention to his appearance. Wilson was already a good
dresser, but Edith injected a bit of flair into his wardrobe. Evidence of her
touch could be seen on June 14, Flag Day, when the president led a big
Preparedness Parade up Pennsylvania Avenue. "How young and vital he
looked," she recalled. "He wore white flannel trousers, a blue sack coat,

white shoes, white straw hat, and carried an American flag about a yard and a half long. What a picture, as the breeze caught and carried out the Stars and Stripes!"[56] That day, Woodrow Wilson was marching along the same route that he had ridden three years earlier at his inauguration. He was hitting his stride toward a second inaugural journey along that route.

TO RUN AGAIN

When Woodrow Wilson ran for reelection in 1916, he faced a daunting task. The increasing likelihood that the Republicans would heal their breach meant that any Democratic nominee, even an incumbent president, would be an underdog. This predicament reflected hard facts of political geography. Since 1896, the Republicans had enjoyed a lock on the Northeast and Midwest, where the population and number of states gave them a prohibitive edge in electoral votes for president and control of both houses of Congress. The Democrats held on to what Bryan liked to call the Great Crescent—the vast expanse that stretched south and west of the Potomac, Ohio, and Missouri rivers. That expanse contained far fewer people and a smaller number of states, and only in the white supremacist South did the Democrats dominate the way their opponents did in their heartland. The Republicans' internecine strife in 1910 and seismic rift in 1912 had given the Democrats openings, first to win the House and then to gain all of Congress and the White House. Many of those gains had proved ephemeral, however. In 1914, Republicans bounced back strongly, particularly in the Northeast and Midwest. If that trend continued in 1916, the Democrats would most likely revert to their habitual minority status on Capitol Hill and banishment from the White House.

Those prospects did not dishearten Wilson. With his penchant for boldness, he liked fights against long odds, and not everything about the political scene looked gloomy. His victories in the preparedness struggle, the submarine crisis, Mexico, domestic reform legislation, and the Brandeis nomination underlined the three major themes of his upcoming campaign: peace, preparedness, and progressivism. There was also a fourth *p:* prosperity. The 1914 elections had occurred during a severe recession, which hit hardest in industrial states from New England to the Great

Lakes—the Republican heartland. Now, thanks to stimulus from Allied war orders, the economy was booming, with robust demand for both manufactured goods and agricultural products. Any president and party in power were bound to take credit for prosperity, and Wilson and his Democrats were no exception. Finally, he had a united, enthusiastic party behind him. Bryan was coming back on board: he was an old campaign warhorse unable to resist the call to action, and he wanted to position himself so that he might have influence in the party. In all, Wilson could face the electorate in good spirits.

Of his three main campaign themes, the president wanted most to stress progressivism. In his Jefferson Day speech in April, he indicated his continued commitment to strong central government: "You cannot draw example from the *deeds* of Thomas Jefferson. . . . There is no parallel in the circumstances of the times of Thomas Jefferson with the circumstances of the time in which we live." Shortly afterward, he began drafting the platform on which he and his party would run, and at the beginning of June he received a suggestion that helped give the document a sharper political focus: Senator Owen of Oklahoma urged him to take ideas from the 1912 Progressive platform "as a means of attaching to our party progressive Republicans who are in sympathy with us in so large a degree."[1] Wilson liked the suggestion and asked Owen to specify the 1912 Progressive ideas to include.

The senator responded by highlighting federal legislation to promote workers' health and safety, provide unemployment compensation, prohibit child labor, establish minimum wages and maximum hours, and require an eight-hour day and six-day workweek. Wilson, in turn, included in his draft platform a plank calling for all work done by and for the federal government to provide a minimum wage, an eight-hour day and six-day workweek, and health and safety measures and to prohibit child labor, and—his own additions—protections for female workers and a retirement program. That plank also expanded on the government's efforts to help workers find employment and extend vocational training from agriculture to other work. In addition, he inserted a separate plank that read, "We recommend the extension of the franchise to the women of the country by the states upon the same terms as to men."[2]

Wilson did not go as far as Owen, who also favored establishment of a department of health and was the author of a bill to outlaw child labor. The expedient of requiring these measures only in federal employment and government contracts was a bow toward the sensibilities of more conservative Democrats. With the president's approval, however, the platform committee at the convention added a statement in favor of a comprehensive child labor law. Wilson's woman suffrage plank fell short of the constitutional amendment that the suffrage organizations wanted and the Progressives had earlier endorsed. Yet for all its shortcomings, his platform marked a great leap forward for the Democrats in social and labor reform, while to recommend woman suffrage by any means was revolutionary in a party that up to now had shunned the issue. In the rest of the platform, Wilson touted the earlier accomplishments of the New Freedom and emphasized aid to farmers, particularly through the rural-credits program.

This courting of Progressives would later lead some interpreters to claim that Wilson was changing his ideological spots. In their view, he was forsaking the New Freedom's limited government progressivism in order to embrace the New Nationalism's more thoroughgoing reforms. Moreover, so they would argue, he did it strictly for reasons of expediency—solely because he needed Progressives' votes in order to beat the Republicans in a two-party contest. Those interpreters misread him badly. Rather than grudgingly doing something he had to do, he was gladly doing something he wanted to do. He was indeed practicing expediency—but to him, as a Burkean, that was a virtue. "I feel sorry for any President of the United States who does not recognize every great movement in the Nation," he avowed early in July. "The minute he stops recognizing, it, he becomes a back number." Most tellingly, he did not embrace Roosevelt's approval of collective bigness and vision of transcendent nationalism. The appointment of Brandeis, the arch-prophet of competition and small-scale enterprise, showed that Wilson had not budged in his devotion to the central tenets of the New Freedom. In his platform draft, he boasted that the Democrats had enacted "reforms which were obviously needed to clear away privilege, prevent unfair discrimination and release the energies of men of all ranks and advantages." He was betting that Roosevelt's followers loved the means of the New Nationalism more than the ends.[3]

This wooing of Progressives got a boost when the Republicans met in Chicago for their convention on June 7. Roosevelt harbored hopes that his former party might overlook his recent apostasy and nominate him again. He based those hopes on his having shelved domestic reform issues in favor of militant foreign policies and heated attacks on Wilson for more than a year. In March, in a remark that became famous, Roosevelt practically dared the Republicans to nominate him: "It would be a mistake to nominate me unless the country has in its mood something of the heroic." The Republicans' convention dashed those hopes. Their platform did strike a belligerent note on Mexico, but it took a vague, equivocal stand on the submarine issue, denouncing Wilson's "shifty expedients" but also demanding "all our rights as a neutral without fear or favor"—a transparent bid for German American support. Domestically, the 1916 Republican platform was more conservative than the one Taft had run on four years earlier: it denounced the lowered tariff, condemned extravagance and incompetence, and ducked most of the current reform issues, as well as immigration restriction and prohibition.4 The delegates brushed aside all talk of picking Roosevelt, and on June 10 they nominated Charles Evans Hughes, who promptly resigned from the Supreme Court to run as their candidate.

The Republicans thought they had the perfect candidate, and given the party's situation in 1916, they were right. The fifty-four-year-old Hughes had all the right qualifications. He was from New York, the state with the biggest electoral vote, and he had served two terms as governor, the office that Roosevelt and Grover Cleveland had held and that had supplied two other major-party presidential nominees in the last half century. Hughes had won the governorship in 1906 by defeating someone not just conservatives but also most respectable people feared and loathed—the demagogic newspaper tycoon William Randolph Hearst. As governor, Hughes had shown himself to be a strong administrator and an energetic public speaker. He had held his party's bosses at arm's length and pushed through a moderate reform program. He first attracted attention as a potential presidential candidate in 1908 and again as a possible compromise choice in 1912. Best of all, from the Republicans' standpoint in 1916, he had sat on the Supreme Court since 1910. That judicial seat had removed him completely from the party's internecine bloodletting and, therefore, made him acceptable in all quarters.5

For Wilson, Hughes promised to be almost as formidable a foe as Roosevelt had been. As with Roosevelt, the two men had known each other and enjoyed pleasant relations for some years. They had first met nine years earlier, when they shared the speakers' platform at the Jamestown, Virginia, tercentenary celebration, and had enjoyed staying together as guests in the same house; years later, in his autobiographical notes, Hughes remembered Wilson reciting a risqué limerick. During the past three years, the two men had met from time to time in Washington, and a special bond arose between them because Wilson's son-in-law Frank Sayre was a law school classmate and close friend of Hughes's son. By coincidence, the Wilsons and the Hugheses had gone to dinner at the McAdoos' the day the president announced Brandeis's nomination to the Supreme Court. Brandeis himself was there too, and Wilson had taken the arm of another of the guests, the irascible and anti-Semitic justice James McReynolds, and said, "Permit me to introduce you to Mr. Brandeis, your next colleague on the Bench."[6]

Personally, the justice and the president had a lot in common. Hughes was also a minister's son with a parent born in England—his father, a Welshman, was a Baptist clergyman with high moral and intellectual standards. Many people who met Hughes compared him to Wilson because he was not a gregarious sort, and professional politicians often found him cold and aloof. Despite those similarities, differences separated them, both physical and intellectual. Hughes had almost as long a jaw as Wilson, but he concealed his with a full beard, which he parted in the middle and combed to the sides. In his earlier years, his rapid-fire delivery and mobile facial expressions on the speaking platform had earned him the nickname of Animated Feather Duster. More recently, his beard had turned gray, giving him a stern look. That look, combined with his reserved manner, earned Hughes such less-fond epithets as "bearded lady" and "bearded iceberg" and, from Roosevelt, "whiskered Wilson." But unlike the president, he had enjoyed law school and had graduated first in his class. He had been a highly successful Wall Street lawyer and had first gained public notice as a special prosecutor in well-publicized investigations of fraud in the insurance industry. As governor, Hughes had sometimes clashed with his state's party bosses but had never battled them in the spectacular way Wilson had battled New Jersey's bosses. Hughes was a warm family man with a well-cloaked sense of humor, but he lacked the playful streak that Wilson showed when he twitted McReynolds at that dinner.

How strong a race Hughes would run in 1916 depended in part on Roosevelt. The Progressives desperately desired their hero to run again— he offered them their only hope of staying afloat as a party. At the Progressive convention, which was meeting in Chicago at the same time as the Republicans, the delegates defied Roosevelt's orders and nominated him a few minutes before the Republicans nominated Hughes. Roosevelt immediately telegraphed to decline, and he added insult to injury by suggesting that the Progressives might nominate a conservative who had opposed their party—Lodge. Angry cries erupted. Delegates took off their Roosevelt badges, threw them on the floor, and stomped out of the hall. Wilson and the Democrats would have preferred to have Roosevelt run again and split the opposition as before, but the bitter taste left by his behavior meant that many Progressives' votes were up for grabs. Roosevelt was already straining to steer them toward Hughes. He announced his endorsement of the Republican nominee, though he told a friend, "I do wish the bearded iceberg had acted a little differently during the last six months so as to enable us to put more heart into the campaign for him."[7]

By contrast, Wilson's emerging campaign was coming together splendidly. The Democrats' national chairman, the unstable William McCombs, could have posed a problem. Wilson delegated the business of getting rid of him to House. The colonel, in turn, enlisted the help of the financier Bernard Baruch, who extracted a letter of resignation from McCombs, to take effect at the end of the convention. As his replacement, House suggested Vance McCormick, a wealthy newspaper publisher from Pennsylvania, who was prominent among the state's more progressive Democrats. After some hesitation and because several other men declined to be considered, Wilson agreed to McCormick's appointment, and the forty-four-year-old bachelor turned out to be an effective campaign manager. With the assistance of two able operatives, Robert Woolley and Daniel Roper, he assembled a large, efficient headquarters in New York. There were also regional offices around the country and divisions that targeted appeals to labor, women, the foreign born, and other interest groups, together with a publicity bureau that produced reams of printed material, sound recordings, and movies.[8]

House's role in McCormick's selection signaled his temporarily renewed involvement in party affairs. For all his conniving and furtiveness, the colonel could be a source and conduit for novel ideas. He showed this when Wilson was in New York in May for Grayson's wedding. In a hurried discussion that included both foreign affairs and party matters, House suggested a cabinet appointment for Martin Glynn, a former governor of New York, who was to be the keynote speaker at the Democratic convention. Wilson, House noted, "thought the country would not approve of his putting a Catholic in the Cabinet." House disagreed "and contended that the country would not object in the slightest. What they do object to is having the President's Secretary a Catholic." To House's surprise, Wilson responded to this slam at Tumulty by asking the colonel to suggest a replacement. "I asked him, when he would make the change," House noted, "and he again surprised me by saying, 'immediately, if I can find the right man. I will offer Tumulty something else.' "[9]

Then, after discussing other party affairs, House made a much bolder suggestion—for the vice presidency:

> We talked of . . . whether we should sidetrack Marshall and give the nomination to [Newton] Baker. He felt that Baker was too good a man to be sacrificed. I disagreed with him. I did not think

that any man was too good to be considered for Vice President of the United States. I thought if the right man took it, a man who has his confidence as Baker has, a new office could be created out of it. He might become Vice President in fact as well as in name, and be a co-worker and co-helper of the President. He was interested in this argument but was unconvinced that Baker should be, as he termed it, sacrificed. He was afraid he could not educate the people in four years up to the possibilities of this office. He reminded me that no Vice President had ever succeeded a President by election.[10]

Neither man could know that three years later Wilson would suffer a stroke and thereby precipitate the worst crisis of presidential disability in the nation's history. That crisis might have been handled better if Wilson had responded differently to House's suggestion. Even without intimations of mortality, he could and should have warmed to the idea. House was speaking for other high-placed Democrats when he proposed dumping Vice President Marshall, who had been practically invisible during the preceding three years. Though no dynamo, Marshall was not entirely to blame for his invisibility. Leaders at both ends of Pennsylvania Avenue largely ignored him, and Wilson saw him only when he addressed a joint session of Congress or attended official functions. Marshall's home state of Indiana was one the Democrats wanted to carry, but Baker's Ohio offered a much richer electoral prize—second only to New York. A month later, Wilson would soon show how much carrying Ohio was on his mind when he filled the vacancy left on the Supreme Court by Hughes's resignation with an Ohioan. After consulting with Newton Baker and the Democratic former governor of Ohio, he named John Hessin Clarke, a federal judge from Cleveland with a reputation as a progressive and friend of labor.

More than short-run political calculations commended replacing Marshall with Baker. The idea of a vice president who might serve as a co-president should have appealed to Wilson. Having spent much of life studying political systems and institutions, he was better equipped than anyone else to grasp the merits of this idea. Having an able and trusted vice president such as Baker at his side during his second term could have made a big difference in management and policy, particularly when it became a wartime presidency. Why Wilson's political imagination failed him at this moment is a troubling question. House left a couple of clues as to possible answers. First, he sprang the suggestion at the end of a hurried meeting. Second, in his last remark Wilson made an elementary error of fact: four vice presidents had gone on to be elected president—John Adams, Thomas Jefferson, Martin Van Buren, and, most recently and most pertinently, Theodore Roosevelt. "The President showed some signs of fatigue," House noted, "and it was time for him to call for Mrs. Wilson to take her to the wedding."[11] It was unfortunate—perhaps tragic—that such great consequences could hang on such ordinary things as timing, fatigue, and personal engagements.

The Democratic convention that opened in St. Louis on June 14 was all Wilson's show. He instructed the convention managers to stress patriotism. Flags festooned the hall where the Democrats met, and there were lots of patriotic songs. He, along with Tumulty and House, read and approved the keynote speech in advance. Ex-governor Glynn of New York, following instructions, played the patriotic card by using the undefined term "Americanism" as a refrain, but Glynn's speech took on a life of its own when he declared that the United States would stay out of war. The delegates exploded in applause. From there on, as Glynn recited times in American history when the nation had not gone to war, shouts arose, "Go on, go on." As he went on, the crowd would roar, "What did we do?" and Glynn would shout, "We didn't go to war."[12]

On the second day of the convention, the delegates' enthusiasm soared, and the peace theme got powerful reinforcement. Senator Ollie James of Kentucky, a burly man with a trumpeting voice, touted "a courage that must be able to stand bitter abuse; a courage that moves slowly, acts coolly, and strikes no blow as long as diplomacy can be employed." As a shining example of such courage, James pointed to Wilson's handling of the submarine challenge: "Without orphaning a single American child, without widowing a single American mother, without firing a single gun, without the shedding of a single drop of blood, he wrung from the most militant spirit that ever brooded above a battlefield an acknowledgment of American rights and an agreement to American demands." Later in the day, cries arose from the floor, "Bryan!" "Bryan!" The Great Commoner was in the press box because enemies among the Nebraska Democrats had denied him a seat as a delegate. The convention suspended the rules to allow him to speak. Literally weeping with joy, Bryan called this convention "a love feast." He brushed aside past differences and praised Wilson for having enacted so many important reforms, and he avowed, "I join the American people in thanking God that we have a President who does not want this nation plunged into this war."[13]

On the third and final day, the delegates dispensed with a roll call and renominated the president and vice president by acclamation. They likewise adopted the platform, to which the committee had added to Wilson's draft the statement: "In particular, we commend to the American people the splendid diplomatic victories of our great President, who has preserved the vital interests of our Government and its citizens, and kept us out of war." This was the origin of the campaign cry "He kept us out of war."[14] In all, Wilson could feel pleased with his party's handiwork at St. Louis. The speakers and the delegates may have beaten the peace drum a bit too hard for his taste, but everything else had gone his way, and he was ready and eager to face the voters.

Before he could plunge into the campaign, he had some welcome business of governing to attend to. The summer months of 1916 offered him a brief reprise of the first year of his presidency, when he had been able to give greater attention to domestic affairs, particularly legislative leadership. Thanks to the resolution of the submarine controversy, the country was no longer teetering on the brink of the world war, and the main diplomatic controversies now involved the British. The greater urgency of the submarine controversy had previously offered cover to the leaders in London as they tightened their blockade, and the main advocate of sensitivity and caution toward the United States, Sir Edward Grey, had lost influence. Others in the government who favored a harder line, particularly Lloyd George, maintained that the Americans would submit to any restrictions so long as they made money from the war. Now the British had to face the consequences of their attitudes and actions.

During the summer of 1916, two of their blockade practices drew angry reactions from the American public and the Wilson administration. One was intercepting and opening mail from Americans who were suspected of having ties with the Germans. The British did not respond to diplomatic protests. The second practice was the compiling of a list of businesses suspected of trading with the Germans. This "blacklist" drew denunciations from the press and objections from the State Department. Wilson shared the widespread disgust with the British. "I am, I must admit, about at the end of my patience with Great Britain and the Allies," he told House in July. "This black list business is the last straw." Evidently presuming that the colonel would contact Grey, he warned, "I am seriously considering asking Congress to authorize me to prohibit loans and restrict exportations to the Allies."[15]

Compounding those troubles for the British was widespread revulsion in America over what was happening in Ireland. On April 24, 1916, revolutionaries had mounted an armed uprising in Dublin that opened what would become a bloody six-year conflict that would lead finally to independence for Ireland. The British army brutally suppressed this Easter Rising and had its leaders shot after summary military proceedings. One incident in particular attracted international attention: the capture and sham trial of the Irish nationalist Sir Roger Casement. Despite appeals for clemency from the pope and a resolution by the U.S. Senate asking that Casement's life be spared, the British executed him. Those acts understandably stirred wrath among Irish Americans, an important Democratic constituency. More generally, British behavior in Ireland ignited latent Anglophobia that stretched back to the Revolution and the War of 1812 and had flared up periodically since then. The British seemed intent on proving that they were only marginally less brutal than the Germans. Ireland damaged their moral standing in American eyes the way Belgium had done for the Germans.

One American felt particularly acute pain at this turn of events. In August, Ambassador Walter Page came home for the first time in three years, hoping to smooth the waters. In Washington, he found negative feelings toward Britain. After several frustrating encounters at the State Department and repeated delays, Page wrangled a private talk in September with his old friend Wilson. It was a painful meeting. Wilson said that he had "started out as heartily in sympathy as any man [could] be," Page recorded immediately afterward. Then, however, England "[h]ad gone on as she wished," ignoring "the rights of others," and that had hurt America's "pride," which was also Wilson's pride. Page also wrote, "He described the war as a result of many causes—some of long origin. He spoke of England's having the earth and Germany's wanting it." For such an impassioned champion of the Allies, these revelations of Wilson's thinking were disheartening. For Page personally, the encounter marked a parting of the ways in a friendship that dated back more than thirty years, to the time when they had been a pair of ambitious young southerners yearning to make their mark in the world.[16]

Actually, diplomatic friction with the British did not rank high among Wilson's concerns. Besides his reelection campaign, he cared most about the reform measures that would round out the second installment of the New Freedom. First on the legislative agenda were child labor and workmen's compensation laws. In February, the House had easily passed a child labor bill, but in the Senate, Democrats stalled action on Robert Owen's version. A measure to provide workmen's compensation for federal employees passed the House virtually without opposition but also languished in the Senate. The Republicans were using the failure to act on those bills in their campaign propaganda. Wilson broke the stalemate by going to the Capitol, where he met with Democratic senators in the President's Room and urged passage of the bills both because they merited passage and because they would honor pledges in the party's platform. The Senate passed the workmen's compensation bill without a recorded vote. Some southern Democrats continued to oppose the child labor bill as an intrusion on state rights and as a blow to their region's cheap labor, but they did not resort to a filibuster, and the bill passed by a vote of 52 to 12. Wilson signed it into law at a White House ceremony on September 1, declaring, "I want to say that with real emotion I sign this bill, because I know . . . what it is going to mean to the health and to the vigor of the country, and also to the happiness of those whom it affects."[17]

Two other pieces of legislation enacted in 1916 were becoming flash points of conflict in the presidential campaign. One was the Revenue Act of 1916, whose curious history involved Wilson only marginally. It stemmed from the preparedness program, which was going to cost $300 million in new spending. The Treasury Department proposed to raise most of that money through excise taxes, which would fall most heavily on middle- and lower-income Americans. Bryanite Democrats on Capitol Hill rose up in revolt, charging that this tax burden was unfair, and besides, the rich and big business should pay for the military spending because they were the ones who were pushing for it. In the House, Claude Kitchin's position as both majority leader and chairman of the Ways and Means Committee gave him the opportunity to write such views into law with a revenue bill that doubled the income tax rate, raised the surtax on high incomes, and levied the first federal inheritance tax. The bill also included a special tax on the profits of the munitions industry. McAdoo pressed Wilson to try to get changes, but the president stayed out of the conflict. In heated debate on the House floor, Republicans denounced the bill as a raid by southerners and westerners on the hard-earned, well-deserved wealth of the Northeast and Midwest; they were raising a sectional argument that would become one of their favorite battle cries in the campaign. On July 10, the House passed the revenue bill by a largely partisan vote of 240 to 140.[18]

In the Senate, La Follette led the fight to keep the revenue bill in the form passed by the House. Acting with Democrats, he succeeded and also got the surcharge on high incomes raised further and the inheritance tax doubled. In angry floor debate, a Democrat and a Republican nearly got into a fistfight, but the bill passed on September 5, by a vote of 42 to 16. All thirty-seven Democrats voting were in favor, and all the negative votes came from Republicans. Also supporting the bill were five Republican insurgents: La Follette, George Norris, Albert Cummins, William Kenyon of Iowa, and Moses Clapp of Minnesota. Wilson involved himself only once, when he got Democratic senators to add amendments empowering the president to retaliate against nations that restricted American trade—a measure aimed at Britain's blockade. Final passage came on September 7, and Wilson signed the bill into law the next day. The debates and votes on the Revenue Act in both houses again showed how party lines continued to be redrawn over progressive issues, as both parties appealed to their sectional core constituencies.[19]

The other piece of legislation that fed conflict in the campaign mandated an eight-hour day for workers on interstate railroads. The eight-hour day had been organized labor's holy grail for nearly half a century, and it was the main demand of railroad unions in negotiations in the summer of 1916. Management refused to consider it, and Secretary of Labor William Wilson tried to mediate. When the secretary's efforts failed early in August, President Wilson met separately with union leaders and railroad presidents. Neither side would budge, and the unions called a strike to begin on September 4. Such a strike spelled disaster for the economy and posed a threat to national security. After conferring briefly with Democratic congressional leaders, the president went to the Capitol on August 29 to address a joint session of Congress. Observers noted that the president seemed informally dressed for such an occasion: he wore a blue jacket and white flannel trousers. In fact, he meant his attire to suggest national security considerations: it was the same outfit he had worn when he marched in the preparedness parade on Flag Day. He told the congressmen and senators that management's intransigence forced him to ask them to establish an eight-hour day for railroad workers by law. He also asked for stronger federal mediation powers, greater ICC oversight of railroads, and presidential authority to take over and run the railroads in the event of military necessity.[20]

Democratic congressional leaders, though generally approving, balked at anything beyond the eight-hour day, and Wilson reluctantly agreed to a stripped-down measure. Bearing the name of the chairman of the House Interstate and Foreign Commerce Committee, William C. Adamson of Georgia, it quickly passed, by a vote of 239 to 56, again mainly along party lines. In the Senate, Republicans denounced the measure as class legislation and a craven surrender to union threats—charges that would become another favorite campaign cry—but it passed quickly by a vote of 43 to 28, even more clearly along party lines. Among Democrats, forty-two favored the bill and only two—both southerners—opposed it. Among Republicans, only one, La Follette, voted in favor, and twenty-six voted against, including such insurgents as George Norris, Albert Cummins, and William Borah. The next day, Wilson signed the

Adamson Act into law aboard his private railroad car at Washington's Union Station. The location was symbolic, as was the timing: Wilson was returning from giving his acceptance speech for the Democratic presidential nomination.[21]

The Adamson Act marked the biggest extension of government power that Wilson ever asked for in peacetime and was the boldest intervention in labor relations that any president had yet attempted. It offered a fitting capstone to the second installment of the New Freedom. None of the measures enacted in 1916 was as monumental as the Federal Reserve, but most of them rivaled tariff revision and the anti-trust law in their lasting significance. Significant income tax rates and the inheritance tax of the Revenue Act would remain in place for the rest of the twentieth century. Aid to farmers and the shipping and tariff boards would likewise remain and pave the way for further action in those areas two decades later under the New Deal. A controversial Supreme Court decision would strike down the child labor law two years later, but that law would serve as the model for a permanent prohibition of child labor, also under the New Deal. Furthermore, the elevation of Brandeis to the Supreme Court rewarded the chief architect, besides Wilson, of the New Freedom, and it gave the Court one of its great justices, one who would open the way for more liberal and more flexible jurisprudence.

Wilson played a different part in passing these measures than he had played in the passage of the first New Freedom legislation. This time, he did not create a program in advance, and he did not involve himself as much in shepherding its parts through Congress. Much of the initiative came from progressive Democrats on Capitol Hill, and Wilson's contribution often lay in giving them their head or stiffening their resolve. Even so, he played a critical role. As before, he kept his congressional supporters at their tasks and on course. Moreover, he had to overcome new obstacles, in addition to the distractions of foreign affairs. Democrats now had a sharply reduced majority in the House, and Bryan no longer stood at the president's side to serve as chief lobbyist and legislative liaison.

Like its predecessor, this installment of the New Freedom was also a party program. Except for La Follette, Republicans did little to help frame, and increasingly opposed, these measures. Some of that was probably unavoidable, given the conservatives' firm control of the party and the collapse of the Progressives. In all, Wilson could take great pride in this second round of legislative accomplishment. The New Freedom was alive and well.

Wilson's looming campaign for reelection made the summer of 1916 different from the preceding months of his presidency. Both he and

Hughes, unlike Roosevelt earlier, observed the old custom of waiting for the notification ceremony to deliver their opening speeches. The challenger got a month's head start, giving his acceptance speech on July 31 to an audience of 3,000 at Carnegie Hall in New York. What should have been a rousing opener to Hughes's campaign fell flat as the candidate droned on, delivering carping criticisms of the Wilson administration and offering few positive alternatives. In foreign policy, he sounded tough but vague; on the league of nations idea, he sounded like Wilson when he called for "the development of international organization" and affirmed that "there is no national isolation in the world of the Twentieth Century." Most observers were disappointed with the speech, but one was delighted. Wilson told Bernard Baruch he was following "the rule never to murder a man who is committing suicide." Later, he softened a bit, saying he felt sorry for Hughes: "He is in a hopelessly false position. He dare not have opinions: He would be sure to offend some important section of his following." Remembering the Animated Feather Duster, some commentators expressed amazement that Hughes could give such a limp performance. He later explained that his campaign skills had grown rusty after six years on the Supreme Court.[22]

Things got better for the Republican candidate when he made a tour in August that took him to the West Coast and back. Hughes made a bold move of his own by going beyond the Republican platform's vague language on woman suffrage to endorse a constitutional amendment. He also recovered some of his wonted vigor as he lambasted Wilson for weakness toward Mexico, and he sometimes made a good personal impression. "Gosh!" one North Dakota farmer reportedly exclaimed. "He ain't so inhuman after all."[23] When the campaign train reached California, however, the trip turned into a comedy of errors. The local managers, who were conservative Republicans, did not serve Hughes well. In San Francisco, they scheduled an event at a hotel where the workers were on strike, and they refused to move to another location. As a result, Hughes wound up crossing a picket line and offending the city's strong union movement.

A still worse misstep in California involved internal party strife. The Republicans' split in 1912 had hurt them there badly because Governor Hiram Johnson, who was the Progressive vice-presidential nominee, had kept Taft and the regular Republicans off the ballot. In 1914, California was the only place where the Progressives did not collapse. Now, in 1916, the pugnacious governor grudgingly followed Roosevelt back into the Republican fold, and he was running hard for the party's nomination for senator. That situation posed a dilemma for Hughes. He did not think he could endorse Johnson's senatorial bid, but he desperately wanted the governor to share the campaign platform with him. Between Johnson's notoriously prickly personality and the machinations of conservatives, no joint appearance or even a meeting came off. Worst of all—in the most notorious incident of the campaign—the nominee and the governor spent several hours on the same day in the same hotel in Long Beach without seeing each other. When he learned of the fiasco, Hughes immediately apologized, but the damage was done. Stories about his "snub" of the governor raced around the state, and Johnson declined all requests for a meeting. The governor won the senate primary and dutifully endorsed the Republican ticket. Hughes later believed that the incident cost him the state—and the election.[24]

Wilson's campaign got off to a later start because he had to stay in Washington to attend to public business, yet the delay gave him an advantage. The last measures of the New Freedom helped his reelection prospects much more than any speeches or tours. Moreover, because he was president, Wilson could speak out in ways that ostensibly were nonpolitical but really advanced his campaign. On July 4, he dedicated the new American Federation of Labor building, and with Gompers and other union leaders present, he lauded labor over capital for being "in immediate contact with the task itself—with the work, with the conditions of the work." Two weeks later, he dropped the nonpartisan mask when he told a convention of patronage-appointed postmasters, "The Democratic party is cohesive. Some other parties are not."[25] Those speeches and his remarks when he signed the rural-credits and child labor laws served as warm-ups for his acceptance of the Democratic nomination. To reestablish his political base in New Jersey, he rented an oceanside estate at Long Branch, called Shadow Lawn, where on September 2, in a setting reminiscent of Sea Girt four years before, he met the delegation from the Democratic convention and delivered his acceptance speech.

As expected, Wilson praised the party's accomplishments and declared that the Democrats had kept the promises they had made in 1912. He also pitched a frank appeal to Roosevelt's erstwhile followers: "This record must equally astonish those who feared that the Democratic Party had not opened its heart to comprehend the demands of social justice. We have in four years come very near to carrying out the platform of the Progressive Party as well as our own; for we also are progressives." Most of the speech covered foreign affairs. With regard to the world war, Wilson reaffirmed neutrality as the bulwark against its hatred and desolation. Regarding Mexico, he deplored the loss of American lives and property but affirmed that Mexicans were seeking emancipation from oppression. He warned that new challenges would come when the world war ended, and he alluded to the league of nations idea without being specific in calling for "joint guarantees" against those who would disturb the peace. He closed by reiterating the basic message of the New Freedom, that people's energies and initiative "should be set free, as we have set them free," and power should never again "be concentrated in the hands of a few powerful guides and guardians."[26]

Immediately afterward, Wilson hit the campaign trail. He signed the Adamson Act in the railroad car, rather than in the White House or at Shadow Lawn, because he was on his way to Kentucky to dedicate Lincoln's birthplace. On this ostensibly nonpolitical occasion, Wilson once again used the example of the nation's greatest self-made man to underline the populist message he had just delivered in his acceptance speech. He then spoke in Atlantic City to the National American Woman Suffrage Association. Mindful that Hughes had stolen a march on him by endorsing a constitutional amendment, Wilson was eager to assure the suffragists that he believed in their cause. He called their movement "one of the most astonishing tides of modern history," and he declared, "We feel the tide; we rejoice in the strength of it, and we shall not quarrel in the long run as to the method of it." Those stirring but vague words made a hit with the 4,000 mostly female delegates, who gave the president a standing ovation.[27]

Wilson intended to give his next speech to an insurance executives' convention in St. Louis, but family misfortune upset those plans. On September 11, he got word that his sister, Annie Howe, was dying in New London, Connecticut. He and Edith traveled there aboard the *Mayflower*, but his sister was heavily sedated and her doctors advised him not to stay. She died on September 16, and Wilson, Edith, and Grayson left for Columbia, South Carolina, for the funeral. This was a doubly sad occasion for Wilson. Of all his siblings, Annie had been closest to him, and her son George had lived with the Wilsons while he was a student at Princeton. Coming just two years after Ellen's death, this funeral and burial at a Presbyterian church in the South could not help but stir painful memories. Edith later remembered the days at Shadow Lawn after their return from the funeral as a peaceful interlude during which her husband read aloud to her in the evening before a fire, but she conceded that such evenings and other quiet moments were rare.[28]

An unceasing stream of visitors came to Shadow Lawn. The first to call after their return from South Carolina was the party chairman, Vance McCormick, who brought good news and bad news. The good news was that he and his assistants had the campaign machinery humming along and that Bryan was barnstorming through the Midwest and West in a manner reminiscent of his own campaign swings, stressing peace—with Mexico rather than in Europe—and progressivism. The bad news concerned Maine and money. Thanks to its September gubernatorial elections, which tended to presage its—and the nation's—returns in the November presidential elections, there had long been a widely bruited maxim: "As Maine goes, so goes the nation." Maine almost always went Republican and had done so again in September 1916. Democratic spokesmen tried to discount the results, but they were worried about a possible trend in the Northeast.

The money problems involved big contributors. Financiers such as Henry Morgenthau and Bernard Baruch gave generously, as did some of the president's Princeton friends, most notably the ever-faithful Cleveland Dodge; otherwise, the pocketbooks of big business and the wealthy opened mostly to the Republicans. The eight-hour railroad law had lent a special edge to this disparity. Referring to business and the Adamson Act, McCormick told Colonel House, "Before this they were lukewarm, but now they are fighting mad and are offering freely their support to Hughes in both money and effort."[29]

The Adamson Act also gave a shot in the arm to the Republican candidate's campaign performance. On the return leg of his speaking tour, Hughes lashed out at the law. "I want what is reasonable for labor," he claimed, but more important is "the willingness to abide by the results of reason . . . and never surrender to any force of any kind." Privately, he told Taft that passing this law was a "most shameful proceeding" and should be made "a fundamental issue. I propose to press it constantly."[30] Hughes was as good as his word. Throughout the rest of the campaign, he lambasted the Adamson Act as proof of Wilson's knuckling under to pressure and granting special privileges to one group. Only foreign policy would receive as much attention in Hughes's speeches, and nothing else would engage his oratorical powers so well.

Hughes's arguments dovetailed with the Republicans' message that Wilson and the Democrats were purveyors of special interest and class legislation. Along with denunciations of the Revenue Act for sectional favoritism, this conservative stance suited the party's increasingly sharp alignment against progressive measures. Another denunciation of the Adamson Act came from Roosevelt. The Republicans were using him as a campaigner the same way the Democrats were using Bryan. The ex-president spent most of his time attacking both Wilson's foreign policy and his personal character as cowardly and debased. But he ventured also into domestic affairs a few times. To him, the Adamson Act epitomized "the policy of craven surrender to whichever side has the superiority of brute force." More broadly, he accused Wilson of lacking "disinterested-ness" and showing "frank cynicism of belief in, and appeal to, what is basest in the human heart."[31] Roosevelt was once more touching upon the core of his philosophy—the need to rise above material desires in order to serve a transcendent national purpose. Wilson's poaching Progressive programs might fool others, but the prophet of the New Nationalism knew that this heretic had not embraced the true faith.

Wilson originally planned to take a leaf from William McKinley's 1896 campaign and give weekly "front porch" speeches to visiting delegations at Shadow Lawn. In each talk, he intended to discuss a single issue in depth and thereby educate the public about his programs and purposes. In his first speech, he defended the Adamson Act by affirming that the bond between capital and labor must be more than "merely a contractual rela-tionship. . . . Labor is not a commodity." He stole Roosevelt's favorite argument when he declared that government must "see that no organiza-tion is as strong as itself" and that no private interest could compete "with the authority of society." He departed from the plan for educational "front porch" speeches, however, when he received a telegram from Jeremiah O'Leary, the head of the American Truth Society, a notorious anti-British, pro-German organization, that accused him of partiality toward the Allies. Wilson shot back publicly: "I would feel deeply mortified to have you or anybody like you vote for me. Since you have access to many dis-loyal Americans, and I have not, I will ask you to convey this message to them."[32] That reply caused a sensation and drew cheers from the press—reminiscent of his reply to George Record in the gubernatorial campaign six years before.

In his next speech at Shadow Lawn, to a group of college-student Democrats, Wilson made a stronger pitch for votes from former Progres-sives. "I myself expected that this campaign would be an intellectual con-test," he told them; "that, upon both sides, men would draw upon some essential questions of politics." But he had been disappointed; except for touting the protective tariff, the Republicans were avoiding any serious discussion of domestic issues. These Republicans were not like the "great body of spirited Republicans" who four years earlier had formed "the great Progressive party—great . . . because it had the real red blood of human sympathy in its veins and was ready to work for mankind." He pointed out that the Democrats had carried out the Progressives' purposes and intentions, and he proclaimed, "I am a progressive. I do not spell it with a capital P, but I think my pace is just as fast as those who do." He also digressed into foreign policy, where, he said, Republicans had taken a clear stand against his own policies and vowed to change them. How would they do that? "There is only one choice as against peace, and that is war." If the Republicans won, he predicted, the country would go to war in Europe and in Mexico, where they wanted to protect American investors.[33]

This was hitting hard and perhaps hitting below the belt. To accuse his opponents of warmongering smacked of the kind of thing Roosevelt was saying about him from the other side. Worse, Wilson was appealing to the "passion" that he deplored in this speech and had warned against for years. Why he said such things is not clear. The sensation caused by his reply to O'Leary may have prompted him to swing heavily to the other side of the "double wish"; perhaps he felt moved by looking at the faces of so many young men in the crowd. This attack did not gibe with his own thinking about "He kept us out of war," at least as the slogan applied to Europe. Josephus Daniels later remembered Wilson telling him, "I can't keep the country out of war. They talk of me as though I were a god. Any little German lieutenant can put us into war at any time by some calculated outrage."[34]

During the last month before the election, Wilson alternated between more speeches at Shadow Lawn and four campaign trips, and he mixed foreign and domestic policies when he spoke. In foreign policy, he took the high road of continuing to advocate a league of nations to maintain peace and the low road of again accusing the Republicans, particularly Roosevelt, of warmongering. In domestic policy, he praised the Adamson Act, appealed to farmers on the basis of rural credits, and opposed immigration restriction. He also denounced the Republicans for reverting to domination by big business and standpat conservatives: the Republicans offer people "masters," whereas the Democrats "offer to go into the fight shoulder to shoulder with them to get the rights which no man has a right to take away from them." Wilson might have been appealing to former Progressives, but he was not diluting or soft-pedaling the New Freedom message of helping ordinary people in their struggle to make their way up in the world. In the last days before the election, after prodding from the campaign managers, he grudgingly made a barnstorming tour of New York, saying privately that he could win with that state. "He thought both McCormick and I had 'New Yorkitis,'" House declared, "and that the campaign should be run from elsewhere."[35]

This campaign showed once more that Wilson was the most articulate person in American politics. Regrettably, it was not, as he said, "an intellectual contest" like the one four years earlier. Unlike Roosevelt, Hughes was not expounding a competing political philosophy. Moreover, as president, Wilson had a record to defend, and the world war and Mexico made foreign affairs compete for attention with domestic concerns. Emotional appeals like the ones he made with his insinuations of warmongering were unusual for him, but they did betoken a new relationship with the public. He was forging the personal bond that he had earlier envied in Roosevelt. People repeatedly yelled out at him, "Woody" and "Woodrow." Crowds lined the tracks when his train passed by. Those moments gratified Wilson. He could end his campaign knowing that he had connected strongly with the voters.

The Republicans did not feel so sanguine about the progress of their campaign. Hughes's performance improved steadily after he began attacking the Adamson Act, and he found an able new manager in Will Hays of Indiana, who brought fresh discipline and focus to the operation. But problems persisted. Hard feelings still divided the party's conservative high command from insurgents and returning Progressives. Foreign policy likewise gave the Republicans headaches because Roosevelt was both an asset and a liability. He drew bigger crowds than anyone else, but his stands on the war made other Republicans uneasy. Hughes sometimes emulated Roosevelt, as when he said that he was not "too proud to fight" and claimed that if he had been president, he would have taken a firm stand on the submarine issue and the *Lusitania* would never have been sunk. Yet he also criticized Wilson for not being tougher on the Allied blockade, and he welcomed support from German American and Irish American groups, meeting in October with some of their leaders, including the man Wilson had denounced as a "disloyal American"—Jeremiah O'Leary. Word of that meeting leaked to the Democrats, who gleefully spread stories about the encounter.

The insinuation of guilt by association was a political dirty trick, but it paled in comparison to the smears and innuendos Republicans were spreading. They tried to revive the Mrs. Peck stories but succeeded mostly in stirring up indignation against the slanders. Rumors circulated that Ellen Wilson had died after her husband pushed her down a flight of stairs in the White House. At Princeton, dirt-seeking emissaries from the Republican campaign approached Hibben for stories about Grover Cleveland's alleged mistrust of Wilson. To his credit, Hibben swallowed hard feelings toward his former friend and angrily rebuffed the approaches. To counteract such stuff, Colonel House asked Stockton Axson to write a magazine article about his brother-in-law. Full of what House called "sob stuff," the article appeared in *The New York Times Magazine* in October under the title "Mr. Wilson As Seen by One of His Family Circle" and was widely reprinted. The Democratic campaign circulated a million copies of it as a pamphlet.[36]

Republicans' gutter tactics exposed a seamy underside to their operation. Things also got rough in public when Lodge brought up the so-
called *Lusitania* postscript, charging that Wilson had told the Germans
not to take his protest seriously. After several cabinet members denied the
story, Lodge responded, "This simply throws an additional light on the
shifty character of this Administration in its foreign policies." Wilson
called Lodge's statement "untrue" and denied that he had written or contemplated any postscript to the *Lusitania* note. That denial was shifty: it
was literally true but left out the proposed "tip" to the press about hoping
for a peaceful outcome to the dispute. Soon afterward, in his final speech
of the campaign, Roosevelt indulged in grisly wordplay on the name of
Wilson's temporary residence: "There are shadows enough at Shadow
Lawn; the shadows of men, women, and children who have risen from the
ooze of the ocean bottom and from graves in foreign lands; . . . the shadows of the tortured dead."[37]

As election day neared, many of the president's prospects looked
good. Farmers were grateful for what his administration had done for
them, and their organizations lined up solidly behind him. Labor was even
more enthusiastic; the Adamson Act had sealed the political engagement
between unions and the Democrats. Following Gompers's lead, AFL
unions were pulling hard for Wilson and his party, particularly in Ohio
and other midwestern states. More generally, the left side of the political
spectrum was shifting in his direction. After Debs decided not to run
again as the Socialist Party's candidate in 1916, many well-known party
members—including John Spargo, John Reed, Max Eastman, and
William English Walling—came out for Wilson. Such prominent social
workers as Jane Addams, Lillian Wald, and Florence Kelley also backed
him, despite his not endorsing a suffrage amendment. *The Nation* supported Wilson's reelection even though its backer, Villard, distrusted him
because of the segregation overture and the about-face on preparedness;
he believed that the Republicans' conservative tilt left him no choice.
Nearly all of those socialists and liberals based their support of the president on both his domestic program and his having stayed out of war in
Europe and Mexico.[38]

Wilson's wooing of former Progressives similarly bore fruit. Most of
the party's few officeholders and professional politicians—such as Governor Johnson of California and Senator Poindexter of Washington—
followed Roosevelt back to the Republicans. They had held office earlier
as Republicans and could not see a political future for themselves in any
other party. Personal closeness to Roosevelt swayed some well-known
Progressives, as with the conservationist Gifford Pinchot and the journal-

ist William Allen White. Other prominent party members backed Wilson, such as Representative William Kent of California, former representative Victor Murdock of Kansas, and Gifford Pinchot's brother, Amos. Where the Progressive rank and file would go would be answered only on election day. Among Republican insurgents, only La Follette tacitly supported Wilson, as he had done in 1912; the rest backed Hughes, though often without enthusiasm.

Given Wilson's wish for "an intellectual contest," two particularly gratifying endorsements came from editors of the erstwhile Progressive house organ, *The New Republic:* Herbert Croly and Walter Lippmann had criticized many of Wilson's actions and policies, but the president's progressivism combined with support for a league of nations and international reform had slowly won them over. In a signed editorial at the middle of October, Lippmann credited Wilson with "remaking his philosophy" and, in the process, "creating, out of the reactionary, parochial elements of the Democracy, the only party which at this moment is national in scope, liberal in purpose, and effective in action." Croly hesitated longer. More fully than anyone else, he shared Roosevelt's belief that individuals and groups must rise above their interests in order to serve the New Nationalism. Yet later in October, Croly produced a signed editorial that endorsed Wilson on the same grounds as Lippmann—for making the Democrats the more progressive of the two parties by changing its ideas: "The New Freedom has been discarded."[39] Wilson may have smiled at the way Croly rationalized his support, but these endorsements and others from Progressives brought a new intellectual respectability and sophistication to the Democrats.

Still, some of the president's prospects did not look good. Opposition from German American organizations and other anti-Allied groups remained sharp. Reports reaching Democratic headquarters indicated that ordinary German Americans were not following their spokesmen, but the concentration of those voters in key midwestern states made them a worrisome piece of the electoral puzzle. Also disturbing was opposition from some Catholics, including members of the church hierarchy. They lambasted Wilson's refusal to intervene in Mexico against Carranza's anticlerical Constitutionalists.[40] Above all, the Republicans still enjoyed two big assets: their apparent stranglehold on much of the electorate in the Northeast, as evidenced by the results in Maine, and their edge in campaign spending, thanks to support from big business and the wealthy, which allowed Hughes's managers to outspend their rivals for advertising, pamphlets, and other publicity.

By mid-October, the president and his campaign managers knew that the election was going to be extremely close and that he might lose. "It is evident, of course, that Mr. Hughes is making very little headway, because he has done so many stupid and insincere things," Wilson told his brother, "but other influences are at work on his behalf which are undoubtedly powerful, chiefly the influence of organized business. I can only conjecture and hope." The chance of losing led him to make an unusual move. House suggested a plan by which Wilson would get Secretary of State Lansing and Vice President Marshall to resign and appoint Hughes to succeed Lansing. Under the law then in force, the secretary of state stood next in the line of succession after the vice president. This meant that if Wilson resigned, Hughes would become president immediately, rather than waiting until the following March 4. "Times are too critical to have an interim of four months between the election and the inauguration of the next President," the colonel wrote in his diary. He broached the plan to Lansing, who went along with it, and then to Wilson. The president said nothing, but two days before the election he drafted a letter in his shorthand, typed it himself, sealed it in an envelope with wax, and had it hand-delivered to Lansing with instructions that no one else was to open it.[41]

In the letter, Wilson outlined the resignation plan to Lansing and observed, "All my life long I have advocated some such responsible government for the United States as other constitutional systems afford as [a matter] of course, and as such action on my part would inaugurate, at least by example." He wanted to avoid a four-month interregnum because these were not "ordinary times. . . . No such critical circumstances in regard to our foreign policy have ever before existed." He believed he had "no right to risk the peace of the nation by remaining in office after I had lost my authority." The "critical circumstances" involved submarines. Confidential reports from Berlin told of growing pressure for unrestricted undersea warfare. Also, Germany's first and as yet only naval submarine with a transatlantic cruising range, the U-53, paid a call at Newport, Rhode Island, in October, and after departing, it sank—after giving warning—six merchant ships, four of them British, one Dutch, and one Norwegian. After discussions about the U-53 in Washington and at Shadow Lawn, Wilson decided to downplay the event. House may have made his suggestion about resignation in part because he was unhappy with the drift of foreign policy and was showing signs of pique. "To hear him talk," House wrote, "you would think the man in the street understood the theory and philosophy of government as he does."[42]

The plan to resign gibed so well with Wilson's thinking that the president almost certainly would have come up with it on his own. Ever since his college days, he had wanted to adapt parliamentary practices to the American system. Nor was he alone in regarding as an outmoded relic the four-month gap between elections and inaugurations that was mandated in the Constitution. Nearly two decades later, the Twentieth Amendment would abolish this calendar and fix January 20 for the inauguration and January 3 for the opening of Congress. Wilson's plan would play no part in that change because no one besides him, House, Lansing, and possibly Edith and Grayson knew about it. House would mention the scheme in passing ten years later in the published edition of his diary, but it would not become public knowledge until Lansing's *War Memoirs* were published posthumously in 1935. It is unfortunate that the plan did not become better known earlier. In 1932, the last election under the old calendar would come at an even more critical time. The defeated president in that election would be Herbert Hoover, who had served under and admired Wilson. If Hoover had known about this plan, he might have adopted it and spared the country four months of governmental paralysis at the nadir of the Great Depression, which has been called the "interregnum of despair."[43]

On November 7, when the returns came in, Wilson thought he might have to implement the plan. On election day, he and Edith drove to Princeton, where he voted once more at the fire station and joked with students and reporters. Back at Shadow Lawn, they spent a quiet afternoon and had dinner with his daughter Margaret, son-in-law Frank Sayre, and cousin Helen Bones, Edith's brother and sister-in-law, and Grayson. They played twenty questions until ten o'clock, when a telephone call from New York brought bad news: *The New York Times* was declaring Hughes the winner. As Edith later recalled, Margaret declared indignantly, "Impossible. They cannot know yet. In the West they are still at the polls." A call to the White House found a gloomy Tumulty repeating the same bad news. According to Edith's recollection, her husband remained calm. He agreed with Margaret that everything was not settled yet, but he was not sanguine. "There now seems little hope that we shall not be drawn into the War," Edith remembered him saying, "though I have done everything I can to keep us out; but my defeat will be taken by Germany as a repudiation of my policy. Many of our own people will so construe it, and will try to force war upon the next Administration." Wilson asked for a glass of milk, and as he left the room to go upstairs to bed, he said, "I might stay longer but you are all so blue."[44]

They were blue at Shadow Lawn and the White House and Democratic headquarters. The returns appeared to be bearing out their worst fears. In the Northeast, the Republican tide swept every state except New Hampshire, which seesawed before finally going to Wilson by 52 votes. In the Midwest, the Republicans did almost as well, although they lost Ohio, and Minnesota remained in doubt. The Democrats' gloom began to brighten during the early hours of the next morning. A tide of their own began to sweep the West, where only South Dakota and Oregon clearly went to Hughes. By noon on November 8, the president had a lead of 4 electoral votes among the declared states. Four states—with a total of 33 electoral votes—remained out: California, with 13; Minnesota, with 12; North Dakota, with 5; and New Mexico, with 3. By noon on November 9, it was clear that Wilson had carried three of those four states; only Minnesota went for Hughes—by 392 votes. Wilson was the winner, with 277 electoral votes to Hughes's 254. In the popular tally, he led by nearly 600,000 votes: 9,129,606 to 8,538,221. Hughes would not formally concede for almost two weeks; after his telegram arrived, the president joked to his brother, "It was a little moth-eaten when it got here but quite legible."[45]

Wilson was the first Democrat since Andrew Jackson to win a second consecutive term. He had increased his popular tally from four years earlier by nearly 3 million votes and his share of the total by a little under eight percentage points. He had beaten an undivided Republican Party, thereby showing that his victory four years earlier had been no fluke owing to his opponents' split. He had outrun his party almost everywhere. On Capitol Hill, the Democrats retained a twelve-seat majority in the Senate. In the House, however, their already-slender majority shrank further, and no one could say which party would have control in the next Congress. Later, some horse-trading of the handful of remaining Progressives and the defection of a few Republicans would keep the Democrats in control, with Champ Clark as Speaker and Claude Kitchin as majority leader and chairman of the Ways and Means Committee. Most glaringly, Wilson had won by a paper-thin margin. His share of the popular vote fell just short of a majority: 49.26 percent. In the Electoral College, if just a single state—California, which was longest in doubt—had gone the other way, he would have lost. He carried California by only 3,806 votes out of nearly 1 million and a plurality of less than four tenths of a percentage point. Hughes was almost certainly right in believing that the misadventure with Hiram Johnson cost him California and the election.[46]

The election of 1916 was one of the closest presidential contests in American history, and questions about why that was so have persisted. Assessing the results presents the classic choice of deciding whether a glass is half-empty or half-full. The half-empty choice, which most interpreters have taken, stresses not that Wilson won but that Hughes almost did. That near-miss was a remarkable feat, especially considering the wounds still carried by the Republicans from 1912 and the mistakes made by Hughes and his managers. One factor above all took him as far as he got: the Republicans' traditional strength in the Northeast and Midwest. Four years before, party conservatives had believed that progressivism was a passing fad and that voters in those regions would return to the allegiances forged in 1896. That homecoming in 1916, coupled with the Republicans' unbroken and overwhelming success in the next three presidential contests, has made such a view seem incontrovertible.

In that view, Wilson's reelection owed everything to his own luck, his personal skill, and the seductive drumbeat of "He kept us out of war." Wilson was an incumbent president, and the White House has nearly always been the best place from which to run for president. He was a successful incumbent with an awesome record of legislative accomplishment, and he could claim credit for peace and prosperity. Yet even with all that going for him, he almost lost. In short, his reelection appears to be the exception that proved the rule of Republican dominance during this era of American politics.

The half-full choice for the 1916 results builds on the half-empty one. The absolutely critical state in 1916 was Ohio. Had Wilson swept the West, including California, he still would have lost if he had not made this one substantial crack in the Republican heartland. This was the first time in a quarter century that a Democrat had carried any state north of the Potomac and Ohio rivers and east of the Missouri in a two-party contest. It was true that except for New Hampshire, Ohio was the only state Wilson won in that region. But he came agonizingly close in Minnesota and reasonably close in Connecticut, Indiana, and Massachusetts. He also improved his share of the vote in every state, often substantially. Furthermore, he won fifteen states outside the South by popular majorities, and several of those majorities in the West were large. Some of this improvement may have reflected the power of incumbency, but bigger factors may also have been at work.47

The two critical components in Wilson's victory, then, were Ohio and a virtually solid West. In both places, more than personal popularity, a good campaign, and the peace issue helped to determine the outcome. In Ohio, as every observer noted, unions went all out for the president and his party; their votes and activity contributed to a sweep that recaptured the governorship and reelected a senator as well. This was a harbinger of the role that labor would later play in swinging big industrial states over to the Democrats. In the West, peace weighed heavily, but so did progressivism. The peace issue there involved Mexico more than Europe, and Republicans never seemed to grasp how deeply repugnant the prospect of war south of the border was in the West. Significantly, too, eleven of the twelve states in which women voted lay west of the Mississippi, and Wilson carried all but one of those states despite not having endorsed a suffrage amendment. Most analysts attributed this result to the peace issue. Likewise, Roosevelt had not done well west of the Mississippi in 1912, except on the coast, and people on the plains and in the Rockies had warmed to the New Freedom, especially the anti-trust and banking reform and aid to farmers and workers. Furthermore, those parts of the West where Roosevelt had not done well were the same places where Debs had realized some of his best showings in 1912, and statistical and anecdotal evidence pointed to Wilson's picking up many of Debs's votes there in 1916. In the nation at large, he also picked up votes from people who had previously favored Roosevelt, but much of the ex-president's earlier support had been personal, and in the Northeast and Midwest the great majority of those supporters followed their leader back to the Republicans.

What Wilson wrought in 1916 was the laying of the foundation for the majority Democratic coalition—one the party would enjoy from the 1930s through the 1960s. Three major elements of that future coalition were now in place: the South, farmers, and labor. Two others were not yet in place. One was aroused and energized white first- and second-generation voters among the immigrant groups. Despite opposing immigration restriction and prohibition, which these recent immigrants and their children loathed, and despite having Tumulty at his side, Wilson had abrasive relations with the mainly Irish urban wing of the party. Some of the coolness toward him sprang from his early battles with the New Jersey bosses, which had made him suspect to Tammany Hall and other machines. Wilson heartily returned their dislike. "He thought New York 'rotten to the core,'" House recorded him saying just before the election, "and should be wiped off the map." Catholic opposition may also have kept these groups from coming aboard Wilson's bandwagon. Yet a new breed of urban Democrat was quietly on the rise. In 1916, that new breed defeated a Republican senator in Rhode Island and two years later would beat another Republican senator in Massachusetts and capture one of the biggest electoral prizes of all—the governorship of New York. Both of the 1918 winners would be Irish Americans, and New York's new governor, Al Smith, would become the party's brightest star—though also its most divisive leader—during the following decade.[48]

The other element in the majority Democratic coalition that was not yet in place was African Americans. No black leaders supported Wilson in 1916, as they had done four years earlier. One of those former supporters, W. E. B. DuBois, wrote to the president during the campaign, challenging him to live up to his assurances to Negroes in 1912: "We received from you a promise of justice and sincere endeavor to forward their interests. We need scarcely to say that you have grievously disappointed us." Wilson did not reply but instructed Tumulty "to answer this letter for me and say that I stand by my original assurances and can say with a clear conscience that I have tried to live up to them, though in some cases my endeavors have been defeated."[49] When African Americans did join the Democratic coalition twenty years later, it would be largely on their own initiative, not the party's.

Racial blindness notwithstanding, Wilson looked forward to building a new party coalition. Soon after the election, he told a former Progressive who had supported him that he wanted to realign the parties in the Democrats' favor, but he admitted, "It is by no means easy to figure it out, but I agree with you that this is the fundamental job in the next four years."[50] That was not to be. Wilson's "irony of fate" was about to reassert itself in the worst possible way. He could not know it, but his domestic presidency was over.

PEACE AND WAR

Less than three months after he was reelected president, Woodrow Wilson's worst fear came to pass. On February 1, 1917, the Germans unleashed their submarines in an onslaught of unrestricted warfare against all shipping, belligerent and neutral, in a broad zone surrounding the British Isles and the coasts of other Allied countries. Wilson now faced the crisis he had been willing to resign over if he had not won the election. How to meet this challenge would be the most important and agonizing decision of his presidency. He had tried to forestall the events that would force this decision with a bolder, more sweeping diplomatic initiative than any he had tried before. As soon as he knew that he would have another term in the White House, he began to lay the groundwork for a multi-pronged peace offensive. At the middle of December 1916, he prepared the way for an offer of American mediation of the war, which he tendered first through proper diplomatic channels and then revealed to the public. He coupled the offer with a proposal to set up a post-war league of nations empowered to maintain peace and in which the United States would be a fully participating member. Then, on January 22, 1917, he escalated this campaign by publicly laying out a program that called for a nonpunitive, compromise peace—"a peace without victory"—together with specific territorial adjustments, international reforms, and a league of nations to enforce peace. This peace offensive of December 1916 and January 1917 would embody his most heartfelt hope and most deeply desired design for the future of the world.

Winning another term as president did not cool Wilson's sense of urgency about the perils of the submarine situation. At the middle of November, he told House he intended to try to mediate the war before America was dragged in. House tried to talk him out of the idea and urged delay, fearing "that the Allies would consider it an unfriendly act." Wilson brushed those objections aside, and later in November he wrote what he called a prolegomenon about the war—probably intended for a speech—and a draft of a diplomatic note. In the prolegomenon, he deplored "this vast, gruesome contest of systematized destruction" and argued that if either "German militarism" or "British navalism" prevailed, there would be no lasting peace: "We see it abundantly demonstrated in the pages of history that the decisive victories and defeats of wars are seldom the conclusive ones." Instead, all nations must recognize the uselessness of this "mechanical slaughter" and join in eliminating war as "a means of attaining national ambition. The world would then be free to build its new peace structure on the solidest foundations it has ever possessed."[1]

In the draft of the diplomatic note, Wilson stressed that the war was disrupting life all over the world and threatened to draw neutrals in. He noted that all the belligerents claimed to be fighting for the same things—self-preservation, security from aggression, and equality of nations—and all disclaimed the goal of conquest or destruction of their foes. Americans sympathized with those objectives and were "ready to join a league of nations that will pledge itself to their accomplishment and definitely unite in the organization not only of purpose but of force as well that will be adequate to assure their realization." The belligerents should, therefore, state their peace terms and agree to come to a conference to be held under neutral auspices. He disavowed any notion of trying to foist a premature peace on the warring nations and maintained that he wanted to know what the belligerents were fighting for so that the United States "can intelligently determine its future course of action."[2] Together with the prolegomenon, this draft note laid out the central ideas for the peace offensive that Wilson was about to launch.

House continued to resist because he thought this note would drive *"the Allies frantic with rage."* The plan also posed a personal problem for the colonel. Wilson wanted him to be in London when the note was presented to the British. House countered that such a move would offend Walter Page, but Edith Wilson suggested that House should replace the ambassador: "She thought I ought to do so during the war. The President also expressed a wish that I accept it."[3] House protested that such a move would hamper his ability to move among the belligerent capitals, but his real reason was that he did not want to be separated from Wilson. He did not seem to recognize what an enemy he had in Edith.

Lansing was equally upset over the planned peace initiative. When Wilson read the draft to him, Lansing likewise advised not to rush things, and he privately brooded that the plan could not be implemented, and "I am not sure that it would be a good thing for the world if it could be." If

America entered the war, *"we must go in on the side of the Allies, for we are a democracy."* Lansing worried what might happen if the Germans accepted the mediation offer and the Allies refused.[4]

Skepticism and foot-dragging by his closest foreign policy advisers did not deter Wilson. He was also abetting a move by the Federal Reserve that showed his newfound appreciation of the intricacies of relations with the warring nations. Huge Allied purchases in the United States had nearly exhausted Britain's capacity to borrow against secured assets. In November 1916, officers of the Morgan firm, the Allies' financial agent, suggested to the Federal Reserve Board that unsecured loans be permitted. The proposal offended the board, which drafted a statement warning against such loans. The chairman of the board, William P. G. Harding, went to the White House on November 25 to show the warning statement to the president. Wilson approved the action and suggested that the board make it a strong, pointed warning, "rather than convey a mere caution." The warning was not lost on the British, whose ambassador reported that the president was probably behind it.[5]

The planned peace move crowded out nearly everything else on Wilson's agenda. Despite his talk about transforming the Democrats into a more progressive party, he neglected domestic politics. He had no plans to shuffle cabinet posts unless McAdoo decided to resign from the Treasury. Edith and House talked him into trying to get rid of Tumulty, who balked at a proposed shift to a U.S. customs board. The journalist David Lawrence, who was also a friend of Tumulty's, went to see the president and told him that "a political cabal" was railroading Tumulty and that his removal would open the president to charges of ingratitude. Wilson relented, and Tumulty would remain his secretary for the rest of his presidency.[6] Wilson also neglected domestic politics in his State of the Union address on December 5, except for appealing to enact provisions to regulate transportation and labor relations that had been left out of the Adamson Act. He did thank the members of the Sixty-fourth Congress for "the measures of constructive policy with which you have enriched the legislative annals of the country"—pallid praise for men who had put through the second installment of the New Freedom.[7]

Wilson resented even minor distractions from preparing the peace note. "Members of Congress have been sucking the life out of me, about appointments and other matters affecting the destiny of the world," he told House, "and I have been prevented from perfecting the document. I shall go out of town (on the MAYFLOWER no doubt) for the purpose, if it can be done in no other way." House was also trying to distract Wilson from the peace initiative with the excuse that a change of government in

Britain had brought Lloyd George in as prime minister and removed Grey as foreign secretary. He suggested reviving his own combined scheme of mediation and promised intervention on the Allied side, but Wilson would have none of it. "The time is at hand for *something!*" he shot back. "We cannot go back to those old plans. We must shape new ones."[8]

In a new draft of the note early in December, Wilson dropped the suggestion for a conference of belligerents and neutrals; otherwise, the document was largely unchanged. Lansing approved the note but recommended omitting the promise of a league of nations because he did not agree with the idea of enforcing peace. He also gingerly aired his concern about how the Allies might reply to this note and said that to enter the war against them would be "a calamity for this nation and for all mankind." House, who was staying at the White House, also tried to warn of the danger of entering the war against the Allies. Again revealing the new strain in their relationship, he wrote, "I am convinced that the President's place in history is dependent to a large degree upon luck. If we should get into a serious war and it should turn out disastrously, he would be one of the most discredited Presidents we have had." The colonel was also back at his old game of collecting complaints from members of the cabinet. "Domestic legislation is the President's forte," he observed. "No one has done that better or perhaps so well. But as an administrator he is a failure, and it is only because of a generally efficient Cabinet that things go as well as they do."[9]

Meanwhile, the Germans made an offer to discuss peace terms with the Allies, and Wilson decided to proceed with his own initiative before a harsh Allied reply might spoil the chances for peace. In the final draft of the note, he partially followed Lansing's advice by dropping the promise to enter a peace-enforcing league but said that Americans stood "ready, and even eager, to cooperate in the accomplishment of these ends" after the war. He also inserted a new sentence: "He [the president] takes the liberty of calling attention to the fact that the objects which the statesmen of the belligerents have in mind in this war are virtually the same." House, who did not see the note before it was sent, despaired over that insertion when he saw it. "That one sentence will enrage them [the Allies]," he wrote. "I find that the President has nearly destroyed all the work I have done in Europe. He knows how I feel about this and how the Allies feel about it, and yet the refrain always appears in some form or another."[10]

Lansing did see the note and suggested only minor verbal changes; with those alterations, the note went out over the State Department cables to the ambassadors in the belligerent capitals on December 18 and was released to the press two days later. Then Lansing tried to undercut the president's move. On December 20, he called in the French ambassador, Jean-Jules Jusserand, and explained that this was not a peace note and that Wilson favored the Allies. Lansing also told Jusserand that he believed France should demand the restoration of Alsace-Lorraine, an indemnity for Belgium, and democratic reforms in Germany. He likewise revealed his skepticism about a league of nations.[11] Two days later, he said the same things to the British ambassador, Cecil Spring-Rice, and he added that the Allies should demand an autonomous Poland, territory for Italy from Austria-Hungary, and the dissolution of Turkey.

Between his meetings with the ambassadors, Lansing went public with his attempt at sabotage. On December 21—the day the peace note appeared in newspapers—he called in reporters and gave them a statement. The reason for sending the diplomatic note was, he explained, "that the situation is becoming increasingly critical. I mean by that that we are drawing nearer the verge of war ourselves, and therefore we are entitled to know exactly what each belligerent seeks, in order that we may regulate our conduct in the future." To underscore the point, he reiterated, "The sending of this note will indicate the possibility of our being forced into the war." This was a blatant act of betrayal and threatened to undo Wilson's peace initiative. Within an hour or so, Tumulty forwarded a copy of Lansing's statement to the president, with part of one sentence underlined: "I mean by that that we are drawing nearer the verge of war ourselves."[12]

Wilson was incensed. "I came very near to asking for his resignation when he gave out that statement to the press," House quoted him saying shortly afterward. Instead, the president immediately told Lansing in a letter, "I quite understand that you did not realize the impression of your statement of this morning would make." He instructed the secretary to tell reporters that his statement "had been radically misinterpreted, . . . and that it was not at all in your mind to intimate any change in the policy of neutrality which the country has so far so consistently pursued in the face of accumulating difficulties." When Wilson saw Lansing later in the day, he repeated what he had said in the letter. Lansing claimed afterward that he agreed to follow the president's orders only if he did not have to contradict his earlier statement. That was retrospective rationalization: his second statement to the press, given out right after his meeting with Wilson, parroted what the president had told him to say.[13]

This was a sorry affair and reflected well on no one involved. Lansing committed a dastardly act of duplicity aimed at destroying Wilson's peace initiative. It was only the latest in a string of betrayals. The difference this time was that he had come out in the open. Previously, Lansing had acted stealthily, such as when he had gone behind Bryan's back after the sinking of the *Lusitania* and when he surreptitiously contradicted the president to the British and French ambassadors. Wilson should have fired him on the spot. He probably did not remove him because this was a delicate moment in international relations. Later, wartime conditions would make the secretary's ouster seem similarly inopportune. Wilson's keeping Lansing on may also have stemmed from the president's extraordinary tolerance for disagreement and disloyalty among subordinates, particularly in foreign policy. He retained Page as ambassador in London out of a comparable combination of convenience and indifference.

Lansing's behavior was even more puzzling than Wilson's. Why had this normally furtive man crept out of the shadows to commit, by his lights, an act of courage? Why, having done that, did he not avail himself of a golden opportunity to stand up for his convictions and follow the example of his predecessor by resigning in protest? Instead, Lansing knuckled under and stayed on. He would betray the president again, and he would continue to fester in disagreement with Wilson's most cherished policies and in resentment at being left out of the biggest decisions and weightiest negotiations. It would have been far better if these two men had parted company at this point.[14]

House likewise busied himself with attempts to undermine the peace initiative, though, characteristically, he did not operate so openly. He was engaging in more of his private diplomacy with the British. After a meeting with the colonel at his apartment in New York on December 22, Sir Horace Plunkett, a friend of Grey's successor as foreign secretary, Arthur James Balfour, cabled Balfour with House's assurance that Wilson was still pro-Allied. Five days later, a pro-Allied newspaper publisher, Roy Howard, cabled the British press baron Lord Northcliffe to say that House had told him Lansing's "verge of war" revealed the real purpose of the peace note. In his diary, House gloomily remarked that he had promised Lansing he would go to Washington and talk to Wilson, "but I have no stomach for it. It is practically impossible to get the President to have a general consultation."[15]

Even without the fireworks surrounding Lansing's statement, the peace note was bound to create a stir at home. Lansing's first pronouncement set off a stock market panic, although his retraction seemed to soothe the nervous men on Wall Street. Most commentators took the note for what it was—a peace move. Democratic senators lauded Wilson as a peacemaker and introduced a resolution commending the note. More belligerent and pro-Allied sorts first privately and then publicly damned him for playing Germany's game. On January 3, Lodge accused the president of siding against the nations that were "fighting the battle of freedom and democracy as against military autocracy." He also condemned Wilson for promising to plunge America into European power politics and break with the nation's traditional isolation. The same day, Roosevelt scorned the note as "profoundly immoral and misleading" and declared that Wilson's "most preposterous absurdity" was the offer to "guarantee the peace of the world." That would require "a policy of violent meddling in every European quarrel, and in return invite Old World nations violently to meddle in everything American."[16]

Attacks from that quarter on grounds of pro-Germanism were predictable. What was unexpected and disturbing was the way they pounced on the idea of enforcing peace. Debate on a Senate resolution to commend the peace note provided a forum for such attacks. That was where Lodge gave this public sign of having shifted his stand and now opposed the league idea, and another Republican senator, William Borah of Idaho, took an even stronger stand against it. Borah was an insurgent orator with a square jaw and flowing hair who had previously said little about foreign policy but now condemned Wilson's implied commitment to a league as requiring automatic entry into foreign wars: "This approaches, to my mind, moral treason." This debate marked the first skirmish in what would grow into the biggest political fight of Wilson's life. Lodge and Borah's stand pointed toward a major realignment of the two parties' foreign policy positions. Up to then, the bulk of resistance to greater involvement abroad, particularly outside the Western Hemisphere, had come from Democrats, whereas Republicans generally—and, most notably, Roosevelt and Lodge in particular—had advocated a bigger, more committed American role in world politics. The Republicans as a whole were not becoming isolationists, but they were beginning to make common cause with isolationists and talk some of their language, and Borah was embarking on a career that would make him the most prominent isolationist in American politics. Now, however, the Senate adopted the resolution commending the peace note, amended to exclude any mention of a league of nations, by a vote of 48 to 17.[17]

Of more pressing concern to Wilson than those political straws in the wind was how the belligerent governments would respond to the peace note. Contrary to House's and Lansing's fears, the Allies did not spurn the overture. The French government was initially inclined to reject the note out of hand, but a different mood prevailed in London. The new prime minister, Lloyd George, believed that rejection would play into the Germans' hands and that it was essential to maintain American goodwill. Why Lloyd George, who had previously taken a harsh line toward the United States, shifted his ground is not clear. Some interpreters have credited

Lansing's statement with keeping Lloyd George and others in the British cabinet in a receptive frame of mind. Others have stressed the warnings of the British Treasury's brilliant young economist, John Maynard Keynes, who held that the Allied war effort was becoming totally dependent on supplies and credit from America. The Federal Reserve Board's statement had also served as a wake-up call to their financial peril. Most important, perhaps, Lloyd George harbored deep suspicions about the promises of his military leaders to win the war by sacrificing still more thousands of men on the Western Front—suspicions that led him to believe that only American intervention could break the stalemate. At any event, after some negotiating, the British and French produced a joint reply at the middle of January stating moderate terms and a desire for peace based upon liberty and justice.[18]

It was a different story in Berlin. Nearly everyone in the highest civilian and military circles was infuriated by Wilson's note, and some took Lansing's statement as proof that this overture was merely a pretext for American intervention against them. The military high command, which now effectively ruled the country, insisted on steering clear of any mediation schemes. The generals were also pressing for unrestricted submarine warfare, and they were about to get their way. As a result, Germany and Austria-Hungary replied on December 26 that only negotiations among the belligerents could end the war and that consideration of new peace-keeping arrangements must await its conclusion. In the polite equivocations of diplomacy, they were telling the Americans to butt out.[19]

That stiff-arm apparently did not register with Wilson. When House came again to stay at the White House on January 3, Wilson told him he wanted to spell out a peace settlement based upon "the future security of the world against wars." House suggested that the president should present his plan in a speech to Congress, and they discussed such peace terms as an autonomous Poland, restoration of Belgium, and dissolution of the Ottoman Empire. House encouraged him to "do this great and dramatic thing. I said, 'you are now playing with what the poker players term "the blue chips," and there is no use sitting by and letting great events swamp you.'" Yet some of Wilson's thinking alarmed House, as when he said, "This country does not intend to become involved in this war. We are the only one of the great White nations that is free from war today, and it would be a crime against civilization for us to go in."[20]

Wilson then drafted a speech and read it to House on January 11. The colonel called it "a noble document and one which I think will live," but he got the president to make some verbal changes and asked if Lansing had seen the speech. Wilson said no, not yet, adding, House noted, that "[h]e thought Lansing was not in sympathy with his purpose to keep out of war." He and House agreed that the text should be cabled in advance to the ambassadors in the belligerent capitals before he delivered it to the Senate. The next day, Wilson read the speech separately to Lansing and Senator Stone and sent it to the State Department for encoding and transmission on January 15. He had to wait a week to deliver the speech, to allow time for the cabled text to be received, decoded, and delivered in the foreign capitals. He worried about leaks, and at a press conference—his third since the election—he declined to say anything about peace. He also said that House had come to town only "to take dinner" and denied having summoned him for "a grand pow-wow." That was misleading, although House had paid two visits in the past month to attend official events, including a gala dinner at the White House that allowed Edith to show her mettle as a hostess and wear one of her fashionable new gowns.[21]

On January 22, Wilson went to the Capitol with only an hour's notice and appeared in the Senate chamber at one o'clock. Speaking at first in an uncharacteristically faint voice but quickly warming up, he declared, "The question upon which the whole future peace and policy of the world depends is this: Is the present war a struggle for a just and secure peace, or only for a new balance of power?" Plainly, the choice must be "not a balance of power, but a community of power; not organized rivalries, but an organized common peace." Just one path pointed to that goal: "It must be a peace without victory. . . . Only a peace between equals can last." With those words, he offered another example of his eloquence, but he did not go beyond a gloss on the peace note until he set out the principles on which he believed a lasting peace must rest, such as equality of rights among nations and freely chosen governments, an example of which would be "a united, independent, and autonomous Poland." He also called again for "freedom of the seas" and limitations on naval and land armaments, which would force world leaders to "plan for peace and nations [to] adjust and accommodate their policy to it as they have planned for war and made ready for pitiless contest and rivalry."[22]

He closed with a plea to heed "the world's yearning desire for peace," and he claimed, "I am speaking for the silent mass of mankind everywhere who have as yet had no place or opportunity to speak their real hearts out concerning the death and ruin they see to have come already upon the persons and homes they hold most dear." He promised that the United States would join in "guaranteeing the permanence of peace upon such terms as I have named," and he maintained that he was proposing that all nations adopt the Monroe Doctrine "as the doctrine of the world," so that they would "henceforth avoid entangling alliances which would draw them into competitions of power, catch them in a net of intrigue and self-ish rivalry. . . . There is no entangling alliance in a concert of power. . . . These are American principles, American policies. We could stand for no others."[23]

Wilson aimed to give a great speech, and he succeeded. The "peace without victory" address anticipated his most important future pronouncements about a just settlement and a new world order. Such components of the Fourteen Points as "freedom of the seas," disarmament, an independent Poland, and national autonomy were here. A league of nations remained deliberately vague and general, although it was hard to miss where the president meant to go. Nor was there any mistaking what kind of peace he wanted and how he wished to attain it. Wilson believed that a lasting settlement could be attained only through compromise on all sides, where no one would be conquered or punished and no one would feel either the intoxication of victory or the vengefulness of defeat. It was a noble vision, and it had huge practical and emotional barriers in the way of its realization. But it was not necessarily an impossible dream. If both sets of belligerents, particularly the Germans, had been as truly chastened and desirous of peace as they professed to be, he might have been able to broker such a grand settlement among the warring powers, guaranteed by a league of nations. This was the fondest wish that he would have as president.

Among the senators who listened to the speech, some warmed to this move toward peace, others scoffed at a deluded dream, and still others recoiled from a nightmare prospect of entanglement in international power politics. Most Democrats applauded and made effusive statements to the press or on the Senate floor. La Follette led in the cheering and said afterward, "We have just passed through a very important hour in the life of the world." His fellow insurgent George Norris also endorsed the idea of a league of nations, and another Republican, Porter J. McCumber of North Dakota, announced himself in favor of "a world-enforced peace organization in which the United States shall take an honored part." Such support from Republican senators was the exception. The party's leader in the chamber, Jacob Gallinger of New Hampshire, dubbed it "ill-timed and utterly impossible of accomplishment," and Lawrence Sherman of Illinois said this speech would "make Don Quixote wish he had not died so soon." Borah warned, "Once in the maelstrom of European politics and it will be impossible to get out." The only way to promote peace was for America to stand apart, Borah declared, "a great, untrammeled, courageous neutral power, representing not bias, not prejudice, not hate, not conflict, but order and law and justice."[24]

Lodge weighed in with a lengthy attack on both "peace without victory" and the league idea. He dismissed Wilson's principles as meaningless and his proposed compromise as fallacious because true peace could come only through military victory and must rest "upon justice and righteousness." Wilson's claim to be extending the Monroe Doctrine was nonsense: "If we have a Monroe doctrine everywhere we may be perfectly certain that it will not exist anywhere." Lodge confessed to have changed his mind about the idea of enforcing peace because coercion would be required. He claimed to have "no superstition" about traditional American isolation, but he saw nothing "but peril in abandoning our long and well-established policies" for the sake of Wilson's proposals, which were "collections of double-dealing words under which men can hide and say they mean anything or nothing."[25] Those reactions to "peace without victory" in the Senate were a dress rehearsal for the full-fledged debate that would come two years later over membership in the League of Nations. Partisan divisions would remain as sharp then as they were now, and Borah and Lodge would emerge again as two of Wilson's strongest opponents.

Reactions in the press likewise divided mainly along party lines, with Democratic newspapers praising the move and Republican journals criticizing it. Exceptions were William Randolph Hearst's nominally Democratic paper, which lambasted the league idea, and Republican organs that backed Taft's work with the LEP, which applauded the speech. Taft announced that all members of his organization "rejoice sincerely" at the president's words and action. In fact, several Republicans who had previously sided with Taft now broke with the LEP. Roosevelt responded with a sneer: "Peace without victory is the natural ideal of the man who is too proud to fight. . . . The Tories of 1776 demanded peace without victory. The Copperheads of 1864 demanded peace without victory. These men were Mr. Wilson's spiritual forbears." By contrast, Bryan told Wilson, "The phrase 'Peace without Victory' was 'a shot heard round the world'—no one can underestimate its power for good." Publicly, Bryan said he believed he and the president could work out their previous differences about a league to enforce peace.[26]

Wilson tried to take reactions at home and abroad in stride. He confessed to Cleveland Dodge that he felt "a little low in my mind" because Republican senators failed to grasp what he meant, but he had "an invincible confidence in the prevalence of the right if it is fearlessly set forth." Foreign reactions concerned him more. As with the peace note, the press and public spokesmen in Britain, France, and Germany had harsh words for "peace without victory," although some British liberals praised the move. The belligerent governments, however, remained silent—not only in communicating with the United States but also in their internal discussions—because for them "peace without victory" was a moot point. One side had already made up its mind to escalate the war, and the other side knew what its adversaries were about to do. The days immediately following Wilson's speech were a time when the leaders of the warring nations were holding their collective breath, waiting for the other shoe to drop.[27]

It dropped on January 31, realizing Wilson's worst fear. At ten minutes after four in the afternoon, Bernstorff called Lansing to deliver a diplomatic note. The note stated that Germany would resume "the full employment of all the weapons which are at its disposal. . . . From February 1, 1917, all sea traffic will be stopped with every available weapon and without further notice . . . around Great Britain, France, Italy and in the Eastern Mediterranean."[28] The note implemented a decision made three weeks earlier. On the evening of January 9, an imperial council had met at the baroque Pless Castle in the hills of Silesia. The hour and a quarter of discussion around a big table there was a charade. The army chiefs, who effectively controlled the government, had already browbeaten the weak-willed kaiser into unleashing the submarines. The naval chief of staff had also swung around and now maintained that the navy had sufficient submarines to knock Britain out of the war long before the United States could transport any forces across the Atlantic. The kaiser himself signed an order to open the submarine campaign at the beginning of February, and he said he expected America to declare war.

That decision would seal Germany's fate in World War I. The men around the table at Pless were acting out of a combination of ignorance, willfulness, deceit, and prejudice. After the war, John Maynard Keynes discovered that his opposite numbers in Berlin had known nothing of Britain's financial plight. Lack of credit was about to crimp and possibly cut off the Allies' stream of munitions and foodstuffs—the job the submarines were expected to do—with no risk of bringing America into the war. Claims about the number and effectiveness of submarines were overly optimistic and sometimes fraudulent. A good chance existed that a limited submarine campaign might not bring the Americans in; yet no one explored that possibility. Most important, the army chiefs demanded a crushing military victory, to be won either in the field or at sea. These military aristocrats disdained such bourgeois, civilian instruments as economics—"a shopkeeper's peace"—and diplomacy. In sum, the Germans would richly deserve their future defeat.[29]

The Germans compounded their blunder by unwittingly tipping their hand to the enemy. In order to make trouble for the United States as a likely future adversary, Foreign Secretary Arthur Zimmermann cabled the German embassy in Mexico on January 16 with instructions to offer a military alliance to Carranza, holding out, as spoils, recovery of Texas, New Mexico, and Arizona. This was the soon-to-be-famous Zimmermann Telegram, and its sender abused a courtesy recently extended by the American embassy that allowed the German foreign office to transmit coded messages over its cables. The telegram began, "It is our purpose on the 1st of February to commence the unrestricted U-boat warfare." Within hours, the telegram was decoded at Room 40 of the Admiralty in London (which had cracked the German diplomatic codes and was tapping nearly every nation's diplomatic cables) and given to the director of naval intelligence, Captain William Reginald Hall. Possession of this intelligence posed a problem for Hall, who had to take extreme care not to reveal his code-breaking operation. When and with whom in the British government Hall shared this news is not clear, but the near total lack of internal discussion about "peace without victory" strongly suggests that a number of people knew they did not have to take Wilson's latest peace overture seriously.[30]

For Wilson, unrestricted submarine warfare turned the world upside down. Now, instead of pressing forward with his peace offensive, he had to grapple with the specter of war. Ironically, earlier on the day that the Germans announced the unrestricted submarine campaign, he rejected an attempt by Lansing to commit him to go to war if they resumed *any* kind of submarine warfare, and he left the clear impression that he might be willing to accept the use of submarines against armed Allied merchant ships. When he heard the news about unrestricted submarine warfare just after 4 p.m. on January 31, he acted the way he did at such critical times— by keeping to himself and taking the time to think. When Lansing came to see him in the evening and pushed for an immediate break in diplomatic relations, Wilson said he was "not sure of that" and "he would be willing to bear all the criticism and abuse which would surely follow our failure to break with Germany."[31]

House rushed to Washington by overnight train and met with Wilson after breakfast the next day. The president seemed sad and depressed, and although he had evidently decided overnight to break relations, he insisted "he would not allow it to lead to war if it could possibly be avoided." Wilson believed it would be "a crime" for the United States to get involved in such a way "as to make it impossible to save Europe afterward." The two men waited "listlessly" for Lansing to join them. Wilson paced around the upstairs study and rearranged books, and the men played two games of pool. When Lansing arrived, just before noon, Wilson agreed to break relations three days hence. The journalist Louis Lochner, who saw the president that afternoon, found him looking "haggard and worried," and when Lochner said he hoped Wilson might find a peaceful way out of the present crisis, the president answered, "[I]f it can be done, I certainly wish it with all my heart."[32]

The following day, February 2, Wilson discussed the situation with the cabinet. He opened the meeting by asking, "Shall I break diplomatic relations with Germany?" and he stated, "With the terrific slaughter taking place in Europe, if we, also, entered the war, what effect would the depletion of man power have upon the relations of the white and yellow races? Would the yellow races take advantage of it and attempt to subjugate the white races?" All of the cabinet members supported a diplomatic break. Secretary of the Treasury McAdoo and Secretary of Agriculture Houston took a tough line against the Germans and wanted to help the Allies, while Secretary of War Baker and Secretary of the Navy Daniels shared the president's wish to avoid war. In the afternoon, he went to the Capitol, where he spent forty minutes alone with Senator Stone in the Foreign Relations Committee's ornate hearing room. Then he walked down the corridor to the President's Room, where he sat in the midst of a hastily gathered group of sixteen senators. Through an open door, reporters could see what was going on—animated talk with much gesturing by senators and the president speaking in a low, grave voice—but they could not distinctly hear what was said.[33]

After the cabinet meeting, Josephus Daniels told the president, "I was glad to hear you say you could not at this time fully trust anybody's judgment, not even your own." He later recalled that Wilson commended him for his strong stand against war and said he based his own opposition on his not wanting to sacrifice the lives of young men and his fear of losing "[e]very reform we have won since 1912." War would require cooperation with "Big Business," which would regain control of government, "and neither you nor I will live to see government returned to the people. More than that—Free Speech and the other rights will be endangered. War is autocratic." The next day, Wilson aired some of his thinking in public when he spoke to a joint session of Congress. In view of the Germans' sudden announcement of unrestricted submarine warfare, he asserted that the United States had "no alternative" but to break diplomatic relations, but he refused to believe that the Germans would do "what they have warned us they will feel at liberty to do. . . . Only actual overt acts on their part can make me believe it even now." If that hope proved wrong, he promised to ask Congress for "any means that may be necessary" to protect Americans on the seas.[34]

The speech lasted just fifteen minutes and got a good reception. Reporters noticed that senators Lodge and Benjamin R. Tillman led the applause at the announcement of the diplomatic break. They also heard Wilson's voice quaver at the end. Lodge soon regretted his applause. "His one desire is to avoid war at any cost," he told Roosevelt, "simply because he is afraid." Roosevelt agreed, telling Hiram Johnson, "Whether we go to war or not, Heaven only knows, and certainly Mr. Wilson does not." Such interventionist voices were few and mostly private. Publicly, editors and others nearly unanimously applauded the break with Germany, but most of them also seconded Wilson's wish to avoid war. The Senate passed a resolution approving the president's action, 78 to 5, with most of the supporters of the resolution likewise claiming that they wanted to stay out of the war. Peace activists held rallies in several cities and staged a march to the Capitol on February 12. Some of them called for the requirement of a popular referendum in order to declare war. The "double wish" remained as strong as ever.[35]

The Germans ignored Wilson's proffered olive branch. Submarines began to sink merchant vessels at an alarming rate, and for the first time in two years they attacked American ships. Those incidents fueled agitation to arm American ships and protect them in convoys with naval vessels. The cabinet discussed the matter six times in February. Wilson held out against hasty action. He was suspicious, he told House, of "the support I am receiving from certain once hostile quarters." Conservatives wanted to "have a coalition cabinet at my elbow. It is the *Junkerthum* trying to creep in under cover of the patriotic feeling of the moment. They will not get in."[36]

During these weeks, Wilson did turn his attention occasionally to domestic matters, as when he continued to press congressional leaders to pass labor legislation and act on measures for government development of hydroelectric power sites, which would become a big political issue during the next decade. Those efforts came to naught. This last, short session of the Sixty-fourth Congress produced only two important legislative results. One was a new revenue bill, initiated by Representative Kitchin, which raised the inheritance tax by 50 percent and levied an excess-profits tax. The other was a bill requiring all adult immigrants to show that they could read and write in their native language—a measure aimed at shutting out immigrants from southern and eastern Europe. Wilson had vetoed a similar literacy-test bill two years earlier, and he did so again at the end of January, stating, "It is not a test of character, of quality, or of personal fitness, but would operate in most cases merely as a penalty for lack of opportunity." Both houses overrode the veto, thereby restricting European immigration for the first time. Immigration restriction would become another big issue during the next decade.[37]

Those matters did not divert Wilson long from the diplomatic crisis. Despite his reluctance, he agreed to arm merchant ships. After the cabinet meeting on February 20, he asked Lansing to prepare a memorandum on the subject, and he spent the afternoon and evening of February 22 writing a speech that he planned to deliver to Congress the following Monday. Making this decision was one thing; liking it was something else. At the cabinet meeting, he lashed out at McAdoo, Houston, and Secretary of the Interior Lane for taking a hard line and charged them, Lane said, "with appealing to the spirit of the *Code Duello*. We couldn't get the idea out of his head that we were bent on pushing the country into war." According to Lane, he also resented Republican efforts to force him to call the next Congress into session: "The President believes, I think, that the munitions makers are back of the Republican plan."[38]

On February 26, after meeting with Senator Stone and Representative Flood, Wilson again went to the Capitol to address Congress. He told the senators and representatives that he believed he already possessed the necessary authority to take defensive measures, but he wanted to know that "the authority and power of Congress are behind me" in order to "defend our commerce and the lives of our people in the midst of the present trying circumstances." Hoping not to have to exercise that authority, he asked Congress only to "authorize me to supply our merchant ships with defensive arms" and said nothing about naval convoys. Wilson maintained, "It is not of material interests merely that we are thinking. . . . I am thinking of those rights of humanity without which there is no civilization." This speech also lasted just fifteen minutes, but it did not get as good a reception as its predecessor. One observer noted that La Follette threw up his hands in despair when the president asked for authority to arm ships, while Lodge sat through the speech tapping his fingers together. Democrats cheered when the president left, but Republicans stood in silence. While Wilson was speaking, word arrived of the sinking of the British liner *Laconia*—without warning, off the coast of Ireland— and the news spread in whispers through the House chamber. The next day, newspapers would report that of the twenty Americans aboard—six passengers and fourteen crewmen—two of the passengers, a mother and daughter from Chicago, died of exposure in an open lifeboat. The reports of the deaths of the two American women helped whip up editorial indignation and support for Wilson's request to arm ships.[39]

On February 28, still more sensational news reached the American press—the text of the Zimmermann Telegram. Behind publication of this document lay intrigue by the British and deliberation by Wilson. Once the Germans unleashed the submarines, the leaders in London started scheming to exploit the telegram's value as propaganda in the United States. To cover the code-breaking operation, they instructed their spies in the German embassy in Mexico City to steal a decoded copy; variations between that copy and the transmitted one would remove any trace of prior interception. Covering their tracks took time, so Balfour had not been able to turn the document over to Page until February 24. Page immediately cabled the text of the Zimmermann Telegram to Washington, and Wilson received it the next day. He decided against immediate publication, and he did not tell Stone and Flood about it when he met with them the next day or drop any hints about it in his speech to Congress. After further reflection, however, he instructed Lansing to release the telegram to the press.[40]

The Zimmermann Telegram stirred up the furor that the British hoped for. Thus far, the controversies with Germany had involved few Americans—crewmen and passengers on foreign ships—and, since February 1, some vessels registered under the Stars and Stripes. Now possible attacks from south of the border and the prospect, though seemingly ludicrous, of losing Texas, New Mexico, and Arizona made the war reach out and touch the United States. Editorial indignation flared across the country. Many newspapers called the Zimmermann Telegram an act of war, and some called for war in response. Some German American leaders claimed that the telegram was a hoax and a British plot, but Zimmermann himself eliminated that defense when he stated publicly on March 3 that he had, indeed, sent it. The furor over the telegram seemed to sweep away resistance to an armed-ships bill on Capitol Hill. The House passed the measure on March 1 by the lopsided margin of 403 to 13. Still, many congressmen who voted for the bill maintained that they did not want war, and an amendment to prohibit armed ships from carrying munitions attracted 125 votes.[41]

Swift Senate passage of the armed-ships bill also looked likely. The Republican effort to force Wilson to call the next Congress into session early by filibustering appropriations bills collapsed in the face of this national uproar. The Senate tried to take up the House bill on March 2, but La Follette blocked unanimous consent, delaying consideration for a day. When debate began on March 3, he and three other midwestern insurgent Republicans—George Norris of Nebraska, Albert Cummins of Iowa, and Asle Gronna of North Dakota—repeatedly blocked attempts to bring the measure to a vote. The Senate stayed in session through the night as the clock ticked toward the constitutionally mandated end of the session at noon on March 4. Anxious to avoid blame for the filibustering tactics, Lodge and other Republicans introduced a petition—called a round-robin—in which they stated that if given the opportunity, they would vote for the bill. Seventy-five senators signed the round-robin; eleven refused: La Follette, Norris, Cummins, Gronna, and two other Republican insurgents—Moses Clapp of Minnesota and John Works of California—along with five Democrats—Stone, William F. Kirby of Arkansas, Harry Lane of Oregon, James O'Gorman of New York, and James K. Vardaman of Mississippi.[42]

The last hours of the debate witnessed one of the wildest scenes ever enacted in the halls of Congress. A flamboyant actor and orator since his youth, La Follette intended to take up the last two hours of the debate with one of his grand speeches. Democrats who supported the bill denied him that chance to take center stage by holding the floor themselves. Fighting Bob was enraged. At several points, he and some Democrats appeared on the verge of violence. La Follette had brought a loaded pistol into the Senate chamber and put it in his desk. One of his supporters, Harry Lane, was prepared to use a small file as a dagger if anyone laid a hand on La Follette. La Follette's son, Robert Junior, surreptitiously removed the pistol and scribbled a note to his father: "You are noticeably extremely excited. For God's sake make your protest & prevent passage of the bill if you like but . . . do not try to fight Senate physically. I am almost sick with worry." At noon, the bill died without a vote when the vice president pronounced the Senate adjourned sine die.[43]

Wilson was nearby, in the President's Room, when that drama transpired. He had come to the Capitol to take the oath of office for his second term in a private ceremony. It was a Sunday, and the public inaugural ceremonies would take place the following day. When Wilson got back to the White House, he railed at the antics in the Senate. Colonel House urged him to "say to the public what he was saying to me, and say it immediately." Wilson thought it would be unseemly to raise the subject in his inaugural address, but House urged him "to strike while the iron is hot." The president spent the afternoon writing a statement, which he showed to McAdoo, Burleson, and Tumulty, who all approved it. That statement, which appeared in newspapers the next day, called for changing Senate rules to cut off debate and affirmed the president's authority under existing laws to arm merchant vessels. Wilson also threw out a stinging rebuke: "A little group of willful men, representing no opinion but their own, have rendered the great Government of the United States helpless and contemptible."[44] His opponents were not the only ones who had let their passions get the better of them.

Inauguration day was cold, windy, and overcast, and the ceremony was subdued. In his address, Wilson noted that "matters lying outside our own life as a nation . . . have drawn us more and more irresistibly into their own current and influence." Despite being "deeply wronged upon the seas," Americans remained determined "to play . . . the part of those who mean to vindicate and fortify peace." He reaffirmed armed neutrality, but he left the door open for "a more active assertion of our rights," without specifying what that might be. Above all, he pledged to serve larger purposes in the world: "We are provincials no longer. The tragical events of the thirty months of vital turmoil through which we have just passed have made us citizens of the world." He reiterated some of his earlier principles for a lasting peace, including equality of nations, freedom of the seas, and reduction of armaments, and he concluded, "The shadows that now lie dark upon our path will soon be dispelled and we shall walk with the light all about us if we be but true to ourselves."[45] If this second inaugural address seemed to sound notes from an uncertain trumpet, it was because the trumpeter was uncertain about the song he wished to play.

Back at the White House, Wilson reviewed the inaugural parade, the first to include women, and afterward he and Edith and House had dinner upstairs and watched the fireworks. "The President was holding Mrs. Wilson's hand and leaning his face against [hers]," House reported. "We talked quietly of the day, and I spoke my joy that we three, rather than the Hughes family, were looking at the fireworks from the White House windows." Wilson insisted that they take a ride around town, where people on the streets recognized them and cheered. The situation made House nervous: "I sat with my automatic in my hand ready to act if the occasion arose." Later, the colonel sat with them and talked until eleven o'clock. Edith again pressed House to become ambassador in London, but Wilson said he had inadvertently promised to keep Page on. That promise saved House from being separated from Wilson, but it did not stop him from soon trying to get someone else who had influence with Wilson sent to London. "I suggested taking Baker from the War Department and sending him to England in place of Page," House wrote, but the president reiterated that "in a misguided moment" he had told Page to stay on.[46]

·   ·   ·

If the world had turned upside down for Wilson in February 1917, the following month brought its weight pressing down on his shoulders. March 1917 became a time of peculiar trial for him. This was the time that would lead Winston Churchill to say "that the action of the United States with its repercussions on the history of the world depended . . . upon the workings of this man's mind and spirit to the exclusion of almost every other factor." Wilson sought an alternative to war, but armed neutrality proved to be a complicated and burdensome business. Naval crews had to outfit merchant ships with guns, and naval vessels assumed some convoy duties. The British, through the Morgan firm, began to disclose hints of their financial straits, and the Federal Reserve Board nullified its earlier warning against foreign loans.[47] On the seas, submarines sank ships in ever mounting numbers, including more American vessels. At the middle of March, a revolution in Russia toppled the czar's autocracy and established a liberal provisional government.

Surprisingly to some, there was no great rise in interventionist sentiment. Roosevelt predictably scorned armed neutrality, and a cadre of northeastern Republicans joined him in pressing for intervention. Metropolitan newspapers such as the *Chicago Tribune* also came out for war, while the revolution in Russia excited progressives by removing an autocratic stain from the Allied cause. Most newspapers and magazines did not take a stand, however, and ordinary citizens did not seem to be in a belligerent mood. In Congress, several observers commented that more than half the members of the House would vote against war if there could be a secret ballot. Clearly, the president was not feeling a push for war from Congress or the public.[48]

Wilson once more kept to himself, receiving few callers and conducting mostly routine correspondence. He declined speaking engagements and usually left the White House only to play golf. Also, for more than a week at the middle of the month, he did not go to his office because he was confined to his bedroom with a bad cold and sore throat. Two matters did intrude on his bed rest. One was the next Congress. The Senate was meeting in special session before the new Congress convened, to consider the treaty of indemnity with, and apology to, Colombia, stemming from the 1903 Panamanian revolution, an issue that had languished through Wilson's first term and then come alive again when Colombia sought to take advantage of America's security concerns. The senators pleased the president by adopting a cloture rule, under which a two-thirds vote could shut off filibusters, but Lodge and other Republicans succeeded in blocking the treaty nevertheless. Because of the urgency of the international situation,

Wilson also issued a call for the Congress to convene on April 16 rather than the following December, as mandated by the Constitution.

The other matter that Wilson had to deal with was a threatened railroad strike, together with the Supreme Court's ruling on the law mandating an eight-hour workday for railway workers. Mediation by McAdoo and Secretary of Labor Wilson averted a strike, and the Court narrowly upheld the law. At one point, McAdoo barged into Wilson's bedroom to talk about the strike. "Damn it, he makes me tired," a White House servant quoted the president as saying. "He's got too much nerve and presumes on the fact that he's my son-in-law to take up with me in my private apartment matters that a Cabinet Officer ought to take up in my office. I'm getting damn sick of it."[49]

Wilson left few clues about what he thought during this time. Given his habits, he almost certainly prayed. He harbored no illusions that God would tell him what to do, but the words with which he ended the speech that he would soon give to Congress indicated that he had reached back to his youth and religious background. Wilson did not write to or send for House. The colonel came to the White House only at the end of the month, on his own initiative and after the president had probably already made his decision about whether to go to war. Wilson did reveal his inner turmoil about that decision to two people in addition to his wife. One was Congressman Adamson, the author of the eight-hour law, who later recalled how passionately Wilson wanted to avoid war. Besides the loss of lives, the president feared the war's effects at home: "He said that a state of war suspended the law, and legal and moral restraints being relaxed," things would get so bad that "it would require a generation to restore normal conditions."[50]

The other person to whom Wilson opened his heart and mind was Frank Cobb, the editor of the New York *World*, who came to the White House on the afternoon of March 19. Cobb later recalled that Wilson believed going to war would mean "there would be a dictated peace, a victorious peace," which would require "an attempt to reconstruct a peacetime civilization with war standards. . . . There won't be any peace standards left to work with. There will be only war standards." The war's effects at home frightened him even more. "Once lead this people into war," Cobb also quoted him as saying, "and they'll forget there ever was such a thing as tolerance. To fight you must be brutal and ruthless, and the spirit of ruthless brutality will enter into the very fibre of our national life, infecting congress, the courts, the policeman on the beat, the man in the street. . . . If there is any alternative, for God's sake, let's take it!" This was possibly the most anguished cry from the heart ever uttered in the White

House by a president. The most eloquent argument against going into this war came from the lips of the man who would take the country into it.[51]

When and how he made that decision is not completely clear. At a cabinet meeting the day after he talked with Cobb, Wilson asked whether he should call Congress into session before April 16 and, if so, what message he should send. The cabinet members were unanimous for war, including Daniels, who was the most reluctant. When Burleson said that people were demanding war, Wilson answered, "I do not care for popular demand. I want to do right, whether popular or not." After everyone had spoken, he said, "Well, gentlemen, I think there is no doubt as to what your advice is. I thank you." When Lansing asked Wilson whether he was going to call Congress into session earlier, he reportedly replied, "Oh, I think I will sleep on it." The following day, March 21, he did issue a call for Congress to meet on April 2. He also authorized Baker and Daniels to federalize the National Guard, increase the size of the regular army, take anti-submarine actions at sea, and explore cooperation with the Royal Navy. Outreach to the British included ordering a senior naval officer, Rear Admiral William S. Sims, and an aide to depart at once for London, traveling in civilian clothes and under assumed names. Yet Lansing lamented to House that he no idea what Wilson was going to do, and he asked the colonel to come to Washington to try to smoke him out.[52]

The colonel arrived late in the afternoon on March 27, and before dinner he and Wilson discussed whether the president should ask for a declaration of war. House said he should, but, curiously, he also told Wilson that he was "not well fitted" to be a war president; "he was too refined, too civilized, too intellectual, too cultivated not to see the incongruity and absurdity of war." Even more curiously, Edith told House that his opinion had encouraged her husband. The colonel argued for replacing Daniels and Baker as unsuited for war, and Wilson listened noncommittally. The next morning, he showed House a memorandum he had written overnight on subjects he wanted to address when he spoke to Congress. House liked the memorandum, "which could not please me better had I written it myself." He particularly liked Wilson's intention to draw a distinction between the German people and their rulers: "This is a war for democracy and it is a war for the German people as well as for other nations." House also had to listen to complaints about Lansing, who Wilson said "was the most unsatisfactory Secretary in his Cabinet; that he was good for a second place but unfitted for the first. That he had no imagination, no constructive ability, and but little real ability."[53]

It is doubtful that Wilson made up his mind to go to war during House's visit. It is more likely that he had already made his decision out of a mixture of practical, temperamental, and philosophical considerations. One practical matter was the unsatisfactory nature of armed neutrality. Daniels had made this point at the cabinet meeting when he reluctantly recommended war. Wilson evidently agreed, because he told a political supporter, "Apparently, to make even measures of defense we must obtain the status of belligerents." Another practical consideration was how to pursue the goal of a league of nations. Lansing noted in his memorandum that he had said at the cabinet meeting that "no League of Peace would be of value with a powerful autocracy as a member." House made the same point when he urged Wilson to say to Congress "that the United States would not be willing to join a league of peace with an autocracy as a member."[54] Whether or not Wilson bought those arguments, they almost certainly struck a responsive chord in his mind.

Yet other aspects of going to war did not strike a responsive chord in him. He had long since gotten over his Roosevelt-style penchant for armed intervention. His horror at the slaughter in Europe was heartfelt, as he had revealed in his "prolegomenon." Moreover, this preacher of self-control viewed this moment as one above all others in which to practice that virtue. The man who had once carried Kipling's poem "If" in his wallet knew by heart the opening lines:

> *If you can keep your head when all about you*
> *Are losing theirs and blaming it on you;*
> *If you can trust yourself when all men doubt you . . .*

When cabinet members maintained that people were demanding war, Lansing noted, "I could almost feel the President stiffen as if to resist and see his powerful jaw set."[55]

Still, other aspects of his mind and spirit did incline him toward war. Despite Roosevelt's and Lodge's aspersions, Wilson was not and never had been a pacifist, and this war repelled him because of its "mechanical slaughter." Moreover, he possessed an incorrigibly activist temperament. Presented with alternatives, he almost always chose the path of boldness. That was what armed neutrality lacked, in addition to its practical shortcomings. It would be complicated, frustrating, and, worst of all, passive and reactive. War, for all its destruction and danger, was active and might lead to better results. Wilson knew full well war's awful consequences, and he was keenly aware of the terrible risk he was taking. Yet given his temperament, it would have been nearly impossible for him not to choose war. Besides, he had a deeper philosophical reason for this choice, which he would implicitly reveal in the speech he was about to give to Congress.

When he closeted himself to write that speech, his labors exacted an emotional cost. Several people noted that he seemed out of sorts. The White House head usher said he never knew the president "to be more peevish. . . . Soon after lunch he went to the study, leaving word that he desired quiet." On April 1, a Sunday, he sent Lansing a sentence from the speech that asked Congress to declare that a state of war existed with Germany, so that it could be used in drafting the necessary legislation. Otherwise, he shared none of the speech with cabinet members or anyone else, except possibly Edith, until he read it to House the next day. The colonel got to hear the speech in advance only because the machinations in organizing the new Congress delayed the president from going to the Capitol until the evening. "Neither of us did anything except 'Kill time' until he was called to the Capitol," House noted.[56]

At eight-thirty, the president entered the House chamber to tumultuous applause. Many senators and congressmen were waving small American flags, although some, most notably La Follette, declined to join in the demonstration. Resting his hands on the desk, Wilson read from his manuscript, neither gesturing nor glancing up. After reviewing events since the Germans unleashed their submarines, he declared this "a war against all nations," to which Americans must respond deliberately in order to seek "only the vindication of right, of human right, of which we are only a single champion." He had hoped that armed neutrality might be enough to meet the challenge, but he now knew that it would not work and "we will not choose the path of submission and suffer the most sacred rights of our nation . . . to be ignored or violated." Up to then, the audience had sat in tense silence. When Wilson rejected "the path of submission," Chief Justice Edward White, who was sitting in the front row, dropped the big hat he was holding and raised his hands above his head to give an explosive clap. That broke the suspense. The chamber erupted into a prolonged roar of applause and then lapsed back into silence.[57]

Wilson now came to the action portion of the speech, which he introduced in a somber tone, noting the "profound sense of the solemn and even tragical character of the step that I am taking." He advised Congress to declare that a state of war existed between the United States and Germany. At this point, the chief justice, with tears streaming down his cheeks, again led the applause with his hands above his head. Wilson proceeded to outline what belligerency would require: large-scale military and industrial mobilization, to be financed "by well conceived taxation," together with continued material aid to the Allies. He also specified what kind of peace he sought, and here he began to inject emotion into the speech. "I have exactly the same things in mind now that I had in mind when I addressed the Senate on the twenty-second of January last. . . . Our object now, as then, is to vindicate the principles of peace and justice in the life of the world as against selfish and autocratic power and to set up amongst the really free and self-governed peoples of the world such a concert of purpose and of action as will henceforth ensure the observance of those principles." He insisted that America had no quarrel with the German people, only with their criminal autocratic rulers. The establishment of democracy would ensure that such crimes as have been committed would never be committed again.[58]

Now, to repeated cheers, he unveiled his vision of democracy and peace. "A steadfast concert for peace can never be maintained except by a partnership of democratic nations," he avowed. It was for this vision that America would fight: "The world must be made safe for democracy." At those words, Senator John Sharp Williams of Mississippi, who was partially deaf and cupping his hands behind his ears to hear, began to clap alone, and the applause turned into an uproar. Of all that Wilson said in this speech, this sentence would take on a life of its own, for better and worse. On other matters, Wilson welcomed the new government in Russia and pointed out that the United States was going to war only with Germany, not with the rest of the Central powers, although relations with Austria-Hungary were strained. He affirmed that most citizens of German extraction were "true and loyal Americans," but he warned that disloyalty "will be dealt with with a firm hand of stern repression."[59]

He was coming to the end of this half-hour speech. He sought to conclude with inspiring words that would encapsulate his message:

It is a distressing and oppressive duty, Gentlemen of the Congress, which I have performed in thus addressing you. There are, it may be, many months of fiery trial . . . ahead of us. It is a fearful thing to lead this great peaceful people into war, into the most terrible and disastrous of all wars, civilization itself seeming to be in the balance. But the right is more precious than peace, and we shall fight for the things which we have always carried nearest our hearts,—for democracy, for the right of those who submit to authority to have a voice in their own governments, for the rights and liberties of small nations, for a universal dominion of right by such a concert of free peoples as shall bring peace and safety to all nations and make the world itself at last free. To such a task we can dedicate our lives and our fortunes, everything that we are and everything that we have, with the pride of those who know that the day has come when America is privileged to spend her blood and her might for the principles that gave her birth and happiness and the peace which she has treasured. God helping her, she can do no other.[60]

Wilson had delivered not only the most important but also the greatest speech of his life. This was no lusty assertion of righteous wrath; this was not Roosevelt crying out to stand at Armageddon and battle for the Lord. The words *solemn, distressing, oppressive,* and *tragical* ran through the speech like a leitmotif. Wilson spoke the language of exalted idealism, but he did it in a humble, circumspect way. America was "only a single champion" of right. "The world must be made safe for democracy"—a world of difference lay in that self-conscious use of the passive voice by this most punctilious of stylists to sit in the White House. He did not say that Americans must make the world safe for democracy; he did not believe that they could. They could only do their part, join with other like-minded nations, and take steps toward that promised land. Above all, this speech was not a call to a holy war. America was making an unsought, inescapable choice. The actions of others had rendered it necessary, he believed, to plunge into the most terrible war yet in human history. After a deliberately downbeat opening, the speech had gradually taken on a somber beauty. The ending, with evocations of fear and cherished values and the shedding of blood, brought back memories of Abraham Lincoln, especially the last words. Its last sentences and last words made this the greatest presidential speech since Lincoln's second inaugural address.

"God helping her, she can do no other"—what a haunting but strange way to close a call to arms. No other speaker would have said those words. Wilson was in the habit of occasionally saying things like "God grant" or "God helping me" at the close of speeches. But this usage was something different. As many people recognized, it was an exact paraphrase of Martin Luther's declaration, "God helping me, I can do no other." Here was possibly the clearest instance of where Wilson's learned, sophisticated Protestant upbringing may have shaped his conduct as a political leader. He was casting America in the same role that Luther cast the Christian believer. For Luther, no one could know God's will; the Christian could rely only on faith and scripture in trying hesitantly, imperfectly, often mistakenly to follow God's will. Nor could the Christian avoid sin; he or she must, Luther declared, "sin boldly." This is what Wilson was asking his country to do. This war was the greatest collective sin in history, and America would be taking part in that sin. And, like Luther, Wilson wanted to sin boldly in hopes of securing a more just and peaceful world. He was taking the boldest gamble of his life, and he knew that he might be doing the wrong thing.

As a piece of public persuasion, Wilson's war address succeeded splendidly. When he finished, the House chamber exploded in an uproar of cheers, rebel yells, and the waving of little flags. Men flocked to congratulate the president as he left the podium. Lodge shook Wilson's hand and said, "Mr. President, you have expressed the sentiments of the American people in the loftiest possible manner." Not everyone joined in the cheering, however. Reporters noticed that Senator La Follette sat with his arms folded in front of his chest as he grimly chewed on a wad of gum. Editorial opinion across the country echoed the cheers in the Capitol, and opponents outside also rushed to heap praise. A flood of letters and telegrams offering congratulations and support swept into the White House. Wilson did not feel entirely comfortable with the way people reacted to his speech. "My message tonight was a message of death for our young men," Tumulty later recalled him saying back at the White House. "How strange it seems to applaud that."[61]

Congress made quick work of declaring war. The Senate acted first. When the war resolution was introduced the next morning, La Follette objected to the suspension of the rules required for immediate consideration, thereby delaying debate for a day. The Senate took up the resolution at ten o'clock on April 4, and debate lasted for thirteen hours. The majority of the speeches expressed support. Some senators were enthusiastic for war; others endorsed the move grudgingly. On the other side, La Follette would not be denied his say this time, and in a four-hour speech he tore apart Wilson's claim to be defending democracy by joining the Allies. Norris was even more bitterly eloquent when he blamed intervention on Wall Street moguls: "We are going into war upon command of gold." When the vote came, at eleven minutes after eleven that night, only six senators opposed the resolution—three insurgent Republicans and three Democrats.[62]

House debate also started on April 4, and it took seventeen hours, spread over two days. Under rules that limited each speech to twenty minutes, 100 representatives spoke in a debate that David Lawrence later described as desultory and at times flippant. Many of those who favored war seemed lukewarm, and almost none of them envisioned American troops fighting on the Western Front. "On the whole," Lawrence also recalled, "the pacifist speeches seemed to be better received than those favoring war." The dramatic high point of the debate came when Claude Kitchin rose to speak. Few knew what Kitchin planned to say, and he drew cheers even from opponents when he broke ranks with his party and remained true to his Bryanite convictions. For his part, Bryan opposed intervention only perfunctorily and declined to come to Washington to lobby against the war resolution. Reporters noticed that La Follette was sitting at the back of the House chamber, smiling broadly, as Kitchin spoke.[63]

When the time came for the roll call vote in the House during the early morning hours of April 6, there was one more moment of drama. All eyes in the galleries were on the first woman elected to Congress, Jeannette Rankin of Montana. She was a pacifist, but she was under pressure from suffrage organizations to vote for the resolution because they planned to use women's patriotic support for the war as another argument for a constitutional amendment. When her name was called the first time, Rankin did not respond. According to one report, she sat staring at the ceiling, clasping and unclasping her hands. An old bull of the House came over and told her, "Little woman you cannot afford not to vote. You represent the womanhood of the country in the American Congress." On the second call, Rankin stood up and said in a cracking voice, reportedly with tears in her eyes, "I want to stand by my country, but I cannot vote for war. I vote no." Speaking during a roll call was against the rules, and some congressmen yelled, "Vote! Vote!" Speaker Clark sent the chief clerk to ask Rankin if she intended to vote no. She nodded, sat down, and threw her head back on her seat and sobbed. When the roll call was completed, at three-twelve in the morning, the clerk handed the tally to the Speaker, who banged down the gavel and announced, "On this motion the Ayes are 373 and the Noes are 50." Voting against the resolution were eighteen Democrats, thirty-one Republicans—nearly all insurgents or midwesterners, including nine of Wisconsin's eleven congressmen—and the lone Socialist, Meyer London of New York.[64]

Only formalities remained before the country officially went to war. The war resolution arrived at the White House at 1 p.m., while the president was having lunch with the First Lady and his cousin Helen Bones. They came out to the main lobby, where Wilson sat down at the head usher's desk and wrote, "Approved 6 April 1917, Woodrow Wilson." With those strokes of a pen, the United States was at war, and Woodrow Wilson was now a war president. War was something he had even less "preparation" for than foreign affairs and something he thought he was ill suited for. He was going to have to harness passion—other people's and his own—and he would be resorting to bloodshed and destruction to try to realize his dream of a just, nonpunitive peace and new world order. God helping him, he could do no other.[65]

WAGING WAR

As he rode up in the White House elevator on the night of April 2, 1917, after delivering his war address to Congress, Woodrow Wilson reportedly remarked to his young cousin, "Fitz, thank God for Abraham Lincoln." Fitz Woodrow, a grandson of Wilson's uncle Jimmy, later recalled asking why he had said that and got the answer, "I won't make the mistakes that he did."[1] Wilson did not explain to Fitz Woodrow what mistakes he thought Lincoln had made, but he would soon use the Lincoln precedent to answer congressional critics. The remark was noteworthy because it gave a clue to how he meant to wage war. He intended to plunge in fully and decisively. Many in Congress and elsewhere appeared to believe that the United States would mostly continue to furnish food, munitions, and money to the Allies. During the next eighteen months, supplies and naval assistance from America would prove essential to enabling the British and French to hold out against repeated and redoubled German onslaughts. But anyone who thought Wilson would limit his country's role in the war to such things had sorely misread this man's mind and spirit. He meant to wage war with every resource at his command, and he meant to do it his way.

America's biggest resource was manpower. Its population of more than 103 million was larger than that of any of the major countries at war except troubled, faltering Russia. Unlike the other belligerents, the United States had barely begun to tap its pool of men of military age. This advantage also posed the biggest problem. In order to field forces of any size on the Western Front, the country would have to expand its army of around 300,000 men, including the National Guard, possibly ten times or more. That would require recruiting, training, and equipping more men than the nation had ever put under arms. Then those men would need to be transported to seaports on the Atlantic coast and shipped to Europe.

Such mobilization would require harnessing agriculture, manufacturing, and transportation on an unprecedented scale—all on top of meeting mounting demands from the Allies for food, machines, and munitions. This president and his administration were facing the biggest wartime challenge since the Civil War, with the added obstacle of having to fight overseas, more than 3,000 miles away.

From the outset, Wilson grasped the immensity of his task. The day after he signed the declaration of war, he wrote a memorandum to himself on his typewriter, which he titled "Programme." Under the heading "Measures for war," he listed additions to the army and navy and "all legislation needed to put the country in a thorough state of defense and preparation for action." Under the heading "Bills for the safeguarding of the nation," he wrote down measures to oversee and restrict public speech and expression and "various restrictions on trading with the enemy." He also had plans for seizing interned enemy ships, securing other maritime provisions, increasing the powers of the Federal Reserve, and taking "control of the Railroads for military purposes." He disclosed a key part of his plan for the armed forces that day when he told Walter Lippmann that "registering all men of military age"—the draft—would be part of the program that the War Department was about to submit.[2]

Wilson tackled each of these items, which he saw as related parts of a unified whole. "We are mobilizing the nation as well as creating an Army," he told Congressman Carter Glass on April 9, "and that means that we must keep every instrumentality at its highest pitch of efficiency and guided by thoughtful intelligence." He believed that public opinion and the economy were essential to such mobilization. "Talked about censorship," Josephus Daniels noted that day. "He will appoint [George] Creel as head." They also talked about munitions, and Wilson asked if Bernard Baruch would do. Daniels asserted that he would, adding, "He is somewhat vain." Wilson reportedly asked, "[D]id you ever see a Jew who was not?" Those two veteran Democratic Party activists would get two of the most important civilian posts in the war effort. Creel got his right away. Some form of censorship to protect national security seemed unavoidable, but thoughts varied widely about how to impose such measures. Creel advised against using the word *censorship* and advocated overlaying control of information with lots of positive publicity, although he did not use the word *propaganda*. That approach appealed to Wilson, who wanted to get people to support the war voluntarily as much as possible. On April 13, he issued an executive order setting up a "Committee on Public Information" (often called the CPI), with Creel as chairman.[3]

Bernard Baruch had to wait awhile for his appointment. Economic mobilization was more complicated and involved competing actors and agencies. War finance came first. With his usual gusto, McAdoo issued a statement to the press on April 9 that included a request to Congress for authority to raise $5 billion in bonds. The Treasury would eventually raise more than $15 billion through five mass subscription drives—soon to be dubbed Liberty Loans. In addition to financing two thirds of war expenditures, the Liberty Loans would feature extensive advertising and big rallies in major cities, with appearances by such movie stars as Charlie Chaplin and Mary Pickford and such sports heroes as Ty Cobb. Liberty Loan advertising and rallies would dovetail with the activities of Creel's CPI in whipping up popular enthusiasm for the war. The remainder of the war financing would come from taxes, particularly from ratcheting up income and inheritance taxes on the wealthy and levies on corporate profits.

Other aspects of economic mobilization took shape more slowly, but Baruch had a hand in most of them. Wilson appointed him to several newly created agencies, including the Allied Purchasing Commission and the General Munitions Board. These appointments, which were mostly advisory, brought Baruch into regular contact with Secretary of War Baker and Secretary of the Navy Daniels and, most important, with Wilson, the last giving him an opportunity to apply his well-honed charm to a man he admired immensely. Daniels correctly spotted Baruch's vanity about his looks; Wilson's retort is the only anti-Semitic remark anyone ever recorded him making. In fact, Wilson found Baruch appealing because he was both a fellow expatriate southerner and a prime example of "the man on the make." He was a close friend McAdoo's and a proudly self-styled "speculator" who had a restless, probing mind that tapped into Wilson's penchant for boldness. Within two months of American entry into the war, Baruch would present comprehensive outlines for control and coordination of shipping and industrial and agricultural production. The president soon gave Baruch still another appointment, to what was as yet only an advisory committee, called the War Industries Board. Later, under Baruch's chairmanship, the WIB would become the spark plug of industrial mobilization.[4]

A little more than a week into the war, the president shared some of his thinking with the public. In a statement to the press—written, as usual, on his own typewriter—he maintained that besides fighting forces, the United States and the Allies required food, shipping, and equipment, which, in turn, demanded greater efficiency from American workers, who would be "serving the country and conducting the fight for peace and freedom just as effectively as the men on the battlefield or in the trenches." He urged farmers to grow bigger crops, and he asked farmers in the South to grow foodstuffs rather than cotton. He admonished businessmen to forgo "unusual profits" and reminded railroad workers and managers that they were maintaining vital arteries for the war effort. "The supreme test of the nation has come," he concluded. "We must all speak, act, and serve together."[5] Except for a few flashes of eloquence, this was not one of his more stirring utterances, and it seems odd that he did not give a speech. He would deliver fewer speeches during the opening year of the war than he had done before, except during the first months after Ellen's death. That would be unfortunate because he was depriving himself of opportunities to educate people about his deep and sophisticated vision of war and peace. Instead, superheated patriotism, fomented and abetted by the CPI and militants outside government, would fill this void in public persuasion.

Oddly, too, this statement made no mention of the centerpiece of comprehensive mobilization—the draft. Four days later, he acknowledged the omission when he told a Democratic congressman that the draft would allow keeping military-age men in critical occupations and would establish "the idea that there is a universal obligation to serve." Backing the draft drew Wilson into a political fight with members of his own party on Capitol Hill. Opposing him in the House were Claude Kitchin and Champ Clark, and in the Senate some leading Democrats likewise expressed doubts. Despite that opposition and skepticism, the draft bill secured passage quickly and easily. Administration supporters in both houses beat back attempts to attach a volunteer alternative. The high point of the debate came when Clark stepped down from the Speaker's chair to deliver an impassioned two-hour oration against the whole concept of conscription, climaxing with the well-remembered line: "In the estimation of Missourians there is precious little difference between a conscript and a convict." Clark was fighting a forlorn battle. Kitchin declined to join him, and Bryan announced that he was supporting the president. Meanwhile, pro-draft organizations were staging big rallies in the Northeast and Midwest. The House approved the draft bill on the evening of April 28 by a vote of 307 to 24, and the Senate followed suit that same night by a margin of 81 to 8.[6]

This easy win masked a sharp, partly personal conflict. The idea of filling army units with volunteers appealed to more than nostalgia for the minutemen of 1776 and many in the blue- and gray-clad ranks of the Civil War. In the Senate, Lodge tried to secure volunteer divisions so that Roosevelt could lead one of them. Military and civilian leaders in the War Department adamantly opposed such divisions. Besides sharing Wilson's concern that such volunteers would wreak havoc in civilian occupations critical to war production, they feared that a unit headed by someone with Roosevelt's fame and glamour would skim away able officers eager for conspicuous chances at combat.7

The old adversary was not easy to put off. On the afternoon of April 10, four days after the declaration of war, Roosevelt came to call at the White House. According to one staff member, Wilson greeted Roosevelt coolly but soon "'thawed out' and was laughing and 'talking back.' They had a real good visit." Roosevelt recalled that he said, "Mr. President, what I have said and thought, and what others have said and thought, is all dust in a windy street, if we can make your [war] message good. . . . [I]f we can translate it into fact, then it will rank as a great state paper, with the great state papers of Washington and Lincoln." He was lathering on flattery by appealing to what he regarded as Wilson's vanity as a "phrasemaker." He also offered Tumulty a commission in the proposed division and toured the White House for sentimental reunions with staff members who fondly remembered him and his family. Wilson bent the rules to allow reporters and photographers with movie cameras to interview Roosevelt on the White House portico. Afterward, Tumulty confessed to being taken with their visitor's high spirits and charm. "Yes," he recalled Wilson replying, "he is a great big boy. I was, as formerly, charmed by his personality. There is a sweetness about him that is very compelling. You can't resist the man."8

Wilson did, in fact, resist Roosevelt, who sensed that he might not be swaying the president. He thought that with anyone else he could count on his request being approved, but he could not tell with Wilson: "He has, however, left the door open." Wilson let others shut the door. Three days later, Secretary of War Baker wrote to inform Roosevelt that the Army War College had unanimously recommended against his proposal for a volunteer division. This was, Baker maintained, "a purely military policy" based on the need to train troops adequately and on the judgment that any expeditionary force to Europe should be commanded by experienced professional officers. Roosevelt believed that the decision came from Wilson, who was spurning him out of jealousy and spite.9 Wilson would not have been human if thoughts of foiling a bitter rival had not crossed his mind. Moreover, Roosevelt could not hide his desire to horn in on running the war—which might have been an argument for trying to co-opt him with a high-level appointment. Lincoln had gathered his main political rivals into his cabinet so that he might watch them and presumably have them work for rather than against him. On the other hand, McKinley's experience did not recommend trying to harness Roosevelt in a subordinate role.

Yet personal motives were only part of the decision. There were diplomatic as well as military reasons not to send Roosevelt to France. He would thunder for an all-out, shoulder-to-shoulder crusade alongside Britain and France against not only Germany but also the other Central powers, and that was not the way Wilson intended to deal with the situation. He wanted to keep his distance from the Allies. On April 14, he told J. H. Whitehouse, a visiting member of Parliament, that he intended to remain "detached from the Allies," particularly because he did not agree with some of their recent pronouncements about peace terms, such as breaking up the Austro-Hungarian Empire. Instead of a sweeping victory, he still wanted "a negotiated settlement, whenever that was possible," with America "at the back of the settlement, a permanent guarantee of future peace." In short, he still clung to the vision he had put forward in his "peace without victory" speech. He also told Whitehouse that he worried that the American press could be irresponsible and might stir up "mob passion."[10]

In such a frame of mind, Wilson preferred to avoid high-level meetings with the principal Allies, but that was not possible. The British immediately asked to send a delegation to Washington, to be headed by Foreign Secretary Balfour. Not to be outdone, the French likewise requested the Americans to receive the minister of justice, René Viviani, who would be accompanied by Marshal Joseph-Jacques-Césaire Joffre, the victor at the battle of the Marne in 1914 and former commander of France's armies. Balfour's ship landed in New York on April 22, and he went to see House in the morning before proceeding to Washington. This was no mere courtesy call. Late in 1916, the British had started using the colonel as their principal channel of communication between their intelligence officers and the president.

One of those officers was Sir William Wiseman. Ingratiating and prone to intrigue, Wiseman resembled his new contact so much that one historian has called him "a young House with an Oxbridge accent." They quickly struck up an intimate friendship reminiscent of the colonel's early relationship with Wilson, and in the fall of 1917 the Englishman rented an apartment in the building where House lived. They soon became co-conspirators in conducting diplomacy, with each one sometimes acting behind the back of his government, as House had done earlier with his House-Grey Memorandum.[11]

Wiseman set up the meeting on April 22 between Balfour and House, who advised the foreign secretary on how to deal with the president, particularly cautioning him to avoid any discussion of an alliance or peace terms. The colonel also advised against replacing Spring-Rice as ambassador in Washington because the present arrangement, relying on his own contacts, was working well. In Washington that afternoon, cheering crowds and a cavalry escort greeted the British visitors. The following day, the French delegation arrived in Hampton Roads, Virginia, and transferred to the *Mayflower*, which brought them up the Potomac to Washington. This began monthlong sojourns for both delegations, replete with dinners, parades, visits to other cities, and meetings with important pro-Allied Americans, most notably Roosevelt. In deference to wartime austerity, official entertaining in Washington was less than sumptuous, and Edith Wilson was usually the only woman present at the formal dinners.

Serious discussions came in Wilson's separate meetings with Balfour and Viviani. Balfour's first visit with Wilson at the White House went stiffly, because, according to House, Lansing was present, along with Spring-Rice. "Lansing has a wooden mind and constantly blocked what I was trying to convey," House said Wilson told him, so the president suggested an after-dinner meeting of just the three of them. That arrangement suited House, who again briefed Balfour on how to deal with Wilson, advising him to disclose the terms of Britain's secret treaties with Italy and other co-belligerents. When the three men met, they pored over a map of Europe and Asia Minor and discussed specific terms of peace involving Poland and the Balkans and the division of Austria—what Balfour called "dividing up the bearskin before the bear was killed." House was delighted because the topics discussed were "exactly the same as Balfour and I had covered." He was also pleased because earlier Balfour had "arranged to keep in constant communication through Wiseman."[12]

With his French visitors, Wilson talked about immediate problems. Viviani agreed with him that the most pressing need was to defeat the submarines by adopting new defensive measures and building more ships. Wilson insisted that the Allies must make their needs known, and he stuck by his vision of a peace settlement, explaining that "annihilation of a nation" only bred desire for revenge. In a separate meeting with Marshal Joffre and an interpreter, Wilson learned how much the French wanted American troops—and the sooner, the better—for a big morale boost. The men talked in detail about how to transport and deploy large numbers of American soldiers.[13] Wilson was getting a better idea of what waging this war would require.

In keeping with his established practice as president, he delegated much of the war effort while setting policies and directions. Baker took care of raising and training the army. No cabinet member enjoyed greater confidence and respect from Wilson than Baker, whom Wilson would stand by steadfastly. The war secretary set about immediately implementing the draft, which the administration called Selective Service. Baker and the man he picked to run this new system, Enoch Crowder, the army's provost marshal general, strove to overcome bad memories of the Civil War draft. Crowder kept military officers out of the actual process of selecting draftees and set up a network of more than 4,000 boards composed of local civilians. Baker also enlisted mayors, governors, and civic leaders to support the kickoff of the draft on June 5, when all eligible young men were required to register. Wilson lent his voice to the occasion with a brief speech, in which he asserted that the spirit of obligation ran even deeper than the spirit of voluntarism.

Between the dash of presidential admonition and the elaborate public relations campaign, registration day went off smoothly. Ten million men between the ages of twenty-one and thirty reported to their local draft board, and everyone from Baker on down felt relieved. Two weeks later, a blindfolded secretary of war drew from a big glass bowl capsules containing numbers randomly assigned to groups of registrants. During the summer, local boards used those numbers to call up the first 687,000 draftees, who reported to hastily built training camps in September. At the outset, problems arose from exemptions granted to farmers and workers in industries deemed critical to the war effort. One such well-publicized exemption went to the heavyweight-boxing champion Jack Dempsey, who took a job in a shipyard. In the South, all-white local boards tended to call up disproportionate numbers of African Americans. Likewise, neither the Selective Service System nor local boards showed much sensitivity toward conscientious objectors, who were usually jailed, often under brutal conditions. Despite those shortcomings, the draft operated with unforeseen smoothness and set a good tone for mobilization.[14]

This way of raising an army posed the thorny issue of how to deal with criticism and dissent. Free speech now took on an immediately critical dimension: by exhorting young men to evade the draft, opponents of the war could potentially cripple a central element of mobilization. Even without the draft, the need to whip up popular fervor behind the war—to get people to buy bonds, take essential jobs, work harder, forgo pleasures and luxuries—made dissent look dangerous. Yet an administration-sponsored bill to control speech and publications encountered stiff opposition on and off Capitol Hill. The provisions of the bill calling for press censorship, which included a section that would deny the use of the mails to publications deemed disloyal, almost failed to pass in the House. Burleson roved through the corridors of the Capitol lobbying to keep censorship provisions alive, but the Senate struck out everything except the denial of the mails. Wilson tried to keep the House-passed provisions in the final bill, but Congress rejected his pleas, and the Espionage Act he signed on June 15 did not include censorship of the press.

Even without overt censorship, this law hobbled dissent and criticism in print. Burleson exercised with a heavy hand his newly acquired power to deny the mails to publications. Socialist journals came under special attack because the party's majority remained opposed to intervention; its perennial presidential candidate, Eugene Debs, came out of retirement to give speeches against the war. In July, Burleson suspended second-class postage rates, which were indispensable to publications that reached beyond a local readership, for socialist and radical publications, including the voice of cultural bohemianism in New York's Greenwich Village, *The Masses*. Nonsocialist publications likewise fell under the ax, including *Watson's Magazine*, a racist, anti-Semitic, anti-Catholic magazine edited by Georgia's veteran demagogue and Wilson vilifier, Tom Watson. The ban also extended to books, including ones by Thorstein Veblen and former representative Charles Lindbergh, an anti-interventionist Republican progressive from Minnesota and father of the future aviator. The suspension of these journals prompted a protest directly to the president from *The Masses* editor Max Eastman, joined by Amos Pinchot and the journalist John Reed.[15]

Forwarding their protest to Burleson, Wilson observed, "These are very sincere men and I should like to please them." He also instructed Tumulty to tell Pinchot that he was looking into the matter. In fact, he did nothing and accepted the postmaster general's assurances that he was acting in a careful way. In response to Eastman's renewed protests, Wilson confessed that regarding what could be said in wartime, "the line is manifestly exceedingly hard to draw and I cannot say that I have any confidence that I know how to draw it." In October, Burleson extended his bans to the socialist newspapers *The Milwaukee Leader*, *The New York Call*, and *The Jewish Daily Forward*. This move ignited a fresh round of protests, which now came also from the pro-war socialist minority, mainstream newspapers, and *The New Republic* editors Croly and Lippmann. House, who saw Croly and Lippmann regularly, advised Wilson, "[M]ore harm may easily be done by repression. Between the two courses, it is better to err on the side of leniency."[16] He also advised sidelining Burleson and taking charge himself. Wilson did tell Burleson he disagreed with the suspension of *The Milwaukee Leader*, but he did not reverse the action or rein the postmaster in.

The furor died down for a while after those newspaper and magazine suspensions, but Wilson had clearly shown that he would not always protect civil liberties in wartime. He acquiesced in two other big violations of cherished freedoms—violence against and repression of ethnic minorities and radicals. In an ironic twist, intervention in World War I temporarily lifted the burden of anti-immigrant prejudice from the shoulders of southern and eastern Europeans, most of whose homelands were either fighting on the Allied side or trying to break free from the Austro-Hungarian Empire. Instead, that era's model minority, the German Americans, became objects of derision, discrimination, and violence. There were vigilante actions against them and at least one lynching in the Midwest. Municipalities and one state, Nebraska, enacted measures forbidding the teaching of German, and the German-language press came under suspicion and lost readers. There were reports of burning books by German authors, while orchestras fired German-born musicians and banned works by such "German" composers as Mozart, Beethoven, and Brahms. Despite many entreaties, Wilson declined to speak out against these abuses.[17]

He said nothing about actions against radicals either, and he actively condoned some of those actions. The Espionage Act empowered the Justice Department to prosecute anyone who advocated "treason, insurrection, or forcible resistance to any law of the United States." Unlike his fellow Texan Burleson, Attorney General Gregory did not rush to wield his new power against anti-war speakers, but his restraint stemmed from preoccupation with a special perceived source of trouble—the radical Industrial Workers of the World, or Wobblies. The IWW was mounting union organizing drives among loggers, copper miners, and migratory farmworkers—all considered critical to mobilization. In the West, enemies of the IWW took the law into their own hands in violent incidents that summer. The biggest occurred at the middle of July in Bisbee, Arizona, where a posse rounded up more than 1,000 Wobblies who worked in the copper mines, herded them into cattle cars, and dumped them in the middle of the desert without food, water, or shelter. Then, at the beginning of August, masked men in Butte, Montana, snatched Frank Little, a disabled IWW organizer, from his hotel room, tortured him, and hanged him from a railroad trestle.[18]

Wilson received reports of these and other incidents from sources both hostile and sympathetic to the Wobblies. The union's president, William D. "Big Bill" Haywood, sent telegrams demanding redress and threatening strikes. After a cabinet meeting in July, Daniels noted that the president "was indignant, but said what Haywood desires is to be a martyr." Not making martyrs out of dissidents would remain a guiding principle for Wilson, but he deferred to Gregory, who had already instructed his

subordinates to gather material against the IWW. On Gregory's recommendation, Wilson now appointed a special investigating committee to
examine evidence relating to the union. Early in September, agents of the
department's Bureau of Investigation, with the cooperation of local police,
raided IWW offices in thirty-three cities, seizing files and records—more
than five tons of material. At the end of September, the department
secured indictments in Chicago against 166 IWW leaders, including Haywood, while other indictments came down in California, Kansas, and
Nebraska. The government was moving to crush the Wobblies.[19]

Worse violations of civil liberties were to come, and Wilson's actions
and inaction were disturbing. Sometimes he suffered from a defect inherent in his willingness to delegate, as he gave great latitude to lieutenants
whom he might have restrained. With Burleson, he was deferring to a
coarse-grained political operator never known for intellectual discrimination. Gregory seemed different; he was an able attorney and staunch progressive, but like most lawyers of that era, he knew and cared little about
civil liberties. Moreover, he and his U.S. attorneys found themselves constantly bombarded by state and local leaders who demanded action against
dangerous radicals in their midst—in this case, the IWW. Still, freedom of
speech and opinion was something Wilson seemed to care about deeply, as
he had shown when he told Frank Cobb he was afraid of "ruthless brutality" and when he told J. H. Whitehouse that the government must resist
"mob passion."

Why, then, did Wilson do what he did to civil liberties? The best
answer seems to lie in his conflicted attitude toward "passion." He condemned passion in many contexts and tried to overcome it, but he knew
that he had to draw on it to take action. This attitude seems to have
sprung from a fundamental view of himself. The journalist Lincoln Steffens later recalled that Wilson once said to him, "An intellectual—such as
you and I—an intellectual is inexecutive. In an executive job we are dangerous, unless we are aware of our limitations and take measures to stop
our everlasting disposition to think, to listen to—not act." Wilson needed,
Steffens remembered him saying, "when my mind felt like deciding, to
shut it up and act. My decision might be right, it might be wrong. No matter, I would take a chance and do—something." Yet with respect to civil
liberties, his problem seemed to be less taking action himself and more
remaining passive in the face of actions by others. Outwardly, Wilson
affected to be oblivious to the ways his administration was dealing with
dissent. In one of his few statements on the subject, in his State of
the Union speech in December 1917, he asserted, "I hear the voices of
dissent—who does not? I hear the criticism and the clamour of the noisily

thoughtless and troublesome. . . . But I know that none of these speaks for the nation. They do not touch the heart of anything. They may safely be left to strut their uneasy hour and be forgotten."[20] It was a lovely rationalization, but it would not hold up for long.

By the time the president gave that speech, the United States had been a belligerent for nine months, and the fortunes of war were decidedly mixed. Troops for the Western Front remained the most pressing need. More than three years of bloody stalemate in the trenches had bled the French armies nearly dry, and the British forces were not in much better shape. On the war's other fronts, the Allies were winning only in what was then called the Near East, where the British were pushing the Turks out of Arabia, Mesopotamia, and Palestine. By contrast, the Italians suffered a rout at Caporetto in October and only barely succeeded in securing a new front along the Piave River. In Russia, the long-running collapse of the Eastern Front had taken a potential turn for the worse when the Bolsheviks, led by Vladimir Lenin, overthrew the Provisional Government and pledged to withdraw from the war. More than ever, the Western Front was where the war would be won or lost. George M. Cohan's wildly popular new song contained a refrain that promised "the Yanks are coming"—but how soon, and how many?

Until troops could be trained, armed, and transported to France, the United States could not make much difference in the ground war, but there was still a military role to play. Marshal Joffre had impressed upon Wilson what a morale boost it would be to have an American division fighting alongside his armies. Unfortunately, that first division did not go to the front until October, when it was assigned to a quiet sector for further training. In the meantime, the president and the War Department agreed to send over a commander of future forces at once. At the beginning of May, in consultation with the president, Secretary Baker tapped Major General John J. Pershing to lead what would be called the American Expeditionary Forces (AEF). As commander of the Punitive Expedition in Mexico, Pershing had the most recent field experience of any American general. Moreover, unlike the other possible choice, Roosevelt's close friend Leonard Wood, Pershing had refrained from publicly criticizing Wilson's preparedness policies and restraint in Mexico. He also possessed excellent political connections; his recently deceased wife was the daughter of a senior Republican senator, Francis Warren of Wyoming, former chairman of the Military Affairs Committee.[21]

Pershing saw Wilson for the first and only time during the war on May 24, when Baker took him to the White House, where the president told the general he would have complete freedom in conducting operations. Wilson also reviewed Baker's final orders to the AEF commander on May 26, the day before he left for France. Pershing was to work with the Allies but always to remember that he was leading a separate and distinct force, "the identity of which must be preserved." Somewhat contradictorily, Pershing was told that until he had sufficient troops to operate independently, he should "cooperate as a component of whatever army you may be assigned to by the French government." Pershing arrived in France at the middle of June. Parades and lavish ceremonies in Paris and an emotional event at which the AEF commander kissed Napoleon's sword supplied the hoped-for morale boost. Contrary to later legend, however, it was not the laconic general but one of his aides who proclaimed, "Lafayette, we are here!"[22]

Such stirring public gestures notwithstanding, the underlying conflict between an independent force and inter-Allied cooperation quickly surfaced. Ramrod straight in posture and stubborn in personality, Pershing was determined not to allow his men to be amalgamated with British or French forces. Allied commanders began clamoring for company or regimental units of American soldiers, nicknamed doughboys, to replenish their own desperately thin lines, but Pershing gathered his green troops behind the lines for further training. He had a legitimate concern, but he was really putting together a separate army under his sole command. As more doughboys arrived, pressures for amalgamation grew, and at the end of the year Lloyd George interceded with Wilson through House and Wiseman. In response, Wilson had Baker cable Pershing: "We do not desire any loss of identity of our forces but regard that as secondary to the meeting of any critical situation by the most helpful possible use of the troops at your command." Yet Wilson also told Pershing that he had "full authority to use the forces at your command as you deem wise."[23] This was one of Wilson's few interventions in the military operations and the closest he came to communicating directly with Pershing in 1917. Despite diplomatic nods toward the British and French, he was giving his commander everything he wanted.

Any question of how American forces might be used would be moot if ships were not able to transport them across the Atlantic and deliver vital foodstuffs, machines, and munitions to the British and French. The critical elements in this situation were submarines, which had to be combated, and merchant vessels, which had to be commandeered and built. The naval war consisted mainly of submarine attacks and efforts to defend against those attacks. Between March and August 1917, German submarines sank more than 500,000 tons of Allied shipping each month and 921,211 tons in May alone. At that rate, Britain would not be able to stay in the war. Yet as Wilson and his advisers learned when the delegations visited in April, the British were loath to face up to their peril. Nor did their naval leaders seem eager to adopt what promised to be an effective defense—the convoy system, under which destroyers would escort groups of merchant ships. Admiral Sims, who reached London four days after the declaration of war, urged sending all available destroyers immediately, and by June twenty-four American destroyers were operating in British waters.

This move struck Wilson as only a start. He took much greater personal interest in naval affairs than army affairs, and he did not hesitate to deal directly with his commander on the scene. British reluctance to adopt the convoy system prompted him, with Daniels's concurrence, to cable Sims early in July to get the admiral's view of the matter. Sims replied with a review of Britain's naval situation and a recommendation to press the British harder to cooperate in convoy duties. By September, the rate of losses dropped to 300,000 tons, in part because the navy had taken over convoy duties for ships carrying doughboys to France. These improvements gratified Wilson but did not completely satisfy him. In August, he made one of his few trips out of Washington, to visit the Atlantic fleet before it sailed for European waters. Speaking off the record aboard the U.S.S. *Pennsylvania*, he again disparaged British "prudence" and reluctance to try new things: "I should like to see something unusual happen, something that was never done before."[24]

Foiling the submarines solved only half the problem of getting soldiers and supplies to the war. The other half consisted of coming up with enough ships to carry them. During the preceding half century, the once-proud American merchant marine had withered away, the victim of devastation wrought by Confederate raiders during the Civil War and the shift of the economy inward under the impact of the Industrial Revolution. British ships had been carrying most of the massive trade with the Allies since 1914, but Wilson had new tools at hand to try to remedy the situation. The Shipping Act passed in 1916 as part of the second installment of the New Freedom empowered the president to establish the U.S. Shipping Board, which could purchase ships, including interned German vessels, and set up shipyards. The shipbuilding program produced spectacular results, spending $270 million to establish 341 new yards that employed nearly 400,000 workers and launched nearly 100 ships a day after the middle of 1918.[25]

Behind those accomplishments, however, lay conflict and tardiness. A turf battle broke out between William Denman, a businessman and Democratic campaign contributor who was chairman of the Shipping Board, and General George Washington Goethals, the legendary builder of the Panama Canal, who was head of the Emergency Fleet Corporation, the board's operating subsidiary. This pair squabbled about nearly everything, and in July the chairman of the Senate Naval Affairs Committee told Wilson that the "fight between Denman and Goethals is disgusting the Senate, and the House and every sensitive man in the United States."[26] Wilson pulled off a graceful end to this scrap by getting both men to resign quietly. As the new chairman of the Shipping Board, he named Edward N. Hurley, a Chicago businessman and Democratic activist who had no background in shipping but soon brought discipline and harmony to the board. Later, to head the Emergency Fleet Corporation, he appointed the steel tycoon Charles M. Schwab, who supplied the boldness that Wilson valued. Unfortunately, Hurley's and Schwab's efficiency would come too late to make much difference to the outcome of the war. Most of the doughboys would cross the ocean in commandeered private vessels or Allied ships. America's much-ballyhooed "bridge of ships" would serve mainly to bring the doughboys home in 1919.

Overseas shipping was just one transportation problem the Wilson administration faced. Despite the recent proliferation of cars and trucks, the great majority of people and goods in 1917 still moved by rail. Earlier conflicts with railroad management did not stop Wilson from seeking management's voluntary cooperation. In July, a new supervisory agency, the Railroads' War Board, issued an order to expedite shipments by tagging critical items. The order backfired when freight agents tagged everything bound for eastern ports and backed-up freight cars clogged lines as far west as Pittsburgh and Buffalo. In addition, railroads would not allow other lines' engines to operate on their tracks, and most of them squirreled away their freight cars. The tagging mess eventually got straightened out, but delays and bickering grew worse in the fall as industrial production picked up. The railroads demanded rate increases, which the ICC refused to grant, and the unions once more threatened to go out on strike.[27]

The president's closest advisers, particularly McAdoo, pressed him to use his authority under the Adamson Act to take over the railroads. Tumulty likewise lobbied for seizing control of the lines and appointing McAdoo to run them. Wilson resisted outright government ownership, which many progressives had long wanted, but on December 26 he issued a proclamation assuming control of the railroads as a wartime measure.

Speaking to a joint session of Congress a week later, he explained that he was taking this action "only because there were some things which the government can do and private management cannot."[28] Soft-pedal this action as Wilson might, there was no disguising its boldness. This was one of the farthest-reaching assertions of government power in economic affairs in American history. Nothing else in the war at home would go this far, but only because less coercive methods appeared to work elsewhere.

Food also posed a pressing need, for both the troops and the Allies. A bill to deal with food and fuel production and distribution introduced a month into the war stirred up heavy resistance on Capitol Hill. Conservatives in both houses bridled at the extension of presidential power and government interference in the economy. In the Senate, John W. Weeks of Massachusetts succeeded in attaching an amendment to set up a "Joint Committee on Expenditures in the Conduct of the War." This move brought a sharp rejoinder from Wilson. In a public letter to Congressman Asbury Lever of South Carolina, who was chairman of the House Agriculture Committee and the House-Senate conference committee on the bill, he argued that Weeks's proposal would "render my work of conducting the war practically impossible" by usurping functions that belonged to the executive branch. In a barb aimed at Republican critics, he cited "a very ominous precedent in our history" for such interference—namely, the joint congressional committee during the Civil War that "rendered Mr. Lincoln's task all but impossible." Wilson's argument and lobbying succeeded in getting the conference committee to drop the disputed provision, and as finally passed, this law, which came to be called the Lever Act, gave him the powers he had requested.[29]

The food-control measure was the brainchild of the man whom Wilson had already chosen as food administrator—Herbert Hoover. The now forty-three-year-old mining engineer and international businessman had earned a heroic reputation since 1914 as head of the Commission for Relief in Belgium, the multinational group that was feeding the civilian population of German-occupied Belgium, a task that had involved him in diplomacy as much as food delivery. Hoover brought enormous intelligence and energy to his new job, together with a distinctive approach. No friend of bureaucracy, he kept his agency as small as possible while enlisting several thousand volunteers. He also tried to avoid rationing by promoting voluntary restraint in consumption. Because wheat was a critical commodity, the Food Administration promoted "wheatless days." To conserve meat and poultry for military consumption and overseas shipment, it likewise promoted "meatless days." With stories about Hoover appearing regularly in newspapers and magazines, he became what one observer called "the benevolent bogey of the nation." People were supposed to eat foods in specified categories sparingly and thereby "Hooverize" their plates; parents told children they could not have a spoonful of sugar on their cereal "because Mr. Hoover would not like it." One of his own agency's slogans even called him "Herbert Hoover, the Autocrat of the Breakfast Table."[30]

Yet Hoover much preferred to use carrots than sticks, real or implied, in his crusade to get Americans to eat less and produce more. His agency rivaled Creel's CPI in rousing popular sentiment. Housewives, grocers, and restaurateurs, as well as the public in general, became targets for relentless pep talks, posters, and advertisements—with such messages as "Food is sacred. To waste is sinful"; "Wheatless days in America make sleepless nights in Germany"; and "Save beans by all means." Twenty million people signed a pledge to follow Food Administration guidelines in conserving food; in return, they received buttons to wear and stickers to put in their windows. The Food Administration also exhorted people to plant vegetable gardens for home consumption and to raise sheep and knit scarves and mittens for the troops. Edith Wilson set an example by signing the pledge and displaying her sticker in a White House window, planting a "war garden" on the grounds, and, along with her stepdaughters, knitting for the troops. Her husband made a similar gesture by bringing in a flock of much-photographed sheep to graze on the South Lawn. Wilson liked Hoover's go-getting, boosterish methods, and he appreciated the administrator's feats of raising wheat production by nearly half—despite a harsh winter and loss of farmers to the armed forces—and curbing price speculation by setting up a government corporation that bought the entire crop. No other American would come out of World War I with a more stellar public reputation than Hoover.[31]

The Lever Act addressed another critical requirement for the war effort: fuel. That meant coal, which railroads, most ships, offices, homes, and factories still relied on for power. Wilson set up a Fuel Administration and appointed as its head his friend from the Princeton faculty and now president of Williams College, Harry Garfield. Before the fuel administrator took his new post, however, an owner-led Committee on Coal Production forged agreements to stabilize prices and boost production. Suspecting machinations by a "coal trust," Garfield scrapped those agreements and pushed prices down. By the year's end, coal shortages plagued the eastern part of the country, worsened by the coldest winter in three decades. People stole coal, and local authorities would stop coal trains and distribute their cargoes to residents. In January 1918, Garfield tried to meet the crisis by ordering all factories east of the Mississippi to shut down for four days, and he called for "heatless Mondays," which came to be dubbed "Garfield days." The coal shortage and tie-ups in deliveries stirred up a storm of protest and on Capitol Hill roused critics of the administration, who demanded investigations and offered new measures to trim Wilson's authority. The protests would pass, and the fuel crisis would subside, but Garfield, who earned the scornful epithet "the professor," did not come out of the war with much of a public reputation.[32]

Efforts to manage industrial production did not fare well during the summer and fall of 1917 either. The War Industries Board, a shell agency, suffered from weak and divided authority. For that and other reasons, business committees set up under the WIB did little to bring order to the production and distribution of manufactured goods. Unlike the Food and Fuel Administrations, the board had no price-fixing powers and could not enter into contracts—a prerogative that the military and naval procurement bureaus jealously guarded. Confusion reigned, and the board's first and second chairmen quit after a few months in exhaustion and frustration. The WIB would not begin to function with a semblance of effectiveness until Wilson made Baruch its chairman at the beginning of March 1918.[33]

Waging war also affected major social problems at home, particularly in race relations. The migration of African Americans out of the South to northern cities had been growing, partly in response to the rising demand for workers in war-related industries. These newcomers to the North usually found hostility, discrimination, and, increasingly, violence. At the beginning of July, a "race riot"—in reality, a white rampage—raged for a day in East St. Louis, Illinois, leaving thirty-nine blacks and nine whites dead and black neighborhoods burned out. In response to pleas for federal action, Wilson asked Attorney General Gregory, "Do you think we could exercise any jurisdiction in this tragical matter? I am very anxious to have any instrumentality of the Government employed that could . . . effectively . . . check these disgraceful outrages." For once, he seemed to be reacting compassionately in the face of racial injustice.[34]

Wilson did not follow that impulse, however. Gregory advised that no federal action was warranted, although he counseled the president against saying so. Tumulty warned him nevertheless that "[u]ntil some statement is issued by you deprecating these terrible things, I am afraid the pressure will grow greater and greater." The president did not make a statement, but on August 14 he met with four black leaders and allowed them to tell the press that he deplored the violence, was seeking to punish offenders, and would seek to prevent future outbreaks. That tepid response did nothing to quell the violence. On August 23, shooting broke out in Houston, Texas, between black troops and a white mob; fifteen whites and three blacks died before white troops and local police restored order. The next day, Daniels noted some of Wilson's remarks at a cabinet meeting: "Race prejudice. Fight in Houston, Texas. Negro in uniform wants the whole sidewalk." The army summarily hanged thirteen black soldiers and sentenced forty-one to life in prison, while later courts-martial sentenced sixteen more to death.[35]

The incident in Houston highlighted the touchy issue of African Americans in the military. The navy had only 5,000 blacks serving during the war, and the marines had none. The army, however, had 10,000 black enlisted men and some officers in April 1917, and despite misgivings and protests from some white southern politicians, the War Department planned to induct many more. Though born and raised in West Virginia, Newton Baker differed from other cabinet members in his relaxed attitude toward race, and his assistant secretary who oversaw race relations, Frederick Keppel, held liberal views. That was not the case among the army's officers, however, many of whom assumed that black inductees would be put only in labor battalions—as many were—but black leaders moved to forestall such plans. In May, the NAACP called for full black support of, and full black participation in, the war. In the organization's journal, *The Crisis*, W. E. B. DuBois declared, "If this is OUR country, then this is OUR war." In October, after the first African American draftees were called up, Baker appointed a black special assistant, Emmett J. Scott, an administrator at the Tuskegee Institute. Wilson had little to do with these initiatives, and he condoned a move by the army in the opposite direction when it denied a command to the highest-ranking black officer, Colonel Charles Young, a West Point graduate, by imposing a highly suspect medical retirement on him.[36]

Four hundred thousand African Americans would see army service during the war, with a quarter of them going overseas. They served in a single all-black division and other segregated units, all commanded by white officers. Black inductees received training in separate areas of larger camps. The only all-black training facility was an officers' school outside Des Moines, Iowa, which turned out more than 600 graduates at junior ranks. The school lasted only a few months because the military high command decided against black units having black officers—a decision that had adverse consequences. Although some white officers commanding black units acted with fairness and sometimes with goodwill, many of them resented their postings as second-class duty and looked down on their men through the distortions of racist stereotypes. To make matters worse, many black soldiers trained at camps in the South, where segregation prevailed on the base as well as off. Their separate facilities were anything but equal, and as one investigator observed, "Where there was a shortage they were the ones to suffer." Labor battalions suffered most. At one camp in Virginia, soldiers spent the harsh winter of 1917–18 sleeping in tents, without blankets, fresh clothes, bathing facilities, or medical attention. A large number of them died.37

As the NAACP's activity indicates, African Americans played an active role in trying to shape their part in the war. In 1917, they protested against both the "race riots" and the punishment meted out to the soldiers in Houston. After the East St. Louis riot, 1,500 black men, women, and children marched in New York in what they called the Negro Silent Protest Parade, and the marchers petitioned Congress and the president. After the sentencing of the soldiers in Houston, the NAACP gathered 12,000 signatures on a petition requesting investigation and review and sent a delegation to read the petition to the president at the White House on February 19, 1918. The man who read the petition was James Weldon Johnson, the NAACP's executive secretary. Wilson asked his visitors questions and told them a couple of stories about his youth in the South. "When I came out," Johnson later wrote, "it was with my hostility toward Mr. Wilson greatly shaken; however, I could not rid myself of the conviction that at bottom there was something hypocritical about him."38

Wilson would later commute the sentences of some of the men condemned in the Houston riot, and he would spark some hope by the way he addressed an equally ominous cloud on the racial horizon—an epidemic of lynchings. According to reports by the NAACP, nearly 100 black people were lynched in 1917 and 1918, and a number of prominent individuals, black and white, wrote to implore the president to speak out against the crime. The most potent plea came from one of Wilson's few black acquaintances, Robert R. Moton, Booker T. Washington's successor as principal of the Tuskegee Institute. On June 15, 1918, Moton told the president that on recent travels in the South he had found "more genuine restlessness, and perhaps dissatisfaction on the part of colored people than I have ever before known." Lynching was the cause of those attitudes, and Moton urged "a strong word, definitely from you" against it. In reply, Wilson said, "I have been seeking an opportunity to do what you suggest and if I do not find it soon, I will do it without an opportunity."39

On July 26, the president issued a statement "on a subject which so vitally affects the honor of the Nation and the very character and integrity of our institutions." He decried the "mob spirit" of lynching as a blow against liberty and justice: "I say plainly that every American who takes part in the action of a mob or gives it any sort of countenance is no true son of this great Democracy, but its betrayer, and does more to discredit her by that single disloyalty to her standards of law and of rights than the words of her statesmen or the sacrifices of her heroic boys in the trenches can do to make suffering peoples believe her to be their savior." He urged governors and all law-enforcement officers to stamp out "this disgraceful evil."⁴⁰ Wilson's eloquence now tended to be more tinged with passion than his pre-war speaking, and this statement anticipated an argument later generations would make—that racial injustice sullied America's image abroad and efforts to lead the world.

His denunciation of lynching gave a hint of what a powerful civil rights president he might have been if he had put his heart and mind into the cause. But they were not there. His reluctance to enter the war for fear of further depleting the white race disclosed what really moved him. His muttering about black soldiers' wanting "the whole sidewalk" in Houston revealed how readily he accepted the customary racial inequalities and indignities of the time. His friendly meeting with the NAACP leaders shows he had learned from the clash with William Monroe Trotter and the *Birth of a Nation* fiasco—but only that he must maintain his politeness and self-control. His relations with Robert Moton showed that he could work with a moderate black leader, although he had ignored entreaties to make a public statement at the time of Booker T. Washington's death, three years earlier. Wilson had put any ethnic and religious prejudices he ever felt far behind him, and he would soon work easily and sympatheti-cally with nonwhite leaders from other parts of the world. Why, then, did the glaring injustice of racial prejudice on his own doorstep and in his own household not engage his mind and spirit?

Like his acquiescence in wartime repression of civil liberties, this fail-ure of moral conscience remains puzzling. He did leave clues about why did he not take action against racism. When James Weldon Johnson— who was a poet and a black man who read white attitudes with great sensitivity—called the president a hypocrite, he put his finger on some-thing important. Wilson's denunciation of lynching deplored the passion, disorder, and sullied international image of white Americans rather than injury, horror, and death of black Americans. That viewpoint was consis-tent with his earlier depiction of slavery as an economic curse, but not necessarily a moral one, on the South, and it put him in line with other southern critics of slavery, going back to Jefferson, who deplored the peculiar institution's impact on masters and other whites but remained indifferent to the plight of the enslaved.

Wilson's southern birth and upbringing had shaped his approach to race, but not in a simple way. Violence, lynching, and virulent racism, particularly the demagoguery of such firebrands as Vardaman and Watson, grieved him, and he would soon mount a drive to purge southern politics of retrograde actors and influences. His impatience with agitation over race from any quarter made him resemble northern whites of that time more than fellow southerners, but he had grown up despising abolitionists and regarding Reconstruction as an injustice. Further, his southern Presbyterian upbringing made him oppose mixing religion in politics and thereby separated him from the small number of white Christians of that era who came to see racism as a sin. Ironically, his learned, sophisticated Protestantism, which otherwise influenced him profoundly for the better, may have kept him from making the leap of faith of evangelicals who recognized African Americans as fellow children of God. This was perhaps Woodrow Wilson's greatest tragedy: the North Star by which he steered on his life's spiritual and intellectual journey may have prevented him from reaching his full stature as a moral leader and rendering still finer service to his nation and the world.[41]

By the time he made his statement about lynching, Wilson was addressing another issue that he had come to see as part of the war effort—woman suffrage. The two wings of the movement dealt with him in starkly contrasting ways. The militant Alice Paul and the National Woman's Party (NWP) continued to berate him for refusing to endorse a constitutional amendment. The party's picketers outside the White House displayed banners labeling him "Kaiser Wilson"—a hypocrite who professed to promote freedom abroad while not extending it to women at home—and began chaining themselves to the White House fence and disrupting traffic on Pennsylvania Avenue. During the summer of 1917, more than 200 women were arrested, and 97 went to jail. The tense situation exploded on July 14, when District of Columbia policemen arrested sixteen prominent members of the NWP, including the wife of a New Jersey Progressive leader who, with her husband, had recently been a dinner guest at the White House, and the sister-in-law of former Secretary of War Henry Stimson. After being held a few days in jail, these women received presidential pardons, which they indignantly refused.[42]

Wilson did not react to this affair the way he did to some other repressions of dissent. On July 19, he summoned to the White House Louis Brownlow, the D.C. commissioner who oversaw the police. "Mr. Wilson was indignant," Brownlow later recalled. "He told me that we had made a fearful blunder." He wanted the women pardoned and released, but the attorney general had ruled that pardons could not take effect unless accepted. The collector of the Port of New York and a strong suffrage advocate, Wilson's friend Dudley Field Malone, was able to change the prisoners' minds. For Wilson, the main consequence of the July 14 arrests was a painful break with Malone. In September, after a face-to-face argument over whether the president should push Congress to pass a suffrage amendment, Malone resigned and accused Wilson of showing bad faith toward the nation's women. "I know of nothing that has gone more to the quick with me or that seemed more tragical than Dudley's conduct," Wilson told House. "I was stricken by it as I have been by few things in my life." He thought "passion has run away with him," and he quoted Kipling's line about keeping your head when everyone else is losing his. "We must not let the madness touch us. It is the sort of strength I pray for all the time."43

Wilson kept his head on the suffrage issue, with help from leaders of the other, more moderate, wing of the movement. Carrie Chapman Catt and Helen Gardener of the National American Woman Suffrage Association (NAWSA) stayed on the president's good side by distancing themselves from the NWP and conspicuously enlisting themselves and their organization behind the war effort. Catt also artfully suggested to Wilson in May that suffrage might be viewed "possibly as a war measure"—as a way to symbolize the spread of democracy and recognize women's support of the war. Gardener followed up by proposing that the president might inform the chairman of the House Rules Committee that he favored setting up a special committee on suffrage. These women knew the right approach to use with Wilson. He obliged them by telling the chairman, "I am writing this line to say that I would heartily approve. I think it would be a very wise act of public policy and also an act of fairness to the best women who are engaged in the cause of woman suffrage." The Rules Committee complied, and a suffrage committee was established.44

During the rest of 1917, Wilson declined to come out for an amendment, but Catt kept up her campaign of support and flattery and solicited tactical advice from him about suffrage campaigns in the states. In October, he publicly endorsed the effort in New York, linking woman suffrage to the international "struggle between two ideals of government." Those words undoubtedly helped, but the tide was already running strongly in favor of the cause. In November, suffrage prevailed on referenda in New York and Rhode Island—the first states in the Northeast to come over—as well as in North Dakota, Nebraska, and Arkansas—the first southern state. On Capitol Hill, the House scheduled a vote on an amendment in January 1918. The head of the Women's Bureau of the Democratic National Committee, Elizabeth Bass, appealed to Wilson to come out in support of the amendment. She argued that his doing so would help the party in upcoming elections and "would enthrone you forever in the hearts of the women of America as the second Great Emancipator."[45]

Such flattery aside, Wilson now came around to support the suffrage amendment. On January 9, the day before the House voted, he met with Democrats on the suffrage committee and allowed them to release a statement that the president "very frankly and earnestly advised us to vote for the amendment as an act of right and justice to the women of the country and the world."[46] As one of the Democrats recalled two weeks later, the president told them that passing the amendment would send the right message to the world and would acknowledge women's service to the nation. That presidential endorsement, together with the results of the state referenda, did the trick. On January 10, 1918, the amendment squeaked through by a vote of 274 to 136, just two more than the required two-thirds. It was the first time that a house of Congress had endorsed woman suffrage.

The other half of the battle on Capitol Hill proved harder to win. During the spring and summer of 1918, Wilson actively lobbied senators on behalf of the amendment. He wrote to and met with southern Democrats who persisted in opposing suffrage, and he urged the governor of Kentucky to appoint a pro-suffrage successor to replace a Democratic senator who had died. At the middle of June he presented Catt and a delegation from NAWSA with a public letter that saluted women's support of the war and declared that the Senate should acknowledge the debt. As a vote neared at the end of September, Catt wrote to him "in sheer desperation" because the amendment appeared to be two votes short of the necessary two thirds, and she begged him to issue another public appeal. McAdoo also took the drastic step of going to the White House on September 29, knowing, as he later recalled, "that the President did not like to discuss, or consider any public business on Sunday." He urged Wilson to appear in person before the Senate the next day, arguing that even if the amendment fell short, such an appeal would help elect pro-suffrage candidates in November and thereby assure passage in the next Congress. Wilson listened noncommittally, but later that afternoon Edith Wilson telephoned McAdoo to say that he was working on a speech.[47]

Wilson spoke to the Senate on September 30, 1918. He had addressed this chamber only once before, with the "peace without victory" address in January 1917, and once more he gave the senators little warning. This time, however, he brought with him the entire cabinet, except Lansing, who opposed suffrage. He begged the senators' pardon for his unusual move, pleading the "unusual circumstances of a world war in which we stand and are judged in the view of our own people and our own consciences but also in the view of all the nations and peoples. . . . We have made partners of women in this war, shall we admit them only to a partnership of suffering and sacrifice and not to a partnership of privilege and right?" He closed by asking the senators to lighten his burden in waging war and "place in my hands instruments, spiritual instruments, which I do not now possess and sorely need, and which I have daily to apologise for not being able to employ."[48]

This time, his lobbying and eloquence failed to carry the day. On October 1, the suffrage amendment fell short of passage by the predicted two votes. Democrats split, twenty-six in favor and twenty-one against—all but three from southern or border states—while twenty-seven Republicans voted in favor and only ten against. Wilson and the suffragists stuck to their guns. In the 1918 elections, NAWSA targeted four anti-suffrage senators for defeat and succeeded in helping to knock off two of them, including Weeks of Massachusetts. Wilson renewed his plea for the amendment in his State of the Union address in December and lobbied senators, but on February 10, 1919, they again failed to pass the amendment. The president continued to lobby senators, even meeting with a newly elected Democrat during the peace conference in Paris. On May 20, he cabled a message about suffrage to Congress, which made the amendment its first order of business. The House passed it on the same day as his message was conveyed, 304 to 89, and the Senate followed suit on June 4 by a vote of 56 to 25.

Wilson was not able to help much during the drive for ratification. After he returned from the peace conference in July, the fight to secure Senate approval of the Treaty of Versailles and membership in the League of Nations consumed nearly all his time and energy, until he suffered a stroke at the beginning of October. Later, in his semi-invalid condition, he did send messages, drafted by Tumulty, to state legislatures urging ratification. By mid-1920, the amendment stood just one state short of the thirty-six required for ratification. At Catt's request, he telegraphed the governor of Tennessee, asking him to call a special session of the legislature to consider the amendment. The governor complied, and on August 18 Tennessee narrowly approved the amendment, thereby enabling women to vote nationwide for the first time in the 1920 elections. American women, starting with Susan B. Anthony and Elizabeth Cady Stanton, deserved the lion's share of credit for this final, long-belated achievement of nationwide woman suffrage, but among men Woodrow Wilson deserved more approbation than anyone else.[49]

Woman suffrage became the Nineteenth Amendment to the Constitution because in December 1917 Congress had already passed, and in January 1919 the states had ratified, the Eighteenth Amendment, which banned the manufacture and sale of alcoholic beverages in the United States. Prohibition had been gathering strength for several years, and after the country entered the war, supporters used arguments for conserving grain and appeals to crusading idealism and sacrifice to push their cause over the top. Wilson had never backed prohibition, and since his run-ins with "dry" groups in 1912 he had studiously avoided saying anything about the issue. His only real involvement came at the end of the legislative process. In October 1919, just three weeks after suffering the stroke, he vetoed the Volstead Act, the law enforcing prohibition. Tumulty wrote the message, almost certainly with Edith Wilson's consent, and Secretary of Agriculture Houston revised it. Given Wilson's physical weakness and almost total isolation during the first month after the stroke, it is doubtful that he ever saw the message or knew anything about the veto, which Congress promptly overrode.[50]

Domestic problems did not occupy all that much of his time because war leadership brought heavy new burdens. "My days are so full now as to come near to driving me to distraction," he lamented to Harry Fine in May 1917. Edith Wilson similarly recalled, "People descended upon the White House until their coming and going was like the rise and fall of the tides. To achieve anything amid such distractions called for the most rigid rationing of time." Wilson was used to rationing his time, and before long he got his customary routine back in place. He managed to get in golf games, and Edith and Grayson persuaded him to go horseback riding with them. For distraction, he also went to vaudeville shows at Keith's Theater on Fifteenth Street, and after dinner he would sometimes put a record on the player and say to Edith, "Now I'll show you how to do a jig step." He tried to teach her to ride a bicycle, but her lessons with him in the White House basement were not successful. She also recalled that at the end of every evening, "my husband would go back to his study for a look at The Drawer [the day's accumulated official documents]. . . . He would take up one paper after another—and so work until the small hours."[51]

A trip in August to visit the fleet afforded a chance for recreation amid official duties, and in September he and Edith spent a week cruising off the New England coast. In October, Wilson enjoyed a different kind of distraction when John Singer Sargent came to the White House to paint his portrait. The president had not wanted to sit for Sargent; according to House, Wilson was afraid to do so because of Sargent's "alleged faculty of bringing out the latent soul of his sitter." Still, this was an offer he could not refuse. The project had originated early in 1915, when Sargent had come out of retirement to help raise money for the British Red Cross. The director of the National Gallery of Ireland, Sir Hugh Lane, had put up the considerable sum of £10,000 (nearly $50,000 at the exchange rate of the time) for a portrait, but he had not chosen a subject for the portrait before his death in the sinking of the *Lusitania*, and the trustees of the gallery later picked President Wilson. The sittings lasted for more than a week, and Edith recalled, "My husband said he never worked harder than he did to entertain Sargent while he posed."[52]

In the finished portrait, the president is seated with his right hand lightly grasping one arm of the chair and his left hand draped over the other arm in a relaxed manner. The portrait does not highlight Wilson's long jaw and nose, and it gives a true impression of his solid though not stocky physique. His expression is pensive, and his posture conveys an air of calm strength and contained energy. Overall, the portrait is a favorable, perhaps flattering, but not heroic depiction of Wilson—a contrast to Sargent's only other rendition of a president, the one he had done fourteen years earlier of Theodore Roosevelt standing at the foot of a staircase, his right hand resting on a large round finial that is easy to mistake for a globe. Sargent commented on the contrast between the experiences of painting these two presidents. "The White House is empty," he told a friend. "How different from the days of Roosevelt who posed or didn't pose in a crowd."[53]

This portrait drew mixed reactions among Wilson's family and friends. Edith later said it disappointed her because it lacked "virility" and made Wilson look older. House agreed, saying it depicted "an esthetic scholar rather than a virile statesman." By contrast, Bob Bridges, who saw the portrait in New York before it went to Ireland, wrote "Tommy" to say, "I like it hugely. I can see you getting ready to tell a story, with the quirk to the right side of your mouth." Bridges acknowledged that the art critics disliked it: "What they want is a stern-looking Covenanter with a jaw like a pike."[54]

Even with the workload of the wartime presidency, Wilson still kept the most important areas of foreign policy largely to himself. He continued to leave areas he considered less important—such as Asia, Latin America, and, now, Mexico—to Lansing. He also left most of the specific dealings with Britain to others, particularly House and Wiseman. To enhance his cohort's influence at home, the colonel had Wiseman meet the president personally. "It is important that he should be able to say that he has met you," House explained, adding, "Sir William has been the real ambassador over here for some time." The meeting took place on June 26, 1917, at an official reception at the Pan American Building, and onlookers were reportedly goggle-eyed as the president spent so much time with this hitherto unknown person. On a trip back to London, that contact helped Wiseman pursue his and House's agenda, which included the appointment of a special envoy to handle financial matters. The man chosen for that job, Lord Reading, the lord chief justice of England and a Liberal Party insider, came to America in September, temporarily accompanied by John Maynard Keynes. Reading soon forged a good relationship with McAdoo and others in Washington, and at the beginning of 1918 he succeeded the ailing Spring-Rice as ambassador.[55]

Wilson did not spend much time with relations with the other Allies either. France's ambassador, Jean-Jules Jusserand, continued to enjoy pleasant, correct, if not close relations with the president, who had little contact with the Italians beyond formalities and relegated the Japanese to Lansing's sphere. Russia did concern him, however. Immediately after entering the war, Wilson extended a $325 million credit to Russia and dispatched a high-level mission headed by Elihu Root, secretary of state under Roosevelt. The Root mission spent a month in Russia during the summer of 1917 but did little to help the Russian war effort. Part of its purpose was to show what would later be called bipartisanship by enlisting a top Republican, but it accomplished little in that direction too. Root later told his biographer that the mission had been "a grand-stand play"— a show of Wilson's sympathy for the new post-czarist government— "that's all he wanted." George Creel remembered Wilson saying a year and a half after the mission that "its failure was largely due to Russian distrust of Mr. Root."[56]

Wilson's grand design in waging war remained to seek peace without victory. In May, he reminded an Alabama congressman that in the war address he had restated his devotion to a liberal, nonpunitive settlement. In his only major speech during the nation's first six months at war, a Flag Day address on June 14, he declared "that this is a Peoples' War for freedom and self-government amongst all the nations of the world, a war to make the world safe for the peoples who live upon it. . . . [W]oe be to that man or that group of men that seeks to stand in our way in this day of high resolution." That bit of public rhetoric sounded more forthrightly militant than he may have wished, because his private thoughts followed a more twisted path. In July he told House, "England and France *have not the same views with regard to peace that we have* by any means. . . . If there is to be an interchange of views at all, it ought to be between us and the liberals in Germany, with no one else brought in."[57]

Wilson was referring to a resolution just passed in the Reichstag that called for efforts to make peace. Another initiative came from the pope, who in August publicly called for a settlement on the basis of status quo ante bellum, together with future disarmament and international arbitration. To many people, that looked like peace without victory, but Wilson did not agree. In his reply to the pope on August 27, he stated, "Our response must be based upon the stern facts and upon nothing else." America wanted "not a mere cessation of arms . . . [but] a stable and enduring peace," which required saving "the free peoples of the world from the menace and the actual power of a vast military establishment controlled by an irresponsible government" that had "planned to dominate the world." True peace could come only from the people, not from the governments, of the Central powers. "God grant that it may be given soon and in a way to restore the confidence of peoples everywhere in the faith of nations and the possibility of covenanted peace." In walking a fine line between military resolve and generous peace terms, Wilson was establishing himself as the moral and ideological leader of his side in the war.[58]

House prided himself on having a hand in the matter. The colonel had differed with Lansing and others in the State Department and Wilson himself about whether to reply to the pope, and he wrote, "I am sure I have a more complete picture of the situation than either the President or Lansing."[59] That was a dangerous attitude for any presidential adviser, no matter how intimate, to harbor, and it portended eventual trouble. For the present, however, House's relationship with Wilson seemed stronger than ever. Curiously, it did not depend on direct contact. After the British mission to Washington in April, the two men did not see each other again for more than four months, although they wrote to each other frequently.

The separation ended with Wilson's previously mentioned visit to the colonel's summer home during the cruise in September. They engaged in two days of conversation that ranged widely. On the first day, Wilson berated Lansing and discussed a possible cabinet shuffle, as well as shipping and naval matters, and on the second day they discussed peace terms. House noticed that his guest sometimes had difficulty resuming a line of thought after an interruption. "He smiled plaintively," the colonel recorded, "and said: 'You see I am getting tired. This is the way it indicates itself.'" House also brought up a matter that Wiseman had passed on to him—support for a Jewish homeland in Palestine, which the British were about to endorse in what came to be known as the Balfour Declaration. Wilson was sympathetic but did not think it was the right time for any commitment.[60]

During the next two months, House met with Wilson three times for similar broad-ranging talks. The colonel pressed him to speak out again on the future basis of peace, especially the elimination of trade barriers on land and sea, and to demand that a new German government make peace. Wilson gave House two signs of how much he trusted and relied on him: he chose the colonel to represent him at the meeting of the Inter-Allied War Council in November, and he asked him to set up an organization to plan for a peace settlement. The idea for a planning body originated with Wilson, who told House that he wanted to begin systematic work to lay out the American position for post-war negotiations and asked, "What would you think of quietly gathering about you a group of men to assist you to do this?" House jumped at the idea, replying that this was "one of the things I have had in mind for a long while. I shall undertake the work and will go about it at once."[61]

The colonel's activities resulted in the Inquiry, a freestanding organization outside the State Department that would become famous as a covey of experts who brought knowledge and brainpower to the gathering of information and analysis about matters involved in a peace settlement. Actually, in setting up the Inquiry, House acted like the political operator he was. As the organization's head, he picked his brother-in-law, Sidney Mezes, a former president of the University of Texas who was now president of City College of New York. He also enlisted Walter Lippmann, who had taken leave from *The New Republic* to work for Baker in the War Department. More than half of the overwhelmingly male staff found their way into the organization through personal connections to five universities: Harvard, Yale, Princeton, Columbia, and Chicago. Few of the recruits possessed up-to-date knowledge of areas outside western Europe; the academic study of most of the world in the United States was such that expertise in those areas was simply not available. The Inquiry staff strove to make up in enthusiasm and idealism for their lack of knowledge.[62]

The Inquiry played an important role in Wilson's foreign policy much sooner than anyone expected. The last two and a half months of 1917 were a dark hour for the Allies. A two-week period at the end of October and beginning of November witnessed the Italian debacle at Caporetto and the Bolshevik seizure of power in Russia. Elsewhere, signs of war-weariness were manifest. Earlier in the year, mutinies had broken out in French units on the Western Front, and at the end of November a public plea for peace negotiations came from a former British foreign secretary, Lord Lansdowne. At the Inter-Allied War Council meeting in Paris, House supported Lloyd George's successful push for the creation of a supreme war council to provide a unified command on the Western Front.

The colonel also tried to get the Allies to issue a declaration that they were not fighting war for purposes of aggression or indemnity. Wilson backed this move, but his endorsement failed to sway the Allied leaders, and the conference issued no statement of war aims.

Such recalcitrance did not deter Wilson, who was warming up for his own statement. In his State of the Union address in December, he lambasted the rulers of Germany and asked Congress to bring greater force to bear against them by declaring war on Austria-Hungary. At the same time, he insisted that "we do not wish in any way to impair or to rearrange the Austro-Hungarian Empire." In future peacemaking, he eschewed "any such covenants of selfishness and compromise as were entered into at the Congress of Vienna. The thought of the plain people here and everywhere throughout the world, the people who enjoy no privilege and have very simple and unsophisticated standards of right and wrong, is the air governments must henceforth breathe if they would live." Referring specifically to the "peace without victory" address, he affirmed, "We are seeking permanent, not temporary, foundations for the peace of the world and must seek them candidly and fearlessly."[63]

When House returned from Europe, Wilson decided at once, the colonel noted, "to formulate the war aims of the United States. I never knew a man who did things so casually. We did not discuss the matter more than ten or fifteen minutes when he decided he would take the action." House was pleased, although he wished the interallied conference had done it. Wilson asked him to have the Inquiry prepare "a memorandum of the different questions which a peace conference must necessarily take up for solution. I told him I already had this data in my head. He replied that he also had it, but he would like a more complete and definite statement such [as], for instance, a proper solution to the Balkan question."[64] The Inquiry speedily drafted a memorandum that covered the major areas of a peace settlement, and House gave a copy to the president when he was in Washington on December 23.

Wilson does not seem to have consulted that memorandum, in part because other work interfered and in part because he managed to gather his family for Christmas and New Year's at the White House. Jessie and Nell came with their husbands and small children, Stockton Axson journeyed from Texas, where he was teaching at Rice Institute, and Ellen's sister, Madge Axson Elliott, and her husband, Ed Elliott, arrived from California. On Christmas morning, Madge gave Wilson a silk hat, which he set on his head at a jaunty angle and said, "Ha! I see the fine Machiavellian hand of Brooks," meaning the White House valet, who worried about the president's being properly attired. New Year's Eve was not a happy occasion, Madge recalled: "The news from France had been bad, and Woodrow's eyes were grave. He sat a little apart, not sharing our casual talk." He pulled out a volume of Wordsworth's poetry and read aloud "Ad Usque," which he said had been written "when all Europe had fallen to Napoleon and England was threatened." The opening lines are:

> *Another year! Another deadly blow.*
> *Another mighty Empire overthrown.*
> *And we are left, or shall be left, alone,*
> *The last that dare to struggle with the Foe.*[65]

.   .   .

On January 4, House brought with him a revised and expanded memorandum from the Inquiry, and they spent the evening discussing general terms and looking over maps and data. The next day—which House called "a remarkable day"—the men started work at ten-thirty in the morning "and finished remaking the map of the world, as we would have it, at half past twelve o'clock [at night]." They worked from the Inquiry memorandum, on which Wilson made revisions in his handwriting and shorthand notes in the margins. Using his typewriter, he set out a series of fourteen statements, most of them a phrase or single sentence, adapted from the memorandum. When they finished, Wilson asked House to number them in the order he thought they should go. The colonel started with the general terms and ended with the territorial ones. Wilson agreed, "with the exception of the peace association which he thought should come last because it would round out the message properly, and permit him to say some things at the end which were necessary." This numbered sequence would become the salient feature of Wilson's speech—the Fourteen Points.[66]

They talked again the following day, even though it was a Sunday, and Wilson then went into his study alone to write out his speech, first in shorthand and then on his typewriter. The next day, they talked about Russia—a special concern because the Bolsheviks had negotiated an armistice with the Germans and opened peace talks at Brest-Litovsk—as well as Poland and Turkey. A complication arose when news reached them that Lloyd George had just given a speech in London in which he coined the phrase *self-determination* and promised freedom to subject nations under the Austro-Hungarian and Turkish empires. Wilson thought Lloyd George had pre-empted what he wanted to say, but House assured him his speech "would so smother the Lloyd George speech that it would be forgotten and that the President would once more become the spokesman for the Entente, and, indeed, for the liberals of the world." Reassured,

Wilson kept the speech secret from everyone except House and Edith, including the cabinet and Tumulty. The night before he delivered it, he was so keyed up that he talked late into the night and read aloud again from Wordsworth. In the morning, Edith and House persuaded him to play golf before going to the Capitol.[67]

Wilson again wanted to give one of the greatest speeches of his life, and again he succeeded. Appearing in the House chamber just after noon on January 8, he opened by referring to the negotiations between Germany and Russia at Brest-Litovsk, which had just broken off. Those negotiations were significant because they challenged the Allies and America to state their aims in the war. He complimented Lloyd George for having spoken about the Allies' aims and said, "I believe that the people of the United States would wish me to respond, with utter simplicity and frankness." Americans wanted only "that the world be made fit and safe to live in; and particularly that it be made safe for every peace-loving nation which, like our own, wishes to live its own life, determine its own institutions, be assured of justice and fair dealing by the other peoples of the world as against force and selfish aggression."[68]

Now came the Fourteen Points, which took up the rest of the speech, except for the final four paragraphs. Wilson stated each one by number—a Roman numeral in the printed text. The first five were brief and general:

  I.   Open covenants of peace, openly arrived at . . .
  II. Absolute freedom of navigation upon the seas . . .
  III. The removal, so far as possible, of all economic barriers . . .
       among all the nations consenting to the peace . . .
  IV. Adequate guarantees . . . that national armaments will be
       reduced to the lowest point consistent with domestic safety.
  V.   A free, open-minded, and absolutely impartial adjustment
       of all colonial claims . . . [in which] the interests of the pop-
       ulations concerned must have equal weight.

The next nine points treated territorial matters. Point VI, the longest of all, assured Russia of "unhampered and unembarrassed" sovereignty and stated, "The treatment accorded Russia by her sister nations . . . will be the acid test of their good will." Point VII called for the evacuation and restoration of Belgium. Point VIII addressed Alsace-Lorraine as "the wrong done to France . . . which has unsettled the peace of the world for nearly fifty years." Point IX promised Italy borders "along clearly recognizable lines of nationality." Point X offered "[t]he peoples of Austria-Hungary . . . the freest opportunity of autonomous development." Point XI held out independence and security to "the several Balkan states." Point XII promised sovereignty to the Turks and "autonomous development" to other peoples in the Ottoman Empire, along with free navigation through the Turkish straits. Point XIII called for "[a]n independent Poland" with boundaries drawn according to nationality and "a free and secure access to the sea." The final point, XIV, read: "A general association of nations must be formed under specific covenants for the purpose of affording mutual guarantees of political independence and territorial integrity to great and small states alike."[69]

He closed by pledging to fight for those points because they would assure a just and stable peace and remove the main causes of war. He assured the Germans once more of America's goodwill and rejected any notion of forcing them to change their government. "We have spoken now, surely," he declared,

> in terms too concrete to admit of any further doubt or question. An evident principle runs through the whole programme I have outlined. It is the principle of justice to all peoples and nationalities, and their right to live on equal terms of liberty and safety with one another, whether they be strong or weak. Unless this principle be made its foundation no part of the structure of international justice can stand. The people of the United States could stand upon no other principle, and to the vindication of this principle they are ready to devote their lives, their honor, and everything that they possess. The moral climax of this the culminating and final war for human liberty has come, and they are ready to put their strength, their own highest purpose, their own integrity and devotion to the test.[70]

The Fourteen Points speech lived up to House's promise that it would make Wilson the spokesman for "the liberals of the world." He did bring off a remarkable coup with the Fourteen Points. His rhetoric was not as grandiose as Lloyd George's, and he did not use the term *self-determination* nor lay it down as a general principle to be applied at all times and in all places. Later, Wilson would use that term—it was too good to resist—but he would always be circumspect about making excessive promises. Significantly, he continued to spurn the call to break up the Austro-Hungarian and Ottoman empires and urged only "autonomy" for their subject nationalities. This restraint flew in the face of British and French efforts to foment revolts among such peoples as the Slavs of Central Europe and the Arabs and Armenians of Asia Minor, and it reflected an appreciation of how destabilizing the breakup of those empires might be. The Fourteen Points did not express starry-eyed idealism, yet they became a beacon of inspiration, thanks to the president's measured eloquence and moral authority.

What Wilson hoped to accomplish with the Fourteen Points was less than totally clear. One obvious aim was to get the Bolsheviks to stop negotiating with the Germans and possibly woo them back to the Allied side. Whether that overture would succeed remained to be seen. Another goal was to rally critical and war-weary elements in the Allied countries, particularly socialists and other liberals, toward whom Wilson was reaching out informally. Those overtures did seem promising. Most of all, perhaps, Wilson was aiming his words and ideas at the Germans. His repeated assurances of friendship toward them, coupled with condemnation of their government—which he now toned down—extended an invitation to them to make peace on reasonable terms. The Fourteen Points put flesh on the skeleton of peace without victory, and Wilson was once again inviting both friend and foe to accept a liberal, nonpunitive settlement. Such a settlement could end the war without him and millions of others having to tread further down this grim and passion-racked path of waging war.

19

VICTORY

Of the four wartime presidents who preceded him, Woodrow Wilson thought and cared most about Abraham Lincoln. He left no record of saying anything about James Madison, James K. Polk, or William McKinley during the war. Madison was an odd omission because in earlier years he had remarked on how he and Madison were the only "Princeton men" to become president. At the beginning of 1918, he might well have worried about sharing Madison's fate of being a president who failed to lead the nation to victory, but not the "peace without victory" he desired. The Allies' troubles grew when Lenin took Russia out of the war by accepting the humiliating peace terms laid down at Brest-Litovsk. This move freed the Germans to hurl all their might at the Western Front, thereby making the spring of 1918 the Allies' direst hour. The critical question remained, could enough American troops get into combat in time?

Wilson had a special reason for thinking about Lincoln soon after he delivered the Fourteen Points address. Critics on Capitol Hill assailed his administration's conduct of the war and sought to wrest management from the president's hands, much as others in Congress had tried to do half a century earlier. The chairman of the Senate Military Affairs Committee, George E. Chamberlain of Oregon, was a progressive Democrat who usually supported Wilson's policies, but in keeping with his state's political culture, he had a strong maverick streak. At the middle of January 1918, against the backdrop of foul-ups on the railroads and fuel shortages, Chamberlain held hearings that exposed the administration's war managers, particularly Secretary of War Baker, to charges of gross incompetence. Chamberlain introduced a bill to establish a war cabinet of "three distinguished citizens of private ability"—he did not suggest whom—with virtually limitless jurisdiction. This measure would have taken the conduct of the war out of the hands of not only the secretaries of war and the navy but the president himself.[1]

These moves in the Capitol stirred intrigue and anger at the other end of Pennsylvania Avenue. House saw an opportunity to renew his scheme to shove Baker aside, and he bided his time for the right moment to offer his advice. Wilson, however, did not ask House's or anyone else's advice and lashed out in a statement to the press, in which he noted that Chamberlain had not consulted him about the war cabinet proposal. He called the senator's allegations "astonishing and absolutely unjustifiable" and lauded Baker as "one of the ablest public officials I have ever known." In a cabinet meeting the next day, he said the Republicans wanted a war cabinet representing privilege: "They do not think as we do because they wish to act for a class."[2]

Baker thanked Wilson for his support but offered to resign. The president brushed the suggestion aside and encouraged the secretary to fight back. The former mayor had a quick mind and ready tongue, which he had recently displayed when he deftly parried attacks by Chamberlain, Weeks, and others at a Military Affairs Committee hearing earlier in January. Baker bettered that feat when he appeared again before the committee on January 28. He spoke for five hours, dominating the meeting and demolishing charges of mismanagement. He did so well that during the noon recess Senator Ollie James of Kentucky, an administration stalwart, hailed a cab and hurried to the White House. Admitted to the president's office, James forgot himself in his excitement and uttered a sacrilegious expression that Wilson disliked: "Jesus, you ought to see that little Baker. He's eating them up!"[3] Several Republican senators were already having second thoughts about the war cabinet bill, and Baker's performance permanently derailed the drive to hobble his and Wilson's management of the war. But that did not signal any surcease in harsh criticism and scathing attacks from Republicans on and off Capitol Hill, particularly Roosevelt.

The incident in January did prompt Wilson to beef up industrial mobilization. McAdoo was lobbying for Baruch to head the War Industries Board. Secretary of Agriculture Houston and Secretary of Commerce Redfield objected, saying that the financier lacked executive experience; Secretary of the Navy Daniels strongly supported the appointment, while Baker was unsure. Despite his affection for Baruch, Wilson briefly leaned toward appointing Edward R. Stettinius, a partner with J. P. Morgan and Company who was serving in the War Department. Tumulty argued that Stettinius's appointment would send the wrong message to Democrats and labor. Whether that argument was what swayed the president is not clear, but he did decide to go with Baruch, who accepted promptly. The letter of offer spelled out what appeared to be broad authority over production and procurement for both the American armed forces and the Allies, describing the post as "the general eye of all supply departments in the field of industry."[4]

With his genius for self-promotion, Baruch soon made himself one of the most visible and popular figures in the civilian war effort, rivaling Hoover. He publicized himself relentlessly, cultivating not only newspapermen but also movie cameramen. Newsreels now reached big audiences, and the tall, handsome WIB chairman appeared in them regularly, to great applause. Baruch burnished an image of omnicompetence, earning the possibly self-coined nicknames Wizard and Doctor Facts, and he encouraged people to view him as the benevolent czar of American industry. In fact, he possessed neither the authority nor the staff to crack the whip over businesses, and he relied instead mainly on voluntary cooperation. The WIB divided the country into twenty-one production zones, in each of which business leaders were assigned to advisory committees. The approach worked well in promoting conservation of material and standardization of production processes. Baruch got around his lack of authority to set prices through the allocation of priorities. The army's refusal to relinquish control of military procurement complicated matters, but the officer assigned to be the liaison to the WIB, Colonel Hugh S. Johnson, quickly came to see the merits of cooperation and helped get the two bodies to work together.[5]

For all Baruch's public relations success, his agency's substantive record was less than stellar. Small-arms production for the army and the British did improve; even before Baruch took over, factories were turning out more than 5,000 rifles a day. Machine-gun production took hold as well, with Browning automatic rifles and heavy machine guns starting to come out in large numbers early in 1918. Still, most of the doughboys' automatic weapons came from Britain and France until the final weeks of the war. The AEF also had to rely on artillery supplied by the Allies in Europe because of production failures at home. Tanks likewise languished because of Pershing's coolness toward these new combat vehicles and delays in building them. Aircraft production failed dismally, though not for lack of interest and money. Instead, indecision by military commanders and turf wars between the government and private industry stalemated production efforts. Only one American-designed plane even reached the testing stage. Of the nearly 6,400 planes flown by the U.S. Army Air Service, nearly 4,900 were French and the rest mostly British. As with the shipping program, it remains a matter of speculation whether Baruch's leadership of the WIB might have produced better results if the war had lasted longer.

Wilson took so long to name Baruch chairman of the WIB because he had other matters on his mind. He especially wanted to maintain the momentum of his drive for a liberal, nonpunitive peace by keeping up his rhetorical offensive. Germany and Austria-Hungary, against which Congress had now also declared war, replied to the Fourteen Points in polite but unsatisfactory terms, and Wilson believed he needed to answer them with another speech to Congress. The speech that he delivered, on February 11, came to be known as the Four Points Address because in it Wilson laid down four additional elements of his program:

> First, that each part of the final settlement must be based upon the essential justice of that particular case . . . Second, that peoples and provinces are not to be bartered about from sovereignty to sovereignty as if they were mere chattels and pawns in a game . . . Third, every territorial settlement . . . must be made in the interest and for the benefit of the populations concerned. . . . Fourth, that all well defined national aspirations shall be accorded the utmost satisfaction that can be accorded them without introducing new or perpetuating old elements of discord and antagonism.

He condemned the "military and annexationist party in Germany" for standing in the way of achieving a peace based on these principles, and he pledged to throw the whole strength of America into "this war of emancipation."[6]

This was another artful performance. He was enlarging upon the first of the Fourteen Points—"open covenants . . . openly arrived at"—by envisioning an entirely new way of conducting diplomacy. He was likewise enlarging upon the last point—"a general association of nations . . . under specific covenants for the purpose of affording mutual guarantees of political independence and territorial integrity to great and small states alike"—by declaring in this address that such covenants would make the bartering of sovereignty against people's wishes impossible and would be backed by the united force of all peace-loving nations. That was the closest he had come in more than a year to a renewed endorsement of a league of nations empowered to maintain peace. Perhaps most important, he moved toward embracing "self-determination," although he still did not utter the word and he eschewed too ready or too broad an application of the idea, maintaining escape hatches for the sake of peace and stability.

Wilson's recent silence about a league of nations was deliberate. At the time, he was holding the League to Enforce Peace at arm's length—for several reasons. The 1916 election campaign had aggravated partisan animosities between him and the LEP's mostly Republican leaders, particularly Taft. After intervention, the LEP had hitched the league idea to the Allied cause, an approach that did not square with the president's resolve to keep his distance from his new co-belligerents. Wilson also resented distractions from what he privately called this organization's "butters-in" and "woolgatherers." At the beginning of March, he told an LEP activist, "Frankly, I do not feel that it is wise to discuss the formal constitution of a league to enforce peace. The principle is easy to adhere to, but the moment questions of organization are taken up all sorts of jealousies come to the front which ought not to be added to matters of delicacy."[7]

House worried about maintaining outside contacts, and he persuaded Wilson to meet Taft and another LEP leader, President Lowell of Harvard, at the White House on March 28. According to Taft, Wilson began by reiterating his dislike for specific plans for a league: "He said it might embarrass him in dealing with the subject." He believed that nations might come to guarantee others' territorial integrity and hold conferences in case of violations. He acknowledged that this process would be slow, but he reminded his visitors, who were both lawyers, that this was the way the common law had developed. He believed that a series of conferences could ultimately make it possible to create machinery to enforce peace, with precedent and custom dictating the form of such machinery. Wilson also "gave it as his opinion that the Senate of the United States would be unwilling to enter into an agreement by which a majority of other nations could tell the United States when they must go to war."[8]

Taft correctly called this a "minimizing statement." Although it was consistent with Wilson's Burkean proclivity, it sounded odd in view of his well-known taste for bold moves. Lowell challenged Wilson's caution by asking whether at a critical moment such as this more could be accomplished, and he cited the Constitution as an example of going further than anyone except Hamilton had thought possible. Wilson insisted that the circumstances were different, but Lowell persisted in calling for a definite plan. The meeting ended inconclusively, with the parties tacitly agreeing to disagree. The encounter was ironic: in less than a year, Wilson would seize the moment the way Lowell urged him to, and he would push forward the Covenant of the League of Nations against exactly the kind of opposition from the Senate that he was predicting. Despite what he told his visitors, he probably had such a reversal and bold strike in mind in the spring of 1918. Two months earlier, he and House had discussed the possible makeup of the delegation to a peace conference. This discussion, which House called "one of the pleasantest sessions for a long while," revealed that Wilson was thinking ahead and positioning himself for the possibility of big moves.[9]

He was also thinking about how to involve Republicans in the war and the peacemaking. As a student of parliamentary systems, Wilson appreciated the value of coalition governments, and he had the current example of Britain before him. For nearly a year, House had been harping on the need to involve prominent Republicans in the war effort. The appointment of Root to head the mission to Russia had been a gesture in that direction. Wilson made a similar move just a week after his meeting with Taft and Lowell, appointing Taft co-chairman of the newly created National War Labor Board (NWLB). Announced as the "Supreme Court of Labor Relations," this agency brought together representatives of management and unions to formulate and interpret labor policies. Like the Food Administration and WIB, the NWLB relied on patriotic appeals and voluntary cooperation to enforce its rulings. Taft and his co-chairman, the labor lawyer Frank P. Walsh, worked together surprisingly well, and the NWLB instilled a measure of harmony in wartime labor relations. As an experiment in bipartisanship, however, Taft's appointment was less successful. It did not involve the ex-president in high-level policy making, and it did not temper his attacks on the administration during the 1918 election campaign.[10]

Wilson's unwillingness to invite Republicans to join in policy making and management of the war did not extend to those already within the administration. Late in February, House passed along a suggestion to form a "War Board," to consist of the secretaries of war and the navy and the heads of the major support agencies. Wilson liked the idea, and two weeks later he invited Baruch, Harry Garfield, Hoover, and McAdoo, together with Edward Hurley, the head of the Shipping Board, and Vance McCormick, now chairman of the War Trade Board, to come to the White House. This was the first meeting of what came to be called the War Cabinet, which gathered nearly every week for the duration of the war. Although Wilson continued to meet with the full cabinet, this War Cabinet offered him a smaller and more congenial forum for thrashing out supply and transportation problems. In these meetings, Wilson acted much as he did in cabinet meetings: he allowed freewheeling talk, did not dominate discussions, and intimately involved himself in the details of mobilization. He would not have admitted it, but he was probably responding to his Republican critics when he formed his War Cabinet.[11]

After giving the Fourteen Points address, the president had also devoted considerable attention to trying to keep the Bolsheviks from leaving the war. He was likewise working to fend off Allied schemes to intervene in Russia, particularly a Japanese move—which the British and French supported—to occupy the port of Vladivostok and a swath of eastern Siberia. By the time Lenin accepted the final terms of the Treaty of Brest-Litovsk, the Germans were beginning to mount their massive offensive on the Western Front. The British and French pleaded for American troops to be inserted into the gaps in their depleted lines. Lloyd George infuriated Wilson by sending a public message that seemed to imply that the administration was dragging its feet about sending men to Europe. Working through Wiseman, House induced the prime minister to issue another statement, written by Wilson, declaring that the administration was doing everything possible to help.[12]

Wilson temporarily neutralized his domestic critics with a speech he gave on the first anniversary of the American entry into the war. He still hung back from statements except to Congress, but this anniversary, which coincided with the opening of the third Liberty Loan campaign, was an occasion he could not pass up. Speaking to a crowd of 15,000 in Baltimore on April 6, he denounced the Treaty of Brest-Litovsk for showing the German government's true face. The German leaders were trying to erect an empire that had no place for "the principle of free self-determination of nations," and they were seeking "mastery of the World." He insisted that he was ready to discuss a fair and just peace any time, but there was no mistaking where the Germans stood. "There is, therefore, but one response possible from us: Force, Force to the utmost, Force without stint or limit, the righteous and triumphant Force which shall make Right the law of the world and cast every selfish dominion down in the dust."[13] Someone who read rather than heard those words might have thought they came from Roosevelt, not Wilson.

He recognized that he had gone too far and had created the wrong impression—one of militancy and crusading for democracy. Two days later, in off-the-record remarks to a group of reporters from foreign newspapers, he eschewed "the language of braggadocio" and insisted that he had "no desire to march triumphantly into Berlin." Contrary to his apparent embrace of "self-determination," he claimed, "There isn't any one kind of government which we have the right to impose upon any nation. So that I am not fighting for democracy except for the peoples that want democracy."[14] Those remarks lacked the fire of April 6, but they expressed his views far more faithfully.

If Wilson had spoken on the record for public consumption, what he said might have helped quell some of the madness that he saw around him. In April 1918, a young German-born man was lynched in Illinois, and now that the Bolsheviks appeared to be making common cause with the Germans, radicals suffered further repression. Attorney General Gregory and others around him had complained that the Espionage Act did not sufficiently restrict utterances they deemed dangerous. Congress filled the breach by passing a series of amendments, known as the Sedition Act, that broadly prohibited many kinds of expression in speech and print and conferred censorship powers on the postmaster general. Gregory welcomed the measure's new powers, although in a letter to Wilson he questioned the constitutionality of the censorship provisions.[15]

Even before the new law went into effect, fresh prosecutions under the Espionage Act targeted radicals. In April, 113 IWW leaders, including Haywood, went on trial in Chicago. Despite the flimsy and often ludicrous nature of much of the government's case, the six-month-long trial resulted in convictions of all the accused. Other high-profile cases involved members of the Socialist Party. The previous July, a federal court in North Dakota had convicted Kate Richards O'Hare, who had spoken against the war at several public meetings. In May 1918, a Kansas City court convicted Rose Pastor Stokes, who had likewise spoken and written against the war. The most publicized case occurred in September, when the perennial Socialist Party presidential nominee, Eugene Debs, was convicted after a trial in Ohio. In his pre-sentencing statement, Debs avowed, "I say now that while there is a lower class, I am in it; while there is a criminal element I am of it, and while there is a soul in prison, I am not free."[16]

Gregory and Wilson had mixed reactions to these cases. Except for the IWW trial, Gregory left prosecutions to the discretion of federal district attorneys. He later rued that decision because many of those attorneys, as well as the federal district judges, proved prone to hysteria or bowed to local pressures. As earlier with Haywood, the Justice Department leadership tried to avoid making a martyr of Debs—which Debs desperately wished that they would do—and recommended against prosecution, but the U.S. attorney went ahead anyway, probably because he was feeling the heat from patriotic organizations in Ohio. For his part, Wilson did comment to Gregory on "the (very just) conviction of Rose Pastor Stokes" and asked whether the editor of *The Kansas City Star* might not also be indicted. Yet he shared the concern of western progressives that these prosecutions might alienate supporters of his domestic and foreign policies. In October, he told Gregory it might be wise to put enforcement "upon the basis you and I would put it upon if we were handling it ourselves."[17] Those second thoughts came too late to do anything about the repression of civil liberties.

The actions against the socialists look doubly strange in light of some of the president's private thinking. Stockton Axson recalled that in June 1918, Wilson said to him, "Now the world is going to change radically, and I am satisfied that governments will have to do many things which are now left to individuals and corporations. I am satisfied for instance that the government will have to take over all the great natural resources[;] . . . all the water power; all the coal mines; all the oil fields, etc. They will have to be government-owned." Axson remembered him adding, "Now if I should say that outside, people would call me a socialist, but I am not a socialist." He said he was not, but he believed that the next president must take such steps in order to stave off communism. Wilson may have been thinking about himself and a third term. The previous February, he had told House he liked the boldly egalitarian and government-interventionist manifesto just issued by the British Labour Party and talked about forming a new party in America: "He did not believe the Democratic Party could be used as an instrument to go as far as it would be needful to go largely because of the reactionary element in the South."[18] He would soon show that he meant to purge his party of men who were not to his liking.

Before Wilson could move on partisan and progressive fronts, he had to meet other challenges abroad and at home. The greatest danger remained the German onslaught in France. The British kept demanding that AEF units be placed under their command—a scheme called brigading, which Pershing adamantly opposed. Despite repeated face-to-face importuning by the ambassador, Lord Reading, Wilson was reluctant to decide the matter until Baker returned from a tour of the front in Europe. The House-Wiseman axis likewise was active; the Englishman also met with the president and then sailed for home to apprise Lloyd George and Balfour of the situation. When Baker returned, just after the middle of April, he advised Wilson to stick to a tentative agreement to supply the British with 120,000 troops a month from then through July while leaving final decisions to Pershing. After further wrangling involving the French, this deal held, despite efforts by House and Wiseman to undermine Pershing. In the trenches, the last-ditch fortitude of the beleaguered British Tommies and French poilus, combined with German blunders, stalled the great offensive. Units from the First Division of the U.S. Army, which had been brigaded to the French, took part in an attack that captured the town of Cantigny on the Arras sector of the front. Meanwhile, stepped-up shipping across the Atlantic was supplying Pershing with greater numbers of doughboys, and by summer the AEF was ready to operate on its own.[19]

Domestic political infighting mirrored the combat across the ocean. The fiasco of the aircraft production program drew sharp and justified criticism, and Wilson responded by making an unusual choice to investigate the matter: Gutzon Borglum, the sculptor who would later carve the monument at Mount Rushmore. Borglum's qualifications to lead the inquiry lay in his enthusiasm for aviation and his friendship with Roosevelt. The sculptor's haphazard investigation seemed to make problems worse, and in May an angry Senate Military Affairs Committee authorized its own inquiry. To head off this move, Wilson reluctantly asked Charles Evans Hughes to head a new probe. Hughes's report, released just before the end of the war, found evidence of disorganization and incompetence, but not corruption, in the aircraft program. Also in May, McAdoo's call for additional taxes to pay for the war threatened to spark a revolt among Democrats on Capitol Hill. Some of them simply balked at the new taxes, while others feared renewal of the sectional attack that Republicans had leveled against them in 1916—that the improvident South and West were raiding the hard-earned wealth of the Northeast and Midwest. In addition, representatives and senators up for reelection were eager to adjourn and hit the campaign trail rather than stay in Washington for the time-consuming business of passing revenue legislation.[20]

As in the past, Wilson handled trouble at the other end of Pennsylvania Avenue with private and public initiatives. He met several times with agitated Democratic legislators—a chore he did not enjoy—and managed to soothe congressional tempers a bit. At the same time, he spoke out a little more often than he had done recently. Addressing Red Cross volunteers at the Metropolitan Opera House in New York on May 18, he observed, "In my own mind I am convinced that not a hundred years of peace could have knitted this nation together as this single year of war has knitted it together."[21] Five days later, he issued a statement to the press praising foreign-born citizens for their expressions of loyalty and eagerness to serve.

Those statements disclosed a new strain in Wilson's thinking—a belief that this war could become more than a necessary evil and could achieve positive good by uniting the nation and particularly by overcoming ethnic and sectional divisions. They came as a warm-up for a surprise address to a joint session of Congress on May 27. In that speech, Wilson stressed the necessity for new taxes, which would help in planning expenditures, remedy inequities, and prevent speculation and waste. The overriding issue was winning the war, and everything else must go by the boards: "Politics is adjourned. The elections will go to those who think least of it." As earlier, Wilson was striking a note that did not fully reflect his private thinking. "Politics is adjourned" was another of his stirring phrases, which he sometimes made good on, as when he publicly endorsed two Republican senators, William S. Kenyon of Iowa and Knute Nelson of Minnesota, for reelection in the fall. But "politics is adjourned" belied the uses that he was about to make of the politics of loyalty. Back in March, he had written a public letter endorsing Joseph Davies, the Democratic candidate in a special senatorial election in Wisconsin, by praising him for having passed "the acid test" of loyalty. Despite the endorsement, Davies lost to a Republican, Irvine Lenroot, whose election was also a blow to La Follette, who regarded Lenroot as a renegade and had his own candidate in the race.[22]

For a president to endorse his party's candidate over the opposition is standard politics, although Wilson's "acid test" of loyalty did raise the emotional and rhetorical stakes. What was not standard politics was to apply this test to members of his own party. Wilson in fact hesitated at first to intervene in Democratic primaries in 1918. In June, however, he came out in South Carolina's senatorial primary against former governor Coleman Blease, a Bryanite who earlier failed the acid test. A month later, South Carolina Democrats gratified him by rejecting Blease in favor of a pro-administration candidate. His next incursion into primaries in the South came in July in Texas, as a result of some intrigue by Burleson. The postmaster general's brother-in-law was running against Representative James Slayden in the San Antonio district, and Burleson drafted a telegram for the president to send criticizing the congressman. To Burleson's surprise, Wilson sent the telegram, though he soon regretted the move and said that Burleson had gotten him into trouble. Why he went along with the scheme is not clear. Slayden withdrew from the primary, and Burleson's brother-in-law was nominated but later lost to the first Texas Republican to be elected to Congress since Reconstruction. Elsewhere in the state, administration supporters succeeded, without the president's direct intervention, in easily defeating Representative Jeff McLemore, the author of the offending resolution in 1916 against traveling on belligerent merchant ships.[23]

Those successes in Texas prefigured further forays into primaries, though for a while Wilson remained chary about involvement in intraparty contests. Even though he made no secret of his loathing for Senator

John Shields of Tennessee, a Bourbon Democrat who had given the administration trouble on a variety of issues, he did not make a public statement against the senator, who won renomination early in August. He likewise refrained from speaking out against Representative George Huddleston of Alabama, another Bryanite, but then changed his mind and telegraphed a Birmingham newspaper editor: "I think I am justified in saying that Mr. Huddleston's record proved him in every way an opponent of the Administration." The congressman fought back with endorsements from the Democratic leadership in the House and handily prevailed in his primary.[24]

Those disappointments did not deter Wilson from going after what he saw as bigger game: senators James K. Vardaman of Mississippi and Thomas Hardwick of Georgia. No one fit the profile of a failure to pass the "acid test" of loyalty better than Vardaman, who had been one of the six senators to vote against the war resolution. Mississippi's flowing-haired, flamboyant "White Chief" was an agrarian radical and a virulent racist demagogue who embodied everything that respectable whites found so repugnant in southern politics. Wilson needed little prompting to send a public letter that stated, "Senator Vardaman has been conspicuous among the Democrats in the Senate in his opposition to the administration." If Mississippians chose to renominate Vardaman, the president would feel "obliged to accept their action as a condemnation of my administration." Vardaman struck back with his trademark appeal to white supremacy, demanding that black veterans be barred from returning to the South. This time, racism could not trump patriotism, and the senator lost badly in the primary on August 21.[25]

Wilson despised Georgia's Hardwick almost as much as he despised Vardaman. Hardwick was a political cohort of the man who outdid him, and sometimes even Vardaman, as an agrarian race-baiting rabble-rouser and an opponent of Wilson's foreign policy—Tom Watson. Although Hardwick had voted for the war resolution, he stood against most of the administration's policies before and after intervention. Now Georgia's newly enacted "county unit" requirement meant that the winner of a primary or general election had to carry a majority of the state's counties regardless of the popular vote; this rule obviously discriminated against voters in cities, particularly Atlanta, and gave a big boost to Hardwick's and Watson's rural followers. In this race, Wilson publicly called Hardwick a "constant and active opponent of my administration" and urged Georgians to vote for William J. Harris, who had been serving on the FTC. On September 10, Harris swamped Hardwick in the popular vote and carried 114 of Georgia's 152 counties. The news from Georgia was doubly welcome because three weeks earlier Tom Watson had lost in a primary to Representative Carl Vinson, who had denounced the challenger for his opposition to the war.[26]

As a whole, these activities constituted a notable feat of leadership. The failures notwithstanding, Wilson's involvement in the 1918 primaries would become the only successful party purge by a president in American history. Twenty years later, Franklin Roosevelt would try to do the same thing on the same turf and would fail miserably. In 1918, Wilson enjoyed the advantages of acting amid a superheated political atmosphere, thanks to the war, and of being a native southerner, thereby muffling charges of outside interference. He issued his denunciation of lynching just before he intervened in these primaries—which may have been only a coincidence or may have sprung from his confidence that he would not arouse the beast of racism that always lurked in the shadows of southern politics. Vardaman's failure to save himself with a fresh injection of white supremacist demagoguery appeared to prove Wilson right. He was playing for larger stakes than just settling scores with opponents in his own party. This was the final, knockout blow in his fight for supremacy among Democrats. Henceforth, no Democrat would challenge him for mastery, not even in the disheartening days that would befall him and the party in the months to come. Moreover, by purging opponents of his foreign policy, he was taking a giant step toward transforming the South from the most anti-military, anti-interventionist, potentially isolationist section of the country into the most pro-military, interventionist, and at times internationalist section—locating military bases there would help, too.[27]

Domestic politics were not uppermost in the president's mind during the summer of 1918. Above all, there was the fighting in France. In June, the AEF got a bigger taste of what the Germans had been dishing out to the British and the French, first at Chemin des Dames in the Reims-Soissons sector of the front, where two American divisions led the attack, and then on the Aisne-Marne salient. A full corps of doughboys went into action at Château-Thierry, with especially heavy fighting at Belleau Wood, where the U.S. Marines lived up to their reputation as fierce warriors. Their presence was, in the words of a French officer on Marshal Ferdinand Foch's staff, "the magical operation of a transfusion of blood. Life arrived in floods to reanimate the body of a France bled white by the innumerable wounds of four years." As these battles raged through June and July, the AEF took heavy casualties and played its part in foiling the German lunge toward victory on the Western Front. By August, Pershing had enough troops to take over a sector, and he was able to mount independent offensives in September at St.-Mihiel and in the Meuse-Argonne. The Meuse-Argonne offensive struck at the Germans' main supply line and involved the largest number of American troops, and casualties, in any engagement the army ever fought—larger than the Battle of the Bulge in World War II. By November, 2 million American soldiers were in Europe, and Allied war plans called for crossing the Rhine early in 1919, with the bulk of combat in the invasion of Germany to fall on the AEF.[28]

Wilson received regular reports about the fighting, but he almost never discussed any aspect of it with the cabinet or the War Cabinet. One exception occurred in May, when General Leonard Wood—the former army chief of staff, close friend of Roosevelt's, and frequent critic of administration policies—protested his not being sent to France to command a division. Wilson prepared a statement that criticized Wood's erratic temperament and habit of contesting his superiors' decisions, which could be fatal "in the face of the enemy." When he read that statement to the cabinet, most of the members opposed his saying anything about Wood, but they admitted that Pershing did not want Wood and had told Wood so. Wilson met with Wood and listened to his argument for being sent overseas, but he did not budge. Sidelining Wood ignited public criticism, including widespread charges that politics were involved. As earlier with the rejection of Roosevelt's bid to raise a division, personal and political motives may have entered into the decision tangentially, but basically Wilson was sticking to his policy of keeping his hands off military commands and decisions.[29]

Wilson's reluctance to talk about what he considered strictly military matters did not extend to the limited use of American forces for diplomatic purposes. One place posed this problem more than any other— Russia. Entreaties from the Allies to intervene there persisted through the first half of 1918, the most sensitive spot being the Pacific coast of Siberia, where the Japanese remained eager to send in an army. Wilson continued to resist those pleas, but strenuous lobbying for intervention ranged from the Democratic Party to the French—who sent the philosopher Henri Bergson to present their case to the president in person—to American agents in Asia. The most unusual and ultimately influential lobbyist was the Czech leader Tomáš Masaryk, who sought to enlist American support for his people's independence and for his mission to transport Czech soldiers who had been prisoners of war in Russia to Vladivostok so that they might then be shipped to Europe to fight alongside the Allied forces in France. At a meeting on June 19, Wilson and Masaryk discussed intervention strictly as a technical matter, which pleased the president, who was worried about having enough troops to send into Siberia. Ten days later,

Czech soldiers seized control of Vladivostok, giving Wilson the excuse he needed to intervene to support them. In early July, he sent 7,000 American troops, to be matched by 7,000 Japanese troops.³⁰

Meanwhile, small numbers of American troops went into Archangel and Murmansk, in the northern part of European Russia, while British and French troops also operated there and in the Black Sea. These were limited, complicated, messy operations that seemed to defy Wilson's best intentions. "I have been sweating blood over the question of what it is right and feasible *(possible)* to do in Russia," he lamented to House in July. "It goes to pieces like quicksilver under my touch." In August, he issued a statement to the press in which he maintained that these incursions implied no interference with Russian sovereignty and were intended only to help the Russians regain control of their own affairs. In October, he told Wiseman, "My policy regarding Russia is very similar to my Mexican policy. I believe in letting them work out their own salvation, even though they wallow in anarchy for a while." He also told Wiseman that he thought the Russian problems should be held over for the peace conference.³¹

As that reference to a peace conference indicated, post-war settlements occupied a prominent place in Wilson's thinking. Much of that thinking arose on his own initiative, but some of it stemmed from the machinations of House. The relationship between the two men reached a second high point during the summer and fall of 1918—not as warm and intimate as it had been during the months after Ellen Wilson's death, but close and familiar. Yet during the summer, the two men did not see each other for two and a half months. Wilson telephoned occasionally, but he wrote only three letters—something House complained about in his diary. This neglect did not betoken diminished regard for the colonel's counsel. Rather, at the middle of August, Wilson—accompanied by Edith and Dr. Grayson—paid a five-day visit to House in Massachusetts to discuss a number of subjects, especially a league of nations.

Earlier in the summer, House had received the Phillimore Report, prepared for the British government by a commission headed by the jurist Sir Walter Phillimore, which recommended an "alliance" for mutual security and arbitration. House had shared the report with the LEP leaders and had got A. Lawrence Lowell to urge Wilson to set up a comparable commission and work with the British on the project. The president had rebuffed Lowell, and on the first day of the meeting with House he told Wiseman, who was present for part of the discussion, that a public statement by him about a league would only invite attacks. "One section of the Senate, led by Lodge, would cry that he had gone [too] far in committing the United States to a Utopian scheme, and, on the other hand, the

League enthusiasts would attack him for not going far enough," Wiseman paraphrased Wilson saying.[32]

Those discouraging words did not reflect the main line of Wilson's thinking about the league idea. He had revised a paper prepared earlier by David Hunter Miller, the Inquiry's legal expert, on a league covenant. His revisions provided for equality of nations, deleted any mention of an international court, and insisted that all parties guarantee each other's independence and territorial integrity, "subject to the principle of self-determination." Wilson did not show this revised covenant to Wiseman, but he did tell him that a league "must be virile, a reality, not a paper League," and that the one sketched in the Phillimore Report "has no teeth." In their subsequent one-on-one discussion, House could not get Wilson to abandon equality of nations in favor of a great power directorate. They did agree that the league should be part of the peace treaty, and they talked about who should be part of the delegation to the peace conference. Wilson dismissed Roosevelt and Taft out of hand, and he rejected Root as too old and legalistic in his thinking. Lansing would probably have to go, but, as for himself, House wrote in his diary, "I am not certain that I would like to be a delegate, . . . unless, indeed, the President should not go himself."[33]

The discussion of a league of nations on the first day of the visit was their longest and most important one. On the other days, except Sunday, Wilson spent the morning playing golf with Edith and Grayson and saw House in the afternoon. The colonel mentioned the Inquiry and found out Wilson valued its work on details but probably would not use it that much. They also discussed diplomatic appointments, particularly a possible replacement in London for Walter Page, whose health was failing, and considered how best to use McAdoo, who felt overworked and underappreciated. House privately quizzed Grayson about the president's health and his capacity to serve another term. Wilson himself joked to House "that his mind was getting 'leaky,'" and the colonel told Edith that her husband was working too hard and not delegating enough. She answered that "when he delegated to others he found it was not well done."[34]

In Washington, Wilson tried to maintain his accustomed routine, including golf games, car rides, and evenings at the theater, yet the workload continued to pile up, with papers, correspondence, and official functions. Except for brief trips to Mount Vernon for a Fourth of July speech and to Philadelphia for a ship launching, the visit to House gave the president his only chance to escape the heat and humidity of summertime Washington. Some observers then and later said that they detected changes in Wilson's psychology around this time. Brandeis later said he thought Wilson's bold, independent thinking began to slip in August 1918. Whether these were signs of a deeper problem—stemming from his long-dormant arteriosclerosis—is impossible to tell. Still, it was clear that this sixty-one-year-old man, who was burdened with responsibilities that he seemed loath to share, was not at the peak of his powers.[35] That did not bode well for the job of tackling big new challenges.

One task Wilson knew he must tackle was to share his ideas about a postwar world with the public. During the summer of 1918, he did issue press statements on specific subjects, but only in his Fourth of July address at Mount Vernon did he air his larger thinking. There, Wilson declared, "The Past and Present are in deadly grapple." The war's settlement must be final and must rest on four principles, which he enumerated:

> I. The destruction of every arbitrary power anywhere . . . [or] its reduction to virtual impotence. II. The settlement of every question . . . upon the basis of the free acceptance of that settlement by the people immediately concerned . . . III. The consent of all nations to be governed . . . by the same principles of honour and respect that govern individual citizens of all modern states . . . IV. The establishment of an organization of peace which shall make it certain that the combined power of free nations will . . . serve to make peace and justice the more secure.

These "great ends" could not come through high-level intrigues, "with their projects for balances of power and of national opportunity," but must spring from the people, "with their longing hope for justice and social freedom and opportunity."[36] This speech gave a whiff of uplift and again endorsed self-determination, though not by name this time. Otherwise, it marked a retreat into generalities from the Fourteen Points and the four additional points.

Wilson knew he was going to have to do more by way of educating the public. A fine opportunity arose when McAdoo suggested that the president make a trip to the West in September and October as part of a new Liberty Loan campaign. The White House announced a tour to the West Coast and back, but on September 9, Wilson canceled the trip. "I have keenly felt again and again the privation of being confined to the Capital," he explained, "and prevented from having the sort of direct contact with people . . . which would be of so much benefit and stimulation to me."[37] But delicate and critical matters did not allow him to leave. He was not exaggerating: he genuinely regretted having to abort this trip. As he had with his speaking tour on behalf of the preparedness program in 1916, he would have had a chance to explain his aims and plans in homely, compelling language. That was his forte as a leader, and a tour at this time could have done him and his programs a lot of good.

In the fall of 1918, he issued more statements to the press, but he gave just two speeches before the end of the war. One was the appeal to the Senate to pass the woman suffrage amendment, which he linked to the war aim of spreading liberty. The other had come three days earlier, on September 27, when he addressed a Liberty Loan gathering, again at the Metropolitan Opera House in New York. In that speech, Wilson enlarged upon points he had made in July at Mount Vernon. People's free choices of governments and equal rights among strong and weak nations must be backed by an instrument to make peace just and lasting: "a League of Nations formed under Covenants that will be efficacious." He reiterated five of the Fourteen Points—impartial justice, a ban on special interests, a ban on alliances, a ban on economic discrimination, and publicity for all agreements—and he closed by demanding "complete victory," not on Germany's slippery "terms" but a "final triumph of justice and fair dealing."[38]

Wilson made that ringing avowal because he was getting diplomatic feelers that he knew might lead to an end to the war. The Central Powers were crumbling away at the edges. The Turks were retreating from Palestine and Mesopotamia, while Bulgaria was collapsing and about to sue for peace. On September 15, Austria-Hungary had sent out a vaguely worded public appeal for an informal conference to explore "compromise peace." Because the United States was not at war with Turkey or Bulgaria, Wilson declined to take part in negotiations with those countries, and he made a quick, terse reply to the Austro-Hungarian appeal, noting that the United States had stated its terms "repeatedly and with entire candor."[39] House, who was not consulted about that reply, thought Wilson should have waited to answer the Austrians and used the occasion to rally the Allies behind liberal peace terms.

Wilson was conducting diplomacy with an eye toward domestic politics. Lodge, Roosevelt, and other Republicans were thundering about "unconditional surrender" and punitive peace terms. At the beginning of October, he told the financier Thomas Lamont that the whole country was growing "intolerant [and] revengeful," and he worried that the Allied governments, particularly the British, were bent on colonial and commercial aggrandizement. He feared the dangers of a "non-healing peace." Any other kind of peace would leave nations determined to right perceived wrongs: "Providentially I have been placed in a position at this time to have great power for good or ill. I see you smile, Mr. Lamont, when I use the word 'providentially.' I do not mean to indicate that it is necessarily a wise providence that has placed me in this position, but merely that circumstances have done so."⁴⁰

The falling away of Germany's allies foreshadowed a peace move from the main adversary itself. On October 6, the country's newly installed civilian chancellor, Prince Maximilian of Baden, transmitted a public note to Wilson requesting peace negotiations on the basis of the Fourteen Points and principles laid down in the September 27 speech. This note sparked the kind of reaction at home that Wilson feared. Various newspapers lambasted the overture as an insincere ploy by the Germans to evade their complete and richly deserved defeat, and a fierce debate erupted on October 7 in the Senate, where Republicans, particularly Lodge, and some Democrats vied with each other in demands for total, crushing victory. The Senate passed a resolution declaring that there be no armistice until the Germans totally disarmed and agreed to pay reparations and indemnities. Despite those reactions and against House's advice, Wilson sent a prompt reply to the German note in which he asked whether the German government agreed to the Fourteen Points and subsequent principles and would negotiate only "the practical details of their application." He warned that he could not agree to an armistice until German troops evacuated all invaded territory, and he asked whether the chancellor was "speaking merely for the constituted authorities of the Empire who have so far conducted the war."⁴¹

Reaction abroad to the German overture was even fiercer than at home. Before Wilson's reply went out, the three Allied prime ministers—Lloyd George of Britain, Georges Clemenceau of France, and Vittorio Orlando of Italy—met as the Supreme War Council at Versailles and drafted harsh, specific terms for an armistice. In a tense meeting at the White House with Jusserand, the French ambassador, Wilson objected to those terms having been elaborated without the United States being consulted. Jusserand countered by saying that the Allied leaders needed to have "a person who knows the President's thinking and would be in a position to take a real part in debates and decisions." Jusserand himself believed that Wilson was not inclined to delegate power and did not think an armistice was imminent.⁴² Then, on October 12, the Germans responded by agreeing to Wilson's reply and expressing their belief that the Allied governments likewise accepted the Fourteen Points; they also told Wilson that they were speaking for their government and their people.

The German reply set off another explosion in the Senate on October 14, and a Democrat, Henry Ashurst of Arizona, went to the White

House that afternoon. Ushered into the president's office, the senator told Wilson that if he failed to express "the American spirit, you are destroyed." Wilson shot back, "So far as my being destroyed, I am willing if I can serve the country to go into a cellar and read poetry the remainder of my life." He said he was not making armistices, which must be left to the commanders in the field. Ashurst replied that not demanding unconditional surrender would mean that Wilson would have to read poetry in a cellar "to escape the cyclone of the people's wrath." Four days later, Wilson recalled that he told Ashurst, "Senator, it would relieve a great many people of anxiety if they did not start with the assumption that I am a damn fool."[43]

He may have anticipated such senatorial bluster. That morning he closeted himself with House, Lansing, Baker, and Daniels to discuss his answer to the latest German note. He wanted to frame a reply that would not lead to any further dickering, and he and his advisers agreed that if the Germans felt beaten, they would accept any terms. But he did not want vengeful terms. "Neither did we desire to have the Allied armies ravage Germany as Germany has ravaged the countries she has invaded," Wilson wrote after the others had departed. In this note, he left no doubt that Germany must come through the door to peace on bended knee. Only the military commanders could negotiate terms for an armistice, and such terms must maintain Allied military supremacy in the field. Germany's armed forces must also at once stop such "illegal and inhumane practices" as sinking civilian ships, deporting Belgians to work in war industries, and stripping occupied territories of property and people. Finally, any armistice must "come by the action of the German people themselves."[44]

House called October 14 "one of the most stirring days of my life." He was referring not to the discussion of the reply but to what happened that evening. After he had dinner with House and Edith, the president wrote a letter appointing the colonel "my personal representative . . . to take part as such in the conferences of the Supreme War Council and in any other conferences in which it may be serviceable for him to represent me." House exulted at having been given "the broadest powers. It puts me in his place in Europe." They once again arranged a secret code, and as House was leaving, Wilson told him, "I have not given you any instructions because I feel you will know what to do." This lack of instructions suited House fine. "He knows that our mind runs [parallel], and he knows where they diverge. . . . He has his weaknesses, his prejudices and his limitations like other men, but all in all, Woodrow Wilson will probably go down in history as the great figure of his time, and I hope, of all time."[45] The colonel left at once on a rough crossing of the Atlantic. He kept in touch with the president by wireless, but he took no part in the next round of dealings with the Germans.

On October 20, Wilson received a defensive and somewhat ambiguous response from the Germans. After discussing the next move—first with Lansing, Daniels, Baker, and the army chief of staff, then with the cabinet, and finally with the War Cabinet—he told the Germans that he and the Allies could negotiate only with a government that spoke for its own people: any further dealing with "the military masters and the monarchical autocrats" would require "not peace negotiations, but surrender." House thought this move was a blunder. He faulted Wilson for not having consulted with the Allies, risking a stiffened German resistance, and losing a golden opportunity to achieve a liberal, nonpunitive peace. The colonel had sent the journalist Ray Stannard Baker to Europe to sound out opinion among liberals and socialists, and those contacts encouraged his view of the prospects of rallying international opinion behind a nonimperialistic settlement and a league of nations. Despite sharing those hopes and aims, Wilson had still decided to take this harsh line.[46]

Two days after he sent that note to Germany, the president turned to domestic politics. On October 25, he issued a statement to the press in which he appealed to voters to elect Democratic majorities in both houses of Congress. This appeal had been at least a month in the making, and on October 18, he had shown a draft of it to Vance McCormick and Homer Cummings. According to Cummings, McCormick objected to language that might seem bitter, and Wilson deleted it. In the final, published version of the appeal, he observed that the impending elections were occurring at a critical time. He said he was seeking only "undivided support to the government" and was not impugning Republicans' patriotism or support for the war. Rather, he feared the impression that a Republican victory would create abroad: "It is well understood there as well as here that the Republican leaders desire not so much to support the President as to control him." Wilson insisted that he was not appealing for himself or his party: "In ordinary times I would not feel at liberty to make such an appeal to you. But these are not ordinary times." He begged voters to "sustain me with undivided minds" and not embarrass him at home or abroad. "I submit my difficulties and my hopes to you."[47]

No single act of Wilson's as president would spark more criticism at the time and lead to more retrospective repudiation. Of the few people who knew about the appeal in advance, only McCormick expressed doubts about it. Once the appeal went out, members of the cabinet grumbled about not having been consulted, and Franklin Lane commented, "The country thinks that the President lowered himself by his letter." After the Republicans won control of both houses of Congress two weeks later, the second-guessing swelled into a veritable chorus. McCormick, Gregory, and Daniels all later said they thought this was the biggest mistake Wilson made. Burleson and Gregory also claimed afterward that it inflamed partisan passions and that the Democrats would have won if Wilson had just kept his mouth shut.[48]

Why did such an intelligent man do something so universally derided as an act of folly? Part of the explanation lay in pressure to help the party's candidates who were up for reelection. Wilson's aborted speaking tour for the Liberty Loan could have served as a campaign swing and might have obviated the need for this appeal. The night before the appeal went to the press, as Edith later recalled, she tried to talk her husband out of issuing it, but he said it was too late: "I have told them I would do it." Presumably, he was referring to fellow Democrats, and he did feel an obligation to help them, especially after getting such strong support for his intervention in the primaries. It was unlikely, however, that he felt any last-minute qualms. Lane put his finger on the heart of the matter when he noted on November 1, "[H]e likes the idea of personal-party leadership—Cabinet responsibility is still on his mind." The appeal came as a logical outgrowth of Wilson's studies of parliamentary governments and his ideas of making the American system more like them. Those ideas, together with his penchant for taking action, made a move like this well-nigh impossible for him to resist.[49]

Contemporary charges and wise hindsight about the appeal were overworked. Wilson's action made a bad partisan situation marginally worse, but opposition to him already bordered on and sometimes crossed over into hatred. Roosevelt and Lodge defined the far edge of bitterness, but the normally milder-mannered Taft—who had now reconciled with Roosevelt—likewise assailed Wilson and his works with venom. The party's national chairman, Will Hays, displayed superb organizational skills and urged Republicans to stress issues that united rather than divided them. Insurgency and progressivism played almost no part in the campaign, even in Wisconsin, where La Follette and his followers were temporarily eclipsed by war frenzy. Not all Republicans jumped aboard the bandwagon. Senator Norris won reelection in Nebraska despite his vote against the declaration of war, but he was an exception. The run of Republicans gleefully joined in cries for all-out war to the finish and harsh treatment of "traitors."[50]

It would be wrong, however, to read the 1918 election results as a referendum on foreign policy. If the electorate had been as war-mad as many people believed, the opposition party would have scored an even bigger victory. The Republicans picked up thirty-eight seats in the House, to give them a majority of 238 to 193, and twelve seats in the Senate, to give them a two-vote majority. That new Senate majority included La Follette, Norris, and one other war opponent, Asle Gronna of North Dakota, as well as such uneasy supporters of the war as Borah and Hiram Johnson, who had been elected in 1916. The Republicans gained these majorities by further strengthening their traditional dominance in the Northeast and Midwest and by rebounding in the West from a string of losses in the last four elections. Like most midterm contests, this one turned chiefly on domestic and local issues rather than foreign affairs, even though a war was raging.[51]

In the regions where the Republicans picked up seats, they played heavily on sectional feelings. East of the Mississippi, they harped once more on resentment at Democratic tax policies as raids by the South and West. In the West, they exploited feelings of being neglected and discriminated against in different ways. Government price controls had fanned discontent among wheat farmers, who believed they should have been getting better prices and saw favoritism in the higher prices allotted to southern cotton growers. Also in the West, as several observers reported, Republicans and conservatives were exploiting anti-radical hysteria to defeat progressive and pro-labor Democrats. Elsewhere, targeting in senatorial elections by the woman suffrage organizations helped defeat one Democrat and one Republican. More generally, high prices, wartime shortages, and myriad inconveniences worked against the president's party.[52]

Conversely, Democrats could take solace from upset victories in the Northeast, where Al Smith won the governorship in New York and David Walsh won a Senate seat in Massachusetts, defeating Weeks, who was one of the suffragists' targets. Both of those winners were Irish Americans, and their victories offered signs of a rising tide of ethnic voting power in their party, a development that owed nothing to Wilson. Most of the races outside the South were close, and the president's appeal may have contributed to the narrowness of the outcomes, saved some Democrats, and kept the party from suffering a worse defeat. If nothing else, Wilson's action earned him gratitude among his party followers: he had shown that he was willing to stick out his neck for them and suffer the consequences.

Although it was not a foreign policy referendum, this election did have foreign policy consequences. Republican control of the Senate meant that Lodge—perhaps Wilson's worst enemy in that chamber— would become both majority leader and chairman of the Foreign Rela-

tions Committee. In those capacities, particularly as the committee chairman, he would exert great influence over consideration of any peace
treaties or other pacts that might come out of post-war conferences.
Lodge and his friend Roosevelt—who now looked like a sure bet to be the
party's next presidential nominee—started at once to flex their newfound
foreign policy muscles by crowing that the American people had rejected
Wilson's leadership. "[I]n any free country, except the United States,"
Roosevelt told Foreign Secretary Balfour, "the result of the Congressional
elections on November 5th would have meant Mr. Wilson's retirement
from office and return to private life. He demanded a vote of confidence.
The people voted a want of confidence."53 Still, the Republicans would
almost certainly have said the same things if he had not made his appeal.

Roosevelt and Lodge's public utterances amounted to little more than
spiteful after-the-fact campaign talk. What counted for much more were
the actions they soon took. Between the election and the end of 1918, they
made overtures to foreign leaders. Roosevelt wrote to Lloyd George, Balfour, and Clemenceau, telling them to disregard Wilson and impose a
harsh peace on Germany. His party stood, he told Balfour, "for absolute
loyalty to France and England in the peace negotiations . . . to stand with
the allies at the Peace Conference and present an undivided front to the
world." Lodge wrote to Balfour in the same vein and warned against making "an almost hopelessly impossible" scheme for a league of nations part
of a peace treaty. The senator also visited the British and French
embassies to tell the envoys there that their governments should not follow Wilson's lead in dealing with Germany. These were blatant violations
of the principle—albeit more often honored in the breach—that politics
should stop at the water's edge. If the party situation had been reversed, if
the Republicans had been in power, particularly if Roosevelt had been
president, he and Lodge would have damned such actions as treason.
Wisely, the British and French understood that they still had to deal with
Wilson and did not respond to those overtures.54

For his part, Wilson put a public brave face on the outcome of the
election, but in private he was less sanguine. Right afterward, he had an
hour-long meeting with Homer Cummings. "He told me frankly that it
made his difficulties enormously greater," Cummings wrote. It would
encourage opposition at home to his foreign policies, and he felt hurt that
people had rejected his appeal.55 Wilson's parliamentary proclivities
notwithstanding, he gave no thought to stepping aside, even though he
knew his path of leadership was going to get much rougher. Also, it is
worth asking what might have happened in the 1918 elections if the war

had ended a week earlier. Would public relief and joy have tipped the scales just enough to retain a Democratic majority, at least in the Senate?

As matters transpired, the Armistice did not come until six days after voters had gone to the polls. It took that long to arrange in part because of another exchange with the Germans but more because of arguments with the Allies. As soon as House reached Paris, on October 27, he moved into negotiations with Lloyd George, Clemenceau, and the military commanders. A constant flow of cables kept Wilson informed of their discussions, and he did not like what he was hearing about French unwillingness to accept the Fourteen Points and British caviling at freedom of the seas. "It is my solemn duty to authorize you to say that I cannot consent to take part in the negotiation of a peace which does not include freedom of the seas," he cabled back on October 30, "because we are pledged to fight not only to do away with Prussian militarism but with militarism everywhere. Neither could I participate in a settlement which did not include a league of nations because peace would be without any guarantee except universal armament which would be intolerable. I hope I shall not be obliged to make this decision public."[56]

In response to Lloyd George's and Clemenceau's objections, House suggested that the president might have to share those differences with Congress. That seemed to have an impact. "Everything is changing for the better since yesterday," House cabled on October 31, and he asked for a free hand in dealing with these matters.[57] Taking Wilson's silence as assent, he busied himself discussing armistices with Austria-Hungary and Turkey and fending off a last-minute push by Pershing for unconditional surrender. The British continued to balk at freedom of the seas, and Wilson cabled House instructing him to tell them that if they could not accept this principle, the United States would build a bigger navy than theirs. Before House received that cable, he met with Lloyd George, Clemenceau, Orlando, and other Allied representatives for a conference that formally accepted the Fourteen Points as the basis for making peace. But their resolution stated that freedom of the seas was open to unacceptable interpretations and they would reserve to themselves complete freedom on this subject at the peace conference. In short, the British had not budged. Yet Wilson thought this was half a loaf worth having, and he planned to take up freedom of the seas later, when he had a chance to bring other countries around to his point of view. He did not cable his acceptance, and again House took his silence as assent.

For his part, the colonel was ecstatic at what he took to be the Allies' acceptance of the American position. He made light of British dissent on freedom of the seas and said he had straightened out the British on the importance of the League of Nations. This resolution, which would later be known as the Pre-Armistice Agreement, had to remain secret until the Germans heard and accepted the specific provisions that the generals were about to impose on them. November 5 was election day in the United States, which meant that this step toward peace could bring no political profit to the president and his party. The negotiations that led to the Pre-Armistice Agreement exposed major differences between Wilson and House. The colonel favored a softer touch in negotiating, in part because of his personality and in part because he was the one on the scene dealing with the Allied leaders face-to-face. The president was more confrontational. The two men were not polar opposites, however. It was House who originally favored pushing for more liberal peace terms and privately suggested to the British that America might outbuild them in the navy even before Wilson raised that as a possible threat. On his side, Wilson cabled House to stress flexibility and trust over freedom of the seas, and he implicitly assured Wiseman that his country had little to fear about the disposition of Germany's colonies.

Yet their differences went deeper than style and circumstance. House was not only willing to get into the details of the settlement sooner, but he was also steadily becoming more accommodating to the wishes of the Allies. An illustration of how deep those differences were came when House solicited a quick exegesis of the Fourteen Points and their application to the armistice negotiations from Frank Cobb and Walter Lippmann, who were also in Paris. Wilson liked their memorandum but warned that it should be used "as merely illustrative and reserved for [the] peace conference." The difference in interpreting the Fourteen Points may have spawned what many critics would later identify as the source of a fatal flaw in the peace settlement. The British diplomat Harold Nicolson, despite great admiration for House, described that flaw when he argued that the colonel's use of Cobb and Lippmann's memorandum led to a "fundamental misunderstanding"—that is, that the Germans accepted Wilson's principles as stated, whereas the Allies accepted them as filtered through House's interpretation.[58]

The end of the fighting came six days after the Pre-Armistice Agreement. German morale sagged as news of negotiations leaked out. Sailors mutinied when the admirals attempted to mount a final attack in the North Sea. Riots and uprisings broke out in a number of cities, and rumors of Bolshevik-incited revolution were rife. The kaiser abdicated on November 9 and fled to exile in the Netherlands. German envoys met in a railway car in a forest near Compiègne with a delegation headed by Foch and, except for two British liaison officers, composed entirely of French representatives. Foch's terms called for the Germans to disarm completely on land and sea, surrender much of the rolling stock of their railways, and withdraw their forces to the right bank of the Rhine, ceding the Rhineland to immediate Allied occupation. The harshness of those terms and the uncertain governmental situation in Germany delayed final signing until three o'clock in the morning of November 11. Orders went out from the high commands to cease operations at eleven o'clock, thus lending the symbolic litany of the eleventh hour of the eleventh day of the eleventh month to what would afterward be called the Armistice.[59]

Wilson got the news in a series of cables from House that began to arrive around midnight Washington time. He and Edith had not gone to bed, and, as she recalled, final confirmation of the end of the hostilities came at three in the morning. "Many persons have asked me what we did," she later wrote, "and all I can say is, we stood mute—unable to grasp the significance of the words." The president immediately issued a statement to the press: "A supreme moment of history has come. The eyes of the people have been opened and they see. The hand of God is laid upon the nations. He will show them favour, I devoutly believe, only if they rise to the clear heights of His own justice and mercy." Wilson did not often invoke the name of God, and he did so now to strike a note of humility and caution. His words stood in stark contrast to the reactions of other leaders. "Autocracy is dead," House cabled from Paris. "Long live democracy and its immortal leader." In London, Lloyd George told the House of Commons, "I hope we may say that thus, this fateful morning, came to an end all wars"—thereby giving rise to the phrase "war to end all wars," which Wilson did not coin, although it would later be widely and mistakenly attributed to him.[60]

Just after noon, the president went to Capitol Hill to address a joint session of Congress. The speech consisted almost entirely of a solemn, half-hour reading of the terms of the Armistice. Despite the drab presentation, when Wilson read the second clause, which mandated evacuation of Alsace and Lorraine, the tension in the House chamber broke and tumultuous applause broke out. He devoted the remainder of the speech to sober reflections on the meaning of victory, urging patience, forbearance, and generosity.[61] This circumspect tone brought him back to where he had begun when he took the country into the war. Passion and its control remained his greatest concern. The unleashing of passions at home, as in anti-German and anti-radical hysteria, race rioting, and bloodthirsty cries for war to the finish, was the worst price that the country paid for fighting this war—worse even than the 126,000 men who died in combat, of wounds, and from disease, making this the third deadliest war in all of American history, despite its being the second shortest. Failure to try to control those passions would stand as Wilson's greatest failure as a war leader.

The Armistice of November 11 would be his cruelest irony of fate in foreign affairs. It was at once his greatest triumph and his greatest tragedy. Without question, his proclamation of the Fourteen Points and subsequent statements of what he called a "healing peace" shortened the war. A quarter century later, roughly the same coalition of Allies—augmented by a more powerful Russia—would fight under the banner of "unconditional surrender," which itself would be a reaction against alleged flaws in the ending of this war. Then Germany would hold out against that more crushing coalition—in spite of being led by a genocidal Satan—until totally crushed. The Armistice saved hundreds of thousands, perhaps millions, of lives and untold physical destruction. For such salvation, Wilson deserved honor and gratitude, but he would seldom get much of either in generations to come.

His achievement with the Armistice would go largely unsung because it contained the elements of its own destruction. From many standpoints, World War I ended too soon. If it had gone on longer, it would have taken on a different character at home and abroad. Domestically, a longer war would have afforded Wilson opportunities to rein in the excesses of repression and reconnect with the public, strengthen his hand politically, and make his case for a liberal peace. He might not have succeeded, but his leadership would look better for his having tried. In mobilization, he and his War Cabinet would have had more time to try different techniques of management, which might have led to more efficient procurement and production. Militarily, if World War I had lasted even a few months longer, it would have begun to resemble World War II. The British and American armies were finally perfecting tank warfare, and the future supreme commander in Europe and president of the United States, Dwight Eisenhower, was still stateside, training with those tanks. The British were also developing aircraft with longer flying ranges and the capacity to carry heavier payloads of explosives, thus opening possibilities for providing tactical support of ground forces and bombing targets behind the battle lines. Above all, the steady weakening of German forces and the ever-mounting number of doughboys meant that the coming months would have featured a war of movement instead of further deadlock in the trenches. Much of the sweep and dash that would make World War II a more satisfying and more fondly remembered war were in the offing at the end of 1918.

The worst consequences of this foreshortened war lay in diplomacy. Some interpreters would criticize Wilson and his supporters for making a soft peace that allowed Germany to rise again and menace the world a final time. Others would criticize him for abetting a hard peace that left Germans embittered and bent on revenge. Those criticisms would miss the point that Wilson was in the worst possible position to go far in either of those directions. The only chances for a peace that might have reconciled the Germans had come when he offered "peace without victory" at the beginning of 1917 and when he proclaimed the Fourteen Points a year later—both of which they spurned in the nastiest possible way. The only chance for a peace that might have tamed the Germans would have come if the war had gone on longer and resulted in a crushing defeat for them. That outcome would have conferred the added benefit of putting the president in the position he most desired. America would have been in the war longer and demonstrably contributed much more to a bigger victory. The Allies would have been utterly dependent on America and Wilson would have been able to dictate the terms of the settlement. Either of those alternatives might have led to lasting peace. Instead, Wilson was going to have to try to make bricks without straw.

20

COVENANT

On December 28, 1918, Woodrow Wilson celebrated his sixty-second birthday in London, where he and Edith were staying at Buckingham Palace as guests of the king and queen. King George came to the guest suite to congratulate the president and give him a present, and later Wilson went to the American embassy to greet well-wishers. Sentimentally, the next day was an even more momentous day for him. After an overnight train trip, Wilson visited Carlisle, where he was—as he told the pastor of the church where his grandfather had preached—"making a pilgrimage of the heart." He went to see the Woodrow family's house and walked through the room where his mother was born. Then he attended Sunday services at the church, where, at the invitation of the congregation, he spoke briefly at the end of the service. He said the memories of his mother that came to him now moved him, and her "quiet character and sense of duty" always remained with him as he strove to do right in the world.[1]

It was appropriate for Wilson to mix personal feelings with public purpose. He had come to England, after stopping first in France, for a largely ceremonial tour before the opening of the peace conference. He was deeply suspicious about the intentions of the British and French leaders, but his wildly enthusiastic reception by huge crowds in Paris and London had heartened him. Moreover, he had just received sketches along lines similar to his own ideas for a league of nations from Lord Robert Cecil, a minister in the British cabinet, and Jan Christiaan Smuts, a South African delegate to the peace conference. These circumstances, together with Wilson's own taste for bold action, were about to impel him on the biggest venture of his life, and it would look as if he might bring off the feat of leading the world down new paths of international justice and peace.

Some people had tried to talk the president out of going to Europe and playing a leading role in shaping the post-war settlement. Three days after the Armistice, House cabled from Paris that unnamed Americans "whose opinions are of value" thought he should not come because "it would involve a loss of dignity and your commanding position." Clemenceau and Lloyd George suggested Wilson might appear at part of the conference but should hold himself aloof from the negotiating sessions. He exploded in response, "I infer that the French and English leaders desire to exclude me from the Conference for fear I might there lead the weaker nations against them. . . . I believe that no one would wish me to sit by and try to steer the conference from the outside." House did not directly try to talk Wilson out of going to Paris, but he confided to his diary, "I wish in my soul the President had appointed me as Chairman of the Peace Delegation with McAdoo and Hoover as my associates." He believed that this dream team of negotiators could achieve great and speedy results. House later admitted that he liked to be the principal negotiator, and regarding the presidency, "there have been times when I would have like[d] the office itself instead of being an adviser to him who held it."[2] Those were troubling thoughts for him or any adviser to harbor.

Not everyone in Washington wanted Wilson to go to Paris either, and after Lansing met privately with him the day after the Armistice, he wrote in a memorandum, "I told him frankly that I thought the plan to attend was unwise and would be a mistake . . . [and] that he could practically dictate the terms of peace if he held aloof." Wilson did not take kindly to that advice. "His face assumed that harsh, obstinate expression which indicates resentment at unacceptable advice. He said nothing, but looked volumes." Wilson did seek other opinions about whether he should go to Paris. He asked two Democratic senators, Key Pittman of Nevada and Peter Gerry of Rhode Island, to seek their colleagues' views about the matter. Pittman reported that the senators were about equally divided. Some feared domestic affairs would be neglected—a point Lansing had also raised—and some thought he could dominate the negotiations "as a superman residing afar off in a citadel of power beyond that of all nations." Others argued that he alone could bring about a just settlement and new ways to maintain peace.[3]

Wilson agreed with those who wanted him to go, and he itched to be in the thick of things. Soon afterward, he laughingly told a visiting Swiss politician, "I'm going over to Europe because the Allied governments don't want me to. . . . I want to tell Lloyd George certain things I can't write to him. I'll tell him: Are you going to grant freedom of the seas? If not, are you prepared to enter into a race with us to see who will have the

larger navy, you or we?" Wilson also wanted to extend the Monroe Doctrine to a mutual security pact, as he had tried to do earlier with the Pan-
American pact: "Not a big-brother affair, but a real partnership." He
admitted, "The solutions cannot be ideal and I know that everybody will
be disgusted with me."[4] On November 18, the White House issued a
statement to the press that the president would leave for France early in
December, immediately after the opening of the next session of Congress,
but that it was unlikely he would stay for the whole conference.

Curiously, this decision raised little public reaction, even from such
critics as Roosevelt and Lodge. Wilson's next decision, however, stirred up
a furious outcry that would leave a near-unanimous legacy of later condemnation. That decision involved the four men whom he picked as the
other members of the delegation to the peace conference. Several objectives needed to be served in choosing this delegation. Foremost came
diplomacy, which put a premium on negotiating skill and experience and
considerations of prestige. Those criteria made two choices well-nigh
inescapable. Wilson presumed from the outset that House would accompany him, and by virtue of his position, Lansing must go, too. Since military matters would loom large in the settlement, an expert in that field
ought to be included. Wilson offered that slot to Baker, but the secretary
of war countered that since McAdoo was about to resign as secretary of
the Treasury, it would not be wise to have two cabinet members out of
the country for an extended period. On Baker's recommendation, the
appointment went instead to General Tasker H. Bliss, who had been serving as the American representative to the Allied Supreme War Council.
Of these choices, only House caused any criticism. Critics regularly
accused the colonel of being nothing more than Wilson's crony, and
Republicans had made his closeness to the president a minor campaign
issue in 1916.

The real controversy arose because representatives from two categories were not chosen: senators and prominent Republicans. The Constitution's requirement that two thirds of the Senate consent to a treaty
made it seem wise, if not imperative, to include members of that body.
The last time the United States had negotiated a peace treaty, with Spain
in 1898, President McKinley had named three senators among the
negotiators—two from the Republican majority and one from the Democratic minority—and those senators had reputedly facilitated approval of
the treaty. Twenty years later, however, the president faced an apparently
insuperable obstacle in the Senate: Henry Cabot Lodge. Because Lodge
was soon to become chairman of the Foreign Relations Committee and
majority leader, to invite any senators without including him would have

been both bad politics and an insult to that prerogative-conscious chamber. Perhaps if Wilson had felt his gambler's instinct more keenly, he might have bet that Lodge would decline an invitation in order to preserve his freedom to criticize and oppose what might come out of the peace conference. Unfortunately, he found the senior Democrat and current chairman of the Foreign Relations Committee, Gilbert Hitchcock of Nebraska, only slightly less obnoxious than Lodge. In view of so much bad blood and such unappetizing choices, Wilson understandably, though not wisely, gave little thought to choosing senators.[5]

Failure to include a prominent Republican was less understandable or excusable. The previous summer, Wilson and House had bandied about several possibilities, particularly Root, and the colonel and Tumulty continued to push for him to be included. Other possibilities were Taft and Hughes, but their attacks during the recent campaign had left hard feelings. When a cabinet member asked if Hughes might be appointed, Wilson answered, "No—there is no room big enough for Hughes & me to stay in."[6] Finally, at Lansing's suggestion, Wilson chose Henry White to be the delegation's token Republican. White was a retired diplomat who was close to Roosevelt, Lodge, and Root, and he evidently expected to act as a liaison with those men, because he accepted the appointment only after clearing it with Roosevelt and Lodge.

The complete lineup of delegates—House, Lansing, Bliss, and White—drew heated criticism when it was announced on November 29. "Our delegation with the exception of Mr. White are merely mouthpieces of the President," Lodge told Lord Bryce, "and if Mr. White should differ he will be overridden." By not including Republicans, Lodge believed the delegation included no persons of stature who might challenge the president's views. Wilson explained this omission to a newspaper editor by noting that except for Taft—"I have lost all confidence in [Taft's] character"—all the leading Republicans who had been suggested "are already committed to do everything possible to prevent the Peace Conference from acting upon the peace terms which they have already agreed to." He told another correspondent that the delegates should represent "the country as a whole," not any particular group or interest.[7]

Those were rationalizations. Wilson knew he would need Republican support for a peace settlement, but he was balking once more at practicing the kind of partnership with the opposition party that he should have understood from his study of coalition governments under parliamentary systems. The real reason for his failure to reach out to the opposition was that he wanted a free hand in the peace negotiations. Having powerful but unsympathetic men at his elbow might restrict the freedom of movement he craved in order to be ready to strike out in bold and unconventional directions. Wilson left leading Republicans off the delegation not because they were Republicans but because they might get in his way.

The exclusion of prominent Republicans from the delegation to the peace conference would later become almost as widely condemned as had been his appeal for a Democratic Congress. Wilson would come to be charged with a failure to practice bipartisanship—in sharp contrast to the next two Democratic presidents, who would serve during and after World War II. As with the election appeal, such charges would be overworked. Both the term *bipartisanship* and its practice would arise twenty years later as another "lesson" learned from Wilson's supposed mistakes, and the later successes of bipartisanship would depend more on the willingness of the opposition party to cede primacy in foreign policy than on presidential outreach. At the end of 1918, Republicans had repeatedly shown that they had no intention of following Wilson's lead in peacemaking. Subsequent debates over the peace treaty and membership in the League of Nations would show what a wide gulf separated the two parties; bridging that gulf would have required much more constructive thinking and goodwill than all but a few leading Republicans were willing to show. Wilson can and should be faulted for not reaching out to the opposition party, but taking Root or Hughes with him to Paris would probably not have brought enough of their fellow partisans on board to guarantee success. This sin of omission—like his sin of commission with the appeal for a Democratic Congress—made an already bad situation a bit worse.[8]

Wilson's decision to go to Paris required assembling a staff to accompany him and wrapping up affairs at home as much as possible. The staff question did not receive a great deal of attention from him and caused further tensions with Lansing. In Paris, House already had a group of advisers, headed by the Foreign Service officer Joseph C. Grew. Wilson evidently planned to have House use this group as the nucleus of the delegation staff. Lansing, meanwhile, appointed Grew secretary—chief of staff—and chose two other Foreign Service officers as his deputies, all without consulting the president. This angered Wilson, although he acquiesced, on advice from House. Also on the colonel's advice, the president appointed twenty-three members of the Inquiry to the staff, while the State Department, the Navy Department, and various boards also got representation. Most of these appointees accompanied the presidential party and the delegates to Europe aboard the U.S.S. *George Washington*. Such casualness about assembling the staff and the simmering feud between the president and the secretary of state did not augur well for the negotiations.[9]

A stab by Wilson at wrapping up affairs at home did not augur well either. The war's sudden, unexpected end raised a host of problems. Doughboys' families were clamoring for their sons to be brought home— a task that proved easier than expected, thanks to reversing the flow of men on the "bridge of ships." On the home front, business groups and Republicans in general demanded the immediate suspension of wartime regulations and controls and the return of railroads and telegraph lines to private ownership. Progressive groups and organized labor saw those measures as great gains and wanted them incorporated into a peacetime program of "reconstruction." Within the administration, two cabinet members, McAdoo and Gregory, announced their intentions to resign as soon as the war was over. Mac had been smarting under what he regarded as his father-in-law's lack of appreciation of his considerable contributions to the victorious war effort, and he was laying plans to run for president in 1920. He insisted on leaving immediately after the Armistice, and at the beginning of December, Wilson appointed Carter Glass of Virginia, the chairman of the House Banking Committee and an author of the Federal Reserve Act, to be secretary of the Treasury. Two months later, he picked Walker D. Hines for McAdoo's other post, director general of the railroads. Gregory stayed on until March 1919, to be succeeded by former congressman A. Mitchell Palmer of Pennsylvania.[10]

Wilson mainly tried to sidestep domestic questions. Between the Armistice and his departure for Europe, he devoted far more time to international matters. When he delivered the State of the Union address on December 2, he sent mixed signals about where he stood on major domestic concerns. He opened with a celebration of the victory Americans had just won, praising both the soldiers who had fought and the civilians who had worked on the home front. He singled out the contribution of women and asked again for passage of the suffrage amendment. He said he had seen no plan for industrial "reconstruction" that would suit "our spirited businessmen and self-reliant labourers," although he thought the government should help returning servicemen find work and should mount a public works program to create jobs. He said he had "no answer ready" about the railroads and invited Congress to study the problem. He closed by talking about the upcoming peace conference, promising to stay in touch with Congress and affairs at home and asking, "May I not hope . . . [that] I may have the encouragement and the added strength of your united support?"[11]

When Wilson asked for united support from Congress, he was indulging in wishful thinking, and he knew it. Josephus Daniels noted that Republicans said they would "give him an ice bath," and they sat in sullen silence except when he mentioned the troops. The next day, Senator Phi-lander C. Knox of Pennsylvania, who had been Taft's secretary of state, introduced a resolution to restrict the peace settlement to the reasons for which the United States had gone to war and postpone for separate con-sideration any discussion of a league of nations. Knox's resolution set off a debate in which Wilson's longtime Democratic nemesis, James Reed of Missouri, denounced the league idea as "the old Holy Alliance all over again"—a reference to Czar Alexander's scheme to suppress independence and republics a hundred years earlier—and William Borah seconded the charge. Wilson was well aware of the hornet's nest of opposition on Capi-tol Hill; it was one reason why, despite much criticism, he refused to dis-cuss specific plans for a league of nations.[12]

The evening after he spoke to Congress, he and Edith boarded an overnight train to Hoboken, New Jersey, where they boarded the *George Washington* for the ten-day voyage across the Atlantic. Those days at sea offered him a wonderful interlude and a chance to rest up for the peace conference. The weather was mild, and the ocean was calm, and he and Edith took walks on the decks and played shuffleboard. They mingled with the sailors and went to movies with them and the enlisted personnel in the theater belowdecks, not the upper-deck theater reserved for first-class passengers. The musical accompaniment to the silent films included loud, raucous singing, in which the president joined with gusto. The Wilsons took their meals in their stateroom suite, usually with two or three guests. The food was excellent, but Wilson was chagrined to learn that a leading New York chef was cooking only for them and select other dignitaries. "His disbelief in special privilege was aroused," Edith recalled, "and on our second trip to the Conference this culinary artist was left behind."[13]

For all the relaxation and joviality, Wilson never forgot that this was a working trip with a major struggle awaiting him at its end. He spent sev-eral hours each day going over papers. These included regular telegraphic reports from House about the machinations of the Allied leaders, which disturbed him. Roosevelt had responded to the State of the Union address by claiming that Britain had won the war and should dictate the peace without interference from the United States, particularly over what he sneeringly referred to as "freedom of the seas." On the first day at sea, Wilson shot back with off-the-record remarks to reporters who were accompanying him on the voyage. "I don't believe our boys who fought over there will be inclined to feel just that way about it," he declared. He also observed, "Militarism is equally dangerous when applied to sea forces as to land forces," and if Britain refused to reduce naval armaments, "the United States will show her how to build a navy."[14]

Despite the mutual hard feelings between him and the Republicans, Wilson tried to convey some reassurances to them. He took Henry White aside to explain that his views on a league of nations were different from Taft's. "I was much relieved to find that the President's idea as to the League is a rather general one," White noted. He was pleased that it would be restricted to reporting on possible breaches of the peace and might impose a boycott, but there would be no authority, in the event of war, "to take further joint action of a punitive character." Another time, Wilson unburdened himself, as he would do often in the coming months, to Grayson. Reports from House of demands made at a meeting of the three Allied premiers, Clemenceau, Lloyd George, and Orlando, made him suspect that they sought "a peace of loot or spoliation," and if they did, he said, "I will withdraw personally and with my commissioners return home." He also thought problems "under this principle of self-determination" might prove thorny, and he intended to make the League of Nations part of the peace treaty. He did not plan to stay at the conference for long because he would have to return home at the close of Congress in March, but he believed he might have to go back to Paris later.[15]

The most extended and best-recorded statement of the president's thinking came on December 10, when ten members of the Inquiry gathered in his stateroom office. They and others had been complaining of being kept in the dark about plans for the conference, and one of them, William C. Bullitt, a brash and self-confident young man, approached the president before one of the movies and asked him to explain to them his approach to the conference and plans for a league of nations. Seated on chairs in a semicircle around the president's desk, his visitors listened to him talk for nearly an hour. He was in good form, covering a range of problems and questions, beginning with the League of Nations. "The President does not believe that any hard and fast constitution of the 'League to Enforce Peace,' can be established at the present time," Bullitt noted in his diary. Wilson again envisioned a minimal organization, although he insisted on its upholding independence and territorial integrity, and he believed that it would develop to meet changing conditions, just as the Monroe Doctrine had done; he also insisted it would not be a great power directorate or a balance of power. He impressed his listeners with the spirit in which he approached the conference and his beliefs that America was the only disinterested nation and the Allied leaders did not represent their people. The same words stuck in the mind of nearly everyone who wrote an account of the meeting: they were, as one of them, Isaiah Bowman, recorded, "Tell me what's right and I'll fight for it; give me a guaranteed position."[16]

Those words—"Tell me what's right and I'll fight for it"—would come back to haunt Wilson. In the coming months and in later years, a profound disillusionment and sense of betrayal would cause many people to hurl those words back in his face. This may have been another instance of Wilson's eloquence appearing to promise too much. In fact, he voiced grave doubts about how much he could accomplish. The next day, Bullitt said that Raymond Fosdick, Wilson's friend and protégé from Princeton, told him, "The President replied that it frightened him to think how much the common people of the world expect of him." George Creel, who was also part of the mission, later remembered that as they walked on the deck one evening, Wilson told him, "[Y]ou know, and I know, that these ancient wrongs, these present unhappinesses, are not to be remedied in a day or with the wave of a hand. What I seem to see—with all my heart I hope I am wrong—is a tragedy of disappointment."[17]

The urgency of expectations struck Wilson from the moment he was in Europe. The *George Washington* landed at Brest, on France's Atlantic coast, on December 13. The vessel's most distinguished passenger regarded that as a good omen since he thought of thirteen as his lucky number—the number of letters in his name. As soon as he set foot on French soil, an explosion of celebrations began. French and American soldiers lined the streets of Brest as the Wilsons rode in an open car under triumphal arches of flowers. Throngs packed the sidewalks and leaned out windows, many of them in the folk costumes of Brittany, shouting, *"Vive l'Amérique!"* and *"Vive Vilson!"* His arrival in Paris the following day was spectacular. After ceremonial greetings at the railroad station by President Raymond Poincaré, Premier Clemenceau, and the French cabinet, a mounted contingent of breast-armored Gardes républicaines escorted the two presidents, who rode together in an open horse-drawn carriage down the Champs Élysées to la place de la Concorde and on to the Murat Palace, where the Wilsons would be living. Hordes of cheering people packed the sidewalks and hung out every window. "The French think that with almost a magic touch he will bring about the day of political and industrial justice," Raymond Fosdick noted. "Will he? Can he?"[18]

For Edith Wilson, the cheers of the crowds in Brest were enthralling, and the next seven months would mark the high point of her years as First Lady. She luxuriated in the splendor of their accommodations at Murat Palace, and, best of all, she could shed her wartime austerity wardrobe. In the coming months, she would revel in the rounds of official entertaining, and she would seize the opportunity that the extended time in Paris offered her to order new dresses, coats, hats, and shoes, particularly from her favorite, the leading fashion house of Worth. Still, she recognized that ceremony, entertaining, and fashion were not the reasons why she and her husband were in Paris. "Woodrow is busy here every moment," she wrote to her family, "& feels he must put through the big thing he came to do first."[19]

On the first day in Paris, he talked with House for two hours, going over plans for the peace conference. They agreed to make the League the first order of business; House thought this move might keep Wilson out of the negotiations and allow the president to go home after a month. On his second day in Paris, Wilson had his first talk with Clemenceau. The seventy-seven-year-old premier had lived as a political exile in the United States during the Civil War and spoke English, and House had coached him before he visited Wilson at Murat Palace. Their encounter went smoothly, and they had another pleasant meeting the next day, when Wilson called on Clemenceau, who told House afterward that meeting Wilson had made him change his mind and want him to be at the peace conference. For his part, Wilson did not let public or private charm turn his head. "I have not been deceived by the acclaim which I have received," he told a journalist friend. "It is based upon the trust that I will stand fast to the principles and purpose which I have avowed."[20]

Wilson had hoped that the peace conference could begin as soon as he arrived. With leaders from all over the world and representatives of racial and ethnic groups and subject peoples descending on Paris, however, a host of logistic problems had arisen. Wilson also suspected that the Allied leaders were in no hurry to sit down with him at the bargaining table, and there were entreaties that he visit the other main Allied capitals. As a result, he and Edith spent the last five days of December in England and the first week of January 1919 going to and from Rome, with stops on the return trip in Genoa, Milan, and Turin. Before he embarked on those journeys, Wilson received a steady stream of visitors at Murat Palace, laid a wreath on the tomb of the Marquis de Lafayette, visited an American military hospital and cemetery, spent Christmas with General Pershing and the troops, and gave a few brief talks. He and Edith also took a few automobile rides but were not able to play golf until the first day of the new year.

Wilson decided to use this interlude before the conference to pave the way for the kind of peace he wanted. He pursued this strategy both openly and behind the scenes. While in Paris, he issued a statement to the press on December 18 denying reports that he had endorsed the program of the League to Enforce Peace but also declaring, "I am, as every one knows, not only in favor of a League of Nations, but believe the formation of such a League absolutely indispensable to the maintenance of peace." In a private talk, the British ambassador, Lord Derby, found his ideas for a league "of the haziest description . . . apparently to be a sort of general parliament of Ambassadors." Equality of nations was the one point on which Derby found him "very definite." Wilson also "rather horrified" him by stating that the League should take control of Germany's colonies. House reassured Derby a bit by saying that he "need pay no attention to what the President said . . . about each of the Nations having the same representation."[21]

On December 26, the Wilsons crossed the English Channel and arrived at midafternoon in London, where the king and queen met them at Charing Cross Station. The two heads of state then rode in an open carriage to Buckingham Palace, over a route packed with spectators on sidewalks, in windows, and on rooftops. In the afternoon, the president and Grayson called on the Queen Mother, and in the evening there was an informal dinner at the palace, which Grayson described as "entirely without stiffness," as the king and Wilson swapped stories. The next day, he met Lloyd George for the first time when the prime minister and Balfour came to Buckingham Palace for a three-hour discussion. The two men seemed to hit it off well and discussed a variety of subjects. According to Lloyd George, Wilson gave the impression that the League was all he really cared much about, and the prime minister was inclined to let him make it the first order of business and thereby take pressure off such matters as freedom of the seas and colonial claims. Lloyd George also thought Wilson would not stay long at the peace conference. After that meeting, they went to lunch at 10 Downing Street, where Wilson met other British leaders for the first time, including Winston Churchill. He brought off the rare feat of leaving Churchill speechless by teasing him about his recent aspersions on the role of the U.S. Navy in winning the war.[22]

Wilson gave more speeches in England and talked more confidentially with his hosts than he had done in France. On his birthday, he responded to a resolution of support presented by British Methodist and Baptist leaders: "I think one would go crazy if he did not believe in Providence. It would be a maze without a clue. Unless there were some supreme guidance we would despair of the results of human counsel." The same day, in the City of London, he maintained that what was essential was a guarantee of the terms of peace, a permanent concert of power for their maintenance, and he pledged to remain as steadfast in pursuing that goal as were his Scottish forbears in pursuing theirs: "The stern Covenanter tradition that is behind me sends many an echo down the years." In the evening, before he boarded the train for Carlisle, he warned a top British intelligence officer against thinking of Americans "as cousins, still less as brothers; we are neither. Neither must you think of us as Anglo-Saxons, for that term can no longer be rightly applied to the peoples of the United States." About Bolshevism, he professed no fear of it in America and said Russians should be free to settle their own affairs as long as they did not menace anyone else. The following day, he kept the Sabbath by giving no speeches except for the impromptu remarks at his grandfather's church and a brief talk in Manchester, but he privately reiterated to the editor of *The Manchester Guardian* that the most important thing about the peace settlement was its ability to evolve and change through "a machinery of adjustment."[23]

The Wilsons spent the last day of 1918 traveling back to France. They greeted the new year by playing their first round of golf in Europe, on the links at St.-Cloud. At lunch with House, who had not gone across the Channel with them, Wilson read from Smuts's draft of a league of nations and then went to the Hôtel de Crillon, the headquarters of the American delegation, to brief the other delegates on his trip and Smuts's draft, which he studied again the next day as his train traveled toward Rome. On the Wilsons' arrival on the morning of January 3, the king and queen and the Italian cabinet met the Wilsons at the station, and a splendidly uniformed troop of cavalry escorted the open carriages that transported the party to the Quirinal Palace. Banners festooned buildings along the route, and sidewalks and windows were again packed with people. That evening, there was another state dinner hosted by royalty, and afterward the president visited Capitoline Hill. Between ceremonial events, Wilson spoke to the Italian parliament, using the occasion to declare that the peacemakers must "organize the friendship of the world, to see to it that all the moral forces that make for right and justice are united and given a vital organization . . . [to be] substituted for the balance of power."[24]

The Wilsons' second day in Rome included a visit fraught with significance and delicacy. At midafternoon, the president, First Lady, and Dr. Grayson called on Pope Benedict XV at the Vatican. Wilson knew well the extent of anti-Catholic sentiment in the United States, but he was nevertheless determined to be the first president to visit the pope. Swiss Guards lined the corridors as the party walked to the papal throne room. Pope Benedict led the president alone into his study before inviting Grayson and a military aide to join them. They then returned to the throne room, where the pope blessed everyone with the sign of the cross.

"It is for you, your family and your dear ones," Grayson recorded him saying. Later in the day, Wilson attended a reception given at St. Paul's
Within the Walls, the American Episcopal church serving the Protestant
community of Rome. In the evening, before the presidential train left
Rome, Wilson talked with Leonida Bissolati, a liberal Italian leader who
had recently resigned from the cabinet in protest over the demands for the
port city of Fiume and the Dalmatian coast. Bissolati urged Wilson to
resist those demands, as well as "the excessive pretensions of French and
English nationalism."[25]

The next day was a Sunday, but Wilson bent his Sabbatarian scruples
to make public appearances and speeches and attend a performance at
Milan's famed La Scala, where a cast of 400 performed one act of
Giuseppe Verdi's *Aïda*. On Monday, after a stop for a speech in Turin, a
telegram from Tumulty informed Wilson that Roosevelt had died. The
president sent a telegram of condolence to Mrs. Roosevelt and rewrote
the proclamation prepared by the State Department, adding, "As President he awoke the Nation to the dangers of private control which lurked
in our financial and industrial systems. It was by thus arresting the attention and stimulating the purpose of the country that he opened the way
for subsequent necessary and beneficent reforms." The ex-president
stayed on the president's mind; the following evening, Wilson read aloud
to Edith and her secretary an essay about Roosevelt.[26]

Wilson would have been less than human if he had not wondered to
himself how the death of this man, his greatest adversary, might affect his
own political fortunes and his programs. By nearly everyone's reckoning,
Roosevelt was going to be the Republican candidate for president in 1920.
The war had wrought an astounding resurrection of his standing with the
public and the Republican Party, and old foes as well as erstwhile followers were jumping aboard the bandwagon for his nomination. He had been
acting like a president-in-waiting, and some foreign leaders wanted to
treat him as such. Roosevelt had meant to bolster other powers' intentions
to impose a harsh victors' peace on Germany and give a lower priority to a
league of nations. Now, Roosevelt's death relieved Wilson of some of that
pressure, although Lodge would guide much of his own conduct in the
coming months according to what he believed his fallen friend would have
done. On the other hand, the possibility of Roosevelt's becoming the next
president had guaranteed greater Republican receptivity to a league or
some kind of alliance and certainly to a greater American role in world
politics. The death of this adversary was not necessarily a gain for Wilson.[27]

· · ·

Uppermost in his mind during the trip to Italy was the League of Nations. On the night he learned of Roosevelt's death, he told some American reporters off the record that he had a definite program in mind and was going to rely on Smuts's draft in order to give the British a sense of authorship. As soon as he got back to Paris, he typed another "Covenant" on twenty-two sheets of paper, adding handwritten emendations. He gave this document to House in the afternoon on January 8, and the two men discussed it at Murat Palace that evening. This document, which later became known as the First Paris Draft, contained thirteen articles and six supplementary provisions. It sketched out the organization's structure, calling for a "Body of Delegates" to include all members and an "Executive Council" made up of the "Great Powers," with other countries rotating on and off. It called for arms reduction, laid down procedures to settle disputes, and stipulated that any member not following those procedures would be subject to an economic and financial boycott; the council could also recommend use of military or naval force by the members of the League. The draft likewise provided for blockades of offending nations, asserted the League's concern in all threats of war, and outlined procedures to admit new members. The supplementary provisions dealt with former German colonies and Austro-Hungarian and Turkish territories, over some of which the League might assume "mandatory" authority.[28]

For Wilson, the essence of the League in this draft lay in Article III: "The Contracting Powers unite in guaranteeing to each other political independence and territorial integrity." He added that territorial readjustments "pursuant to the principle of self-determination" could be effected by a three-fourths vote of the members. Finally, he affirmed, "The Contracting Powers accept without reservation the principle that the peace of the world is superior in importance to every question of political jurisdiction or boundary."[29] Some of the ideas and language in this draft drew upon Smuts's draft, but its overall tone and phrasing were distinctly Wilson's, as was its central tenet, Article III. This commitment to independence and territorial integrity and the pledge to boycott or even resort to military force to punish violators showed that Wilson intended his league of nations to be essentially a political, not a judicial or consultative, organization. That was where he parted company with Root, Taft, and the League to Enforce Peace, who wanted a peace-enforcing organization to follow set rules and conduct judicial proceedings. By contrast, Wilson wanted the experience and deliberations of the members to guide the organization in responding to changing circumstances.

He sent copies of his Paris draft to the other members of the American delegation and discussed it with them on January 10. Lansing privately scoffed that Wilson "rejoices in catchy phrases" and deplored the president's vain, curt "manner of refuting valid objections to the document which he has drawn. House says that he must have been feeling unwell." Soon afterward, General Bliss suggested softening the implied commitment in the preamble to maintaining existing regimes and using the word *covenant* throughout the document, and he recommended that the guarantee of territorial integrity in Article III should read "as against external aggression." He also cautioned against identifying the League too closely with the settlement of the war, so as to avoid "the appearance of being a new form of the old Holy Alliance." Contradicting Lansing's aspersion on Wilson's presumed vanity, the president gladly accepted nearly all of Bliss's suggestions and produced a new version on January 18, which became known as the Second Paris Draft. This would become his outline in upcoming negotiations, but it could be only an outline. In an interview with the president of Switzerland, he affirmed that "only the essential lines could be immediately traced and that the rest will be the fruit of long labor and repeated experiences."[30] The scholar in politics had not forgotten what he had learned from Edmund Burke.

Much as Wilson might have liked to devote all his attention to the League of Nations project, he knew he must deal with the pressing problems of the peace settlement. In fact, he was eager for negotiations to begin and for those problems to be addressed. To Edith and her secretary, he vented his "contempt for [Allied leaders] and the things for which they stood. . . . [Their] people are eager for peace and are resenting bitterly this delay." Not surprisingly, Wilson did not enjoy his first discussions with the assembled Allied leaders. Although the peace conference had not yet convened, he attended meetings of the Supreme War Council on January 12 and 13 in the main conference room of the Quai d'Orsay, the headquarters of the French Foreign Ministry. Grayson wrote that Wilson found the atmosphere "exotic," both because the attendees included Indians in turbans and the Arab leader Emir Faisal "in picturesque costume" and because liveried servants came in to serve tea. "The President remarked to me afterward that it was with a little difficulty that he restrained himself from voicing his surprise, that with the great affairs and future of the world under discussion, this conference should be interrupted by what he considered a tea party."[31]

The content of the discussions at these meetings did not please him either. The first meeting degenerated into a haggle over renewal of the Armistice agreement and arguments about which countries should be represented at the conference and how many representatives they should have. The second one touched briefly on one matter of substance—reparations—but then reverted to representation, particularly regarding the British dominions and India, with numbers finally agreed upon. The council finally set January 18 for the opening of the conference. Wilson proposed that governments should submit recommendations to the major powers on the League, reparations, new nations, boundary changes, and colonies. The European leaders wanted smaller powers at a preliminary meeting, and the president agreed. Grayson noted that Bernard Baruch, who was present, told him afterward that Wilson was "a complete master of the whole performance and that he entirely dominated the meeting."[32]

Those preliminary meetings, which came to be called the Council of Ten, took place during three days before the opening of the conference; they gathered the delegations of ten nations and would continue to meet as the executive committee of the conference until March. These first meetings dealt with several matters of procedure. One was the official language. Pride and diplomatic tradition impelled the French to insist upon their language, while Wilson championed English as the most widely spoken tongue; as a compromise, both languages were adopted. Another matter was the agenda. The French wanted to add a number of specific items to the subjects Wilson had proposed, and the matter was left in abeyance. The most controversial matter involved publicity. Wilson had just appointed the journalist Ray Stannard Baker as press officer to the delegation, and a small army of American reporters had descended on Paris, hungry for news. The president wanted to admit reporters to the council's general meetings because delicate and weighty questions would be handled beforehand. Lloyd George objected to "a Peace settled by public clamour."[33] Finally, Wilson acquiesced to a restrictive policy that would cause him trouble in the future.

The official opening, on January 18 in the Hall of the Clock at the Quai d'Orsay, was an almost strictly ceremonial affair. President Poincaré's brief welcoming remarks closed with references to "punishment of the guilty" and guarantees against a "return of the spirit by which they were tempted." President Wilson then nominated Premier Clemenceau to be permanent chairman of the conference. This move honored the custom of having the leader of the host country preside, but Wilson said he also intended it as a tribute to France and to Clemenceau's leadership. After his unanimous election, the premier demanded "reparation for acts committed—material reparation, if I may say so, which is due to all of us—but the higher and nobler reparation" of security against renewed aggression. The only items of business at this session were receipt of the memoranda requested on pressing questions and the announcement that the question of the League of Nations would be the first item taken up at the next meeting of the full conference.[34]

The opening of the peace conference made an already busy schedule for Wilson even more demanding. He and Edith had gotten in one more game of golf, but his car rides now consisted mostly of trips between Murat Palace and the Quai d'Orsay for the Council of Ten. On the diplomatic front, he was receiving reports of unofficial talks with representatives of the Bolshevik government in Russia, and he was trying to overcome obstacles to getting food shipments to Europe. From home, he was hearing protests against restrictions on publicity surrounding the conference—to which he replied to Tumulty that publicity for his talks with Allied leaders "would invariably break up the whole thing." The pace of activity naturally worried Grayson, who on the day of the conference's opening had to treat the president for a bad cold. The next day, Sunday, Grayson recorded, "I persuaded him to stay in bed during the morning and take a ride in the country in the afternoon: We passed a very quiet day and the rest did the President a great deal of good."[35]

Wilson needed that rest. In the evening he spent three hours meeting at Murat Palace with the authors of the latest British plans for a league, Lord Robert Cecil and Jan Smuts. Neither man had met Wilson except in passing, and Cecil quickly formed an unfavorable impression of him, although he seems to have masked his dislike, for the meeting went well. The three of them went over Wilson's latest draft, which the Englishman described as "almost entirely Smuts and Phillimore combined, with practically no new ideas in it." Wilson told them that he wanted an informal Anglo-French-American group to draft a plan to submit to the conference. He hoped that they could finish the job in two weeks, a time frame that Cecil sniffed at as "fantastic," although he did not say so. Wilson confided in them how difficult he found it to be to work with the French and Italians. "He is evidently disillusioned about those two nations," Cecil noted.[36]

Wilson had to attend meetings of the Council of Ten, sometimes twice daily, and sessions of the Supreme War Council. Several times he put in fifteen-hour workdays. This was probably the most intensely busy time in his life. Council of Ten sessions particularly tried his patience as between thirty and forty people crowded into the dark-paneled, stuffy, overheated office of the French Foreign Minister at the Quai d'Orsay. He did get the council to propose to the full conference that the plans drafted by Cecil, Smuts, and him be considered by a League of Nations Commission consisting of fourteen members. There would be two members from each of the great powers and one apiece from other countries, with Wilson as chairman and Cecil as vice chairman. The Council of Ten approved the creation of the League Commission and charged it, together with others, with examining war guilt and penalties, reparations, international labor conditions, and international control of transportation. At that session, Wilson declared that the conference was under "a solemn obligation to make permanent arrangements that justice shall be rendered and peace maintained. This is the central object of our meeting. Settlements may be temporary, but the actions of the nations in the interests of peace and justice must be permanent. We can set up permanent processes . . . [to be] the eye of the nations to keep watch upon the common interest."[37]

During its second week of meetings, the Council of Ten dealt mostly with Germany's former colonies in Africa and the Pacific. Wilson argued strongly for making those territories mandates of the League of Nations, and he told Grayson that the British and their dominions and the Japanese "wanted to 'divide the swag,'" and then have the League of Nations created to perpetuate their title." A member of the Inquiry staff, Charles Seymour, who was a professor at Yale, wrote to his family after attending one of these meetings, "Everything reminded me of a faculty committee meeting, rather than a gathering of statesmen." Seymour commented on the way Clemenceau, who wore gray gloves all the time, looked "expressionless, even rather bored," whereas Wilson seemed "absolutely at home," spoke easily, and liked "to make a humorous allusion and Balfour, Lloyd George and Clemenceau are evidently glad of some excuse to smile."[38]

The League Commission did not meet until February 3, the beginning of the third week of the conference. Having already packed the commission's membership, Wilson now sought to stack the agenda with a draft of a covenant that embodied his, Cecil's, and Smuts's views. These machinations brought House—who had been ill from an attack of gallstones and did not attend the Council of Ten meetings—back into the thick of things. House met with Cecil on January 30 and the following day with Cecil, Smuts, and Wilson at his suite at the Hôtel de Crillon, where they decided to have legal experts from their staffs, C. J. B. Hurst from Britain and David Hunter Miller from the United States, prepare a more formal draft. When Wilson read what the two lawyers produced over the weekend, he did not like it. "He said the document had 'no warmth or color in it,'" but House advised accepting this draft anyway. To add punch to the language, Wilson made handwritten changes. Miller then stayed up all night on February 2 to incorporate them into what would be called the Third Paris Draft.[39]

This new draft almost unhorsed the scheme for a prearranged plan for

a league. Wilson met with Cecil and House the next afternoon, just before
the League Commission convened for the first time. "The meeting bade
fair to be stormy for the first seven or eight minutes," House noted, but it
calmed down when Wilson agreed to accept the Hurst-Miller draft. Cecil
felt particularly miffed because the president accepted this draft "as a
skeleton, reserving to himself the right to clothe it in flesh and blood."
Cecil disliked Wilson's autocratic manner, as shown, he noted, in his
"abruptly tearing up a draft which we had jointly agreed to have prepared
as our working text. He seemed mildly surprised that I should resent it."
Cecil may have thought Wilson was being rigid and egotistical, but the
president's wish to change the Third Paris Draft sprang from his deep
feeling for language and concern with the wording of the League
Covenant. To Herbert Hoover, he said, "We must have a great state
instrument which will be like the Declaration of Independence and the
Constitution of the United States, and mark a great step forward in international relations." In his eyes, these drafts fell far short of that exalted
standard. Ironically, his presumed authorship of this new document would
later lay him open to a reputed gibe by Senator Lodge: "As an English
production it does not rank high. It might get by at Princeton, but certainly not at Harvard."[40]

In the first meetings of the League Commission, Wilson, Cecil, and
the French member, Léon Bourgeois, did most of the talking. "The Japs
never speak," House noted. "General Smuts speaks so seldomly that it is
practically not at all." House believed he and Cecil kept the discussion on
course by doing "nearly all the difficult work between meetings." Those
meetings took place at night, from eight-thirty until around midnight—
after a full day of work for Wilson. A matter of contention arose early
because the Japanese wanted a statement of racial equality in the
Covenant. House advised the Japanese members to draft a mildly worded
resolution, which Wilson watered down further. Cecil added to the contention by moving to drop from the guarantee of member states' independence and territorial integrity the words "and preserve against
external aggression." Wilson countered with a compromise amendment
saying that the League Council would advise on how to meet this obligation. For his part, Cecil was afraid of trouble "with the Dominions, who
do not appreciate the idea of having to fight for the integrity of Bohemia,
or some such place"—an example that eerily forecast Neville Chamberlain's words about the same place (Czechoslovakia) during the Munich crisis of 1938: "a faraway country of which we know little." Cecil also sniffed
that the "smaller powers, who seemed singularly perverse," backed the

president: "It is annoying to find all these foreigners quite keen for the guarantee."[41]

A clash came with the French when Bourgeois made an impassioned plea for the League to have its own army to enforce its decisions. Responding at length, Wilson tried to bridge the gap between national sovereignty and international commitment. "We must make a distinction between what is possible and what is not," he maintained. The U.S. Constitution would not allow international control, and an international army in peacetime would seem to be trading "international militarism for national militarism." America could only promise to maintain its military forces and come to the aid of countries threatened by aggression, "but you must trust us. We must all depend on our mutual good faith."[42]

On February 13, Wilson was attending a meeting of the Council of Ten when Baron Nobuaki Makino of Japan introduced a revised resolution promising equal treatment of citizens of all members of the League and disavowing all discrimination, "either in law or in fact, on account of their race or nationality." Makino conceded that this was a difficult and complicated problem, but in the war "different races have fought together on the battlefield, in the trenches, on the high seas, . . . and they have saved the lives of their fellow men irrespective of racial differences." Cecil, who was presiding in Wilson's absence, responded that this matter "raised extremely serious problems within the British Empire" and said discussion of it was best postponed.[43] House was pleased with this outcome because the British had borne the onus of opposing the racial equality declaration, but his relief was premature. With that controversy temporarily averted, the work of the League Commission was complete.

At the meeting of the Council of Ten on February 13, Wilson secured approval to present the League Commission's product, which would be called the Draft Covenant, to the full conference the next day. Getting this approval was no small feat, inasmuch as the meetings of this council and the Supreme War Council during the preceding two weeks had been contentious. When the Council of Ten discussed the borders of Czechoslovakia, Edvard Beneš, that country's foreign minister, appealed for retaining the frontier of the Austro-Hungarian Empire with Germany, even though he conceded that doing so would incorporate a large number of Germans—who would later provide the pretext for the Munich crisis. The council also heard Emir Faisal—speaking through his English interpreter, the celebrated Lawrence of Arabia—present the aspirations of the Arab peoples. When Wilson asked him about possible League mandates in the Near East, Faisal answered that the Arabs had fought for their unity and independence and would feel betrayed with anything less. But the council also heard an American, Howard S. Bliss, president of the Syrian Protestant College (later American University) in Beirut, maintain that the Arabs lacked "balance" and "political fairness" and needed to grow gradually toward self-determination.44

The discussions in the Council of Ten were mild compared with the arguments in the Supreme War Council over the Armistice terms and disarmament of Germany. Wilson found Clemenceau shifty and unreliable and thought House had sized him up wrong. "The French people are the hardest I ever tried to do business with," he told Grayson, and attacks on him in French newspapers for alleged softness toward the Germans led him to plan to have Ray Stannard Baker plant a story with the American reporters in Paris to the effect that these attacks might require the conference to move to a neutral capital. House objected, but Wilson insisted on sending the story out. "To my mind it was a stupid blunder," House noted in one of the first signs at Paris of dissension between him and the president.45 Clearly, the volume of work and the emotional tension were taking a toll on Wilson.

The president's weariness showed on February 14, when he presented the Draft Covenant to the full conference in the Hall of the Clock of the Quai d'Orsay. Cecil may have found Wilson's two-week timetable "fantastic," but it had taken only two weeks longer than that to produce this document. He read it article by article, occasionally stopping to offer a few words of explanation. William Allen White found the content of the recitation "as gray and drab and soggy as his reading. Slowly, as he read, the hearers realized that they were getting some new declaration of independence, of the world's national independence, . . . that a super-nation had been created and that the President's words were of tremendous import; he droned on like one reading a list at a receiver's sale."46

Still, there was no disguising the great step forward in world politics this document proposed to take. Despite Wilson's dissatisfaction with its language, the substance of the Draft Covenant gave him what he most desired. The guarantee of independence and territorial integrity was there in Article X, almost exactly as he had written it, while Article XI asserted the right of the League of Nations to concern itself about "war or threat of war" anywhere in the world. Articles XII through XV established procedures for mediation and arbitration and called for a "Permanent Court of International Justice." Article XVI laid down the League's authority to impose economic boycotts and recommend the use of force against offending nations. Disarmament, mandates over former enemy's colonies and territories, concern for labor conditions, an assembly in which each nation would have an equal vote, an executive council with the five great powers as permanent members and other countries rotating on and off—all these features of Wilson's earlier programs were in the Draft Covenant. Most important of all for him, this would be an essentially political body with the potential for enforcing peace and order in strong and far-reaching ways. It was a remarkable achievement, and the lion's share of the credit belonged to Wilson.[47]

Despite his fatigue, he could not keep gleams of enthusiasm and momentousness from flickering through his explanation of the Draft Covenant to the conference. "Armed force is in the background in this program," he asserted, "but it *is* in the background, and if the moral force of the world will not suffice, the physical force shall. But that is the last resort, because this is intended as a constitution of peace, not as a league of war." As a constitution, "it is not a straitjacket, but a vehicle of life. A living thing is born, and we must see to it that the clothes we put upon it do not hamper it—a vehicle of power, but a vehicle of power in which power may be varied at the discretion of those who exercise it and in accordance with the changing circumstances of the time."[48]

The Draft Covenant of the League of Nations seemed to vindicate handsomely Wilson's decision to go in person to the peace conference and dominate his country's delegation. If he had not been there or if he had needed to answer to Elihu Root or some senator at his side, he almost certainly could not have moved as swiftly and boldly as he did. Yet that freedom of maneuver came at a price. Aside from House, no American had known what the president was about to propose, which meant there had been no chance to prepare any groundwork for support. Democratic senators, sympathetic journalists, and the delegation's press officer, Ray Stannard Baker, had urged him to share some of his plans for the League with them, but he had rebuffed them.

The Wilsons left Paris on the evening of February 14 to return to the United States, and the president cabled Tumulty to request members of the House Foreign Affairs and Senate Foreign Relations committees not to discuss the Draft Covenant until he had had a chance to explain it to them in detail.[49] Wilson was about to open a second front in the struggle for a peace settlement—a home front, where he would have to fight for approval of his vision and program in his own land among his own people.

21

PEACEMAKING ABROAD AND AT HOME

When Woodrow Wilson sailed for the United States on February 15, 1919, he had been abroad for more than two months. After an eight-day crossing, he would spend just ten days at home before leaving again for Europe. That second trip to Paris would last four months, with the president not returning to America until July 8. These twin sojourns would make him not just the first president to leave the country while in office but the only one to stay away anywhere near so long. Later, improved communications and swifter transportation, especially air travel, would permit high-level diplomacy to transpire by telephone exchanges, frequent visits of foreign leaders to Washington, short jaunts abroad by presidents, and, occasionally, intense, concentrated "summit" meetings. The Paris Peace Conference of 1919 would become the last prolonged international conclave of its kind—harking back to such earlier gatherings as the Congress of Vienna in 1814–15—and it would bring forth the last set of sweeping, general peace treaties.

Back in the United States, the president had to be present to sign bills passed in the last days of the third session of the Sixty-fifth Congress. This voyage of the *George Washington* from Europe was as rough as the earlier voyage had been smooth, but Wilson was not affected. He spent most of his first days at sea resting and sleeping in his cabin. Business from the peace conference intruded from time to time: a call by Churchill for large-scale intervention in Russia brought a sharp rebuke from the president; he also sent a message of sympathy to Clemenceau, who had just survived an assassination attempt—which brought high-level negotiations to a halt for a while. As on the previous voyage, he and Edith got out on deck for walks, watched movies with the ship's crew, and dined with a few fellow passengers, including Assistant Secretary of the Navy Franklin Roosevelt and his wife, Eleanor.

Wilson felt both eager and apprehensive about what awaited him at home. Reactions in the press to the Draft Covenant were largely positive, although they varied according to party affiliation and region. Democratic and southern newspapers usually applauded Wilson's accomplishment, while Republican journals, particularly those in the Midwest and West, more often took a critical stance. Taft came out enthusiastically in support, and he swung the League to Enforce Peace behind Wilson's program. Attacks had also started. "If the Saviour of mankind should revisit the earth and declare for a League of Nations, I would be opposed to it," William Borah had stated even before the unveiling of the Draft Covenant. When he and several other senators read the document, they immediately denounced it for spelling destruction of the Monroe Doctrine and drowning America in the cauldron of European and Asian power politics. Henry Cabot Lodge and other prominent Republicans honored the president's request to suspend debate until he had had a chance to explain the document, though their silence did not reassure Wilson. On his last night at sea, he told Dr. Grayson, "The failure of the United States to back [the League] would break the heart of the world."[1]

Troubles dogged the visit home from the outset. Because of a longshoreman's strike in New York, the *George Washington* docked in Boston in the evening of February 23, but only after almost running aground in heavy fog. Boston's being Lodge's hometown meant that a low-key visit, without any appearance of campaigning, was in order. Local officials foiled that plan when, against Wilson's wishes, they staged an elaborate welcome the next day, which included a big parade and a rally attended by an enthusiastic crowd of 7,000 or 8,000 people. Speaking extemporaneously, the president avoided any reference to the Draft Covenant, but he did mention his reception in Europe and the national aspirations of the Poles, Czechs, Yugoslavs, and Armenians. Later, in brief remarks at the railroad station in Providence, Rhode Island, he maintained that the people of Europe trusted America, "and if America disappoints them the heart of the world will be broken."[2] In New York, he came out onto the platform only to wave. The railroads cleared the tracks for the presidential train, which reached Washington early in the morning on February 25.

Wilson held meetings in the afternoon with the cabinet and in the evening with Democratic leaders in the Senate. They discussed how to deal with the Republicans on Capitol Hill, who were reportedly holding up appropriations bills in order to force the president to call an early session of the next Congress—which they would control. The Republicans' aim was to debate the peace proceedings, but Wilson responded that he would not call Congress into session until the conference was over; the White House also announced that the president would not make a speech to Congress about the conference and the League. Instead, he met with members of Congress in different venues. On February 26, he did something no president had ever done before: he had the members of the Foreign Affairs and Foreign Relations committees to dinner at the White House and afterward discussed the Draft Covenant with them for more than two hours. The question of the president appearing before a congressional committee raised constitutional issues involving the separation of powers; having the committees come to the White House rather than the president going formally to them evidently sidestepped the constitutional problem.

All but three members of the committees went to the White House that evening. According to some of them, the dinner was awkward and uncomfortable. One Republican senator and announced League opponent, Frank Brandegee of Connecticut, complained that no alcohol was served, and he gossiped that Edith Wilson's fingernails were dirty. After dinner, the president and the thirty-four senators and representatives adjourned to the East Room, where Wilson answered questions. No stenographer was present, and a minor war of words about the discussion broke out in the press as soon as the meeting ended. Pro-League papers such as *The New York Times* and *The World* stressed Wilson's "good humor" and quoted several senators, including Brandegee, who said they appreciated his openness and knowledge in answering their questions. The conservative New York *Sun*, however, quoted anonymous senators, probably Brandegee and Lodge, who expressed "great astonishment" at the president's "lack of information" about how the Draft Covenant would affect the Monroe Doctrine and rights to withdraw from the League and refuse mandates. Those anonymous sources also claimed that Wilson brushed aside a question about self-rule for Ireland as strictly an internal affair for Britain, which Democratic senators denied.[3]

Privately, Lodge scorned Wilson's ignorance about the League and told Henry White, "We learned nothing." But a Republican congressman from Massachusetts, John Jacob Rogers, praised the president to White for being informative and good-humored: "I never saw Mr. Wilson appear so human or so attractive as he did that night." The following afternoon, Wilson spent two hours at the Capitol talking with members of Congress and reporters in the President's Room off the Senate chamber. He stood most of the time, and some of his visitors thought he looked tired. He discussed domestic concerns, such as the woman suffrage amendment and appropriations, as well as the peace conference. He also met with several

Democratic senators and told them that the Monroe Doctrine was not impaired under the League and that national sovereignty would not be curtailed.4

Wilson gave three speeches during these ten days at home. Tumulty had persuaded him to speak in Washington at a banquet given by the Democratic National Committee on February 28 and to a conference of governors and mayors on March 3. He also got Wilson to agree to a joint appearance with Taft at the Metropolitan Opera House in New York on the evening of March 4, just before he sailed back to Europe. The day Wilson gave the first of those speeches, Lodge attacked the Draft Covenant in the Senate, particularly charging that the League would destroy the Monroe Doctrine and take away control of immigration. Lodge wanted a harsh peace and an alliance of Europeans only: "We must not lose by an improvident attempt to reach eternal peace all that we have won by war and sacrifice." The following day, the Republicans' other foreign policy expert in the Senate besides Lodge, Philander Knox, delivered an even harsher blast, dismissing the proposed League as "merely an offensive and defensive alliance, . . . [which] absolutely requires that every future war will be a potential world war, and that we shall be an active participant in every such war."5

Those attacks did not bode well for cooperation with the Senate, and they made it hard for Wilson to curb his combative streak. Speaking at the Democratic dinner the evening after Lodge had spoken, he teasingly appeared to rule out a third term by noting that in two years he would "begin again to be a historian instead of an active public man" and would be able to say what he really thought about his opponents. He did allude to "all the blind and little provincial people," but he worried that "the world placed in America a tragical hope— . . . it is so great, so far-reaching, it runs out to such depths that we cannot in the nature of things satisfy it." Still, the League of Nations would set up processes to banish war and must be part of the peace treaty. In his meetings and speeches, he did make some conciliatory moves. Congressman Rogers told White that he got the clear impression at the White House meeting that the president believed the Draft Covenant could be changed. Wilson also promised others that he would bring up the Monroe Doctrine before the League Commission.6

His opponents in the Senate now moved to thwart those efforts at conciliation and persuasion, which the League to Enforce Peace was augmenting with a massive publicity campaign. On Sunday, March 2, Brandegee, Knox, and Lodge met to write a statement protesting the Draft Covenant. The next day they gathered signatures from Republican colleagues. Just before midnight on March 3, Lodge took the Senate floor to read a resolution stating that the League "in the form now proposed by the peace conference" was unacceptable to the Senate and that the conference should promptly conclude a treaty with Germany. When a Democratic senator objected to the introduction of this resolution, Lodge replied, "I merely wish to add by way of explanation the following." He then read the names of thirty-seven Republican senators and senators-elect who had signed the document, adding that four others whom he had been unable to contact would probably also sign it. Newspapers used a 200-year-old term to dub this statement a round-robin. Lodge said he knew the resolution could not come to a vote and that by reading the list of signers, "our purpose, however, had been served."[7]

Lodge's action wiped out all notions of swift or easy approval of American membership in the League of Nations. Its authors deliberately kept it an all-Republican affair, but one Democrat, James Reed of Missouri, had also damned the Draft Covenant. Two absent Republicans immediately telegraphed their support of Lodge's resolution. Added to the thirty-seven signers, this total of forty comfortably exceeded the one third of the ninety-six-member Senate needed to block consent to a treaty. The authors of the round-robin were also sending a message to Paris. Brandegee, Knox, and Lodge favored a harsh settlement, and they wanted to encourage the Allied leaders to forge ahead and separate the League from the peace treaty. Lodge claimed later that he had aimed the round-robin at provoking an intemperate reaction from Wilson. Such a degree of wily premeditation sounds far-fetched, although the senator had made friends in recent years with Wilson's old enemy from Princeton, Andrew West, and was glad to do him dirt.[8]

Wilson initially ignored the round-robin. When he went to the Capitol shortly before the expiration of the Congress at noon on March 4, he made no mention of it as he chatted with reporters. He did issue a statement about Republican senators reminiscent of his excoriation of "a little group of willful men" exactly two years before and reiterated that he would not call Congress into session until he returned from the peace conference. Early in the afternoon, the presidential party boarded the train for New York and the voyage to Europe. The Wilsons stopped in Philadelphia to see the president's daughter Jessie, who had given birth a few days earlier to her second son, whom she and her husband named Woodrow Wilson Sayre. The president reportedly said to a nurse, "With his mouth open and his eyes shut, I predict he will make a Senator when he grows up."[9] The party had dinner on the train, and on arrival in New York they went directly to the Metropolitan Opera House for the joint appearance with Taft. People jammed every seat, aisle, corridor, and corner of the hall, and a crowd of 15,000 filled the streets outside.

Taft hailed the League of Nations as "what I have ever regarded as 'the promised land.'" It would erect a bulwark against Bolshevism and offer insurance against the "world suicide" of another war fought with still more terrible weapons. He devoted most of his speech to detailed answers to criticisms of the Draft Covenant, including the charge that Article X imposed obligations to intervene in faraway places: instead, he declared, nations closer to conflicts would be called upon to act. Most important, perhaps, he extended an olive branch to Republican senators: he did not mention the round-robin, but he called speeches such as Lodge's "useful" for offering "suggestions that should prove especially valuable in the work of revising the form of the Covenant and making changes."[10]

Wilson gave a shorter speech, in which he came out swinging at his opponents. He saluted the sacrifices of the troops and vowed not "to permit myself for one moment to slacken in my effort to be worthy of them and their cause." He did not mention the round-robin by name either, but he announced that the League Covenant would be so tightly bound up in the peace treaty "that you cannot dissect the Covenant from the treaty without destroying the whole vital structure." He dismissed his critics as having made no constructive suggestions but only carping, "'Will it not be dangerous to us to help the world?' It would be fatal to us not to help it." The crowd went wild when Wilson hurled defiance at his opponents, but a number of observers, particularly Republicans, believed he had committed a blunder. This seems to be another case of his emotions getting the better of him, as had happened a year earlier with "Force, Force to the utmost" in response to the Germans' actions at Brest-Litovsk. He did feel angry and frustrated. The fatigue that he sometimes complained about and others remarked on was undoubtedly affecting him. Grayson had examined him the night before this speech and found him in good health, but his emotional equilibrium was another story.[11]

Wilson had to deal with one other matter of conflict before the *George Washington* sailed that night. After the speech, he met in an office in the opera house for twenty-five minutes with a delegation of Irish Americans who pressed him to gain a hearing at the peace conference for representatives of an independent Ireland. Tumulty, George Creel, and other Democrats had been warning that discontent over Ireland could hurt the party. At this meeting, Wilson listened politely and told his visitors that when Ireland's case did come before the conference, he would use his best judgment to determine how to proceed, but to Grayson he said, "[T]he Irish as a race are very hard to deal with owing to their inconsiderateness, their unreasonable demands and their jealousies." He predicted that dissatisfaction among Irish Americans and German Americans "might defeat the Democratic party in 1920."[12]

Wilson's defiant mood ebbed a bit on the nine-day voyage across the Atlantic. The seas were calmer, and he was able to rest, although his stomach bothered him and he ran a fever for three days because of a gum infection. He spent time on the voyage reading and discussing memoranda that Ray Stannard Baker had prepared on American opinion of the League and how to promote the Covenant to the public. Baker recommended greater publicity for the negotiations and an educational campaign at home. Supporters in the Senate were also telling Wilson that the round-robin did not mean all was lost and that changes in the Covenant, especially regarding the Monroe Doctrine and later, perhaps, reservations to American ratification, could turn things around. The rest and reflection seemed to help Wilson. When the *George Washington* reached Brest on March 13, one of the reporters aboard cabled back, "If he felt any resentment at the Washington opposition and anxiety about Paris, there was nothing to indicate it."[13]

That report exaggerated Wilson's mellowing. On the train from Brest to Paris the next day, he blamed House for "[y]our dinner" with the men from Capitol Hill because it was "a failure as far as getting together was concerned."[14] In Paris, Lord Robert Cecil also found him truculent and determined to make no concessions to Republican senators. Yet he soon set to work on changes in the Draft Covenant. Discussions with Cecil and David Hunter Miller, the American delegation's legal expert, revealed, however, that mentioning the Monroe Doctrine might offend the Europeans, who had never recognized it, and might tempt the Japanese to claim similar suzerainty in the Pacific; also, altering Article X would be difficult, and the right of withdrawal seemed already implicit.

Meanwhile, Wilson had been soliciting views from Republicans about changes in the Draft Covenant. From shipboard, he had sent a request through Tumulty to Taft, and from Paris he sent a request through Henry White to Root. Taft replied with his usual generosity, stressing the need to mention the Monroe Doctrine, which he believed would bring most Republican senators around. Root responded with his usual guardedness. Through intermediaries, he declined to render "matured" judgment but said he regretted the lack of an international court, would like an exemption for the Monroe Doctrine, and worried that Article X committed the United States to intervention in distant conflicts.[15] In fact, Root was being more than guarded.

White, acting on his own while the president was still at sea, had cabled Lodge to ask what changes the senator wanted. Reporters learned about White's cable, and the New York *Sun* contacted Lodge before he received it. Lodge immediately met with Brandegee and sent an intermediary to consult Root. In a reply to White drafted by Root—which Lodge used verbatim—the senator stated: "The President expressed no willingness to receive any communication from the Senate when that body was in session. If he now wishes to have amendments drafted which the Senate will consent to, the natural and necessary course is to convene the Senate in the customary way." Cold reactions like those did not make prospects for cooperation with leading Republicans look promising.[16]

As before, cooperation with the Allied leaders was more immediately pressing and equally vexing. While Wilson was away, Lloyd George had gone back to London to attend to parliamentary business, and Clemenceau was recuperating from the assassination attempt on February 19 by a deranged anarchist—one shot hit the premier in the chest between the ribs, leading him to joke about "a Frenchman who misses his target six times out of seven at point-blank range." House had sat in Wilson's place at the Council of Ten and planned to use the time to speed things up. Just before Wilson left, House had told him he could "button everything up in the next four weeks" by reaching a preliminary agreement that dealt with such matters as boundaries, colonies, and reparations: the colonel asked the president "to bear in mind while he was gone that it is sometimes necessary to compromise in order to get things done."[17]

If Wilson did agree to the colonel's plan, he was sowing seeds of misunderstanding. While he was away, House and Arthur James Balfour conducted negotiations concerning German boundaries. They attempted to deal with French efforts to tear away and possibly annex the Rhineland, which Wilson adamantly opposed. They grappled with the conundrum posed by the Bolsheviks in Russia. Churchill, Marshal Foch, and others were pushing for large-scale military intervention against them, which Wilson also opposed. Others wanted to expand tentative, low-level talks with them. Under House and Balfour's direction, the council approved sending the junior American diplomat William Bullitt to Moscow—a move that would later backfire and harm Wilson and his program. Most sensitively of all, House proposed, with Cecil's and Balfour's backing, that the League of Nations start to function at once. This may have been a ploy to separate the League from the peace treaty, and Wilson had cabled that the plan bothered him and would offend the Senate.[18]

How House's doings in his absence sat with Wilson is a matter of dispute. Edith later wrote that her husband's appearance after his first meet-

ing with the colonel on their return shocked her: "He seemed to have
aged ten years and his jaw was set in that way it had when he was making a
superhuman effort to control himself." When she asked what the matter
was, he said with a bitter smile, "House has given away everything I had
won before we left Paris." That account may have been skewed by Edith's
long-festering dislike of House and her memories of her husband's later
attitude toward him. Yet Wilson's gibe at House about "[y]our meeting"
with the congressional committees was consistent with her account, and
the two men had talked for only a short time on the train from Brest to Paris.
Grayson also noted that the next day Wilson reproved the delegation—
meaning House—"for apparently failing to keep the League of Nations
covenant to the fore" and for not maintaining a firm stand on German
boundaries. Ray Stannard Baker and others who later studied this relationship would conclude that things were never the same between them
again. There was no dramatic break at this point or later, but Wilson was
now in a frame of mind that allowed him to believe the worst about his
onetime intimate friend.[19]

Other circumstances added to his troubles on his return to Paris. The
Wilsons did not resume residence at the Murat Palace but had to move to
a house at 11 place des États-Unis. The location, with its statue of
Lafayette and Washington, had a nice symbolism, but as Grayson noted in
his diary, "The new quarters were by no means so commodious and were
far less comfortable." Edith, however, remembered the house as "less
ornate . . . and more homey." She particularly liked the garden outside her
husband's window and her bathtub, which was "almost like a small pool"
and had faucets made of gold.[20] Wilson's rooms included a comfortable
study with a fireplace, which would become the most important meeting
place of the conference. These new quarters were across the street from
the residence assigned to Lloyd George, who came over as soon as the
Wilsons arrived and stayed for more than an hour. After lunch, Wilson
spent the afternoon at the Crillon with the American delegation, and in
the evening he met with Premier Orlando, who as usual pressed Italian
claims to the Dalmatian coast, and with Admiral Sims, who discussed
naval aspects of the settlement. The work and the tension had resumed
without a missing a beat.

During Wilson's first full week back in Paris, the Council of Ten met
three times, the Supreme War Council twice, and the League of Nations
Commission once. These sessions proved as protracted and fruitless as
ever. The Council of Ten resorted to the delaying tactic of deferring consideration of Poland's borders with Germany until an investigative commission could issue a report. "It is hard to keep one's temper when the

world is on fire, and we find delegates, such as those of the French, blocking all of the proceedings," Wilson told Grayson. "It is bad enough to waste time just talking but these men give us no constructive suggestions whatever. They simply talk." In the League Commission, he was able to get the right of withdrawal specified in the Draft Covenant, but he did not yet propose an exemption for the Monroe Doctrine. Cecil privately broached that question to Lloyd George, who objected strongly and planned to use the matter as a bargaining chip. This dickering quickly undid the good effects of the voyage on Wilson. "The President looked worn and tired," House noted, but his sympathy sprang from more than concern for the president's health: he thought negotiations were moving too slowly, and he could not decide questions "on my own initiative as I did when the President was away." He told Lansing, "It was a mistake for [Wilson] to come at all. However we must make the best of it."[21]

Self-serving though House's complaints were, the colonel made a point that the president and others had already grasped. On March 19, Wilson, Lloyd George, and Clemenceau decided to constitute the Council of Four, comprised solely of them and Orlando. This council replaced the Council of Ten, which met for the last time on March 24, and excluded foreign ministers and advisers and, at first, even a secretary to take minutes. For a while, only one other person sat with them: because Orlando spoke no English, Professor Paul Mantoux of the Sorbonne interpreted into French what Wilson, Lloyd George, and Clemenceau (when he was speaking English) said. At the middle of April, Orlando brought in a senior Italian diplomat, Count Luigi Aldrovandi Maresotti, to serve as his own interpreter. On Clemenceau's orders, Mantoux secretly kept notes of the meetings, which were the only record of the discussions until mid-April, when the negotiators decided to call in the secretary to the British cabinet, Sir Maurice Hankey, to take minutes. During the next three months, this group would meet 148 times—almost every weekday, frequently twice or three times a day, and sometimes on Sundays—mostly in Wilson's study in the house on la place des États-Unis. Wilson normally sat upright in an armchair; Clemenceau wore his gloves and lounged back in his chair while Lloyd George fidgeted, gesticulated, and often stood up. Those three were on one side of the fireplace, while on the other side, next to Mantoux and Aldrovandi Maresotti, sat Orlando, looking at the others and taking less part in the discussion. Except for drafting the Covenant of the League of Nations, this Big Four, as they were soon dubbed, did the real work of peacemaking in 1919.[22]

Wilson got their meetings off to a brisk start. First, he proposed taking up reparations, French security, and the Adriatic coast. Reparations sparked a clash between Clemenceau, who held out for big, undefined payments spread over many years, and Wilson, who wanted prompt payment of a fixed sum of between $25 billion and $35 billion. Lloyd George played an equivocal game, holding out for big indemnities but also circulating a memorandum that deplored an overly harsh peace with Germany. French security proved even more fractious, as Clemenceau held out for both taking away the Rhineland and annexing the coal-rich Saarland. When Wilson maintained that the League of Nations would provide security, Clemenceau scoffed that America was "far away, protected by an ocean," and derided the "excellent intentions of President Wilson." The president responded by noting the worldwide "passion for justice" and declaring, "I wish to do nothing that would be said of us, 'They profess great principles, but they admitted exceptions everywhere.'"[23]

These clashes struck House and Lansing as unnecessary. The colonel told Lloyd George that Wilson was "the most difficult man I ever knew when aroused." The prime minister asked him to try to soothe Wilson, but House evidently did not, because the next day the president said to Grayson over lunch that "it was a time for courage and audacity" and that he intended to confront both Lloyd George and Clemenceau that afternoon. He must have been letting off steam, because the notes of that afternoon's meeting do not record any confrontation. Rather, the four discussed the Baltic port of Danzig, which had a German population but provided an outlet to the sea for Poland; Hungary, where Bolsheviks led by Béla Kun had seized power; and reparations again, with questions raised about what damages to compensate.[24]

In fact, Wilson was working toward compromises with the French over their security and the German borders. He suggested that the left bank of the Rhine and fifty kilometers beyond the right bank be demilitarized, and he proposed a "military guarantee" by Britain and the United States to France. In his own hand, he wrote out and signed a statement pledging himself "to propose to the Senate of the United States . . . an engagement, subject to the approval of the Council of the League of Nations, to come immediately to the assistance of France in case of unprovoked attack by Germany." On the Saar, he soon suggested turning administration of the coal mines over to the French for a period of time. Along with Lloyd George, he proposed that Danzig become a free city under League of Nations administration. He resisted efforts by Clemenceau and Lloyd George to demand that the Dutch turn over the former German emperor for trial and likely execution. Wilson responded, "He has drawn universal contempt upon himself; is that not the worst punishment for a man like him?" The French did not warm to these proposals, and their reserve frustrated the president.[25]

Grayson noted the stress caused by this frustration, and he had cause to worry. The Council of Four was making the strain and an already difficult workload even worse for Wilson. On March 31, Ray Stannard Baker had breakfast with him at eight and commented in his diary, "He is working fearfully hard." The press secretary noted that the president's schedule that day included two hours of correspondence, two meetings of the council, lunch with House, evening meetings with him and Secretary of the Navy Daniels, who was visiting Paris, and at the end, "[s]tudying maps & reports of experts &c &c."[26] Such a schedule left no time for golf, and Wilson could take only an occasional evening ride in a limousine with Edith.

Besides French security and reparations—which involved reports from and meetings with financial advisers—and Hungary, the council took up Russia, Poland, and Italy's claims in the Adriatic. Russia caused a flare-up in the press at home when anti-administration newspapers published garbled stories about Bullitt's mission to Moscow, with allegations that Wilson was planning to recognize the Bolsheviks. The Adriatic question brought Orlando out of his usual silence to argue passionately for his country's right to annex Fiume and a large slice of the Dalmatian coast, on top of other border claims from the South Tirol up to the Brenner Pass.

Wilson's health gave out on April 3 during an afternoon meeting of the council. He abruptly left the room and summoned Grayson. He had made himself sit through most of the meeting in spite of intense pains in his back, stomach, and head, but he had given in to an uncontrollable coughing spell. Grayson found that the president was running a fever of 103 degrees, and he coughed violently throughout the night. Grayson avoided the word *influenza* until he issued a statement to the press two days later, yet it seems clear that this was what ailed Wilson. It was almost certainly not the notorious Spanish flu of the pandemic that had raged worldwide in recent months. Unlike much of the White House staff, the president had escaped that plague the previous autumn, but his fatigued condition now made him susceptible to a different strain. He spent the next four and a half days confined to his bedroom, the first two in bed. He did not attend sessions of the Council of Four, although he did meet with Bernard Baruch and called in House, Lansing, White, and General Bliss for a two-hour conference on Sunday, April 6.[27]

As he usually did when forced to be idle, Wilson brooded. He told Grayson he was fed up with the French, and he thought he might have to threaten to leave the conference: "And when I make this statement I do not intend it as a bluff." He asked Grayson to get the navy to send the *George Washington* to Brest: "When I decide, doctor, to carry this thing through, I do not want to say that I am going as soon as I can get a boat. I want the boat to be here." Reports of the order to bring back the *George Washington* immediately appeared in the press—probably because Grayson leaked the story to a *New York Times* reporter—stirring consternation in some quarters. But Baker welcomed the move: "He will fight for his principles. . . . He has reached the point where he will give no further."[28]

Not wanting to delay the negotiations while he was sick, Wilson designated House to sit in his place at the Council of Four. This could have been taken as a sign of trust, but it was not. Wilson said to him, "[I]t is very hard not to go to the full length with you in concessions." House did not make significant concessions during the president's illness, but his contrasting style was such that Baker commented, "The colonel sides with the group which desires a swift peace on any terms." House indiscreetly made his differences with Wilson public when he told reporters that the order to bring over the *George Washington* was, in fact, a bluff, a gesture for home consumption. According to Grayson, this ploy of the colonel's backfired with the newspapermen, and the doctor had to discourage one of them from writing an article about House titled "The Great American Acquiescor." Yet Grayson noted that "no one has yet heard Colonel House say NO . . . and in any event he never refuses."[29]

None of this was lost on the man in the sickbed, and Grayson's view of House reflected his patient's attitude. Grayson also wrote that when Edith asked whether House should telephone the other delegates about the Sunday conference in the sickroom, Wilson emphatically said no, because House would have his son-in-law, Gordon Auchincloss, do it, "and he (Auchincloss) has such an exalted opinion of himself these days that I don't care to have him do any business in my name." The next day, Wilson asked Grayson, "Do you see any change in House; I don't mean a physical change; he does not show the same free and easy spirit; he seems distant with me as if he has something on his conscience." Wilson later added that House, "whose specialty had been saying YES," had allowed the French to staff his and Edith's new residence with spies.[30]

Although Wilson was what Grayson called "'wabbly' [*sic*] on his feet" and "markedly showing the effects" of his illness, he insisted on rejoining the Council of Four on the afternoon of April 8. They met in his bedroom rather than the study, but that was the only concession he or anyone else made to his recent indisposition. Wilson again resisted Lloyd George and Clemenceau's push to bring the former German emperor to trial. "The worst punishment will be that of public opinion," he said—to which Clemenceau shot back, "Don't count on it." Turning to the Saar, the president continued to stand against tearing the region away from Germany while once more offering the French control of the coal there. This meeting and the one the next morning in the study took a toll on Wilson, who told Grayson he felt tired, but he was pleased that he had worked out a compromise on the matter of bringing the emperor to trial: his surrender would be "requested" but not demanded from the Dutch, who were not likely to comply; any trial would not be for "a violation of the criminal law, but as a supreme offense against international morality and the sanctity of treaties," and no penalties would be specified. In the afternoon, Wilson presented a proposal drafted by British and American experts to place the Saar under French rule for fifteen years, to be followed by a plebiscite to determine ultimate sovereignty; Clemenceau seemed receptive to this approach, although he later appeared to renege.[31]

Notwithstanding those apparent agreements, neither the pace nor the emotional tenor of the discussions was doing Wilson any good. The problems included what struck him as a contradictory back-and-forth about whether to set a fixed sum for reparations. "I must confess I do not know where I am," he said. The League Commission meeting also troubled him, as he had to make an impassioned plea for amending the Draft Covenant to recognize the Monroe Doctrine as a regional understanding unaffected by the League. Then the Japanese reintroduced their racial-equality amendment; Jan Christiaan Smuts was not present, and Cecil, as he later wrote, had "to grapple with the Japanese as best I could, which was not very well." Eleven members of the commission voted for the amendment, with Cecil and the Polish delegate voting against it. Wilson ruled that the motion failed because it had not carried unanimously. Cecil privately faulted him for not showing "quite as much courage as I could have hoped in resisting the amendment" and called him "a very curious mixture of the politician and the idealist. . . . He is not to me very attractive."[32]

If Cecil faulted Wilson for not sticking up for racial inequality, nearly everyone else afterward would fault him for not striking a blow against it. He wanted to avoid giving offense to the Japanese and smaller nations, but he knew that any statement hinting at racial equality would bring outcries not just from the British and their dominions but from his own countrymen as well. He told the League Commission that he wanted "to quiet discussion that raises national differences and racial prejudices" and see such matters "forced as much as possible into the background." He had dealt with, or ignored, race relations at home in this manner, and his approach was not working any better now in the international arena. He tried to reassure the Japanese by affirming, "The League is obviously based upon the principle of the equality of nations."33 For the moment, they accepted his decision, but they would soon exact a stiff price from him. This was not one of his finer hours, but he did come out of the meeting with a revised version of the Covenant, which he hoped would mollify critics at home.

The next few days brought him no respite. After meeting again with his financial advisers, Baruch and Thomas Lamont, he decided that no fixed sum of reparations should be stated but that a commission set up under the peace treaty should work out the amount, schedule, and kinds of payments. This decision soon drew particularly harsh condemnation from John Maynard Keynes, who would resign from the British delegation in May. Keynes then spent the summer furiously writing his excoriation of the settlement and the president's role in it, which would be published in December 1919 as *The Economic Consequences of the Peace*. Failure to set a sum for reparations may have been a mistake, but Wilson's reliance on a reparations commission did reflect his preference for processes over fixed terms, not only in peacemaking but in politics generally. Much of the blame for the way wrangling over reparations would poison the post-war environment would lie in American nonparticipation in those deliberations, something neither Wilson nor anyone else could have foreseen.34

Monday, April 14, was a rare day off for the council, but not for Wilson, who spent much of his time in other meetings. Orlando came to press Italy's claims in the Adriatic once more. Taking his stand on the Fourteen Points, Wilson did not relent in his opposition. "I do not feel at liberty to suggest one basis of peace with Germany and another for peace with Austria," he stated in a memorandum that he gave to Orlando. Yet he also made an important concession in that memorandum. He said he was willing for Italy to have the South Tirol up to the Brenner Pass, a region populated by German-speaking Austrians. He was violating the same principle that he was upholding in resisting Italy's demands for Fiume and the Dalmatian coast, something for which he would soon be roundly condemned. Several weeks later, when Baker asked him about the South Tirol, he regretted the move: "I was ignorant of the situation when the decision was made." He was also tired and wanted to show sympathy toward Italy.35

In the afternoon on April 14, Wilson dealt with the home front of peacemaking. Frank Hitchcock, who had been postmaster general under Taft, came to assure the president of his support. Wilson thanked Hitchcock but told him that Taft and Lowell were objecting to the wording of the Monroe Doctrine amendment; Hitchcock said he would work on them. Meanwhile, House was receiving a visit from Clemenceau, who said he would agree to Wilson's terms for the protection of France and the west bank of the Rhine: "It was not what he wanted but with the [guarantee] of the United States he thought it sufficient." It was interesting that Clemenceau chose to tell House first. "Colonel House is practical, I can understand him," the colonel recorded Clemenceau saying to someone else, "but when I talk with President Wilson, I feel as if I am talking to Jesus Christ." Clemenceau added, "The Almighty gave us Ten Commandments, but Wilson has given us Fourteen."[36] Despite such cracks, it was clear that the president's firm stand and possibly his implied threat to withdraw from the conference were what had brought the Tiger of France to heel. This French concession would ease relations between Wilson and Clemenceau during the rest of the conference.

The Council of Four now moved with dispatch through the Saar and Rhineland arrangements. Wilson, Clemenceau, and Balfour, who was substituting temporarily for Lloyd George, felt confident enough to lay plans for inviting the Germans to come to Paris to receive preliminary terms later in the month. Other areas, however, continued to be worrisome: Italy, Russia, eastern Europe, Syria and Mesopotamia, and East Asia. The Japanese were pressing for cession of the German possessions in China that they had conquered and now occupied: the port of Kiaochow and the Shantung Peninsula. The Chinese delegation, led by the young Columbia-educated V. K. Wellington Koo, had already made representations to Lansing and Wilson for the return of those territories. "My sympathies are on the side of China," Wilson declared in the council on April 15, "and we must not forget that in the future the greatest dangers for the world can arise in the Pacific." Two days later, he received a visit from Koo and the Chinese delegation, who presented him with an eighty-seven-page memorandum stating their nation's case for the restoration of Shantung.[37]

The Chinese were not the president's only visitors on April 17, which Grayson called "the busiest day which he has put in since he left Washington, having approximately eighteen engagements, which covered every conceivable problem dealing with the Peace situation." The doctor did not exaggerate. The Big Four did not meet, but Wilson's foreign visitors that day included officials from Syria, Dalmatia, Albania, Greece, Portugal, Serbia, and Armenia, the Greek Orthodox patriarch of Constantinople, and an English journalist. From home, a delegation of Irish Americans urged the president to push for an independent Ireland, something a group of Democratic senators had also just written to him to advocate. Secretary of War Newton Baker came to lunch and shared his assessment of League support at home, prohibition enforcement, and small matters, such as repainting the White House and the lonesomeness of the sheep on the grounds. When Baker asked how he was handling the workload, Wilson smiled and said, "After all this ocean of talk has rolled over me, I feel that I would like to return to America and go back into some great forest, amid the silence, and not hear any argument or speeches for a month."[38]

Starting on April 19, Orlando and Italy's foreign minister, Baron Giorgio Sidney Sonnino, argued and re-argued their case for Fiume for six days. "Orlando finally broke down and wept copiously," Wilson told House. Wilson did not budge, but House suggested to the Italians that Fiume and Dalmatia might be set aside for future negotiations. The suggestion backfired. Ray Stannard Baker noted in his diary, "The rift between the President & Col. House seems to be widening. The Colonel compromises everything away." Baker thought House had "such immature ideas, not thought out, poorly considered," and his suggestion "served to fan the flame of Italian nationalism & make it harder for Wilson." Baker did not present these remarks as Wilson's views, but it seems certain that he picked them up in the house on la place des États-Unis. Edith later recalled that around this time she had exploded to her husband, "Oh, if Colonel House had only stood firm while you were away none of this would have to be done over. I think he is a perfect jellyfish." To this, she said he replied, "Well, God made jellyfish, so, as Shakespeare said about a man, therefore to let him pass, and don't be too hard on House."[39] That sounds like a gentler version of what Baker was writing in his diary.

Wilson got some rest during the Easter weekend. On Saturday night, he and Edith saw a play, and on Sunday afternoon they took a ride in the countryside. The following morning, he stayed in his study to draft a public statement about the Adriatic dispute. Although he repeatedly expressed profound sympathy for Italy's sacrifices in the war, he asserted that Fiume was necessary as a seaport for "the states of the new Jugo-Slav group."[40] Before he released the statement to the press, he consulted with Clemenceau and Lloyd George, who told him that they felt obliged to stand by their treaty obligations to Italy. He nevertheless issued the statement on April 23. Orlando and Sonnino in turn made good on their earlier privately aired threats to withdraw from the conference, and after an emotional meeting of the council they left Paris the following day. This was the first public break among the leaders at the conference.

The day after the Italians left, what some observers now called the Big Three took up the Shantung question. In the morning, the Japanese delegates made their case, and in the afternoon the Chinese delegates made theirs. To the Japanese, Wilson said there was "a lot of combustible material in China" and warned them against inflaming it. Baron Makino answered that it would be a very grave matter if his country's claims were not met. To the Chinese, Wilson maintained that he had presented their case forcefully. Koo answered that with regard to the peace commission, his people were "now at the parting of the ways." After the Chinese left, Wilson admitted to Lloyd George and Clemenceau that he might have to seem to contradict his resistance to Italy's claims because having Japan join the League was of paramount importance. Lloyd George, who had told the Japanese that he would stand by Britain's treaty obligations to them, now called this "one of the most unscrupulous proceedings in all history, especially against a gentle and defenseless people." Wilson agreed but said he did not want a rift with the Japanese.[41]

Shantung confronted him with the most anguished choice of the whole peace conference. He told Grayson that if he followed "the principles of what is just and right," the Japanese would refuse to sign the peace treaty. When Baker pointed out to him the similarity between the Adriatic and Shantung, he replied, "[W]hen you lay down a general truth it may cut anywhere," adding that "he could not see clearly just where his principles applied." Baker reminded him that public opinion at home and abroad favored China, and Wilson asked, if the Italians and Japanese pull out, "what becomes of the League of Nations?" As Baker put it, "He is at Gethsemane." On April 30, after wrestling with this dilemma for more than a week and suffering at least one sleepless night, he decided in favor of Japan. He told Baker he knew the decision would be unpopular and that he would "be accused of violating his own principles—but never-the-less he *must* work for world order & organization against anarchy & a return to the old [unilateralism]."[42]

Wilson did suffer for this decision. Shantung would hurt his campaign to gain support in America for the treaty and the League more than any other single issue, with the possible exception of Ireland. In the longer run, this decision would open him to the charge that he placed too much faith in the League of Nations. When the preliminary terms of the peace treaty became known two weeks later, critics would maintain that he had given away too much on territorial, colonial, and financial matters in order to gain support for the League. Those charges would be wrong. Shantung offered the sole example of Wilson's consciously making a concession for the League, and he also decided as he did because of the realistic calculation that he could not force the Japanese out. He did compromise on other matters but, except for this one time, never for the sake of his new institution for maintaining peace.

Unfortunately for Wilson, the Shantung decision overshadowed the unveiling of the final version of the League Covenant on April 28. This document incorporated the revisions intended to appease critics at home: a clearly specified procedure for withdrawal, exemption of the Monroe Doctrine, and the right to declare domestic questions off-limits. In presenting this Covenant to the full conference, the president confined himself to a drab recital of those and a few other changes, and he made some factual slips in discussing them, which caused him to backtrack. Those slips were not like Wilson, nor were his abrupt delivery and his failure to toss out even a morsel of eloquence, as he had done with the Draft Covenant. The omission of eloquence was doubly curious because just the week before, he had said at a Big Three meeting, "The central idea of the League of Nations was that States must support each other even when their interests were not involved. When the League of Nations was formed then there would be established a body of partners covenanted to stand up for each other's rights." Some interpreters would later speculate that Wilson's slip and omissions in presenting the Covenant stemmed from his having suffered a small stroke.[43]

The beginning of May brought no relief. Although May Day was a holiday in Paris, the Big Three met to discuss some difficult questions. They considered the rights of minorities in eastern Europe, with Wilson expressing concern about Germans and Jews who would be living in Poland. When Lloyd George remarked on Jews' reported lack of loyalty to Poland, Wilson shot back, "It is the result of a long persecution. The Jews of the United States are good citizens."[44] They also discussed the Italians and the Germans, and Lloyd George's erratic behavior particularly irked Wilson. All the wrangling wore on him, and Grayson persuaded him not to attend services the next day in the cold, damp Scottish church in Paris. Instead, after sleeping late, he joined Edith, Grayson, and Baker for a long ride in the country and went to bed early.

Wilson needed to be well rested because the inner circle was again about to be the Big Four, and the Germans were coming to receive the preliminary peace terms. Public opinion in Italy appeared to support Orlando and Sonnino's walkout, and, having said they felt vindicated, they were returning to Paris. The real reason the Italians came back was that they wanted to be present for the appearance of the Germans. How the Germans would react worried Wilson. He admitted to Grayson that the terms were harsh, "but I have striven my level best to make them fair."

He told Baker, "If I were a German I think I should never sign [the treaty]."45 He tried and failed to get reporters admitted to the session at which they received the terms.

The presentation occurred on May 7, on a beautiful spring afternoon, with chestnut trees and lilacs blooming in the gardens of the Trianon Palace at Versailles; by coincidence, not design, this was the fourth anniversary of the sinking of the *Lusitania*. The German delegation took seats in the middle of a horseshoe arrangement of tables, which they later claimed made them feel like prisoners in the dock. Clemenceau stood and crisply outlined the terms, giving the Germans two weeks to respond. The German foreign minister, Count Ulrich Graf von Brockdorff-Rantzau, a slender, haughty Prussian aristocrat, replied, "We know the force of the hatred which confronts us here. . . . We are required to admit that we alone are war-guilty; such an admission on my lips would be a lie." This demonstration of defiance made a bad impression, as did the rest of the speech and, especially, Graf von Brockdorff-Rantzau's remaining seated while he spoke. Some observers thought—correctly—that this was a deliberate insult; others noted—also correctly—that he gripped the table tightly and his knees trembled the whole time. Despite the lovely setting, this first encounter between victors and vanquished set an ugly tone for the last phase of peacemaking in Paris.46

Some on the American delegation recoiled at the preliminary terms. Baker called it "a document of retribution to the verge of revenge." Herbert Hoover was so upset when he read an advance copy early in the morning on May 7 that he went out for a walk, on which he met up with Keynes and Smuts, who reacted the same way he did to the terms. A dozen younger members of the staff, some of whom remembered Wilson's promises on board the *George Washington*, resigned in protest. Most kept their disagreements private, but not the irrepressible William Bullitt, who was back from his abortive mission to Moscow and now gave a letter to reporters in which he charged the president with having "consented now to deliver the suffering peoples of the world to new oppressions, subjections and dismemberments—a new century of war." Some reactions in America echoed those sentiments. *The Nation* had already accused Wilson of dealing in "intrigue, selfish aggression, and imperialism." *The New Republic* had condemned Article X of the Draft Covenant as a pledge "to uphold injustices." When the preliminary terms were published, *The Nation* issued a series of we-told-you-so editorials, while *The New Republic* emblazoned the cover of its May 24 issue with the headline THIS IS NOT PEACE. Those magazines' reactions did not reflect wider editorial sentiment, most of which approved of these peace terms, but they revealed an erosion of support in quarters where Wilson had formerly enjoyed enthusiastic backing, and their defection would add intellectual firepower to the opponents of the League in the upcoming debate at home.[47]

Wilson could have anticipated those reactions. He had worried about excessive expectations, and he had largely refrained from appearing to promise a brave new world; yet his wartime rhetoric and moral standing had fed high hopes, and he had played upon those hopes. Baker had tried to forestall disillusionment by urging Wilson to negotiate more openly and take reporters into his confidence. The president had responded not only by pointing to the other leaders' insistence on secrecy but also by arguing that such delicate matters as the Japanese push for a racial-equality clause could not be discussed in public. He was following the same instinct that had led him to cancel press conferences after the sinking of the *Lusitania*. Whether greater publicity would have arrested the loss of support from progressives and idealists is an open question, but there was no doubt that Wilson was once more passing up an opportunity to educate the public about his programs and the obstacles he faced—omissions that would hurt him on the domestic front of peacemaking.

Disillusionment with Wilson for infidelity to the Fourteen Points and hopes for a peace of forgiveness would shape future views of what he and the other leaders had wrought at Paris in 1919. Their negative model, and Wilson's, was the Congress of Vienna—an example of how not to make peace—yet those perfumed aristocrats and reactionaries of the preceding century had crafted a settlement that lasted for many decades. By contrast, the handiwork of these men would crumble in little more than one decade and give way to another world war exactly twenty years later. Their settlement would come to bear the stigma of "the peace that failed." In the eyes of many future interpreters, much of the blame for the failure would fall on Wilson's head: he had not prevented the Allies from exacting vengeance and dividing the spoils, and he had compounded these iniquities with lofty rhetoric and excessive reliance on the feeble, doomed instrument of the League of Nations.

Most of Wilson's detractors forgot how limited and specific most of the Fourteen Points were. They forgot, too, that he had not coined the term *self-determination* or laid it down as a general principle. His most glaring violations of that line of policy occurred either as a mistake, as with the South Tirol, or as a calculated risk, as with Shantung. Widespread severing of ethnic and linguistic groups from their homelands in Central and eastern Europe came from conditions created by the new states there: Poland, Czechoslovakia, and the Yugoslav kingdom. Wilson's preferred solution—to replace the Austro-Hungarian Empire with a federation of autonomous nationalities—might have mitigated some of that splintering and preserved greater stability, but it had become impossible because of factors over which the peacemakers had little or no control. The "acid test," Russia, was already what Churchill would later call "a riddle wrapped in a mystery inside an enigma," and it should have surprised nobody that the peacemakers merely fumbled with the situation there. The idea of talks with the Bolsheviks, which Wilson initially favored, drew vehement opposition from Clemenceau and Lloyd George. Wilson did not try hard to rebut them, but he did stand firm against schemes for military intervention hatched by Churchill and Foch and the food blockade put forward by Hoover.[48]

Outside Europe, the mandate system struck many critics as a fig leaf to cover an imperialist grab for colonies. Like Shantung, other former German possessions wound up in the hands of the respective Allied belligerents that had seized them during the war, and those conquerors were not about to give them up. The designation of those territories as mandates under the League was, however, more than empty symbolism. The mandatory powers promised to improve transportation, utilities, sanitation, health care, and education for the indigenous peoples, and they pledged to prepare them for eventual independence. Such a pledge was something that no power besides the United States had yet made regarding its own colonies. The mandate system sufficiently impressed W. E. B. DuBois—who had been in Paris earlier in 1919 organizing the first Pan-African Congress—that he would support the League and the treaty in spite of his own history of bitter disappointment with Wilson. With former parts of the Ottoman Empire, mandates did mainly cloak a division of territory between the British and the French, although Wilson worked to prevent the Allies from carving up Turkey proper, and at times he considered an American mandate in Constantinople and Armenia.[49]

His decisions on nonterritorial matters such as reparations, disarmament, and the League sprang from his deep-seated preference for dynamic processes over fixed terms. Despite Keynes's excoriation, leaving amounts and schedules of reparations payments to regular review by an international commission was a reasonable approach. Another economic aspect of the settlement that Keynes would condemn, severing the coalfields of the Saar from the iron deposits of Lorraine, was addressed by the arrangement to keep the Saar and its mines under French administration. Some observers might be disappointed that the peace settlement did not prescribe set reductions of arms on land and sea, but all the peacemakers agreed that the wiser course lay in future negotiations, some of which would bear fruit. In his approach to reparations and disarmament, Wilson was not sweeping problems under the rug or betraying principles. If he had wanted to do those things or if he had really cared only about the League of Nations, he would not have subjected himself to the grueling negotiations among the Big Four.[50]

Wilson regarded the League as more important than the specific terms of the treaty because he grasped where the core problem in maintaining the peace lay: the defeated must bow to their defeat, and the victors must uphold their victory. This war had left sore losers and disgruntled, divided winners. The Germans' real complaint was that they had lost the war, and since crushing them was now no longer an option, it was doubtful that gentler terms would have made them more willing to accept their defeat. Conversely, Italy and Japan harbored unsatisfied expansionist urges, and they would switch sides in the next war. Nor were the Big Three of one mind about how to uphold the peace terms. The only way out of this situation lay, Wilson believed, in establishing a new forum for dealing with these problems. In the coming months, he would readily admit that the settlement had flaws that would need mending, but he would argue that only vigilant, constructive engagement by all nations, especially the great powers and most especially the United States, could manage this situation and thereby maintain peace. For him, the sole available path to such engagement lay through the League of Nations.

The pace of negotiations in Paris slackened for a while after presentation of the preliminary terms. On May 8, Wilson accepted a suggestion by Grayson to go to the famous Longchamp racecourse. He also attended his first formal dinner in weeks and gave his first speeches in more than two months. On May 9, at an international gathering attended by dignitaries interested in international law, he showed signs of fatigue as he rambled and inadvertently seemed to insult his formally clad listeners: "And when I think of mankind, I do not always think of well-dressed persons. Most persons are not well-dressed. The heart of the world is under very plain jackets." The following afternoon, however, to a group of French academics, he spoke crisply and quipped, "[I]f a man is a fool, the best thing is to encourage him to advertise the fact by speaking."[51]

While they awaited the Germans' reply to the preliminary terms, the Big Four turned to other matters, chief among them Italy. Orlando pressed claims not only to the Adriatic coast but also to islands in the Aegean with Greek populations, parts of Turkey, and territories in Africa. Although House continued to believe he could easily resolve things, Wilson remained adamant about not giving in to the Italians. Eastern Europe, particularly the borders of Austria, Hungary, and Poland, likewise demanded their attention, as did Russia. Lloyd George and Clemenceau wanted to reach out to the Whites, the Bolsheviks' adversaries in the civil war raging there, but Wilson disagreed, telling Grayson the Whites were "a pig in a poke."[52] Over all those discussions hung the question of how the Germans would respond. Their delegation asked for and got a one-week extension, which pushed the deadline to May 28.

Concerns from home also intruded. A delegation of Irish Americans came to Paris and met with Wilson, and Congress demanded his attention. The need to enact appropriations legislation and the prospect of completing the peace treaty impelled him to call the new Republican-controlled Congress into session on May 19. Regretting that for the first time he was not addressing the two houses in person, Wilson sent a message announcing that he hesitated "to venture any opinion or press any recommendation with regard to domestic legislation" and then did just that. He urged passage of legislation to aid labor and help job seekers and maintain taxation along progressive lines. He warned the Republicans not to try to raise the tariff, pleaded for passage of the woman suffrage amendment, and recommended an end to the wartime prohibition on wine and beer. He made only one glancing allusion to foreign policy because, as he told Grayson, "I am leaving my real message until my return home."[53]

Wilson did not stick to that resolve. On May 30, Decoration Day, he went to the American military cemetery on a hillside outside Paris at Suresnes, where he appealed to the spirit of these honored dead: "The thing that these men left us . . . is the great instrument of the League of Nations. The League of Nations is the covenant of governments that these men shall not have died in vain." He asked the soldiers at the cemetery what their fallen comrades would say to the peacemakers, and he answered: "Be ashamed of the jealousies that divide you." Echoing the words and spirit of both Luther and Lincoln, he vowed, "Here stand I, consecrated in spirit to the men who were once my comrades and who are now gone, and who have left me under eternal bonds of fidelity." Baker saw tears in the eyes of people around him and felt them in his own eyes, and he called this Wilson's greatest speech. It was also the opening gun of his rhetorical campaign on the peacemaking home front.[54]

At first, his health appeared to be bearing up better. Although the Big Four met as often as before, he made time to take rides with Edith and Grayson, and the doctor persuaded him to go for morning walks. Family visits heartened him too. His daughter Margaret had come earlier, between singing engagements, and Stockton Axson arrived and reportedly added to the spice of after-dinner conversations. Those measures of relief could go only so far. Baker noticed that Wilson looked tired and that he had a facial tic and often could not recall the day's discussions among the Big Four. The facial tic was probably less serious than Baker thought, but the memory lapses may have stemmed from effects of arteriosclerosis. Grayson, on the other hand, made no comment about his health at this time, and the president clearly rallied his powers for the Decoration Day speech at Suresnes.[55]

The German foreign minister's written reply to the preliminary terms on May 29—a day late—touched off the final crisis of the peace conference. Graf von Brockdorff-Rantzau charged the victors with reneging on their promised peace of justice and maintained that the exactions of the treaty were more than the German people could bear. This reply reinforced doubts and second thoughts that had been percolating in Paris during the past three weeks. No criticisms carried greater weight than the ones that came from Smuts, who put them in writing to Wilson and Lloyd George. Conveniently overlooking his own part in reparations decisions and colonial issues, the South African denounced those and other provisions and threatened not to sign the treaty. Wilson promised to restudy the treaty, while Lloyd George—who had qualms of his own and was hearing doubts from members of his cabinet—called his delegation together on June 1 to reconsider the terms. Smuts's impassioned arguments carried the day. The British delegates unanimously instructed the prime minister to seek to soften the terms on German borders and reparations, the Rhineland occupation, and other matters and to propose early membership for Germany in the League.[56]

Lloyd George tried to prepare the way for his about-face by meeting with Wilson and asking the president to serve as mediator between him and Clemenceau. Wilson would sometimes serve in that capacity in the Big Four during the next two weeks, but he had no intention of playing into Lloyd George's hands. On June 3, he met for two hours with the entire American delegation to hear their views, which inclined mostly against changes in the treaty and deplored the British loss of nerve. Their stance suited Wilson, who declared, "I have no desire to soften the treaty," and said about the British, "[I]t makes me a little tired for people to come and say now that they are afraid that the Germans won't sign, and their fear is based upon things that they insisted upon at the time of the treaty; that makes me very sick."[57]

The ensuing debates in English among the Big Three—Orlando attended only occasionally, to discuss Italy's claims in the Adriatic—pitted Lloyd George against an alternately icy and acerbic Clemenceau, with Wilson considering but rarely favoring changes in the treaty. The one modification that did emerge from these tense discussions was to order a plebiscite to determine whether Upper Silesia would go to Germany or Poland. Why Wilson did not side with Lloyd George is a pertinent question. After all, the prime minister was trying to rewrite the treaty along lines that were closer to the president's own thinking. Wilson's resistance to making changes stemmed in part from impatience with Lloyd George's constant shifts of position and more from his ever-present bane—fatigue.

That fatigue got striking visual confirmation in a portrait painted at this time. An artist commissioned by the British government to paint portraits of leaders at the conference, Sir William Orpen, told House early in June that the president was refusing to sit for him because he did not have time. "What damned rot!" House answered. "He's got a damned sight more time than I have. What day do you want him to come to sit?" The colonel did arrange four or five half-hour sittings, but his remark gave another indication of his estrangement from Wilson. House's loss of influence was common knowledge and a topic of gossip among the staff of the American delegation.⁵⁸ Orpen's portrait depicts Wilson from the waist up against a light background that makes his long jaw and nose stand out, although his glasses are nearly invisible. In contrast to the Sargent portrait of eighteen months earlier, his face appears less smooth, and lines of age and fatigue are striking. His expression is calm and determined, almost but not quite grim. Wilson did not like this second portrait, but it would become one of the best known and most widely reproduced portraits of him.

Impatient and tired though he was, Wilson held out against revisions in the settlement, and finally, on June 16, after last-minute delays during what Baker called "dull but expectant days," the Council of Four dispatched the terms, only slightly revised, to Graf von Brockdorff-Rantzau and his delegation. The Germans were given a deadline of three days— later extended to a week—to accept the treaty. The interlude offered a chance for Wilson to make a two-day state visit to Belgium. Met at the border by the king and queen, he and Edith spent the first day with the royal couple on a long, often dusty motor ride through some of the most war-ravaged parts of Flanders, viewing the ruins of Ypres and other towns. Crowds once more packed the streets and lined the roads. Children thrust flowers at the First Lady and the queen, who, Edith recalled, sneezed violently because of her allergies. In the evening, a train took them from Bruges to Brussels, where the Wilsons stayed at the royal palace.⁵⁹

The next day, the Wilsons witnessed more evidence of German destruction, including the ruins of the library at the University of Louvain, and they called at the home of Cardinal Mercier, the hero of the occupation, who showed them where he had sheltered wounded and orphaned children during the war. The Belgian trip had especially great emotional impact because accompanying them was Hoover, whose leadership of the Commission for Relief in Belgium from 1914 to 1917 had made him the most beloved American in the country. As on his earlier visits to Britain and Italy, Wilson gave only short speeches and confined himself mainly to praising the part played by his hosts in the war—with one exception. Speaking to the Belgian parliament, he declared, "The League of Nations is the child of this great war for right . . . and any nation which declines to adhere to this Covenant deliberately turns away from the most telling appeal that has ever been made to its conscience and its manhood."[60] He was aiming those words at America.

The trip did him good, and he needed these newfound good spirits because nearly all signs indicated that the Germans would refuse to accept the peace terms. The government in which Graf von Brockdorff-Rantzau served resigned rather than sign the treaty, and the commanders of the German fleet anchored at Scapa Flow, off the Scottish coast, scuttled their ships rather than turn them over to the Allies. The Big Four met at least twice, and sometimes four times, a day to discuss contingency plans if the Germans would not sign the treaty and to deal with eastern Europe, Turkey, and, as usual, Italy and the Adriatic. Finally, on June 23, just two hours before the deadline, a newly formed German government cabled its acceptance. Wilson issued a brief statement commending the treaty for compensating victims of the war and providing security against another war, but he added that its greater work lay ahead, with the League.[61]

The French took great pride in their arrangements for the signing of the peace treaty. The event was to be an exercise of two qualities at which they excelled—grandeur and revenge. On June 24, Clemenceau took Wilson on a tour of Louis XIV's palace at Versailles, showing the president where he had given his first speech as an officeholder in 1871. That was the year the victors had crowned the first emperor of the newly unified German Empire in the Hall of Mirrors; this grandest room in the palace was where the Germans, now the vanquished, would sign the new peace treaty. To underscore the symbolism, the French arranged for them to sign the treaty on Louis XIV's council table, the same table on which the Germans had made the French sign the peace treaty after their defeat in 1871.[62]

The Council of Four continued to meet regularly, mostly in a last, fruitless stab at untangling the Adriatic imbroglio. The main business of Paris, however, was celebration, and Wilson nearly marred the festive mood by refusing to attend a formal dinner given on June 26 by the president of France, but Henry White got him to relent. At the dinner, he saluted the friendship between France and America. Giving measured praise to the work of the conference, he concluded, "As I go away from these scenes, I think I shall realize that I have been present at one of the most vital things that has happened in the history of nations."[63]

The signing was to be on June 28: by another coincidence, this was the fifth anniversary of the assassination in Sarajevo that had sparked the crisis that led to the war. The day before, Wilson at last did what Baker had been begging him to do for months: he met for more than an hour with fifty American reporters. The meeting harked back to the easy give-and-take of the press conferences during his first two years in the White House. He gave bantering replies to some questions and conceded about Shantung, "That seemed the best that could be got out of a complicated situation." He said the treaty was "rough on Germany," but he also emphasized that it should never be forgotten "that Germany did an unpardonable wrong." He answered the only query about the League by saying that the question of American forces under its command had never been raised, and he claimed that the treaty adhered to the Fourteen Points "more closely than I had a right to expect." Baker was delighted and wrote, "I wish he would do this oftener: but he dreads it." This performance could have helped in informing opinion back home, but like all of his press conferences, it was off the record and served only to enlighten the journalists who were there.[64]

The appointed day for the signing of the Treaty of Versailles started out overcast but turned sunny and warm by afternoon. Delegates, reporters, photographers, movie cameramen, and spectators holding coveted tickets began to gather in the Hall of Mirrors before two in the afternoon. Of the Big Four, Clemenceau arrived first and shook hands as he made his way to the center seat at the arrangement of tables. Wilson arrived next and jovially made his way through a throng of autograph seekers. Then came the British and the Italian representatives. Taking his place and chatting with people nearby, the president noticed a stir around the entrance as French officers escorted a four-man party of Germans to seats facing the Big Four. Clemenceau stood and spoke briefly, stating that the treaty was ready and the Germans should sign it. After his remarks were translated into English and German, the moment arrived.[65]

Two members of the new government, Foreign Minister Hermann Müller and Transportation Minister Johannes Bell, went and sat at the Louis XIV table to affix their signatures to the document. "It was as if men were called upon to sign their own death warrants," Lansing noted. "With pallid faces and trembling hands they wrote their names quickly and were then conducted back to their places." In the painting he made of the ceremony, Orpen caught the moment as one of the Germans slumped in a chair with an anxious-looking aide hovering beside him while the Big Four and others stared at them. At a signal, cannons on the palace grounds began booming, followed by guns all over France. The victors then came up to sign the treaty, starting with Wilson. "I did not know I was excited until I found my hand trembling when I wrote my name," he told Lansing. The delegates spent the better part of an hour taking their turn signing while the rest milled around and chatted. The painter Orpen for one found the scene repellent; using a figure of speech he had picked up from soldiers at the front that referred to statesmen by the coats they favored, he wrote later, "All the 'frocks' did their tricks to perfection."[66]

Not all the victors signed the treaty or did so cheerfully. The seats assigned to the Chinese delegation remained empty; its members refused to sign because they were not allowed to register their reservations about Shantung. Smuts stated his dissatisfaction with some of the clauses regarding Germany but signed because he held hopes for the League of Nations and future cooperation in the rebuilding of Europe. Wilson did not speak at the ceremony, but he issued a brief statement to the press to be released in the United States: "It is a severe treaty in the duties and penalties it imposes upon Germany, but it is severe only because great wrongs done by Germany are to be righted and repaired." He stressed that it was much more than a peace treaty with Germany: it liberated peoples, abolished the right of conquest, put small nations on an equal footing with great ones, established the League of Nations, and was withal "a great charter for a new order of affairs."[67]

After everyone present had signed the treaty, the Big Four walked out onto the terrace for photographs. Then Wilson, Lloyd George, and Clemenceau went inside for a final meeting, at which they issued an appeal to Italy to settle the Adriatic dispute. When the three came out into the square in front of the palace, the crowd shouted "Vive Wilson" and rushed forward to shake the president's hand while women cried out that they just wanted to touch him. The crowd nearly pushed the president into a fountain, and bodyguards had to surround him. The Wilsons drove back through cheering crowds to the house on la place des États-Unis, where they ate a quiet dinner and Lloyd George came over to say a private and effusive farewell. Shortly after nine o'clock, they went to la gare des Invalides for the overnight train to Brest, where the *George Washington* waited to take them back to America. French dignitaries filled the platform to see them off. "In saying good-bye to the President I am saying good-bye to my best friend," Clemenceau gushed to Grayson. As a military band played "The Star-Spangled Banner," the doctor noted, "[W]e steamed slowly out of Paris, the work of seven months finally accomplished."[68]

Wilson may have thought that too, but his mind was already on affairs at home. Earlier that day, he had cabled Tumulty about issuing an amnesty for anyone convicted during the war of expressing a dissenting opinion. Tumulty replied that the new attorney general, A. Mitchell Palmer, advised waiting until the president returned. In the evening, House had been among the party at the station, where the two men had what turned out to be their final face-to-face meeting. With unconscious prescience, the colonel recorded in his diary, "My last conversation with the President yesterday was not reassuring." He urged Wilson to adopt the same conciliatory approach and spirit of compromise that he claimed both of them had used with foreign leaders in Paris. Wilson had replied, "House, I have found one can never get anything in life that is worth while without fighting for it."[69] He knew he had as hard a struggle awaiting him as the one he was leaving behind, and he was girding himself for the home front of peacemaking.

22

THE LEAGUE FIGHT

When Woodrow Wilson used the word *fighting* in talking about the Senate and the League of Nations with Colonel House, he was not indulging in a spasm of pugnacity. He was voicing his considered view of the upcoming debates over the peace treaty. Republican attacks on his foreign policy in the previous fall's campaign and the reception given the Draft Covenant in March by Senator Lodge and others had left little doubt that he would have a fight on his hands when he went back with this treaty incorporating the League Covenant. In April, he had urged William Allen White to "get into the fight at home" for the League. Nothing that would happen in coming months would change his mind about this fight and what he thought was at stake in it. On the speaking tour that he would make in September 1919, he would look at the children who flocked to see him and say, "I know, if by chance, we should not win this great fight for the League of Nations, it would be their death warrant." This was going to be the fight of his life—one that would cost him more dearly than any other and would, if he lost it, he believed, "break the heart of the world."[1]

All evidence pointed to a hard fight against great odds in an unpromising arena. Public opinion, as well as positions in the Senate, had hardened since Wilson's trip home in March. A rival organization to the League to Enforce Peace had entered the field: the League for the Preservation of American Independence. Usually called the Independence League, this organization would mobilize anti-League opinion and send oratorical stars such as senators Borah and Hiram Johnson and former senator Albert J. Beveridge out on speaking tours. Meanwhile, Lodge and Elihu Root had adopted a strategy of attacking provisions of the Covenant, particularly Article X, and demanding "reservations"—binding statements in the instrument of ratification—to limit American commitments and participation. Revisions to the Covenant after Wilson's return to Paris had not won over Republican senators, and in May, once Congress convened, senators Borah, Brandegee, and Philander Knox had attacked the Covenant root and branch. In June, four days before the signing of the treaty, the *Chicago Tribune* published a lineup of senators, which showed forty as pro-League—all but one of them Democrats—forty-three as reservationists, eight as die-hard opponents—who proudly called themselves irreconcilables—and four as undecided. Months later, when the Senate came to vote on the treaty, this forecast would prove remarkably accurate.[2]

Wilson faced a choice at the outset between an inside and an outside strategy. An inside strategy required him to stay in Washington and try to deal with the senators. An outside strategy required him to make speaking tours and try to educate the public. He had been getting advice both ways. Tumulty and McAdoo had written and cabled urging him to take his case to the public soon after his return home; in Paris, Thomas Lamont had recommended the same course. Democratic senators and Postmaster General Burleson had counseled the opposite, urging him to respect the sensibilities on Capitol Hill and let some time elapse before making any appeal to the public. Simple logistics favored staying put initially, and the two strategies dovetailed with the presentation of the treaty to the Senate early in July, which everyone expected to be a widely watched event.

Wilson wanted to deliver a great speech that would rank beside "peace without victory," the war address, and the Fourteen Points. He started working on this speech on the second day of the voyage home. As usual, he enjoyed the respite offered by the ten-day crossing on the *George Washington*. He slept late, dined with a few fellow passengers, watched movies with the crew, and walked on the deck with Edith. Yet the upcoming speech vexed him as none had ever done before. He excused the difficulty to Grayson by saying that "he had very little respect for the audience."[3] That was a lame rationalization. By this time, he had addressed joint sessions of Congress or the Senate twenty-two times, and never before had he had any trouble preparing a speech. He also did something now he had never done before with a speech: he rehearsed with a small group of advisers, including Baruch, Lamont, and Vance McCormick. Oddly, however, he did not consult with the one person on board the *George Washington* who could have given him sound advice—Ray Stannard Baker. As press secretary to the delegation, Baker had been in daily contact with American journalists, and he had stayed abreast of opinion about the League and the treaty. Nor did Wilson consult with Tumulty or others in Washington, except about whether to speak to a joint session of Congress or to the Senate alone.

The presidential party enjoyed a festive homecoming on July 8. Crowds packed the sidewalks of New York, where a ticker tape parade took Wilson to Carnegie Hall for a brief speech. A train then took the Wilsons to Washington, where a crowd estimated at 100,000 gathered around Union Station to greet their arrival at midnight. The president did not speak to the crowd, but on the way to the White House he said he was touched by the reception. After a day of seclusion to work further on the speech, Wilson opened his campaign for the League and the treaty on July 10. In the morning, he held a press conference with more than 100 reporters in the East Room of the White House. Speaking on the record for a change, he gave newspaper readers a taste of the way he performed at press conferences; he was clear, to the point, and informative while holding his ground and remaining noncombative. Some of his answers were just a few words, but on Article X and proposed reservations he gave longer explanations. Asked if he would discuss criticisms of the article, he replied, "No, only to say that if you leave that out, it is only a debating society, and I would not be interested in a debating society." He maintained that reservations would be "a complicated problem," but he did not rule them out. He closed by affirming, "The Senate is going to ratify the treaty." It looked like a promising opener to his effort to gain acceptance of the treaty.[4]

At noon, he went to the Capitol to present the document to the Senate and give his speech. Grayson noted in his diary that as Wilson entered the chamber, Lodge asked him, "Mr. President, can I carry the Treaty for you?" To that, Wilson smiled and answered, "Not on your life." That exchange and Borah's presence among the escort committee drew laughs in the chamber. This was the first time a president had presented a treaty to an open session of the Senate. Even though it was raining heavily and only ticket holders could enter the building, a large crowd had been milling around the Capitol for hours. When Wilson came into the Senate chamber, loud applause greeted him, mixed with rebel yells, but reporters noted that nearly all the applause came from the galleries and Democratic senators. Only a few Republicans joined in, and at the end only one, Porter McCumber of North Dakota, an outspoken supporter of the League, applauded again. The chamber was silent during the thirty-seven-minute speech, and the senators appeared to be listening intently.[5]

Wilson maintained that the treaty was too complicated to explain in this address, although he did talk in general terms about some parts of the settlement. He paid tribute to the American forces, and he expatiated on the hopes raised for a better, more peaceful world, which the League of Nations was a first step toward fulfilling. "Shall we or any other free people hesitate to accept this great duty?" he asked rhetorically. "Dare we reject it and break the heart of the world?" He answered that such was impossible, and he closed with what he thought was a burst of eloquence by intoning, "The stage is set, the destiny disclosed. It has come about by no plan of our conceiving, but by the hand of God who led us this way. We cannot turn back. We can only go forward, with lifted eyes and a freshened spirit, to follow the vision. It was of this that we dreamed at our birth. America shall show the way. The light streams upon the path ahead, and nowhere else."[6]

The speech was a flop. In comments to reporters, Democratic senators sounded upbeat while Republicans were often scathing. "Soap bubbles and a soufflé of rhetorical phrases," snorted Brandegee, while George Norris of Nebraska called it "a fine lot of glittering generalities." The senators had anticipated explanations of such things as the Shantung settlement, the workings of Article X, and the future of Ireland. A Democrat, Henry Ashurst of Arizona, thought it was as if the head of a business had been asked to explain its obligations to his board of directors "and tonefully read Longfellow's Psalm of Life. . . . His audience wanted red meat, he fed them cold turnips." Why Wilson did so badly is puzzling. His health may have played a part. One reporter noted that he skipped several words in reading from his typewritten text and then reread the sentences. Ashurst noted tight muscles in his neck and the paleness of his ears. Those were signs of tension, probably a headache, and perhaps insufficient blood to the brain—possibly symptoms of the underlying condition that would bring on a stroke three months later. Even more than poor delivery, the speech suffered from poor judgment. Ashurst was not alone in thinking that Wilson had given the wrong speech at the wrong time in the wrong place. Something more along the lines of what he had said in the press conference would have better filled the bill. He was showing impaired political judgment, which did not augur well for his performance in the League fight.[7]

When the president finished his speech, he placed the bound copy of the treaty on the vice president's lectern. He left the chamber in good spirits and went into a reception room to meet with some senators, all but one of whom were Democrats. In what newspaper accounts described as a frank, open discussion, Wilson talked about reservations, which he again called complicated and perilous; the Monroe Doctrine, which he explained was now recognized by the European powers for the first time; the Shantung settlement, which he admitted he disliked; Ireland, which he called one of the most difficult problems of the conference; and Article X, which he believed did not infringe on Congress's power to declare war.

This exchange went some way toward repairing omissions in the speech, and on advice from Burleson and others, he decided to have meetings with individual senators. That meant again shelving plans for a speaking tour, which relieved a number of people close to him.[8]

Staying in Washington spared Wilson the rigors of summer travel, but it did not offer him a pleasant respite. The summer of 1919 was torrid even by the capital city's standards, and racial violence exploded there as in other urban centers. This came to be called the Red Summer, because of the blood that figuratively and literally flowed in the streets. Before this time, race riots had occurred almost entirely in the South, but now, thanks to the migration of African Americans to northern cities, these white-instigated attacks on blacks in their neighborhoods spread to such places as Chicago, Philadelphia, and Washington. More than 100 people were killed and thousands injured, the great bulk of them African Americans. Homes and stores went up in flames. Soldiers from National Guard units and the regular army patrolled thoroughfares and gradually restored order. In Washington, much of the violence broke out in African American neighborhoods less than a mile from the White House, and troops patrolled Lafayette Square and the Mall and around the Capitol. In all, it was a frightening and unnerving spectacle.[9]

The president seemed removed from the racial violence as well as other serious domestic problems, such as a rash of strikes, unemployment, inflation, and the continuing anti-radical crusade that would culminate in a full-fledged Red scare at the end of the year. His posture may have stemmed from concern about his health. On July 19, Wilson fell ill after a meeting at the Capitol and canceled his other appointments. A cruise on the *Mayflower* the next day did not help, and Grayson told the press that the president was suffering from dysentery. Whether something more serious was involved cannot be determined.

When he was not resting in the White House, Wilson was meeting with senators. Between July 18 and August 1, he saw twenty-six of them: twenty-two Republicans and four Democrats; two other Republicans were invited but declined. The meetings took place one-on-one in the East Room and lasted about an hour apiece. Afterward, each Republican senator told waiting reporters that his conversation with the president had been cordial but that he had not changed his mind about the need for reservations. In private, accounts of the meetings contradicted one another. Taft's chief informant in the capital told the ex-president that Wilson's "attitude had been courteous and even gracious . . . and I believe he has done some good." On the same day, Truman H. Newberry, a newly elected Republican from Michigan, told the state's other Republican senator he had had an agreeable meeting but said to a Washington lawyer that Wilson had given "the impression of a spoiled society belle, who considered herself irresistible to me." Wilson's usual persuasiveness in personal encounters evidently did not change any senator's mind, and the meetings took a lot out of him.[10]

He broke off these meetings at the beginning of August because domestic problems finally demanded his attention. He had resumed cabinet meetings, and on July 31 the discussion for the first time dealt exclusively with troubles at home: inflation and another threatened railroad strike. Inflation, which had earned the initials HCL (for "high cost of living"), was particularly troubling, and the Republicans were trying to reap partisan gain from it. In response, Wilson spoke to a joint session of Congress on August 8. As with the speech to the Senate a month earlier, this one gave him great trouble in writing, and his delivery was rambling and disorganized. Substantively, aside from vigorous enforcement of laws and the dissemination of economic information, he had little to recommend: "We must, I think, freely admit that there is no complete immediate remedy from legislation and executive action." He digressed with a description of the destruction wrought by the war, he attempted to link problems at home with delay in ratifying the peace treaty, and he delivered vague injunctions. It was the last address he would deliver to Congress in person.[11]

The threatened strike posed only one part of the railroad problem. Management, business groups, and conservatives were demanding an end to wartime control of the lines, while railroad unions, organized labor in general, and progressives were demanding continued government control under the Plumb plan, named after the rail unions' lawyer, Glenn Plumb. The night after his speech to Congress, Wilson read aloud a summary of the Plumb plan to Edith and Stockton Axson, who was visiting. "There is nothing radical in this," Axson recalled him saying. "It is a proposition for serious consideration." Another evening, while sitting on the rear portico of the White House, Wilson said he did not want to run for a third term, and as possible successors he mentioned Newton Baker, David Houston, and McAdoo. He did not think Baker and Houston were abler than McAdoo, but they were "both *reflective* men—and I am not sure Mac is a reflective man." He linked having a "reflective" successor to his openness to the Plumb plan. He believed that a measure of socialism was necessary to ensure opportunity for individuals: "I am perfectly sure that the state has got to control everything that everybody needs and uses," and the next president must therefore be "a man who reflects long and deeply on these complicated relationships of our time."[12] Wilson might have said he did not want a third term, but he sounded as if he was leaving the door open to the possibility.

Ironically, he had first expressed those views about the need for a greater government role in the economy at the same time that his administration was cracking down on socialists and other radicals for opposing the war. Now he was expressing these views again, after he had proposed releasing those dissidents from prison with the signing of the peace treaty. This issue had not faded away since his return home. During the summer of 1919, such prominent figures as the novelist Upton Sinclair and the attorney Clarence Darrow wrote to urge the president to pardon Eugene Debs, but no supplicant on behalf of imprisoned dissenters carried greater weight with the president than John Nevin Sayre, the Episcopal clergyman who had performed the wedding ceremony in the White House between his brother Frank and Jessie Wilson. At the beginning of August, Sayre wrote on behalf of the National Civil Liberties Board to ask for release of all persons convicted under the Espionage Act as a gesture of healing and reconciliation. Forwarding Sayre's letter to Attorney General Palmer, Wilson said he knew and trusted Sayre, and he affirmed, "I am anxious to act at an early date." Palmer had already recommended against releasing Debs and others until the peace treaty was ratified, and he never responded directly to the president—possibly because he was already hatching his plans for an anti-radical crusade. Failure to move now toward freeing Debs and other dissenters was a fateful missed opportunity.[13]

Another missed opportunity was the failure to deal with reservations to the peace treaty. The Republican senators who came to the White House all told Wilson that reservations were essential to Senate approval. Likewise, Taft impulsively—and, in the view of some, unwisely—broke the LEP's united front in favor of outright ratification of the treaty and proposed some fairly mild reservations. Hughes also put forward some of his own, which were more stringent than Taft's but less stringent than the ones Root had earlier proposed.[14] Tumulty, McAdoo, and Lamont recommended that Wilson regain the initiative by speaking out about acceptable reservations to the Monroe Doctrine, Shantung, and Article X. At mid-July, Sir William Wiseman reported to the Foreign Office that the president admitted he might have to agree to some reservations. Yet Wilson waited until the beginning of August, when he fretted for a week about what to say in a public statement, and finally let Tumulty draft most of it for him. Such fretting, like his difficulty in writing speeches, was out of character for him and also probably stemmed from his deteriorating health. Where Wilson had joked in the past about his "single-track mind" while easily attending to multiple tasks, he now seemed to have real problems dealing with domestic and foreign policy at the same time.

At the other end of Pennsylvania Avenue, the Senate appeared to be in no hurry to deal with the peace treaty. In July, the only notable speech on the floor came from Norris, who spent three days denouncing the settlement as infected with "the germs of wickedness and injustice" and heaping special scorn on the Shantung cession and Japan's treatment of Korea. The Foreign Relations Committee took its time too. In his capacity as Republican leader, Lodge had packed the committee at the beginning of this Congress with other critics and opponents of the League, who now included Borah, Brandegee, Albert Fall of New Mexico, Hiram Johnson, and Knox. In his capacity as chairman, Lodge ruled that the treaty must be read aloud to the committee, which consumed several days, and then he got a majority to request all confidential documents from the negotiations and to block appointments to the Reparations Commission set up under the treaty.[15]

Lodge did not begin to hold hearings in the committee's ornate room in the Capitol until August. The first witnesses were members of the delegation to the peace conference, including Lansing, who laconically and unemotionally underwent five hours of mostly hostile interrogation. It was a "disagreeable experience," Lansing noted, but mainly because "I felt I could not tell the truth as to the negotiations"—meaning his disagreements with Wilson, especially about the League, which he disliked. Hiram Johnson told his sons that the secretary's performance was "the picture of indifference, vacillation, hesitation and downright ignorance." Lodge found Lansing's performance pathetic and told his daughter, "One of the Democratic Senators turned around to me and said, 'What do you suppose Lansing did while he was in Paris?'" The person the committee most wanted to hear from was the president, and Lansing's uninformative testimony only whetted their appetite to grill him.[16]

On his side, Wilson was wrestling with how to deal not only with the Foreign Relations Committee but also, apparently more promisingly, with a group of nine Republican senators known as mild reservationists, who supported the League but wanted some safeguards and needed political cover for siding with a Democratic president. Two LEP representatives, A. Lawrence Lowell and Oscar Straus, who had served as secretary of commerce and labor under Roosevelt, met with Wilson on August 6 and found him willing to get in touch with the milder reservationists but unsure about the best way to go about it. McAdoo later recalled suggesting compromise on reservations to his father-in-law at this time and getting the answer, "Mac, I am willing to compromise on anything but the

Ten Commandments." But Wilson also feared that willingness to accept mild reservations might open the door to stronger and more objection-able ones.[17]

On Capitol Hill, prospects for bipartisan cooperation briefly looked bright. Some mild reservationists were reaching across party lines, although the New York *World* reported that "a get-together movement" between them and Democrats was "still in the conference stage." Key Pittman of Nevada, a Democrat, later recalled that he felt confident about reaching an agreement. That confidence was excessive. The mild reserva-tionists were divided among themselves; a few blew hot and cold about how far to go in accommodating the Democrats, and some of them sup-ported reservations that were not so mild. At the middle of August, Lodge enlisted Root's help in trying to bring two of them, LeBaron Colt of Rhode Island and Frank Kellogg of Minnesota, back into line behind "a real reservation" on Article X—one that would limit American commit-ments to enforce collective security actions by the League Council. In the end, those two senators and all but one of the mild reservationists— McCumber of North Dakota—would support Lodge's position on Arti-cle X and the whole treaty.[18]

Wilson dashed these hopes for bipartisan cooperation. On August 11, when Lansing also suggested an accommodation with the mild reserva-tionists, the president "would have none of it, and his face took on that stubborn and pugnacious expression which comes whenever anyone tells him a fact which interferes with his plans."[19] Four days later, Wilson authorized the ranking Democrat on the Foreign Relations Committee, Gilbert Hitchcock, to tell the press that the president did not believe any compromise should be discussed or negotiated yet, although one might be eventually. Wilson's reasons for this intransigent turn evidently sprang from the fear he expressed to McAdoo about opening the door to more stringent reservations. He was making a serious mistake: an accommoda-tion with the mild reservationists could have strengthened his hand with the Senate and put pressure on other Republicans. This was another sig-nificant missed opportunity, and the likeliest explanation lay once again in the effects of fatigue and nervous strain. Also, these overtures came just when Wilson had to turn from dealing with the Senate over the treaty to address domestic problems. His mind did appear to be having trouble shifting gears.

Curiously, no howl of protest greeted Wilson's rejection of reserva-tions. The silence in the Capitol seems to have stemmed from distraction by the anticipation of an encounter that dominated almost everyone's attention: Wilson's upcoming meeting with the Foreign Relations Committee, which the president had authorized Hitchcock to announce. Previously, he had planned to release his statement on reservations as a public letter to Lodge. Instead, showing a flash of his old boldness, he decided to read the statement to the committee and submit to questioning by its members. This was a historic break with precedent and with the constitutional separation of powers. The only comparable encounter between a president and a congressional committee had been his inviting the Foreign Affairs and Foreign Relations committees to the White House in February to discuss the Draft Covenant. That meeting, however, had been an informal gathering, with no stenographer present, and it had not involved any business before Congress. Wilson had never liked the separation of powers, although he did assert executive privilege in refusing the Foreign Relations Committee's request to turn over the documents from the peace negotiations. In this case, he again observed constitutional niceties by inviting the committee to the White House rather than going to the Capitol himself.[20]

At ten o'clock in the morning on August 19, the senators gathered with the president around a large table in the East Room. Wilson sat at one corner, between Lodge and John Sharp Williams of Mississippi, opposite Borah and Brandegee. Two stenographers and the head usher of the White House were the only others present during the three-and-a-half-hour meeting, which was followed by lunch. The president opened the discussion by reading his statement on reservations. He asserted that the only barrier to ratification of the peace treaty lay in "certain doubts with regard to the meaning and implication of certain articles of the covenant of the league of nations," which he found groundless. Article X imposed "a moral, not a legal obligation" and left Congress to interpret what actions to take. He did not object to reservations so long as they were not "part of the instrument of ratification"—incorporating them into that instrument would require the agreement of other nations and would create ambiguity about America's obligations.[21]

Though largely drafted by Tumulty, the statement captured Wilson's thought and language, and the distinction between a legal and a moral obligation under Article X could have offered an opening to a compromise between his insistence on international commitment and Lodge and other Republicans' insistence on freedom of action. Yet the statement was not adequate to the occasion. Agreeing to reservations that were not part of the instrument of ratification was a meager sop that did not satisfy even the mild reservationists. If Wilson had been willing to work with them earlier, he might have been able to unveil an agreement on a specific set of reservations. That would have been a stupendous coup and would have sent his critics and opponents reeling. Instead, he was adding to the pile of missed opportunities.

Lodge opened for the committee by stating that he and his fellow senators had "no thought of entering into an argument as to interpretations" but sought only information. He asked specific questions about other treaties besides the one with Germany and about the drafting of the Covenant. Wilson answered him crisply and knowledgeably. Other senators quickly got into interpretations of the Covenant. Borah asked who besides the United States, in the event of American withdrawal from the League, would judge whether the United States had fulfilled its obligations; Wilson answered, "Nobody." Several senators probed him about Article X, and he reiterated his distinction between a legal and moral obligation—"Only we can interpret a moral obligation"—and he maintained that a reservation attached to the instrument of ratification would make it "necessary for others to act upon it." Lodge disagreed, saying that only an amendment to the treaty required such action; a reservation did not—and Knox concurred. Warren Harding of Ohio reportedly tried the president's patience by going on at length about obligations under Article X. "Now a moral obligation is of course superior to a legal obligation," Wilson snapped, "and, if I may say so, has a greater binding force."[22]

Questioning by Borah then led him to stumble. Asked about the French security treaty, he maintained incorrectly that it also imposed only a moral obligation: "In international law, 'legal' does not mean the same thing as in national law, and the word hardly applied." Asked when he first learned about the Allies' wartime secret treaties, he answered that he had not known about them until the peace conference. Some critics would call that answer a lie, but Hiram Johnson, who had learned from Walter Lippmann that the president had known about the treaties in 1917, told his sons only that Wilson's "memory played him false." When Johnson and Brandegee asked about Shantung, he first denied and then admitted that he had agreed to the cession because Japan threatened not to sign the treaty. Brandegee and Harding further badgered him about Article X, but Wilson stuck by its moral obligation, which "steadies the whole world by its promise that it will stand with other nations of similar judgment and maintain the right in the world." By all accounts, the tensest time in the meeting came when Brandegee relentlessly, and at times insolently, needled the president about Article X, but Wilson maintained his poise and good humor. When the senator pushed the idea of separating the treaty from the Covenant, the president called that an "unworkable peace, because the league is necessary to the working of it." Brandegee countered that the United States could opt out of any obligations under the treaty, and Wilson replied, "We could, sir, but I hope the people of the United States would never consent to it." Brandegee shot back, "There is no way by which the people can vote on it."[23]

The meeting had now gone on for more than three hours, and Lodge broke up this confrontation by inquiring about the resumption of trade with Germany. Other Republicans asked about eastern Europe and mandates over former German colonies. In response, Wilson stated erroneously that America was not involved in those matters. Harry New of Indiana, a Republican, asked how the Covenant might have affected the United States during the War of 1812 and the Spanish-American War, to which Wilson responded, "I have tried to be a historical student, but I could not quite get the league back to those days clearly enough in my mind to form a judgment." Lodge then interjected, "Mr. President, I do not wish to interfere in any way, the conference has now lasted about three hours and a half, and it is half an hour after the lunch hour." Wilson replied, "Will not you gentlemen take luncheon with me? It will be very delightful." All but two of the senators accompanied the president into the State Dining Room, where, according to newspaper reports, the president genially played host and told his guests stories from the peace conference; this time, although no alcohol was served, no senator complained about the meal.[24]

Memory lapses and mistakes aside, Wilson had stood up well under a barrage of hostile questions. Democrats on the committee took next to no part, although an occasional friendly question came from Pittman, as well as from the mild reservationist McCumber, a Republican. Lodge privately told friends that Wilson's performance "amounted to nothing" and that he "displayed ignorance and disingenuousness in his slippery evasions." By contrast, a League opponent, Fall, publicly praised Wilson for his frankness and manliness. Johnson said privately, "I rather think the day was his." That praise was strictly backhanded: Johnson thought Lodge and their colleagues should have seen through Wilson's "foxy and cunning manner." He found the president's expression "quite wicked" and his face "hard, and cold, and cruel. . . . His ponderous lower jaw gives a very vague appearance of a vicious horse."[25]

The delayed outcry in the Senate at Wilson's rejection of reservations exploded the day after his meeting with the Foreign Relations Committee. Pittman introduced a resolution stating four propositions as the basis for interpretation of the treaty; they covered withdrawal, domestic questions, the Monroe Doctrine, and Article X, which imposed a moral obligation subject to voluntary construction and compliance. The mild reservationists immediately repudiated Pittman's scheme; with the exception of McCumber, they demanded that any reservations be part of the instrument of ratification. The White House likewise pulled the rug out from under Pittman, authorizing Hitchcock to tell reporters, "The President had no knowledge of the resolution or its introduction." It was a case of a good intention gone awry.[26]

Meanwhile, Wilson's enemies were not idle. Lodge turned his committee's hearings into a sounding board for representatives of groups and nationalities that harbored grievances against the peace treaty, especially regarding Shantung and Ireland. After a delegation of leading Irish Americans spent six hours regaling the senators with stories about their frustration in trying to gain the president's support for Irish independence, Ashurst privately lamented, "These Irishmen, alas, are *lost* to the Democratic party in the next election."[27] Floor debate in the Senate also quickened, with twelve speeches on the treaty and the League during August. The most important of those came from Lodge on August 12 and Knox on August 29. Lodge self-consciously aimed at oratorical distinction and larded his long speech with literary allusions. Knox took a clear stand against the League—now definitively aligning himself with the irreconcilables—and other features of the treaty as well. He also unexpectedly condemned the settlement with Germany as a "hard and cruel peace," and he excoriated the economic clauses in a way that uncannily anticipated Keynes's as yet unpublished denunciation.

For Wilson, the unkindest cut of all came four days after his meeting with the Foreign Relations Committee. Right after the lunch at the White House, the irreconcilables on the committee—Borah, Brandegee, Johnson, and George Moses of New Hampshire—huddled to plot strategy. The following day, they met again in Knox's office, with reporters correctly reading the conclave as a sign that the former secretary of state was about to come out as an irreconcilable. The cabal decided to press Lodge and other Republicans to amend the text of the treaty, a move that if successful in the full Senate would indisputably require new negotiations and delay ratification. On August 23, they scored their first victory when the Republican majority on the committee, minus McCumber, voted to strike the Shantung clauses from the treaty. Democrats protested that the Allies, especially Japan, would never agree to this amendment, but Knox chortled, "The committee decided it would take independent action." Lodge gladly accepted the amendment and said he also wanted a reservation to Article X that was "much more drastic than anything hitherto drafted," declaring that "no compromise was possible."[28]

An angry Wilson was not slow to respond to what he saw as a slap in the face. On August 27, the White House announced that the president would undertake a speaking tour that would begin early in September and take him across the country and back. This decision struck some people as an impulsive act committed in anger, and some interpreters would read it as yet another sign of Wilson's declining health. Both Edith and Grayson tried to talk him out of making this trip, but according to Edith's recollection, he said, "I promised our soldiers, when I asked them to take up arms, that this was a war to end wars; and if I do not do all in my power to put the Treaty into effect, I will be a slacker and never able to look those boys in the eye. I must go."[29]

Although his wife's recollection may have embellished his words, Wilson probably did say something like that. This did not mean, however, as some interpreters would later claim, that he was courting martyrdom, seeking to sacrifice himself in a holy cause. Roosevelt might have wanted to do that, but Wilson did not think that way. He had always enjoyed campaigning, and he believed that a democratic leader—like the mythical figure Antaeus, who renewed his strength through contact with the earth—renewed his strength through contact with his people. He may have decided quickly to make the tour, but he was not acting impulsively. Twice before, he had postponed such a trip in order to deal with senators, and Tumulty evidently had arrangements more or less in place against the day when the president gave him the green light.

The decision to make the tour did not rule out continuing to deal with senators. On August 25, Wilson spent forty-five minutes in the office of one of the Democrats on the Foreign Relations Committee, Claude Swanson of Virginia, while Edith waited outside in the limousine. Swanson urged the president to accept reservations in the instrument of ratification. At that meeting and another one a week later, Wilson reiterated his opposition to amendments or anything that might require renegotiation of the treaty, but he authorized Swanson to tell reporters, "If interpretative reservations were deemed imperative, the President said he would not oppose them." He also met at the White House with one of the mild reservationists, Irvine Lenroot of Wisconsin, who later recalled that he spent an hour trying to persuade the president to accept a reservation relieving the United States of obligations under Article X, but Wilson refused, declaring that Article X was the heart of the treaty.[30]

Wilson also drafted four reservations of his own. Just before he boarded the train for the speaking tour, he summoned Hitchcock to the White House and gave him a paper titled "Suggestion," which he had typed himself and revised in his own hand. In a preamble, he asserted that the Senate should consent "with the following understanding" of certain articles. What followed were one-sentence reservations covering withdrawal, domestic questions such as "immigration, naturalization or tariffs," and the Monroe Doctrine. Those reservations were like the ones that had been proposed by Taft and Hughes and others and were being circulated by the mild reservationists. The fourth reservation, on Article X, asserted that action by the League Council was "to be regarded only as advice and leaves each Member State free to exercise its own judgment as to whether it is wise or practicable to act upon that advice or not." This was a significant concession, but it differed from other reservations in making no mention of Congress. Wilson was trying to retain presidential flexibility and his notion of "a moral obligation." It is doubtful that those reservations would have satisfied the mild reservationists or other Republicans, and it is not clear what Wilson hoped to accomplish with them. He forbade Hitchcock to tell anyone he had written them, again fearing that his opponents would demand further concessions; in any case, no one but the president could bargain with the senators, and he was going away for a month.[31]

Wilson's health seemed to take a turn for the better in the last part of August, but he was having trouble coordinating his political moves. Before he left on the tour, he had to turn his attention to the threatened railroad strike. On August 25, he met with union leaders and told them, "Our common enemy is the profiteer." By appealing for cooperation and agreeing to a modest wage hike, he was able to head off a strike. That same day, he and Edith gave their only party of the summer, a reception on the White House lawn for wounded soldiers. When one of the soldiers took a photograph of the president carrying a cake and some ice cream, as Edith recalled, the doughboy remarked "that he guessed that was the first time a President had ever been caught doing K. P."—slang for "kitchen police" duty.[32] It was the last party the Wilsons would give at the White House.

On the night of September 3, the presidential train left Washington. At the rear, Wilson's private car, also called the Mayflower, contained a sitting room, where the president and Edith ate at a folding table; a bedroom for each of them plus one for Edith's maid and another for Dr. Grayson; and a kitchen staffed by White House cooks. The rest of the train consisted of a dining car, a club car, and sleeping cars for Tumulty, stenographers, Secret Service agents, and twenty-one members of the press, as well as the servants and train crew. Tumulty would regularly spend time with the reporters in the club car, and Wilson would also sometimes go back to talk to them. The train functioned as a miniature mobile White House, and for the Wilsons, except for three nights when they slept in a hotel, it would be their rolling, jostling home for three and a half weeks.[33]

The arrangements made the tour look like one of Wilson's presidential campaigns. As usual, he spoke without notes, although now he resorted to outlines. At some time, probably shortly before he left Washington, he had typed an eight-page outline on particular subjects, such as the nature and scope of the treaty and the League Covenant. Sometime on the trip, probably while he was in California or just afterward, he would type another outline, including extracts from the treaty and Covenant to use as quotations. Wilson had never done anything like that before, and it may have betrayed waning confidence in his once-formidable memory and gifts as an extemporaneous speaker. As in the presidential campaigns, stenographers took down his speeches, which they promptly typed, copied, and distributed, not just to the traveling press but also to local reporters who covered the event at each stop. Nor did the distribution end there. Assisted by the LEP, Tumulty sent out texts of the president's speeches to 1,400 smaller newspapers throughout the country—at a cost of $1,000 a day, financed mostly by the automobile tycoon Henry Ford. Tumulty kept the train's telegraph lines humming with requests for information to use in the speeches, reports on opinion in Washington and around the country, and "personal" messages supposedly from the president to individual senators.[34]

The first stop on the tour came when the train pulled into Columbus, Ohio, at eleven in the morning on September 4. Dignitaries greeted the presidential party, and a motorcade took them to a municipal auditorium. Crowds along the streets were friendly but, because of a streetcar strike, not large. Still, at the auditorium, 4,000 people packed the seats and aisles, and another 2,000 reportedly tried to get in. Wilson launched into a defense of the treaty and an attack on his opponents. In an implicit reply to Knox's recent speech, he declared, "The terms of the treaty are severe, but they are not unjust." After touching on various aspects of the settlement, he spent most of the hour-long speech talking about the League. He professed astonishment at the ignorance and "radical misunderstanding" of the League, which was intended not "merely to end this war. It was intended to prevent any similar war. . . . [T]he League of Nations is the only thing that can prevent the recurrence of this dreadful catastrophe and redeem our promises." He closed by saluting "our boys in khaki . . . because I have done the job the way I promised I would do it. And when this treaty is accepted, men in khaki will not have to cross the seas again. That is the reason I believe in it." The crowd loved the speech.[35]

The train then made its way to Indianapolis, with whistle-stop appearances along the way. Again, dignitaries were on hand to greet the president and First Lady, and a motorcade took them to the state fair-

grounds, where between 16,000 and 20,000 people swelled the auditorium. The size of the crowd and poor acoustics made it hard for the audience to hear Wilson, who spoke in a husky voice. As he had done earlier in
the day, he jumped around in discussing different parts of the treaty, but
he devoted much of the speech to Article X, and he eschewed partisanship
in his advocacy of the peace settlement. This speech also made a big hit,
with frequent applause and people shouting, in reference to Indiana's two
Republican senators, "Better tell that to Harry New and Jim Watson."[36]

That first day revealed the pattern and problems that would shape and
plague the tour. Unlike the presidential campaigns, this swing around the
circle was not well paced. Wilson would give forty speeches in twenty-one
days, and the original plan called for even more. Never before had he spoken so often and made so many public appearances in so short a time—not
in his gubernatorial or presidential campaigns, not on the New Jersey and
1916 preparedness speaking tours, which were his models for what he
intended to do now. Wilson was trying to do too much too fast to educate
the public about his ideas and his program in a belated attempt to make up
for time lost. Moreover, the extent and complexity of the subjects he
needed to cover strained his explanatory powers—small wonder, then,
that he jumped around in these speeches.

Overshadowing those problems was Wilson's health. The wonder of
this speaking tour was that he did as well, and lasted as long, as he did.
Some of his initial fumbling stemmed from a slowness in hitting his stride
on the trail, a trait he had first shown when he ran for governor. The first
week of the tour took him through Ohio, Missouri, Iowa, Indiana,
Nebraska, South Dakota, and Minnesota as he made two speeches a day,
except for a break on Sunday. State and local officials greeted the party at
each stop, and a motorcade or bigger parade took them to the site of the
speech. Grayson clashed with Tumulty about Wilson's speaking at whistle-
stops. The doctor vetoed such talks, but even shaking hands with people
who crowded the rear platform tired Wilson, as did the late-summer heat
in the nation's heartland. "I believe I lost at least two pounds," the president joked to reporters on the third day of the tour.[37]

As in his earlier campaigns, once Wilson hit his stride, his speaking improved during most of the rest of the tour. Beginning in St. Louis
on the second day, he emphasized a few basic points in each speech, usually explanations of how the League and Article X were going to work.
He also made greater use of his outline, and his performance varied with
his level of fatigue. In his best speeches, he blended his well-worn talent
for appealing to people's minds through clear explanations with his more
recent penchant for appealing to their hearts. To businessmen in St.

Louis, he extolled the benefits they would reap from the restoration of international trade, while to his audience in Omaha, which presumably included farmers, he compared the international system without Article X to a community where everyone had to defend his own land. He conceded that the League would bring "no absolute guarantee" against another world war, but "I can predict with absolute certainty that, within another generation, there will be another world war if the nations of the world—if the League of Nations—does not prevent it by concerted action."[38]

Wilson also made pointed emotional appeals. In Sioux Falls, South Dakota, he singled out mothers who had lost their sons in the war, and in St. Louis he warned that without the League and Article X, America would have to stay on a permanent war footing and be ruled by "Prussian" military despotism. In Kansas City, he avowed that he was fighting for something "as great as the cause of mankind" and added that he was descended from "troublesome Scotchmen" known as Covenanters: "Very well here is the Covenant of the League of Nations. I am a Covenanter!"[39] It was no accident that he made that declaration of defiance in the adopted hometown of Senator Reed, his persistent antagonist in the Democratic Party and now one of his fiercest foes on the League.

In the supercharged political and social atmosphere of the summer of 1919, emotional appeals carried the danger of demagoguery. Wilson leaned in that direction just a few times on this speaking tour. Anti-German sentiment offered the greatest temptation, and some League advocates, most notably Taft, touted the organization as a way to keep Germany downtrodden. Wilson used that argument only sparingly in his speeches. An almost equally great temptation lay in the rising tide of anti-Bolshevik and anti-radical sentiment that would soon erupt into Attorney General Palmer's Red scare. At Kansas City, Wilson scorned the Bolsheviks and slyly linked their destructive spirit to some anti-League spokesmen. Later on the tour, he would take a few more passing swipes at the Bolsheviks, but that was the single time he tried to tar his opponents with the anti-Bolshevik brush. Again, it was noteworthy that Wilson stooped toward demagoguery in the hometown of Reed, who had recently hurled blatantly racist denunciations at the League.

Most of the president's sins and errors on the tour fell under the heading of omission. He showed his two most glaring kinds of omission in his speeches during the first week. In his explanations of the treaty, he continued to shy away from responding to criticism. He also failed to suggest possible compromises and reach out to senators. Only once on the tour did he mention any senators by name: in Omaha, he thanked Hitchcock for his support and expressed the hope—in vain—that Norris would join him. Otherwise, in a senator's state, friend, foe, and fence-sitter alike went unmentioned by name and, with a few exceptions, by implication. Tumulty's "personal" telegrams from the presidential train were efforts to repair such omissions.

Wilson was aiming his oratory at an audience beyond the people who came to hear him. The press coverage, which included the texts of the speeches, enabled him to try to influence opinion throughout the country, which, in turn, he hoped would sway senators. This was not a vain hope. Despite Brandegee's sneer that people could not vote on the treaty, his colleagues paid attention to public opinion and made their own efforts to influence it. Borah, Johnson, and Reed set out on speaking tours of their own, arranged and financed by the Independence League, to trail the president. In Washington, on the first day of Wilson's tour, Lodge marshaled the Republicans on the Foreign Relations Committee, except McCumber, to pass four reservations. Three of them asserted the absolute right to withdraw from the League and exempt domestic questions and the Monroe Doctrine from its jurisdiction. The fourth declined "any obligation to preserve territorial integrity or political independence of any other country," join in economic boycotts, employ American armed forces, or accept a mandate except by act of Congress. The public impact of the committee's action delighted Lodge, who told a friend, "Our reservations made a hit and shared the front page with Wilson."[40]

The senator soon savored a much bigger publicity coup. On September 12, his committee heard testimony from William Bullitt, the young diplomat who had resigned publicly in protest from the peace conference delegation. After two hours of leisurely questioning, Bullitt produced a memorandum of a conversation in which Secretary of State Lansing had condemned much of the treaty, especially the parts dealing with Shantung and the League. Bullitt quoted Lansing as stating, "I consider that the league of nations at present is entirely useless," and if the Senate and the people really understood the treaty, "it would unquestionably be defeated." This bombshell made headlines in every major newspaper. Lansing refused to comment and left for a fishing trip on Lake Ontario. After he returned, he stonewalled reporters with the feeble excuse that he could not say anything until he had read the full, official transcript of Bullitt's testimony. His real reason for not speaking, he privately explained, was that Bullitt's "garbled" account contained "enough truth so that I would have to explain my statements as quoted by the little traitor. I could not flatly deny the testimony."[41]

Wilson was furious. For five days after Bullitt's testimony, Lansing did not contact him, and then he telegraphed a brief account of the conversation in Paris, calling Bullitt's conduct "most despicable and outrageous." Tumulty later recalled that Wilson summoned him to the private car and showed him Lansing's telegram: "Read this and tell me what you think of a man who was my associate on the other side and who expressed himself to an outsider in such a fashion: Were I in Washington I would at once demand his resignation. Think of it! This from a man whom I raised from the level of a subordinate to the great office of Secretary of State of the United States. My God! I did not think it was possible for Lansing to act in this way."[42] Given his own attitude and their past relations, Lansing's behavior should not have surprised Wilson. On his return to Washington, Lansing circulated to cabinet colleagues a letter of resignation in which he expressed bitter disappointment at the president's failure to fulfill the Fourteen Points and live up to the idealism of the war. Only the president's stroke would prevent Lansing from staging a dramatic, damaging exit.

As the presidential train made its way across the Great Plains, the sparse, scattered population meant fewer stops and speeches during the second week of the tour and more time for Wilson to rest. Grayson continued to worry about the accumulating effects of heat, fatigue, and the noise and motion of the train, and he commented in his diary that his patient was having headaches that lasted several days and kept coming back. Wilson was also having trouble breathing, which may have been because of the thinner air and dry heat of the Plains and Rockies. Whether or not these ailments were warning signs of an impending stroke, they showed that the rigors of the tour were harming Wilson's health.[43]

With his usual mix of determination and denial, he soldiered on, but his speeches seemed to suffer from his deteriorating health. In North Dakota and Montana, he delivered disjointed, rambling remarks, and once he abruptly switched to domestic affairs, expressing "my shame as an American citizen at the race riots that have occurred in some places." This was Wilson's only public statement on the racial violence of the summer of 1919. He made no separate, extended statement condemning the violence, as he had done against lynching a year before. His absorption in the League fight probably explained this silence and neglect, but it was a lamentable failure of presidential leadership, especially for someone as eloquent as Wilson. He added insult to injury by linking this brief, passing mention of the race riots with the strike by the police force in Boston, which he called "a crime against civilization."[44]

When the train reached the Pacific Northwest, with its lower altitude and higher humidity, Wilson's health seemed to improve, and his speeches grew more hard-hitting. He called Article X "the heart of the pledge we

have made to other nations in the world" and said he could accept interpretative reservations but not ones "which give the United States a position of special privilege or special exemption." He began to make his most
poignant emotional appeal when he noted that at every station there were
"little children—bright-eyed little boys, excited little girls"—who might
have to fight another world war. He began to praise the LEP and Taft, and
he quoted Lodge's 1915 espousal of the league idea. In doing that, he was
following advice from Tumulty to reach out to the other party. He also
asked his audience to give no thought to the 1920 election and asked them
to "forget, if you please, that I had anything to do with . . . [the League]."[45]

Was Wilson suggesting that he would not run again and hinting at
what might happen if he disavowed a third term? Most political wisdom
counseled against disavowing a third term—at least then. The threat of
running in 1920 was the biggest stick he could wield. With Roosevelt
gone, no one commanded anything like Wilson's stature, and he was making this tour to remind friend and foe of his public appeal. Reports were
reaching him that Democrats in the Senate might defect to support reservations, and taking himself out of the presidential race would rob him of
the best way to keep them in line. Yet an announcement that he would not
run would have reshaped the League fight. It would instantly have made
people forget the Bullitt-Lansing fiasco, and it could have had a healthy,
air-clearing impact on the larger debate. It would have allowed the president to put himself forward as the totally disinterested seeker of peace.

He enjoyed his longest, most restful respite from the grind of the tour
when the train traveled two nights and a day through scenic woods and
mountains in Oregon and California on the way to San Francisco. The
tour was now in its third week, and he would spend the next six days in
California. Two days and nights in San Francisco marked the longest stop
on the trip, and one of the three times when he and Edith slept in a hotel.
The speeches he gave in California were the best of the tour, and a few
ranked among the finest Wilson ever gave. In San Francisco, he explained
the obligation under Article X and charged his opponents with wanting
"to make it [the League] a matter of opinion merely." In Oakland, he
pointed again to the "little children who [seem] to be my real clients,"
because unless the League works, "there will be another and final war just
about the time these children come to maturity."[46] Wilson got a lift from
giving those speeches and from the enthusiastic reception in Hiram Johnson's adopted hometown. Grayson believed that this tonic effect offset the
headaches. A restful day with only short stops and no speeches on the way
to San Diego further refreshed him.

Perhaps as a result, Wilson went on to give the finest speech of the tour. On September 19 in San Diego, he addressed a crowd of 30,000 in an outdoor stadium. The speaker's platform had a glass box with a "voice phone" inside and electric wires connected to megaphones aimed at the audience. This early use of a microphone and electric amplifiers offered a taste of things to come: the Democrats' gathering the next year in San Francisco would be the first national political convention to use such technology. Now, Wilson did not enjoy the experience because he could not move around, yet the constraint did not seem to affect his performance. He declared that "the great heart of humanity beats in this document," and he answered criticisms, again rejecting reservations that sought "an unjust position of privilege." He ended with another reference to the children: "I know, if by any chance, we should not win this great fight for the League of Nations, it would mean their death warrant." They would have to fight "that final war" in which the "very existence of civilization would be in the balance," and to reject the League would betray the sacrifices of mothers of sons who had laid down "their lives for an idea, for an ideal, for the only thing that is worth living for—the spiritual redemption that rests in the hearts of humanity."[47]

That night and the next, he and Edith slept in a hotel in Los Angeles and spent Sunday there before starting on the return leg of the trip. The day of rest included a reminder of a painful part of Wilson's past: Mary Allen Hulbert, formerly Mrs. Peck, came to have lunch at the hotel with him, Edith, and Grayson. This was the first time the two women met. "She came," Edith later wrote, "—a faded, sweet-looking woman who was absorbed in an only son." According to Edith, Mary Hulbert told tales of her difficulties and took up time Wilson needed to spend with other visitors, but he insisted on hearing about her troubles. When the talk turned to the stories about the two of them, Wilson cried out, "God, to think that you should have suffered because of me." In parting, as Edith went to get her coat, Wilson asked, "Mary, is there nothing we can do?" She asked only if he could help her son. Edith walked her to the elevator, which, Mrs. Hulbert would write, "quickly dropped me out of the life of my friend Woodrow Wilson."[48]

The rest of the third week of the speaking tour brought an ascent in altitude and a decline in performance. The distances between cities in the Rockies gave Wilson more time to rest, but the thinner, drier air caused him breathing problems again. Grayson noted in his diary that the president had constant headaches and coughing spells. Five years later, the doctor would claim that in Los Angeles he had seen a more alarming sign: "Little drops of saliva appeared at the corners of Mr. Wilson's mouth. The saliva continued. His pallor increased." That recollection smacked of a face-saving claim on Grayson's part that he had diagnosed his patient's true condition earlier than he did. News from Washington did not help either. When the train made a stop in Ogden, Utah, on September 23, Wilson received a telegram informing him that Lodge had reached an agreement with McCumber and other senators on the Foreign Relations Committee about a reservation on Article X. At first, the president appeared to react calmly, instructing Tumulty to telegraph back to the White House for more information. The calm was deceptive. In brief remarks after a motorcade in Ogden, Wilson lashed out, saying that "all the elements that tended toward disloyalty are against the League, and for a very good reason. If this League is not adopted, we will serve Germany's purpose."[49]

When he spoke that evening at the Mormon Tabernacle in Salt Lake City, a crowd estimated at between 13,000 and 15,000 packed the unventilated hall. "The fetid air we encountered was unlike anything I have ever experienced," Edith recalled. She nearly fainted, and she found that her husband's suit jacket was soaked with perspiration. Wilson gave his worst performance on the tour. He equated—erroneously—reservations with amendments and claimed they would require the assent of all signatories to the treaty, including Germany. Then he read the text of the reservation that the committee members had just agreed to, and when the audience applauded, he lashed out, "Wait until you understand the meaning of it, and if you have a knife in your hand with which you intend to cut out the heart of the Covenant, applaud." Recovering his poise, he maintained that nothing in the Covenant impaired Congress's sole power to declare war. Furthermore, common sense would prevent sending American forces to faraway fights: "If you want to put out a fire in Utah, you don't send to Oklahoma for the fire engine." He argued that reservations like that one undermined the moral obligation under Article X, and, thereby, "by holding off from the League, they serve the purposes of Germany."[50]

The speech was so bad that even the normally uncritical Tumulty told him, "Frankly, your 'punch' did not land last night." He advised Wilson to stick to a few main points, particularly the assertion that failure to enter the League wholeheartedly would betray the sacrifices of the men who had fallen in the war. Tumulty also took the unusual step of drafting a speech that included a comparison between Article X and the last statement on the league idea by Roosevelt. Wilson did not adopt Tumulty's suggestion, but the next day in Cheyenne, Wyoming, he declared that Article X "cuts at the taproot of war," and he urged senators who supported reservations— "men whom I greatly respect"—to realize that they would "make no general promise" and leave other nations to guess what they felt obligated to do in each instance. On September 25 in Denver, he painted a picture of the next war: the last war's weapons "were toys as compared with what would be used in the next war." That war "would be the destruction of mankind. And I am for any kind of insurance against it and the barbarous reversal of civilization." Wilson bobbed on reservations. He still maintained, "Qualified adoption is not adoption," but he added that it was legitimate "to say in what sense we understand certain articles." He also pointed out that contrary to what people thought, the Senate did not ratify a treaty but gave only advice and consent: final ratification lay with the president.[51]

In the afternoon of September 25, Wilson spoke at the Colorado state fairgrounds in Pueblo. Grayson noted that the president had a splitting headache all day, but he gave a strong, moving speech. This time, he followed Tumulty's suggestion and quoted Roosevelt on the need for organized peace, which he equated with Article X, which the United States could not adopt "on a special privilege basis." He again painted a picture of a militarized America in the event that America did not enter the League, and he closed with an avowal that Americans had seen "the truth of justice and of liberty and of peace. We have accepted that truth, and we are going to be led by it, and it is going to lead us, and, through us, the world out into the pastures of quietness and peace such as the world has never dreamed of before."[52]

Those were Wilson's last words on the speaking tour, and they ended the last extended speech he would ever give. They would be the closing lines of one of the greatest speaking careers in American history—a final burst of eloquence from a dying star. Daniel Patrick Moynihan, who would later make himself the most shining example of the scholar in politics since Wilson, would deem the speech at Pueblo "as moving as anything in the language of the American presidency," and he would call it a "speech from the cross."[53] Laudatory as that comparison is, it would not have entirely pleased Wilson. He never thought of himself as a messiah, and he did not entertain any intimations of finality as he spoke in Pueblo. The tour was only three quarters completed, and the schedule included five more stops with major speeches before the return to Washington. Wilson planned to make another speaking tour in October that would take him to the Northeast and include a stop in Boston, where he would pull Lodge's pointed beard in his own hometown. None of that was to be.

On the train, Grayson noted that Wilson was tired and in pain. He suggested a walk, and about twenty miles outside Pueblo the train stopped. With Edith and Grayson, Wilson walked briskly for about an hour. Along the way, an old farmer driving his car recognized the president and stopped to shake his hand and give him a cabbage and some apples. Later, Wilson spotted a sick-looking soldier in a private's uniform sitting on the porch of a house, and he climbed over a fence to shake hands with him. At dinner, he said he thought the walk had done him good, and his appetite was better than it had been for several days. Wilson insisted on staying up until ten o'clock, when the train made a last stop in Colorado, at Rocky Ford. The doctor tried to keep the president from going out on the platform, but as the train pulled out, Wilson did get in some hand shaking and then waved to the people lined up beside the tracks.[54] It was the last flesh-pressing public appearance Wilson would make.

Later that night, as Edith recalled, her husband knocked on the door of her compartment and told her he could not sleep because his headache was "unbearable." She called Grayson, who found Wilson "in a highly nervous condition, the muscles of his face were twitching, and he was completely nauseated." The doctor did what he could to relieve the pain and suggested that the rest of the trip be canceled; Wilson protested that his enemies would call him a quitter. Edith and Grayson propped him up on pillows in the study in an effort to get him to sleep, and he finally did around five. "That night was the longest and most heart-breaking of my life," Edith later wrote.[55]

While Wilson slept, Grayson went to see Tumulty and told him that the rest of the trip must be canceled. Tumulty in turn sent word to the engineer to stop the train in the yards outside Wichita, Kansas. Whether Grayson immediately suspected something more serious than exhaustion is not clear, but at some point he did. Six weeks later, he told Ray Stannard Baker that on the way eastward he had seen "a curious drag or looseness at the left side of his mouth—a sign of danger that could no longer be obscured."[56] That may have been a symptom of what neurologists now term a transient ischemic attack—a temporary blockage in the smaller capillaries of the brain that often prefigures a stroke. Grayson was not trained in neurology, and at no time in his diary did he use the word *stroke*. Still, he must have suspected something was wrong in the president's circulatory system, because he asked two specialists from Philadelphia to examine the president. But Grayson did not summon those doctors until after the party had returned to Washington.

When Wilson woke the next morning in Wichita, he tried to resist the plans to cancel the trip, but Grayson insisted. When Tumulty came to talk to him about arrangements, he admitted, "I don't seem to realize it, but I seem to have gone to pieces. The Doctor is right. I am not in condition to go on. I have never been in a condition like this, and I just feel as if

I am going to pieces." Then he looked out the window and wept. Tumulty issued a statement to the press that the rest of the trip was being canceled because the president's exertions had brought on "a nervous reaction in his digestive organs." The railroad cleared the tracks so that the train could proceed directly to Washington. Wilson stayed in his compartment; twice Grayson had railroad officials slow the train in an attempt to ease his patient's suffering. When the train arrived at Union Station, a photographer snapped a picture that shows the president's face haggard and his mouth fixed in a grimace.[57]

The speaking tour had unquestionably taken a toll on Wilson, and serious questions arose immediately about whether it had been worth the price he paid. Critics and opponents predictably scoffed at his effort to influence public opinion and the Senate while supporters praised it. The most balanced assessment came from Secretary of War Baker, who told a friend at the end of the tour that Wilson had gotten an enthusiastic reception but, "[a]s one of the Senators said to me the other day, 'Nearly every Senator has from four to six years to serve, and they are perfectly willing to let future events cover up any present disapproval of their course of action.'" Most interpreters since then have echoed that assessment, although some have gone further and maintained that Wilson went on a fool's errand that produced no results and left him a broken man. By contrast, one of the veteran reporters on the tour, Charles Grasty of *The New York Times*, told a friend soon afterward "that the President would have produced an enormous effect if he had continued." Grasty probably meant not just the rest of this tour but also the next one Wilson planned, in the Northeast.[58]

Wilson made mistakes on the tour, particularly in failing to target senators for praise or criticism, and his speeches often suffered from his deteriorating health. Yet with all due allowance for such shortcomings, he put on a remarkable performance. Taken together, his speeches put forward the most compelling case for his side in the League fight. He effectively answered the major criticisms of the League and the treaty, especially those aimed at Article X and Shantung, and he delivered deeply moving appeals to spare that generation's children from the horrors of another world war. He did tread occasionally on the verge of demagoguery, as when he pointed to the specter of Bolshevism, cast aspersions on the motives of his opponents, and played on anti-German sentiment. In fact, he might have stirred up public opinion more and put greater heat on senators by resorting to more of those appeals. But that was not like Wilson: he rarely chose to stoop to conquer.

Instead, he chose to make the most extensive effort any president has ever made to try to educate the public about foreign policy. He was doing the job of democratic leadership that he valued most and did best; he was trying to reach the minds of the people and draw forth thoughtful, considered support from them. He had done this throughout his political career, most notably in his first presidential campaign, and it is interesting to speculate how well he might have done now if he had been younger and more vigorous. It is also interesting to speculate on what he might have accomplished if he had enjoyed the benefit of an impending technological breakthrough. His encounter with the microphone in San Diego presaged the advent of radio. Some interpreters have wondered whether he could have rallied greater support if he had been able to use the radio. Wilson was the kind of speaker who might have developed something akin to Franklin Roosevelt's Fireside Chats and used them with great effectiveness in making his case for the treaty and the League.[59]

The League fight marked the last flowering of a great oratorical tradition that had flourished in America in the nineteenth century and again in the first two decades of the twentieth century. Bryan, Roosevelt, La Follette, Albert Beveridge, William Borah, and Hiram Johnson, as well as Wilson, had sought to educate the public about great domestic reform issues. With World War I, those men and others had turned their efforts to foreign policy, thereby ensuring a level of public debate that would never be matched again. Political contests had always featured manipulation and heated emotional appeals, and the rise of marketing and advertising had added to those elements. Moreover, a new oratorical approach borrowed from Protestant evangelism was coming into vogue. Both Bryan and Roosevelt had proudly proclaimed themselves "political evangelists." Nor was Wilson immune to such evangelism, as he had shown particularly on this speaking tour. Soon, new media—first radio, then newsreels, and finally television—would vastly expand politicians' reach, but at the price of shorter exposures that offered fewer chances for education and more for exhortation and manipulation. Wilson and his cohorts and adversaries in the League fight were practicing a dying art.[60]

Back at the White House, the president went into seclusion. Rest was the only treatment that Grayson or any physician could then prescribe, but as Edith recalled, "My husband wandered like a ghost between the study at one end of the hall and my room at the other. The awful pain in his head that drove him relentlessly back and forth was too acute to permit work, or even reading." They took short rides in the limousine, and on the third day back, October 1, they watched a movie in the East Room. Edith thought Wilson seemed better, and she took it as a good sign that he insisted on reading aloud from the Bible. The next morning, however, she noticed that his left hand hung limply. "I have no feeling in that hand," she remembered him saying. "Will you rub it? But first help me to the bathroom." Edith recalled that he got there with difficulty and pain, and while she went to telephone Grayson, he fell and lost consciousness. Other accounts closer to the time said that when he got up in the morning, he felt numbness and weakness in his left leg and sank to the bedroom floor when he tried to make his way to the bathroom. Either way—as Grayson immediately suspected when he arrived—Wilson had suffered a stroke.[61]

After talking with two other physicians who consulted at the White House, Grayson telephoned Francis X. Dercum, a Philadelphia neurologist who was to see the president the next day, and asked him to come at once. When Dercum's train arrived at Union Station, Grayson met him and briefed him in the car on the way to the White House. Dercum began his examination at four-thirty in the afternoon. He found Wilson's left arm and leg completely paralyzed and the lower part of the left side of his face drooping. Wilson was conscious but somnolent and answered questions slowly but clearly. Dercum's diagnosis, which he confirmed after another examination nine days later, "was that of a severe organic hemiplegia, probably due to a thrombosis of the middle right hemisphere." He ruled out an ingravescent hemorrhage "because of the extremely gradual onset of the symptoms" and because the patient had not lost consciousness or died. That was the neurologist's way of saying that Wilson had not suffered a stroke caused by a hemorrhage, often called an apoplectic stroke, which has a sudden onset, causes loss of consciousness, and is often fatal. Instead, he had suffered what would later be called an ischemic stroke, one caused by clotting, which has a gradual onset, does not cause loss of consciousness, and is rarely fatal.[62]

That was good news, comparatively speaking, and a few other factors also held out hope. Because Wilson was right-handed, a stroke on the right side of the brain would not impair his ability to write or perform tasks with his dominant hand. An ischemic stroke on the right side of the brain does not affect intellectual functioning or speech. Recovery of function is common in the affected leg, but less so in the arm; the degree of recovery depends upon the severity of the brain damage done by the stroke and the patient's age and physical condition. The bad news was that this kind of stroke usually leaves some physical impairment and can cause other problems. It can affect eyesight by reducing the visual field, as George de Schweinitz, the ophthalmologist, found had occurred when he examined Wilson on October 4. In addition, some of the stroke's worst consequences can be emotional and psychological, limiting the sufferer's attention span and ability to adapt to changing circumstances and exercise judgment. How much those consequences would affect Wilson would soon become apparent.

At first, the president appeared to be bearing up reasonably well. On October 3, Dr. Dercum told reporters, "He is very cheerful and takes an interest in what is going on." That was true, but Dercum, Grayson, and the other physicians attending Wilson would issue only upbeat statements to the press, never mention or hint at a stroke, and refer only and vaguely to nervous exhaustion. The following day, Wilson said to Grayson, "I'll show you my temper if you keep me in this bed much longer." On October 6, when Wilson found out that cabinet members had called a meeting without consulting him, Grayson told the cabinet members, "The President wanted to know why a meeting of Cabinet was held—did not like it." If the stroke had not dampened Wilson's temper, it had not stifled his sense of humor either. He recited limericks to the doctors and accused one of them who was drawing blood of doing to him what the Senate wanted to do.[63]

Those were good signs and might have pointed to a rapid recovery if another illness had not intervened. The stroke did not threaten to kill Wilson, but a probably unrelated infection of the prostate gland, which he developed on October 14, did put his life in danger. The infection caused an alarming urinary blockage and high fever. Surgery offered the only sure way to relieve the blockage, but it would be dangerous for someone in Wilson's condition. After hesitating and consulting with other physicians, Grayson called in a leading urologist, who examined the president on October 17 and recommended the continued application of hot compresses. After four days, this treatment succeeded in reducing the swelling and relieving the blockage. Wilson had hovered near death for more than a week, and he emerged from the ordeal more weakened than ever.

If there had ever been any question about the president's resuming an active role in the League fight after his return to Washington, the combination of the stroke and this life-threatening illness laid all such notions to rest. Yet the cancellation of Wilson's speaking tour did not signify the end of his part in this political conflict: he still had a final, decisive role to play. Nevertheless, the train had brought back a sick man who could no longer act as the principal combatant in the League fight or fully function as president. Nearly a year and a half of Woodrow Wilson's term in the White House remained, but he would never again occupy his office and wield its powers as he had done before.

23

DISABILITY

The stroke and illness Woodrow Wilson suffered in October 1919 brought on the worst crisis of presidential disability in American history. Nothing like it had ever happened before. Five presidents had died in office and had been succeeded by their vice presidents. In all but one of those instances, the fallen president had died within hours, as Lincoln did, or within a few days. The sole exception was in 1881, when James A. Garfield had lingered for two months after a would-be assassin shot him. Though weakened, Garfield had remained alert and in command of his faculties, and little pressing public business had required his attention. Things were totally different now: it was plain from the first that Wilson's disability was going to create problems and raise questions that the nation had not yet faced.[1]

At the outset, the question of whether the president should resign or be removed from office came to several people's minds. Not surprisingly, the one person who does not seem to have contemplated that prospect was Wilson himself. Just a few times during the rest of his presidency would he mention resigning, and those would be months after he suffered the stroke and had begun to recover. For the first three weeks, the White House head usher recalled, "[h]e just lay helpless. . . . He was lifted out of bed and placed in a comfortable chair for a short while each day. He gradually seemed to kind of get used to his helpless condition. At times Mrs. Wilson would read to him."[2] The thoughts that passed through Wilson's mind as he lay in bed in that upper room in the White House almost certainly did not include resignation. He had always dealt with illnesses and obstacles by denying their existence or minimizing their severity. Moreover, he was in the middle of the biggest political fight of his life, and he had resisted abandoning the speaking tour because he did not want his enemies to call him a "quitter." In that frame of mind, stepping down would never have occurred to him.

Edith supposedly did think about his resignation. As she later told the story, Dr. Dercum spoke reassuringly about her husband's condition, citing the scientist Louis Pasteur, "who had been stricken exactly in this way, but had recovered and did his most brilliant work afterwards." Recovery would depend on relieving the president of stress, the neurologist told her: "But always keep in mind that every time you take him a new anxiety or problem to excite him, you are turning a knife in an open wound." Edith asked whether he should resign, and the doctor responded with an emphatic no: "He has staked his life and made his promise to the world to do all in his power to get the Treaty ratified and make the League of Nations complete. If he resigns, the greatest incentive to recovery is gone; and as his mind is clear as crystal he can still do more with even a maimed body than any one else." Edith said Dercum also advised her to act as a clearinghouse and to judge whether matters really needed to come to the president's attention.3

That recollection suffered from the embroidery of memory. It is highly unlikely that Dercum or any responsible physician would have talked to Mrs. Wilson that way. None of the doctors' records of their consultations contains any comment on how resignation might affect the president's recovery. They did share the diagnosis of a stroke with Edith and with Wilson's daughter Margaret, but Grayson noted that everyone agreed they should issue "only a general statement regarding the President's case. . . . Mrs. Wilson, the President's wife[,] was absolutely opposed to any other course." She seems to have latched onto the uncertainty about the extent of her husband's impairment and the likelihood of some recovery to rule out resignation and forbid any mention of a stroke.4

Edith Wilson would later come in for harsh criticism for those decisions. Some interpreters would fault her for putting wifely concern about her husband's health ahead of the good of the country and the world. She probably did think that staying on as president would help him recover, but that was not the main reason why she rejected resignation. She must have believed that she was speaking for him, doing what he wanted to do, and she read his mind right. Edith would receive even harsher criticism for another decision. She had already started to act as the gatekeeper for the president when, two days before the stroke, she had barred Wiseman from seeing Wilson. After the stroke, supposedly on Dercum's advice, she continued the practice. Her "stewardship," as she called it, included reading all the papers that came to the office and deciding which ones to pass on to her husband.5

Except for her, Wilson's daughters Margaret and Jessie (Nell was on the West Coast and came later), doctors and nurses, and a few White House servants, no one got to see the president for nearly a month after the stroke. Thereafter, Edith continued to act as gatekeeper, restricting access to her husband until well into 1920. Tumulty would not get to see the president until mid-November; afterward, he would gain access only for occasional meetings and would usually go through Edith. In screening Wilson from outside contact the way they did, Edith and Grayson were following the medical thinking of the time about treating stroke patients. Moreover, the life-threatening prostate infection and urinary blockage reinforced the decision to isolate him. Later, physicians would reverse themselves because they would discover that such isolation worsens the psychological impact of a stroke. Patients need the stimulation of outside contacts to recover their capacity for dealing with reality and to keep them from entertaining illusions about how things were before the stroke. Ironically, and with the best intentions, the president's wife and doctor were doing one of the worst things possible for him.

In later years, Edith Wilson would defend herself against charges that she had usurped the powers of the presidency. "I, myself, never made a single decision regarding the disposition of public affairs," she declared. The First Lady did protest too much. In one case, she probably did make an important policy decision. In late October, three weeks after the stroke, Congress passed the Volstead Act, the law to enforce prohibition under the recently ratified Eighteenth Amendment. Most likely with Edith's consent and without Wilson's knowledge, Tumulty wrote a veto message, which Secretary of Agriculture Houston revised. This action was consistent with Wilson's views on prohibition, but given that the measure had passed by big majorities in both houses of Congress, an override seemed foreordained. Nor was Edith's gatekeeper role as small or benign as she maintained. The person who controls access to the president is, to a degree, president. Many people believed that was just what she was. There were charges that the country had a woman president, that the nation was afflicted with "government by petticoat." What no one seemed to ask was, if there was going to be a surrogate president, who was better qualified than this woman, who was her husband's closest confidant, who knew his mind better than anyone else?[6]

Whether there should have been a surrogate president at all was a different matter. Many people did not think there should be, and some of them made moves toward removing Wilson from office. The first person to raise the issue was Lansing. On October 3, the day after the stroke, he met for two hours with Tumulty and Grayson in the Cabinet Room of the

White House. Before Grayson joined them, Lansing asked Tumulty what was the matter with the president. Lansing would later write, "He did not answer me in words, but he significantly put his hand to his left shoulder and drew it down along the left side. Of course the indication was that the President had had a shock [a stroke] and was paralyzed." When Grayson came, he would say little about what ailed Wilson. They discussed the possibility of the vice president filling in temporarily, which infuriated Tumulty. They did agree that the cabinet should discuss the situation, and Lansing talked afterward with Secretary of War Baker, who concurred. Over the weekend, Lansing discussed the situation with Secretary of the Interior Lane as well.[7]

The following Monday, October 6, the cabinet met and had a brief discussion. Lansing raised the question of calling on the vice president to fill in and referred "to the Constitutional provision 'in case of the inability of the President.'" Further, he asked, "What constitutes 'inability' & who is to decide it[?]" He was referring to Article II, Section 1: "In case of the removal of the President from office, or of his death, resignation, or inability to discharge the powers and duties of the said office, the same shall devolve on the Vice President"—which was all the Constitution had to say about a situation like this one. Grayson then joined the meeting, and, he recorded, "Secretary Lansing asked me the direct questions as to what was the matter with the President, what was the exact nature of the President's trouble, how long he would be sick and was his mind clear or not. My reply was that the President's mind was not only clear but very active, and that he clearly showed that he was very much annoyed when he found out that [the] Cabinet had been called and that he wanted to know by whose authority the meeting had been called and for what purpose. Secretary Lansing was somewhat astounded when I spoke thus." Secretary of War Baker thereupon broke in to assert that the cabinet had "only met as a mark of affection" and said, "Please convey our sympathy to the President and give him our assurance that everything is going all right."[8]

Lansing's motives in raising the question of presidential disability are open to question. The recent brouhaha over Bullitt's testimony and his tepid response had left him sore and resentful toward the president. Stories were circulating in Washington that Lansing was anxious to have the vice president take over, and even before the stroke he had told a Republican lawyer that cabinet members had conferred and agreed to go about their business "without attempting to consult with the President." That seems doubtful, because no one else left any record of such conferring, but Colonel House learned from State Department sources that in calling the cabinet meeting on October 6, "Lansing had in mind more than the interchange of ideas on departmental matters."9

What did Lansing have in mind? Was he plotting a coup to make himself president? If the vice president replaced Wilson, the secretary of state would be next in line of succession and could step up if the vice president resigned. As Lansing knew, Wilson had hatched such a plan three years earlier to make Hughes president if he had won the election. A scheme of that sort might have suited Lansing's nature, but it did not ring true with much else in the man's character. The secretary of state was timid and unimaginative, and he was not in good health. Nor did he enjoy close relations with the vice president. At worst, he may have been trying to get rid of a superior who pursued policies he disliked and who, he believed, had neglected and humiliated him.10

If this tense, badly handled business had an unsung, unlikely hero it was the forgotten man of the Wilson administration, Vice President Thomas R. Marshall. This folksy, low-keyed Hoosier enjoyed a reputation as a small-bore party hack and was best known for his quip, "What this country needs is a really good five-cent cigar." In fact, Marshall resembled others who survived and got ahead in the cutthroat, faction-ridden politics of the Midwest of that time—most notably Ohio's Warren Harding—by encouraging people to underestimate them. He was still vice president only because in 1916 Wilson had rejected efforts to dump him in favor of Newton Baker. Marshall had stayed on as before, an invisible figure in Washington, never consulted by Wilson or the cabinet or anyone else in the administration and not even playing much part in relations with Democrats on Capitol Hill.

Marshall still seemed invisible during these days after Wilson's return from the speaking tour. He made no contact with the White House, and he refused to talk to reporters. Behind that pose of detachment, he was much more involved than all but a few people knew. A political reporter, J. Fred Essary of *The Baltimore Sun*, later recounted that someone at the White House—most likely Tumulty acting on Edith's orders—informed him about the president's condition right after the stroke and asked him to pay a secret visit to the vice president. As Essary told the story, when he went to Marshall's office in the Capitol, the vice president sat dumbfounded and silently stared down at his hands clasped on his desk. "It was the first great shock of my life," Marshall said later.11 Other shocks were to follow because rumors about the president's illness were circulating on Capitol Hill. On October 12, newspapers published a letter in which Senator George Moses of New Hampshire, a Republican irreconcilable, told a constituent that Wilson's illness was a cerebral lesion. Grayson immediately brushed the assertion aside, joking to reporters that Moses must have his own sources of information.

Grayson's denial of the gravity of Wilson's illness and his and the other physicians' vague but upbeat reports did not satisfy a number of men on Capitol Hill. Senators twice attempted to persuade Marshall to take over from Wilson. One overture reportedly came from two prominent but unnamed Democrats; the second came from four Republicans, probably including Moses and James Watson of Indiana. Marshall spurned both moves and kept the matter almost entirely to himself. His secretary tried to get him to think about replacing Wilson, but the vice president answered that the only way he might agree to become president was if Congress passed a resolution declaring the office vacant and Mrs. Wilson and Dr. Grayson agreed to it in writing. The vice president steadfastly refused to take any initiative. Later, when he wrote his memoirs, Marshall would inject an implied criticism of Wilson and his role in the League fight: "I have sometimes thought that great men are the bane of civilization; that they are the real cause of all the bitterness and contention that amounted to anything in the world."[12]

As it turned out, Wilson played no role in the League fight during October and the first part of November. He was in such bad physical shape, particularly at the time of the prostate infection, that he could not pay attention to public business. There is never a good time to suffer a stroke, and Wilson's stroke and illness came at a particularly bad time in the League fight. As he lay in his bed in the White House, at the other end of Pennsylvania Avenue senators were voting on the amendments to the treaty that had come out of the Foreign Relations Committee. Republican senators were also negotiating among themselves over reservations. Aside from a few dissidents who backed reservations, Democrats did not take part in those negotiations. They felt both loyal and indebted to Wilson, and they were afraid to act in his absence. On October 24, most of the Democratic senators met in a caucus and voted to take no action on reservations unless and until they heard from the president. Their absence from the negotiations put the mild reservationist Republicans in a bind. One of them, Charles McNary of Oregon, told a reporter, "The proponents of the treaty among the Democrats missed a great opportunity. The mild reservationists were forced to deal with the radicals of their own side." What McNary meant was that in the absence of competing suggestions and counterpressure from Democrats, he and his fellow mild reservationists had to acquiesce in stronger reservations than they liked in order to defeat the proposed amendments.[13]

As a result, Lodge won a sweeping victory. Also on October 24, he sent out from the Foreign Relations Committee a set of reservations—which numbered fourteen. These reservations withheld assent to the Shantung clauses of the treaty, allowed the United States to maintain relations with Covenant-breaking nations and exceed arms limitations set by the League, prohibited American mandates for former German colonies, and stingingly asserted exclusive rights to exempt questions deemed to be vital national interests or matters of national honor. The Article X reservation was just as restrictive as, and only slightly less offensively worded than, the one Wilson had denounced in Salt Lake City: this one disclaimed obligations "under provisions" of the article unless authorized by Congress "by act or joint resolution." In addition, a preamble to these fourteen reservations required three of the four leading Allies—Britain, France, Italy, and Japan—to assent to them.[14]

In this situation, two questions stood uppermost. First, for Wilson and League advocates, did these reservations concede too much? Were they really a compromise, or did they mask a surrender? Second, could there have been a compromise closer to the convictions of the president and like-minded people if he or Democratic senators had taken part in the negotiations? Wilson would soon answer the first question, and his supporters in the Senate would have to decide whether they agreed with his answer. No one could answer the second question because it involved a might-have-been. Still, it is worth pondering. Democratic senators might have succeeded in modifying the language and softening the thrust of some of the reservations, thereby saving face for themselves and the president.[15]

As always, however, Article X formed the crux on which everything depended. Here, it would have required a truly gifted dialectician to reconcile Wilson's insistence on an obligation and Lodge's demand to gut any such obligation. No Democrat in the Senate filled that bill; the only Republican senator who possessed such gifts was Philander Knox of Pennsylvania, and he had joined the irreconcilables. Outside the Senate, Elihu Root could have played such a role, but he had absented himself since offering his earlier suggestions for reservations. In the end, any meeting of minds on Article X would have required Wilson's active involvement. If he had returned from the speaking tour a healthy man and if he been able to use another resounding tour, of the Northeast, to strengthen his hand for bargaining, then he might have been able to bring off a grand, mutually acceptable compromise. He had done something comparable in 1916 with military preparedness, although then his political circumstances had been more favorable and he had been dealing with his own party. Now the hour was late, and he had missed more promising opportunities to reach out and shape the terms for a bargain that could bring him some semblance of victory in the Senate. Wilson was no longer capable of that kind of thinking and action, as he would soon demonstrate in a devastating way.

On October 30, Edith finally allowed a visitor into her husband's sickroom. Albert, king of the Belgians, and his queen, Elizabeth, accompanied by their son Prince Leopold, called at the White House, and the president insisted on seeing the king. Grayson took him upstairs, where Wilson shook his visitor's hand and beckoned him to sit to the right of the bed; they had a ten-minute talk. Two weeks later, on November 14, the president received another royal visitor when the Prince of Wales came to call. Propped up in bed, Wilson pointed out that it was the same bed in which the prince's namesake and grandfather, the future King Edward VII, had slept in 1860 and in which Lincoln had later slept. "I was much relieved to find him looking better than I had expected from the published reports," Prince Edward later wrote to Edith. Wilson was looking better because two days earlier he had allowed himself to be shaved, and the previous day he had marked the first anniversary of the Armistice by leaving the bedroom for the first time. Grayson had ordered a wheelchair, but the ones then available proved clumsy and hard to maneuver, so the doctor had procured one of the wicker chairs on wheels used to transport tourists on the Atlantic City boardwalk. On the day of the Prince of Wales's visit, Wilson spent some time sitting in the open air on the South Portico.[16]

Those royal visits were brief and strictly ceremonial, but between them Wilson received his first caller to talk business. Senator Hitchcock of Nebraska was Lodge's opposite number as the ranking Democrat on the Foreign Relations Committee and party leader, in an acting capacity, substituting for the ailing senator Thomas Martin of Virginia. In late October, Hitchcock had come to the White House, conferred with Grayson, and requested a meeting with the president. Edith finally relented, and on November 7 the senator spent half an hour with Wilson. "I beheld an emaciated old man with a thin white beard which he had permitted to grow," Hitchcock later recalled. Wilson asked him how many senators would vote for the treaty without reservations: "I told him not over forty-five out of ninety-six. He fairly groaned: 'It is possible, it is possible.'" Talking with reporters immediately afterward, Hitchcock said Wilson would accept compromises to save the treaty but believed "that the Lodge reservations would kill the treaty."[17]

Attending to public business appeared to do Wilson good. His excursions in the wheeled chair now included some time out on the White House lawn, and after examining him on November 15, Dr. Dercum told Edith and Margaret that the president was making a good recovery. Probably at her husband's request, Edith asked Hitchcock to send reports on the situation in the Senate, which she read to Wilson. On November 13, Hitchcock characterized the Article X reservation as less "obnoxious" than earlier but still bad. He said the Democrats planned to block consent to the treaty with the Lodge reservations and then introduce five reservations of their own, which he enclosed. "The first four are substantially in accordance with the suggestions made to me by the President," Hitchcock said, "and the last one is, I think, in accordance with his views on the true meaning of the league covenant."[18] Two days later, Hitchcock restated the plan to block consent with the Lodge reservations and requested another meeting with the president to get his approval.

It is clear that Wilson did think this was the proper course, because Edith wrote on the envelope containing Hitchcock's second report, "Program [Hitchcock] out lines has [Wilson's] approval. He could not accept Lodge Reservations in any case." He agreed to see Hitchcock, who came again on November 17. The senator found a changed man, stronger and more assertive. "I would give anything if the Democrats, in fact, all the Senate, could see the attitude that man took this morning," he told Grayson afterward. "Think of how effective it would be if they could see the picture you and I saw." When the senator asked about Lodge's set of reservations, which Grayson had previously read to him, the president replied, "I consider it a nullification of the Treaty and utterly impossible." He deliberately used the pejorative term *nullification*, because he compared these reservations to South Carolina's efforts to nullify the federal laws before the Civil War—which was like waving a red flag in the face of Republicans. When Hitchcock asked about the Article X reservation, Wilson shot back, "That cuts the very heart out of the Treaty."[19]

Wilson meant to play a blame game. "If the Republicans are bent on defeating the treaty," he said,

> I want the vote of each, Republican and Democrat, recorded, because they will have to answer to the people. I am a sick man, lying in this bed, but I am going to debate this issue with these gentlemen in their respective states whenever they come up for re-election if I have breath enough in my body to carry on the fight. I shall do this even if I have to give my life to it. And I will get their political scalps when the truth is known to the people.

They have got to account to their constituents for their actions in
this matter. I have no doubts as to what the verdict of the people
will be. Mind you, Senator, I have no hostility towards these gentlemen but an utter contempt.

When Hitchcock mentioned compromise, Wilson dismissed the idea and
then asked the senator to describe the situation in detail. Hitchcock's rendition stretched the meeting to over an hour, and he apologized for tiring
the president. Grayson recorded that Wilson smiled and said, "No, Senator, you have strengthened me against the opponents."[20]

The president's performance awed Hitchcock, but it should have
appalled him. The transformation of the wispy-bearded wraith of ten days
before was striking, but the psychological effects of the stroke were even
more striking. Wilson's emotions were unbalanced, and his judgment was
warped. Whereas he had formerly been able to offset his driving determination, combativeness, and overweening self-confidence with detachment, reflection, and self-criticism, those compensations were now largely
gone. Worse, his denial of illness and limitations was starting to border on
delusion, particularly when he talked about fighting senators for reelection. Yet when he called himself "a sick man, lying in this bed," he was displaying a trait that he had never shown before—self-pity. Worst of all, he
had said he wanted to "pick up the threads that were left when I was put to
bed," but that—adjusting to changing political realities—was something
he was no longer capable of doing.[21]

Starting with his meeting with Hitchcock, Wilson threw an insur-
mountable obstacle into the path of the Senate. In a guarded account to
reporters waiting outside the White House, the senator invoked the
threat of refusing to ratify: "President Wilson will pocket the treaty if the
Lodge program of reservations is carried out." Contradictorily and mis-
leadingly, however, he added that Wilson had not totally rejected the
Lodge reservations. Hitchcock and Edith Wilson were going to let the
president appear to speak for himself. Later in the day, the senator sent to
the White House a draft of a letter—which Edith read to her husband and
edited at his dictation—to go out ostensibly from the president dated the
next day, November 18. The letter stated that the Lodge reservations did
not "provide for ratification but for nullification. I sincerely hope that the
friends and supporters of the treaty will vote against the Lodge resolution
of ratification."[22]

This bombshell blasted away all hopes for compromise. Since the
beginning of November, various people inside and outside the Senate had

been scurrying to find some middle ground between Lodge's reservations and milder ones. LEP lobbyists had busied themselves meeting with senators; ex-president Taft and Harvard's president Lowell had persuaded the organization's executive board to announce that, if necessary, it could accept the Lodge reservations as the price of entering the League. Even Lodge made a stab at compromise. Stephen Bonsal, formerly a member of House's staff in Paris and a friend of the Lodge family, later revealed that he met twice with the senator at the middle of November and secured his agreement to changes in Article X. According to Bonsal, a draft of those changes went to House, who supposedly forwarded them to the White House but never got a reply. If the colonel had forwarded those changes—which is doubtful—Wilson probably would have spurned them. "The Colonel's stock has fallen to zero," Ray Stannard Baker noted after talking with Grayson early in November. "He is no longer a factor."[23]

On the morning of November 19, Democratic senators met in caucus, where Hitchcock read the letter putatively from the president. Either he or the White House also released the letter to the press, and newspapers carrying its text were circulating in the chamber soon after the Senate convened at noon. Lodge read the letter aloud to his colleagues and said, "I think comment is superfluous, and I shall make none." Privileged spectators packed the galleries and others milled around in the corridors as the Senate spent ten hours in final debate and then voted on the Treaty of Versailles. On consent with the Lodge reservations, the treaty fell short, with thirty-nine senators in favor—thirty-five Republicans and four Democrats—and fifty-five against—forty Democrats and fifteen irreconcilables. Then, after futile attempts to buy time in order to introduce compromise reservations, Lodge allowed a vote on the treaty without reservations. This too fell short, with thirty-eight in favor—thirty-seven Democrats and one Republican, Porter McCumber of North Dakota—and fifty-three against—thirty-three Republicans, five Democrats, and fifteen irreconcilables. Afterward, just before adjournment, a Democratic senator asked whether the president should be informed. Pennsylvania's corpulent, cynical conservative Republican Boies Penrose responded, "Oh, he'll know about it well enough."[24]

The president did know. When Edith told him the news, he lay silent and then said, "All the more reason I must get well and try to bring this country to a sense of its great opportunity and greater responsibility." He tried to draft a statement but managed to dictate to Edith only a few disjointed remarks. Lodge made no public statement either. The next day, however, the senator indulged his malice when he privately told George

Harvey, Wilson's erstwhile patron now turned bitter enemy, "Brandegee and I thought of you last night after the thing was over and wished we could have an opportunity to exchange with you a few loving words."[25]

If Lodge and Wilson had gotten their way, the League fight would have been over. The senator snapped at a friend who urged compromise, "It is for [Wilson] to move—not for us." The president did not answer letters from Democrats who urged compromise, although Edith evidently did read or describe two letters to that effect from House. In response, he did try again to draft a statement to the press but left it unfinished and directed Edith to strike out all but a few oblique references to the treaty in the State of the Union message that Tumulty was drafting for the opening of the next session of Congress on December 2. Not being able to speak in person and having someone else write an address for him hurt Wilson deeply. The message admitted that he could not deal directly with some problems and was relying on cabinet members. It presented a list of suggestions for legislation along progressive lines, including a unified federal budget, continuation of income and excess-profits taxes, an unaltered tariff, aid to veterans and farmers, and better procedures for labor relations. It sidestepped the pressing issue of whether to keep the railroads under government control and blamed current domestic problems on the failure to ratify the peace treaty.[26]

Nine years at Wilson's side had taught Tumulty how to capture his boss's thought and language reasonably well. The message sounded like the last speech the president had been able to give to Congress, the one on the high cost of living four months earlier, which had also been long on rhetoric and short on solutions to burning problems. This message's references to domestic problems glaringly understated the troubles that plagued the country at the end of 1919. Inflation, or HCL, still ran rampant, unemployment was soaring as veterans returned to the workforce, and strikes were disrupting major industries, including coal and steel. A radical-led general strike earlier in the year in Seattle, explosions of bombs in May at the homes of public officials, including one on the doorstep of the home of Attorney General Palmer himself, and the police strike in Boston in September—these events had made many people shudder at the specter of revolution. Palmer was beginning his crackdown on "Reds" by having 249 noncitizens suspected of radical connections deported to Russia aboard a former troopship that was dubbed the Soviet Ark.[27]

If there have been times in the nation's history that have cried out for strong presidential leadership, this was one of them. Instead, from

1600 Pennsylvania Avenue came silence, occasionally punctuated by a vague but always upbeat report about the president's condition. Rumors rushed in to fill the information vacuum. Besides complaining about "government by petticoat," some people were saying that Wilson had gone insane and bars on some first-floor windows proved that the White House was harboring a lunatic. The bars had, in fact, been installed during Roosevelt's presidency, to keep his young sons from breaking windows with their baseballs. Rumblings about Wilson's condition broke out on Capitol Hill after an infuriated Hitchcock told reporters that Wilson had refused to see him on November 29. Tumulty tried to make light of the incident, explaining to reporters that the president was improving but Mrs. Wilson did not think he should have any long conferences just now.[28]

When Congress reconvened on December 2, newspapers reported that Wilson's refusal to see Hitchcock had stirred disquiet and led many in Congress to believe that the president's condition was worse than his physicians were letting on. Senators soon found a way to assuage their curiosity. Tensions with Mexico had flared up again in October when Carranza's Constitutionalists seized and detained an American citizen, William O. Jenkins, thereby sparking new cries for military intervention. The loudest and most relentless advocate of intervention was Senator Fall of New Mexico, who owned land in Mexico and was close to conservatives there. On December 1, Lansing told Fall privately that he had not discussed Mexico with Wilson since August, and three days later he publicly repeated that admission in testimony before the Senate Foreign Relations Committee. The committee then voted, along party lines, to send two of their members, Fall and Hitchcock, to discuss the Mexican situation with the president. Some senators privately admitted that their real motive was to check up on Wilson. Wags immediately dubbed the two senators the "smelling committee."[29]

Grayson thought something like this might happen, and he had laid plans. Doctor and patient now put on a show designed to hide the nature and extent of Wilson's disability. When Fall and Hitchcock telephoned on December 5, Grayson told them the president would see them at two-thirty that afternoon. When they arrived, he told them to stay as long as they needed, and he escorted the two senators upstairs to the president's bedroom, where they found him propped up in his bed. It was a gloomy day, with the December sun low in the sky, and Wilson had instructed that all the lights in the room be turned on so that his visitors could get a good look at him. He lay with his paralyzed left side cloaked in the bedcovers; papers lay on a table to the right of the bed, where he could reach them with his good hand. Edith sat to one side with a writing pad. Wilson shook hands with both senators, and Fall said, "I hope you will consider me sincere. I have been praying for you[,] Sir." Edith later recalled that her husband shot back, "Which way, Senator?" That was Wilson's wit at its best. Unfortunately, he almost certainly did not say it, since neither Edith's notes nor Grayson's memorandum, written the same day, recorded the remark.[30]

Even without that comeback, the president performed beautifully. Hitchcock told reporters afterward that Fall had done most of the talking and Wilson listened attentively for forty minutes. He also reached out and took some papers from the senators and took papers off the bedside table. At one point, Grayson left the room, and when he came back he announced, "Secretary Lansing has asked me to tell you immediately that Jenkins has been released." Grayson afterward admitted "that he felt like an actor making a sensational entrance." In the ensuing discussion, Wilson counseled against haste in dealing with Mexico. According to Hitchcock, he repeated a joke made by one of Finley Peter Dunne's characters: "Mexico is so contagious to us that I'm thinkin' we'll have to take it." As for the peace treaty, Hitchcock reported, "The President said that he regarded responsibility . . . as having been shifted from his shoulders to others, and that he was disposed to let it rest there awhile."[31]

The show achieved the desired effect. Hitchcock told reporters, "The President looks much better than when I last saw him. He was sitting up in bed, wearing a dark brown sweater. His color was good. . . . He was mentally most alert, and physically seemed to me to have improved greatly." Fall agreed, telling the reporters that Wilson was perfectly capable of handling the Mexican situation and "seemed to me to be in excellent trim, both mentally and physically, for a man who has been in bed for ten weeks. Of course, I am not an expert, but that's how it appeared to me."[32] Wilson's performance before the "smelling committee" ended talk of removing him from office.

He was recovering a bit. On December 14, he stood up and took his first steps since the stroke, and the physical therapist assigned to him reported to Dr. Dercum that he would soon be able to sit in a chair for one meal a day and use the toilet instead of a bedpan. Wilson's defiance was also growing stronger. When Hitchcock finally got to see him alone and urged compromise, Wilson shot back, "Let Lodge compromise. Let Lodge hold out the olive branch." The same day that he took his first steps, he dictated a press release "from the highest authority in the executive department," declaring that the president had "no compromise or concession of any kind" in mind and intended to let blame for the failure of the peace treaty remain with the Republican senators.[33]

Wilson's attitude was starting to cross the line between defiance and delusion. Also at the middle of December, he had Tumulty draft a statement—which he revised by dictating changes to Edith—in which he again asserted with respect to the peace treaty, "There is but one way to settle such questions, and that is by direct reference to the voters." Because the Constitution does not provide for a referendum, he challenged fifty-six senators, listed by name, to resign and run for reelection. "For myself I promise if all of them or a majority of them are re-elected, I will resign the presidency." The vice president would also resign, and he would "invite one of the acknowledged leaders of the Republican party" to become secretary of state and thereby become president.[34]

If this fantastic scheme had come to light, fresh calls might have arisen for Wilson's removal from office. He was mixing a crazy brew of his youthful notions about adopting parliamentary practices with his more recent ideas about appealing to the people over the heads of legislators and his plan to resign if Hughes had won in 1916. Moreover, his list of senators was bizarre; it included three Democrats who had supported him on the treaty and the two mildest reservationist Republicans, McCumber and Knute Nelson of Minnesota, and it omitted one of the irreconcilables, George Norris of Nebraska. Fortunately for him, Wilson lacked the will and energy to pursue the scheme, but he had the referendum idea in his head, and he would soon air it again in a slightly less drastic way.[35]

Wilson's statement to the press rejecting compromise backfired because it flew in the face of efforts to bring the treaty back before the Senate and work out a way to achieve consent with reservations. Democratic and Republican party leaders wanted to put the controversy behind them before the next election, while the LEP's lobbyists and the American Federation of Labor were exerting influence in the direction of compromise. Senators themselves made the most important moves toward breaking the stalemate by starting to conduct the kind of bipartisan talks that should have preceded the earlier votes on the treaty. Now the mild reservationists took more initiative, and Democrats started talking about concessions.[36]

Meanwhile, in the White House the Wilsons passed a subdued Christmas without a tree, and Tumulty tried to cheer the president on his sixty-third birthday by saying, "Be of good cheer Governor, the clouds are going to pass away." Tumulty was trying to lift his own spirits as well. He was being barraged with complaints that cabinet and diplomatic appointments were not being filled. Likewise, the British were miffed because Wilson had refused to meet with their temporary ambassador, the former foreign secretary, who was now Viscount Grey. The alleged reason was that Grey's private secretary, Major Charles Kennedy Craufurd-Stuart, had spread stories about Dr. Grayson, the First Lady's premarital involvement with the president, and Bernard Baruch's relations with an attractive woman suspected of spying for the Germans.[37]

As the new year began, Wilson made a new attempt to scuttle plans for compromise on the treaty by reviving the referendum idea. Two days before the Democrats' Jackson Day dinner on January 8, he ordered Tumulty to draft a letter charging that the Senate's failure to act threatened to undo the victory over Germany and that the only way to avoid a calamity was "by a direct referendum; . . . it is our duty as a party to give the next election the form of a great and solemn referendum to the voters of the country in this great matter." Tumulty showed again that he could mimic Wilson's style, coining the ringing slogan "great and solemn referendum," which sounded typical of the president. Tumulty evidently felt uneasy about the tone and content of the letter, however, because he asked several people to go over it with him. Those he consulted thought the letter was unwise but also thought it fruitless to try to talk Wilson out of it. One of them, Secretary of Agriculture Houston, revised the letter to eliminate errors of fact and give it a slightly more conciliatory tone. Wilson accepted Houston's revisions, but he dictated to Edith another sentence declaring, "We have no moral right to refuse now to take part in the execution & administration of these settlements."[38]

When the letter was read at the dinner, it did less damage than some feared and Wilson hoped. Bryan, who was the featured speaker, sought to soften its impact by arguing that too much had been made of Article X and urging compromise. Much as many Democrats liked that message, some questioned the motives of the messenger. Some Democrats in the Senate grumbled about a revolt against Wilson, although one of them scoffed at such "cloakroom courage." On January 15, a group of them got together with Lodge and a few Republicans and began a series of meetings that came to be called the bipartisan conference. The going was tough in those meetings, but by January 23 the conferees appeared to be on the verge of an agreement to a reservation on Article X. At that point, the Republican irreconcilables hauled Lodge into a stormy meeting at which they threatened to depose him as majority leader unless he broke off the negotiations. Lodge readily complied, thereby casting doubt on his true desire for a compromise, and he told the bipartisan conference that he would accept no modification of his previous reservations.[39]

Back at the White House, another move toward compromise was afoot, although not one instigated by Wilson. It was Tumulty who opened a behind-the-scenes campaign to get the president to take part in compromise negotiations. On January 14, he drafted a letter for Wilson to send to Hitchcock, and he circulated it to secretaries Baker, Houston, and Lansing and to Edith. The next day, he told her that in view of talk of compromise in the Senate, this was the "psychological moment" for action and the president should put forward his own interpretation of the treaty. The cabinet secretaries approved the draft letter; so did Edith, who seems to have encouraged Tumulty to send it to her husband, as he did the next day.[40]

The draft set out twelve numbered points, which covered most of the Lodge reservations. On all but three of the points, it took no issue with the intent behind a reservation and often said, "I see no objection." It did disagree with two reservations, those that covered withdrawal from the League and appointments to the Reparations Commission. On "the much-discussed Article X," it stated that it was necessary that the president's "moral influence . . . for the preservation of peace shall not be diminished," while keeping "inviolate" Congress's power to accept or reject League recommendations. The letter also expressed a sincere hope that these interpretations would assist "in bringing about an early ratification of the Peace Treaty." Tumulty was trying to get around the question of whether an obligation remained under Article X. Coincidentally, he was following the same line that the bipartisan conference would come close to adopting. The effect of listing numbered points corresponding to reservations and giving agreeable responses left an impression of reasonableness and accommodation. Tumulty had high hopes and told Edith that the bipartisan conference would "give the President, in my opinion, his great opportunity."[41]

Unfortunately, Tumulty did not reckon on Wilson's physical and emotional state. He made only a few marks beside the more accommodating points, and he deleted an implied acceptance of reservations as part of the instrument of ratification. Grayson told Ray Stannard Baker, who was then visiting the White House, that Wilson was "perfectly calm about everything that comes up *except* the treaty. That stirs him: makes him restless." Baker told Edith "as diplomatically as I could" that people were blaming her husband for the stalemate over the treaty. "I know," she replied, "but the President still has in mind the reception he got in the west, and he believes the people are with him." Edith was unwittingly describing the effects of her husband's isolation in the White House bedroom and a psychological consequence of the stroke—an inability to adjust to reality—which together made it impossible for him to seize the opportunity that Tumulty was trying to offer.[42]

At this point, Wilson's physical health made matters still worse. On

January 20 or 21, he came down with what Grayson called "a sharp attack of the 'flu,'" which gave him a high fever, accompanied by headaches and vomiting. He got over this episode fairly quickly, but it depressed him. "It would probably have been better if I had died last fall," he said to Grayson. As earlier, a bit of recovery heightened his combativeness. On January 26, he wrote to Hitchcock that the reservation to Article X proposed in the bipartisan conference must not "create the impression that we are trying to escape obligations." The closest he could come to appearing accommodating was to have Edith attach a note to the letter leaving it up to Hitchcock's judgment whether to publish his letter. Hitchcock would not release the letter for two weeks, and in the meantime Wilson would revive the referendum scheme. He had Edith send Albert Burleson a list of the names and states of fifty-four senators, Democrats and Republicans, and asked him to consult with the Democratic leaders in the Senate about whether those men had opposed the treaty. Burleson, after consulting on Capitol Hill, replied by simply reciting which senators had taken which stands on the treaty during the previous session of Congress. That deadpan reply may have dampened Wilson's ardor, but it is more likely that another brief bout of influenza at the beginning of February distracted him and sapped his limited energies.[43]

Coming so soon after the previous illness, this one worsened the mood swings that were afflicting Wilson after the stroke. Renewed depression evidently made him think, uncharacteristically, of resigning, and Grayson seems to have tried to engineer that resignation. During coming months, Grayson would sometimes whisper to close friends about this effort. At one point, he would dictate a note to himself: "Look up notes re President Wilson's intention to go before the Senate in a wheeled chair for the purpose of resigning." In his whispered confidences, Grayson would blame Edith for scotching the resignation scheme, but it seems more likely that Wilson's quick recovery from this bout of flu again spurred his determination and combativeness.[44]

Wilson's recovery from this second illness at the beginning of February 1920 triggered his most destructive behavior in the League fight and in his whole presidency. It started with a well-intentioned gesture by an outsider. Foreign leaders also felt dismayed at the stalemate over the treaty, although the governments in London and Paris and their ambassadors in Washington studiously avoided comment for fear of offending Wilson. Lord Grey, who had returned to London, believed he could help to break the deadlock. On January 31, *The Times* published a letter from him— reprinted the next day in American newspapers—stating that the Allies should welcome American participation in the League of Nations on almost any terms. The letter infuriated Wilson. On February 5, he dictated a press release excoriating this attempt at outside influence, saying that if Grey were still ambassador, his recall would be demanded. That rebuke understated Wilson's anger. Grayson told Ray Stannard Baker that the White House was "all in a state of utter confusion heightened by the President's illness & his stubborn temperament. He does not want to hear what is going on apparently."[45]

Wilson did hear, possibly from Tumulty, that Lansing liked Grey's letter, and he chose this occasion to stage a showdown with the secretary of state. On February 7, Wilson sent Lansing a stinging letter—which he dictated—asking whether it was true that Lansing had convened cabinet meetings in his absence. "If it is, I feel it my duty to call your attention to considerations which I do not care to dwell upon until I learn from yourself that this is the fact." For a change, Lansing did not shrink from confrontation. The letter's "brutal and offensive" language sounded to him like the product of "a species of mania, which seems to approach irrationality. . . . It sounded like a spoiled child crying out in rage at an imaginary wrong." He felt relieved because it gave him "the very opportunity I have been looking for to leave the Cabinet." He replied on February 9 with a coolly worded letter noting that he had always kept the president informed of cabinet meetings and had only tried to serve him. If Wilson was questioning his loyalty or lacked confidence in him, "I am of course ready, Mr. President, to relieve you of any embarrassment by placing my resignation in your hands."[46]

Lansing did not immediately release the exchange of letters to the press, and he allowed Undersecretary of State Frank Polk to go to the White House the next day and talk to Grayson. Polk warned that this incident would make the president look bad, and Grayson agreed and talked to Edith and Tumulty. They also agreed, and they tried to talk Wilson out of firing Lansing. Edith recalled that she told her husband his "letter as written made him look small," and Tumulty remembered telling the president that "it was the wrong time to do the right thing." Wilson answered both of them the same way. "Well, if I am as big a man as you think me I can well afford to do a generous thing," he laughingly told Edith, adding that he had to put a stop to disloyalty. Likewise, he told, Tumulty, "[I]t is never the wrong time to spike disloyalty. When Lansing sought to oust me, I was upon my back. I am on my feet now and I will not have disloyalty about me."[47]

Delusions of potency prompted Wilson to take further action. Urged by Hitchcock and Carter Glass—who had resigned as secretary of the

Treasury to fill the Senate seat for Virginia left vacant by Thomas Martin's death—the president now released his statement on reservations. Some thought this a good move, but Glass told him that every Democratic senator he talked to wanted the president to accept a reservation to Article X like the one proposed earlier by Taft and feared that the voters would punish them if they did not appear conciliatory. Again, Wilson would have none of it. On February 9, Edith wrote to Glass that the president's "judgment is decidedly against the course Sen. G. proposes. Article 10 is the backbone of the Covenant & Mr. Taft[']s proposed reservation is not drawn in good faith." Wilson still believed that the Republicans should take the initiative to compromise, and he "attached little importance to party strategy at this juncture."[48]

The next day, Wilson decided to take diplomatic matters into his own hands for the first time since the stroke. He had a public note sent rebuking the British and French for what he viewed as appeasement of Italy's Adriatic ambitions. He put language back into the note that Lansing and Polk had tried to soften, stating that this dispute "raises the fundamental question as to whether the American Government can on any terms cooperate with the European associates in the great work of maintaining peace by removing the causes of war . . . [through] a concert of powers the very existence of which must depend upon a new spirit and new order." The note also stated that many Americans were "fearful lest they become entangled in international policies and committed to international obligations foreign alike to their ideals and their traditions," and to give way to Italy "would be to provide the most solid ground for such fears."[49] This all-or-nothing, isolationist-sounding language would soon damage further efforts at compromise in the Senate.

More immediately, fallout from Lansing's resignation did greater damage to Wilson. On February 11 and 12, the president and the secretary of state engaged in a duel by letter. Wilson said he was "very much disappointed" with Lansing's explanations and accused him of disloyalty. Lansing replied with a letter of resignation in which he denied the charges of disloyalty and recited a series of cases in which he had been ignored or met with "frequent disapproval of my suggestions." Assistant Secretary Breckinridge Long, a former student of Wilson's at Princeton, believed this exchange of letters would hurt the president and went to the White House and talked with Grayson, who evidently got Wilson to send a brief note simply accepting Lansing's resignation. The secretary had already had the previous letters mimeographed, and the State Department gave them to reporters at seven-thirty in the evening. *Friday, the 13th!*" Lansing exulted. "This is my lucky day for I am free from the intolerable situation in which I have been so long."[50]

Despite Wilson's fondness for the number thirteen, this was one of his unluckiest days. As predicted, the Lansing affair cast him in a terrible light. Dismissing the secretary of state ostensibly because he had convened the cabinet angered and puzzled even Democratic newspapers, while Republican journals excoriated the action. The editors did not support Lansing so much as they condemned Wilson. "It seems the petulant & irritable act of a sick man," Baker noted. That view had received reinforcement on February 10, when the urologist from Johns Hopkins who had treated Wilson earlier told a reporter that the president had suffered a "cerebral thrombosis." This was the first admission by any of his physicians that Wilson had had a stroke, and it set off a flurry of comment by other physicians, including a statement by a former president of the American Medical Association that the president had a "permanently damaged brain." Grayson did not directly deny the urologist's statement, but he and Dercum insisted that Wilson was improving.[51]

The furor over the secretary's resignation and the urologist's disclosure ignited doubts about the president's ability to govern that had been simmering among the public for the past four months. During the third week in February, *The Literary Digest* collected newspaper opinion, and nearly every comment it cited expressed qualms about Wilson's fitness to remain president. Up to this time, to the extent that public opinion can be gauged, it appears that people blamed the Republican senators just as much as Wilson for the deadlock over the treaty and were showing increasing impatience and boredom with the business. Now sentiment was beginning to focus on Wilson's ability to hold office, especially in view of such domestic problems as strikes, inflation, unemployment, and Palmer's campaign against Reds. McAdoo warned a Texas Democrat that "a drifting course is the worst possible thing for the party. We have had too much of it. This is due, primarily, I believe to the President's unfortunate illness."[52]

Wilson sowed further doubt about his competence when he appointed a successor to Lansing. It would be his fifth cabinet appointment in three months. He had already picked Representative Joshua W. Alexander, a Missouri Democrat, to replace William Redfield, who had retired, at Commerce. He had moved Houston from Agriculture to replace Glass at the Treasury, and he had named Edwin T. Meredith, an Iowa Democrat and publisher of a farm journal, to replace Houston. He had chosen John Barton Payne, a Chicago lawyer and member of the

Shipping Board, to replace Lane (who had resigned to pursue a private career) at Interior. All were reasonable, though not stellar, appointments. The State Department was another matter. On February 25, he asked Grayson, "Do you know of any reason why I should not appoint Bainbridge Colby Secretary of State?" Grayson guardedly observed, "It would really be an unusual appointment." Wilson replied, "We do not want to follow precedents and stagnate. We have to do unusual things in order to progress."[53]

This was a bizarre appointment. The fifty-year-old Colby was a New York lawyer, a former Progressive who had supported Wilson in 1916, and a member of the Shipping Board. Colby had no experience in foreign affairs, and Wilson did not know him well. The president was passing over the undersecretary of state, Polk, another New York lawyer and an anti-Tammany Democrat who had served as a Wilson loyalist in the department for the past four years. Polk blamed Tumulty for being passed over, but it is doubtful he was responsible. Colby probably owed his appointment to the twisted version of Wilson's thinking about doing bold things. Editorial reaction to Colby's appointment ran the gamut from puzzlement to outrage. Privately, some observers thought it gave further proof of Wilson's incompetence. Lodge would not comment publicly to reporters, but off the record he called the appointment the worst he'd ever seen and "a political plum handed to a man who is willing to serve as a rubber stamp."[54]

Other signs of the president's weakness came from Capitol Hill. When the Senate took up the treaty again, Borah delighted in reading extensive quotations from Keynes's *Economic Consequences of the Peace*, which had been published in the United States at the beginning of February and earlier serialized in *The New Republic*. In it, Keynes called the president "a blind and deaf Don Quixote" and portrayed him as not just a naïve and ignorant idealist "bamboozled" by wily Europeans but also a hypocrite who possessed "all the intellectual apparatus of self-deception." This view of Wilson would soon strike a chord among such self-styled American disillusionists as H. L. Mencken. Democratic senators were also growing restive. On February 27, Tumulty told Wilson that in the Senate "there is no doubt our forces are rapidly disintegrating" and warned that the treaty with the Lodge reservations might be approved by a two-thirds vote that would include a majority of the Democratic senators. He urged the president to accept that outcome but also issue a statement "showing wherein those reservations weaken the whole Treaty and make it a useless instrument."[55]

Others also made abortive attempts to get through to the president and urge him to compromise. On February 29, a conclave of leading Democrats gathered at the Chevy Chase Club: they included Tumulty, six cabinet members, and senators Glass and Hitchcock, as well as Homer Cummings, the party's national chairman; Edward Hurley, chairman of the Shipping Board; and Vance McCormick, chairman of the War Trade Board. Evidently, everyone at the meeting agreed that Wilson should yield in some way. Hurley recalled that the group agreed that the president should accept the Lodge reservations, but Glass interjected, "I would like to know, in the present condition of the President's mind and his state of health, who among us will be willing to go to him and tell him that he should accept the reservations." After Glass spoke, Hurley recalled, "There was a hush. . . . There was no volunteer."[56]

If any of those Democrats had approached Wilson, he would have been on a fool's errand. The day before they met, the president started to draft a statement, in the form of a letter to Hitchcock, about the "so-called Lodge reservations." He said he was willing to accept some of them, but "if the treaty should be returned to me with such a reservation on Article X, I would be obliged to consider it a rejection of the treaty and of the Covenant of the League of Nations. Any reservation seeking to deprive the League of Nations of the virility of Article X cuts at the heart of the Covenant itself." He maintained that Article X was essential to assuring peace and preventing another world war. "Every imperialistic influence in the chancelleries of Europe opposed the embodiment of Article X in the League of Nations, and its defeat now would mark the complete consummation of their efforts to nullify the treaty."[57]

This stepped-up defiance once more sprang from Wilson's growing sense of his own strength. This was the first long letter that he appears to have dictated to a stenographer and the first long letter he wrote without relying on a draft by Tumulty. He also made changes and additions in his own handwriting—another first since the stroke. A different sign of recovery came a few days later, when he left the White House for the first time in five months. On March 3, he rode with Edith for more than an hour in the presidential limousine, which traveled along the Potomac and up Pennsylvania Avenue to Capitol Hill. Many people recognized the car and waved at the president. Rides in the limousine would again be Wilson's favorite way to relax for the rest of his days in office. At this time, he was also reworking his statement about the Lodge reservations. Tumulty showed the president's draft to some cabinet members, and they made suggestions. Wilson accepted some of those suggestions, made shorthand notes, and dictated a final version to a stenographer and Edith. This was his longest piece of speaking or writing since the speech at Pueblo, and even people who disagreed with him conceded that it was an impressive rhetorical performance.

The statement—released as a letter to Hitchcock at the end of the day on March 8—thundered with righteous defiance and focused almost entirely on Article X: "For myself, I could not look the soldiers of our gallant armies in the face again if I did not do everything in my power to remove every obstacle that lies in the way of this particular Article of the Covenant. . . . Any reservation which seeks to deprive the League of Nations of the force of Article X strikes at the very heart of the Covenant itself." Without its guarantees, the League would be merely "a futile scrap of paper," like the guarantee of Belgium that Germany had violated in 1914. Instead of quibbling about obligations, America should fearlessly embrace "the role of leadership which we now enjoy, contributing our efforts towards establishing a just and permanent peace." The letter ended with a sting: "I have been struck by the fact that practically every so-called reservation was in effect a nullification of the terms of the treaty itself. I hear of reservationists and mild reservationists, but I cannot understand the difference between a nullifier and a mild nullifier."[58]

This bombshell did its destructive work. All but a few staunchly Democratic newspapers recoiled from Wilson. *The Washington Post* labeled him "an affirmative irreconcilable," and the New York *World* carried an editorial titled "Ratify!" which called his position "weak and untenable." His opponents on Capitol Hill were delighted. Senator Brandegee told reporters, "The President strangled his own child." On the Senate floor, Lodge mockingly thanked the president for having "justified the position that we on this side, all alike, have taken, that there must be no obligation imposed on the United States to carry out the provisions of article 10." Mild reservationists bristled at the "mild nullifier" label, and Democrats openly defied Wilson, with Robert Owen of Oklahoma declaring, "I will not follow any leader who is leading to [the treaty's] defeat or delay." During the next ten days, the senators voted to attach the same fourteen reservations as they had voted for earlier, plus one more, offered by a Democrat, Peter Gerry of Rhode Island, affirming self-determination for Ireland and expressing sympathy for an independent Ireland. With that, the Senate was ready to vote again on consent to the Treaty of Versailles.[59]

The vote came on March 19, exactly four months after the earlier votes on the treaty. This time, debate lasted just six hours, and the senators considered only the treaty with the Lodge reservations plus the Gerry reservation. Several Democrats usually loyal to Wilson announced that they would vote for the treaty with those reservations. At six in the evening, when the roll call began, it looked as if enough Democrats might break with the president to supply the two thirds necessary for consent. Three of the first four answered aye, and next came Charles Culberson of Texas, who had not announced his intentions. There was talk that if he voted in favor, most other Democrats would join him. Culberson reportedly hesitated and looked perplexed before he answered nay. Everything then went as predicted. The vote was 49 in favor and 35 against, seven votes short of two thirds of the members present. A majority of Democrats voted for consent, which was a rebuke to Wilson. All but three of those who stayed with him were from the southern or border states; many of those "loyal" Democrats appeared to be afraid of reprisals by the president. A final bit of business was to return the treaty to the president. The following day, the secretary of the Senate carried back to the White House the same bound volume of the Treaty of Versailles that Wilson had presented to the Senate eight months earlier.[60]

This was the end of the League fight. Wilson had lost. The United States would never ratify that treaty and would never join the League of Nations. Many newspapers and commentators expressed regret at the outcome, and most of them laid the blame on Wilson—properly so. Brandegee's cruel remark about Wilson's strangling his own child was not far off the mark. Wilson had blocked every effort at compromise, and only his active intransigence prevented more Democrats from voting for the treaty with the Lodge reservations. Even though he threatened to refuse to ratify the treaty, the Senate's consenting to the treaty with those reservations would have put pressure on the Republicans to take a stand for League membership on those terms in the 1920 election and, when they won, to complete the process of ratification. As things now stood, the Republicans were free to wipe the foreign policy slate clean and go their own way, which was what Lodge wanted and what they soon would do.[61]

One question has haunted Wilson's defeat in the League fight: what, in the larger scheme of things, did it mean? Did it, as he said, "break the heart of the world"? The outbreak of another world war almost exactly twenty years after the ceremony in the Hall of Mirrors at Versailles would lead many people to elevate Wilson to the stature of a prophet whose words had gone unheeded. Others, however, would claim that Wilson had made a mountain out of a molehill in his fixation on Article X. With or without stringent reservations like Lodge's, the United States was going to consult its own interests and convenience every time an international conflict threatened—just as the European powers would do in the League. Yet membership in the League, even though restricted by Lodge's or some other reservations, would at least have given the United States a larger, more active role and a generation of experience as a leading power in the international arena.[62]

This bad, even tragic, outcome of the League fight turned on Wilson's stroke. Even more than in the earlier round, his emotional imbalance and skewed judgment blocked a more constructive outcome. At times in the first three months of 1920, he did seem to verge on mental instability, if not insanity. Edith Wilson, Dr. Grayson, and Tumulty did the best they could by their lights, but they were frightened, limited people who should not have been trying to keep Wilson's presidency afloat. He should not have remained in office. If he had not, the League fight would have turned out differently, and the nation and the world would have been better off.

Wilson did not take the end of the League fight well. According to one story, Edith did not break the news of the Senate vote to him until the next morning, and a depressed Wilson said to Grayson, "I feel like going to bed for a week and staying there." By another account, Wilson got the news immediately after the vote and spent a sleepless night, calling Grayson to his bedside several times and telling him, "Doctor, the devil is a very busy man." Grayson later recalled that the president asked him to read to him from the Bible, 2 Corinthians 4:8—"We are troubled on every side, yet not distressed; we are perplexed, but not in despair"—and then said, "If I were not a Christian, I think I should go mad, but my faith in God holds me to the belief that He is in some way working out His own plan through human perversity and mistakes." That sounds more like something he would say later. The other reactions rang true to Wilson's thoughts and feelings as he faced his last, worst year in the White House.[63]

24

DOWNFALL

March 1920 was a cruel month for Woodrow Wilson. After his defeat in the League fight, his delusions and mood swings grew worse. Six days after the Senate voted, he told Grayson that the League should be the main issue in the presidential election and the Democratic convention might decide that "I am the logical one to lead—perhaps the only one to champion this cause." Other times, he sounded philosophical, telling Grayson it was "too soon for the country to accept the League—not ready for it. May have to break the heart and the pocketbook of the world before the League will be accepted and appreciated." Yet at the end of March, the doctor found him depressed over the defeat of the treaty and complaining, "I feel that I would like to go back to bed and stay there until I either get well or die."[1]

Physically, Wilson continued to show signs of recovery, although only modestly. He paid some attention to politics, and he intended to veto the Republicans' resolution authored by Senator Knox that would end the state of war with Germany without a peace treaty. He told Grayson he intended to make his veto message so "extremely distasteful to the Senate" that they might "try to impeach me for it."[2] He also scoffed at Herbert Hoover's decision to run for president as a Republican, saying he lacked the courage to stand by the Democrats. Yet when Tumulty urged him to make a public statement about such domestic issues as inflation, taxes, and prohibition and drafted a statement for him, he did not respond. Similarly, he did not answer pleas by Secretary of War Baker and Tumulty to issue a general amnesty for all persons convicted under the wartime laws against dissent.

April brought additional mixed signs of physical recovery and emotional fragility. At two o'clock in the morning on April 13, he summoned Grayson to his bedroom, where they talked for two hours. Wilson dwelled on the "double-dealing of some of the Senators," particularly Hoke Smith, James Reed, and Lodge, and on how much he wanted to fight them. Yet he also mentioned resigning: "If I am only half-efficient I should turn over the office to the Vice-President . . . the country cannot afford to wait for me." This time, Grayson did not encourage that thought but told him that meeting with the cabinet would reassure him about his ability to handle his office, and Wilson responded, "I will try not to be discouraged even as it is and I shall make the best of the circumstances."[3]

He took the doctor's advice, and in his study the next day, April 14, he held his first cabinet meeting in seven and a half months. Wilson sat at his desk and did not stand up when the cabinet members came in, as he had done in the past, and his only contribution to the discussion was to deplore public criticism of Burleson and to tell Palmer "not to let the country see red." This was the first time any of the cabinet members had seen Wilson since his stroke, and their reactions to him varied. "He looked fuller in the face, lips seemed thicker & face longer," Daniels noted, "but he was bright and cheerful." Palmer thought he "looked like a very old man and acted like one," while Houston later recalled that his voice was weak and his jaw drooped: "It was enough to make one weep to look at him."[4]

Wilson would hold cabinet meetings almost weekly until early in June, and his appearance and performance at them would wax and wane. Domestic matters came up again at the later meetings, but foreign affairs dominated most of them, particularly the situation with the Senate and the peace treaty. Wilson's most energetic performance came at the second cabinet meeting, when Burleson tried unsuccessfully to persuade him to resubmit the treaty with reservations that he would accept. In later meetings, he continued to fulminate about the perfidy of the British and French and his determination to veto the Knox resolution, but despite efforts by Burleson and others, he provided no guidance on most matters, especially domestic concerns. Cabinet members continued to act largely on their own, as they had done since the president's stroke. This practice had the virtue of keeping the government going after a fashion, but it also allowed Palmer to conduct his anti-radical rampage without the president's knowledge. In early June, the new British ambassador, Sir Auckland Geddes, painted a painfully accurate picture of the situation in Washington: "The deadlock is so complete that one would almost be justified in saying that the United States had no Government." Geddes blamed the deadlock equally on the Democrats—"the President has been the whole show"—and the Republicans—"[t]he President is regarded as antichrist or something worse."[5]

Wilson's foes did not have a strong or energetic antichrist to fight against. Grayson thought the president was making slow but steady progress, as evidenced by the nineteen pounds he had gained since February. In May, the doctor described Wilson's daily routine to Cleveland Dodge: at nine in the morning, he walked from the bedroom to the study and worked at his desk until ten-thirty or eleven, when he was wheeled into the garden; at noon, he often watched a movie for an hour; after lunch in the bedroom, he napped for an hour and then attended to some matters and sometimes took a ride in the car with Edith. Grayson also reported to Dercum that the president's walking had improved to the point where for the first time he could come to the dining room to eat lunch.[6] This cheered him, but the doctor was grasping at straws. By any reasonable standard, Wilson was not functioning as president.

Some matters that did engage his attention seemed strange and often petty. He told Grayson that the new secretary of state, Colby, was "the flower of the cabinet" and said House had made "a fizzle" at Paris. He still nursed his grudge against Jack Hibben, complaining to a Princeton classmate about the shortcomings of the university's administration. After one of his rides, he became obsessed with trees that were being cut down in Rock Creek Park and called the superintendent "a liar" for saying that only dead trees were being thinned out. Ten years later, the stenographer Charles Swem reminisced to Tumulty about how the president would sit wrapped in blankets in the wheeled chair "and brood, and when a thing struck him he would send for me and dictate it." It might be the trees in the park or a plan to spend the summer in England or a scheme for the presidential campaign.[7] Yet Burleson complained that he got no response from Wilson to a draft platform for the Democratic convention. Edith Wilson did not falter during these dark days in the White House. She continued to shield her husband from whatever she thought might hurt him, and she showed him fierce loyalty and uncritical devotion. Her love and loyalty unquestionably made his affliction easier to bear, but they did not help him face up to the troubles and dangers that confronted him, his party, and the nation.

As spring came to Washington, Wilson became more active, and he began to receive the new ambassadors who came to present their credentials to him. The new Swiss minister noted that his open mouth "gives him an air of senility, which, however disappears once he speaks and his eyes light up." The minister also noted that his left arm did not move and he did not stand up or leave his chair; he worried that Wilson might suffer another stroke and noted that the White House "has become for him an ivory tower." Geddes, the new British ambassador, was a physician by training, and he likewise noted that Wilson's immobility indicated paralysis. He found the president mentally alert and given to telling stories—an old habit—but he concluded, "I should say he is a typical case of hemiplegia. He is not really able to see people and ought to be freed from all the cares of office." More than anything else and despite Burleson's complaint about the draft platform, Wilson tried to deal with the way the Democrats stood on the League. Late in May, he drafted in his shorthand a model plank on the treaty, which called for "the unqualified ratification of the Treaty of Versailles" and full and immediate American participation in the League. What Wilson meant to do with this shorthand draft is not clear. He did not have it transcribed, and he does not appear to have shared this model plank with anyone.[8]

At the same time, Wilson did make public his thoughts on one aspect of peacemaking by calling the bluff of his adversaries on Capitol Hill. On May 14, the Senate had passed, unanimously by voice vote, a resolution authored by Warren Harding expressing sympathy for the Armenians, whose massacre at the hands of the Turks had become a prominent international cause. Wilson responded by urging Congress to accept an American mandate over Armenia: "I believe that it would do nothing less than arrest the hopeful processes of civilization if we were to refuse the request to become helpful friends and advisers." The Republicans in the Senate gave Wilson's request the back of their collective hand. On June 1, the Senate adopted a resolution, drafted by Philander Knox, rejecting the mandate by a vote of 52 to 23. Every Republican voting opposed the mandate, including Lodge, who had earlier championed the cause of the Armenians.[9]

Wilson also had a chance to air his views when he rejected the Republicans' move to end the state of war. Starting in April, the two houses of Congress, voting almost strictly along party lines, passed resolutions declaring the war at an end. On May 27, the president vetoed the final version of what was called the Knox resolution. In a stinging message, he affirmed, "I can not bring myself to become party to an action which would place an ineffaceable stain upon the honor and gallantry of the United States. . . . Such a peace with Germany—a peace in which none of the essential interests which we had when we entered the war is safeguarded—is, or ought to be, inconceivable, is inconsistent with the dignity of the United States, with the rights and liberties of her citizens, and with the very fundamental conditions of civilization." The veto held. On May 28, a motion in the House to override fell twenty-nine votes short of the necessary two thirds—once more almost strictly along party lines. This outcome pleased Lodge and other Republican leaders because they could continue to charge the president with being the main obstacle to peace.[10]

Clashing with his adversaries over Armenia and the Knox resolution seemed to invigorate Wilson. Four days after the veto, while sitting in his wheeled chair on the rear portico of the White House, he had a long talk with Homer Cummings, the chairman of the Democratic National Committee. When they went over the draft of the keynote speech that Cummings was to deliver at the convention, Wilson made only one criticism. Cummings recalled, "I spoke of his being many times at the point of death. He said that wasn't true. I shall never forget the way he looked at me with his big eyes when he said that and I looked at Mrs. Wilson and I knew then that the President did not fully realize how sick he had been or how near death he had been." On matters related to the convention, Wilson objected to Senator Thomas Walsh of Montana because he had voted for the peace treaty with the Lodge reservations, and he gave Cummings a draft plank on prohibition, which condemned the Volstead Act. He also worked out a way of communicating with the chairman, using the same code he had arranged earlier with House. When Cummings mentioned potential nominees, Wilson expressed no preference and said he wanted "a free and open convention." He also declared, "It is dangerous to stand still. The government must move, and be responsive to the wishes of the people."[11]

Between expressing no preference for a nominee and talking about the need for responsive, dynamic government, it might be thought that Wilson wanted to run again. He did indeed. He was beginning to indulge in his greatest delusion of all following the stroke. Early in June, he wrote two notes in shorthand and his own hand. One, titled "The Great Referendum and Accounting of Your Government," enumerated three questions, the last labeled "chiefly" in capital letters: "Do you wish to make use of my services as President for another four years? Do you approve of the way in which the Administration conducted the War? Do you wish the Treaty of Versailles ratified? Do you, in particular, approve of the League of Nations as organized and empowered under the Treaty of Versailles, and do you wish the United States to play a responsible part in it?" The other note, titled "3rd Administration," listed cabinet officers, with Colby staying on as secretary of state and Burleson as postmaster general, McAdoo possibly returning as secretary of the Treasury, and Bernard Baruch becoming secretary of commerce.[12]

Some of the people closest to Wilson struggled to keep this flight of fancy from getting off the ground. At the middle of June, Grayson told Senator Glass that the president was seriously contemplating a third term but he was not up to a campaign, which would "probably kill him." Grayson begged him to do everything possible to prevent this, and Tumulty expressed the same concerns. Grayson also went to see another Democratic activist, his friend Robert Woolley, and unburdened himself, telling Woolley how feeble and moody the president was. The doctor was particularly worried because Wilson had scheduled an interview with Louis Seibold of the New York *World*.[13]

The interview with Seibold, one of *The World*'s star reporters, sprang from a scheme by Tumulty that went awry. Since March, Tumulty had been trying to get the president to announce that he was not going to run for a third term, and he believed that this interview might smoke him out. Wilson completely foiled those intentions. Seibold's stories, which appeared on June 18, opened, "Nine months of courageous battling to repair the consequences of illness resulting from the profligacy with which all earnest men draw upon their balance in the bank of nature has neither daunted the spirit nor impaired in the slightest degree the splendid intellect of Woodrow Wilson." The reporter spent three hours with the president on June 15 and "saw him transact the important functions of his office with his old-time decisiveness, method and keenness of intellectual appraisement." He recounted how Wilson told jokes, dictated letters, and worked through a basket of documents "with characteristic Wilsonian vigor." The following day, Seibold saw the president again as he was about to take one of his afternoon rides. "From the distance of a dozen feet he suggested a man ready to sally forth for a stroll on the beach," Seibold wrote. Though Wilson walked with a cane, "there was no hesitancy in his step, or apparent lack of confidence. His movements, while slow, were not those of a man whose lower limbs have become paralyzed."[14]

In the interview, Wilson claimed, "I am coming around in good shape and could do a lot more more things now if Mrs. Wilson and Dr. Grayson would kindly look the other way once in a while." He said he was concentrating better than ever on public business, and he declined to discuss candidates for the nomination. He did say he wanted the party to adopt a progressive platform on domestic issues and make a forthright defense of the League of Nations, calling again for a referendum on the League: "No one will welcome a referendum on that issue more than I." With this interview, Wilson staged a show comparable to the one he had put on earlier for the "smelling committee." Most observers read these stories as a bid for a third term, and Democrats around the country started expressing support for the president to run again.[15]

The day after the first story appeared, Wilson talked with Glass, who was about to leave for the convention. About the leading candidates, he thought McAdoo—who had just published a letter announcing that he was dropping out of the race—had still left the door open to being nominated, Palmer would be a weak candidate, and the nomination of Governor James Cox of Ohio "would be a fake." He said nothing about his own prospects, but when Glass regretted that the president's health would not permit him to lead "a great fight for the League of Nations, . . . [n]either the President nor Mrs. Wilson responded to this." Glass added that he "would rather follow the President's corpse through a campaign than the live bodies of some of the men mentioned for the nomination. This seemed to please the President." It did not please Tumulty and Grayson. They rode with Glass to Union Station and pumped him to say whether Wilson was thinking of a third term. Grayson got on board with Glass and talked until the train started moving. The doctor's final words to the senator were "If anything comes up save the life and fame of this great man from the juggling of false friends." Glass evidently heeded Grayson's warning, because in a newspaper interview at a stopover in Chicago, he noted that Democrats on the train were convinced that the president was not thinking of a third term and would be surprised if the convention nominated him.[16]

It took more than such gentle splashes of cold water to awaken Wilson from his dream. The same day that he talked with Glass, he summoned Colby to the White House and deputized the secretary of state to put his name before the convention. Newspaper reports were already circulating that the president was seeking renomination. Cummings sent a steady stream of telegrams back to the White House, using the code Wilson had worked out with him. Most of the pre-convention maneuvering centered on the League plank in the platform. Glass and Colby held out for a strong endorsement, but Senator Walsh succeeded in leaving the door open to reservations. That concession angered Wilson, but Cummings assured him that the League plank was a victory for him, and Wilson sent a telegram congratulating the delegates.

The Democratic convention that opened in San Francisco on June 28, 1920, featured several firsts. It was the first major party convention to be held on the West Coast—a circumstance that disgruntled many of the delegates, who endured several days of dusty, hot, bumpy train rides to get there. It was the first convention to use microphones and electrical amplifiers—a circumstance that infuriated Bryan, who brushed the microphone aside as if it were an instrument of the devil when he spoke. It was the first convention to be broadcast in part on the radio—a medium that was in its infancy and did not yet reach many listeners. As it played out, the convention had a Janus face: its seemingly interminable ballots harked back to the stalemate of 1912 that had finally broken in Wilson's favor, and they looked forward to a much worse deadlock four years later that would come close to tearing the party apart.[17]

Wilson seemed to own the convention. During the opening cere-monies, winches lifted the huge flag behind the speaker's platform to reveal a gigantic portrait of the president. The delegates went wild, and when a spotlight played on the portrait, they exploded again. Delegates marched up and down the aisles waving their state placards in a show of support. New York's Tammany-dominated delegation conspicuously refrained from joining in, whereupon Franklin Roosevelt wrestled the state placard from a Tammany delegate and paraded in the aisles. The thirty-eight-year-old assistant secretary of the navy attracted a lot of pub-licity with that gesture, which would soon redound to his political benefit. The pro-Wilson mood persisted as the days wore on, and Burleson told another Democratic insider that without the general impression of Wil-son's physical incapacity, nothing could have kept him from being nomi-nated, "notwithstanding the third-term bogey."[18]

The impression of Wilson's unfitness to run prevailed at the conven-tion because at a crucial moment Burleson and others made sure that it did. When the balloting began, Palmer faded, and McAdoo and Cox became the leading contenders. Prohibition emerged as an issue between them; McAdoo had come out as a "dry," favoring strict enforcement, whereas Cox was a long-standing "wet," opposing prohibition and favor-ing relaxation of enforcement. McAdoo's status as Wilson's son-in-law and his presumed closeness to the president had earned him the nickname of Crown Prince, but people greatly exaggerated his ties to his father-in-law. Indeed, the president cast a jaundiced eye on the leading contenders. He thought a vastly better person had a chance to win the nomination— himself. On July 2, Colby telegraphed that since the convention appeared deadlocked, he would put the president's name in nomination. Wilson gave Colby the go-ahead by telephone.[19]

This scheme sowed consternation on opposite sides of the country. Tumulty learned about it from Ray Stannard Baker, who was in San Fran-cisco. Taking his political life in his hands, Tumulty wrote to tell Edith that the president's true friends all opposed his seeking a third term, adding, "As his devoted friend, I am still of the same view, for I firmly believe it would mar his place in history." Curiously, Edith did not resent this stand by Tumulty, whom she had never grown to like. On Sunday, July 4, Colby unveiled the scheme before a conclave in San Francisco that included Cummings, Burleson, Daniels, Glass, Senator Joseph T. Robin-son of Arkansas, Representative Cordell Hull of Tennessee, Ray Stannard

Baker, and Vance McCormick. Except for Colby, everyone at the meeting believed that any move to nominate Wilson would be a mistake and would hurt the party. Colby seemed taken aback and said the others made him feel like a criminal. But that was the end of Wilson's dream of another nomination, and he blamed the cabinet members at that meeting, particularly Burleson, for killing it. According to the recollection of a well-informed journalist from New Jersey, he wanted to fire Burleson, and Tumulty had to work hard to prevent that. The White House head usher recalled that the cabinet members got a cold reception when they returned. With Grayson's help, Daniels got back in Wilson's good graces, but "poor old Burleson . . . became sort of an outcast around the White House."[20]

When Cox won the nomination, on the forty-fourth ballot on July 6, Wilson took the news hard. He sent Cox a perfunctory telegram of congratulations, and when Franklin Roosevelt won the vice-presidential nomination, he sent him an equally perfunctory telegram. He felt depressed and complained to Grayson that everyone had lost interest in him, but his spirits lifted a little when the party's nominees came to call on him on Sunday, July 18. Cox and Roosevelt went to the South Portico of the White House, where Wilson was waiting in his wheeled chair with a shawl over his left arm and shoulder. When Cox shook the president's hand, Wilson said in a weak voice, "Thank you for coming. I am very glad you came." Roosevelt later remembered that he noticed tears in Cox's eyes. Edith recalled that her husband brought up stories about Warren Harding's having an African American ancestor and said they should not use those stories; "we must base our campaign on principles, not back-stairs gossip." The meeting lasted fifty minutes. Wilson's talk about the League moved Cox, who told him, "Mr. President, we are going to be a million per cent with you and your Administration and that means the League of Nations." Wilson replied in a whisper, "I am very grateful. I am very grateful."[21]

The lift from the candidates' visit did not last long. The next night, Wilson had difficulty breathing, and when Cummings came to see him a week later, he noticed that the president's eyes filled with tears when Cummings assured him of his continued loyalty. The same day, Swem noted, "The President's mind is not like of old." Instead of being able to dictate more than one letter at a time, "he lapsed into a sort of coma." Edith had to remind him what to do next. Wilson fretted about the size of his envelopes and the proper way to fold letters, and he flew into a rage about automobiles passing the presidential limousine when he was out for a ride. The head of the Secret Service found him irascible and had trouble getting around his unreasonable orders. Even a visit from Jessie and Frank Sayre and their children failed to cheer him up.[22]

He gave his surest sign of depression when the presidential campaign failed to rouse his old combativeness. From the beginning, the Republicans made him their main issue. They denounced "Wilson's league," blamed all the country's troubles on him, and promised a return to "normalcy"—a word their nominee, Warren Harding, had made their chief slogan. Tumulty repeatedly begged the president to speak out, but Wilson rebuffed him. The most he would do was grant a confidential interview at the end of September to a reporter, William Hawkins of the United Press, who found him "only the shattered remnant of the man" he had been before, with "a timidity, almost an apologetic effect in his [manner]." Still, Wilson had some praise for Cox, declared "Harding is nothing," and showed a spark of humor when he said, "I suppose at that distance, I look like a damn fool."[23]

Early in October, he roused himself to write a lengthy public statement on the campaign. Breathing his old fire and overruling advice from Tumulty and George Creel, he avowed, "This election is to be a genuine national referendum. . . . The chief question that is put to you is, of course: Do you want your country's honor vindicated and the Treaty of Versailles ratified?" Wilson maintained that people had been "grossly misled" about the treaty by the "gross ignorance and impudent audacity" of opponents of the treaty and the League. They would "substitute America for Prussia in the policy of isolation and defiant segregation." He dismissed the charge that Article X would impair Congress's authority to declare war as "absolutely false," and he said that the framers of the Covenant would be "amazed and indignant at the things that are now being ignorantly said about this great and sincere document." The whole world, he concluded, awaited the voters' verdict on the shape of the future.[24]

Immediately after the release of that statement, Wilson became even more of a campaign issue. A Republican senator running for reelection, Selden Spencer of Missouri, claimed that Tumulty had acted as president and issued orders in his own name. Tumulty denied the charge, and Wilson publicly telegraphed a denial to Spencer. The senator also claimed that at Paris, Wilson had promised military aid to Romania and Serbia. Wilson answered, "I am perfectly content to leave it to the voters of Missouri to determine which of us is telling the truth." The flurry of charges and countercharges following this exchange received extensive coverage in newspapers all over the country, temporarily crowding the presidential campaign off the front pages. Wilson did not enjoy the attention, and he continued to resist Tumulty's pleas to involve himself more actively. Visiting the president again early in October, Cummings told him that the campaign should have focused more on the League. "Yes, that is the pity of it," Wilson answered. "You and men like you are Crusaders. The other people are politicians."[25]

Viewing the election as a crusade for the League of Nations finally prompted him to get into the campaign, though in a limited way. On October 18, he addressed a public letter to Harding, rejecting the Republican candidate's claim that the French had asked him, Wilson, to "lead the way to a world fraternity." Wilson asserted, "I need not point out to you the grave and extraordinary inferences to be drawn from such a statement." That was a warm-up to his biggest foray into the campaign. Nine days later, on October 27, he spoke to fifteen pro-League Republicans who had bolted their party and were supporting the Democratic ticket. This was Wilson's first speech in more than a year, and he had written it himself. He apologized for sitting while he spoke and for reading from a text, "what my dear father called 'dried tongue.'" He affirmed that the League offered the only way to redeem the sacrifices made by the husbands, sons, and brothers who had fallen in the war and that Article X would prevent another world war. "This is the true, the real Americanism." This was the "supreme choice" that transcended parties: "The nation was never called upon to make a more solemn choice than it must now make."[26]

Two days later, he made one last foray into the campaign. Cox invited him to attend a large rally in New York, but he declined, using infirmity as an excuse. In fact, although Cox and Roosevelt had issued statements endorsing the League, they had also talked favorably about reservations, and that distressed Wilson. He recognized, though, that the candidates still offered a sterling alternative to Harding, and on October 29, four days before the election, he wrote a public letter praising Cox for having "spoken truly and fearlessly about the great issue at stake." Wilson predicted victory and signed the letter, "Your gratified and loyal supporter."[27] Still, the endorsement lacked warmth and came far too late.

As things turned out, earlier, more enthusiastic endorsements by Wilson and speeches, if he had been able to make them, would have done little good. The only surprise in the election results was the Republicans' truly titanic victory. Harding captured more than 60 percent of the popular vote, more than 16 million, to 9 million for Cox. His electoral margin was 404 to 127—almost as big as Wilson's in 1912. This tidal wave swept away almost everything the Democrats held outside the South. Beyond the borders of the Confederacy, not a single one of the party's candidates for senator or governor won, not even New York's rising star, Al Smith. Except for Kentucky, all the border states went Republican, as did such usually safe states as Oklahoma and Arizona. Even in the South, despite whispering campaigns about Harding's alleged "black blood," Tennessee fell to the Republicans. New York City and Boston went Republican for the first time since the Civil War. The party's majority in the House of Representatives rose to 303 seats to the Democrats' 131, while in the Senate they gained ten seats to hold 70 to the Democrats' 26.[28]

Wilson had wanted this election to be a referendum, and many people were delighted to read its outcome as such. Senators Borah and Johnson gleefully proclaimed that the American people had spoken resoundingly against League membership, and later historians would echo their judgment and call this election a "referendum for isolation." Actually, the League and foreign policy in general played far less of a role in the results than did discontent with post-war troubles. Another influence was "reform fatigue." In their national campaign, Republicans hewed to an unabashedly conservative line. They slammed Wilson's domestic policies, and they almost never uttered the name of Theodore Roosevelt. That was a deliberate omission. The governor of Kansas told William Allen White, "I have a feeling that we have had all the superman business the party is likely to want."[29] For the Republicans, Harding's "normalcy" meant implicitly, and sometimes explicitly, a return to the days of McKinley.

In the only apparent contradiction, Eugene Debs, running from his cell in the federal prison in Atlanta, racked up more than 900,000 votes— a few thousand more than he had gotten eight years earlier. Actually, the Socialist's showing was perfectly consonant with Harding's triumph: either way, people were voting against Wilson. If the election of 1920 was a referendum, it was a referendum on him. As one historian has put it, Harding offered the perfect foil to Wilson: "modest mediocrity rather than arrogant genius; . . . warm humanity rather than austere intellectualism; genial realism rather than strenuous idealism." There was no question which half of that antinomy the electorate chose.[30]

The object of this repudiation had oscillating reactions to the event, as was typical with most of his reactions since the stroke. Wilson spent part of election day, November 2, as he did every day now, trying to climb a set of little steps Grayson had ordered built for him. The next day, he told Swem that the "Republicans had committed suicide"—by which he evidently meant that their conservative domestic policies would doom their future political prospects. He also believed that the result had hurt the country in the eyes of the world. Yet Stockton Axson told Jessie, "He has never been finer than he is today, serene, steady, his patriotism sublime." Axson thought Wilson looked better than he had in months, "and this evening he was almost merry, laughed more than I have seen him laugh for a year." Talking about the election and the fate of the country, Axson found "not a suggestion of bitterness, rather loving-kindness." Yet a few days later, Cummings noted that the president seemed "mournful," and his "whole household seems tired." Wilson asked Colby to write a Thanksgiving proclamation for him because "although I have no resentment in my heart I find myself very much put to it to frame a proper proclamation."[31]

The Republicans' romp in 1920 left Wilson the lamest of lame ducks. He would pass his final four months in the White House as an often-embittered caretaker. A special target of his bitterness was Debs. Earlier, in August, the subject of pardons for persons convicted under the wartime laws had come up again. Changing his mind, Palmer now favored them, as did Newton Baker and Josephus Daniels, but Wilson said no. Appeals to pardon Debs continued to come, particularly from labor leaders, including Samuel Gompers, and at the end of January 1921, Palmer sent the president a formal legal argument—replete with references to Supreme Court opinions, particularly ones written by Justice Oliver Wendell Holmes, Jr.—in favor of executive clemency. "Debs is now approaching 65 years of age," Palmer concluded. "If not adequately, he surely has been severely punished." Wilson wrote on the document, "Denied. W.W." He would carry his refusal to forgive to his grave. A year later, after Harding did pardon Debs, Ida Tarbell recorded Wilson saying, "Debs should never have been released. Debs was one of the worst men in the country. He should have stayed in the penitentiary."[32]

The president's engagement with affairs of state picked up after the election. Edith let down her guard over access to her husband, and Tumulty resumed his former role of chief adviser. The government still functioned with surprising smoothness, thanks to the delegation of authority to cabinet members. As he had done before the stroke, Wilson interested himself in foreign affairs, although he deferred to Colby far more than he had ever done with Lansing. He insisted upon nonrecognition and noninterference toward the Bolsheviks in Russia, he resisted Allied incursions in Asia Minor, and he favored nonintervention in the Caribbean and Mexico. Wilson adamantly rejected all suggestions to resubmit the peace treaty to the Senate, and he feared that when the Republicans came in, they would, as he told an old friend from Princeton, "take us into the League in such a niggardly fashion, with 'if's' and 'but's' which so clearly proceed from prejudice and a desire to play a lone hand and think first and only of the United States."33

This increased activity reflected continued recovery, but Wilson was nowhere near fully functioning as president. When Ray Stannard Baker saw him at the end of November, the sight shook him: "A broken, ruined old man, shuffling along, his left arm inert, the fingers drawn up like a claw, the left side of his face sagging frightfully. His voice is not human: it gurgles in his throat, sounds like that of an automaton. And yet his mind seems as alert as ever." Baker watched newsreels of the European tour with the Wilsons, and he noted that the president sat silent except for making a few remarks "in a dead, hollow, weary voice." Baker was visiting the White House to write a magazine article, but after reading the draft, Edith and Grayson blocked publication. Edith told Baker she feared readers might receive "a great shock, but to us who have been constantly in touch and seen great improvement it would seem to strike the wrong note."34

Such improvement led Wilson to want to give the State of the Union speech in person again when Congress reconvened in December. Grayson had to talk him out of it. He reminded the president that the ovation at the Capitol might overcome him and that his voice might give out. Grayson told Baker that Wilson "easily loses control of himself" and that "when he talks he is likely to break down and weep." Although he did not go to Capitol Hill, Wilson did meet with congressional leaders at the White House on the day the session of Congress opened. The staff ushered into the Blue Room senators Lodge and Underwood, who was now the Democratic leader, and representatives Joseph W. Fordney of Michigan, chairman of the Ways and Means Committee, and Champ Clark, the former Speaker. Wilson walked in, holding his cane in his right hand; he did not shake hands with the men. He whispered to Underwood, "I used the excuse of this 'third leg,' as I did not want to shake hands with Lodge." After the meeting, he told Grayson, "Can you imagine what kind of a hide Lodge has got, coming up here in these circumstances and wanting to appear familiar and talk with me. His hide has a different anatomical arrangement than any I have heard of."35

Wilson dictated and edited his last State of the Union message, which sparkled with his eloquence and opened with "an immortal sentence of Abraham Lincoln's, 'Let us have faith that right makes might, and in that faith let us dare to do our duty as we understand it.'" He depicted democracy being put to the test in the world, and he wanted the United States to uphold democracy at home and champion weak nations abroad. Specifically, he called for a unified government budget, simplified taxes, loans to Armenia, and independence for the Philippines. "I have not so much laid before you a series of recommendations, gentlemen," he concluded, "as sought to utter a confession of faith, of the faith in which I was bred and which it is my solemn purpose to stand by until my last fighting day. I believe this to be the faith of America, the faith of the future."[36]

Lame-duck sessions of Congress usually enact little legislation, and this Republican-controlled body was in no mood to please a partisan adversary in the dying days of his administration. In those circumstances, Wilson would have had little to do even if he had been in good health. He did veto some bills passed by the Republican-controlled Congress, including a measure to raise tariff rates back to pre-1913 levels. In a veto message written by Secretary of the Treasury Houston, the president warned that higher tariffs would hurt American farmers and that the United States had now become the world's leading creditor nation, which meant that European nations must sell goods here in order to be able to pay their debts.[37] This Congress still contained enough Democrats to sustain the veto, but the tariff bill offered a foretaste of a government in which the Republicans controlled both the executive and the legislative branches. This veto message accurately predicted the damage that higher tariffs would do to the American and international economy in the coming decade.

Some of the time, Wilson occupied himself with thoughts about his future. Back in July, after the Democratic convention, he had talked about entering a new career, and he also occasionally thought about academic life and writing. Edith later recalled that shortly before they left the White House, she found him at his typewriter. He looked up at her and smiled as he said, "I have written the dedication to the book on Government for which I have been preparing all my life and which now I will have leisure to do." The dedication began, "To E. B. W. I dedicate this book because it is a book in which I have tried to interpret life, the life of a nation, and she has shown me the full meaning to life." Edith added in her memoir, "The tragedy is that this was the only page of that book ever written."[38]

Money worried her and her husband because Congress did not then provide an ex-president with a pension. In fact, they were in good shape financially. Wilson had saved money from his $75,000-a-year presidential salary, and a newspaper report later stated that he had $250,000 in the bank—a handsome sum in those days.[39] A welcome addition to their assets came in December, when the Norwegian Nobel Committee awarded Wilson the Nobel Prize for Peace for his role in founding the League of

Nations. He was the second American president so honored—the first was Theodore Roosevelt, for his role in mediating the Russo-Japanese War. In addition to the honor, the Nobel Prize brought him a cash award of $40,000.

Larger and still more welcome additions to the Wilsons' finances would soon come from their wealthy friends. A group led by Cleveland Dodge and Bernard Baruch would raise money for them to purchase one of the White House limousines and a house in Washington. Over the next three years, these financial angels would establish a trust that would pay an annuity of $10,000 a year; Wilson would receive the first quarterly payment less than a month before his death. In the meantime, Wilson made a surprising move, apparently dictated by concerns about money. In February, he asked Secretary of State Colby what he planned to do after leaving office. Colby replied that he was going to practice law again; although the prospect did not excite him, he had to make a living. "Well, I, too, must make a living," Wilson said. "As I was once a lawyer, why not open an office together here in Washington?" Although Edith soon told Colby that this was just a momentary impulse and not something to take seriously, the arrangements went forward, and Wilson casually remarked one day, "Oh, that reminds me, Tumulty—you can tell [reporters] I have decided to open a law office in partnership with Colby."40

Wilson made this move after he and Edith had decided where they would live after they left the White House. She later recalled that in Paris they had begun to consider various places. She drew up a list that included Baltimore, Washington, Richmond, Boston, and New York, and they scored those cities for "Climate," "Friends," "Opportunities," "Freedom," and "Amusements." Washington came out lowest, but they chose it anyway because he wanted to use the Library of Congress in writing his book, and, she said, "it was home to me." Wilson wanted to build a house on a site overlooking the Potomac beyond Georgetown, and he had clipped articles and illustrations from architectural magazines. When the project proved impracticable, they considered several houses in the district and nearby Virginia, including Woodlawn, a plantation that had belonged to George Washington's stepchildren. Edith did most of the house hunting, assisted by her brother Wilmer Bolling, who was in the real estate business. Eventually, she settled on a large, recently built house at 2340 S Street N.W., half a block off Massachusetts Avenue. Their benefactors put up $100,000 toward the purchase price of $150,000, and Wilson signed the deed on December 14. This would be home to both of the Wilsons for the rest of their lives.41

During the new year, Edith busied herself with renovations to the house, adding an elevator and bookshelves for her husband's library. In February, for the first time since his stroke, Wilson went to the theater, where the audience cheered him before and after the performance and between acts. His moods still seesawed. He was reliving past glories by watching newsreels of the European tour over and over. One last unpleasant duty remained before Harding's inauguration on March 4. At six-thirty in the preceding evening, the president-elect and his wife paid the customary call on the outgoing president and First Lady. The visit, which lasted only twenty minutes, was cool and correct. Earlier, Edith had invited Florence Harding to the White House to discuss domestic arrangements. Given Wilson's health, questions arose about whether he would attend the inauguration. At a cabinet meeting in January, Daniels recorded Newton Baker saying, "I hope you will not go if it is a cold & sleety day." Wilson answered, "O that will not matter. I will wear a gas mask anyhow."[42]

Inauguration day, March 4, 1921, was clear and cold. Wilson rode from the White House to the Capitol beside Harding in an open car, with two old-line Republicans, Senator Knox and Representative Joseph G. Cannon of Illinois, the former speaker, sitting in front of them. People who lined up along Pennsylvania Avenue got their first glimpse of the president since his return from the speaking tour. One reporter described "the pathetic picture" of him limping out of the White House to the car; beside the ruddy-faced, smiling Harding, the reporter wrote, Wilson looked like a living ghost.[43] Harding was solicitous, helping him in and out of the car, but at the Capitol the younger man reinforced the contrast by bounding up the steps while Wilson had to use a wheeled chair to enter the building. Once inside, Wilson walked with his cane to the elevator that took him to the ornate President's Room off the Senate chamber.

One last painful encounter awaited Wilson in that room. Senator Lodge entered and informed the president that the houses of Congress had concluded their business and asked if he had any further communication to make to them. "Tell them I have no further communication to make," Wilson replied. "I thank you for the courtesy. Good morning, Sir." A reporter who was in the room noted, "There was something in the voice of the President and the way he uttered those words. . . . The President's response was not uttered curtly or discourteously, but there was no mistaking the rigidity of the response." Wilson then told Harding and the incoming vice president, Calvin Coolidge, that he could not attend the inaugural ceremony because the stairs were too steep for him. He joked to Knox, "Well, the Senate threw me down before, and I don't want to fall down myself now." Shortly before noon, the Wilsons, accompanied by

Tumulty, Grayson, and a valet, left the Capitol and drove to S Street. A crowd cheered his arrival, and a group of League supporters marched up the street at three o'clock. Wilson came out several times and waved, but he declined calls to speak.[44]

On that quiet, subdued note, the eight years of Wilson's presidency ended. No one tried to look for silver linings in the clouds that had over-hung his last year in the White House. He did receive many messages · wishing him well, and public tributes usually hailed him as a prophet who had pointed the way toward a better world. No one tried, either, to dis-guise the struggle and conflict that had marked his time in office from the beginning or to pretend that he had not failed in his final quest. The most affecting valedictory came from the journalist who, besides Baker, knew Wilson best—Frank Cobb, the person to whom the president had bared his soul as he agonized over his decision to enter the war. Cobb closed his editorial in the New York *World* by affirming,

> Woodrow Wilson on this morning of the fourth of March can say, in the words of Paul the Apostle to Timothy:
>
> "For I am now ready to be offered, and the time of my depar-ture is at hand.
>
> "I have fought a good fight. I have finished my course, I have kept faith."

Those words pleased Wilson as he departed from the public arena and faced the prospect of the rest of his life.[45]

25

TWILIGHT

Woodrow Wilson lived the rest of his life in twilight. He lived a month short of three years in the house on S Street, which Edith made into a refuge for and shrine to him. A replica of the big Lincoln bed took up much of his second-floor bedroom, at the back of the house. At his insistence, the bedroom harbored one object that Edith disliked and replaced after he died: over the mantel, where his eye alighted when he lay in bed, hung a painting he had bought of a young woman who reminded him of Ellen. On bright days, sunlight flooded through the bedroom's south-facing windows, which looked out on a terraced backyard and garden and offered a verdant, flower-filled view in the spring and summer. On the first floor, between the library and the dining room, there was a solarium reminiscent of the White House portico where Wilson had spent many hours; in the dining room, French doors opened onto a large terrace. The weakness of Wilson's left leg prevented him from walking on the grass in the yard.[1]

The ex-president's family worked to make the move to his new home as easy as possible for him. When the Wilsons arrived from the Capitol on inauguration day, familiar faces surrounded him at lunch. After the meal, as Edith recalled, Grayson said, "Mr. President—" to which her husband replied with a smile, "Just Woodrow Wilson." He disliked being called Mr. President now, and he would henceforth discourage people from addressing him in that way. Catching himself, the doctor responded, "Mr. Wilson, I think you should excuse yourself and get some rest." President Harding generously permitted Grayson, who was still an active-duty naval officer, to continue to serve as the ex-president's physician. A succession of private nurses would care for him during the next three years. In place of Arthur Brooks, the thoughtful and efficient valet at the White House,

Edith secured the services of a highly recommended couple, Isaac and Mary Scott, who soon became essential to Wilson's comfort.[2]

After a few days, Edith established a household routine. She brought in her bachelor younger brother, John Randolph Bolling, to be Wilson's secretary. In frail health since childhood and hunchbacked, Randolph knew shorthand and typing and had helped out during the last months in the White House. He handled the voluminous correspondence at a desk in the hall outside Wilson's bedroom and responded to most letters on Wilson's behalf. Tending to the mail was Wilson's first activity in the morning, followed by walking in the hall and being shaved by Isaac Scott. Unless guests came, he would stay in his bathrobe and slippers, having lunch in the bedroom and taking a nap in the early afternoon. Then, he would dress for the daily ride in the Pierce-Arrow and afterward receive a few visitors by the fireside in the library. He usually ate dinner on a small table in the bedroom while Edith read to him; later, she would have dinner with Randolph and come back to read to her husband again until nine or ten. Family visitors included his daughters Margaret, Jessie, and Nell and Stockton Axson, together with Edith's relatives. The Wilsons and their visitors often watched movies in the library. Starting in April, they also went out each Saturday night to Keith's Theater on Fifteenth Street, where the audience and sometimes even the actors applauded Wilson.[3]

Despite this care, he did not make the transition well. He grew tired more easily, and he suffered a recurrence of the prostate problems. When Ray Stannard Baker visited two and a half weeks after they moved into the house, Wilson struck him as "lon[e]lier, more cut-off, than ever before. His mind still works with power, but with nothing to work upon!" When Baker told him that audiences at movie theaters were cheering him in the newsreels more than Harding, Wilson grumbled that once when he was in a theater, people had cheered Roosevelt louder. He managed a flash of humor. About hostile accounts of the peace conference in a recently published book and magazine article by Lansing he quipped, "I think I can stand it if Lansing can!"[4]

The coming of spring in 1921 brought little cheer or solace to Wilson. In May, Tommy—as Wilson was still known to some—had to beg off a nearby reunion of the Witherspoon Gang from Princeton, telling one of them that newspapers exaggerated his improvement: "I have not yet the physical strength to venture so far afield." When Baker visited again in May, Edith told him her husband had resisted suggestions that he do some work and was reading mostly mystery stories, and in the car he always wanted to ride along the same route. In June, Stockton Axson secretly reported to Hibben, who hoped to reconcile with Wilson, that he saw no improvement in the arm and leg and that Wilson could not seem to get interested in writing.[5]

Practicing law with Bainbridge Colby did not occupy his mind the way he had thought it might. After going abroad briefly in the spring of 1921, Colby began to set up the practice, renting and furnishing offices in New York and Washington. According to Edith's recollection, Grayson advised his patient not to take up work for a while, and remodeling problems delayed the opening of the Washington office until August. Wilson went there on the opening day, but that would be his only visit. A ceremonial appearance before a judge to be admitted to the District of Columbia bar would be his only other venture outside the house for the law practice. Colby sought to remedy his partner's absence by installing three telephone lines from the office to the house, but there was little traffic on those lines at first. An ex-president and former secretary of state should have dazzled as rainmakers, but high-paying clients did not immediately flock to their practice.[6]

When business finally picked up, another obstacle loomed. Wilson nearly always found something ethically objectionable about prospective clients. Approached in February 1922 about a boundary dispute between Costa Rica and Panama, he told Colby, "I am sure you will agree with me that we should accept no business which might involve us in dealings with the Government of Costa Rica." Four months later, in a matter involving Ecuador and American banks, he said, "Frankly, my dear Colby, I am not willing to have my name associated with this transaction." He did agree to represent the bid of the breakaway Western Ukrainian National Republic for recognition by the League of Nations. Colby went to Europe in the fall of 1922 to look into the matter, but he found that they could do little on behalf of the Ukrainians.[7]

In one instance, Wilson's ethical qualms saved the partners from a painful embarrassment. In August 1922, representatives of the oil company owned by Harry Sinclair asked the firm to represent them in an upcoming Senate investigation into the leasing of the Teapot Dome oil reserves in Wyoming. They were offering a retainer that would, Colby noted, "swamp the inadequate financial returns that are involved in the Ukrainian business." He did not give a figure, but Edith recalled that it was $100,000—a huge amount at the time. Wilson smelled a rat. "Colby must be a child not to see through such a scheme," he told Edith. Because exploding political scandals soon made Teapot Dome a byword for corruption under the Harding administration, her memory may have exaggerated Wilson's reaction—but not by much. He composed a letter to Colby stating that he did not know what the oil companies were up to, but reading the newspapers gave him "the impression that some ugly business is going on in respect to Teapot Dome." Instead of sending the letter, however, he telegraphed to say that they should talk in person, and when Colby came to Washington and heard Wilson's objections, he agreed to withdraw.[8]

At that meeting, Wilson probably also broached the idea of ending the partnership. Three months later, he reminded Colby of "the suggestion I made to you in the summer . . . to leave you free individually to take business such as has frequently come to us but with which I, because of my years of public service and conduct of national affairs,—cannot associate myself as counsel." Colby demurred, but after his return from Europe he bowed to financial reality and suggested closing the Washington office. Wilson responded by renewing his offer to leave the practice. This time, Colby agreed. At the middle of December, he announced the end of the partnership. Although he mentioned "the long interruption of [Wilson's] active work in the bar," Colby insisted that Wilson had "shown the same effectiveness that he has displayed in every field to which he has turned his energies." Their parting was completely amicable.[9]

This second foray of Wilson's into the law proved only a little more remunerative and no more satisfying to him than his youthful sojourn in Atlanta had been forty years before. This time, despite Colby's polite disclaimer at the time of the dissolution of their partnership, the ex-president's health obviously had hobbled his work. His lack of physical energy and his difficulty concentrating might not have raised an insuperable obstacle if his stiff ethical scruples and regard for his former office had not barred the door to most prospective clients. Yet as in his long-ago encounter with legal practice, the real fault lay in his attitude and desires. Soon after he suggested dissolving the partnership, he told McAdoo, "The members of the [American Bar] Association constitute the most reactionary and pig-headed group in the nation."[10] Also, Wilson did not take much interest in the practice; the partners' correspondence usually dealt with Democratic party politics rather than legal business. In every other field to which he had dedicated himself—as scholar, writer, teacher, college president, governor, president of the United States—Wilson had succeeded brilliantly. The law was the only endeavor where he fell short. He failed at it in his old age for the same reason he had in his young manhood—his heart was not in it.

The physical and mental handicaps that kept him from actively practicing law hampered him in other pursuits as well. In November 1921, the public got a painful reminder of how feeble Wilson was. The third anniversary of the Armistice witnessed the dedication of the Tomb of the

Unknown Soldier, containing unidentified remains of a serviceman killed in the war. Because he could not walk from the White House to the cemetery in Arlington, Wilson asked permission to go in a horse-drawn carriage, which the War Department denied. Instead, he and Edith rode in the procession that took the remains from the Capitol to the White House, and then they returned to S Street. Loud cheers along Pennsylvania Avenue heartened Wilson, as did more cheers and tributes from people gathered in front of his house. After hobbling inside and waving from the upstairs window, he came to the front door and told the throng, "I wish I had the voice to reply and thank you for the wonderful tribute you have paid me. I can only say God bless you." When someone shouted, "Long live the best man in the world!" Wilson's eyes filled with tears, and he reached out to hold hands with Edith, who was weeping too.[11]

Now, scholarship and writing no longer seemed open to him either. The paralysis in his left hand made it hard to hold a book, and his limited vision made reading on his own slow and laborious. During the second half of 1921, Stockton Axson stayed with the Wilsons, and he often took Edith's place, reading to his brother-in-law from more serious works, including the novels of Jane Austen and the essays of his old inspiration, Edmund Burke, who interested him anew. In 1922, he commended to Colby "the word expediency as Burke would have used it, to mean the wisdom of circumstances." Soon afterward, Baker noted, "We got on the subject of Edmund Burke of whom he is a great admirer: & he was positively brilliant in his comments on Burke's service."[12]

Not long after he talked with Baker, Wilson dictated to Edith some notes for a book to be titled "The Destiny of the Republic." Under the heading "The Vision and Purpose of the Founders," he observed that unlike every other nation, the United States had been founded "for the benefit of mankind as well as for the benefit of its people." Yet, others in the world had not welcomed this experiment. Under other headings he outlined reactions and effects abroad, and, echoing Burke, he observed, "France caught in a luminous fog of political theory, was groping her way from revolution to revolution in bewildered search of firm ground upon which to build a permanent government." Two weeks after dictating those notes, Wilson told J. Franklin Jameson, his onetime teacher at Johns Hopkins, that he was thinking about making a study of the impact of the American republic on European politics, "and I would be greatly indebted to you if you would direct me to the books which are likely to be of most service to me in carrying out that purpose."[13]

Despite Jameson's prompt offer to help, the project fell by the wayside. The only fruit to come from these musings was an abbreviated essay that Wilson finally produced in April 1923, "The Road Away From Revolution." Typed by Wilson himself, the essay opens by asking what had caused the present unsettled state of the world and by noting that the Russian Revolution was part of a widespread reaction against "capitalism" and the way it treated people. "The world has been made safe for democracy," Wilson asserted. "But democracy has not yet made the world safe against irrational revolution. That supreme task, which is nothing less than the salvation of civilization, now faces democracy, insistent, imperative." The clearly marked road away from revolution lay through the reassertion of the highest standards and ideals: "The sum of the whole matter is, that our civilization cannot survive materially unless it be redeemed spiritually. It can be saved only by becoming permeated with the spirit of Christ and being made free and happy in the practices which spring out of that spirit."[14]

Barely 1,000 words long, vague and evangelical in tone and message, this essay sounded like some of Wilson's immature writing during and just after college. When he sent the essay to George Creel, the journalist wrote back—not to him but to Edith—that it was not up to Wilson's usual standard. Creel was telling this to her rather than her husband because he worried that it would crush his spirit and bring back "all of the old depression with possible effect upon his physical state." When Edith gently tried to convey that assessment during a ride in the car with Wilson and Axson, he said to Axson, "They kept after me to do this thing, and I did it." Edith responded, "Now don't get on your high horse about this. I am just telling you that they say that what the article needs is expansion, reasoning out the case more." Wilson shot back, "I have done all I can, and all I am going to do."[15]

Back at the house, after Wilson retired to his bedroom, Axson found Edith sobbing in the hallway. "All I want to do is help in any way I can," she said. "I just want to help and I don't know what to do." Axson offered to read the essay and then told her it needed to be shorter, not longer: "This is not an argument, it is a challenge." Edith asked Axson to talk to her husband, who readily agreed to his suggested cuts.[16] Wilson sent the revised essay to *The Atlantic*, which published it in the August issue and later as a short book.

"The Road Away From Revolution," which would be Wilson's next-to-last published work, contained the germ of later analyses of totalitarianism. The seizure of power in Italy by Benito Mussolini's Fascists had recently troubled him, and his stress on ideals and spiritual values to combat such creeds anticipated later anti-Communist and anti-Fascist views.

But a few intellectual nuggets and rhetorical sparks did not make up for the essay's shortcomings. For someone who had once written so easily and confidently to produce such a slight piece of writing after so much effort and anguish marked a sad finish to a formerly great literary career.

Other pursuits did beckon Wilson. He attracted constant public attention as an ex-president and champion of the League of Nations. Early in 1921, a group of friends and admirers set about to organize and endow the Woodrow Wilson Foundation, which would promote his ideas and annually honor a person who made contributions to world peace. Prominent among the organizers and donors were the League advocate Hamilton Holt and Wilson's wealthy Princeton classmates Cleveland Dodge and Cyrus McCormick. The main energy behind the effort, however, came from Franklin D. Roosevelt. Roosevelt corresponded with Wilson in 1921 and came to visit during the summer, not long before he contracted polio. Roosevelt's subsequent paralysis would be the basis for a bond between him and Wilson, who would send regular messages of encouragement. With his soon-to-be-famous determination, Roosevelt plunged ahead with work on the foundation. Even though Wilson refused to lend his name to any appeal for money, the organizers had raised most of the $1 million endowment by the end of 1922. Formal incorporation took place on December 27 at Roosevelt's home in New York. The next day, on the ex-president's sixty-sixth birthday, a delegation visited to inform him that the Woodrow Wilson Foundation had been established.[17]

Wilson received another birthday tribute when a resolution arrived from the Capitol expressing "the pleasure and joy of the Senate of the United States because of his rapid recovery to good health." Newspaper reports noted that the senators had passed the resolution unanimously by voice vote, with Democrats shouting aye and most Republicans appearing occupied with other business. "Think of them passing it and not meaning it," Wilson chuckled to Grayson. "I would much rather have had three Senators get together and have it passed with sincerity." The senators had heard correctly about his health. Six weeks earlier, he had displayed his newfound vigor on the fourth anniversary of the Armistice. In contrast to his tearfulness and his inability to say more than a few words the year before, he spoke forcefully and at some length to some 5,000 people gathered in front of his house. He excoriated the Senate for blocking the path to permanent peace and avowed, "Puny persons who are standing in the way will find that their weakness is no match for the strength of a moving Providence." Reporters observed that he looked good and seemed to have put on weight. Although Isaac Scott helped him out through the front door, Wilson stood without support and tucked the crook of his cane into his coat pocket. His voice did not ring out as strongly as in days past, but most in the crowd could hear him.[18]

Concern about world affairs and the League helped pull Wilson out of his prolonged slump in 1921. In October, when the Harding administration submitted a treaty with Germany that copied the Treaty of Versailles without the League Covenant, he privately scorned Democratic senators who voted "to accept national disgrace in the form of a separate treaty with Germany which repudiated every obligation to our allies." Soon afterward, he sent Justice Brandeis a statement on foreign policy for a possible Democratic platform. Reclaiming the motto he had first coined and the Republicans had taken up in 1920, Wilson declared, "'AMERICA FIRST' is a slogan which does not belong to any one political party." For Republicans, it meant America "must render no service to any other nation or people," whereas for Democrats it meant "that in every organization for the benefit of mankind America must lead the world by imparting to other peoples her own ideals of Justice and of Peace."[19] That statement marked the beginning of consultation and collaboration with Brandeis and other prominent Democrats, such as Frank Cobb of the New York *World* and the diplomat Norman Davis about what they came to call "The Document."

Not everyone chose to pursue American membership in the League through party channels. Hamilton Holt and John Hessin Clarke, Wilson's appointee to the Supreme Court, who resigned in 1922 partly because of ill health, began to plan an organization to promote League membership outside politics. They attracted a number of prominent Republicans, including former leaders of the League to Enforce Peace, but when Clarke approached Wilson, the ex-president said that he preferred to concentrate his influence upon Democrats to get a strong League plank in the next party platform and nominate someone who would rectify "the gross and criminal blunder of failing to ratify the Treaty of Versailles." Yet he told Holt that he and Clarke were doing good work, "and it will always be a pleasure to cooperate with you."[20] Taking that message as assent, Holt and Clarke formed the League of Nations Non-Partisan Association, which eventually grew into a large, well-funded organization but, like the LEP, would never succeed in reaching its goal.

As Wilson's health improved, he devoted his gradually increasing energies mainly to defending his actions as president and involving himself in Democratic politics. Veterans of his administration were quick to tell their tales, particularly about the peace conference. Lansing had jumped in first with an article in *The Saturday Evening Post* and a book titled *The Peace Negotiations: A Personal Narrative*, both published in

March 1921. Wilson himself had already moved to get out his side of the story by enlisting Baker to write an account of the time in Paris. Baker worked with Wilson's files, first in the White House and then during the spring of 1921 at S Street. He found the material so massive that he persuaded the Wilsons to have the files moved to his home, in Amherst, Massachusetts. There, Baker labored to produce three volumes of narrative and documents. Excerpts were serialized in newspapers and magazines, and the complete work was published late in 1922 as *Woodrow Wilson and World Settlement.*[21] Before those volumes appeared, Tumulty published magazine articles about Wilson and his memoir, *Woodrow Wilson As I Know Him.* His accounts were sentimentalized and often inaccurate.

Wilson evidently did not read Tumulty's book, but he soon found reasons for being vexed with his former secretary. At the beginning of April 1922, Tumulty asked Wilson to give him a statement that he could read at the Democrats' Jefferson Day dinner in New York. Wilson, who was working behind the scenes on "The Document," declined, saying he did not think this an appropriate occasion "for breaking my silence." According to Edith, Tumulty telephoned her the next day to ask her to get "the Governor" to make the statement, which she refused to do. She recalled that Tumulty then asked to see Wilson about "an important *personal* matter." She put down the telephone to ask her husband, who agreed to see Tumulty before he went for his ride in the afternoon. She was out when Tumulty came to the house, but she recalled that her brother cautioned Tumulty not to mention the statement. When Edith got back, Wilson told her Tumulty had not mentioned it.[22]

After the dinner, at which Tumulty did issue a statement on Wilson's behalf, he described the incident differently. "As I stood up to go," he explained, "you took hold of my arm and in substance said what was contained in the message." He admitted that Wilson had not told him to make the remarks at the dinner, "but I think I was justified by every fair implication from what you said to me." The statement read, "Say to the Democrats of New York that I am ready to support any man who stands for the salvation of America, and the salvation of America is justice to all classes"—which the press took as an endorsement of Cox, who was at the dinner. When Wilson read the newspaper accounts, he wrote to *The New York Times,* "I did not send any message whatever to that dinner nor authorize anyone to convey a message." As for Cox, Wilson gibed privately that the party would "commit suicide" if it nominated him again. He did not answer Tumulty's letters of explanation and profuse apology. "Tumulty will sulk for a few days, then come like a spanked child to say he is sorry and wants to be forgiven," Edith recalled him saying. He took no lasting hard feelings away from this incident, and he later recommended Tumulty as a possible Senate candidate in New Jersey in 1924. The hard feelings were on Tumulty's side. He did not come to the house until the ex-president lay dying, and then Edith would not allow anyone but family members into the sickroom.²³

Wilson cared about maintaining his silence in early 1922 because he wanted to control his reentry into Democratic politics. Besides repeatedly working over and consulting on "The Document," he endorsed and opposed candidates for the Senate in Democratic primaries in 1922. In Missouri, he backed a challenge to James Reed by Breckinridge Long, his former student who had served in the State Department. He felt keenly disappointed when Reed narrowly won the primary, and he seriously considered endorsing Reed's Republican opponent. In Mississippi, he denounced Vardaman, who was attempting a comeback, as "thoroughly false and untrustworthy," and he applauded Vardaman's defeat. In Maryland, he endorsed former representative David J. Lewis, and he lamented Lewis's loss to William Cabell Bruce, his nemesis from the University of Virginia. Despite those disappointments, Wilson took heart from the election results in November 1922. In New York, Al Smith won back the governorship, and in Congress the Democrats picked up seventy-six seats in the House and five in the Senate—enough to give them effective control of both houses in combination with newly energized Republican insurgents. "I believe with you that Tuesday's elections make it easier to turn the thoughts of the country in the right direction," Wilson told former justice Clarke, "and to make ready for the great duty of 1924."²⁴

Wilson had something in mind for 1924 more personal than a renewed push for League membership. His earlier remark to Clarke about the need to nominate someone to rectify "the gross and criminal blunder of failing to ratify the Treaty of Versailles" sounded suspiciously like a description of himself. Writing around the same time to an Alabama newspaper editor and influential state Democrat, Wilson asserted, "[M]y principles and purposes are known and sympathetically interpreted in every part of the world,—particularly among the plainer and simpler kind of people. The selfish conspiracy against the realization of my ideals is confined to a few highbrows who have their own ends to seek. I think I am justified in saying that I am perhaps the only public man in the world who does not need to be interpreted to anybody."²⁵ Incredible as it might seem, Wilson wanted to run again for president in 1924.

The intervening year, 1923, marked the best time in his life since the stroke. Nearly everyone who saw him commented on how much better he looked. In June, a senior reporter for *The New York Times*, Richard Oula-han, wrote a long story about him. Oulahan noted that he still limped but did not drag his left foot, and he used a cane but could stand without it and could get in and out of a car without help. "He has good color, his eyes are clear, his voice is strong, his cheeks are filled out, and he has lost that ema-ciated appearance of face and body which shocked those who saw him on his first outing after his long siege of confinement to the White House." The reporter noted that from all reports, mentally he was "the Woodrow Wilson of the stirring days of September, 1919." He compensated for lack of paid work with attention to public affairs. Oulahan dismissed rumors that Wilson was personally interested in the race for the Democratic nomination in 1924, and he noted that Wilson had not committed himself to any of the contenders, not even his son-in-law McAdoo.[26] This news-paper story read a lot like the one by Louis Seibold in *The World* three years earlier, which had set the stage for the abortive stab at a third-term bid.

As in 1920, McAdoo's drive for the nomination pained Wilson. Mac had moved his family to California in 1922 to establish a new political base, and he appeared to be the front-runner. Wilson's silence notwith-standing, McAdoo might have secured a lock on the nomination except for damaging publicity growing out of legal work he had done for the Teapot Dome oilmen—the kind of guilt by association that Wilson had had the wit to avoid. This setback made McAdoo covet an endorsement from his father-in-law all the more. He sent warm, newsy letters regularly, and in November he and Nell and their two daughters came to Washing-ton for a ten-day visit. Wilson did not want to talk about the campaign with McAdoo, and he asked Edith not to leave him alone with his son-in-law. On the last day of the visit, McAdoo asked Edith if he could talk about the campaign with Wilson. She declined the request and once more the Crown Prince went away empty-handed—with dire consequences for his candidacy and the prospect of a deadlocked convention.[27]

During the summer of 1923, Americans got a macabre reminder of Wilson's improved health. On August 2, the news flashed across the wires that President Harding had died in San Francisco while on an official tour of the West. Wilson had found his successor amiable and felt grateful to him for permitting Grayson to continue as the ex-president's doctor, but he held Harding's intellect in contempt. In May 1922, he had told Ida Tar-bell that Harding "has nothing to think with," and he remembered that at his meeting with the Senate Foreign Relations Committee "nobody [but Harding] asked such unintelligent questions."[28] Also, like other critics, Wilson had winced at his successor's use of language. Such aspersions paled, however, in the face of what Wilson saw as his official duty. On August 8, he rode in the funeral procession that carried Harding's casket from the White House to the Capitol. The irony was not lost on reporters and spectators: the living ghost from the inauguration of two years earlier was riding down Pennsylvania Avenue behind the body of the seemingly hale younger man who had bounded up the Capitol steps.

During the summer and fall of 1923, Wilson gave other signs of increasing strength and vigor, and three weeks after Harding's funeral, Edith left for a short vacation in Newport, Rhode Island, and Buzzards Bay, Massachusetts. Although visitors usually noted how well she was bearing up, the strain of caring for her invalid husband had taken a toll on her. This was the first time in their seven and a half years of marriage that the couple had been apart even for one night, except during Wilson's visit to the Atlantic fleet in 1917. Edith's decision to get away sprang from confidence that her husband was well enough to stand a brief separation, and he raised no objections. She wrote loving letters to him every day, and with one hand he typed two letters to her, which were speckled with errors, and then, at the end of the second one, he wrote by hand, "I do not feel equal to the typewriter to-day but must send a line to say *I love you.*"29 Edith went away again in October for a weekend in New York.

His spirits were good during the summer and fall of 1923, and he was rediscovering some of his old-time cheerful fatalism. In September, Bernard Baruch told the British diplomat Lord Riddell that Wilson had recently said to him, "Perhaps it was providential that I was stricken down when I was. Had I kept my health I should have carried the League. Events have shown that the world was not ready for it." That was not the only time he expressed that belief. His daughter Margaret later recalled him saying that when America joined the League, it would be because the people were convinced it was right "and then will be the *only right* time for them to do it." With a smile, he added, "Perhaps God knew better than I did after all."30

In September, Jessie came with her husband, Frank Sayre, and their three children. They were bidding good-bye before leaving for Asia, where Sayre would spend a year as a legal adviser to the king of Siam. The other members of the Big Three at the peace conference also came to call, Clemenceau the previous December and Lloyd George in October. Those were pleasant personal visits, and Lloyd George particularly enjoyed hearing Wilson recite limericks.

Wilson's mind went back to his academic days. In October he asked his former student Raymond Fosdick, who was now working for the

Rockefeller Foundation, to see him about "an educational matter." When Fosdick arrived the following week, Wilson told him that he had made his greatest contributions not in politics but as a teacher and college administrator and wanted to do more there. He believed that American colleges and universities could yet rise to the levels of scholarship of Oxford and Cambridge, and he asked for help from the Rockefeller Foundation so that he could become "president of some university which would take the initiative in the new reformation." Fosdick suggested that on account of his health Wilson might not be up to such a task, but he insisted he was "ready for any kind of work." Fosdick noted that Wilson had tears in his eyes when he talked about his ideas, and he spoke bitterly about their alma mater: "Princeton was bought once with Ivory Soap money, and I suppose she is for sale again."[31]

Fosdick later confessed to Baker that he was "considerably embarrassed by his request," but he promised to take it up with his colleagues in New York. A month later, he wrote diplomatically that the foundation found Wilson's ideas attractive but it was "necessarily reluctant to initiate enterprises of an experimental character in education." Unappeased, Wilson fired back, "Please do not let the idea get rooted in the minds of the Rockefeller trustees that what I have in mind is experimental. . . . I can honestly say that my plans are so thoroughly thought out in detail that there is nothing experimental about them." Fosdick promised to talk further with Wilson, but thirty years later he would write, "It was, of course, the nostalgic dream of an old and crippled warrior as he thinks over the battles of his younger days—a knight with his armor laid aside, sitting by the fire in the autumn of his life and remembering the blows he had struck for causes that had inspired his youth."[32]

That characterization of Wilson was not entirely on the mark. More than nostalgia, Wilson was showing the same delusions of potency he had demonstrated when he hatched his third-term scheme in 1920. Nor, despite what he said to Fosdick, had he forsaken politics. Twice in November 1923, he spoke out forcefully on current affairs. On the day before the fifth anniversary of the Armistice, he gave his first and only talk over the radio. Standing before a microphone in the library of his house, he spoke in a voice that quavered a bit at first and betrayed more of a southern accent than in the past. He excoriated America's failure to live up to the responsibilities to maintain peace, but he believed that the nation would "retrieve that fatal error and assume once more the role of courage, self-respect and helpfulness which every true American must wish to regard as our natural part in the affairs of the world." Stations across the country carried the talk, and some towns set up loudspeakers in auditoriums, allowing thousands of people to hear the ex-president's voice for the first time. It might have served as a kickoff for a campaign.[33]

The following day brought another public appearance that looked even more like a campaign event. This year, the Armistice Day crowd on S Street numbered an estimated 20,000 people. A band played, and Senator Glass spoke for a delegation of Democratic dignitaries, assuring the ex-president of the American people's loyalty to and affection for him. Visibly moved, Wilson faltered and stopped as he began to speak. The band struck up the hymn "How Firm a Foundation," but he raised his hand and started speaking again. After paying tribute to the doughboys and General Pershing and condemning the Armistice again as "an armed standstill," Wilson concluded, "I am not one of those who have the least anxiety about the triumph of the principles I have stood for. I have seen fools resist Providence before and I have seen the destruction, as will come upon these again—utter destruction and contempt. That we shall prevail is as sure as that God reigns." The crowd did not disperse after he stopped speaking, and the band played on until the car pulled out of the driveway to take Wilson for his afternoon ride, accompanied by Edith and her mother.[34] This would be his last speech and public appearance.

Another moving experience awaited him six weeks later, on his sixty-seventh birthday. On December 28, as he and Margaret were about to go out for his daily ride, Cleveland Dodge and other wealthy friends surprised Wilson with a Rolls-Royce. The car, which reportedly cost $15,000, had a removable top for open rides; it also sported orange and black stripes on the trim and the monogram *W.W.* on the rear doors. Wilson was delighted, and a photograph of him sitting in the Rolls-Royce would be the last one taken of him. That same day in New York, Franklin Roosevelt spoke at a luncheon of the Woodrow Wilson Foundation and announced its annual $25,000 prize for service to the world. Someone who had seen Wilson the week before told reporters at the luncheon that his mind was active, but he was no longer up to the strains of the presidency.[35]

Wilson thought otherwise. Earlier in December, he had told Baker, "You may be sure that I will keep my eye out for every opportunity to guide the Democrats, and I hope and believe that the opportunity will not now be long deferred." On January 16, 1924, the Democratic National Committee made a pilgrimage to S Street, where Wilson shook hands and said something personal to each of the 200 visitors. The party chairman, Representative Cordell Hull of Tennessee, announced that the next convention would meet in New York and presented Wilson with a resolution from the committee pledging a campaign "inspired by the incomparable achievements of his great Administration and confident of the compelling power of the high ideals which he brought to the service of his country." Four days later, Wilson took a step toward guiding that upcoming campaign by sending Newton Baker a "confidential document"—the latest version of "The Document"—for Baker to use in the platform committee. Wilson did not trust the Document to the mails but had Randolph Bolling hand it over more than nine days later, on Baker's next visit to Washington.[36]

The same day that Wilson wrote to Newton Baker, Raymond Fosdick stopped by for an impromptu visit. Fosdick had come earlier in January to put a polite quietus to the university scheme. On this second visit, the conversation rambled over many topics, including the League, and Wilson commented on current affairs, telling Fosdick, "Mussolini is a coward. Somebody should call his bluff. Dictators are all cowards," and "Some day another Bismarck will arise and the Germans will wipe the French off the face of the earth—and I hope they do." He thought the 1920 campaign had been "fought with lies. Sick as I was, I wish I had consented to run. I think I could have won." He liked Newton Baker as a future president but thought he "ought not to run in 1924. He ought to be saved for 1928."[37]

The person Wilson wanted to run in 1924 was himself. Around the time of the letter to Newton Baker and Fosdick's last visit, he made notes in shorthand and on his typewriter for a speech accepting the Democratic nomination and a third inaugural address. For the acceptance speech, he praised the Democrats as "an effective instrument of public service . . . (See Burke on party)" while lambasting the "complete and disastrous failure of the Republicans," as well as their "deep and heinous treason," which had betrayed "a deep and holy cause whose success has been bought by the blood of thousands of your fellow countrymen." In "3rd Inaugural," he admonished Americans "[t]o fight and defeat all—aggression—all Reaction and thus bring light and hope back into the world of affairs. . . . Present objects and motives: to establish an order in which labour shall have assumed greater dignity and capital acquired greater vigour and advantage by the practice of justice." "Justice," in capital letters, headed "Closing passage of third Inaugural," which read, "[Justice] is the only, certain insurance against revolution. . . . Without justice society must break up into hostile groups—even into hostile individuals and go utterly to pieces."[38]

Those fragmentary notes show that Wilson had not retreated from his progressivism at home and internationalism abroad. Together with his other comments at the time, they prefigured essential elements of the next

Democratic presidency a decade later, under Franklin Roosevelt, particularly in its vigorous government intervention in economic affairs and resistance to aggression and dictatorship overseas. Even if Wilson had been healthier, he almost certainly would have had no real chance to move his party and country in those directions. The Democrats were retreating from the League and international commitments almost as fast as the Republicans. Worse, they were on the verge of tearing themselves apart over such red-hot social issues as immigration restriction, prohibition, and the rise of the Ku Klux Klan. Those conflicts—which pitted big-city Catholics from the Northeast and Midwest against small-town and rural Protestant whites from the South and West—had intruded on Democratic conventions as early as 1912, and they burst out in force in 1920. The looming deadlock in 1924 between the two sides' respective champions, Al Smith and William McAdoo, would come close to wrecking the party. That Wilson's presence could have made much difference seems doubtful. Yet with radio at his disposal, even as a semi-invalid he might have made a better compromise candidate than the one the party finally picked—the obscure and lackluster John W. Davis.

How much hope Wilson invested in these notions is hard to tell. He had a long-practiced capacity for denial of obstacles and limitations, and this would have been his second stab at a third-term bid. Yet reminders of mortality haunted him. A month earlier, Frank Cobb, his journalist friend and collaborator on "The Document," had died, and Cobb's widow, in answering Wilson's letter of condolence, had written, "Speaking of you a few days before he died he ended up triumphantly—'He never lowered his Standard.'" Those words could have served as Wilson's epitaph. In a brief foreword to a collection of Cobb's writings, which included an account of how the president had bared his agony of soul on the eve of entering the war, Wilson wote early in January, "I recognized in him a peculiar genius for giving direct and effective expression to the enlightened opinions which he held." That was Wilson's last published piece of writing, and it could have served as another epitaph for him. On his last visit, Fosdick found him in poor shape, and when Fosdick asked him how he was, Wilson quoted a presidential predecessor: "John Quincy Adams is all right, but the house he lives in is dilapidated, and it looks as if he would soon have to move out."[39]

Another indication that Wilson may have recognized that time was running out came in his dealings with Ray Stannard Baker. Several people had obliquely approached him about writing his biography, including Creel and the University of Chicago historian William E. Dodd, who was both a fervent admirer and a fellow southern academic expatriate. Early in

January 1924, Baker tried the direct approach, reminding Wilson that he had once spoken to him "about going forward with a further and more complete study of your whole career. I have a great ambition to do this and do it thoroughly." At first, Wilson put him off, saying his papers were "scattered and inaccessible" and he had doubts about "making too much of a single man." On January 25, however, he wrote to Baker that he would give him exclusive access to his papers: "I would rather have your interpretation of them than that of anybody else I know."[40]

The would-be biographer would later get cold feet about undertaking the task. As an editor friend predicted to Baker—correctly, as it turned out—"It will swallow up your whole life." Early in 1925, Baker shared his second thoughts in long talks with Edith Wilson, explaining the need for "my own complete freedom as a writer. If I should undertake such a task, I must put down exactly what I found, and take my own time in doing it." For her part, Edith was, as Baker recalled, "as level-headed and far-sighted as I could wish." Still, he wrote, he might not have agreed to take on the task "if Mrs. Wilson had not shown me a letter written to me by Mr. Wilson only a few days before his death. It was dated January 25, 1924, and was the last letter he ever wrote to anyone. He was too ill to sign it." Baker could not resist what he took to be a deathbed entreaty.[41]

The day after Wilson dictated that letter, everyone thought him well enough to allow Grayson to leave on a hunting trip to South Carolina. He seemed about as well as usual until January 29, when the night nurse told Randolph Bolling that she thought Wilson was very sick, and after midnight Edith instructed her brother to send a telegram to Grayson. When the doctor received the telegram the next day, he telephoned Edith and said he would come back as soon as possible but thought Wilson was just suffering from his recurrent digestive troubles. When Grayson arrived on January 31, he examined Wilson and did not find his condition alarming. Still, Edith was concerned enough to call in Dr. Sterling Ruffin, who had also attended her husband after the stroke, and he and Grayson issued a joint statement to the press that Wilson had a digestive complaint that confined him to bed.[42]

Behind the walls at S Street, apprehension was mounting. On February 1, Edith told Randolph Bolling she thought her husband was dying, and she asked him to contact Wilson's children. Bolling telephoned Margaret, who took the train from New York and arrived in the afternoon. He telegraphed Nell; she and McAdoo started out immediately but would not reach Washington until the day of the funeral. Jessie and her family were in Bangkok, and she got the news of her father's illness by a cablegram that Bolling sent through the Siamese embassy. That same day, the physicians began giving their patient oxygen and morphine, and they issued regular updates on his condition to reporters who gathered outside the house. Wilson was only intermittently conscious. He spoke his last sentences that Friday. When Grayson read him a note from President Calvin Coolidge, he said, "He is a fine man." When the doctor talked to him about his condition, he said, "I am ready. When the machinery is broken—" He stopped and then repeated, "I am ready." Stirring once more later, he told Grayson, "You have been good to me. You have done everything you could." The next day, Saturday, February 2, he briefly regained consciousness in the afternoon and called out faintly, "Edith." That was his last word.[43]

Woodrow Wilson died at eleven-fifteen in the morning of Sunday, February 3, 1924. Besides Grayson and two nurses, only Edith and Margaret were in the bedroom when he breathed his last. Other family members and friends were in the house, and hundreds of people were outside in the street, some kneeling in prayer. Grayson came out the front door and announced, with tears streaming down his cheeks and his voice trembling, "The end came at 11:15." In a brief statement, he explained, "His heart action became feebler and feebler and the heart muscle was so fatigued that it refused to act any longer." Grayson attributed the remote cause of death to the stroke and the immediate cause to "exhaustion following a digestive upset which began in the early part of this week and reached an acute state until the early morning hours of February first." On the official death certificate, Grayson listed "General Arterio-sclerosis with hemiplegia"—hardening of the arteries and paralysis—as the cause of death, with "Asthenia"—weakness and loss of strength—as a contributory cause. In lay terms, the stroke and its underlying pathology had finally worn him out and killed him.[44]

The funeral and burial that came three days later were Edith's choices. She declined President Coolidge's offer to use his influence with Congress to have Wilson's body lie in state in the Capitol Rotunda, as Harding's had done six months earlier, or to have her husband buried at Arlington— Wilson had reportedly believed that the land for the cemetery had been taken unfairly from the family of Robert E. Lee. Nor, with his unhealed resentments toward Princeton, had he wanted to be buried in the cemetery on Witherspoon Street, which contained the graves of other presidents of the college. Edith did not want him to be buried alongside Ellen in Rome, Georgia, or with his parents in Columbia, South Carolina. Instead, she accepted an offer from James Edward Freeman, the Episcopal bishop of Washington, to inter her husband's remains in the basement chapel of the newly begun cathedral. Freeman had visions of his cathedral becoming America's Westminster Abbey, and he had previously persuaded the family of Admiral George Dewey to bury the victor of Manila Bay in the same chapel. That ambition of Freeman's appalled the now only living ex-president, Taft, who, according to his granddaughter, implored his wife, "[D]on't let those body snatchers at the Cathedral get me."45

The funeral service took place in the house on S Street, where family, officials, and old friends crowded in. Edith allowed Tumulty to attend, but she had word sent to House that there would not be room for him. Also, after learning that the Senate had named Lodge to attend, she wrote, "As the funeral is private, and not an official one, and realizing that your presence there would be embarrassing to you and unwelcome to me I write to request that you do not attend." President and Mrs. Coolidge came, but Taft, who was now chief justice, was ill and could not be present. Most of the members of Wilson's cabinet were in attendance. Two lines of uniformed servicemen decorated for bravery in the war flanked a pathway to the door, but there was no military presence inside. The ministers of the Presbyterian churches where Wilson had most recently worshipped, Sylvester Beach from Princeton and James Taylor of the Central Presbyterian Church in Washington, conducted most of the fifteen-minute service. Beach read from Psalm 23 and offered a brief tribute to Wilson for "his unswerving devotion to duty; for his courage to do the right as God gave him to see the right." Bishop Freeman closed the service by reading biblical verses from a devotional book that Wilson had kept at his bedside.46

A hearse followed by cars carrying the funeral party proceeded up Massachusetts Avenue to the site of the cathedral on Mount St. Alban. More officials attended this service, including Secretary of State Hughes, Wilson's opponent in 1916, and others from the Coolidge cabinet, as well as Harding's widow. After the choir and clergy processed in, Freeman performed the Episcopal ritual of the order of the burial of the dead, with Beach and Taylor assisting in the responsive readings. At the end, the congregation recited the Lord's Prayer, with Episcopal "trespasses" rather than Presbyterian "debts," and the Apostles' Creed. After the benediction, the choir recessed to the hymn "The Strife Is O'er, the Battle Done." The only military touches came when a bugler outside played taps as the honor guard lowered the casket into the crypt. At the same moment, another bugler sounded the same notes at the Tomb of the Unknown Soldier in the amphitheater at Arlington.47

Those services marked the end of Wilson's earthly days in ways that were at once ironic and fitting. The most Presbyterian of presidents now lay at rest in an Episcopal cathedral, interred with the rites of the church his forebears had rebelled against. Yet for all his pride in his heritage, Wilson had never made much of sectarian differences. He had once joined a Congregational church, and he had taught at colleges founded by Quakers and Methodists. At Princeton, he had labored to loosen lingering Presbyterian orthodoxy, and Fosdick remembered that when Wilson had led chapel services, he had always closed with the same reading from the Book of Common Prayer, which began, "Almighty and most merciful Father; we have erred and strayed from thy ways like lost sheep. We have followed the devices and desires of our own hearts," and included the plea, "Spare those, O God, who confess their faults."[48] At Princeton, in Trenton, and in Washington, he had appointed Jews and Catholics to important posts, and he had counted Catholics and Jews among his closest political associates. When he came to marry a second time, he wed an Episcopalian, and he never asked her to leave her church for his. His middle daughter also married an Episcopalian, and her older son would one day serve as dean of the cathedral where his grandfather lay buried.

Wilson's interment in what would later rise to become a great stone edifice in the nation's capital suited him. Almost alone among truly notable presidents, he had no strong association with a single home or place: no Mount Vernon; no Monticello; no Sagamore Hill, as with his rival Roosevelt; no Hyde Park, as with his successor Roosevelt. Son and grandson of immigrants; born in Virginia; raised in Georgia, South Carolina, and North Carolina; educated in North Carolina, New Jersey, Virginia, and Maryland; working as a private citizen in Pennsylvania, Connecticut, and New Jersey; elected to office from New Jersey; holding office in New Jersey and Washington, D.C.—Wilson came closer to epitomizing the mobile, rootless American of the nineteenth and twentieth centuries than any other president. Likewise, he spent more time working within nongovernmental institutions than others who ascended to the White House, and he had risen to the top rank in two private professions. Wilson never thought of himself as a cosmopolitan, but he had about him a breadth and catholicity that made a great building in a city that is home to everyone and no one in America a fitting place for his remains.

The chapel in the basement of that building would not be Wilson's final resting place. Three decades after his burial, when the cathedral's soaring nave was finally finished, his remains would come up to the tomb there in time for the centennial of his birth. There, on his birthday, a military honor guard would yearly lay a wreath, and the light streaming through the stained glass windows would cast bright patches of color on his stone sarcophagus. This last move resonated with the ups and downs and controversies that would continue to swirl around his memory.

Wilson, along with Lincoln and Jefferson, would come to be one of the best remembered and most argued over of all presidents. Like Jefferson, but unlike Lincoln or even such once-controversial figures as the two Roosevelts, he would not ascend into a glow of warm and near universal, though often contradictory, adulation. Just as Jefferson's thought, actions, and aftermath formed an ideological battleground in the nineteenth century and beyond, so Wilson's words, deeds, ideas, and legacies would furnish fodder for debate and conflict throughout the twentieth century and beyond. The man whose bones lie in the cathedral would leave behind a mind and spirit that live on in everything he touched.

Notes

Abbreviations used in notes

ASL	Arthur S. Link
CTG	Cary T. Grayson
CTGD	Cary T. Grayson diary
EA; EAW	Ellen Axson; Ellen Axson Wilson
EBG; EBGW	Edith Bolling Galt; Edith Bolling Galt Wilson
EMH	Edward M. House
EMHD	Edward M. House diary
HCL	Henry Cabot Lodge
HCLP	Henry Cabot Lodge Papers, Massachusetts Historical Society
HWB	Henry W. Bragdon
HWBC	Henry W. Bragdon Papers, Woodrow Wilson Collection, Seeley G. Mudd Library, Princeton University
JD	Josephus Daniels
JDD	Josephus Daniels diary
JPT	Joseph Patrick Tumulty
LC	Library of Congress
MAH; MAHP	Mary Allen Hulbert; Mary Allen Hulbert Peck
Memoir	Edith Bolling Galt Wilson, *My Memoir* (Indianapolis, 1939)
NDB	Newton D. Baker
PWW	Woodrow Wilson, *The Papers of Woodrow Wilson*, ed. Arthur S. Link et al., 69 vols. (Princeton, N.J., 1966–1993)
RB	Robert Bridges
RL	Robert Lansing
RSB	Ray Stannard Baker
RSBD	Ray Stannard Baker diary
RSBP	Ray Stannard Baker Papers, Library of Congress
SA	Stockton Axson
TR	Theodore Roosevelt
WHT	William Howard Taft
WHTP	William Howard Taft Papers, Library of Congress
WJB	William Jennings Bryan
WW	Woodrow Wilson
WWP	Woodrow Wilson Papers, Library of Congress

PROLOGUE　"THIS MAN'S MIND AND SPIRIT"

1.　Winston S. Churchill, *The World Crisis*, vol. 3, *1916–1918* (London, 1927), p. 229. On the nine decades of argument and analysis of American intervention, see John Milton Cooper, Jr., "The United States," in *The Origins of World War I*, ed. Richard F. Hamilton and Holger H. Herwig (New York, 2003), pp. 415–42.

2.　Charles E. Swem diary, entry for 1915, *PWW*, vol. 33, p. 138; WW speech at Pittsburgh, Oct. 24, 1915, *PWW*, vol. 31, p. 221.

3.　WW remarks, Apr. 8, 1918, *PWW*, vol. 47, p. 288.

4.　WW speech, June 13, 1914, *PWW*, vol. 29, p. 177. In 2008, a faculty committee at Princeton rated the twenty-five most influential alumni and the twelve alumni who have had the greatest impact on Princeton. On the first list, Wilson ranked third, behind James Madison and the mathematician Alan Turing, and on the second list he ranked first. He and Fitzgerald were the only two to appear on both lists. See *Princeton Alumni Weekly*, Jan. 23, 2008, pp. 30–49.

5.　WW speech, Mar. 20, 1914, *PWW*, vol. 29, p. 362.

I　TOMMY

1.　The story is told in Eleanor Wilson McAdoo, *The Woodrow Wilsons* (New York, 1937), p. 195.

2.　The birth is recorded in the Wilson family Bible, *PWW*, vol. 1, p. 3. There is some dispute about whether Wilson was born on December 28 or 29. See *PWW*, vol. 1, p. 3, n. 7.

3.　On Joseph Ruggles Wilson, see *PWW*, vol. 1, p. 34, n. 1, and John M. Mulder, *Woodrow Wilson: The Years of Preparation* (Princeton, N.J., 1978), pp. 3–6.

4.　Harriet Woodrow Welles to RSB, Sept. 28, 1925, RSBP, box 124.

5.　On the Woodrows, see Mulder, *Years of Preparation*, pp. 4–5, and RSB, *Woodrow Wilson: Life and Letters*, vol. 1, *Youth, 1856–1890* (Garden City, N.Y., 1927), pp. 14–23.

6.　Janet Woodrow Wilson to Thomas Woodrow, Apr. 27, 1857, *PWW*, vol. 1, p. 7.

7.　On the Augusta church and Joseph Wilson's move there, see Mulder, *Years of Preparation*. p. 7. It is not possible to determine from the slave schedules of the census for Richmond County, Georgia, the number, age, or sex of the slaves who worked for the Wilsons.

8.　The proportion of slaves in the population is based on U.S. Bureau of the Census, *Population of the United States: Eighth Census* (Washington, D.C., 1861), pp. iv, xiii, 60–61, 64–65, 68–69, 73–74. Richmond County, in which Augusta is located, also had 490 "Free Colored" residents, 386 of whom lived in Augusta.

9.　WW speech, Feb. 12, 1909, *PWW*, vol. 19, p. 33.

10.　On Joseph Wilson's wartime service, see *PWW*, vol. 1, p. 11, and Florence Fleming Corley, *Confederate City: Augusta, Georgia, 1860–1865* (Columbia, S.C., 1960), pp. 39–40, 63–64, 67–68.

11.　On the relations with the respective families, see Harriet Woodrow Welles to RSB, Sept. 28, 1925, RSBP, box 124, and J. Wilson Woodrow to RSB, Feb. 10, 1926, RSBP, box 124.

12.　WW shorthand note, July 19, 1880, *PWW*, vol. 1, pp. 664–65; EMHD, entry for Feb. 14, 1913, *PWW*, vol. 27, p. 113.

13.　Jessie W. Wilson to WW, Aug. 23, 1880, *PWW*, vol. 1, p. 674; WW to EAW, Apr. 19, 1888, *PWW*, vol. 5, p. 719; Pleasant A. Stovall to RSB, June 8, 1925, RSBP, box 122. The recollection of cockfighting is in EMHD, entry for May 11, 1914, *PWW*, vol. 30, p. 21.

14. WW to EAW, Apr. 19, 1888, *PWW*, vol. 5, pp. 719–20.

15. CTG, interviews by RSB, Feb. 18–19, 1926, RSBP, box 109; McAdoo, *The Wilsons*, p. 40; WW to EAW, Mar. 9, 1889, *PWW*, vol. 6, p. 139. On Josie Wilson, see RSB, Memorandum of a Conversation with J. R. Wilson, Feb. 19, 1926, RSBP, box 124.

16. On the left-handed writing, see Edwin A. Weinstein, *Woodrow Wilson: A Medical and Psychological Biography* (Princeton, N.J., 1981), pp. 142–45.

17. WW shorthand diary, entry for June 10, 1876, *PWW*, vol. 1, p. 137; SA comments on manuscript of RSB biography of WW, vol. 1, [ca. 1926], RSBP, box 100. On Wilson's teaching himself shorthand, see Editorial Note, "Wilson's Study and Use of Shorthand, 1872–1892," *PWW*, vol. 1, pp. 8–19. For the interpretation that Wilson suffered from dyslexia, see Weinstein, *Medical and Psychological Biography*, pp. 15–18.

18. Jessie W. Wilson to WW, Feb. 6, 1877, *PWW*, vol. 1, p. 250; David Bryant, quoted in William Allen White, *Woodrow Wilson: The Man, His Times, and His Task* (Boston, 1924), p. 59.

19. WW speech, May 29, 1914, *PWW*, vol. 30, p. 106; CTG, interviews by RSB, Feb. 18–19, 1926, RSBP, box 109.

20. WW to James Edwin Webster, July 23, 1878, *PWW*, vol. 1, pp. 384–85. On the work with his father in denominational meetings, see Mulder, *Years of Preparation*, p. 9.

21. WW speech, Dec. 27, 1907, *PWW*, vol. 17, p. 578; Joseph R. Wilson to WW, Mar. 27, 1877; Nov. 5, 1877, *PWW*, vol. 1, p. 254; unnamed niece quoted in Margaret Axson Elliott, *My Aunt Louisa and Woodrow Wilson* (Chapel Hill, N.C., 1944), p. 122. See also CTG, interviews by RSB, Feb. 18–19, 1926, RSBP, box 109.

22. The best account of this incident is in Mulder, *Years of Preparation*, pp. 13–17.

23. WW notebook, Apr. 5, 1874, *PWW*, vol. 1, p. 33.

24. Douglas McKay to WW, June 25, 1875, *PWW*, vol. 6, p. 66. Jessie Bones Brower to RSB, May 9, 1926, RSBP, box 102. The historian who has studied Wilson's early life most closely has argued that Joseph Wilson did want his son to follow him into the ministry and that Tommy showed some interest, attending lectures at the seminary. See Mulder, *Years of Preparation*, pp. 40–41.

25. WW to RB, Aug. 22, 1881, *PWW*, vol. 2, pp. 770–78; WW confidential journal, entry for Dec. 28, 1889, *PWW*, vol. 6, p. 462.

26. On Wilson's lack of a southern accent by the time he went to college, see responses to questionnaires sent to his Princeton classmates by Henry W. Bragdon in the late 1930s and early 1940s, HWBC. On Wilson's use of a broad *a*, see WW, *The Priceless Gift: The Love Letters of Woodrow Wilson and Ellen Axson Wilson*, ed. Eleanor Wilson McAdoo (New York, 1962), pp. 121–22. On his effort to wean Ellen from her southern accent, see WW to EA, Feb. 17, 1885, *PWW*, vol. 4, p. 263.

27. Robert H. McCarter, interview by HWB, July 14, 1940, HWBC; WW speech, Jan. 19, 1909, *PWW*, vol. 18, p. 631.

28. WW quoted in Edith Gittings Reid, *Woodrow Wilson: The Caricature, the Myth and the Man* (New York, 1934), p. 22. The only biographer who interviewed any of the family's African American servants was William Allen White, who wrote a brief and fundamentally hostile book about Wilson (*The Man, His Times, and His Task*). It is odd that Ray Stannard Baker, who was assiduous in seeking material about Wilson's early life, did not seem to have sought out any of the family's black servants. It is doubly odd because Baker was one of the few white journalists of the time who was interested in race relations. In 1907, he wrote a series of magazine articles that was published as *Following the Color Line: An Account of Negro Citizenship in the American Democracy* (Garden City, N.Y., 1908).

29. WW to Andrew J. Graham, [ca. Apr. 24], 1875, *PWW*, vol. 1, p. 62. Mulder views Wilson's year at Davidson as a time of spiritual and vocational turmoil for him and

speculates about his ill health. See Mulder, *Years of Preparation*, pp. 38–41. I do not agree with that interpretation.

30. On the founding and early history of Princeton, see Thomas Jefferson Wertenbaker, *Princeton, 1746–1896* (Princeton, N.J., 1946).

31. On McCosh and his presidency of Princeton, see J. David Hoeveler, Jr., *James McCosh and the Scottish Intellectual Tradition: From Glasgow to Princeton* (Princeton, N.J., 1981), pp. 215–349.

32. Robert H. McCarter, interview by HWB, July 15, 1940, HWBC; RB, *Woodrow Wilson* (Princeton, N.J., 1931), pp. 2–3.

33. WW shorthand diary, entries for June 12, 1876; Oct. 27, 1876, *PWW*, vol. 1, pp. 139, 217; WW, quoted in SA, *Brother Woodrow: A Memoir of Woodrow Wilson* (Princeton, N.J., 1993), p. 15. For a similar version of the "mind" discovery, see CTG, interviews by RSB, Feb. 18–19, 1926, RSBP, box 109.

34. WW shorthand diary, entry for June 9, 1876, *PWW*, vol. 1, p. 137.

35. Jessie Wilson Sayre, interview by RSB, Dec. 1, 1925, RSBP, box 121; WW to EA, Oct. 11, 1883, *PWW*, vol. 2, p. 466.

36. WW shorthand diary, entry for July 4, 1876, *PWW*, vol. 1, p. 149.

37. WW to Albert Bushnell Hart, June 3, 1889, *PWW*, vol. 6, p. 243.

38. "W" [WW] to *Princetonian*, Jan. 25, 1877, *PWW*, vol. 1, pp. 238–39. About the Witherspoon Gang, Wilson later said, "He [Bridges] and Charlie Talcott and Hiram Woods were the *real* friends whom college life gave me for an inspiring possession; and if I keep any friends, I shall, before all others keep them." WW to EA, Nov. 20, 1884, *PWW*, vol. 3, p. 466.

39. Robert H. McCarter, interview by HWB, July 15, 1940, HWBC; *Princetonian* editorials, Jan. 30, 1879; Feb. 6 and 27, 1879, *PWW*, vol. 1, pp. 450–51, 461. Also, in contrast to his successor, Fine, Wilson had nothing to say about the place of science in the curriculum. See the cited editorials.

40. "Junius" [WW], "Some Thoughts on the Present State of Public Affairs," *PWW*, vol. 1, pp. 347–54.

41. William F. Magie, interview by HWB, June 12, 1940, HWBC. For speculation on why Wilson was not elected to a class officership, see HWB, *Woodrow Wilson: The Academic Years* (Cambridge, Mass., 1967), pp. 41–42. See also Editorial Note, "Wilson's Refusal to Enter the Lynde Competition," *PWW*, vol. 1, pp. 480–81.

42. WW draft to William M. Sloane, [ca. Dec. 5, 1883], *PWW*, vol. 2, p. 567.

43. WW, "Cabinet Government in the United States," *PWW*, vol. 1, pp. 493–500.

44. WW, "Cabinet Government," *PWW*, vol. 1, pp. 501–10.

45. On the composition and its influences, see Editorial Note, "'Cabinet Government in the United States,'" *PWW*, vol. 1, pp. 492–93.

46. WW to EA, Oct. 30, 1883, *PWW*, vol. 2, pp. 499–500; RB, *Wilson*, p. 10. In 1913, when the two men met shortly after Wilson's inauguration as president, Wilson told Lodge, "Senator, . . . a man never forgets the first editor who accepts one of his articles. You were the first editor who accepted an article written by me." HCL, *The Senate and the League of Nations* (New York, 1925), p. 2.

47. WW to EA, Oct. 30, 1883, *PWW*, vol. 2, pp. 501–2.

2 WOODROW

1. Dumas Malone, *Jefferson and His Time*, vol. 1, *Jefferson the Virginian* (Boston, 1948), p. vii; WW to RB, Nov. 7, 1879, *PWW*, vol. 1, pp. 581–82.

2. WW, "Self Government in France," [ca. Sept. 4, 1879], *PWW*, vol. 1, pp. 515–39; WW, "Congressional Government," [ca. Oct. 1, 1879], *PWW*, vol. 1, pp. 548–74.

3. WW, "John Bright," *PWW*, vol. 1, pp. 608–21.

4. William Cabell Bruce, *Recollections* (Baltimore, 1936), p. 71; WW to EA, May 14, 1885, *PWW*, vol. 4, p. 590.

5. Jefferson Society debate, Apr. 2, 1880, *PWW*, vol. 1, pp. 643–46; Braxton Gibson, recollection to HWB, ca. Dec. 1941, HWBC.

6. Richard Heath Dabney, interview by HWB, Mar. 22, 1941, HWBC; Samuel B. Woods to HWB, Jan. 15, 1942, HWBC; WW to Cordell Hull, Sept. 12, 1922, *PWW*, vol. 68, pp. 134–35.

7. WW to Charles Talcott, Dec. 31, 1879, *PWW*, vol. 1, p. 591; WW to RB, Feb. 15, 1880, *PWW*, vol. 1, p. 604; Joseph R. Wilson to WW, Dec. 22, 1879, *PWW*, vol. 1, p. 589.

8. Harriet Woodrow Welles to RSB, Sept. 28, 1925, RSBP, box 124.

9. WW to RB, Jan. 1, 1881, *PWW*, vol. 2, p. 10; WW, "Stray Thoughts from the South," *PWW*, vol. 2, pp. 19–25. See also Editorial Note, "Wilson's Withdrawal from the University of Virginia," *PWW*, vol. 2, p. 704.

10. WW to Harriet Woodrow, Jan. 15, 1881; Apr. 22, 1881; May 10, 1881, *PWW*, vol. 2, pp. 17, 46, 66.

11. WW to Harriet Woodrow, [Sept. 25, 1881], *PWW*, vol. 2, p. 83; WW to EA, Oct. 11, 1883, *PWW*, vol. 2, p. 467; on the incident in Chillicothe, see also Editorial Note, "Wilson's Proposal to Hattie Woodrow," *PWW*, vol. 2, pp. 84–85.

12. WW to RB, Mar. 15, 1882, *PWW*, vol. 2, p. 107. Wilson and Hattie later became friends again. In 1894, on his first trip to the West, he visited her and her husband, Eddie Welles, at their home in Colorado. In 1913 and 1917, Harriet Woodrow Welles attended Wilson's presidential inaugurations, and she visited him and his family in the White House several times. Many years later, after Wilson's and Welles's deaths, one of her grandsons married one of his granddaughters. See Helen Welles Thackwell, "Woodrow Wilson and My Mother," *Princeton University Library Chronicle*, Autumn 1950, pp. 6–18.

13. WW, "Government by Debate," *PWW*, vol. 2, pp. 159–275. See also Editorial Note, " 'Government by Debate,' " *PWW*, vol. 2, pp. 152–57.

14. WW to editor, *International Review*, [ca. Apr. 30, 1881], *PWW*, vol. 2, p. 48.

15. WW to RB, Oct. 28, 1882, *PWW*, vol. 2, p. 148.

16. WW testimony, Sept. 23, 1882, *PWW*, vol. 2, pp. 140–43; New York *World*, Sept. 24, 1882.

17. Joseph R. Wilson to WW, Aug. 14 and 20, 1882, *PWW*, vol. 2, p. 135; WW to RB, Oct. 28, 1882, *PWW*, vol. 2, p. 148; WW to Hiram Woods, May 9 [10], 1883, *PWW*, vol. 2, p. 349; WW to Richard Heath Dabney, May 11, 1883, *PWW*, vol. 2, pp. 350–51.

18. WW to RB, May 12, 1883, *PWW*, vol. 2, p. 353; WW to EA, Oct. 30, 1883, *PWW*, vol. 2, p. 501.

19. WW to EA, Oct. 30, 1883, *PWW*, vol. 2, p. 501; WW to RB, Feb. 24, 1881, *PWW*, vol. 2, p. 31.

20. Joseph R. Wilson to WW, Feb. 14, 1883, *PWW*, vol. 2, p. 304; James Woodrow to Jessie Woodrow Wilson, Mar. 13, 1883, *PWW*, vol. 2, p. 317.

21. On this typewriter, see Editorial Note, "Wilson and His Caligraph," *PWW*, vol. 2, pp. 366–67. The editors of *The Papers of Woodrow Wilson* speculate that Wilson purchased this model rather than its rival, the Remington 2, which was simpler and faster, because it cost $40 less.

22. WW to EA, Oct. 11, 1883, *PWW*, vol. 2, p. 468. See also Editorial Note, "Wilson's Introduction to Ellen Axson," *PWW*, vol. 2, pp. 333–35, and Frances Wright Saunders, *Ellen Axson Wilson: First Lady between Two Worlds* (Chapel Hill, N.C., 1985), pp. 3–4.

23. WW to EA, Oct. 11, 18, and 23, 1883, *PWW*, vol. 2, pp. 468–69, 481, 485. See also Editorial Note, "Wilson's Early Courtship of Ellen Axson," *PWW*, vol. 2, pp. 361–63, and Saunders, *Ellen Axson Wilson*, pp. 5–6.

24. EA to WW, Nov. 5, 1883, *PWW*, vol. 2, p. 517; Rosalie Anderson to Ellen Axson, July 5, 1877, WWP, microfilm ed., reel 4. On her "man-hater" reputation, see Saunders, *Ellen Axson Wilson*, p. 4.

25. Rosalie Anderson to EAW, June 29, 1877, WWP, microfilm ed., reel 4. On the Axson family and Ellen Axson's early years, see Saunders, *Ellen Axson Wilson*, pp. 9–25.

26. On Axson's mother's death and her father's depression, see Saunders, *Ellen Axson Wilson*, pp. 26–29.

27. WW to EA, July 16, 1883, *PWW*, vol. 2, pp. 388–89; WW to RB, July 26, 1883, *PWW*, vol. 2, p. 393.

28. EA to WW, Sept. 21, 1883, *PWW*, vol. 2, p. 435. On this encounter, see Editorial Note, "The Engagement," *PWW*, vol. 2, pp. 426–27, and Saunders, *Ellen Axson Wilson*, pp. 6–8.

29. WW to EA, Nov. 27, 1883, *PWW*, vol. 2, p. 551. On the founding and early years of Johns Hopkins, see Hugh Hawkins, *Pioneer: A History of the Johns Hopkins University, 1874–1889* (Ithaca, N.Y., 1960), esp. pp. 3–125.

30. WW to EA, Oct. 30, 1883, *PWW*, vol. 2, p. 503; minutes of the seminary of history and political science, Apr. 18, 1884, *PWW*, vol. 2, p. 136. Taking the opposing side was John Dewey, who cited statistics to show that illiteracy was rising in the South. Long afterward, the dry, understated Dewey could still recall Wilson's "vigorous attack" on the bill, "not exactly on old southern states rights lines, but against anything looking toward 'encroachment.'" John Dewey to HWB, July 14, 1941, HWBC.

31. WW to EA, Oct. 16 and 30, 1883, *PWW*, vol. 2, pp. 479, 503–4.

32. WW to EA, Nov. 27, 1883; Jan. 1, 1884, *PWW*, vol. 2, pp. 552, 642.

33. WW to EA, Sept. 18, 1883, *PWW*, vol. 2, p. 427; EA to WW, Sept. 21 and 25, 1883; June 21, 1885, *PWW*, vol. 2, pp. 434, 441; vol. 4, p. 730. Their youngest daughter later published a collection of these letters. See WW, *The Priceless Gift: The Love Letters of Woodrow Wilson and Ellen Axson Wilson*, ed. Eleanor Wilson McAdoo (New York, 1962).

34. WW to EA, Oct. 30, 1883, *PWW*, vol. 2, pp. 499–505.

35. WW to EA, Oct. 16, 1883; Jan. 1, 1884, *PWW*, vol. 2, pp. 480, 641–42. On the beginning of the new book, see Editorial Note, "*Congressional Government*," *PWW*, vol. 4, pp. 6–10.

36. For the writing of this book, see the chronology provided in Editorial Note, "*Congressional Government*," *PWW*, vol. 4, pp. 10–11.

37. WW to EA, Nov. 28, 1884, *PWW*, vol. 3, p. 493; EA to WW, Jan. 24, 1884 [1885], *PWW*, vol. 4, p. 181.

38. WW to RB, Nov. 19, 1884, *PWW*, vol. 3, p. 465; WW, *Congressional Government*, *PWW*, vol. 4, pp. 13–14, 17, 40. The entire book is reprinted in *PWW*, vol. 4, pp. 13–179. The original edition runs to 333 pages.

39. WW, *Congressional Government*, *PWW*, vol. 4, pp. 77–78, 111, 114.

40. Ibid., pp. 140, 154, 155.

41. Ibid., pp. 168, 172, 178–79.

42. Gamaliel Bradford review, [Feb. 12, 1885], *PWW*, vol. 4, pp. 236–37. For other reviews, see *PWW*, vol. 4, pp. 284, 288–93, 309–15, 372–75, 403–49. On later criticisms, see HWB, *Woodrow Wilson: The Academic Years* (Cambridge, Mass., 1967), pp. 137–48.

43. A. Lawrence Lowell, interview by HWB, May 23, 1939, HWBC; WW, "Responsible Government and Constitutionalism," *PWW*, vol. 5, pp. 107–24.

44. Lowell, interview by HWB, May 23, 1939, HWBC; WW to EA, Feb. 24, 1885, *PWW*, vol. 4, p. 287.

45. WW to EA, Feb. 13, 1885, *PWW*, vol. 4, p. 245. Wilson's friend and faculty colleague Winthrop Daniels made a similar observation. See Winthrop M. Daniels memoir, summer 1924, RSBP, box 105.

46. WW to EA, May 17, 1884, *PWW*, vol. 3, pp. 184–85; Joseph R. Wilson to WW, May 17, 1884, *PWW*, vol. 3, p. 183. On Edward Axson's condition, see Saunders, *Ellen Axson Wilson*, pp. 41–44.

47. WW to EA, May 1, 1884, *PWW*, vol. 3, pp. 155–56; EA to WW, June 5, 1884, *PWW*, vol. 3, p. 208; SA, *Brother Woodrow: A Memoir of Woodrow Wilson* (Princeton, N.J., 1993), pp. 33–34.

48. SA to RSB, RSBP, box 100; WW to EA, June 29, 1884, *PWW*, vol. 3, p. 221.

49. WW to EA, Mar. 27, 1885, *PWW*, vol. 4, p. 421; EA to WW, Mar. 28, 1885, *PWW*, vol. 4, p. 428.

50. WW to EA, Nov. 8, 1884, *PWW*, vol. 3, p. 415. On the collaboration with Richard Ely, see Editorial Note, "Wilson's Research for a 'History of Political Economy in the United States,'" *PWW*, vol. 3, pp. 447–48, and Editorial Note, "Wilson's 'History of Political Economy in the United States,'" *PWW*, vol. 4, pp. 628–31. Wilson's section is reproduced in *PWW*, vol. 4, pp. 631–63.

51. EA to WW, Nov. 28, 1884, *PWW*, vol. 3, p. 494; WW to EA, Dec. 1, 1884, *PWW*, vol. 3, p. 504.

52. WW to EA, Nov. 9, 1884; Mar. 3 and 14, 1885, *PWW*, vol. 3, p. 417; vol. 4, pp. 324, 364.

53. WW to EA, Mar. 21, 1885, *PWW*, vol. 4, p. 394.

54. For descriptions of the wedding, see *Savannah Morning News*, June 25, 1885, *PWW*, vol. 4, p. 735, and Saunders, *Ellen Axson Wilson*, pp. 62–63.

3 PROFESSOR

1. On the founding of Bryn Mawr, see Edith Finch, *Carey Thomas of Bryn Mawr* (New York, 1947), pp. 132–60; Cornelia Meigs, *What Makes a College? A History of Bryn Mawr* (New York, 1956), esp. pp. 34–47; and Helen Lefkowitz Horowitz, *The Power and Passion of M. Carey Thomas* (New York, 1994), pp. 156–59, 163–65, 183–91.

2. Mary Tremain to RSB, Jan. 26, 1926, RSBP, box 116; Effie S. Spalding to Satie Leslie, Jan. 10, 1926, RSBP, box 115; Helen A. Scribner to RSB, Mar. 13, 1926, RSBP, box 115; WW to RB, Nov. 30, 1887, *PWW*, vol. 5, p. 633; WW to Richard Heath Dabney, Jan. 25, 1887, *PWW*, vol. 5, pp. 437–38; WW journal, entry for Oct. 20, 1887, *PWW*, vol. 5, p. 619.

3. WW to Charles Talcott, Nov. 14, 1886, *PWW*, vol. 5, p. 389; Lucy Maynard Salmon to RSB, Jan. 6 and 15, 1925, RSBP, box 121.

4. For the story of Wilson's shaving his mustache, see SA, *Brother Woodrow: A Memoir of Woodrow Wilson* (Princeton, N.J., 1993), p. 35. On the births of the first two Wilson daughters and the family's domestic arrangements, see Frances Wright Saunders, *Ellen Axson Wilson: First Lady between Two Worlds* (Chapel Hill, N.C., 1985), pp. 67–76.

5. WW to EAW, May 29, 1886, *PWW*, vol. 5, p. 267; WW talk, Mar. 23, 1886, *PWW*, vol. 5, pp. 137–41. See also Editorial Note, "Wilson's 'First Failure' at Public Speaking," *PWW*, vol. 5, pp. 134–37.

6. WW journal, entry for Oct. 20, 1887, *PWW*, vol. 5, p. 619. Wilson was not the only person at Bryn Mawr who entertained such thoughts. At the time of his appointment, Dean Martha Carey Thomas had rejected the idea of hiring a woman to teach

history and political science, sneering, "How can a political zero teach politics, an ineligible statesman, statecraft?" Quoted in Horowitz, *Power and Passion*, p. 195.

7. WW to James Bryce, Mar. 6, 1888, *PWW*, vol. 5, p. 709; WW to RB, Nov. 5, 1887, *PWW*, vol. 5, p. 625.

8. WW to James E. Rhoads, June 7, 1888, *PWW*, vol. 5, p. 736; WW to RB, Aug. 26, 1888, *PWW*, vol. 5, p. 764.

9. WW, "The Study of Administration," [ca. Nov. 1, 1886], *PWW*, vol. 5, pp. 359–80.

10. WW notes, [ca. Dec. 1–20, 1885], *PWW*, vol. 5, pp. 58–59; WW, "The Modern Democratic State," [ca. Dec. 1–20, 1885], *PWW*, vol. 5, pp. 61–92; WW to Horace Scudder, May 12, 1886, *PWW*, vol. 5, pp. 218–20.

11. WW to Hiram Woods, Sept. 16, 1886, *PWW*, vol. 9, p. 577; WW to EA, Mar. 12, 1885, *PWW*, vol. 4, p. 356.

12. WW, "Socialism and Democracy," [ca. Aug. 22, 1887], *PWW*, vol. 5, pp. 559–62; WW, "The Functions of Government," [ca. Feb. 17, 1888], *PWW*, vol. 5, pp. 669–77.

13. Ibid.

14. C. F. Price, quoted in RSB, *Woodrow Wilson: Life and Letters*, vol. 1, *Youth, 1856–1890* (Garden City, N.Y., 1927), pp. 300–301; H. Monmouth Smith to HWB, Mar. 1941, HWBC.

15. WW to Horace Scudder, Mar. 31, 1889, *PWW*, vol. 8, p. 658.

16. RB to WW, Nov. 5, 1889, *PWW*, vol. 6, p. 411.

17. Frances Landey Patton to WW, Feb. 18, 1890, *PWW*, vol. 6, p. 527; WW to Albert Shaw, May 5, 1890, *PWW*, vol. 6, p. 625.

18. WW, "Bryce's American Commonwealth," *PWW*, vol. 6, pp. 61–76.

19. WW to Munroe Smith, Jan. 7, 1889, *PWW*, vol. 6, p. 45; WW, "Bryce's American Commonwealth," *PWW*, vol. 6, p. 76.

20. WW, *The State* (Boston, 1889), in *PWW*, vol. 6, pp. 253–311 (this volume of *The Papers of Woodrow Wilson* reprints only some of the chapters, not the entire book). One high estimate of *The State* came from Edward S. Corwin. See Corwin, "Departmental Colleague," in *Woodrow Wilson: Some Princeton Memories*, ed. William Starr Myers (Princeton, N.J., 1946), p. 26. The lead editor of *The Papers of Woodrow Wilson*, Arthur S. Link, also told me on several occasions that he considered *The State* Wilson's best work.

21. WW, "Leaders of Men," [June 17, 1890], *PWW*, vol. 6, pp. 646–71.

22. WW speech, Jan. 30, 1891, *PWW*, vol. 7, pp. 161–62; Alfred P. Dennis, *Gods and Little Fishes* (Indianapolis, 1931), p. 89; Robert McNutt McElroy, interview by HWB, Nov. 20, 1940, HWBC.

23. Ernest Poole, *The Bridge: My Own Story* (New York, 1940), pp. 65–66; Booth Tarkington, interview by HWB, Nov. 27, 1940, HWBC; *Baltimore Sun*, Feb. 2, 1894, *PWW*, vol. 8, p. 450.

24. WW, "University Training and Citizenship," *PWW*, vol. 7, pp. 587–96.

25. WW to Albert Shaw, July 14, 1891, *PWW*, vol. 7, p. 191; WW to Patton, Mar. 28, 1897, *PWW*, vol. 10, p. 196.

26. WW to Shaw, Nov. 3, 1890, *PWW*, vol. 7, pp. 62–63; WW speech at Chicago, July 26, 1893, *PWW*, vol. 7, pp. 285–92.

27. EAW to WW, June 22, 1892, *PWW*, vol. 8, p. 16.

28. WW to Charles W. Kent, Apr. 22, 1898, *PWW*, vol. 10, p. 523; Francis Landey Patton to Cyrus McCormick, Apr. 4, 1898, *PWW*, vol. 10, p. 497.

29. WW to EAW, Mar. 10, 1892; Feb. 12, 1898, *PWW*, vol. 7, p. 467; vol. 10, p. 389.

30. SA, interviews by RSB, Feb. 8–11, 1925; Mar. 12, 1925, RSBP, box 99; Bliss Perry, *And Gladly Teach: Reminiscences* (Boston, 1935), p. 156.

31. Jessie Wilson Sayre, interview by RSB, Dec. 1, 1925, RSBP, box 115; SA and George Howe, interviews by RSB, Feb. 8–11, 1925, RSBP, box 99.

32. On the Wilson daughters, see Eleanor Wilson McAdoo, *The Woodrow Wilsons* (New York, 1937), esp. pp. 1–60, and Saunders, *Ellen Axson Wilson,* esp. pp. 96–98. For the game of tag in the White House, see SA, interviews by RSB, Feb. 8–11, 1925, RSBP, box 99.

33. Margaret Axson Elliott, *My Aunt Louisa and Woodrow Wilson* (Chapel Hill, N.C., 1944), p. 139. On the circle of friends, see pp. 158–59.

34. EAW to Anna Harris, June 1, 1895, *PWW,* vol. 9, p. 281.

35. EAW to Frederick Jackson Turner, Dec. 15, 1896, *PWW,* vol. 10, p. 80.

36. For speculation about a stroke, see *PWW,* vol. 9, p. 507, n. 2, and Edwin A. Weinstein, *Woodrow Wilson: A Medical and Psychological Biography* (Princeton, N.J., 1981), pp. 141–49.

37. WW, "Princeton in the Nation's Service," *PWW,* vol. 10, pp. 13, 14, 22–23, 30, 30–31. The entire address is on pp. 11–31.

38. EAW to Mary Hoyt, Oct. 27, 1896, *PWW,* vol. 10, p. 37. For descriptions of the event and Wilson's speech, see *New York Tribune,* Oct. 22, 1896, *PWW,* vol. 10, pp. 10–11, and Horace Elisha Scudder diary, entry for Oct. 21, 1896, *PWW,* vol. 10, p. 31. On the disappointment of the Princeton presidential aspirant, see George McLean Harper, "A Happy Family," in Myers, *Princeton Memories,* p. 3.

39. WW to Albert Shaw, July 18, 1893, *PWW,* vol. 8, p. 281; WW to EAW, Aug. 3, 1896, *PWW,* vol. 9, p. 556.

40. WW to Caleb Winchester, May 13, 1893, *PWW,* vol. 8, p. 211; WW, "Edmund Burke: The Man and His Times," [ca. Aug 31, 1893], *PWW,* vol. 8, pp. 328, 341–43.

41. WW, "A Calendar of Great Americans," Feb. 1894, *PWW,* vol. 8, pp. 368–80; WW, "Mere Literature," [Dec. 1893], *PWW,* vol. 8, pp. 240–52. See also Editorial Note, "'Mere Literature,'" *PWW,* vol. 8, pp. 238–40.

42. WW to EAW, Jan. 24, 1894, *PWW,* vol. 9, p. 124; WW to Albert Shaw, Feb. 28, 1893, *PWW,* vol. 8, p. 141.

43. WW to EAW, Mar. 15, 1900, *PWW,* vol. 11, p. 515; WW speech, Oct. 13, 1899, *PWW,* vol. 11, p. 253; EAW to WW, [July 13, 1902], *PWW,* vol. 14, p. 8.

44. SA, "Mr. Wilson As Seen by One of His Family Circle," [ca. 1916], RSBP, box 99; SA, interviews by RSB, Feb. 8–11, 1925; Mar. 12, 1925, RSBP, box 99.

45. WW, "Leaderless Government," Aug. 5, 1987, *PWW,* vol. 10, pp. 288–304; Bliss Perry, interview by RSB, Nov. 12, 1925, RSBP, box 119; SA comments on manuscript of RSB biography of WW, Sept. 1931, RSBP, box 100; *Chicago Inter-Ocean,* Jan. 14, 1899, *PWW,* vol. 11, p. 93.

46. WW, Introduction, Aug. 15, 1900, *PWW,* vol. 11, pp. 570–71; WW, "Democracy and Efficiency," [Mar. 1901], *PWW,* vol. 12, pp. 6–20. On the Wilsons' fondness for Kipling, see EAW to WW, Feb. 11, 1897, *PWW,* vol. 10, p. 158, and WW to EAW, Feb. 14, 1897, *PWW,* vol. 10, p. 161.

47. WW to EAW, Feb. 4 and 17, 1898, *PWW,* vol. 10, pp. 374–75, 399.

48. WW to RB, Jan. 12, 1900, *PWW,* vol. 11, p. 368; Edward S. Corwin, interview by HWB, June 6, 1939, HWBC, box 1.

49. WW to Frederick Jackson Turner, Jan. 21, 1902, *PWW,* vol. 12, p. 240.

50. John Hibben to WW, July 20, 1899, *PWW,* vol. 11, p. 180; WW to EAW, July 31, 1899; Mar. 8, 1900, *PWW,* vol. 11, pp. 197, 493.

51. Samuel B. Dod to WW, June 25, 1902, *PWW,* vol. 12, p. 457.

52. Annie B. Perry to EAW, June 10, 1902, *PWW,* vol. 12, pp. 405–6; EAW to Florence Hoyt, June 28, 1902, *PWW,* vol. 12, p. 464; WW speech, June 11, 1902, *PWW,* vol. 12, p. 424.

4   BOLD LEADER

1. TR to Cleveland H. Dodge, June 16, 1902, in TR, *Letters*, ed. Elting E. Morison, vol. 3, *The Square Deal, 1901–1905* (Cambridge, Mass., 1951), p. 275. For a description of the inaugural ceremony, see *PWW*, vol. 14, pp. 191–95.

2. WW, "The Making of a Nation," [July 1897], *PWW*, vol. 10, p. 230; Jessie Wilson Sayre, interview by RSB, Dec. 1, 1925, RSBP, box 121; Jessie Wilson Sayre to RSB, [Apr. 25, 1927], RSBP, box 121. The female representatives in the procession were the president of Mount Holyoke, the dean of Radcliffe, and a professor from Wellesley. Neither President M. Carey Thomas nor anyone else from Bryn Mawr was present. Examination of records at Princeton and Bryn Mawr does not reveal whether Thomas received an invitation, but it seems likely that she did.

3. WW, "Princeton for the Nation's Service," *PWW*, vol. 14, pp. 170–85.

4. On George Harvey's spotting Wilson as a presidential possibility, see ASL, *Wilson*, vol. 1, *The Road to the White House* (Princeton, N.J., 1947), p. 98.

5. WW to EAW, July 19, 1902, *PWW*, vol. 14, p. 27; SA, "The Princeton Controversy," [Feb. 1925], RSBP, box 99.

6. SA, "The Princeton Controversy."

7. WW, Report to the Board of Trustees, Oct. 21, 1902, *PWW*, vol. 14, pp. 150–61.

8. Ibid., p. 161.

9. WW draft to Benjamin F. Jones, Jr., [Mar. 30, 1904], *PWW*, vol. 15, p. 221.

10. Mary W. Hoyt memoir, Oct. 1926, RSBP, box 111; WW to Peyton Harrison Hoge, Jan. 31, 1903, *PWW*, vol. 14, p. 336; WW to TR, Feb. 1, 1903, *PWW*, vol. 14, p. 337.

11. Henry B. Fine, interview by RSB, June 18, 1925, RSBP, box 108. On Wilson as a recruiter, see Edward Grant Conklin, "As a Scientist Saw Him," in *Woodrow Wilson: Some Princeton Memories*, ed. William Starr Myers (Princeton, N.J., 1946), p. 59, and Robert K. Root, "Wilson and the Preceptors," in Myers, *Princeton Memories*, pp. 114–15.

12. Bliss Perry, *And Gladly Teach: Reminiscences* (Boston, 1935), p. 159.

13. The Catholic was David McCabe, in Wilson's own department, Politics, and the Jew was Horace M. Kallen, in English.

14. WW, Report to the Board of Trustees, Dec. 10, 1903, *PWW*, vol. 15, pp. 69–75.

15. WW to Edward Graham Elliott, July 15, 1902, *PWW*, vol. 14, p. 12. On his befriending Fosdick, see Raymond B. Fosdick, *Chronicle of a Generation: An Autobiography* (New York, 1958), p. 42.

16. On the changes at Princeton, see SA, "The Princeton Controversy"; Hardin Craig, *Woodrow Wilson at Princeton* (Norman, Okla., 1960), pp. 34–37, 39–41; and HWB, *Woodrow Wilson: The Academic Years* (Cambridge, Mass., 1967), pp. 203–5, 272–74.

17. Mary W. Hoyt memoir, Oct. 1926, RSBP, box 111.

18. WW, "Statement of the Tutorial System," [ca. Feb. 18, 1905], *PWW*, vol. 16, pp. 6–7; WW, "The Princeton Preceptorial System," [ca. June 1, 1905], *PWW*, vol. 16, p. 109. On the use of the term *preceptor*, see *PWW*, vol. 16, p. 8, n. 1 and 2.

19. Charles H. McIlwain, interview by HWB, Jan. 2, 1940, HWBC; Norman S. Mackie, interviews by HWB, Feb. 21–22, [1940?], HWBC. On the first group of preceptors, see WW reports to trustees, [ca. June 12], 1905; [ca. Oct. 21], 1905; Dec. 14, 1905; *PWW*, vol. 16, pp. 131–32, 198, 249–59.

20. WW speech at Morristown, N.J., Feb. 23, 1903, *PWW*, vol. 14, pp. 366–67; WW speech at Chicago, Nov. 22, 1902, *PWW*, vol. 14, p. 239; Roland S. Morris, interviews by RSB, Mar. 7–8, 1926, RSBP, box 117; WW to John Rogers Williams, Sept. 2, 1904, *PWW*, vol. 15, p. 462. No African American would receive an undergraduate degree from Princeton until 1947.

21. On the death of Edward Axson and his family and its impact on Ellen Wilson, see

Frances Wright Saunders, *Ellen Axson Wilson: First Lady Between Two Worlds* (Chapel Hill, N.C. 1985), pp. 161–64.

22. Margaret Axson Elliott, *My Aunt Louisa and Woodrow Wilson* (Chapel Hill, N.C., 1944), pp. 221–23; J. Duncan Spaeth, "Wilson As I Knew Him and View Him Now," in Myers, *Princeton Memories*, p. 87.

23. Henry B. Fine, quoted in Elliott, *My Aunt Louisa*, p. 261. On Wilson's losing the sight in his left eye, see Editorial Note, *PWW*, vol. 16, p. 412, n. 1, and Edwin A. Weinstein, *Woodrow Wilson: A Medical and Psychological Biography* (Princeton, N.J., 1981), pp. 165–67.

24. EAW to Florence Hoyt, June 27, [1906], *PWW*, vol. 16, p. 430; WW to EAW, Sept. 2, 1906, *PWW*, vol. 16, pp. 445–46.

25. Andrew West, "A Narrative of the Graduate College of Princeton University from Its Proposal in 1896 until Its Dedication in 1915," Princeton University Archives, Seeley G. Mudd Manuscript Library, Princeton University. That MIT offered its presidency to West, who had even less interest in or acquaintance with science than Wilson, seemed odd at the time and has remained a mystery ever since. According to one story, the delegation from MIT intended to make the offer to Fine, who would have been a natural choice and was subsequently offered the job, but they called at the wrong dean's office and mistakenly delivered the offer to West. For the story of the mistaken offer, see Winthrop M. Daniels, interview by HWB, Mar. 30, 1940, HWBC; Jacob Beam, interview by HWB, May 3, 1941, HWBC.

26. WW, supplementary report to Princeton University trustees, [ca. Dec. 13, 1906], *PWW*, vol. 16, pp. 519–25.

27. Harry A. Garfield, interview by HWB, Feb. 14, 1940, HWBC; WW report to the Graduate School Committee, [ca. May 30, 1907], *PWW*, vol. 16, pp. 164–68.

28. WW, "Report on the Social Coordination of the University," [ca. June 6], 1907, *PWW*, vol. 17, pp. 176–86; WW address to Princeton University trustees, June 10, 1907, *PWW*, vol. 17, pp. 199–203.

29. WW speech at Harvard University, June 26, 1907, *PWW*, vol. 17, pp. 226–28.

30. George Harvey speech, [Feb. 3, 1906], *PWW*, vol. 16, p. 300; WW to St. Clair McKelway, Mar. 11, 1906, *PWW*, vol. 16, p. 330.

31. WW speech at Cleveland, May 19, 1906, *PWW*, vol. 16, p. 408; WW speech to the South Carolina Society of New York, Mar. 18, 1907, *PWW*, vol. 17, p. 82.

32. WW to Adrian H. Joline, Apr. 29, 1907, *PWW*, vol. 17, p. 124. On Wilson's Senate candidacy, see *PWW*, vol. 17, p. 561, n. 1.

33. Andrew West to WW, July 10, 1907, *PWW*, vol. 17, pp. 270–71; Henry van Dyke, "The 'Residential Quad' Idea at Princeton," *Princeton Alumni Weekly*, Sept. 25, 1907, *PWW*, vol. 17, pp. 276–79.

34. WW to John Hibben, July 10, 1907, *PWW*, vol. 17, pp. 268–69; WW to Cleveland Dodge, July 1, 1907, *PWW*, vol. 17, p. 240.

35. Elliott, *My Aunt Louise and Woodrow Wilson*, p. 237. See also SA, "The Princeton Controversy"; Jessie Wilson Sayre, interview by RSB, Dec. 1, 1925, RSBP, box 121; Hibben, interviews by RSB, June 18, 1925; Oct. 27, 1926, RSBP, box 111; Charles H. McIlwain, interview by HWB, Jan. 2, 1940, HWBC; William Magie, interview by HWB, June 13, 1939, HWBC; Ralph Barton Perry, interview by HWB, May 29, 1945, HWBC.

36. WW to MAHP, Feb. 12, 1911, *PWW*, vol. 22, p. 426; Margaret Wilson, quoted in Edith Gittings Reid, *Woodrow Wilson: The Caricature, the Myth and the Man* (New York, 1934), p. 108.

37. William Starr Myers diary, entry for Sept. 30, [1907], *PWW*, vol. 17, pp. 408–9. For the vote, see faculty minutes, Sept. 30, 1907, *PWW*, vol. 17, p. 408.

38. David B. Jones to WW, Mar. 15, 1904, *PWW*, vol. 14, pp. 191–92.

39. Henry B. Fine, interview by RSB, June 18, 1925, RSBP, box 108; WW draft statement, [ca. Oct. 4, 1907], *PWW,* vol. 17, p. 418. See also trustees' minutes, Oct. 17, 1907, *PWW,* vol. 17, p. 442.

40. WW shorthand draft, [Oct. 17, 1907], *PWW,* vol. 17, pp. 443–44; WW to Melancthon William Jacobus, Oct. 23, 1907, *PWW,* vol. 17, p. 451; New York *Evening Sun,* Oct. 18 and 23, 1907, *PWW,* vol. 17, pp. 445, 451; WW talk, [Oct. 24, 1907], *PWW,* vol. 17, p. 455.

41. Moses Pyne to WW, Dec. 24, 1907, *PWW,* vol. 18, p. 568.

42. WW, *Constitutional Government in the United States, PWW,* vol. 18, pp. 69–70. The entire volume is reprinted on pp. 69–216.

43. WW, *Constitutional Government, PWW,* vol. 17, pp. 94, 101, 105–6, 196–97.

44. Ibid., pp. 114–16, 132, 141, 158, 162.

45. Ibid., pp. 163, 177, 179–80, 186, 189, 195, 200, 204–5, 207, 209–10.

46. WW speech, Nov. 12, 1907, *PWW,* vol. 18, p. 493; Jessie Wilson Sayre, interview by RSB, Dec. 1, 1925, RSBP, box 121; WW, "A Credo," Aug. 6, 1907, *PWW,* vol. 18, pp. 335–38.

47. This was not the first recurrence of the condition: during the summer of 1904, Wilson had complained of a weakness in his right hand that hampered his writing. The 1904 and 1907 incidents, like the first one, may have been the result of small strokes caused by arteriosclerosis, but the length of time between the incidents and the fact that they affected Wilson's right side whereas the hemorrhage affected his left eye have raised questions about the exact nature of his condition. For speculation on the cause of these incidents, see *PWW,* vol. 17, p. 550, n. 1, and Weinstein, *Medical and Psychological Biography,* pp. 158–59, 179.

48. WW to MAHP, Feb. 6, 1907; Mar. 27, 1907, *PWW,* vol. 17, pp. 29, 94; Florence Hoyt interview by RSB, Oct. 1926, RSBP, box 121.

49. WW shorthand note, [ca. Feb. 1, 1908], *PWW,* vol. 17, p. 611; WW to MAHP, Sept. 26, 1909, *PWW,* vol. 17, p. 394.

50. WW to EAW, June 26, 1908, *PWW,* vol. 18, p. 346; TR, quoted in William Allen White essay [1924], William Allen White Papers, series E, box 1, LC.

51. WW to EAW, July 20, 1908, *PWW,* vol. 18, p. 372. The editors of *The Papers of Woodrow Wilson* observe that the first quoted sentence probably refers to Mrs. Peck. See *PWW,* vol. 18, p. 372, n. 8.

52. CTG, quoted in Breckinridge Long diary, entry for Jan. 11, 1924, *PWW,* vol. 68, p. 527.

53. WW shorthand draft, [ca. Sept. 20, 1915], *PWW,* vol. 34, p. 496; WW to EBG, Sept. 21, 1915, *PWW,* vol. 34, p. 500.

54. WW speech, Mar. 12, 1908, *PWW,* vol. 18, p. 23.

5   ACADEMIC CIVIL WAR

1. SA, "The Princeton Controversy," [Feb. 1925], RSBP, box 99; EAW to John Hibben, Feb. 10, 1912, *PWW,* vol. 24, p. 150.

2. Frederick W. Yates to EAW, Sept 1, 1908, *PWW,* vol. 24, p. 417.

3. Charles Grosvenor Osgood, interview by HWB, Apr. 12, 1939, HWBC.

4. WW, preface to *The Proposed Graduate College of Princeton University,* Feb. 17, 1903, *PWW,* vol. 14, p. 361.

5. For descriptions of Merwick, see Raymond B. Fosdick, *Chronicle of a Generation: An Autobiography* (New York, 1958), pp. 61–62, and Maxwell Struthers Burt, "Life at Merwick," *Princeton Alumni Weekly,* May 8, 1907, p. 512.

6. SA, "The Princeton Controversy."

7. Harlow Shapley, interview by HWB, Mar. 6, 1967, HWBC.

8. Cleveland quoted in Andrew West, "A Narrative of the Graduate College of Princeton University from Its Proposal to Its Dedication in 1915," Princeton University Archives, Seeley G. Mudd Manuscript Library, Princeton University, p. 37.

9. WW speech, Oct. 16, 1908, *PWW*, vol. 18, pp. 463–65; WW speech, Nov. 6, 1908, *PWW*, vol. 18, p. 488.

10. WW speeches, Apr. 3 and 13, 1908, *PWW*, vol. 18, pp. 222, 266. On the faculty debate, see William Starr Myers diary, entry for May 8, [1908], *PWW*, vol. 18, pp. 293–94. The preceptor who rebutted Wilson's arguments was Edward S. Corwin. See Corwin, "Departmental Colleague," in *Woodrow Wilson: Some Princeton Memories*, ed. William Starr Myers (Princeton, N.J., 1946), pp. 27–28.

11. WW speech, Nov. 16, 1907, *PWW*, vol. 17, p. 500.

12. WW to MAHP, Nov. 2, 1908, *PWW*, vol. 18, pp. 479–80.

13. For examples supporting the interpretation that Wilson's turn toward progressivism was reflected in his struggles at Princeton, see ASL, *Wilson*, vol. 1, *The Road to the White House* (Princeton, N.J., 1947), pp. 22–23, and John M. Mulder, *Woodrow Wilson: The Years of Preparation* (Princeton, N.J., 1978), p. 252.

14. WW, *Constitutional Government in the United States*, *PWW*, vol. 18, pp. 147–48.

15. WW speeches, Feb. 12 and 19, 1909; Nov. 2, 1909, *PWW*, vol. 19, pp. 41, 60, 477.

16. WW speech, Oct. 8, 1908, *PWW*, vol. 18, p. 441; WW speeches, May 6, 1909; Oct. 29, 1909, *PWW*, vol. 19, pp. 187, 465–66; WW, "The Tariff Make-Believe," *PWW*, vol. 19, pp. 359, 371.

17. Mary Yates diary, entry for July 31, [1908], *PWW*, vol. 18, p. 386, *Daily Princetonian*, Apr. 3, 1909, *PWW*, vol. 19, p. 149; WW memorandum, ca. Dec. 3, 1909, *PWW*, vol. 18, p. 550.

18. On the digestive problems see Edwin A. Weinstein, *Woodrow Wilson: A Medical and Psychological Biography* (Princeton, N.J., 1981), pp. 127, 146, 149.

19. WW speech, Mar. 20, 1909, *PWW*, vol. 19, p. 113.

20. WW to Frank A. Vanderlip, Feb. 1, 1909, *PWW*, vol. 19, p. 18; WW to MAHP, July 18, 1909, *PWW*, vol. 19, p. 312.

21. WW speech, Mar. 11, 1910, *PWW*, vol. 20, p. 233. On the Procter offer, see also William Cooper Procter to Andrew West, May 8, 1909; June 7, 1909, *PWW*, vol. 19, pp. 189–90, 237–38. On Cram's change of mind, see also Ralph Adams Cram, interview by HWB, May 8, 1940, HWBC.

22. WW to MAHP, Oct. 24, 1909, *PWW*, vol. 19, pp. 442–43.

23. WW to Moses Pyne, Dec. 22 and 25, 1909, *PWW*, vol. 19, pp. 620, 628–30.

24. Pyne to William Cooper Procter, Jan. 15, 1910, *PWW*, vol. 19, pp. 17–18. The editors of *The Papers of Woodrow Wilson* have observed, "[T]here can be no doubt that Wilson's statement that the site of the Graduate College was not important was one of the great strategic errors of his career." Editorial Note, "Wilson at the Meeting of the Board of Trustees of January 13, 1910," *PWW*, vol. 20, p. 9. By contrast, Cyrus McCormick later recalled that this statement was "an illustrative comparison to clinch his point that the kind of organization adopted be in close sympathy between teacher and scholar was the main goal to be reached." McCormick to William Allen White, William Allen White Papers, series E, box 83, LC.

25. Pyne to Wilson Farrand, Jan. 25, 1910, *PWW*, vol. 20, pp. 56–57; Procter to Pyne, Jan. 30, 1910, *PWW*, vol. 20, p. 65.

26. WW to Herbert B. Brougham, Feb. 1, 1910, *PWW*, vol. 20, p. 70; *New York Times*, Feb. 3, 1910, *PWW*, vol. 20, pp. 74–76. For Farrand's account, see Princeton University Archives, Seeley G. Mudd Manuscript Library, Princeton University. For the reactions of alumni and Pyne, see *PWW*, vol. 20, p. 77, n. 1; p. 84, n. 1.

27. WW to Cleveland H. Dodge, Feb. 7, 1910, *PWW*, vol. 20, p. 83.

28. WW to Melancthon William Jacobus, Apr. 2, 1910, *PWW,* vol. 20, p. 312; WW speech, Apr. 7, 1910, *PWW,* vol. 20, pp. 337–48.

29. WW to MAHP, Apr. 19, 1910, *PWW,* vol. 20, p. 370; *Pittsburgh Dispatch,* Apr. 17, 1910, *PWW,* vol. 20, p. 366; Pittsburgh *Gazette-Times,* Apr. 17, 1910, *PWW,* vol. 20, pp. 364–65.

30. On the Wyman bequest, see Andrew West, "A Narrative of the Graduate College of Princeton University from Its Proposal in 1896 until Its Dedication in 1916," Princeton University Archives, Seeley G. Mudd Manuscript Library, Princeton University, pp. 51–54, 87–88, 105–7, and John F. Raymond to West and WW, May 22, 1910, *PWW,* vol. 20, p. 464.

31. Margaret Axson Elliott, *My Aunt Louisa and Woodrow Wilson* (Chapel Hill, N.C., 1944), pp. 241–42; Eleanor Wilson McAdoo, *The Woodrow Wilsons* (New York, 1937), p. 101; West, "Narrative of the Graduate College," p. 108; WW to Hiram Woods, May 28, 1910, *PWW,* vol. 20, p. 482.

32. WW to MAHP, June 5, 1910, *PWW,* vol. 20, p. 501; SA, "The Princeton Controversy."

33. For speculation about strokes' affecting Wilson's behavior, see HWB, *Woodrow Wilson: The Academic Years* (Cambridge, Mass., 1967), pp. 381–82, and Weinstein, *Medical and Psychological Biography,* p. 216. The comparison between the Graduate College and the League of Nations arose early. In 1925, both Stockton Axson and a faculty supporter of Wilson's drew the comparison privately. See SA, "The Princeton Controversy," and George McLean Harper, interview by RSB, Nov. 12, 1925, RSBP, box 107.

34. WW speeches, May 25, 1911; Sept. 2, 1912, *PWW,* vol. 23, p. 93; vol. 25, p. 68; EMHD, entries for Dec. 12, 1913; Jan. 22, 1914, *PWW,* vol. 29, pp. 33–34, 163.

35. WW to MAHP, Oct. 8, 1911, *PWW,* vol. 23, p. 425; EMHD, entry for Jan. 24, 1913, *PWW,* vol. 26, p. 71.

36. Henry B. Fine, interview by RSB, June 18, 1925, RSBP, box 105. For a superb account and interpretation of the rise of Princeton to the top rank of universities, see James Axtell, *The Making of Princeton University: From Woodrow Wilson to the Present* (Princeton, N.J., 2006).

6 GOVERNOR

1. On Smith and his role in New Jersey politics, see ASL, *Wilson,* vol. 1, *The Road to the White House* (Princeton, N.J., 1947), pp. 140–41.

2. George Harvey quoted in Editorial Note, "Colonel Harvey's Plan for Wilson's Entry into Politics," *PWW,* vol. 20, p. 147.

3. WW statement, July 15, 1910, *PWW,* vol. 20, p. 581. On the meeting with the party bosses, see Editorial Note, "The Lawyers' Club Conference," *PWW,* vol. 20, pp. 565–66.

4. WW to Edgar Williamson, Aug. 25, 1910, *PWW,* vol. 21, p. 60; WW speech, Aug. 31, 1910, *PWW,* vol. 21, p. 65.

5. Audience member's remark, quoted in SA comments, n.d., on manuscript of RSB biography of WW, RSBP, box 100. For accounts of the convention by people who were there, see James Kerney, *The Political Education of Woodrow Wilson* (New York, 1926), pp. 51–54, and JPT, *Woodrow Wilson As I Know Him* (Garden City, N.Y., 1921), pp. 16–22.

6. WW speech, Sept. 15, 1910, *PWW,* vol. 21, pp. 91–94.

7. Dan Fellows Platt to WW, Sept. 19, 1910, *PWW,* vol. 21, pp. 141–42. See also JPT, *Wilson As I Know Him,* p. 22.

8. Kerney, *Political Education*, pp. 62–64; Eleanor Wilson McAdoo, *The Woodrow Wilsons* (New York, 1937), p. 110; WW, *The Priceless Gift: The Love Letters of Woodrow Wilson and Ellen Axson Wilson*, ed. Eleanor Wilson McAdoo (New York, 1962), p. 263.

9. For the estimate of campaign spending, see ASL, *Wilson*, vol. 1, pp. 187–88.

10. *Philadelphia Record*, Oct. 2, 1910, *PWW*, vol. 21, p. 223; WW speech at Long Branch, Oct. 3, 1910, *PWW*, vol. 21, p. 227.

11. Vivian Lewis speech, Sept. 20, 1910, quoted in *PWW*, vol. 21, p. 219, n. 1; WW speech, Oct. 3, 1910, *PWW*, vol. 21, pp. 229–30. On the New Idea Republicans, see Ransom E. Noble, Jr., *New Jersey Progressivism before Wilson* (Princeton, N.J., 1946), pp. 65–99.

12. WW speeches, Oct. 13, 20, and 22, 1910, *PWW*, vol. 21, pp. 318, 376, 400.

13. George Record to WW, Oct. 17, 1910, *PWW*, vol. 21, pp. 338–47.

14. WW to Record, Oct. 24, 1910, *PWW*, vol. 21, pp. 406–11. Wilson originally wrote some of his answers in shorthand on Record's letter and later produced several drafts on his own typewriter. See *PWW*, vol. 21, p. 411, n. 1.

15. Record, quoted in ASL, *Wilson*, vol. 1, p. 195; Record, interview by RSB, Apr. 6, 1928, RSBP, box 114; WW speech, Nov. 5, 1910, *PWW*, vol. 21, pp. 575–76.

16. WW to Lawrence C. Woods, Oct. 27, 1910, *PWW*, vol. 21, p. 444. On the trustees' action, see minutes of the Board of Trustees, Oct. 20, 1910, *PWW*, vol. 21, pp. 364–66, and editorial comment, *PWW*, vol. 21, p. 362, n. 1.

17. WW, quoted in ASL, *Wilson*, vol. 1, p. 201. For an analysis of the returns, see *PWW*, vol. 21, p. 584, n. 1. At that time, New Jersey elected governors to three-year terms, so the two previous elections had taken place in 1904 and 1907.

18. See *PWW*, vol. 22, p. 73, n. 3, for both the quotations and the judgment of the editors of *The Papers of Woodrow Wilson*.

19. WW to George Harvey, Nov. 15, 1910, *PWW*, vol. 22, pp. 46–48.

20. WW, quoted in *PWW*, vol. 21, p. 142, n. 1; WW statement, Dec. 8, 1910, *PWW*, vol. 22, p. 154.

21. WW to MAHP, Dec. 9, 1910, *PWW*, vol. 22, p. 141; WW to Thomas Jones, Dec. 8, 1910, *PWW*, vol. 22, p. 154; WW speeches, Jan. 5 and 16, 1911, *PWW*, vol. 22, pp. 296, 337.

22. WW to MAHP, Jan. 29, 1911, *PWW*, vol. 22, p. 392. For an account of the caucus and legislative actions, see ASL, *Wilson*, vol. 1, pp. 233–35.

23. New York *World*, Jan. 28, 1911; WW to MAHP, Jan. 3, 1911, *PWW*, vol. 23, p. 293.

24. *Trenton Evening Times*, Nov. 10, 1910, *PWW*, vol. 22, p. 5; WW speech, Nov. 29, 1910, *PWW*, vol. 22, p. 109.

25. On the family affairs, see Frances Wright Saunders, *Ellen Axson Wilson: First Lady between Two Worlds* (Chapel Hill, N.C., 1985), pp. 212–14.

26. Much later, there would be two governors' mansions in Princeton: from 1945 to 1981, Morven, the home of Richard Stockton, a signer of the Declaration of Independence; then, from 1981 to the present, Drumthwacket, which had been the home of Momo Pyne, Wilson's nemesis on the board of trustees.

27. On Tumulty, see John M. Blum, *Joe Tumulty and the Wilson Era* (Boston, 1951). Tumulty's memoir, *Woodrow Wilson As I Know Him*, tends toward sentimental exaggeration, but it has useful parts.

28. *New York Evening Post*, Jan. 19, 1911, *PWW*, vol. 22, pp. 357–58. For an eyewitness account of the meeting, see Kerney, *Political Education*, pp. 103–4.

29. WW speech, Jan. 17, 1911, *PWW*, vol. 22, pp. 345–54.

30. Ida B. Taylor to RSB, Nov. 11, 1927, RSBP, box 116; WW to MAHP, Feb. 12, 1911, *PWW*, vol. 22, p. 424.

31. WW to MAHP, Apr. 2, 1911, *PWW*, vol. 22, p. 532.

32. On the Geran bill, see ASL, *Wilson*, vol. 1, pp. 245–48.

33. WW speech at Harrison, Feb. 28, 1911, *PWW*, vol. 22, pp. 461, 464.

34. WW to MAHP, Mar. 5, 1911, *PWW*, vol. 22, p. 477; WW, quoted in *PWW*, vol. 22, p. 505, n. 1.

35. *Trenton Evening Times* and Trenton *True American*, Mar. 14, 1911, *PWW*, vol. 22, pp. 504; 505, n. 1.

36. WW statement, Mar. 20, 1911, *PWW*, vol. 22, pp. 512–13; WW to MAHP, Mar. 26, 1911, *PWW*, vol. 22, p. 518. On Tumulty's activities, see Blum, *Tumulty and the Wilson Era*, pp. 27–28.

37. On the passage of the Geran bill, see ASL, *Wilson*, vol. 1, pp. 256–58.

38. On these bills, see, ASL, *Wilson*, vol. 1, pp. 259–64, and *PWW*, vol. 22, pp. 546, n. 5; 579, n. 3; 580, n. 4.

39. On these measures, see ASL, *Wilson*, vol. 1, pp. 264–67, and *PWW*, vol. 22, p. 550, n. 2.

40. WW to MAHP, Apr. 23, 1911, *PWW*, vol. 22, pp. 581–82.

41. James Nugent, quoted in *PWW*, vol. 23, p. 235, n. 1. On the committee meeting, see p. 262, n. 3. For another account of Nugent's behavior, see Kerney, *Political Education*, pp. 148–49.

42. WW speeches, Sept. 19 and 21, 1911, *PWW*, vol. 23, pp. 338–345; *Newark Evening News*, Oct. 4, 1911, *PWW*, vol. 23, p. 386.

43. WW speeches, Oct. 5 and 7, 1911, *PWW*, vol. 23, pp. 398–99, 416.

44. Eleanor Wilson McAdoo, *The Wilsons*, p. 145.

45. Kerney, *Political Education*, pp. 193–94.

46. SA, *Brother Woodrow: A Memoir of Woodrow Wilson* (Princeton, N.J., 1993), pp. 217–18.

47. Saunders, *Ellen Axson Wilson*, p. 217.

7   NOMINEE

1. On Walter Page's activities on Wilson's behalf, see John Milton Cooper, Jr., *Walter Hines Page: The Southerner as American, 1855–1918* (Chapel Hill, N.C., 1977), pp. 235–37.

2. WW to MAHP, Mar. 26, 1911; Apr. 2, 1911, *PWW*, vol. 22, pp. 479, 519, 533.

3. WJB to WW, Jan. 5, [1911], *PWW*, vol. 22, p. 307; WW to MAHP, Mar. 12, 1911, *PWW*, vol. 22, p. 501; EAW, quoted in James Kerney, *The Political Education of Woodrow Wilson* (New York, 1926), p. 163.

4. WW to MAHP, Apr. 9, 1911, *PWW*, vol. 22, pp. 544–45.

5. WW speech, Feb. 21, 1911, *PWW*, vol. 22, pp. 443, 449–50; Archibald Butt to Clara Butt, Mar. 11, 1911, in Archibald Butt, *Taft and Roosevelt: The Intimate Letters of Archie Butt* (Garden City, N.Y., 1930), vol. 2, p. 601; WW to MAHP, Mar. 13 [12], 1911, *PWW*, vol. 22, pp. 500–501.

6. WW speech, Apr. 13, 1911, *PWW*, vol. 22, pp. 559, 565.

7. On Jefferson's legacy, see Merrill D. Peterson, *The Jefferson Image in the American Mind* (New York, 1960), esp. pp. 222–26, 333–45.

8. WW speeches, Nov. 2, 1910; May 12, 1911, *PWW*, vol. 21, p. 510; vol. 23, pp. 34, 36.

9. Portland *Oregonian*, May 19, 1911, *PWW*, vol. 23, p. 63; WW speeches, May 25, 1911; June 2, 1911, *PWW*, vol. 3, pp. 94, 120–21.

10. *Nebraska State Journal*, May 27, 1911, *PWW*, vol. 23, p. 100; WW to Walter Page, June 7, 1911, *PWW*, vol. 23, p. 135. On the meeting in Washington, see Frank Stockbridge, interview by RSB, Nov. 2, 1927, RSBP, box 122.

11. William McCombs to WW, Sept. 26, 1911, *PWW*, vol. 23, p. 360. On McCombs's role, see ASL, *Wilson*, vol. 1, *The Road to the White House* (Princeton, N.J., 1947), pp. 336–37.

12. On McAdoo, see his autobiography, *Crowded Years: The Reminiscences of William G. McAdoo* (Boston, 1931), and a contemporary biography, Mary Synon, *McAdoo: The Man and His Times, a Panorama in Democracy* (Indianapolis, 1924).

13. WW speech, Oct. 26, 1911, *PWW*, vol. 23, p. 491; WW to MAHP, Apr. 30, 1911, *PWW*, vol. 22, p. 598.

14. *Charlotte Observer*, Dec. 7, 1911, quoted in ASL, *Wilson*, vol. 1, pp. 329–30; George Fred Williams, quoted in ASL, *Wilson*, vol. 1, p. 330.

15. WW statement, Dec. 5, 1911, *PWW*, vol. 23, pp. 565–66; EAW to Richard Heath Dabney, Feb. 12, 1912, *PWW*, vol. 24, p. 149.

16. WW to MAHP, *PWW*, vol. 23, p. 590. The original letter from WW to Adrian Joline, Apr. 29, 1907, is in vol. 17, p. 124.

17. Dudley Field Malone, interview by RSB, Nov. 1, 1927, RSBP, box 111. On Daniels's influence on Bryan, see JD, *The Wilson Era*, vol. 1, *Years of Peace, 1910–1917* (Chapel Hill, N.C., 1944), p. 32.

18. Malone, interview by RSB, Nov. 1, 1927, RSBP, box 116; WW speech, Jan. 8, 1912, *PWW*, vol. 24, pp. 10, 13–14, 16; WW to MAHP, Jan. 12, 1912, *PWW*, vol. 24, p. 43.

19. EAW to Robert Ewing, Jan. 12, 1912, *PWW*, vol. 24, p. 41; WW to George Harvey, Dec. 21, 1911, *PWW*, vol. 23, p. 603; *Commoner*, Jan. 26, 1912, quoted in ASL, *Wilson*, vol. 1, p. 373. On this incident, see also SA, interview by RSB, Mar. 12, 1925, RSBP, box 99, and Malone, interview by RSB, Nov. 1, 1927, RSBP, box 111.

20. On James Beauchamp Clark, see ASL, *Wilson*, vol. 1, pp. 398–99, 401. There is no biography of Clark, and his autobiography, *My Quarter Century of American Politics* (New York, 1920), is singularly unreflective and uninformative, even in a genre noteworthy for those failings.

21. On the division of support in the South, see John Milton Cooper, Jr., *The Warrior and the Priest: Woodrow Wilson and Theodore Roosevelt* (Cambridge, Mass., 1983), pp. 182–83. On the presidential candidacy of Oscar W. Underwood, see ASL, *Wilson*, vol. 1, pp. 408, 415–17, and Evans C. Johnson, *Oscar W. Underwood: A Political Biography* (Baton Rouge, La., 1980), pp. 170–83.

22. WW, quoted in ASL, *Wilson*, vol. 1, p. 382.

23. For an excellent account of these primaries, see ASL, *Wilson*, vol. 1, pp. 406–20.

24. On the appeal of James Beauchamp Clark, see ASL, *Wilson*, vol. 1, pp. 400–402.

25. New York *World*, Dec. 24, 1911; WW speeches, Jan. 12, 1912; Apr. 17, 1912; May 23, 1912, *PWW*, vol. 24, pp. 55, 58, 341, 414–15, 424.

26. WW public letter, May 24, 1912, *PWW*, vol. 24, p. 433; *Newark Evening News*, May 28, 1912, *PWW*, vol. 24, p. 448. On the near encounter with Roosevelt, see William Starr Myers, "Wilson in My Diary," in *Woodrow Wilson: Some Princeton Memories*, ed. William Starr Myers (Princeton, N.J., 1946), p. 43. On the primary results, see ASL, *Wilson*, vol. 1, p. 427.

27. New York *World*, Apr. 25, 1912; May 28, 1912; WW to MAHP, June 9, 1912, *PWW*, vol. 24, p. 466.

28. On Wilson's organization and contributors, see ASL, *Wilson*, vol. 1, pp. 392–93, 402–3.

29. TR speech, June 17, 1912, Theodore Roosevelt, *The Works of Theodore Roosevelt*, ed. Hermann Hagedorn (New York, 1926), vol. 17, p. 231; WW to Edith Gittings Reid, May 26, 1912, *PWW*, vol. 24, p. 446. Of the many accounts of the 1912 Republican convention, the best is Lewis L. Gould, *Four Hats in the Ring: The 1912 Election and the Birth of Modern American Politics* (Lawrence, Kan., 2008), pp. 66–74.

30. On Roosevelt's thinking, see Cooper, *Warrior and Priest*, pp. 159–61.
31. WW speech, Feb. 12, 1912, *PWW*, vol. 24, p. 153; Kermit Roosevelt, quoted in JD, "Wilson and Bryan," *Saturday Evening Post*, Sept. 5, 1925, p. 48.
32. On these ballots, see ASL, *Wilson*, vol. 1, pp. 447–49.
33. WJB to WW, June 21, 1912, *PWW*, vol. 24, p. 492; WW to WJB, June 22, 1912, *PWW*, vol. 24, p. 493; *New York Times*, July 4, 1912. On these incidents, see ASL, *Wilson*, vol. 1, pp. 434–37, 442–43.
34. WW telephone messages, June 29, 1912, *PWW*, vol. 24, pp. 508–9; *New York Times*, June 30, 1912. For Joseph Tumulty's recollection and William McCombs's claim, see *PWW*, vol. 24, p. 509, n. 1.
35. WW to MAHP, July 6, 1912, *PWW*, vol. 24, p. 541; New York *World*, June 30, 1912. On the back and forth among Wilson, McCombs, and McAdoo, see McAdoo, *Crowded Years*, pp. 153–55, and *PWW*, vol. 24, p. 524, n. 3.
36. On the Wilson managers' tactics and Sullivan's switch, see ASL, *Wilson*, vol. 1, pp. 459–61.
37. *New York Times*, July 3, 1912.
38. Eleanor Wilson McAdoo, *The Woodrow Wilsons* (New York, 1937), pp. 164–65; WW to MAHP, July 6, 1912, *PWW*, vol. 24, p. 541.

8   THE GREAT CAMPAIGN

1. Soon after Wilson's nomination, a Democratic senator told him that Robert La Follette, who nursed a grudge against Roosevelt for snatching away the insurgent Republican leadership, had said that "the real fight would be between you [Wilson] and Roosevelt in November and that Taft would not win the electoral vote of more than six states—a view very generally shared by the shrewdest of the Washington correspondents and by many well-informed members of Congress." Luke Lea to WW, July 13, 1912, *PWW*, vol. 24, p. 546.
2. TR speech at Chicago, Aug. 6, 1912, in TR, *The Works of Theodore Roosevelt*, ed. Hermann Hagedorn (New York, 1926), vol. 17, pp. 276–77, 292, 299.
3. WW speech, Aug. 7, 1912, *PWW*, vol. 25, pp. 3–18.
4. TR to Hiram Johnson, Oct. 27, 1911, in TR, *Letters*, ed. Elting E. Morison, vol. 7, *The Days of Armageddon, 1900–1914* (Cambridge, Mass., 1954), p. 420. On Roosevelt's attitude toward Wilson, see also John Milton Cooper, Jr., *The Warrior and the Priest: Woodrow Wilson and Theodore Roosevelt* (Cambridge, Mass., 1983), pp. 130–33, 160.
5. WW to MAHP, Dec. 17, 1911, *PWW*, vol. 23, p. 597. On the discussion of the New Nationalism, see Winthrop M. Daniels to WW, Oct. 13, 1910, *PWW*, vol. 21, p. 322, and WW to Daniels, Oct. 17, 1910, *PWW*, vol. 21, p. 337. On Wilson's attitude toward Roosevelt, see Cooper, *Warrior and Priest*, pp. 133–36.
6. On the early visits and arrangements, see ASL, *Wilson*, vol. 1, *The Road to the White House* (Princeton, N.J., 1947), pp. 469–72.
7. Eleanor Wilson McAdoo, *The Woodrow Wilsons* (New York, 1937), p. 154; WW to MAHP, Aug. 25, 1912, *PWW*, vol. 25, pp. 55–56.
8. McAdoo, *The Wilsons*, p. 172; WJB to WW, Aug. [1]8, 1912, *PWW*, vol. 25, p. 46.
9. On Brandeis, see Alpheus T. Mason, *Brandeis: A Free Man's Life* (New York, 1946), and Philippa Strum, *Louis D. Brandeis: Justice for the People* (Cambridge, Mass., 1984).
10. *New York Times*, Aug. 29, 1912; Louis Brandeis, interview by RSB, Mar. 3, 1929, RSBP, box 102.
11. WW to Brandeis, [Nov. 12, 1912], *PWW*, vol. 25, p. 545. On the meeting and Bran-

deis's influence, see ASL, *Wilson*, vol. 1, pp. 488–89, and Cooper, *Warrior and Priest*, pp. 193–94.

12. WW speech, Sept. 2, 1912, *PWW*, vol. 25, pp. 69–92.

13. TR speech at Fargo, Sept. 6, 1912, *Outlook*, Sept. 11, 1912, pp. 105–7.

14. Oscar King Davis, *Released for Publication: Some Inside Political History of Theodore Roosevelt and His Times, 1898–1918* (Boston, 1925), pp. 360–61.

15. WW speech, Sept. 9, 1912, *PWW*, vol. 25, p. 124; TR speech at San Francisco, Sept. 14, 1912, in TR, *Works of Roosevelt*, vol. 17, pp. 306–7, 313–14.

16. Charles Willis Thompson to Bernice M. Thompson, Oct. 6, 1912, *PWW*, vol. 25, p. 361. On this point, see also WW, *A Crossroads of Freedom: The 1912 Campaign Speeches of Woodrow Wilson*, ed. John Wells Davidson (New Haven, Conn., 1956), pp. 122–23.

17. WW speeches, Sept. 17, 18, and 20, 1912, *PWW*, vol. 25, pp. 152, 179, 206–7.

18. WW speeches, Sept. 23 and 25, 1912, *PWW*, vol. 25, pp. 224–25, 236, 250.

19. *New York Times*, Sept. 27, 1912.

20. WHT to Myron T. Herrick, June 20, 1912, quoted in Henry F. Pringle, *The Life and Times of William Howard Taft* (New York, 1939), vol. 2, p. 808; *New York Times*, Sept. 29, 1912.

21. Wilson speech at Boston, Sept. 27, 1912, quoted in WW, *Crossroads of Freedom*, pp. 291–92, 293. See also Louis Brandeis memoranda, Sept. 30, 1912, *PWW*, vol. 25, pp. 289–304.

22. WW speeches, Oct. 3 and 5, 1912, *PWW*, vol. 25, pp. 327, 329, 359; Charles Willis Thompson to Bernice M. Thompson, Oct. 6, 1912, *PWW*, vol. 25, p. 361.

23. WW speeches, Oct. 8, 9, and 11, 1912, *PWW*, vol. 25, pp. 379, 390, 393, 411; WW to MAHP, *PWW*, vol. 25, p. 496.

24. TR speech at Chicago, Oct. 12, 1912, quoted in TR to WJB, Oct. 22, 1912, TR, *Letters*, vol. 7, pp. 630–31.

25. TR speech at Milwaukee, Oct. 14, 1912, TR, *Works of Roosevelt*, vol. 17, pp. 320, 322–23. For speculation on Roosevelt's feelings about the situation, see Cooper, *Warrior and Priest*, pp. 201–2; 391, n. 30.

26. McAdoo, *The Wilsons*, p. 173.

27. WW speeches at Wilmington, Del., Oct. 17, 18, and 19, 1912, *PWW*, vol. 25, pp. 424–25, 429, 458, 464–65; speech at Clarksburg, W. Va., Oct. 18, 1912, WW, *Crossroads of Freedom*, p. 449.

28. *Crisis*, [Aug 1912], quoted in David Levering Lewis, *W. E. B. DuBois: Biography of a Race, 1868–1919* (New York, 1993), p. 424. On the overtures to Wilson, see pp. 423–24 and ASL, *Wilson*, vol. 1, pp. 501–5.

29. WW to Alexander Walters, [Oct. 21, 1912], *PWW*, vol. 25, p. 449.

30. *New York Times*, Oct. 20, 1912.

31. On the conflicts in New Jersey and New York and the campaign organization, see ASL, *Wilson*, vol. 1, pp. 481–84, 494–98.

32. On the campaign's finances, see ASL, *Wilson*, vol. 1, pp. 485–86.

33. WW speeches, Oct. 28, 1912, *PWW*, vol. 25, pp. 463–64; WW speech, Oct. 28, 1912, WW, *Crossroads of Freedom*, pp. 489, 491; *Trenton True American*, Nov. 5, 1912, evening ed., *PWW*, vol. 25, p. 518.

34. Dudley Field Malone, interview by RSB, Dec. 1, 1927, RSBP, box 116.

35. New York *World*, Nov. 6, 1912; Malone, interview by RSB, Dec. 1, 1927, RSBP, box 116; WW speech, Nov. 6, 1912, *PWW*, vol. 25, pp. 520–21.

36. For analyses of the 1912 vote, see ASL, *Wilson*, vol. 1, p. 525, and Cooper, *Warrior and Priest*, pp. 204–5, 207.

37. On Debs's vote, see Cooper, *Warrior and Priest*, p. 391, n. 37.

38. William Allen White, *Woodrow Wilson: The Man, His Times, and His Task* (Boston, 1924), p. 264. For a comparison of the Democrats' and the Progressives' 1912 platforms, see TR, *Letters*, vol. 7, p. 593, n. 3.

39. On the early drift toward Wilson, see ASL, *Wilson*, vol. 1, pp. 467–69.

40. On the contest in California and Roosevelt's chances in a two-man race, see David Sarasohn, *The Party of Reform: Democrats in the Progressive Era* (Jackson, Miss., 1989), pp. 149–54. The only state that Wilson campaigned in but did not carry was Pennsylvania, which, along with Vermont, was one of the most solidly Republican states in the country. The last election in which a Democrat had carried Pennsylvania was 1856, when a native son, James Buchanan, was the nominee and the Republicans were still a fledgling party. Pennsylvania would not go Democratic again until 1936.

41. This analysis and the following paragraphs follow the interpretation I have presented in somewhat different form in *Warrior and Priest*, p. 211ff.

42. On these later developments, see Cooper, *Warrior and Priest*, pp. 345–58.

43. WW speech, Dec. 28, 1912, *PWW*, vol. 25, pp. 627, 629.

44. WW speech, Dec. 28, 1912, *PWW*, vol. 25, pp. 638–39. The reference was to Representative Hal Flood, a leader of the Virginia machine.

45. Ibid., p. 628.

9   PREPARATION

1. Edward Grant Conklin, interview by RSB, June 3, 1925, RSBP, box 104.

2. Edward House still needs a full biography—a need that will be filled by the work of Charles Neu. The best work thus far on his earlier life is Rupert N. Richardson, *Colonel Edward M. House: The Texas Years, 1858–1912* (Abilene, Tex., 1964).

3. EMHD, entries for Nov. 8 and 16, 1912, *PWW*, pp. 532, 550.

4. EMH to WW, Nov. 22, 28, 1912, *PWW*, vol. 25, pp. 563–65.

5. *Trenton Evening Times*, Dec. 16, 1912, *PWW*, vol. 25, pp. 589–90; WW speech, Dec. 17, 1912, *PWW*, vol. 25, p. 595.

6. WJB to WW, Dec. 25, 1912, *PWW*, vol. 25, pp. 622–23. See also WJB and Mary Baird Bryan, *The Memoirs of William Jennings Bryan* (Philadelphia, 1925), pp. 187–89.

7. WJB to WW, Dec. [22 and] 25, 1912, *PWW*, vol. 25, pp. 616, 622–23. In later years, Brandeis's protégé, Felix Frankfurter, would often quote with contempt a statement of Bryan's: "Any man with real goodness of heart can write a good currency law." See Arthur M. Schlesinger, Jr., *The Age of Roosevelt*, vol. 3, *The Politics of Upheaval* (Boston, 1960), p. 223.

8. WW speech, Jan. 11, 1913, *PWW*, vol. 27, pp. 29–39, 40.

9. Carter Glass to H. Parker Willis, Dec. 29, 1912, *PWW*, vol. 25, p. 644.

10. WW speech, Jan. 28, 1913, *PWW*, vol. 27, p. 86; *New York Times*, Jan. 29, 1913.

11. On these legislative wrangles, see ASL, *Wilson*, vol. 2, *The New Freedom* (Princeton, N.J., 1956), pp. 41–48.

12. John Dos Passos, *U.S.A.*, pt. 2, *Nineteen Nineteen* (New York, 1940), p. 244.

13. Their meetings and telephone calls are recounted in EMHD entries, *PWW*, vol. 27. Correspondence between the two men was sparse at this time, probably because they were meeting so often. House's letters contain some matters of substance; Wilson's are strictly routine.

14. The list is in EMH to WW, Jan. 9, 1913, *PWW*, vol. 27, pp. 26–27. See also EMHD, entry for Jan. 8, 1913, pp. 20–24.

15. EMHD, entry for Feb. 13, 1913, *PWW*, vol. 27, pp. 110–11. On the machinations against Brandeis, see ASL, *Wilson*, vol. 2, pp. 10–14.

16. A. Mitchell Palmer to WW, Feb. 24, 1913, *PWW*, vol. 27, p. 132; EMHD, entry for Feb. 22, 1913, *PWW*, vol. 27, p. 126. On Garrison's appointment, see *PWW*, p. 133, n. 3.

17. WW to JD, *PWW*, vol. 27, p. 128; Oscar W. Underwood to WW, Jan. 13, 1913, *PWW*, vol. 27, p. 144. On these appointments, see ASL, *Wilson*, vol. 2, pp. 15–16.

18. EMHD, entry for Jan. 8, 1913, *PWW*, vol. 27, p. 22. On these appointments, see ASL, *Wilson*, vol. 2, pp. 16–19.

19. EMHD, entry for Dec. 12, 1912, *PWW*, vol. 25, p. 610.

20. EMHD, entry for Aug. 16, 1913, *PWW*, vol. 28, p. 178.

21. JD to NDB, Feb. 3, 1936, NDB Papers, box 62, LC.

22. WW to EBG, Aug. 28, 1915, *PWW*, vol. 34, pp. 352–53.

23. EMHD, entry for Jan. 8, 1913, *PWW*, vol. 27, p. 21.

24. EMHD, entries for Jan. 8, 1913; Feb. 23, 1913, *PWW*, vol. 27, pp. 23, 130.

25. Helen Woodrow Bones to Jesse Bones Brower, Feb. 12, 1913, *PWW*, vol. 27, p. 553.

26. On the proposed amendment and Wilson's response, see ASL, *Wilson*, vol. 2, pp. 22–23, and *PWW*, vol. 27, p. 101, n. 1.

27. WW to A. Mitchell Palmer, Feb. 5, 1913, *PWW*, vol. 27, pp. 98–101.

28. On the handling of the amendment, see ASL, *Wilson*, vol. 2, p. 23.

29. WHT to EAW, Jan. 3, 1913, *PWW*, vol. 27, p. 12; WHT to WW, Jan. 6, 1913, *PWW*, vol. 27, pp. 16–18. See also Frances Wright Saunders, *Ellen Axson Wilson: First Lady between Two Worlds* (Chapel Hill, N.C., 1985), pp. 232–344.

30. WW to MAHP, Mar. 2, 1913, *PWW*, vol. 27, p. 146. For descriptions of the departure, see ASL, *Wilson*, vol. 2, pp. 55–56, and Saunders, *Ellen Axson Wilson*, pp. 237–38. For a recollection of the event by an eyewitness who was then a Princeton freshman, see Hamilton Fish Armstrong, *Peace and Counterpeace: From Wilson to Hitler* (New York, 1971), p. 15.

10 BEGINNINGS

1. For descriptions of the inauguration, see New York *World*, Mar. 5, 1913; *New York Times*, Mar. 5, 1913.

2. WW inaugural address, Mar. 4, 1913, *PWW*, vol. 27, pp. 148–52.

3. For a description of the family's first evening in the White House, see Frances Wright Saunders, *Ellen Axson Wilson: First Lady between Two Worlds* (Chapel Hill, N.C., 1985), p. 239.

4. See Saunders, *Ellen Axson Wilson*, pp. 218–19, 239–42, 250–51.

5. For Ellen's activities and the toll on her health, see Saunders, *Ellen Axson Wilson*, pp. 242–48.

6. For descriptions of Wilson's office routine and workday, see John M. Blum, *Joe Tumulty and the Wilson Era* (Boston, 1951), pp. 58–60, and ASL, *Wilson*, vol. 2, *The New Freedom* (Princeton, N.J., 1956), p. 72.

7. Enclosure, John Reed to JPT, June 30, 1914, *PWW*, vol. 30, pp. 232–33. This interview did not appear in print. The editors of *The Papers of Woodrow Wilson* speculate that Wilson may have refused permission to publish it because he spoke too frankly about Mexico. *PWW*, vol. 30, p. 231, n. 2.

8. WW statement, Mar. 22, 1913, *PWW*, vol. 50, pp. 3–5. For an account of the first press conference, see Robert C. Hilderbrand, *Power and the People: Executive Management of Public Opinion in Foreign Affairs, 1897–1921* (Chapel Hill, N.C., 1981), pp. 95–96.

9. Press conference, Mar. 19, 1914, *PWW*, vol. 50, pp. 418–19. No transcripts of the press conferences were made for nearly seventy years, until the editors of *The Papers of Woodrow Wilson* had Charles Swem's shorthand notebooks transcribed.

10. Richard V. Oulahan to RSB, Mar. 15, 1929, RSBP, box 112.

11. On the cessation of the press conferences, see Hilderbrand, *Power and the People*, p. 103.

12. JD, *The Wilson Era*, vol. 1, *Years of Peace, 1910–1917* (Chapel Hill, N.C., 1944), pp. 136–37.

13. JDD, entry for Apr. 11, 1913, *PWW*, vol. 27, p. 291.

14. On the effort to introduce segregation and the appointment of African Americans, see ASL, *Wilson*, vol 2, pp. 246–52; Kathleen Long Wolgemuth, "Woodrow Wilson's Appointment Policy and the Negro," *Journal of Southern History* 24 (Nov. 1958), pp. 457–71, and Morton Sosna, "The South in the Saddle: Racial Politics During the Wilson Years," *Wisconsin Magazine of History* 54 (1970), pp. 30–49.

15. Oscar Garrison Villard to WW, July 21, 1913, *PWW*, vol. 28, pp. 60–61; WW to Villard, July 23, 1913, *PWW*, vol. 28, p. 64.

16. John Palmer Gavit to Villard, Oct. 1, 1913, *PWW*, vol. 28, pp. 349–50; WW statement, Nov. 6, 1913, *PWW*, vol. 28, pp. 496–99.

17. The ascribing of blame to Franklin K. Lane first appeared in RSB, *Woodrow Wilson: Life and Letters*, vol. 4, *President, 1913–1914* (Garden City, N.Y., 1931), pp. 297–98, and was based on interviews with several cabinet members. It is also supported by McAdoo in his memoir, *Crowded Years: The Reminiscences of William G. McAdoo* (Boston, 1931), pp. 193–94. This interpretation is followed in ASL, *Wilson*, vol. 2, p. 75. It is disputed in Keith W. Olson, *Biography of a Progressive: Franklin K. Lane, 1864–1921* (Westport, Conn., 1979), pp. 122–24. Olson notes the lack of direct evidence of Wilson's reaction and Lane's not having the only loose tongue in the cabinet.

18. The stationery struck at least one New York acquaintance of House's as an affectation. Hamilton Fish Armstrong, who later knew the colonel through the Council on Foreign Relations and the magazine *Foreign Affairs*, observed: "He prided himself on the variety of his contacts and the fact that they were spread all across the country and were not limited to the Eastern seaboard. Long after he had installed himself definitely in New York, his notepaper was still embossed, 'Edward M. House, Austin, Texas.'" Armstrong, *Peace and Counterpeace: From Wilson to Hitler* (New York, 1971), p. 446.

19. EMHD, entry for Dec. 2, 1913, *PWW*, vol. 29, p. 12.

20. CTG, interviews by RSB, Feb. 18–19, 1926, RSBP, box 106.

21. WW to EAW, Aug. 10, 1913, *PWW*, vol. 28, pp. 133–34. On Cary Grayson's care for Ellen, see Saunders, *Ellen Axson Wilson*, p. 248. The Wilsons evidently chose not to attend the New York Avenue Presbyterian Church, which was nearer the White House, because it was affiliated with the northern branch of the denomination.

22. Eleanor Wilson McAdoo, *The Woodrow Wilsons* (New York: 1937), p. 240. On Grayson's early care for Wilson and Wilson's difficulty with golf, see Edwin A. Weinstein, *Woodrow Wilson: A Medical and Psychological Biography* (Princeton, N.J., 1981), pp. 251–52.

23. EMHD, entry for Aug. 16, 1913, *PWW*, vol. 28, p. 178. On the intraparty problems in New York and elsewhere, see ASL, *Wilson*, vol. 2, pp. 164–68.

24. On diplomatic appointments, see ASL, *Wilson*, vol. 2, pp. 98–110.

25. WW statement, Mar. 12, 1913, *PWW*, vol. 27, p. 172.

26. WW statement, Mar. 18, 1913, *PWW*, vol. 27, pp. 193–94.

27. WW message to president of China, U.S. Department of State, *Papers Relating to the Foreign Relations of the United States, 1913* (Washington, 1920), p. 110.

28. WW to James D. Phelan, Apr. 9, 1913, *PWW*, vol. 27, p. 277. On the effect of the withdrawal from the loan consortium, see Tien-yi Li, *Woodrow Wilson's China Policy, 1913–1917* (New York, 1952), pp. 45–46.

29. On the controversy with Japan, see ASL, *Wilson*, vol. 2, pp. 288–304.
30. WW, *Constitutional Government in the United States, PWW*, vol. 18, pp. 120, 121.

11   TAKEN AT THE FLOOD

1. JDD, entry for Apr. 8, 1913, *PWW*, vol. 27, p. 268; WW speech, Apr. 8, 1913, *PWW*, vol. 27, pp. 269–70.
2. Eleanor Wilson McAdoo, *The Woodrow Wilsons* (New York, 1937), p. 248.
3. Albert S. Burleson, interviews by RSB, Mar. 17–19, 1927, RSBP, box 103.
4. Burleson, interviews by RSB, Mar. 17–19, 1927, RSBP, box 103.
5. WW speeches, Apr. 14, 1913; May 2, 1913, *PWW*, vol. 27, pp. 307, 394; *Financial World*, Apr. 12, 1913, quoted in ASL, *Wilson*, vol. 2, *The New Freedom* (Princeton, N.J., 1956), p. 155.
6. WW to MAH, Sept. 21, 1913, *PWW*, vol. 28, p. 311; WW speech, Apr. 8, 1913, *PWW*, vol. 27, pp. 270–71.
7. WW press statement, May 26, 1913, *PWW*, vol. 27, p. 473.
8. *La Follette's Weekly*, July 12, 1913, p. 1. On reaction to the statement and the investigation, see ASL, *Wilson*, vol. 2, pp. 187–90.
9. WW to Furnifold Simmons, Sept. 4, 1913, *PWW*, vol. 28, p. 254.
10. WW statement, Oct. 3, 1913, *PWW*, vol. 28, p. 351.
11. EAW to WW, Oct. 5, 1913, *PWW*, vol. 28, pp. 363–64.
12. WW to MAH, June 22, 1913, *PWW*, vol. 28, p. 556.
13. William Gibbs McAdoo to EMH, June 18, 1913, EMH Papers, Yale University Library. On the June 17 meeting, see also *New York Times*, June 18, 1913, and New York *World*, June 18, 1913. On the positions and machinations of the various actors, see ASL, *Wilson*, vol. 2, pp. 206–11.
14. Louis Brandeis to WW, June 14, 1913, *PWW*, vol. 27, pp. 520–21; WW press conference, June 16, 1913, *PWW*, vol. 27, p. 522.
15. WW speech, June 23, 1913, *PWW*, vol. 27, pp. 570–73. On the meetings at the White House, see ASL, *Wilson*, vol. 2, pp. 212–14.
16. New York *Sun*, June 21, 1913, quoted in ASL, *Wilson*, vol. 2, p. 216; WW quoted in Carter Glass, *An Adventure in Constructive Finance* (Garden City, N.Y., 1927), p. 116. On the bankers' and conservative opposition, see ASL, *Wilson*, vol. 2, pp. 214–18.
17. WW to EAW, July 27, 1913, *PWW*, vol. 28, p. 85. On the revolt of the agrarians, see ASL, *Wilson*, vol. 2, pp. 218–22.
18. On the House maneuvering and the bankers' opposition, see ASL, *Wilson*, vol. 2, pp. 222–27, and Glass, *Adventure in Constructive Finance*, pp. 139–40.
19. WW to EAW, Sept. 9, 1913, in *PWW*, vol. 28, pp. 267–68; WW to MAH, Sept. 28, 1913, *PWW*, vol. 28, pp. 336–37. Gilbert Hitchcock headed the faction of Nebraska Democrats that opposed Bryan, and he kept up a relentless battle with the secretary over patronage in that state. James O'Gorman was a Tammany man, and despite being Dudley Field Malone's father-in-law, he resented Wilson's friendliness toward the machine's reformist opponents. James Reed, a flowery orator and ally of the machine in his hometown of Kansas City, also conducted patronage fights with the administration.
20. WW to Oscar W. Underwood, Oct. 20, 1913, *PWW*, vol. 28, p. 419. On the meeting with the senators, see *New York Times*, Oct. 17, 1913, and New York *World*, Oct. 17, 1913.
21. WW to Frank A. Vanderlip, Oct. 24, 1913, *PWW*, vol. 28, p. 430. On the Vanderlip plan and its presentation, see ASL, *Wilson*, vol. 2, pp. 231–34.

22. On the last debates and final passage of the Federal Reserve Act, see ASL, *Wilson*, vol. 2, pp. 234–37.

23. WW speech, Dec. 23, 1913, *PWW*, vol. 29, pp. 63–66.

24. Formally, there were two sessions, the first, which adjourned in November 1913, and the second, which began in December. In fact, Congress had never taken such a brief recess between sessions before.

25. On how Glass's approach came out, see *Adventure in Constructive Finance*, pp. 124–25. A decade later, under Republican presidents, the Federal Reserve Bank of New York would effectively become the nation's central bank, and its chairman—a collaborator of Vanderlip's in 1913 with the fitting surname of Strong—would become a European-style central banker.

26. For an excellent characterization and analysis of these approaches, see Marc Winerman, "The Origins of the FTC: Concentration, Cooperation, Control, and Competition," *Antitrust Law Journal* 71, no. 1 (2003), pp. 15–48.

27. WW to MAH, Oct. 12, 1913, *PWW*, vol. 28, p. 395; WW address, Dec. 2, 1913, *PWW*, vol. 29, p. 7.

28. WW address, Jan. 20, 1914, *PWW*, vol. 29, pp. 153–58.

29. On Wilson's desire for flexibility and his divergent thoughts, see WW to John Sharp Williams, Jan. 27, 1914, *PWW*, vol. 29, pp. 184–85.

30. On the final vote, see *New York Times*, June 6, 1914. Nearly all of the Republicans voting for the bill were insurgents from the Midwest and West; one Progressive, from New York, opposed the bill.

31. On Wilson's meeting with labor leaders and his refusal to go further, see *New York World*, Apr. 14, 1914; May 1, 1914.

32. Samuel Gompers to WW, Oct. 16, 1914, *PWW*, vol. 31, p. 168. On the Senate's actions and Gompers's reaction, see ASL, *Wilson*, vol. 2, pp. 432–33.

33. On the Senate action and final passage, see ASL, *Wilson*, vol. 2, pp. 442–44. On the first Senate vote, every Democrat favored the bill, joined by seven Republicans and one Progressive. On the second vote, three Democrats broke ranks—Harry Lane of Oregon, James Martine of New Jersey, and James Reed of Missouri—and all the Republicans who voted were opposed.

34. See George Rublee, "The Original Plan and Early History of the Federal Trade Commission," *Proceedings of the Academy of Political Science* 11 (Jan. 1926), p. 116, and ASL, *Wilson*, vol. 2, pp. 425–26.

35. Norman Hapgood to WW, Apr. 21, 1914, *PWW*, vol. 29, pp. 481–82. Why Brandeis did not involve himself more in advising Wilson on the anti-trust issue is a matter of disagreement among scholars. Thomas K. McCraw argues that this was an "abdication" on Brandeis's part. McCraw, *Prophets of Regulation: Charles Francis Adams, Louis D. Brandeis, James M. Landis, Alfred E. Kahn* (Cambridge, Mass., 1984), p. 122. McCraw offers no explanation, however, for Brandeis's behavior. The historian of the Federal Trade Commission, Marc Winerman, believes that Hapgood was correct in saying that Brandeis was simply too busy with other matters to advise Wilson closely. See Winerman, "Origins of the FTC," p. 66, n. 398. On Rublee, see Marc Eric McClure, *Earnest Endeavors: The Life and Public Work of George Rublee* (Westport, Conn., 2003).

36. WW to Henry F. Hollis, June 2, 1914, *PWW*, vol. 29, p. 134. On Murdock's criticisms of the Covington bill and later support of the Stevens bill, see Winerman, "Origins of the FTC," pp. 60–62. Starting late in 1913, Colonel House had been wooing one of the Progressives' leading publicists and financial backers, William Rockhill Nelson, owner of *The Kansas City Star.* See EMHD, entry for Jan. 16, 1914, *PWW*, vol. 29, p. 135.

37. George Rublee memoir, Dec. 1950–Feb. 1951, pp. 112–14, Microfiche Collection, Oral History Research Office, Columbia University Libraries; WW to Charles A. Culberson, July 30, 1914, *PWW*, vol. 29, p. 320.

38. WW to William C. Adamson, Aug. 5, 1914, *PWW*, vol. 30, pp. 348–49. On the votes, see Winerman, "Origins of the FTC," pp. 90, 91–92. On final passage of the Federal Trade Commission bill, see ASL, *Wilson*, vol. 2, pp. 440–42.

39. WW to Oscar W. Underwood, Oct. 17, 1914, *PWW*, vol. 31, pp. 170–71.

40. On the early history of the FTC, see Winerman, "Origins of the FTC," pp. 93–97.

41. Winerman, "Origins of the FTC," p. 93. McCraw also uses the term "rocky start" and stresses the ambiguity of the agency's charter. See *Prophets of Regulation*, p. 125. Among historians, the leading proponent of the "reluctant progressive" view of Wilson is Arthur Link in his earlier work. See "The South and the 'New Freedom,'" *American Scholar* 20 (summer 1951), pp. 314–24, and *Woodrow Wilson and the Progressive Era, 1910–1917* (New York, 1954), esp. pp. 80, 224–25. In the volume of his larger work that treats this legislation, he modifies this view. See *Wilson*, vol. 2, pp. 241–42, 444, 471. In one of the later volumes, *Wilson*, vol. 3, *The Struggle for Neutrality, 1914–1915* (Princeton, N.J., 1960), pp. 322–23, he downplays the view, and in the final volume, *Wilson*, vol. 5, *Campaigns for Progressivism and Peace, 1916–1917* (Princeton, N.J., 1965), he abandons it altogether.

42. *New Republic*, Jan. 9, 1915, p. 8; Winerman, "Origins of the FTC," p. 48. The claim of Wilson's gradual conversion to the New Nationalism is advanced by Link in the works cited in n. 41, above.

12 TRIUMPH AND TRAGEDY

1. JDD, entry for Apr. 18, 1913, *PWW*, vol. 27, pp. 331–32.

2. Ibid. On British policy toward Mexico and the influence of oil interests there, see Peter Calvert, *The Mexican Revolution, 1910–1914: The Diplomacy of Anglo-American Conflict* (Cambridge, U.K., 1968).

3. Memorandum enclosed with Delbert J. Haff to WW, May 12, 1913, *PWW*, vol. 27, pp. 419–25.

4. WW press conference, May 26, 1913, *PWW*, vol. 27, p. 471.

5. William Bayard Hale report, July 9, 1913, *PWW*, vol. 28, p. 31. There was also a secret mission by a friend of William Jennings Bryan's to make contact with and assess the Constitutionalists, but it turned into a fiasco. See ASL, *Wilson*, vol. 2, *The New Freedom* (Princeton, N.J., 1956), p. 355.

6. Hale report, July 9, 1913, *PWW*, vol. 28, p. 33.

7. WW instructions, [Aug. 4, 1913], *PWW*, vol 28, p. 110.

8. WW speech, Aug. 27, 1913, *PWW*, vol. 28, pp. 227–31.

9. WW to EAW, Sept. 9, 1913, *PWW*, vol. 28, p. 268; WW draft diplomatic note, Oct. 24, 1913, *PWW*, vol. 28, pp. 431–32.

10. On William Tyrrell's meeting with Wilson, see EMHD, entries for Nov. 12 and 13, 1913, *PWW*, vol. 28, pp. 530–33; Tyrrell to Sir Edward Grey, Nov. 14, 1913, *PWW*, vol. 28, pp. 543–45.

11. WW speech, Dec. 2, 1913, *PWW*, vol. 29, pp. 4–5; EMHD, entry for Oct. 30, 1913, *PWW*, vol. 28, p. 478.

12. On these developments, see ASL, *Wilson*, vol. 2, pp. 382–92.

13. WW press conference, Nov. 14, 1914, *PWW*, vol. 32, p. 351. On this incident and its repercussions, see Robert E. Quirk, *An Affair of Honor: Woodrow Wilson and the Occupation of Vera Cruz* (Lexington, Ky., 1962).

14. Samuel G. Blythe, "Mexico: The Record of a Conversation with President Wilson," *Saturday Evening Post*, May 23, 1914, *PWW*, vol. 29, pp. 516–17; WW speech, Apr. 20, 1914, *PWW*, vol. 29, pp. 471–74.

15. Venustiano Carranza, quoted in George C. Carothers to WJB, Apr. 22, *PWW*, vol. 29, p. 485. The only Mexican leader who seemed to approve the action was the guileful Pancho Villa, who privately told a State Department agent that "no drunkard, meaning Huerta, was going to draw him into war" and he would try to change Carranza's mind. Carothers to WJB, Apr. 23, 1914, *PWW*, vol. 29, p. 494.

16. H. J. Forman to RSB, RSBP, box 109; WW press conference, Apr. 23, 1914, *PWW*, vol. 29, p. 511.

17. For a sample of reactions, see ASL, *Wilson*, vol. 2, pp. 403–7.

18. New York *World*, May 19, 1914; WW to Lindley M. Garrison, Aug. 8, 1914, *PWW*, vol. 30, p. 362.

19. For this characterization, see Samuel G. Blythe, "A Talk with the President," *Saturday Evening Post*, Jan. 9, 1915, *PWW*, vol. 30, pp. 402–3: "He showed me why a writer was wrong who said he could not be a progressive Democrat if he admired Edmund Burke." Unfortunately, Blythe did not record how Wilson explained his synthesis of Burke and progressivism.

20. WJB to WW, Aug. 16, 1913, *PWW*, vol. 28, p. 176; TR to William J. Stone, July 11, 1914, in TR, *Letters*, ed. Elting E. Morison, vol. 7, *The Days of Armageddon, 1900–1914* (Cambridge, Mass., 1954), p. 777. Ironically, in 1921, after Roosevelt's death, Lodge would manage Senate approval of a similar treaty under Wilson's successor, a Republican—a treaty that dropped mention of regret but paid the same indemnity and had strong backing from American oil interests. On the Colombian treaty, see ASL, *Wilson*, vol. 2, pp. 321–24.

21. WW speech, Oct. 27, 1913, *PWW*, vol. 28, pp. 448–51.

22. EMHD, entry for Dec. 16, 1914, *PWW*, vol. 31, p. 469; WW draft of Pan-American pact, [Dec, 16, 1914], *PWW*, vol. 30, pp. 471–72. On the Pan-American pact, see Thomas J. Knock, *To End All Wars: Woodrow Wilson and the Quest for a New World Order* (New York, 1992), pp. 39–45. On James Slayden, see Ellen Maury Slayden, *Washington Wife: Journal of Ellen Maury Slayden from 1897–1919* (New York, 1963).

23. New York *World*, Aug. 3, 1913. On the Nicaraguan affair, see ASL, *Wilson*, vol. 2, pp. 331–46.

24. On Wilson's involvement in the Dominican affair, see ASL, *Wilson*, vol. 2, pp. 496–516, 538–48.

25. WW to RL, Aug. 4, 1915, *PWW*, vol. 34, p. 78. On the Haitian affair, see ASL, *Wilson*, vol. 3, *The Struggle for Neutrality, 1914–1915* (Princeton, N.J., 1960), pp. 516–38.

26. For the phrase and the interpretation, see ASL, *Woodrow Wilson and the Progressive Era, 1910–1917* (New York, 1954), pp. 81–106.

27. WW statement, Aug. 29, 1916, *PWW*, vol. 38, p. 102. On the legislative wrangle and passage of the Jones Act, see ASL, *Wilson*, vol. 4, *Confusion and Crises, 1915–1916* (Princeton, N.J., 1960), pp. 351–56.

28. WW to Walter Page, Jan. 6, 1914, *PWW*, vol. 29, p. 104.

29. WW to William L. Marbury, Feb. 5, 1914, *PWW*, vol. 29, p. 220; WW speech to Congress, Mar. 5, 1914, *PWW*, vol. 29, pp. 312–13. On congressional repeal of the tolls exemption, see ASL, *Wilson*, vol. 2, pp. 311–14.

30. WW speech, June 13, 1914, *PWW*, vol. 30, p. 177; WW to James Bryce, July 6, 1914, *PWW*, vol. 30, p. 260.

31. EMH to WW, May 29, 1914; June 19, 1914; July 3, 1914, *PWW*, vol. 30, pp. 109, 189–90, 247–48.

32. WW to EMH, June 16 and 23, 1914, *PWW*, vol. 30, pp. 187, 201; EMHD, entry for Aug. 30, 1914, *PWW*, vol. 30, p. 465.

33. WW to John Sharp Williams, Apr. 2, 1914, *PWW*, vol. 29, p. 394. On the Terrell appointment, see George C. Osborn, "Woodrow Wilson Appoints a Negro Judge," *Journal of Southern History* 24 (Nov. 1958), pp. 481–93. On Wilson's broader appointments record, see Kathleen Long Wolgemuth, "Woodrow Wilson's Appointment Policy and the Negro," *Journal of Southern History* 24 (Nov. 1958), pp. 457–71.

34. WW remarks, June 30, 1914, *PWW*, vol. 30, pp. 226–28.

35. WW speech, May 11, 1914, *PWW*, vol. 30, p. 14.

36. Arthur Krock memorandum of conversation with WW, Apr. 30, 1915, Henry Watterson Papers, LC. For an account of this complicated and sometimes ludicrous situation, see ASL, *Wilson*, vol. 2, pp. 259–60. The veto of the Volstead Act occurred after Wilson's stroke. Tumulty wrote the veto message, and there is some question about whether Wilson was aware of the action. Mrs. Wilson did review and approve the veto message, and it was consistent with his views.

37. WW speech, Dec. 2, 1913, *PWW*, vol. 29, p. 5.

38. Wilson later shifted his stands on this issue and child labor. Interestingly, Arthur Link is less categorical in viewing his position on rural credits as insufficiently progressive: "Wilson would not adhere forever to New Freedom doctrines that denied the demands of the organized farmers, politically the most powerful pressure group in the United States." ASL, *Wilson*, vol. 2, p. 264.

39. WW speech, June 25, 1914, *PWW*, vol. 30, pp. 211–12; WW to Frank E. Doremus, Sept. 4, 1914, *PWW*, vol. 30, pp. 475–76; EMHD, entry for Sept. 28, 1914, *PWW*, vol. 31, p. 94.

40. On passage of the seamen's act, see ASL, *Wilson*, vol. 2, pp. 269–72, and Belle Case La Follette and Fola La Follette, *Robert M. La Follette, June 14, 1855–June 18, 1925* (New York, 1953), vol. 1, pp. 521–35.

41. WW quoted in La Follette and La Follette, *Robert La Follette*, vol. 1, pp. 535–36; WW to NDB, Mar. 5, 1915, *PWW*, vol. 32, p. 324.

42. WW speeches, Mar. 20, 1914; May 29, 1914; June 13, 1914, *PWW*, vol. 29, pp. 362–64; vol. 30, pp. 107–8, 177.

43. WW speech, July 4, 1914, *PWW*, vol. 30, pp. 248–55.

44. For Wilson's borrowing from the Library of Congress, see William W. Bishop to WW, Nov. 14, 1914, *PWW*, vol. 31, pp. 316–17. Given the pressures on him in the fall of 1914, it is doubtful that he read all or many of the books Bishop listed, but the list does show where his interests ran.

45. On the summer in Cornish, see Frances Wright Saunders, *Ellen Axson Wilson: First Lady between Two Worlds* (Chapel Hill, N.C., 1985), pp. 249–60. Harlakenden was owned by the popular novelist and Progressive Party activist Winston Churchill—no relation to the rising British political star of the same name.

46. WW to EAW, July 27, 1914, *PWW*, vol. 28, p. 84; EAW to WW, July 28, 1914, *PWW*, vol. 28, p. 91.

47. *New York Times*, Nov. 26, 1913.

48. EMHD, entry for Nov. 29, 1913, *PWW*, vol. 28, p. 596. See also *New York Times*, Nov. 30, 1913.

49. WW to Benjamin M. King, Mar. 22, 1914, *PWW*, vol. 29, p. 371. On Ellen's health, see Saunders, *Ellen Axson Wilson*, pp. 267–69, 270–71.

50. EAW to Jessie Wilson Sayre, Feb. 20, 1914, quoted in Saunders, *Ellen Axson Wilson*, p. 270. On the romance and engagement, see pp. 268–70.

51. *New York Times*, May 8, 1914; WW to MAH, May 10, 1914, *PWW*, vol. 30, p. 12. See

also Eleanor Wilson McAdoo, *The Woodrow Wilsons* (New York, 1937), pp. 285–87, and Saunders, *Ellen Axson Wilson*, pp. 271–72.

52. McAdoo, *Crowded Years: The Reminiscences of William G. McAdoo* (Boston, 1931), pp. 521, 525.

53. SA, *Brother Woodrow: A Memoir of Woodrow Wilson* (Princeton, N.J., 1993), p. 218.

54. McAdoo, *Crowded Years*, p. 512.

55. WW to MAH, July 12, 1914, *PWW*, vol. 30, p. 277. On the final weeks of Ellen's illness, see Saunders, *Ellen Axson Wilson*, pp. 273–76.

56. *New York Times*, Aug. 7, 1914; CTG, interviews by RSB, Feb. 18–19, 1926, RSBP, box 106.

57. McAdoo, *The Wilsons*, pp. 300–301.

58. WW to MAH, [Aug. 7, 1914], *PWW*, vol. 30, p. 357. A moving tribute to Ellen came sixty-five years later, when the editors of *The Papers of Woodrow Wilson* stated in their preface, "In this volume, we say farewell to Ellen Axson Wilson, whom, over the years we have come to know, admire, and love." *PWW*, vol. 30, p. viii.

13   IRONY AND THE GIFT OF FATE

1. Henry James to Howard Sturgis, Aug. 5, 1914, in Henry James, *The Letters of Henry James*, vol. 2, ed. Percy Lubbock (New York, 1920), p. 384; *New York Times*, Sept. 27, 1914. For a survey of American reactions to the outbreak of World War I that is both comprehensive and incisive, see ASL, *Wilson*, vol. 3, *The Struggle for Neutrality, 1914–1915* (Princeton, N.J., 1960), pp. 1–56.

2. For a description of the funeral services and burial, see Frances Wright Saunders, *Ellen Axson Wilson: First Lady between Two Worlds* (Chapel Hill, N.C., 1985), pp. 276–79.

3. WW to MAH, Aug, 23, 1914, *PWW*, vol. 30, p. 437; Walter Page to WW, July 29, 1914, *PWW*, vol. 30, p. 316. On Hoover's work, see George H. Nash, *The Life of Herbert Hoover*, vol. 2, *The Humanitarian, 1914–1917* (New York, 1988), pp. 3–14.

4. WW statement, [Aug. 18, 1914], *PWW*, vol. 30, p. 394.

5. On the economic issues, see ASL, *Wilson*, vol. 3, pp. 76–91.

6. WJB to WW, Aug. 10, 1914, *PWW*, vol. 30, p. 372; *New York Times*, Aug. 16, 1914.

7. On the reversal of the loan ban, see Vanderlip testimony, Jan. 7, 1936, U.S. Senate, *Hearings before the Special Committee on Investigation of the Munitions Industry*, 73rd Congress (Washington, D.C., 1936), esp. pp. 7529–31, and Charles A. Beard, "New Light on Bryan and the Wilson War Policies," *New Republic* June 17, 1936, pp. 177–78. The committee before which Vanderlip testified was the Senate subcommittee chaired by Gerald Nye of North Dakota and popularly known as the Nye Committee.

8. EMHD, entry for Sept. 27, 1914, *PWW*, vol. 31, pp. 86–87.

9. EMHD, entry for Sept. 30, 1914, *PWW*, vol. 31, p. 109; SA, interviews by RSB, Feb. 8, 10, and 11, 1925, RSBP, box 99.

10. Sir Cecil Spring-Rice to Sir Edward Grey, Oct. 1, 1914, *PWW*, vol. 31, p. 118. See also George M. Trevelyan, *Grey of Fallodon: The Life and Letters of Sir Edward Grey* (Boston, 1937), pp. 351–52, and ASL, *Wilson*, vol. 3, pp. 117–32.

11. EMHD, entry for Nov. 6, 1914, *PWW*, vol 31, p. 320,

12. EMH to WW, Dec. 26, 1914, *PWW*, vol. 31, p. 535.

13. WW to Nancy Saunders Toy, Dec. 12, 1914, *PWW*, vol. 31, p. 455; *New York Times*, Oct. 16, 1914.

14. WW press conference, Oct. 19, 1914, *PWW*, vol. 50, p. 613; *New York Times*, Oct. 20, 1914; WW speech, Dec. 8, 1914, *PWW*, vol. 31, p. 423. On Wilson's look-

ing Gardner in the eye, see Gus J. Karger to WHT, July 27, 1915, WHTP, box 316 (general correspondence). On the response to Wilson's declaration, see ASL, *Wilson*, vol. 3, pp. 140–43, and John Milton Cooper, Jr., *The Vanity of Power: American Isolationism and the First World War, 1914–1917* (Westport, Conn., 1969), pp. 23–25.

15. For the survey of editorial opinion, see *Literary Digest*, Nov. 14, 1914, pp. 939–41, 974–78. There was considerable regional variation in sentiment, with the South and Northeast registering the strongest pro-Allied feelings. In no region did sentiment favoring the Central powers (pro-German sentiment) register above 9 percent.

16. EMHD, entry for Aug. 30, 1914, *PWW*, vol. 30, pp. 462–63; Sir Cecil Spring-Rice to Sir Edward Grey, Sept. 3, 1914, *PWW*, vol. 30, p. 472; WW to WJB, Sept. 4, 1914, *PWW*, vol. 30, p. 476.

17. *Literary Digest*, Nov. 14, 1914, p. 939; *New Republic*, Jan. 9, 1915, p. 3. For the assessment of public sentiment, see Mark Sullivan, *Our Times: The United States, 1900–1925*, vol. 5 (New York, 1926), p. 59. On the arms-embargo drive, see ASL, *Wilson*, vol. 3, pp. 163–70, and Cooper, *Vanity of Power*, pp. 28–32.

18. Bryan may have reacted so readily against the idea because of past clashes in Nebraska with brewing interests over prohibition and because his home-state foe, Senator Gilbert Hitchcock, was sponsoring an embargo resolution. For the vote on the embargo amendment, see 63rd Cong., 3rd Sess., *Congressional Record* 4916 (Feb. 15, 1915).

19. WW speech, Jan. 8, 1915, *PWW*, vol. 32, p. 33. On the ship-purchase fight, see ASL, *Wilson*, vol. 3, pp. 143–60.

20. William Monroe Trotter statement, Nov. 12, 1914, *PWW*, vol. 31, p. 300; transcript of meeting, Nov. 12, 1914, *PWW*, vol. 31, pp. 301–8.

21. *New York Times*, Nov. 13, 1914; JD to Franklin D. Roosevelt, June 10, 1933, quoted in *PWW*, vol. 3, p. 309, n. 2. The exchange between Trotter and Wilson survived only because Wilson had his stenographer, Charles Swem, record what was said. No published transcript would appear until the editors of *The Papers of Woodrow Wilson* deciphered Swem's shorthand sixty-five years later.

22. WW remarks, [Dec. 15, 1914], *PWW*, vol. 31, pp. 464–65.

23. Thomas Dixon to JPT, May 1, 1915, *PWW*, vol. 32, p. 142, n. 5.

24. The "history with lightning" remark appeared in Milton MacKaye, "The Birth of a Nation," *Scribner's Magazine*, Nov. 1937, p. 69. The recollection of the last survivor of the showing, Marjorie Brown King, comes from an interview by Arthur Link. See *PWW*, vol. 32, p. 267, n. 1.

25. WW to JPT, Apr. [24 and] 28, 1915, *PWW*, vol. 33, pp. 68, 86; WW to JPT, [ca. Apr. 22, 1918], *PWW*, vol. 47, p. 388, n. 3.

26. TR to William Allen White, Nov. 7, 1914, TR, *Letters*, ed. Elting E. Morison, vol. 8, *The Days of Armageddon, 1900–1914* (Cambridge, Mass., 1954), p. 836.

27. WW to Nancy Saunders Toy, Nov. 9, 1914; Jan. 31, 1915, *PWW*, vol. 31, p. 290, vol. 32, pp. 165–66; WW speeches, Dec. 8, 1914; Jan. 8, 1915, *PWW*, vol. 31, pp. 420–21; vol. 32, pp. 30–36.

28. On the *Dacia* affair, see Ross Gregory, "A New Look at the Case of the *Dacia*," *Journal of American History* 55 (Sept. 1968), pp. 292–96. On the Asian controversy, see ASL, *Wilson*, vol. 3, pp. 267–308.

29. The best discussions in English of the background to the submarine declaration are ASL, *Wilson*, vol. 3, pp. 309–20, and Ernest R. May, *The World War and American Isolation, 1914–1917* (Cambridge, Mass., 1959), pp. 113–22.

30. WJB to James W. Gerard, Feb. 10, 1915, *PWW*, vol. 32, pp. 208–9; WW to MAH, Feb. 14, 1915, *PWW*, vol. 32, p. 233. For an analysis of "strict accountability," see May, *World War and American Isolation*, pp. 137–42.

31. Herbert B. Brougham, memorandum, Dec. 14, 1914, *PWW*, vol. 31, pp. 458–59.

32. SA, interviews by RSB, Feb. 8, 10, and 11, 1925, RSBP, box 99. I agree with Thomas Knock in dating this statement February 1915, not August 1914. See Thomas J. Knock, *To End All Wars: Woodrow Wilson and the Quest for a New World Order* (New York, 1992), pp. 35–36.

33. EMHD, entry for Jan. 25, 1915, *PWW*, vol. 32, p. 121; WW to EMH, Jan. 29, 1915, *PWW*, vol. 32, pp. 157–58.

34. WW to WJB, Apr. 3, 1915, *PWW*, vol. 32, pp. 486–89; WJB to WW, Apr. 6 and 7, 1915, *PWW*, vol. 32, pp. 487, 489–90.

35. WW speech, Apr. 20, 1915, *PWW*, vol. 33, pp. 38–40.

36. WW to WJB, Apr. 22, 1915, *PWW*, vol. 33, pp. 61–62, 81; WJB to WW, Apr. 23, 1915, *PWW*, vol. 33, p. 67.

37. Nancy Saunders Toy diary, entry for Jan. 3, 1915, *PWW*, vol. 33, p. 10.

38. EMHD, entry for Jan. 13, 1915, *PWW*, vol. 33, p. 66; WW to Nancy Saunders Toy, Dec. 12, 1914, *PWW*, vol. 21, p. 455; Toy diary, entry for Jan. 3, 1915, *PWW*, vol. 32, pp. 8–9.

39. WW speech, [Oct. 24, 1914], *PWW*, vol. 31, p. 221.

40. *Memoir*, p. 56. The exact date of the meeting is not known.

41. On Edith Galt's background, see *Memoir*, pp. 1–20, and Phyllis Lee Levin, *Edith and Woodrow: The Wilson White House* (New York, 2001), p. 58.

42. *Memoir*, p. 22. See also Levin, *Edith and Woodrow*, pp. 58–73.

43. CTG, *Woodrow Wilson: An Intimate Memoir* (New York, 1960), p. 50; EBG to Annie Litchfield Bolling, Mar. 23, 1915, *PWW*, vol. 32, p. 423; *Memoir*, p. 58.

44. *Memoir*, pp. 60–61.

45. Ibid., p. 61.

46. EBG to WW, May 4 [*sic*], 1915, *PWW*, vol. 33, pp. 108–10.

47. WW to EBG, May 7, 1915, *PWW*, vol. 33, pp. 124–25.

14   THE SHOCK OF RECOGNITION

1. See Mark Sullivan, *Our Times, 1900–1925*, vol. 5, *Over Here, 1914–1918* (New York, 1933), p. 120, n. 5.

2. WW to WJB, June 7, 1915, *PWW*, vol. 33, p. 349. On the newspaper poll and public reactions, see David Lawrence, *The True Story of Woodrow Wilson* (New York, 1924), pp. 197–98.

3. WW to EBG, [May 8, 1915], *PWW*, vol. 33, p. 129. See also *New York Times*, May 8, 1915; New York *World*, May 8, 1915.

4. For the statement, see *New York Times*, May 10, 1915.

5. Charles E. Swem diary, entry for May 10, [1915], *PWW*, vol. 33, p. 138.

6. WW speech, May 10, 1915, *PWW*, vol. 33, pp. 147–49.

7. WW to EBG, May 11, 1915, *PWW*, vol. 33, p. 162; WW press conference, May 11, 1915, *PWW*, vol. 33, pp. 153–54; Frank Parker Stockbridge memorandum, RSBP, box 11. Wilson tried to unsay the words, after a fashion. In the fall of 1915, when a publisher printed a volume of his presidential speeches, he deleted the sentence that contained "too proud to fight." See *PWW*, vol. 33, p. 149, n. 3

8. EMH to WW, May 9, 1915, *PWW*, vol. 33, p. 134; WW to WJB, May 11, 1915, *PWW*, vol. 33, p. 155; WW draft diplomatic note, [May 11, 1915], *PWW*, vol. 33, pp. 155–58. For an account of the cabinet meeting by Attorney General Thomas Gregory, see EMHD, entry for June 20, 1915, *PWW*, vol. 33, p. 425.

9. WW to WJB, May 13, 1915, *PWW*, vol. 33, pp. 181–82.

10. For accounts of this affair, see EMHD, entry for Nov. 3, 1916, Yale University

Library, Lindley M. Garrison to RSB, Nov. 12, 1928, RSBP, box 1, and memorandum on "postscript," RSB chronology, RSBP, box 63. The speculation that Wilson may have changed his mind on his own comes from Joseph V. Fuller, a historian who advised Ray Stannard Baker.

11. Johann von Bernstorff to Theobald von Bethmann Hollweg, May 29, 1915, *PWW*, vol. 33, p. 283. On Wilson's planting the newspaper stories, see WW to WJB, May 14, 1915, *PWW*, vol. 33, p. 191. For the interpretation of Bernstorff's dispatch by the editors of *The Papers of Woodrow Wilson*, see *PWW*, vol. 33, p. 280, n. 1.

12. EBG to WW, May 24, 1915, *PWW*, vol. 33, p. 249; WW to EBG, May 28, [1915], *PWW*, vol. 33, p. 278. On the encounter in the automobile, see *PWW*, vol. 33, p. 278, n. 1.

13. EBG to WW, [May 28, 1915], *PWW*, vol. 33, pp. 278–79. For Edith's admission of attraction to the presidency, see *Memoir*, p. 62.

14. Johann von Bernstorff to German Foreign Office, June 2, 1915, *PWW*, vol. 33, pp. 318–19.

15. Draft of second *Lusitania* note [June 4, 1915], *PWW*, vol. 33, p. 320; WW to WJB, June 7, 1915, *PWW*, vol. 33, p. 349. For the visit from Senator Martin and Congressman Flood, see WJB to WW, June 4, 1915, *PWW*, vol. 33, p. 337.

16. WJB to WW, June 5, 1915, *PWW*, vol. 33, pp. 342–43; WW to WJB, June 5, 1915, *PWW*, vol. 33, p. 343.

17. EBG to WW, May [June] 5–6, 1915, *PWW*, vol. 33, p. 346; McAdoo, *Crowded Years: The Reminiscences of William G. McAdoo* (Boston, 1931), pp. 337–38.

18. EBG to WW, May [June], 5–6, 1915, *PWW*, vol. 33, p. 346. On Tumulty's advice, see James Kerney, *The Political Education of Woodrow Wilson* (New York, 1926), p. 354.

19. EMHD, entry for June 24, 1915, *PWW*, vol. 33, p. 449. The story about Bryan's spilling the water comes from RSB, *Woodrow Wilson: Life and Letters*, vol. 5, *Neutrality, 1914–1915* (Garden City, N.Y., 1935), p. 356.

20. WJB to George Derby, Aug. 1, 1924, RSBP, box 103; WW, quoted in David F. Houston, *Eight Years with Wilson's Cabinet, 1913 to 1920* (Garden City, N.Y., 1926), vol. 1, p. 141.

21. Grace Bryan Hargreaves manuscript biography of Bryan, WJB Papers, box 65, LC; WJB quoted in Houston, *Wilson's Cabinet*, vol. 1, p. 146.

22. WW to EBG, June 19, 1915, *PWW*, vol. 33, p. 422.

23. SA comments on manuscript of RSB biography of WW, Aug. 29, 1928, RSBP, box 100.

24. WHT to Mabel T. Boardman, May 10, 1915, WHTP, series 8, letterbook 31. For the story of Wilson's holding up his fingers, see Gus J. Karger to WHT, May 12, 1915, WHTP, box 309.

25. EMHD, entries for June 14 and 24, 1915, *PWW*, vol. 33, pp. 397, 449; EMH to WW, June 16, 1915, *PWW*, vol. 33, p. 409. See also Houston, *Wilson's Cabinet*, vol. 1, p. 141.

26. Lansing later wrote that when Wilson offered him the post, he objected that he had no political influence, to which the president replied, "By experience and training you are especially equipped to conduct the foreign affairs of the United States. This, under present conditions, is far more important than political influence." RL, *War Memoirs of Robert Lansing, Secretary of State* (Indianapolis, 1935), p. 16. Lansing was also the son-in-law of John W. Foster, who had served as secretary of state under President Benjamin Harrison. Two of Lansing's nephews, John Foster Dulles and Allen Dulles, would later play large roles in foreign policy.

27. EMHD, entry for June 24, 1915, *PWW*, vol. 33, p. 450.

28. *Memoir*, 71–72.

29. WW to EMH, July 7, 1915, *PWW,* vol. 33, p. 480.

30. Lindley M. Garrison memorandum, July 20, 1916, *PWW,* vol. 33, pp. 536–37; WW to EBG, July 20, 1916, *PWW,* vol. 33, p. 540.

31. WW statement, July 21, 1915, *PWW,* vol. 34, pp. 3–4.

32. *New York Times,* July 25, 1915.

33. On the navy proposals, see ASL, *Wilson,* vol. 4, *Confusion and Crises, 1915–1916* (Princeton, N.J., 1964), p. 15. The best treatment of the cultural conflict and personal divisions surrounding Josephus Daniels is the part memoir, part history of this time by his son, Jonathan Daniels, *The End of Innocence* (Philadelphia, 1954).

34. WW to EBG, Aug. 31, 1915, *PWW,* vol. 34, p. 392. On the army plan, see ASL, *Wilson,* vol. 4, pp. 15–18.

35. WW to EBG, Aug, 5, 1915, *PWW,* vol. 34, p. 101; EBG to WW, Aug. 26, 1915, *PWW,* vol. 34, p. 338.

36. WW to EBG, Aug. 28, 1915, *PWW,* vol. 34, pp. 351–53.

37. EMHD, entry for July 31, 1915, EMH Papers, Yale University Library.

38. On the cotton affair, see ASL, "The Cotton Crisis, the South, and Anglo-American Diplomacy, 1914–1915," in *Studies in Southern History in Memory of Albert Ray Newsome,* ed. J. Carlyle Sitterson (Chapel Hill, N.C., 1957), pp. 122–38. For assessments of public opinion, see *New York Times,* Aug. 20 and 21, 1915, and "The Attack on the Arabic," *Literary Digest,* Aug. 28, 1915, pp. 387–88.

39. New York *World,* Aug. 23, 1915. On the German response, see ASL, *Wilson,* vol. 3, *The Struggle for Neutrality, 1914–1915* (Princeton, N.J., 1960), pp. 570–87.

40. *New York Evening Post,* Sept. 2, 1915.

41. JD, *The Wilson Era,* vol. 1, *Years of Peace, 1910–1917* (Chapel Hill, N.C., 1944), p. 454. For the story of McAdoo's confrontation, see EMHD, entry for Sept. 25, 1915, *PWW,* vol. 34, p. 507. According to Edith's recollection, McAdoo later told her that the story about the anonymous letter had been House's idea. *Memoir,* p. 78.

42. WW shorthand drafts, [ca. Sept. 20, 1915], *PWW,* vol. 34, p. 496; WW to EBG, Sept. 18 and 19, 1915, *PWW,* vol. 34, pp. 489, 491. The editors of *The Papers of Woodrow Wilson* admit that the dating of the shorthand drafts is "somewhat conjectural." *PWW,* vol. 34, p. 497, n. 1.

43. EBG to WW, Sept. 19, 1915, *PWW,* vol. 34, p. 490.

44. WW to EBG, Sept. 19, 1915, *PWW,* vol. 34, p. 492; Edmund W. Starling with Thomas Sugrue, *Starling of the White House: The Story of the Man Whose Secret Service Detail Guarded Five Presidents from Woodrow Wilson to Franklin D. Roosevelt* (New York, 1946), p. 56.

45. EMHD, entries for Sept. 22 and 24, 1915, *PWW,* vol. 34, pp. 506–8, 518; EBG to WW, Sept. 24, *PWW,* vol. 34, p. 518.

46. A good deal of preparation preceded the announcement. Stockton Axson wrote a draft of the statement, and Wilson privately told Mary Hulbert and his friend Edith Gittings Reid in advance. The draft and letters are in *PWW,* vol. 35, pp. 23–24, 153–54.

47. WW statement, Oct. 6, 1915, *PWW,* vol. 35, p. 28.

48. WW to EMH, Sept. 20, 1915, *PWW,* vol. 34, p. 493. On the submarine negotiations, see ASL, *Wilson,* vol. 3, pp. 645–81.

49. On the anti-preparedness activity, see ASL, *Wilson,* vol. 4, pp. 23–33; on Villard's activities, see Oswald Garrison Villard, *Fighting Years: Memoirs of a Liberal Editor* (New York, 1939), p. 308.

50. WW speeches, Oct. 6 and 28, 1915; Nov. 4, 1915, *PWW,* vol. 35, pp. 29, 122–25, 173.

51. WW speech, Dec. 7, 1915, *PWW,* vol. 35, pp. 292–310.

52. WW speeches, Dec. 8 and 10, 1915, *PWW,* vol. 35, pp. 314, 326–27.

53. Starling, *Starling of the White House,* p. 62. For descriptions of the wedding, see *New*

York Times, Dec. 19, 1915; *Memoir*, p. 86; and Irwin Hood Hoover, *Forty-Two Years in the White House* (Boston, 1934), pp. 70–75.

54. JPT memorandum, Jan. 4, 1916, *PWW*, vol. 35, p. 424.

15　SECOND FLOOD TIDE

1. JPT memorandum, Jan. 4, 1916, *PWW*, vol. 35, p. 424.
2. On these negotiations, see ASL, *Wilson*, vol. 4, *Confusions and Crises, 1915–1916* (Princeton, N.J., 1964), pp. 76–100.
3. JPT to WW, Jan. 17, 1916, *PWW*, vol. 35, pp. 492–94.
4. Wilson speeches, Jan. 27 and 29, 1916, *PWW*, vol. 36, pp. 26–48, 41–48.
5. Arthur Capper to Oswald Garrison Villard, Feb. 3, 1916, Oswald Garrison Villard Papers, Houghton Library, Harvard University. For a description of the tour, see ASL, *Wilson*, vol. 4, pp. 46–48.
6. WW speeches, Feb. 1 and 3, 1916, *PWW*, vol. 36, pp. 78, 117, 118, 119–20. Wilson seems to have realized that he got carried away in speaking about the navy: he changed the officially published text of the speech to read "incomparably the most adequate navy in the world." The original wording could have been interpreted as a challenge to Britain. See p. 120, n. 2.
7. WJB to JD, Feb. 4, 1916, JD Papers, box 37, LC; Claude Kitchin to WJB, Feb. 9, 1916, Claude Kitchin Papers, box 8, Southern Historical Collection, University of North Carolina Library, Chapel Hill. On the congressional opposition to Wilson's preparedness program, see John Milton Cooper, Jr., *The Vanity of Power: American Isolationism and the First World War, 1914–1917* (Westport, Conn., 1969), pp. 87–105.
8. The main advocate of the armor-plate factory was South Carolina's aging senator Pitchfork Ben Tillman. On the navy bill, see ASL, *Wilson*, vol. 4, pp. 35–39, 335–38.
9. On the role of James Hay, see George C. Herring, Jr., "James Hay and the Preparedness Controversy, 1915–1916," *Journal of Southern History* 30 (Nov. 1964), pp. 383–404.
10. Lindley M. Garrison to WW, Feb. 9, 1916, *PWW*, vol. 36, p. 144; WW to Garrison, Feb. 10, 1916, *PWW*, vol. 36, pp. 62–64.
11. James Hay to WW, Feb. 11, 1916, *PWW*, vol. 36, pp. 170–71. On the subsequent fortunes of the army bill, see ASL, *Wilson*, vol. 4, pp. 327–34. The nitrate plant, with a hydroelectric power–generating facility, would be located on the Tennessee River at Muscle Shoals, Alabama. This power-generating facility would become a political football in the 1920s when successive Republican administrations tried to sell it to private utilities. A coalition of Democrats and Republican insurgents, led by Senator George Norris, successfully prevented the sale, and this plant would later serve as the nucleus of the Tennessee Valley Authority.
12. EMH to RL, Feb. 14, 1916, in U.S. Department of State, *Papers Relating to the Foreign Relations of the United States: The Lansing Papers, 1914–1920* (Washington, D.C., 1939), vol. 1, p. 342. On the modus vivendi, see ASL, *Wilson*, vol. 4, pp. 142–66, and Ernest R. May, *The World War and American Isolation, 1914–1917* (Cambridge, Mass., 1959), pp. 184–88.
13. *New York Times*, Feb. 23, 1916. See also William J. Stone to WW, Feb. 23, 1916, *PWW*, vol. 36, p. 210.
14. *New York Times*, Feb. 26, 1916; Mar. 3, 1916.
15. WW to William J. Stone, Feb. 24, 1916, *PWW*, vol. 36, pp. 213–15; WW to Edward W. Pou, Feb. 29, 1916, *PWW*, vol. 36, pp. 231–32; WW to Albert S. Burleson and William Gibbs McAdoo, Mar. 2, 1916, *PWW*, vol. 36, p. 239. For an analysis of these moves, see ASL, *Wilson*, vol. 4, pp. 173–75.

16. WW to William Gordon, Mar. 2, 1916, *PWW*, vol. 36, p. 240. For the vote on the Gore resolution, see Cooper, *Vanity of Power*, pp. 112–13.

17. Statement by Cyrus Cline, Democrat of Indiana, 64th Cong., 1st Sess., *Congressional Record* 3706 (Mar. 7, 1916). See also *New York Times*, Mar. 8, 1916. For an analysis of the vote on the McLemore resolution, see Cooper, *Vanity of Power*, pp. 113–15, 229–32.

18. EMHD, entry for Mar. 7, 1916, *PWW*, vol. 36, p. 267.

19. House-Grey Memorandum, Feb. 22, 1916, *PWW*, vol. 36, p. 180, n. 2.

20. Participants and historians alike have written extensively about the House-Grey Memorandum, including not only House in his subsequently published diary but also Sir Edward Grey and David Lloyd George in their memoirs. The most incisive historical accounts and analysis are in ASL, *Wilson*, vol. 4, pp. 101–42, and Patrick Devlin, *Too Proud to Fight: Woodrow Wilson's Neutrality* (New York, 1975), pp. 392–471. Devlin lays particular stress on personal and psychological elements in the relationship between House and Wilson.

21. Walter Hines Page diary, entry for Feb. 13, 1916, Houghton Library, Harvard University; Jonathan Daniels, *The End of Innocence* (Philadelphia, 1954), p. 89. On House's dealings with Clifford Carver, see John Milton Cooper, Jr., *Walter Hines Page: The Southerner as American, 1855–1918* (Chapel Hill, N.C., 1977), pp. 305–6, 353.

22. It is not clear how much of a personal stake Edward Grey felt he had in the scheme. When he brought the plan up before the cabinet's War Committee, he argued for it somewhat tepidly, but he later revised the meeting's minutes to show himself backing it more vigorously, though not wholeheartedly. See John Milton Cooper, Jr., "The British Response to the House-Grey Memorandum: New Evidence and New Questions," *Journal of American History* 59 (Mar. 1973), pp. 958–71. This article reproduces the minutes of the meeting and Grey's revisions, which are in "Addendum to the Proceedings of the War Committee on March 21, 1916," CAB [Cabinet] 22, 13 (1), Public Record Office, London.

23. "Conversation du Colonel House avec M. Jules Cambon," Feb. 2, 1916, *PWW*, vol. 36, p. 126, n. 1; EMH to WW, Feb. 3, 1916, *PWW*, vol. 36, p. 125; WW to EMH, Dec. 24, 1915, *PWW*, vol. 35, pp. 387–88.

24. EMH to WW, Feb. 9, 1916, *PWW*, vol. 36, p. 148.

25. "Deuxieme Entrevue du Colonel House," Feb. 7, 1916, *PWW*, vol. 36, p. 148, n. 1; Jonathan Daniels to John Milton Cooper, Jr., Sept. 6 and 22, 1977, Jonathan Daniels Papers, Southern Historical Collection, University of North Carolina Library, Chapel Hill.

26. EMHD, entry for Mar. 6, 1916, *PWW*, vol. 36, pp. 262–63. Wilson wrote House no letters while he was abroad and sent him just four telegrams. Only the first of those telegrams, right after House arrived in London, concerned his mission: "Would be glad if you would convey my assurance that I shall be willing and glad when the opportunity comes to cooperate in a policy seeking to bring about and maintain permanent peace among the civilized nations." WW to EMH, Jan. 9, 1916, *PWW*, vol. 35, p. 457. The other three telegrams dealt with submarine and blockade matters.

27. Lloyd George, *War Memoirs of David Lloyd George* (Boston, 1933), vol. 2, p. 141. On the intelligence interception and code breaking, see Devlin, *Too Proud to Fight*, p. 455, and on Grey's equivocation, see n. 22 above.

28. For an account of the raid, see Friedrich Katz, *The Life and Times of Pancho Villa* (Stanford, Calif., 1998), pp. 564–66. Army reports of the raid are reproduced in *PWW*, vol. 36, pp. 281–84.

29. WW statement, [Mar. 10, 1916], *PWW*, vol. 36, p. 287. See also *New York Times*, Mar. 10 and 11, 1916, and ASL, *Wilson*, vol. 4, pp. 205–9.

30. "Memorandum to the Adjutant General," *PWW*, vol. 36, p. 285.

31. Much has been written about the Punitive Expedition and the political and diplomatic circumstances surrounding it. The most detailed account from the American side is found in ASL, *Wilson*, vol. 4, pp. 194–221, 280–318, and ASL, *Wilson*, vol. 5, *Campaigns for Progressivism and Peace, 1916–1917* (Princeton, N.J., 1965), pp. 120–23, 131–34, 328–38. For an account that takes in the Mexican side, see Katz, *Pancho Villa*, pp. 566–614.

32. For an estimate of Villa, see Katz, *Pancho Villa*, pp. 800–818. A junior officer on the expedition would also find future glory in combat: Lieutenant George S. Patton, Jr. He typified many of his fellow officers when he chafed at not being able to wage a wider war, and he unleashed the sharp tongue, if not the foul mouth, for which he would later become famous when he complained to his father about Wilson, "He has not the soul of a louse nor the mind of a worm or the backbone of a jellyfish." George S. Patton, Jr., to George S. Patton, Sept. 28, 1916, in Martin Blumenson, ed., *The Patton Papers* (Boston, 1972), vol. 1, p. 351. Ironically, the senior Patton was running on the same ticket with Wilson as the Democratic nominee for senator in California.

33. JPT, *Wilson As I Know Him* (Garden City, N.Y., 1921), pp. 157–60. The remarks about valor are from a speech the president had given at the Gridiron Club dinner in Washington two weeks earlier.

34. RSB memorandum, [May 12, 1916], *PWW*, vol. 37, p. 36.

35. WW speech, June 30, 1916, *PWW*, vol. 37, pp. 333–35.

36. EMHD, entry for Mar. 17, 1916, *PWW*, vol. 36, p. 335.

37. On the attack on the *Sussex* and Wilson's routine, see *New York Times*, Mar. 25, 26, and 27, 1916.

38. RL to WW, Mar. 27, 1916, *PWW*, vol. 36, p. 372; EMHD, entry for Mar. 29, 1916, *PWW*, vol. 36, p. 388. See also WW draft, [Apr. 10, 1916], *PWW*, vol. 36, p. 456.

39. On House's effort, see EMHD, entry for Apr. 11, 1916, *PWW*, vol. 36, pp. 459–60. On Lansing's activities, see ASL, *Wilson*, vol. 4, pp. 248–52.

40. WW speech, Apr. 13, 1916, *PWW*, vol. 36, p. 472.

41. WW speech, Apr. 19, 1916, *PWW*, vol. 36, pp. 506–10. See also *New York Times*, Apr. 20, 21, and 22, 1916, and ASL, *Wilson*, vol. 4, pp. 254–55.

42. On the German debates and decision, see ASL, *Wilson*, vol. 4, pp. 257–79.

43. WW statement, [May 7, 1916], *PWW*, vol. 36, pp. 649–50. For Lansing's amended version, see *PWW*, vol. 36, pp. 650–51.

44. WW statement, May 8, 1916, in Charles Swem transcript of meeting, *PWW*, vol. 36, p. 645.

45. HCL, *War Addresses, 1915–1917* (Boston, 1917), p. 40; WW speech, May 27, 1916, *PWW*, vol. 37, pp. 113–14. Ironically, as it turned out, Lodge's phrase would lead to the later internationalist watchwords and the title of a future international peacekeeping organization: "united nations."

46. WW speech, May 27, 1916, *PWW*, vol. 37, pp. 114–16.

47. WW speech, May 27, 1910, *PWW*, vol. 37, p. 116. The best exposition of the difference between Wilson and the LEP, or "conservative internationalists," and Wilson's affinity for socialist- and progressive-inspired "liberal internationalists" is found in Thomas J. Knock, *To End All Wars: Woodrow Wilson and the Quest for a New World Order* (New York, 1992).

48. WW speech, May 30, 1916, *PWW*, vol. 37, p. 126; draft of Democratic Party platform, [June 10, 1916], *PWW*, vol. 37, pp. 195–96. On Democrats' and insurgent Republicans' attraction to Bryan's isolationism, see Cooper, *Vanity of Power*, pp. 86–124.

49. Asbury F. Lever to RSB, Mar. 22, 1927, RSBP, box 109.

50. Gus Karger to WHT, Jan. 29, 1916, WHTP, microfilm ed., reel 162. House was reportedly appalled when he heard the news. See Chandler P. Anderson diary, entry for Feb. 10, 1916, Chandler P. Anderson Papers, LC.

51. On the House Democrats' program, see *PWW*, vol. 36, p. 366, n. 1.

52. On the public and senatorial controversies over Brandeis's nomination, see ASL, *Wilson*, vol. 4, pp. 356–62, Alpheus T. Mason, *Brandeis: A Free Man's Life* (New York, 1946), pp. 465–508, and Philippa Strum, *Louis D. Brandeis: Justice for the People* (Cambridge, Mass., 1984), pp. 291–99. The following paragraphs are based on those accounts.

53. WW to Charles Culberson, May 5, 1916, *PWW*, vol. 36, pp. 609–11.

54. WW to Henry Morgenthau, June 5, 1916, *PWW*, vol. 37, p. 163; Hapgood, *The Changing Years: Reminiscences of Norman Hapgood* (New York, 1930), p. 193.

55. *Memoir*, p. 95. On their early months together in the White House, see pp. 89–101.

56. *Memoir*, p. 101.

16   TO RUN AGAIN

1. WW speech, Apr. 13, 1916, *PWW*, vol. 36, p. 474; Robert Owen to WW, June 2, 1916, *PWW*, vol. 37, p. 151.

2. WW draft platform, [ca. June 10, 1916], *PWW*, vol. 37, pp. 198–99.

3. WW speech, July 4, 1916, *PWW*, vol. 37, p. 357; WW draft platform, [ca. June 10, 1916], *PWW*, vol. 37, p. 193. For statements of the interpretation of the conversion from the New Freedom to the New Nationalism, see ASL, "The South and the 'New Freedom,'" *American Scholar* 20 (summer 1951), pp. 314–24, and *Woodrow Wilson and the Progressive Era, 1910–1917* (New York, 1954), esp. pp. 80, 224–25. In the volumes of his full-scale biography produced later, Link modified, downplayed, and finally abandoned this interpretation. For a counterargument see John Milton Cooper, Jr., *The Warrior and the Priest: Woodrow Wilson and Theodore Roosevelt* (Cambridge, Mass., 1983), pp. 253–54; 400, n. 9.

4. TR statement, Mar. 9, 1916, in TR, *The Works of Theodore Roosevelt*, ed. Hermann Hagedorn (New York, 1926), vol. 17, p. 410. The Republican platform is in Kirk H. Porter and Donald Bruce Johnson, eds., *National Party Platforms, 1840–1956* (Urbana, Ill., 1956), pp. 204–7.

5. The best biography of Hughes is Merlo J. Pusey's two-volume *Charles Evans Hughes* (New York, 1951).

6. *Daily News Bulletin*, Feb. 4, 1924, quoted in Alpheus T. Mason, *Brandeis: A Free Man's Life* (New York, 1946), p. 466. For Hughes's recollection of meeting Wilson, see Hughes, *The Autobiographical Notes of Charles Evans Hughes*, ed. David J. Danelski and Joseph S. Tulchin (Cambridge, Mass., 1973), pp. 153–56.

7. TR to Austin Wadsworth, June 23, 1916, in TR, *Letters*, ed. Elting E. Morison, vol. 8, *The Days of Armageddon, 1900–1914* (Cambridge, Mass., 1954), p. 1078. Roosevelt's biographers have described the Progressive convention and his treatment of the delegates many times. For two good recent treatments, see Kathleen Dalton, *Theodore Roosevelt: A Strenuous Life* (New York, 2002), pp. 464–67, and Patricia O'Toole, *When the Trumpets Call: Theodore Roosevelt after the White House* (New York, 2005), pp. 295–97. The fullest treatment of this convention is in John A. Gable, *The Bull Moose Years: Theodore Roosevelt and the Progressive Party Movement* (Port Washington, N.Y., 1978), pp. 246–69.

8. On the Democratic campaign organization, see ASL, *Wilson*, vol. 5, *Campaigns for Progressivism and Peace, 1916–1917* (Princeton, N.J., 1965), pp. 98–100.

9. EMHD, entry for May 24, 1916, *PWW*, vol. 37, p. 104.

10. Ibid., p. 105.

11. EMHD, entry for May, 24, 1916, *PWW*, vol. 34, p. 106. On the possible impact of this decision on the later crisis of disability, see John Milton Cooper, Jr., *Breaking the*

Heart of the World: Woodrow Wilson and the Fight for the League of Nations (New York, 2001), pp. 211–12.

12. Martin Glynn speech, June 14, 1916, official reporter's transcript of the Democratic convention, copy in WWP, series 2, box 136. See also *New York Times* and New York *World,* June 15 and 16, 1916. For an account of the convention, see ASL, *Wilson,* vol. 5, pp. 42–48.

13. Ollie James and WJB speeches, June 15, 1916, in official reporter's transcript of the Democratic convention, copy in WWP, series 2, box 136.

14. Democratic Party platform, June 16, 1916, in official reporter's transcript of the Democratic convention, copy in WWP, series 2, box 136.

15. WW to EMH, July 23, 1916, *PWW,* vol. 37, p. 467. On these controversies, see ASL, *Wilson,* vol. 5, pp. 65–71.

16. "About Washton," [ca. Sept. 1916], Walter Hines Page diary, Houghton Library, Harvard University; Page memorandum, [Sept. 23, 1916], *PWW,* vol. 38, p. 241. For an account of Page's visit home, see John Milton Cooper, Jr., *Walter Hines Page: The Southerner as American, 1855–1918* (Chapel Hill, N.C., 1977), pp. 337–49.

17. WW statement, Sept. 1, 1916, *PWW,* vol. 38, pp. 123–24. Ten of the no votes in the Senate came from southern Democrats, but nine other senators from the South voted in favor. Two Republicans, George Oliver and Boies Penrose of Pennsylvania, also voted no.

18. Among Democrats, 196 voted for the bill and only one voted against it. Among Republicans, 139 voted against it and 37 voted for it. All but four of the Republican dissidents came from the West or the farther reaches of the Midwest, and most of them were insurgents. On the framing and passage of the revenue bill, see ASL, *Wilson,* vol. 4, *Confusions and Crises, 1915–1916* (Princeton, N.J., 1964), pp. 60–64.

19. The senators who nearly came to blows were Henry Ashurst, Democrat of Arizona, and Charles Curtis, Republican of Kansas. On the retaliatory measures, see ASL, *Wilson,* vol. 5, pp. 65–71.

20. On Wilson's appearance, see *New York Times,* Aug. 30, 1916. On the bargaining that led to the strike threat, see ASL, *Wilson,* vol. 5, pp. 83–88.

21. Of House Democrats voting, 167 supported the bill and only 3 opposed it. Republicans split almost down the middle: 70 in favor and 53 against, with most of the no votes coming from northeasterners. For the signing of the bill, see *New York Times,* Sept. 4, 1916.

22. Hughes speech, July 31, 1916, Charles Evans Hughes Papers, box 182, LC; WW to Bernard Baruch, Aug. 19, 1916, *PWW,* vol. 38, p. 51; WW to RL, Oct. 2, 1916, *PWW,* vol. 38, p. 319. For Hughes's explanation, see Hughes, *Autobiographical Notes,* p. 181.

23. Farmer's remark quoted in Pusey, *Hughes,* vol. 1, p. 339.

24. For accounts of the Long Beach incident, see Hughes, *Autobiographical Notes,* pp. 182–85, and Pusey, *Hughes,* vol. 1, pp. 344–49.

25. WW speeches, July 4 and 20, 1916, *PWW,* vol. 37, pp. 355, 442.

26. WW speech, Sept. 2, 1916, *PWW,* vol. 38, pp. 126–39.

27. WW speech, Sept. 8, 1916, *PWW,* vol. 38, pp. 161–63.

28. See *Memoir,* pp. 105–6.

29. Vance McCormick to EMH, Sept. 11, 1916, EMH Papers, Yale University Library.

30. *New York Times,* Sept. 6, 1916; Charles Evans Hughes to WHT, Sept. 16, 1916, WHTP microfilm ed., reel 169.

31. *New York Times,* Sept. 30, 1916, Oct. 1, 1916; TR speech, Nov. 3, 1916, in TR, *Works of Roosevelt,* vol. 18, pp. 447–48.

32. WW speech, Sept. 23, 1916, *PWW,* vol. 38, pp. 213–17; WW to Jeremiah O'Leary, Sept. 29, 1916, *PWW,* vol. 38, p. 286.

33. WW speech, Sept. 30, 1916, *PWW,* vol. 38, pp. 302–7. Before making this speech, Wilson spent an hour and a half talking with the young *New Republic* editor Walter Lippmann, who evidently advised him to make such an appeal to Progressives. On Lippmann's visit and influence, see WW to Lippmann, Sept. 29, 1916, *PWW,* vol. 38, p. 295; WW to NDB, Sept. 30, 1916, *PWW,* vol. 38, p. 312; and Ronald Steel, *Walter Lippmann and the American Century* (Boston, 1980), pp. 103–6.

34. JD, interview by RSB, Mar. 20, 1929, RSBP, box 103. For the speculation that it was the sight of the young men that moved Wilson to make those statements, see ASL, *Wilson,* vol. 5, p. 106.

35. WW speech, Nov. 4, 1916, *PWW,* vol. 38, pp. 608–15; EMHD, entry for Nov. 2, 1916, *PWW,* vol. 38, pp. 606–7.

36. EMHD, entry for Sept. 30, 1916, Yale University Library. On the smears and efforts to counteract them, see ASL, *Wilson,* vol. 5, pp. 143–45.

37. *New York Times,* Oct. 28, 1916; WW to Walter [*sic;* i.e., Jonas] Lippmann, Oct. 30, 1916, *PWW,* vol. 38, p. 559; TR speech at New York, Nov. 3, 1916, in TR, *Works of Roosevelt,* vol. 18, pp. 451–52.

38. On socialist and other liberal support for Wilson, see Thomas J. Knock, *To End All Wars: Woodrow Wilson and the Quest for a New World Order* (New York, 1992), pp. 93–94.

39. *New Republic,* Oct. 14, 1916, p. 203, and Oct. 21, 1916, p. 286.

40. On the Catholic opposition to Wilson, see ASL, *Wilson,* vol. 5, pp. 130–34.

41. WW to J. R. Wilson, Jr., Oct. 16, 1916, *PWW,* vol. 38, p. 452; EMHD, entry for Oct. 19, 1916, *PWW,* vol. 38, p. 493. See also ASL, *Wilson,* vol. 5, pp. 153–54.

42. WW to RL, Nov. 5, 1916, *PWW,* vol. 38, pp. 617–18; EMHD, entry for Nov. 2, 1916, *PWW,* vol. 38, p. 607.

43. Curiously, the plan did not begin to become well known until Arthur Link reproduced Wilson's letter to Lansing in "President Wilson's Plan to Resign in 1916," *Princeton University Library Chronicle* 23 (summer 1962), pp. 167–72. At some point, Hughes obtained a copy of the letter. It is in the Charles Evans Hughes Papers, LC. Edith Wilson makes no mention of the plan in her memoirs. In 1926, excerpts from House's diary and his letter to Wilson about possibly resigning were published in EMH, *The Intimate Papers of Colonel House,* ed. Charles Seymour (Boston, 1926), vol. 2, pp. 378–80. In 1937, Ray Stannard Baker also published Wilson's letter to Lansing, in RSB, *Woodrow Wilson: Life and Letters,* vol. 6, *Facing War, 1915–1917* (Garden City, N.Y., 1937), pp. 292–93. On the later interregnum, see Jordan A. Schwarz, *The Interregnum of Despair: Hoover, Congress, and the Depression* (Urbana, Ill., 1970).

44. *Memoir,* pp. 114–15.

45. WW to J. R. Wilson, Jr., Nov. 27, 1916, *PWW,* vol. 40, p. 90.

46. Hiram Johnson won his race for the Senate by more than 300,000 votes, defeating the father of Lieutenant George S. Patton.

47. Hughes believed that he carried Michigan only because he did some last-minute campaigning there. See Hughes, *Autobiographical Notes,* p. 185. This seems exaggerated, because he carried Michigan by a comfortable margin. Wilson's least impressive showings came in New York and New Jersey, where he barely increased his share of the vote over 1912. The result in New York was not surprising because it was Hughes's home state, and Democrats there were divided, as usual. New Jersey, however, was a big disappointment.

48. EMHD, entry for Nov. 2, 1916, *PWW,* vol. 38, p. 607. The Rhode Island winner, Peter Gerry, had a name that sounded Irish, but he was an old-stock Yankee and a descendant of Elbridge Gerry, the vice president and Massachusetts politician for whom the gerrymander was named.

49. W. E. B. DuBois to WW, Oct. 10, 1916, *PWW*, vol. 38, p. 459; WW to JPT, [ca. Oct. 17, 1916], *PWW*, vol. 38, p. 459.

50. WW to J.A.H. Hopkins, Nov. 16, 1916, *PWW*, vol. 38, p. 663.

17   PEACE AND WAR

1. EMHD, entry for Nov. 14, 1916, *PWW*, vol. 38, pp. 646–47; WW, Prolegomenon to a Peace Note, [ca. Nov. 25, 1916], *PWW*, vol. 40, pp. 67–70.

2. WW draft peace note, [ca. Nov. 25, 1916], *PWW*, vol. 40, pp. 70–74.

3. EMHD, enties for Nov. 26, 1916; Jan. 3, 1917, *PWW*, vol. 40, pp. 656, 658.

4. RL memorandum, "What Will the President Do?" Dec. 3, 1916, RL Papers, LC.

5. WW to W.P.G. Harding, Nov. 26, 1916, *PWW*, vol. 40, p. 77. On these machinations with the Federal Reserve Board, see ASL, *Wilson*, vol. 5, *Campaigns for Progressivism and Peace, 1916–1917* (Princeton, N.J., 1965), pp. 200–206, and John Milton Cooper, Jr., "The Command of Gold Reversed: American Loans to Britain, 1915–1917," *Pacific Historical Review* 45 (May 1976), pp. 209–30.

6. David Lawrence, *The True Story of Woodrow Wilson* (New York, 1924), pp. 333–35. On the attempt to remove Tumulty, see also John M. Blum, *Joe Tumulty and the Wilson Era* (Boston, 1951), pp. 120–22, and ASL, *Wilson*, vol. 2, *The New Freedom* (Princeton, N.J., 1956), pp. 142–44.

7. WW speech, Dec. 5, 1916, *PWW*, vol. 40, p. 159.

8. WW to EMH, Dec. 8, 1916, *PWW*, vol. 40, p. 189.

9. RL to WW, Dec. 10, 1916, *PWW*, vol. 40, pp, 209–11; EMHD, entry for Dec. 14, 1916, *PWW*, vol. 40, p. 238.

10. WW draft, Dec. 17, 1916, *PWW*, vol. 40, pp. 256–59; EMHD, entry for Dec. 20, 1916, *PWW*, vol. 40, p. 304–5.

11. Jean-Jules Jusserand's reports to Paris are paraphrased in ASL, *Wilson*, vol. 5, pp. 223–34.

12. *New York Times*, Dec. 22, 1916; JPT to WW, Dec. 21, 1916, *PWW*, vol. 40, p. 306.

13. WW to RL, Dec. 21, 1916, *PWW*, vol. 40, p. 307. See also RL, *War Memoirs of Robert Lansing, Secretary of State* (Indianapolis, 1935), p. 187.

14. The closest Lansing came to explaining his actions was when he wrote to a friend a month later, "I will one of these days tell you the whole story. The inside facts are most interesting, and I believe that you will find my course was justified." RL to E. N. Smith, Jan. 21, 1917, RL Papers, LC. In a memorandum to himself, Lansing justified his statement by saying that he wanted to dissociate the United States from the German overture and reassure the Allies. He explained his backing down by saying that after Wilson wrote and talked to him, "I saw that my words were open to such an erroneous interpretation" (i.e., that America was abandoning neutrality). RL, "Confidential Memorandum in re: The Two Statements I Issued to the Press on December 21, 1916," RL Papers, Princeton University Library.

15. Sir Horace Plunkett to Arthur James Balfour, Dec. 22, 1916, *PWW*, vol. 40, p. 307, n. 1; Roy Howard, quoted in Lord Northcliffe to David Lloyd George, Dec. 27, 1916, *PWW*, vol. 40, p. 307, n. 1; EMHD, entry for Dec. 23, 1916, *PWW*, vol. 40, p. 326. On House's dealings with Plunkett, see also Sir Horace Plunkett diary, entry for Dec. 21, 1916, *PWW*, vol. 40, p. 294, n. 2, and Plunkett to EMH, Dec. 27, 1916, *PWW*, vol. 40, pp. 339–42.

16. 64th Cong., 2nd Sess., *Congressional Record* 792–97 (Jan. 3, 1917); *New York Times*, Jan. 4, 1917.

17. 64th Cong., 2nd Sess., *Congressional Record* 792–97 (Jan. 3, 1917); 892–95 (Jan. 5,

1917). The senators voting in favor included thirty-eight Democrats and ten Republicans; eight of those Republicans were insurgents, including Borah. Lodge had been privately edging away from the league idea for several months. See HCL to W. Sturgis Bigelow, Apr. 5, 1916, HCLP; HCL to TR, Dec. 21, 1916, TR Papers, LC, box 316. On Borah's conversion to isolationism, see John Milton Cooper, Jr., *The Vanity of Power: American Isolationism and the First World War, 1914–1917* (Westport, Conn., 1969), pp. 137–42.

18. For two expressions of these conflicting views of Lloyd George's response, see ASL, *Wilson*, vol. 5, pp. 227–33, 237–39, and Patrick Devlin, *Too Proud to Fight: Woodrow Wilson's Neutrality* (New York, 1975), pp. 583–92.

19. On the German reply, see ASL, *Wilson*, vol. 5, pp. 233–37.

20. EMHD, entries for Jan. 3 and 4, 1917, *PWW,* vol. 40, pp. 408–9.

21. EMHD, entry for Jan. 11, 1917, *PWW,* vol. 40, p. 445; WW press conference, Jan. 15, 1917, *PWW,* vol. 40, pp. 470, 474–75. Some question has arisen about whether, in writing this speech, Wilson was influenced by *The New Republic* editors. House had sent him two editorials from the magazine: "Peace without Victory" (Dec. 23, 1916) and an unsigned piece (Jan. 6, 1917). Wilson later told Herbert Croly, "I was interested and encouraged, when preparing my recent address to the Senate, to find an editorial in the New Republic which was not only written along the same lines but which served to clarify and strengthen my thought not a little." WW to Croly, Jan. 25, 1917, *PWW,* vol. 41, p.13. Wilson may have taken the speech's signature phrase, "peace without victory," from *The New Republic,* but its main ideas were ones that he had formulated on his own. Walter Lippmann later doubted that he and Croly had much influence on Wilson, and he believed there was only a coincidental congruence of thinking. See Lippmann, "Notes for a Biography," *New Republic,* July 16, 1930.

22. WW speech, Jan. 22, 1917, *PWW,* vol. 40, pp. 535–38.

23. Ibid., pp. 538–39.

24. *New York Times,* Jan. 23 and 27, 1917; 64th Cong., 2nd Sess. *Congressional Record* 1950 (Jan. 25, 1917); 2361–64 (Feb. 1, 1917); 2749 (Feb. 7, 1917). Other senators who attacked the league idea were James Reed, Democrat of Missouri, and Albert Cummins, Republican of Iowa.

25. 64th Cong., 2nd Sess., *Congressional Record* 2364–70 (Feb. 1, 1917).

26. *New York Times,* Jan. 27 and 29, 1917; WJB to WW, Jan. 26, 1917, *PWW,* vol. 41, p. 29. On Republican defections from the LEP and other unfavorable reactions to "peace without victory," see Cooper, *Vanity of Power,* pp. 156–57.

27. WW to Cleveland Dodge, Jan. 25, 1917, *PWW,* vol. 41, p. 1. On foreign reactions to "peace without victory," see ASL, *Wilson,* vol. 5, pp. 271–77.

28. Johann-Heinrich von Bernstorff to RL, Jan. 31, 1917, *PWW,* vol. 41, pp. 76–77.

29. Comment about "a shopkeeper's peace" quoted in von Bernstorff to RL, Jan. 31, 1917, *PWW,* vol. 41, pp. 76–77. For analyses of this decision, see Cooper, "Command of Gold Reversed," and "The United States," in *The Origins of World War I,* ed. Richard F. Hamilton and Holger H. Herwig (New York, 2003), pp. 415–42.

30. Arthur Zimmermann to Heinrich von Eckhardt, Jan. 16, 1917, in *Official German Documents Relating to the World War* (New York, 1923), vol. 2, p. 1337. The classic work on this affair is Barbara W. Tuchman, *The Zimmermann Telegram* (New York, 1958). Tuchman follows William Reginald Hall's biographer in maintaining that the captain sat on the telegram until after February 1 in order to protect his operation. That is extremely doubtful. See John Milton Cooper, Jr., *Walter Hines Page: The Southerner as American, 1855–1918* (Chapel Hill, N.C., 1977), pp. 362–63.

31. RL memorandum, Feb. 4, 1917, *PWW,* vol. 41, pp. 120–21. On Wilson's possible

acceptance of limited submarine warfare, see WW to RL, Jan. 31, 1917, *PWW,* vol. 41, p. 71. See also the interpretation of this exchange in ASL, *Wilson,* vol. 5, p. 284.

32. EMHD, entry for Feb. 1, 1917, *PWW,* vol. 41, pp. 87–88; Louis Lochner memorandum, Feb. 1, 1917, *PWW,* vol. 41, pp. 89, 92. House did not come to Washington at Wilson's request. The number two person in the State Department, Frank L. Polk, had telephoned and asked the colonel to come.

33. David F. Houston, *Eight Years with Wilson's Cabinet, 1913–1920* (Garden City, N.Y., 1926), vol. 1, pp. 229–30; William B. Wilson to RSB, Sept. 17, 1932, RSBP, series 1, box 58. For an account of the meetings at the Capitol, see New York *World,* Feb. 3, 1917. Evidently the most energetic gesticulator was Hoke Smith of Georgia.

34. JD to WW, Feb. 2, 1917, *PWW,* vol. 41, p. 94; JD, *The Wilson Era,* vol. 1, *Years of Peace, 1910–1917* (Chapel Hill, N.C., 1944), p. 582; WW speech, Feb. 3, 1917, *PWW,* vol. 41, pp. 109–12. Daniels incorrectly recalled this conversation taking place in January.

35. HCL to TR, Feb. 13, 1917, TR Papers, LC; TR to Hiram Johnson, Feb. 17, 1917, Hiram Johnson Papers, Bancroft Library, University of California, Berkeley, part 2, box 28. For a description of the speech, see *New York Times,* Feb. 4, 1917. The no votes on the Senate resolution came from three insurgent Republicans—La Follette, Asle Gronna of North Dakota, and John Works of California—and two Bryanite Democrats, William F. Kirby of Arkansas and James K. Vardaman of Mississippi; another Democrat, Harry Lane of Oregon, announced that he also opposed the resolution.

36. WW to EMH, Feb. 12, 1917, *PWW,* vol. 41, p. 201. The *Junkerthum* was Germany's militarist big business clique.

37. WW veto message, Jan. 29, 1917, *PWW,* vol. 41, pp. 51–52. On this legislative session, see ASL, *Wilson,* vol. 5, pp. 325–28.

38. Franklin K. Lane to George W. Lane, Feb. 25, 1917, Lane, *The Letters of Franklin K. Lane, Personal and Political,* ed. Anne W. Lane and Louise H. Wall (Boston, 1922), pp. 239–41.

39. WW speech, Feb. 26, 1917, *PWW,* vol. 41, pp. 283–87. On the scene in the Capitol, see *New York Times,* Feb. 27, 1917, and RSBD, entry for Feb. 26, 1917, RSBP. On the *Laconia* sinking, see *New York Times,* Feb. 27, 1917. On editorial reactions to the speech and the sinking of the *Laconia,* see ASL, *Wilson,* vol. 5, pp. 349–50.

40. On the British operation to cover the tracks of their interception, see Tuchman, *Zimmermann Telegram,* pp. 143–46, and on the decision to publish the telegram, see ASL, *Wilson,* vol. 5, pp. 353–54.

41. For a survey of editorial opinion, see *Literary Digest,* Mar. 17, 1917, pp. 687–90. For an analysis of the votes on the armed-ships bill and the amendment to bar munitions shipments, see Cooper, *Vanity of Power,* pp. 179–81, 233–35.

42. See *New York Times,* Mar. 4 and 5, 1917.

43. Robert M. La Follette, Jr., to Robert M. La Follette, [Mar. 4, 1917], La Follette Family Papers, LC. This note and others exchanged between La Follette and his son are reprinted, along with a description of the scene, in Belle Case La Follette and Fola La Follette, *Robert M. La Follette, June 14, 1855–June 18, 1925* (New York, 1953), vol. 1, pp. 623–24.

44. EMHD, entry for Mar. 5, 1917, *PWW,* vol. 41, pp. 331–32; WW statement, Mar. 4, 1917, *PWW,* vol. 41, pp. 318–20.

45. WW speech, Mar. 5, 1917, *PWW,* vol. 41, pp. 322–25.

46. EMHD, entries for Mar. 5 and 28, 1917, *PWW,* vol. 41, pp. 341, 497.

47. Winston S. Churchill, *World Crisis,* vol. 3, *1916–1918* (London, 1927), p. 234. On armed neutrality and the financial situation, see ASL, *Wilson,* vol. 5, pp. 372–83.

48. For estimates of congressional opinion, see Gus J. Karger to WHT, Apr. 6, 1917, WHTP, box 374; David Starr Jordan to Jessie Jordan, Apr. 6, 1917, David Starr Jordan Papers, Hoover Institution on War, Revolution, and Peace, Stanford University; David Starr Jordan, *The Days of a Man: Being Memories of a Naturalist, Teacher, and Minor Prophet of Democracy* (Yonkers, N.Y., 1922), vol. 2, p. 733, n. 1; Arthur Wallace Dunn, *From Harrison to Harding: A Personal Narrative, Covering a Third of a Century, 1888–1921* (New York, 1922), vol. 2, p. 357, and Fiorello H. La Guardia, *The Making of an Insurgent: An Autobiography, 1882–1919* (Philadelphia, 1948), pp. 138, 140.

49. Thomas W. Brahany diary, entry for Mar. 26, 1917, *PWW*, vol. 41, pp. 474–75. Brahany, a member of the stenography staff, got the story from John Mays, the president's barber.

50. William C. Adamson memorandum, RSBP, box 99.

51. Frank Irving Cobb, *Cobb of "The World,"* ed. John L. Heaton (New York, 1924), pp. 268–70. A heated academic debate has raged over the authenticity of Cobb's recollection. In 1965, Arthur Link pointed out that the meeting took place on March 19, not April 1, as Cobb had stated. See ASL, *Wilson*, vol. 5, p. 399, n. 33. Two years later, Jerold S. Auerbach called much of the interview into question, particularly the prediction of the repression of civil liberties. See Auerbach, "Woodrow Wilson's 'Prediction' to Frank Cobb: Words Historians Should Doubt Ever Got Spoken," *Journal of American History* 54 (Dec. 1967), pp. 608–17. Several other historians subsequently weighed in, and one uncovered the manuscript of Cobb's account. Link eventually rejoined the debate, upholding the authenticity of the interview in his presidential address to the Organization of American Historians. See ASL, "That Cobb Interview," *Journal of American History* 72 (June 1985), pp. 7–17. On balance, Link has the better of the argument, not only because of his unparalleled knowledge of Wilson but also because Cobb's recollection is consonant with what Wilson said to other people in February and March 1917.

52. JDD, entry for Mar. 20, 1917, *PWW*, vol. 41, pp. 444–45; RL, "Memorandum of the Cabinet Meeting, 2:30–5 p.m., Tuesday, March 20, 1917," *PWW*, vol. 41, pp. 438, 443–44. For Attorney General Thomas Gregory's brief account of the meeting, see EMHD, entry for Mar. 22, 1917, *PWW*, vol. 41, p. 454. For a later recollection of this meeting, see Houston, *Wilson's Cabinet*, vol. 1, pp. 242–44.

53. EMHD, entries for Mar. 27 and 28, 1917, *PWW*, vol. 41, pp. 482–83, 497–98.

54. WW to Matthew Hale, Mar. 31, 1917, WWP, series 2, box 148; RL memorandum, Mar. 20, 1917, *PWW*, vol. 41, p. 440; EMHD, entry for Mar. 29, 1917, *PWW*, vol. 41, p. 498.

55. RL memorandum, Mar. 20, 1917, *PWW*, vol. 41, p. 443.

56. Irwin Hood Hoover, quoted in Thomas W. Brahany diary, entry for Mar. 31, 1917, *PWW*, p. 515; EMHD, entry for Apr. 2, 1917, *PWW*, vol. 41, p. 529.

57. WW speech, Apr. 2, 1917, *PWW*, vol. 41, pp. 519–21. For the description of the scene and Edward White's clapping, see *New York Times*, Apr. 3, 1917.

58. WW speech, Apr. 2, 1917, *PWW*, vol. 41, pp. 521–23; *New York Times*, Apr. 3, 1917.

59. WW speech, Apr. 2, 1917, *PWW*, vol. 41, pp. 524–26; *New York Times*, Apr. 3, 1917.

60. WW speech, Apr. 2, 1917, *PWW*, vol. 41, pp. 526–27. Wilson made a slip when he said "Gentlemen of the Congress." Representative Jeannette Rankin of Montana had just taken her seat as the first woman to serve in either house.

61. JPT, *Wilson As I Know Him* (Garden City, N.Y., 1921), p. 256. On the reactions to the speech, see also *New York Times*, Apr. 3, 1917; *New York World*, Apr. 3, 1917; and ASL, *Wilson*, vol. 5, pp. 427–28.

62. 65th Cong., 1st Sess., *Congressional Record* 261 (Apr. 4, 1917). The Republicans were Robert La Follette, George Norris, and Asle Gronna, and the Democrats were

William Stone, James K. Vardaman, and Harry Lane. One other Democrat, Thomas Gore, announced against the war but did not vote.

63. Lawrence, *True Story*, pp. 208–9. For a description of Claude Kitchin's speech, see *New York Times*, Apr. 7, 1917, and New York *World*, Apr. 7, 1917. On Bryan's opposition to intervention, see WJB to Louis Lochner, Apr. 2, 1917, Louis Lochner Papers, Wisconsin Historical Society, box 52, and WJB to David Starr Jordan, Mar. 28, 1917, David Starr Jordan Papers.

64. *New York Times*, Apr. 7, 1917. Four representatives also announced against the resolution.

65. For a description of Wilson signing the war resolution, see Thomas W. Brahany diary, entry for Apr. 6, 1917, *PWW,* vol. 41, p. 557.

18   WAGING WAR

1. Fitz W. Woodrow to Arthur C. Walworth, Apr. 12, 1948, quoted in Walworth, *Woodrow Wilson* (New York, 1958), vol. 2, p. 101. Walworth claimed that Woodrow verified this statement in May 1956. See p. 101, n. 1, and "Interview with Col. FitzWilliam McMaster Woodrow at his home, 4409 Que St., Washington, D.C., April 12, 1948, March 16, 1955, and over the phone on March 15, 1956," Arthur C. Walworth Papers, Yale University Library, folder 61. The original of the letter is not among these papers. Wilson had not criticized Lincoln's war leadership in any of his published work.

2. WW, "Programme," Apr. 7, 1917, *PWW,* vol. 42, p. 3; WW to Walter Lippmann, Apr. 7, 1917, *PWW,* vol. 42, p. 4.

3. WW to Carter Glass, Apr. 9, 1919, *PWW,* vol. 42, p. 21; JDD, entry for Apr. 9, 1917, *PWW,* vol. 42, p. 2; WW executive order, [Apr. 13, 1917], *PWW,* vol. 42, p. 59. On George Creel, see his autobiography, *Rebel at Large: Recollections of Fifty Crowded Years* (New York, 1947).

4. On Baruch's personality and background, see Jordan A. Schwarz, *The Speculator: Bernard Baruch in Washington, 1917–1965* (Chapel Hill, N.C., 1981), pp. 3–22.

5. WW statement, Apr. 15, 1917, *PWW,* vol. 42, pp. 71–75.

6. WW to Guy T. Helvering, Apr. 19, 1917, *PWW,* vol. 42, p. 97; 65th Cong., 1st Sess., *Congressional Record* 1120 (Apr. 25, 1917). On the passage of the draft act, see John Whiteclay Chambers II, *To Raise an Army: The Draft Comes to Modern America* (New York, 1987), pp. 151–67.

7. Their fears were justified. As soon as word got out that the ex-president wanted to lead a division to fight on the Western Front, officers of all ranks scrambled to climb aboard, including a young lieutenant from Kansas less than two years out of West Point—Dwight Eisenhower.

8. Thomas W. Brahany diary, entry for Apr. 10, 1917, *PWW,* vol. 42, p. 31; Roosevelt to J. Callan O'Laughlin, Apr. 13, 1917, TR, *Letters,* ed. Elting E. Morison, vol. 8, *The Days of Armageddon, 1900–1914* (Cambridge, Mass., 1954), p. 1173; JPT, *Woodrow Wilson As I Know Him* (Garden City, N.Y., 1921), pp. 286–88.

9. John J. Leary, Jr., *Talks with T.R.* (Boston, 1920), pp. 95–98; NDB to TR, Apr. 10, 1917, *PWW,* vol. 42, pp. 56–57.

10. J. H. Whitehouse, "The House Report, 14 November 1916 to 14 April 1917," *PWW,* vol. 42, pp. 65–69.

11. W. B. Fowler, *British-American Relations, 1917–1918: The Role of Sir William Wiseman* (Princeton, N.J., 1969), p. 17. On Wiseman and the beginning of his relationship with House, see pp. 12–25. For an example of their conspiring together, see pp. 74–75.

12. EMHD, entries for Apr. 26, 28, and 30, 1917, *PWW,* vol. 42, pp. 142, 155–56, 169, 171–72.

13. Jean-Jules Jusserand to council of ministers, May 1 and 3, 1917, *PWW,* vol. 42, pp. 184, 213.

14. On the draft registration and the choosing of the first inductees, see Chambers, *To Raise an Army,* pp. 184–86.

15. On the suspension of these publications, see also Harry N. Scheiber, *The Wilson Administration and Civil Liberties, 1917–1921* (Ithaca, N.Y., 1960), pp. 143–45, and James Weinstein, *The Decline of Socialism in America, 1912–1915* (New York, 1967), pp. 29–41.

16. WW to Max Eastman, Sept. 13, 1917, *PWW,* vol. 44, pp. 210–11; EMH to WW, Oct. 17, 1917, *PWW,* vol. 44, p. 393.

17. On the plight of German Americans during World War I, see Frederick C. Luebke, *Bonds of Loyalty: German-Americans and World War I* (Dekalb, Ill., 1974).

18. On these incidents, see Melvyn Dubofsky, *We Shall Be All: A History of the Industrial Workers of the World* (Chicago, 1969), pp. 385–92.

19. JDD, entry for July 31, 1917, *PWW,* vol. 43, p. 336. On the raids and indictments, see Dubofsky, *We Shall Be All,* pp. 405–9.

20. Steffens, *The Autobiography of Lincoln Steffens* (New York, 1931), p. 739; WW speech, Dec. 4, 1917, *PWW,* vol. 44, p. 195.

21. On the choice of Pershing and the internal politics of the military, see Edward M. Coffman, *The War to End All Wars: The American Military Experience in World War I* (New York, 1968), pp. 43–46, and Frank E. Vandiver, *Black Jack: The Life and Times of John J. Pershing* (College Station, Tex., 1977), vol. 2, pp. 682–96.

22. NDB to Pershing, May 26, 1917, *PWW,* vol. 42, pp. 464–65. On Pershing's arrival in France, see Vandiver, *Black Jack,* vol. 2, pp. 714–24.

23. NDB to Pershing, Dec. 18, 1917, *PWW,* vol. 45, p. 328.

24. WW speech, Aug. 11, 1914, *PWW,* vol. 43, p. 430. On William Sims's dealings with the British over the convoy system, see Elting E. Morison, *Admiral Sims and the Modern American Navy* (Boston, 1942), pp. 341–62.

25. For a concise account of the shipbuilding program, see Robert H. Ferrell, *Woodrow Wilson and World War I, 1917–1921* (New York, 1985), pp. 98–102.

26. Benjamin Tillman to WW, July 17, 1917, *PWW,* vol. 43, p. 198.

27. On the railroad situation, see David M. Kennedy, *Over Here: The First World War and American Society* (New York, 1982), pp. 252–54.

28. WW speech, Jan. 4, 1918, *PWW,* vol. 45, p. 449.

29. WW to Asbury F. Lever, July 23, 1917, *PWW,* vol. 43, p. 245. On the debate over the Lever Act, see Seward W. Livermore, *Politics Is Adjourned: Woodrow Wilson and the War Congress, 1916–1918* (Middletown, Conn., 1966), pp. 55–56. On Hoover's role in drafting the Lever Act, see Witold S. Sworakowski, "Herbert Hoover, Launching the Food Administration," in *Herbert Hoover—the Great War and Its Aftermath, 1914–1923,* ed. Lawrence E. Gelfand (Iowa City, Iowa, 1979), pp. 40–60.

30. Charles Seymour, *Woodrow Wilson and the World War: A Chronicle of Our Own Times* (New Haven, Conn., 1921), p. 164.

31. Slogans quoted in Ferrell, *Wilson and World War I,* p. 93. On Hoover's work as food administrator, see George H. Nash, *The Life of Herbert Hoover,* vol. 3, *Master of Emergencies, 1917–1918* (New York, 1996).

32. On the coal crisis, see James P. Johnson, "The Wilsonians as War Managers: Coal and the 1917–18 Winter Crisis, "*Prologue* 9 (winter 1977), pp. 193–208.

33. On the early months of the War Industries Board, see Robert D. Cuff, *The War Industries Board: Business-Government Relations during World War I* (Baltimore, 1973), pp. 86–148.

34. WW to Thomas W. Gregory, July 7, 1917, *PWW*, vol. 43, p. 116. On this incident, see Elliott M. Rudwick, *Race Riot at East St. Louis, July 2, 1917* (Carbondale, Ill., 1964).

35. JPT to WW, Aug. 1, 1917, *PWW*, vol. 43, p. 342; JDD, entry for Aug. 24, 1917, *PWW*, vol. 44, p. 49. For the black leaders' statement, see *Washington Post*, Aug. 17, 1917. On the violence in Houston, see Robert V. Haynes, *A Night of Violence: The Houston Riot of 1917* (Baton Rouge, La., 1976).

36. *Crisis*, August 1917. On the army's rare policies, see Coffman, *War to End All Wars*, pp. 69–70, and Kennedy, *Over Here*, pp. 158–60. For Wilson's involvement in the Charles Young incident, see WW to NDB, June 28, 1917, *PWW*, vol. 43, p. 78, and WW to John Sharp Williams, June 28, 1917, *PWW*, vol. 43, p. 78. Young was called back from retirement for active duty in late 1918 but was never given the opportunity to serve in Europe.

37. Charles H. Williams, quoted in Coffman, *War to End All Wars*, p. 71. On the labor battalion's experience, see p. 71.

38. Johnson, *Along This Way: The Autobiography of James Weldon Johnson* (New York, 1933), pp. 324–25. The petition is reprinted on pp. 323–24 and in *PWW*, vol. 48, pp. 383–84.

39. Robert R. Moton to WW, June 15, 1918, *PWW*, vol. 48, p. 323; WW to Moton, June 18, 1918, *PWW*, vol. 48, p. 346.

40. WW statement, July 26, 1918, *PWW*, vol. 49, pp. 97–98.

41. For an examination of Wilson's political thought that emphasizes southern influences, see Stephen Skowronek, "The Reassociation of Ideas and Purposes: Racism, Liberalism, and the American Political Tradition," *American Political Science Review* 100 (Aug. 2006), pp. 385–401, and for an examination that puts him in a larger context of "racial nationalism," see Gary Gerstle, "Race and Nation in the Thought and Politics of Woodrow Wilson," in *Reconsidering Woodrow Wilson: Progressivism, Internationalism, War, and Peace*, ed. John Milton Cooper, Jr. (Washington, D.C., 2008), pp. 93–123.

42. For accounts of the NWP incident see *Washington Post*, July 15, 18, 19, and 20, 1917, and *New York Times*, July 17 and 19, 1917.

43. Louis Brownlow, *A Passion for Anonymity: The Autobiography of Louis Brownlow, Second Half* (Chicago, 1958), pp. 78–79; WW to EMH, July 29, 1917, *PWW*, vol. 43, pp. 313–14. On the break with Malone, see also EMHD, entry for July 26, 1917, *PWW*, vol. 43, p. 290; WW to EMH, July 26 1917, *PWW*, vol. 43, p. 293; and Dudley Field Malone to WW, Sept. 7, 1917, *PWW*, vol. 44, p. 167.

44. Carrie Chapman Catt to WW, May 7, 1917, *PWW*, vol. 42, p. 237; WW to Edward W. Pou, May 14, 1917, *PWW*, vol. 42, p. 293. See also Helen Hamilton Gardener to WW, May 10, 1917, *PWW*, vol. 42, p. 269. For an account of how Catt, Gardener, and other NAWSA leaders skillfully appealed to Wilson, see Victoria Brown, "Did Woodrow Wilson's Gender Politics Matter?" in Cooper, *Reconsidering Wilson*, pp. 125–62.

45. WW statement, [Oct. 25, 1917], *PWW*, vol. 44, pp. 441–43; Elizabeth Merrill Bass to WW, Jan. 8, 1918, *PWW*, vol. 45, p. 542.

46. WW statement, Jan. 10, 1918, *PWW*, vol. 45, p. 544.

47. Carrie Chapman Catt to WW, Sept. 29, 1918, *PWW*, vol. 49, pp. 157–59; McAdoo, *Crowded Years: The Reminiscences of William G. McAdoo* (Boston, 1931), pp. 496–97.

48. WW speech, Sept. 30, 1918, *PWW*, vol. 50, pp. 159–61. See also *New York Times*, Oct. 1, 1918.

49. This assessment agrees with the one in the excellent treatment in Christine A. Lunardini and Thomas J. Knock, "Woodrow Wilson and Woman Suffrage: A New Look," *Political Science Quarterly* 95 (winter, 1980–81), pp. 655–71.

50. On the veto and Wilson's likely lack of knowledge about it, see *PWW*, vol. 63, p. 602, n. 3.
51. WW to Henry B. Fine, May 14, 1917, *PWW*, vol. 42, p. 292; *Memoir*, pp. 134–35.
52. EMHD, entry for Nov. 15, 1916, vol. 38, p. 659; *Memoir*, p. 149. On the conversations between Wilson and John Singer Sargent, see also Sargent to WW, Nov. 6, 1917, WWP, series 2, box 473, and WW to Sargent, Nov. 8, 1917, *PWW*, vol. 44, p. 536.
53. Sargent to Mary Hale, Oct. 20, 1917, quoted in Evan Charteris, *John Sargent* (New York, 1927), p. 162. Cf. Sargent to Isabella Stewart Gardner, n.d., also quoted on p. 162.
54. *Memoir*, p. 149; EMHD, entry for Dec. 30, 1917, *PWW*, vol. 45, p. 400; RB to WW, Feb. 2, 1918, *PWW*, vol. 46, p. 219.
55. EMH to WW, June 27, 1917, *PWW*, vol. 43, p. 24. On Wiseman's meeting with Wilson, see Arthur Willert, *The Road to Safety: A Study in Anglo-American Relations* (London, 1952), p. 61, and on Reading's appointment and work in Washington, see Fowler, *British-American Relations*, pp. 53–60.
56. Root, quoted in Philip C. Jessup, *Elihu Root* (New York, 1938), vol. 2, p. 358; Creel, *Rebel at Large*, p. 253. On the Root mission, see Jessup, *Root*, vol. 2, pp. 352–68, and George F. Kennan, *Soviet-American Relations, 1917–1920*, vol. 1, *Russia Leaves the War* (Princeton, N.J., 1956), pp. 19–23.
57. WW speech, June 14, 1917, *PWW*, vol. 42, pp. 502–4; WW to EMH, July 21, 1917, *PWW*, vol. 43, p. 238.
58. WW reply to Pope Benedict XV's peace appeal, Aug. 27, 1917, *PWW*, vol. 44, pp. 57–59.
59. EMHD, entry for Aug. 15, 1917, *PWW*, vol. 43, pp. 486–87.
60. EMHD, entries for Sept. 9 and 10, 1917, *PWW*, vol. 45, pp. 175–79, 184–86.
61. WW to EMH, Sept. 2, 1917, *PWW*, vol. 44, pp. 120–21; EMH to WW, Sept. 4, 1917, *PWW*, vol. 44, p. 149.
62. On the beginning of the Inquiry, see the excellent account in Lawrence E. Gelfand, *The Inquiry: American Preparations for Peace, 1917–1919* (New Haven, Conn., 1963), pp. 32–78.
63. WW speech, Dec. 4, 1917, *PWW*, vol. 45, pp. 197–99.
64. EMHD, entry for Dec. 18, 1917, *PWW*, vol. 45, pp. 323–24.
65. Margaret Axson Elliott, *My Aunt Louisa and Woodrow Wilson* (Chapel Hill, N.C., 1944), p. 288.
66. EMHD, entries for Jan. 4 and 9, 1918, *PWW*, vol. 45, pp. 458, 550–51. On the Inquiry memorandum, see Gelfand, *Inquiry*, pp. 136–53.
67. EMHD, entry for Jan. 9, 1918, *PWW*, vol. 45, pp. 556–58.
68. WW speech, Jan. 8, 1918, *PWW*, vol. 45, pp. 534–36.
69. Ibid., pp. 536–38.
70. Ibid., pp. 538–39.

19   VICTORY

1. On the senatorial attacks and the Chamberlain bill, see Seward W. Livermore, *Politics Is Adjourned: Woodrow Wilson and the War Congress, 1916–1918* (Middletown, Conn., 1966), pp. 65–104. On Oregon's political culture, see Robert D. Johnston, *The Radical Middle Class: Populist Democracy and the Question of Capitalism in Progressive Era Portland, Oregon* (Princeton, N.J., 2003).
2. WW press release, Jan. 21, 1918, *PWW*, vol. 46, pp. 55–56; JDD, entry for Jan. 22, 1918, *PWW*, vol. 46, p. 79.

3. Ollie James quoted in RSB, *Woodrow Wilson: Life and Letters*, vol. 7, *War Leader, April 6, 1917–February 28, 1918* (Garden City, N.Y., 1966), p. 504.

4. WW to Bernard Baruch, Mar. 4, 1918, *PWW*, vol. 46, p. 522.

5. On the WIB under Baruch, see Robert D. Cuff, *The War Industries Board: Business-Government Relations during World War I* (Baltimore, 1973). In the 1930s, Johnson drew upon his experience with the WIB as director of the National Recovery Administration under the New Deal.

6. WW speech, Feb. 11, 1918, *PWW*, vol. 46, pp. 318–24.

7. WW to Theodore Marburg, Mar. 8, 1918, *PWW*, vol. 46, pp. 85–86. For the cracks about "butters-in" and "woolgathers," see WW to EMH, Mar. 20, 1918, *PWW*, vol. 47, p. 85. On the LEP's wartime activities, see Ruhl J. Bartlett, *The League to Enforce Peace* (Chapel Hill, N.C., 1944), pp. 83–112. See also John Milton Cooper, Jr., "The Not So Vital Center: The League to Enforce Peace and the League of Nations, 1919–1920," in *Gesellschaft und Diplomatie im transatlantischen Kontext: Festschrift für Reinhard R. Dorries*, ed. Michael Wala (Stuttgart, Germany, 1999), pp. 119–32.

8. WHT memorandum, [ca. Mar. 29, 1918], *PWW*, vol. 47, pp. 200–201.

9. EMHD, entry for Jan. 27, 1918, *PWW*, vol. 46, pp. 115–17. During this discussion, Edith chimed in, "I thought you and Woodrow would go alone," *PWW*, vol. 46, p. 115.

10. On William Howard Taft and the NWLB, see Valerie Jean Conner, *The National War Labor Board: Stability, Social Justice, and the Voluntary State in World War I* (Chapel Hill, N.C., 1983).

11. No minutes were taken at the meetings of the War Cabinet, and virtually the only record of its deliberations comes from Josephus Daniels's diary. On the War Cabinet, see Robert D. Cuff, "We Band of Brothers—Woodrow Wilson's War Managers," *Canadian Review of American Studies* 5 (fall 1974), pp. 135–48.

12. On the efforts to appease the Bolsheviks and deter the Japanese, see George F. Kennan, *Soviet-American Relations, 1917–1920*, vol. 1, *Russia Leaves the War* (Princeton, N.J., 1956), pp. 312–29. and on the flap with David Lloyd George, see W. B. Fowler, *British-American Relations, 1917–1918: The Role of Sir William Wiseman* (Princeton, N.J., 1969), pp. 139–40.

13. WW speech, Apr. 6, 1918, *PWW*, vol. 47, pp. 267–70.

14. WW remarks, Apr. 8, 1918, *PWW*, vol. 47, pp. 264–69.

15. On the Sedition Act, see Harry N. Scheiber, *The Wilson Administration and Civil Liberties, 1917–1921* (Ithaca, N.Y., 1960), pp. 22–26. Gregory's doubts about censorship are expressed in Thomas Gregory to WW, May 14, 1918, *PWW*, vol. 48, pp. 12–14.

16. Eugene V. Debs, "Statement to the Court," [Sept. 14, 1918], in Debs, *Writings and Speeches of Eugene V. Debs* (New York, 1948), p. 437.

17. WW to Thomas Gregory, Oct. 7, 1918, *PWW*, vol. 51, p. 257. The recommendation against prosecuting Debs is in John Lord O'Brian to E. S. Wertz, June 20, 1919, Records of the Department of Justice, record group 60, box 687, file 77175, National Archives, College Park, Md.

18. SA, interview by RSB, Sept. 2, 1931, RSBP, box 99; EMHD, entry for Feb. 24, 1918, *PWW*, vol. 46, pp. 435–36. Wilson made the same statement about government ownership a year later to Bernard Baruch and Vance McCormick. See Vance McCormick diary, entry for July 1–2–3, 1919, in *PWW*, vol. 63, p. 366.

19. The intricacies of dealing with the manpower crisis are ably covered in Fowler, *British-American Relations*, pp. 127–63. See also Edward M. Coffman, *The War to End All Wars: The American Military Experience in World War I* (New York, 1968), pp. 168–77.

20. On both Gutzon Borglum and the congressional restiveness, see Livermore, *Politics Is Adjourned*, pp. 124–30.

21. WW speech, May 18, 1918, *PWW*, vol. 48, p. 54.

22. WW address, May 27, 1918, *PWW*, vol. 48, pp. 162–65; WW to Joseph E. Davies, Mar. 18, 1918, *PWW*, vol. 47, p. 52. Davies would later serve as ambassador to the Soviet Union and would write a controversial memoir about his experience, which was made into a Hollywood movie.

23. James Slayden, who had originated the idea of the Pan-American Pact, had voted for the McLemore resolution, and he had run afoul of both Albert Burleson and Colonel House in Texas politics. His wife, as a young woman in Charlottesville, had known Wilson when he was a law student at Virginia and had disliked him ever since. In her diary, she wrote that the president had never forgiven her husband for having "committed the unpardonable sin of not wanting him nominated." Ellen Maury Slayden, entry for July 25, 1918, in Slayden, *Washington Wife: Journal of Ellen Maury Slayden from 1897–1919* (New York, 1963), p. 334. Her nephew, Maury Maverick, later served as congressman from the same district and as mayor of San Antonio.

24. WW to Frank P. Glass, Aug. 9, 1918, *PWW*, vol. 49, p. 224. On the campaigns against John Shields and George Huddleston, see Livermore, *Politics Is Adjourned*, pp. 161–64.

25. WW to Myron S. McNeil, Aug. 5, 1919, *PWW*, vol. 49, p. 180. On Vardaman's campaign, see William F. Holmes, *The White Chief: James Kimble Vardaman* (Baton Rouge, La., 1970), pp. 339–58.

26. WW to Clark Howell, Aug. 7, 1918, *PWW*, vol. 49, p. 206. On Watson's bid for a House seat, see C. Vann Woodward, *Tom Watson: Agrarian Rebel* (New York, 1938), pp. 451–63. Georgia politics had not seen the last of Thomas Hardwick and Tom Watson. Two years later, they brought off a spectacular comeback, with Hardwick winning the governorship and Watson a Senate seat, defeating Wilson's sometime supporter and onetime nemesis Hoke Smith.

27. The transformation of the Democrats on foreign policy is insightfully recounted and analyzed in Anthony Gaughan, "Woodrow Wilson and the Rise of Militant Interventionism in the South," *Journal of Southern History* 65 (Nov. 1999), pp. 771–808.

28. Jean le Pierrefeu, quoted in Winston Churchill, *The World Crisis*, vol. 4, *1916–1918* (London, 1927), p. 454. On the AEF operations, see Coffman, *War to End All Wars*, pp. 212–61.

29. On the controversy over Wood, see Hermann Hagedorn, *Leonard Wood: A Biography* (New York, 1931), vol. 2, pp. 282–302, and Jack McCallum, *Leonard Wood: Rough Rider, Surgeon, Architect of American Imperialism* (New York, 2006), pp. 172–74.

30. On the Czechs in Russia and the seizure of Vladivostock, see George F. Kennan, *Soviet-American Relations, 1917–1920*, vol. 2, *The Decision to Intervene* (Princeton, N.J., 1958), pp. 136–65, 393–94.

31. WW to EMH, July 8, 1918, *PWW*, vol. 48, p. 550; William Wiseman, "Notes of an Interview with the President at the White House, Wednesday, October 16th, 1918," *PWW*, vol. 51, pp. 348–49.

32. Wiseman to Lord Reading, Aug. 16, 1918, *PWW*, vol. 49, p. 273.

33. Ibid.; EMHD, entry for Aug. 15, 1918, *PWW*, vol. 49, pp. 265–67.

34. EMHD, entry for Aug. 18, 1918, *PWW*, vol. 49, p. 294.

35. For Brandeis's speculation, see Louis Brandeis, interview by RSB, Jan. 23, 1929, RSBP, box 102. For speculation about Wilson's health at this time, see Edwin A. Weinstein, *Woodrow Wilson: A Medical and Psychological Biography* (Princeton, N.J., 1981), pp. 320–23.

36. WW speech, July 4, 1918, *PWW*, vol. 48, pp. 514–18.

37. WW press statement, Sept. 9, 1918, *PWW*, vol. 49, p. 490.

38. WW speech, Sept. 27, 1918, *PWW*, vol. 51, pp. 127–33.

39. WW statement, Sept. 16, 1916, *PWW*, vol. 51, p. 11.

40. Thomas Lamont memorandum of interview with WW, Oct. 4, 1918, *PWW,* vol. 51, pp. 221–26. Lamont must have had a near-photographic memory, because right after this meeting he dictated an eight-page typewritten account that reads like a steno-graphic transcript. The typewritten-manuscript account of the interview is in the Thomas W. Lamont Papers, Baker Library, Harvard Business School.

41. RL to Frederich Oederlin, Oct. 8, 1918, *PWW,* vol. 51, p. 268. For the Senate debate, see 65th Cong., 2nd Sess., *Congresisonal Record* 11155–63 (Oct. 7, 1918).

42. Jean-Jules Jusserand to French foreign ministry, enclosed in Jusserand to Colville Barclay, Oct. 11, 1918, *PWW,* vol. 51, pp. 307–8.

43. Henry F. Ashurst diary, entry for Oct, 14, 1918, *PWW,* vol. 51, pp. 339–40; Homer Cummings diary, entry for Oct. 20, 1918, *PWW,* vol. 51, p. 391.

44. WW note, [Oct. 14, 1918], *PWW,* vol. 51, p. 333.

45. EMHD, entry for Oct. 15, 1918, *PWW,* vol. 51, pp. 340–42.

46. WW diplomatic note, Oct. 23, 1918, *PWW,* vol. 51, pp. 417–19. For an incisive and detailed treatment of House's views and negotiations in Europe, see Inga Floto, *Colonel House in Paris: A Study of American Diplomacy at the Paris Peace Conference, 1919* (Princeton, N.J., 1980), pp. 25–60.

47. WW statement, [Oct. 25, 1918], *PWW,* vol. 51, pp. 381–82. On the meeting with Cummings and McCormick, see Homer Cummings memorandum, Oct. 20, 1918, *PWW,* vol. 51, pp. 390–92; Vance McCormick, interview by RSB, July 21, 1926, RSBP, box 116; and Cummings memorandum, Nov. 21, 1928, RSBP, box 104.

48. Franklin K. Lane memorandum, Nov. 1, 1918, *PWW,* vol. 51, p. 546. For McCormick's and Daniels's judgments, see McCormick, interview by RSB, July 21, 1926, RSBP, box 116, and Josephus Daniels memorandum, Aug. 8, 1936, RSBP, box 105. For the claim that the Democrats might have won without the appeal, see Albert S. Burleson, interview by RSB, Mar. 27, 1927, RSBP, box 103, and Thomas Gregory, interviews by RSB, Mar. 14–15, 1927, RSBP, box 109.

49. EBGW, interview by RSB, Jan. 4, 1926, RSBP, box 124; Franklin K. Lane memoran-dum, Nov. 1, 1918, *PWW,* vol. 51, p. 548. On party machinations leading up to the appeal, see Livermore, *Politics Is Adjourned,* pp. 213–33.

50. On the campaign and salient issues, see Livermore, *Politics Is Adjourned,* pp. 169–205.

51. For an analysis of the results, see Livermore, *Politics Is Adjourned,* pp. 224–47.

52. For contemporary analyses that stress Republican use of patriotic appeals, particu-larly in the West, see memorandum enclosed with Homer Cummings to WW, Nov. 7, 1918, *PWW,* vol. 49, pp. 628–33, and George Creel to WW, Nov. 8, 1918, *PWW,* vol. 49, pp. 645–46.

53. TR to Arthur James Balfour, Dec. 15, 1918, TR, *Letters,* ed. Elting E. Morison, vol. 8, *The Days of Armageddon, 1900–1914* (Cambridge, Mass., 1954), p. 1415.

54. TR to Balfour, Dec. 15, 1918, TR, *Letters,* vol. 8, p. 1415; HCL to Balfour, Nov. 25, 1918, HCLP. For Lodge's visits to the embassies, see Colville Barclay to Balfour, Nov. 21, 1918, Arthur James Balfour Papers, British Museum. These contacts are also covered in Fowler, *British-American Relations,* pp. 229–31.

55. Homer Cummings memorandum, Nov. 8 or 9, 1918, *PWW,* vol. 51, pp. 646–48.

56. WW to EMH, [Oct. 30, 1918], *PWW,* vol. 51, p. 513.

57. EMH to WW, [Oct. 31], 1918, *PWW,* vol. 51, p. 534.

58. WW to EMH, [Oct. 30, 1918], *PWW,* vol. 51, p. 511; Harold Nicolson, *Peacemak-ing, 1919* (London, 1933), p. 16. Frank Cobb and Walter Lippmann's memorandum is in EMH to WW, Oct. 29, 1918, *PWW,* vol. 51, pp. 495–504.

59. On the final negotiations, see Harry R. Rudin, *Armistice, 1918* (New Haven, Conn., 1944), pp. 320–91.

60. *Memoir,* p. 170; WW statement, [ca. Nov. 11, 1918], *PWW,* vol. 53, p. 24; EMH to WW, [Nov. 11, 1918], *PWW,* vol. 53, p. 24; David Lloyd George, *Parliamentary*

Debates, H.C. Deb., 110, 2463 (Nov. 11, 1918). Lloyd George appears to have taken the phrase from the title of a book by H. G. Wells: *The War That Will End War* (London, 1914).

61. WW address, Nov. 11, 1918, *PWW*, vol. 53, pp. 24–43. For a description of the scene in the House chamber, see Henry F. Ashurst diary, entry for Nov. 11, 1918, *PWW*, vol. 51, p. 24

20 COVENANT

1. CTGD, entry for Dec. 28, 1918, *PWW*, vol. 53, p. 526; WW remarks, Dec. 29, 1918, *PWW*, vol. 53, p. 541.

2. EMH to WW, Nov. 14, 1918, *PWW*, vol. 53, pp. 71–72; WW to EMH, Nov. 16, 1918, *PWW*, vol. 53, pp. 96–97; EMHD, entry for Dec. 3, 1918, and EMH, "Memories," ca. 1928, EMH Papers, Yale University Library.

3. RL memorandum, "Will the President Go to the Peace Congress?" Nov. 12, 1918, *PWW*, vol. 53, pp. 65–66; Key Pittman to WW, Nov. 15, 1918, *PWW*, vol. 53, pp. 93–95. The editors of *The Papers of Woodrow Wilson* raise doubts about whether Lansing did confront Wilson the way he said he did. See *PWW*, vol. 53, p. 66, n. 1.

4. William Emmanuel Rappard memorandum of conversation with WW, [Nov. 20, 1918], *PWW*, vol. 53, pp. 626–27.

5. One appealing choice might have been the second-ranking Republican on the Foreign Relations Committee, Porter J. McCumber of North Dakota, who would be his party's strongest advocate of League membership in the Senate. This possibility is discussed in John Milton Cooper, Jr., *Breaking the Heart of the World: Woodrow Wilson and the Fight for the League of Nations* (New York, 2001), pp. 34–35.

6. Thomas Gregory, interviews by RSB, Mar. 14–15, 1927, RSBP, box 109.

7. HCL to James Bryce, Dec. 14, 1918, HCLP; WW to Richard Hooker, Nov. 29, 1918, *PWW*, vol. 53, pp. 243–44; WW to Frank Morrison, Nov. 22, 1918, *PWW*, vol. 53, p. 165.

8. For a discussion of this failure of bipartisanship, see Cooper, *Breaking the Heart of the World*, pp. 36–37. FDR's first major bipartisan overture—appointing Henry Stimson secretary of war and Frank Knox secretary of the navy—did not result in any appreciable rise in Republican support for his foreign policies. Such support came only after Pearl Harbor, when the Republicans felt badly burned by their earlier support for isolationism.

9. On assembling the staff, see Arthur Walworth, *America's Moment, 1918: American Diplomacy at the End of World War I* (New York, 1977), pp. 75–84.

10. On the post-war situation at home, see Burl Noggle, *Into the Twenties: The United States from Armistice to Normalcy* (Urbana, Ill., 1974), pp. 13–65.

11. WW address, Dec. 2, 1918, *PWW*, vol. 53, pp. 274–86.

12. JDD, entry for Dec. 2, 1918, *PWW*, vol. 53, p. 301; 65th Cong., 3rd Sess., *Congressional Record* 23 (Dec. 3, 1918); 189–197 (Dec. 6, 1918). On these attacks on the league idea in the Senate, see Cooper, *Breaking the Heart of the World*, pp. 39–42.

13. *Memoir*, pp. 172–74.

14. CTGD, entry for Dec. 4, 1918, *PWW*, vol. 53, p. 314.

15. Henry White memorandum, Dec. [18], 1918, quoted in Allan Nevins, *Henry White: Thirty Years of American Diplomacy* (New York, 1930), p. 359; CTGD, entry for Dec. 8, 1918, *PWW*, vol. 53, pp. 337–40.

16. William C. Bullitt diary, entry for Dec. 10, 1918, *PWW*, vol. 53, p. 350; Isaiah Bowman memorandum, Dec. 10, 1918, *PWW*, vol. 53, p. 356. For other accounts of this meeting, see Charles Seymour to family, Dec. 10, 1918, *PWW*, vol. 53, pp. 356–57;

Clive Day to Elizabeth Day, Dec. 10, 1918, *PWW,* vol. 53, pp. 348–49; George Louis Beer diary, entry for Dec. 10, 1918, Rare Book and Manuscript Library, Columbia University; and William Linn Westermann diary, entry for Dec. 10, 1918, William Linn Westermann Papers, Rare Book and Manuscript Library, Columbia University. All these accounts agree on what Wilson said.

17. Bullitt diary, entry for [Dec. 11, 1918], *PWW,* vol. 53, p. 367; George Creel, *The War, the World and Wilson* (New York, 1920), p. 163. See also Raymond Fosdick diary, entry for Dec. 11, 1918, *PWW,* vol. 53, pp. 365–66.

18. Fosdick diary, entry for Dec. 14, 1918, *PWW,* vol. 53, p. 384.

19. EBGW to family, Dec 15 [and 17], 1918, *PWW,* vol. 53, pp. 398–99.

20. WW to Herbert B. Brougham, Dec. 17, 1918, *PWW,* vol. 53, p. 412.

21. Lord Derby to Arthur James Balfour, Dec. 22 and 24, 1918, *PWW,* vol. 53, pp. 471–72, 498.

22. CTGD, entry for Dec. 26, 1918, *PWW,* vol. 53, p. 511. For the encounter with Churchill, see Edith Benham Helm diary, entry for Jan. 27, 1919, *PWW,* vol. 54, p. 307. The impression that Wilson cared only about the League comes from "Draft Minutes of a Meeting held at 10 Downing Street, S.W., on Monday, December 30, 1918, at 3:30 p.m.," *PWW,* vol. 53, pp. 558–59. That was a meeting of the Imperial War Cabinet, and the record states that Wilson discussed such matters as intervention in Russia, financial reparations, disarmament, the Turkish straits, and the Dalmatian coast. See Imperial War Cabinet minutes, Dec. 30, 1918, *PWW,* vol. 53, pp. 558–69.

23. WW speeches, Dec. 28, 1918, *PWW,* vol. 53, pp. 530, 534; Frank Worthington, "Statements made by President Wilson to me on the evening of Saturday, the 28th of December, 1918," *PWW,* vol. 53, pp. 574–76; C. P. Scott diary, entry for Dec. 29, 1918, *PWW,* vol. 53, p. 576, n. 1.

24. WW speech, Jan. 3, 1918, *PWW,* vol. 53, p. 598.

25. CTGD, entry for Jan. 4, 1919, *PWW,* vol. 53, p. 607; "Digest of the President's Conference with On. Bissolati," [Jan. 4, 1919], *PWW,* vol. 53, pp. 641–44.

26. State Department proclamation, Jan. 7, 1919, *PWW,* vol. 53, p. 635. For WW's rewriting the proclamation, see CTGD, entry for Jan. 7, 1919, *PWW,* vol. 53, p. 634, and for his reading the essay about Roosevelt, see Edith Benham diary, entry for Jan. 10, 1919, *PWW,* vol. 53, p. 708.

27. On what Roosevelt's death meant for the conflict over the League of Nations, see Cooper, *Breaking the Heart of the World,* pp. 43–45.

28. WW draft, [ca. Jan. 8, 1919], *PWW,* vol. 53, pp. 678–86. A facsimile copy of this draft is reproduced in *PWW,* vol. 53, pp. 655–77. Colonel House claimed that the draft embodied what "I wrote at Magnolia [his summer home], embellished with some of General Smuts' ideas and a paragraph or two of the President's own." EMHD, entry for Jan. 8, 1919, *PWW,* vol. 53, p. 694. House was both egotistic and mistaken. Wilson had written that earlier draft, and this "First Paris Draft" was largely his own.

29. WW draft, [ca. Jan. 8, 1919], *PWW,* vol. 53, p. 679.

30. RL memorandum, Jan. 11, 1919, *PWW,* vol. 54, pp. 3–4; Tasker H. Bliss, "Suggestions in Regard to the Draft of the Covenant," Jan. 14, 1919, *PWW,* vol. 54, pp. 85–88; Gustav Ador, interview with WW [Jan. 23, 1919], *PWW,* vol. 54, p. 233.

31. Edith Benham diary, entry for Jan. 10, 1919, *PWW,* vol. 53, pp. 707–8; CTGD, entry for Jan. 12, 1919, *PWW,* vol. 54, p. 5.

32. CTGD, entry for Jan. 13, 1919, *PWW,* vol. 54, p. 35.

33. [Sir Maurice Hankey], minutes of the Council of Ten, Jan. 17, 1919, *PWW,* vol. 54, p. 111.

34. Protocol of the plenary session of the Paris Peace Conference, Jan. 18, 1919, *PWW,* vol. 54, pp. 128–32.

35. WW to JPT, Jan. 20, 1919, *PWW*, vol. 54, p. 158; CTGD, entry for Jan. 19, 1919, *PWW*, vol. 54, p. 150.
36. Robert Cecil diary, entry for Jan. 19, 1919, *PWW*, vol. 54, p. 152.
37. WW quoted in minutes of the protocol of the Paris Peace Conference, Jan. 25, 1919, *PWW*, vol. 54, pp. 265–67. For a description of meetings of the Council of Ten, see Margaret MacMillan, *Paris 1919: Six Months That Changed the World* (New York, 2002), pp. 53–54.
38. CTGD, entry for Jan. 28, 1919, *PWW*, vol. 54, p. 308; Charles Seymour to family, Jan. 30, 1919, *PWW*, vol. 54, pp. 383–84.
39. EMHD, entry for Feb. 3, 1919, *PWW*, vol. 54, p. 459. See also David Hunter Miller diary, entry for Feb. 2 [3], [1919], *PWW*, vol. 54, p. 439.
40. EMHD, entry for Feb. 3, 1919, *PWW*, vol. 54, pp. 468–69; Robert Cecil diary, entry for Feb. 3, [1919], *PWW*, vol. 54, p. 469; Herbert Hoover quoted in Henry L. Stimson diary, entry for Mar. 18, 1920, Henry L. Stimson Papers, Department of Manuscripts and Archives, Yale University Library; HCL, quoted in Stephen Bonsal, *Unfinished Business* (Garden City, N.Y., 1944), p. 275.
41. EMHD, entry for Feb. 4, 1919, *PWW*, vol. 54, pp. 484–85; Robert Cecil diary, entry for Feb. 6, [1919], *PWW*, vol. 54, p. 514. About Wilson himself, Cecil wrote, "I am coming to the conclusion that I do not personally like him. I do not quite know what it is that repels me: a certain hardness coupled with vanity and an eye for effect. He supports idealistic causes without being in the least an idealist himself." *PWW*, vol. 54, p. 522.
42. WW, quoted in minutes of the League of Nations Commission, Feb. 11, 1919, *PWW*, vol. 55, pp. 75–80.
43. Minutes of the League of Nations Commission, Feb. 13, 1919, *PWW*, vol. 55, pp. 138–40.
44. Minutes of the Council of Ten, Feb. 6 and 13, 1919, *PWW*, vol. 54, p. 509; vol. 55, p. 141.
45. CTGD, entry for Feb. 10, 1919, *PWW*, vol. 55, p. 41; EMHD, entry for Feb. 11, 1919, *PWW*, vol. 55, pp. 88–89.
46. New York *World*, Feb. 15, 1919.
47. For the Draft Covenant as Wilson read it to the conference, see *PWW*, vol. 55, pp. 164–73.
48. WW remarks, Feb. 14, 1919, *PWW*, vol. 55, pp. 175–77.
49. WW to JPT, Feb. 14, 1919, *PWW*, vol. 55, p. 184.

21 PEACEMAKING ABROAD AND AT HOME

1. William E. Borah, quoted in New York *World*, Feb. 1, 1919; CTGD, entry for Feb. 22, 1919, *PWW*, vol. 55, p. 224. On reactions to the Draft Covenant, see John Milton Cooper, Jr., *Breaking the Heart of the World: Woodrow Wilson and the Fight for the League of Nations* (New York, 2001), pp. 57–61.
2. WW speech, Feb. 24, 1919, *PWW*, vol. 55, p. 238, n. 2.
3. *New York Times*, Feb. 27, 1919; Mar. 1, 1919; New York *World*, Feb. 27, 1919; New York *Sun*, Feb. 27, 1919. See also 65th Cong., 3rd Sess., *Congressional Record* 4528–30 (Feb. 28, 1919), 4881 (Mar. 1, 1919). For Frank Brandegee's account and complaints, see Chandler P. Anderson diary, entry for Mar. 13, 1919, Chandler P. Anderson Papers, LC. For a retrospective account of the meeting, see Tom Connally and Alfred Steinberg, *My Name Is Tom Connally* (New York, 1954), p. 96.
4. HCL to Henry White, Apr. 8, 1919, HCLP; John Jacob Rogers to White, Mar. 3, 1919, quoted in Allan Nevins, *Henry White: Thirty Years of American Diplomacy* (New

York, 1930), p. 392. See also WW to Thomas J. Walsh, Feb. 26, 1919, *PWW,* vol. 55, p. 280, and *New York Times,* Feb. 28, 1919.

5. 65th Cong., 3rd Sess., *Congressional Record* 4520-28 (Feb. 28, 1919); 4687–94 (Mar. 1, 1919). For an analysis of these speeches, see Cooper, *Breaking the Heart of the World,* pp. 64–66.

6. WW speech, Feb. 28, 1919, *PWW,* vol. 55, pp. 309–24. On the promise to bring up the Monroe Doctrine, see WW to Samuel McCall, Feb. 28, 1919, *PWW,* vol. 55, pp. 328–29; on changes in the Draft Covenant, see John Jacob Rogers memorandum, [ca. Mar. 1, 1919], Henry White Papers, Rare Book and Manuscript Library, Columbia University, box 1.

7. 65th Cong., 3rd Sess., *Congressional Record* 4974 (Mar. 4, 1919). On the round-robin, see Cooper, *Breaking the Heart of the World,* pp. 56–57, 67–68.

8. See *New York Times,* Mar. 4 and 5, 1919; New York *World,* Mar. 4 and 5, 1919. On Lodge's motives, see HCL, *The Senate and the League of Nations* (New York, 1925), pp. 62–63, and HCL to Robert E. Annin, Apr. 4, 1924, HCLP.

9. CTGD, entry for Mar. 4, 1919, *PWW,* vol. 55, p. 410.

10. WHT speech, Mar. 4, 1919, in WHT, *Taft Papers on League of Nations,* ed., Theodore Marburg and Horace Flack (New York, 1920), pp. 262–80.

11. WW speech, Mar. 4, 1919, *PWW,* vol. 55, pp. 413–21. For Republican criticisms of the speech, see Nicholas Murray Butler to Alfred Holman, Mar. 4, 1919, Nicholas Murray Butler Papers, Rare Book and Manuscrip Library, Columbia University, and George W. Wickersham to Henry White, Mar. 9, 1919, Henry White Papers, LC, box 40.

12. CTGD, entry for Mar. 5, 1919, *PWW,* vol. 55, p. 443.

13. *New York Times,* Mar. 15, 1919.

14. EMHD, entry for Mar. 14, 1919, *PWW,* vol. 55, p. 499.

15. Root quoted in enclosure, Thomas W. Lamont to WW, Mar. 19, 1919, *PWW,* vol. 56, pp. 99–100.

16. HCL to Henry White, Mar. 15, 1919, HCLP. On these contacts, see Cooper, *Breaking the Heart of the World,* pp. 72–74.

17. Georges Clemenceau, quoted in Margaret MacMillan, *Paris 1919: Six Months That Changed the World* (New York, 2002), p. 151; EMHD, entry for Feb. 14, 1919, *PWW,* vol. 55, p. 193.

18. For the speculations of the editors of *The Papers of Woodrow Wilson* about this proposal, see *PWW,* vol. 55, p. 305, n. 1. For an exhaustive examination of House's activities during this time, see Inga Floto, *Colonel House in Paris: A Study of American Diplomacy at the Paris Peace Conference, 1919* (Princeton, N.J., 1980), pp. 99–163.

19. *Memoir,* pp. 245–46; CTGD, entry for Mar. 14, 1919, *PWW,* vol. 55, p. 498. For evaluations of this incident and relations between Wilson and House, see *PWW,* vol. 55, p. 488, n. 2, and Floto, *Colonel House in Paris,* pp. 164–70.

20. *Memoir,* p. 247; CTGD, entry for Mar. 14, 1919, *PWW,* vol. 55, p. 497.

21. CTGD, entry for Mar. 22, 1919, *PWW,* vol. 56, pp. 164–65; EMHD, entry for Mar. 22, 1919, *PWW,* vol. 56, pp. 179–80; RL memorandum, Mar. 28, 1919, *PWW,* vol. 56, p. 352.

22. For a description of the Council of Four, see MacMillan, *Paris 1919,* pp. 273–74. On Mantoux's notes, see Paul Mantoux, Author's Preface, in *Paris Peace Conference, the Deliberations of the Council of Four (March 24–June 28, 1919): Notes of the Official Interpreter,* trans. and ed. ASL and Manfred F. Boemeke (Princeton, N.J., 1992), vol. 1; *To the Delivery to the German Delegation of the Preliminaries of Peace,* pp. xxxiii–xl; and "Mantoux and His Notes," pp. xiii–xviii.

23. Mantoux notes, Mar. 24 and 27, 1919, *PWW,* vol. 56, pp. 208, 319, 366, 368. Mantoux's notes are reproduced in this and successive volumes of *The Papers of Woodrow*

Wilson and in *Paris Peace Conference, the Deliberations of the Council of Four*. Wilson was in the habit of telling his wife and Grayson about the meetings, and his view of what transpired is often reproduced in the excerpts from Grayson's diary, in *The Papers of Woodrow Wilson*.

24. EMHD, entry for Mar. 28, 1919, *PWW*, vol. 56, p. 350; CTGD, entry for Mar. 29, 1919, *PWW*, vol. 56, p. 498. For Mantoux's notes of the afternoon meeting, see pp. 408–20.

25. Mantoux notes, Mar. 27, 1919; Apr. 1, 1919, *PWW*, vol. 56, pp. 323, 510; WW statement, [May 6, 1919], *PWW*, vol. 57, p. 58. The dating of the statement in *The Papers of Woodrow Wilson* is speculative.

26. RSBD, entry for Mar. 31, 1919, *PWW*, vol. 56, p. 441.

27. CTGD, entry for Apr. 3, 1919, *PWW*, vol. 56, pp. 556–57. There would be speculations that the president suffered a small stroke or an attack of encephalitis, but medical specialists who recently examined his symptoms concluded that the illness was almost certainly a viral infection and probably a strain of influenza. For the examination of his symptoms by physicians and review of previous speculations, see *PWW*, vol. 56, p. 557, n. 2.

28. CTGD, entry for Apr. 6, 1991, *PWW*, vol. 57, pp. 50–51; RSBD, entry for Apr. 7, 1919, *PWW*, vol. 57, p. 68. On the press leak about the *George Washington*, see p. 63, n. 1.

29. WW to EMH, [ca. Apr. 7, 1919], *PWW*, vol. 57, p. 90; RSBD, entries for [Mar. 31, 1919]; Apr. 4, [1919], *PWW*, vol. 56, pp. 441, 589. On Colonel House's dealing with reporters, see p. 65, n. 2. On his performance as Wilson's substitute, see Floto, *Colonel House in Paris*, pp. 194–205.

30. CTGD, entries for Apr. 6, 7, and 8, 1919, *PWW*, vol. 57, pp. 51, 62, 100.

31. CTGD, entry for Apr. 8, 1919, *PWW*, vol. 57, p. 98; notes of the Council of Four, Apr. 8 and 9, 1919, *PWW*, vol. 57, pp. 123, 130, 163–65.

32. League Commission minutes, Apr. 10, 1919, *PWW*, vol. 57, p. 226; Robert Cecil diary, entry for Apr. 11, [1919], *PWW*, vol. 57, p. 274. For the debates, see League Commission minutes, Apr. 11, 1919, *PWW*, vol. 57, pp. 248–66.

33. WW remarks, [Apr. 11, 1919], *PWW*, vol. 57, pp. 268–69.

34. On Keynes's resigning and writing *The Economic Consequences*, see Robert Skidelsky, *John Maynard Keynes*, vol. 1, *Hopes Betrayed, 1883–1920* (New York, 1986), pp. 371–81.

35. WW memorandum, [Apr. 14, 1919], *PWW*, vol. 57, pp. 343–44; RSBD, entry for May 28, [1919], *PWW*, vol. 57, p. 575.

36. EMHD, entries for Apr. 14, 15, and 28, 1919, *PWW*, vol. 57, pp. 335, 353; vol. 58, p. 186.

37. Notes of the Council of Four, Apr. 15, 1919, *PWW*, vol. 57, p. 358. On the Chinese memorandum, see p. 431, n. 1.

38. CTGD, entry for Apr. 17, 1919, *PWW*, vol. 57, pp. 426–28.

39. RSBD, entries for April 19 and 20, [1919], *PWW*, vol. 57, pp. 508, 527–28; *Memoir*, p. 252.

40. WW statement, [Apr. 21, 1919], *PWW*, vol. 57, pp. 542–44.

41. Minutes of the Council of Four, Apr. 22, 1919, *PWW*, vol. 57, pp. 603, 606, 620, 623, 625–26.

42. RSBD, entries for Apr. 25 and [Apr. 30], 1919; May 1, [1919], *PWW*, vol. 58, pp. 142–43, 270–71, 327.

43. WW remarks, Apr. 28, 1919, *PWW*, vol. 58, p. 201; minutes of the Council of Four, Apr. 22, 1919, *PWW*, vol. 57, p. 606. On possible physical causes for the shortcomings of the remarks, see *PWW*, vol. 58, p. 202, n. 1, and for three neurologists' speculation about a small stroke, see Bert E. Park, "The Impact of Wilson's Neurologic

Disease during the Paris Peace Conference," *PWW*, vol. 58, pp. 611–30; Edwin A. Weinstein, "Woodrow Wilson's Neuropsychological Impairment at the Paris Peace Conference," *PWW*, vol. 58, pp. 630–35; and James F. Toole, "Some Observations on Wilson's Neurological Illness," *PWW*, vol. 58, pp. 635–38.

44. Minutes of the Council of Four, May 1, 1919, *PWW*, vol. 58, p. 287.

45. CTGD, entry for May 2, 1919, *PWW*, vol. 58, p. 332; RSBD, entry for May 3, 1919, *PWW*, vol. 58, p. 419.

46. Ulrich Graf von Brockdorff-Rantzau remarks, [May 7, 1919], *PWW*, vol. 58, p. 514. For firsthand accounts of the session, see RSBD, entry for May 7, [1919], *PWW*, vol. 58, pp. 529–30; CTGD, entry for May 7, 1919, *PWW*, vol. 58, pp. 501–3; and EMHD, entry for May 7, 1919, *PWW*, vol. 58, pp. 520–21. For a description of the session, see MacMillan, *Paris 1919*, pp. 463–64.

47. RSBD, entry for May 3, [1919], *PWW*, vol. 58, p. 419; William C. Bullitt to WW, May 17, 1919, *PWW*, vol. 59, pp. 232–33; *Nation*, Apr. 26, 1919, pp. 646–47; *New Republic*, Mar. 29, 1919, pp. 263–65; May 24, 1919, pp. 100–106. See also Herbert Hoover, *The Ordeal of Woodrow Wilson* (New York, 1958), p. 234. For other examples of disappointment with the terms, see MacMillan, *Paris 1919*, pp. 467–68. On the resignations, see also Cooper, *Breaking the Heart of the World*, pp. 95–96. On progressives' attacks on the League and the peace terms, see Thomas J. Knock, *To End All Wars: Woodrow Wilson and the Quest for a New World Order* (New York, 1992), pp. 252–56, and Cooper, *Breaking the Heart of the World*, pp. 85–86, 97–100.

48. These matters are all covered in MacMillan, *Paris 1919*; my views agree largely with hers.

49. On the mandates, see MacMillan, *Paris 1919*, pp. 83–106. For DuBois's assessment, see *Crisis*, May 1919, pp. 10–11, and also Manning Marable, *W. E. B. DuBois, Black Radical Democrat* (Boston, 1986), pp. 91–103, and David Levering Lewis, *W. E. B. DuBois: Biography of a Race, 1868–1919* (New York, 1993), pp. 535–80.

50. Despite John Maynard Keynes's stature as one of the greatest economists in history, his analysis of the settlement has not gone without attack. See Etienne Mantoux, *The Carthaginian Peace; or, the Economic Consequences of Mr. Keynes* (New York, 1946).

51. WW speeches, May 9 and 10, 1919, *PWW*, vol. 58, pp. 598–99; vol. 59, p. 5. Two of the neurologists consulted by the editors of *The Papers of Woodrow Wilson* detect in the May 9 speech signs of a serious underlying condition. See Park, "Wilson's Neurological Disease," *PWW*, vol. 58, p., 627, and Weinstein, "Wilson's Neuropsychological Impairment," *PWW*, vol. 58, p. 634.

52. CTGD, entry for May 24, 1919, *PWW*, vol. 59, p. 453.

53. RSBD, entry for May 21, 1919, *PWW*, vol. 59, p. 368; WW message to Congress, [May 20, 1919], *PWW*, vol. 59, pp. 289–97; CTGD, entry for May 13, 1919, *PWW*, vol. 59, p. 79.

54. WW speech, May 30, 1919, *PWW*, vol. 59, pp. 606–10; RSBD, entry for May 30, 1919, *PWW*, vol. 59, p. 622.

55. See RSBD, entry for May 28, [1919], *PWW*, vol. 59, p. 574. For speculation about the significance of Ray Stannard Baker's observations, see p. 575, n. 1.

56. On David Lloyd George and the meeting of the British delegation, see MacMillan, *Paris 1919*, pp. 468–69.

57. Transcript of the meeting of the American delegation, [June 3, 1919], *PWW*, vol. 60, pp. 67–71. For eyewitness descriptions of this meeting, see Vance McCormick diary, entry for June 3, [1919], *PWW*, vol. 60, pp. 72–79; Charles Seymour to family, June 3, 1919, *PWW*, vol. 60, pp. 75–79; and RSBD, entry for June 3, 1919, *PWW*, vol. 60, pp. 79–80.

58. William Orpen, *An Onlooker in France, 1917–1919* (London, 1921), p. 104. For evidence of how well known Colonel House's loss of influence was, see William Linn

Westermann diary, entry for June 13, [1919], *PWW,* vol. 60, p. 492, and RL memorandum, Aug, 21, 1919, *PWW,* vol. 62, pp. 454–55.

59. RSBD, entry for June 19, [1919], *PWW,* vol. 60, p. 374. See also *Memoir,* pp. 261–64.

60. WW speech, June 19, 1919, *PWW,* vol. 60, pp. 17–18.

61. On the events and conflict in Germany, see MacMillan, *Paris 1919,* pp. 471–74.

62. On the visit to Versailles, see CTGD, entry for June 24, 1919, *PWW,* vol. 61, pp. 118–19.

63. WW speech, June 26, 1919, *PWW,* vol. 61, pp. 189–91.

64. Walter E. Weyl, notes of press conference, June 27, 1919, *PWW,* vol. 61, pp. 242–45. Other accounts of the conference are in CTGD, entry for June 27, 1919, *PWW,* vol. 61, pp. 236–37, and Charles T. Thompson report, [June 27, 1919], *PWW,* vol. 61, pp. 246–52.

65. For eyewitness accounts of the scene, see EMHD, entry for June 28, 1919, *PWW,* vol. 61, pp. 352–53; William Linn Westermann, "The Signing of the Treaty of Versailles," *PWW,* vol. 61, pp. 328–32; and *New York Times,* June 29, 1919. For a historian's description, see MacMillan, *Paris 1919,* pp. 474–78.

66. RL memorandum, June 28, 1919, *PWW,* vol. 61, pp. 323–24; Orpen *Onlooker in France,* p. 119.

67. WW statement, June 27, 1919, *PWW,* vol. 61, pp. 292–93.

68. CTGD, entry for June 28, 1919, *PWW,* vol. 61, pp. 304–5.

69. WW to JPT and JPT to WW, June 28, 1919, *PWW,* vol. 61, p. 352; EMHD, entry for June 29, 1919, *PWW,* vol. 61, pp. 354–55.

22   THE LEAGUE FIGHT

1. WW to William Allen White, Apr. 2, 1919, *PWW,* vol. 56, p. 545; WW speech, Sept. 19, 1919, *PWW,* vol. 63, p. 382.

2. For the senatorial lineup, see *Chicago Tribune,* June 24, 1919. On the developments in opinion since March, see John Milton Cooper, Jr., *Breaking the Heart of the World: Woodrow Wilson and the Fight for the League of Nations* (New York, 2001), pp. 74–86, 90–94, 99–108.

3. CTGD, entry for July 1, 1919, *PWW,* vol. 61, pp. 360–61.

4. WW press conference, July 10, 1919, *PWW,* vol. 61, pp. 417–24. Wilson might have felt less touched by his reception if he had known that Alice Roosevelt Longworth, Roosevelt's daughter, had made the sign of the evil eye as his limousine passed and muttered a curse: "A murrain on him, a murrain on him." Alice Roosevelt Longworth, *Crowded Hours: Reminiscences of Alice Roosevelt Longworth* (New York, 1933), p. 285.

5. CTGD, entry for July 10, 1919, *PWW,* vol. 61, p. 417. See also *New York Times,* July 11, 1919.

6. WW speech, July 10, 1919, *PWW,* vol. 61, pp. 426–36.

7. New York *World,* July 11, 1919; Henry F. Ashurst diary, entry for July 11, 1919, *PWW,* vol. 61, pp. 445–46. See also *New York Times,* July 11, 1919.

8. See *New York Times,* July 11, 1919.

9. On the race riots of 1919, see especially William M. Tuttle, Jr., *Race Riot: Chicago in the Red Summer of 1919* (New York, 1970).

10. Gus J. Karger to WHT, July 19, 1919, WHTP, microfilm ed., reel 211; Chandler P. Anderson diary, entry for July 30, 1919, Chandler P. Anderson Papers, microfilm ed., reel 2, LC.

11. WW speech, Aug. 8, 1919, *PWW,* vol. 62, pp. 209–19. On Wilson's difficulty composing the speech and possible effects of his health on this speech, see p. 209, n. 1.

12. SA memoir, quoted in *PWW,* vol. 61, p. 228, n. 1; SA memorandum, *PWW,* vol. 67, pp. 605–7.

13. WW to A. Mitchell Palmer, Aug. 4, 1919, *PWW,* vol. 62, p. 126. For Palmer's recommendation to wait until ratification, see Palmer to WW, July 30, 1919, *PWW,* vol. 6, p. 58.

14. On William Howard Taft's and Charles Evans Hughes's espousal of reservations, see Cooper, *Breaking the Heart of the World,* pp. 114–16, 131–32.

15. 66th Cong., 1st Sess., *Congressional Record* 2592–2600 (July 15, 1919). On the committee's actions, see Cooper, *Breaking the Heart of the World,* pp. 138–40.

16. RL diary, entry for Aug. 7, 1919, RL papers, LC; Johnson to Hiram Johnson, Jr., and Arch M. Johnson, Aug. 7, 1919, in Johnson, *The Diary Letters of Hiram Johnson,* vol. 3, *1919–1921* (New York, 1983); HCL to Constance Lodge Gardner, Aug. 9, 1919, HCLP. Lansing's testimony is in U.S. Senate, Committee on Foreign Relations, *Treaty of Peace with Germany Hearings,* 66th Cong., 1st Sess. (Washington, D.C., 1919), pp. 139–214.

17. McAdoo, *Crowded Years: The Reminiscences of William G. McAdoo* (Boston, 1931), p. 514. On the mild reservationists, see Herbert F. Margulies, *The Mild Reservationists and the League of Nations Controversy in the Senate* (Columbia, Mo., 1989), pp. xii, xiv, 60–61.

18. New York *World,* Aug. 11, 1919; HCL to Elihu Root, Aug. 15, 1919, Elihu Root Papers, LC. On these dealings, see Margulies, *Mild Reservationists,* pp. 90–91, and Cooper, *Breaking the Heart of the World,* pp. 147–49.

19. RL diary, entry for Aug. 11, 1919, *PWW,* vol. 62, pp. 258–59.

20. On Wilson's sparring with the Senate Foreign Relations Committee over the documents from the peace conference, see Cooper, *Breaking the Heart of the World,* pp. 140–41. During the Civil War, Lincoln met twice at the White House with a "committee" named by the Republican caucus in the Senate. These were strictly private meetings and did not involve either a standing committee of either house of Congress or any items of legislation. See James G. Randall, *Lincoln, the President,* vol. 2, *Springfield to Gettysburg* (New York, 1945), pp. 243–47; Phillip Shaw Paludan, *The Presidency of Abraham Lincoln* (Lawrence, Kans., 1994), pp. 173–77; and David Herbert Donald, *Lincoln* (New York, 1995), pp. 403–5. In the twentieth century, presidents met informally with members of committees, and in the 1950s and '60s, presidents Truman, Eisenhower, Kennedy, and Johnson would often consult with members of the Foreign Relations Committee, sometimes the whole committee, especially in times of crisis.

21. WW statement, Aug. 19, 1919, *PWW,* vol. 62, pp. 340–44. For descriptions of the scene, see New York *World,* Aug. 20, 1919, and *New York Times,* Aug. 20, 1919.

22. Transcript of meeting, Aug. 19, 1919, *PWW,* vol. 62, pp. 345–52.

23. Ibid., pp. 353–406; Hiram Johnson to Hiram Johnson, Jr., and Arch Johnson, Aug. 23, 1991, in Johnson, *Diary Letters,* vol. 3. On what the president knew and when he knew it about the secret treaties, see *PWW,* vol. 62, p. 365, n. 27.

24. Transcript of meeting, Aug. 19, 1919, *PWW,* vol. 62, pp. 407–11. On the lunch, see *New York Times,* Aug. 20, 1919.

25. HCL to James T. Williams, Jr., Aug. 20, [1919], HCLP; HCL to W. Sturgis Bigelow, Aug. 25, 1919, HCLP; Hiram Johnson to Hiram Johnson, Jr., and Arch Johnson, Aug. 23, 1919, in Johnson, *Diary Letters,* vol. 3.

26. *New York Times,* Aug. 21, 1919. The editors of *The Papers of Woodrow Wilson* speculate, based on circumstantial evidence, that Wilson may have authorized Pittman's resolution as a trial balloon. See *PWW,* vol. 62, p. 432, n. 2. Pittman, however, later said, "I purposely refrained from consulting with the president with regard to such resolution, as I realized it was not proper or advisable for him to approve . . . any

reservation at that time." Key Pittman to William Hard, July 27, 1926, Key Pittman Papers, LC.

27. Entry for Aug. 30, 1919, in Henry Fountain Ashurst, *A Many-Colored Toga: Diary*, ed., George F. Sparks (Tucson, Ariz., 1962), p. 164.

28. New York *World*, Aug. 24, 1919; HCL, quoted in Chandler P. Anderson diary, entry for Aug. 22, 1919, Chandler P. Anderson Papers, microfilm ed., reel 2, LC.

29. *Memoir*, p. 274. For the view that the decision was "made without much thought, in anger, and on the spur of the moment" and was, therefore "irrational," see *PWW*, vol. 62, p. 507, n. 2. For a contrary view, see John Milton Cooper, Jr., "Fool's Errand or Finest Hour? Woodrow Wilson's Speaking Tour in September 1919," in *The Wilson Era: Essays in Honor of Arthur S. Link*, ed. John Milton Cooper, Jr., and Charles E. Neu (Arlington Heights, Ill., 1991), pp. 199–205.

30. *New York Times*, Sept. 3, 1919. For Irvine Lenroot's recollection, see *Washington Post*, Mar. 4, 1945.

31. WW, "Suggestion," [Sept. 3, 1919], *PWW*, vol. 62, p. 621. This is a draft; the original is enclosed with Hitchcock to EBGW, Jan. 5, 1920, *PWW*, vol. 64, p. 244. See also Hitchcock, "Events Leading to the World War," [Jan. 13, 1925], Gilbert M. Hitchcock Papers, LC. On the unlikelihood that the mild reservationists would have accepted these reservations, see Margulies, *Mild Reservationists*, pp. 72, 88–89.

32. WW remarks, Aug. 25, 1919, *PWW*, vol. 62, p. 491; *Memoir*, p. 274.

33. On the train arrangements, see CTGD, entry for Sept. 3, 1919, *PWW*, vol. 62, pp. 626–27, and *Memoir*, p. 275.

34. On the use of outlines, see Editorial Note, "Wilson's Speeches on His Western Tour," *PWW*, vol. 63, p. 6. On the distribution of speeches and on finances, see Cooper, *Breaking the Heart of the World*, p. 164.

35. WW speech, Sept. 4, 1919, *PWW*, vol. 63, pp. 7–18. For reports of the speech, see CTGD, entry for Sept. 4, 1919, *PWW*, vol. 63, p. 3, and New York *World*, Sept. 5, 1919.

36. CTGD, entry for Sept. 4, 1919, *PWW*, vol. 63, p. 4.

37. *Kansas City Star*, Sept. 6, 1919.

38. WW speech, Sept. 8, 1919, *PWW*, vol. 63, p. 102.

39. WW speeches, Sept. 5 and 6, 1919, *PWW*, vol. 63, pp. 48, 75.

40. 66th Cong., 1st Sess., *Congressional Record* 5113 (Sept. 10, 1919); HCL to James T. Williams, Jr., Sept. 6, 1919, HCLP. On the reservations and the speaking tour, see Cooper, *Breaking the Heart of the World*, pp. 166–69.

41. U.S. Senate, Committee on Foreign Relations, *Treaty of Peace Hearings*, document 106, 1276–77; RL to Frank L. Polk, Oct. 1, 1919, *PWW*, vol. 63, p. 540. On William Bullitt's testimony and Robert Lansing's reaction, see Cooper, *Breaking the Heart of the World*, pp. 168–71.

42. RL to WW, Sept. 17, 1919, *PWW*, vol. 63, p. 337; JPT, *Wilson As I Know Him* (Garden City, N.Y., 1921), p. 442. Tumulty's version of events is often unreliable, but this account is supported by Breckinridge Long memorandum, 1924, *PWW*, vol. 63, p. 339, n. 4.

43. In his diary, Grayson made comments about Wilson's condition retrospectively, suggesting that he was covering himself after the fact. For a diagnosis of Wilson's symptoms as stemming from hypertension and congestive heart failure, see Bert E. Park, "Woodrow Wilson's Stroke of October 2, 1919," *PWW*, vol. 63, p. 640.

44. WW speech, Sept, 11, 1919, *PWW*, vol. 63, p. 196.

45. WW speeches, Sept. 13 and 15, 1919, *PWW*, vol. 63, pp. 247, 262, 277–85. For Tumulty's advice, see JPT to WW, Sept. 12, 1919, *PWW*, vol. 63, pp. 221–22.

46. WW speeches, Sept. 18 and 19, 1919, *PWW*, vol. 63, pp. 311–22, 352–61.

47. WW speech, Sept. 19, 1919, *PWW*, vol. 63, pp. 371–82. On Wilson's experience with the microphone, see CTGD, entry for Sept. 18, 1919, *PWW*, vol. 63, p. 340. As one of Bryan's biographers pointed out, this innovation robbed him of an advantage he had hitherto enjoyed: his powerful voice. See Paolo E. Coletta, *William Jennings Bryan*, vol. 3, *1915–1925* (Lincoln, Neb., 1969), pp. 128, 121.

48. *Memoir*, p. 281; Mary Allen Hulbert, *The Story of Mrs. Peck: An Autobiography* (New York, 1933), pp. 267–77.

49. CTG, quoted in Breckinridge Long memorandum, 1924, *PWW*, vol. 63, p. 339, n. 4; WW speech, Sept. 23, 1919, *PWW*, vol. 63, p. 448.

50. *Memoir*, p. 282; WW speech, Sept. 23, 1919, *PWW*, vol. 63, pp. 449–63.

51. WW speeches, Sept. 24 and 25, 1919, *PWW*, vol. 63, pp. 467–82, 493–95.

52. WW speech, Sept. 25, 1919, *PWW*, vol. 63, pp. 500–513.

53. Daniel Patrick Moynihan, *On the Law of Nations* (Cambridge, Mass., 1990), pp. 52–53.

54. See CTGD, entry for Sept. 25, 1919, *PWW*, vol. 63, pp. 488–90.

55. CTGD, entry for Sept. 26, 1919, *PWW*, vol. 63, pp. 518–19; *Memoir*, p. 284.

56. RSBD, entry for Nov. 5, 1919, *PWW*, vol. 63, p. 620.

57. CTGD, entry for Sept. 26, 1919, *PWW*, vol. 63, pp. 518–19; JPT statement, Sept. 26, 1919, *PWW*, vol. 63, p. 520. There are also accounts of the cancellation of the trip in *Memoir*, pp. 284–85, and JPT, *Wilson As I Know Him*, pp. 446–48. Edith's account agrees with Grayson's; Tumulty's is doubtful because he says Wilson was paralyzed on his left side during the night. The paralysis did not begin until after Wilson suffered a stroke on October 2.

58. NDB to Hugh C. Wallace, NDB Papers, box 11, LC; Charles Grasty, quoted in Gilbert Parker to Theodore Marburg, Dec. 18, 1919, in Marburg, *The Development of the League of Nations Idea: Documents and Correspondence of Theodore Marburg*, ed. John H. Latané (New York, 1932), vol. 2, p. 61. For other assessments of the tour's effectiveness, see Cooper, *Breaking the Heart of the World*, p. 190, n. 58.

59. On the possibilities of radio, see Thomas A. Bailey, *Woodrow Wilson and the Great Betrayal* (New York, 1945), p. 104, and Cooper, *Breaking the Heart of the World*, p. 191.

60. For an excellent exposition of Wilson in this great oratorical tradition, see Robert A. Kraig, *Woodrow Wilson and the Lost World of the Oratorical Statesman* (College Station, Tex., 2004). See also Cooper, *Breaking the Heart of the World*, pp. 431–32.

61. *Memoir*, pp. 268–88. For the accounts closer to the event, see Francis X. Dercum memorandum [Oct. 20, 1919], *PWW*, vol. 64, pp. 500–501; CTG memorandum, ca. Jan. 1920, *PWW*, vol. 64, p. 508. The White House head usher, Ike Hoover, also later claimed that Wilson fell in the bathroom, lost consciousness, and gashed his head. See Irwin Hood Hoover, "The Facts about President Wilson's Illness," *PWW*, vol. 63, pp. 634–35. It seems odd that neither physician mentioned such a traumatic fall.

62. Frances X. Dercum memorandum, [Oct. 20, 1919], *PWW*, vol. 64, pp. 501, 503. In a memorandum probably written in January 1920, Grayson stated, "THE DIAGNOSIS made October 2nd and confirmed in subsequent examinations was that of a thrombosis [*thrombosis* crossed out] involving the internal capsule of the right cerebral hemisphere." *PWW*, vol. 64, p. 510. For a discussion of the cause of the stroke aided by consultation with neurologists, see Cooper, *Breaking the Heart of the World*, p. 199, n. 3.

63. *Washington Post*, Oct. 4, 1919; JDD, entries for Oct. 4 and 6, 1919, *PWW*, vol. 63, pp. 552–55.

23 DISABILITY

1. For a discussion of Wilson's case in light of previous and subsequent instances of presidential incapacity, see John Milton Cooper, Jr., "Disability in the White House: The Case of Woodrow Wilson," in *The White House: The First Two Hundred Years*, ed. Frank Freidel and William Pencak (Boston, 1994), pp. 75–99.
2. Irwin Hood Hoover, "The Facts about President Wilson's Illness," *PWW*, vol. 63, pp. 635–36.
3. *Memoir*, pp. 288–89.
4. CTG memorandum, [ca. late 1919 or early 1920], *PWW*, vol. 64, p. 510. For the judgment of a distinguished neurologist that neither Dercum nor any other physician would have said what Edith Wilson remembered, see Edwin A. Weinstein, *Woodrow Wilson: A Medical and Psychological Biography* (Princeton, N.J., 1981), p. 360.
5. *Memoir*, p. 286.
6. *Memoir*, p. 289. The editors of *The Papers of Woodrow Wilson* agree that Wilson knew nothing about this veto. See *PWW*, vol. 63, p. 602, n. 3.
7. RL, "Cabinet Meetings during the Illness of the President," Feb. 23, 1920, *PWW*, vol. 64, pp. 455–56. In JPT, *Woodrow Wilson As I Know Him* (Garden City, N.Y., 1921), pp. 443–44, Tumulty depicts Lansing as actively seeking Wilson's removal and Grayson and himself angrily quashing the idea. Lansing's recollection seems closer to the truth. At the time, he recorded in his diary, "Conferred with Tumulty and Grayson in Cabinet room. Tumulty pointed to left side significantly. Discussed V. P. acting as Prest. Decided to call Cabinet meeting Monday." RL diary, entry for Oct. 3, 1919, *PWW*, vol. 63, p. 547.
8. CTG memorandum, Oct. 6, 1919, *PWW*, vol. 63, p. 496; JDD, entry for Oct. 6, 1919, *PWW*, vol. 63, p. 555.
9. Chandler P. Anderson diary, entry for Sept. 27, 1919, Chandler P. Anderson Papers, microfilm ed., reel 2, LC; EMHD, entry for Mar. 28, 1920, *PWW*, vol. 65, p. 139.
10. In May 1996, Arthur Link suggested to me in a private conversation that Lansing may have been scheming to make himself president.
11. J. Fred Essary, quoted in Charles M. Thomas, *Thomas Riley Marshall, Hoosier Statesman* (Oxford, Ohio, 1939), p. 207. The account of Essary's visit to Marshall is based upon correspondence with Marshall's secretary in July 1937. See Thomas, *Marshall*, pp. 206–7, 266.
12. Marshall, *Recollections of Thomas R. Marshall, Vice-President and Hoosier Philosopher: A Hoosier Salad* (Indianapolis, 1925), p. 363. The account of the senators' approaching Marshall in Thomas's biography appears to be based upon correspondence with the vice president's secretary, his wife, and senators George Moses and James Watson in August 1937. See Thomas, *Marshall*, p. 266.
13. *St. Louis Post-Dispatch*, Oct. 24, 1919, quoted in Herbert F. Margulies, *The Mild Reservationists and the League of Nations, Controversy in the Senate* (Columbia, Mo., 1989), p. 145. On these negotiations, see p. 147, and John Milton Cooper, Jr., *Breaking the Heart of the World: Woodrow Wilson and the Fight for the League of Nations* (New York, 2001), pp. 221–26.
14. 66th Cong., 1st Sess., *Congressional Record* 7417 (Oct. 24, 1919). On the bargaining in the Foreign Relations Committee that produced these reservations, see Lloyd E. Ambrosius, *Woodrow Wilson and the American Diplomatic Tradition: The Treaty Fight in Perspective* (New York, 1987), pp. 199–201.
15. Porter J. McCumber, who was by far the mildest of the reservationists, made the point about the absence of input from Democrats: "If we make the reservations as mild as I would wish to have them, the treaty would be defeated. I wish to concede as

little as possible and still be certain of ratification. To accomplish this, I must agree to a compromise, even though that compromise is far from my convictions of what should be done." McCumber to Courtenay Crocker, Oct. 26, 1919, A. Lawrence Lowell Papers, Harvard University Archives.

16. Prince Edward to EBGW, Nov. 14, 1919, *PWW*, vol. 64, p. 36. On the visits and the wheeled chair, see *New York Times*, Oct. 31, 1919; Nov. 12 and 16, 1919, and *Washington Post*, Nov. 14, 1919. Two years later, after being paralyzed with poliomyelitis, Franklin Roosevelt also found current wheelchairs unsatisfactory and designed a smaller, more mobile version using a kitchen chair.

17. Hitchcock memoir, "Wilson's Place in History," Gilbert M. Hitchcock Papers, LC; *New York Times*, Nov. 8, 1919. The editors of *The Papers of Woodrow Wilson* claim that Hitchcock met with Wilson around October 20, but that was a visit on which he talked with Grayson and did not see the president. See *PWW*, vol. 64, p. 45, n. 1.

18. Hitchcock to EBGW, Nov. 13, 1919, *PWW*, vol. 64, pp. 28–29.

19. EBGW note, [ca. Nov. 15, 1919], *PWW*, vol. 64, p. 38; CTG memorandum, Nov. 17, 1919, *PWW*, vol. 64, pp. 43, 45.

20. CTG memorandum, Nov. 17, 1919, *PWW*, vol. 64, pp. 43–44.

21. On possible psychological effects of the stroke on Wilson, see Bert E. Park, "Woodrow Wilson's Stroke of October 2, 1919," *PWW*, vol. 63, pp. 639–46.

22. *New York Times*, Nov. 18, 1919; WW to Gilbert Hitchcock, Nov. 18, 1919, *PWW*, vol. 64, p. 58. On the drafting of the letter, see Hitchcock to EBGW, Nov. 17, 1919, *PWW*, vol. 64, p. 50, and letter draft with her emendations and additions, p. 51.

23. RSBD, entry for Nov. 5, 1919, *PWW*, vol. 63, p. 621. On these efforts at compromise, including a detailed analysis of the Bonsal affair, see Cooper, *Breaking the Heart of the World*, pp. 247–57. It was to Stephen Bonsal that Henry Cabot Lodge reportedly made his crack about the League Covenant as a literary performance: "It might get by at Princeton but certainly not at Harvard." See also chapter 20, n. 40.

24. 66th Cong., 1st Sess., *Congressional Record* 8768, 8803 (Nov. 19, 1919). The four Democrats who voted for consent with reservations included Hoke Smith; those four voted against consent without reservations, joined by Park Trammell of Florida, who did not explain his vote. Another Republican, Knute Nelson of Minnesota, probably would have joined McCumber in voting for the treaty without reservations, but he had left the chamber. A sixteenth irreconcilable, Albert Fall of New Mexico, was not present but was recorded as against the treaty on both votes. On this last day of debating, maneuvering, and voting, see Cooper, *Breaking the Heart of the World*, pp. 264–69.

25. *Memoir*, p. 297; HCL to George Harvey, Nov. 20, 1919, HCLP.

26. HCL to John H. Sherburne, Dec. 4, 1919, HCLP; WW message, Dec. 2, 1919, *PWW*, vol. 64, pp. 106–16.

27. For a recent treatment of the troubles of this year, see Ann Hagedorn, *Savage Peace: Hope and Fear in America, 1919* (New York, 2007).

28. On Wilson's refusal to see Hitchcock, see JPT to EBGW, Dec. 1, 1919, *PWW*, vol. 64, p. 103; Gilbert Hitchcock to WJB, Nov. 30, 1919, WJB Papers, box 32, LC; and Charles D. Warner memorandum, Nov. 29, 1919, RL Papers, vol. 49, LC.

29. On the "smelling committee," see *New York Times*, Dec. 5, 1919. On November 29, someone at the White House had also admitted Wilson's lack of involvement in the Mexican business. See *New York Times*, Nov. 30, 1919.

30. EBGW notes, [Dec. 5, 1919], *PWW*, vol. 64, p. 133; *Memoir*, p. 299. See also CTG memorandum, Dec. 5, 1919, *PWW*, vol. 64, pp. 136–37. The closest thing to

"Which way, Senator?" was Houston's recollection that sometime afterward Wilson told him, "If I could have got out of bed, I would have hit the man. Why did he want to put me in bad with the Almighty?" David F. Houston, *Eight Years with Wilson's Cabinet, 1913–1920* (Garden City, N.Y., 1926), vol. 2, p. 141.

31. *New York Times*, Dec. 6, 1919. Finley Peter Dunne was the satirical newspaper columnist, best known for his fictional Chicago Irish American bartender, "Mr. Dooley."

32. Ibid.

33. Gilbert Hitchcock pamphlet, "Brief View of the Late War and the Struggle for Peace Aims," Jan. 13, 1925, Gilbert W. Hitchcock Papers, LC; *New York Times*, Dec. 15, 1919.

34. Draft statement, [ca. Dec. 17, 1919], *PWW*, vol. 64, pp. 199–202.

35. On the list of senators, see *PWW*, vol. 64, p. 202, n. 1.

36. On the efforts to reconsider the treaty, see Cooper, *Breaking the Heart of the World*, pp. 290–96.

37. JPT to WW, Dec. 28, 1919, *PWW*, vol. 64, p. 253. On Edward Grey's mission and Charles Kennedy Craufurd-Stuart, see *PWW*, vol. 63, p. 606, n. 1. For a detailed rendition of the incident, see Phyllis Lee Levin, *Edith and Woodrow: The Wilson White House* (New York, 2001), pp. 399–408.

38. JPT draft, [Jan. 6, 1920], *PWW*, vol. 64, pp., 247–49; EBGW handwritten addition, [Jan. 7, 1920], *PWW*, vol. 64, p. 254. See also Houston, *Wilson's Cabinet*, vol. 2, pp. 47–48.

39. Philadelphia *Public Ledger*, Jan. 11, 1920; *New York Times*, Jan. 23, 1920. On the bipartisan conference, see Cooper, *Breaking the Heart of the World*, pp. 302–14.

40. JPT to EBGW, Jan. 15, 1920, *PWW*, vol. 64, pp. 276–77. See also RL desk diary, entries for Jan. 14 and 15, 1920, *PWW*, vol. 64, pp. 276, 282, and EBGW notes, [ca. Jan. 14, 1920], *PWW*, vol. 64, p. 277, n. 1.

41. JPT draft, Jan. 15, 1920, *PWW*, vol. 64, pp. 278–82; JPT to EBGW, Jan. 17, 1920, *PWW*, vol. 64, p. 287.

42. RSBD, entry for Jan. 23, 1920, *PWW*, vol. 64, p. 321. The neurologist, Bert E. Park, uses the terms "focal psychosyndrome" and "caricature of himself" to describe Wilson's condition. See Park, "The Aftermath of Wilson's Stroke," *PWW*, vol. 64, pp. 525–28. Other neurologists are less categorical about divorcing such conditions from the effects of isolation.

43. CTG to SA, Jan. 24, 1920, *PWW*, vol. 64, p. 325; RSBD, entry for Jan. 23, 1920, *PWW*, vol. 64, p. 321; WW to Gilbert Hitchcock, Jan. 26, 1920, *PWW*, vol. 64, pp. 329–30. The editors of *The Papers of Woodrow Wilson* state that Tumulty wrote this letter to Hitchcock. See *PWW*, vol. 64, p. 328, n. 1. Its tone and approach persuade me, however, that Wilson either dictated it or substantially revised it. On this new referendum scheme, see EBGW to Albert S. Burleson, with enclosed list, Jan. 28, 1920, *PWW*, vol. 64, pp. 336–37, and Burleson to EBGW, Jan. 28, 1920, *PWW*, vol. 64, pp. 338–39.

44. CTG note, n.d., quoted in *PWW*, vol. 64, p. 363, n. 1. For Grayson's divulgences about the resignation scheme, see EMHD, entry for June 10, 1920, *PWW*, vol. 65, p. 384; John W. Davis diary, entry for Sept. 2, 1920, quoted in *PWW*, vol. 64, p. 363, n. 1; and RSBD, entry for Nov. 28, 1920, *PWW*, vol. 66, p. 436. For the treatment of the matter by the editors of *The Papers of Woodrow Wilson*, see *PWW*, vol. 64, p. 363, n. 1.

45. RSBD, entry for Feb. 5, [1920], *PWW*, vol. 64, p. 365. On British and French attitudes toward the deadlock, see George W. Egerton, *Great Britain and the Creation of the League of Nations: Strategy Politics, and International Organization, 1914–1919* (Chapel Hill, N.C., 1978), pp. 177–98.

46. WW to RL, Feb. 7, 1920, *PWW*, vol. 64, p. 383; RL memorandum, Feb. 7, 1920, *PWW*, vol. 64, pp. 385–86; RL to WW, Feb. 9, 1920, *PWW*, vol. 64, pp. 388–89. In his memorandum, Lansing also speculated that Tumulty, a Catholic, might have conspired against him because he was active in the Inter Church World Movement, a Protestant organization.

47. *Memoir*, p. 301; JPT, *Wilson As I Know Him*, p. 445.

48. Carter Glass to WW, Feb. 9, 1920, *PWW*, vol. 64, p. 387; EBGW to Glass, [Feb. 11, 1920], *PWW*, vol. 64, p. 405. Edith Wilson's letter is a handwritten draft; a reply from Glass indicates that he received a more polished version.

49. Diplomatic note sent by RL to Hugh C. Wallace, Feb. 10, 1920, *PWW*, vol. 64, pp. 401–2. For Wilson's restoration of harsh language, see p. 402, n. 1.

50. WW to RL, Feb. 11, 1920, *PWW*, vol. 64, p. 404; RL to WW, Feb. 12, 1920, *PWW*, vol. 64, pp. 409–10; RL memorandum, Feb. 13, 1920, *PWW*, vol. 64, p. 415. On Long's visit to the White House, see Breckinridge Long diary, entry for Feb. 13, 1920, Breckinridge Long Papers, box 2, LC.

51. RSBD, entry for Feb. 15, [1920], *PWW*, vol. 64, p. 434; *New York Times*, Feb. 11, 1920; *Philadelphia Press*, Feb. 16, 1920.

52. *Literary Digest*, Feb. 28, 1920, pp. 13–15; McAdoo to Zach Lamar Cobb, Feb. 25, 1920, William Gibbs McAdoo Papers, box 230, LC.

53. CTG memorandum, Feb. 25, 1920, *PWW*, vol. 64, pp. 473–74.

54. HCL, quoted in Raymond Clapper diary, entry for Feb. 25, 1920, Raymond Clapper Papers, box 6, LC.

55. Keynes, *The Collected Writings of John Maynard Keynes*, ed. Elizabeth Johnson, vol. 2, *The Economic Consequences of the Peace* (Cambridge, U.K., 1971), pp. 25, 32; JPT to WW, Feb. 27, 1920, *PWW*, vol. 64, p. 479. Whether Tumulty sent this letter is not clear. The only copy is in Tumulty's papers, not Wilson's, and there is no record of a reply from Wilson. On the publication of Keynes's book in America, see Cooper, *Breaking the Heart of the World*, pp. 326–27.

56. Edward N. Hurley, *The Bridge to France* (Philadelphia, 1927), pp. 325–27. On this meeting and whether there was any follow-up, see Homer Cummings diary, entry for Feb. 29, 1920, *PWW*, vol. 64, p. 14; Albert S. Burleson to JPT, Mar. 5, 1920, *PWW*, vol. 65, pp. 56–57; and Cooper, *Breaking the Heart of the World*, pp. 337–39.

57. WW draft, [ca. Feb. 28, 1920], *PWW*, vol. 6, pp. 7–9.

58. WW to Gilbert Hitchcock, Mar. 8, 1920, *PWW*, vol. 65, pp. 67–71.

59. *Washington Post*, Mar. 9, 1920; New York *World*, Mar. 10, 1920; 66th Cong., 2nd Sess., *Congressional Record* 4050–51 (Mar. 9, 1920). On the final debate and vote on reservations, see Cooper, *Breaking the Heart of the World*, pp. 348–62.

60. On this final day and the voting, see Cooper, *Breaking the Heart of the World*, pp. 362–70.

61. On the repercussions of the vote and Lodge's intentions, see Cooper, *Breaking the Heart of the World*, pp. 371–73.

62. For a consideration of the meaning of the League fight, see Cooper, *Breaking the Heart of the World*, pp. 412–33.

63. CTG memoranda, Mar. 20 and 25, 1920, *PWW*, vol. 65, pp. 108, 125; CTG, *Woodrow Wilson: An Intimate Memoir* (New York, 1960), p. 109.

24 DOWNFALL

1. CTG memoranda, Mar. 25, 26, and 31, 1920, *PWW*, vol. 65, pp. 123, 125, 149.

2. CTG memoranda, Mar. 25 and 31, 1920, *PWW*, vol. 65, pp. 124, 149.

3. CTG memorandum, Apr. 13, 1920, *PWW*, vol. 65, pp. 179–80.

4. JDD, entry for Apr. 14, 1920, *PWW*, vol. 65, pp. 186–87; RL desk diary, entry for April 14, 1920, *PWW*, vol. 65, p. 188; David F. Houston, *Eight Years with Wilson's Cabinet, 1913–1920* (Garden City, N.Y., 1926), vol. 2, pp. 69–70. See also CTG memorandum, Apr. 14, 1920, *PWW*, vol. 65, p. 186.

5. Sir Auckland Geddes to David Lloyd George, June 4, 1920, *PWW*, vol. 65, pp. 371–72.

6. See CTG to Cleveland H. Dodge, May 29, 1920, *PWW*, vol. 65, p. 342; CTG to Frances X. Dercum, June 7, 1920, *PWW*, vol. 65, p. 380.

7. CTGD, entries for Apr. [20], 1920; May 3, 1920, *PWW*, vol. 65, pp. 212, 244; WW to William Royal Wilder, May 3, 1920, *PWW*, vol. 65, p. 246; Charles E. Swem to JPT, June 3, 1930, quoted in *PWW*, vol. 65, p. 347, n. 4.

8. Marc Peter to Giuseppe Motta, May 28, 1920, *PWW*, vol. 65, pp. 338–40; Sir Auckland Geddes to David Lloyd George, June 4, 1920, *PWW*, vol. 65, p. 369; WW draft statement, [May 24, 1920], *PWW*, vol. 65, p. 319.

9. WW message, May 24, 1920, *PWW*, vol. 65, p. 322. On the Senate action, see John Milton Cooper, Jr., *Breaking the Heart of the World: Woodrow Wilson and the Fight for the League of Nations* (New York, 2001), pp. 379–80.

10. WW veto message, May 27, 1920, *PWW*, vol. 65, pp. 328–29. On the override vote, seventeen Democrats voted in favor, and two Republicans voted against. On the Knox resolution, see Cooper, *Breaking the Heart of the World*, pp. 376–79.

11. Homer Cummings diary, entry for May 31, [1920], *PWW*, vol. 65, pp. 344–50.

12. WW notes, [ca. June 10, 1920], *PWW*, vol. 65, p. 382.

13. Carter Glass memorandum, June 16, 1920, *PWW*, vol. 65, p. 400. See also Woolley, "Politics Is Hell," Robert W. Woolley Papers, box 44, LC.

14. New York *World*, June 18, 1920. On Tumulty's intentions, see *PWW*, vol. 65, p. 401, n. 1.

15. New York *World*, June 18, 1920.

16. Carter Glass memorandum, June 19, 1920, *PWW*, vol. 65, p., 435. For Glass's discouragement of a third term, see *New York Times*, June 21, 1920.

17. On this convention, see Wesley Marvin Bagby, *The Road to Normalcy: The Presidential Campaign and Election of 1920* (Baltimore, 1962), pp. 102–22.

18. Albert S. Burleson to Daniel C. Roper, July 12, 1920, quoted in *PWW*, vol. 65, p. 511, n. 3. See also *New York Times*, June 29, 1920.

19. See CTGD, entries for July 3 [and July 6] 1920, *PWW*, vol. 65, pp. 491, 498; Charles E. Swem diary, entry for [ca. July 6, 1920], *PWW*, vol. 65, p. 499; Bainbridge Colby to WW, July 2, 1920, *PWW*, vol. 65, p. 490. Colby used Homer Cummings's code in the telegraph to Wilson. Swem claimed that Wilson dictated to Edith a telegram in reply approving Colby's plan (see Swem diary, entry for [ca. July 6, 1920], *PWW*, vol. 65, p. 498), but no copy of such a telegram survives, and Colby did not mention it in his communications with Wilson.

20. JPT to EBGW, July 4, 1920, *PWW*, vol. 65, p. 494; Irwin Hood Hoover, *Forty-two Years in the White House* (Boston, 1934), quoted in *PWW*, vol. 65, p. 511, n. 2. On the meeting in San Francisco, see Colby to WW, July 4, 1920, *PWW*, vol. 65, p. 496; Cummings memorandum, [July 3 and 4, 1920], *PWW*, vol. 65, pp. 580–81. Cummings recalled that two meetings took place on July 4, and not all the men named may have been present at both of them. On the move to fire Albert Burleson, see James Kerney, *The Political Education of Woodrow Wilson* (New York, 1926), pp. 456–57. Ike Hoover's memoir also states that Tumulty kept Burleson "afloat."

21. Franklin D. Roosevelt to Claude G. Bowers, quoted in James M. Cox, *Journey through My Years* (New York, 1946), pp. 241–44; *Memoir*, pp. 305–6. See also CTGD, entries for July 18 and 19, 1920, *PWW*, vol. 65, pp. 520–21, 529.

22. Charles E. Swem diary, entry for July 26, 1920, *PWW*, vol. 65, p. 550. See also Edmund W. Starling with Thomas Sugrue, *Starling of the White House: The Story of the Man Whose Secret Service Detail Guarded Five Presidents from Woodrow Wilson to Franklin D. Roosevelt* (New York, 1946), p. 157.

23. William W. Hawkins interview, [Sept. 27, 1920], *PWW*, vol. 66, pp. 153, 156–57.

24. WW statement, [Oct. 3, 1920], *PWW*, vol. 66, pp. 181–83.

25. WW to Selden P. Spencer, Oct, 6, 1920, *PWW*, vol. 66, p. 198; Homer Cummings memorandum, Oct. 5, 1920, *PWW*, vol. 66, p. 195.

26. WW to Warren G. Harding, Oct. 18, 1920, *PWW*, vol. 66, p. 239; WW speech, Oct. 27, 1920, *PWW*, vol. 66, pp. 277–80.

27. WW to James M. Cox, Oct. 29, 1920, *PWW*, vol. 66, pp. 290–91.

28. Voters had not so much turned against the Democrats as they had stayed home. Thanks to the Nineteenth Amendment, nationwide woman suffrage boosted the total vote, but in percentages, participation fell. For the first time in American history, less than half of all eligible voters cast ballots in a presidential election. For a good assessment of the election results, see Bagby, *Road to Normalcy*, pp. 159–67.

29. Henry J. Allen to White, Mar. 23, 1920, William Allen White Papers, series E, box 51, LC.

30. Bagby, *Road to Normalcy*, p. 161. On the role of foreign policy in the election, see Cooper, *Breaking the Heart of the World*, pp. 396–97.

31. Charles E. Swem diary, entry for Nov. 3, 1920, *PWW*, vol. 66, p. 306; SA to Jessie Wilson Sayre, Nov. 4, 1920, *PWW*, vol. 66, pp. 319–20; Homer Cummings memorandum, [Nov. 6, 1920], *PWW*, vol. 66, p. 331; WW to Bainbridge Colby, Nov. 6, 1920, *PWW*, vol. 66, p. 331.

32. A. Mitchell Palmer to WW, Jan. 30, 1921, *PWW*, vol. 67, pp. 98–102; WW notation, *PWW*, vol. 67, p. 102, n. 8; Ida M. Tarbell memorandum, May 22, 1922, *PWW*, vol. 68, p. 48.

33. WW to Lawrence C. Woods, Dec. 1, 1920, *PWW*, vol. 66, p. 447. On Tumulty's role and the functioning of the government, see editors' comments, *PWW*, vol. 63, p. 638, n. 6, and vol. 66, pp. vi–viii.

34. RSBD, entry for Nov. 28, 1920, *PWW*, vol. 66, pp. 435–36; EBGW to RSB, Nov. 30, 1920, *PWW*, vol. 66, p. 446.

35. RSBD, entry for Dec. 1, 1920, *PWW*, vol. 66, p. 451; CTG memorandum, Dec. 6, 1920, *PWW*, vol. 66, p. 479.

36. WW message, Dec. 7, 1920, *PWW*, vol. 66, pp. 484–90.

37. See WW veto message, Mar. 3, 1921, *PWW*, vol. 67, pp. 191–94.

38. *Memoir*, pp. 309–10.

39. For the figure on Wilson's savings, see *New York Tribune*, Sept. 27, 1921.

40. *Memoir*, pp. 326–27. On the Wilsons' finances, see Phyllis Lee Levin, *Edith and Woodrow: The Wilson White House* (New York: 2001), pp. 459–60.

41. *Memoir*, 308. On the house hunting, see pp. 310–12.

42. JDD entry on Jan. 17, 1921, *PWW*, vol. 67, p. 71.

43. *New York Times*, Mar. 5, 1921.

44. Ibid.

45. New York *World*, Mar. 4, 1921. For Wilson's expression of appreciation, see WW to Frank Cobb, Mar. 7, 1921, *PWW*, vol. 67, p. 230.

25   TWILIGHT

1. In her memoir, Edith insisted that the painting in the bedroom was a portrait of herself. See *Memoir*, p. 306. For descriptions of the house, see pp. 323–24 and RSB,

"Memorandum of a Talk with Mrs. Woodrow Wilson, January 27, 1925," RSBP, box 124.

2. *Memoir*, pp. 320, 322.

3. On the routine, see *Memoir*, pp. 324–26.

4. RSBD, entry for Mar. 22, [1921], *PWW*, vol. 67, pp. 237–38.

5. WW to Robert S. Henderson, May 7, 1921, *PWW*, vol. 67, p. 281; RSBD, entry for May 25, [1921], *PWW*, vol. 67, p. 288. See also SA to John Hibben, June 11, 1921, *PWW*, vol. 67, p. 310.

6. On the law partnership, see *Memoir*, pp. 328–29; RSB, "Memorandum of a Talk with Mrs. Woodrow Wilson at 2340 S St., N.W., Washington, D.C., on December 7, 1925," RSBP, box 124; and Bainbridge Colby, interview by RSB, June 19, 1930, RSBP, box 103.

7. WW to Colby, Feb. 17, 1918, *PWW*, vol. 67, p. 548; WW to Colby, June 10, 1918, vol. 68, p. 74.

8. Colby to WW, Aug. 22, 1922, *PWW*, vol. 68, p. 119; WW draft letter and telegram to Colby, Aug. 23, 1922, *PWW*, vol. 68, pp. 120–21; RSB, "Memorandum of a Talk with Mrs. Woodrow Wilson at 2340 S St., N.W., Washington, D.C., on December 7, 1925," RSBP, box 124. Edith erroneously recalled that Wilson telephoned Colby; she also recalled that Colby had already entertained second thoughts of his own.

9. WW to Colby, Nov. 29, 1922; Dec. 14, 1922, *PWW*, vol. 68, pp. 202, 232. Almost eight years later, when Baker interviewed Colby, he found him almost worshipful in his attitude toward Wilson. See Colby, interview by RSB, June 19, 1930, RSBP, box 103.

10. WW to William Gibbs McAdoo, Sept. 17, 1922, *PWW*, vol. 68, p. 129.

11. *New York Times*, Nov. 12, 1921.

12. WW to Bainbridge Colby, Feb. 24, 1922, *PWW*, vol. 67, p. 556; RSBD, entry for Apr. 4, [1922], *PWW*, vol. 67, p. 585.

13. WW notes, Apr. 26, 1922; [ca. May 1], 1922, *PWW*, vol. 68, pp. 40–42; WW to J. Franklin Jameson, May 11, 1922, *PWW*, vol. 68, p. 52.

14. WW, "The Road Away from Revolution," [ca. Apr. 8, 1923], *PWW*, vol. 68, pp. 322–24.

15. George Creel to EBGW, Apr. 19, 1923, *PWW*, vol. 68, p. 342; SA, interview by RSB, Sept. 2, 1931, *PWW*, vol. 68, p. 349, n. 1.

16. SA, interview by RSB, Sept. 2, 1931, *PWW*, vol. 68, p. 349, n. 1.

17. On the formation of the Woodrow Wilson Foundation, see *New York Times*, Dec. 29, 1922, and *PWW*, vol. 68, p. 249, n. 2.

18. *New York Times*, Nov. 12, 1922; Dec. 29, 1922; CTG memorandum, [ca. Dec. 28, 1922], *PWW*, vol. 68, pp. 250–51.

19. WW statement, [ca. Oct. 20, 1921], *PWW*, vol. 68, p. 428; WW statement, Nov. 6, 1921, *PWW*, vol. 67, p. 443.

20. WW to John Hessin Clarke, Oct. 27, 1922, *PWW*, vol. 68, pp. 166–67; WW to Hamilton Holt, Nov. 5, 1922, *PWW*, vol. 68, pp. 177–78.

21. For Baker's account of writing *Woodrow Wilson and the World Settlement*, see RSB, *American Chronicle: The Autobiography of Ray Stannard Baker* (New York, 1945), pp. 488–98.

22. WW to JPT, Apr. 6, 1922, *PWW*, vol. 67, p. 460; "Dictated by Mrs. Woodrow Wilson, to Give Her Memory of the Tumulty Incident," Nov. 21, 1924, RSBP, box 124.

23. JPT to WW, Apr. 10, 1922, *PWW*, vol. 68, p. 15; *New York Times*, Apr. 9, 1922; WW to editor, *New York Times*, Apr. 12, 1922, *PWW*, vol. 68, p. 14; WW to Arthur Krock, Apr. 12, 1912, *PWW*, vol. 68, p. 14; *Memoir*, p. 339. On the recommendaton of

Tumulty for the Senate, see WW to James Kerney, Oct. 30, 1923, *PWW*, vol. 68, p. 459, and Kerney, "Last Talks with Woodrow Wilson," *Saturday Evening Post*, Mar. 29, 1924, *PWW*, vol. 68, p. 595.

24. Wilson to James F. McCaleb, July 8, 1922, *PWW*, vol. 68, p. 93; WW to John Hessin Clarke, Nov. 13, 1922, *PWW*, vol. 68, p. 189. After William Cabell Bruce's victory in the primary, Wilson wrote a bitter letter about him to the chairman of the Democratic National Committee. See WW to Cordell Hull, Sept. 12, 1922, *PWW*, vol. 68, pp. 134–35.

25. WW to Frederick I. Thompson, Nov. 4, 1922, *PWW*, vol. 68, p. 175.

26. *New York Times*, June 10, 1923.

27. On the McAdoo visit, see RSB, "Memorandum of an Interview with Mrs. Woodrow Wilson—January 4, 1926," RSBP, box 124.

28. Ida Tarbell memorandum, May 5, 1922, *PWW*, vol. 68, p. 46.

29. WW to EBGW, [Aug.] 31, 1923, *PWW*, vol. 68, p. 415.

30. Lord Riddell diary, entry for [Sept. 10, 1923], *PWW*, vol. 68, p. 422; Margaret Wilson, quoted in Edith Gittings Reid, *Woodrow Wilson: The Character, the Myth and the Man* (New York, 1934), p. 236.

31. WW to Raymond Fosdick, Oct. 22, 1923, *PWW*, vol. 68, p. 451; Fosdick to RSB, June 23, 1926, RSBP, box 108.

32. Fosdick to WW, Nov. 27, 1923, *PWW*, vol. 68, p. 493; WW to Fosdick, Nov. 28, 1923, *PWW*, vol. 68, p. 493; Raymond B. Fosdick, *Chronicle of a Generation: An Autobiography* (New York, 1958), pp. 230–31.

33. WW speech, Nov. 10, 1923, *PWW*, vol. 68, p. 466.

34. *New York Times*, Nov. 12, 1923. See also Arthur Link's description of the scene in *PWW*, vol. 68, pp. viii–ix.

35. *New York Times*, Dec. 29, 1923.

36. WW to RSB, Dec. 13, 1923, *PWW*, vol. 68, p. 499; WW to NDB, Jan. 20, 1924, *PWW*, vol. 68, p. 534; *New York Times*, Jan. 17, 1924. On the delivery of "The Document," see Randolph Bolling to NDB, Jan. 21, 1924, *PWW*, vol. 68, pp. 541, n. 1; 544.

37. Raymond Fosdick to RSB, June 23, 1926, RSBP, box 103.

38. WW notes, [ca. Jan. 21, 1924], *PWW*, vol. 68, pp. 541–43.

39. Margaret H. Cobb to WW, Dec. 27, 1923, *PWW*, vol. 68, p. 508; WW foreword, [Jan. 6, 1924], to Frank Irving Cobb, *Cobb of "The World,"* ed. John L. Heaton (New York, 1924), in *PWW*, vol. 68, p. 520; Raymond Fosdick to RSB, Jan. 23, 1924, RSBP, box 103.

40. RSB to WW, Jan. 7, 1924, *PWW*, vol. 68, p. 523; WW to RSB, Jan. 8 and 25, 1924, *PWW*, vol. 68, pp. 524, 547.

41. RSB, *American Chronicle*, pp. 507–8. Two other letters Wilson dictated that day were condolences to an old friend and supporter among the Princeton trustees, Thomas Jones, on the death of his brother David, another friend and supporter, and a brief reply to an inmate in a federal prison who had requested help in having his sentence commuted.

42. On these days, see Randolph Bolling, "A Brief History of the Last Illness of Honorable Woodrow Wilson," [Feb. 7 or 8, 1924], *PWW*, vol. 68, pp. 548–49.

43. Bolling memorandum, *PWW*, vol. 68, pp. 549–50; White House staff memorandum to Calvin Coolidge, Feb. 2, 1924, *PWW*, vol. 68, p. 553; *New York Times*, Feb. 3 and 4, 1924.

44. *New York Times*, Feb. 4, 1924; CTG statement, [Feb. 3, 1924], CTG Papers, Woodrow Wilson Presidential Library, Staunton, Va.; death certificate, CTG Papers. See also, "Memorandum of Interview with Dr. Cary T. Grayson on February 18, 19, 1926 at Washington," RSBP, box 109.

45. Helen Manning Hunter, quoting WHT in Lewis L. Gould to John Milton Cooper, Jr., June 13, 2008.
46. EBGW to HCL, Feb. 4, 1924, *PWW,* vol. 68, p. 574; *New York Times,* Feb. 7, 1924.
47. *New York Times,* Feb. 7, 1924.
48. Raymond Fosdick to RSB, June 23, 1926, RSBP, box 103.

Sources and Acknowledgments

In a display of excessive modesty, Sir Isaac Newton said, "If I have seen further, it is by standing on the shoulders of giants." I make the same claim with no modesty whatever. If I have seen further into Woodrow Wilson and his times, it is entirely by standing on the shoulders of giants. Some of those giants come from the time I have written about, so the debts I wish to acknowledge include men and women from Wilson's time as well as my own.

The first and greatest debt owed by any Wilson biographer is to the man himself. He remains perhaps the most self-revealing of all American presidents. He was not secretive or elusive, and he shared his thoughts and motives with others, particularly with the women in his life. Fortunately for the biographer, he began his life when people communicated mainly by letters, and despite the inroads of the telephone and more rapid transportation later in his life, he and his contemporaries continued to rely on written communication for important and intimate matters.

The letters Wilson exchanged with his first wife, Ellen, before and after their marriage stand alongside the correspondence of John and Abigail Adams as the frankest, deepest, and most touching exchanges between a president and his spouse. The letters he wrote to his second wife, Edith, before their marriage offer comparable views into his mind and spirit, but they do not cover as long a period, and her responses are not as insight-filled as Ellen's. Likewise, his letters to Mary Hulbert (also Peck) reveal his thoughts and emotions at a particularly significant juncture in his life. Unfortunately, her letters to him do not survive, most likely because he destroyed them for fear of potential scandal. Those were among the few papers Wilson ever discarded—much to the gratitude of biographers and historians. He also wrote what seem to be astonishingly revealing letters from a president to a variety of friends, colleagues, and acquaintances. Earlier, at different times in his life, he bared his plans, dreams, and feelings to close friends, most notably Robert Bridges during his first decade out of college. These letters alone would suffice to make Wilson a biographer's dream subject.

His contemporaries also contributed greatly to making him accessible to future generations. Fortunately, the great tradition of diary keeping had not yet died out—as it largely would later in the twentieth century—and several of Wilson's closest associates served as a small team of Boswells for him. First, foremost, and most controversially comes Colonel House. His deviousness and his agendas, both open and hidden, require the reader to approach his diary and correspondence with caution. Although House could lie and often shade the truth to suit his listener, he kept a diary that was usually accurate on the facts as far as it went. The main problems in using this diary come from its shades of meaning—which magnify House's importance and sagacity—and its aspersions on others—although those afford important, though unintended, insight into House himself. Another problem is having only House's side of the story for most of the time until the peace conference; then other important figures also kept diaries, against which his accounts can be checked. Only once, in a letter to Edith before they were married, did Wilson speak for himself about House and their relationship. Still, despite those pitfalls and drawbacks, House's diary remains an indispensable source from the time of Wilson's election as president in 1912 to the end of the peace conference in 1919.

Wilson's physician, Cary Grayson, likewise kept a diary during the conference and on the speaking tour in September 1919, and he wrote frequent memoranda relating particularly to his patient's health. Grayson's diary entries in Paris recount what Wilson told him and Edith, usually at the end of each day. The president evidently did the same thing with the press secretary to the American delegation, Ray Stannard Baker, who was long practiced at keeping a diary. Grayson and Baker include information about others at Paris, and Baker often makes shrewd comments on the principal negotiators, members of the delegation, and the progress of the conference. Grayson's diary entries during the speaking tour are open to question about whether he altered them later to cover himself in diagnosing the president's deteriorating physical condition. Unlike the earlier diary, there are no manuscripts of this one, only a typescript. The memoranda that he wrote after Wilson's stroke are more reliable.

Another diary keeper during his presidency was Secretary of the Navy Josephus Daniels, whose entries often give the only account of cabinet meetings. Daniels's entries tend to be brief, sometimes almost like shorthand, but they are always valuable. He and other members of the cabinet conducted voluminous, frequently revealing correspondence, most of which is preserved in the collections of their papers at the Library of Congress. Many of those cabinet secretaries also wrote memoirs of their service under Wilson; these are most valuable when they can be checked against contemporary letters and diary entries.

Joe Tumulty, the ever-faithful Horatio of Wilson's political career, likewise contributed greatly to illuminating the thoughts and actions of his boss. Even though they were in daily personal contact, the two men exchanged frequent notes and memoranda, which illuminate the workings of the president in his White House office. Suffering as he did from the machinations of House and the dislike of Edith Wilson, Tumulty was sometimes not privy to important matters, but his perseverance at the "governor's" side affords a view of the personality dynamics surrounding Wilson. Tumulty, too, wrote a memoir—one of the first to appear after Wilson left the White House—but, either through faulty memory or a highly sentimentalized view of events, he left accounts that often have to be regarded with skepticism.

One other contemporary who also provided great insight into Wilson was his brother-in-law Stockton Axson. He later titled his memoir *Brother Woodrow*, and he was closer to Wilson than his own brother or than any other person except his two wives. As a young man, Axson frequently lived with his sister and brother-in-law, and as a fellow faculty member at Princeton he came to their house practically every day. Later, he was a frequent visitor to the White House and the house on S Street. Besides his memoir, which was not published until 1993, Axson left extensive written accounts of parts of Wilson's life, annotations on the manuscript of the first biography of him, and extended interviews, which are in Ray Stannard Baker's papers at the Library of Congress. Two other family memoirs are also valuable. The youngest Wilson daughter, Eleanor (Nell), who married William Gibbs McAdoo, wrote a memoir of her parents and later edited their letters, and Ellen's sister, Margaret (Madge) Axson Elliott, likewise wrote an account of the family, with whom she lived from the age of ten until her marriage. The Elliott memoir contains some inaccuracies, but it offers an intimate look at life in the home of the professor and university president.

The biographer's good fortune with Wilson does not end with him and his contemporaries. Other biographers and scholars who have come afterward have continued to shed light on him and his career. Two of them have stood out from all the others. The first of them, Ray Stannard Baker, straddled the roles of contemporary observer and biographer. Wilson's own deathbed anointment of him and Edith's cajolery brought him to his task while memories were still fresh. As a journalist, Baker reflexively sought out reminiscences of his subject through correspondence and interviews. This was fortunate because academic historians still remained in the thrall of strictly contemporary documents and would not come to appreciate the value of oral history for another generation. Baker did not neglect documents, and he collected a number of letters that might otherwise have gone astray, but his greatest contribution was to gather recollections of Wilson dating back to his childhood. The transcripts of his interviews and the commentary Stockton Axson produced as Baker wrote the biography, together with the other material he collected, make his papers in the Library of Congress second only to Wilson's own papers in value to the biographer and to historians of this era.

The other outstanding contributor to the illumination of this man and his times was Arthur S. Link. Born three years before Wilson died, Link did not know him, but he began work on him soon after Baker completed his multivolume authorized biography. Link approached Wilson differently, as a historian of the era rather than as a biographer. Over the course of twenty years, Link produced a five-volume history of Wilson's political career up to intervention in World War I. The four volumes dealing with Wilson's time in the White House constitute the fullest, most insightful history of a presidential administration ever written. Their only rivals are Arthur Schlesinger, Jr.'s two volumes on the first Franklin Roosevelt administration and Henry Adams's eight volumes on the Jefferson and Madison administrations. My notes to the chapters dealing with the years from 1910 to 1917 begin to indicate my reliance on Link's work. Having used many of the same sources that he did, I continually marvel at how he "got it right." Link's work can be corrected only where evidence to which he did not have access has come to light, and the instances of that are infrequent.

Link also made a second, still greater contribution to an understanding of Wilson. Starting in the 1950s, the Woodrow Wilson Foundation dedicated its assets and Princeton University provided institutional support for a comprehensive multivolume edition of *The Papers of Woodrow Wilson*. Link was the editor of this edition from start to finish, which came with the publication of the final volume in 1993. He enjoyed able assistance throughout most of the project from his associate editors, John Wells Davidson, David W. Hirst, and John Little, as well as his wife, Margaret Douglas Link. There was also an editorial advisory committee, which included Richard W. Leopold, William H. Harbaugh, and Arthur Schlesinger, Jr., among others, for the duration. About twenty years into the project I also joined that advisory committee, and I was proud to serve to its completion. In the process, I became a close friend of Arthur and Margaret Link, and I regret that I began this biography when they were no longer alive to help me with their counsel and criticism.

Important as the assistance of others was, what Link always called *The Papers* was his work: it perfectly fulfills Emerson's dictum, "An institution is the lengthened shadow of one man." The sixty-nine volumes of *The Papers of Woodrow Wilson* constitute one of the great editorial achievements in all history. Of the great documentary editions that began to flourish in the second half of the twentieth century, this is the only one that has been completed and the only one that has had only one editor. Second only to Wilson himself and equal to Baker, Link deserves the greatest credit for making this man so accessible to anyone who wants to know a little or a lot about him.

These volumes bring together and reproduce nearly all the significant contemporary documents by and about Wilson and the events in which he played a major role. Much of the material comes from the Wilson manuscripts in the

Library of Congress, but, particularly for his earlier life—when people wrote longhand letters and did not make copies—this edition gathers material from widely scattered sources. Those volumes also contain extensive editorial notes that add up to a biography of Wilson in those years. For the presidency, the selection sometimes leaves out material and requires consulting the manuscripts—which are available on microfilm—but those instances are rare. All relevant diary entries are included, and when foreign affairs are involved there is material from archives in other countries. Again, my notes indicate my heavy reliance on *PWW*, as they are abbreviated there. They are the indispensable source for anyone who studies Wilson or this era. For the biographer, it is amazing how seldom he or she needs to venture beyond *PWW*, except to Baker's collection and a few other sources.

I have likewise relied on the work of other historians and biographers. The notes give some indication of those whose work I found most helpful. One whose work is frequently cited deserves additional thanks. Henry Bragdon served as a bridge between Baker and Link. In the 1930s, he also interviewed people who had known Wilson during his years as a student, professor, and college president. He was able to talk with some people whom Baker missed or could not get much out of, and even when he repeated interviews, these elicited fresh information and provided a second take on the person's memories. Bragdon then produced an excellent biography of Wilson's "academic years," prior to his entry into politics in 1910. It is also a fine contribution to the history of higher education in America, although it has been supplemented and in some instances supplanted by a still better work in that field, James Axtell's history of Princeton in the century that started with Wilson's presidency there. Axtell tells the story of what Wilson attempted in the way of transforming Princeton into one of America's and the world's great universities and how, by fits and starts and over a long time, his vision came to be a reality. It is the finest history of an American university yet written.

Other works on Wilson that I found helpful and are cited in the notes, though not often enough, are John Mulder's account of Wilson's life to 1910, Edwin Weinstein's medical and psychological biography of Wilson, Neils Thorsen's study of his pre-presidential political thought, and Robert Kraig's study of Wilson's rhetoric. All are excellent works. Mulder emphasizes the religious environment of Wilson's youth. Weinstein brings matters of Wilson's health into perspective, as do notes in *PWW* for the time surrounding his stroke in 1919. Thorsen probes into what a truly gifted student of politics Wilson was. Kraig places Wilson in the Western rhetorical tradition dating back to classical times and illuminates the influences and contributions that he made to that tradition—now horribly eroded by modern techniques of political manipulation and appeals through mass media. Thomas Knock's book on Wilson's foreign policy and Margaret MacMillan's account of the peace conference also guided me through these aspects of Wilson's life and work. At the risk of immodesty, I should mention two of my previous books, a comparative biography of Wilson and his great rival Theodore Roosevelt and a study of the League Fight. The first puts Wilson in an indispensable context that sheds light on both him and his greatest rival; the second examines not only him but also his friends and foes in the last great debate over American foreign policy—the culmination of what Kraig aptly terms "the lost world of oratorical statesmanship." There are many other fine works on Wilson and the momentous events of his time, and a good way to approach them is through the comprehensive bibliography published in 1997 by John Mulder and his associates.

Finally comes the happiest task of all, thanking the individuals and institutions that have aided and speeded me along the path to this book. Early on Frank Smith and my children, John M. Cooper III and Elizabeth Cooper Doyle, together with my wife, Judith Cooper, encouraged and prodded me to write a biography of Wilson. I resisted, but not for long, because they were asking me to do something I really wanted to do. Along the way, several people have helped me find material, including Robert Cullinane, Kathleen Dalton, Lewis Gould, Arthur S. Link III, Samuel Schaffer, William Walker, and Katherine Wilkins. At Princeton's Mudd Library, Dan Linke and Chris Kitto aided me in gathering illustrations, and at the National Gallery of Ireland, Adrian Le Harivel afforded me the opportunity of a close-up examination of the Sargent portrait of Wilson and helped arrange its reproduction. Others have read and commented on portions of the manuscript, including Anthony Gaughan, Bruce Freed, Christine Schillig, Marc Winerman, Victoria Brown, Edward Coffman, and Michael Dickens. Three people have read everything in one version of this work and sometimes more. My wife, Judy, has patiently gone over several incarnations line by line, constantly raising questions about what I meant, how I said things, and how I interpreted a number of Wilson's and others' motives and actions. Jim Axtell performed the same service, reading and writing comments on everything and raising constant questions. Since he was writing his history of Princeton at the same time, we became something like co-conspirators as we read each other's chapters and traded opinion and lore. Justus Doenecke took great pains to spot numerous errors. To all these friends and loved ones, I can offer only small thanks for making a lonely job far more enjoyable and stimulating.

Two institutions provided greatly appreciated aid toward the end of this work. The University of Wisconsin–Madison granted me a sabbatical for the academic year 2007–8, which allowed me to write full-time. I would like to thank the university for this opportunity. The Woodrow Wilson International Center for Scholars made me a Policy Scholar for five months in 2008. Besides time, a pleasant place for writing, and proximity to sources, the Wilson Center furnished me with the services of an intern, Colin Biddle, who found material for me, read portions of the manuscript, and checked references for the first part. In addition, the Wilson Center provided a most enjoyable and stimulating place to be, living up to its mission of bringing together scholars and persons in public life. I would like to thank its director, Lee Hamilton, and its associate director, Samuel Wells, for making this possible.

From manuscript to book, this biography has enjoyed the indispensable services of giants in the world of publishing. My agent, Alexander Hoyt, navigated the waters of this industry for me, landing me with a superb publisher and aiding and encouraging me all along the way. At Alfred A. Knopf, I have profited from the gifts of two outstanding editors, who have proven that the truly noble work of the golden age of American publishing is not dead. I began first with Ashbel Green, who is a legend in his own time for his work with a long line of distinguished historians. If I had written faster, Ash could have seen this through to the end, but he graciously read the rest of the work in retirement and gave me the benefit of his eagle eye for infelicities of wording and curbed my tendency toward slanginess. His retirement meant that I also benefited from the services of another equally gifted editor, Andrew Miller, who reinforced Ash's oversight and went on to suggest ways to streamline and improve the work. As I have told him, Andrew really knows how to make a book move, and the flow of this one owes a great deal to him. In addition, Andrew was a fount of ideas for how to improve the interpretations and depictions of persons and events. Sara Sherbill and Andrew Michael Carlson patiently and cheerfully shepherded me through the indispensable tasks of transforming a piece of writing into a book. Finally, Abigail Winograd copyedited the book with truly extraordinary skill and insight—I have never had a more attentive and helpful reader. My deepest thanks to each of them.

In the end, all remaining errors, bad uses of words, quirks, and dubious interpretations remain entirely my own. This book comes out of a companionship with its subject that goes back a long way, and I hope it reflects some of his virtues.

Index

Adams, Abigail, 46
Adams, Herbert Baxter, 45–6, 47, 54, 58
Adams, John, 46, 341
Adams, John Quincy, 594
Adamson, William C., 345, 382
Adamson Act of 1916, 345–6, 349, 350–4, 364, 404, 637n21
Addams, Jane, 171, 354
Adriatic Coast issue, 485, 487, 490, 492, 502, 554
"Ad Usque" (Wordsworth), 421
Aeneid (Virgil), 39
African Americans, 11, 24, 88, 109, 170–1, 200, 273, 397, 610n20
    lynching of, 409–10
    migration of, 407, 510
    in military, 407–9
    1916 election and, 360–1
    in Wilson administration, 205–6, 252
    see also race, race relations
Agassiz, Louis, 15
Agriculture Department, U.S., 191, 555
Alabama, 151
Albania, 491
Albert, King of the Belgians, 501, 542
Aldrich-Vreeland Act, 220–1, 223
Aldrovandi Maresotti, Luigi, 485
Alexander, Joshua W., 555
Alexander I, Czar of Russia, 460
Allied Purchasing Commission, 392
Alligators club, 27, 28–9, 30
Alsace-Lorraine, 315, 317, 366, 422, 451

American Bankers' Association, 222, 223
American Bar Association, 330, 582
American Commonwealth, The (Bryce), 58, 63
American Expeditionary Forces (AEF), 401–2, 427
    in Europe, 433–4, 437–8
American Federation of Labor (AFL), 191, 230, 234, 329, 348, 354, 549
American Medical Association, 555
American Railway Union, 230
American Review of Reviews, The, 66, 74
American Revolution, 25
ancien régime, L' (Tocqueville), 34
Ancona, 307–8
Anthony, Susan B., 414
anti-Semitism, 330, 391, 392
anti-trust legislation, 216, 226–34, 254, 346, 360
Arabic, 300, 303–4
Argentina, 244
Arizona, 374, 378, 572
Arlington National Cemetery, 290, 328, 596, 597
Armenia, 317, 491, 497, 564–5, 575
Armistice, 449, 450–3, 455
    assessment of, 452–3
    terms of, 451
Army Air Service, U.S., 427–8
Army War College, 298, 394
Art Students League, 52–3

Ashurst, Henry, 443–4, 509, 518, 637n19
Atlanta Constitution, 38
Atlantic, 50, 70, 74, 76, 79, 584
Auchincloss, Gordon, 488
Austro-Hungarian Empire, 6, 191, 308, 317, 366, 369, 386, 395, 396, 399, 420, 421, 422, 423–4, 428, 442, 449, 473, 496–7, 498
Axson, Edward, 43, 58, 61, 69, 88, 89, 99
Axson, Ellen, *see* Wilson, Ellen Axson
Axson, Isaac Stockton, 55
Axson, Margaret, *see* Elliott, Margaret Axson
Axson, Margaret Jane Hoyt, 43
Axson, Samuel Edward, 41, 43–4
    decline and death of, 51–2
Axson, Stockton, 19–20, 43, 52, 57, 61, 68, 69, 70, 75, 80–1, 94, 102, 104, 115, 116, 129, 139, 172–3, 199, 257, 260, 262, 266, 267, 276, 306, 353, 420, 433, 499, 511, 572–3, 583, 584, 632n46

Bagehot, Walter, 30, 32, 47, 48, 51, 59, 71, 98, 99
Baker, Hobart (Hobey) Amory Hare, 117–18
Baker, Newton D., 185, 311–12, 339–40, 375, 380, 383, 392, 394, 396–7, 401–2, 408, 418, 425, 491, 511, 531, 538, 539, 551, 561, 573, 577, 578, 583, 587, 593
Baker, Ray Stannard, 203, 215, 322–3, 326, 426, 433–4, 444–5, 456, 469, 474, 475, 482, 484, 487, 488, 490, 492, 493, 495–6, 499–500, 503, 507, 529, 545, 551, 553, 555, 568–9, 574, 591, 594–5, 603n28
Balfour, Arthur James, 316, 367, 378, 395, 396, 448, 464, 483, 491
Balfour Declaration, 418
Bancroft, Jane Marie, 57
banking reform, 186–7, 219–26, 360
    central bank debate and, 219–20
    opposition to, 222–3
    see also Federal Reserve Act

Bank War, 219
Baruch, Bernard, 172, 339, 347, 350, 391–2, 407, 430, 469, 487, 490, 507, 550, 565, 576, 590
    WIB led by, 426–8
Bass, Elizabeth, 412–13
Beach, Sylvester, 257, 262, 597
Beerbohm, Max, 215
Belgium, 6, 269, 315, 317, 366, 369, 405, 422, 501–2
    German invasion of, 268, 558
Bell, Johannes, 503
Belleau Wood, Battle of, 437
Benedict XV, Pope, 418, 465–6
Beneš, Edvard, 473
Benham, Edith, 332
Bergson, Henri, 438
Bermuda, 89, 98–9, 101, 180, 182
Bernstorff, Johann-Heinrich von, 266, 289, 300, 304, 324, 373
Beveridge, Albert J., 506–7, 532
Bill of Rights, U.S., 25
Bill of Rights, Virginia, 181
Birth of a Nation, 272–3, 410
Bissolati, Leonida, 466
Blease, Coleman, 435, 487
Bliss, Howard S., 474
Bliss, Tasker H., 456–7, 468
Blythe, Samuel G., 203, 626n19
Bolling, John Randolph, 580, 593, 595
Bolling, Wilmer, 576
Bolsheviks, Bolshevism, 5, 401, 419, 421, 424, 432, 465, 483, 486, 487, 497, 499, 523, 573
Bones, Helen Woodrow, 69, 195, 196, 279, 280–3, 289, 306, 357, 389
Bonsal, Stephen, 545
Borah, William E., 331, 345, 368, 372, 447, 460, 477, 506, 507, 513, 515–16, 518, 524, 532, 556, 572, 640n17
Borglum, Gutzon, 434
Bourgeois, Léon, 472, 473
Bowman, Isaiah, 462
Bradford, Gamaliel, 49
Brandegee, Frank, 478, 480, 483, 509, 513, 515–18, 524, 546, 558–9

Brandeis, Louis D., 5, 8, 176, 213, 221,
223, 227, 228, 232, 233, 235,
440–1, 586, 620n7, 624n35
  cabinet post considered for, 183, 185,
  189–90, 194
  1912 election and, 162–3, 167, 169
  Supreme Court nomination of, 190,
  329, 330–2, 334, 336, 338, 346
Brazil, 244
"Breaking the Money Trust" (Brandeis),
228
Brest-Litovsk, Treaty of, 425, 431
Briand, Aristide, 317
Bridges, Robert (Bob), 26, 28, 32, 33,
35–9, 40, 48, 56, 58, 59, 62, 70, 74,
76, 79, 416, 604n38
Brockdorff-Rantzau, Ulrich Graf von,
495, 500–2
Brooks, Arthur, 196–7, 420, 579
Brougham, Herbert, 275
Browning, Elizabeth Barrett, 46
Browning, Robert, 173
Brownlow, Louis, 411
Bruce, William Cabell, 34–5, 588, 667n24
Bryan, Charles, 145
Bryan, Grace, 293
Bryan, Mary, 145, 291
Bryan, William Jennings, 4–5, 73, 87, 92,
98, 106, 127, 140, 186, 190, 195,
196, 198, 199, 203, 204, 205, 209,
210–11, 212, 213, 215, 218, 220–1,
230, 244–5, 247–9, 255, 266, 267,
269, 275, 277, 278, 279, 295, 296,
300, 308, 309, 312, 314–15, 323,
325, 328, 334, 372, 389, 393, 532,
550, 567, 620n7, 623n19, 629n18
  cabinet appointment of, 183, 185, 189,
  194
  Cross of Gold speech of, 152
  Lusitania crisis and, 286, 287, 290–4
  Mexico crisis and, 238–9, 243
  military preparedness issue and, 297,
  304, 307, 310
  1912 election and, 141–9, 151, 154,
  162, 166, 168, 173–4, 176
  1916 election and, 335, 341, 349–50
  resignation of, 291–4
Bryant, David, 20

Bryce, James, 44, 58, 63, 71, 98, 250, 457
Bryn Mawr College, 53–4, 56–8
Bullitt, William C., 461, 462, 495
  in Moscow mission, 483, 487
  Senate testimony of, 524–5, 538
Bureau of Investigation, U.S., 400
Burleson, Albert S., 171, 183, 191, 205,
214–15, 217, 238, 250, 288, 313,
331, 379, 383, 397–400, 435, 446,
507, 510, 552, 562–5, 568–9
Burke, Edmund, 8, 26, 28, 30, 59, 73, 77,
98, 108, 213–14, 245, 468, 583
Burr, Aaron, 25
Butt, Archie, 143

"Cabinet Government in the United
States" (Wilson), 30–2, 38
"Calendar of Great Americans, A" (Wilson), 74
Calhoun, John C., 39
California, 135, 173, 174, 175–6, 274, 400
  anti-Asian legislation of, 211–12
  1916 election and, 358–9
Cambon, Jules-Martin, 316–17
Cannon, Joseph G., 51
Caporetto, Battle of, 401, 419
Carden, Lionel, 241
Carnegie, Andrew, 82, 85, 87, 110, 147
Carranza, Venustiano, 241–5, 319–21,
355, 374, 547, 626n15
Carrizal, fight at, 320–1, 322
Carroll, Lewis, 166
Carver, Clifford, 316
Casement, Roger, 343
Catt, Carrie Chapman, 412–14
Cecil, Robert, 454, 470–3, 474, 482, 483,
489, 652n41
Chamberlain, George, 314, 425–6
Chamberlain, Neville, 472
Château-Thierry, Battle of, 437
Chicago, University of, 119, 419
Chicago Tribune, 381, 507
child labor, 253, 335–6, 346, 627n38
  1916 election and, 343–4, 348,
  637n17
Chile, 244, 246

China, 209, 211, 274–5, 491, 493, 504

Churchill, Winston, 4, 381, 464, 476, 483, 497

Civil War, U.S., 16–18, 24, 26, 97, 143, 152, 175, 178, 184, 225, 391, 393, 397, 403, 405

Clansman, The (Dixon), 272

Clapp, Moses, 344, 379

Clark, James Beauchamp, 149, 151–6, 157, 161, 213, 250, 304, 312, 358, 389, 393, 574

Clarke, John Hessin, 340, 586

Clayton, Henry D., 196, 229

Clayton Anti-Trust Act, 229–31, 234

Clemenceau, Georges, 443, 448, 449, 455, 461–3, 469, 471, 474, 476, 483, 485–6, 488–9, 491, 492, 493, 495, 497, 499, 500, 503, 504–5, 590

Cleveland, Grover, 54, 72, 74, 79, 90, 100, 104, 129, 187, 216, 337, 353

Cobb, Frank, 382–3, 400, 450, 578, 586, 594, 642n51

Cohan, George M., 401

Colby, Bainbridge, 556, 562, 565, 567, 568–9, 573, 576, 583, 666n8

Colombia, 245–6, 381

Colt, LeBaron, 514

Columbia University, 96, 419

Commerce Department, U.S., 190, 555

Commission for Relief in Belgium, 405, 502

Committee on Coal Production, 406

Committee on Public Information (CPI), 391–2, 406

"Committee or Cabinet Government?" (Wilson), 38

Confederate States of America, 17

"Confession of Faith" speech, 159–60

Congress, U.S., 24, 29, 31, 39, 47, 50, 76, 98, 146, 183, 184, 187, 200, 213, 214, 221–2, 227, 240, 243, 263, 270, 300, 304, 310–14, 324, 334, 342, 381, 409, 449, 456, 459, 477, 499, 520, 547, 574, 624n24

Armenian mandate issue and, 564

army bill in, 310–12

immigration ban and, 253

lame-duck legislation in, 575

McLemore resolution in, 313–14

Seaman's Act passed by, 254–5

Sedition Act passed by, 432

ship-purchasing bill in, 270

Sixty-third, 235–6, 254

Sixty-fourth, 364, 376

Sixty-fifth, 416, 418, 642n62

Wilson's Fourteen Points speech to, 422–3, 428

Wilson's last address to, 511

Wilson's legislative leadership and, 215–16

Wilson's war address to, 385–8

see also House of Representatives, U.S.; Senate, U.S.

Congressional Government (Wilson), 47–51, 53, 63, 74, 75–7, 96–8, 196, 284

"Congressional Government" (Wilson), 34, 38

Congress of Vienna, 420, 476, 496

Conklin, Edward Grant, 182

Constitution, U.S., 34, 38, 50, 184, 429, 456, 473, 549

Article II of, 538

proposed term-limits amendment of, 195–6

Sixteenth (income tax) Amendment of, 135, 187–8

Seventeenth Amendment of, 188

Eighteenth Amendment of, 253, 415, 537

Nineteenth Amendment of, 414–15

Twentieth Amendment of, 357

Wilson on, 48, 97

Constitutional Government in the United States (Wilson), 97–8, 107, 129, 196, 212

Constitutionalists, Mexican, 238, 239, 241, 242, 245, 319, 320, 355, 547, 625n5

Continental Army proposal, 298, 310–11, 312

Continental Congress, 25

Coolidge, Calvin, 577, 596

Cooper, James Fenimore, 26

Costa Rica, 581

Council of Four, 485–9, 491, 494, 499, 501–2, 504
Council of Ten, 468–71, 473, 483–5
Covington, James, 232
Cowdray, Lord, 241
Cox, James, 567–71, 587
Cram, Ralph Adams, 87, 111
Crane, Charles R., 172
Craufurd-Stuart, Charles Kennedy, 550
"Credo, A" (Wilson), 98
Creel, George, 391–2, 406, 417, 462, 481, 570, 584, 594
Crisis, 170, 408
Croly, Herbert, 143–4, 161, 235, 355, 398, 640n21
Crowder, Enoch, 397
Culberson, Charles A., 331, 559
Cummings, Homer, 445, 448, 557, 565, 567, 568, 571, 573
Cummins, Albert, 230, 269, 330, 344, 345, 379, 640n24
Cuyler, Cornelius, 77
Czechoslovakia, 472, 473, 496

Dacia, S.S., 274
Daily Princetonian, The, 93
Dalmatia, 484, 487, 490, 491, 492
Daniels, Jonathan, 316, 318
Daniels, Josephus, 148, 150, 154, 183, 185, 189, 190–3, 204, 205, 214, 238, 243, 271, 289, 297–8, 301, 352, 375, 383–4, 391, 392, 399, 408, 426, 444–5, 446, 459, 487, 568, 569, 573, 577
Daniels, Winthrop, 131
Darrow, Clarence, 512
Davidson College, 25
Davies, Joseph, 435
Davis, Jefferson, 18
Davis, John W., 594
Davis, Norman, 586
Debs, Eugene Victor, 159, 174, 230, 354, 360, 398, 432, 512, 572, 573
Declaration of Independence, 25

democracy, 60, 98, 386, 431–2
  promotion of, 5–6, 248
  Wilson on, 59, 63, 98, 584
Democracy in America (Tocqueville), 39, 63
Democratic National Committee, 305, 412, 479, 567–9, 592–3
Democratic National Conventions:
  of 1912, 139, 145, 146, 155–8
  of 1916, 341–2
  of 1920, 527, 561, 563, 565–7
  of 1924, 592–3
Democratic Party, New Jersey, 120–1, 126, 134, 137, 141
Democratic Party, New York, 135–6
Democratic Party, U.S., 4, 24, 35, 54, 75, 91, 92, 98, 108–9, 127, 138, 149, 155, 160, 164, 175, 184, 195, 234, 254, 268, 292, 312, 315, 325, 328–9, 334, 348, 351, 433, 594
  Bourbon faction of, 150
  conservative, 105–6
  immigration issue and, 252–3
  organized labor and, 231
  Philippine independence and, 249
  progressive, 105–6
  tariff reform and, 187
  see also specific elections
Dempsey, Jack, 397
Denman, William, 404
Derby, Lord, 464
Dercum, Francis X., 533–4, 536, 543, 548, 555
de Schweinitz, George, 89, 533
"Destiny of the Republic, The" (Wilson), 583
Dewey, George, 597
Division and Reunion, 1829–1889 (Wilson), 73–4
Dix, John A., 140, 171
Dixon, Thomas, 272–3
"Document, The," 586–8, 593, 594
Dodd, William E., 594
Dodge, Cleveland, 30, 62, 86, 93, 95, 110, 113, 154, 172, 238, 350, 372, 563, 576, 585, 592
dollar, U.S., 263
"dollar diplomacy," 210–11, 245, 249
Dominican Republic, 247–8, 249

Dos Passos, John, 189
Douglas, Stephen, 178
draft, 391, 393–7
Draft Covenant, 473–5, 485
  Article X of, 495, 506, 508–9, 512, 514,
    515–16, 517, 519, 522–3, 526,
    528–9, 531, 541, 543–5, 550–2, 554,
    557–8, 559, 570, 571, 661n23
  in League fight, 506–7
  Monroe Doctrine in, 477–9, 482, 485,
    489, 490–1, 494
  Republican opposition to, 477–80, 481,
    482
DuBois, W. E. B., 170–1, 361, 408, 497
Dunne, Finley Peter, 548, 662n31

Easter Rising, 342–3
Eastman, Max, 326, 354, 398
Economic Consequences of the Peace, The
  (Keynes), 490, 556
Edison, Thomas A., 304
Edward, Prince of Wales, 542
Edward VII, King of England, 542
Edwards, Jonathan, 25
eight-hour workday, 345, 350, 382
Eisenhower, Dwight D., 452, 643n7
election of 1910, New Jersey, 120–9, 140,
    144, 149, 161, 165, 351
  results of, 126–7
  Wilson's campaign in, 123–5
  Wilson's nomination in, 120, 122–3
election of 1912, U.S., 13, 100, 117, 139,
    140–81, 183, 195, 213, 218, 230,
    252, 259, 270–1, 273, 274, 307,
    309, 334, 335, 337, 347, 348, 354,
    359, 360, 361, 594, 620n40
  attempted assassination of T. Roosevelt
    in, 169–70
  Brandeis's influence in, 162–3, 167, 169
  Bryan and, 141–9, 151, 154, 162, 166,
    168, 173–4, 176
  Clark's candidacy in, 149–50, 151
  "Confession of Faith" speech in,
    159–60
  conservatism issue in, 164–5
  Democratic convention in, 155–8

Democratic platform in, 160–1
Electoral College vote in, 173
New Freedom in, 163, 168, 175
New Nationalism slogan in, 161, 163,
    165, 167
New York *World*'s endorsement in,
    153–4
primaries in, 151–3, 187–8
race issue in, 170–1
Republican convention in, 154–5
results of, 173–4
T. Roosevelt in, 143, 152, 154, 159–60,
    166, 168–9, 171, 173–4, 175–80
trusts issue in, 163–4, 167, 174, 176
Underwood's candidacy in, 150
Wilson-Bryan meetings in, 141–2
Wilson-Harvey break in, 148–9
Wilson-Roosevelt encounter in, 166
Wilson's campaign in, 163–9
Wilson's nomination in, 158, 160–1,
    618n1
woman suffrage issue in, 171, 174
election of 1916, 223, 249, 273, 279, 303,
    305, 330–1, 334–61, 429, 434, 447,
    456, 522, 539, 556, 597
  African Americans and, 360–1
  Bryan and, 335, 341, 349–50
  child labor issue in, 335–6, 348
  Democratic platform in, 328, 335–6,
    341–2
  economy and, 334–5
  Hughes's California misstep in, 347–8
  Hughes's campaign in, 346–51, 353
  "kept us out of war" theme in, 341–2,
    352, 359–60
  labor and, 343–5, 350–1, 352, 354,
    359–60
  major themes of, 334–5
  Mexico intervention issue in, 322–3
  Progressive national convention in, 338
  Progressives in, 354–5
  Republican convention in, 336–7
  Republican smears, 353–4
  resignation scheme in, 356–7, 549,
    638n43
  results of, 357–8, 638n47
  rural credits issue in, 348, 352
  T. Roosevelt in, 336, 338–9, 348–54

war issue in, 307–8, 322
Wilson's campaign in, 346–53
woman suffrage issue in, 335–6, 347, 360
election of 1918, U.S., 360, 430, 435–50
Armistice and, 448–9, 450
results of, 446–8
Wilson's appeal to voters in, 445–6, 448, 458
Wilson's primary interventions in, 435–7
elections, U.S.:
of 1844, 156
of 1858, 178
of 1860, 16
of 1884, 54
of 1896, 73, 141, 152, 230, 334, 351, 359
of 1900, 75, 249
of 1904, 126, 156
of 1906, 337
of 1907, 92
of 1908, 106, 173, 174, 175–6, 230, 337
of 1910, 334
of 1911, 137–8
of 1912, *see* election of 1912
of 1913, 208
of 1914, 232, 249, 273, 304, 334, 347
of 1916, *see* election of 1916
of 1918, *see* election of 1918
of 1920, 414, 459, 466, 482, 526, 527, 559, 561, 563, 565–7, 570–2, 573, 588, 665n28
of 1924, 588–9, 592–3, 594
of 1928, 593
of 1932, 357
Eliot, Charles William, 80, 91, 119, 209, 330
Elizabeth, Queen of the Belgians, 501, 542
Elliott, Edward, 89, 109, 129, 420
Elliott, Margaret Axson (Madge), 43, 69, 88, 114, 129, 260, 420–1
Ely, Richard T., 45–6, 53
Emergency Fleet Corporation, 404
English Constitution (Bagehot), 48
Epochs of American History (Hart, ed.), 73
Espionage Act, 11, 398–9, 432, 512
Essary, J. Fred, 539

Faisal, Emir, 468, 473–4
Falaba, 277, 278, 288
Fall, Albert, 513, 517, 547–8
Federalist Papers, The, 25
Federal Reserve, 8, 222–4, 228, 253–4, 346, 364, 369, 381, 391, 624n25
Federal Reserve Act, 222–7, 253, 459
Federal Trade Commission (FTC), 8, 232, 233–5, 436, 624n35
Fielder, James, 188–9
Fine, Henry (Harry) Burchard, 29, 70, 82–3, 84, 86, 88, 89, 90–1, 94, 95, 104, 109, 116, 204, 209, 415, 604n39, 611n25
First Paris Draft, 467–8, 651n28
Fitzgerald, F. Scott, 8, 118
Fiume, 487, 490, 492
Flood, Henry (Hal) De La Warr, 291, 312–13, 324, 377, 378, 620n44
Foch, Ferdinand, 437, 450–1, 483, 497
Folk, Joseph W., 190
Food Administration, U.S., 405–6, 407, 430
Ford, Henry, 521
Fordney, Joseph W., 574
Fosdick, Raymond, 84, 462, 590–1, 593, 594, 598
Four Points Address, 428–9
Fourteen Points, 6, 7, 276, 327, 371, 420–4, 425, 428–9, 431, 441, 442, 443, 449, 450, 452, 453, 490, 496, 503, 507, 525
goals of, 424
House and, 421–2, 423
"peace without victory" and, 371
Wilson's speech on, 422–3
France, 34, 48, 59, 191, 207, 219, 245, 274, 315, 366, 368, 390, 395–6, 401, 402, 417, 433, 469, 473, 487, 502–3, 541, 554, 562, 571, 583
House's wartime mission to, 316–17
loan ban and, 264–5
"peace without victory" and, 372–3
proposed Russia intervention and, 431, 438
Freeman, James Edward, 596–7
French Revolution, 34, 245

Fuel Administration, U.S., 407
Furuseth, Andrew, 254–5

Gallinger, Jacob, 371
Galt, Edith Bolling, *see* Wilson, Edith
    Bolling Galt
Galt, Norman, 281–2
Gardener, Helen, 412
Gardner, Augustus Peabody, 267–8
Garfield, Harry, 99, 406–7, 430
Garfield, James A., 535
Garrison, Lindley M., 190, 194, 212, 238,
    243, 245, 275, 288, 296–7, 298,
    310, 311–12
Garrison, William Lloyd, 170
Geddes, Auckland, 562, 563–4
George V, King of England, 454, 464–5
George Washington, U.S.S., 458, 460, 462,
    476, 477, 481, 482, 488, 495, 504,
    507
George Washington (Wilson), 76
Georgia, 39, 40, 51, 151, 436–7, 648n26
Geran, Elmer, 132
Gerard, James W., 209
German Americans, 355, 378, 399,
    482
Germany, Imperial, 6–7, 75, 203, 207,
    209, 219, 251, 308, 318, 324, 325,
    326, 356, 365, 366, 417, 422–4,
    428, 442, 528
    Armistice signed by, 450–1
    Belgian neutrality violated by, 268, 558
    British naval blockade of, 265–6,
        299–300
    "peace without victory" and, 372–4
    preliminary peace treaty and, 494–5
    submarine warfare and, *see* submarine
        warfare
    U.S. declaration of war against, 385–6,
        388–9
    see also Lusitania; World War I
Germany, Nazi, 452
Gerry, Peter, 455, 558, 638n48
Gilman, Daniel Coit, 67, 119
Gladden, Washington, 114
Gladstone, William Ewart, 22

Glass, Carter, 183, 186–7, 219, 221–2,
    225, 226, 391, 459, 533–4, 555,
    557, 565–7, 568, 592
Glynn, Martin, 339, 341
Goethals, George Washington, 404
gold standard, 73
Gompers, Samuel, 191, 230–1, 329, 348,
    354, 573
Good Neighbor policy, 246–7
Gordon, Alice Gertrude (Altrude), 280,
    282, 289, 306, 332
Gore, Thomas, 312–13, 314, 643n62
"Government by Debate" (Wilson), 38
Grasty, Charles, 531
Grayson, Cary T., 19, 100, 200, 201, 267,
    280, 295–6, 306, 339, 349, 357,
    461, 477, 481, 505, 507, 508, 519,
    536, 543, 545, 550, 569, 578, 585,
    589, 658n43
    Ellen Wilson's death and, 260–1
    in League speaking tour, 520, 525,
        526–31
    marriage of, 332
    "smelling committee" visit and, 547–8
    with Wilson for Paris talks, 468–71,
        474, 484–8, 493–5, 499–500
    Wilson's death and, 595–6
    in Wilson's disability and recovery
        period, 537–8, 540, 542, 547–8,
        552, 553, 555, 556, 560, 561–3,
        565–7, 572, 574
    in Wilson's European tour, 464, 465–6
    Wilson's recreational activities with,
        256, 258, 279, 281, 289, 415, 440,
        498
    Wilson's stroke and, 532–4
Great Adventure project, 251–2, 315
Great Britain, 27, 34, 48, 50, 59, 190, 207,
    209, 219, 237, 241, 251–2, 278,
    291, 365, 383, 390, 395–6, 401,
    403, 416–17, 431, 448, 541, 554,
    562
    Easter Rising and, 342–3
    freedom of the seas issue and, 449–50,
        460–1
    House's mission to, 315–17
    intelligence operation of, 318, 374
    Irish independence issue and, 342–3

naval blockade of, 265–6, 299–300, 346, 353

Panama Canal tolls controversy and, 249–50

"peace without victory" and, 372–3

precarious finances of, 364, 373, 381

ship-purchasing plan opposed by, 263–4

Great Depression, 179–80, 357

"Great Referendum and Accounting of Your Government" (Wilson), 565

Gregory, Thomas W., 273, 295–6, 329, 331, 399–400, 407, 432–3, 446, 459

Grew, Joseph C., 458

Grey, Edward, 251, 266, 269, 277, 300, 315, 342, 365, 549–50, 552–3, 634n22

Griffith, D. W., 272–3

Gronna, Asle, 379, 447, 641n35, 642n62

Gulf War, 4

Hague, Frank, 153, 189

Haiti, 248–9

Hale, William Bayard, 239, 240, 242

Hall, William Reginald, 374

Hamilton, Alexander, 28, 39, 74, 96, 143, 144, 175, 179, 214, 429

Hamlet (Shakespeare), 21

Hankey, Maurice, 485

Hapgood, Norman, 232, 331–2, 624n35

Harding, Florence, 577

Harding, Warren, 516, 539, 564, 569, 570–2, 577, 589–90, 596

Harding, William P. G., 364

Harding administration, 581, 586

Harmon, Judson, 140, 155

Harper, William Rainey, 119

Harper's, 76, 296

Harper's Weekly, 79, 80, 92, 149, 228

Hart, Albert Bushnell, 73

Harvard University, 80, 87, 91, 119, 159, 162, 330, 419

Harvey, George, 79, 80, 92, 106, 120–2, 123, 127, 141, 545–6

Wilson's break with, 148–9

Hay, James, 310–11

Hay-Pauncefote Treaty of 1901, 249–50

Hays, Will, 353, 446

Haywood, William D. "Big Bill," 399–400, 432

Hearst, William Randolph, 147, 151, 152, 158, 337, 372

Hesperian, 301

Hibben, Jennie, 70, 102

Hibben, John (Jack) Grier, 70–1, 77, 83, 89, 90, 99, 112, 113, 117, 118, 138, 173, 193, 194, 353, 563

Wilson's break with, 93–4, 102

History of England (Macaulay), 26

"History of Political Economy in the United States" (unpublished), 53

History of the American People, A (Wilson), 76, 79, 151, 266, 296

Hitchcock, Gilbert, 223, 224, 226, 269, 457, 490–1, 514–15, 518, 519, 523, 542–5, 547–8, 553, 557, 623n19, 629n18

Hofstadter, Richard, 5

Hollis, Henry, 232–3, 329

Holmes, Oliver Wendell, Jr., 573

Holt, Hamilton, 585–6

Hoover, Herbert, 201, 263, 357, 405–6, 427, 430, 455, 472, 497, 502, 561

Houghton Mifflin, 47, 59, 74

House, Edward M., 117, 182–3, 185, 201, 208, 209, 212, 214, 216, 221, 227, 254, 258, 268, 273, 279, 292, 300, 304, 306, 308, 315, 318, 323, 329, 341, 342, 350, 356, 360, 369–70, 430, 433, 442, 443, 444, 451, 506, 622n18, 632n41, 634n26, 641n32

administration appointments and, 189–90

Clemenceau's meeting with, 491

Edith Wilson's dislike of, 299, 302–3, 484, 597

Fourteen Points and, 421–2, 423

Great Adventure project and, 251–2, 315

House-Grey Memorandum and, 315–19

influence of, 191–4, 323

Inter-Allied War Council and, 419–20

Lansing appointment and, 294–5

Mexico crisis and, 210, 238, 241–2

House, Edward M. *(continued)*
  naval blockade and, 265–6
  1912 election and, 171–2
  Pan-American pact and, 246
  Paris peace talks and, 430, 433,
     449–50, 453, 455–8, 460, 461,
     463–5, 468, 471, 472, 474, 475,
     483–8, 491, 498, 553
  peace offensive and, 362–5, 367
  Phillimore Report and, 439–40
  submarine controversy and, 323–6
  vice president choice and, 339–41
  war question and, 374–5
  wartime missions of, 276–7, 315–19
  Wilson's relationship with, 189–92,
     206–7, 266–7, 294, 316, 365,
     418–19, 439, 483–4, 488, 492, 501,
     505, 545
House-Grey Memorandum, 315–19, 394
House of Commons, British, 451
House of Representatives, U.S., 48, 50,
     51, 97, 149, 184, 191, 223, 232–4,
     249, 250, 305, 334, 344, 378–9
  Agriculture Committee, 405
  Armed Services Committee, 297, 304
  Banking and Commerce Committee,
     183, 186, 220, 221, 222, 228, 459
  child labor issue in, 253, 343
  Clinton bill in, 229–30, 231
  Commerce Committee, 228, 232, 233
  draft bill in, 393
  Foreign Affairs Committee, 291, 312,
     475, 478
  Insular Affairs Committee, 249
  Interstate and Foreign Commerce
     Committee, 345
  Judiciary Committee, 196, 228–30
  McLemore resolution in, 314
  Rules Committee, 313, 412
  ship-purchasing bill in, 270
  war debate in, 388–9
  Ways and Means Committee, 216, 228,
     304, 344, 574
  woman suffrage in, 412–13, 414
  see also Congress, U.S.; *specific elections*
Houston, David F., 189, 191, 192, 194,
     204, 253, 292–3, 294, 329, 375, 377,
     415, 511, 550, 551, 555, 562, 575

Howe, Anne Josephine Wilson, 15, 22, 43,
     69–70, 82, 129, 172–3, 208, 283,
     289, 349
Howe, Annie, 129
Howe, George, 22, 69, 262, 349
Howe, Margaret, 257
Howells, William Dean, 79
How the Other Half Lives (Riis), 65
Hoyt, Florence, 78, 89, 99
Hoyt, Mary, 58, 72, 82, 85
Huddleston, George, 436
Huerta, Victoriano, 210, 237–40, 241,
     242–3, 245, 626n15
Hughes, Charles Evans, 136, 337, 338,
     352, 356, 357, 358–9, 434, 457,
     458, 512, 520, 539, 549, 597
  1916 campaign of, 346–50, 638n47
Hulbert, Mary Allen Peck, 98–101, 102,
     135, 146, 147, 148, 168, 197, 199,
     201, 220, 223, 263, 275, 280, 282,
     301–2, 353, 632n46
  Edith Wilson's meeting with, 527
  Wilson's correspondence with, 101,
     110, 113–14, 115, 117, 127, 128,
     131, 132, 133, 141, 142, 143, 154,
     157, 158, 161, 162, 259, 260,
     261
Hull, Cordell, 568, 592
Hungary, 486, 487, 498
Hurley, Edward N., 404, 557
Hurst, C. J. B., 471–2
Hutchins, Robert M., 119

"If" (Kipling), 76, 384
Illinois, 151, 152, 158, 273, 309
Illinois, University of, 67
immigration, 253, 305, 352, 360, 376–7,
     594
imperialism, 6, 75–6, 247
Independence League, 506, 524
India, 469
Indiana, 157, 340, 359
Industrial Workers of the World (IWW),
     399–400, 432
Inquiry, 419–21, 440, 458, 461, 471
Inter-Allied War Council, 419–20

Interstate Commerce Commission (ICC), 191, 222, 228–9, 231–2, 234, 345, 404
Iraq War, 4
Ireland, 342–3, 478, 491–2, 493, 509, 518, 558
Irish Americans, 343, 447, 481–2, 491–2, 499, 518
isolationism, 278, 328, 368
Italy, 317, 366, 373, 396, 401, 417, 419, 422, 487, 490–2, 494, 498, 500, 502, 541, 554, 584
 Wilson's visit to, 465–6

Jackson, Andrew, 74, 159, 219, 358
Jaffray, Elizabeth, 196–7, 332
James, Henry, 262
James, Ollie, 341, 426
Jameson, John Franklin, 45–6, 583
Japan, 211–12, 249, 274–5, 417, 431, 472, 473, 482, 489–91, 493–4, 498, 513, 516, 518, 541
Japanese Americans, 11
Jefferson, Thomas, 11, 33, 74, 92, 97, 143, 153, 159, 166, 179, 214, 328, 335, 341, 410, 599
Jefferson Society, 34–5
Jenkins, William O., 547–8
Joffre, Joseph-Jacques-Césaire, 395, 396, 401
Johns Hopkins University, 41, 44, 53, 58, 59, 60, 62, 63, 118
Johnson, Hiram, 135, 161, 175, 212, 274, 347–8, 354, 358, 376, 447, 506, 513, 516–18, 524, 526, 532, 572, 638n46
Johnson, James Weldon, 409–10
Johnson, Lyndon B., 9, 51, 204, 213
Joint Committee on Expenditures in the Conduct of the War, 405
Joline, Adrian, 92, 148
J. P. Morgan and Company, 264, 426
Jusserand, Jean-Jules, 264–5, 366, 417, 443
Justice Department, U.S., 189, 399, 432

Kansas, 151, 309, 400
Kansas City Star, 154, 432–3
Keith's Theater, 415, 580
Kellogg, Frank, 514
Kennedy, Anderson Ross, 52
Kennedy, Marion Williamson Wilson, 15, 52, 70
Kentucky, 349, 413, 572
Kenyon, William, 344, 435
Kern, John W., 213, 312
Kerney, James, 123
Keynes, John Maynard, 369, 373, 417, 490, 497, 518, 556
King, Benjamin Mandeville, 199, 258
Kipling, Rudyard, 76, 384, 412
Kirby, Rollin, 294
Kirby, William F., 379, 641n35
Kitchin, Claude, 304, 310, 312, 313, 314, 344, 358, 376, 388–9, 393
Knox, Philander C., 460, 479–80, 507, 513, 516, 518, 521, 541, 561–2, 564, 565, 577
Koo, V. K. Wellington, 491, 493
Korea, 513
Korean War, 4
Ku Klux Klan, 272, 594
Kun, Béla, 486

labor, labor unions, 11, 231, 234, 329, 430, 459, 499, 511, 520, 546
 anti-trust reform and, 229–31
 child, *see* child labor
 1916 election and, 343–5, 348, 350–1, 352, 354, 359–60
Labour Party, British, 433
Laconia, 377–8
La Follette, Robert, Jr., 379
La Follette, Robert M., 121, 122, 132, 135, 146, 152, 163, 168, 170, 210, 218, 220, 227, 233, 254–5, 268, 269, 274, 310, 329, 330, 331, 344, 345, 354, 371, 377, 378–9, 385, 388, 389, 435, 446, 447, 618n1, 641n35, 642n62
Lamont, Thomas, 442–3, 490, 507, 512

Lane, Franklin K., 191, 192, 194, 206, 238, 377, 446, 538, 556

Lane, Harry, 379, 641n35, 643n62

Lansdowne, Lord, 419

Lansing, Robert, 288, 300, 303–4, 306, 308, 319, 323–6, 356, 357, 363–70, 373–5, 377, 378, 383–5, 396, 413, 416, 418, 440, 444–5, 503–4, 551, 573, 631n26, 639n14
    League of Nations condemned by, 524–5
    memoir of, 586–7
    in peace talks delegation, 455–7, 468, 485, 486, 487, 491
    resignation of, 553–5, 663n46
    Senate testimony of, 513
    "smelling committee" and, 547–8
    Wilson's ability to govern doubted by, 537–40, 650n7

Latin America, 59, 209–10
    Wilson policy in, 245–8

Lawrence, David, 289, 364, 388

Lawrence of Arabia, 473

"Leaders of Men" (Wilson), 64

League Commission, 470–3, 484–5, 489

League fight, 506–34, 614n33
    amendments initiative in, 518–19, 540
    Article X debate in, 506, 508–9, 512, 514, 515–16, 522–3, 526, 528–9, 531, 541, 543–5, 550–2, 554, 557–8, 559, 570, 571
    compromise urged in, 544–6, 548, 550–1, 554
    Draft Covenant in, 506–7
    Lodge's reservations in, 543–6, 557–60
    Monroe Doctrine in, 477–9, 482, 485, 489, 490–1, 494, 512, 517, 520, 524
    presentation of treaty to Senate in, 508–9
    reservations issue in, 512–15, 517–20, 524, 528–9, 542–4, 554, 556–7, 559–60, 571
    Senate hearings on, 513–17
    Shantung issue in, 512–13, 516, 524, 532, 541
    speaking tour in, *see* speaking tour of September 1919
    votes on treaty in, 545, 558–9

    Wilson's health in, 509, 510, 512, 519, 520, 526–34
    Wilson's "mild nullification" statement in, 557–8
    Wilson's referendum scheme and, 549, 552
    Wilson's Senate testimony in, 515–17
    Wilson's strategy for, 507

League for the Preservation of American Independence, 506

League of Nations, 7, 8, 94, 117, 118, 246, 276, 326–8, 347, 352, 355, 372, 414, 429–30, 442, 449, 450, 458, 461, 463, 496, 498, 504, 521, 536, 564, 573–6, 585, 594
    Draft Covenant of, *see* Draft Covenant
    First Paris Draft of, 467–8
    Lansing's condemnation of, 524–5
    Paris peace talks and, 467–73
    Phillimore Report and, 439–40
    Republican opposition to, 372, 460–1
    Second Paris Draft of, 468
    Third Paris Draft of, 471–2
    U.S. debate on, *see* League fight
    in Wilson's peace initiative, 362–3, 365–7

League of Nations Non-Partisan Association, 586

League to Enforce Peace (LEP), 326–7, 328, 372, 429–30, 439, 461, 464, 467, 477, 479, 506, 512, 513, 521, 526, 545, 549, 586

Lee, Robert E., 596

Lenin, V. I., 401, 425

Lenroot, Irvine, 435, 519

Leopold, Prince of Belgium, 542

Lever, Asbury, 329, 405

Lever Act, 406

Liberty Loans, 392, 431, 441, 442, 446

Library of Congress, 256, 576

Lincoln, Abraham, 11, 16, 74, 79, 110, 114, 153, 155, 168, 178, 225, 349, 387, 394, 405, 425, 499, 535, 574, 599

Lincoln, Robert Todd, 79

Lind, John, 240, 243

Lindbergh, Charles, 398

Lippmann, Walter, 194, 256, 355, 391, 398, 418, 450, 516, 638n33, 640n21

Literary Digest, 268, 269, 555

Lloyd George, David, 6, 316, 318, 342, 364–5, 368–9, 402, 419, 421, 422, 423, 431, 433, 443, 448, 449, 451, 455, 461, 464, 469, 483, 484, 485–6, 488–9, 491, 492–4, 497, 499, 500–1, 504, 590

Lodge, Henry Cabot, 31, 32, 74, 75, 143, 246, 267–8, 314, 326, 328, 329, 338, 354, 377, 381, 393, 439, 456–7, 466, 472, 482–3, 508, 524, 526, 528, 556, 562, 564, 574, 597, 604n46, 626n20
   Draft Covenant debate and, 477–81, 506
   in League fight, 513–18, 540–1, 543–6, 550
   League of Nations opposed by, 372, 378–9
   punitive peace favored by, 442, 443
   treaty reservations of, 543–6, 557–60
   war question and, 285, 367–8, 376, 384, 388, 640n17
   Wilson's last encounter with, 577

Long, Breckinridge, 554, 588

London, Meyer, 389

Lotos Club, 91–2

Louisiana, 187, 217, 218

Lowell, A. Lawrence, 50–1, 330, 429–30, 439, 490–1, 513, 545

Lusitania, 203, 276, 290, 300, 307, 308, 323, 324, 325, 353, 366–7, 416, 495, 496
   U.S.-German diplomatic exchanges on, 285–91, 294, 296–7

Luther, Martin, 387–8, 499

lynching, 409–10, 411, 437, 525

McAdoo, Eleanor Randolph Wilson, 62, 68–9, 88, 114–15, 123, 138, 139, 158, 162, 170, 173, 199, 208, 214, 256, 261, 279, 420, 537, 589, 595

McAdoo, William Gibbs, 145–6, 154, 157, 161, 169–70, 171, 192, 194, 204, 206, 221–2, 225, 258–9, 263, 279, 291–4, 301, 313, 329, 331, 364, 375–7, 379, 382, 392, 404, 413, 417, 426, 430, 434, 440, 441, 455, 507, 511–14, 555, 565, 595
   appointed Treasury secretary, 183, 185, 189–90
   1920 election and, 566–7, 568
   1924 election and, 589, 594
   resignation of, 459
   Wilson's relationship with, 259–60

McCarter, Robert, 26, 29

McCombs, William F., 141, 145–6, 148, 154, 156, 157, 161, 171, 185, 191, 207, 209, 339

McCorkle, Walter, 141, 145

McCormick, Cyrus, 30, 62, 68, 72, 77, 585

McCormick, Vance, 339, 349, 352, 430, 445–6, 507, 557, 568–9

McCosh, James, 26, 62, 65, 85, 87, 103

McCumber, Porter J., 371, 508, 514, 517–18, 524, 528, 545, 549, 650n5, 660n15

McKinley, William, 73, 75, 351, 394, 425, 456, 572

McLemore, Jeff, 312–13, 435

McReynolds, James, 183, 185, 189, 190, 192, 194, 227, 232, 338
   as Supreme Court choice, 273

Madero, Francisco, 210, 239, 322

Madison, James, 25, 266, 278, 425

Magie, William F., 30, 64, 70, 94

Makino, Nobuaki, 473, 493

Malone, Dudley Field, 209, 412, 623n19

Mantoux, Paul, 485

Marne, Battle of the, 395

Marshall, John, 96

Marshall, Thomas R., 155, 157, 198, 340, 356, 539–40

Martin, Thomas S., 291, 542, 554

Martine, James E. "Farmer Jim," 127–8, 138

Marx, Karl, 6

Masaryk, Tomáš, 438

Massachusetts, 32, 329, 359, 447

Maximilian, Prince of Baden, 443

Mayflower (presidential yacht), 279, 289, 324, 332, 349, 396, 510

Mencken, H. L., 556

Mercier, Désiré-Joseph Cardinal, 501–2
"Mere Literature" (Wilson), 36, 74
Meuse-Argonne offensive, 438
Mexico, 5, 183, 227, 237–45, 248, 299,
    318, 319, 326, 334, 336, 347, 348,
    350, 352–3, 354–5, 360, 416, 418,
    573
  arms embargo and, 241–2
  Huerta coup in, 209–10, 213
  Jenkins incident and, 547–8, 661n29
  U.S. punitive expedition into, 320–3
  Zimmermann Telegram and, 374
Michigan, 173, 510–11, 638n47
military preparedness, 268, 297–8, 301–5,
    307–10, 313–14, 326, 334
  Bryan and, 297, 304, 307, 310
  Wilson's speaking tour on, 308–9
Miller, David Hunter, 440, 471–2, 482
Minnesota, 173, 358–9
Missouri, 226, 309, 588
"Mr. Wilson As Seen by One of His
    Family Circle" (Axson), 353
Monroe Doctrine, 241, 370–1, 372, 456,
    461, 509, 520
  in Draft Covenant, 477–89, 482, 485,
    489, 490–1, 494, 512, 517, 520,
    524
  T. Roosevelt's corollary to, 210
Morgan, J. P., 79, 82, 164, 219
Morgenthau, Henry, 172, 350
Morley, John, 157
Moses, George, 518, 539–40
Moton, Robert R., 409–10
Moynihan, Daniel Patrick, 529
Munich crisis of 1938, 472, 473
Murdock, Victor, 233, 355
Murphy, Charles, 155–6, 157
Mussolini, Benito, 584, 593

Napoleon I, Emperor of France, 322, 402
Nation, 40, 49, 154, 205, 304, 354, 495
National American Woman Suffrage
    Association (NAWSA), 349, 412
National Association for the Advancement
    of Colored People (NAACP), 170,
    205, 271–2, 409, 410, 413–14

National City Bank of New York, 224, 264
National Civil Liberties Board, 512
National Colored Democratic League,
    170
National Guard, U.S., 137, 138–9, 298,
    310, 383, 390
National Park Service, 186
National War Labor Board (NWLB), 430
National Woman's Party (NWP), 411–12
Navy Department, U.S., 190–1, 289, 458
Nebraska, 151, 399–400, 412, 446
Negro Silent Protest Parade, 409
Nelson, Knute, 435, 549
Netherlands, 265, 450
New, Harry, 517, 522
Newberry, Truman H., 510–11
New Deal, 213, 225, 346
New Freedom, 163, 167, 175, 186, 205,
    213, 227, 228, 235, 237, 246, 249,
    250, 305, 329, 336, 343, 346,
    348–9, 352, 355, 360, 364, 403,
    627n38
New Idea Republicans, 124, 125, 134
New Jersey, 8, 92, 117, 187, 615n17,
    615n26, 638n47
  Geran bill of, 132–4
  jury reform in, 188
  1910 election of, *see* election of 1910,
    New Jersey
  1912 election and, 187
  Nugent-Wilson confrontation in,
    133
  Sixteenth Amendment and, 187–9
  Wilson and state politics of, 120–2
  Wilson inaugurated as governor of,
    130–1
  Wilson's legislative agenda for, 130–2,
    134–8
  Wilson's resignation as governor of,
    189
New Jersey Public Utility Commission,
    131, 132, 134
Newlands, Francis, 331
New Mexico, 358, 374, 378
New Nationalism, 161, 163, 175, 177,
    235, 336, 351, 355
New Republic, 235, 355, 398, 418, 495, 556
New South, 38, 39

New York Democratic Club, 92
New York Evening Post, 37, 154, 170, 205,
    289, 300, 304
New York State, 32, 128, 140, 151, 152,
    171, 174, 209, 273, 360, 412, 447,
    568, 638n47
  progressive reform movement in, 135–6
New York *Sun*, 147–8, 222, 478, 483
New York Times, 112–13, 149, 188, 217,
    259, 275–6, 289, 357, 478, 488,
    531, 587, 589
New York Times Magazine, 353
New York *World*, 39, 128, 136, 153–4, 239,
    245, 478, 514, 558, 566, 578, 586,
    589
  Wilson interviewed by, 382–3, 566
Niagara Falls conference, 244, 245
Nicaragua, 247–8
Nicolson, Harold, 450
Nobel Peace Prize, 575–6
Norris, George W., 310, 331, 344, 345,
    371, 379, 388, 446, 447, 509,
    523–4, 549, 642n62
Northcliffe, Lord, 367
Nugent, James, 121–2, 132, 133, 136–8,
    146, 153, 189

Oglethorpe University, 16
O'Gorman, James, 223, 224, 226, 258,
    314, 379, 623n19
O'Hare, Kate Richards, 432
Ohio, 140, 152, 273, 340, 354, 358
O'Leary, Jeremiah, 351–3
Oregon, 134, 162, 189, 358
Orlando, Vittorio, 443, 449, 461, 484, 485,
    490, 492, 494, 498, 500
Orpen, William, 501, 504
Ottoman Empire, 6, 317, 366, 369, 401,
    421, 422–4, 442, 449, 467, 497, 502
Owen, Robert, 220–1, 222, 225, 255, 335,
    343, 558

Page, Walter Hines, 39, 70, 74, 79, 141,
    145, 154, 189–90, 191, 194, 209,

    239, 250, 263, 299, 300, 316, 343,
    363, 366, 380, 440
Palestine, 401, 418, 442
Palmer, A. Mitchell, 190, 191, 195–6, 459,
    505, 512, 523, 546, 555, 562, 567,
    568, 573
Pan-African Congress, 497
Panama, 245–6, 381, 581
Panama Canal, 241, 248, 404
  tolls controversy and, 249–51
Pan-American pact, 246
Paris peace conference, 7, 201, 203, 430,
    439, 454–504
  Adriatic in, 485, 487, 490, 492, 498,
    502, 554
  Arab interests and, 473–4
  Council of Four in, 485–9, 491, 494,
    499, 501–2, 504
  Council of Ten in, 468–71, 473, 483–5
  Dalmatia in, 484, 487, 490, 491, 492
  and fate of Wilhelm II, 486–9
  Fiume in, 487, 490, 492
  French security in, 485–6, 489
  German boundaries in, 483–6, 489,
    500, 501
  Irish independence in, 481, 491–2
  Italy's withdrawal from, 492
  League Commission and, 470–3
  league of nations question in, 460–1,
    463
  mandate system and, 497
  as "peace that failed," 496
  presentation of preliminary terms in,
    494–6
  racial equality amendment in, 473,
    489–90
  reparations in, 469, 471, 485–6, 489,
    490, 497–8, 500
  revisions debate in, 500–1
  Rhineland in, 483, 486, 500
  Saar in, 486, 489, 497
  self-determination principle in, 461,
    467, 474, 496
  Shantung in, 491, 493–4, 496, 503
  U.S. delegation to, 440, 455–8
  war guilt in, 471
  White-Lodge cable and, 482–3
  Wilson in prelude to, 463–4

Paris peace conference *(continued)*
  Wilson's health in, 487–9, 499–500
  Wilson's journey to Europe for, 454–5,
    460–2, 476, 482
  see also League fight; League of
    Nations; Versailles, Treaty of
Parliament, British, 44, 48, 50, 395
Pasteur, Louis, 536
Patton, Francis Landey, 62, 63, 65, 67–8,
    72, 77–8, 83, 85, 94, 103
Payne, John Barton, 555–6
Payne-Aldrich tariff, 121
*Peace Negotiations, The: A Personal
    Narrative* (Lansing), 586–7
peace initiative of December 1916–
    January 1917, 362–71
  Lansing's sabotage of, 363–70
  league of nations idea in, 362–3, 365–7
  Wilson's prolegomenon on, 362–3
  Wilson's Senate speech on, 370–1
"peace without victory" speech, 370–4,
    507, 640n21
  foreign reactions to, 372–3
  Fourteen Points and, 371
  Republican criticism of, 371–3
Pearl Harbor attack, 4, 285
Peck, Mary Allen, *see* Hulbert, Mary Allen
    Peck
Pennsylvania, U.S.S., 403
Perry, Bliss, 68, 70, 74, 75, 77, 78, 79, 83
Pershing, John J., 320–1, 401–2, 427,
    433–4, 437–8, 463, 592
Persia, 306, 307–8
Philippines, 75, 76, 190, 249, 311, 575
Phillimore, Walter, 439, 470
Phillimore Report, 439–40
Pinchot, Amos, 326, 355, 398
Pinchot, Gifford, 354–5
Pitney, Mahlon (May), 29, 138
Pittman, Key, 455, 514, 517–18, 657n26
Plunkett, Horace, 367
Poincaré, Raymond, 462, 469
Poindexter, Miles, 218, 331, 354
Poland, 6, 317, 366, 369–71, 396, 421, 422,
    484, 486, 487, 494, 496, 498, 501
Polk, Frank, 553–4, 556, 641n32
Polk, James K., 425
Poole, Ernest, 65

Portugal, 491
Pound, Roscoe, 330
Pre-Armistice Agreement, 449–50
Preface to Politics (Lippmann), 256
Princeton Alumni Weekly, 93, 95, 112
Princetonian, The, 28–9, 30, 64, 93
"Princeton in the Nation's Service"
    (Wilson), 72, 80
"Princeton Preceptorial System, The"
    (Wilson), 86
Princeton University, 3, 8, 58, 62–3,
    79–119, 138, 419, 591, 596
  assessment of Wilson's presidency at,
    115–16
  country club image of, 117–18
  curriculum reform at, 84–5
  faculty practice of, 83–4
  fraternities at, 85
  graduate school controversy of, 77,
    90–1, 96, 99, 103–5, 107, 111–15,
    116, 119, 613n24, 614n33
  history of, 25–6
  law school of, 82
  name of, 65, 71–2
  preceptorial system proposed for, 85–7,
    116
  Presbyterianism of, 84–5
  Procter's pledge and, 111–13
  Quad Plan controversy of, 89–95, 96,
    99, 101–5, 107, 109, 110–11, 116,
    119
  Wilson as student at, 25–32
  Wilson elected president of, 78
  Wilson-Hibben break and, 93–4
  Wilson inaugurated as president of,
    78–80
  Wilson as lecturer at, 65, 67
  Wilson-Pyne conflict and, 95–6
  Wilson's law school plan for, 66–7
  Wilson's leadership at, 80–3
  Wilson's legacy at, 118–19
  Wilson's resignation as president of,
    126
  Wilson-West clash and, 90–1, 93–5,
    116
  Wyman bequest and, 114–15, 117
Procter, William Cooper, 111–13
Procter and Gamble, 111

"Professor Wilson Visiting Congress" (Beerbohm), 215
Progressive National Convention of 1916, 338
Progressive Party, U.S., 159–60, 170, 220, 233, 268, 274, 314, 329, 338, 346, 348, 352
   in 1912 election returns, 173–4
progressivism, 5, 105–7, 142, 143, 150, 165–6, 185–6, 254–5, 351, 355, 593
prohibition, 4, 5, 140, 252, 253, 269, 360, 492, 537, 568, 594
   Eighteenth Amendment and, 415
Promise of American Life, The (Croly), 143–4, 161
Pyle, Howard, 76
Pyne, Moses Taylor, 62, 72, 77, 95–6, 104, 111–14, 117, 126, 615n26

race, race relations, 170–1, 237, 252, 436, 510, 523, 525
   Birth of a Nation and, 272–3
   in Paris peace talks, 473, 489–90
   Red Summer riots, 510
   in Wilson administration, 204–6
   Wilson-Trotter confrontation and, 270–2
   World War I and, 407–11
   see also African Americans
railroads, 345–6, 350, 382, 404–5, 459, 511, 520, 546
Rankin, Jeannette, 389, 642n60
Rayburn, Sam, 51
Reading, Lord, 417, 433
Reconstruction, 24, 37, 411
Record, George, 125–6, 130–2, 134, 351
Red Cross, 416, 434
Redfield, William C., 189–90, 192, 227, 426, 555
Red scares, 11, 510, 523, 546
Reed, James, 223, 224, 226, 231, 331, 460, 480, 523, 524, 562, 588, 623n19, 640n24
Reed, John, 201, 354, 398
Reed, Thomas B. "Czar," 50, 51, 76, 79
Reichstag, German, 418

Renick, Edward I., 38–9
Reparations Commission, 513, 551
Republican National Conventions:
   of 1912, 154–5
   of 1916, 336–7
Republican Party, New Jersey, 124–5, 134, 138
Republican Party, U.S., 50, 75, 108, 109, 121, 138, 143, 149, 152, 167, 180, 195, 216, 244, 254, 314, 328, 334, 346, 351–2, 506, 511, 512, 594
   Draft Covenant opposed by, 477–80
   League of Nations opposed by, 459–60; *see also* League fight
   military preparedness issue and, 268
   punitive peace sought by, 442–4, 448, 459–60, 480
   tariff reform and, 187
   war policies and, 430–1
   see also specific elections
Revenue Act of 1916, 344–5, 346, 637n18, 637n19
Rhineland, 451, 483, 486, 491, 500
Rhoads, James E., 59
Rhode Island, 360, 412, 638n48
Riddell, Lord, 590
Riis, Jacob, 65
"Road Away From Revolution, The" (Wilson), 584–5
Rockefeller, John D., 110
Rockefeller Foundation, 590–1
Rogers, John Jacob, 478, 479
Roosevelt, Eleanor, 155, 476
Roosevelt, Franklin D., 9, 151, 155, 179–80, 196, 203, 204, 213, 246–7, 297–8, 437, 476, 594, 598, 599, 650n8
   1920 election and, 568–9, 571
   Woodrow Wilson Foundation and, 585, 592
Roosevelt, Kermit, 86–7, 155
Roosevelt, Theodore, 4, 5, 9, 32, 73–6, 79, 82, 86, 88–9, 92, 98, 100, 106, 126, 127, 136, 140–1, 153, 180, 184, 186, 192, 195, 196, 197, 208, 209, 214, 226, 232–4, 247, 262, 274, 285, 298, 300, 307, 311, 314, 323, 325, 328, 329, 341, 360, 368, 372,

Roosevelt, Theodore *(continued)*
    376, 381, 384, 387, 396, 417, 426,
    434, 435, 440, 442, 446, 448, 456,
    519, 528, 529, 532, 547, 572, 598,
    599, 643n7
  attempted assassination of, 169–70
  "Confession of Faith" speech of, 159–60
  death of, 466
  management style of, 204
  military preparedness and, 268
  Monroe Doctrine Corollary of, 210
  1912 election and, 143, 152, 154,
    159–60, 166, 168–9, 171, 173–80,
    618n1
  1916 election and, 336, 338–9, 348–54
  Nobel Peace Prize of, 576
  Panama affair and, 246
  Sargent's portrait of, 416
  voluntary division proposal of, 393–5
  Wilson contrasted with, 177–8
Root, Elihu, 192, 244, 417, 430, 440, 457,
    458, 467, 475, 482–3, 506, 512,
    514, 541
Roper, Daniel, 339
Rublee, George, 232–3
rural credits, 222, 253–4, 329, 330, 336,
    348, 352
Russia, 5, 6, 75, 245, 315, 317, 386, 390,
    422, 439, 452, 470, 483, 487, 491,
    497, 499
  Allied intervention proposals and, 431,
    438–9
  Bolshevik takeover in, 401, 419, 421,
    424
  Brest-Litovsk Treaty and, 425, 431
  Root's mission to, 417, 430
Russian Revolution, 381, 584
Russo-Japanese War, 576

Saarland, 486, 489, 491, 497
Salmon, Lucy Maynard, 57
Sargent, John Singer, 415–16, 501
Sayre, Eleanor Axson, 323
Sayre, Francis (Frank) Bowes, 199–200,
    256, 259, 260, 296, 337, 357, 512,
    570, 590

Sayre, Francis Bowes, Jr., 279
Sayre, Jessie Woodrow Wilson, 57, 68–9,
    79, 88, 98, 139, 199–200, 219, 256,
    260, 261, 279, 296, 306, 323, 420,
    480, 537, 570, 572, 590, 595
  White House wedding of, 257, 512
Sayre, John Nevin, 257, 512
Sayre, Woodrow Wilson, 480
Schiff, Jacob, 172
Scott, Isaac, 580, 585–6
Scribner's Magazine, 28, 74, 79
Scudder, Horace, 59, 62, 74
Seamen's Act, 254–5
Secret Service, U.S., 290, 296, 302, 569
Sedition Act, 432
Seibold, Louis, 566, 589
Selective Service System, 397
  see also draft
self-determination, principle of, 6, 421,
    423, 428–9, 431, 441, 461, 467,
    474, 496
"Self-Government in France" (Wilson), 34
Senate, U.S., 32, 48–9, 51, 97, 127, 138,
    171, 173, 178, 184, 195, 227, 246,
    250, 255, 343, 388, 397–8, 439,
    483, 554, 562, 624n33, 640n17
  Adamson Act passed by, 345–6
  Appropriations Committee, 291
  Armed Services Committee, 297, 304
  arming of merchant ships and, 378–80
  army bill in, 310–12
  Banking and Currency Committee of,
    220–1, 223–4, 228
  banking reform in, 223–4
  Brandeis nomination in, 330–1
  Clayton Act passed by, 231
  Colombia indemnity in, 381
  Commerce Committee, 228, 233–4
  draft bill in, 393
  Finance Committee, 217, 218, 228
  Foreign Relations Committee, 247,
    312, 447–8, 456–7, 475, 478,
    513–17, 524, 528, 540–1, 542, 547,
    589, 657n30
  FTC bill passed by, 233–4
  Harding resolution in, 564
  Judiciary Committee, 217–18, 231,
    330–1

League of Nations opposed in, *see*
League fight
Military Affairs Committee, 310, 401,
425, 434
Naval Affairs Committee, 310, 404
navy bill in, 310
Philippine independence and, 311
popular election of, 188
punitive peace sought by, 443–4
revenue bill of 1916 in, 344–5
rural credits in, 254
Simmons bill in, 218
tariff reform in, 216–18
treaty debate in, 513–16, 556, 573–4
treaty votes in, 545, 558–9
Wilson's peace initiative and, 370–1
woman suffrage amendment in,
413–14, 441
see also Congress, U.S.; *specific elections*
September 11, 2001, attacks of, 4, 285
Serbia, 491, 570
Shakespeare, William, 219
Shantung question, 491, 493–4, 496, 503,
504, 509
in League fight, 512–13, 516, 524, 532,
541
Shaw, Albert, 66, 74
Sherman, William Tecumseh, 17–18
Sherman Anti-Trust Act, 105, 226–7, 229,
235
Shields, John K., 331, 435–6
Shipping Act of 1916, 403
Shipping Board, 403, 404, 430, 555–6, 557
Simmons, Furnifold, 217–18
Sims, William S., 383, 403, 484
Sinclair, Harry, 581
Sinclair, Upton, 512
slavery, 73–4, 602n7
Slayden, James L., 246, 435, 648n23
"smelling committee," 547–8, 566
Smith, Al, 360, 447, 572, 588, 594
Smith, Hoke, 74, 150, 331, 562, 648n26
Smith, James, 120–1, 122, 123, 125–8,
130, 133, 136, 146, 150, 151, 152,
153, 171, 187–8, 218
Smuts, Jan Christiaan, 454, 456, 467,
470–2, 489, 500, 504
socialism, 60, 64, 92, 511–12

Socialist Party, U.S., 159, 354, 432, 572
"Some Thoughts on the Present State of
Public Affairs" (Wilson), 29
Sonnets from the Portuguese (Browning), 46
Sonnino, Giorgio Sidney, 492, 494
South Carolina, 16, 109, 151, 435, 543
South Dakota, 173, 176, 358
Southern Society of New York, 141, 184–5
Spain, 59, 456
Spanish-American War, 74–5, 169, 517
speaking tour of September 1919,
518–32
cancellation of, 530–1
Lansing fiasco and, 524–5, 526
press coverage of, 524
Wilson's declining health in, 522, 525,
526–31
Spring-Rice, Cecil, 265–6, 269, 366,
395–6, 417
Standard Oil, 227
Stanton, Elizabeth Cady, 414
State, The (Wilson), 61, 63–4
State Department, U.S., 54, 189, 238, 243,
254–5, 265, 288, 295, 342, 343,
365, 370, 418, 458, 466, 538, 554,
556, 588
State of the Union addresses:
of 1913, 241–2, 249, 253
of 1914, 268, 274
of 1915, 305
of 1916, 364
of 1917, 400–1, 420
of 1918, 414, 459–60
of 1919, 546
of 1920, 574–5
state rights, 28, 96, 98, 344
Staunton, Va., 13–14, 180–1, 185–6
Steffens, Lincoln, 400
Stengel, Alfred, 89
Stettinius, Edward R., 426
Stevens, Raymond, 232–3
Stimson, Henry, 411, 650n8
Stockbridge, Frank Parker, 141, 142, 144,
145, 287
Stone, William J., 312–13, 314, 324, 370,
375, 377, 378, 379, 643n62
"Stray Thoughts from the South"
(Wilson), 37

"Study of Administration, The"
    (Wilson), 59
submarine warfare, 277–8, 290–1, 300,
    303–4, 307, 308, 312–15, 323–6,
    334, 353, 402–3
    Arabic incident in, 300, 302–4
    and arming of merchant ships, 377–81,
        384
    Falaba incident in, 277–8
    Laconia incident and, 377–8
    1916 election and, 336–7
    Sussex incident in, 323–5
    unrestricted warfare campaign in, 362,
        373–4, 376
    see also Lusitania
suffrage, 171, 447
    universal, 28, 29, 30–1
    woman, *see* woman's suffrage
Sullivan, Roger, 121, 158
Sunrise Conference, 313–14
Supreme Court, U.S., 5, 8, 29, 162–3
    Brandeis nominated to, 190, 329,
        330–2, 338, 346
    child labor law and, 346
    Clarke nominated to, 340
    Debs case and, 230
    Hughes's resignation from, 337, 340
    McReynolds appointed to, 273
    Pitney nomination to, 138
    Standard Oil ruling of, 229
Supreme War Council, Allied, 443, 444,
    456, 468, 470, 473, 474, 484
Sussex, 323
Swem, Charles, 201, 202, 286, 329, 330,
    332, 563, 569, 572, 629n21
Switzerland, 59, 468
Syria, 491

Taft, William Howard, 138, 152, 153, 184,
    187, 192, 195, 198, 208, 209, 210,
    214, 216, 226, 244, 247, 258, 268,
    326, 327, 337, 347, 350, 372, 429,
    440, 457, 460, 461, 467, 481, 482,
    490–1, 510, 512, 520, 523, 526,
    554, 597
    Draft Covenant supported by, 477, 479

    1908 election and, 175–6
    1912 election and, 161, 164, 166–8,
        170, 173–6, 179, 618n1
    White House staff advice of, 196–7
    Wilson LEP meeting with, 429–30
Taft administration, 121, 149, 210, 247
Talcott, Charles (Charlie), 28, 57,
    604n38
Tammany Hall, 92, 106, 128, 136, 151,
    155, 156–7, 209, 360, 568, 623n19
Tarbell, Ida, 203, 573, 589
Tariff Commission, 39
tariff reform, 186–7, 216–19, 346
    previous attempts at, 187, 216
tariffs, 108, 160, 175, 308, 329, 330, 351,
    499, 546, 575
    Payne-Aldrich, 121, 216
    Underwood-Simmons, 218–19
    Wilson-Gorman, 216
Taylor, Ida, 131
Taylor, James, 262, 306, 597
Teapot Dome scandal, 581–2
Texas, 374, 378, 435
Thackeray, William M., 70
"3rd Administration" (Wilson), 565
Third Paris Draft, 471–2
Thomas, Norman, 84
Thresher, Leon, 277
Tillman, Benjamin R., 376
Times (London), 552–3
Titanic, 254, 262, 285
Tocqueville, Alexis de, 34, 39, 63
Tomb of the Unknown Soldier, 582–3, 597
Treasury Department, U.S., 183, 185,
    189–90, 344, 364, 392, 459, 555,
    565
Trotter, William Monroe, 206, 270–2,
    410, 629n21
Tumulty, Joseph, 123, 127–30, 131, 133,
    139, 151, 156, 158, 190–2, 196,
    203, 206, 253, 255, 261, 272, 273,
    288, 289, 292, 294, 296–7, 300,
    306, 307–11, 313, 319, 321, 322,
    339, 341, 357, 360, 361, 364, 366,
    379, 388, 394, 397, 404, 407, 414,
    415, 422, 426, 457, 466, 470, 475,
    479, 481, 482, 505, 507, 512, 515,
    519, 578, 597, 627n36

Edith Wilson's dislike of, 299
in League speaking tour, 520–2, 524,
    525, 528–31
memoir of, 587–8
secretarial duties of, 200–1
in Wilson's disability and recovery
    period, 537–8, 546, 549–51, 553,
    556–7, 560, 561, 566, 567, 568–71,
    573
Wilson's rift with, 587–8
Turkey, *see* Ottoman Empire
Turner, Frederick Jackson, 62, 66, 67, 73,
    76–7
Tuskegee Institute, 79, 109, 408–9
Twain, Mark, 18, 98
Tyrrell, William, 241

unconditional surrender policy, 7, 452
Underwood, Oscar W., 150, 151, 154–5,
    157–8, 191, 213, 216–17, 223–4,
    250, 304, 574
University Commission on the Southern
    Race Question, 271–2
"University Training and Citizenship"
    (Wilson), 66
Untermyer, Samuel, 172
U.S.A. (Dos Passos), 189

Van Buren, Martin, 341
Vanderbilt, William Henry, 146
Vanderlip, Frank A., 224, 264–5, 628n7
van Dyke, Henry, 93–4
Vardaman, James K., 150, 205, 379, 411,
    436–7, 588, 641n35
Vatican, 5, 465
Veblen, Thorstein, 119, 398
Versailles, Treaty of, 7, 414, 508–9, 536,
    564, 586
    Reparations Commission of, 513, 551
    Senate votes on, 545, 558–9, 661n24
    signing of, 502–4
    U.S. debate on, *see* League fight
Vienna, Congress of, 420, 476, 496
Vietnam War, 4

Villa, Francisco "Pancho," 242, 319–21,
    626n15
Villard, Oswald Garrison, 170–1, 205,
    300–1, 304, 354
Vinson, Carl, 437
Virginia, 181, 554
Virginia, University of, 33–4, 67–8, 588
Viviani, René, 395–6
Volstead Act, 253, 415, 537, 565, 627n36

Wald, Lillian, 326, 354
Wallas, Graham, 256
Walsh, Thomas J., 217, 565, 567
Walters, Alexander, 170–1
War Cabinet, 425–6, 438, 445, 452
War Department, U.S., 190, 320, 380,
    391, 393, 401, 408, 426, 583
War Industries Board (WIB), 392, 407,
    426–8, 430
War Memoirs (Lansing), 357
War of 1812, 266, 319, 343, 517
War Trade Board, 430, 557
Washington, Booker T., 79–80, 109, 409,
    410
Washington, George, 76
    Farewell Address of, 328
Washington State, 173, 174
Watson, James, 522, 540
Watson, Tom, 150, 151, 398, 411, 436–7,
    648n26
Watterson, Henry, 148–9
Webster, Daniel, 14
Weeks, John W., 329, 405, 414, 426
Welles, Edward, 37, 605n12
Welles, Harriet (Hattie) Woodrow, 37, 40,
    144, 180, 605n12
Wesleyan University, 58–9, 61, 62
West, Andrew Fleming, 72, 77, 78, 82, 83,
    84, 94, 96, 117, 119, 129, 138, 192,
    480, 611n25
    Wilson's clash with, 90–1, 93, 103–5,
    110–15, 116
Western Ukrainian National Republic, 581
Whig (debating society), 27–8
White, Andrew D., 119
White, Edward, 198, 385–6

White, Henry, 457, 461, 478, 479, 482–3,
    487, 502
White, William Allen, 175–6, 274, 354–5,
    474, 506, 572
Whitehouse, J. H., 395, 400
Wilhelm II, Kaiser of Germany, 251, 373,
    450
    Paris peace talks on fate of, 486–9
Williams, John Sharp, 386, 515
Willis, H. Parker, 186–7
Wilson, Anne Josephine, *see* Howe, Anne
    Josephine Wilson
Wilson, Edith Bolling Galt, 280–4, 287,
    291–5, 297, 309, 315, 323, 324,
    357, 363, 364, 370, 380, 383, 385,
    396, 406, 413, 415, 416, 422, 494,
    501, 507, 511, 519, 520, 540, 549,
    553, 562, 565, 567, 568, 569, 584,
    589, 592, 595
  blackmail threat and, 302
  description of, 281
  as First Lady, 332
  House disliked by, 299, 302–3,
    484
  memoir of, 290, 296, 332
  as presidential gatekeeper, 536–7, 542,
    546–8, 557, 562
  S Street home of, 576–7
  in Versailles Treaty speaking tour, 520,
    526–30
  Wilson accompanied to Paris talks by,
    460–3, 468, 484, 485, 488
  Wilson described by, 483–4
  Wilson's courtship of, 283–4, 289–90,
    295–6, 298–9, 301–3
  Wilson's disability and, 535–6
  Wilson's love letters to, 283–4, 286,
    289–90, 298–9, 302, 590
  Wilson's marriage to, 306
  Wilson's recovery period and, 542–4,
    546–8, 554, 557, 560, 567, 573,
    574, 576
Wilson, Eleanor Randolph, *see* McAdoo,
    Eleanor Randolph Wilson
Wilson, Ellen Axson, 24, 67, 68, 72, 76,
    78, 79, 85, 86, 89, 93, 109, 110, 121,
    129, 139, 156, 158, 173, 180, 208,
    219, 222, 224, 228, 241, 279, 280,

    284, 290, 295, 299, 307, 349, 353,
    393, 439, 579, 596
  children of, 57, 61–2
  death of, 203, 231, 260–3
  depression of, 88, 99, 261
  father's death and, 51–3
  as First Lady, 199, 256
  House and, 189, 192, 207
  illness of, 258
  marriage of, 54–5
  in move to White House, 196–7
  Peck affair and, 100–1, 102
  Princeton house of, 70–1
  Wilson-Bryan meeting and, 141–3
  Wilson's correspondence with, 32, 37,
    40–8, 51, 52–3, 60–1, 68–9, 73, 74,
    75, 77, 80, 100, 256–7, 261
  Wilson's courtship of, 41–4
Wilson, Henry Lane, 210, 237, 239–40
Wilson, Janet "Jessie" Woodrow, 15, 17,
    36, 61
  Wilson's relationship with, 18–19, 20
Wilson, Jessie Woodrow (daughter), *see*
    Sayre, Jessie Woodrow Wilson
Wilson, Joseph Ruggles, 13–17, 20–2, 27,
    33, 39, 55, 75, 603n24
  death of, 82
  Wilson's correspondence with, 21,
    29–30, 35–6
  Wilson's relationship with, 30, 35–6
Wilson, Joseph Ruggles, Jr., 19, 199, 262
Wilson, Margaret Woodrow, 57, 68–9, 88,
    94, 139, 199, 256, 257, 258, 260,
    261, 283, 289, 296, 357, 499, 536,
    537, 543, 590, 595–6
Wilson, Marion Williamson, *see* Kennedy,
    Marion Williamson Wilson
Wilson, William B., 191–2, 345, 382
Wilson, Woodrow:
  academic background of, 8–9
  academic career of, 40–1, 53–4, 63,
    64–7, 71, 84, 603n24, 604n39
  academic life and, 57–8
  administrations of, *see* Wilson presi-
    dency, first term of; Wilson presi-
    dency, second term of
  "America First" statement of, 278,
    586

Bagehot's influence on, 30, 32, 47, 48,
    51, 59, 97
birth of, 13–14
blindness episode of, 89
boldness of, 5, 81, 116, 125, 212, 327,
    334, 384, 405, 515
Burke as model for, 8, 28, 30, 73, 77,
    108, 213–14, 587
as campaigner, 123–5
childhood of, 18, 22–3
children of, 57, 61–2
civil liberties abuses and, 11, 398–401,
    410, 432–3, 512
college education of, 25–7
conservatism of, 72, 93, 94–5, 98, 164,
    165
daily White House routine of, 332
death of, 595–6
delegating practice of, 204, 212, 396–7
on democracy, 59, 63
descriptions of, 11, 15, 483–4, 574, 577
drinking habits of, 9, 27, 253
dyslexia of, 19–20
education of, 22
Ellen Wilson's death and, 261
facial tic of, 499–500
family background of, 14–15
finances of, 58–9, 62, 71, 76, 147, 197,
    575–6
first foreign policy speech of, 240–1
first inaugural address of, 198–9
first marriage of, *see* Wilson, Ellen
    Axson
first political foray of, 92
foreign policy vision of, 240–1, 244
Fourteen Points speech of, 422–3
funeral of, 596–8
on government, 60–1, 63–4, 73
as governor, *see* New Jersey
as graduate student, 40, 44–6, 53
hand paralysis of, 71, 75, 98–9, 612n47
at Harding's inauguration, 577–8
Hattie Woodrow courted by, 36–8, 40
health problems of, 71, 89, 95, 109,
    116, 208, 256, 381, 440–1, 481,
    485, 487–8, 489, 494, 498–500, 509,
    510, 512, 519, 520, 522, 525,
    526–33, 534, 537, 551–2, 654n27

home life of, 22, 57–8, 82, 88, 129,
    139, 199, 256, 278–9, 332, 420–1,
    580
Icarus compared with, 7–8
imperialism of, 75–6
intellectual awakening of, 26–7, 32
interventionist streak of, 242–4, 384
in journeys to Europe, 454–5, 460–2,
    464–6, 476, 482
as lame-duck president, 573
last public appearance of, 592
law practice of, 38–40, 581–2
law studies of, 33–6
leadership style of, 9–10, 29, 82–3,
    107–8, 116, 131–2, 136, 177–8, 192,
    309
as lecturer, 56, 61, 64, 65–6
legislative accomplishments of, 8, 10,
    214–15
literary success of, 73–4, 76
management style of, 204
media and, 201–3
mental and memory lapses of, 440–1,
    500, 509, 512–13, 517, 546–7, 560,
    561–2, 570, 582–3
mood swings of, 552, 561–2, 570, 577
mother's relationship with, 18–19, 20
in mourning for Ellen Wilson, 262,
    267, 278–9
name change of, 36
in 1910 gubernatorial campaign, *see*
    election of 1910, New Jersey
1922 election and, 588
Nobel Peace Prize awarded to, 575–6
as orator, 20, 44–7, 123, 529, 606n30,
    659n47
Orpen's portrait of, 501
parliamentary institutions favored by,
    10, 27–8, 30–3, 48–50
party affiliation of, 24, 105–6, 107, 109
"peace without victory" declaration of,
    276–7, 507
Peck affair and, 98–101, 102
Ph.D. degree earned by, 58
Philadelphia July 4 speech of, 255–6
"Philosophy of Politics" synthesis of,
    73, 76–7, 96
physical paralysis of, 582–3, 585–6

Wilson, Woodrow (*continued*)
   playful nature of, 69, 131, **338**
   political cartoon of, 215
   political interest of, 21–2, **32**, **45**, 73,
      76, 91
   political views of, 4–5, 8–9, 27–8, 38
   postpresidency projects of, 583–7
   on presidency, 97–8
   presidential ambition of, 128
   progressivism of, 105–7, 165–6, 185–6,
      254–5, 351, 355, 593
   psychological effects of stroke and,
      544, 551, 560
   public administration writings of, 59
   public speaking and, 44–7
   race issues and, 11, 24–5, 68, 79–80,
      87–8, 109, 205–6, 252, 270–2, 361,
      407–11, 437, 489–90, 629n21
   radio talk of, 591–2
   reading difficulty of, 19–20
   readings of, 23, 256, 627n44
   in recovery from stroke, 542–3, 546–9,
      586, 589
   religious faith of, 3, 4–5, 23, 61, 70, 74,
      208, 279–80, 382, 411, 464, 560,
      598, 622n21
   resignation question and, 535–6
   Sargent's portrait of, 415–16, 501
   as scholar, 8
   second inaugural address of, 380
   second marriage of, *see* Wilson, Edith
      Bolling Galt
   sexual appetite of, 289
   shorthand learned by, 11–12, 20
   siblings of, 15
   small stroke suspected in, 494, 654n27
   "smelling committee" visit to, 547–8,
      566
   smoking avoided by, 27
   on socialism, 511–12
   Southern background of, 16–18, 23–5
   speechwriting of, 201
   sports interests of, 9, 22, 27, 57, 61,
      65–6, 87, 201, 208, 256, 258, 279,
      281, 306, 323, 415, 440, 470
   S Street home of, 576–7, 579, 665n1
   State of the Union addresses of, *see*
      State of the Union addresses

   stroke suffered by, 7, 115, 203, 204,
      261, 340, 530, 533–4, 659n61,
      659n62
   teaching career of, 56–8
   third-term ambition of, 565–7, 588,
      591
   tomb of, 3, 12, 598–9
   "too proud to fight" statement of, 287,
      290, 303, 309–10, 321–2, 324
   in transition to private life, 579–86
   T. Roosevelt contrasted with, 177–8
   typewriter used by, 41–2, 68, 131,
      605n21
   as visionary, 119
   war decision of, 4, 5–7, 374–5, 382–5
   Wesleyan job offer and, 58–9
   women and, 9–10, 19, 58, 280
   women students and, 56, 57–8, 607n6
   working habits of, 10, 195, 201, 237,
      415
   writing method and style of, 20, 31, 60
Wilson-Gorman tariff, 216
Wilson presidency, first term of
      (1913–1917):
   Adamson Act in, 345–6
   administration appointments in, 183,
      185, 189, 191–2, 207, 209, 234–5
   African American appointments in, 252
   ambassadorial appointments in, 185,
      191
   anti-trust legislation in, 216, 226–34
   army bill in, 310–12, 315
   banking reform in, *see* banking reform
   Brandeis nomination in, 329–32
   cabinet appointments in, 183, 185,
      189–91
   California's anti-Asian legislation in,
      211–12
   child labor issue in, *see* child labor
   Continental Army proposal in, 298,
      310–12
   Covington bill in, 232–4
   diplomatic appointments in, 209
   "dollar diplomacy" in, 210–11
   domestic issues in, 186, 252–4, 329–30,
      376–7
   first days in White House in, 199–200
   FTC in, 232–4

ICC issue in, 227–9
Latin America policy in, 245–8
legislative initiatives in, 183–4, 186, 213–16, 329–30
McLemore resolution in, 312–14
Mexico crisis in, *see* Mexico
military preparedness issue in, *see* military preparedness
New Jersey governorship and, 187–8
oath of office in, 198
peace initiative in, *see* peace initiative of December 1916–January 1917
preparation for, 182–6, 194–5
press corps and, 201–3
proposed term-limit amendment in, 195–6
race and, *see* race, race relations
Revenue Act in, 344–6, 637n18, 637n19
segregation controversy in, 204–6, 270–1
submarine issue in, *see* submarine warfare
Sunrise Conference in, 313–14
tariff reform in, *see* tariff reform
tolls controversy in, 249–50
trade commission legislation in, 231–2
typical workday in, 201
Wilson's inaugural address in, 198–9
Wilson presidency, second term of (1917–1921):
aircraft production in, 427–8, 434
cabinet appointments in, 553–6
censorship in, 391, 397–9, 432–33
civil liberties abuses in, 397–401, 410, 432–3, 512
domestic issues in, 382, 511, 537, 546, 555, 561, 562
draft in, 391, 393–7
Edith Wilson's gatekeeper role in, 536–7
Espionage Act in, 398
food and fuel crises in, 405–7
foreign policy in, 416–19
inaugural address in, 380
inauguration in, 379–80
Knox resolution in, 564–5, 664n10
lame-duck status of, 573, 575

Lansing's resignation in, 553–5
Lever Act in, 405–6
mobilization in, 390–2, 426
munitions production in, 427–8
1920 campaign in, 568–71
oath of office in, 379
presidential disability issue in, 535–6
race relations in, 407–11
railroad management in, 404–5
resignation question in, 535–6
royal visit in, 542
shipbuilding program in, 403
Shipping Act in, 403
taxes in, 434–5
war address in, 385–8
War Cabinet in, 425–6, 430–1, 438, 445, 452
Wisconsin, 135, 151, 189, 274, 309, 435, 446
Wiseman, William, 395, 402, 416–17, 418, 431, 433, 439–40, 450, 512, 536
Witherspoon, John, 25, 62, 72, 87
Witherspoon Gang, 28, 30, 580, 604n38
woman suffrage:
constitutional amendment on, 412–15, 441, 459, 478, 499
1916 election and, 335–6, 347, 360
World War I and, 411–15
Wood, Leonard, 401, 438
Woodrow, Fitz, 390
Woodrow, Harriet (Hattie), *see* Welles, Harriet (Hattie) Woodrow
Wilson's courtship of, 36, 37–8
Woodrow, James, 15, 16, 17, 21, 22, 23, 41
Woodrow, Thomas, 15
Woodrow, Thomas, Jr., 36
Woodrow Wilson and World Settlement (Baker), 587
Woodrow Wilson As I Know Him (Tumulty), 587
Woodrow Wilson Foundation, 585, 592
Woods, Hiram "the Cow," 28, 60, 604n38
Woolley, Robert, 339, 566
Wordsworth, William, 421, 422
workmen's compensation, 343–4
World Series, 258, 303
World's Work, 79, 154, 239
Works, John, 330, 379, 641n35

World War I, 3, 235, 452–3, 532
  AEF in, 433–4, 437–8
  Allied cooperation in, 395–6, 402
  Armistice in, *see* Armistice
  arms embargo in, 269–70
  Belgian neutrality violated in, 268, 558
  blacklist issue in, 342
  Brest-Litovsk Treaty in, 425, 431
  British finances in, 364, 373, 381
  British naval blockade in, 265–6, 268,
    288, 290, 299–300, 325, 342
  casualties in, 451–2
  consequences of, 452–3
  Eastern Front in, 401
  German atrocities in, 269
  German peace overture in, 418, 443–5
  House's missions in, 276–7, 315–19
  loan ban in, 264–5, 269–70
  Lusitania problem in, 285–91, 296–7
  Meuse-Argonne offensive in, 438
  munitions production in, 427–8
  onset of, 182, 231, 248–9, 262
  "peace without victory" speech in, 395,
    417–18
  Pre-Armistice Agreement in, 449–50
  race relations in, 407–11
  railroads in, 404–5
  "secret counsels" as cause of, 327
  ship-purchasing plan in, 263–4, 270
  submarine issue in, *see* submarine
    warfare
  transportation problem in, 403–4,
    427–8
  U.S. debate on war question and,
    374–6
  U.S. declaration of war in, 388–9
  U.S.-Japanese relations and, 274–5
  U.S. mobilization in, 390–2
  U.S. neutrality in, 263–4, 326
  U.S. war aims in, 420
  War Cabinet in, 425–6
  Western Front in, 401, 425, 431, 437
  Wilson's congressional address on,
    385–8
  Wilson's decision for war in, 4, 5–7,
    382–5
  Wilson's Four-Point Program for,
    276
  Wilson's grand strategy for, 417–18
  Wilson's *New York Times* interview in,
    275–6
  Wilson's peace initiative of December
    1916–January 1917 in, 362–71,
    373–4, 376
  Wilson's prolegomenon on, 362–3
  World War II and, 452
  Zimmermann Telegram and, 374,
    378
  see also Paris peace conference;
    Versailles, Treaty of
World War II, 4, 7, 11, 438, 452, 458
Wyman, Isaac, 114

Yale University, 119, 159, 419
Yates, Fred, 89, 102, 109
Young, Charles, 408, 645n36
Young Men's Christian Association,
  279–80
Yugoslav kingdom, 496

Zapata, Emiliano, 245
Zimmermann, Arthur, 374
Zimmermann Telegram, 374, 378

CRUSADER NATION
The United States in Peace and the Great War
by David Traxel

With World War I on the horizon, the struggles to end child labor, improve public health, advance education, win votes for women, and rid cities of corrupt political machines brought forth passionate responses from millions of Americans. There was a demand for reform and a desire for a more efficient and compassionate society. From wide-eyed dreamers to hard-line politicians, seasoned reporters to diary-keeping soldiers, these crusaders—Jack Reed, Theodore Roosevelt, Woodrow Wilson, Margaret Sanger, and "Mother" Jones to name a few—come alive in these pages.

History/978-0-375-72465-7

A GODLY HERO
The Life of William Jennings Bryan
by Michael Kazin

Politician, evangelist, and reformer William Jennings Bryan was the most popular speaker of his time. In this acclaimed biography—the first major reconsideration of Bryan's life in forty years—award-winning historian Michael Kazin illuminates his astonishing career and the richly diverse and volatile landscape of religion and politics in which he rose to fame.

Biography/978-0-385-72056-4

THEODORE ROOSEVELT
A Strenuous Life
by Kathleen Dalton

In Theodore Roosevelt, historian Kathleen Dalton reveals a man with a personal and intellectual depth rarely seen in our public figures. She shows how Roosevelt's struggle to overcome his frailties as a child helped to build his character, and offers new insights into his family life, uncovering the important role that Roosevelt's second wife, Edith Carow, played in the development of his political career. She also shows how TR flirted with progressive reform and then finally committed himself to deep reform in the Bull Moose campaign of 1912. Incorporating the latest scholarship into a vigorous narrative, Dalton reinterprets both the man and his times to create an illuminating portrait that will change the way we see this great man and the Progressive Era.

Biography/978-0-679-76733-6

EUROPE'S LAST SUMMER
Who Started the Great War in 1914?
by David Fromkin

When war broke out in Europe in 1914, it surprised a European population enjoying the most beautiful summer in memory. For nearly a century since, historians have debated the causes of the war. In Europe's Last Summer, David Fromkin provides a different answer: hostilities were commenced deliberately. In a riveting re-creation of the run-up to war, Fromkin shows how German generals, seeing war as inevitable, manipulated events to precipitate a conflict waged on their own terms. He moves deftly between diplomats, generals, and rulers across Europe, making the complex diplomatic negotiations accessible and immediate. Examining the actions of individuals amid larger historical forces, this is a gripping narrative and a dramatic reassessment of a key moment in the twentieth century.

History/World War I/978-0-375-72575-3

AND THE DEAD SHALL RISE
The Murder of Mary Phagan and the Lynching of Leo Frank
by Steve Oney

In 1913, thirteen-year-old Mary Phagan was found brutally murdered in the basement of the Atlanta pencil factory where she worked. The factory manager, a college-educated Jew named Leo Frank, was arrested, tried, and convicted in a trial that seized national headlines. When the governor commuted his death sentence, Frank was kidnapped and lynched by a group of prominent local citizens. Steve Oney's acclaimed account re-creates the entire story for the first time, from the police investigations to the gripping trial to the brutal lynching and its aftermath. Oney vividly renders Atlanta as a city enjoying newfound prosperity a half century after the Civil War but still rife with barely hidden prejudices and resentments. Combining investigative journalism and sweeping social history, this is the definitive account of one of American history's most repellent and most fascinating moments.

History/978-0-679-76423-6

VINTAGE BOOKS AND ANCHOR BOOKS
Available from your local bookstore, or visit
www.randomhouse.com